TREATIES AND OTHER INTERNATIONAL ACTS
OF THE UNITED STATES OF AMERICA

TREATIES

AND OTHER

INTERNATIONAL ACTS
OF THE UNITED STATES
OF AMERICA

EDITED BY

HUNTER MILLER

VOLUME 4

DOCUMENTS 80–121 : 1836–46

UNITED STATES
GOVERNMENT PRINTING OFFICE
WASHINGTON : 1934

PUBLICATIONS OF THE DEPARTMENT OF STATE

No. 645

PREFACE

The scheme of this work as a whole is fully described in volume 1. It may be said here that the arrangement of the documents is chronological according to date of signature; each document has a serial number, but the numbers are merely for convenience and have no other significance. All international acts of the United States which have gone into force are in general included, whether now in force or not; but postal conventions and treaties with Indian tribes are not included. Extrinsic and related papers which are referred to in the documents proper are also printed, so far as possible.

The headnote to each document gives the relevant dates; the notes which follow each document are mainly textual and procedural but treat to some extent of the diplomatic history of the document.

As the document volumes are to be globally indexed, there is no separate index for this volume.

The print of the documents and of the quotations in the notes is literal and thus includes any peculiarities and even any errors of the original. Certain texts are reproduced in facsimile.

This volume contains forty-two documents of the treaty edition, numbered 80 to 121, inclusive. The period covered is from 1836 to 1846.

H. M.

April 6, 1934.

v

CONTENTS OF VOLUME 4

VII

LIST OF DOCUMENTS IN VOLUME 4

x

List of Documents in Volume 4

LIST OF DOCUMENTS IN VOLUME 4—Continued

MAP IN VOLUME 4

WRITINGS CITED IN VOLUME 4

(Citations abbreviated in the text are included, with cross references where necessary.)

Acts and Resolves Passed by the Legislature of Massachusetts, in the Years 1839, 1840, 1841, 1842. Together with the Rolls and Messages. Published by the Secretary of the Commonwealth. Boston, Dutton & Wentworth, printers to the State, 1842.

Acts and Resolves Passed by the Twenty-second Legislature of the State of Maine, A.D. 1842. Augusta, William R. Smith & Co., printers to the State, 1842.

Adams, Ephraim Douglass. "Lord Ashburton and the Treaty of Washington". *In* American Historical Review (q.v.), XVII.

Adams, Herbert Baxter. The Life and Writings of Jared Sparks, Comprising Selections from His Journals and Correspondence. Boston and New York, Houghton, Mifflin & Co., 1893. 2 vols.

Albert, Thomas. Histoire du Madawaska d'après les recherches historiques de Patrick Therriault et les notes manuscrites de Prudent L. Mercure. Quebec, Imprimerie Franciscaine Missionnaire, 1920. xxiii+448 pp.

American Historical Review, The. New York, The Macmillan Co.; London, Macmillan & Co., 1896–.

American Secretaries of State and Their Diplomacy, The. Edited by Samuel Flagg Bemis. New York, A. A. Knopf, 1927–29. 10 vols.

American State Papers. Documents, Legislative and Executive, of the Congress of the United States. . . . Selected and Edited under the Authority of Congress. . . . Class 1. Foreign Relations. Washington, Gales & Seaton, 1832–59. 6 vols.

An Account of the Receipts and Expenditures of the United States . . . 1791–. Washington [etc.], 1793–.

Anderson, Chandler Parsons. Canadian Questions. Northern Boundary of the United States. The Demarcation of the Boundary between the United States and Canada, from the Atlantic to the Pacific, with Particular Reference to the Portions Thereof Which Require More Complete Definition and Marking. Report Prepared for the Department of State. Washington, Government Printing Office, 1906. 85 pp.

Annual Report of the American Historical Association for the Years 1884–. New York and London, G. P. Putnam's Sons, 1885–89; Washington, Government Printing Office, 1890–.

Aranda, Ricardo. Republica del Peru: Coleccion de los tratados, convenciones, capitulaciones, armisticios y otros actos diplomaticos y politicos celebrados desde la independencia hasta el dia, precedida de una introduccion que comprende la epoca colonial. Lima, Imprenta del Estado. 1890–.

Baring-Gould, Sabine, and C. A. Bampfylde. A History of Sarawak under Its Two White Rajahs, 1839–1908. London, Henry Sotheran & Co., 1909. xxiii+464 pp.

Barrows, David Prescott. History of the Philippines. Rev. ed. Yonkers-on-Hudson, N.Y., and Chicago, World Book Co., 1925. viii+406 pp.

Benton, Thomas Hart. Thirty Years' View; or, a History of the Working of the American Government for Thirty Years, from 1820 to 1850. Chiefly Taken from the Congress Debates, the Private Papers of General Jackson, and the Speeches of Ex-Senator Benton, with His Actual View of Men and Affairs: with Historical Notes and Illustrations, and Some Notices of Eminent Deceased Contemporaries. New York and London, D. Appleton & Co., 1856. 2 vols.

Blue Books, 1838, 1840, 1843. North American Boundary. . . . London, Printed by J. Harrison & Son [etc., 1838–43]. 7 vols. in 3.

British and Foreign State Papers, 1812–. London, 1825[?]–.

Burrage, Henry Sweetser. Maine in the Northeastern Boundary Controversy. Portland, Me., Printed for the State, 1919. xiv+398 pp.

Calvo, Carlos. Le droit international théorique et pratique; précédé d'un exposé historique des progrès de la science du droit des gens. 5th ed. Paris, Arthur Rousseau, 1896. 6 vols.

Canada and Its Provinces: A History of the Canadian People and Their Institutions, by One Hundred Associates. Edinburgh ed. Edited by Adam Shortt and Arthur G. Doughty. Toronto, T. and A. Constable at the Edinburgh University Press for the Publishers Association of Canada, Ltd., 1914–17. 23 vols.

Catalogue of Maps, Prints, Drawings, etc. Forming the Geographical and Topographical Collection Attached to the Library of His Late Majesty King George the Third, and Presented by His Majesty King George the Fourth to the British Museum. London, Printed by order of the Trustees of the British Museum, by G. Woodfall, 1829. 2 vols.

Clercq, Alexandre Jehan Henry de. Recueil des traités de la France, publié sous les auspices du Ministère des Affaires Etrangères. Paris, 1864–.

Code of the Laws of the United States of America of a General and Permanent Character in Force December 7, 1925, The. Volume 44—part 1 of the United States Statutes at Large. Washington, Government Printing Office, 1926.

Codificación nacional de todas las leyes de Colombia desde el año de 1821, hecha conforme a la ley 13 de 1912, por la Sala de Negocios Generales del Consejo de Estado. Bogotá, Imprenta Nacional, 1924–.

Collecção de decretos e regulamentos mandados publicar por Sua Magestade Imperial o Regente do Reino desde a sua entrada em Lisboa até á instalação das Camaras Legislativas. 3d series. Lisbon, Imprensa Nacional, 1840. xix+263+82 pp.

Colvocoresses, George M.   Four Years in a Government Exploring Expedition; to the Island of Madeira—Cape Verd Islands—Brazil—Coast of Patagonia—Chili—Peru—Paumato Group—Society Islands—Navigator Group—Australia—Antarctic Continent—New Zealand—Friendly Islands—Fejee Group—Sandwich Islands—Northwest Coast of America—Oregon—California—East Indies—St. Helena, &c., &c.   New York, Cornish, Lamport & Co., 1852. 371 pp.

Congressional Globe, The.   [23d to 42d Congress, December 2, 1833, to March 3, 1873.]   Washington, Office of the Globe, 1834–73.   46 vols. in 111.

Curtis, George Ticknor.   Life of Daniel Webster.   2d ed.   New York, D. Appleton & Co., 1870.   2 vols.

Daily National Intelligencer, Washington, April 4, 1843.

Dennett, Tyler.   Americans in Eastern Asia; a Critical Study of the Policy of the United States with Reference to China, Japan and Korea in the 19th Century. New York, The Macmillan Co., 1922.   xvi+725 pp.

Diary of James K. Polk during His Presidency, 1845 to 1849, The.   Edited by Milo Milton Quaife.   Chicago, A. C. McClurg & Co., 1910.   4 vols.

Dingle, Edwin John.   Across China on Foot; Life in the Interior and the Reform Movement.   New York, Henry Holt & Co., 1911.   xvi+446 pp.

Douglas, Edward Morehouse.   Boundaries, Areas, Geographic Centers, and Altitudes of the United States and the Several States, with a Brief Record of Important Changes in Their Territory and Government.   (U.S. Geological Survey Bulletin 817.)   2d ed.   Washington, Government Printing Office, 1930. vii+265 pp.

D.S.   (Archives of the Department of State.)   *See* Manuscript, Department of State Archives, for a list of the volumes cited.

Dublan, Manuel, and José María Lozano.   Legislacion mexicana ó coleccion completa de las disposiciones legislativas expedidas desde la independencia de la republica.   Edicion oficial.   Mexico City, Dublan y Lozano, hijos, 1876–90. 19 vols.

Edwards, Thomas.   Reports of Cases Argued and Determined in the High Court of Admiralty; Commencing with the Judgments of the Right Hon. Sir William Scott, Easter Term, 1808 [–1812].   London, Printed by A. Strahan, for J. Butterworth [etc.], 1812.   417+xcix pp.

English Reports, The.   Edinburgh, William Green & Sons, Ltd. [etc.], 1900–.

Executive Journal.   *See* Journal of the Executive Proceedings of the Senate of the United States of America.

Featherstonhaugh, George William.   Observations upon the Treaty of Washington, Signed August 9, 1842; with the Treaty Annexed.   Together with a Map, to Illustrate the Boundary Line as Established by the Treaty between Her Majesty's Colonies of New Brunswick and Canada and the United States of America.   London, John W. Parker, 1843.   119 pp.

Ficklen, John R.   "Was Texas Included in the Louisiana Purchase?"   *In* Publications of the Southern History Association (q.v.), V.

Fitzmaurice, Edmond George Petty-Fitzmaurice.   Life of William, Earl of Shelburne, Afterwards First Marquess of Lansdowne.   With Extracts from His Papers and Correspondence.   London, Macmillan & Co., 1875–76.   3 vols.

Fuess, Claude Moore.   The Life of Caleb Cushing.   New York, Harcourt, Brace & Co., 1923.   2 vols.

Gallatin, Albert.   A Memoir on the North-eastern Boundary, in Connexion with Mr. Jay's Map, . . . together with a Speech on the Same Subject, by the Hon. Daniel Webster . . . Delivered at a Special Meeting of the New-York Historical Society, April 15th, 1843.   Illustrated by a Copy of the "Jay Map".   New York, Printed for the Society, 1843.   (2) + 74 pp.

Garrison, George P.   "Diplomatic Correspondence of the Republic of Texas".   *In* Annual Report of the American Historical Association for the Years 1907 and 1908 (q.v.).   3 vols.

Gibert, Eugène.   L'Espagne et la question de Bornéo et de Joló.   Interpellation de M. Francisco Cañamaque, Député aux Córtes, . . . au Congrès des Députés des Córtes espagnoles.   Avec une préface par M. le Mis. de Croizier.   (Société Académique Indo-Chinoise.)   Paris, 1882.   38 pp.

Globe, The, Washington, May 28, 1839.

Greville, Charles Cavendish Fulke.   A Journal of the Reign of Queen Victoria from 1837 to 1852.   (The Greville Memoirs, second part.)   Edited by Henry Reeve.   London, Longmans, Green & Co., 1885.   3 vols.

Hansard's Parliamentary Debates, Third Series, Commencing with the Accession of William IV.   Comprising the Period from [October 26, 1830, to August 5, 1891].   London, 1831–91.   356 vols.

Haswell, John H.   Treaties and Conventions Concluded between the United States of America and Other Powers since July 4, 1776.   Containing Notes, with References to Negotiations Preceding the Several Treaties, to the Executive, Legislative, or Judicial Construction of Them, and to the Causes of the Abrogation of Some of Them; a Chronological List of Treaties; and an Analytical Index.   Washington, Government Printing Office, 1889.   xiii + 1434 pp.   (Senate Executive Document No. 47, 48th Congress, 2d session.)

Hertslet, Edward.   The Map of Europe by Treaty; Showing the Various Political and Territorial Changes Which Have Taken Place since the General Peace of 1814.   With Numerous Maps and Notes.   London, Butterworths [etc.], 1875–91.   4 vols.

House of Representatives Document No. 145, 24th Congress, 2d session, 1836–37 (serial 304).

———   Report No. 239, 24th Congress, 2d session, 1836–37 (serial 306).

———   Document No. 64, 25th Congress, 2d session, 1837–38 (serial 322).

———   Document No. 74, 25th Congress, 2d session, 1837–38 (serial 323).

House of Representatives Document No. 302, 25th Congress, 2d session, 1837–38 (serial 329).

——— Document No. 451, 25th Congress, 2d session, 1837–38 (serial 331).

——— Document No. 351, 25th Congress, 2d session, 1837–38 (serial 332).

——— Document No. 183, 25th Congress, 3d session, 1838–39 (serial 347).

——— Document No. 169, 26th Congress, 1st session, 1839–40 (serial 366).

——— Document No. 33, 26th Congress, 2d session, 1840–41 (serial 383).

——— Report No. 162, 26th Congress, 2d session, 1840–41 (serial 388).

——— Document No. 128, 27th Congress, 2d session, 1841–42 (serial 403).

——— Document No. 2, 27th Congress, 3d session, 1842–43 (serial 418).

——— Document No. 31, 27th Congress, 3d session, 1842–43 (serial 420).

——— Documents Nos. 271 and 278, 28th Congress, 1st session, 1843–44 (serial 444).

——— Document No. 69, 28th Congress, 2d session, 1844–45 (serial 464).

——— Documents Nos. 144 and 158, 28th Congress, 2d session, 1844–45 (serial 466).

——— Report No. 160, 28th Congress, 2d session, 1844–45 (serial 468).

——— Document No. 2, 29th Congress, 1st session, 1845–46 (serial 480).

——— Document No. 16, 29th Congress, 1st session, 1845–46 (serial 482).

——— Documents Nos. 110 and 133, 29th Congress, 1st session, 1845–46 (serial 483).

——— Document No. 169, 29th Congress, 1st session, 1845–46 (serial 485).

——— Executive Document No. 7, 30th Congress, 1st session, 1847–48 (serial 514).

——— Executive Document No. 132, 39th Congress, 1st session, 1865–66 (serial 1263).

International Boundary Commission: Joint Report upon the Survey and De-marcation of the Boundary between the United States and Canada from the Northwesternmost Point of Lake of the Woods to Lake Superior in Accordance with the Provisions of Article V of the Treaty Signed at Washington, April 11, 1908, and Article I of the Treaty Signed at Washington, February 24, 1925. Washington, Government Printing Office, 1931.   xiv+621 pp.   Box volume of "Triangulation and Traverse Sketches".

International Boundary Commission: Joint Report upon the Survey and De-marcation of the Boundary between the United States and Canada from the Source of the St. Croix River to the St. Lawrence River in Accordance with the Provisions of Article III of the Treaty Signed at Washington, April 11, 1908. Washington, Government Printing Office, 1925.   xv+512 pp.

Jennings, Louis John. The Croker Papers. The Correspondence and Diaries of the Late Right Honourable John Wilson Croker, LL.D., F.R.S., Secretary to the Admiralty from 1809 to 1830. London, John Murray, 1884. 3 vols.

Johns Hopkins University Studies in Historical and Political Science. Baltimore, The Johns Hopkins Press, 1883–.

Jones, Anson. Letters Relating to the History of Annexation. Galveston, Printed at the Civilian Office, 1848. 30 pp.

———— Memoranda and Official Correspondence Relating to the Republic of Texas, Its History and Annexation. Including a Brief Autobiography of the Author. New York, D. Appleton & Co., 1859. 648 pp.

Journal of the Executive Proceedings of the Senate of the United States of America. Printed by Order of the Senate. Washington, Duff Green and Government Printing Office, 1828–.

Kaeckenbeeck, Georges Silvain François Charles. International Rivers. A Monograph Based on Diplomatic Documents. (Grotius Society Publications, No. 1.) London, Published for the Society by Sweet & Maxwell, Ltd., 1918. xxvi+255 pp.

Laws of the Commonwealth of Massachusetts Passed by the General Court at Their Session Which Commenced on Wednesday, the Twenty-sixth Day of May and Ended on the Nineteenth of June, One Thousand Eight Hundred and Nineteen. Boston, 1819.

Laws of the Republic of Texas. . . . Houston, Printed at the Office of the Telegraph [etc.], 1838–39. 4 vols. in 1.

Laws of the State of New Hampshire, Passed June Session, 1842. Published by Authority. Concord, Carroll & Baker, State printers, 1842.

Laws of the United States of America, from the 4th March 1789, to [March 3, 1845], Including the Constitution of the United States, the Old Act of Confederation, Treaties, and Many Other Valuable Ordinances and Documents; with Copious Notes and References. Arranged and Published under the Authority of an Act of Congress. Philadelphia, John Bioren & W. John Duane; Washington, R. C. Weightman [etc.], 1815–45. 10 vols. in 11.

Lossing, Benson J. The Pictorial Field-Book of the War of 1812; or, Illustrations, by Pen and Pencil, of the History, Biography, Scenery, Relics, and Traditions of the Last War for American Independence. New York, Harper & Bros., 1869. 1084 pp.

Malloy, William M. Treaties, Conventions, International Acts, Protocols, and Agreements between the United States of America and Other Powers, 1776–[1923]. Washington, Government Printing Office, 1910–23. 3 vols. (Vols. 1–2, Senate Document No. 357, 61st Congress, 2d session; vol. 3, Senate Document No. 348, 67th Congress, 4th session.)

Manuscript, *Archivo Histórico Nacional. Legajo* 6609, Doc. 2362.

Manuscript, Department of State Archives. Boundary, Article 7, Treaty of Ghent (unbound manuscript).

———— Brazilian Claims (unbound manuscript).

Manuscript, Department of State Archives.   Colombian Claims (unbound manuscript).

———— Communications from Agents of Texas.   Vol. 1.

———— Communications to Foreign Sovereigns and States.   Vol. 1.

———— Consular Despatches, Guayaquil.   Vol. 1.

———— Consular Despatches, Hamburg.   Vol. 3.

———— Consular Despatches, Lima.   Vols. 3, 5.

———— Consular Despatches, Pará.   Vol. 1.

———— Consular Despatches, Santa Marta.   Vol. 1.

———— Consular Despatches, Tangier.   Vol. 5.

———— Credences.   Vols. 2, 3.

———— Despatches, Belgium.   Vol. 3.

———— Despatches, Brazil.   Vols. 10, 11, 12, 14, 15.

———— Despatches, Chile.   Vols. 1, 5, 6, 7, 8.

———— Despatches, China.   Vols. 1, 2, 3.

———— Despatches, Colombia.   Vols. 8, 9, 10, 11, 12.

———— Despatches, Germany.   Vol. 9.

———— Despatches, Great Britain.   Vols. 44, 49, 50, 57.

———— Despatches, Italy.   Vols. 2 (Naples), 4 (Sardinia).

———— Despatches, Mexico.   Vols. 9, 11, 12.

———— Despatches, Netherlands.   Vols. 9, 11.

———— Despatches, Peru.   Vols. 3, 4, 5, 6, 7, 8, 9, 10, 11.

———— Despatches, Portugal.   Vol. 13.

———— Despatches, Prussia.   Vols. 1, 2, 3, 4.

———— Despatches, Texas.   Vols. 1, 2.

———— Despatches, Venezuela.   Vols. 1, 2.

———— Domestic Letters.   Vols. 29, 30, 32, 36.

———— File 124.416/147.

———— File 852.412/19.

———— Instructions, Austria.   Vol. 1.

———— Instructions, Barbary Powers.   Vol. 14.

———— Instructions, Belgium.   Vol. 1.

———— Instructions, Brazil.   Vol. 15.

———— Instructions, China.   Vol. 1.

———— Instructions, Colombia.   Vol. 15.

———— Instructions, France.   Vol. 14.

Manuscript, Department of State Archives. Instructions, Great Britain. Vols. 14, 15.

———— Instructions, Mexico. Vol. 15.

———— Instructions, Netherlands. Vol. 14.

———— Instructions, Peru. Vol. 15.

———— Instructions, Portugal. Vol. 14.

———— Instructions, Prussia. Vol. 14.

———— Instructions, Texas. Vol. 1.

———— Instructions to Consuls. Vol. 9.

———— Instructions, Two Sicilies. Vol. 14.

———— Instructions, United States Ministers. Vols. 10, 12, 14.

———— Instructions, Venezuela. Vol. 1.

———— Journal of All the Proceedings of the Commissioners on the Part of His Britannic Majesty and of the United States of America Appointed to Carry into Effect the Sixth and Seventh Articles of the Treaty of Peace and Amity Made and Concluded at Ghent on the Twenty-fourth Day of December in the Year of Our Lord One Thousand Eight Hundred and Fourteen in Execution of the Sixth Article.

———— Legation Archives, China. No. 199.

———— Miscellaneous Letters, May–September 1839; January–February 1842; May–July 1842; July–August 1844; April–July 1845; November–December 1845; April–June 1846; July–September 1846; July–September 1848; May–June 1849.

———— Miscellaneous Papers Relative to Claims "on file in Bureau of Rolls and Library . . . August 1, 1887" (unbound manuscript).

———— Netherland Claims (unbound manuscript).

———— Northeastern Boundary. Envelopes 18, 19½.

———— Notes from the British Legation. Vols. 21, 22, 23, 24.

———— Notes from the French Legation. Vols. 11, 12.

———— Notes from the Mexican Legation. Vol. 4.

———— Notes from the Netherland Legation. Vol. 2.

———— Notes from the Peruvian Legation. Vol. 1.

———— Notes to Foreign Legations. Vol. 5.

———— Notes to the British Legation. Vols. 6, 7.

———— Notes to the French Legation. Vol. 6.

———— Notes to the Mexican Legation. Vol. 6.

———— Notes to the Netherland Legation. Vol. 6.

———— Notes to the Peruvian Legation. Vol. 1.

Manuscript, Department of State Archives. Notes to the Texan Legation. Vol. 6.

——— Report Book. Vol. 6.

——— Special Agents. Vols. 12, 14.

——— Special Missions. Vol. 1.

——— Unperfected. Original treaties in the archives of the Department of State which have not gone into force.

Manuscript, Library of Congress. Facsimiles of papers in the Public Record Office, London, Foreign Office Records, America, 5, vols. 340, 378, 379, 380.

Manuscript, Naval Records and Library. Wilkes Exploring Expedition. Vols. 1, 2. Area 9.

Manuscript, Texas State Library. Foreign Letters to Department, 1844, 5 and 6. Vol. 2.

Manuscript, Treasury Department. Circulars, October 10, 1843–February 4, 1848.

——— Miscellaneous, 1801–48.

Marshall, Thomas Maitland. A History of the Western Boundary of the Louisiana Purchase, 1819–1841. (University of California Publications in History.) Berkeley, University of California Press, 1914. xiii+266 pp.

Martens, Georg Friedrich von. Nouveau recueil de traités d'alliance, de paix, de trève . . . et de plusieurs autres actes servant à la connaissance des relations étrangères des puissances . . . de l'Europe . . . depuis 1808 jusqu'à présent. Gottingue, Dieterich, 1817–42. 16 vols. in 20.

——— Nouveau recueil général de traités, conventions, et autres transactions remarquables, servant à la connaissance des relations étrangères des puissances et états dans leurs rapport mutuels. Rédigé sur des copies authentiques, par Frédéric Murhard [etc.]. Continuation du grand recueil de feu M. de Martens. Gottingue, Dieterich, 1843–75. 20 vols. in 22.

——— Recueil des principaux traités d'alliance, de paix, de trève . . . conclus par les puissances de l'Europe . . . depuis 1761 jusqu'à présent. . . . [1st ed.] Gottingue, Jean Chretien Dieterich, 1791–1801. 7 vols.

Martin, Lawrence. Mitchell's Map, an Account of the Origin and Uses of the Most Important Map in American History. [Draft of an unpublished book.]

Middleton, Annie. "Donelson's Mission to Texas in Behalf of Annexation". *In* Southwestern Historical Quarterly (q.v.), XXIV.

——— "The Texas Convention of 1845". *In* Southwestern Historical Quarterly (q.v.), XXV.

Miller, Hunter. "An Annotated Dashiell's Map". *In* American Historical Review (q.v.), XXXVIII.

Mills, Dudley A. "British Diplomacy and Canada". *In* United Empire, the Royal Colonial Institute Journal, new series (q.v.), II.

Montero y Vidal, José.   Historia de la piratería malayo-mahometana en Mindanao, Joló y Borneo.   Madrid, Manuel Tello, 1888.   2 vols.

———— Historia general de Filipinas desde el descubrimiento de dichas islas hasta nuestros días.   Madrid, Manuel Tello, 1887–95.   3 vols.

Moore, John Bassett.   A Digest of International Law.   Washington, Government Printing Office, 1906.   8 vols.

———— History and Digest of the International Arbitrations to Which the United States Has Been a Party, Together with Appendices Containing the Treaties Relating to Such Arbitrations, and Historical and Legal Notes. Washington, Government Printing Office, 1898.   6 vols.

———— International Adjudications, Ancient and Modern: History and Documents, Together with Mediatorial Reports, Advisory Opinions, and the Decisions of Domestic Commissions, on International Claims.   Modern series. New York, London [etc.], Oxford University Press, 1929–.

———— The Works of James Buchanan, Comprising His Speeches, State Papers, and Private Correspondence.   Philadelphia and London, J. B. Lippincott Co., 1908–11.   12 vols.

Niles' Weekly Register, Containing Political, Historical, Geographical, Scientific, Statistical, Economic, and Biographical Documents, Essays, and Facts: Together with Notices of the Arts and Manufactures, and a Record of the Events of the Times.   Baltimore [etc.], 1811–48.   73 vols.

North American Review, The.   Boston, Wells & Lilly [etc.], 1815–77; New York, D. Appleton & Co. [etc.], 1878–1908.   188 vols. in 191.

Official Opinions of the Attorneys General of the United States, Advising the President and Heads of Departments in Relation to Their Official Duties. . . . Washington, Government Printing Office [etc., 1852–].

Oliphant, Laurence.   La Chine et le Japon.   Mission du Comte d'Elgin pendant les années 1857, 1858 et 1859.   Traduction nouvelle.   Précédée d'une introduction par M. Guizot.   Paris, Michel Lévy frères, 1860.   2 vols.

———— Narrative of the Earl of Elgin's Mission to China and Japan in the Years 1857, '58, '59.   Edinburgh and London, William Blackwood & Sons, 1859.   2 vols.

Pan American Union.   American Nation Series.   Washington, 1926–.

Pasinomie.   Collection complète des lois, décrets, arrêtés et règlements généraux. . . .   Brussels, 1789–.

Paullin, Charles Oscar.   Atlas of the Historical Geography of the United States. Edited by John K. Wright.   Washington, Carnegie Institution; New York, American Geographical Society, 1932.   xv + 162 pp. + 166 plates.

Poore, Benjamin Perley.   A Descriptive Catalogue of the Government Publications of the United States, September 5, 1774–March 4, 1881.   Compiled by Order of Congress.   Washington, Government Printing Office, 1885.   iv + 1392 pp.

Primer rejistro auténtico nacional.   (Año de 1830–[39]).   [Quito?], 18—.   2 vols.

Publications of the Southern History Association.   Washington, The Association, 1897–1907.   11 vols.

Regular Confidential Printed Documents before the Senate of the United States in Executive Session during the 18th . . . Congresses, from December 15, 1824, to . . . .   Washington, Government Printing Office, 1914–.

Report of the Commission on Extraterritoriality in China.   Presented by the Secretary of State for Foreign Affairs to Parliament by Command of His Majesty. ([Great Britain Foreign Office], China, No. 3, 1926; Cmd. 2774.)   London, His Majesty's Stationery Office, 1926.   130 pp.

Reports upon the Survey of the Boundary between the Territory of the United States and the Possessions of Great Britain from the Lake of the Woods to the Summit of the Rocky Mountains, Authorized by an Act of Congress Approved March 19, 1872. . . .   Published in Accordance with an Act of Congress Approved March 3, 1877.   Washington, Government Printing Office, 1878.   624 pp.   (Senate Executive Document No. 41, 44th Congress, 2d session.)

Resolves of Maine, 1895.   Augusta [1895?].

Resolves of the State of Maine, from 1829 to 1835 Inclusive.   Vol. 2.   Augusta, William R. Smith & Co., printers to the State, 1842.

Revised Statutes of the United States, Passed at the First Session of the Forty-third Congress, 1873–'74. . . .   Reprinted, with Amendments, under Authority of an Act of Congress Approved the Second Day of March, in the Year One Thousand Eight Hundred and Seventy-seven, with an Appendix.   Edited . . . under the Direction of the Secretary of State [by George S. Boutwell].   2d ed. Washington, Government Printing Office, 1878.   xv+1394 pp.

Richardson, James Daniel.   A Compilation of the Messages and Papers of the Presidents, 1789–1897.   Published by Authority of Congress.   Washington, Government Printing Office, 1896–99.   10 vols.

Rives, George Lockhart.   The United States and Mexico, 1821–1848; a History of the Relations between the Two Countries from the Independence of Mexico to the Close of the War with the United States.   New York, Charles Scribner's Sons, 1913.   2 vols.

Robertson, William Spence.   History of the Latin-American Nations.   Rev. ed. New York and London, D. Appleton & Co., 1925.   xxi+630 pp.

Ryden, George Herbert.   The Foreign Policy of the United States in Relation to Samoa.   New Haven, Yale University Press; London, Humphrey Milford, Oxford University Press, 1933.   xviii+634 pp.

St. John, Spenser Buckingham.   Rajah Brooke; the Englishman as Ruler of an Eastern State.   New York, Longmans, Green & Co., 1899.   xxiv+302 pp.

Saleeby, Najeeb M.   The History of Sulu.   (Bureau of Science, Division of Ethnology Publications, IV, pt. 2.)   Manila, Bureau of Printing, 1908.   283 pp.

Scott, Winfield.   Memoirs of Lieut.-General Scott, LL.D.   Written by Himself. New York, Sheldon & Co., 1864.   2 vols.

Senate Confidential Documents.   *See* Regular Confidential Printed Documents before the Senate of the United States.

Senate Documents Nos. 1 and 13, 25th Congress, 2d session, 1837–38 (serial 314).

———— Document No. 1, 25th Congress, 3d session, 1838–39 (serial 338).

———— Document No. 1, 27th Congress, 2d session, 1841–42 (serial 395).

———— Document No. 199, 27th Congress, 2d session, 1841–42 (serial 397).

———— Document No. 1, 27th Congress, 3d session, 1842–43 (serial 413).

———— Document No. 99, 27th Congress, 3d session, 1842–43 (serial 415).

———— Documents Nos. 341, 345, and 349, 28th Congress, 1st session, 1843–44 (serial 435).

———— Document No. 1, 28th Congress, 2d session, 1844–45 (serial 449).

———— Documents Nos. 58 and 67, 28th Congress, 2d session, 1844–45 (serial 450).

———— Document No. 138, 28th Congress, 2d session, 1844–45 (serial 457).

———— Document No. 1, 29th Congress, 1st session, 1845–46 (serial 470).

———— Documents Nos. 118 and 139, 29th Congress, 1st session, 1845–46 (serial 473).

———— Document No. 405, 29th Congress, 1st session, 1845–46 (serial 477).

———— Executive Document No. 58, 31st Congress, 1st session, 1849–50 (serial 561).

———— Executive Document No. 103, 34th Congress, 1st session, 1855–56 (serial 824).

———— Executive Document No. 58, 35th Congress, 1st session, 1857–58 (serial 930).

———— Report No. 391, 35th Congress, 2d session, 1858–59 (serial 994).

———— Executive Document No. 41, 44th Congress, 2d session, 1876–77 (serial 1719).

———— Executive Document No. 38, 44th Congress, 2d session, 1876–77 (serial 1720).

———— Document No. 136, 56th Congress, 1st session, 1899–1900 (serial 3851).

Smith, Justin Harvey.   The Annexation of Texas.   New York, The Baker & Taylor Co., 1911.   ix+496 pp.

Soulsby, Hugh G.   "The Right of Search and the Slave Trade in Anglo-American Relations, 1814–1862".   *In* Johns Hopkins University Studies in Historical and Political Science (q.v.), LI, No. 2, 1933.

Southwestern Historical Quarterly, The.   Austin, Texas, The Texas State Historical Association, 1898–.

Sparks, Jared. "The Treaty of Washington". *In* North American Review (q.v.), LVI.

Statutes at Large of the United States of America, The.   Boston, C. C. Little & J. Brown, 1845–51; Boston, Little, Brown & Co., 1855–73; Washington, Government Printing Office, 1875–.

Statutes of the United Kingdom of Great Britain and Ireland, The.   With Notes, References, and an Index. . . .   From A.D. 1801; 41 George III.—To [32 and 33 Victoria; 1868–69].   London, Printed by G. Eyre and A. Strahan, printers to the King [etc.], 1804–69.   29 vols. in 34.

Story, Joseph.   Commentaries on the Conflict of Laws, Foreign and Domestic, in Regard to Contracts, Rights, and Remedies, and Especially in Regard to Marriages, Divorces, Wills, Successions, and Judgments.   8th ed.   Edited by Melville M. Bigelow.   Boston, Little, Brown & Co., 1883.   xxxix+ 901 pp.

Supreme Court Reporter, The.   Permanent ed.   Cases Argued and Determined in the United States Supreme Court, October Term, 1882–.   St. Paul, West Publishing Co., 1883–.

Surville, Fernand, and F. Arthuys.   Cours élémentaire de droit international privé conforme au programme des facultés de droit.   Droit civil—Procédure— Droit commercial.   5th ed.   Paris, Arthur Rousseau, 1910.   viii+807 pp.

Tanner, Henry Schenck.   New Universal Atlas Containing Maps of the Various Empires, Kingdoms, States and Republics of the World with a Special Map of Each of the United States, Plans of Cities &c.   Comprehended in Seventy Sheets and Forming a Series of One Hundred and Seventeen Maps Plans and Sections.   Philadelphia, Published by the author, 1836.

Texas National Register, Washington, Texas, April 24, 1845.

Thorpe, Francis Newton.   The Federal and State Constitutions, Colonial Charters, and Other Organic Laws of the States, Territories, and Colonies Now or Heretofore Forming the United States of America.   Washington, Government Printing Office, 1909.   7 vols.   (House Document No. 357, 59th Congress, 2d session.)

Tratados y convenciones celebrados y no ratificados por la Republica Mexicana, con un apendice que contiene varios documentos importantes.   Edicion oficial.   (Derecho internacional Mexicano, pt. 2.)   Mexico, Gonzalo A. Esteva, 1878.   xiii+408 pp.

Treaty Series.   Washington, Government Printing Office, 1908–.

Tyler, Lyon Gardiner.   The Letters and Times of the Tylers.   Richmond, Va., Whittet & Shepperson [etc.], 1884–96.   3 vols.

United Empire, the Royal Colonial Institute Journal.   New series.   Edited by Archibald R. Colquhoun.   London, 1910–11.   2 vols.

United States Code.   *See* Code of the Laws of the United States.

United States Reports: Cases Adjudged in the Supreme Court.   Vol. 5 (*cited* 1 Cranch).

Weiss, André. Traité élémentaire de droit international privé. Paris, L. Larose et Forcel, 1886. xxxviii+996 pp.

Wharton, Francis. The Revolutionary Diplomatic Correspondence of the United States. Edited under Direction of Congress . . . with Preliminary Index, and Notes Historical and Legal. Published in Conformity with Act of Congress of August 13, 1888. Washington, Government Printing Office, 1889. 6 vols.

Wheaton, Henry. Elements of International Law. 8th ed. Edited by Richard Henry Dana, Jr. Boston, Little, Brown & Co., 1866. xlvii+749 pp.

White, James. "Boundary Disputes and Treaties". *In* Canada and Its Provinces (q.v.), VIII.

Wilkes, Charles. Narrative of the United States Exploring Expedition. During the Years 1838, 1839, 1840, 1841, 1842. Quarto ed. Philadelphia, Lea & Blanchard, 1845. 5 vols. and atlas.

——— Narrative of the United States Exploring Expedition. During the Years 1838, 1839, 1840, 1841, 1842. Octavo ed. Philadelphia, Lea & Blanchard, 1845. 5 vols.

——— United States Exploring Expedition. During the Years 1838, 1839, 1840, 1841, 1842. Under the command of Charles Wilkes, U.S.N. Quarto ed. On half titles: "By authority of Congress." Philadelphia, C. Sherman, 1844–74. 18 vols. in 19. 11 atlases.

Willoughby, Westel Woodbury. Foreign Rights and Interests in China. Rev. and enl. ed. Baltimore, The Johns Hopkins Press, 1927. 2 vols.

Wooten, Dudley Goodall. A Comprehensive History of Texas, 1685 to 1897. Dallas, William G. Scarff, 1898. 2 vols.

Wriston, Henry Merritt. Executive Agents in American Foreign Relations. (The Albert Shaw Lectures on Diplomatic History, 1923.) Baltimore, The Johns Hopkins Press; London, Humphrey Milford, Oxford University Press, 1929. xii+874 pp.

Writings and Speeches of Daniel Webster, The. National ed. Boston, Little, Brown & Co., 1903. 18 vols.

Yela Utrilla, Juan Francisco. España ante la independencia de los Estados Unidos. 2d ed. Lérida, Gráficos Academia Mariana, 1925. 2 vols.

DOCUMENTS 80–121 : 1836–46

Treaty Series No. 366
8 Statutes at Large, 466–83
18 *ibid.*, pt. 2, Public Treaties, 787–95

80

VENEZUELA : JANUARY 20, 1836

Treaty of Peace, Friendship, Navigation, and Commerce, signed at Caracas January 20, 1836. Original in English and Spanish. Submitted to the Senate March 7, 1836. Resolution of advice and consent March 23, 1836. Ratified by the United States April 20, 1836. Ratified by Venezuela May 25, 1836. Ratifications exchanged at Caracas May 31, 1836. Proclaimed June 20, 1836.

Treaty of Peace, Friendship, Navigation and Commerce between the United States of America and the Republic of Venezuela

The United States of America and the Republic of Venezuela desiring to make lasting and firm the friendship and good understanding which happily prevails between both nations have resolved to fix in a manner clear, distinct, and positive the rules which shall in future be religiously observed between the one and the other, by means of a treaty of friendship, commerce and navigation.

For this most desirable object the President of the United States of America has conferred full powers on John G. A. Williamson a citizen of the said States, and their Chargé d'affairs to the said republic, and the President of the Republic of Venezuela on Santos Michelena a citizen of the said Republic, who after having ex-

Tratado de Paz, Amistad Navegacion y Comercio entre la Republica de Venezuela y los Estados Unidos de America

La Republica de Venezuela y los Estados Unidos de America, deseando hacer duradera y firme la amistad y buena inteligencia que felizmente existe entre ambas potencias, han resuelto fijar de una manera clara, distinta y positiva, las reglas que deben observar relijiosamente en lo venidero, por medio de un tratado de paz, amistad, comercio y navegacion.

Con este muy deseable objeto el Presidente de la Republica de Venezuela ha conferido plenos poderes á Santos Michelena ciudadano de la misma y el Presidente de los Estados Unidos de America á John G. A. Williamson ciudadano de dichos Estados y su encargado de negocios cerca de la dicha Republica: quienes despues

3

4

Document 80

changed their said full powers, in due and proper form, have agreed to the following articles:

ARTICLE 1.

There shall be a perfect, firm, and inviolable peace and sincere friendship between the United States of America and the Republic of Venezuela in all the extent of their possessions and territories, and between their people and citizens respectively, without distinction of persons or places.

ARTICLE 2.

The United States of america and the Republic of Venezuela desiring to live in peace and harmony with all the other nations of the earth, by means of a policy frank, and equally friendly with all, engage mutually not to grant any particular favor to other nations in respect of commerce and navigation which shall not immediately become common to the other party, who shall enjoy the same freely, if the concession was freely made, or on allowing the same compensation if the concession was conditional.

ARTICLE 3.

The two high contracting parties being likewise desirious of placing the commerce and navigation of their respective countries on the liberal basis of perfect

de haber canjeado sus espresados plenos poderes en debida y buena fcrma han convenido en los articulos siguientes.

ARTICULO 1.

Habrá una paz perfecta, firme, é inviolable y amistad sincera entre la Republica de Venezuela y los Estados Unidos de America, en toda la estension de sus posesiones y territorios, y entre sus pueblos y ciudadanos respectivamente, sin distincion de personas ni lugares.

ARTÍCULO 2.

La Republica de Venezuela y los Estados Unidos de America deseando vivir en paz y en armonia, con las demas naciones de la tierra, por medio de una politica franca é igualmente amistosa con todas, se obligan mútuamente á no conceder favores particulares á otras naciones, con respecto á comercio y navegacion, que no se hagan inmediatamente comunes á una ú otra, quien gozará de los mismos, libremente, si la concesion fúe hecha libremente, ó prestando la misma compensasion si la concesion fuere condicional.

ARTÍCULO 3.

Las dos altas partes contratantes deseando tambien establecer el comercio y navegacion de sus respectivos paises sobre las liberales bases de perfecta igual-

equallity and reciprocity, mutually agree that the citizens of each may frequent all the coasts and countries of the other and reside and trade there in all kinds of produce manufactures and merchandize. And they shall enjoy all the rights, privileges and exemptions, in navigation and commerce which native citizens do or shall enjoy, submitting themselves to the laws, decrees, and usages there established, to which native citizens are subjected. But it is understood that this article does not include the coasting trade of either country, the regulation of which is reserved by the parties respectively according to their own separate laws.

Article 4.

They likewise agree that whatever kind of produce, manufactures or merchandize, of any foreign country, can be from time to time lawfully imported into the United States in their own vessels, may be also imported in vessels of the Republic of Venezuela, and that no higher or other duties upon the tonnage of the vessel and her cargo shall be levied and collected, whether the importation be made in the vessels of the one country or of the other. And in like manner that whatever kind of produce manufactures or merchandize, of any foreign country, can be from time to time lawfully imported

dad y reciprocidad convienen mutuament en que los ciudadanos de cada una podrán frecuentar todas las costas y paises de la otra y residir y traficar en ellos con toda clase de producciones, manufacturas y mercaderías, y gozarán de todos los derechos, privilegios y exenciones, con respecto á navegacion y comercio, de que gozan ó gozaren los ciudadanos naturales, sometiendose á las leyes, decretos y usos establecidos á que estan sujetos dichos ciudadanos. Pero debe entenderse que este articulo no comprende el comercio de cabotage de cada uno de los dos paises cuya regulacion queda reservada á las partes respectivamente segun sus leyes propias y peculiares.

Articulo 4.

Ygualmente convienen en que cualquiera clase de producciones, manufacturas ó mercaderias de cualquier pais estranjero que puedan ser en cualquier tiempo legalmente introducidas en la Republica de Venezuela en sus propios buques, puedan tambien ser introducidas en los buques de los Estados Unidos, y que no se impondrán ó cobrarán otros ó mas altos derechos de tonelada, ó por el cargamento, ya sea que la importacion se haga en buques de la una ó de la otra. De la misma manera cualquiera clase de producciones, manufacturas ó mercaderias de cualquiera pais estranjero que puedan ser en

into the Republic of Venezuela in its own vessels may be also imported in vessels of the United States, and that no higher or other duties, upon the tonnage of the vessels and her cargo, shall be levied or collected, whether the importation be made in vessels of the one country or of the other. And they agree that whatever may be lawfully exported or reexported from the one country in its own vessels to any foreign country, may in like manner be exported or reexported in the vessels of the other country. And the same bounties, duties, and drawbacks shall be allowed, and collected, whether such exportation or reexportation be made in vessels of the United States, or of the Republic of Venezuela.

cualquiere tiempo legalmente introducidas en los Estados Unidos en sus propios buques, podrán tambien ser introducidas en los buques de la Republica de Venezuela, y no se impondran ó cobrarán otros ó mas altos derechos de tonelada ó por el cargamento, ya sea que la importacion se haga en buques de la una ó de la otra. Y convienen que todo lo que pueda ser legalmente exportado ó reexportado de uno de los dos paises en sus propios buques para un pais estrangero, pueda de la misma manera ser exportado ó reexportado en los buques del otro. Y los mismos derechos, premios, ó descuentos se concederán y cobrarán, sea que la exportacion ó reexportacion se haga en los buques de la Republica de Venezuela ó en los de los Estados Unidos.

ARTICLE 5.

For the better understanding of the preceding article, and taking into consideration the actual state of the commercial marine of the Republic of Venezuela, it has been stipulated and agreed that all vessels belonging exclusively to a citizen or citizens of said Republic and whose captain is also a citizen of the same, though the construction or crew are or may be foreign, shall be considered for all the objects of this treaty as a venezuelean vessels.

ARTICULO 5.

Para cabal inteligencia del artículo precedente y en consideracion al estado de la marina comercial de la Republica de Venezuela, se ha estipulado y convenido que todo buque perteneciente exclusivamente á ciudadano ó ciudadanos de dicha Republica y cuyo capitan sea tambien ciudadano de ella, aunque su construccion y tripulacion sean estranjeras, será considerado, para todos los efectos de este tratado, como buque Venezolano.

ARTICLE 6.

No higher or other duties shall be imposed on the importation into the United States of any articles the produce or manufactures of the Republic of Venezuela, and no higher or other duties shall be imposed on the importation into de Republic of Venezuela of any articles, the produce or manufacture of the United States, than are or shall be payable on the like articles beeing the produce or manufactures of any other foreign country, nor shall any higher or other duties, or charges be imposed in either of the two countries, on the exportation of any articles to the United States, or to the Republic of Venezuela respectively than such as are payable on the exportation of the like articles to any other foreign country; nor shall any prohibition be imposed on the exportation or importation of any articles the produce or manufactures of the United States or of the Republic of Venezuela to or from the territories of the United States, or to or from the territories of the Republic of Venezuela, which shall not equally extend to all other nations.

ARTICLE 7.

It is likewise agreed that it shall be wholly free for all merchants, commanders of ships and other citizens of both countries to

ARTICULO 6.

No se impondrán otros ó mas altos derechos á la importacion en la Republica de Venezuela de cualquiera articulo, produccion ó manufactura de los Estados Unidos, ni se impondrán otros ó mas altos derechos á la importacion de cualquier articulo, produccion ó manufactura de la Republica de Venezuela, en los Estados Unidos, que los que se paguen ó pagaren por iguales articulos, produccion ó manufactura de cualquier pais estrangero; ni se impondrán otros ó mas altos derechos ó impuestos en cualquiera de los dos paises á la exportacion de cualesquiera articulos para la republica de Venezuela ó para los Estados Unidos respectivamente, que los que se paguen ó pagaren á la exportation de iguales articulos para cualquiera otro pais extrangero; ni se prohibirá la importacion ó exportacion en los territorios ó de los territorios de la Republica de Venezuela y de los Estados Unidos de cualesquiera articulos, produccion ó manufactura de la una ó de la otra, á menos que esta prohibision sea igualmente extensiva á todas las otras naciones.

ARTICULO 7.

Se conviene á demas que será enteramente libre y permitido á los comerciantes, comandantes de buques, y otros ciudadanos

manage themselves their own business in all the ports and places subject to the jurisdiction of each other, as well with respect to the consignment and sale of their goods and merchandize by wholesale or retail, as with respect to the loading, unloading, and sending off their ships, they being in all these cases to be treated as citizens of the country in which they reside or at least to be placed on a footing with the subjects or citizens of the most favoured nation.

Article 8.

The citizens of neither of the contracting parties shall be liable to any embargo, nor be detained with their vessels, cargos, merchandizes or effects, for any military expedition, nor for any public or private purpose whatever, without allowing to those interested a sufficient indemnification.

Article 9.

Whenever the citizens of either of the contracting parties, shall be forced to seek refuge or asylum in the rivers, bays, ports or dominions of the other with their vessels, whether merchant, or of war, public or private, through stress of weather, pursuit of pirates or enemies, they shall be received and treated with humanity, giving to them all favour and protection for repairing their ships,

de ambos paises, el manejar sus negocios por si mismos, en todos los puertos y lugares sujetos á la jurisdiccion de uno ú otro, así respecto de las consignaciones, y ventas por mayor y menor de sus efectos, y mercaderias, como de la carga y descarga, y despacho de sus buques, debiendo en todos casos, ser tratados como ciudadanos del pais en que residan, ó al menos puestos sobre un pié igual con los súbditos ó ciudadanos, de las naciones mas favorecidas.

Articulo 8.

Los ciudadanos de una ú otra parte no podrán ser embargados, ni detenidos con sus embarcaciones, tripulaciones, mercaderias, y efectos comerciales de su pertenencia, para alguna expedicion militar, usos publicos, ó particulares cualesquiera que sean, sin conceder á los interesados una suficiente indemnizacion.

Articulo 9.

Siempre que los ciudadanos de alguna de las partes contratantes se vieren precisados á buscar refujio ó asilo en los rios, bahias, puertos, ó dominios de la otra, con sus buques ya sean mercantes ó de guerra publicos ó particulares, por mal tiempo, persecucion de piratas ó enemigos, serán recibidos y tratados con humanidad, dandoles todo favor y proteccion, para reparar sus buques,

procuring provisions, and placing themselves in a situation to continue their voyage, without obstacle or hindrance of any Kind.

ARTICLE 10.

All the ships, merchandize, and the effects belonging to the citizens of one of the contracting parties, which may be captured by pirates, whether within the limits of its jurisdiction, or on the high seas, and may be carried or found in the rivers, roads, bays, ports, or dominions of the other, shall be delivered up to the owners, their proving in due and proper form their rights before the competent tribunals, it being well understood that the claim should be made within the term of one year by the parties themselves, their attorneys, or agents of the respective Governments.

ARTICLE 11.

When any vessel belonging to the citizens of either of the contracting parties, shall be wrecked, foundered, or shall suffer any damage on the coasts, or within the dominions of the other, there shall be given to them all assistance and protection in the same manner, which is usual and customary with the vessels of the nation, where the damage happens, permitting them to unload the said vessel, if necessary of its merchandize and effects, without exacting for it any duty, impost,

procurar viveres, y ponerse en situacion de continuar su viaje sin obstáculo ó estorbo de ningun genero.

ARTICULO 10.

Todos los buques, mercaderias, y efectos pertenecientes á los ciudadanos de una de las partes contratantes, que sean apresados por piratas, bien sea dentro de los límites de su jurisdiccion, ó en alta mar, y fueren llevados, ó hallados en los rios, radas, bahias, puertos ó dominios de la otra, serán entregados á sus dueños, probando estos en la forma propia y debida, sus derechos ante los tribunales competentes; bien entendido, que el reclamo ha de hacerse dentro del término de un año, por las mismas partes, sus apoderados, ó agentes de los respectivos Gobiernos.

ARTICULO 11.

Cuando algun buque perteneciente á los ciudadanos de alguna de las partes contratantes, naufrague, encalle, ó sufra alguna averia en las costas, ó dentro de los dominios de la otra, se les dará toda ayuda y proteccion, del mismo modo que es uso y costumbre con los buques de la nacion en donde suceda la averia; permitiéndoles descargar el dicho buque, si fuere necesario, de sus mercaderias y efectos, sin cobrar pr esto hasta que sean exportadas, ningun derecho, impuesto, ó con-

or contribution whatever, until they may be exported, unless they be destined for consumption.

ARTICLE 12.

The citizens of each of the contracting parties shall have power to dispose of their personal goods within the jurisdiccion of the other by sale, donation, testament or otherwise, and their representatives, being citizens of the other party, shall succeed to their said personal goods, whether by testament, or *ab intestato*, and they may take possession thereof, either by themselves or others acting for them, and dispose of the same at their will, paying such dues only as the inhabitants of the country, wherein the said goods are, shall be subject to pay in like cases. And if in the case of real state, the said heirs would be prevented from entering into the possession of the inheritance, on account of their caracter of aliens; there shall be granted to them, the term of three years to dispose of the same, as they may think proper, and to withdraw the proceeds without molestation, nor any other charges than those which are imposed by the laws of the country.

ARTICLE 13.

Both the contracting parties, promise, and engage formally, to give their special protection to the persons and property of the citi-

ARTICULO 12.

Los ciudadanos de cada una de las partes contratantes tendrán pleno poder para disponer de sus bienes personales, dentro de la jurisdiccion de la otra, por venta, donacion, testamento, ó de otro modo; y sus representantes, siendo ciudadanos de la otra parte, succederán á sus dichos bienes personales, ya sea por testamento ó *ab intestato*, y podrán tomar posesion de ellos, ya sea por sí mismos, ó por otros que obren por ellos, y disponer de los mismos segun su voluntad, pagando aquellas cargas solamente, que los habitantes del pais en donde estan los referidos bienes estuvieren sujetos á pagar en iguales casos. Y si en el caso de bienes raices los dichos herederos fuesen impedidos de entrar en la posesion de la herencia, por razon de su caracter de extrangeros, se les dará el termino de tres años, para disponer de ella como juzguen conveniente, y para extraer su producto sin molestia, ni otros impuestos que los establecidos por las leyes del pais.

ARTICULO 13.

Ambas partes contratantes se comprometen y obligan formalmente á dar su proteccion especial á las personas y propiedades de

zens of each other, of all occupations, who may be in the territories subject to the jurisdiction of the one or the other, transient or dwelling therein, leaving open and free to them the Tribunals of Justice for their judicial recourse on the same terms which are usual and costumary with the natives or citizens of the country in which they may be; for which they may employ in defence of their rights such advocates, solicitors, notaries, agents, and factors, as they may judge proper in all their trials at law; and such citizens or agents, shall have free opportunity to be present at the decissions and sentences of the Tribunals in all cases, which may concern them, and likewise at the taking of all examinations and evidence which may be exhibited on the said trials.

ARTICLE 14.

The citizens of the United States residing in the territories of the Republic of Venezuela, shall enjoy the most perfect and entire security of conscience without being annoyed, prevented, or disturbed on account of their religious belief. Neither shall they be annoyed, molested, or disturbed in the proper exercise of their religion in private houses, or in the chapels or places of worship appointed for that purpose, with the decorum due to divine worship, and with

los ciudadanos de cada una reciprocamente, transeuntes ó habitantes, de todas ocupaciones, en los territorios sujetos á la jurisdiccion de una y otra, dejándoles abiertos y libres los tribunales de justicia para sus recursos judiciales, en los mismos terminos que son de uso y costumbre para los naturales ó ciudadanos del pais en que residan; para lo cual, podrán emplear en defensa de sus derechos, aquellos abogados, procuradores, escribanos, agentes, ó factores que juzguen conveniente, en todos sus asuntos y litijios; y dichos ciudadanos ó agentes tendrán la libre facultad de estar presentes en las decisiones y sentencias de los tribunales, en todos los casos que conciernan á aquellos, como igualmente al tomar todos los exâmenes y declaraciones que se ofrezcan en los dichos litijios.

ARTICULO 14.

Los ciudadanos de la Republica de Venezuela residentes en los territorios de los Estados Unidos, gozarán una perfecta é ilimitada libertad de conciencia sin ser molestados, inquietados ni perturbados por su creencia religiosa. Ni serán molestados, inquietados ó perturbados en el egercicio de su religion en casas privadas, en las capillas, ó lugares de adoracion designados al efecto con el decoro debido á la divinidad y respeto á las leyes, usos y costumbres del

due respect to the laws, usages, and customs of the country. Liberty shall also be granted to bury the citizens of the United States who may die in the territories of the Republic of Venezuela, in convenient and adequate places to be appointed and established by themselves for that purpose, with the knowledge of the local authorities, or in such other places of sepulture as may be chosen by the friends of the deceased. Nor shall the funerals or sepulcres of the dead be disturbed in any wise nor upon any account.

In like manner the citizens of Venezuela shall enjoy within the Government and territories of the United states a perfect and unrestrained liberty of conscience, and of exercising their religion publicly or privately within their own dwelling houses, or in the chapels and places of worship appointed for that purpose agreeable to the laws, usages and customs of the United States.

pais. Tambien tendrán libertad para enterrar los ciudadanos de Venezuela que mueran en los territorios de los Estados Unidos, en los lugares convenientes y adecuados, designados y establecidos por ellos con acuerdo de las autoridades locales, ó en los lugares de sepultura que elijan los amigos de los muertos; y los funerales y sepulcros no serán trastornados de modo alguno ni por ningun motivo.

De la misma manera los ciudadanos de los Estados Unidos gozarán en los territorios de la Republica de Venezuela perfecta é ilimitada libertad de conciencia; y egercerán su religion publica ó privadamente en sus mismas habitaciones, ó en las capillas y lugares de adoracion designados al efecto, de conformidad con las leyes, usos y costumbres de la Republica de Venezuela.

ARTICLE 15.

It shall be lawful for the citizens of the United States of America and of the Republic of Venezuela to sail with their ships with all manner of liberty and security, no distinction being made who are the proprietors of the merchandizes laden thereon, from any port to the places of those, who now are, or hereafter shall be,

ARTICULO 15.

Será lícito á los ciudadanos de la Republica de Venezuela y de los Estados Unidos de America navegar con sus buques con toda seguridad y libertad, de cualquier puerto, á las plazas ó lugares de los que son ó fueren en adelante enemigos de cualquiera de las dos partes contratantes, sin hacerse distincion de quienes son los

at enmity with either of the contracting parties. It shall likewise be lawful for the citizens aforesaid to sail with their ships and merchandizes before-mentioned, and to trade with the same liberty and security from the places, ports, and havens of those who are enemies of both or either party, without any opposition or disturbance whatsoever, not only directly from the places of the enemy before-mentioned to neutral places, but also from one place belonging to an enemy to another place belonging to an enemy, whether they be under the jurisdiction of one power or under several. And it is hereby stipulated that free ships shall also give freedom to goods, and that every thing shall be deemed to be free and exempt, which shall be found on board the ships belonging to the citizens of either of the contracting parties, although the whole lading or any part thereof should appertain to the enemies of either; contraband goods being always excepted. It is also agreed in like manner that the same liberty shall be extended to persons who are on board a free ship, with this effect, that although they be enemies to both or either party, they are not to be taken out of that free ship, unless they are officers or soldiers, and in the actual service of the enemies. Provided, however, and it is hereby agreed, that the

dueños de las mercancias cargadas en ellos. Será igualmente lícito á los referidos ciudadanos navegar con sus buques y mercaderias mencionadas, y traficar con la misma libertad y seguridad, de los lugares, puertos y ensenadas de los enemigos de ambas partes, ó de alguna de ellas, sin ninguna oposicion, ó disturbio cualquiera, no solo directamente de los lugares del enemigo arriba mencionados á lugares neutros, sino tambien de un lugar perteneciente á un enemigo, á otro enemigo ya sea que esten bajo la jurisdiccion de una potencia ó bajo la de diversas. Y queda aqui estipulado que los buques libres dan tambien libertad á las mercaderias, y que se ha de considerar libre y exento todo lo que se hallare á bordo de los buques pertenecientes á los ciudadanos de cualquiera de las partes contratantes, aunque toda la carga, ó parte de ella, pertenezca á enemigos de una ú otra, exceptuando siempre los articulos de contrabando de guerra. Se conviene tambien del mismo modo en que la misma libertad se extienda á las personas que se encuentren ábordo de buques libres, con el fin de que aunque dichas personas sean enemigos de ambas partes, ó de alguna de ellas, no deban ser extraidos de los buques libres, á menos que sean oficiales ó soldados en actual servicio de los enemigos á condicion no obstante, y se conviene aqui en esto, que

stipulations in this article contained, declaring that the flag
shal cover the property, shall be
understood as applaying to those
powers only, who recognise this
principle; but if either of the two
contracting parties, shall be at
war with a third, and the other
neutral, the flag of the neutral,
shall cover the property of enemies, whose governments acknowledge this principle, and not
of others.

las estipulaciones contenidas en el
presente articulo, declarando que
el pabellon cubre la propiedad, se
entenderán aplicables solamente
á aquellas potencias que reconocen este principio; pero si alguna
de las dos partes contratantes
estuviese en guerra con una
tercera, y la otra permaneciese
neutral, la bandera de la neutral,
cubrirá la propiedad de los enemigos cuyos gobiernos reconozcan
este principio, y no de otros.

ARTICLE 16.

It is likewise agreed that in the
case where the neutral flag of one
of the contracting parties shall
protect the property of the enemies of the other by virtue of the
above stipulations, it shall always
be understood that the neutral
property found on board such
enemies' vessels, shall be held and
considered as enemies' property,
and as such, shall be liable to
detention and confiscation, except
such property as was put on board
such vessel before the declaration
of war, or even afterwards, if it
were done without the knowledge
of it: but the contracting parties
agree, that two months having
elapsed after the declaration,
their citizens shall not plead
ignorance thereof. On the contrary if the flag of the neutral
does not protect the enemies'
property, in that case the goods
and merchandizes of the neutral

ARTICULO 16.

Se conviene igualmente que en
el caso de que la bandera neutral
de una de las partes contratantes,
proteja las propiedades de los
enemigos de la otra, en virtud de
lo estipulado arriba, deberá siempre entenderse, que las propiedades neutrales encontradas á
bordo de tales buques enemigos,
han de tenerse y considerarse
como propiedades enemigas, y
como tales estarán sujetas á detencion y confiscacion, exceptuando
solamente aquellas propiedades que hubiesen sido puestas á
bordo de tales buques, antes de la
declaracion de la guerra, y aun
despues, si hubiesen sido embarcadas en dichos buques sin tener
noticia de la guerra; y se conviene
que pasados dos meses despues de
la declaracion, los ciudadanos de
una y otra parte no podrán alegar
que la ignoraban Por el contrario si la bandera neutral no

embarked in such enemy's ship, shall be free.

ARTICLE 17.

This liberty of navigation and commerce shall extend to all kinds of merchandize, excepting those only, which are distinguished by the name of contraband, and under this name of contraband or prohibited goods, shall be comprehended:

1st. Cannons, mortars, howitzers, swivels, blunderbusses, muskets, fusees, rifles, carbines, pistols, pikes, swords, sabres, lances, spears, halberds, and granades, bombs, powder, matches, balls, and all other things belonging to to the use of these arms.

2d. Bucklers, helmets, breastpleates, coats of mail, infantry-belts, and clothes made up in the form, and for military use.

3d. Cavalry-belts, and horses with their forniture.

4th. And generally all Kinds of arms and instruments of iron, steel, brass and copper, or of any other materials, manufactured, prepared, and form expressly to make war by sea or land.

ARTICLE 18.

All other merchandises and things not comprehended in the articles of contraband, explicitly

protegiese las propiedades enemigas, entonces serán libres los efectos y mercaderias de la parte neutral embarcadas en buques enemigos.

ARTICULO 17.

Esta libertad de navegacion y comercio se estendera á todo genero de mercaderias exceptuando aquellas solamente que se distinguen con el nombre de contrabando; y bajo este nombre de contrabando ó efectos prohibidos, se comprenderán:

1º Cañones, morteros, obuces, pedreros, trabucos, mosquetes, fusiles, rifles, carabinas, pistolas picas, espadas, sables, lanzas, chuzos, alabardas y granadas, bombas, pólvora, mechas, balas, con las demas cosas correspondientes al uso de estas armas.

2º Escudos, casquetes, corazas, cotas de malla, fornituras y vestidos hecho en forma y á usanza militar.

3º Bandoleras y caballos junto con sus armas y arneses.

4º Y generalmente, toda especie de armas ó instrumentos de hierro acero, bronce, cobre y otras materias cualesquiera, manufacturadas preparadas y formadas espresamente para hacer la guerra por mar ó tierra.

ARTICULO 18.

Todas las demas mercaderias y efectos no comprendidos en los articulos de contrabando explíci-

enumerated and classified as
above, shall be held and considered as free, and subjects of free
and lawful commerce, so that they
may be carried and transported
in the freest manner by the citizens of both the contracting parties, even to places belonging to
an enemy, excepting only those
places which are at that time besieged or blockaded; and to avoid
all doubt in this particular, it is
declared that those places only
are besieged or blockaded, which
are actually attacked by a belligerent force, capable of preventing
the entry of the neutral.

ARTICLE 19.

The articles of contraband before enumerated and classified,
which may be found in a vessel
bound for an enemy's port, shall
be subject to detention and confiscation, leaving free the rest of
the cargo and the ship, that the
owners may dispose of them as
they see proper. No vessel of
either of the two nations shall be
detained on the high seas on account of having on board articles
of contraband: whenever the master, captain or supercargo of said
vessel, will deliver up the articles
of contraband to the captor, unless the quantity of such articles
be so great, or of so large a bulk,
that they cannot be received on
board the capturing ship without

tamente enumerados y clasificados en el artículo anterior, serán
tenidos y reputados por libres, y
de lícito y libre comercio, de modo
que ellos puedan ser transportados y llevados de la manera mas
libre por los ciudadanos de ambas
partes contratantes aún á los
lugares pertenecientes á un enemigo de una ú otra, exceptuando
solamente aquellos lugares ó plazas que están al mismo tiempo
sitiadas ó bloqueadas; y para
evitar toda duda en el particular
se declaran sitiadas ó bloqueadas
aquellas plazas que en la actualidad estuviesen atacadas por una
fuerza de una beligerante, capaz
de impedir la entrada del neutral.

ARTICULO 19.

Los articulos de contrabando
antes enumerados y clasificados,
que se hallen en un buque destinado á puerto enemigo, estarán
sujetos á detencion y confiscacion,
dejando libre el resto del cargamento, y el buque, para que los
dueños puedan disponer de ellos
como lo crean conveniente. Ningun buque de cualquiera de las
dos naciones, será detenido, por
tener á bordo articulos de contrabando, siempre que el maestre,
capitan ó sobrecargo de dicho
buque quiera entregar los articulos de contrabando al apresador,
á menos que la cantidad de estos
articulos sea tan grande y de
tanto volúmen, que no puedan ser
recibidos á bordo del buque apre-

great inconvenience; but in this and in all other cases of just detention, the vessel detained shall be sent to the nearest convenient and safe port, for trial and judggment according to law.

Article 20.

And whereas it frequently happens, that vessels sail for a port or places belonging to an enemy, without knowing that the same is besieged, blockaded, or invested; it is agreed that every vessel so circumstanced may be turned away from such port or place, but shall not be detained, nor shall any part of her cargo, if not contraband, be confiscated, unless, after warning of such blockade or investment, from any officer commanding a vessel of the blockading forces, she shall again attempt to enter; but she shall be permitted to go to any other port or place she shall think proper. Nor shall any vessel of either, that may have entered into such port, before the same was actually besieged, blockaded, or invested by the other, be restrained from quitting such place with her cargo, nor if found therein after the reduction and surrender, shall such vessel or her cargo be liable to confiscation, but they shall be restored to the owners thereof.

sador, sin grandes inconvenientes; pero en este, como en todos los otros casos de justa detencion, el buque detenido será enviado al puerto mas inmediato, cómodo y seguro, para ser juzgado y sentenciado conforme á las leyes.

Articulo 20.

Y por cuanto frecuentemente sucede que los buques navegan para un puerto ó lugar perteneciente á un enemigo sin saber que aquel este sitiado, bloqueado, ó envestido, se conviene en que todo buque en estas circunstancias se pueda hacer volver de dicho puerto ó lugar, pero no será detenido, ni confiscada parte alguna de su cargamento, no siendo contrabando; á menos que despues de la intimacion de semejante bloqueo ó ataque, por cualquier comandante de un buque de las fuerzas bloqueadoras, intentase otra vez entrar; pero le será permitido ir á cualquiera otro puerto ó lugar que juzgue conveniente. Ni ningun buque de una de las partes que haya entrado en semejante puerto ó lugar antes que estuviese sitiado, bloqueado ó envestido, por la otra, será impedido de dejar el tal lugar con su cargamento, ni si fuere hallado alli despues de la rendicion y entrega de semejante lugar, estará el tal buque ó su cargamento sujeto á confiscacion, sino que serán restituidos á sus dueños.

ARTICLE 21.

In order to prevent all kind of disorder in the visiting and examination of the ships ands cargos of both the contracting parties on the high seas, they have agreed mutually, that whenever a vessel of war public or private shall meet with a neutral of the other contracting party, the first shall remain out of cannonshot, and may send its boat with two or three men only, in order to execute the said examination of the papers concerning the ownership and cargo of the vessel without causing the least extortion, violence, or ill-treatment, for which the commanders of the said armed ship, shall be responsible with their persons and property: for which purpose the commanders of said private armed vessels shall, before receiving their commissions, give sufficient security to answer for all the damages they may commit; and it is expressly agreed that the neutral party shall in no case be required to go on board the examining vessel for the purpose of exhibiting his papers or for any other purpose whatever.

ARTICLE 22.

To avoid all kind of vexation and abuse in the examination of the papers relating to the ownership of the vessels, belonging to

ARTÍCULO 21.

Para evitar todo genero de desorden en la visita y exâmen de los buques y cargamentos de ambas partes contratantes, en alta mar, han convenido mútuamente, que siempre que un buque de guerra público, ó particular, se encontrase con un neutral de la otra parte contratante, el primero permanecerá fuera de tiro de cañon, y podrá mandar su bote con dos ó tres hombres solamente, paga egecutar el dicho exâmen de los papeles concernientes á la propiedad y carga del buque, sin ocacionar la menor extorcion, violencia ó mal tratamiento, por lo que los comandantes del dicho buque armado serán responsables con sus personas y bienes; á cuyo efecto, los comandantes de buques armados por cuenta de particulares, estarán obligados, antes de entregarseles sus comisiones ó patentes, á dar fianza suficiente para responder de los perjuicios que causen. Y se ha convenido expresamente que en ningun caso se exijirá á la parte neutral que vaya á bordo del buque exâminador con el fin de exîbir sus papeles ó para cualquier otro objeto, sea el que fuere.

ARTÍCULO 22.

Para evitar toda clase de vejamen y abuso en el examen de los papeles relativos á la propiedad de los buques pertenecientes á

the citizens of the two contracting parties, they have agreed and do agree, that in case one of them should be engaged in war, the ships and vessels belonging to the citizens of the other, must be furnished with sea-letters or passports expressing the name, property and bulk of the ship, as also the name and place of habitation of the master or commander of said vessel, in order that it may thereby appear that said ship really and truly belongs to the citizens of one of the parties: they have likewise agreed, that such ship, being laden, besides the said sea-letters or passports, shall also be provided with certificates, containing the several particulars of the cargo, and the place whence the ship sailed, so that it may be known, whether any forbidden or contraband goods be on board the same; which certificates shall be made out by the officers of the place, whence the ship saild, in the accustomed form; without such requisites said vessels may be detained to be adjudged by the competent tribunal, and may be declared legal prize, unless the said defect shall be proved to be owing to accident and satisfied or supplied by testimony entirely equivalent.

Article 23.

It is further agreed that the stipulations above expressed, relative to the visiting and examina-

los ciudadanos de las dos partes contratantes, han convenido y convienen que en caso de que una de ellas estuviere en guerra, los buques y bajeles pertenecientes á los ciudadanos de la otra, serán provistos con letras de mar ó pasaportes, espresando el nombre, propiedad y tamaño del del buque, como tambien el nombre y lugar de la residencia del maestre ó comandante, á fin de que se vea que el buque real y verdaderamente pertenece á los ciudadanos de una de las partes; y han convenido igualmente, que estando cargados los espresados buques, ademas de las letras de mar ó pasaportes, estarán tambien provistos de certificatos que contengan los pormenores del cargamento y el lugar de donde salío el buque, para que asi puedo saberse si hay á su bordo algunos efectos prohibidos ó de contrabando, cuyos certificatos serán hechos por los oficiales del lugar de la procedencia del buque en la forma acostumbrada; sin tales requisitos el dicho buque puede ser detenido para ser juzgado por el tribunal competente, y puede ser declarado buena presa, á menos que prueben que la falta emana de accidente y satisfagan ó suplan el defecto, con testimonios enteramente equivalentes.

Articulo 23.

Se ha convenido ademas, que las estipulaciones anteriores relativas al exâmen y visita de buques, se

tion of vessels shall apply only to those which sail without convoy, and when said vessels shall be under convoy, the verbal declaration of the commander of the convoy on his word of honour, that the vessels, under his protection, belong to the nation whose flag he carries, and, when they are bound to an enemy's port, that they have no contraband goods on board, shall be sufficient.

Article 24.

It is further agreed that in all cases, the established courts for prize causes, in the country to which the prizes may be conducted, shall alone take cognizance of them; and whenever such tribunals of either party shall pronounce judgment against any vessel or goods, or property, claimed by the citizens of the other party, the sentence or decree shall mention the reason or motives, on which the same shall have been founded, and an authenticated copy of the sentence or decree, and of all the proceedings in the case, shall, if demanded be delivered to the commander or agent of said vessel, without any delay, he paying the legal fees for the same.

Article 25.

Whenever one of the contracting parties shall be engaged in war with another state, no citizen of the other contracting party shall accept a commission or let-

aplicarán solamente á los que navegan sin convoy, y cuando los dichos buques estuviesen bajo de convoy, será bastante la declaracion verbal del comandante del convoy bajo su palabra de honor, de que los buques que estan bajo su proctecion pertenecen á la nacion cuya bandera llevan, y cuando se dirijen á un puerto enemigo que dichos buques no tienen á su bordo articulos de contrabando de guerra.

Artículo 24.

Se ha convenido ademas, que en todos los casos que ocurran, solo los tribunales establecidos para causas de presas en el pais á que las presas sean conducidas, tomarán conocimiento de ellas. Y siempre que semejante tribunal de cualquiera de las partes, pronunciase sentencia contra algun buque, ó efectos, ó propiedad reclamada por los ciudadanos de la otra parte, la sentencia ó decreto hará mencion de las razones ó motivos en que aquella se haya fundado, y se entregará sin demora alguna, al comandante ó agente de dicho buque, si lo solicitase, un testimonio autentico de la sentencia ó decreto, ó de todo el proceso, pagando por él los derechos legales.

Artículo 25.

Siempre que una de las partes contratantes estuviese empeñada en guerra con otro estado, ningun ciudadano de la otra parte contratante, aceptará una comision ó

ter of marque, for the purpose of assisting or cooperating hostilely with the said enemy, against the said party so at war, under the pain of being considered as a pirate.

ARTICLE 26.

If by any fatality, which cannot be expected, and which God forbid the two contracting parties should be engaged in a war with each other, they have agreed, and do agree now, for then, that there shall be allowed the term of six months to the merchants residing on the coasts and in the ports of each other, and the term of one year to those who dwell in the interior, to arrange their business and transport their effects wherever the please, giving to them the safe conduct necessary for it, which may serve as a sufficient protection until they arrive at the designated port. The citizens of all other occupations, who may be established in the territories or dominions of the United States and of the Republic of Venezuela, shall be respected and maintained in the full enjoyment of their personal liberty and property, unless their particular conduct shall cause them to forfeit this protection, which in consideration of humanity, the contracting parties engage to give them.

letra de marca, para el objeto de ayudar ó cooperar hostilmente con el dicho enemigo contra la dicha parte que esté así en guerra, bajo la pena de ser tratado como pirata.

ARTICULO 26.

Si por una fatalidad que no puede esperarse, y que Dios no permita, las dos partes contratantes se viesen empeñadas en guerra una con otra, han convenido y convienen de ahora para entonces, que se concederá el término de seis meses á los comerciantes residentes en las costas y en los puertos de entrambas, y el término de un año á los que habitan en el interior, para arreglar sus negocios y transportar sus efectos á donde quieran, dandoles el salvo-conducto necesario para ello, que les sirva de suficiente proteccion hasta que lleguen al puerto que designen. Los ciudadanos de otras ocupaciones que se hallen establecidos en los territorios y dominios de la Republica de Venezuela ó de los Estados Unidos, serán respetados, y mantenidos en el pleno goce de su libertad personal y propiedad, á menos que su conducta particular les haga perder esta proteccion, que en consideracion á la humanidad, las partes contratantes se comprometen á prestarles.

ARTICLE 27.

Neither the debts due from individuals of the one nation to the individuals of the other, nor shares, nor moneys which they may have in public funds, nor in public, or private banks, shall ever in any event of war or of national difference, be sequestered or confiscated.

ARTICLE 28.

Both the contracting parties being desirous of avoiding all inequality in relation to their public communications and official intercourse, have agreed, and do agree, to grant to the envoys, ministers, and other public agents, the same favours, immunities, and exemptions, which those of the most favoured nation do or shall enjoy; it being understood, that whatever favours, immunities, or privileges the United States of America, or the Republic of Venezuela may find it proper to give to the ministers and other public agents of any other power, shall by the same act be extended to those of each of the contracting parties.

ARTICLE 29.

To make more effectual the protection which the United States and the Republic of Venezuela shall afford in future to the navigation and commerce of the citizens of each other they agree to

ARTÍCULO 27.

Ni las deudas contraidas por los individuos de una nacion con los individuos de la otra, ni las acciones ó dineros que puedan tener en los fondos publicos, ó en los bancos públicos ó privados, seran jamas secuestrados ó confiscados en ningun caso de guerra ó de diferencia nacional.

ARTÍCULO 28.

Deseando ambas partes contratantes evitar toda diferencia relativa á etiqueta en sus comunicaciones y correspondencia diplomaticas, han convenido asi mismo y convienen, en conceder á sus enviados y ministros y otros agentes diplomáticos los mismos favores, inmunidades y exenciones de que gozan ó gozaren en lo venidero los de las naciones mas favorecidas; bien entendido, que cualquiera favor, inmunidad, ó privilegio que la Republica de Venezuela ó los Unidos Estados de america tengan por conveniente dispensar á los enviados, ministros y agentes diplomáticos de otras potencias, se haga por el mismo hecho extensivo á los de una y otra de las partes contratantes.

ARTICULO 29.

Para hacer mas efectiva la proteccion que la Republica de Venezuela y los Estados Unidos de América darán en adelante á la navegacion y comercio de los ciudadanos de una y otra, se

receive and admit Consuls and Vice-Consuls in all the ports open to foreign commerce, who shall enjoy in them all the rights, prerogatives, and immunities, of the Consuls and Vice-consuls, of the most favoured nation; each contracting party, however, remaining at liberty to exept those ports and places, in which the admission and residence of such consuls may not seem convenient.

ARTICLE 30.

In order that the consuls and Vice-consuls, of the two contracting parties may enjoy the rights, prerogatives, and immunities, which belong to them by their public character, they shall, before entering on the exercise of their functions, exhibit their commission or patent in due form, to the government to which they are accreditated, and having obtaind their *exequatur*, they shall be held and considered as such, by all the authorities, magistrates and inhabitants in the Consular district in which they reside.

ARTICLE 31.

It is likewise agreed that the consuls, their Secretaries, officers, and persons attached to the service of Consuls, they not being citizens of the country in which the Consul resides, shall be

convienen en recibir y admitir Cónsules y Vice-Cónsules en todos los puertos abiertos al comercio extrangero, quienes gozarán en ellos de todos los derechos, prerrogativas ó inmunidades de los Cónsules y Vice-cónsules de la nacion mas favorecida; quedando no obstante en libertad cada parte contratante para exceptuar aquellos puertos y lugares en que la admision y residencia de semejantes Cónsules y Vice-consules no parezca conveniente.

ARTÍCULO 30.

Para que los Cónsules y Vice-cónsules de las dos partes contratantes, puedan gozar de los derechos, prerrogativas, é inmunidades que les correspondan por su caracter público, antes de entrar en el egercicio de sus funciones, presentarán su comision ó patente en la forma debida al gobierno con quien estén acreditados, y habiendo obtenido el *exequatur*, serán tenidos y considerados como tales por todas las autoridades, magistrados, y habitantes del distrito consular en que residan.

ARTICULO 31.

Se ha convenido igualmente, que los cónsules, sus secretarios oficiales y personas agregadas al servicio de los consulados (no siendo estas personas ciudadanos del pais en que el consul reside)

exempt from all Kind of taxes, imposts, and contributions, except those, which they shall be obliged to pay on account of commerce or their property, to which the citizens and inhabitants, native and foreign, of the country in which they reside, are subject, being in every thing besides subject to the laws of the respective States. The archives and papers of the consulates shall be respected inviolably, and under no pretext whatever, shall any magistrate seize or in any way interfere with them.

ARTICLE 32.

The said Consuls shall have power to require the assistance of the authorities of the country for the arrest, detention and custody of deserters from the public and private vessels of their country, and for that purpose, they shall address themselves to the courts, judges, and officers competent, and shall demand the said deserters in writing; proving by an exhibition of the registers of the vessels, or ships-roll, or other public documents, that those men were part of the said crews, and on this demand so proved (saving however, where the contrary is proved) the delivery shall not be refused. Such deserters, when arrested, shall be put at the disposal of said consuls, and may be put in the public prisons, at the

estarán exentos de todo servicio publico, y tambien de toda especie de pechos, impuestos y contribuciones, exceptuando aquellos que estén obligados á pagar por razon de comercio ó propiedad, y á los cuales estan sugetos los ciudadanos y habitantes, naturales y extrangeros del pais en que residen, quedando en todo lo demas sujetos á las leyes de los respectivos Estados. Los archivos y papeles de los consulados serán respetados inviolablemente, y bajo ningun pretesto los ocupará magistrado alguno, ni tendrá con ellos ninguna intervension

ARTICULO 32.

Los dichos consules tendrán poder de requerir el auxílio de las autoridades locales para la prision, detension y custodia de los desertores de los buques públicos y particulares, de su pais, y para este objeto se dirijirán á los tribunales, jueces y oficiales competentes, y pedirán los dichos desertores por escrito, probando por una presentacion de los registros de los buques, rol del equipage ú otros documentos publicos, que aquellos hombres erán parte de las dichas tripulaciones, y á esta demanda asi probada (menos, no obstante, cuando se probase lo contrario) no se reusará la entrega. Semejantes desertores luego que sean arrestados se pondrán á disposicion de los dichos cónsules, y pueden ser depositados en las

request and expence of those who reclaim them, to be sent to the ships to which they belonged, or to others of the same nation. But if they be not sent back within two months, to be counted from the day of their arrest, they shall be set at liberty, and shall be no more arrested for the same cause.

ARTICLE 33.

For the purpose of more effectually protecting their commerce and navigation, the two contracting parties do hereby agree, as soon hereafter as circumstances will permit them, to form a Consular convention, which shall declare especially the powers and immunities of the Consuls and Vice-consuls of the respective parties.

ARTICLE 34.

The United States of America and the Republic of Venezuela desiring to make as durable as circumstances will permit, the relations which are to be established between the two parties, by virtue of this Treaty of Peace, Amity, Commerce, and Navigation, have declared solemnly, and do agree to the following points:

1st: The present Treaty shall remain in full force and virtue for the term of twelve years to be counted from the day of the exchange of the ratifications and further until the end of one year

prisiones publicas á solicitud y expensas de los que lo reclamen, para ser enviados á los buque á que corresponden ó á otros de la misma nacion. Pero si no fueren mandados dentro de dos meses, contados desde el dia de su arresto, serán puestos en libertad, y no volverán á ser presos por la misma causa.

ARTICULO 33.

Para proteger mas efectivamente su comercio y navegacion, las dos partes contratantes se convienen en formar, luego que las circunstancias lo permitan, una convencion Consular, que declare mas especialmente los poderes é inmunidades de los Cónsules y Vice-consules de las partes respectivas.

ARTICULO 34.

La Republica de Venezuela y los Estados Unidos de America, deseando hacer tan duraderas y firmes, como las circunstancias lo permitan, las relaciones que han de establecerse entre las dos potencias, en virtud del presente Tratado de Paz, Amistad, Navegacion, y Comercio, han declarado solemnemente y convienen en los puntos siguientes:

1º El presente tratado permanecerá en su fuerza y vigor por el termino de doce años, contados desde el dia del cange de las ratificaciones, y ademas hasta un año despues que cualquiera de

after either of the contracting parties shall have given notice to the other of its intention to terminate the same; each of the contracting parties reserving to itself the right of giving such notice to the other at the end of said term of twelve years; and it is hereby agreed between them that on the expiration of one year after such notice shall have been received by either from the other party, this Treaty in all its parts relative to commerce and navigation, shall altogether cease and determine, and in all those parts which relate to peace and friendship it shall be perpetually and permanently binding on both powers.

2d. If any one of more of the citizens of either party, shall infringe any of the articles of this Treaty, such citizen shall be held personally responsible for the same, and harmony and good correspondence between the two nations, shall not be interrupted thereby, each party engaging in no way to protect the offender, or sanction such violation.

3d. If (what, indeed, cannot be expected) unfortunately any of the articles in the present Treaty shall be violated or infringed in any other way whatever, it is expressly stipulated, that neither of the contracting parties will order or authorize any act of reprisal, nor declare

las partes contratantes haya notificado á la otra su intension de terminarlo: reservandose las partes contratantes el derecho de hacer tal notification la una á la otra al fin de dicho termino de doce años. Y ademas se ha convenido que este tratado en todo lo relativo á comercio y navegacion quedará sin efecto transcurrido que sea un año despues de recibida dicha notificacion por cualquiera de los partes, y en todo lo relativo á paz y amistad será perpetuamente obligatorio á ambos poderes.

2º Si alguno ó algunos de los ciudadanos de una ú otra parte, infrinjieren algunos de los artículos contenidos en el presente tratado, dichos ciudadanos serán personalmente responsables, sin que por esto se interrumpa la armonia y buena correspondencia entre las dos naciones, comprometiendose cada una, á no proteger de modo alguno al ofensor, ó sancionar semejante violacion.

3º Si (lo que á la verdad no puede esperarse) desgraciadamente algunos de los articulos contenidos en el presente Tratado fuesen en alguna otra manera violados ó infringidos, se estipula expresamente, que ninguna de las dos partes contratantes, ordenará, ó autorizará ningunos actos

war against the other on complaints of injuries, or damages, until the said party considering itself offended, shall first have presented to the other, a statement of such injuries or damages, verified by competent proofs, and demanded justice, and the same shall have been either refused or unreasonably delayed.

4d. Nothing in this Treaty contained shall, however, be constructed, or operate contrary to former and existing public Treaties With other Sovereigns and States.

The present Treaty of Peace, Amity, Commerce and Navigation, shall be approved and ratified by the President of the United States of America, by and with the advice and consent of the Senate thereof, and by the President of the Republic of Venezuela with the consent and approbation of the Congress of the same, and the ratifications shall be exchanged in the city of Caracas within eight months, to be counted from the date of the signature hereof, or sooner if possible.

In faith whereof, we the Plenipotentiaries, of the United States of America and of the Republic of Venezuela have signed and sealed these presents.

Done in the city of Caracas on the twentieth day of January, in the year of our Lord one thousand

de represalia, ni declarará la guerra contra la otra, por quejas de injurias ó daños, hasta que la parte que se crea ofendida, haya presentado á la otra, una esposicion de aquellas injurias ó daños, verificada con pruebas y testimonios competentes, exîjiendo justicia y satisfaccion, y esto haya sido negado ó diferido sin razon.

4º Nada de cuanto se contiene en el presente tratado se construirá, sin embargo, ni obrará en contra de otros Tratados publicos, anteriores y existentes con otros Soberanos ó Estados.

El presente Tratado de Paz, Amistad, Comercio y Navegacion, será ratificado por el Presidente ó Vice-Presidente de la republica de Venezuela encargado del Poder Egecutivo, con consentimiento y aprobacion del Congreso de la misma, y por el Presidente de los Estados Unidos de America con consejo y aprobacion del Senado de los mismos; y las ratificaciones serán cãgeadas en la ciudad de Caracas dentro de ocho meses contados desde este dia, ó antes si fuere posible.

En fé de lo cual, nosotros los Plenipotenciarios de la Republica de Venezuela y de los Estados Unidos de America, hemos firmado y sellado las presentes.

Dadas en la ciudad de Caracas el dia veinte de Enero, del año del Señor mil ochocientos treinta

eight hundred and thirty six, and
in the sixtieth year of the Independence of the United States of
America, and the twenty-sixth of
that of the Republic of Venezuela.

y seis—Vigesimo sexto de la Independencia de Venezuela y sexâ-
gesimo de la de los Estados
Unidos de America.

JOHN. G. A WILLIAMSON   [Seal]
SANTOS MICHELENA   [Seal]

SANTOS MICHELENA   [Seal]
JOHN. G. A. WILLIAMSON [Seal]

NOTES

Venezuela, previously united with New Granada and Ecuador in the
Republic of Colombia, "was formally recognized by the United States
as an independent state by the issuance of an exequatur to Mr.
Nicholas D. C. Moller, as Venezuelan Consul at New York, February
25, 1835" (Moore, Digest, I, 90).

In the instructions of April 15, 1835, to John G. A. Williamson,
who on the previous March 3 had been appointed Chargé d'Affaires
to the Republic of Venezuela, Secretary of State Forsyth wrote regarding the attitude of the United States as follows (D. S., 1 Instructions, Venezuela, 2–3):

A recognition of the Republic of Venezuela has been delayed under the expectation that a reunion might be effected between the States once forming the Republic
of Colombia. Desiring only that the neighbouring nations might adopt and
pursue such a policy as would be most calculated in their own opinions to promote and secure their permanent interests, the United States have been at all
times prepared to acquiesce in whatever has been done by them, confidently
believing that separated into independent Governments or confederated under
one, justice will be equally done to their desire to promote mutual interests by
acts of reciprocal good will and the faithful observance of all the obligations of
good neighbourhood. While it appeared probable that the several States composing the Republic of Colombia, with whom a treaty had been formed, would
re-unite, it was due to consistency to refrain from recognising formally the separated portions of the Republic: as it is now ascertained that the separation is to
be permanent, and the parties have themselves amicably arranged the terms of
it, the President is happy to congratulate them on the event, and to proceed to
welcome each on its entrance into the great American family of nations. The
President considers the treaty with Colombia [Document 47] as forming the basis
of our commercial and navigating intercourse with Venezuela, New Granada and
Equador, and obligatory upon each and all of them. This is understood to be
acknowledged by Venezuela, from the tenor of the Report of the Minister of
Foreign Affairs to the Congress of Venezuela of the 20ᵗʰ of January, last. That
Minister, with great prudence and propriety suggests, that the dismemberment
of the Republic and the new order of things produced by that event, required the
conclusion of other compacts. Mr Michelena, the Envoy of Venezuela at Bogotá
has expressed the same sentiment to Mr McAfee, adding that his government
would promptly and cheerfully empower him to enter upon the negotiation of a
treaty, should the disposition of Venezuela be reciprocated by the United States,
and Mr McAfee be authorized to carry that disposition into effect. Obvious
reasons, however, having led the President to prefer Caraccas to Bogotá as the
seat of the negotiation, the duty of concluding the compact will devolve upon
you, and you are herewith provided with a full power for that purpose.

THE FILE PAPERS

Three originals of this treaty were signed; John G. A. Williamson, Chargé d'Affaires at Caracas, the United States Plenipotentiary, wrote of "a second original" in his despatch of February 11, 1836 (D. S., 1 Despatches, Venezuela, No. 16); and the instructions to Williamson of April 20, 1836 (D. S., 1 Instructions, Venezuela, 20), mention "both the copies [meaning originals] of the Treaty sent by you"; but only one of those two originals for this Government has been found. It seems that the other original was sent to Bogotá with instructions of April 21, 1836, to Robert B. McAfee, Chargé d'Affaires to New Granada (D. S., 15 Instructions, Colombia, 29–30), for in that instruction, authorizing the negotiation of a treaty with Ecuador on the basis of this treaty with Venezuela, there is written: "The copy of the Treaty with Venezuela which accompanies this letter, being a duplicate, need not be returned, but may be deposited among the archives of your Legation."

The signed original of this treaty which is in the file is written in English and Spanish, with the English text in the left columns. The *alternat* was properly observed, as the printed texts show.

The treaty file is complete, including the attested resolution of the Senate of March 23, 1836 (Executive Journal, IV, 525). All the documents are in customary form. The duplicate United States instrument of ratification of April 20, 1836, is bound with the original proclamation of June 20, in which is embodied the signed original of the treaty. The Venezuelan instrument of ratification of May 25, 1836, contains both texts of the treaty, the Spanish in the left columns. There are two originals of the certificate of the exchange of ratifications at Caracas on May 31, 1836, each written in both languages.

The texts above printed, English and Spanish, have, in accordance with the rule for this edition, been collated with the signed original of the treaty which is in the file and which is quite carelessly written. It appears, however, that certain corrections were made in the United States instrument of ratification, although precisely what they were cannot be stated, as no facsimile thereof is available. In the instructions of April 20, 1836 (D. S., 1 Instructions, Venezuela, 20), with which was transmitted the United States instrument of ratification, is the following:

I regret to say that in both the copies of the Treaty sent by you, there was a general inaccuracy of accentuation and punctuation and there were some material errors in the words, all of which, however, have been corrected in the ratified copy.

It appears that no papers accompanied this treaty when it was transmitted to the Senate with the presidential message of March 7, 1836 (Executive Journal, IV, 517), and no papers are with the Senate print of the treaty (Senate Confidential Document, March 7, 1836, 24th Congress, 1st session, Regular Confidential Documents, VI, 647–66).

The treaty was communicated to Congress with the presidential message of June 30, 1836 (Richardson, III, 231).

The Full Powers

The full power given to John G. A. Williamson, Chargé d'Affaires at Caracas, is dated March 21, 1835, and is in customary form, although it included power to treat regarding "claims of the citizens of the two countries respectively upon the Governments of the United States and the said Republic of Venezuela" (D. S., 2 Credences, 230).

Whether the original full powers were exchanged is not expressly stated in the despatches. In his despatch of January 30, 1836 (D. S., 1 Despatches, Venezuela, No. 15), Williamson wrote of the "exchange" thereof which was to have been made on January 8 and also that they were "exhibited"; but with that despatch was enclosed a copy in Spanish, with an English translation, of a certified copy of the full power, dated January 5, 1836, to Santos Michelena, the Venezuelan Plenipotentiary (formerly Secretary of State for Foreign Relations) to negotiate and conclude the treaty. The translation reads as follows:

The President of the Republic of Venezuela

To all whom these presents may concern, Greeting:

Whereas relations of friendship, navigation, and commerce have existed for some years past between the Republic of Venezuela and the United States of North America, which, for their respective interests, it is proper to regulate, consolidate, and fix in a manner clear, distinct, and positive by means of a formal and express treaty; therefore, and reposing entire confidence in the integrity, capacity, and other qualities of Santos Michelena, we have thought fit to appoint him, and by these presents do appoint, commission, and authorize him with special and ample powers, to negotiate, adjust, and conclude said treaty, in conformity with the instructions given him, with the Chargé d'Affaires of the United States residing in this capital and invested by the President of said States with the necessary power and authority *ad hoc.*

In faith whereof we give these presents, signed with our hand, sealed in due form, and countersigned by the Secretary of State for Foreign Affairs in Caracas the 5th of January, 1836, seventh of the law and twenty-sixth of independence.

[Seal]   José Vargas

By the President:
José E. Gallegos

José E. Gallegos, Secretary of State for Foreign Affairs. I certify that this copy in all respects agrees with the original.

Caracas, 5th of January, 1836, seventh of the law and twenty-fifth of independence.

José E. Gallegos

The original full powers to exchange the ratifications were perhaps also exchanged. In his despatch of May 31, 1836 (D. S., 1 Despatches, Venezuela, No. 19), Williamson wrote that his "special power . . . was required by this [the Venezuelan] Government". The record copy thereof is in D. S., 2 Credences, 245; and a copy of that given by the Government of Venezuela under date of May 30, 1836, to José Eusebio Gallegos, Secretary of State for the Departments of the Treasury and of Foreign Relations, is in the treaty file.

TERMS OF THE TREATY

While this Government regarded the treaty with Colombia of October 3, 1824 (Document 47), as binding on Venezuela, that treaty was not, in 1835, a very lasting basis of relations, as it was to terminate "in all the parts relating to commerce and navigation" on May 27, 1837, twelve years after the exchange of ratifications; and the instructions to Williamson of April 15, 1835 (D. S., 1 Instructions, Venezuela, 2–13), contemplated "a more liberal basis":

As the treaty with Colombia [Document 47], though in many respects mutually beneficial, does not secure for our commerce and navigation all the advantages which are at once desirable and not incompatible with the interests and obligations of the States of which that Republic was formed, the President desires that a more liberal basis should be proposed to the Venezuelan Government.

[Here follow seven paragraphs copied almost literally from the instructions to John Hamm of October 15, 1830; see the first eight paragraphs quoted in the note to Document 73 on "Commercial Policy".]

The principle upon which you will first endeavour to negotiate with the Venezuelan Government is that on which the Act of 1828 [act of May 24, 1828, 4 Statutes at Large, 308–9] was based. You will find it unfolded in the third, fourth and fifth articles of the Treaty concluded in 1828 with Brazil, which adopts our system in its full extent, as to the equalization of duties on tonnage and imports, whatever may be the nature and origin of the cargoes or from whence imported.

.   .   .   .

The rule of our relations, by the second article of the treaty with Colombia [Document 47], is that of the most favored nation in respect to commerce and navigation: if either party grant special favors to another nation, it becomes common to the other party, who shall enjoy the same freely, if the concession was freely made, or on allowing the same compensation, if the concession was conditional. This stipulation leaves either government at liberty to burthen vexatiously the commerce and navigation of the other, to foster its own mercantile and navigating interest. Independently of this great objection, which leaves the relations between the parties liable to be constantly trammelled or overloaded by restrictions on one side, counteracted by retaliatory restrictions on the other, the rule of the most favored nation, even explained as it is in the second article, has been found in practice to be uncertain and illusory in effecting the avowed objects of the parties; that is, to give to each a fair competition in the ports of the other with all foreign nations. Favors may be granted to some nations by one party, for which the same compensation cannot be allowed by the other. With the best intentions on both sides, this may occur; with a desire to disregard the spirit of the article by either, it will constantly happen. . . .

If, therefore, you should not find the Venezuelan administration disposed to treat upon the basis first mentioned, it is the wish of the President that you should represent to them that he considers the Treaty with Colombia [Document 47] as reciprocally binding, and that as it is so considered by Venezuela, he deems it unnecessary to enter upon the negotiation of a treaty upon the same basis—at least until our Convention with Colombia [Document 47] shall expire. You will also represent that as it is presumed Venezuela likewise deems the treaties of Colombia with Central America and Peru as obligatory upon her, it is considered, for the reasons specified, that the United States under the second article of their treaty with Colombia, have a clear right to the same advantages which are secured to those Republics in Venezuelan ports, and that if discriminating duties upon our vessels and their cargoes should not be repealed, the President will be constrained to cause the privileges now enjoyed in our ports by vessels of the Colombian States, to be abolished.

Should you induce the Venezuelan Government to assent to a treaty placing the commerce and navigation of the parties on the basis of our Act of 1828, for the other articles you will adopt as a model the treaty with Brazil, with the following exceptions.

It is understood that the people of Venezuela are less bigoted in their attachment to the predominant religion than those of any of the Spanish American
States, and that the authorities of that country tolerate protestant worship.   As
this liberal feeling, however, may change, you will propose to substitute the 12th
article of the treaty between Great Britain and Colombia [British and Foreign
State Papers, XII, 661–73] for the 11th of ours, with the following additions.   In
the second sentence of the article, after the words 'private houses,' add 'or in the
chapels or places of worship appointed for that purpose'; omitting the words
'provided that this take place.'   In the third sentence, after the words 'local
authorities,' add, 'or in such other places of sepulture as may be chosen by the
friends of the deceased.'   If you should not obtain the assent of the Venezuelan
Government to the substitution of the British article as thus modified, you may
propose that that article be inserted as it now stands.

The treaty with Colombia [Document 47] was to continue in force twelve years,
but no provision like that contained in the treaties with Prussia, Austria, Sweden,
Russia and Brazil, is made for its continued duration.   You may propose twelve,
ten, or eight years for the duration of the treaty, and a clause for its continuance
similar to that in the treaties referred to.

In all essentials, and even in language, this treaty is very much the
same as the treaty with Brazil of December 12, 1828 (Document 64).
The exceptions in that treaty (Article 2) in favor of Portugal are
naturally omitted; Article 5 of the treaty with Venezuela is somewhat
fuller than the corresponding clause of Article 4 of the treaty with
Brazil; Article 13 of this treaty has a final clause which is omitted from
Article 12 of the treaty with Brazil; Article 14, regarding religious
freedom, is here more complete; the concluding sentence of Article 19
of the treaty with Brazil is here omitted; and in wording Article 21
of this treaty differs from Article 20 of the treaty with Brazil; but
those differences, even in their totality, are minor and unimportant;
and there was a still earlier American treaty—that with the Central
American Federation of December 5, 1825 (Document 50)— in which
were written the bases of both that treaty with Brazil and this with
Venezuela.   But it is of course not intimated that the clauses in the
Central American treaty were themselves the beginning of a policy;
rather, they expressed a policy which began earlier and the development of which is described in the extract from the instructions of
Secretary of State Van Buren of October 15, 1830, quoted in the note
to Document 73 on "Commercial Policy".   The difference between
the policy of this treaty and that of the treaty with Colombia (Document 47) which, as to Venezuela, it replaced, may be best seen by
noting that the most-favored-nation clauses of Article 2 of both
treaties are entirely similar, and then reading Article 2 along with the
nondiscriminatory and national-treatment clauses of Articles 3, 4,
and 6 of this treaty in contrast with Article 2 plus the most-favored-
nation clauses of Article 3 of the treaty with Colombia.

Treaty Series No. 244—2
8 Statutes at Large, 484-87
18 *ibid.*, pt. 2, Public Treaties, 521-25

81

MOROCCO : SEPTEMBER 16, 1836

Treaty of Peace, signed at Meccanez (Meknès or Mequinez) September 16, 1836 (3 Jumada II, A.H. 1252). Original in Arabic.

A document including a copy of the treaty in Arabic and an English translation, followed by a clause of conclusion under the seal of the United States consulate at Tangier, was signed by James R. Leib, consul and agent of the United States, on October 1, 1836.

Submitted to the Senate December 26, 1836. (Message of December 20, 1836.) Resolution of advice and consent January 17, 1837. Ratified by the United States January 28, 1837. As to the ratification generally, see the notes. Proclaimed January 30, 1837.

The following twenty-six pages of Arabic text are a reproduction of the pages of the original treaty; but they are arranged in left-to-right order of pagination. Then, from the above-mentioned document signed by James R. Leib on October 1, 1836, is printed the English translation, with the clause of conclusion reserving the treaty for the ratification of the President by and with the advice and consent of the Senate.

33

بسم الله الرحمٰن الرحيم

الحمد لله هذا تفصيل شروط الصلح التي جعلناها مع الماركانوس وأثبتناها بهذا الدفتر ووضعنا عليها طابعنا الشريع لتبقى مستمرة إنشاء الله وكتب بحضرة مكناسة الزيتون في ثالث جمادى الأخيرة عام اثنين وخمسين ومايتين وألف

الشــــــرط الاوّل

إِنَّ هٰذِهِ الشُّروطَ المَذْكورَةَ
في هٰذا الدَّفْتَرِ وَهِيَ خَمْسَةٌ
وَعِشْرونَ شَرْطاً قَدْ قَبِلْناها مِنَ
الجانِبَيْنِ وَذٰلِكَ عَلى يَدِ والوافِيَ
عَلى أُمورِهِمْ وَكيلِهِمْ وَفَوَّضْتُهُمْ
جيشُنا أَعيبُ المُعَيَّنِ وَفَتَّقَهْ
بِمُحَرَّمٍ لِسَنَةِ طَنْجَة
ة

2

الشَّرْطُ الثَّانِي أَنَّهُ مَهْمَا
كَانَتِ القِرَاءَةُ مَعَ أَيِّ جِنْسٍ
كَانَ وَلَا تَخْرُجُ مَعِينَةٌ مِنْ إِحْدَى
الجَانِبَيْنِ وَتَعْمَلُ تَنْبُوا العَدُوّ
وَتَذْهَبُ تَعْيِينَ العَدُوِّ وَالمَاسِى
جِهَتِهَا وَإِمَّا مِنْ جِهَةِ المَازِكَانُوسِ

a

٣ الشَّرْطُ الثَّالِثُ أَقَدَمْتَى

جَعَلَتِ الْقِتْرَة مَعَ أَتِى جَنْسٍ كَانَ

وَقَبَضَتْ سَفِينَة مِنْ أَهْلِ الكِ

الجِنْس وَوُجِدَ مِعْهَا مُسْلِمًا آفْ

نَصْرَانِيًّا وَلَمْ سَلْعَة بِأَنَّهُمْ

يَتَرَحَّوْن بِسِلَعِهِمْ وَحَتَّى إِذَ اَكَانُوا

حَامِلِينَ سِلْعَة لِجِنْسٍ وَبَيْنَمَا وَبَيْنَهَ

الْقِتْرَة بَلَا تُوخَذْ مِنْ ايْدِيهِمْ وَأَيَكَلَّفُوا

بِمَرِّ لِهَا حَا بَيْنَنَا وَيَسْتَمِرْ مِنَ الْقَلْه

الشرط الرابع تكون

٤

بعينها علامة يعرف بها بعضنا

بعضاً به البيع ومما العينى أصدقاً

معينة القيمة لا ينجعث عنها

وإنما يكيبه كلاغ التراييس

بينا بقلامع شعبى اُختِز

الشرط الخامس أنه مهما
تخلّفت الشعوب في البرّ وكانت العزلة
وإن كل واحد من الجهتين ما يبعث
لاختبار السفينة التي أراد اختبارها
لا لملوكة واحدة بينهما اثنان
أو ثلاثة بقعا ومهما خرجت بحمارة
ولا كسرت شيئا من أحد الجمعتين
من غيركم به وإن صاحب العمارة
التي خرجت يصلح للاخر ما قبض
له

الشرط السادس أن أقف منا فيض

٦

المسلمون أهل جميعا أو سلعتهم

وأقنوا بهم يسير دانص إذ الله

مانه يصرح وكذ إلك إذ انقض

مسلمون من غير إذا ابتنا وذ خلوا

بهم لأحدى مراسينا قا انهم

يسم حور إ انهم تحت إما ننا وما

تحيّر معنا

٧

الشَّرْطُ السَّابِعُ أنَّهُ مَتَى
وَرَدَتْ سَفِينَةٌ لِأَحَدَى مَرَاسِ
انجلاننير تَغتيم كمانينة أوْ
غَيرهَا بإنَّها تَغتير وَذلِكَ
مِنْ غَيرِ مَشَقَّةٍ وَلَا حَرَجٍ

الشرط الثامن أقدمتي وقع
٨ بإحدى الشعبى شيئًا ومالت إلى البحر
ووضعت ونسفها حتى اضطحت ما
يسر منها فإنها فإنما أرادت تحمل
ذلك البط الوثنى الذى وضعت فإنها
تحمله من غير طاكتة ولا غيرها

الشرط التاسع أنه متى حرثت سفينة
بحاجبة من نواجبنا وإنما تبغى على حالها
حتى تمدها ما يصلح لها إما الخروج من
موضع آخر أو نغل المتاع أو غير ذلك
مما لوجوه التي تليق بها ولا يغنى بها
أحدًا لا نساء أمانتا وكذلك إذا دخلت
سفينة للمرسية أو أجاها الريح حتى
دخلت للمرسية ولا تكلف بنزول
متاعها بل تبغى على أمان حتى تخرج
برضاها

١٥

الشرط العاشر إنه قد متى وقع قتال من
إحدى الجانبين مع بعض أجناس النصرى
وكان القتال فرضا من بعض مدرا الجانبين
بإننا نعين بعضنا على داخل الجنس
حتى يغلب أو يبذ جميع أو حرثت
معينته ؏ وإذ نون أو ثمين ؏ فإن
النصرى الذي يرى بهاي ذما ان حتى
يطلبون بلاد ثمم إن شاء الله

الشَّرْطُ الحَادِي عَشَرَ أَنَّهُ مَتَى كَانَتِ الغَزْوُ

11

بَيْنَنَا وَيَخْرُجُ جِنْسٌ مِنْ أَجْنَاسِ النَّصَارَى وَكُنَّا

بِالمَرْسَةِ وَأَرَادَتْ سَفِينَتُنَا الخُرُوجَ مِنَ المَرْبِيَّة

وَأَرَادَتْ سَفِينَةُ العَدُوِّ وَتَتْبَعُهَا فَلَا تَخْرُجُ

تَتْبَعُهَا حَتَّى تَمْضِيَ مِنَ الزَّمَانِ أَرْبَعَةٌ

وَعِشْرُونَ سَاعَةً وَكَذَلِكَ سُفُنُ التُّجَّارِ كَانُوا

إِذَا كَانَتْ بِالمَرْسَةِ وَقْتَ زَمَانِ الغَزْوِ وَأَرَا

دَتِ الخُرُوجَ فَلَا تَتْبَعُهَا سَفِينَةٌ حَتَّى تَمْضِيَ

أَرْبَعَةٌ وَعِشْرُونَ سَاعَةً سَوَاءٌ كَانَتْ مِنْ

سُفُنِ المُسْلِمِينَ أَوْ مِنْ سُفُنِ النَّصَارَى

١٢ الشروط الثالث عشر أنّه متى وردت
سفينة الكرة على أحد مراسينا
بأنها تفتش بل أتبقى على حالها
ومهما كان بها أسير أهاربا فإنّه
لا يُنزل منه كرهًا ولا يطلب عامل
تلك البلاد الذي به السفينة من
ربّ السفينة قيمة ذلك الأسير

الشرط الثالث عشر أنه متى

13

وردت سفينة العثور على إيرواب
وردت وأخرجت المدا مع بإنما
لا تخرج عليها من تلك المرسى
إلا مثل ما أخرجت من غير زيـــــــادة
زيــادةٍ ولا نقْـــصـانٍ

14

الشرط الرابع عشر أن قسمها
التجار يكونون على عادة
تجار اصطنبول ويكونون
معتبرين ويكونون مثل
الجمس العزيز عند نا ج
ألوفت ويذهبون ج أخرى
والمواسي حيث شاء ولا
يتعرض لهم أحـــد

١٥

الشرط الخامس عشر أن التجار يكونوا
مشتغلين بالشبان وإذا أرادوا و—أ
يتعلمون من يثق معهم أو ترجمان بلا
بأمر بذلك وكل يغلب وسوسعينة
إلى أخرى ولا تنفع سعينة إحدى مسة
وإذا أرادوا يعلمون من يعاونهم
على أمور الوسق أو غيرها فإنهم
ما يعطون سوى ألغذ زاللي يعطوا
الأجناس من قبلهم —

١٦

الشرط السادس من عشر أنه متى كان
النصراء من الجانبين هان الأساري
يكونون رأسا برأس والترابيس بالترابيس
ومنهم رابيس بسوقة رابيس والبحر
بالبحر وهاكذا وإن لم يكمل
العده بيننا فنقطعي في كل رأس من
الجانبين مائة ريال بشرط أن لا يبقى
الأسير من الجانبي الثم من سنة وحتى
إذه أراد مراءه من كانكج أو تاجر من
الجانبين يقرب يه بالملئة ريال المذكوره

الشرط السابع عشر أن التجار
لا تُكلَّفُ عليهم السلع ويشتروا
إلا ما أرادوا على حسب أنفسهم
وكذلك أبيع إلا إذا كانت
هناك مسائل جارية ميها
العادة مع من قبلهم من أجناس
النصارى يحملونها بلا باس كذلك

الشرط الثامن عمر أن اصطلح أنّ
18
تو سق تو زن وتقلب قبل وضعها في
السفينة لاجل أن لا تتعقب السفينة
من اجل إذا لحفوا أن بها كمر بينه
و إذا اكار كر الك بزاك ألفى جعل
الكر بينه موا أو يو اضن بزالك
وخيرة على العادة الجارية به مى
قبله واما السفينة والاصطلح وما
معه جانها بريئة من ذلك

الشهر التاسع عشر

وَأَنَّهُ لَا تُتَّفَقُ مَدِينَةٌ وَمَرْسَيَةٌ

وَلَا تُحْمَلُ شَيْئًا يَكْرَهُهَا إِلَّا إِذَا

كَانَ عَزِيبٌ بِنَفْسِهِ مِنْ رَوِيسِهَا

بِإِنَّهُ يَتَهَاوَدُ مَعَهُ عَلَى

حَمِيلِ مَا أَرَادَ حَمْلَهُ

الشهرُ العشرونَ أنَّهم

15 مهما جنا جانٍ أحدٌ من أهل جنسنا

جنايةٌ أو من هو داخلٌ تحتَ

سنجفنا وإن أردنا نحكمُ فيه

فوّضوا جنسَه وإذا احتاجَ

ألعوّضوا إلى أصحابٍ باشة

إبلاه ويعينه على ذلك

21

الشرط الحادى والعشرون

أنه إذا اقتلاتم نضراً او اوالعكس
او وجعه وإنه يحكم عليه بالقانون
الشرعى من غير زيادة وانقطاع
ويكون الحكم بحضر القونصوا
ولاهرب قبل موضع الحكم
بالا يوا عذوجد القونصوا والرابط
جنى ٢

الشرط الثاني والعشرون أقدمهما

22 مات أحد من جنس التجار كان نزل في
بلدنا ولم يوص بإبن فوضعنا
مع مال يقف على متروكه وسلعته
وإن لم يكن قد نصوا فتوضع عند
أمين حتى يقدم من يستحقها
ولدا كان منزله من تم قد يتعكى
لورثته من غير تعسر أو أوصى
بحق يبره لمن يصرف ماله والنظر
بعد إلك لمن يقبضه

23

الشَّرْطُ الثَّالِثُ وَالْعِشْرُونَ أَنَّ
الْقُونْصُوات يَكُونُون أَنْ مَرْسَيَة
أَرَاهُوا وَيَكُونُون مُوَفِّرِين مِثْل
أَجْنَا مِنْ قَبْلِهِم مِن النَّصَارَى وَإِذَا
تَعَامَلَ أَحَدٌ مِنْ جِنْسِهِم مَعَ مُسْلِم بِالْ
وَاتْلُفَهُ لَهُ جَلَّا يُوَاخِذُ بِهِ الْقُونْصُو
وَلَا يَضْمَنَهُ إِلَّا إِذَا كَانَ الْقُونْصُوا
أَعْطَى بِزَالِك خَطَّ يَدِهِ وَبِيَغْرَمُه
وَأَمَّا إِذَا لَمْ يَعْطِ خَطَّ يَدِهِ جَلَّا كَلَام
مَعَهُ مِثْلَ جَمِيعِ الْقُونْصُوات

الشرط الرابع والعشرون أفذ منهما تنازع
٢٤
أحدهم شروط من شروط الظلم بإزالة عمى
أحدٍ منهما وادعى الأخر مملكة وقال
إنما ليست بإلشركة وحال الترازع
بينهما فإن الصلح يبقى على حاله
ويبحث كل واحدٍ منهما على ما ينبغي
هتزراة اليوم يوم أحدهم طوع الصلح
ومنع منه كل الامتناع بأن العترة
تعمل حسنين وجميع التجار قضوا لمن
قضعة أثرٍ أهلاً إلى أن يرفعوا بلعلم وإذا
تبقط سيدنا على جنس من أجناس النصر وقضي
من جملتهم

الشرطُ الخَامِسُ وَالعِشْرُون

25

أَزَهَذَا الصُّلْحُ يَبْقَى مُسْتَمِرًّا إِنْ
شَاءَ اللهُ بِحَوْلِ اللهِ وَقُوَّتِهِ
مُدَّةً مِنْ خَمْسِينَ سَنَةً وَيَبْقَى يَجْرِ
بَيْنَ الدَّوْلَتَيْنِ عَلَى الْقَانُونِ الجَارِ حَتَّى
يُخْبِرَ أَحَدُ الجَانِبَيْنِ الأَخَرَ قَبْلَ مُدَّةٍ مِنْ
سَنَةٍ بِأَنْ مُرَاحَةً قَطْعَهُ فَحِينَئِذٍ
يَنْقَطِعُ بَعْدَ تَمَامِ تِلْكَ السَّنَةِ

[Translation]

In the name of God, the merciful and Clement!

(Abd Errahman Ibenu Kesham whom God exalt!)

Praise be to God!

This is the copy of the Treaty of peace which we have made with the Americans; and written in this book; affixing thereto our blessed Seal, that, with the help of God, it may remain firm for ever.

Written at Meccanez, the City of Olives, on the 3ᵈ day of the month Jumad el lahhar, in the year of the Hegira 1252.   (corresponding to Sept. 16. A.D. 1836.)

ART. I. We declare that both Parties have agreed that this Treaty, consisting of Twenty five Articles, shall be inserted in this Book, and delivered to James R. Leib, Agent of the United States, and now their Resident Consul at Tangier, with whose approbation it has been made, and who is duly authorized on their part, to treat with us, concerning all the matters contained therein.

ART. 2. If either of the parties shall be at war with any nation whatever, the other shall not take a commission from the enemy, nor fight under their colors.

ART. 3. If either of the parties shall be at war with any nation whatever, and take a prize belonging to that nation, and there shall be found on board subjects or effects belonging to either of the parties, the subjects shall be set at biberty, and the effects returned to the owners.   And if any goods, belonging to any nation, with whon either of the parties shall be at war, shall be loaded on vessels belonging to the other party, they shall pass free and unmolested, without any attempt being made to take or detain them.

ART. 4. A signal, or pass, shall be given to all vessels belonging to both parties, by which they are to be known when they meet at sea: and if the Commander of a ship of war of either party shall have other ships under his convoy, the declaration of the Commander shall alone be sufficient to exempt any of them from examination.

ART. 5. If either of the parties shall be at war, and shall meet a vessel at sea belonging to the other, it is agreed, that if an examination is to be made, it shall be done by sending a boat with two or three men only: and if any gun shall be fired, and injury done, without reason, the offending party shall make good all damages.

ART. 6. If any Moor shall bring citizens of the United States, or their effects, to his Majesty, the citizens shall immediately be set at liberty, and the effects restored: and, in like manner, if any Moor, not a subject of these dominions, shall make prize of any of the citizens of America or their effects, and bring them into any of the ports of his Majesty, they shall be immediately released, as they will then be considered as under his Majesty's protection.

ART. 7 If any vessel of either party, shall put into a port of the other, and have occasion for provisions or other suplies, they shall be furnished without any interruption or molestation.

ART. 8. If any vessel of the United States, shall meet with a disaster at sea, and put into one of our ports to repair, she shall be at biberty to land and reload her cargo, without paying any duty whatever.

ART. 9. If any vessel of the United States, shall be cast on shore on any part of our coasts, she shall remain at the disposition of the owners, and no one shall attempt going near her without their approbation, as she is then considered particularly under our protection; and if any vessel of the United States shall be forced to put into our ports by stress of weather, or otherwise, she shall not be compelled to land her cargo, but shall remain in tranquility until the commander shall think proper to proceed on his voyage.

ART. 10. If any vessel of either of the parties shall have an engagement with a vessel belonging to any of the Christian powers, within gun-shot of the forts of the other, the vessel so engaged, shall be defended and protected as much as possible, until she is in safety: and if any American vessel shall be cast on shore, on the coast of Wadnoon,[1] or any coast thereabout, the people belonging to her, shall be protected and assisted, until by the help of God, they shall be sent to their country.

ART. 11. If we shall be at war with any Christian power, and any of our vessels sails from the ports of the United States, no vessel belonging to the enemy shall follow, until twenty-four hours after the departure of our vessels: and the same regulation shall be observed towards the American vessels sailing from our ports, be their enemies Moors or Christians.

ART. 12. If any ship of war belonging to the United States, shall put into any of our ports, she shall not be examined on any pretence

[1] Or Ouadnoun, on the Atlantic coast, about latitude 29° N.

whatever, even though she should have fugitive slaves on board, nor shall the governor or commander of the place compel them to be brought on shore on any pretext, nor require any payment for them.

ART. 13. If a ship of war of either party shall put into a port of the other, and salute, it shall be returned from the fort with an equal number of guns, not more or less.

ART. 14. The commerce with the United States, shall be on the same footing as is the commerce with Spain, or as that with the most favored nation for the time being; and their citizens shall be respected and esteemed, and have full liberty to pass and repass our country and sea-ports whenever they please, without interruption.

ART. 15. Merchants of both countries shall employ only such interpreters, and such other persons to assist them in their business, as they shall think proper. No commander of a vessel shall transport his cargo on board another vessel: he shall not be detained in port longer than he may think proper; and all persons employed in loading or unloading goods, or in any other labor whatever, shall be paid at the customary rates, not more and not less.

ART. 16. In case of a war between the parties, the prisoners are not to be made slaves, but to be exchanged one for another. Captain for Captain, Officer for Officer, and one private man for another; and if there shall prove a deficiency on either side, it shall be made up by the payment of one hundred Mexican dollars for each person wanting. And it is agreed, that all prisoners shall be exchanged in twelve months from the time of their being taken, and that this exchange may be effected by a merchant, or any other person, authorized by either of the parties.

ART. 17. Merchants shall not be compelled to buy or sell any kind of goods but such as they shall think proper: and may buy and sell all sorts of merchandise but such as are prohibited to the other Christian nations.

ART. 18. All goods shall be weighed and examined before they are sent on board; and to avoid all detention of vessels, no examination shall afterwards be made, unless it shall first be proved that contraband goods have been sent on board; in which case, the persons who took the contraband goods on board, shall be punished according to the usage and custom of the country, and no other person whatever

shall be injured, nor shall the ship or cargo incur any penalty or damage whatever.

ART. 19. No vessel shall be detained in port on any pretence whatever, nor be obliged to take on board any article without the consent of the Commander, who shall be at full liberty to agree for the freight of any goods he takes on board.

ART. 20. If any of the citizens of the United States, or any persons under their protection, shall have any dispute with each other, the Consul shall decide between the parties; and whenever the Consul shall require any aid, or assistance from our government, to enforce his decisions, it shall be immediately granted to him.

ART. 21. If a citizen of the United States should kill or wound a Moor, or, on the contrary, if a Moor shall kill or wound a citizen of the United States, the law of the Country shall take place, and equal justice shall be rendered, the Consul assisting at the trial; and if any delinquent shall make his escape, the Consul shall not be answerable for him in any manner whatever.

ART. 22. If an American citizen shall die in our country, and no will shall appear, the Consul shall take possession of his effects; and if there shall be no Consul, the effects shall be deposited in the hands of some person worthy of trust, until the party shall appear who has a right to demand them; but if the heir to the person deceased be present, the property shall be delivered to him without interruption; and if a will shall appear the property shall descend agreeably to that will, as soon as the Consul shall declare the validity thereof.

ART. 23. The Consul of the United States of America, shall reside in any seaport of our dominions that they shall think proper: and they shall be respected, and enjoy all the priviliges which the Consuls of any other Nation enjoy: and if any of the citizens of the United States shall contract any debts or engagements, the Consul shall not be in any manner accountable for them, unless he shall have given a promise in writing for the payment or fulfilling thereof; without which promise in writing, no application to him for any redress shall be made.

ART. 24. If any differences shall arise by either party infringing on any of the Articles of this treaty, peace and harmony shall remain notwithstanding, in the fullest force, until a friendly application shall be made for an arrangement; and until that application shall be rejected,

no appeal shall be made to arms. And if a war shall break out between the parties, nine months shall be granted to all the subjects of both parties, to dispose of their effects and retire with their property. And it is further declared, that whatever indulgence, in trade or otherwise, shall be granted to any of the Christian powers, the citizens of the United States shall be equally entitled to them.

ART. 25. This Treaty shall continue in force, with the help of God, for fifty years; after the expiration of which term, the Treaty shall continue to be binding on both parties, until the one shall give twelve months notice to the other of an intention to abandon it; in which case, its operations shall cease at the end of the twelve months.

CONSULATE OF THE UNITED STATES OF AMERICA.

For The Empire of Morocco.

TO ALL WHOM IT MAY CONCERN.

BE IT KNOWN.

Whereas the undersigned, James R. Leib, a Citizen of the United States of North America, and now their Resident Consul at Tangier, having been duly appointed Commissioner, by *letters patent*, under the signature of the President and Seal of the United States of North America, bearing date, at the City of Washington, the Fourth day of July A.D. 1835, for negotiating and concluding a Treaty of *peace and friendship* between the United States of North America and the Empire of Morocco; I, therefore, James R. Leib, Commissioner as aforesaid, do conclude the foregoing Treaty and every Article and clause therein contained; reserving the same, nevertheless, for the final ratification of the President of the United States of North America, by and with the advice and consent of the Senate.

In testimony whereof, I have hereunto affixed my signature, and the Seal of this Consulate, on the First day of October, in the year of our Lord One Thousand eight hundred and *Thirty six*, and of the Independence of the United States the *Sixty First*.

[Seal]   JAMES R. LEIB

NOTES

The stated date of the signature of this treaty is September 16, 1836; but according to the chronological tables, 3 Jumada II, A.H. 1252, was September 15; and in the despatch of James R. Leib, consul at Tangier, of the following October 11 (D. S., 5 Consular Despatches, Tangier, No. 39), which transmitted the treaty, he gives the equiva-

lent date as September 17. (See vol. 2, pp. xxi–xxii, for a statement regarding the Mohammedan calendar.)

This treaty was in substance, and, indeed, almost literally, a renewal of the treaty with Morocco of 1786 (Document 14). The additional article of the earlier treaty is not embodied in the renewal; and while Article 25 of each treaty provides that it shall continue in force for fifty years, this treaty adds that thereafter the treaty shall continue unless and until twelve months' notice of denunciation is given by one party or the other. In this connection the interesting question arises as to whether the terms of fifty years and of twelve months are to be calculated according to the Mohammedan calendar or according to our calendar.

The Negotiations

The instructions to Leib were dated August 10, 1835 (D. S., 14 Instructions, Barbary Powers, 5–7). The bearer of the communication was William B. Hodgson, who took with him on the U.S. frigate *Constitution* the presents "to the Emperor of Morocco and his officers upon the renewal of the Treaty with the United States".

The instructions regarding the terms of the treaty were as follows:

If there should appear to be a disposition on the part of the Emperor, so far to extend the privileges of the former arrangement, as to place the vessels of the two countries upon the same footing, you will not fail to take advantage of it. If, on the other hand, there should be an indisposition to grant more favourable terms than before, you will obtain a renewal of the old treaty exactly as it stands, for the further period of fifty years; with the addition of a stipulation, that after the expiration of that term the treaty shall continue to be binding on both parties, until the one shall give twelve months' notice to the other of an intention to abandon it; in which case, its operation shall cease at the end of the twelve months. This stipulation is not to be considered indispensable; but you are to make every effort to procure its insertion, and not to relinquish the point until you find it absolutely necessary to do so.

The full power to Leib varied slightly from the usual form, its clauses of substance being the following (D. S., 2 Credences, 235):

Know Ye; That reposing special trust and confidence in the integrity, prudence and ability of *J. R. Leib*, a citizen of the United States, and now their Resident Consul at Tangier, I have appointed him agent of the United States to meet, confer, treat and negotiate with His Majesty the Emperor of Morocco and his Government, or with any person or persons duly authorized in his or its behalf, of and concerning all matters of Navigation and Commerce between the United States and the said Government of Morocco, with full power to conclude and sign a treaty therewith transmitting the same to the Government of the United States for his final ratification by and with the advice and consent of the Senate.

Leib acknowledged receipt of the instructions in his despatch from Gibraltar of September 19, 1835 (D. S., 5 Consular Despatches, Tangier, No. 26). While Leib had some discussions with Moroccan officials, most of the negotiations were by correspondence, and during them he did not see the Emperor of Morocco at all. Finally, on August 22, 1836, Leib sent from Tangier the acting vice consul, John F. Mullowny, and the interpreter of the consulate, Peter Boyn, on a

mission to the Court of Morocco at Meknès. The instructions of Leib to Mullowny of August 21 (D. S., 5 Consular Despatches, Tangier, No. 36, enclosure) included the following:

You are provided with a copy of the old Treaty [the treaty of 1786, Document 14], procured from the Department of State; and a copy of the New Form, which has been proposed. The number of Articles in each is the same; & the principal modifications are to be found in Article 10, & 25, which can be easily pointed out to the Minister. The modification in Art. 10 is merely an incorporation of the *Additional Article*, attached to the old Treaty, into the body of the New:—and that in Article 25, the insertion of a clause providing that, at the expiration of the term of the new Treaty, either party shall give the other twelve months notice of an intention to abandon it. These modifications, it is presumed, will not be deemed of sufficient consequence to give rise to difficulty; but, as some importance is attached to them by Government, my instructions are, not to abandon them, until every effort has been made to procure their insertion.

You are also furnished with two blank books, to serve as models, for engrossing the New Treaty; or into which, if immediately concluded, it may be copied.

It was doubtless in the two blankbooks furnished by Leib that the two originals of the treaty were written; and the result of the negotiations is thus stated by Leib in his despatch from Tangier of September 26, 1836 (D. S., 5 Consular Despatches, Tangier, No. 38):

I have the honor to inform you that my Vice-Consul & Interpreter have this moment returned from Mequinas, bringing with them the new Treaty sealed by the Emperor. Every effort was made to introduce the additional points, but without success; with the exception of the clause in the last article by which *twelve months notice* is to be given by either party when disposed to abandon its provisions. The Treaty will be conveyed to the United States by a Special Messenger.

The most remarkable feature in the negotiation of the present Treaty is the fact that it was sealed by the Emperor *before* giving him his present, & without stipulating to give him any thing;—a circumstance unknown hitherto in the history of Morocco. Further information will be transmitted as soon as the necessary papers can be prepared. In the mean time, this note is sent by express to Gibraltar, in order that the Department may be possessed of the earliest intelligence.

The File Papers

The original treaty with the seal of the Emperor of Morocco is in the file. It is written in a book in the usual Arabic order, with the preamble on a right page, the first of the twenty-five articles on the opposite left page, and the remaining articles on left pages, one on a page.

Also in the file is a copy of the treaty in Arabic, with an English translation. This document is a book very similar to the book which contains the original. The Arabic is on the right pages and the English translation on the corresponding left pages. Most of the English is written on very thin sheets of paper which are generally the alternate sheets of the book. The Arabic articles are not numbered. Following Article 25, or, as we would say, preceding it, is the certificate or clause of conclusion (which is printed), under the seal of the United States consulate at Tangier and signed by James R. Leib, consul and agent of the United States, on October 1, 1836.

The original and the copy were transmitted with the despatch of Leib of October 11, 1836, above mentioned, in which he wrote:

> The Treaty, it will be observed, being sealed by the Emperor according to the diplomatic custom observed in this Empire, bears the form of a grant. Hence, it would be out of rule to deface the original with my signature or seal. I have therefore attached these to the copy and translation which will accompany the original, according to the usage observed by Diplomatic Agents in other parts of Barbary.
>
> There are two original copies, sealed by the hands of the Emperor, the one being the counterpart of that which is now transmitted, destined to remain in this Consulate, the other to be deposited in the archives of the Department of State.

It thus appears that there were two originals under the seal of the Emperor of Morocco, one of which remained in the consulate at Tangier. No further record of that other original has been found.

In the copy of the treaty above described, on the page next to the back cover, is written the duplicate United States instrument of ratification, signed by President Jackson, sealed with the Great Seal, and attested by Secretary of State Forsyth. The first part of the original proclamation is on the page next preceding, and its final clauses are on the page opposite the certificate or clause of conclusion signed by Leib.

Also in the treaty file is the attested resolution of the Senate of January 17, 1837 (Executive Journal, IV, 598).

Another paper in the treaty file is a manuscript in pamphlet form which is clearly the draft submitted by Leib, which was called the "New Form" in his above-quoted instructions of August 21 to Mullowny. This has the twenty-five articles in Arabic and English, but not the preamble. The English of the draft is almost identical with Leib's translation of the treaty, except that Article 7 of the draft adds a clause of reciprocity in respect of vessels in commercial transactions and that Article 10 has incorporated in it the substance of the additional article of the treaty of 1786 (Document 14).

The original Arabic text is first reproduced above; but the twenty-six pages of Arabic are arranged in left-to-right order of pagination; then follows the text of the English translation with the clause of conclusion signed by Leib, collated with the copy in the file. It is this translation which is printed in the Statutes at Large and in treaty collections generally.

RATIFICATION AND PROCLAMATION

In the notes to Document 14 are some observations regarding the general practice in Morocco in respect of ratification of treaties.

It was on January 30, 1837, that the United States instrument of ratification was transmitted to Leib for delivery to the Emperor of Morocco. The following is an extract from the instructions of that date (D. S., 14 Instructions, Barbary Powers, 9):

> The new Treaty between the United States and the Empire of Morocco, sealed by the Emperor, together with a copy and translation, signed by you, which were

transmitted by the hands of Mr. John F. Mullowny, accompanied by a despatch from you of the 11th. of October, has been received, and a transcript of the copy in English ratified by the President with the advice and consent of the Senate is herewith returned by the same bearer for the purpose of being delivered to the Emperor.

It thus seems that the United States instrument of ratification included the English translation only. The receipt of the ratification was acknowledged by Leib in his despatch of March 20, 1837 (D. S., 5 Consular Despatches, Tangier), in which he wrote that it would "be conveyed to the Emperor together with his presents, without any unnecessary delay". Accordingly, it is to be presumed that the United States ratification was duly delivered some time shortly after the date of that despatch.

The proclamation of January 30, 1837, did not await the delivery of the United States instrument of ratification to the Emperor of Morocco; it recites that "the said Treaty has been duly ratified by the respective Governments"; and printed copies of the proclamation were transmitted to Congress by President Jackson with his message of February 9, 1837 (Richardson, III, 279; House Document No. 145, 24th Congress, 2d session, serial 304).

THE ARABIC TEXT

The writings in Arabic have been examined by Professor C. Snouck Hurgronje, of Leiden. From his report it appears that the differences in the Arabic between the original and the copy are of the most trifling character. The introduction, except for the seal, and fifteen articles, are exactly the same, and in the other articles there are a few verbal or orthographical differences of no moment.

Having compared the original of this treaty with that of the treaty of 1786 (Document 14), Professor Snouck Hurgronje finds that aside from the preamble and the opening and closing articles, the Arabic of the treaty of 1836 is almost exactly the same as that of the earlier treaty. Of the twenty-three articles numbered 2 to 24, eighteen are identical. Article 14 differs only in the order of the sentences; in Articles 5, 8, and 9, the trifling differences are merely orthographical; and in Article 11 one Arabic word for "twenty" is used in the early treaty and another word in the later.

Accordingly, the comments of Dr. Snouck Hurgronje on the English translation of the treaty of 1786, with his notes and translation of various articles, which follow the text of Document 14 in volume 2 at page 220, should be consulted.

In respect of the few real differences between the Arabic text of this treaty and that of the treaty of 1786, Dr. Snouck Hurgronje writes as follows:

The preamble differs from that of the treaty of 1786 in having a superscription, "In the name of God, the Compassionate, the Merciful"; and after the word "seal" is the word "al-sharîf", meaning "the blessed, the noble".

The second sentence of the preamble of this treaty, which gives the date, may be thus translated: "Written at Miknâsah of the Olives on the third of Jumâda al-Akhîrah [Jumada II], one thousand two hundred and fifty-two."

The seal of this treaty (which is not legible) naturally differs from that of the former treaty.

In Article 1 the second sentence of the later treaty may be translated thus: "That took place in the presence of their Agent and Plenipotentiary and consul general, James Leib, residing at this time in the well-preserved Tangier."

Article 25 of this treaty is thus translated: "This treaty shall continue in full force, if God please, by God's might and power, a period from [*sic*] fifty years, and it shall continue to be in force between the two Governments in accordance with the prevailing rule until either of the parties gives notice to the other in a period from [*sic*] a year, of his intention to abandon [break] it, in which case it will cease at the end of that year."

Treaty Series No. 274
8 Statutes at Large, 487–96
18 *ibid.*, pt. 2, Public Treaties, 602–10

82

PERU-BOLIVIAN CONFEDERATION
NOVEMBER 30, 1836

*Treaty of Peace, Friendship, Commerce, and Navigation, signed at Lima
November 30, 1836. Original in English and Spanish.
Submitted to the Senate September 7, 1837. Resolution of advice and
consent October 10, 1837. Ratified by the United States October 14,
1837. Ratified by the Peru-Bolivian Confederation January 10, 1837.
Ratifications exchanged at Lima May 28, 1838. Proclaimed October
3, 1838.*

General Convention of Peace, Friendship, Commerce and Navigation, between the United States of America and the Peru-Bolivivian Confederation.

The United States of America and the Peru-Bolivian Confederation, desiring to make firm and permanent the peace and friendship which happily subsist between them,—have resolved to fix, in a clear, distinct, and positive manner, the rules which shall in future be religiously observed between the one and the other, by means of a Treaty, or General Convention of Peace, Friendship, Commerce and Navigation.

For this desirable purpose, the President of the United States of America has conferred full powers on Samuel Larned, Chargé d'Affaires of the said States near the Government of Peru, and the Supreme Protector of the North

CONVENCION JENERAL de Paz, Amistad, Comercio y Navegacion, entre la Confederacion Peru Boliviana, y los Estados Unidos de America.

La Confederacion Peru-Boliviana y los Estados Unidos de America, deseando establecer firme y permanentemente la páz y Amistad que afortunadamente subsisten entre ellos, han resuelto fijar, de una manera clara, distinta y positiva, las reglas que en lo futuro han de observarse relijiosamente entre ambos, por medio de un tratado ó convencion jeneral de páz, amistad, comercio y navegacion.

Para este deseable objeto, el Supremo Protector de los Estados Nor y Sur-Peruanos, Presidente de la Republica de Bolivia, encargado de dirijir las relaciones exteriores de la Confederacion Peru-Boliviana, ha conferido Plenos

and South Peruvian States, President of the Republic of Bolivia, encharged with the direction of the foreign relations of the Peru-Bolivian Confederation,—has conferred like powers on John Garcia del Rio, Minister of State in the Department of Finance, of the North Peruvian State:—who after having exhibited to each other their respective full powers,—found to be in due and proper form,—and exchanged certified copies thereof, have agreed to the following articles, to wit,—

Poderes á Don Juan Garcia del Rio, Ministro de Estado en el departamento de Hacienda del Estado Nor-Peruano; y el Presidente de los Estados Unidos de America ha conferido iguales Plenos Poderes á Don Samuel Larned Encargado de Negocios de los Estados predichos cerca del Gobierno del Perú, los cuales despues de haber presentado el uno al otro sus respectivos plenos Poderes, encontradolos en propia y debida forma, y canjeado copias certificadas de ellos, han convenido en los Articulos siguientes—Á saber:

ARTICLE I.

There shall be a perfect, firm, and inviolable peace, and sincere friendship, between the United States of America and the Peru-Bolivian Confederation;—in all the extent of their respective territories and possessions;—and between their people and citizens, respectively, without distinction of persons or places.

ARTICULO 1º

Habrá perfecta, firme é inviolable páz, y sincera amistad, entre la Confederacion Perú-Boliviana y los Estados Unidos de America, en toda la estension de sus respectivos territorios y posesiones, y entre sus pueblos y ciudadanos respectivamente, sin distincion de personas ó lugares.

ARTICLE II.

The United States of America and the Peru-Bolivian Confederation, desiring to live in peace and harmony, as well with each other as with all the Nations of the earth, by means of a policy frank and equally friendly with all, engage, mutually, not to concede any particular favor to other nations, in respect of commerce and navigation,—which shall not im-

ARTICULO 2º

La Confederacion Peru-Boliviana y los Estados Unidos de America, deseando vivir en páz y armonia, tanto entre si, como con todas las naciones de la tierra, por medio de una politica franca, é igualmente amistosa para con todas, se comprometen, mutuamente, á no conceder ningun favor particular á otras naciones, en punto á comercio y navega-

mediately become common to the other party to this Treaty; who shall enjoy the same freely, if the concession was freely made, or on allowing the same compensation, if the concession was conditional.

ARTICLE III.

The two high contracting parties, being likewise desirous of placing the commerce and navigation of their respective countries on the liberal basis of perfect equality with the most favored nation, mutually agree, that the citizens of each may frequent with their vessels all the coasts and countries of the other, and may reside and trade there, in all kinds of produce, manufactures and merchandize, not prohibited to all; and shall pay no other or higher duties, charges, or fees, whatsoever, either on their vessels or cargoes, than the citizens or subjects of the most favored are, or shall be, obliged to pay, on their vessels and cargoes:— and they shall enjoy, respectively, all the rights, privileges and exemptions, in navigation and commerce, which the citizens or subjects of the most favored nation do, or shall enjoy; they submitting themselves to the laws, decrees and usages there established, to

cion, que no se haga inmediatamente comun á la otra parte de este tratado; la cual disfrutará libremente de aquel favor, si la concesion se hizo libremente, ó concediendo la misma compensacion, si fué condicional la concesion.

ARTICULO 3º

Las dos altas partes contratantes, estando asimismo deseosas de colocar el comercio y navegacion de sus paises respectivos, sobre la base liberal de perfecta igualdad con la nacion mas favorecida, convienen, mutuamente que los ciudadanos de cada una puedan frecuentar con sus buques todas las costas y paises de la otra, y residir y comerciar en ellos, en todo jenero de productos, manufacturas y mercaderias, que no estén prohibidos á todas; que no pagarán distintos ó mas subidos derechos, cargas ó emolumentos de ninguna especie, ni sobre sus buques, ni sobre sus cargamentos, que los que están ó estuvieren obligados á pagar, sobre sus buques ó cargamentos, los ciudadanos ó subditos de la nacion mas favorecida; y que gozaran, respectivamente, de todos los derechos, privilejios y esenciones, en punto á navegacion y comercio, que gozan ó gozaren los ciudadanos ó subditos de la nacion

which such citizens or subjects are, of right, subjected.

But it is understood that the stipulations contained in this article, do not include the coasting trade of either of the two countries; the regulation of this trade being reserved by the parties, respectively, according to their own separate laws.

Article IV.

It is likewise agreed that it shall be wholly free for all merchants, commanders of ships, and other citizens, of both countries, to manage, themselves, their own business;—in all the ports and places subject to the jurisdiction of the other, as well with respect to the consignment and sale of their goods and merchandize, as to the purchase of their returns, unloading, loading, and sending off, of their vessels. The citizens of neither of the contracting parties shall be liable to any embargo, nor to be detained with their vessels, cargoes, merchandize or effects, for any military expedition, nor for any public or private purpose whatever,—without being allowed therefor a sufficient indemnification. Neither shall they be called upon for any forced loan, or occasional contributions—

mas favorecida; sometiendose á las leyes, decretos y usos allí establecidos, á que están, de derecho, sujetos los tales ciudadanos ó subditos.

Pero debe entenderse, que las estipulaciones contenidas en este Artículo, no incluyen el comercio costanero de ninguno de los dos paises, pues que la regulacion de este comercio está reservada, respectivamente, á las partes contratantes, conforme á sus propias y separadas leyes.

Articulo 4º

Se conviene asimismo en que todos los negociantes, comandantes de buques, y otros ciudadanos de los dos paises, tendrán entera libertad para manejar, por si mismos, sus negocios, en todos los puertos y lugares sometidos á la jurisdiccion de uno ú otro, tanto con respecto á la consignacion y venta de sus efectos y mercaderias, como á la compra de sus retornos, y á la descarga, carga, y despacho de sus buques. Los ciudadanos de las partes contratantes no estarán sujetos á ningun embargo, ni á ser detenidos con sus buques, cargamentos, mercaderias y efectos, para ninguna espedicion militar, ni para ningun objeto publico ó privado, sea el que fuere; sin que por ello se les conceda una indemnizacion suficiente. Tampoco se les ecsijirá ningun emprestito forzoso, ni con-

nor be subject to military service, on land or sea.

ARTICLE V.

Whenever the citizens of either of the contracting parties, shall be forced to seek refuge, shelter or relief, in the rivers, bays, ports, and dominions of the other, with their vessels, whether of war, (public or private) of trade, or employed in the fisheries,— through stress of weather, want of water or provisions, pursuit of pirates or enemies,—they shall be received, and treated with humanity; and all favor and protection shall be given to them, in the repairing of their vessels, procuring of supplies, and placing of themselves in a condition to pursue their voyage, without obstacle or hindrance.

ARTICLE VI.

All ships, merchandize, and effects, belonging to citizens of one of the contracting parties, which may be captured by pirates, whether on the high seas, or within the limits of its jurisdiction, and may be carried or found in the rivers, roads, bays, ports, or dominions of the other,— shall be delivered up to the owners; they proving, in due and proper form, their rights, before the competent tribunals: it being understood, that the claim should be made within the term of two

tribucion ocacional, ni estarán sujetos á servicio militar, por mar ó por tierra.

ARTICULO 5º

Cuando los ciudadanos de una de las dos partes contratantes se vean obligados á buscar refujio, abrigo ó aucilio, en los rios, bahias, puertos y dominios de la otra, con sus buques, ya sean de guerra, publicos ó particulares, ya de comercio, ó ya de los que se emplean en la pesca, por causa de temporal, falta de agua ó provisiones, y persecucion de piratas ó enemigos, serán recibidos, y tratados con humanidad; y se les concederá todo favor y proteccion, para que reparen sus buques, se proporcionen aucilios, y se coloquen en estado de proseguir su viaje, sin obstaculo ó molestia.

ARTICULO 6º

Todos los buques, mercaderias y efectos pertenecientes á ciudadanos de una de las partes contratantes, que sean apresados por piratas, bien en alta mar, ó dentro de los limites de su jurisdiccion, y que fueren llevados ó encontrados en los rios, radas, ó bahias, puertos ó dominios de la otra, serán entregados á los dueños; con tal que prueben en propia y debida forma, sus derechos, ante los Tribunales competentes; debiendo entenderse, que el reclamo ha de hacerse dentro del termino de dos años, por

years; by the parties themselves, their attornies, or the agents of their respective governments.

ARTICLE VII.

Whenever any vessel belonging to the citizens of either of the contracting parties shall be wrecked, founder, or suffer damage, on the coasts, or within the dominions, of the other, all assistance and protection shall be given to the said vessel, her crew, and the merchandize on board;—in the same manner as is usual and customary with vessels of the nation, where the accident happens, in like cases: and it shall be permitted to her, if necessary, to unload the merchandize and effects on board, with the proper precautions to prevent their illicit introduction, without exacting, in this case, any duty impost, or contribution, whatever; provided the same be exported.

ARTICLE VIII.

The citizens of each of the contracting parties, shall have power to dispose of their personal effects, within the jurisdiction of the other, by sale, donation, testament, or otherwise; and their representatives, being citizens of the other party, shall succeed to their said personal effects, whether by testament or *ab intestato*; and may take possession thereof, either themselves, or by others acting for them; and dis-

las mismas partes, sus procuradores, ó los Ajentes de sus Gobiernos respectivos.

ARTICULO 7º

Siempre que algun buque perteneciente á ciudadanos de una de las partes contratantes, naufrague, encalle, ó sufra daño en las costas ó dentro de los dominios de la otra, se dará todo aucilio y proteccion al predicho buque, á su tripulacion, y á las mercaderias que tenga á su bordo, del mismo modo que es uso y costumbre, en semejantes casos, con los buques de la nacion donde sobrevenga el accidente; y se le permitirá, si fuere preciso, descargar las mercaderias y efectos que traiga á bordo, con las precauciones que sean necesarias para impedir su ilicita introduccion, sin ecsijir en este caso ningun derecho, impuesto ni contribucion, de ninguna especie; con tal que sean esportados.

ARTICULO 8º

Los ciudadanos de cada una de las partes contratantes, podrán disponer de sus efectos personales, dentro de la jurisdiccion de la otra, por venta, donacion, testamento ó de cualquier otro modo; y sus representantes, si son ciudadanos de la otra parte, succederán á los susodichos efectos personales, ya sea por testamento, ó *ab intestato;* y pueden tomar posecion de ellos, bien por si mismos, ó por otros que obren en su nombre, y

pose of the same at their will;— paying such dues, only, as the inhabitants of the country wherein said effects are, shall be subject to pay in like cases. And if, in the case of real estate, the said heirs should be prevented from entering into possession of the inheritance, on account of their character as aliens, there shall be granted to them the term of three years, in which to dispose of the same, as they may think proper, and to withdraw the proceeds; which they may do without obstacle, and exempt from all charges, save those which are imposed by the laws of the country.

Article IX.

Both the contracting parties solemnly promise and engage, to give their special protection to the persons and property of the citizens of each other, of all classes and occupations, who may be in the territories subject to the jurisdiction of the one or the other, transient or dwelling therein:—leaving open & free to them the tribunals of justice, for their judicial recourse, on the same terms as are usual and customary with the natives, or citizens, of the country in which they may be: for which purpose they may employ in defence of their rights, such advocates, solicitors, notaries, agents and factors as they may judge proper, in all their trials at law: and such citizens

disponer de ellos á su voluntad; pagando unicamente aquellos derechos, á que en tales casos, están sujetos los habitantes del pais donde se hallan los efectos precitados. Y si, en el caso de ser bienes raizes, estuviesen impedidos los susodichos herederos de entrar en posecion de la herencia en razon de ser extranjeros, se les concederá el termino de tres años, para que dispongan de ellos, segun lo estimen conveniente, y para esportar su producto; lo cual podrán hacer sin obstaculo, y esentos de todas cargas, con escepcion de aquellas que imponen las leyes del pais.

Articulo 9º

Las dos partes contratantes prometen solemnemente, y se empeñan en dar su especial proteccion á las personas y propiedades de los ciudadanos de una ú otra, de todas clases y ocupaciones, que puedan estar en los territorios sujetos á la jurisdiccion de una ú otra, ya sean transeuntes ó domiciliados; dejandoles abiertos y libres los Tribunales de justicia para sus recursos judiciales, en los mismos terminos que son de uso y costumbre con los naturales ó ciudadanos del pais en donde se hallen; para cuyo objeto podrán emplear, en defenza de sus derechos, los Abogados, procuradores, escribanos, ajentes y factores que estimen oportuno en todos sus juicios ó pleitos; y los

or agents shall have free opportunity to be present at the decisions and sentences of the tribunals, in all cases that may concern them; and, likewise, at the taking of all evidence and examinations that may be exhibited in the said trials.

And to render more explicit, and make more effectual, the solemn promise and engagement herein before mentioned,—under circumstances to which one of the parties thereto has heretofore been exposed,—it is hereby further stipulated and declared, that all the rights and privileges which are now enjoyed by, or may hereafter be conferred on, the citizens of one of the contracting parties by, or in virtue of the Constitution and laws of the other, respectively;—shall be deemed and held to belong to, and inhere in, them, until such rights and privileges shall have been abrogated or withdrawn by an authority constitutionally or lawfully competent thereto.

Article X.

It is likewise agreed, that perfect and entire liberty of conscience shall be enjoyed by the citizens of both the contracting parties, in the countries subject to the jurisdiction of the one and the other; without their being liable to be disturbed or molested on account of their religious belief, so long as they respect the

tales ciudadanos ó Ajentes podrán asistir con entera libertad, á las decisiones y sentencias de los Tribunales, que les conciernan; como tambien á la toma de todas las declaraciones y ecsamenes á que haya lugar en los predichos juicios ó pleitos.

Y á fin de hacer mas esplicitos y efectivos la solemne promesa y el comprometimiento arriba mencionados, bajo de las circunstancias á que una de las partes ha estado espuesta hasta aqui, se estipula ademas y se declara, que todos los derechos y privilejios de que ahora disfrutan, ó que en adelante pudieran conferirse á ciudadanos de una de las partes contratantes por, ó á virtud de, la constitucion y leyes de la otra, respectivamente, se juzgarán y se tendrán como pertenecientes é inherentes á ellos, hasta que los tales derechos y privilejios hubieren sido derogados ó retirados por una autoridad que constitucional ó legalmente sea competente para hacerlo

Articulo 10º

Se conviene asimismo en que los ciudadanos de las dos partes contratantes, disfrutarán entera y perfecta libertad de conciencia en los paises sometidos á la jurisdiccion de la una y de la otra, sin estar sujetos á ser perturbados ó molestados á causa de su creencia relijiosa, en tanto que respeten las leyes y usos esta-

laws, and established usages of the country. Moreover, the bodies of the citizens of one of the contracting parties who may die in the territories of the other, shall be buried in the usual burying grounds, or in other decent and suitable places; and shall be protected from violation or disturbance.

Article XI

It shall be lawful for the citizens of the United States of America and of the Peru-Bolivian Confederation, to sail with their ships, with all manner of liberty and security,—no distinction being to be made who are the proprietors of the merchandize laden therein, —from any port or place, whatever, to the ports and places of those who are now, or hereafter shall be, at enmity with either of the contracting parties. It shall likewise be lawful for the citizens aforesaid, to sail with the ships and merchandize before mentioned, and to trade, with the same liberty and security, from the places, ports and havens of those who are enemies of both, or of either party,—without any opposition or disturbance whatsoever,—not only directly from the places of the enemy, before mentioned, to neutral places; but, also, from one place belonging to an enemy to another place belonging to an enemy; whether they be under the jurisdiction of one power or under that of several. And it is

blecidos del pais. Ademas, los cuerpos de los ciudadanos de una de las partes contratantes, que murieren en los territorios de la otra, serán enterrados en los acostumbrados cementerios, ó en otros lugares acomodados y decentes, y protejidos de toda violacion ó perturbacion.

Articulo 11 º

Será licito á los ciudadanos de la Confederacion Peru-Boliviana y de los Estados Unidos de America, navegar con sus buques en perfecta libertad y seguridad, sin que se haga distincion de quienes sean los dueños de las mercaderias que tengan á su bordo, de cualquier puerto ó lugar, á los puertos y lugares de aquellos que en la actualidad són, ó fueren en lo sucsecivo, enemigos de una de las partes contratantes. Será asimismo licito á los predichos ciudadanos, navegar con los buques y mercaderias arriba mencionados, y comerciar con la misma libertad y seguridad, de los lugares, puertos y bahias de aquellos que son enemigos de una de las dos partes, ó de ambas, sin ninguna oposicion ó impedimento, no solo directamente de los lugares del enemigo ya nombrados, á lugares neutrales, sino tambien de un lugar perteneciente á un enemigo á otro lugar perteneciente á un enemigo, bien sea que estén bajo la jurisdiccion de una potencia, ó bajo la de

hereby stipulated, that free ships shall give freedom to goods; and that every thing shall be deemed to be free and exempt which shall be found on board of the ships belonging to the citizens of either of the contracting parties, although the whole lading, or any part thereof, should appertain to the enemies of either,—goods contraband of war being always excepted. It is also agreed, in like manner, that the same liberty shall be extended to persons who are on board of a free ship;—with this effect, that, although they be enemies to both or either of the parties, they shall not be taken out of that free ship, unless they are officers or soldiers, and in the actual service of the enemy:—provided, however; and it is hereby further agreed, that the stipulations in this article contained, declaring that the flag shall cover the property, shall be understood as applying to those Powers, only, who recognise this principle: but if either of the contracting parties shall be at war with a third, and the other be neutral, the flag of the neutral shall cover the property of those enemies whose governments acknowledge this principle, and not that of others.

varias. Y por la presente se estipula, que los bajeles libres darán libertad á los efectos, y que se estimará libre y esento todo lo que se encuentre á bordo de los buques pertenecientes á los ciudadanos de cualquiera de las partes contratantes, aunque todo el cargamento, ó una parte de él, pertenesca á enemigos de la otra, esceptuandose siempre los efectos de contrabando de guerra. Tambien se conviene, del mismo modo, que la misma libertad se estenderá á los individuos que estén á bordo de un buque libre; con este efecto, que aunque sean enemigos de una de las dos partes, ó de ambas, no serán estraidos del buque libre, á menos que sean oficiales ó soldados, y en actual servicio del enemigo; con tal que, segun se conviene aqui, se entienda que las estipulaciones contenidas en este articulo, declarando que el Pabellon cubrirá la propiedad, son aplicables á aquellas Potencias, solamente, que reconocen este principio: pero si alguna de las partes contratantes estuviese en guerra con una tercera, y la otra fuese neutral, el pabellon del neutral cubrirá la propiedad de aquellos enemigos, cuyos Gobiernos reconocen este principio, y no la de los otros.

Article XII.

It is likewise agreed, that in cases where the neutral flag of one of the contracting parties

Articulo 12º

Se conviene asimismo que, en los casos en que el pabellon neutral de una de las partes contra-

shall protect the property of the enemies of the other, in virtue of the above stipulation,—it shall always be understood, that the neutral property found on board of such enemy's vessel, shall be held and considered as enemy's property; and as such shall be liable to detention and confiscation;—except such property as was put on board of such vessels before the declaration of war, or even afterwards, if it were done without the knowledge of such declaration: but the contracting parties agree, that six months having elapsed, after the declaration, their citizens shall not be allowed to plead ignorance thereof. On the contrary, if the flag of the neutral does not protect the enemy's property on board, in this case, the goods and merchandize of the neutral, embarked in such enemy's ship, shall be free.

Article XIII

This liberty of navigation and commerce shall extend to all kinds of merchandize; excepting, only, those which are distinguished by the name of contraband, or prohibited, goods:—under which name shall be comprehended,— 1st cannons, mortars, howitzers, swivels, blunderbusses, muskets, fusees, rifles, carbines, pistols, pikes, swords, sabres, lances, spears, halberds, granades and bombs; powder, matches, balls,

tantes proteja la propiedad de los enemigos de la otra, en virtud de la precedente estipulacion, se entenderá siempre que la propiedad neutral, que se hallare á bordo de los buques de tal enemigo, se estima y considera como propiedad enemiga, y como tál estará sujeta á detencion y confiscacion; escepto aquella propiedad que hubiere sido puesta á bordo de tales buques, antes de la declaracion de la guerra, ó aun despues, si se hubiere hecho sin conocimiento de la tal declaracion: pero las partes contratantes convienen que, pasados seis meses despues de la declaracion, no se permitirá á sus ciudadanos alegar ignorancia de ella. Por el contrario, si el pabellon del neutral no proteje la propiedad enemiga que haya á bordo, en este caso, los efectos y mercaderias del neutral, embarcados en tales buques enemigos, serán libres.

Articulo 13º

Esta libertad de navegacion y comercio se estenderá á toda especie de mercaderias; esceptuandose, unicamente, aquellas que se distinguen con el nombre de efectos prohibidos ó de contrabando, bajo cuya denominacion se comprenden :—1º Cañones, morteros, obuses, pedreros, trabucos, mosquetes, fusiles, rifles, carabinas, pistolas, picas, espadas, sables, lanzas, chuzos, alabardas, granadas y bombas; polvora, me-

and all other things belonging to the use of these arms. 2^{ndly} Bucklers, helmets, breastplates, coats-of-mail, infantry belts, and clothes made up in a military form, and for a military use. 3^{rdly} Cavalry belts, and horses with their furniture. 4^{thly} and generally, all kinds of arms and instruments of iron, steel, brass and copper, or of any other materials, manufactured, prepared and formed expressly for the purposes of war—either by sea or land.

ARTICLE XIV

All other merchandize and things, not comprehended in the articles of contraband explicitly enumerated and classified as above, shall be held and considered as free, and subjects of free and lawful commerce; so that they may be carried and transported, in the freest manner, by both the contracting parties;— even to places belonging to an enemy;—excepting, only, those places which are at that time, besieged or blockaded: and, to avoid all doubt in this particular, it is declared, that those places, only, are besieged, or blockaded, which are actually attacked by a force capable of preventing the entry of the neutral.

chas, balas con las demas cosas correspondientes al uso de estas armas:—2° escudos, casquetes, corazas, cotas de malla, fornituras y vestidos hechos en forma y para uso militar:—3° bandoleras, y caballos junto con sus arneses:— 4° y jeneralmente toda especie de Armas é instrumentos de hierro, acero, bronce, cobre y otras materias cualesquiera, manufacturadas, preparadas y formadas espresamente para hacer la guerra, por mar ó por tierra.

ARTICULO 14°

Cualesquiera otras mercaderias y cosas no comprendidas en los articulos de contrabando esplicitamente enumerados y clasificados arriba, se tendrán y considerarán libres, y materia de libre y lejitimo comercio; de manera que, puedan ser llevadas y trasportadas en el modo mas libre por las dos partes contratantes, aún á los lugares pertenecientes á un enemigo, esceptuando unicamente, aquellos lugares que estén en aquel tiempo, sitiados ó bloqueados: y para evitar toda duda sobre el particular, se declara que unicamente son sitiados ó bloqueados aquellos lugares que están actualmente atacados por una fuerza capáz de impedir la entrada del neutral.

ARTICLE XV

The articles of contraband, of those before enumerated and classified, which may be found in a vessel bound for an enemy's port, shall be subject to detention and confiscation; but the rest of the cargo, and the ship, shall be left free, that the owners may dispose of them as they see proper. No vessel, of either of the contracting parties, shall be detained on the high seas, on account of having on board articles of contraband, whenever the master, captain, or supercargo of said vessel will deliver up the articles of contraband to the captor; unless, indeed, the quantity of such articles be so great, and of so large a bulk, that they cannot be received on board of the capturing vessel without great inconvenience:—but in this, and all other cases of just detention, the vessel detained shall be sent to the nearest convenient and safe port, for trial and judgment, according to law.

ARTICLE XVI

And whereas it frequently happens, that vessels sail for a port or place belonging to an enemy, without knowing that the same is besieged, blockaded or invested,—it is agreed, that every vessel so circumstanced, may be turned away from such port or place, but shall not be detained;—nor shall

ARTICULO 15º

Los articulos de contrabando de los ya enumerados y clasificados, que se encuentren en un buque destinado á un puerto enemigo, estarán sujetos á detencion y confiscacion; pero el resto del cargamento, y el buque, se dejarán libres, para que los dueños puedan disponer de ellos, segun estimen conveniente. Ningun buque, de ninguna de las partes contratantes, será detenido en alta mar por tener á bordo articulos de contrabando, siempre que el Maestre, capitan ó sobrecargo del susodicho buque, entregue los articulos de contrabando al apresador; á menos que sea tan grande, y de tanto volumen, la cantidad de los tales articulos, que no puedan recibirse á bordo del buque apresador sin grande inconveniente: pero en este, y en todos los otros casos de justa detencion, el buque detenido será enviado al puerto mas inmediato, comodo y seguro, para ser juzgado con arreglo á las leyes.

ARTICULO 16º

Y como frecuentemente sucede que navegan buques para un puerto ó lugar perteneciente á un enemigo, sin saber que él mismo está sitiado, bloqueado ó embestido, se conviene que todo buque, que se halle en este caso, sea rechazado del tal puerto, ó lugar, pero no detenido, ni con-

any part of her cargo,—if not contraband,—be confiscated; unless, after being warned of such blockade or investment, by the commanding officer of a vessel forming part of the blockading forces,—she shall again attempt to enter:—but she shall be permitted to go to any other port or place the master or supercargo shall think proper. Nor shall any vessel, of either party, that may have entered into such port or place before the same was actually besieged, blockaded, or invested, by the other, be restrained from quitting it, with her cargo; nor if found therein, before or after the reduction and surrender, shall such Vessel, or her cargo, be liable to seizure, confiscation, or any demand on the score of redemption or restitution:—but the owners thereof shall be allowed to remain in the undisturbed possession of their property. And if any vessel, having thus entered the port before the blockade took place, shall take on board a Cargo, after the blockade be established, and attempt to depart; she shall be subject to being warned by the blockading forces, to return to the port blockaded, and discharge the said cargo; and if, after receiving said warning, the vessel shall persist in going out with the cargo, she shall be liable to the same consequences to which a vessel attempting to enter a blockaded port, after being

fiscada ninguna parte de su cargamento, que no sea contrabando; á menos que, despues de ser avisado del tal bloqueo ó embestidura, por el oficial que mande un buque, que forme parte de las fuerzas bloqueadoras, intentase de nuevo entrar: pero se le permitirá ir á cualquiera otro puerto, ó lugar, que juzgue oportuno el maestre ó sobrecargo. Y á ningun buque, de una ú otra parte, que hubiere entrado en tal puerto, ó lugar, antes de que el mismo estuviese actualmente sitiado, bloqueado, ó embestido por la otra, se le impedirá que salga, con su cargamento; ni si se encontrase alli, antes ó despues de la reduccion y entrega, estará sujeto el tal buque, ó su cargamento, á apresamiento, confiscacion ó demanda alguna, por causa de redencion ó restitucion, sino que se dejará á sus dueños en tranquila posecion de su propiedad. Y si algun buque que hubiere entrado en el puerto, antes de tener lugar el bloqueo, tomase carga á bordo despues de establecido el bloqueo, é intentase salir, estará sujeto á ser intimado por las fuerzas bloqueadoras, que vuelva al puerto bloqueado, y descargue su cargamento: y si despues de recibir la susodicha intimacion, insistiere el buque en salir con el cargamento, estará sujeto á las mismas consecuencias á que lo estaria una embarcacion que intentase entrar

warned off by the blockading forces, would be liable.

en un puerto bloqueado, despues de ser intimada por las fuerzas bloqueadoras.

Article XVII

To prevent all kinds of disorder and irregularity in the visiting and examining of the ships and cargos, of both the contracting parties, on the high seas, they have agreed, mutually, that whenever a vessel of war, public or private, shall meet with a neutral, of the other contracting party, the first shall remain at the greatest distance compatible with the possibility and safety of making the visit, under the circumstances of wind and sea, and the degree of suspicion attending the vessel to be visited; and shall send one of her small boats, with no more men than those necessary to man it, for the purpose of executing the said examination,—of the papers concerning the ownership and cargo of the vessel,—without causing the least extortion, violence, or ill treatment; in respect of which, the commanders of said armed vessels shall be responsible, with their persons and property; for which purpose, the commanders of said private armed vessels shall, before receiving their commissions,—give sufficient security, to answer for all the injuries and damages they may commit. And it is expressly agreed, that the neutral party shall in no case be required to go on board the exam-

Articulo 17º

Para impedir todo jenero de desorden é irregularidad en la visita y ecsamen de los buques y cargamentos de las dos partes contratantes en alta mar, han convenido mutuamente, que cuando un buque de guerra, publico ó particular, encontrare á un neutral de la otra parte contratante, el primero permanecerá á la mayor distancia que sea compatible con la posibilidad y la seguridad de hacer la visita, atendidas las circunstancias del viento y de la mar, y el grado de sospecha que acompañe al bajel que ha de ser visitado, y enviará uno de sus botes pequeños, sin mas gente que la necesaria para tripularlo, con el objeto de ejecutar el predicho ecsamen de los papeles relativos á la propiedad y cargamento del buque, sin causar la menor estorcion, violencia ó maltratamiento; respecto á lo cual, los Comandantes de los susodichos buques armados, serán responsables, con sus personas y propiedades; para cuyo fin, los Comandantes de los predichos buques particulares armados, antes de recibir sus comisiones, darán la suficiente seguridad, para responder por todos los daños y perjuicios que cometieren. Y se conviene espresamente, que en

ining vessel, for the purpose of exhibiting the ships papers; nor for any other purpose whatever.

Article XVIII

To avoid all vexation and abuses in the examination of the papers relating to the ownership of the vessels belonging to the citizens of the contracting parties;— they have agreed, and do agree, that, in case one of them should be engaged in war, the ships and vessels of the other must be furnished with sea-letters, or passports;— expressing the name, property and burden of the ship; as also the name and place of residence of the master or commander thereof; in order that it may thereby appear that the said ship really and truly belongs to the citizens of one of the parties. They have likewise agreed, that such ships, being laden, besides the said sea-letters or passports, shall be provided with certificates containing the several particulars of the cargo, and the place whence the ship sailed;—so that it may be known whether any contraband or prohibited goods are on board of the same:—which certificates shall be made out by the officers of the place whence the ship sailed, in the accustomed form, without which requisites, the said Vessel may be detained, to be adjudged by the competent

ningun caso se requerirá que la parte Neutral vaya á bordo del buque ecsaminador, ni para exhibir los papeles del buque, ni para ningun otro objeto cualquiera.

Articulo 18º

Para evitar toda vejacion y abusos en el ecsamen de los papeles relativos á la propiedad de los buques pertenecientes á los ciudadanos de las partes contratantes, han convenido, y convienen, que en el caso que una de ellas estuviere empeñada en guerra, los buques de la otra deben estar provistos de letras de mar, ó pasaportes, en que se espresen el nombre, la propiedad y tamaño del buque, como tambien el nombre, y el lugar de la residencia de su maestre ó comandante, á fin de que aparesca por ellos que el susodicho buque pertenece real y verdaderamente á ciudadanos de una de las partes. Han convenido asimismo, en que los predichos buques, estando cargados, llevarán, ademas de las mencionadas letras de már ó pasaportes, certificados que contengan los diferentes pormenores del cargamento, y el lugar de donde salio el buque; de manera que se sepa si hay á su bordo efectos prohibidos ó de contrabando; cuyos certificados serán espedidos por los oficiales del lugar de donde salio el buque, en la forma acostumbrada, sin cuyos requisitos el

tribunals: and may be declared a legal prize,—unless the said defect shall be proved to be owing to accident, or be satisfied or supplied by testimony entirely equivalent, in the opinion of said tribunals; to which ends, there shall be allowed a sufficient term of time for its procurement.

Article XIX.

And it is further agreed, that the stipulations above expressed, relative to the visiting and examining of vessels, shall apply to those, only, which sail without convoy, and when said Vessels shall be under convoy, the verbal declaration of the commander of the convoy, on his word-of-honor, that the vessels under his protection belong to the nation whose flag he carries, and, when they are bound to an enemy's port, that they have no contraband goods on board, shall be sufficient.

Article XX.

It is moreover agreed, that, in all cases, the established Courts for prize causes, in the country to which the prize may be conducted, shall, alone, take cognizance of them. And whenever such tribunal, or court, of either party, shall pronounce judgment against any vessel, goods, or prop-

susodicho bajel puede ser detenido, para ser adjudicado por los Tribunales competentes, y puede ser declarado Presa legal, á menos que se pruebe, que el precitado defecto proviene de accidente, ó sea satisfecho ó suplido por un testimonio del todo equivalente, en la opinion de los susodichos Tribunales; á cuyo fin, se concederá un termino suficiente para proporcionarselo.

Articulo 19º

Y ademas se conviene, que las estipulaciones arriba espresadas, relativas á la visita y ecsamen de los buques, se aplicarán solamente á aquellos que navegan sin convoi; y que cuando los predichos buques fueren convoyados, será suficiente la declaracion verbal del Comandante del convoi, bajo su palabra de honor, de que los bajeles que están bajo su proteccion, pertenecen á la nacion cuya bandera tremola él, y, cuando su destino sea á un puerto enemigo, de que no tienen á bordo efectos de contrabando.

Articulo 20º

Se conviene asimismo, que, en todo caso, los Tribunales establecidos para causas de presas, en el Pais á que puedan ser conducidas las presas, serán los unicos que tomen conocimiento de ellas. Y siempre que semejante Tribunal de una ú otra parte, pronunciare juicio contra

erty, claimed by citizens of the other party,—the sentence, or decree, shall mention the reasons, or motives, in which the same shall have been founded:—and an authenticated copy of the sentence, or decree, and of all the proceedings in the case, shall, if demanded, be delivered to the commander, or agent, of said Vessel or property; without any excuse or delay;—he paying the legal fees for the same.

Article XXI

Whenever one of the contracting parties shall be engaged in war with another State, no citizen of the other contracting party, shall accept a commission, or letter-of-marque, for the purpose of assisting, or cooperating hostilely with the said enemy, against the said party so at war; under pain of being treated as a pirate.

Article XXII

If at any time a rupture should take place between the two contracting Nations, and (which God forbid) they should become engaged in war with each other; they have agreed, and do agree now, for then, that the merchants, traders, and other citizens, of all occupations of each of the two parties, residing in the Cities, ports and dominions of the other, shall have the privilege of remain-

algun buque, efectos, ó propiedad reclamados por ciudadanos de la otra parte, la sentencia ó decreto mencionará las razones ó motivos en que se ha fundado, y se entregará al Comandante ó Ajente del Predicho buque ó propiedad, sin escusa ó demora alguna, si él lo pidiere, una copia autentica de la sentencia ó decreto, y de todos los procedimientos del caso, con tal que pague por ello los derechos ó emolumentos legales.

Articulo 21º

Siempre que una de las partes contratantes estuviere empeñada en guerra con otro Estado, ningun ciudadano de la otra parte contratante, aceptará comision ó letra de marca, con el objeto de ayudar ó cooperar hostilmente con el susodicho enemigo contra la predicha parte que está en guerra, só pena de ser tratado como pirata.

Articulo 22º

Si en cualquier tiempo tuviere lugar un rompimiento entre las dos naciones contratantes, y (lo que Dios no permita) se empeñaren en guerra una con otra, han convenido, y convienen, ahora para entonces, que los comerciantes, traficantes, y otros ciudadanos de todas profesiones, de cada una de las partes, que residan en las ciudades, puertos y dominios de la otra, tendrán el privi-

ing and continuing their trade and business therein, and shall be respected and maintained in the full and undisturbed enjoyment of their personal liberty and property; so long as they behave peaceably and properly, and commit no offence against the laws. And in case their conduct should render them suspected of malepractices, and, having thus forfeited this privilege, the respective Governments should think proper to order them to depart; the term of twelve months from the publication, or intimation of this order therefor, shall be allowed them, in which to arrange and settle their affairs, and remove with their families, effects and property; to which end, the necessary safe conduct shall be given to them, and which shall serve as a sufficient protection until they arrive at the designated port and there embark. But this favor shall not be extended to those who shall act contrary to the established laws. It is nevertheless to be understood, that the persons so suspected, may be ordered, by the respective Governments, to remove forthwith into the interior, to such places as they shall think fit to designate.

Article XXIII.

Neither the debts, due from individuals of the one Nation to the individuals of the other, nor shares, nor money, which they

lejio de permanecer alli, y de continuar su comercio y negocio, y serán respetados y mantenidos en el pleno y tranquilo goze de su libertad personal y de su propiedad, en tanto que se conduscan pacificamente, de un modo arreglado, y no cometan ofenza alguna contra las leyes. Y en caso de que su conducta los hiciere sospechosos de malas practicas, y por haber perdido así este privilejio, juzgaren oportuno los Gobiernos respectivos mandarles partir, se les concederá el termino de doce meses, contados desde la publicacion ó intimacion de la orden, para que en él puedan arreglar y ordenar sus negocios, y retirarse con sus familias, efectos y propiedades; á cuyo fin, se les dará el necesario salvo-conducto, que sirva de suficiente proteccion hasta que lleguen al puerto designado, y en él se embarquen. Pero este favor no se estenderá á aquellos que obraren de un modo contrario á las leyes establecidas. Debe, no obstante, entenderse, que á las personas asi sospechadas, pueden los Gobiernos respectivos mandarlas retirar inmediatamente á lo interior, á aquellos lugares que tengan por conveniente designar.

Articulo 23º

Ni las deudas, que debieren individuos de una nacion á individuos de la otra, ni las acciones, ni el dinero que puedan tener en los

may have in public funds, nor in public or private Banks, shall ever, in any event of war or national difference, be sequestered or confiscated.

Article XXIV.

Both the contracting parties being desirous of avoiding all inequality in relation to their public communications and official intercourse, they have agreed, and do agree, to grant to their Envoys, Ministers, and other public Agents the same favors, immunities and exemptions as those of the most favored Nation do, or shall enjoy:—it being understood, that whatever favors, immunities, or privileges the United States of America, or the Peru-Bolivian confederation, may find it proper to grant to the Envoys, Ministers, and public Agents of any other Power, shall by the same act, be granted and extended to those of the contracting parties respectively.

Article XXV.

To make more effectual the protection which the United States of America and the Peru-Bolivian confederation shall afford in future to the navigation and commerce of the citizens of each other;—they agree to receive and admit Consuls and Vice Consuls, in all the ports open to foreign commerce; who shall enjoy within

fondos Publicos, ó en bancos publicos ó particulares, se secuestrarán ó confiscarán, en ningun caso de guerra, ó de otra diferencia nacional.

Articulo 24º

Deseando las dos partes contratantes evitar toda desigualdad con relacion á sus comunicaciones públicas, y á su correspondencia oficial, han convenido, y convienen, en conceder á sus Enviados, Ministros, y otros Ajentes públicos, los mismos favores, inmunidades y esenciones, que hoy disfrutan, ó en adelante disfrutaren, los de la Nacion mas favorecida; entendiendose, que cualesquiera favores, inmunidades ó privilejios que la Confederacion Peru-Boliviana y los Estados Unidos de America tuvieren por conveniente conceder á los Enviados, Ministros, y Ajentes Publicos de cualquiera otra potencia, serán por el mismo acto, estendidos y concedidos á los de las partes contratantes, respectivamente.

Articulo 25º

A fin de hacer mas efectiva la proteccion que la Confederacion Peru-Boliviana y los Estados Unidos de America concedieren en lo futuro á la Navegacion y comercio de los ciudadanos de cada una de las dos partes, convienen en recibir y admitir Consules y Vice-Consules en todos los puertos abiertos al comercio extranjero; los

their respective consular districts, all the rights, prerogatives and immunities of the Consuls and Vice Consuls of the most favored Nation; each contracting party however, remaining at liberty to except those ports and places in which the admission and residence of such functionaries may not seem convenient.

cuales disfrutarán, dentro de sus respectivos distritos consulares, todos los derechos, prerrogativas é inmunidades de los Consules y Vice-Consules de la Nacion mas favorecida; quedando, sin embargo, cada una de las partes contratantes en libertad de esceptuar aquellos puertos y lugares en donde no se crea conveniente la admision y residencia de tales funcionarios.

Article XXVI.

In order that the Consuls and Vice-Consuls of the two contracting parties may enjoy the rights, prerogatives and immunities which belong to them by their public character, they shall before entering on the exercise of their functions, exhibit their commission, or patent, in due form, to the government to which they are accredited, and having received their *exequatur*, they shall be held and considered as such Consuls and Vice Consuls, by all the authorities, magistrates and inhabitants in the Consular district in which they reside.

Articulo 26º

Para que los Consules y Vice-Consules de las dos partes contratantes, puedan disfrutar de los derechos, prerrogativas, é inmunidades, que les pertenecen por su caracter publico, exhibirán, antes de ejercer sus funciones, su comision ó patente, en debida forma, al Gobierno cerca del cual están acreditados; y habiendo recibido su *execuatur*, serán tenidos y considerados como tales Consules ó Vice Consules, por todas las Autoridades, Majistrados y habitantes del distrito consular donde residan.

Article XXVII.

It is likewise agreed that the consuls, Vice Consuls, their secretaries, officers, and persons attached to their service;—they not being Citizens of the country in which the Consul, or Vice Consul resides, shall be exempt from all public service, and also from all

Articulo 27º

Se conviene, asimismo, que los Consules, Vice-Consules, sus Secretarios, Oficiales, y personas agregadas á su servicio, con tal que no sean ciudadanos del Pais en donde resida el Consul ó Vice-Consul, estarán esentos de todo servicio publico, y tambien de

kinds of taxes, imposts and contributions, except those which they shall be obliged to pay on account of commerce, or their property; and from which the Citizens of their respective country, resident in the other, are not exempt, in virtue of the stipulations contained in this treaty:—they, being, in every thing besides, subject to the laws of the respective States. The archives and Papers of the Consulates shall be respected inviolably, and under no pretext, whatever, shall any magistrate, or other person, seize, or in any way interfere with them.

Article XXVIII.

The said Consuls and Vice-Consuls shall have power to require the assistance of the authorities of the country, for the arrest, detention and custody, of deserters from the public and private vessels of their country; and for this purpose, they shall address themselves to the Courts, Judges, or officers competent, and shall demand the said deserters in writing; proving, by an exhibition of the ship's roll, or other public document, that the men so demanded, are part of the crew of the vessel from which it is alledged they have deserted: and, on this demand, so proved, (saving however, when the contrary is more conclusively proved) the delivery

todo jenero de contribuciones, pechos, é impuestos, escepto aquellos que estuvieren obligados á pagar, á causa de su comercio, ó de su propiedad, y de los cuales no están esentos, á virtud de las estipulaciones contenidas en este tratado, los ciudadanos de su respectivo pais residentes en el otro; entendiendose, que en todo lo demas están sujetos á las leyes de los respectivos Estados. Los archivos y papeles de los Consulados, serán inviolablemente respetados; y bajo de ningun pretesto se apoderará de ellos, ó intervendrá en manera alguna con ellos, ningun majistrado, ni cualquiera otra persona.

Articulo 28º

Los susodichos Consules y Vice-Consules tendrán la facultad de requerir el aucilio de las autoridades del pais, para el arresto, detencion y custodia de los desertores de los buques públicos y particulares de su pais; y al efecto, se dirijirán á los Tribunales, Juezes, ú oficiales competentes, y pedirán, por escrito, los susodichos desertores; manifestando el ròl del buque, ú otros documentos publicos, para probar con ellos que los hombres asi pedidos forman parte de la tripulacion del buque, de donde se alega que se desertaron; y sobre esta peticion, asi probada (esceptuandose, no obstante los casos en que lo contrario se pruebe de un modo mas

shall not be refused. Such deserters, when arrested, shall be put at the disposal of the said Consuls or vice-Consuls, and may be put in the public prisons, at the request and expense of those who reclaim them, to be sent to the ships to which they belong;— or to others of the same nation: but if they should not be so sent within two months, to be counted from the day of their arrest,—they shall be set at liberty, and shall be no more arrested for the same cause.

Article XXIX

For the purpose of more effectually protecting their commerce and Navigation, the two contracting parties do hereby agree to form, as soon hereafter as may be mutually convenient, a Consular convention, which shall declare, specially, the powers and immunities of the Consuls and Vice Consuls of the respective parties.

Article XXX

The United States of America and the Peru-Bolivian Confederation, desiring to make as durable as circumstances will permit, the relations which are established between the two parties in virtue of this Treaty, or General Convention of Peace, Friendship, Commerce and Navigation, have declared solemnly, and do agree, as follows:

concluyente), no se reusará la entrega. Una vez arrestados los tales desertores, se tendrán á disposicion de los susodichos Consules ó Vice-Consules, y pueden ponerse en las prisiones publicas, á peticion y costo de aquellos que los reclaman, para ser enviados á los buques á que pertenecen, ú á otros de la misma nacion: pero si no fueren así enviados dentro de dos meses, que deberán contarse desde el dia de su arresto, serán puestos en libertad, y no volverán á ser arrestados por la misma causa.

Articulo 29º

Con el objeto de protejer de un modo mas efectivo su comercio y navegacion, las dos partes contratantes, convienen por la presente, en formar mas adelante, tan pronto como á ambas les convenga, una convencion consular, en que se declaren especialmente los poderes é inmunidades de los Consules y Vice-Consules de las partes respectivas.

Articulo 30º

La Confederacion Peru-Boliviana y los Estados Unidos de America, deseando hacer tan duraderas, cuanto lo permitan las circunstancias, las relaciones que están establecidas entre las dos partes en virtud de este tratado, ó convencion jeneral de Páz, Amistad, comercio y navegacion, han declarado solemnemente, y convienen en lo que sigue:

1ˢᵗ The present Treaty shall be in force for twelve years, from the day of the exchange of the ratifications thereof; and, further, until the end of one year after either of the contracting parties shall have given notice to the other of its intention to terminate the same each of them reserving to itself the right of giving such notice to the other, at the end of said term of twelve years. And it is hereby agreed between the parties, that, on the expiration of one year after such notice shall have been received by either of them, from the other, as above mentioned;—this Treaty shall, in all points relating to commerce and navigation, altogether cease and determine;—and in all those parts which relate to peace and friendship, it shall be permanently and perpetually binding on both Powers.

2ⁿᵈˡʸ If any, one or more, of the citizens of either party shall infringe any of the articles of this Treaty, such citizen, or citizens, shall be held personally responsible therefor; — and the harmony and good correspondence between the two nations shall not be interrupted thereby; each party engaging, in no way to protect the offender or offenders, or to sanction such violence;—under pain of rendering itself liable for the consequences thereof.

I. El presente tratado subsistirá en toda su fuerza por el espacio de doce años contados desde el dia en que se canjeen sus ratificaciones, y ademas, hasta el fin de un año despues que una de las partes contratantes haya dado aviso á la otra de su intencion de que el mismo termine; reservandose cada una de ellas el derecho de dar á la otra el susodicho aviso al fin del precitado termino de doce años. Y por la presente se conviene entre las partes, que al espirar un año despues de haber recibido una de ellas, de parte de la otra, el tal aviso, segun se ha mencionado arriba, cesará y terminará este Tratado en todos los puntos relativos á comercio y Navegacion; y en todas aquellas partes que son referentes á la Páz y Amistad, será permanente y perpetuamente obligatorio á las dos Potencias.

II. Si uno, ó mas, de los ciudadanos de una ú otra parte, infrinjiese alguno de los articulos de este tratado, el tal ciudadano ó ciudadanos serán personalmente responsables por ello, y no se interrumpirá por esto la armonia y buena correspondencia entre las dos Naciones, comprometiendose cada parte á no protejer en manera alguna al ofensor ú ofensores, ni á sancionar la tal violencia, só pena de hacerse responsable por sus consecuencias.

3^{rdly} If, (which indeed cannot be expected) unfortunately, any of the stipulations contained in the present Treaty shall be violated, or infringed, in any other way whatever, it is expressly covenanted and agreed, that neither of the contracting parties will order or authorize, any act of reprizals, nor declare or make war against the other, on complaint of injuries or damages resulting therefrom, until the party considering itself aggrieved shall first have presented to the other a statement or representation of such injuries or damages, verified by competent proofs,—and have demanded redress and satisfaction;—and the same shall have been either refused or unreasonably delayed.

4^{thly} Nothing in this treaty contained shall, however, be construed to operate contrary to former and existing public Treaties with other States or Sovereigns.

The present Treaty of Peace, Friendship, Commerce and Navigation shall be approved and ratified by the President of the United States of America, by and with the advice and consent of the Senate thereof; and by the Supreme Protector of the North and South Peruvian States, President of the Republic of Bolivia, encharged with the direction of the foreign relations of the Peru-

III. Si desgraciadamente, y contra lo que en verdad debe esperarse, alguna de las estipulaciones contenidas en el presente tratado, fuere violada ó infrinjida de cualquiera otra manera, se estipula y conviene espresamente, que ninguna de las partes contratantes ordenará, ni autorizará, acto alguno de represalia, ni declarará, ò hará la guerra á la otra, por quejas de injurias ó daños que de ello resulten, hasta que la parte que se considera agraviada, haya primero presentado á la otra una esposicion ó representacion de tales daños ó injurias, comprobandolos competentemente, y hasta haber pedido satisfaccion y reparacion, y haberse negado estas, ó demorado mas tiempo del racional.

IV. Sin embargo, nada de lo que en este tratado se contiene, se construirá de manera que obre de un modo contrario á anteriores y ecsistentes tratados publicos, celebrados con otros Estados ó Soberanos.

El presente tratado de páz, amistad, comercio y navegacion, será aprobado y ratificado por el Supremo Protector de los Estados Nor y Sur-Peruanos, Presidente de la Republica de Bolivia, encargado de la direccion de las Relaciones Exteriores de la Confederacion Peru-Boliviana, y por el Presidente de los Estados Unidos de America, con anuencia y consentimiento del Senado de los

Bolivian Confederation;—and the ratifications shall be exchanged within eighteen Months from the date of the signature hereof;—or sooner if possible.

predichos Estados Unidos de America; y las ratificaciones serán canjeadas dentro del termino de diez y ocho meses, contados desde la fecha en que este tratado está firmado, ó antes, si fuese posible.

In faith whereof, we, the Plenipotentiaries of the United States of America, and the Peru-Bolivian Confederation, have signed and sealed these presents.

Done, in the City of Lima, on the thirtieth day of November in the year of Our Lord, One thousand eight hundred and thirty Six.

En feé de lo cual, nosotros los Plenipotenciarios de la Confederacion Perú Boliviana, y de los Estados Unidos de America, lo hemos firmado y sellado.

Fecho en la Ciudad de Lima, el dia treinta de Noviembre del Año de Nuestro Señor de Mil ochocientos treinta y seis.

SAM. LARNED.   [Seal]
J. GARCIA DEL RIO   [Seal]

(L. S.)   J. GARCIA DEL RIO.
(L. S.)   SAMUEL LARNED.

NOTES

There is the same unimportant question here as in certain other cases (e.g., Documents 47, 50, 64, and 73) whether the agreement should be called a treaty or a convention. The expression "Treaty, or General Convention" is in the preamble and in Article 30, but in Article 30 the words "the present treaty" or "this treaty" are used six times; both the presidential message of September 7, 1837 (Executive Journal, V, 28), and the Senate resolution of the following October 10 (*ibid.*, 42) refer to the "general convention"; but the word "treaty" is used in these notes, following its use in the declaration of February 9, 1848, which is printed below.

The textual date of this treaty is November 30, 1836, but the actual date of its signature is uncertain; probably it was not signed until some time in January 1837. The original in the treaty file was enclosed with the despatch of Samuel Larned, Chargé d'Affaires to Peru, of January 14, 1837 (D. S., 4 Despatches, Peru, No. 201). On November 19, 1836, Larned wrote that he had "arranged and agreed upon a treaty with this country of the most advantageous description; and that it only awaits being done into Spanish (which, also, is already far advanced) and copied out, to receive our signatures" (*ibid.*, No. 192); and in his despatch of December 4 (*ibid.*, No. 195) he added:

The thirtieth of last month, was the day agreed upon for the signing of the Treaty of Friendship, Commerce and navigation with this country, in the terms mentioned in my communication Nº 192:—and it would have been signed on that day, had the Peruvian Plenipotentiary been ready with his copies; but a number of errors and omissions having been found in them, upon examination

and collation, it became necessary to make out new copies. This, it will take them some days to effect; but so soon as they are ready with correct ones, we shall proceed to the signature of this Treaty:—in the meantime, the whole is arranged and agreed upon; and the Treaty is to bear the date mentioned, out of compliment to the President and the Supreme Protector, (under whose immediate auspices it was negotiated) that being S⁺ Andrew's day, and consequently their *Jour d' fete.* I fear it will not be ready in season to be got home and acted on at the present Session of Congress.

THE FILE PAPERS

While this treaty was signed in the two languages, the procedure adopted was that one original, in English only, was signed for the Government of the United States, and another original, in Spanish only, for the Government of the Peru-Bolivian Confederation. Accordingly, both the duplicate United States instrument of ratification of October 14, 1837, and the original proclamation of October 3, 1838, which are attached to the original treaty in the file, include the English text of the treaty only; and similarly the ratification on the part of the Peru-Bolivian Confederation of January 10, 1837, includes the Spanish text only. It is from that instrument of ratification that the Spanish text above printed is taken. As the printed texts show, the *alternat* was properly observed.

The treaty file is complete, including the attested Senate resolution of October 10, 1837 (Executive Journal, V, 42), and the certificate of the exchange of ratifications at Lima on May 28, 1838, which is in Spanish and in customary form.

It appears that no papers accompanied this treaty when it was submitted to the Senate with the presidential message of September 7, 1837 (*ibid.*, 28). It was communicated to Congress with the presidential message of December 3, 1838 (Richardson, III, 483, 489).

THE BASIS OF THE TREATY

The basis of this treaty was that with Colombia of October 3, 1824 (Document 47); in large part the provisions are similar, although there are not a few changes of wording and some of substance.

Regarding the terms of the treaty and its advantages as he saw them, Larned wrote (D. S., 4 Despatches, Peru, No. 192, November 19, 1836):

The basis of this treaty is that with Colombia, or of equality with the most favored nation:—but it contains several valuable and important provisions not in that, or any of our treaties with these new States; and which are essential to the security of our interests, and the safety of our citizens, in these continually embroiled countries: such as, their exemption from forced loans, occasional contributions and military service, by land and sea: a stipulation, that, even in the event of war, they may continue to reside and carry on their business, without molestation in their persons or property. . . .

The treaty is for twelve years fixed, and until one year after notice by either of the parties. It is made, at the suggestion of General Santa Cruz, and as now a matter of course, with the Peru-Bolivian Confederation; which extends its benefits to the ports of Bolivia; where, in consequence of its provisions, we shall be placed on the same advantageous footing as French citizens occupy, since the

negotiation of the treaty between France and Bolivia [of December 9, 1834; Spanish text, with translation, in British and Foreign State Papers, XXIII, 165–89]. A stipulation is inserted, that our vessels employed in the fisheries shall be allowed to enter the ports of Peru for refreshments &c. to which obstacles have heretofore been interposed. It contains, also, all the stipulations making the flag cover the property—touching the meaning of blockade &c., embraced in our treaty with Colombia; by virtue of which, and the similar ones in that with Chile,—in the event of war between Peru and Chile, our vessels will be enabled to perform their carrying, and even coasting, trade. Our commercial fellow-citizens here, are highly gratified at the happy conclusion of this interesting negotiation; which secures our flour-trade to this country,—thereby greatly facilitating our trade to it, in general;—and defeats the application of the odious principle of special privileges, consigned in that with Chile;—and which she is so earnest to establish.

As this treaty was initiated directly with the Supreme Protector, so have most of these valuable provisions been obtained by personal negotiation with him:—for my friend Mr Garcia del Rio, the Plenipotentiary *ad hoc*, although exceedingly well inclined, did not feel himself authorized to yield them; and requested me, therefore, to "speak to the General about them myself." It is very gratifying to me, to be able to say, that I succeeded in every instance, save one, and that of little moment,—namely, obtaining for our citizens the privilege of carrying on the *retail* trade; which, he said, he did not dare to grant,—as he had been compelled to refuse it to the French, in Bolivia: we therefore concluded to say nothing about it, one way or the other;—and let it stand on the footing of tolerance, as at present. Not one of our citizens is, however, here engaged in this business, at present.

RELATIONS WITH BOLIVIA AND PERU

Prior to this treaty the United States had made no treaty with either Bolivia or Peru. The independence of Peru was proclaimed on July 15, 1821 (Aranda, Tratados del Perú, I, 260–61); and James Cooley, of Pennsylvania, was commissioned Chargé d'Affaires at Lima on May 2, 1826. On January 13, 1823, John B. Prevost, of New York, had been nominated to that post, but his nomination was recalled in a message of March 1 of the same year (Executive Journal, III, 320, 340).

Under Spanish rule Bolivia (Upper Peru) was within the Viceroyalty of Peru until 1776, and thereafter part of the Viceroyalty of Buenos Aires. The contest for independence began on May 25, 1809, and was decided by the battle of Ayacucho of December 9, 1824. A constitutional congress which met at Chuquisaca on August 6, 1825, declared that Upper Peru should be an independent state and adopted the name of Bolivia; the constitution was formally proclaimed on November 19, 1826 (see Pan American Union, American Nation Series, No. 2, Bolivia, 5–7).

The first appointment of a diplomatic representative of the United States to the Republic of Bolivia was that of John Appleton, of Maine, on March 30, 1848, as Chargé d'Affaires; but James B. Thornton, when appointed Chargé d'Affaires to Peru, was given a full power under date of July 7, 1836 (D. S., 2 Credences, 251), to treat with the Government of Bolivia upon the subjects of commerce and claims, and also instructions in that regard and a letter of credence to that Government. Thornton, however, died on January 25, 1838, three days after his arrival at Callao.

The *de facto* union of Peru and Bolivia commenced in 1836 and did not last beyond January 1839.   In the despatch of James C. Pickett of March 27, 1839, from Quito (D. S., 5 Despatches, Peru, No. 6), is the following about the Peru-Bolivian Confederation:

The Peru-Bolivian Confederation is certainly at an end, and General Santa-Cruz, the *Protector* of it, is now in Guayaquil.   Instead of finding support and cooperation in the South, as he expected, and of returning to Lima, in three or four months, with eight or nine thousand troops, as he said he could do, when he left it, he found every where, revolutionary movements against himself, and was fortunate to be able to escape from Arequipa, (which he did with difficulty) to the port of Islay, where a British vessel of war received him and eight or ten officers on board, and brought them to Ecuador.   In Bolivia, also, there has been a revolution fatal to his authority and influence, and in that state, Genⁱ Ballivian, his enemy, is now at the head of affairs.

The Full Powers

The Plenipotentiary of the United States who signed this treaty was Samuel Larned, who was appointed Chargé d'Affaires to Peru on May 15, 1830, following an earlier commission in the same capacity, of December 29, 1828, on which day his full power was issued, authorizing him to "agree treat, consult and negotiate of and concerning commerce and Navigation between the United States, and the Republic of Peru, and claims of the Citizens of the two Countries respectively upon the Governments of the United States, and the said Republic of Peru, and all matters and subjects connected therewith, and to conclude and sign a Treaty or Treaties, Convention or Conventions touching the premises" (D. S., 2 Credences, 97).   The second commission to Larned was given because of the death of his intended successor as Chargé d'Affaires to Peru, Emanuel J. West, who had been appointed on October 22, 1829, but who died while on his way to Lima; but at no time was Larned accredited to the Government of the Peru-Bolivian Confederation; and efforts on the part of Larned to open negotiations with Bolivia were emphatically disapproved (D. S., 15 Instructions, Peru, 6–8, August 26, 1835).

The decree of General Santa Cruz, Article 1 of which declared that "The Peru-Bolivian Confederation, composed of the North Peruvian State, of the South Peruvian State, and of the Republic of Bolivia, is established", was dated October 28, 1836.   A copy and translation of that decree are with the despatch of Larned of January 14, 1837 (D. S., 4 Despatches, Peru, No. 201).

It is specifically stated in the preamble of this treaty that certified copies of the full powers were exchanged.   The certified copy of the full power of Don Juan Garcia del Rio was an enclosure to the despatch of Larned of January 14, 1837 (D. S., 4 Despatches, Peru, No. 201).   The accompanying translation thereof is as follows:

Andrew Santa Cruz, Captain General, Restorer, Great Citizen and President of Bolivia, General of Brigade of Colombia, Grand Marshal Pacificator of Peru, Supreme Protector of the South and North Peruvian States, Encharged with the Direction of the Foreign Relations of the Peru-Bolivian Confederation, etc.

For as much as the Government of the United States of America has authorized their Chargé d'Affaires near this to arrange and celebrate a treaty of peace, friendship, commerce, and navigation; the epoch having arrived for celebrating it in consequence of the invitation which the said Chargé d'Affaires has made in his note of the 11th of October of this year; and it being necessary to invest, on the part of the States composing the Peru-Bolivian Confederation, a sufficient Minister Plenipotentiary for this object; meriting our confidence Don Juan Garcia del Rio, Minister of State in the Department of Finance of the North Peruvian State, I have, therefore, named him Minister Plenipotentiary for the expressed purpose, conferring on him full and especial power to negotiate and celebrate the treaty of peace, friendship, commerce, and navigation above mentioned.

In faith whereof we have caused these presents to be issued, signed with our hand, sealed with the great seal of the Confederation, and countersigned by our Secretary General, Minister of Foreign Relations, in the Protectoral Palace in Lima, the thirty-first day of October, one thousand eight hundred and thirty-six.

[Seal]   ANDREW SANTA CRUZ

By order of His Excellency:
PIO DE TRISTAN

Instructions regarding the negotiation of a treaty with Peru were given as early as April 15, 1828 (D. S., 12 Instructions, U. S. Ministers, 89–95), to James Cooley, the predecessor of Samuel Larned as Chargé d'Affaires at Lima; and the early instructions were renewed; but the occasional discussions with the Government of Peru from 1832 on reached no result (D. S., 3 Despatches, Peru, No. 167, April 13, 1836).

This treaty was negotiated after General Santa Cruz, President of Bolivia, had assumed the rule over both countries, with the titles given in the full power above quoted.

THE EXCHANGE OF RATIFICATIONS

Serious procedural difficulties arose in effecting the exchange of ratifications of this treaty. By its terms (Article 30) the exchange was to take place within eighteen months of the date of signature, or by May 30, 1838; the place of exchange was not stated.

The United States instrument of ratification was transmitted with instructions of October 14, 1837 (D. S., 15 Instructions, Peru, 17–18), by the hands of William B. Hodgson as bearer of despatches; the instructions were directed to James B. Thornton, Chargé d'Affaires, and with them was a power authorizing him to make the exchange. Hodgson arrived at Lima on April 2, 1838, and learned that Thornton had died more than two months earlier. The American consul at Lima, Edwin Bartlett, to whom the ratification, the despatches, and other papers were delivered by Hodgson, wrote as follows (D. S., 3 Consular Despatches, Lima, No. 11, April 5, 1838):

Immediately on the receipt of the Treaty I called upon the acting Minister of Foreign affairs to state the fact & to learn whether the ratifications could be at once exchanged here, or whether it would be necessary to refer the case to H. E the Protector, now in Bolivia. I thought this better than to lose time in correspondence when the term within which the ratifications must be exchanged, was so near expiring. I found one of the original copies of the treaty in the office of the Minister of Foreign Affairs, ratified by H. E the Protector; but wanting the usual form of the Preamble & conclusion. No special powers or instructions to

exchange the ratifications had been left by the Protector and the minister expressed his wish to have another copy of the Treaty made out in the usual form, to be sent to the Protector for his ratification; & promised to have it ready in four or five days, intimating a wish that a vessel of war of the U States might take the bearer of it to the nearest point of communication with the Protector, & there await his return.

Under these circumstances I did not hesitate to request Commander McKeever of the Falmouth to offer his ship which he has done & I have today informed the Minister that she will be ready on the 7th inst to convey the messenger with the treaty, to any port he may designate.

I stated to the Minister that the instructions from you & authority from the President to exchange the ratifications were directed to the late Mr Thornton: but he assures me that his Gov't will readily admit my authority, subject to the future approval of the President to do all that may be required to effect the exchange.

But the effort to have a new ratification executed by General Santa Cruz and returned to Lima by May 30, 1838, failed; and in his despatch of July 5, 1838, Bartlett thus describes the procedure finally adopted (D. S., 3 Consular Despatches, Lima, No. 17):

Finding by information received from Mr Hodgson, on his arrival at Arequipa, that there was no probability that the copy of the Treaty sent to the Protector, would be returned here previous to the 30th May, the last day allowed by the 30th Article, for the Exchange of the ratifications, I addressed a note on the 17 of May . . . to the acting Minister of Foreign affairs, proposing a provisional exchange of the copy I held for that left here by the Protector. After submitting my Note to the Ministers in Council, and the President of the State of North Peru, who is invested by the Protector with extraordinary powers, my proposal was agreed to. . . . I called upon D^n Juan Garcia del Rio who was authorized to exchange the ratifications, compared the copy of the Treaty sent by you with the original & delivered it, taking, at the same time, the original copy in Spanish, having the ratification of the Protector annexed, signing four copies of the Certificate of Exchange, two in English and two in Spanish . . . thus complying with the strict letter of the 30th article of the Treaty.

On the 30th June, the bearer of the Copy sent to the Protector returned with it to Lima, having a letter to me from the Acting Minister of Foreign Affairs of the Peru Bolivian Confederation, dated Cochabumba 25 May . . . and on the same day, I rec^d from the Acting Minister of Foreign Affairs in Lima, a note ; . . informing me that the treaty had been received and sent to D^n Juan Garcia del Rio, the Commissioner named by the Protector, to be exchanged. I replyed . . . and called immediately upon Garcia del Rio taking with me the original treaty received on the 28 May, and after comparing it with the newly ratified Copy, exchanged the one for the other, leaving it to appear upon the face of the Certificate of exchange, as if the copy now held by me had been delivered on the 28 May.

Official approval of that procedure was given by Aaron Vail, Acting Secretary of State, in his communication to Bartlett under date of October 6, 1838, from which the following is extracted (D. S., 9 Instructions to Consuls, 329):

The President approves the course you took at the delicate and critical juncture occasioned by the decease of Mr Thornton with respect to the exchange of the ratifications of the treaty. The accompanying power is deemed the best mode of giving the formal sanction to your action for that purpose in behalf of the United States, which the Acting Minister of Foreign Affairs, in his note to you of the 25th of May last, says would be expected by that Government. You will accordingly transmit the power to that functionary with a letter stating the

purpose for which it is designed and the lively sense entertained by the President of the fresh proof of friendly regard for the United States shown by waiving punctilio as to your wanting of special powers to make the exchange. If however Mͬ Pickett should have arrived at Lima, you will request him to perform this service, as he will be the most proper organ of communication.

James C. Pickett, named in the foregoing instruction, was appointed on June 9, 1838, as Chargé d'Affaires to the Peru-Bolivian Confederation (D. S., 2 Credences, 301); but his actual post was that of Chargé d'Affaires to Peru, as he did not arrive at Lima until August 6, 1839 (D. S., 5 Despatches, Peru, No. 1, August 23, 1839).

The full power to exchange the ratifications is recorded in D. S., 2 Credences, 307. It recites the fact of the issuance of a power to James B. Thornton under date of October 14, 1837, and also that "the said James B. Thornton died before that power arrived at Lima". Its concluding words are merely, "Given under my hand at the city of Washington", followed by the signature of President Van Buren and the countersignature of Aaron Vail as Acting Secretary of State. The following note is appended to the record:

The above power was signed on the 6th of October, 1838, and sent to Mr Bartlett with a letter of that date, to be communicated to the Minister of Foreign Affairs of the Peru-Bolivian Confederation, in compliance with the wish of that government that Mͬ Bartlett's action in the place of Mr Thornton for the exchange of the ratifications of the Convention, should be formally sanctioned by the government of the United States.

That power, however, was not delivered, as it did not reach Lima until after the Peru-Bolivian Confederation had ceased to exist in any sense. Bartlett reported as follows (D. S., 5 Consular Despatches, Lima, No. 52, May 18, 1839):

I have the honor to acknowledge the receipt of your letter of 6 Octͬ last transmitting a power from the President, sanctioning, and confirming what I had done in Exchanging the treaty between the United States, and the Peru Bolivian Confederation, and am gratified to find that the course I pursued in that business has met with his approval.

As the Peru Bolivian Confederation is dissolved De facto and as the present Government in Peru has shewn a disposition to deny the existence of the treaty, on the ground that the Confederation never Existed I have thought it best to retain the power now sent, until further instructions from you, or the arrival of Mͬ Pickett. The treaty having been proclaimed and published here, and (I presume) at Washington, is binding on both parties without this document & it may give rise to a new question with this Government if transmitted now.

DURATION OF THE TREATY

The Peru-Bolivian Confederation came to an end in 1839, and the separate existence of the two Republics of Bolivia and Peru was then resumed. The question of the later validity of this treaty as to the Republic of Peru was raised by the note of Joaquin José de Osma, Minister of Peru, dated April 22, 1847, as follows (D. S., 1 Notes from the Peruvian Legation, translation; see Senate Confidential Document No. 17, 31st Congress, 1st session, Regular Confidential Documents, XXIII, 989–1049):

The undersigned, Minister Plenipotentiary of Peru near the United States of America, has the honor to enclose, for the consideration of the Honorable Secretary of State, a copy of a resolution voted by the Congress of Peru, declaring that it does not recognize as binding to the nation, the treaties entered into by General Andres Santa Cruz, President of Bolivia, when he usurped the authority of Peru after having invaded that country in 1836.

In the interview which the undersigned had with the Honorable Secretary of State for the purpose of explaining, in pursuance of instructions received from his Government, the motives and causes which have operated in inducing the latter to declare as null the treaty which had been agreed upon with the United States by General Santa Cruz in the name of the projected Peruvian-Bolivian Confederacy, the Honorable Secretary of State declared that he had no knowledge of such resolution and that consequently he could not express the opinion of his Government relative to said treaty, but that he believed it to be in force in consequence of its having been consummated by a government *de facto*. In forwarding on this occasion the above-mentioned resolution, the undersigned begs that the Honorable Secretary of State will permit him to reiterate the reasons which he had expressed to him verbally, in order that, by examining them at leisure, he may be able to judge whether they are sufficient to justify the resolution of the Peruvian Congress and whether they can contribute to a mutual understanding on the subject between the two Governments.

General Santa Cruz, President of Bolivia, invaded Peru towards the end of the year 1835, under the pretext of rendering assistance to one of the parties which contended for the supremacy of power in that country; and as soon as the campaign of 1836 was terminated, he usurped that power on his own account, and in order to consolidate it he issued a proclamation dividing Peru into two States—North and South Peru—and exhibited a disposition to form through them and Bolivia a confederation which he was to rule by the name of "Protector". Without any other title—without this confederacy having become anything but a project, merely a political speculation—General Santa Cruz, in order to give the moral weight of public treaties to his authority, consummated one in the name of a confederacy which had no existence, with Mr. Larned, Chargé d'Affaires of the United States near the Republic of Peru. The undersigned is ignorant whether Mr. Larned was then accredited near the Peruvian-Bolivian Confederation, but he believes not, because at that time the Confederacy was nothing but a political scheme which General Santa Cruz had in contemplation. In April 1837 a conference was held at Tacna by order of that Chief, composed of three Plenipotentiaries for each State, whom he himself appointed and through whom he decreed a federal compact for the organization of the government of the Confederacy, but with a condition expressed in the same document that this law would not be in force until it was approved by the Congresses of the several States. That of Bolivia, the only one that General Santa Cruz convened for this object, rejected the federal compact; those of North and South Peru were not assembled and consequently the Confederacy never was organized nor established. In the meanwhile, in October 1837, the south of Peru was occupied by some Peruvian forces commanded by the chiefs who always resisted the authority of the President of Bolivia, aided by some troops from Chile; and during the war, which was abetted by the downright opposition of the people of Peru to the Government of Santa Cruz and to his own projects for establishing the Confederacy, the capital shook off his power (in July 1838), and shortly after (in January 1839), he was himself put down and driven from the country.

The undersigned finds himself obliged to refer to these facts in order to convince the Honorable Secretary of State that the so-called Peru-Bolivian Confederation was nothing more than a project; that such Confederacy never was established nor attained the character of those political bodies with which other nations can solemnize public compacts; and that the authority of General Santa Cruz, who styled himself the Chief of that Confederation, never implied in Peru the quiet and undisturbed exercise of the supreme power which is required from governments *de facto* in order that their stipulations may be considered capable of producing the effects of international obligations.

The establishment of the Peru-Bolivian Confederation, as it was projected by General Santa Cruz, would have required that the three States of which it was supposed to be constituted, had had a previous existence; and it was, moreover, necessary that the governments of such States should themselves have agreed to enter into some federal compact according to the forms generally adopted in those cases.   Peru had proclaimed its independence in 1821; Bolivia did the same in 1825 at the expiration of Spanish dominion in South America; the independence of both countries had been recognized by other nations, but none of them—not even those which had entered into treaties with Santa Cruz in the name of the Confederation—had ever recognized in Peru the existence of two independent States, but a single Republic near which they had accredited agents, and the institutions of which, although occasionally interrupted by the troubles of the times, could not be unknown to them.   But, even supposing for a moment that the Confederation had existed according to the project of federal compact mentioned before and published at Tacna in 1837, even then General Santa Cruz (by the Article 23) had no authority to make treaties without the permission and consent of the Senate; and that body was never assembled nor appointed, because the project of the federal compact had never passed into a law nor contributed to organize the government of the Confederacy; so that, even supposing that it had existed, still the treaty with the United States had been solemnized by an incompetent authority and without those formalities required by its political code.

The undersigned is ready to acknowledge with the Honorable Secretary of State the principle that treaties entered into with governments *de facto* should be considered as binding on those nations in the name of which they were made; but he cannot designate as a government *de facto* in Peru the unsettled authority of General Santa Cruz—a foreign chieftain who invaded that country without cause, ruled it by force of arms, and who was incessantly engaged in hostilities to maintain his power.   The acts of governments *de facto* are considered valid because their authority is presumed to be legitimate; but when all the circumstances attending the existence of such governments demonstrate the reverse, there is no reason, in the opinion of the undersigned, for giving to their public acts a character which is denied by the facts themselves.   None of the qualities which are thought indispensable to constitute a government *de facto* out of any authority—viz., the entire submission of the country, the undisturbed possession of the supreme power, strengthened and consolidated by time—constituted the power of General Santa Cruz in Peru.   The only point of view in which the Government of the latter can be considered is that of a conqueror, because, being the Chief of another independent State, he invaded Peru with his forces, usurped there the supreme power, and maintained himself in possession of it for a short time with the aid of the Bolivian Army; and such being the case, the undersigned is of opinion that Peru cannot be denied the right of repudiating obligations contracted in its name by a foreign power during a brief period of his usurpation.

The Government of Peru has no objections to offer to the stipulations of the treaty itself; the principal features which it contains are the exposé of the policy adopted by Peru in its intercourse with friendly nations; and it is owing to this that for the past years there has been no cause on the part of the United States to have resort to the fulfilment of the said stipulations, which might have agitated the question whether the treaty was lawful and binding on Peru.   The same conduct which the Peruvian Government has pursued till now, will be adhered to in its future relations with the United States—relations which it desires to cultivate and strengthen every day; but it cannot allow that this conduct should be imposed upon it by a treaty which its own legitimate authority never has solemnized.

The undersigned hopes that the Honorable Secretary of State will appreciate how great the importance to Peru must be the principle that any authority established on its soil—whatever may be its origin, whatever may have been the means employed to maintain it, and however destitute it may have been of that character of permanency which alone could imply the consent of the nation—can be considered legitimate enough to bind it towards other nations.   Nowhere would this principle be more fatal than in those states that are exposed through various causes to the evils of political vicissitudes; and no principle would be more

apt to endanger the interests and independence of the South American nations, and even to establish in the course of time on our own continent the influence of any European power. Peru, which has adopted very different principles as the foundation of the legitimacy of its Government and as the source of its public obligations—which have already involved so many sacrifices, and for the consolidation of which it still puts forth all its energies—can do no less than denounce a sinister precedent which might be authorized by her silence.

The undersigned expects that the opinion of the Government of the United States on this subject will be in unison with that of the Government of Peru, because on another occasion, when the latter refused to recognize the validity of the ratification signed by General Vivanco to the convention of 1841 [the convention of March 17, 1841 (Document 97), the notes to which treat of the "occasion"], in consequence of the unlawful authority exercised by that General, the Government of the United States, listening with deference to the representations made by the Government of Peru, called for another ratification, giving thus a proof of the respect that it entertains for those principles which it has promulgated throughout America.

To that note Secretary of State Buchanan replied in the following terms under date of June 9, 1847 (D. S., 1 Notes to the Peruvian Legation, 2–5):

The Undersigned Secretary of State of the United States, has the honor to acknowledge the receipt of the note of Mr Osma, Minister Plenipotentiary of Peru, of the 22nd of April, last, accompanied by a copy of a law of the Peruvian Congress, passed on the 23d November, 1839, declaring that "the Nation does not acknowledge the Treaties concluded by the invader Don Andres Santa Cruz with Great Britain [of June 5, 1837; English and Spanish texts in British and Foreign State Papers, XXVI, 1202–17] and the United States of America."

It appears that this law, although passed on the 23d November, 1839, was not ordered to be published until the 31st May, 1845, and the first knowledge which this Government ever acquired of its existence was derived from Mr Osma himself in the month of April, last, more than seven years after its passage.

The Convention which this law refuses to recognize, was Concluded at Lima on the 30th November, 1836, between a Plenipotentiary of the President of the United States and a Plenipotentiary of "the Supreme Protector of the North and South Peruvian States, President of the Republic of Bolivia, encharged with the direction of the foreign Relations of the Peru Bolivian Confederation." This Convention was duly ratified by both parties and the ratifications were exchanged at Lima on the 28th May, 1838. The President, on the 3d October, 1838, proclaimed this Treaty, and under the Constitution of the United States it became "the supreme law of the land," and a guide for such of our citizens as might have intercourse with the States of which the Peru-Bolivian Confederation was composed. As such, it has ever since been published in the different editions of the laws of the United States.

After more than seven years and six months have elapsed from the date of this proclamation, the Government of the United States have been informed for the first time by Mr Osma that the Peruvian nation does not acknowledge this Convention. That this Government could not have acquired any such knowledge from the conduct of the Peruvian Government, is substantially admitted by Mr Osma himself, who states that his Government has always acted and still intends to act in conformity with the provisions of the Convention.

Under these circumstances, Mr Osma in his note of the 22nd April, last, has gone into an extended argument for the purpose of proving that the Government of General Santa Cruz, by which this Convention was concluded, was not such a Government *de facto* as was capable to binding Peru by Treaties with foreign nations.

It is not the intention of the Undersigned at present to reply to this argument. If this were his purpose, he might contend with great force that the long acquiescence of the Peruvian Government in the terms of this Convention, without any notice or intimation to the contrary, precluded it at this late day from objecting

to the authority by which that Convention was concluded. In addition, he might urge, even from the note of Mr Osma, without any other historical reference, that General Santa Cruz invaded Peru towards the end of the year, 1835, that he had acquired the supreme power over that country in the campaign of the year 1836, and before the conclusion of the Convention; that he maintained himself in possession of this power until after the exchange of the ratifications of this Convention at Lima in May, 1838; and that it was not until January, 1839, that he was 'put down and driven from the country.'

The undersigned might further insist that the conduct of the Government of the United States in regard to the Convention with Peru of the 17th March, 1841, cited by Mr Osma as a precedent, is not applicable to the present case, that Convention having expressly required that it should be approved by the Congress of Peru, whilst the Convention in question contains no such stipulation, doubtless because it was concluded with an individual who had himself acquired, or, as Mr Osma observes, had usurped the supreme power.

But the Undersigned would willingly avoid any such discussion. The President desires to cultivate the most friendly relations with the Government of Peru and to avoid every point of controversy which can be honorably avoided. In proof of this, he is willing to conclude a new Commercial Convention with Peru and thus leave the validity of the present Convention undecided, unless some practical question should arise which might render such decision necessary. He does not perceive what objection can exist against this course of proceeding, as it is admitted that the terms of the present Convention are unobjectionable. This will obviate every difficulty.

On February 9, 1848, concurrently with the signature at Washington of a treaty between the United States and Peru (a treaty which, because of the refusal of the Peruvian Congress to assent to the ratification thereof, did not go into force), this declaration was signed by the same representatives of the two Governments (original in the file of this treaty).

Declaration.

Whereas a Treaty between the Government of the United States and the Government of the Peru-Bolivian Confederation, was concluded and signed on the 30th November, 1836, and was subsequently duly ratified by both parties; and whereas, since the dissolution of that Confederacy, the Government of the Republic of Peru, for reasons set forth in the note of Mr Osma to Mr Buchanan of the 22nd April, 1847, has denied the validity of this Treaty, to which Mr Buchanan, in his note to Mr Osma, of the 9th of June, 1847, has responded; in consequence of which a new and separate Treaty has this day been signed by the subscribers on behalf of their respective Governments: Now, therefore, with a view to avoid future misunderstanding, they declare, that any rights under the Treaty between the Government of the United States and the Government of the Peru-Bolivian Confederation which citizens of the United States may have acquired prior to this date, shall be considered as perfect and shall be decided as if the said Treaty were in force with the approbation of both Governments.

In witness whereof, we have hereunto set our hands and seals at Washington, this ninth day of February, A D 1848.

JAMES BUCHANAN [Seal]
JOAQⁿ J. DE OSMA [Seal]

It is to be observed in this connection that this treaty, in all the "points relating to commerce and navigation", was subject to termination upon one year's notice by either of the contracting parties on May 28, 1850, twelve years after the date of the exchange of ratifications (Article 30).

Treaty Series No. 147
8 Statutes at Large, 498–509
18 *ibid.*, pt. 2, Public Treaties, 373–77

83

GREECE : DECEMBER 22, 1837

Treaty of Commerce and Navigation, signed at London December 22, 1837 (December 10, Old Style). Original in English and French. Submitted to the Senate March 14, 1838. Resolution of advice and consent March 26, 1838. Ratified by the United States April 12, 1838. Ratified by Greece April 18, 1838 (April 6, Old Style). Ratifications exchanged at London June 25, 1838. Proclaimed August 30, 1838.

Treaty of Commerce and Navigation between The United States of America, and His Majesty The King of Greece

The United States of America and His Majesty The King of Greece, equally animated with the sincere desire of maintaining the relations of good understanding which have hitherto so happily subsisted between their respective States, of extending also and consolidating the Commercial intercourse between them; and convinced that this object cannot better be accomplished than by adopting the system of an entire freedom of Navigation, and a perfect reciprocity, based upon principles of equity equally beneficial to both Countries; Have, in consequence, agreed to enter into negotiations for the conclusion of a Treaty of Commerce and Navigation, and for that purpose have appointed Plenipotentiaries; The

Traité de Commerce et de Navigation entre les Etats-Unis d'Amerique et Sa Majesté le Roi de la Grèce.

Les Etats Unis d'Amérique et Sa Majesté le Roi de la Grèce, également animé du desir sincère de maintenir les rapports de bonne intelligence qui ont si heureusement subsisté jusqu'ici, entre leurs etats respectifs, et d'en etendre et consolider les relations commerciales; et convaincus que cet objet ne saurait être mieux rempli qu'en adoptant le système d'une entière liberté de Navigation, et d'une parfaite reciprocité, basée sur des principes d'équité également avantageux aux deux pays; sont, en conséquence convenus d'entrer en négociation pour conclure un Traité de Commerce et de Navigation, et ont nommé, à cet effet des Plenipotentiaires; le President des Etats-Unis d'Amérique Andrew

President of the United States of America Andrew Stevenson, Envoy Extraordinary, and Minister Plenipotentiary of the United States, near the Court of Her Britannic Majesty, and His Majesty The King of Greece Spiridion Tricoupi Councillor of State on Special Service, His Envoy Extraordinary, and Minister Plenipotentiary near the same Court, Grand Commander of the Royal Order of the Saviour, Grand Cross of the American Order of Isabella the Catholic, who after having exchanged their full Powers, found in good and due form, have agreed upon the following Articles.

Stevenson Envoyé Extraordinaire, et Ministre Plenipotentiaire des Etats Unis près la Cour de Sa Majesté Britannique, et Sa Majesté le Roi de la Grèce, le Sieur Spiridion Tricoupi, Son Conseiller d'Etat en service Extraordinaire, son Envoyé Extraordinaire, et Ministre Plenipotentiaire, près la même Cour, Grand Commandeur de l'Ordre Royal du Sauveur, Grand Croix de l'Ordre Americain de l'Isabelle la Catholique, lesquels, après avoir échangé leurs pleins Pouvoirs, trouvés en bonne et due forme, ont arrêté les Articles suivans.

ARTICLE I

The Citizens and Subjects of each of the two High Contracting Parties, may, with all security for their persons, vessels, and cargoes, freely enter the ports, places, and rivers of the Territories of the other, wherever Foreign Commerce is permitted. They shall be at liberty to sojourn and reside in all parts whatsoever of said territories;—to rent and occupy houses and warehouses for their commerce, and they shall enjoy generally, the most entire security and protection in their Mercantile Transactions, on conditions of their submitting to the Laws and Ordinances of the respective Countries.

ARTICLE I.

Les Citoyens et Sujets de chacune des deux Hautes Parties Contractantes, pourront, avec toute sureté pour leurs personnes, vaisseaux et cargaisons, aborder librement dans les ports, places, et rivières, des territoires de l'autre, partout où le commerce étranger est permis. Ils pourront s'y arrêter et résider dans quelque partie que ce soit, des dits territoires; y louer et occuper des maisons et des magazins pour leur commerce, et jouiront généralement de la plus entière sécurité et protection pour les affaires de leur négoce, à charge de se soumettre aux lois et ordonnances des pays respectifs.

Article II.

Greek Vessels arriving either laden or in ballast, into the Ports of the United States of America, from whatever place they may come, shall be treated on their entrance, during their stay, and at their departure upon the same footing as National Vessels coming from the same place, with respect to the duties of tonnage, light houses, pilotage, and port charges, as well as to the perquisites of Public Officers, and all other duties or charges of whatever kind or denomination, levied in the name, or to the profit of the Government, the Local Authorities, or of any Private Establishment whatsoever.

And, reciprocally, the Vessels of the United States of America arriving either laden, or in ballast, into the Ports of the Kingdom of Greece, from whatever place they may come, shall be treated on their entrance, during their stay, and at their departure upon the same footing as National Vessels coming from the same place, with respect to the duties of tonnage, light-houses, pilotage, and port charges, as well as to the perquisites of Public Officers; and all other duties or charges, of whatever kind or denomination, levied in the name, or to the profit of the Government, the Local Authorities, or of any Private Establishments whatsoever

Article II.

Les batimens Grecs qui arriveront sur leur lest, ou chargés dans les Ports des Etats-Unis d'Amérique, de quelque lieu qu'ils viennent, seront traités à leur entrée, pendant leur séjour, et à leur sortie, sur le même pied que les batimens Nationaux venant de même lieu, par rapport aux droits de tonnage, de fanaux, de pilotage, et de port, ainsi qu'aux vacations des officiers publics, et à tout autre droit ou charge, de quelque espèce ou dénomination que ce soit, perçus au nom ou au profit du Gouvernement, des Administrations Locales, ou d'Etablissemens particuliers quelconques.

Et, reciproquement, les batimens des Etats-Unis d'Amérique qui arriveront sur leur lest ou chargés dans les Ports du Royaume de la Grèce, de quelque lieu qu'ils viennent, seront traités à leur entrée, pendant leur sejour, et à leur sortie, sur le même pied que les batimens nationaux venant de même lieu, par rapport aux droits de tonnage, de fanaux, de pilotage, et de port, ainsi qu'aux vacations des officiers publics, et à tout autre droit ou charge de quelque espèce ou dénomination que ce soit, perçus au nom, ou au profit du Gouvernement, des Administrations Locales, ou d'Etablissemens particuliers quelconques.

ARTICLE III.

All that may be lawfully imported into the United States of America in Vessels of the said States, may also be thereinto imported in Greek Vessels, from whatever place they may come, without paying other or higher duties or charges of whatever kind or dénomination, levied in the name, or to the profit of the Government, the Local Authorities, or of any Private Establishments whatsoever, than if imported in National Vessels.

And, reciprocally, all that may be lawfully imported into the Kingdom of Greece, in Greek Vessels, may also be thereinto imported, in Vessels of the United States of America, from whatever place they may come, without paying other or higher duties or charges, of whatever kind or denomination, levied in the name, or to the profit of the Government, the Local Authorities, or of any Private Establishments whatsoever, than if imported in National Vessels

ARTICLE IV.

All that may be lawfully exported from the United States of America, in Vessels of the said States, may also be exported therefrom in Greek Vessels, without paying other or higher duties

ARTICLE III.

Tout ce qui pourra légalement être importé dans les Etats-Unis d'Amerique, par batimens des dits Etats pourra également y etre importé par batimens Grecs, de quelque lieu qu'ils viennent, sans payer d'autres ou plus hauts droits ou charges, de quelque espèce ou dénomination que ce soit, perçus au nom, ou au profit du Gouvernement, des Administrations Locales, ou d'Etablissemens Particuliers quelconques, que si l'importation avait lieu en batimens Nationaux.

Et, réciproquement tout ce qui pourra légalement être importé dans le Royaume de la Grèce, par batimens Grecs, pourra également y être importé par batimens des Etats Unis d'Amerique de quelque lieu qu'ils viennent, sans payer d'autres ou plus hauts droits ou charges, de quelque espèce ou dénomination que ce soit, perçus au nom ou au profit du Gouvernement, des Administrations Locales, ou d'Etablissemens particuliers quelconques que si l'importation avait lieu en batimens nationaux.

ARTICLE IV.

Tout ce qui pourra légalement être exporté des Etats-Unis d'Amérique, par batimens des dits Etats, pourra également en être exporté par batimens Grecs, sans payer d'autres ou plus hauts droits

or charges of whatever kind or denomination, levied in the name or to the profit of the Government, the Local Authorities or of any Private Establishments whatsoever, than if exported in National Vessels.

And, reciprocally, all that may be lawfully exported from the Kingdom of Greece in Greek Vessels, may also be exported therefrom in Vessels of the United States of America, without paying other or higher duties or charges, of whatever kind or denomination, levied in the name or to the profit of the Government, the Local Authorities, or of any Private Establishments whatsoever, than if exported in National Vessels.

Article V.

It is expressly understood that the foregoing second, third, and fourth Articles are not applicable to the Coast-wise Navigation from one Port of the United States of America, to another Port of the said States; nor to the navigation from one port of the Kingdom of Greece to another port of the said Kingdom, which navigation each of the two High Contracting Parties reserves to itself.

ou charges, de quelque espèce ou dénomination que ce soit, perçus au nom ou au profit du Governement, des Administrations Locales ou d'Etablissemens particuliers quelconques, que si l'exportation avait lieu en batimens nationaux

Et, réciproquement, tout ce qui pourra légalement être exporté du Royaume de la Grèce par batimens Grecs, pourra également en être exporté par batimens des Etats - Unis d'Amérique, sans payer d'autres ou plus hauts droits ou charges, de quelque espèce ou dénomination que ce soit, perçus ou nom ou au profit du Governement, des Administrations Locales, ou d'Etablissements particuliers quelconques, que si l'exportation avait lieu en batimens nationaux.

Article V.

Il est expressement entendu, que les Articles précédens deux, trois, et quatre, ne sont point applicables à la Navigation de côte, ou de cabotage d'un Port des Etats-Unis d'Amérique à un autre Port des dits Etats, ni à la Navigation d'un port du Royaume de la Grèce à un autre Port du même Royaume, Navigation que, chacune des deux hautes Parties Contractantes se réserve.

ARTICLE VI.

Each of the two High Contracting Parties engages not to grant, in its purchases, or in those which might be made by Companies or Agents, acting in its name, or under its authority, any preference to importations made in its own vessels, or in those of a third Power, over those made in the vessels of the other Contracting Party.

ARTICLE VII.

The two High Contracting Parties engage not to impose upon the Navigation between their respective Territories, in the vessels of either, any tonnage or other duties of any kind or denomination, which shall be higher or other than those which shall be imposed on every other Navigation, except that which they have reserved to themselves respectively by the fifth Article of the present Treaty.

ARTICLE VIII.

There shall not be established in the United States of America, upon the products of the soil or industry of the Kingdom of Greece, any prohibition or restriction of importation or exportation, nor any duties of any kind or denomination whatsoever, unless such prohibitions, restrictions, and duties shall likewise be established upon articles of like nature, the growth of any other Country;

ARTICLE VI.

Chacune des deux hautes Parties Contractantes s'engage à ne donner dans ses achats, ou dans ceux qui seraient faits par des Compagnies ou des Agens, agissant en son nom ou sous son autorité aucune préférence aux importations faites par ses batimens, ou par ceux d'une Nation tierce, sur celles faites dans les batimens de l'autre Partie Contractante

ARTICLE VII.

Les deux Hautes Parties Contractantes s'engagent à ne pas établir sur la navigation entre leurs territoires respectifs, par les batimens de l'une ou de l'autre, des droits de tonnage ou autres de quelque espèce ou dénomination que ce soit, plus hauts ou autres que ceux qui seront établis sur toute autre Navigation, excepté celle qu'elles se sont respectivement reservée par l'article cinque du présent Traité.

ARTICLE VIII.

Il ne pourra pas être établi dans les Etats-Unis d'Amérique, sur les productions du sol ou de l'industrie de la Grèce, aucune prohibition ou restriction d'importation ou d'exportation, ni aucuns droits de quelque espèce ou dénomination que ce soit, qu'autant que ces prohibitions, ces restrictions et ces droits seraient également établis sur les objets de même nature provenant de toute autre Contrée

And, reciprocally, there shall not be established in the Kingdom of Greece on the products of the soil or industry of the United States of America, any prohibition or restriction of importation or exportation, nor any duties of any kind or denomination whatsoever, unless such prohibitions, restrictions, and duties be likewise established upon articles of like nature, the growth of any other Country.

Article IX.

All privileges of transit and all bounties and drawbacks which may be allowed within the territories of one of the High Contracting Parties, upon the importation or exportation of any article whatsoever, shall, likewise, be allowed on the articles of like nature, the products of the soil or industry of the other Contracting Party, and on the importations and exportations made in its vessels.

Article X.

The Citizens or Subjects of one of the High Contracting Parties, arriving with their Vessels on the Coasts belonging to the other, but not wishing to enter the Port, or after having entered therein, not wishing to unload any part of their cargo, shall be at liberty to depart and continue their voyage, without paying any other duties,

Et, réciproquement, il ne pourra pas être établi dans le Royaume de la Grèce, sur les productions du sol ou de l'industrie des Etats-Unis d'Amérique aucune prohibition ou restriction d'importation ou d'exportation, ni aucuns droits, de quelque espèce ou dénomination que ce soit, qu'autant que ces prohibitions, ces restrictions, et ces droits, seraient également établis sur les objets de même nature, provenant de toute autre Contrée.

Article IX.

Toute faculté d'entrepôt, et toutes primes et remboursemens de droits, qui seraient accordés dans les territoires d'une des Hautes Parties Contractantes, à l'importation ou à l'exportation de quelque objet que ce soit, seront également accordés aux objets de même nature produits du sol ou de l'industrie de l'autre Partie Contractante, et aux Importations et Exportations faites dans ses batimens.

Article X.

Les Citoyens ou Sujets de l'une des Hautes Parties Contractantes arrivant avec leurs batimens à l'une des côtes appartenants à l'autre, mais ne voulant pas entrer dans le port, ou, après y être entrés, ne voulant décharger aucune partie de leur cargaison, auront la liberté de partir et de poursuivre leur voya-

imposts, or charges whatsoever, for the vessel and cargo, than those of pilotage, wharfage, and for the support of Light-houses, when such duties shall be levied on National Vessels in similar cases.   It is understood, however, that they shall always conform to such regulations and ordinances concerning navigation, and the places and ports which they may enter, as are, or shall be, in force with regard to National Vessels, and that the custom house officers shall be permitted to visit them, to remain on board, and to take all such precautions as may be necessary to prevent all unlawful Commerce, as long as the Vessels shall remain within the limits of their Jurisdiction.

Article XI.

It is further agreed that the Vessels of one of the High Contracting Parties, having entered into the ports of the other, will be permitted to confine themselves to unloading such part only of their cargoes as the Captain or Owner may wish, and that they may freely depart with the remainder, without paying any duties, imposts, or charges whatsoever, except for that part which shall have been landed, and which shall be marked upon, and erased from, the manifest exhibiting the enumeration of the articles with

ge, sans payer d'autres droits, impôts, ou charges quelconques, pour le batiment ou la cargaison que les droits de pilotage, de quayage, et d'entretien de fanaux, quand ces droits sont perçus sur les batimens nationaux dans les mêmes cas.   Bien entendu, cependant qu'ils se conformeront toujours aux réglemens et ordonnances concernant la navigation et les places ou ports dans lesquels ils pourront aborder, qui sont, ou seront en vigueur pour les batimens nationaux, et qu'il sera permis aux officiers des douanes de les visiter, de rester à bord, et de prendre telles précautions qui pourraient être necessaires, pour prévenir tout commerce illicite, pendant que les batimens resteront dans l'enceinte de leur jurisdiction.

Article XI.

Il est aussi convenu que les batimens de l'une des Hautes Parties Contractantes, etant entrés dans les ports de l'autre, pourront se borner à ne décharger qu'une partie de leur cargaison, selon que le Capitaine ou Proprietaire le désirera, et qu'ils pourront s'en aller librement avec le reste, sans payer de droits, impôts, ou charges quelconques, que pour la partie qui aura été mise à terre, et qui sera marquée et biffée sur le manifeste, qui contiendra l'énumeration des effets dont le batiment était chargé, lequel mani-

which the vessel was laden, which manifest shall be presented entire at the Custom House of the place where the vessel shall have entered. Nothing shall be paid on that part of the cargo which the vessel shall carry away, and with which it may continue its voyage, to one, or several other ports of the same Country, there to dispose of the remainder of its cargo, if composed of articles whose importation is permitted, on paying the duties chargeable upon it; or it may proceed to any other Country. It is understood, however, that all duties, imposts, or charges whatsoever, which are or may become chargeable upon the vessels themselves, must be paid at the first port where they shall break bulk, or unlade part of their cargoes; but that no duties, imposts, or charges, of the same description shall be demanded anew in the ports of the same Country, which such vessels, might, afterwards wish to enter, unless National Vessels, be in similar cases, subject to some ulterior duties.

ARTICLE XII.

Each of the High Contracting Parties grants to the other, the privilege of appointing in its commercial ports and places, Consuls, Vice Consuls, and Commercial Agents, who shall enjoy the full protection, and receive every assistance necessary for the due

feste devra être presenté en entier à la douane du lieu, où le batiment aura abordé. Il ne sera rien payé pour la partie, de la cargaison que le batiment remportera, et avec laquelle il pourra continuer sa route pour un ou plusieurs autres ports du même pays, et y disposer du reste de sa cargaison, si elle est composée d'objets dont l'importation est permise, en payant les droits qui y sont applicables, ou bien il pourra s'en aller dans tout autre pays. Il est, cependant, entendu que les droits, impôts, ou charges quelconques, qui sont ou seront payables pour les batimens mêmes doivent être acquittés au premier port où ils rompraient le chargement ou en déchargeraient une partie, mais qu'aucuns droits, impôts, ou charges pareils, ne seront démandés de nouveau, dans les ports du même pays, ou les dits batimens pourraient vouloir entrer, après, à moins que les batimens nationaux ne soient sujets à quelques droits ultérieurs dans le même cas.

ARTICLE XII.

Chacune des Hautes Parties Contractantes, accorde à l'autre la faculté d'entretenir dans ses ports et places de commerce, des Consuls, Vice Consuls, ou Agens de Commerce, qui jouiront de toute la protection, et recevront toute l'assistance necessaire, pour

exercise of their functions; But it is expressly declared that in case of illegal or improper conduct, with respect to the laws or government of the Country, in which said Consuls, Vice Consuls, or Commercial Agents shall reside, they may be prosecuted and punished conformably to the laws, and deprived of the exercise of their functions by the offended Government, which shall acquaint the other with its motives for having thus acted; it being understood, however, that the archives and documents relative to the affairs of the Consulate shall be exempt from all search; and shall be carefully preserved under the seals of the Consuls, Vice Consuls, or Commercial Agents, and of the authority of the place where they may reside.

The Consuls, Vice Consuls, or Commercial Agents, or the persons duly authorized to supply their places, shall have the right as such, to sit as Judges and Arbitrators in such differences as may arise between the Captains and Crews of the vessels belonging to the Nation whose interests are committed to their charge, without the interference of the Local Authorities, unless the conduct of the Crews, or of the Captain should disturb the order or tranquillity of the Country, or the said Consuls, Vice Consuls, or Commercial Agents should require their assistance to cause their decisions

remplir duement leur fonctions; Mais il est expressément déclaré que dans le cas d'une conduite illégale ou impropre envers les lois ou le Gouvernement du pays dans lequel, les dits Consuls, Vice Consuls, ou Agens de commerce résideraient, ils pourront être poursuivis et punis conformément aux lois et privés de l'exercise de leurs fonctions, par le Gouvernement offensé, qui fera connoitre à l'autre ses motifs pour avoir agi ainsi, Bien entendu, cependant, que les archives et documens relatifs aux affaires du Consulat seront à l'abri de toute recherche, et devront être soigneusement conservés sous le scellé des Consuls, Vice Consuls, ou Agens Commerciaux, et de l'autorité de l'endroit ou ils résideràient.

Les Consuls, Vice Consuls, et Agens Commerciaux, ou ceux qui seraient duement autorisés à les suppléer auront le droit, comme tels, de servir de Juges et d'Arbitres dans les differens qui pourraient s'élever entre les capitaines et les équipages des batimens de la Nation dont ils soignent les interêts, sans que les Autorités Locales puissent y entrevenir, à moins que la conduite des équipages ou du capitaine ne troublat l'ordre ou la tranquillité du pays, ou que les dits Consuls, Vice Consuls, ou Agens Commerciaux ne réquissent leur intervention pour faire

to be carried into effect or supported— It is, however, understood, that this species of judgment or arbitration shall not deprive the contending parties of the right they have to resort on their return to the judicial authority of their Country.

ARTICLE XIII.

The said Consuls, Vice Consuls, or Commercial Agents are authorized to require the assistance of the Local Authorities for the arrest, detention, and imprisonment of the Deserters from the ships of War, and Merchant Vessels of their Country; and for this purpose, they shall apply to the competent Tribunals Judges, and Officers, and shall in writing demand said Deserters, proving by the exhibition of the registers, of the vessels, the rolls of the Crews, or by other Official Documents that such Individuals formed part of the Crews;—and on this reclamation being thus substantiated, the surrender shall not be refused.

Such Deserters, when arrested, shall be placed at the disposal of the said Consuls, Vice Consuls, or Commercial Agents, and may be confined in the Public Prisons, at the request and cost of those who claim them, in order to be sent to the vessels to which they belonged, or to others of the same Country. But if not sent back within the space of two months,

exécuter ou maintenir leurs décisions. Bien entendu que cette espèce de jugement ou d'arbitrage ne saurait pourtant priver les parties contendants du droit qu'elles ont, à leur retour de recourir aux autorités judiciaires de leur patrie.

ARTICLE XIII.

Les dits Consuls, Vice Consuls, ou Agens Commerciaux seront autorizés à réquérir l'assistance des Autorités Locales pour l'arrestation, la détention, et l'emprisonnement de déserteurs des navires de guerre et marchands, de leur pays, et ils s'adresseront pour cet objet aux tribunaux, juges, et officiers compétens, et réclameront par écrit les déserteurs sus-mentionnés, en prouvant par la communication des régistres des navires, ou rôles de l'equipage, ou par d'autres documens officiels que de tels Individus ont fait partie des dits équipages, et cette reclamation ainsi prouvée l'extradition ne sera point refusée.

De tels Déserteurs, lorsqu'ils auront été arrêtés, seront mis à la disposition des dits Consuls Vice Consuls, ou Agens Commerciaux et pourront être enfermés dans les prisons publiques à la réquisition et aux frais de ceux que les réclament, pour être envoyés aux navires aux quels ils appartenaient; ou à d'autres de la même Nation. Mais s'ils

reckoning from the day of their arrest, they shall be set at liberty, and shall not be again arrested for the same cause.

It is understood, however, that if the deserter should be found to have committed any crime or offence, his surrender may be delayed, until the Tribunal before which the case shall be depending, shall have pronounced its sentence, and such sentence shall have been carried into effect.

ARTICLE XIV.

In case any vessel of one of the High Contracting Parties shall have been stranded or shipwrecked, or shall have suffered any other damage on the Coasts of the Dominions of the other, every aid and assistance shall be given to the persons shipwrecked, or in danger, and passports shall be granted to them to return to their Country. The shipwrecked vessels and merchandize or their proceeds, if the same shall have been sold, shall be restored to their owners, or to those entitled thereto, if claimed within a year and a day, upon paying such costs of salvage as would be paid by National vessels in the same circumstances; and the Salvage Companies shall not compel the acceptance of their services, except in the same cases, and after the same delays as shall be granted to the captains and

ne sont pas renvoyés dans l'espace de deux mois, à compter de jour de leur arrestation, ils seront mis en liberté, et ne seront plus arrêtés pour la même cause.

Il est entendu, toutefois, que si le déserteur se trouvoit avoir commis quelque crime ou délit, il pourra être sursis à son extradition, jusqu'à ce que le tribunal nanti de l'affaire, aura rendu sa sentence, et que celle-ci ait reçu son exécution.

ARTICLE XIV.

Dans le cas où quelque batiment de l'une des Hautes Parties Contractantes aura échoué, fait naufrage, ou souffert quelqu'autre dommage sur les côtes de la domination de l'autre, il sera donné tout aide et assistance aux personnes naufragées, ou qui se trouveraient en danger, et il leur sera accordé des passeports pour retourner dans leur patrie. Les batimens et les marchandises naufragés, ou leurs produits s'ils ont été vendus, seront restitués à leurs propriétaires ou ayant cause, s'ils sont réclamés dans l'an et jour, en payant les frais de sauvetage que payeroient les batimens nationaux dans les mêmes cas, et les compagnies de sauvetage ne pourront faire accepter leurs services, que dans les mêmes cas, et après les mêmes délais qui seraient accordés aux capitaines et aux

crews of National vessels. Moreover, the respective Governments will take care that these companies do not commit any vexatious or arbitrary acts.

ARTICLE XV.

It is agreed that vessels arriving directly from the United States of America, at a port within the dominions of His Majesty The King of Greece, or from the Kingdom of Greece at a port of the United States of America, and provided with a bill of Health, granted by an Officer, having competent power to that effect, at the port whence such vessels shall have sailed, setting forth that no malignant or contagious diseases prevailed in that port, shall be subjected to no other Quarantine than such as may be necessary for the visit of the Health Officer of the Port where such vessels shall have arrived, after which said vessels shall be allowed immediately to enter, and unload their cargoes— Provided always that there shall be on board no person who during the voyage, shall have been attacked with any malignant or contagious Diseases; that such vessels shall not, during their passage, have communicated with any vessel liable itself, to undergo a Quarantine, and that the Country whence they came shall not, at that time, be so far infected or suspected, that before their arriv-

ARTICLE XV.

Il est convenu que les batimens qui arriveront directement des Etats-Unis d'Amérique, à un port de la domination de Sa Majesté le Roi de la Grece, ou du Royaume de la Grèce à un port des Etats-Unis d'Amérique, et qui seroient pourvus d'un certificat de santé donné par l'Officier compétent à cet égard du port d'où les batimens sont sortis, et assurant qu'aucune maladie maligne ou contagieuse n'existait dans ce port, ne seront soumis à aucune autre Quarantaine que celle qui sera nécessaire pour la visite de l'Officier de santé du port où les batimens seroient arrivés, après laquelle il sera permis à ces batimens d'entrer immédiatement et de décharger leurs cargaisons;— Bien entendu, toutefois, qu'il n'y ait eu personne à leur bord qui ait été attaqué pendant le voyage d'une maladie maligne, ou contagieuse;—que les batimens n'aient point communiqué dans leur traversée avec un batiment qui serait lui même dans le cas de subir une quarantaine, et que la Contrée d'où ils viendraient ne fut pas, a cette époque si généralement infectée ou suspecté qu'on ait rendu avant leur arrivée, une

al an ordinance had been issued, in consequence of which all vessels coming from that Country should be considered as suspected, and consequently subject to Quarantine.

Article XVI.

Considering the remoteness of the respective Countries of the two High Contracting Parties, and the uncertainty resulting therefrom, with respect to the various events which may take place; It is agreed that a Merchant vessel belonging to either of them, which may be bound to a Port supposed at the time of its departure to be blockaded, shall not, however, be captured or condemned, for having attempted a first time to enter said port, unless it can be proved that said vessel could and ought to have learned during its voyage that the blockade of the place in question still continued. But all Vessels which after having been warned off once, shall, during the same voyage attempt a second time to enter the same blockaded port, during the continuance of said Blockade, shall then subject themselves to be detained, and condemned.

Article XVII.

The present Treaty shall continue in force for ten years, counting from the day of the exchange of the ratifications; and if before the expiration of the first nine years, neither of the High Con-

ordonnance d'après laquelle tous les batimens venant de cette Contrée seraient régardés comme suspects, et, en conséquence, assujettis à une Quarantaine.

Article XVI.

Vû l'éloignement des Pays respectifs des deux Hautes Parties Contractantes, et l'incertitude qui en résulte sur les divers événemens qui peuvent avoir lieu, il est convenu, qu'un batiment marchand appartenant à l'une d'elles qui se trouverait destiné pour un port supposé bloqué au moment du départ de ce batiment, ne sera cependant pas capturé ou condamné pour avoir essayé une prémière fois d'entrer dans le dit port, à moins qu'il ne puisse être prouvé que le dit batiment avait pu et du apprendre en route que l'Etat de blocus de la place en question durait encore; Mais les batimens qui après avoir été renvoyés une fois essayeraient, pendant le même voyage, d'entrer une seconde fois dans le même port bloqué, durant la continuation de ce blocus, se trouveront alors sujet à être détenus et condamnés.

Article XVII

Le présent Traité sera en vigueur pendant dix années à partir du jour de l'échange des ratifications; et si avant l'expiration des neufs premières années l'une ou l'autre des Hautes Parties

tracting Parties shall have announced by an Official Notification to the other its intention to arrest the operation of said Treaty, it shall remain binding for one year beyond that time, and so on, until the expiration of the twelve months which will follow a similar Notification, whatever the time at which it may take place.

Contractantes n'avait pas annoncée à l'autre, par une notification officielle, son intention d'en faire cesser l'effet, ce Traité restera obligatoire une année au dela, et ainsi de suite jusqu'a l'expiration des douze mois, qui suivront une semblable notification à quelque époque qu'elle ait lieu.

ARTICLE XVIII.

The present Treaty shall be ratified by the President of the United States of America, by and with the advice and consent of the Senate, and by His Majesty The King of Greece, and the ratifications to be exchanged at London within the space of twelve months from the signature, or sooner if possible.

In faith whereof the respective Plenipotentiaries of the High Contracting Parties, have signed the present Treaty, both in English and French, and have affixed thereto their seals

Done in duplicate at London the tenth/twenty second of December in the year of our Lord One thousand eight hundred and thirty seven.

ARTICLE XVIII.

Le présent Traité sera ratifié par le Président des Etats-Unis d'Amérique, par et avec l'avis et le consentement du Sénat, et par Sa Majesté le Roi de la Grèce, et les ratifications en seront échangés à Londres, dans l'espace de douze mois, ou ploutôt si faire se peut.

En foi de quoi les Plénipotentiaires respectifs des deux Hautes Parties Contractantes ont signé le présent Traité en Anglais et en Français et y ont apposé leurs scéaux.

Fait en duplicate à Londres, le dix/vingt deux de Décembre, l'an de Grâce mil huit cent trente sept.

A: STEVENSON [Seal]
S TRICOUPI [Seal]

S TRICOUPI [Seal]
A: STEVENSON [Seal]

NOTES

Dates in the headnote and in these notes are, unless otherwise stated, in the New Style or present calendar, which was then twelve days later than the Old Style.

THE FILE PAPERS

The file papers of this treaty are complete, except for the attested resolution of advice and consent of the Senate of March 26, 1838 (Executive Journal, V, 95). The treaty, according to the final clauses thereof, was signed in duplicate; and one original was transmitted to the Department of State with the despatch of Andrew Stevenson, Minister at London, of December 27, 1837 (D. S., 44 Despatches, Great Britain, No. 40). That original, which is in the treaty file, has the English in the left columns and the French in the right; in both texts of the original the United States has precedence, although the *alternat* was observed in the order of the signatures. That original is embodied in the original proclamation of August 30, 1838, which is bound with the duplicate United States instrument of ratification of April 12, 1838; both documents are in customary form.

The Greek instrument of ratification of April 18, 1838, is written in French; it contains both texts of the treaty, the French in the left columns; in those texts the King of Greece is named first throughout. The protocol of the exchange of ratifications at London on June 25, 1838, is in both languages and in customary form; it is signed by the Ministers of the respective Governments at that capital, Andrew Stevenson and Prince Michel Soutzo.

Accompanying this treaty when it was submitted to the Senate with the presidential message of March 14, 1838, were "documents relating to the negotiations" (Executive Journal, V, 91). These were printed in Senate Confidential Document No. 6, 25th Congress, 2d session (Regular Confidential Documents, IX, 111–14). The proclamation of the treaty was transmitted to Congress with the presidential message of December 3, 1838 (Richardson, III, 483, 489; printed with accompanying papers in Senate Document No. 1, 25th Congress, 3d session, serial 338).

THE NEGOTIATIONS

The first proposal for the making of a treaty between the United States and Greece came from the Greek Minister at London, Spiridion Tricoupi, in a note to the American Minister, Andrew Stevenson, under date of April 26, 1837, containing the following (translation, enclosure to despatch of May 4, 1837, D. S., 44 Despatches, Great Britain, No. 23):

The Greek Government has already adopted the principle of receiving, in regard to port duties, on the same footing as national vessels, all those of every nation which has extended similar advantages to Greek vessels entering their ports. It is also understood that the Government of the United States of America professes and applies the same principles, on similar occasions, in favor of the vessels of such nations as have declared that those of the United States should be received in their ports on the same conditions.

Upon this information the Government of the King, desiring to establish relations of navigation on this footing with the United States, has hastened to sign a declaration to this effect and to cause its insertion in the Government Journal No. 9, under date March 6/18, 1837.

I have been directed to transmit to Your Excellency a copy of this sheet and to solicit your mediation in presenting it to the attention of your Government, in order that, on its part, it may be pleased to make a similar declaration in favor of Greek vessels.

With the view of introducing greater facilities into our commercial relations with the United States by means of a broader and more important understanding, His Majesty will regard with pleasure the conclusion of a treaty of commerce and navigation between the Kingdom of Greece and the United States. For this purpose I have just been authorized to make overtures towards negotiating and concluding such a treaty in my capacity as the Plenipotentiary of His Majesty, if he finds that His Excellency the President of the United States entertains the same opinions upon the subject. In this case the Greek Government proposes that the treaty in question be based, and even formed, on that which has been made and concluded at Stockholm between the United States of North America and the Kingdom of Sweden and Norway, the 4th of July, 1837 [July 4, 1827, Document 55].

The response of this Government was made in the instructions of November 7, 1837, the substance of which follows (D. S., 14 Instructions, Great Britain, 263–64):

A copy of the communication made to you in April last, by Mʳ Tricoupi, the Greek Minister at London, expressing a desire on the part of His Majesty the King of Greece to enter into a treaty of commerce and navigation with the United States of America, was duly received at this Department. . . . The proposition has been laid before the President for consideration, and I am now directed to convey to you his cheerful concurrence in the wish of His Majesty regarding this subject. I am, at the same time, instructed to authorize and empower you immediately to enter upon the negotiation of a treaty of commerce and navigation between the United States and His Majesty the King of Greece, upon the basis proposed by His Majesty's Minister, vizᵗ our treaty with Sweden and Norway, dated 4ᵗʰ of July 1827 [Document 55]. It is not, however, distinctly understood here, whether or not the Government of Greece wishes to embrace, in the negotiation now offered, the stipulations of certain articles of a previous treaty with the same Power, as referred to in the 17ᵗʰ article of the existing treaty. In either event the President is willing to entertain the proposition—but should it be the intention of His Greek Majesty to adopt, generally, those articles of the treaty of 1783 [Document 10] designated in the 17ᵗʰ article of that of 1827, some modifications will be found necessary, in a few cases, to render them consonant to the language and doctrine of our conventional agreements of more recent date—for instance, the definition of blockade, as contained in the two last lines of the 10ᵗʰ article of the treaty of 1783 . . . conflicts with that contained in the 18ᵗʰ article of the treaty of 1827, and ought of course to be omitted. A careful examination will probably discover other inaccuracies, of a similar character.

Articles XV and XVI of the old treaty, making commanders of armed vessels answerable for injuries done, on either side, &c. and requiring persons fitting out privateers to give bond to answer all damages, &c. are objectionable and useless, and cannot therefore be agreed to.

A full power to conclude a treaty of commerce and navigation with Greece, in conformity to the preceding instructions, is herewith transmitted to you.

In the French text the provisions of Articles 1–17 of this treaty were copied almost literally from those of Articles 1–4, 6–16, 18, and 19 of the treaty with Sweden and Norway of July 4, 1827 (Document 55), which was signed in French only; and the English text was copied from the English translation of that treaty which was included in the original proclamation thereof and which has been printed in the Statutes at Large and in treaty collections generally.

There appears in the despatches no mention of the full power of the Greek Plenipotentiary. That given by this Government to Andrew Stevenson, Minister at London, was under date of November 7, 1837, and in customary form (D. S., 2 Credences, 285).

RELATIONS WITH GREECE

For an account of events leading up to Greek independence and the acknowledgment thereof by the United States, see Moore, Digest, I, 110–12. Proceedings in Congress during the period 1822–27 are noted in Haswell, 1341–42.

The Greek war for independence which commenced in 1821 was followed by various public acts, to which Great Britain, France, and Russia were parties, guaranteeing the independence of Greece; among these may be mentioned the treaty signed at London July 6, 1827 (British and Foreign State Papers, XIV, 632–39), the agreement of December 12, 1828 (*ibid.*, XVII, 405–31), and the protocol of London of March 22, 1829 (*ibid.*, 131–61). The last-named instrument was accepted by Turkey by Article 10 of the Treaty of Peace with Russia signed at Adrianople on September 14, 1829 (*ibid.*, XVI, 647–59).

By the convention signed at London on May 7, 1832, between Great Britain, France, and Russia on the one hand and Bavaria on the other, the Crown of Greece was offered to Prince Frederick Otho of Bavaria (*ibid.*, XIX, 33–41). Formal notice of that convention and of its execution was given by the Ministers of the three powers to the United States under date of April 18, 1833, in a joint note which included a formal invitation to the Government of the United States to acknowledge Prince Otho of Bavaria as King of Greece (D. S., 11 Notes from the French Legation).

The answering note of Secretary of State Livingston, under date of April 30 (D. S., 5 Notes to Foreign Legations, 101–2), did not announce a present compliance with the request of the three powers, as may be seen from this extract therefrom:

This note has been laid before the President of the United States, who has directed the Undersigned to inform the Ministers Plenipotentiary of the said three Powers that it has been the principle, and the invariable practice of the U. S. to recognise that as the legal Government of another nation, which, by its establishment in the actual exercise of political power might be supposed to have received the express or implied assent of the people, and that he is therefore happy that the assurance given by the three mediating powers, that they were duly authorised to make the arrangement they announce, by the people of Greece, will enable him on the part of the United States, without departing from their known principles in similar cases, to acknowledge the Prince Otho of Bavaria, as the King of Greece, and to comply with the request of the high mediating powers, on his reception by the people of that Country as their Sovereign.

Diplomatic intercourse between the United States and Greece did not begin until the negotiations for this treaty were initiated at London in 1837.

Treaty Series No. 355
8 Statutes at Large, 510
18 *ibid.*, pt. 2, Public Treaties, 753

84

TEXAS : APRIL 11, 1838

Convention to Terminate Reclamations of the Government of the United States, signed at Houston April 11, 1838. Original in English. Submitted to the Senate May 7, 1838. Resolution of advice and consent June 13, 1838. Ratified by the United States June 21, 1838. Ratified by Texas May 3, 1838. Ratifications exchanged at Washington July 6, 1838. Proclaimed July 6, 1838.

Convention between the Government of the United States of America and the Government of the Republic of Texas, to terminate the reclamations of the former Government for the capture, seizure and detention of the Brigs Pocket and Durango, and for injuries suffered by American citizens on board the Pocket.

Alcée La Branche, Chargé d'Affaires of the United States of America, near the Republic of Texas, acting on behalf of the said United States of America, and R. A. Irion, Secretary of State of the Republic of Texas, acting on behalf of the said Republic, have agreed to the following articles.

ART. 1. The Government of the Republic of Texas, with a view to satisfy the aforesaid reclamations for the capture, seizure and confiscation of the two vessels aforementioned, as well as for indemnity to American citizens who have suffered injuries from the said Government of Texas, or its officers, obliges itself to pay the sum of eleven thousand, seven hundred and fifty dollars, ($11750.), to the Government of the United States of America, to be distributed amongst the claimants, by the said Government of the United States of America.

ART. 2. The sum of eleven thousand, seven hundred and fifty dollars, ($11750.), agreed on in the 1st. Art., shall be paid in gold or silver, with interest at six per cent., one year after the exchange of the ratifications of this convention. The said payment shall be made, at the seat of Government of the Republic of Texas, into the hands of such person or persons as shall be duly authorized by the Government of the United States of America to receive the same.

125

ART. 3. The present convention shall be ratified, and the ratifications thereof shall be exchanged in the city of Washington, in the space of three months from this date, or sooner if possible.

In faith whereof the parties above-named have respectively subscribed these articles, and thereto affixed their seals.

Done at the city of Houston, on the eleventh day of the month of April, one thousand, eight hundred and thirty eight.

ALCÉE LA BRANCHE   [Seal]
[Seal]   R. A. IRION

NOTES

Three documents in the treaty file are bound together, namely, a signed original of the convention (with which the text here printed has been collated), the duplicate United States instrument of ratification of June 21, 1838, and the original proclamation of the following July 6; the two documents last mentioned are in customary form. Other papers in the file are the attested Senate resolution of June 13, 1838 (Executive Journal, V, 132), and the certificate of the exchange of ratifications at Washington on July 6, 1838.

The document which served as the Texan instrument of ratification is another signed original of the convention, to which is appended an attested resolution of the Senate of Texas under date of May 3, 1838, reading as follows:

IN SENATE OF TEXAS.   (Secret Session)
May 3rd 1838.

Ordered, That the Senate advise and consent to the ratification of the Convention entered into on the 11th day of April, *ultimo,* between the Hon! R. A. Irion, secretary of State of the Republic of Texas, and the Hon! Alcée La Branche, Chargé D'Affaires of the United States of America, acting on behalf of their respective Governments, to terminate the reclamations of the Government of the United States, for the capture, siezure, and detention of the Brigs Pocket and Durango; and for injuries suffered by citezens of the United States, on board the Pocket.

Ordered, That the injunction of secrecy in relation to the confirmation of the Convention above named, be removed.

Extract from the Secret Journal of the Senate of Texas.

W. F. GRAY
Secretary.

To such an informal instrument of ratification objections were at first raised. In his despatch of June 22, 1838, Fairfax Catlett, Chargé d'Affaires of Texas, thus described them (Garrison, Diplomatic Correspondence of Texas, pt. 1, 332):

I have the honor to acknowledge the receipt of your despatches of date 18th and 19th. ultimo, addressed to Genl. Hunt, together with the convention of indemnity to American citizens for losses sustained by the brigs Pocket and Durango.

I have had several interviews with the Secretary of State on the subject of the treaty of indemnity and although he evinced a disposition from the first to accept it and have it ratified on the part of the United States, he seemed to be in much doubt as to whether it would be received, on account of its not having been ratified by the President under the great seal of the Republic of Texas;—both of which were indispensable to the full and formal completion of the treaty and were of course necessary, before the ratifications could be regularly exchanged. Another difficulty in the way of the exchange of the ratifications was my having no specific power for the purpose.

In consideration however of the smallness of the amount involved and the unimportance of the transaction, (there being no danger of the act being hereafter disavowed on the part of Texas) he yesterday agreed to waive these objections and accept the treaty as it now stands. He told me that he would have the necessary papers prepared and send for me when they were ready.

In his next despatch Catlett wrote regarding the exchange of ratifications as follows (*ibid.*, 336, July 7, 1838):

In exchange for the copy of the convention which I placed in his hands, being the same as was transmitted by you, Mr. Forsyth gave me a formally ratified copy on the part of the United States;—this copy being handsomely bound in black velvet, and having the great seal of the United States suspended from it with large tassels, and the whole, when enclosed in its case, presenting the form and appearance of a splendidly bound folio volume. A similar ceremonial was expected to have been observed on the part of Texas, but this being impracticable under the circumstances, he had agreed to waive any difficulties on this score as I mentioned in my last despatch.

The two signed originals are almost literally alike; one immaterial comma appears in each which is not in the other; there are the differences naturally due to the observance of the *alternat;* and the words appearing in the preamble as above printed, "near the Republic of Texas", are not in the original which served as the Texan instrument of ratification.

The certificate of the exchange of ratifications is in the following form:

We, John Forsyth, Secretary of State of the United States of America and Fairfax Catlett, Chargé d'Affaires of the Republic of Texas accredited to the Government of the said United States certify that the Ratifications of the Convention between the Government of the United States of America and the Government of the Republic of Texas to terminate the reclamations of the former Government for the capture, seizure and detention of the brigs Pocket and Durango, and for injuries suffered by American citizens on board the Pocket, signed at Houston on the eleventh day of April, one thousand eight hundred and thirty eight, have, this day, with all suitable solemnities and after due comparison each with the other and both with the original example of said Convention been exchanged by Us.

In witness whereof, we have signed this Act, in duplicate, and have sealed the same with our respective seals at Washington, this sixth day of July, in the year of our Lord, one thousand eight hundred and thirty eight.

                  [Seal]   JOHN FORSYTH
                  [Seal]   FAIRFAX CATLETT

It appears from the following message of President Van Buren of May 7, 1838 (Executive Journal, V, 108), which transmitted this convention to the Senate, that the convention was signed before the representative of the United States was in possession of any full power for the purpose; and it is to be observed that the convention makes no mention of full powers:

I transmit to the Senate, for their consideration, with a view to its ratification, a convention signed at Houston, on the 11th ult., by Alcée La Branche, chargé d'affaires of the United States, and R. A. Irion, secretary of state of the Republic of Texas, stipulating for the adjustment and satisfaction of claims of citizens of the United States on that Government in the cases of the brigs Pocket and Durango. This convention having been concluded in anticipation of the receipt from the Department of a formal power for that purpose, an extract from a dispatch of Mr. La Branche to the Secretary of State, explanatory of his motives for that act, is also transmitted for the information of the Senate.

The extract from the despatch of Alcée La Branche which is mentioned in the above message was the only accompanying paper transmitted to the Senate with the convention; that extract, which was printed with the convention as Senate Confidential Document No. 19G, 25th Congress, 2d session (Regular Confidential Documents, XI, 167–70), was the following paragraph from the despatch of La Branche of April 16, 1838 (D. S., 1 Despatches, Texas, No. 9):

I, herewith, transmit you a convention stipulating for the payment of the indemnity which I was charged to obtain from the Texian Government. Although my instructions did not directly authorize me to sign this document, yet I thought, under the circumstances of the case, it might fairly be implied, and I determined to act accordingly, in order that the matter might finally be settled without further delay. I am induced to believe there will be no difficulty in confirming the arrangement I have made, as the sums for the claimants have been fully acknowledged, and the terms are as favorable as I possibly could exact. This government is totally unable to pay at present, and hence I felt constrained to extend the period for payment one year after the exchange of the ratifications, with an interest of six per cent. The formation of a convention was the only alternative I had to secure the amount in the time and manner agreed upon. This government also desired that the usual formalities should be observed. The whole amount recognized is 11750 dollars of which 8050$ is for the insurance company, 1500$ for Somers and the same for Taylor, and 700$ for Hogan. It was only after repeated efforts that I succeeded in removing the objections urged against the claims for the Pocket, and I trust the President will have cause to be satisfied with the course I have pursued, in coming to what I hope he may consider a prompt and happy termination of the demand.

After that despatch of April 16 was written, but before it was received at Washington, a full power in the customary form, dated April 28, 1838 (D. S., 2 Credences, 300), was sent to La Branche with instructions of May 2, 1838, from which the final paragraph is extracted (D. S., 1 Instructions, Texas, 9–11):

As that government may desire a formal convention for the adjustment of our claims upon it, I transmit a power authorizing you to conclude one for that purpose. You need not, however, use the power unless it should be required. Claims, where they are few in number and inconsiderable in amount, are frequently adjusted by an informal agreement between the diplomatic agent and the minister of foreign affairs, recognizing the amounts to be paid and the time and manner of payment. Another common method for transacting such business is for the diplomatic agent and the minister first to agree as to the accountability of the government and then for each of them to name a Commissioner to examine and decide upon the details. You may adopt either course if it should be consented to by that government, and no objection is entertained to your allowing a liberal time for them to pay such sums as they may engage for. This is left to your own discretion.

The Pocket and Durango Claims

The payment of $11,750 agreed to by Article 1 of this convention was, as stated in its heading, for the settlement of the claims arising from "the capture, seizure and detention of the Brigs Pocket and Durango, and for injuries suffered by American citizens on board the Pocket". The claims are thus described in the instructions to Chargé d'Affaires Alcée La Branche under date of July 22, 1837 (D. S., 1 Instructions, Texas, 1–4):

It will be your duty to embrace the first favorable opportunity to present the claims of citizens of the United States who have suffered injury from the Texian government or officers. The only cases of this description for the prosecution of which the aid of this Department has been solicited, are those of the brig Pocket and brig Durango. The former sailed from New Orleans on the 28th of March, 1836, bound to Matamoros. On the voyage, she was taken by the armed schooner Invincible sailing under the Texian flag and commanded by one Brown, carried to Galveston and, with her cargo, appropriated without trial or condemnation by persons claiming to act under the authority of the government of Texas. Her officers, passengers and crew were also treated with great harshness. The facts are detailed in the protest of her master, mate and two seamen and in an affidavit of Daniel Somers and James Taylor before a Judge at New Orleans. An authenticated copy of these papers and of others relating to the case, is herewith sent.

The brig Durango was seized in Matagorda bay on the 22nd of March, 1836, by an armed force acting under the orders of John A. Wharton, Adjutant General of Texas and ——— Brown, commander of the Texian schooner Invincible. She was consequently abandoned by her master, who in his protest, an authenticated copy of which is herewith transmitted, states the particulars of the outrage. The claimant in these cases is the Sea Insurance Company of New York. The accompanying copy of a letter to this Department from the President of that Company contains a statement of the amount claimed, which you will accordingly demand of the Texian government. It is also expected that the individuals on board the vessels referred to, particularly Somers and Taylor, will be indemnified for the property taken from them and for the other injuries they received.

A more detailed description of the claims is in the note of Chargé d'Affaires La Branche to R. A. Irion, Secretary of State of Texas, dated November 29, 1837 (D. S., 1 Despatches, Texas, No. 5, January 1, 1838, enclosure; Garrison, Diplomatic Correspondence of Texas, pt. 1, 270–72):

As I had the honor of apprizing you a few days ago, it becomes my duty to submit formally the claims of citizens of the United States, who have suffered injury from your government or its officers, with a request that the same be laid before his excellency the President.

I would, I apprehend, do injustice to your intelligence and sense of equity, were I to conceive that more than a mere statement of the facts were necessary to convince you of the validity of these claims, and the propriety of acknowledging them. I will, therefore, confine myself to a brief recital of the circumstances of the case.

On the 20th of March 1836, the brig Pocket sailing under american colors, and belonging to Citizens of the United States, left New Orleans, bound for Matamoras. On the voyage, she was captured by the Texian armed Schooner Invincible, commanded by Jeremiah Brown, carried to Galveston, and with her cargo appropriated without trial or condemnation by persons acting under the authority of the Texian government. The officers and passengers on board

were treated with great violance. The captain and crew, with the exception of the second mate, who was still more severely dealt with, were detained nineteen days at that place, after which they were released and suffered to embark for New Orleans. Permission was given them to take such articles of private property as belonged to them, but after a general search they were unable to find any thing, their clothing, hats, books, quadrants, charts were all missing, having been already secured by the captors. Previous to this, the passengers were all transferred on board of a Texian armed schooner called the Brutus, where they were all stripped and searched by a order of a person named Damon, who acted as the lieutenant, and four of them, to wit, Hill, Hogan, Murje and Campo were immediately put in double irons by him. One of the passengers, Taylor, had his trunks broken open by this Damon, and four hundred and ninety seven dollars, together with other property taken therefrom, amounting in value in all to eight hundred dollars. When he desired to obtain a simple receipt for the money alone, he was also put in double irons. Hogan and Campo received one hundred lashes on the bare back, with a cat o' nine tails, stretched on an eighteen pound cannon, and were threatened by Hurd, acting as captain of the Brutus, and Damon, that they should be hanged. The foreyard was accordingly loosened and braced for that purpose, and these inoffending victims were actually brought on deck with ropes around their necks, and tortured with their impending fate. Somers and Taylor were kept in double irons, the former for the space of twenty five days, and the latter for seven weeks. At the expiration of those periods, instead of being released, they were forcibly detained without any legal pretext or excuse for upwards of four months, and seven months separately, when they were permitted to depart for the United States. Somers, during all this latter period, was compelled to perform various works, such as unloading vessels &c and had all his clothing and instruments of navigation taken from him. As american citizens, proud of a title honored and respected by all nations, and under the protection of their flag, they had a right to expect exemption from violence or outrage from any quarter, but most of all from officers acting under the authority of the people of Texas, whose reminiscences of a common country, consanguinity and sympathy should still be so vividly entertained and afford such constant sources of pleasing emotions.

The brig Durango, commanded by James C. Ryan, also an american vessel, was seized in Matagorda Bay and pressed into the Texian service by the orders of John A. Wharton, adjutant general of the Texian forces, and William S. Brown, commander of the Texian armed schooner Liberty. Said vessel sailed from the port of New Orleans bound for the port of Matagorda. Captain Ryan finding himself deprived of his vessel, and being unable to reclaim her in a legal way was compelled to abandon her, but recorded his dissent to this proceeding by entering his protest in due form before Charles Wilson, primary judge of the department of Brassos, and jurisdiction of Matagorda on the 22ᵈ of March 1836.

The facts, above mentioned, in relation to these vessels, are made known to me by documents in my possession duly attested, and which I am ready to communicate to you, should you desire it.

The amount claimed for the vessels is eight thousand and fifty dollars, which I am instructed to demand of the Texian government, and also to require an indemnity for the property taken from the individuals on board and for the other injuries they received. For the latter claim, I refer to future consultation with you to determine what shall be deemed fair and equitable; and I doubt not we shall agree upon that point, as well as upon the justice and propriety of the present application for redress.

In his despatch of April 16, 1838, La Branche wrote that the total of $11,750 recognized was made up of $8,050 for the Sea Insurance Company, $1,500 for Somers, $1,500 for Taylor, and $700 for Hogan (D. S., 1 Despatches, Texas, No. 9). Regarding the individual claims, La Branche had previously written (*ibid.*, No. 5, January 1, 1838):

I have now the honor to inform you, that I have been enabled to obtain from Mr Somers, one of the claimants, and s^d mate of the Pocket, residing at present in Houston, such information as makes me familiar with the whole question. From a conversation with him, it seems that he had originally taken steps through the medium of an attorney for the recovery of 1500 dollars, the amount of his demand against the Texian government. Taylor is likewise in the country, and is expected here every day; twelve or fifteen hundred dollars would be an ample indemnity for him. As to Capt Howes, who is since dead, he has received the amount claimed as damages for himself and crew from the agent of Texas in N. Orleans. Hogan, the only other American citizen on board, who was also detained seven months, is now dead. He has left a wife and children and I think it no more than proper that the indemnity to which he would have been entitled, were he living, should be allowed to them. Seven hundred dollars, I conceive, would be a fair remuneration for his detention.

Under date of December 12, 1838, the Department of State was informed that the convention had been published at Houston (*ibid.*, No. 14); and the amount due, with interest, in all $12,455, was duly paid (*ibid.*, No. 24, July 8, 1839; 1 Instructions, Texas, 19, August 7, 1839).

RELATIONS WITH TEXAS

For a summary of the early relations between the United States and the Republic of Texas, see the notes to Document 85, the convention of April 25, 1838, with Texas, for the partial demarcation of the boundary between the two countries.

Treaty Series No. 356
8 Statutes at Large, 511
18 *ibid.*, pt. 2, Public Treaties, 754

85

TEXAS : APRIL 25, 1838

Convention for Marking the Boundary between the United States of America and the Republic of Texas, signed at Washington April 25, 1838. Original in English.
Submitted to the Senate May 7, 1838. (Message of April 27, 1838.) Resolution of advice and consent May 10, 1838. Ratified by the United States October 4, 1838. Ratified by Texas May 25, 1838. Ratifications exchanged at Washington October 12, 1838. Proclaimed October 13, 1838.

Convention between the United States of America and the Republic of Texas, for marking the boundary between them.

Whereas the treaty of limits made and concluded on the twelfth day of January in the year of our Lord one thousand eight hundred and twenty eight between the United States of America on the one part and the United Mexican States on the other is binding upon the Republic of Texas, the same having been entered into at a time when Texas formed a part of the said United Mexican States:

And whereas it is deemed proper and expedient in order to prevent future disputes and collisions between the United States and Texas in regard to the boundary between the two countries as designated by the said treaty, that a portion of the same should be run and marked without unnecessary delay:

The President of the United States has appointed John Forsyth their plenipotentiary, and the President of the Republic of Texas has appointed Memucan Hunt its plenipotentiary:

And the said plenipotentiaries having exchanged their full powers, have agreed upon and concluded the following articles:

ART. 1. Each of the contracting parties shall appoint a commissioner and surveyor, who shall meet before the termination of twelve months from the exchange of the ratifications of this Convention at New Orleans and proceed to run and mark that portion of the said boundary which extends from the mouth of the Sabine, where that river enters the Gulph of Mexico to the Red River. They shall make out plans and

133

keep journals of their proceedings and the result agreed upon by them shall be considered as part of this Convention and shall have the same force as if it were inserted therein. The two governments will amicably agree respecting the necessary articles to be furnished to those persons and also as to their respective escorts, should such be deemed necessary.

ART. 2. And it is agreed that until this line shall be marked out as is provided for in the foregoing article, each of the contracting parties shall continue to exercise jurisdiction in all territory over which its jurisdiction has hitherto been exercised, and that the remaining portion of the said boundary line shall be run and marked at such time here-after as may suit the convenience of both the contracting parties, until which time each of the said parties shall exercise without the inter-ference of the other within the territory of which the boundary shall not have been so marked and run, jurisdiction to the same extent to which it has been heretofore usually exercised.

ART. 3. The present Convention shall be ratified and the ratifica-tions shall be exchanged at Washington within the term of six months from the date hereof, or sooner if possible.

In witness whereof, we, the respective Plenipotentiaries, have signed the same, and have hereunto affixed our respective seals. Done at Washington, this twenty fifth day of April in the year of our Lord one thousand eight hundred and thirty eight, in the sixty second year of the Independence of the United States of America, and in the third of that of the Republic of Texas.

[Seal]   MEMUCAN HUNT
[Seal]   JOHN FORSYTH

NOTES

The file of this convention is complete, and the documents are in customary form. They include a signed original of the convention, the attested resolution of the Senate of May 10, 1838 (Executive Journal, V, 109), a duplicate of the United States instrument of rati-fication of October 4, 1838, the Texan instrument of ratification of May 25, 1838, a certificate of the exchange of ratifications at Wash-ington on October 12, 1838, and the original proclamation of the following day.

In the text of the convention the *alternat*, it seems, was not observed, as the United States is named first both in the original in the file and in the text included in the Texan instrument of ratification; but in the latter the name of John Forsyth appears above that of Memucan Hunt, and not below it, as in the original in the file.

It appears that no papers accompanied this convention when it was transmitted to the Senate on May 7 with the presidential message of April 27, 1838; and the resolution of advice and consent was adopted by the Senate three days after the receipt of the convention (Executive Journal, V, 107, 109).

The convention was communicated to Congress with the presidential message of December 3, 1838 (Richardson, III, 483, 489).

Under date of December 12, 1838, La Branche reported, "The conventions [this convention and that of April 11, 1838, Document 84] entered into between the two governments have been published and a proclamation of the President declaring the treaty [of amity, commerce, and navigation] with Mexico [of April 5, 1831, Document 70] binding on the Republic of Texas" (D. S., 1 Despatches, Texas, No. 14).

THE FULL POWERS

The full power to Secretary of State Forsyth was dated April 13, 1838, and was in customary form (D. S., 2 Credences, 299). A copy of that given by the Government of Texas to General Memucan Hunt, Minister at Washington, under date of February 23, 1838, to negotiate and conclude the convention, is in the treaty file; it follows the American form, reading as follows:

Sam. Houston, President of the Republic of Texas.

To all to whom these presents shall come, greeting.

Know ye, That, for the purpose of confirming between the Republic of Texas and the Government of the United States perfect harmony and good correspondence, and of removing all grounds of dissatisfaction, and reposing especial trust and confidence in the integrity, prudence, and ability of Memucan Hunt, appointed Envoy Extraordinary and Minister Plenipotentiary of the Republic of Texas near the said Government of the United States, I have invested him with full and all manner of power and authority, for and in the name of the Republic of Texas, to meet and confer with any person or persons, duly authorized by the said Government of the United States, being furnished with like power and authority, and with him or them to agree, treat, consult, and negotiate of and concerning Amity, Commerce, Navigation, Annexation and Limits between the two countries, and of all matters and subjects connected therewith, and to conclude and sign a treaty or treaties, convention or conventions, touching the premises, transmitting the same to the President of the Republic of Texas for his final ratification, by and with the advice and consent of the Senate of the Republic of Texas.

In testimony whereof, I have caused the Seal of the Republic of Texas to be hereunto affixed.

(L. S.) Given under my hand, at the City of Houston, this twenty-third day of February A.D. one thousand eight hundred and thirty-eight, and of the Independence of Texas the [second.]

(Signed)   SAM. HOUSTON.

By the President:
(Countersigned)   R. A. IRION,
Secretary of State.

THE NEGOTIATIONS

Each of the two Governments from the beginning of their relations regarded the boundary fixed by the earlier treaties of the United

States with Spain and with Mexico (Documents 41 and 60) as binding, so far as concerned the line between the United States and the Republic of Texas. The Government of the United States was so informed by the representatives of Texas as early as January 11, 1837 (Garrison, Diplomatic Correspondence of Texas, pt. 1, 175); the attitude of that Government at no time varied in that regard (*ibid.*, 232, 279, 295); indeed, the Government of Texas appointed a. commissioner to run the line accordingly (*ibid.*, 252, August 4, 1837; 279, December 31, 1837). The boundaries of Texas, as claimed by that Government, were thus described in the instructions of March 21, 1838, from R. A. Irion, Secretary of State of Texas, to Memucan Hunt (*ibid.*, 318–20):

> The present boundaries of Texas as fixed by an act of Congress are as follows, viz,—Beginning at the mouth of the Sabine River and running west along the Gulf of Mexico three leagues from land to the mouth of the Rio Grande; thence up the principal branch of said river to its source, thence north to the forty second degree of north latitude; thence along the boundary line as defined in the treaty between the United States and Spain to the beginning.

That description of the boundaries of Texas was taken almost literally from the Texan act of December 19, 1836, "to define the Boundaries of the Republic of Texas", which contained the following provisions (Laws of the Republic of Texas, I, 133–34):

> That from and after the passage of this act, the civil and political jurisdiction of this republic be, and is hereby declared to extend to the following boundaries, to wit: beginning at the mouth of the Sabine river, and running west along the Gulf of Mexico three leagues from land, to the mouth of the Rio Grande, thence up the principal stream of said river to its source, thence due north to the forty-second degree of north latitude, thence along the boundary line as defined in the treaty between the United States and Spain, to the beginning: and that the president be, and he is hereby authorized and required to open a negotiation with the government of the United States of America, so soon as in his opinion the public interest requires it, to ascertain and define the boundary line as agreed upon in said treaty.

Secretary of State Forsyth, as reported by the Texan Minister, took the position that the eastern boundary of Texas ran from the Gulf of Mexico up the Neches, instead of the Sabine (Garrison, *op. cit.*, pt. 1, 287, January 31, 1838):

> In regard to the running of the boundary line, I have had an additional conversation with Mr. Forsyth, in which he again insisted upon the Neches, as the true eastern limit of Texas; although I had invariably declared, and again took occasion to say, that the words of the treaty of 1819 were too explicit to admit of so forced a construction, and that the Sabine River, referred to in the treaty, was the identical stream, to which we claimed and the same that was laid down upon Mellish's Map of 1818;—and that by no manner of means would the government of Texas renounce its claim to a portion of territory, to which it was so clearly entitled by the specific and express words of the treaty itself.

Owing to the resulting uncertainty as to the proper location of the line running due north to the Red River, from latitude 32°, there were conflicts of jurisdiction over Red River County, or Miller County, in southwestern Arkansas (see D. S., 1 Despatches, Texas,

No. 6, January 30, 1838; and Garrison, *op. cit.*, pt. 1, 291–313). The act of June 15, 1844 (5 Statutes at Large, 674), was one result of that uncertainty.

The contention that the River Sabine named in the earlier treaties (Documents 41 and 60) was not the Sabine, but the Neches, was one that involved an area of nearly 10,000 square miles. The question itself, the arguments on the one side and the other, and their relation to the negotiations, are fully treated in Marshall, A History of the Western Boundary of the Louisiana Purchase, 1819–1841, 206–24, and the writings there cited.

The Texan Minister at Washington reported that the disposition of this Government was to delay a settlement (Garrison, *op. cit.*, pt. 1, 312, March 3, 1838):

This Government has, manifestly, been disposed to delay the fixation of the boundary line; notwithstanding my note of the 4th. of August to Mr. Forsyth on the subject, and my repeated communications relative thereto; nor did he apprise me until just before my Despatch No 29. [January 31, 1838], that the time limited by a treaty with Mexico and the United States for that purpose, had expired; nor had he replied to my note on the subject up to that time. He then made a verbal statement saying, that the treaty on the subject was at an end, and must be renewed, with Texas, before commissioners for that purpose could act.

Some of the alleged delay was due to the lack of full powers on the part of the Texan Minister (*ibid.*, 288), and perhaps also to the discussions regarding running the line "as far as the Pacific Ocean" (*ibid.*), an ambition which the Texan Government wholly disavowed (*ibid.*, 327–28).

It was the desire of the Government of Texas to limit the demarcation so that it would not go beyond the Red River, for reasons stated in the instructions to Hunt of March 21, 1838, enclosing his full power to treat (*ibid.*, 319–20):

This Government does not wish to run the line at present farther than the 100dth. degree of West longitude to a point on Red River in latitude nearly 33° 30', leaving a distance of eight or nine degrees to be run at a future time when it can be done with less hazard and expense.

The region north of Red River through which the line will pass is inhabited by hostile Indians, which circumstance would render it necessary to send a considerable guard to accompany the Commissioners and Surveyors. It is hoped that the Government of the U. States will not insist on running the line beyond the point above indicated on Red River.

The report of Hunt of the opening of the negotiations was made very shortly thereafter (*ibid.*, 323–25, April 13, 1838), from which it appears that the final discussions were had verbally:

I have just received your letter of the 21st of March, accompanied by a full power from the President for various purposes. I communicated the fact to the Secretary of State of the United States immediately after their receipt, and am happy to inform you, that he has been instructed by the President, to open a negotiation with me immediately, for the renewal of an agreement, to appoint commissioners and time, and place, for their meeting, to establish the boundary line permanently, between the two Republics, in conformity with the treaty of

the Spanish Government of 1819 and as renewed by the Government of Mexico in 1828. Mr. Forsyth has receded from his demand to establish the line the whole distance to the Pacific, and thinks it will be best for both parties to make it only so far as it is desired to be done by the Texian Government at this time.

The Government of the United States, is very desirous, I have no doubt, to procure the Bay of St. Francisco, on the Pacific, and I apprehended and have now additional evidence to convince me of the fact that, Mr. Forsyth's apparently anxious desire to make the line the whole distance to the Pacific, was to procure from me, the relinquishment of the claim of the Government of Texas, to the right of an extention of its boundary beyond what it was under the Mexican Government. And he expects, I imagine, to be enabled to pass over the claim in the arrangements which we are now making to establish the boundary, in such a manner, as to leave an impression, that the Government of Texas claimed its original boundary, only on its Northern and Eastern frontier. But I will take care in the wording of an article on the subject, that this claim to additional territory, be not overlooked. As a seperated Power, the splendid harbours on the South Sea or Pacific Ocean, will be indespensable for us; and apart from the great increase of territory by an extention of the line, the possession of the harbour of St. Francisco alone, is amply sufficient, for any increased difficulties or expence, should there be any in regard to a claim of territory to the Pacific, in a final treaty of Peace with Mexico.

My impression is that, nothing short of coercion, will afford us peace with that nation, and in the exercise of this means, to acquire it eventually, a claim to a large territory, will be as readily conceded to us, when they do so yield, as the former limits of Texas would be; and believing this, it is my duty as minister, to act accordingly, in my claim of territory for Texas, in the absence of instructions from my Government on the subject.

In my intercourse with Mr. Forsyth on the subject of limits, he mentioned, what you had written to me on the subject of, and relative to, the interchanges between the Chargé of the United States and Yourself at Houston.

I smoothed matters over as well as I could, and turned the circumstance to an argument in favour of settling, with as little delay as possible, the boundary question, which I insisted, would terminate all causes for misconceptions and misapprehensions between the two Governments relative thereto, which he conceded, and, as I have no doubt, will prove to be the case.

Mr. Forsyth mentioned to me on yesterday that, he wished to set out this evening, on a short trip to Philadelphia; I expressed a disposition to go to New York for one day, myself, and he proposed, and we agreed, to make the trip together, and complete verbally our negotiations during the progress of our travel; and that so soon as we should return, they should be finally agreed upon, and reduced to writing, and signed for the confirmation of the senate, at the earliest date practicable. The exchange of ratifications will be made in Texas, and so soon as it occurs, and the fact can be communicated officially to this Government, a commissioner will be despatched, for the purpose of complying with the terms of the treaty of limits, with as little delay as possible.

That report was followed by the despatch of Hunt of April 28, 1838, which included the following (*ibid.*, 325–26):

I, herewith, transmit a copy of the treaty of limits, which I have effected with this Government. It would have been forwarded the day after it was signed, but for the delay in procuring a copy of a form of ratification. I objected to the power which it confers on the commissioners, and desired that a clause should be inserted, which would leave it discretionary with either Government, to object to the agreement of the commissioners within three months or less, after they might fix and report the boundary line; but the President of the United States objected to any change in the terms of the original treaty, on the ground that, it would be necessary to make an entirely new treaty, should any portion of it be altered. I hope it may be satisfactory to the President and Senate.

RELATIONS WITH THE REPUBLIC OF TEXAS

By Article 3 of the treaty with Spain of February 22, 1819 (Document 41), a treaty which went into force on February 22, 1821, the boundary between the United States and Spanish territory on this continent was fixed from the Gulf of Mexico north and west to the Pacific Ocean; and as that line began in the Gulf of Mexico at the mouth of the Sabine River, the area which was later the Republic of Texas and which became the State of Texas was without the limits of the United States.

The *de facto* independence of Mexico, which dated from 1821, made that boundary of the United States one between the United States and Mexico; and on December 12, 1822, the United States recognized the independent Government of Mexico, when President Monroe received José Manuel Zozaya as Minister of Mexico at Washington.

The line which, by the treaty of 1819 with Spain, had been one between the United States and Spanish territory, was adopted as the line between the United States and Mexico by the Treaty of Limits of January 12, 1828, with Mexico (Document 60), which, however, did not go into force until April 5, 1832.

Each of those treaties, that with Spain of 1819 (Document 41) and that with Mexico of 1828 (Document 60), contained provisions for the demarcation of the boundary fixed from the mouth of the Sabine River to the Pacific Ocean; but in neither case were those provisions executed, although in respect of Mexico a convention further providing for their execution was signed as late as April 3, 1835 (Document 79), which went into force on April 20, 1836.

The struggle for Texan independence began in 1835; the independence of Texas was declared by a convention which met at the town of Washington in that state on March 2, 1836; the decisive battle of San Jacinto was fought on April 21, 1836; an act of March 3, 1837 (5 Statutes at Large, 170), made an appropriation for the salary of a diplomatic agent to the Republic of Texas; a Senate resolution of an earlier date expressed the opinion that Texas should be recognized by the United States; and just before the close of his term of office, President Jackson acquiesced in what he regarded as "a virtual decision of the question" by his nomination of Alcée La Branche on March 3, 1837, to be Chargé d'Affaires to the Republic of Texas; that nomination was sent to the Senate with the following message (Executive Journal, IV, 631):

In my message to Congress of the 21st of December last I laid before that body, without reserve, my views concerning the recognition of the independence of Texas, with a report of the agent employed by the Executive to obtain information in respect to the condition of that country. Since that time the subject has been repeatedly discussed in both branches of the Legislature. These discussions have resul ed in the insertion of a clause in the general appropriation law passed by both Houses providing for the outfit and salary of a diplomatic agent to be sent to the Republic of Texas, whenever the President of the United States may receive satisfactory evidence that Texas is an independent power and shall deem it expedient to appoint such minister, and in the adoption of a resolution by the Senate, the constitutional advisers of the Executive on the diplomatic

intercourse of the United States with foreign powers, expressing the opinion that "the State of Texas having established and maintained an independent government, capable of performing those duties, foreign and domestic, which appertain to independent governments, and it appearing that there is no longer any reasonable prospect of the successful prosecution of the war by Mexico against said State, it is expedient and proper, and in conformity with the laws of nations and the practice of this Government in like cases, that the independent political existence of said State be acknowledged by the Government of the United States." Regarding these proceedings as a virtual decision of the question submitted by me to Congress, I think it my duty to acquiesce therein, and therefore I nominate Alcée La Branche, of Louisiana, to be charge d'affaires to the Republic of Texas.

On the same evening, apparently, President Jackson "sent for Genl Hunt [Memucan Hunt] and myself [William H. Wharton] and requested the pleasure of a glass of wine, and stated that Mr. Forsyth would see us officially on Monday [March 6, 1837]" (Garrison, *op. cit.*, pt. 1, 201).

William H. Wharton had been commissioned as Minister Plenipotentiary from Texas to the United States on November 18, 1836 (*ibid.*, 140–41), and General Memucan Hunt as Minister Extraordinary on December 31 (*ibid.*, 165–66); but neither was formally received at the time, because of their informal credentials, which were returned (D. S., 6 Notes to the Texan Legation, 1–2, March 13, 1837). As to Hunt, that defect was remedied by new papers, and he was received by President Van Buren on July 6, 1837 (Garrison, *op. cit.*, pt. 1, 236).

The nomination of Alcée La Branche to be Chargé d'Affaires to the Republic of Texas was duly confirmed by the Senate on March 7, 1837 (Executive Journal, V, 17), in the beginning of the administration of President Van Buren, and his commission was issued on the same day.

Both Governments agreed that the Treaty of Amity, Commerce, and Navigation of April 5, 1831, between the United States and Mexico (Document 70), was binding as between the United States and Texas; such was the position of the United States from the beginning (D. S., 6 Notes to the Texan Legation, 1–2, March 13, 1837). The similar attitude of the Republic of Texas was formally stated in the note of June 23, 1838, from Irion to La Branche, as follows (Garrison, *op. cit.*, pt. 1, 334–35):

With regard to your note of the 23rd March, transmitting a copy of the Treasury Circular, of the United States, dated 2nd February, by which the fifth and Sixth Articles, of the Treaty of Amity, Navigation, and Commerce, existing between the said U. States and Mexico, are declared to be binding on Texas.

I have the honor to state, that the President, having considered the subject, directs me to inform you, that the stipulations indicated by the Circular will be observed by this Government.

The application on the part of the U. States relative to the treaty aforesaid, calling on this Government, for a declaration, whether or not it considers the whole treaty obligatory, has also been submitted to His Excellency, for consideration, respecting which, I am likewise directed to state, that it will be observed by this Government, till a new treaty shall be formed.

The pendency, of the proposition for the annexation of Texas, to the U. States, and a desire on the part of this Government, should the proposition not succeed, to form at the earliest practicable period, a new treaty, with that Government, induced the President, to hope, that no emergencies would again arise, while that

question remained undetermined, requiring further action on the said treaty, believing at the same time, in as much as the condition of Texas, in many important respects, differs materially, from that of Mexico, that the commercial interests of the United States, and this Republic, could be more satisfactorily arranged, by a new one, framed with a view to the relative position, political organization, extent, resources etc, of both Governments.

The clauses of the treaty with Mexico of particular concern were those of Article 33, regarding "hostilities and incursions on the part of the Indian nations living within their respective boundaries"; those provisions gave rise to considerable correspondence.

That treaty, however, by Article 34 thereof, "in all its parts, relating to Commerce and Navigation", was subject to termination by either party on one year's notice from and after April 5, 1840. Such notice was duly given on behalf of the Republic of Texas on May 19, 1841 (D. S., 1 Communications from Agents of Texas; see also 1 Instructions, Texas, 31–33, June 14, 1841).

THE BOUNDARY DEMARCATION

The boundary between the United States and the Republic of Texas was only a part of the line fixed first by the treaty of 1819 with Spain (Document 41) and later adopted as the boundary between the United States and Mexico by the Treaty of Limits of 1828 (Document 60); and it is to be particularly observed, moreover, that this convention provided for the immediate demarcation of only a portion of the boundary between the United States and the Republic of Texas, namely, that "which extends from the mouth of the Sabine, where that river enters the Gulph of Mexico to the Red River", a distance of less than 300 miles.

An act of Congress of January 11, 1839 (5 Statutes at Large, 312–13), provided for the carrying into effect of this convention; and the boundary (to the extent mentioned) was duly surveyed and marked according to its description in Article 2 of the Treaty of Limits of January 12, 1828, with Mexico (Document 60), a description which had been adopted from Article 3 of the treaty of 1819 with Spain (Document 41):

The Boundary Line between the two Countries, West of the Mississippi, shall begin on the Gulph of Mexico, at the mouth of the River Sabine in the Sea, continuing North, along the Western Bank of that River, to the 32ᵈ degree of Latitude; thence by a Line due North to the degree of Latitude, where it strikes the Rio Roxo of Nachitoches, or Red-River.

The result of that demarcation is thus described in Douglas, Boundaries, Areas, Geographic Centers, and Altitudes of the United States, 2d edition, 169–70:

The eastern boundary of the Republic of Texas, which followed the west bank of the Sabine River, was surveyed in 1840 by a joint commission representing the United States and Texas from the Gulf to Logans Ferry, the observed latitude of which was found to be 31°58′24″ and the longitude 94°00′02.4″. The initial mark of this survey was a mound of earth 50 feet in diameter and about 7 feet high on the shore of the Gulf, the position of which was reported as latitude 29°41′27.5″, longitude 93°50′14.2″.

In the following year another commission ran the line northward along the Sabine River to the 32d parallel as determined from astronomic observations, thence along a true north line to the south bank of the Red River.   Mounds were erected at 1-mile intervals on the meridian boundary, the measured length of which was found to be a little less than 106½ miles.   The original plats of this survey are on file in the United States State Department, and the General Land Office has copies.   The field notes were probably filed in the War Department. The approximate longitude of the meridian line at latitude 33°06′30″ is 94°02′ 35.1″.

The original journal and maps of the commission are in the archives of the Department of State; the journal is printed, with reproductions of the maps, and with correspondence accompanying the presidential messages to the Senate of March 17 and April 12, 1842, in Senate Document No. 199, 27th Congress, 2d session, serial 397.

A full account of "The Survey of the Texas-Louisiana Boundary", with numerous citations, is in Marshall, A History of the Western Boundary of the Louisiana Purchase, 1819–1841, chapter XII.

The attitude of the Government of Mexico was formally declared on June 18, 1839, when the Mexican Minister at Washington, Francisco Pizarro Martinez, wrote to Secretary of State John Forsyth as follows (D. S., 4 Notes from the Mexican Legation, translation):

His Excellency the Acting President of the Mexican Republic, being informed of the appointment made by His Excellency the President of the United States in February last of a commission to lay off the boundary between Texas and this Republic, has directed me to declare to you, as I now have the honor to do, that nothing which may be now settled with the Texans will in any manner bind Mexico if she should recover Texas, or whenever the Republic should treat on the subject of limits with the United States.

The historical diagram of Texas on page 143 shows clearly the relevant portion of the treaty line of 1819 and the part thereof dealt with by this convention, as well as the State boundaries in that region. In connection with that diagram, however, it is to be observed that the boundaries of the State of Texas were in some respects, subsequent to 1845, modified by agreement and legislation and more definitely determined by judicial decision.   Such changes and decisions are described in detail in Douglas, *op. cit.*, 171–76, and in the writings there cited.

The various phases of the boundaries of Texas are elaborately and learnedly treated, with abundant citations, in Paullin, Atlas of the Historical Geography of the United States.   The relevant plates are 93G, 93H, 94A, 94B, 95A, 95B, 95C, 95D, 97H, and 101C.   The relevant text is at pages 63–69, 78, and 87.

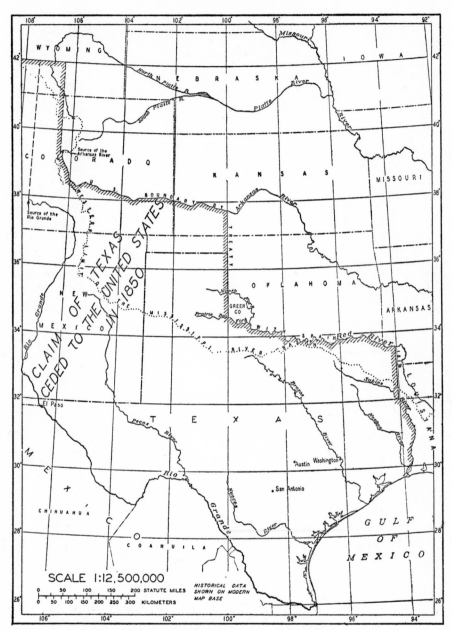

HISTORICAL DIAGRAM OF TEXAS

143

Treaty Series No. 316
8 Statutes at Large, 512–23
18 *ibid.*, pt. 2, Public Treaties, 684–89

86

SARDINIA : NOVEMBER 26, 1838

*Treaty of Commerce and Navigation, with separate article, signed at
Genoa November 26, 1838. Original in English and French.
Submitted to the Senate January 28, 1839. (Message of January 24,
1839.) Resolution of advice and consent March 2, 1839. Ratified
by the United States March 8, 1839. Ratified by Sardinia December
1, 1838. Ratifications exchanged at Washington March 18, 1839.
Proclaimed March 18, 1839.*

The United States of America and His Majesty the King of Sardinia desirous of consolidating the relations of good understanding which have hitherto so happily subsisted between their respective States and of facilitating and extending the Commercial intercourse between the two Countries, have agreed to enter into negotiations for the conclusion of a Treaty of Commerce and Navigation, for which purpose the President of the United States has conferred full Powers on Nathaniel Niles their special Agent near His Sardinian Majesty and His Majesty the King of Sardinia has conferred like Powers on the Count Clement Solar de la Marguerite, Grand Cross of the Military and Religious Order of S. Maurice and S. Lazarus, of Isabella the Catholic of Spain, and Knight of the Order of Christ,

Les Etats Unis d'Amérique, et Sa Majesté le Roi de Sardaigne désirant consolider les rapports de bonne intelligence qui ont si heureusement subsisté jusqu'ici entre leurs Etats respectifs, et de faciliter et étendre les relations commerciales entre les deux pays, sont convenus d'entrer en négociation pour conclure un Traité de commerce et de navigation. À cet effet Le Président des Etats-Unis a muni de Pleinspouvoirs Nathaniel Niles, leur Agent spécial auprès de Sa Majesté Sarde; et Sa Majesté le Roi de Sardaigne le Comte Clément Solar de la Marguerite Chevalier Grand Cordon de l'Ordre Religieux et Militaire de St Maurice et St Lazare, Grand Croix de l'Ordre d'Isabelle la Catholique d'Espagne, et Chevalier de L'Ordre du Christ, son Premier Secrétaire d'Etat pour les Affaires

145

His First Secretary of State for the foreign Affairs;

And the said Plenipotentiaries having exchanged their full Powers, found in good and due form, have concluded and signed the following Articles.

ARTICLE I

There shall be between the territories of the High Contracting Parties a reciprocal liberty of Commerce and Navigation. The inhabitants of their respective States shall mutually have liberty to enter the Ports and commercial places of the territories of each party, wherever foreign commerce is permitted. They shall be at liberty to sojourn and reside in all parts whatsoever of said territories in order to attend to their affairs and they shall enjoy to that effect the same security and protection as the natives of the country wherein they reside, on condition of their submitting to the laws and ordinances there prevailing.

ART: II

Sardinian Vessels arriving either laden or in ballast in the Ports of the United States of America, and reciprocally vessels of the United States arriving either laden or in ballast in the Ports of the dominions of His Sardinian Majesty, shall be treated on their entrance, during their stay and at their departure upon the same footing as national vessels coming from

Etrangères; Lesquels Plénipotentiaires après avoir échangé leurs Pleinspouvoirs trouvés en bonne et due forme, ont arrêté et signé les articles suivans.

ARTICLE I

Il y aura entre les Territoires des hautes parties contractantes, liberté et réciprocité de Commerce et de Navigation. Les habitans de leurs Etats respectifs pourront entrer librement dans les ports des territoires de chacune d'elles, partout où le Commerce étranger est permis. Ils pourront séjourner ou résider librement dans quelque partie que ce soit des dits territoires, pour y vaquer à leurs affaires, et ils jouiront à cet effet de la même sécurité et protection que les habitans du pays dans lequel ils resident, à la condition toutefois de se soumettre aux loix et aux règlemens qui y sont en vigueur.

ART: II

Les bâtimens Sardes arrivant chargés ou sur lest dans les Ports des Etats-Unis d'Amérique, et réciproquement les bâtimens des Etats-Unis d'Amérique arrivant chargés ou sur Lest dans les Ports de Sa Majesté le Roi de Sardaigne, seront traités à leur entrée, pendant leur séjour et à leur sortie, sur le même pied que les bâtimens nationaux venant

the same place, with respect to the duties of tonnage lighthouses, pilotage and port charges as well as to the fees and perquisites of public Officers and other duties or charges of whatever kind or denomination, levied in the name or to the profit of the Government, the local authorities or of any private establishment whatsoever.

ART: III

All kind of merchandise and articles of commerce either the produce of the soil or the industry of the United States of America or of any other country, which may be lawfully imported into the Ports of the dominions of Sardinia in Sardinian Vessels, may also be so imported in vessels of the United States of America without paying other or higher duties or charges of whatever kind or denomination levied in the name or to the profit of the Government, the local authorities or of any private establishment whatsoever, than if the same merchandise or produce had been imported in Sardinian vessels. And reciprocally all kind of merchandise and articles of commerce, either the produce of the soil, or of the industry of the dominions of Sardinia or of any other country, which may be lawfully imported into the ports of the United States, in vessels of the said

des mêmes parages, par rapport aux droits de tonnage, de fanaux, de pilotage, de péage, aux droits de port, vacations d'officiers Publics, ainsi qu'à toutes les taxes et charges de quelque espèce ou dénomination que se soit, perçues au nom ou au profit du Gouvernement, des autorités locales, ou d'établissemens particuliers quelconques.

ART III

Toute espèce de marchandises et objets de commerce provenant du Sol ou de l'industrie des Etats-Unis d'Amérique, ou de tout autre pays, qui pourront légalement être importés dans les Ports des Etats de Sa Majesté le Roi de Sardaigne par des bâtimens Sardes, pourront également y être importés par des bâtimens des Etats-Unis sans être tenus à payer d'autres ou de plus forts droits de quelque espèce ou dénomination que ce soit, perçus au nom ou au profit du Gouvernement, des autorités locales, ou d'établissemens particuliers quelconques, que ceux que ces mêmes marchandises ou produits payeraient dans le même cas s'ils étaient importés sur des batimens Sardes. Et réciproquement, toute espèce de marchandises et objets de commerce provenant du Sol ou de l'industrie du Royaume de Sardaigne ou de tout autre pays, qui pourront être légale-

States, may also be so imported in Sardinian vessels, without paying other or higher duties or charges of whatever kind or denomination levied in the name or to the profit of the Government, the local authorities, or of any private establishment whatsoever, than if the same merchandise or produce had been imported in Vessels of United States of America.

ART IV.

To prevent the possibility of any misunderstanding, it is hereby declared that the stipulations contained in the two preceding Articles are to their full extent applicable to Sardinian vessels and their cargoes arriving in the Ports of the United States of America. And reciprocally to vessels of the said States, and their cargoes arriving in the ports of the dominions of Sardinia, whether the said vessels clear directly from the ports of the country to which they respectively belong, or from the ports of any other foreign country.

ART V.

All kind of merchandise and articles of commerce, which may lawfully be exported from the Ports of the United States of

ment importés dans les Etats-Unis d'Amérique par des bâtimens de ces mêmes Etats, pourront également y être importés par des bâtimens Sardes, sans payer d'autres ou de plus forts droits de quelque espèce ou dénomination que ce soit, perçus au nom ou au profit du Gouvernement, des autorités locales, ou d'un établissement particulier quelconque, que ceux que ces mêmes marchandises ou produits payeraient dans le même cas s'ils étaient importés sur des bâtimens des Etats-Unis d'Amérique.

ART IV.

Afin de prévenir toute espèce de mésentendu, il est convenu que les dispositions contenues dans les articles 2 et 3 sont applicables dans toute leur étendue aux Bâtimens Sardes et à leurs cargaisons, arrivant dans les Ports des Etats-Unis d'Amérique, et réciproquement aux Bâtimens des dits Etats et à leurs cargaisons arrivant dans les Ports de Sa Majesté le Roi de Sardaigne, soit que ces Bâtimens viennent directement des Ports du pays auquel ils appartiennent, soit de ceux de tout autre pays étranger.

ART: V.

Toute espèce de marchandises et objets de commerce qui pourront être légalement exportés des Ports des Etats-Unis d'Amérique

America in national vessels, may also be exported therefrom in Sardinian vessels without paying other or higher duties or charges of whatever kind or denomination levied in the name or to the profit of the Government, the local authorities, or of any private establishment whatsoever, than if the same merchandise or Articles of commerce had been exported in vessels of the United States of America. And reciprocally all kind of merchandise and articles of commerce which may be lawfully exported from the Ports of the Kingdom of Sardinia in national vessels, may also be exported therefrom in vessels of the United States of America, without paying other or higher duties, or charges of whatever kind or denomination levied in the name, or to the profit of the Government, the local authorities or of any private establishment whatsoever, than if the same merchandise or articles of commerce had been exported in Sardinian vessels.

sur des bâtimens nationaux, pourront en être également exportés sur des bâtimens Sardes, sans payer d'autres ou de plus forts droits ou charges, de quelque espèce ou dénomination que ce soit, perçus au nom ou au profit du Gouvernement, des autorités locales, ou d'un établissement particulier quelconque que ceux qui seraient payés pour les mêmes marchandises et objets de commerce qui auraient été exportés sur des Bâtimens des Etats-Unis d'Amérique; et réciproquement toute espèce de marchandises ou objets de commerce qui pourront être légalement exportés des Ports de Sa Majesté le Roi de Sardaigne sur des bâtimens nationaux pourront également en être exportés sur des bâtimens des Etats-Unis d'Amérique, sans payer d'autres ou de plus forts droits ou charges, de quelque espèce ou dénomination que ce soit, perçus au nom ou au profit du Gouvernement, des autorités locales, ou d'établissemens particuliers quelconques, que ceux qui seraient payés pour les mêmes marchandises ou objets de commerce, s'ils avaient été exportés sur des bâtimens Sardes.

Art: VI.

No higher or other duties shall be imposed on the importation into the United States of any article the produce or manufacture of Sardinia: and no higher or

Art: VI

Il ne sera imposé d'autres ou de plus forts droits sur l'importation dans les Etats-Unis d'Amérique de tout article provenant du sol ou de L'industrie du Royaume

other duties shall be imposed on the importation into the Kingdom of Sardinia of any article the produce or manufacture of the United States than are or shall be payable on the same article being the produce, or manufacture of any other foreign country. Nor shall any prohibition be imposed on the importation or exportation of any article the produce of, or the manufacture of the United States or of Sardinia, to or from the ports of the United States, or to or from the ports of the Kingdom of Sardinia which shall not equally extend to all other nations

ART: VII.

It is expressly understood, and agreed that the preceding Articles do not apply to the coastwise navigation of either of the two countries, which each of the two High Contracting Parties reserves exclusively to itself.

ART: VIII.

No priority or preference shall be given directly or indirectly by either of the High Contracting Parties, nor by any company corporation or agent acting in their behalf, or under their authority in the purchase of any article of commerce lawfully imported on account of, or in reference to the character of the vessel, whether it be of the one

de Sardaigne, et il ne sera imposé d'autres ou de plus forts droits sur l'importation dans le Royaume de Sardaigne de tout article provenant du Sol ou de l'industrie des Etats-Unis, que ceux qui sont ou seront imposés sur de semblables articles provenant du Sol ou de l'industrie de tout autre pays étranger. De même on ne mettra aucune entrave ou prohibition quelconque à l'importation ou à l'exportation de tout article provenant du Sol ou de l'industrie des Etats-Unis d'Amérique ou du Royaume de Sardaigne, à l'entrée ou à la sortie des Ports de chaque pays, qui ne soit pas également applicable à toute autre Nation.

ART: VII.

Il est expressément entendu que les articles, précédens ne sont point applicables à la navigation de côte ou cabotage de chacun des deux pays que l'une et l'autre des deux nations se reservent exclusivement.

ART: VIII.

Aucune priorité ou préférence quelconque ne sera accordée directement ou indirectement par l'une ou l'autre des parties contractantes, ni par aucune compagnie, corporation ou agent agissant en son nom ou par son autorité, pour l'achat d'aucun objet de commerce, légalement importé, par considération ou préférence pour la nationalité du bâtiment

party or the other, in which such article was imported, it beeing the true intent and meaning of the Contracting Parties, that no distinction or difference whatever shall be made in this respect.

qui aurait importé les dits objets, soit qu'il appartienne à l'une ou à l'autre des parties dans les Ports de laquelle ces objets de commerce auront été importés, l'intention el la volonté précise des hautes parties contractantes étant qu'aucune différence ou distinction quelconque n'ait lieu à cet égard.

Art: IX.

If either Party shall hereafter grant to any other nation any particular favor in commerce or navigation, it shall immediatly become common to the other party, freely where it is freely granted to such other Nation, or on yielding the same or an equivalent compensation when the grant is conditional.

Art: IX.

Si par la suite l'une des parties contractantes accordait quelque faveur spéciale à d'autres nations en fait de commerce ou de navigation, cette faveur deviendra immédiatement commune à l'autre partie qui en jouira sans charge d'aucune espèce, si elle a été accordée gratuitement à l'autre nation, ou en accordant la même compensation ou une autre équivalente, si la concession a été conditionnelle.

Art: X.

Vessels of either of the High Contracting Parties arriving on the coasts of the other, but without the intention to enter a Port, or having entered not wishing to discharge the whole, or any part of their cargoes shall enjoy in this respect the same privileges, and be treated in the same manner as the Vessels of the most favored nations.

Art: X.

Les bâtimens de l'une des deux parties contractantes abordant à quelque côte de la dépendance de l'autre, mais n'ayant pas l'intention d'entrer au Port, ou y étant entrés ne voulant pas y décharger tout ou une partie de leur cargaison, jouiront des mêmes privilèges et seront traités à cet égard de la même manière que les bâtimens des Nations les plus favorisées.

Art: XI.

When any Vessel belonging to either of the Contracting Parties, or to their citizens, or subjects shall be wrecked, foundered, or otherwise suffer damage on the coasts, or within the dominions of the other, there shall be given to such vessel and all persons on board every aid and protection, in like manner as is usual and customary to vessels of the nation where such shipwreck or damage happens, and such shipwrecked vessel, its merchandise, and other effects, or their proceeds, if the same shall have been sold, shall be restored to their owners, or to those entitled to receive them, upon the payment of such costs of salvage as would have been paid by national vessels in the same circumstances.

Art XII.

Sardinian merchant vessels beeing forced from stress of weather, or other unavoidable causes to enter a Port of the United States of America, and reciprocally, merchant vessels of the said states, entering the ports of His Sardinian Majesty from similar causes, shall be exempt from port charges and all other duties levied to the profit of the Government, in case the causes which have rendered such entry necessary are real and evident, provided such vessel does not

Art. XI.

S'il arrivait qu'un vaisseau appartenant à l'une des deux parties contractantes ou bien à ses citoyens ou sujets, fit naufrage, sombrât, ou souffrit quelqu'autre dommage sur les côtes ou dans les Etats soumis à l'autre partie, il sera accordé à ces navires et à toutes les personnes qui seront à bord le même secours et la même protection dont jouissent ordinairement les bâtimens de la nation où le naufrage a eu lieu; et ces vaisseaux naufragés, les marchandises ou autres effets qu'ils contiendront, ou leur produit, si ces objets avaient été déjà vendus, seront restitués à leurs propriétaires ou à leurs ayant droit, en payant un droit de sauvetage égal à celui qui serait payé dans le même cas, par un Vaisseau national.

Art: XII.

Tout bâtiment de commerce Sarde entrant en relâche forcée dans un Port des Etats-Unis d'Amérique; et réciproquement tout bâtiment de commerce des dits Etats entrant en relâche forcée dans un Port de Sa Majesté le Roi de Sardaigne, y sera exempt de tout droit de Port et de navigation, perçu ou à percevoir au profit de l'Etat, si les causes qui ont nécessité la relâche sont réelles et évidentes, pourvu qu'ils ne se livrent dans le port de relâche à aucune opération de

engage in any commercial operation while in port, such as loading and unloading merchandise, it beeing understood nevertheless that the unloading, and reloading rendered necessary for the repair of the said Vessel shall not be considered an act of commerce affording ground for the payment of duties, and provided also that the said vessel shall not prolong her stay in Port beyond the time necessary for the repair of her damages.

commerce en chargeant où déchargeant des marchandises; bien entendu toutefois que les déchargemens et rechargemens motivés par l'obligation de réparer le bâtiment ne seront point considérés comme opérations de commerce donnant ouverture au payement des droits, et pourvu que le bâtiment ne prolonge pas son séjour dans le port au de-là du tems nécessaire d'après les causes qui auront donné lieu à la relâche.

ART: XIII.

Considering the remoteness of the respective countries of the two High Contracting Parties, and the uncertainty resulting therefrom with respect to the various events which may take place, it is agreed that a merchant vessel, belonging to either of them which may be bound to a port supposed, at the time of its departure to be blockaded, shall not however be captured, or condemned for having attempted a first time to enter said port, unless it can be proved that said Vessel could, and ought to have learned during its voyage, that the blockade of the place in question still continued. But all vessels which after having been warned off once, shall, during the same voyage, attempt a second time to enter the same blockaded Port during the continuance of the said blockade, shall then subject themselves to be detained and condemned.

ART XIII.

Vu l'éloignement des pays respectifs des deux hautes parties contractantes et l'incertitude qui en résulte sur les divers évènemens qui peuvent avoir lieu; il est convenu qu'un bâtiment marchand appartenant à l'une d'elles qui se trouverait destiné pour un port supposé bloqué au moment du départ de ce bâtiment, ne sera cependant pas capturé ou condamné pour avoir essayé une première fois d'entrer dans le dit port, à moins qu'il ne puisse être prouvé que le dit bâtiment avait pu et dû apprendre en route que l'état du blocus de la place en question durait encore. Mais les bâtimens qui, après avoir été renvoyés une première fois, essayeraient pendant le même voyage d'entrer une seconde fois dans le même port bloqué durant la continuation de ce blocus, se trouveront alors sujets à être détenus et condamnés.

Art: XIV.

All Articles of commerce the growth or manufacture of the United States of America, and the products of their fisheries, with the exception of Salt, Gunpowder and Tobacco manufactured for use, shall be permitted to pass in transitu from the free port of Genoa through the territories of His Sardinian Majesty to any point of the inland frontier of the said territories, and vice-versa, all Articles of commerce coming from any one point of the Sardinian inland frontier destined for the United States, shall be permitted to pass the territories of His Sardinian Majesty to the free Port of Genoa without being liable to the payment of any duty whatever levied in the name or to the profit of the Government, the local authorities or of any private establishment whatsoever, other than such as are required to meet the expenses of the necessary precautionary measures against smuggling, which precautionary measures to be observed in regard to transit to the frontier shall be the same whether the said articles of commerce are imported by the Vessels of the one or of the other of the High Contracting Parties. But if peculiar circumstances or considerations should render the reestablishment of transit duties necessary on the said Articles of commerce directed to any one point of the Sardinian frontier,

Art XIV.

Les articles de Commerce, produits du Sol ou des manufactures des Etats-Unis d'Amérique, et des pêches de ce pays, excepté le sel, la poudre à Canon et le tabac fabriqué, pourront librement passer du Port-franc de Gênes à travers le territoire de Sa Majesté Sarde à un point quelconque de la frontière intérieure du dit territoire; et vice-versa tous les articles de commerce venant par un point quelconque de la frontière intérieure Sarde, qui seront destinés pour les Etats-Unis, pourront traverser les Etats de Sa Majesté le Roi de Sardaigne jusqu'au Port-franc de Gênes sans être tenus de payer aucune espèce de droit perçus au nom ou au profit du Gouvernement, des autorités locales ou d'un établissement particulier quelconque excepté ceux nécessaires pour couvrir les frais qu'exigent les précautions et les mesures contre la fraude et la Contrebande, et qui ne seraient pas également applicables au transit des mêmes articles importés par les Bâtimens de l'une ou l'autres des hautes parties contractantes Mais si par des circonstances et des motifs particuliers il était jugé convenable ou nécessaire de retablir des droits de transit sur les articles susmentionnés dirigés par un point de la frontière Sarde, le Gouvernement de S. M. le Roi de Sardaigne s'en reserve le plein droit, s'engageant

the Sardinian Government, in reserving to itself the full right to establish such duty, engages to notify to the Government of the United States such determination six months before any such transit duty shall be exacted. It is also understood that all articles of commerce imported directly from the United States of America shall be taken and considered as the products of the said States, and shall be entitled equally and in like manner, with the exceptions above mentioned in the present article, to a free transit through the territories of His Sardinian Majesty.

ART: XV.

The two High Contracting Parties reciprocally grant to each other the liberty of having each in the Ports and other commercial places of the other, Consuls, Vice consuls and commercial Agents of their own appointment, who shall enjoy the same privileges powers and exemptions as those of the most favored nations. But if any of such Consuls shall exercise commerce, they shall be subjected to the same laws and usages to which the private individuals of their nation, or subjects or citizens of the most favored nations are subject in the same places, in respect to their commercial transactions.

toutefois à notifier cette détermination au Gouvernement des Etat-Unis six mois avant son exécution. Il est aussi convenu que tous les articles de commerce importés directement des Etats Unis d'Amérique seront reçus et considérés comme des produits des dits Etats et en cette qualité auront également droit au libre transit à travers les Etats de Sa Majesté le Roi de Sardaigne, sauf les exceptions mentionnées dans le présent article.

ART: XV.

Les deux hautes parties contractantes s'accordent mutuellement le droit d'envoyer dans les ports et villes commercantes de leurs Etats respectifs des Consuls, Vice Consuls et agens commerciaux nommés par Elles qui jouiront des mêmes privilèges, pouvoirs et exemptions dont jouissent ceux des nations les plus favorisées; mais dans le cas où quelques uns de ces Consuls voudraient exercer le commerce, ils seront tenus de se soumettre aux mêmes loix et usages auxquels sont soumis dans le même lieu par rapport à leurs transactions commerciales, les particuliers de leur nation, et les sujets des états les plus favorisés.

Art: XVI.

It is specially understood that whenever either of the two Contracting Parties shall select for a Consular Agent to reside in any Port or commercial place of the other party a subject or citizen of this last, such Consul or Agent shall continue to be regarded, notwithstanding his quality of a foreign Consul, as a subject or citizen of the nation to which he belongs, and consequently shall be submitted to the laws and regulations to which natives are subjected in the place of his residence. This obligation however shall in no respect embarass the exercise of his Consular functions, or affect the inviolability of the consular archives.

Art: XVII.

The said Consuls, Vice consuls and commercial Agents are authorised to require the assistance of the local authorities for the search, arrest, detention, and emprisonment of the deserters from the ships of war and merchant vessels of their country. For this purpose they shall apply to the competent tribunals, judges, and officers, and shall, in writing, demand said deserters, proving by the exhibition of the registers of the vessels, the rolls of the crews, or by other official documents that such individuals formed part of the crews: and

Art: XVI.

Il est spécialement entendu que lorsqu'une partie contractante choisira pour son Agent consulaire pour resider dans un port ou une ville commerçante de l'autre partie un sujet ou citoyen de celle-ci, ce Consul ou Agent continuera à être considéré, malgré sa qualité de Consul étranger, comme sujet ou citoyen de la nation à laquelle il appartient et qu'il sera par conséquent soumis aux loix et règlemens qui régissent les nationaux dans le lieu de sa résidence, sans que cette obligation puisse cependant gêner en rien l'exercice de ses fonctions consulaires, ni porter atteinte à l'inviolabilité des archives consulaires.

Art: XVII.

Les dits Consuls, Vice Consuls et Agens commerciaux seront autorisés à requérir l'assistance des autorités locales pour la recherche, l'arrestation, la détention et L'emprisonnement des déserteurs des bâtimens de guerre et marchands de leur pays. Ils s'adresseront à cet effet aux Tribunaux, Juges, et Officiers compétens, et reclameront par écrit les déserteurs susmentionnés en prouvant par la comunication des régistres des bâtimens ou rôles des Equipages, ou par d'autres documens officiels que ces individus ont fait partie des dits équipages. Cette recla-

this reclamation thus substantiated, the surrender shall not be refused. Such deserters when arrested shall be placed at the disposal of the said Consuls, Vice Consuls or commercial Agents and may be confined in the public prisons at the request and cost of those who shall claim them in order to be detained until the time when they shall be restored to the vessels to which they belonged, or sent back to their own country by a vessel of the same nation or any other vessel whatsoever. But if not sent back within three months from the day of their arrest, they shall be set at liberty and shall not again be arrested for the same cause.

If however the deserter should be found to have committed any crime or offence, his surrender may be delayed until the tribunal before which his case should be depending shall have pronounced its sentence and such sentence shall have been carried into execution.

Art: XVIII

The citizens and subjects of each of the Contracting Parties shalle have power to dispose of their personal goods within the jurisdiction of the other, by testament, donation, or otherwise, and their representatives, being citizens or subjects of the other party, shall succeed to their said personal goods whether by testa-

mation ainsi prouvée, l'extradition ne sera point refusée. Ces déserteurs lorsqu'ils auront été arrêtés seront mis à la disposition des dits Consuls Vice Consuls ou Agens Commerciaux et pourront être enfermés dans les prisons publiques à la requisition et aux frais de ceux qui les reclament pour être retenus jusqu'au moment ou ils pourront être rendus aux bâtimens auxquels ils appartiennent, ou pour être renvoyés dans leur pays sur des bâtimens nationaux ou autres. Mais s'ils ne sont pas renvoyés dans l'espace de trois mois, à compter du jour de leur arrestation, ils seront mis en liberté et ne pourront plus être arrêtés pour la même cause. Toutefois si le déserteur se trouvait avoir commis quelque crime ou delit, il pourra être sursis à son extradition jusqu'à ce que le Tribunal saisi de l'affaire ait rendu sa sentence, et que celle-ci ait reçu son exécution.

Art: XVIII

Les sujets ou Citoyens de chacune des parties contractantes pourront librement disposer par Testament, donation, ou autrement, des biens personnels qu'ils posséderont dans les Etats de l'autre, et leurs heritiers qui seront sujets ou citoyens de l'autre nation pourront succeder à leurs biens personnels soit en vertu d'un

ment or *ab intestato*, and may take possession thereof either by themselves or by others acting for them and dispose of the same at will, paying such taxes and dues only as the inhabitants of the country wherein the said goods are, shall be subject to pay in like cases.

And in case of the absence of the representatives such care shall be taken of the said goods as would be taken of the goods of a native of the same country in like case until the lawfull owner may take measures for receiving them. And if a question should arise among several claimants as to which of them said goods belong, the same shall finally be decided by the laws and judges of the land wherein the said goods are. And where on the death of any person holding real estate within the territories of one of the Contracting Parties such real estate would by the laws of the land descend on a Citizen or subject of the other party who by reason of alienage may be incapable of holding it, he shall be allowed a reasonable time to sell such real estate, and to withdraw and export the proceeds without molestation and without paying to the profit of the respective Governments any other dues taxes or charges than those to which the inhabitants of the country wherein said real estate is

Testament soit *ab intestato* et en prendre possession, soit en personne soit par d'autres agissant en leur nom: ils pourront en outre en disposer à leur gré, en ne payant à cet effet que les mêmes impositions taxes ou droits auxquels sont assujettis dans des cas semblables les habitans du pays où se trouvent les dits biens. En cas d'absence des heritiers, on donnera pour la conservation des dits biens les mêmes dispositions qu'on prendrait en pareil cas pour les propriétés des natifs du pays jusqu'à ce que le Propriétaire ait fait les arrangemens nécessaires pour recueillir l'héritage. S'il s'élevait des contestations entre différens prétendans quant aux droits que chacun d'eux soutiendrait avoir sur la succession, elles seront décidées en dernier ressort par les Juges et selon les loix du pays où ces biens seront situés. Et si par la mort d'une personne possédant des biens fonds sur le territoire d'une des deux parties contractantes, ces biens fonds venaient à passer par la dernière volonté de leur possesseur, à un citoyen ou sujet de l'autre partie qui par sa qualité d'étranger serait inhabile à les posséder on lui accordera un délai convenable pour les vendre, pour en retirer et emporter le produit sans obstacles d'aucune sorte et sans qu'on lui

situated shall be subject to pay in like cases.

Art: XIX.

The present Treaty shall continue in force for ten years counting from the day of the exchange of the ratifications, and if twelve months before the expiration of that period, neither of the High Contracting Parties shall have announced to the other by an official notification its intention to arrest the operation of the said Treaty, it shall remain obligatory one year beyond that time, and so on, until the expiration of the twelve months which will follow a similar notification, whatever is the time at which it may take place.

Art XX.

The present Treaty shall be approved and ratified by the President of the United States of America by and with the advice and consent of the Senate thereof, and by His Majesty the King of Sardinia, and the Ratifications shall be exchanged in the City of Washington within ten months from the date of the signature thereof or sooner if possible.

In faith whereof the Plenipotentiaries of the Contracting Parties have signed the present Treaty

impose au profit du Gouvernement respectif aucune taxe, imposition ou droit plus forts que ceux auxquels seraient soumis en pareils cas les habitans du pays où ces biens sont situés.

Art XIX.

Le présent traité sera en vigueur pendant dix années à compter du jour de l'échange des Ratifications et si un an avant ce terme l'une des parties contractantes n'avait pas annoné à l'autre par une notification officielle, son intention d'en faire cesser l'effet le dit Traité restera obligatoire pendant douze mois au delà de ce terme et ainsi de suite jusqu'à l'expiration des douze mois qui suivront une semblable déclaration quelle que soit l'époque à laquelle elle aurait eu lieu

Art: XX.

Le présent Traité sera approuvé et ratifié par le President des Etats-Unis d'Amérique, par et avec l'avis et le consentement du Senat des dits Etats, et par Sa Majesté le Roi de Sardaigne, et les Ratifications en seront échangées à Washington dans dix mois de la date de la signature ou plutôt si faire se peut.

En foi de quoi les Plénipotentiaires respectifs ont signé le présent Traité et y ont apposé leurs

and thereto affixed their respective Seals.

Done at Genoa this 26. November 1838.

NATHANIEL NILES
[Seal]

SOLAR DE LA MARGUERITE
[Seal]

Cachets respectifs. Fait à Gênes le 26 Novembre 1838.

NATHANIEL NILES

SOLAR DE LA MARGUERITE

SEPARATE ARTICLE.

Circumstances of a peculiar nature rendering it necessary for His Sardinian Majesty to continue for a time differential duties to the disadvantage of foreign Flags, on grain, Olive Oil and Wine, imported directly from the Black Sea, the Ports of the Adriatic, and of those of the Mediterranean, as far as Cape Trafalgar, notwithstanding the general provisions of the Articles N⁰ 2. 3. and 4 of the present Treaty, it is distincty understood and agreed by the High Contracting Parties, that the United States shall have full and entire liberty to establish countervailing differential duties on the same Articles imported from the same places to the disadvantage of the Sardinian Flag, in case the existing or any other differential duties on the said Articles, shall be continued in force to the disadvantage of the Flag of the United States of America by His Sardinian Majesty, beyond a period of four years, counting from the day of the exchange of the ratifications of the present Treaty

ARTICLE SÉPARÉ.

Sa Majesté Sarde jugeant convenable par des motifs particuliers de continuer à percevoir pour à présent des droits différentiels au détriment des Pavillons étrangers sur les Bleds, l'huile d'Olive et le Vin importé directement de la Mer Noire, des Ports de la Mer Adriatique et de ceux de la Méditerannée jusqu'au Cap Trafalgar nonobstant les articles 2. 3. et 4 du présent Traité il est spécialement entendu et établi entre les Hautes parties contractantes que les Etats-Unis auront pleine et entière liberté d'établir des droits différentiels équivalens sur les mêmes articles importés des mêmes pays au détriment du Pavillon Sarde dans le cas où la perception des droits différentiels continuerait à être exercée au détriment du Pavillon des Etats-Unis d'Amérique par Sa Majesté le Roi de Sardaigne au delà de l'espace de quatre ans à compter du jour de l'échange des ratifications du présent Traité et article séparé. Mais ces droits différentiels équivalens de quelque espèce

and separate article, but all countervailing differential duties on the said articles shall cease to be exacted from the time the United States Government shall have been informed officially of the discontinuance of differential duties on the part of His Sardinian Majesty.

The present separate Article shall have the same force and value as if it where inserted word for word in the Treaty signed this day and shall be ratified in the same time.

In faith whereof, we the Undersigned, by virtue of our full Powers, have signed the present separate Article and thereto affixed Our respective Seals

Done at Genoa the 26 November 1838.

NATHANIEL NILES
SOLAR DE LA MARGUERITE
[Seal]   [Seal]

qu'ils soyent sur les dits Articles de Commerce cesseront d'être perçus du moment où le Gouvernement des Etats-Unis aura été informé d'office de la cessation des droits différentiels de la part de Sa Majesté Sarde.

Le présent article séparé aura la même force et valeur que s'il avait été inséré mot à mot dans le Traité signé aujourd'hui et sera ratifié en même tems. En foi de quoi Nous soussignés en vertu de Nos Pleinspouvoirs avons signé le présent article séparé et y avons apposé nos Cachets respectifs. Fait à Gênes le 26 Novembre 1838.

NATHANIEL NILES
SOLAR DE LA MARGUERITE

NOTES

The treaty file is complete. The signed original of the treaty and the separate article is in English and French, with the English in the left columns. The other documents are in customary form; they include the attested resolution of the Senate of March 2, 1839 (Executive Journal, V, 219), the duplicate United States instrument of ratification of March 8, 1839, the Sardinian instrument of ratification of December 1, 1838, the certificate of the exchange of ratifications at Washington on March 18, 1839 (in English), and the original proclamation of the same date. The Sardinian instrument of ratification is in French, including both texts of the treaty and the separate article, with the French in the left columns; and in each of those texts the King of Sardinia is named first throughout.

Certain original documents accompanied this treaty when it was submitted to the Senate, although not mentioned in the presidential message of January 24, and were ordered printed with the treaty and returned (*ibid.*, 185, 187, 219–20); they comprise a considerable por-

tion of the relevant correspondence (Senate Confidential Document E, 25th Congress, 3d session, Regular Confidential Documents, IX, 398–424); a more complete collection of papers, with some of later date, is in Senate Document No. 118, 29th Congress, 1st session, serial 473.

The treaty was communicated to Congress with the presidential message of December 2, 1839 (Richardson, III, 529, 532).

The Full Powers

The full power to Nathaniel Niles, the American Plenipotentiary, was under date of May 3, 1838, and in customary form (D. S., 2 Credences, 298); it ran to "Nathaniel Niles, Special Agent of the U. S. to the Kingdom of Sardinia", and had as its subject a convention or treaty "respecting the admission of American tobacco into the ports of Sardinia, and in regard to the trade generally between the two nations". In this case it appears that the original full powers were exchanged; that given to the Plenipotentiary of the King of Sardinia is in the treaty file; it is written in French and reads as follows in translation:

Charles Albert, by the Grace of God King of Sardinia, of Cyprus, and of Jerusalem, Duke of Savoy, of Genoa, etc., Prince of Piedmont, etc.

To all those who shall see these presents, Greeting:

Animated by a constant solicitude for all that may render closer and consolidate Our friendly relations with the different powers, We have welcomed with complete satisfaction the overtures which Nathaniel Niles, Esquire, Special Agent of the United States of America, has made to Count Clement Solar de la Marguerite, Our First Secretary of State for Foreign Affairs, for the conclusion of such treaty or commercial convention as shall be judged of reciprocal interest for the two states; wishing on Our part to give to the Government of the United States of America every proof of Our friendship and of the desire which We share with it to favor the connections and relations of every sort between its nationals and Our subjects; for these reasons We, trusting entirely in the knowledge, zeal, and devotion of the said Count Clement Solar de la Marguerite, Knight Grand Cordon of Our Religious and Military Order of Saint Maurice and Saint Lazarus, Grand Cross of the American Order of Isabella the Catholic, Knight of the Order of Christ, Our First Secretary of State for Foreign Affairs, Notary of the Crown, Chief Intendant General of Posts, We have chosen, delegated, and authorized him, and by these presents, signed by Our hand and countersigned by the Knight Eloi de Buttet, Lieutenant Colonel of Cavalry, Our First Officer at the Ministry of Foreign Affairs, We choose, delegate, and authorize him, to follow the proposed negotiation; to stipulate and sign with the said Nathaniel Niles, Esquire, such treaty or convention as may contribute toward strengthening the relations of commerce between the respective states; conferring on him for those ends the full powers and the authority necessary, and reserving on Our part the issuance of Our ratification thereof within the agreed term.

Given at Turin the thirtieth of the month of October, the year of grace one thousand eight hundred and thirty-eight, and of Our reign the eighth.

[Seal]   C. Albert

de Buttet

Special Agents

In the preamble of the treaty it is said that "the President of the United States has conferred full Powers on Nathaniel Niles their special Agent near His Sardinian Majesty".

Numerous treaties have been negotiated on the part of the United States by special agents appointed by the President without nomination to the Senate. This is not the first instance of such a negotiation; Charles Rhind, who negotiated the treaty of 1830 with Turkey (Document 69), was a special agent, as was also Edmund Roberts, who negotiated the treaties of 1833 with Siam and Muscat (Documents 76 and 77); and in the clause of conclusion of the document last mentioned Roberts referred to himself as having been "duly appointed a Special Agent by Letters Patent".

The constitutional practice is now entirely settled that the President may, without nomination to the Senate, grant full powers to negotiate and sign treaties either to "constitutional officers", that is to say, those who have been appointed by and with the advice and consent of the Senate, or to officials not within that class, or to individuals not in the public service. In the past the practice varied, as many such full powers were issued with, and many others without, the advice and consent of the Senate. Moreover, at times great divergence of view has found expression in both Houses of Congress on the general subject. The whole question is treated exhaustively in Wriston, Executive Agents in American Foreign Relations; and chapter IV of that work, with the numerous writings there cited, is particularly in point here.

In this case there is no record of any discussion in the Senate of the question of special agents; the treaty was referred to the Committee on Foreign Relations on January 28, 1839, the day of its receipt; it was reported and debated on February 28; and the resolution of advice and consent in simple form was adopted unanimously on March 2 (Executive Journal, V, 185, 187, 215, 219–20).

The case of Nathaniel Niles as Special Agent, however, has some features which distinguish it from most other cases of special agents.

The letter under date of June 7, 1837, addressed to the Minister of Foreign Affairs at Vienna, which was given to Niles for presentation as a letter of credence, begins as follows (D. S., 2 Credences, 276):

The Congress of the U. S. having at their last session made an appropriation with a view to the appointment of Special Agents to the several countries of Europe in which this Government has not accredited Agents, for the purpose of endeavoring to procure a removal or modification of the duties and restrictions to which the importation or consumption of American Tobacco is subjected in those countries, the President has thought proper to appoint Nathaniel Niles a Special Agent for that purpose to the Empire of Austria.

While in the statute to which reference is therein made (act of March 3, 1837, 5 Statutes at Large, 163–76), there is no specific reference to special agents, as there is in the act of May 8, 1840 (*ibid.*, 371, 379), it seems that a portion of the sums appropriated for contingent expenses by the act of 1837 (*ibid.*, 170) was intended to provide for the appointment of special agents.

In the instructions of April 20, 1838, to Henry A. Muhlenberg, appointed Minister to Austria (D. S., 1 Instructions, Austria, 12–16), Secretary of State Forsyth wrote as follows:

Accompanying this despatch you will find the Report of a Select Committee of the House of Representatives at the 2ᵈ session of the 24th Congress upon this subject. The joint resolution recommended by that Committee, which will be found appended to their Report, from want of time or some other cause, was not acted upon by the Senate; yet it was passed as a separate resolution by the House of Representatives, and it is not doubted that the Senate concurred with that body in its wishes upon the subject, as a considerable sum was allowed by Congress in the General Appropriation Bill, with a view, as was understood, to the appointment of Special Agents, to negotiate with the Governments of those countries in which American tobacco is subjected to duties and restrictions, and in which the U. States have no accredited Representatives;—and provision was also made for missions to Austria and Prussia, it is believed, with a special view to the extension of this particular trade. Since that period circumstances have transpired which plainly show that there is no abatement of the interest felt upon the subject, and that the benefits expected to flow from successful negotiations respecting this commodity are deemed to be of no ordinary value.

The Committee report to which reference is made in the instruction cited is House Report No. 239, 24th Congress, 2d session, serial 306, and the resolution recommended by the Committee and which passed the House of Representatives reads as follows:

That the President be requested to instruct the ministers and other representatives of this country in France, England, Russia, Prussia, Holland, and Germany, to negotiate with the respective Governments to which they are accredited, for a modification of the duties and restrictions upon tobacco imported from the United States; and that he be also requested to appoint special agents to negotiate in like manner with the Governments of those countries into which tobacco is imported under similar restrictions, that have no accredited representatives from the United States.

It appears, accordingly, that the appointment of Niles and of his successors in a similar capacity received the advance approval of Congress (see Wriston, *op. cit.*, 634–35, 822).

THE NEGOTIATIONS

The important clauses of the treaty were those of Article 14 and of the separate article; Niles discussed these particularly under date of December 1, 1838, in his account of the negotiations contained in his despatch transmitting the treaty, which, with slight omissions, is as follows (D. S., 4 Despatches, Italy: Sardinia):

In communicating the Treaty of Commerce, herewith transmitted, concluded & signed at Genoa on the 26th ult, it is proper for me to accompany it by a brief notice, at least, of those circumstances & considerations which have given to it the peculiar stipulations you will observe in the 14th & Separate Article.

The annexation of the ancient Republic of Genoa to the Kingdom of Sardinia imposed upon the Government the necessity of giving to this newly acquired & most important possession, the most convincing proofs of its disposition to encourage & foster its leading interests, those of navigation & Commerce, in every possible way and by that means to tranquilize & render harmless that general dissatisfaction with which the Genoese witnessed the loss of their independence. This

paramount object of Governmental policy, it was falsely thought, at the time, would be attained by the adoption of a system of differential duties, to the disadvantage of foreign flags, applied to tonnage & to the principal articles of commerce of which Genoa was then the Centre, such as grain, Breadstuffs, Wine, Olive Oil, Spirits, of all kinds & some other articles of minor importance.   An extraordinary development of all branches of business connected with navigation, properly speaking, was the first & only result of this policy.   But measures of retaliation adopted by other countries, soon presented the unexpected consequence of a constantly decreasing general Commerce with an augmenting national navigation, employed in particular privileged branches of trade.   The Commercial & navigating interests became divided; the first attributing to the differential system the decline of that varied and general Commerce which formerly made Genoa the Commercial Emporium of the Mediterranean: the other disclaiming against this view of the subject and pertinaciously defending those interests which had grown up under, & depended upon, the encouragement of the differential duties.   A warm contest has been carried on for years past on this subject between the mercantile classes on the one hand, and Ship owners, ship builders & sailors on the other, the latter altho' the weakest in argument having the immense advantage of defending acquired interests which had become important under the encouraging influence of existing laws.

The Government has listened to the representations & counter representations of the contending parties; but altho' long since fully satisfied of the pernicious effects of the differential system of duties on the commercial prosperity of Genoa, it has not been able to devise a policy which would, at the same time, save the interests of navigation, supposed to be in danger, by opening new channels for its employment, and ensure the return of that general commerce for which Genoa is so particularly well placed.

This Sir is a succinct account of the state of feelings & opinions, touching the differential system of duties up to the time when I arrived here—a state of things which has hitherto isolated the commerce of Sardinia & prevented her Government from entering into Commercial Treaties with other nations and rendered impossible the immediate, full & entire application of the broad principles of free trade & perfect reciprocity advocated by the United States.

On examining into the course of Mediterranean Commerce I found that the differential duties imposed on importation in foreign Vessels, could with few exceptions, rarely if ever affect American Shipping, particularly in regard to those Articles imported into Genoa from the Mediterranean ports.   Vessels engaged in the Corn, Wine & oil trade are required to be of a small description, fitted to enter the almost numberless small ports of the Mediterranean & adjacent seas, where these articles are sought for & disposed of by Sardinian vessels.   The minister of foreign affairs to whom a project of a Commercial Treaty was early submitted, avowed his willingness to abandon all differential duties on imports from beyond the Straits of Gibraltar & to limit them to grain Wine & Oil, imported from the Ports of the Mediterranean, the Adriatic & the Black Sea, at the same expressing the determination of his Government to give them up altogether, by slow degrees, as soon as it could be done without exposing the ship owning interest to any violent shock; but he could not fix a time when this object would be accomplished.

In this state of the case the idea occurred to me that we might take advantage of the necessity in which the Sardinian Government was placed of continuing the differential duties on grain Wine & Oil, and by conceding to it the benefit of them for a time, without any act of retaliation on our part, secure in this way of offset to our products, tobacco included, the right of a free transit through the territories of His Sardinian Majesty to the Markets of Parma, Lombardy & Switzerland, and at the same time, reserve the right of imposing countervailing duties on the same articles, imported into the United States in Sardinian vessels from the Mediterranean the Adriatic & the Black Sea, if the Sardinian Government should not wholly abandon then, the differential duties, within a given period.   The Minister was evidently pleased with the outline of this idea, but said that in regard to transit it would be necessary for him to consult with the other members of the Government before an answer could be given to my proposition.

Many conferences were held between this Minister & myself in reference to this subject in which I did not omit to urge upon him all the arguments in favor of the encouragement of a transit trade to the Countries mentioned, as well in the political interest of Sardinia in regard to the immense commercial advantages which Genoa would derive from it. The Minister at length consented to stipulate for the free transit of all all articles of commerce the produce the United States with the exception of gun powder salt & Tobacco, and was evidently desirous of concluding a Treaty on this basis

This was the state of our negotiations on the first of November, when the King & his Ministers set off for Genoa which is the official residence of the Government for a part of the year. Count Solar de la Marguerite took it for granted, that I should follow the Government in common with all the other members of the Diplomatic Corps, & that he would be able to conclude a Treaty without conceding the free transit of Tobacco. I however remained in Turin and on the 5th November addressed to the Minister a letter. . . . Anterior to doing this, I wrote to our Consul, M Campbell, who deservedly stands very high, both as a man & a Merchant, with all the influential classes at Genoa, empressing upon him the importance of the present moment as one particularly favorable for the Mercantile interests of that City to bring all their influence to bear on the Government in favor of encouraging a transit trade from the free Port of Genoa to Parma, Lombardy and Switzerland & through that Country into the south of Germany, particularly in the great staples of transatlantic Commerce, Cotton & Tobacco, pointing out the advantages which must inevitably result from it to Genoa. M Campbell lost not a moment in disposing influential Merchants, natives of the City, to make personal representations on the subject both to the King & his Ministers.

A first note from Count Solar de la Marguerite dated at Genoa on the 10th Nov, . . . without alluding to my letter, in terms, informed me, as you will see, that the negotiations were to be continued by M de Buttet, Chief of the foreign office who remained in Turin. But through this Gentleman the Minister soon learned my indisposition to proceed further unless a free transit of Tobacco should be accorded. I have reason also, to believe, that the King, a most active & intelligent business man, anxious to see our negotiations brought to a definitive conclusion, had inquired particularly into the cause of the apparent delay & required an exact account of the state of the matter to be made to him. The suggestions made in my letter of the 5th, to Count Solar, of which the King became in this way possessed, were not, I believe, wholly without effect on the royal mind. At any rate the result of further consideration on the subject of my letter was the admission of Tobacco in an unmanufactured state to a free transit. . . .

In the mean time, observing the evident anxiety of the Ministers mind to conclude a Treaty of Commerce with the United States, in the manner I had suggested of getting round the differential duties, I determined to go to Genoa, so as to be ready to profit by circumstances, and I arrived there the very day the Ministers letter reached my House in Turin.

The only remaining difficulty was to provide for the eventual reestablishment of transit duties to & from Parma, which it appears is a bad neighbor, should circumstances require; but as it would evidently have been improper to particularly indicate the frontier of that Dutchy in a public Treaty, in reference to such a provision, the proviso for imposing transit duties for *any one point* of the inland frontier took the form in which it is inserted in the 14th Article.

This proviso I think cannot be considered as in any way invalidating the general conceded privilege of a free transit. At any rate many ways are presented to prevent the abuse of that proviso. In the first place those interests which are to spring up, connected with the transit trade will soon effectually control the dispositions of the Government itself, to say nothing of the power we have of affecting the determinations of the Government in the state of the silk trade. So deeply does the Commerce in silk affect the whole cisalpine population of Sardinia that the United States, of all other Countries, is that which this Government will be the least likely to offend by giving an abusive interpretation to a Treaty stipulation, while we are as large consumers of that article as at present on the liberal conditions on which it is now renewed. The right to a free transit

may, therefore, be considered, as I am sure it was intended, a perfect grant, except it should become necessary to impose transit duties on goods to & from Parma, as a means of carrying on an equal Custom House war with that Dutchy. But even if difficulties with Parma may be anticipated, it must be seen that the Sardinian Government will after all, obey its clear political instructive policy, that of conquering the interests and affections of her population by habituating them to transact their Commercial business through Genoa, on the easiest possible terms.

In conceding to Sardinia the right to continue differential duties on grain wine & olive oil, imported from ports within the Mediterranean & dependant waters, for a period of four years, we make no sacrifice whatever of our own interests, since we can never have either a motive or a capacity to compete with Sardinian vessels in carrying on a coasting trade in these, or any other articles, to Sardinian ports.

By thus limiting the exceptions to a mutually perfect free trade, to the three Articles mentioned, imported into Sardinian ports from within the Mediterranean, the general principles of a reciprocal free commerce are adhered to, while the right of reprisals, in a way that will turn to our advantage, is stipulated for, if their application is not made universal by the Sardinian Government within the time agreed on.

The 14th Article which is really the offset to the Separate Article, altho' care was taken to prevent its having that appearance, secures to us, directly, & to commerce generally, by its necessary consequences on the policy of other countries, advantages of the greatest & most substantial value. The port of Genoa is much nearer to every part of Switzerland, Wurtemberg & a great portion of Bavaria than any of the maritime Cities of France, Belgium, Holland, Germany, or Austria. Several great public routs over the Alps are at all times kept in a perfect state of repair by the Sardinian Government. The snows which impede trade in the Winter, equally embarass the communications over the Jura mountains in France. The transit of goods up the Rhine is obstructed by ice for about the same length of time. In a word, the greater proximity of Genoa to the countries mentioned, with a parity of difficulties in reaching them, renders that City their natural Channel of Communication with the sea. This is particularly true of the greater part of the immense & incomparably fertile plains of Lombardy which lie between the Alps & the Appenines.

But an easy means of getting at the markets of these several countries & supplying them with our Tobacco, Cotton Rice Fish &c, affords no just measure of the value of the concession made by the 14th Article. In order to prevent the trade of Lombardy from taking a direction through Sardinia, Austria must encourage Commerce through Venice by new facilities, or the affections & the hopes of her Italian population will naturally be turned to this Government whose policy, as avowed in this Treaty, is more in harmony with their interests.

The heavy duties & other obstructions, such as municipal taxes for the use of roads & bridges, which now embarass the transit trade through Belgium Holland the German Custom House Union, as well as of the Rhine, must, if this Treaty goes into effect, be abolished or favorably modified or the entire supplies of transatlantic Merchandize for Switzerland & the whole southern section of Germany will ultimately be obtained through Genoa.

Should the peace of northern Europe be disturbed either by conflicting armies or a maritime war between Russia & England, an event in all probability not very remote, we have here a free & an unobstructed Channel open to the Centre of the Continent, guaranteed by a Treaty stipulation with a formidable power which will have every possible interest to adhere to this liberal policy, a policy which places her far in advance of all the other Continental Countries with regard to the freedom of inland Commerce.

The provisions of the Separate Article are highly important to Sardinia, as they expose a basis on which she can now enter into Commercial Treaties with other maritime Countries & thus open new channels for the employment of her overgrown navigation and avoid exciting that discontent which she would have just reason to apprehend from a sudden withdrawal of that protection to her own shipping which has been thought so necessary There is indeed good

reason to believe that both parties will be permanently & extrinsically benefitted by the Treaty.

The Quarantines on transatlantic arrivals having been given up, & the differential duties on Tonnage as well as on all articles which can possibly be imported by American ships done away with by the present Treaty if it should be approved by the President & the Senate, of which I flatter myself there can be no doubt, it may be fairly calculated that Genoa will soon become the great depot in the Mediterranean for the products of American industry, while her established relations with every port in the Black Sea & on the shores of the Mediterranean & Adriatic, will afford her every facility for carrying on a profitable trade in transporting them to new & remote markets.

The other articles of the Treaty, being similar to those which enter into most of our Commercial Treaties & so perfectly in accordance with the universally acknowledged public Law, require, I take it, neither explanation nor defence.

RELATIONS WITH SARDINIA

The Kingdom of Sardinia as reconstituted by the Congress of Vienna under Victor Emmanuel I of the House of Savoy (see the Final Act of the Congress of Vienna, June 9, 1815, British and Foreign State Papers, II, 3–180), comprised Piedmont (with Savoy and Nice) and the island of Sardinia, and also the former Republic of Genoa. The capital of the Kingdom of Sardinia was Turin. With certain territorial changes (the cession of Savoy and Nice to France) the territories of the Kingdom of Sardinia were included in the Kingdom of Italy in 1860–61 under Victor Emmanuel II, who had been King of Sardinia since 1849, when he succeeded to the throne of his father, Charles Albert, King of Sardinia from 1831 to 1849.

The following account of the relations of the United States and the Kingdom of Sardinia is from Wriston, *op. cit.*, 342–44):

Nathaniel Niles was sent to Austria early in the Van Buren administration to exploit possibilities for increasing the American tobacco business. In the course of his work on that mission he had an interview with the Minister of Sardinia at Vienna. The United States had no diplomatic representative at the Sardinian court, and had no treaty. Hitherto the commercial relations had been governed by domestic regulations which, however, were founded upon a mutual agreement between the two governments (Eighth annual message of Monroe, December 7, 1824, Richardson, Messages and Papers, II, 251). The minister pointed out to Niles that diplomatic relations would be advantageous to both countries. The opinions of the two men were then embodied in notes which Niles transmitted to Secretary of State Forsyth in 1838 (Niles to Forsyth, Feb. 18, 1838, MS. Desp. Austria, I; Serial 473, 29 Cong. I Sess., Sen. Doc. 118, 3–7; credence, MS. Credences, II, 298; Niles's reports, Sept. 26, 1838, July 29, 1839, MS. Desp. Sardinia (Italy); there is also a letter in MS. Special Agent Bundle, Department of State). It was as a direct result of this episode that Niles was instructed to "repair to Sardinia, and endeavor to conclude a commercial arrangement, securing upon the most advantageous terms, the admission of American tobacco into the ports of that country, and, if practicable, to extend it so as to embrace the general trade between the two nations." It was anticipated that in the event of a successful negotiation, a diplomatic officer would be accredited to the Sardinian court; in case of the failure of the negotiation, matters would continue as theretofore (Forsyth to Niles, May 2, 1838, MS. Inst. Italy, I, 3–4; Serial 473, Doc. 118, 8).

When, however, the treaty was made, it did not result in an immediate exchange of diplomatic representatives. Sardinia soon sent a chargé (Solar de la Marguerite, secretary of foreign affairs, to Niles, Sept. 29, 1838, ibid., 13), but an American chargé was not sent as promptly. President Van Buren said that it was his

intention to express his appreciation of the cordial spirit of the Sardinian government in making with the United States its first commercial treaty, by the immediate appointment of a diplomatic officer to reside at the Sardinian court.   The failure of the Senate to consent promptly to ratification postponed the request of the President for the necessary appropriation, and a special agent, Abraham Van Buren, was directed to go to Turin to explain that when Congress next met the President would request the appropriation (Forsyth to Van Buren, April 18, 1839, MS. Inst. Italy, I, 1–2).   Van Buren failed to carry out his instructions and the explanations were made instead to the Sardinian chargé (Van Buren to Forsyth, Nov. 29, 1839, MS. Desp. Sardinia (Italy); Forsyth to Van Buren, loc. cit.).   In May, 1840, H. Gold Rogers was appointed chargé and the relations of the two countries were put on a regular footing (Sen. Ex. Jol., V, 284; Forsyth to Rogers, June 6, 1840, Serial 473, Doc. 118, 26).

Treaty Series No. 251
8 Statutes at Large, 524-27
18 *ibid.*, pt. 2, Public Treaties, 542-44

87

NETHERLANDS : JANUARY 19, 1839

Treaty of Commerce and Navigation, signed at Washington January 19, 1839. Original in English and Dutch.
Submitted to the Senate January 21, 1839. Resolution of advice and consent January 31, 1839. Ratified by the United States February 1, 1839. Ratified by the Netherlands March 19, 1839. Ratifications exchanged at Washington May 23, 1839. Proclaimed May 24, 1839.

The United States of America and His Majesty the King of the Netherlands, anxious to regulate the commerce and navigation carried on between the two countries in their respective vessels, have, for that purpose, named Plenipotentiaries, that is to say:

The President of the United States has appointed John Forsyth, Secretary of State of the said United States; and His Majesty the King of the Netherlands, Jonkheer Evert Marius Adrian Martini, Member of the body of Nobles of the Province of North Brabant, Knight of the order of the Netherland Lion, and His Chargé d'Affaires near the United States, who having exchanged their respective full powers, found in good and due form, have agreed to the following articles:

Zyne Majesteit de Koning der Nederlanden en de Vereenigde Staten van Amerika, den handel en de scheepvaart wenschende te regelen, welke tusschen de twee landen in derzelver schepen respectivelyk wordt gedreven, hebben daartoe Gevolmagtigden benoemd, te weten:

Zyne Majesteit de Koning der Nederlanden heeft benoemd: Jonkheer Evert Marius Adriaan Martini, Lid van de Ridderschap van de Provincie Noord Braband, Ridder der orde van den Nederlandschen Leeuw en Hoogstdeszelfs Zaakgelastigde by de Vereenigde Staten; en de President der Vereenigde Staten: John Forsyth, Secretaris van Staat van gezegde Vereenigde Staten; dewelke na hunne wederzydsche volmagten te hebben uitgewisseld, die in goede en behoorlyke orde bevonden zyn, over de volgende artikelen zyn overeengekomen.

171

172   *Document 87*

Article I.

Goods and merchandise, whatever their origin may be, imported into or exported from, the ports of the United States, from or to the ports of the Netherlands in Europe, in vessels of the Netherlands, shall pay no higher or other duties than shall be levied on the like goods and merchandise so imported or exported in national vessels. And reciprocally, goods and merchandise, whatever their origin may be, imported into, or exported from, the ports of the Netherlands in Europe, from or to the ports of the United States, in vessels of the said States, shall pay no higher or other duties, than shall be levied on the like goods and merchandise so imported or exported in national vessels. The bounties, drawbacks, or other favors of this nature, which may be granted in the States of either of the Contracting Parties, on goods imported or exported in national vessels, shall also and in like manner be granted on goods directly exported or imported in vessels of the other country, to and from the ports of the two countries; it being understood, that in the latter as in the preceding case, the goods shall have been loaded in the ports from which such vessels have been cleared.

Artikel I.

Goederen en koopwaren onverschillig welke derzelver herkomst zy, ingevoerd of uitgevoerd wordende, in of uit de havens der Nederlanden in Europa van of naar de havens der Vereenigde Staten, in Nederlandsche schepen zullen geene hoogere of andere regten betalen, dan zullen worden geheven op gelyke goederen en koopwaren ingevoerd of uitgevoerd in nationale schepen. En wederkeerig zullen goederen en koopwaren, onverschillig welke derzelver herkomst zy, ingevoerd of uitgevoerd wordende, in of uit de havens der Vereenigde Staten van of naar de havens der Nederlanden in Europa, in de schepen dier Staten geene hoogere of andere regten betalen, dan zullen worden geheven op gelyke goederen en koopwaren ingevoerd of uitgevoerd in nationale schepen. De premien, teruggave van regten of andere begunstigingen van dien aard, in de Staten van eene der contracterende partyen aan den in- of uitvoer met nationale schepen toegekend, zullen insgelyks bewilligd worden, wanneer de regtstreeksche in- of uitvoer tusschen de havens der twee Landen zal geschieden met schepen van den anderen Staat, met dien verstande, dat zoowel in dit, als in het vorige geval, de goederen werkelyk zullen moeten zyn ingeladen in de havens, van waar die schepen respectivelyk zyn uitgeklaard.

ARTICLE II.

Neither party shall impose upon the vessels of the other, whether carrying cargoes between the United States and the ports of the Netherlands in Europe, or arriving in ballast from any other country, any duties of tonnage, harbour dues, light-houses, salvage, pilotage, quarantine, or port charges of any kind or denomination which shall not be imposed in like cases on national vessels.

ARTICLE III.

It is further agreed between the two contracting parties, that the Consuls and Vice Consuls of the United States in the ports of the Netherlands in Europe; and reciprocally the Consuls and Vice Consuls of the Netherlands in the ports of the said States, shall continue to enjoy all privileges, protection and assistance, as may be usual and necessary for the duly exercising of their functions, in respect also of the deserters from the vessels, whether public or private, of their countries.

ARTICLE IV.

The Contracting Parties agree to consider and treat as vessels of the United States and of the Netherlands, all such as, being furnished by the competent au-

ARTIKEL II.

Geene der partyen zal op de schepen der andere, hetzy dezelve ladingen tusschen de havens der Nederlanden in Europa en die der Vereenigde Staten overbrengen, of wel in ballast aankomen van eenig ander land, eenige regten heffen voor tonnen- haven- baken- berg- of reddingloon, (:salvage:) loods- quarantaine- of havengelden van welke soort of benaming ook, welke in gelyke gevallen niet zullen worden gelegd op nationale schepen.

ARTIKEL III.

Verder is tusschen de beide contracteerende partyen overeengekomen, dat de Nederlandsche Consuls en Vice Consuls in de havens der Vereenigde Staten, en wederkeerig de Consuls en Vice Consuls dier Staten in de Nederlandsche havens in Europa, voortdurend al zoodanige voorregten, bescherming en bystand zullen genieten, als gebruikelyk zyn, en vereischt worden tot de behoorlyke waarneming hunner ambtspligten, ook met betrekking tot de deserteurs van de schepen hunner landen, zoowel oorlogschepen als koopvaarders.

ARTIKEL IV.

De contracteerende partyen komen overeen, om als schepen der Nederlanden en der Vereenigde Staten te beschouwen en te behandelen al dezulke, welke, door

thority with a passport or sea letter, shall, under the then existing laws and regulations, be recognised as national vessels by the country to which they respectively belong.

ARTICLE V.

In case of shipwreck or damage at sea, each party shall grant to the vessels, whether public or private, of the other, the same assistance and protection which would be afforded to its own vessels in like cases.

ARTICLE VI.

The present treaty shall be in force for the term of ten years, commencing six weeks after the exchange of the ratifications; and further until the end of twelve months after either of the Contracting Parties shall have given to the other notice of its intention to terminate the same: Each of the Contracting Parties reserving to itself the right of giving such notice to the other, after the expiration of the said term of ten years. And it is hereby mutually agreed, that in case of such notice this treaty, and all the provisions thereof, shall, at the end of the said twelve months, altogether cease and determine.

de bevoegde autoriteit voorzien van een paspoort of zeebrief, onder de in der tyd bestaande wetten en verordeningen als nationale schepen zullen worden erkend door het land, tot hetwelk zy respectivelyk behooren.

ARTIKEL V.

In geval van schipbreuk of zeeschade zal elke party aan de schepen van de andere, hetzy dezelve oorlogschepen of koopvaarders zyn, dezelfde hulp en bystand verleenen, welke in gelyke gevallen aan hare eigene schepen zouden worden verstrekt.

ARTIKEL VI.

Het tegenwoordige Traktaat zal van kracht zyn voor den tyd van tien jaren, te beginnen zes weken na de uitwisseling der ratificatien; en verder tot aan het einde van twaalf maanden, nadat eene der contracteerende Partyen aan de andere kennis zal gegeven hebben van haar voornemen om hetzelve te doen ophouden: behoudende elk der contracterende Partyen zich het regt voor, om zoodanige kennisgeving aan de andere te doen na het einde van het voornoemde tydperk van tien jaren: en is men hierby onderling overeengekomen dat, ingeval van zoodanige kennisgeving, dit Traktaat en al deszelfs bepalingen gezamenlyk, na verloop der gestelde twaalf maanden, zullen ophouden en eindigen.

ARTICLE VII.

The present treaty shall be ratified, and the ratifications shall be exchanged at Washington, within six months of its date, or sooner, if practicable

In witness whereof, the respective Plenipotentiaries have signed the same, and have affixed thereto the seals of their arms.

Done in duplicate, at the city of Washington, this nineteenth day of January in the year of our Lord one thousand eight hundred and thirty-nine.

    [Seal] JOHN FORSYTH
    [Seal] ADR. MARTINI.

ARTIKEL VII.

Het tegenwoordige Traktaat zal bekrachtigd worden, en de bekrachtigingen zullen worden uitgewisseld te Washington binnen zes maanden na de dagteekening, of zoo mogelyk vroeger.

Ter oorkonde waarvan de wederzydsche Gevolmagtigden deze hebben geteekend, en met het zegel hunner wapenen voorzien.

Gedaan in duplikaat, te Washington, den negentienden dag van January in het Jaar Onzes Heeren een duizend acht honderd negen en dertig.

    [Seal] ADR. MARTINI.
    [Seal] JOHN FORSYTH

NOTES

The treaty file is complete. The signed original of the treaty is in English and Dutch, with the English in the left columns; as the printed texts show, the *alternat* was duly observed. The duplicate United States instrument of ratification of February 1, 1839, omits the usual words of reference to the text or tenor of the treaty, though mentioning its place and date of signature; but the instrument is bound with the original and the proclamation. The other papers, all in customary form, are the attested Senate resolution of January 31, 1839 (Executive Journal, V, 190), the Netherland instrument of ratification of March 19, 1839, the certificate of the exchange of ratifications at Washington on May 23, 1839 (in English), and the original proclamation of the following day. The Netherland instrument of ratification is in the Dutch language and includes both texts of the treaty, the Dutch in the left columns.

It appears that no papers accompanied this treaty when it was submitted to the Senate with the presidential message of January 21, 1839 (*ibid.*, 180); only the texts of the treaty are printed with the message in Senate Confidential Document, January 21, 1839, 25th Congress, 3d session (Regular Confidential Documents, IX, 295–99).

With the presidential message of December 2, 1839, the treaty was communicated to Congress by President Van Buren, who wrote (Richardson, III, 528, 532–33):

That [treaty of commerce] with the Netherlands happily terminates a long-existing subject of dispute and removes from our future commercial intercourse

all apprehension of embarrassment. The King of the Netherlands has also, in further illustration of his character for justice and of his desire to remove every cause of dissatisfaction, made compensation for an American vessel captured in 1800 by a French privateer, and carried into Curaçoa, where the proceeds were appropriated to the use of the colony, then, and for a short time after, under the dominion of Holland [see Document 88].

THE NEGOTIATIONS

The negotiations for this treaty took place in Washington and were in part verbal. Bases of agreement were, it seems, agreed on in conversations of February 6 and 10, 1838 (D. S., 2 Notes from the Netherland Legation, June 6, 1838); a draft with five substantive articles, in Dutch and English, was submitted by the Plenipotentiary of the Netherlands, Adriaan Martini (*ibid.*, June 10, 1838); Secretary of State Forsyth, in his note of July 17, 1838, transmitted a draft in six articles (D. S., 6 Notes to the Netherland Legation, 10–13). Doubts as to the wording of Article 1 caused the Plenipotentiary of the Netherlands to ask for further instructions (D. S., 2 Notes from the Netherland Legation, July 18, 1838); when these were received, the American draft was accepted, with some changes in the language of Article 1 and with the addition of the provisions of Article 3 regarding consuls, and so forth (*ibid.*, January 2, 1839).

Questions of form were among those discussed. In transmitting the project of June 10, 1838, the Plenipotentiary of the Netherlands wrote (*ibid.*, translation from the French):

> This treaty is to be concluded in the Dutch and English languages, written opposite in the two examples, alternately to the right and the left, so that the original for the ratification of the King, my master, shall have the Dutch text at the left, while that text will be at the right in the original to be ratified by the President.

In his note of January 14, 1839, the Plenipotentiary of the Netherlands acknowledged receipt from Mr. Derrick (William S. Derrick, then a clerk in the Department of State) of the two examples for signature, which had been sent in order that the Dutch text might be therein written; but the two papers were returned by Martini, who pointed out that in each the English text was written at the left, while in one of them, that for the Government of the Netherlands, the Dutch text should be at the left. He called attention to his note of the previous June 10, added that it was customary that each contracting party should have precedence in the text of its own language, and referred to a recent treaty between the Netherlands and Great Britain as evidence of the practice, and he concluded by saying that he would send to the Department of State two days later for examples written according to the form suggested.

THE FULL POWERS

In this case it seems that while the respective full powers were communicated, the originals were not exchanged. That of Secretary of State Forsyth was dated June 14, 1838, and was in customary form

(D. S., 2 Credences, 302). A copy of that of the Plenipotentiary of the Netherlands was enclosed with his note of June 6, 1838 (D. S., 2 Notes from the Netherland Legation); translated from the French it reads as follows:

William, by the Grace of God King of the Netherlands, Prince of Orange-Nassau, Grand Duke of Luxemburg, etc.

To all who shall see these presents, Greeting:

Considering that the Government of the Republic of the United States of America is disposed to come to an understanding with Us regarding an arrangement intended to regulate the commerce and navigation between the two countries under the respective flags of the two powers, and as We on Our part desire nothing more ardently than to draw more closely the bonds of good intelligence and amity so happily existing between Us and the Government of the United States of America, by the conclusion of a convention in that regard, based on reciprocal interests, We have given and to this end do give by these presents full power, commission, and special mandate to the Sieur Evert Marius Adriaan Martini, Knight of the Order of the Lion of the Netherlands, member of the Equestrian Order of the Province of North Brabant, and Our Chargé d'Affaires near the Government of the Republic of the United States of America, to enter into negotiation with the plenipotentiary or plenipotentiaries of the said Government, in like manner furnished with full powers in good and due form, regarding the above-stated object, reserving to Ourselves the approval and ratification of that which shall be agreed by Our said Plenipotentiary or which shall have been negotiated by him in virtue of the present full power, in conformity with the instructions which We have given to him.

In faith whereof We have signed these presents with Our own hand and have caused to be affixed to them Our royal seal. Given at The Hague this sixteenth of April in the year of grace one thousand eight hundred and thirty-eight, and of Our reign the twenty-fifth.

[Seal] WILLIAM

By the King:
The Minister of Foreign Affairs,
VERSTOLK DE SOELEN

It appears that the Department of State had suggested the necessity of full powers for the exchange of ratifications; while the Government of the Netherlands acceded to this suggestion, Chargé d'Affaires Martini, in his note of May 14, 1839 (D. S., 2 Notes from the Netherland Legation), which enclosed a copy of his full power for the exchange (dated the previous March 19), wrote as follows on the point (translation from the French):

Although it is not at all customary in Europe to give special full powers in order to effectuate such an exchange, and is considered sufficient that the qualities of the persons by whom the exchange is made be mentioned in the *procès-verbal* which ordinarily is drawn up following the execution of that act, the custom of the United States has none the less been willingly complied with in this instance, and His said Majesty has had sent to me for that end the full power or authorization desired.

88

NETHERLANDS : MARCH 25, 1839

Settlement of the Claim for the Ship "Mary" and Her Cargo, signed at The Hague March 25, 1839. Original in English.
Not subject to ratification and not proclaimed. It seems that the only writing evidencing the settlement was the acquittance given on behalf of the United States, the text whereof follows.

I, Auguste Davezac, Chargé d'affaires of the United-States of America, near the Government of His Majesty the King of the Netherlands, acting by authority of the President of the United States, and under instruction from the Secretary of State of the Said United-States, do hereby acknowledge to have received from the Government of His Said Majesty, by the means of a mandate of payment upon His Majesty's Consul General, in England, for and in behalf of the owners or parties intrested in the Ship "Mary" of Baltimore, and her Cargo, the Sum of Sixty Two Thousand Six Hundred and ninety two Dollars, in full Satisfaction of all demands on their part upon the Government of His Said Majesty, for the proceeds of Said Vessel and Cargo, to be paid over and distributed among them by the Government of the United States, according to their Legal title to the Same: And acting under the Same authority, I do hereby assume, in the name of the Government of the United-States, the obligation towards that of His Majesty the King of the Netherlands, to Answer all demands or applications which may in future be addressed to the Government of His Said Majesty, either by the owners or parties interested in the Ship "Mary" and her Cargo, or their representatives, the owners of the French Privateer by which Said Ship was captured, or their representatives, or the French Government in their behalf, whenever such demands or applications may be referred for that purpose by the Netherlands' Government to that of the United States; the latter hereby engaging to Stand in the place and Stead of the Netherlands' Government, in all respects and for all purposes and liabilities connected with, or arising from the Seizure and detention of the property referred to

Given under my Hand and the Seal of the Legation of the United States of America, at the Hague, this twenty fifth day of March One

179

thousand eight Hundred and thirty nine, and the Sixty Third Year of American Independence.

Auguste Davezac   [Seal]

NOTES

The source text for the document printed above is a facsimile of the original, obtained from the archives at The Hague.

It seems that the acquittance of March 25, 1839, was the only writing evidencing the settlement; the offer of the Government of the Netherlands was made in a note (cited below) of October 16, 1838, addressed by Baron Verstolk de Soelen, Minister of Foreign Affairs, to Auguste Davezac, Chargé d'Affaires at The Hague; that offer was the basis of the settlement; but the discussions subsequent thereto appear to have been verbal; and the terms of the offer, with some necessary elaboration, were embodied in the acquittance.

It is, however, to be mentioned that some of the notes of Davezac to the Minister of Foreign Affairs of the Netherlands are lacking; for his remissness in failing to transmit copies to the Department of State, Davezac was more than once reproved (D.S., 14 Instructions, Netherlands, 34–36, 38–39, August 4, 1837, and July 28, 1838), but to no avail; and the archives of the Legation at The Hague include copies of no notes to the Foreign Office from April 1830 to July 12, 1839; for nearly eight years of that period (from 1831) Davezac was Chargé d'Affaires of the United States.

The form of the acquittance is highly unusual, in that it embodies an engagement of the United States to hold the Government of the Netherlands harmless, not only against further claims by those deemed interested (as was doubtless implicit in the settlement), but also against any claims by the owners of the captor or the French Government in their behalf.   The reason for that obligation appears from the facts which were the basis of the claim.

Mention of the settlement was made in the annual message of President Van Buren to Congress of December 2, 1839 (Richardson, III, 532–33).

The Claim and the Settlement

The available relevant papers are mostly in D.S., Netherland Claims, Miscellaneous, folder *Mary;* the following account is largely based thereon, without specific citation; some of the correspondence (but none later than 1837) is printed in Senate Document No. 13, 25th Congress, 2d session, serial 314, hereafter cited as "Senate Document".

On February 4, 1800, the ship *Mary*, Isaac Phillips, master, while on a voyage from Batavia to Baltimore, her home port, laden chiefly with coffee, was captured by the French privateer *Renommée*, Captain Joseph Rodignan, and taken to the island of Curaçao (Dutch West Indies); of both vessel and cargo Jeremiah Yellott, of Baltimore, was sole owner, except for an adventure of coffee and indigo owned by

Captain Phillips and insured for $10,000; the vessel and cargo were afterwards sold by the Curaçao Government, which ordered that the proceeds thereof be retained in the public treasury "until the Executive Directory of the Batavian Republic, or such Court of Justice as might be competent, should decide upon the merits of the capture". At the time the Netherland Government (the Batavian Republic, 1795–1806) was dominated by the Government of France under Napoleon Bonaparte as First Consul.

The insurance on the vessel and cargo, amounting to $95,000, was paid (see D.S., 14 Instructions, Netherlands, 23–24, June 27, 1836; printed in Senate Document, pp. 2–3); the insurers were the United Insurance Company of New York ($40,000 on cargo), the Baltimore Insurance Company ($20,000 on the vessel), and the Marine Insurance Company of Baltimore ($25,000 on cargo owned by Yellott and $10,000 on cargo owned by Phillips); but notwithstanding payment by the underwriters, the owner, Jeremiah Yellott, retained a substantial interest in the claim; his share was afterwards deemed to be four twenty-thirds of the whole.

The claim was for the proceeds of the sale by the Curaçao Government ($62,692), interest, and expenses. By the settlement the principal sum only was allowed.

Application to the Netherland Government was made by the interested parties during the regime of the brother of Napoleon, Louis Bonaparte, as King of Holland (the United States had no diplomatic representative at The Hague from September 2, 1801, when William Vans Murray took leave as Minister Resident, until 1815); the decision rendered in May 1808 was as follows (translation printed in Senate Document, p. 5):

The Minister Secretary of State [W. F. Roell] having received a decision of the King, doth hereby inform the petitioners that they are referred to the competent judge in order to have the legality or illegality of the capture of the ship *Mary* and cargo, brought to Curaçao, previously decided, as in good justice shall be found right, with leave to renew their petition for the delivery of the proceeds of the prize when a final decision of the competent judge shall have adjudged them the right to the same; without, however, that this permission shall be esteemed as containing any acknowledgment in favor of the legality of the petitioners' claim, and such, with restitution of the exhibit annexed to the said petition.

Following that decision no further steps were taken, it seems, for more than twenty years. On September 22, 1829, a memorial (printed in Senate Document, pp. 4–5) of John Connell, of Philadelphia, agent of the claimants, was addressed to the King of the Netherlands and submitted, it seems, through the Chargé d'Affaires of the United States, Christopher Hughes, Jr.; the prayer of the memorialist was "that Your Majesty may be graciously pleased to order the competent Tribunal in Holland, to take cognizance of the merits of this claim, and render such a decision as may be consistent with Public Law & Public Justice". The decision (February 18, 1831) was in substance the same as that of 1808 (translation printed in Senate Document, pp. 5–6; D.S., 9 Despatches, Netherlands, No. 32, March 3, 1831, enclosure):

That the Government of the Netherlands, before it can decide upon the application of the petitioners, must await the decision of the competent tribunal as to the validity of the capture; and that, therefore, the claimants, conformably to what was intimated to them in 1808, must apply to that end to the tribunal, and especially to the Superior Court of Justice sitting at The Hague, which appears to have the right of judging in the last resort in matters of maritime prizes.

Legal proceedings were accordingly commenced; John Cuthbert, consul at Hamburg, acting for Connell (with the permission of the Department of State), retained "the first counsel" of The Hague (D.S., 3 Consular Despatches, Hamburg, October 26, 1832); but the decision of the High Court of Justice at The Hague (March 16, 1836; a translation is among the papers of the case) was unsatisfactory to the claimants; it is thus described in a letter of the counsel, D. Donker Curtius, to Cuthbert, of March 27, 1836 (printed in Senate Document, p. 13; the following text, from a copy in Connell's handwriting in D.S., Netherland Claims, Miscellaneous, folder *Mary*, has been revised as to capitalization, punctuation, and spelling):

Our business of the *Mary* has taken an unfavorable turn. The court has adopted the exception proposed by the Government and decided that before they can be called to account, the legality or illegality of the capture must first be decided by a competent court.

The court looks upon the Government of Curaçao as a place of deposit, in whose hands the privateers and the owners of the *Mary* have placed the ship and cargo, and which deposit will only be given up to the persons to whom it shall be legally adjudged. This reasoning leads to nothing, as the privateersman was summoned before the court to support his claim and to adjudge our property. It appears that if this extraordinary system had not been adopted, an equally unfavorable judgment would have been given into, and our endeavors at recovery would have been proscribed.

The court does what the Government proposes, and declares the capture illegal, although neither in this country, Curaçao, nor France do they say one word where we are to find a competent judge to decide upon the legality or illegality of the capture.

There remains but one mode of recovery in this business, and that is diplomatic. I am sorry that my exertions have been unsuccessful until now, but hope that you will deprive the Government that would send us to that tribunal of the means of subterfuge.

It is not easy to understand the refusal of the High Court of Justice at The Hague to take jurisdiction and decide the merits; that tribunal, it seems, was generally competent in matters of prize; the Netherland Government at no time put forward any contention that it was entitled in its own right to retain the fund derived from the sale of the *Mary* and her cargo; the French privateersman had, according to the quoted letter of counsel, been summoned; and the evidence of American ownership was clear; however, one point seems to have been overlooked at the time; by Article 4 of the convention between the United States and France of September 30, 1800 (Document 25), it was provided that "Property captured, and not yet definitively condemned, or which may be captured before the exchange of ratifications . . . shall be mutually restored"; that convention made any question of the legality of the capture immaterial and was thus a complete answer to any claim on the part of the French privateer (see *United States* v. *Schooner "Peggy"*, 1 Cranch, 103–9).

Within a few months after the decision of the High Court of Justice at The Hague the claim was brought before the Government of the Netherlands pursuant to the instruction of June 27, 1836, from Secretary of State Forsyth to Davezac (D.S., 14 Instructions, Netherlands, 23–24; printed, with the enclosures, in Senate Document, pp. 2–6):

I have the honor to transmit to you, herewith, the copy of a letter from Mᵣ John Connell, dated the 24ᵗʰ instant, together with the papers to which it refers, in relation to a claim on the Government of the Netherlands, in the case of the ship "Mary" and cargo, of Baltimore, (belonging solely to American citizens,) Phillips, Master,—unlawfully captured in the year 1800, by the French privateer "Renommée"—carried into the Island of Curaçoa, and the proceeds of the vessel and cargo appropriated, by the local authorities of that Island, to the use of the colony, without even the form of a trial. The particulars regarding this claim, as well as the steps taken to procure indemnification for those interested, will be found in the papers now sent and those relating to the subject already in the Legation, to which you are referred. Mᵣ John Cuthbert, the Consul of the United States at Hamburg, is the agent in Europe for the present claimants, is perfectly conversant with all the facts of the case, and will, it is presumed, cheerfully furnish you with any information relative to it, which may not be contained in the documents above mentioned.

The apparent justice of this claim, the amount involved,—$95,000 having been insured and paid on the ship and cargo more than thirty years ago, by certain insurance companies of the cities of New York and Baltimore,—and the length of time which has elapsed since this outrage was committed upon our commerce, render it proper, and you are accordingly authorized by direction of the President, to bring the subject distinctly before the Government of the Netherlands for consideration. You will urge a prompt settlement of the claim, the adjustment and liquidation of which, the President cannot but think, has been unnecessarily, if not unreasonably, protracted.

The "eventuality of a Claim in behalf of the French Captors" seems to have been the chief, if not the only, ground of objection raised by the Government of the Netherlands to the American claim (D.S., 11 Despatches, Netherlands, No. 187, May 6, 1837; extract only printed in Senate Document, p. 11); and a convincing argument on the point was made in the instruction of April 4, 1837 (D.S., 14 Instructions, Netherlands, 31–32; printed in Senate Document, pp. 6–7):

I regret the necessity that again compels me to address you relative to the claim on the Dutch Government for indemnification for the ship "Mary" and cargo, of Baltimore,—a case to which your attention was first directed by the instructions of this Department dated the 27ᵗʰ of June of the past year. Since your acknowledgment of the receipt of that despatch, much interest has been felt, both on the part of the American claimants and Government in the expected decision of His Netherlands' Majesty on the subject—and a corresponding degree of disappointment has been experienced, that no answer, down to the date of the last communication received from you at this Department,—had been given to your written and verbal representations in regard to a claim, the justice of which appears to be uncontroverted and incontrovertible. The principal, if not the only, objection made to the restitution of the proceeds of this vessel and cargo to the agent of the owners, when the case was brought before the Dutch judicial tribunals, which admitted that the money was in the possession of the government of Curaçoa,—was, that the owners of the French privateer might hereafter prefer a claim to it. The utter groundlessness of this objection is apparent, since the capture of the "Mary" was effected in February, 1800, and on the 30ᵗʰ of September following a Convention was concluded between the French Repub-

lic and the United States, the fourth article of which expressly stipulated that property captured, and not yet definitively condemned, or which might be captured before the exchange of ratifications, (contraband goods destined to an enemy's port excepted,) should be mutually restored on the exhibition of certain proofs of ownership: a fact which accounts for the circumstance, alleged by the agent, that there never has been any claim to the money interposed in behalf of the owners of the French privateer.

It is the wish of the President, that immediately upon the receipt of this despatch, you should address a note to the Minister of Foreign Affairs of His Majesty the King of the Netherlands, again calling his attention to the case in question, and in firm but respectful terms, urging a prompt decision upon this claim. It has now been before the Dutch Government for about thirty years, and the President trusts that there will be no further unnecessary delay in bringing it to a satisfactory adjustment.

.   .   .   .

It is not known to the Department whether the application of the article of the treaty referred to in this despatch, to the subject of this claim, has not been before made. If it should not have been, it cannot fail, upon being properly presented to the Dutch Government, to have a controlling effect upon their reply to your renewed appeal.

It was stated in the instruction of July 28, 1838, "that the claim to which this instruction has reference, has been made the subject of separate Executive communications to each house of Congress; and that a decided sense of the justice of the claim has been expressed by the appropriate committee of each" (D.S., 14 Instructions, Netherlands, 38–39; see Richardson, III, 476, message to the House of Representatives of May 30, 1838); and Davezac was directed to renew his application.

The offer of settlement made by the Netherland Government was in the note of the Minister of Foreign Affairs, Baron Verstolk de Soelen, of October 16, 1838, as follows (D.S., 11 Despatches, Netherlands, No. 207, October 19, 1838, enclosure, translation from the French):

In the despatch (*office*) which you did me the honor to address to me on May 9 of last year you were good enough to make several observations relative to the case of the ship the *Mary*, of Baltimore, which you also recalled to my attention in our last conversations.

The purpose of the said despatch was to set forth the unsuccessful steps with the Netherland judicial authorities which the Americans concerned took in the interest of their claims, and to express the desire of the Government of the United States of America that, in view of this state of things, a prompt decision in the case be made by the Government of the Netherlands.

If the Cabinet of The Hague has constantly shared the wish expressed by that of Washington to see a settlement of the matter reached, the new study which it again undertook of the circumstances, both numerous and complicated, relating thereto, has strengthened its conviction that it followed right principles in laying down the basis that before relinquishing possession of the deposit placed by the force of events in the hands of the colonial authorities, it was necessary that a competent tribunal of the Kingdom should have rendered a decision as to the rightful claimants.

Independently, however, of this basis, and without abandoning it, the Cabinet took up the task of determining whether a means could be devised of reconciling the necessary guaranty presented by this basis with a political formula; and, guided by its eagerness to find a solution agreeable to the Washington Cabinet, compatible with its own safety, and offering an unequivocal token of its disposition to adjust on an equitable footing, by an arrangement as between one nation and another, the claim resulting from the seizure of the vessel, the *Mary*, of Baltimore, it has decided on the following offer, which I am instructed to address

to you, Sir, as I have the honor to do in this despatch: "The Government of the Netherlands would discharge the deposit in the amount of 62,692 piasters. The delivery and the payment of this sum would be made to the Government of the United States, in view of the fact that it would be impossible to judge properly here as to the personal rights of the claimants. The American Government would furnish that of the Netherlands with a full act of guaranty with respect to any possible claim which might be presented against the latter on the part of the owners, outfitters, insurers, or of any other party interested in the said vessel, as well as on the part of the privateer or of his representatives and claimants under him (*ayants droit*), and of the French Government itself, with the declaration that by the payment of the sum of 62,692 piasters the Government of the Netherlands shall also be guaranteed against and indemnified for any claim which might have some connection with the seizure of the vessel, or with the consequences thereof; so that the American Government would undertake not only to protect the Government of the Netherlands at all times against the above-mentioned claims, but to indemnify it also, if occasion should arise, fully and without restriction."

I beg you, Sir, to be good enough to bring this proposal to the knowledge of the Washington Cabinet, and I avail myself of this occasion to renew to you the assurance of my distinguished consideration.

By a letter to the Secretary of State dated December 4, 1838, signed by John Connell as agent of the claimants, consent was given to the acceptance of the sum offered by the note of the previous October 16; Davezac was accordingly authorized to agree to that amount (if he could obtain no more) and also to sign the clause of guaranty required by the terms of the offer; the instruction was as follows (D.S., 14 Instructions, Netherlands, 43–45, December 3, 1838):

Your despatch N? 207, was, on the 18th ultimo, received at the Department, and conveyed the decision of the Netherlands' Government in the case of the ship "Mary". The amount offered to the claimants by that decision falls so far short of the losses sustained by them, as well in consequence of the original seizure of their property as on account of the long lapse of time during which it has been withheld from them, that the expectation of a further allowance on the ground of interest, if not on account of the principal, cannot but appear as constituting a fair claim on the justice of the Dutch Government. You are, therefore, instructed to use your best exertions in endeavoring to obtain such an additional allowance, the amount of which may be regulated by your own knowledge of the case, and the expectations of the claimants which are fully known to you. Should your efforts in this, however, prove unsuccessful, and you become convinced of the inutility of a renewal of them, you are authorized to inform Baron Verstolk that, actuated by their desire to bring the matter to a close, the claimants have through their accredited Agents, consented to accept the sum offered, in full discharge of their demands upon the Netherlands Government.

The readiest mode which suggests itself of effecting the liquidation of the claim, in a manner calculated at once to meet the wishes of the claimants and the views of the Dutch Government, is the payment of the sum allowed, whatever it may ultimately be, to the Government of the United States, to be paid over to the rightful claimants; and the President has consented, agreeably to the suggestions of Baron Verstolk in his note of the 16th October last, that this Government shall, on receipt of the money, give a full acquittance for the same, and assume towards all persons having a title to the property in this country, towards the original captors, and towards the French Government, all liabilities justly growing out of the transaction. You will acquaint Baron Verstolk with this decision, and state to him that, on being furnished with a certificate of the deposit of the money in the hands of the banker of the United States at London, to the credit of the Secretary of the Treasury, you will deliver to him a full acquittance for the same, containing a clause so worded as to impose upon the United States Government the obligation of answering all demands or applications which might in future be made upon that of the Netherlands in relation to the subject either by the owners

of the property, or their representatives, in this country; the owners of the privateer by which the "Mary" was captured, or their agents or representatives, or by the French Government in their behalf. If, which is to be hoped, this arrangement prove agreeable to the Netherlands, you will, without delay, transmit the required certificate of deposit to this Department, with all such documents in the Legation, or in the hands of Mᵣ Cuthbert as may facilitate the distribution of the proceeds of the claim among the parties interested.

To avoid the possibility of mistake, a model of such an acquittance as you are to deliver, as above-stated, is herein enclosed.

The "model" enclosed with the foregoing instruction was followed very literally in the acquittance signed on March 25, 1839; aside from such necessary insertions as the means of payment and the amount, and verbal elaboration of the testimonium clause, the wording of the original is the same as that of the draft; and Davezac reported the closing in his despatch of April 16, 1839, from which the following is extracted (D.S., 11 Despatches, Netherlands, No. 211):

Having found it useless to persevere in my efforts to obtain, as I had been directed by the Department, an addition, (as interest,) to the Sum offered by this Government as an indemnity to the owners of the "Mary", the Minister of foreign affairs furnishing in His asseveration, that the Sum deposited had produced no interest; I have accepted the Sum of Sixty two Thousand Six Hundred and Ninety two dollars, proposed, by this Government: The receipt of which Sum, by N M. Rothchild, to the credit of the Secretary of the Treasury of the United States of America, I have the honor to transmit here with, pursuant to your instructions.

.   .   .   .

I Send all the papers of the "Mary", which I had—Baron Verstolk said they had none in their possession.

It will be observed that Davezac enclosed, not the "mandate of payment" for $62,692, mentioned in the acquittance, but the receipt of the London bankers of the United States, N. M. Rothschild & Sons, for the equivalent thereof, £13,452 13s. 3d., placed to the credit of the Secretary of the Treasury of the United States.

DISTRIBUTION OF THE FUND

There was no real doubt as to who the parties entitled to the fund were; their representations had been for years before the Department of State and had been accepted as ground for the diplomatic steps taken. However, and doubtless out of abundant caution, the Secretary of State caused an item to be inserted in the Washington Globe of May 28, 1839, in which the fact of the payment of $62,692 was stated and which gave "notice to all whom it may concern, that the person[s] interested can apply at the Treasury Department, for the purpose of entering into the necessary arrangements, to enable them to receive their respective portions of the proceeds of said claim" (see D.S., 30 Domestic Letters, 258–59, Secretary of State Forsyth to Levi Woodbury, Secretary of the Treasury, May 27, 1839).

Objection was made to the procedure proposed by the Department of State, on the ground that if the money were paid into the Treasury, statutory authority would be required to pay it out (D.S., Miscellane-

ous Letters, May–September 1839, Woodbury to Forsyth, June 3, 1839); the difficulty was met by an authorization of the Secretary of the Treasury to the London bankers "to pay the money referred to, over to the holders of such certificates as may be issued by the Department of State establishing the title of the claimants to their respective shares" (*ibid.*, the same to the same, June 8, 1839); and each recipient was required to give bond, with approved sureties, indemnifying the Secretary of the Treasury and the United States "against any future demands by other parties, for the amount which may be paid" (D.S., 30 Domestic Letters, 305–6, Aaron Vail, Acting Secretary of State, to George Law, July 24, 1839).

The first certificate issued was to Alexander Lardner, second assistant cashier of the Bank of the United States at Philadelphia, as attorney for John Connell, for £3,363 3s. 4d., or one fourth of the whole fund, obviously for the costs and expenses (*ibid.*, 268–69, 303, June 13 and July 23, 1839). The remainder of the fund, or £10,089 9s. 11d., was, pursuant to agreement of the parties in interest, paid over ratably to the underwriters and to the estate of the owner (the latter receiving a share of four twenty-thirds) as stated in the letter of Secretary of State Forsyth to Samuel T. Thompson (*ibid.*, 355–56, October 19, 1839); the respective payees and amounts were as follows:

George Griswold, attorney of the trustees of the United Insurance Company of New York	£3, 509 7s. 10d.
George Law, president of the Marine Insurance Company of Baltimore	3, 070 14s. 3d.
Samuel T. Thompson, president of the Baltimore Insurance Company	1, 754 13s. 11d.
Charles Worthington, administrator *de bonis non* of Jeremiah Yellott	1, 754 13s. 11d.

Treaty Series No. 205
8 Statutes at Large, 526–33
18 *ibid.*, pt. 2, Public Treaties, 487–90

89

MEXICO : APRIL 11, 1839

Convention for the Adjustment of Claims of Citizens of the United States of America upon the Government of the Mexican Republic, signed at Washington April 11, 1839. Original in English and Spanish. Submitted to the Senate March 4, 1840. (Message of February 27, 1840.) Resolution of advice and consent March 17, 1840. Ratified by the United States April 6, 1840. Ratified by Mexico January 11, 1840. Ratifications exchanged at Washington April 7, 1840. Proclaimed April 8, 1840.

Convention for the adjustment of claims of citizens of the United States of America upon the Government of the Mexican Republic.

Whereas a Convention [1] for the adjustment of claims of citizens of the United States upon the Government of the Mexican Republic was concluded and signed at Washington on the 10th day of September 1838, which Convention was not ratified on the part of the Mexican Government on the alleged ground that the consent of His Majesty the King of Prussia to provide an arbitrator to act in the case provided by said Convention could not be obtained:

And whereas the Parties to said Convention are still, and equally, desirous of terminating the discussions which have taken place

Convencion para el arreglo de reclamaciones de ciudadanos de los Estados Unidos de America contra el Gobierno de la República Mexicána.

Por cuanto en 10. de Septiembre de 1838 fue concluida y firmada en Washington una Convencion [1] para el arreglo de reclamaciones de ciudadanos de los Estados Unidos de America contra el Gobierno de la Republica Mexicána, cuya convencion no fue ratificada por parte del Gobierno Mexicano, fundandose en que no podia obtenerse de Su Magestad el Rey de Prúsia que consintiese en nombrar un Arbitradór que actuáse en el caso prevenido en dicha Convencion:

Y por cuanto las Partes interesadas en ella continuan igualmente deseosas de terminar las discusiones que han tenido, con

[1] For the English text of the convention of September 10, 1838, see the notes following the texts of this convention.

between them in respect to said claims arising from injuries to the persons and property of citizens of the United States by Mexican authorities, in a manner equally advantageous to the citizens of the United States by whom said injuries have been sustained and more convenient to Mexico than that provided by said Convention, the President of the United States has named for this purpose, and furnished with full powers, John Forsyth, Secretary of State of the said United States and the President of the Mexican Republic has named His Excellency Señor Don Francisco Pizarro Martinez, accredited as Envoy Extraordinary and Minister Plenipotentiary of the Mexican Republic to the United States, and has furnished him with full powers for the same purpose: And the said plenipotentiaries have agreed upon and concluded the following articles.

Article I.

It is agreed that all claims of citizens of the United States upon the Mexican Government, statements of which, soliciting the interposition of the government of the United States have been presented to the Department of State or to the diplomatic agent of the United States at Mexico until the signature of this Convention, shall be referred to four Commissioners who shall form a board, and be appointed in the following

respecto á las espresadas reclamaciones por daños causados á las personas y propiedades de ciudadanos de los Estados Unidos por autoridades Mexicanas, de una manera igualmente ventajosa á los ciudadanos de los Estados Unidos que han sufrido dichos daños, y mas conveniente para Mexico que la estipulada en la mencionada Convencion; ha conferido el Presidente de la República Mexicana plenos poderes, á este efecto, á Francisco Pizarro Martinez, Enviado Estraordinario y Ministro Plenipotenciario de la misma Republica cerca de los Estados Unidos, y el Presidente de estos ha nombrado y autorizado plenamente, con el propio fin, al Honorable Señor Juan Forsyth, Secretario de Estado de dichos Estados Unidos, quienes han ajustado y convenido en los articulos siguientes.

Articulo I.

Todas las reclamaciones de ciudadanos de los Estados Unidos contra el Gobierno Mexicana, á cerca de las cuales se haya representado, solicitando la interposicion del de los Estados Unidos, y hayan sido exhibidas al Departamento de Estado ó al Agente Diplomatico de los mencionados Estados Unidos en Mexico hasta que esta Convencion sea firmada, se pasarán á cuatro Comisionados, que formarán una junta, y serán

manner, namely: two Commissioners shall be appointed by the President of the United States, by and with the advice and consent of the Senate thereof, and two Commissioners by the President of the Mexican Republic. The said Commissioners so appointed, shall be sworn impartially to examine and decide upon the said claims according to such evidence as shall be laid before them on the part of the United States and the Mexican Republic respectively.

ARTICLE II.

The said board shall have two Secretaries versed in the English and Spanish languages, one to be appointed by the President of the United States, by and with the advice and consent of the Senate thereof, and the other by the President of the Mexican Republic. And the said Secretaries shall be sworn faithfully to discharge their duty in that capacity.

ARTICLE III.

The said board shall meet in the City of Washington within three months after the exchange of the ratifications of this Convention, and within eighteen months from the time of its meeting shall terminate its duties. The Secretary of State of the United States shall, immediately after the exchange of the ratifications of this Convention, give

nombrados de la manera siguiente: á saber, dos de ellos lo serán por el Presidente de la República Mexicána, y los otros dos por el de los Estados Unidos, con consentimiento y aprobacion del Senado de los mismos. Los dichos Comisionados, nombrados segun se ha espresado, prestarán juramento de ecsáminar y fallár imparcialmente sobre dichas reclamaciones, con arreglo á las pruebas que se les presentáren por parte de la República Mexicána y de los Estados Unidos.

ARTICULO II.

La mencionada junta tendrá dos Secretarios, versados en los idiomas Castelláno é Ynglés; uno de los cuales será nombrado por el Presidente de la República Mexicána y otro por el de los Estados Unidos, con consentimiento y aprobacion del Senado de los mismos, y dichos Secretarios prestarán juramento de cumplir fielmente los deberes de su destino.

ARTICULO III.

Se reunirá la mencionada Comision en la Ciudad de Washington, dentro del termino de tres meses, contados desde el cánge de las ratificaciones de este Convénio, y á los diez y ocho meses despues del dia en que se reunire, terminarán sus funciones. Ynmediatamente despues de que las ratificaciones de esta Convencion hayan sido cangeadas, anunciará

notice of the time of the meeting of the said board, to be published in two newspapers in Washington and in such other papers as he may think proper.

ARTICLE IV.

All documents which now are in, or hereafter, during the continuance of the Commission constituted by this Convention, may come into the possession of the Department of State of the United States, in relation to the aforesaid claims, shall be delivered to the board.   The Mexican Government shall furnish all such documents and explanations as may be in their possession, for the adjustment of the said claims according to the principles of justice, the law of nations, and the stipulations of the treaty of Amity and Commerce[1] between the United States and Mexico of the 5th of April, 1831; the said documents to be specified when demanded at the instance of the said Commissioners.

ARTICLE V.

The said Commissioners shall, by a report under their hands and seals, decide upon the justice of the said claims, and the amount of compensation, if any, due from the Mexican Government in each case.

el Secretario de Estado de los Estados Unidos, en dos de los periodicos de Washington y otros que le parezca conveniente, la epoca en que dicha Comision se reunirá.

ARTICULO IV.

Todo documento que en la actualidad se halle ó que en lo succesivo viniere á poder del Departamento de Estado de los Estados Unidos, durante la ecsistencia de la Comision establecida por este convénio, y sea relativo á las mencionadas reclamaciones, se entregará á la Comision.   El Gobierno Mexicano subministrará cuantos documentos y aclaraciones estén á su alcance, para el ajuste de las espresadas reclamaciones, segun los principios de justicia, el derécho de gentes, y las estipulaciones del tratádo de Amistad y Comercio[1] entre Mexico y los Estados Unidos de 5 de Abril de 1831; y se especificará cuales sean dichos documentos, al tiempo de pedirlos, á instancia de los mencionados Comisionados.

ARTICULO V.

Los dichos Comisionados fallarán por médio de una relacion autorizada con sus firmas y séllos respectivos, sobre la justicia de las mencionadas reclamciones y el importe á que pueda ascender la compensacion de que resulte deudor, en cada caso, el Gobierno Mexicano.

---

[1] Document 70.

Article VI.

It is agreed that if it should not be convenient for the Mexican Government to pay at once the amount so found due, it shall be at liberty, immediately after the decisions in the several cases shall have taken place, to issue Treasury notes receivable at the Maritime Custom Houses of the Republic in payment of any duties which may be due or imposed at said Custom Houses upon goods entered for importation or exportation: said Treasury notes to bear interest at the rate of eight per centum per annum from the date of the award on the claim in payment of which said Treasury notes shall have been issued until that of their receipt at the Mexican Custom Houses. But as the presentation and receipt of said Treasury notes at said Custom Houses in large amounts might be inconvenient to the Mexican Government, it is further agreed that, in such case, the obligation of said Government to receive them in payment of duties as above stated, may be limited to one half the amount of said duties.

Article VII.

It is further agreed that in the event of the Commissioners differing in relation to the aforesaid claims, they shall, jointly or severally, draw up a report stating, in detail, the points on which they

Articulo VI.

Se ha convenido igualmente, que si al Gobierno Mexicáno no lo fuere cómodo satisfacer al contado el importe de que resultáre deudor, podrá inmediatamente despues de pronunciados los fállos en los diversos casos, emitir Libranzas recibidéras en las Aduanas Maritimas de la República en pagamento de cuales quiera derechos que en ellas se adeudáren ó se impusieren á los efectos, tanto á su importacion, como á su esportacion. Dichas Libranzas estarán sujetas á un interés anual de ocho por ciento, desde la fecha en que se dén los decretos sobre las reclamaciones en cuya satisfaccion hayan sido emitidas dichas Libranzas, hasta la en que se perciban en las espresadas Aduanas. Pero como la presentacion y recibo de dichas Libranzas en las mencionadas Aduanas en grandes sumas, podria no convenir al Gobierno Mexicáno, se ha acordado, ademas, que en tal caso la obligacion de recibirlas dicho Gobierno, en pagamento de derechos, segun se ha espresado arriba, pueda limitarse á una mitad del importe á que asciendan dichos derechos.

Articulo VII.

Se ha convenido ademas que, en caso de no estar conformes los Comisionodas con respecto á las precitadas reclamaciones, estiendan junta ó separadamente, una relacion circunstanciada de

differ, and the grounds upon which their respective opinions have been formed. And it is agreed that the said report or reports, with authenticated copies of all documents upon which they may be founded, shall be referred to the decision of His Majesty the King of Prussia.

But as the documents relating to the aforesaid claims are so voluminous that it cannot be expected His Prussian Majesty would be willing or able personally to investigate them, it is agreed that he shall appoint a person to act as an arbiter in his behalf; that the person so appointed shall proceed to Washington; that his travelling expenses to that City and from thence on his return to his place of residence in Prussia, shall be defrayed, one half by the United States and one half by the Mexican Republic; and that he shall receive as a compensation for his services a sum equal to one half the compensation that may be allowed by the United States to one of the Commissioners to be appointed by them, added to one half the compensation that may be allowed by the Mexican Government to one of the Commissioners to be appointed by it. And the compensation of such arbiter shall be paid, one half by the United States and one half by the Mexican Government.

los puntos en que sean de opinion contraria y de las razones sobre que funden sus respectivos juicios. Y se ha acordado que dicha relacion ó relaciones, acompañadas de copias auténticas de todos los documentos en que se apoyen, se refieran á la decision de Su Magestad el Rey de Prusia. Pero como los documentos relativos á las precitadas reclamaciones son tan voluminosos que no puede esperarse que Su Magestad Prusiana quiera ó pueda ecsaminarlos por si, se ha convenido en que nombre una persona que como árbitro le represente; que la persona nombrada del modo que va espresado se trasladará á Washington; que los gastos de su viage á esta Ciudad y de ella al punto de su residencia en Prúsia, serán costeádos una mitad por la Republica Mexicána y otra por los Estados Unidos, y que recibirá como honorarios por sus servicios, una suma igual á la mitad de la que el Gobierno Mexicano señaláse á uno de los Comisionados que ha de nombrar, con otra mitad de la que por los suyos señaláren los Estados Unidos á uno de los Comisionados que por su parte han de nombrarse: cuyos honorarios serán satisfechos una mitad por la Republica Mexicána y la otra por los Estados Unidos.

Article VIII.

Immediately after the signature of this Convention, the Plenipotentiaries of the contracting parties (both being thereunto competently authorized) shall, by a joint note, addressed to the Minister for Foreign Affairs of His Majesty the King of Prussia, to be delivered by the Minister of the United States at Berlin, invite the said Monarch to appoint an umpire to act in his behalf in the manner above mentioned, in case this Convention shall be ratified respectively by the governments of the United States and Mexico.

Article IX.

It is agreed that, in the event of His Prussian Majesty's declining to appoint an umpire to act in his behalf, as aforesaid, the contracting parties, on being informed thereof, shall, without delay, invite Her Brittannic Majesty, and, in case of her declining, His Majesty the King of the Netherlands to appoint an umpire to act in their behalf, respectively, as above provided.

Article X.

And the contracting parties further engage to consider the decision of such umpire to be final and conclusive on all the matters so referred.

Articulo VIII.

Ynmediatamente despues que los Plenipotenciarios de las partes contratantes hayan firmado esta Convencion, dirigirán de mancomun (para lo cual estan ambos competentemente autorizados), por conducto del Sr. Enviado de los Estados Unidos á Berlin, á Su Escelencia el Ministro de Relaciones Estrangeras de Su Magestad el Rey de Prusia, una nota invitando á dicho Monarca para nombrar una persona que como Arbitro lo represente de la manera arriba mencionada, en caso de que esta Convencion sea ratificada respectivamente por los Gobiernos de Mexico y los Estados Unidos.

Articulo IX.

Se ha convenido ademas que si Su Magestad Prusiana rehusáre hacer el nombramiento de que habla el articulo anterior, procederán al momento que lo sepan las partes contratantes á invitar á Su Magestad Britanica, y si tambien ella se rehusaré, á Su Magestad el Rey de Holanda, á fin que nombre un Arbitrador que le represente segun queda pactado.

Articulo X.

Las partes contratantes se obligan ademas á considerar como finál y decisivo el fallo del mencionado arbitrador, en todas las materias que se hayan sujetado á su ecsámen.

ARTICLE XI.

For any sums of money which the umpire shall find due to citizens of the United States by the Mexican Government, Treasury notes shall be issued in the manner aforementioned.

ARTICLE XII.

And the United States agree for ever to exonerate the Mexican Government from any further accountability for claims which shall either be rejected by the board or the arbiter aforesaid, or which, being allowed by either, shall be provided for by the said Government in the manner before mentioned.

ARTICLE XIII.

And it is agreed that each Government shall provide compensation for the Commissioners and Secretary to be appointed by it; and that the contingent expenses of the board shall be defrayed, one moiety by the United States and one moiety by the Mexican Republic.

ARTICLE XIV.

This Convention shall be ratified and the ratifications shall be exchanged at Washington within twelve months from the signature hereof, or sooner, if possible.

In faith whereof, we, the Plenipotentiaries of the United States of America and of the Mexican

ARTICULO XI.

Se emitirán Libranzas, en los terminos arriba espresados, por el importe del dinero que el Arbitrador encuentre que sea deudor á ciudadanos de los Estados Unidos el Gobierno Mexicano.

ARTICULO XII.

Y los Estados Unidos convienen en descargar para siempre al Gobierno Mexicáno de toda responsabilidad último, por reclamaciones que sean rechazadas, bien por la junta ó por el mencionado arbitrador, ó que admitidas por cualquiera de ellos, haya dicho Gobierno provisto á su compensacion en los terminos antes espresados

ARTICULO XIII.

Se ha convenido en que cada gobierno señále á los Comisionados y Secretarios que ha de nombrar, los honorarios respectivos; y que los gastos contingentes de la junta sean costeados, una mitad por la Republica Mexicana y otra por los Estados Unidos.

ARTICULO XIV.

La presente Convencion será ratificada, y las ratificaciones serán cangeadas en Washington dentro de doce meses desde este dia, ó antes si fuere posible.

En fé de lo cual, nosotros los plenipotenciarios de la República Mexicana y de los Estados Unidos

Republic have signed and sealed these presents.

Done in the City of Washington, on the eleventh day of April, in the year of our Lord one thousand eight hundred and thirty nine, in the sixty third year of the Independence of the United States of America, and the nineteenth of that of the Mexican Republic.

JOHN FORSYTH   FRAN. PIZARRO
[Seal]   MARTINEZ
              [Seal]

de America, hemos firmado y sellado las presentes.

Fecho en la Ciudad de Washington á los once dias de Abril del año del Sõr. mil ochocientos treinta y nueve, decimo nono de la Yndependencia de la Republica Mexicana, y el sexagesimo tercio de la de los Estados Unidos de America.

FRAN. PIZARRO   JOHN FORSYTH
MARTINEZ   [Seal]
[Seal]

NOTES

The file of this convention is complete. The signed original of the convention is written in English and Spanish, with the English on the left pages; as the printed texts show, the *alternat* was duly observed. The other documents are in customary form, including the attested Senate resolution of March 17, 1840 (Executive Journal, V, 269), the duplicate United States instrument of ratification of April 6, 1840, the Mexican instrument of ratification of January 11, 1840, the certificate (in English) of the exchange of ratifications at Washington on April 7, and the original proclamation of April 8, 1840. The Mexican instrument of ratification of January 11, 1840, includes both texts of the convention, the Spanish in the left columns.

The sending of the Mexican instrument of ratification to Washington was delayed; the messenger carrying that document and the Mexican full power to exchange the ratifications, John Black, American vice consul at Mexico City, left there on March 11, 1840, sailed from Veracruz for New Orleans on the U.S. revenue cutter *Woodbury* on March 15, and reached Washington in time for the exchange of ratifications to take place on April 7 (D. S., 9 Despatches, Mexico, No. 15, March 10, 1840, enclosures; No. 17, March 28, 1840).

From the message of President Van Buren of February 27, 1840, transmitting this convention to the Senate, it seems that it was withheld until information of ratification by the Government of Mexico had been received (Executive Journal, V, 260); the accompanying correspondence was printed (*ibid.*, 261), but the document is not now available.

The convention was communicated to Congress with the presidential message of April 15, 1840 (Richardson, III, 590).

THE FULL POWERS

The full powers of the Plenipotentiaries are mentioned in the preamble of the convention, but without statement of their exchange. The full power given to Secretary of State Forsyth was in customary

form and under date of March 18, 1839. Its subject matter was limited to "the reclamations of citizens of the United States against the government of the Mexican Republic" (D. S., 2 Credences, 312). The original full power of the Mexican Plenipotentiary, dated June 13, 1838, is in the file. As its date is earlier than that of the unratified convention of September 10, 1838 (discussed below), it was doubtless the authorization of the Plenipotentiary of Mexico in respect of both that convention and this. In translation the Mexican full power reads as follows:

Anastasio Bustamente, President of the Republic of Mexico

Know all to whom these presents may come, that:

Animated by a sincere desire to reestablish friendly relations with the United States of America, and the proposal having been accepted by the Government of the latter to refer to a friendly power the decision of pending claims, for which purpose it is necessary to conclude in advance a convention in which the bases of arbitration shall be established by common agreement; and having full confidence in the zeal and knowledge of His Excellency Señor Don Francisco Pizarro Martinez, Minister Plenipotentiary of the Republic of Mexico near the Government at Washington, I have appointed and authorized him, and by these presents do appoint and authorize him, to conclude and sign the said convention with the plenipotentiary or plenipotentiaries duly appointed and authorized by the President of the United States of America, promising to hold as valid and binding and to fulfil and execute whatever the said Minister Plenipotentiary may agree to, and also to ratify it during the stipulated period.

In faith whereof I have ordered the issuance of these presents, signed by my hand, attested by the seal of the nation, and countersigned by the Minister of Foreign Relations, in the National Palace of Mexico on the thirteenth day of the month of June in the year one thousand eight hundred and thirty-eight, and the eighteenth year of the independence of the Republic.

[Seal]　Anast⁰ Bustam.

Luis G. Cuevas

As stated in the certificate of exchange, the ratifications were exchanged by "William Hunter, Jr, of the Department of State of the United States and Angel M. Cos, Acting Secretary of the Mexican Legation in the United States, having full powers therefor from our respective Governments". A copy of the full power of Hunter is of record (D. S., 2 Credences, 320, April 6, 1840). The original of the Mexican full power for the exchange is in the file. It is dated February 4, 1840, and ran primarily to the Mexican Minister at Washington, Francisco Pizarro Martinez, and in the alternative, to the Mexican Secretary of Legation. Señor Martinez died at Washington on February 9, 1840.

The Convention of 1838

In the preambie of this convention reference is made to a previous convention for the adjustment of American claims which was signed at Washington on September 10, 1838, and which did not go into force, as it was not ratified by the Government of Mexico. The reason given for the nonratification of that convention is stated in the English text of the preamble as "the alleged ground that the consent of His Majesty the King of Prussia to provide an arbitrator to act in the case provided by said Convention could not be obtained"; but

the corresponding Spanish has no equivalent of the word "alleged". The facts in the matter are somewhat obscure (Moore, International Arbitrations, II, 1218; and see Executive Journal, V, 193–94); the explanation given by the Mexican Minister at Washington in his note of March 3, 1839, is in the following terms (D. S., 4 Notes from the Mexican Legation, translation):

I have received by today's post an official communication from Señor Don Manuel Eduardo de Gorostiza, Minister of Foreign Relations of the Republic, dated January 5 last. His Excellency informs me therein that when the Government Council took up the examination of the convention of September 10 last, and when its existence had already been called to the attention of Congress, as Your Excellency will see by the copy of the message of the President which I have the honor to enclose, it was found that the Chargé d'Affaires of His Majesty the King of Prussia had notified that Ministry on the 6th of November last, in a note of which I enclose a copy for Your Excellency, that his Sovereign did not believe that he should accept the functions of arbitrator for the reasons therein expressed. This important document had been received just at the time of the arrival at Veracruz of the French squadron, and when the attention of the Government was completely absorbed by the grave and decisive events which were then in preparation and which afterwards happened with such rapidity. The result, therefore, was that it was reserved in one of the letter cases of the Ministry, that its contents were not brought to the attention of the President, nor did it come to the knowledge of Señor Gorostiza, until the 2d of January. His Excellency, however, lost no time, since that same morning he sought an interview with Mr. Gerolt with the purpose of finding out whether the latter had received any communication from his Government subsequent to that date which might lead him to believe that His Prussian Majesty might change his resolution regarding his refusal, after receiving more exact information as to the conditions of the arbitration agreed upon in this capital. Mr. Gerolt replied in the negative, and thereupon reiterated to Señor Gorostiza his opinion that there remained no hope that the King might yield to any new solicitation on the part of Mexico, because, he added, His Majesty, having conferred with his Minister of Justice, had become convinced that it was impossible for him to respond to the trust placed in him.

In view thereof, the President found himself under the regrettable necessity of directing the Minister of Foreign Relations not to present the convention for the approval of Congress, in order that the latter might not be obliged to disapprove it by reason of the fact that the arbitration of the King of Prussia constituted an integral part thereof by the provision of Article 7.

The President directed, moreover, that I should negotiate a new convention with the Government of the United States, for which I am fully authorized and prepared.

I hasten to bring the above to the knowledge of Your Excellency for reasons of expediency, assuring you at the same time of my very sincere regret that I did not receive earlier the communication to which the present refers, although, in order that it might reach me with the greatest security and promptness Señor Gorostiza took the precaution to entrust its delivery to a messenger dispatched to this country on the said 5th of January last by the consul of the United States residing in the city of Mexico.

It is not clear, however, that the King of Prussia had declined to act under the convention of September 10, 1838. It appears that the proposal of "a mediation" by the King of Prussia had been made in a note of the Mexican Government of March 15, 1838, addressed to the Prussian Chargé d'Affaires at Mexico City; and from the tenor of the note of the Prussian Chargé d'Affaires of November 6, 1838 (a copy of which, in French, is with the note of the Mexican Minister at Washington of March 3, 1839, above quoted), it seems that it had not been made plain to the Government of Prussia that the task of

the King of Prussia was proposed to be limited to the appointment of "a person to act as an arbiter in his behalf".

However, there is no reason to doubt that the Mexican Government acted in entire sincerity and under the belief that the convention of 1838 would be ineffectual; that convention did not reach Mexico City until November 12, 1838, during a period of great difficulty; some delay was natural enough, under the circumstances; and the offer then made to negotiate a new convention to the same end is in itself convincing evidence of the good faith of the Government of Mexico in the matter (see D. S., 4 Notes from the Mexican Legation, March 17, 1839, answering the note of Secretary of State Forsyth of March 16, 6 Notes to the Mexican Legation, 123–26).

That convention of September 10, 1838, the United States was prepared to accept; it was submitted to the Senate on January 21, 1839, and the usual resolution of advice and consent was unanimously adopted by that body ten days later (Executive Journal, V, 180, 190). Furthermore, following a presidential message of February 2, with a report from the Secretary of State regarding the necessity of an extension of the time allowed for the exchange of ratifications (*ibid.*, 193–94), the Senate on March 2 unanimously adopted a resolution of advice and consent to the exchange of ratifications "at any time prior to" December 10, 1839 (*ibid.*, 220); by the terms of that convention the exchange was to take place within five months after the date of signature, or by February 10, 1839. On that day the Mexican Minister at Washington was informed that the convention had been ratified by the President and was "now ready for exchange" (D. S., 6 Notes to the Mexican Legation, 122).

That convention, like this, was written in English and Spanish and provided for the adjustment of the same American claims as here, except that it was of earlier date, so that claims presented to the Department of State or to the diplomatic agent of the United States at Mexico City after September 10, 1838, but not later than April 11, 1839, were covered by the terms of this convention, though not by those of the earlier one. The texts of the convention of 1838 are printed in Senate Confidential Document, January 21, 1839, 25th Congress, 3d session (Regular Confidential Documents, IX, 289–94); the English text, collated with the original which is bound with the duplicate United States instrument of ratification (D. S., Unperfected G2), follows:

Convention for the adjustment of claims of citizens of the United States of America upon the Government of the Mexican Republic.

The United States of America and the Mexican Republic being equally desirous of terminating the discussions that have taken place between them in respect to claims of citizens of the United States for injuries to their persons and property by Mexican authorities, the President of the United States has named for this purpose, and furnished with full powers, John Forsyth, Secretary of State of the said United States, and the President of the Mexican Republic has named His Excellency Señor Don Francisco Pizarro Martinez, accredited as Envoy Extraordinary and Minister Plenipotentiary of the Mexican Republic to the United States, and has furnished him with full powers for the same purpose: And the said plenipotentiaries, after having exchanged their full powers, found in good and due form, have agreed upon and concluded the following articles:

ARTICLE 1.

It is agreed that all claims of citizens of the United States upon the Mexican Government, statements of which, soliciting the interposition of the Government of the United States, have been presented to the Department of State, or to the diplomatic agent of the United States at Mexico, until the signature of this Convention, shall be referred to four Commissioners who shall form a board and be appointed in the following manner, namely: two Commissioners shall be appointed by the President of the United States, by and with the advice and consent of the Senate thereof, and two Commissioners by the President of the Mexican Republic. The said Commissioners, so appointed, shall be sworn impartially to examine and decide upon the said claims according to such evidence as shall be laid before them on the part of the United States and the Mexican Republic respectively.

ARTICLE 2.

The said board shall have, versed in the English and Spanish languages, two Secretaries, one to be appointed by the President of the United States, by and with the advice and consent of the Senate thereof, and the other by the President of the Mexican Republic. And the said Secretaries shall be sworn faithfully to discharge their duty in that capacity.

ARTICLE 3.

The said board shall meet in the City of Washington within three months after the exchange of the ratifications of this Convention, and within eighteen months from the time of its meeting shall terminate its duties. The Secretary of State of the United States shall immediately after the exchange of the ratifications of this Convention give notice of the time of the meeting of the said board, to be published in two newspapers in Washington, and in such other papers as he may think proper.

ARTICLE 4.

All documents which now are in, or hereafter, during the continuance of the Commission constituted by this Convention, may come into, the possession of the Department of State of the United States, in relation to the aforesaid claims, shall be delivered to the board. The Mexican Government shall furnish all such documents and explanations as may be in their possession, for the adjustment of the said claims according to the principles of justice, the law of nations, and the stipulations of the treaty of Amity and Commerce between the United States and Mexico, of the 5th of April, 1831 [Document 70]; the said documents to be specified when demanded at the instance of the said Commissioners.

ARTICLE 5.

The said Commissioners shall, by a report under their hands and seals, decide upon the justice of the said claims, and the amount of compensation, if any, due from the Mexican Government in each case.

ARTICLE 6.

And it is agreed that, should it not be convenient for the Mexican Government to pay at once the amounts so found due, it shall, immediately after the decisions in the several cases shall have taken place, issue certificates of debt, bearing the usual interest of Mexico, in favor of the United States, or of the persons interested in the claims found due,—which certificates shall be for an amount sufficient, according to the price of Mexican securities in the London market, to enable the holders to realize by a sale of them an amount equal to the sums found to be due in the several cases.

ARTICLE 7.

It is further agreed that, in the event of the Commissioners differing in relation to the aforesaid claims, they shall, jointly or severally, draw up a report stating, in detail, the points on which they differ, and the grounds upon which their respec-

tive opinions have been formed. And it is agreed that the said report or reports, with authenticated copies of all documents upon which they may be founded, shall be referred to the decision of His Majesty the King of Prussia.

But as the documents relating to the aforesaid claims are so voluminous that it cannot be expected His Prussian Majesty would be willing or able personally to investigate them, it is agreed that he shall appoint a person to act as an arbiter in his behalf; that the person so appointed shall proceed to Washington; that his travelling expenses to that city, and from thence on his return to his place of residence in Prussia, shall be defrayed one-half by the United States and one-half by the Mexican Republic; and that he shall receive as a compensation for his services a sum equal to one-half the compensation that may be allowed by the United States to one of the Commissioners to be appointed by them, added to one-half the compensation that may be allowed by the Mexican Government for one of the Commissioners to be appointed by it. And the compensation of such arbiter shall be paid one-half by the United States and one-half by the Mexican Government. It is further agreed that immediately after the signature of this Convention proper measures shall be adopted by the contracting parties to procure from His Prussian Majesty the provisional appointment of an umpire to act in his behalf in the manner before mentioned, if this Convention shall be ratified, respectively, by the Governments of the United States and Mexico.

ARTICLE 8.

And the contracting parties further engage to consider the decision of such umpire to be final and conclusive on all the matters so referred.

ARTICLE 9.

For any sums of money which the umpire shall find due to citizens of the United States by the Mexican Government, certificates of debt shall be issued in the manner aforementioned.

ARTICLE 10.

And the United States agree for ever to exonerate the Mexican Government from any further accountability for claims which shall either be rejected by the board or the arbiter aforesaid, or which, being allowed by either, shall be provided for by the Mexican Government, in the manner before mentioned.

ARTICLE 11.

And it is agreed that each Government shall provide compensation for the Commissioners and secretary to be appointed by it; and that the contingent expenses of the board shall be defrayed, one moiety by the United States and one moiety by the Mexican Republic.

ARTICLE 12.

This Convention shall be ratified, and the ratifications shall be exchanged at Washington within five months from the signature hereof, or sooner, if possible.

In faith whereof, we, the Plenipotentiaries of the United States of America and of the Mexican Republic, have signed and sealed these presents.

Done in the City of Washington, on the tenth day of September, in the year of our Lord one thousand eight hundred and thirty-eight, in the sixty-third year of the Independence of the United States of America, and the eighteenth of that of the Mexican Republic.

FRAN. PIZARRO MARTINEZ   [Seal]   JOHN FORSYTH   [Seal]

It will be observed that many of the provisions of the convention of 1838 were almost literally the same as those of this convention; but the preamble and the final article were necessarily somewhat different, the mode of payment under Article 6 was changed, and the final clause

of Article 7 of the earlier agreement, regarding the appointment of an umpire by the King of Prussia, was rewritten and became Articles 8 and 9 of this convention.

A full account of the events and negotiations leading up to the convention of 1838 is in Moore, International Arbitrations, II, 1209–17; reference also may be made to the chapter on "Claims against Mexico" in Rives, The United States and Mexico, 1821–1848, I, 417–44. That convention of 1838 had been preceded by a decade of unsettled conditions; the American claims had been the subject of various presidential messages to Congress since 1835; the printed documents are numerous; much of the diplomatic correspondence, instructions, etc., from 1828 on, is printed in House Document No. 351, 25th Congress, 2d session, serial 332 (that document is in two parts, of 23 and 821 pages, respectively); a "solemn and final demand of satisfaction" was made in the note of Secretary of State Forsyth to the Minister of Foreign Affairs of Mexico under date of May 27, 1837 (D. S., 6 Notes to the Mexican Legation, 78–86). Accompanying that note was an elaborate list of fifty-seven causes of complaint. That note was sent to Mexico City by a special messenger (Robert Greenhow, interpreter of the Department of State) and was delivered to the Mexican Government on July 20. It is printed, with the report of the Secretary of State of December 2, 1837, and various other papers, in Senate Document No. 1, 25th Congress, 2d session, serial 314, pp. 29–159. The note concludes as follows:

It is the ardent wish of the President of the United States that the government of the Mexican Republic will give an earnest of its disposition to preserve the relations of concord and good neighbourhood with this country, by bestowing its prompt attention upon this last demand upon its justice and its honor, made according to the forms prescribed by the treaty [of April 5, 1831, Document 70, Article 34, clause 3] between the two governments, that the United States may be justified in the eyes of all nations for any measures they shall be compelled to take, should this appeal to the government of Mexico be made in vain.

Negotiations were made possible by the appointment of Señor Francisco Pizarro Martinez as Minister to the United States. Martinez arrived in Washington in October 1837; offer of arbitration was made in behalf of the Government of Mexico, following an authorizing decree of the Mexican Congress of May 20, 1837, and that offer received the assent of this Government (D. S., 4 Notes from the Mexican Legation, December 23, 1837, and April 7, 1838; 6 Notes to the Mexican Legation, 105–6; these notes are printed in serial 332, first pagination, 7–10, 19–22). Proposal of Prussia as the arbitrating power was made by the Mexican Minister and was at once accepted (*ibid.*, 756–58; D. S., 4 Notes from the Mexican Legation, April 30, 1838; 6 Notes to the Mexican Legation, 107–8, May 10, 1838).

Article 8

Under date of April 18, 1839, a joint note, in French, signed by the Plenipotentiaries of the two Governments, was addressed to Baron de Werther, Minister of State and of Foreign Relations of His Majesty the King of Prussia, enclosing a copy of the convention and conveying

the request of the two Governments for the appointment by the King
of Prussia of an arbiter under the terms of the convention (D. S., 1
Communications to Foreign Sovereigns and States, 183–85). The
original of that note was transmitted to Henry Wheaton, Minister to
Prussia, with the instruction of April 17, 1839, for delivery to Baron
de Werther (D. S., 14 Instructions, Prussia, 28–30). The despatch
of Wheaton of September 20, 1839, enclosed the identic notes of
Baron de Werther dated the previous day, addressed respectively to
Secretary of State Forsyth and to Señor Martinez, the Mexican Plenipotentiary, stating that the King of Prussia had acceded to the request
of the two Governments and had named as arbiter Baron Roenne,
Minister Resident of Prussia at Washington. Only the duplicate of
that despatch, with copies of the identic notes, has been found (D. S.,
2 Despatches, Prussia, No. 133); but it appears that the original was
received (D. S., 6 Notes to the Mexican Legation, 137).

A confidential despatch from Wheaton, also dated September 20,
1839 (D. S., 2 Despatches, Prussia, No. 134), discloses some of the
circumstances surrounding the appointment of Baron Roenne, in the
following terms:

> Finding that another candidate had been proposed to the King for the Office
> of arbitrator under the Mexican convention, in opposition to Mr. de Roenne,
> who had been named by Baron de Werther, I did not hesitate to urge, in such
> quarters as I thought would be likely to influence His majesty's determination,
> my strong conviction that the appointment of Mr. de Roenne would be more
> likely to be satisfactory to our Government, to whom he was personally & advan-
> tageously known, than that of one who was a stranger to our language, laws, &
> manner of doing business. In answer to the question whether I was equally sure
> that the nomination of Mr. de Roenne would be also satisfactory to the Mexican
> Government, I did not hesitate to answer in the affirmative. I have been since
> informed by Mr Eichorn that my assurances had contributed essentially to fix the
> King's final resolution, whose apparent hesitation probably proceeded from His
> Majesty's excessive anxiety to satisfy both parties in the choice he should make
> &, above all, not to lay under the possible imputation of partiality in naming his
> minister in the United States. This will also, in a great measure, account for the
> delay which has occurred in bringing this business to a close. I trust that no
> inconvenience will have occurred from this circumstance which I have done
> everything in my power to obviate.

THE CLAIMS SETTLEMENT

The history of the American claims covered by this convention is
long and complex. It is fully set forth in Moore, International Arbitrations, II, 1209–86, with numerous citations (in that work, also,
various claims under this convention are separately treated; for references to these, see *ibid.*, V, 5181). From that authoritative statement
the following summary of the proceedings under this convention is
written.

The act of June 12, 1840 (5 Statutes at Large, 383–84), provided for
the carrying into effect of this convention and for the appointment by
the President of two commissioners and a secretary pursuant to
Articles 1 and 2 (see also the act of September 1, 1841, *ibid.*, 452).
The commissioners on the part of the United States and those on the
part of Mexico were duly appointed; they organized as a board on
August 25, 1840.

By Article 3 of the convention it was provided that the board "within eighteen months from the time of its meeting shall terminate its duties". The existence of the board accordingly ended on February 25, 1842; but for various reasons thirty of the eighty-four claims presented had not then been decided. The majority of the claims presented, both in number and amount, had, however, been decided either by the board or by the umpire, and the amounts awarded aggregated $2,026,139.68; the interest allowed was, in general, at the rate of 5 percent (see Moore, *op. cit.*, II, 1243); the total amount claimed in the decided cases was $6,648,812.88, and the total amount of claims remaining undecided was $5,201,776.61; of these, claims aggregating $1,864,939.56 (allowed by the American commissioners at $928,627.88) were before the umpire; and the remainder, aggregating $3,336,837.05, had not been passed on by the board of commissioners.

The following statement as to the general character of the claims is quoted from Moore, *op. cit.*, II, 1243–44:

Several claims were presented to the board for supplies of money, arms, and other things to the Mexicans when they were engaged in their struggle for independence, but no objection to the allowance of such claims on the ground of their unneutral character appears to have been made. On the contrary, the Mexican commissioners concurred in their allowance, and the awards upon them were among the earliest made. In three such cases, involving claims for money, arms, and other supplies furnished in 1815, 1816, and 1817, final judgments amounting to nearly $200,000 were made directly by the commissioners themselves. Certain other claims of the same kind were referred to the umpire, not, however, upon international grounds, but only upon questions of fact or of the proper rate of interest.

The liability of the Mexican Government for property seized by the patriot forces before the recognition of Mexican independence by any foreign power was admitted in the awards.

The decisions of the commissioners and the umpire appear under their appropriate heads in the digest. The most of the cases involved the alleged wrongful seizure of property; and in many instances the act complained of was committed by the customs authorities. Several claims were allowed for overcharges of duties. Two claims were allowed for specie seized while in transit through the country by officers of the government, and devoted to the government's use. In certain cases awards were made on account of vessels which the government impressed into its service, while in one case an award was made for the building and in another for the repairing of a vessel for the government. One claim was allowed for the use of houses occupied by troops; one for a forced loan, and one for unjust expulsion. Several awards were rendered in favor of the claimants on the ground of their unlawful imprisonment.

The clauses of this convention for the payment of the allowed claims (Articles 6 and 11) remained ineffective, owing to the condition of the Mexican Treasury; the convention of January 30, 1843 (Document 100, the notes to which should be consulted), made further provision for payment. While some instalments were paid under that convention, the payments ceased in 1844. Two instalments under that convention were taken up by the United States Treasury pursuant to the act of August 10, 1846 (9 Statutes at Large, 85, 94); and by Article 13 of the Treaty of Guadalupe Hidalgo of February 2, 1848, the United States assumed the obligation to pay the balance of the liquidated claims under this convention and the convention of Janu-

ary 30, 1843 (Document 100), an obligation for which appropriation was duly made by the act of July 29, 1848 (*ibid.*, 265).

No adjudication of the unliquidated claims under this convention had then been had, as a convention for that purpose signed on November 20, 1843, failed to go into force; but by Articles 14 and 15 of the Treaty of Guadalupe Hidalgo the United States discharged Mexico "from all claims of citizens of the United States, not heretofore decided against the Mexican Government", and agreed to pay the same to the extent of $3,250,000. The unliquidated claims under this convention were thus included in that blanket obligation of the United States, which was duly fulfilled pursuant to the act of March 3, 1849 (9 Statutes at Large, 393–94; see Moore, *op. cit.*, II, 1248–86).

Treaty Series No. 76
8 Statutes at Large, 534–51
18 *ibid.*, pt. 2, Public Treaties, 187–95

90

ECUADOR : JUNE 13, 1839

Treaty of Peace, Friendship, Navigation, and Commerce, signed at Quito June 13, 1839. Original in English and Spanish.
Submitted to the Senate January 21, 1840. (Message of January 1840.) Resolution of advice and consent July 15, 1840. Ratified by the United States July 31, 1840. Ratified by Ecuador February 19, 1842. Ratifications exchanged at Quito April 9, 1842. Proclaimed September 23, 1842.

Treaty of Peace, Friendship, Navigation and Commerce, between the United States of America and the Republic of Ecuador.

The United States of America and the Republic of Ecuador, desiring to make lasting and firm, the friendship and good understanding which happily prevails between both nations, have resolved to fix, in a manner, clear, distinct and positive, the rules which shall, in future, be religiously observed between the one and the other, by means of a treaty of friendship, commerce and navigation. For this most desirable object, the President of the United States of America, has conferred full powers on James C. Pickett, a citizen of the said States, and the President of the Republic of Ecuador, on Doctor Luis de Saa, Minister of Finance, charged with the Department of the Interior and Foreign Relations; who, after having exchanged

Tratado de Paz, Amistad, Navegacion y Comercio, entre la República del Ecuador y los Estados Unidos de America.

La República del Ecuador y los Estados Unidos de America, deseando hacer duradera y firme la amistad y buena inteligencia que felizmente existe entre ambas potencias, han resuelto fijar de una manera clara, distinta y positíva, las reglas que deben observar religiosamente en lo venidero, por medio de un tratado de paz, amistad, comercio y navegacion. Con este muy deseable objeto, el Presidente de la República del Ecuador ha conferido plenos poderes al Doctor Luis de Saá, Ministro de Hacienda y encargado del Ministerio del Ynterior y Relaciones Esteriores, y el Presidente de los Estados Unidos de America á Santiago C. Pickett, ciudadano de dichos Estados; quienes, despues de haber cangeado sus espresados plenos pode-

their said full powers, in due and proper form, have agreed to the following articles:

ARTICLE 1.

There shall be a perfect, firm and inviolable peace and sincere friendship, between the United States of America and the Republic of Ecuador, in all the extent of their possessions and territories, and between their people and citizens, respectively, without distinction of persons or places.

ARTICLE 2.

The United States of America and the Republic of Ecuador, desiring to live in peace and harmony with all the other nations of the earth, by means of a policy, frank and equally friendly with all, engage mutually, not to grant any particular favor to other nations, in respect of commerce and navigation, which shall not immediately become common to the other party, who shall enjoy the same freely, if the concession was freely made, or, on allowing the same compensation, if the concession was conditional.

ARTICLE 3.

The two high contracting parties, being likewise desirous of placing the commerce and navigation of their respective countries on the liberal basis of perfect equality and reciprocity, mutually agree, that the citizens of

res en debida y buena forma, han convenido en los articulos siguientes.

ARTICULO 1.

Habrá una paz perfecta, firme é inviolable y amistad sincera, entre la República del Ecuador y los Estados Unidos de America, en toda la estension de sus posesiones y territorios, y entre sus pueblos y ciudadanos respectivamente, sin distincion de personas ni lugares.

ARTICULO 2.

La República del Ecuador y los Estados Unidos de America, deseando vivir en paz y en armonia con las demas naciones de la tierra, por medio de una politica franca é igualmente amistosa con todas, se obligan mutuamente á no conceder favores particulares á otras naciones, con respecto á comercio y navegacion, que no se hagan inmediatamente comunes á una ú otra, quien gozará de los mismos, libremente, ó prestando la misma compensacion, si la concesion fuere condicional.

ARTICULO 3.

Las dos altas partes contratantes, deseando tambien establecer el comercio y navegacion de sus respectivos paises sobre las liberales bases de perfecta igualdad y reciprocidad, convienen mutuamente en que los ciudadanos de

each, may frequent all the coasts and countries of the other, and reside and trade there, in all kinds of produce, manufactures and merchandise; and they shall enjoy all the rights, privileges and exemptions, in navigation and commerce, which native citizens do, or shall enjoy, submitting themselves to the laws, decrees and usages there established, to which native citizens are subjected: but it is understood, that this article does not include the coasting trade of either country, the regulation of which is reserved, by the parties respectively, according to their own separate laws. And it is further agreed, that this article shall be subject to the following modification; that whereas by a law of Ecuador of March 21st. 1837,[1] vessels built in the dockyard of Guayaquil, shall be exempted from various charges, therefore, vessels of the United States cannot claim this privilege, but shall enjoy it if it should be granted to vessels belonging to Spain, or to Mexico and to the other Hispano-American Republics.

cada una podrán frecuentar todas las costas y paises de la otra y residir y traficar en ellos con toda clase de producciones, manufacturas y mercaderias, y gozarán de todos los derechos, privilegios y exenciones, con respecto á navegacion y comercio, de que gozan ó gozaren los ciudadanos naturales, sometiendose á las leyes, decretos y usos establecidos, á que estan sujetos dichos ciudadanos. Pero debe entenderse que este articulo no comprende el comercio de cabotage de cada uno de los paises, cuya regulacion queda reservada á las partes respectivamente, segun sus leyes propias y peculiares. Y debe entenderse ademas, que este articulo estará sugeto á la modificacion siguiente;—que por cuanto, una ley del Ecuador, fecha de Marzo 21 de 1837,[1] dispone, que los buques construidos en el astillero de Guayaquil, serán libres de derechos de varias clases, los buques de los Estados Unidos no podrán pretender esta misma libertad; pero la gozarán, si se concediese á los buques de la España, de Mejico y de las demas Repúblicas Hispano-Americanas.

ARTICLE 4.

They likewise agree, that whatever kind of produce, manufactures or merchandise of any foreign country can be, from time to time, lawfully imported into

ARTICULO 4.

Ygualmente convienen en que cualquiera clase de producciones, manufacturas ó mercaderias, de cualquier pais estranjero que puedan ser en cualquier tiempo legal-

---

[1] For a translation of the law of March 21, 1837, see the notes following the texts of this treaty.

the United States, in their own vessels, may be also imported in the vessels of the Republic of Ecuador; and that no higher or other duties upon the tonnage of the vessel and her cargo, shall be levied and collected, whether the importation be made in the vessels of the one country or of the other: and, in like manner, that whatever kind of produce, manufactures or merchandise of any foreign country, can be, from time to time, lawfully imported into the Republic of Ecuador in its own vessels, may be also imported in vessels of the United States; and that no higher or other duties upon the tonnage of the vessel and her cargo, shall be levied or collected, whether the importation be made in vessels of the one country or of the other. And they agree, that whatever may be lawfully exported or re-exported from the one country in its own vessels, to any foreign country, may, in like manner, be exported or re-exported in the vessels of the other country. And the same bounties, duties and drawbacks shall be allowed and collected, whether such exportation, or re-exportation be made in vessels of the United States, or of the Republic of Ecuador.

ARTICLE 5.

For the better understanding of the preceding article, and taking into consideration, the actual

mente introducidas en la República del Ecuador en sus propios buques, puedan tambien ser introducidas en los buques de los Estados Unidos, y que no se impondrán ó cobrarán otros ó mas altos derechos de tonelada, ó por el cargamento, ya sea que la importacion se haga en buques de la una ó de la otra. De la misma manera, cualquiera clase de producciones, manufacturas ó mercaderias de cualquier pais estrangero, que puedan ser en cualquier tiempo legalmente introducidas en los Estados Unidos en sus propios buques, podrán tambien ser introducidas en los buques de la República del Ecuador; y no se impondrán ó cobrarán otros ó mas altos derechos de tonelada ó por el cargamento, ya sea que la importacion se haga en buques de la una ó de la otra. Y convienen que todo lo que pueda ser legalmente esportado ó re-esportado de uno de los dos paises en sus propios buques para un pais estrangero, pueda de la misma manera ser esportado ó re-esportado en los buques del otro. Y los mismos derechos, premios ó descuentos se concederán y cobrarán, sea que la esportacion ó re-esportacion se haga en los buques de la República del Ecuador ó en los de los Estados Unidos.

ARTICULO 5.

Para cabal inteligencia del articulo precedente, y en consideracion al estado de la marina comer-

state of the commercial marine of Ecuador, it has been stipulated and agreed, that all vessels belonging exclusively to a citizen or citizens of said Republic, and whose captain is also a citizen of the same, though the construction or the crew are, or may be foreign, shall be considered for all the objects of this treaty, as an Ecuadorian vessel.

cial de la República del Ecuador, se ha estipulado y convenido que todo buque perteneciente exclusivamente á ciudadano ó ciudadanos de dicha República, y cuyo capitan sea tambien ciudadano de ella, aunque su construccion y tripulacion sean estrangeras, será considerado para todos los efectos de este tratado, como buque Ecuatoriano.

ARTICLE 6.

No higher or other duties shall be imposed on the importation into the United States, of any articles, the produce or manufactures of the Republic of Ecuador; and no higher or other duties shall be imposed on the importation into the Republic of Ecuador, of any articles the produce or manufactures of the United States, than are, or shall be payable on the like articles, being the produce or manufactures of any other foreign country; nor shall any higher or other duties or charges be imposed in either of the two countries, on the exportation of any articles to the United States or to the Republic of Ecuador, respectively, than such as are payable on the exportation of the like articles to any other foreign country; nor shall any prohibition be imposed on the exportation or importation of any articles the produce or manufactures of the United States or of the Republic of Ecuador, to or from the territories of the

ARTICULO 6

No se impondrán otros ó mas altos derechos á la importacion en la República del Ecuador de cualquier articulo, produccion ó manufactura de los Estados Unidos, ni se impondrán otros ó mas altos derechos á la importacion de cualquier articulo, produccion ó manufactura de la República del Ecuador, en los Estados Unidos, que los que se paguen ó pagaren por iguales articulos, produccion ó manufactura de cualquier pais estrangero; ni se impondrán otros ó mas altos derechos ó impuestos en cualquiera de los dos paises, á la esportacion de cualesquiera articulos para la República del Ecuador, ó para los Estados Unidos respectivamente, que los que se paguen ó pagaren á la esportacion de iguales articulos para cualquier otro pais estrangero; ni se prohibirá la importacion ó esportacion en los territorios, ó de los territorios de la República del Ecuador y de los Estados Unidos, de cualesquiera articulos, produccion ó manufac-

United States, or to or from the territories of the Republic of Ecuador, which shall not equally extend to all other nations.

ARTICLE 7.

It is likewise agreed, that it shall be wholly free for all merchants, commanders of ships and other citizens of both countries, to manage themselves, their own business, in all the ports and places subject to the jurisdiction of each other, as well with respect to the consignment and sale of their goods and merchandise by wholesale or retail, as with respect to the loading, unloading and sending off their ships; they being in all these cases to be treated as citizens of the country in which they reside, or, at least, to be placed on a footing with the subjects or citizens of the most favored nation. They shall be subject, however, to such general taxes and contributions, as are, or may be established by law.

ARTICLE 8.

The citizens of neither of the contracting parties, shall be liable to any embargo, nor be detained with their vessels, cargoes merchandises, or effects for any military expedition, nor for any public or private purpose whatever, without allowing to those interested, a sufficient indemnification.

tura de la una ó de la otra, á menos que esta prohibicion sea igualmente estensiva á todas las otras naciones.

ARTICULO 7.

Se conviene ademas, que será enteramente libre y permitido á los comerciantes, comandantes de buques, y otros ciudadanos de ambos paises, el manejar sus negocios por si mismos, en todos los puertos y lugares sujetos á la jurisdiccion de uno ú otro, asi respecto de las consignaciones y ventas por mayor y menor de sus efectos y mercaderias, como de la carga y descarga y despacho de sus buques, debiendo en todos estos casos, ser tratados como ciudadanos del pais en que residan, ó al menos puestos sobre un pie igual con los subditos ó ciudadanos de las naciones mas favorecidas. Estarán sugetos, sin embargo, á los impuestos y contribuciones generales, establecidas por ley, ó que por ella, se establecieren.

ARTICULO 8

Los ciudadanos de una ú otra parte no podrán ser embargados ni detenidos con sus embarcaciones, tripulaciones, mercaderias y efectos comerciales, de su pertenencia, para alguna expedicion militar, usos públicos ó particulares, cualesquiera que sean, sin conceder á los interesados una suficiente indemnizacion.

ARTICLE 9.

Whenever the citizens of either of the contracting parties, shall be forced to seek refuge or asylum, in the rivers, bays, ports or dominions of the other, with their vessels, whether merchant or of war, public or private, through stress of weather, pursuit of pirates or enemies, they shall be received and treated with humanity; giving to them all favor and protection for repairing their ships, procuring provisions, and placing themselves in a situation to continue their voyage, without obstacle or hindrance of any kind.

ARTICLE 10.

All the ships, merchandise, and the effects belonging to the citizens of one of the contracting parties, which may be captured by pirates, whether within the limits of its jurisdiction or on the high seas, and may be carried or found in the rivers, roads, bays, ports or dominions of the other, shall be delivered up to the owners, they proving, in due and proper form, their rights, before the competent tribunals; it being well understood, that the claim should be made within the term of one year, by the parties themselves, their attorneys, or agents of their respective governments.

ARTICULO 9

Siempre que los ciudadanos de alguna de las partes contratantes se vieren precisados á buscar refugio ó asilo en los rios, bahias, puertos ó dominios de la otra con sus buques, ya sean mercantes ó de guerra, publicos ó particulares, por mal tiempo, persecucion de piratas ó enemigos, serán recibidos y tratados con humanidad, dandoles todo favor y proteccion para reparar sus buques, procurar viveres, y ponerse en situacion de continuar su viage, sin obstaculo ó estorbo de ningun genero.

ARTICULO 10.

Todos los buques, mercaderias y efectos pertenecientes á los ciudadanos de una de las partes contratantes, que sean apresados por piratas, bien sea dentro de los limites de su jurisdiccion ó en alta mar, y fueren llevados ó hallados en los rios, radas, bahias, puertos ó dominios de la otra, serán entregados á sus dueños, probando estos, en la forma propia y debida, sus derechos ante los tribunales competentes; bien entendido que el reclamo ha de hacerse dentro del termino de un año, por las mismas partes, sus apoderados, ó agentes de los respectivos Gobiernos.

ARTICLE 11.

When any vessels belonging to the citizens of either of the contracting parties, shall be wrecked, foundered, or shall suffer any damage on the coasts or within the dominions of the other, there shall be given to them, all assistance and protection in the same manner which is usual and customary with the vessels of the nation where the damage happens, permitting them to unload the said vessel, if necessary of its merchandise and effects, without exacting for it, any duty, impost, or contribution whatever, unless they be destined for consumption.

ARTICLE 12.

The citizens of each of the contracting parties shall have power to dispose of their personal goods within the jurisdiction of the other, by sale, donation, testament or otherwise, and their representatives, being citizens of the other party, shall succeed to their said personal goods, whether by testament or *ab intestato*, and they may take possession thereof, either by themselves or by others acting for them, and dispose of the same at their will, paying such duties only, as the inhabitants of the country wherein the said goods are, shall be subject to pay in like cases. And if in the case of real estate, the said heirs would be prevented from entering into the possession of the in-

ARTICULO 11.

Cuando algun buque perteneciente á los ciudadanos de alguna de las partes contratantes, naufrague, encalle, ó sufra alguna averia en las costas ó dentro de los dominios de la otra, se les dará toda ayuda y proteccion, del mismo modo que es uso y costumbre con los buques de la nacion en donde suceda la averia; permitiendoles descargar el dicho buque, si fuere necesario, de sus mercaderias y efectos, sin cobrar por esto, ningun derecho, impuesto ó contribucion, á menos que se destinen al consumo.

ARTICULO 12.

Los ciudadanos de cada una de las partes contratantes tendrán pleno poder para disponer de sus bienes personales dentro de la jurisdiccion de la otra, por venta, donacion, testamento, ó de otro modo; y sus representantes, siendo ciudadanos de la otra parte, sucederán á sus dichos bienes personales, ya sea por testamento ó *ab intestato*, y podrán tomar posesion de ellos, ya sea por si mismos ó por otros que obren por ellos, y disponer de los mismos segun su voluntad, pagando aquellas cargas solamente que los habitantes del pais en donde estan los referidos bienes, estuvieren sujetos á pagar en iguales casos. Y si en el caso de bienes raices los dichos

heritance on account of their character of aliens, there shall be granted to them, the term of three years, to dispose of the same as they may think proper, and to withdraw the proceeds without molestation, nor any other charges than those which are imposed by the laws of the country.

Article 13.

Both the contracting parties promise and engage, formally, to give their special protection to the persons and property of the citizens of each other, of all occupations, who may be in the territories subject to the jurisdiction of the one or the other, transient or dwelling therein, leaving open and free to them, the tribunals of justice, for their judicial recourse, on the same terms which are usual and customary with the natives or citizens of the country, in which they may be; for which they may employ in defence of their rights, such advocates, solicitors, notaries, agents and factors, as they may judge proper, in all their trials at law; and such citizens or agents shall have free opportunity to be present at the decisions and sentences of the tribunals, in all cases which may concern them; and likewise at the taking of all examinations and evidence which may be exhibited on the said trials.

herederos fuesen impedidos de entrar en la posesion de la herencia por razon de su caracter de estrangeros, se les dará el termino de tres años para disponer de ella como juzguen conveniente, y para estraer su producto sin molestia, ni otros impuestos que los establecidos por las leyes del pais.

Articulo 13.

Ambas partes contratantes se comprometen y obligan formalmente á dar su proteccion especial á las personas y propiedades de los ciudadanos de cada una reciprocamente, transeuntes ó habitantes, de todas ocupaciones, en los territorios sujetos á la jurisdiccion de una y otra, dejandoles abiertos y libres los tribunales de justicia para sus recursos judiciales, en los mismos terminos que son de uso y costumbre para los naturales ó ciudadanos del pais en que residan; para lo cual, podrán emplear en defenza de sus derechos, aquellos abogados, procuradores, escribanos, agentes ó factores, que juzguen conveniente, en todos sus asuntos y litijios; y dichos ciudadanos ó agentes tendrán la libre facultad de estar presentes en las decisiones y sentencias de los tribunales, en todos los casos que conciernan á aquellos, como igualmente al tomar todos los examenes y declaraciones que se ofrezcan en los dichos litijios.

ARTICLE 14.

It is likewise agreed that the most perfect and entire security of conscience may be enjoyed by the citizens of both the contracting parties, in the countries subject to the jurisdiction of the one & the other, without their being liable to be disturbed or molested on account of their religious belief, so long as they respect the laws and established usages of the country. Moreover, the bodies of the citizens of one of the contracting parties, who may die in the territories of the other, shall be buried in the usual burying grounds, or in other decent or suitable places, and shall be protected from violation or disturbance.

ARTICLE 15.

It shall be lawful for the citizens of the United States of America and of the Republic of Ecuador, to sail with their ships, with all manner of liberty and security, no distinction being made who are the proprietors of the merchandises laden thereon, from any port, to the places of those who now are, or hereafter shall be at enmity with either of the contracting parties. It shall likewise be lawful, for the citizens aforesaid, to sail with their ships and merchandises before mentioned, and to trade with the same liberty and security from the places, ports

ARTICULO 14.

Se conviene igualmente, en que los ciudadanos de ambas partes contratantes, gozen la mas perfecta y entera seguridad de conciencia en los paises sugetos á la jurisdiccion de una ú otra, sin quedar, por ello, espuestos á ser inquietados ó molestados, en razon de su creencia religiosa, mientras que respeten las leyes y usos establecidos. Ademas de esto, podrán sepultarse los cadáveres, de los ciudadanos de una de las partes contratantes, que fallecieren en los territorios de la otra, en los cementerios acostumbrados, ó en otros lugares decentes y adecuados; los cuales serán protegidos, contra toda violacion ó trastorno.

ARTICULO 15

Será licito á los ciudadanos de la República del Ecuador y de los Estados Unidos de America, navegar con sus buques, con toda seguridad y libertad, de cualquier puerto á las plazas ó lugares de los que son ó fueren en adelante enemigos de cualquiera de las dos partes contratantes, sin hacerse distincion de quienes son los dueños de las mercancias cargadas en ellos. Será igualmente licito á los referidos ciudadanos, navegar con sus buques y mercaderias mencionadas, y traficar con la misma libertad y seguridad, de los lugares, puertos y ensenadas de los enemigos de ambas partes,

and havens of those who are enemies of both,˙ or either party, without any opposition or disturbance whatsoever; not only directly from the places of the enemy before mentioned, to neutral places, but also from one place belonging to an enemy, to another place belonging to an enemy, whether they be under the jurisdiction of one power, or under several. And it is hereby stipulated, that free ships shall also give freedom to goods, and that every thing shall be deemed free and exempt, which shall be found on board the ships belonging to the citizens of either of the contracting parties, although the whole lading, or any part thereof, should appertain to the enemies of either; contraband goods being always excepted. It is also agreed in like manner, that the same liberty shall be extended to persons who are on board a free ship, with this effect, that, although they may be enemies to both, or either party, they are not to be taken out of that free ship, unless they are officers or soldiers, and in the actual service of the enemies. Provided however, and it is hereby agreed that the stipulations in this article contained, declaring that the flag shall cover the property, shall be understood as applying to those powers only, who recognize this principle; but if either of the two contracting parties shall be at war with a

ó de alguna de ellas, sin ninguna oposicion ó disturbio cualquiera, no solo directamente de los lugares del enemigo arriba mencionados á lugares neutros, sino tambien de un lugar perteneciente á un enemigo, á otro enemigo, ya sea que esten bajo la jurisdiccion de una potencia, ó bajo la de diversas. Y queda aqui estipulado, que los buques libres dan tambien libertad á las mercaderias, y que se ha de considerar libre y esento, todo lo que se hallare á bordo de los buques pertenecientes á los ciudadanos de cualquiera de las partes contratantes, aun que toda la carga ó parte de ella pertenezca á enemigos de una ú otra, esceptuando siempre articulos de contrabando de guerra. Se conviene tambien del mismo modo, en que la misma libertad se estienda á las personas que se encuentren á bordo de buques libres, con el fin de que aunque dichas personas sean enemigos de ambas partes ó de alguna de ellas, no deban ser estraidos de los buques libres á menos que sean oficiales ó soldados en actual servicio de los enemigos: á condicion no ostante, y se conviene aqui en esto, que las estipulaciones contenidas en el presente articulo, declarando que el pabellon cubre la propiedad, se entenderán aplicables solamente á aquellas potencias que reconocen este principio; pero si alguna de las dos partes contratantes estuviere en guerra con una tercera, y

third, and the other neutral, the flag of the neutral shall cover the property of enemies, whose governments acknowledge this principle, and not of others.

ARTICLE 16.

It is likewise agreed that in the case where the neutral flag of one of the contracting parties shall protect the property of the enemies of the other, by virtue of the above stipulations, it shall always be understood, that the neutral property found on board such enemy's vessels, shall be held and considered as enemy's property, and as such, shall be liable to detention and confiscation; except such property as was put on board such vessel before the declaration of war, or even afterwards, if it were done without the knowledge of it: but the contracting parties agree, that six months having elapsed after the declaration, their citizens shall not plead ignorance thereof. On the contrary, if the flag of the neutral does not protect the enemy's property, in that case, the goods & merchandises of the neutral, embarked in such enemy's ship, shall be free.

ARTICLE 17.

This liberty of navigation and commerce, shall extend to all kinds of merchandise, excepting those only, which are distinguished

la otra permaneciese neutral, la bandera de la neutral cubrirá la propiedad de los enemigos cuyos Gobiernos reconocen este principio, y no de otros.

ARTICULO 16.

Se conviene igualmente que en caso de que la bandera neutral de una de las partes contratantes, proteja las propiedades de los enemigos de la otra, en virtud de lo estipulado arriba, deberá siempre entenderse, que las propiedades neutrales encontradas á bordo de tales buques enemigos, han de tenerse y considerarse como propiedades enemigas, y como tales estarán sujetas á detencion y confiscacion; esceptuando solamente aquellas propiedades que hubiesen sido puestas á bordo de tales buques antes de la declaracion de la guerra, y aun despues, si hubiesen sido embarcadas en dichos buques sin tener noticia de la guerra: y se conviene que pasados seis meses despues de la declaracion, los ciudadanos de una y otra parte no podrán alegar que la ignoraban. Por el contrario, si la bandera neutral no protegiese las propiedades enemigas, entonces serán libres los efectos y mercaderias de la parte neutral embarcadas en buques enemigos.

ARTICULO 17.

Esta libertad de navegacion y comercio se estenderá á todo genero de mercaderias, esceptuando aquellas solamente que se dis-

by the name of contraband: and under this name of contraband or prohibited goods, shall be comprehended:

1st. Cannons, mortars, howitzers, swivels, blunderbusses, muskets, fusees, rifles, carbines, pistols, pikes, swords, sabres, lances, spears, halberds, and grenades; bombs, powder, matches, balls, and all other things belonging to the use of these arms.

2nd. Bucklers, helmets, breastplates, coats of mail, infantry-belts, and clothes made up in military form and for military use.

3rd. Cavalry belts, and horses with their furniture.

4th. And generally, all kinds of arms and instruments of iron, steel, brass, and copper, or of any other materials, manufactured, prepared and formed expressly to make war, by sea or land.

ARTICLE 18.

All other merchandises and things, not comprehended in the articles of contraband explicitly enumerated and classified as above, shall be held and considered as free, and subjects of free and lawful commerce, so that they may be carried and transported in the freest manner, by the citizens of both the contracting parties, even to places belonging to an enemy; excepting only, those places, which are, at that time, besieged or blockaded: and to avoid

tinguen con el nombre de contra-bando; y bajo este nombre de contrabando ó efectos prohibidos, se comprenderán:

1º Cañones, morteros, obuces, pedreros, trabucos, mosquetes, fusiles, rifles, carabinas, pistolas, picas, espadas, sables, lanzas, chuzos, alabardas, y granadas, bómbas, pólvora, mechas, balas, con las demas cosas correspondientes al uso de estas armas.

2º Escudos, casquetes, corazas, cotas de malla, fornituras, y vestidos hechos en forma y á usanza militar.

3º Bandoleras y caballos, junto con sus armas y arneses

4º Y generalmente, toda especie de armas é instrumentos de hierro, acero, bronce, cobre, y otras materias cualesquiera, manufacturadas, preparadas y formadas espresamente para hacer la guerra por mar ó tierra.

ARTICULO 18.

Todas las demas mercaderias y efectos no comprendidos en los articulos de contrabando esplicitamente enumerados y clasificados en el articulo anterior, serán tenidos y reputados por libres, y de licito y libre comercio, de modo que ellos puedan ser transportados y llevados de la manera mas libre por los ciudadanos de ambas partes contratantes, aun á los lugares pertenecientes á un enemigo de una ú otra, esceptuando solamente aquellos luga-

all doubt in this particular, it is declared that those places only are besieged or blockaded which are actually attacked by a belligerant force capable of preventing the entry of a neutral.

res ó plazas que estan al mismo tiempo sitiadas ó bloqueadas, y para evitar toda duda en el particular, se declaran sitiadas ó bloqueadas aquellas plazas que en la actualidad estuviesen atacadas por una fuerza de un beligerante capaz de impedir la entrada del neutral.

Article 19.

The articles of contraband before enumerated and classified, which may be found in a vessel bound for an enemy's port, shall be subject to detention and confiscation, leaving free the rest of the cargo and the ship, that the owners may dispose of them as they may see proper. No vessel of either of the two nations shall be detained on the high seas, on account of having on board, articles of contraband, whenever the master, captain or supercargo of said vessel, will deliver up the articles of contraband to the captor, unless the quantity of such articles be so great or of so large a bulk, that they cannot be received on board the capturing ship, without great inconvenience; but in this and in all other cases of just detention, the vessel detained shall be sent to the nearest convenient and safe port, for trial and judgment according to law.

Articulo 19

Los articulos de contrabando antes enumerados y clasificados, que se hallen en un buque destinado á puerto enemigo, estarán sujetos á detencion y confiscacion, dejando libre el resto del cargamento y el buque para que los dueños puedan disponer de ellos como lo crean conveniente. Ningun buque de cualquiera de las dos naciones, será detenido por tener á bordo articulos de contrabando, siempre que el maestre, capitan ó sobrecargo de dicho buque, quiera entregar los articulos de contrabando al apresador, á menos que la cantidad de estos articulos sea tan grande y de tanto volúmen que no puedan ser recibidos a bordo del buque apresador sin grandes inconvenientes; pero en este, como en todos los otros casos de justa detencion, el buque detenido será enviado al puerto mas inmediato, comodo y seguro, para ser juzgado y sentenciado conforme á las leyes.

ARTICLE 20.

And whereas it frequently happens, that vessels sail for a port or places belonging to an enemy, without knowing that the same is besieged, blockaded or invested, it is agreed that every vessel so circumstanced, may be turned away from such port or place, but shall not be detained, nor shall any part of her cargo, if not contraband, be confiscated; unless after warning of such blockade or investment, from any officer commanding a vessel of the blockading forces, they shall again attempt to enter; but she shall be permitted to go to any other port or place, she shall think proper. Nor shall any vessel of either, that may have entered into such port before the same was actually besieged, blockaded or invested by the other, be restrained from quitting such place with her cargo; nor, if found therein, after the reduction and surrender, shall such vessel or her cargo be liable to confiscation, but they shall be restored to the owners thereof.

ARTICLE 21.

In order to prevent all kinds of disorder, in the visiting and examination of the ships and cargoes of both the contracting parties, on the high seas, they have agreed, mutually, that, whenever a vessel

ARTICULO 20.

Y por cuanto frecuentemente sucede que los buques navegan para un puerto ó lugar perteneciente á un enemigo, sin saber que aquel esté sitiado, bloqueado ó investido, se conviene en que todo buque en estas circunstancias se pueda hacer volver de dicho puerto ó lugar, pero no será detenido ni confiscado parte alguna de su cargamento, no siendo contrabando; á menos que despues de la intimacion de semejante bloqueo ó ataque por cualquier comandante de un buque de las fuerzas bloqueadoras, intentase otra vez entrar; pero le será permitido ir á cualquier otro puerto ó lugar que juzgue conveniente. Ni ningun buque de una de las partes que haya entrado en semejante puerto ó lugar, antes que estuviese sitiado, bloqueado ó investido por la otra, será impedido de dejar el tal lugar con su cargamento, ni si fuere hallado allí despues de la rendicion y entrega de semejante lugar, estará el tal buque ó su cargamento sujeto á confiscacion, sino que serán restituidos á sus dueños.

ARTICULO 21.

Para evitar todo genero de desorden en la visita y ecsámen de los buques y cargamentos de ambas partes contratantes en alta mar, han convenido mutuamente, que siempre que un buque

of war, public or private, shall meet with a neutral of the other contracting party, the first shall remain out of cannon shot, and may send its boats with two or three men only, in order to execute the said examination of the papers, concerning the ownership and cargo of the vessel, without causing the least extortion, violence or ill-treatment, for which, the commanders of the said armed ships, shall be responsible, with their persons and property: for which purpose, the commanders of the said private armed vessels shall, before receiving their commissions, give sufficient security, to answer for all the damages, they may commit; and it is expressly agreed, that the neutral party shall, in no case, be required to go on board the examining vessel, for the purpose of exhibiting his papers, or for any other purpose whatever.

de guerra público ó particular se encontrase con un neutral de la otra parte contratante, el primero permanecerá fuera de tiro de cañon, y podrá mandar su bote con dos ó tres hombres solamente, para ejecutar el dicho ecsamen de los papeles concernientes á la propiedad y carga del buque, sin ocasionar la menor estorsion, violencia ó mal tratamiento, por lo que los comandantes de dichos buques armados serán responsables con sus personas y bienes; á cuyo efecto los comandantes de buques armados, por cuenta de particulares, estarán obligados antes de entregarseles sus comisiones ó patentes, á dar fianza suficiente para responder de los perjuicios que causen. Y se ha convenido espresamente, que en ningun caso se ecsigirá á la parte neutral que vaya á bordo del buque ecsaminador con el fin de ecsibir sus papeles, ó para cualquier otro objeto, sea el que fuere.

ARTICLE 22.

To avoid all kind of vexation and abuse, in the examination of the papers relating to the ownership of the vessels belonging to the citizens of the two contracting parties, they have agreed and do agree, that in case one of them should be engaged in war, the ships and vessels belonging to the citizens of the other, must be furnished with sea-letters or passports, expressing the name, prop-

ARTICULO 22.

Para evitar toda clase de vejamen y abuso en el ecsamen de los papeles relativos á la propiedad de los buques pertenecientes á los ciudadanos de las dos partes contratantes, han convenido y convienen que en caso de que una de ellas estuviere en guerra, los buques y bajeles pertenecientes á los ciudadanos de la otra, serán provistos con letras de mar ó pasaportes, espresando el nom-

erty and bulk of the ships; as also, the name and place of habitation of the master and commander of said vessel, in order that it may thereby appear that said ship truly belongs to the citizens of one of the parties; they have likewise agreed, that such ships being laden, besides the said sea-letters or passports, shall also be provided with certificates containing the several particulars of the cargo, and the place whence the ship sailed, so that it may be known whether any forbidden or contraband goods be on board the same; which certificates shall be made out by the officers of the place whence the ship sailed, in the accustomed form: without such requisites said vessels may be detained, to be adjudged by the competent tribunal, and may be declared legal prize, unless the said defect shall be proved to be owing to accident, and satisfied or supplied by testimony entirely equivalent.

ARTICLE 23.

It is further agreed that the stipulations above expressed relative to the visiting and examination of vessels, shall apply only to those which sail without convoy, & when said vessels shall be under convoy, the verbal declaration of the commander of the convoy, on his word of honor, that the vessels

bre, propiedad y tamaño del buque, como tambien el nombre y lugar de la residencia del maestre ó comandante, á fin de que se vea que el buque real y verdaderamente pertenece á los ciudadanos de una de las partes; y han convenido igualmente, que estando cargados los expresados buques, ademas de las letras de mar ó pasaportes, estarán tambien provistos de certificados, que contengan los por menores del cargamento y el lugar de donde salió el buque, para que asi pueda saberse si hay á su bordo algunos efectos prohibidos ó de contrabando, cuyos certificados serán hechos por los oficiales del lugar de la procedencia del buque en la forma acostumbrada; sin tales requisitos el dicho buque puede ser detenido, para ser juzgado por el tribunal competente, y puede ser declarado buena presa á menos que prueben que la falta emana de accidente y satisfagan ó suplan el defecto con testimonios enteramente equivalentes.

ARTICULO 23.

Se ha convenido ademas, que las estipulaciones anteriores relativas al ecsamen y visita de buques, se aplicarán solamente á los que navegan sin convoy, y cuando los dichos buques estuviesen bajo de convoy, será bastante la declaracion verbal del comandante del convoy, bajo

under his protection belong to the nation whose flag he carries; and when they are bound to an enemy's port, that they have no contraband goods on board, shall be sufficient.

su palabra de honor, de que los buques que estan bajo su proteccion pertenecen á la nacion cuya bandera llevan; y cuando se dirijen á un puerto enemigo, que dichos buques no tienen á su bordo articulos de contrabando de guerra.

ARTICLE 24.

It is further agreed, that in all cases, the established courts for prize causes, in the country to which the prizes may be conducted, shall alone take cognizance of them; and whenever such tribunals, of either party, shall pronounce judgment against any vessel, or goods or property claimed by the citizens of the other party, the sentence or decree shall mention the reasons or motives, on which the same shall have been founded, and an authenticated copy of the sentence or decree, and of all the proceedings in the case, shall, if demanded, be delivered to the commander or agent of said vessel, without any delay, he paying the legal fees for the same.

ARTICULO 24.

Se ha convenido ademas, que en todos los casos que ocurran, solo los tribunales establecidos para causas de presas en el pais á que las presas sean conducidas tomarán conocimiento de ellas. Y siempre que semejante tribunal de cualquiera de las partes, pronunciase sentencia contra algun buque, ó efectos ó propiedad reclamada por los ciudadanos de la otra parte, la sentencia ó decreto hará mencion de las razones ó motivos en que aquella se haya fundado, y se entregará sin demora alguna al comandante ó agente de dicho buque, si lo solicitase, un testimonio autentico de la sentencia ó decreto, ó de todo el proceso, pagando por él los derechos legales.

ARTICLE 25.

Whenever one of the contracting parties shall be engaged in war with another State, no citizen of the other contracting party shall accept a commission or letter of marque, for the purpose of assisting or co-operating hostilely with the said enemy, against the said

ARTICULO 25.

Siempre que una de las partes contratantes estuviere empeñada en guerra con otro estado, ningun ciudadano de la otra parte contratante aceptará una comision ó letra de marca para el objeto de ayudar ó cooperar hostilmente con el dicho enemigo contra la

party so at war, under the pain of being considered as a pirate.

ARTICLE 26.

If, by any fatality, which cannot be expected, and which God forbid, the two contracting parties should be engaged in a war with each other, they have agreed, and do agree, now for then, that there shall be allowed the term of six months to the merchants residing on the coasts and in the ports of each other, and the term of one year to those who dwell in the interior, to arrange their business and transport their effects, wherever they please, giving to them, the safe-conduct necessary for it, which may serve as a sufficient protection, until they arrive at the designated port. The citizens of all other occupations, who may be established in the territories or dominions of the United States and the Republic of Ecuador, shall be respected, and maintained in the full enjoyment of their personal liberty and property, unless their particular conduct shall cause them to forfeit this protection, which, in consideration of humanity, the contracting parties engage to give them.

ARTICLE 27.

Neither the debts due from individuals of the one nation to the individuals of the other, nor shares, nor moneys which they may have in public funds, nor in

dicha parte que esté asi en guerra, bajo la pena de ser tratado como pirata.

ARTICULO 26

Si por alguna fatalidad que no puede esperarse, y que Dios no permita, las dos partes contratantes se viesen empeñadas en guerra una con otra, han convenido y convienen de ahora para entonces, que se concederá el termino de seis meses á los comerciantes residentes en las costas y en los puertos de entrambas, y el termino de un año á los que habitan en el interior, para arreglar sus negocios y transportar sus efectos á donde quieran, dandoles el salvo conducto necesario para ello, que les sirva de suficiente proteccion hasta que lleguen al puerto que designen. Los ciudadanos de otras ocupaciones que se hallen establecidos en los territorios y dominios de la República del Ecuador, ó de los Estados Unidos, serán respetados y mantenidos en el pleno gozo de su libertad personal y propiedad, á menos que su conducta particular les haga perder esta proteccion, que en consideracion á la humanidad, las partes contratantes se comprometan á prestarles.

ARTICULO 27

Ni las deudas contraidas por los individuos de una nacion con los individuos de la otra, ni las acciones ó dineros que puedan tener en los fondos publicos ó en

public nor private banks, shall ever, in any event of war, or of national difference, be sequestered or confiscated.

ARTICLE 28.

Both the contracting parties being desirous of avoiding all inequality in relation to their public communications and official intercourse, have agreed and do agree, to grant to the envoys, ministers and other public agents, the same favors, immunities and exemptions, which those of the most favored nation do or shall enjoy: it being understood, that whatever favors, immunities or privileges, the United States of America or the Republic of Ecuador may find it proper to give to the ministers and other public agents of any other power, shall, by the same act be extended to those of each of the contracting parties.

ARTICLE 29.

To make more effectual the protection which the United States and the Republic of Ecuador shall afford in future, to the navigation and commerce of the citizens of each other, they agree to receive and admit consuls and vice-consuls, in all the ports open to foreign commerce, who shall enjoy in them, all the rights, prerogatives and immunities of the consuls and vice-consuls of the most

los bancos publicos ó privados, serán jamas secuestrados ó confiscados en ningun caso de guerra ó de diferencia nacional.

ARTICULO 28

Deseando ambas partes contratantes evitar toda diferencia relativa á etiqueta en sus comunicaciones y correspondencias diplomaticas, han convenido así mismo, y convienen en conceder á sus enviados y ministros y otros agentes diplomaticos, los mismos favores, inmunidades y esenciones de que gozan ó gozaren en lo venidero los de las naciones mas favorecidas; bien entendido, que cualquier favor, inmunidad ó privilegio que la República del Ecuador ó los Estados Unidos de America tengan por conveniente dispensar á los enviados, ministros y agentes diplomaticos de otras potencias, se haga por el mismo hecho estensivo á los de una y otra de las partes contratantes.

ARTICULO 29.

Para hacer mas efectiva la proteccion que la República del Ecuador y los Estados Unidos darán en adelante á la navegacion y comercio de los ciudadanos de una y otra, se convienen en recibir y admitir consules y vice-consules en todos los puertos abiertos al comercio estrangero, quienes gozarán en ellos de todos los derechos, prerogativas é inmunidades de los consules y vice-

favored nation; each contracting party, however, remaining at liberty to except those ports and places, in which the admission and residence of such consuls and vice-consuls, may not seem convenient.

ARTICLE 30.

In order that the consuls and vice-consuls of the two contracting parties, may enjoy the rights, prerogatives and immunities which belong to them by their public character, they shall, before entering on the exercise of their functions, exhibit their commission or patent in due form to the Government to which they are accredited, and, having obtained their *exequatur*, they shall be held and considered as such, by all the authorities, magistrates and inhabitants in the consular district in which they reside.

ARTICLE 31.

It is likewise agreed that the consuls, their secretaries, officers and persons attached to the service of consuls, they not being citizens of the country in which the consul resides, shall be exempted from all kinds of taxes, imposts and contributions, except those which they shall be obliged to pay on account of commerce or their property, to which the citizens and inhabitants, native and foreign, of the country in

consules de la nacion mas favorecida; quedando no ostante en libertad cada parte contratante, para esceptuar aquellos puertos y lugares en que la admision y residencia de semejantes consules y vice-consules no parezca conveniente.

ARTICULO 30.

Para que los consules y vice-consules de las dos partes contratantes puedan gozar de los derechos prerogativas é inmunidades que les correspondan por su caracter publico, antes de entrar en el ejercicio de sus funciones, presentarán su comision ó patente, en la forma debida, al Gobierno con quien esten acreditados, y habiendo obtenido el *exequatur*, serán tenidos y considerados como tales por todas las autoridades, magistrados y habitantes del distrito consular en que residan.

ARTICULO 31.

Se ha convenido igualmente que los consules, sus secretarios, oficiales y personas agregadas al servicio de los consulados, (no siendo estas personas ciudadanos del pais en que el consul reside,) estarán escentos de toda clase de pechos, impuestos y contribuciones, esceptuando aquellos que estén obligados á pagar por razon de comercio ó propiedad, y á los cuales estan sujetos los ciudadanos y habitantes naturales y es-

which they reside, are subject; being in every thing besides, subject to the laws of the respective States. The archives and papers of the consulates shall be respected inviolably, and, under no pretext whatever, shall any magistrate seize, or in any way interfere with them.

trangeros del pais en que residen, quedando en todo lo demas sujetos á las leyes de los respectivos Estados. Los archivos y papeles de los consulados serán respetados inviolablemente, y bajo ningun pretesto los ocupará magistrado alguno, ni tendrá con ellos ninguna intervencion.

ARTICLE 32.

The said consuls shall have power to require the assistance of the authorities of the country, for the arrest, detention and custody, of deserters from the public and private vessels of their country, and for that purpose, they shall address themselves to the courts, judges and officers competent, and shall demand the said deserters in writing; proving by an exhibition of the register of the vessel's or ship's roll, or other public documents, that those men were part of the said crews, and on this demand so proved, (saving, however, where the contrary is proved,) the delivery shall not be refused. Such deserters, when arrested, shall be put at the disposal of said consuls, and may be put in the public prisons, at the request and expense of those who reclaim them, to be sent to the ships to which they belonged, or to others of the same nation. But if they be not sent back within two months, to be counted from the day of their arrest, they shall

ARTICULO 32.

Los dichos consules tendrán poder de requerir el ausilio de las autoridades locales para la prision, detencion y custodia de los desertores de los buques publicos y particulares, de su pais, y para este objeto se dirijirán á los tribunales, jueces y oficiales competentes, y pedirán los dichos desertores por escrito, probando por una presentacion de los registros de los buques, rol de equipage ú otros documentos públicos, que aquellos hombres, eran parte de las dichas tripulaciones, y á esta demanda así probada (menos, no ostante, cuando se probase lo contrario) no se recusará la entrega. Semejantes desertores luego que sean arrestados, se pondrán á disposicion de los dichos consules, y pueden ser depositados en las prisiones publicas, á solicitud y espensas de los que los reclamen, para ser enviados á los buques á que correspondan ó á otros de la misma nacion. Pero sino fueren mandados dentro de dos meses con-

be set at liberty, and shall be no more arrested for the same cause.

Article 33.

For the purpose of more effectually protecting their commerce and navigation, the two contracting parties do hereby agree, as soon hereafter as circumstances will permit them, to form a consular convention, which shall declare especially, the powers and immunities of the consuls and vice-consuls of the respective parties.

Article 34.

It is further agreed, that the words, 'most favored nation', that occur in this treaty, shall not be so construed as to prevent either of the contracting parties, from concluding any treaty or convention, with any other nation or state, it may think proper, as freely and as fully as though said words were not used: Provided however, that notwithstanding any such treaty or convention, the citizens of the United States shall be placed in Ecuador, with respect to navigation and commerce, upon an equal footing with the subjects of Spain and with the citizens of Mexico and of the other Hispano-American States, with which treaties have been, or may be, concluded; and that the citizens of Ecuador shall be entitled to enjoy, in the United

tados desde el dia de su arresto, serán puestos en libertad, y no volverán á ser presos por la misma causa.

Articulo 33.

Para proteger mas efectivamente su comercio y navegacion, las dos partes contratantes se convienen en formar luego que las circunstancias lo permitan, una convencion consular, que declare mas especialmente los poderes ó inmunidades de los consules y vice-consules de las partes respectivas.

Articulo 34.

Se conviene ademas, que las palabras, 'la nacion mas favorecida', que se encuentran en este tratado, no serán entendidas de modo, que impidan á la una ó á la otra, de las partes contratantes, celebrar el tratado ó convenio, con cualquier nacion ó estado, que tenga por conveniente, tan libre y estensamente, como si dichas palabras no ecsistiesen; con tal que, no ostante tal tratado ó convenio, los ciudadanos de los Estados Unidos, estén puestos, en el Ecuador, con respecto á navegacion y comercio, sobre un pie igual con los subditos de la España, y con los ciudadanos de Mejico y de los otros estados Hispano-Americanos, con quienes haya de tratar ó tenga tratados ecsistentes; y que los ciudadanos del Ecuador sean admitidos á

States, the same rights and privileges, with respect to navigation and commerce, that the citizens of the United States enjoy, or shall enjoy, in Ecuador.

gozar, en los Estados Unidos, de los mismos derechos y privilegios, respecto de navegacion y comercio, que gozan ó gozaren los ciudadanos de los Estados Unidos en el Ecuador.

ARTICLE 35.

The United States of America and the Republic of Ecuador, desiring to make as durable, as circumstances will permit, the relations which are to be established between the two parties, by virtue of this treaty of peace, amity, commerce and navigation, have declared solemnly, and do agree to the following points:

1st. The present treaty shall remain in full force and virtue for the term of twelve years, to be counted from the day of exchange of the ratifications, and further, until the end of one year, after either of the contracting parties shall have given notice to the other, of its intention to terminate the same; each of the contracting parties reserving to itself, the right of giving such notice to the other at the end of said term of twelve years: And it is hereby agreed between them, that on the expiration of one year, after such notice shall have been received by either, from the other party, this treaty, in all its parts relative to commerce and navigation, shall altogether cease and

ARTICULO 35

La República del Ecuador y los Estados Unidos de America, deseando hacer tan duraderas y firmes como las circunstancias lo permitan, las relacionas que han de establecerse entre las dos potencias en virtud del presente tratado de paz, amistad, navegacion y comercio, han declarado solemnemente, y convienen en los puntos siguientes.

1º El presente tratado permanecerá en su fuerza y vigor por el termino de doce años, contados desde el dia del cange de las ratificaciones, y ademas hasta un año despues que cualquiera de las partes contratantes haya notificado á la otra su intencion de terminarlo; reservandose las partes contratantes el derecho de hacer tal notificacion la una á la otra al fin de dicho termino de doce años. Y ademas se ha convenido que este tratado, en todo lo relativo á comercio y navegacion, quedará sin efecto transcurrido que sea un año despues de recibida dicha notificacion por cualquiera de las dos partes, y en todo lo relativo á paz y amistad, será perpetua-

determine, and in all those parts which relate to peace and friendship, it shall be perpetually and permanently binding on both powers.

2nd. If any one or more of the citizens of either party, shall infringe any of the articles of this treaty, such citizen shall be held personally responsible for the same, and harmony and good correspondence between the two nations shall not be interrupted thereby, each party engaging in no way to protect the offender, or sanction such violation.

3rd. If, (what indeed cannot be expected) unfortunately, any of the articles contained in the present treaty, shall be violated or infringed in any way whatever, it is expressly stipulated, that neither of the contracting parties will order or authorize any act of reprisal, nor declare war against the other on complaints of injuries or damages, until the said party considering itself offended, shall first have presented to the other, a statement of such injuries or damages, verified by competent proofs, and demanded justice, and the same shall have been either refused or unreasonably delayed.

4th. Nothing in this treaty shall, however, be construed or operate contrary to former and existing public treaties with other sovereigns and states.

mente obligatorio á ambos poderes.

2º Si alguno ó algunos de los ciudadanos de una ú otra parte infringiesen algunos de los articulos contenidos en el presente tratado, dichos ciudadanos serán personalmente responsables, sin que por esto se interrumpa la armonia y buena correspondencia entre las dos naciones, comprometiendose cada una á no protejer de modo alguno al ofensor, ó sancionar semejante violacion.

3º Si, (lo que á la verdad no puede esperarse) desgraciadamente algunos de los articulos contenidos en el presente tratado fuesen en alguna otra manera violados ó infringidos, se estipula espresamente que ninguna de las dos partes contratantes ordenará ó autorizará ningunos actos de represalia, ni declarará la guerra contra la otra, por quejas de injurias ó daños, hasta que la parte que se crea ofendida, haya presentado á la otra una esposicion de aquellas injurias ó daños, verificada con pruebas y testimonios suficientes, ecsigiendo justicia y satisfaccion, y esto haya sido negado ó diferido sin razon.

4º Nada de cuanto se contiene en el presente tratado, se construirá sin embargo, ni obrará en contra de otros tratados publicos anteriores, y ecsistentes con otros Soberanos ó Estados.

The present treaty of peace, amity, commerce and navigation, shall be approved and ratified by the President of the United States of America, by and with the advice and consent of the Senate thereof, and by the President of the Republic of Ecuador, with the consent and approbation of the Congress of the same; and the ratifications shall be exchanged in the city of Quito, within three years, to be counted from the date of the signature hereof, or sooner, if possible.

In faith whereof, we, the Plenipotentiaries of the United States of America and of the Republic of Ecuador, have signed and sealed these presents.

Done in the city of Quito, on the thirteenth day of June, in the year of our Lord, one thousand eight hundred and thirty-nine, and in the sixty third year of the Independence of the United States of America and the twenty ninth of that of the Republic of Ecuador.

[Seal] J. C. PICKETT

[Seal] LUIS DE SAA

El presente Tratado de Paz, Amistad, Comercio y Navegacion será ratificado por el Presidente ó Vice Presidente de la República del Ecuador, encargado del Poder Ejecutivo, con consentimiento y aprobacion del Congreso de la misma, y por el Presidente de los Estados Unidos de America, con consejo y aprobacion del Senado de los mismos; y las ratificaciones serán cangeadas en la ciudad de Quito dentro de tres años contados desde este dia, ó antes si fuere posible.

En fe de lo cual, nosotros los plenipotenciarios de la República del Ecuador y de los Estados Unidos de America, hemos firmado y sellado las presentes.

Dadas en la ciudad de Quito, el dia trece de Junio, del año del Señor, mil ochocientos treinta y nueve, vigesimo nono de la Yndependencia de la República del Ecuador y sexagesimo tercero de la de los Estados Unidos de America.

[Seal] LUIS DE SAA

[Seal] J. C. PICKETT

NOTES

The file of this treaty is complete. The signed original consists of two documents, each signed by the Plenipotentiaries, one being the English and the other the Spanish text of the treaty; both are now bound with the duplicate United States instrument of ratification of July 31, 1840, and the original proclamation of September 23, 1842. As the printed texts show, the *alternat* was duly observed. The instrument of ratification on the part of Ecuador of February 19, 1842, includes the Spanish text only.

Other papers in the file are the attested resolution of the Senate of July 15, 1840 (Executive Journal, V, 302), and the certificate or act

of the exchange of ratifications at Quito on April 9, 1842, in two originals, one in English and one in Spanish, in somewhat different forms; the latter recites the examination of the respective powers to exchange the ratifications and the delivery of copies thereof.

Various papers were submitted to the Senate on January 21, 1840, with the presidential message, the exact date of which is not given; those papers, which were printed, included a copy of the instructions to James C. Pickett, the United States Plenipotentiary, and his original despatches (Executive Journal, V, 250); the latter were returned more than a year later, March 11, 1841 (*ibid.*, 374).

The Senate print mentioned is Confidential Document C, 26th Congress, 1st session (Regular Confidential Documents, XI, 271–333). In that document are printed all the various despatches from Pickett which are hereafter cited from D. S., 5 Despatches, Peru.

The treaty was communicated to Congress with the presidential message of December 6, 1842 (Richardson, IV, 194, 198).

Terms of the Treaty

This was the first treaty made between the United States and the Republic of Ecuador; however, the treaty of October 3, 1824 (Document 47), had been made with the Republic of Colombia, then embracing New Granada and Venezuela as well as Ecuador, a union which terminated as to Ecuador in 1830; that treaty with the Republic of Colombia had expired twelve years after the exchange of its ratifications, or on May 27, 1837, except as to "all those parts, which relate to peace and friendship" (Article 31).

This treaty differs essentially in its commercial clauses (Articles 3–6 and 34) from the earlier one with the Republic of Colombia; the immediate basis of this treaty was that with Venezuela of January 20, 1836 (Document 80, the notes to which give some account of the origin of the provisions); regarding its terms Pickett wrote as follows in the despatch transmitting the treaty (D. S., 5 Despatches, Peru, No. 8, July 3, 1839):

The treaty between the United States and Venezuela was adopted as a basis for the present one, and there is a perfect conformity between them, in all that is material, with the following exceptions:—

To the 3rd article of the treaty with Ecuador, a clause is added, securing certain privileges to vessels built at Guayaquil. These privileges they have enjoyed, since the passage of the law of the 21st of March 1837, referred to in the treaty.

In the 7th article, a clause is inserted subjecting the citizens of the United States and of Ecuador, to such general taxes and contributions as may be established by law. To these they are subject, no doubt, without any such clause; but as the insertion of it was desired by the Government at Quito, and as it is mere surplusage, I made no objection.

In the 11th article, the words "until they may be exported", are omitted, as suggested in your instructions: Consequently the article will not be liable to the misconstruction placed upon a similar one, by the Brazilian authorities, in the treaty between the United States and Brazil [of December 12, 1828, Document 64, Article 10].

The 14th article, on the subject of religion and liberty of conscience, is taken from the treaty between the United States and the former republic of Colombia; and if it does not secure all that is desirable, it secures all that is at present, essential. The Ecuadorian Plenipotentiary said frankly, that the state of public

opinion in Ecuador, would not, at present, tolerate chapels and houses of public worship for any form of religion, except the Roman catholic; and that a concession similar to that contained in the treaty with Venezuela, would probably cause the rejection of the one with Ecuador, when it came to be submitted to the Congress. And of this, I was so fully satisfied, from all I could see and hear, that I thought it prudent not to press the point; but that it would be better to accept what could be certainly secured, than to endanger the whole treaty by insisting upon what would, very probably, be disapproved by the Congress, as it most assuredly would be, by the community.

. . . .

In the 16th article, six months (instead of two) are allowed, after which, ignorance of a declaration of war in a certain case, cannot be pleaded. This time is allowed in the treaty with the Peru-Bolivian Confederation [Document 82]; and if not too long in that instance, (and I do not think it is) it is not in the present.

The 34th article of the treaty is an additional one, and is inserted in consequence of the Resolution of the Congress of Ecuador, approved by the President the 20th of April last, . . . As the Resolution declares, that "to no nation shall be conceded privileges, as to the most favored nation", it became necessary to insert an article shewing precisely, upon what footing the United States would be placed, in Ecuador, which will be that upon which Spain, Mexico and the other Hispano-American states will be placed; and as these will undoubtedly be the most favored nations, in Ecuador, this article, taken with the third and fourth articles, appears to me, to secure all that can be expected; and as much, as though the United States were placed explicitly & in so many words, upon a footing with the most favored nation.

From some cause or other, (inadvertence probably) Spain is omitted in the Resolution, and if it were literally construed, she would be classed with the other European nations: But it is well understood, and is notorious, that it was the intention originally, to grant commercial privileges to her, not to be granted to any other nation; provided she would acknowledge the independence of Ecuador. But the Gov't. at Quito determined finally to have but two classes of treaties; those with Spain and the American states (including the United States) to form the first, and all others to form the second.

. . . .

The . . . decree . . . of the last Congress, concerning the vessels and productions of Spain, shews conclusively, that a very friendly feeling now prevails in Ecuador, towards that nation, which will be much strengthened, no doubt, should she recognise, formally, the independence of this country, as she has already done, virtually, by receiving diplomatic and consular agents from Ecuador, and by establishing commercial relations with her.

I inserted Mexico specially, in the 34th article, because a treaty[1] between Ecuador and that state has been approved by the Congress of the former, and will, I have no doubt, be ratified and carried into effect. This treaty (which has not yet been published) is a copy, to a great extent, of the one between the United States and Mexico. Even the words, *'the most favored nation'*, are used and will be retained, the late decree prohibiting them, not being intended, I apprehend, to have a retrospective effect.

. . . .

In the 5th article of the treaty, is inserted a concession in favor of the commercial marine of Ecuador, similar to that in favor of the marine of Venezuela. The condition of the former authorises such a concession, at least as fully as that of the latter.

It is provided that the ratifications of the treaty shall be exchanged at Quito, within three years. As the Congress of Ecuador, to which it must be submitted,

---

[1] Treaty of June 21, 1838, which was ratified by Ecuador but did not go into force; the text, in Spanish, is in Tratados y convenciones celebrados y no ratificados por la Republica Mexicana, 235–46.

does not meet until the 15th of January 1841, the time allowed, though long, may not be too much.

The duration of the treaty is limited to twelve years, to which the Gov't. at Quito consented finally, to extend it, though disposed at first, to insist upon a much shorter term.

The resolution of the Congress of Ecuador, approved April 20, 1839, to which reference is made in the foregoing despatch, contained five clauses reading as follows in translation (D.S., 5 Despatches, Peru, No. 8, enclosure 8):

The Senate and Chamber of Representatives of the Republic of Ecuador, in Congress assembled,

Having attentively examined the note of the Minister of Foreign Relations, in which is considered whether the favors and privileges conceded to the Hispano-American states shall be extended to the United States of the North, as their Plenipotentiary, Mr. Pickett, has proposed, declare:

ARTICLE 1. That all the Hispano-American Republics shall be entitled, in their public treaties with Ecuador, to greater favors and privileges than the European nations.

ARTICLE 2. That the United States ought to be considered as a sister republic entitled to the same favors and privileges as the Hispano-American states.

ARTICLE 3. That the convenience of the state should be the measure of those favors.

ARTICLE 4. That to no nation shall be conceded privileges as to the most favored nation.

ARTICLE 5. That, therefore, those words should be excluded from every public treaty.

It appears that in Article 3 of the English text of the treaty, after "1837" and before "vessels", the words "it is provided that" were omitted by the copyist at Quito (D. S., 6 Despatches, Peru, No. 78, April 26, 1843).

In Article 3 of the treaty (and also in the despatch of July 3, 1839, quoted above) mention is made of a law of Ecuador of March 21, 1837; the text of that law is in Primer rejistro auténtico nacional, 1837, 263–64; its four articles read as follows in translation:

ARTICLE 1. The products and manufactures of the Republic that are exported in vessels constructed in the Guayaquil shipyard shall be free from export duty for two years; and while these vessels fly the national flag they shall be exempt from port, anchorage, and tonnage duties.

ARTICLE 2. All naval and construction supplies that are imported for specified workshops or vessels into the said shipyard shall be free from import duties in such quantity or weight as in the judgment of the treasury board of its province may be considered sufficient for the workshop in question. The surplus quantity, however, shall be subject to such duties.

ARTICLE 3. Vessels constructed abroad, that are sold in the ports of the Republic, shall pay 30 percent on the price for which they may be sold; but if the alienation thereof is the result of a court order, only 4 percent of the export duty shall be collected.

ARTICLE 4. The law of August 28, 1835 [*ibid.*, 1835, 64–65], regarding privileges and exemptions for vessels built or careened in the Guayaquil shipyard, is repealed in so far as it may be inconsistent with the provisions hereof.

THE FULL POWERS

The full power given to James C. Pickett, who had been appointed Chargé d'Affaires of the United States near the Government of the Peru-Bolivian Confederation, was dated June 15, 1838. It gave

authority "to agree, treat, consult and negotiate of and concerning Amity, Commerce and Navigation between the two countries and of all matters and subjects connected therewith, and to conclude and sign a treaty or treaties, Convention or Conventions touching the premises" (D. S., 2 Credences, 303).

Pickett arrived at Quito on December 21, 1838; soon thereafter he opened negotiations with the Ecuadoran Minister of Foreign Relations, General Daste, "a Frenchman", and full powers were exchanged (D. S., 5 Despatches, Peru, No. 2, January 9, 1839); then another Plenipotentiary was named, Dr. Mariano Miño, but his appointment was not confirmed; and upon a change of administration the successor Minister of Foreign Relations, Dr. Luis de Saá, became the Plenipotentiary of Ecuador who signed the treaty (*ibid.*, No. 3, January 30, 1839; No. 5, February 27, 1839).

A copy and translation of the full power of the Ecuadoran Plenipotentiary are with the despatch of Pickett of July 3, 1839 (*ibid.*, No. 8, enclosures 9 and 10). The latter reads as follows:

Juan José Flores, President of the Republic of Ecuador:

To all who shall see these presents, Greeting:

Whereas we have special confidence in the abilities, honor, and patriotism of Dr. Luis de Saá, Minister of State in the Department of Finance and charged with that of the Interior and Foreign Relations of the Republic, we have thought proper to appoint him, as by these presents we do appoint and constitute him, our Minister Plenipotentiary, giving and conferring on him full power and a special commission, that, meeting J. C. Pickett, Plenipotentiary of the United States of the North, he may conclude a new convention between the Republic of Ecuador and the United States, in conformity with the instructions which have been given him to that effect.

JUAN J. FLORES

By His Excellency:
The colonel in charge of the Department of War and Marine,
J. H^to SOULIN

THE EXCHANGE OF RATIFICATIONS

It is provided in one of the final clauses of the treaty that the ratifications should be exchanged at Quito. A quite unusually long time was allowed for this purpose, three years from the date of signature; but the Congress of Ecuador then met biennially; the 1839 session had terminated when the treaty was signed; the next session was to begin on January 15, 1841; and the treaty, by its final clause, was subject to "the consent and approbation of the Congress" of Ecuador.

There being then no diplomatic representative of the United States at Quito, Benjamin Tappan, Jr., was appointed Special Agent to exchange the ratifications and was also instructed thereafter to treat regarding the claims of citizens of the United States in the cases of the *Josephine* and the *Ranger* (D. S., 1 Special Missions, 171–74, September 16, 1840; as to the claims, see the notes to Document 67, the convention with Colombia of November 25, 1829).

Tappan arrived at Quito on February 21, 1841, and left there on the following June 15 without having accomplished his mission. It

appears that the 1841 session of the Congress of Ecuador did not take place, and conflicting views were expressed as to whether the treaty could be ratified by the Government of Ecuador under the circumstances (D. S., 12 Special Agents, Tappan to Secretary of State Webster, December 6, 1841).

The papers were turned over by Tappan to Seth Sweetser, American consul at Guayaquil, to whom alternative instructions had been issued regarding the exchange of ratifications and to whom a full power had been given for that purpose (*ibid.*, letter of December 6, 1841, above cited, and enclosures thereto; 2 Credences, 322–23).

Sweetser arrived at Quito on January 8, 1842, and the exchange of ratifications took place on the following April 9. It seems to have been finally decided by the Government of Ecuador that approval of the treaty by the Ecuadoran Congress was not essential. Sweetser's reports of his mission are in D. S., 1 Consular Despatches, Guayaquil (January 10, February 28, and September 20, 1842, and enclosures). Among those papers are a certified copy and translation of the full power to exchange the ratifications given by Juan José Flores, President of Ecuador, to José Felix Valdivieso, President of the Senate, dated February 19, 1842 (*ibid.*, September 20, 1842, enclosure 18). Sweetser himself brought the Ecuadoran instrument of ratification to the United States (*ibid.*, September 20, 1842; see also Wriston, Executive Agents in American Foreign Relations, 642–45).

Relations with Ecuador

Robert B. McAfee was commissioned Chargé d'Affaires to New Granada on February 9, 1833. While at no time during his service at Bogotá did McAfee go to Quito, on June 3, 1835, he addressed a note to the Ecuadoran Minister of Foreign Relations, enclosing an authenticated copy of the commission of Seth Sweetser as consul at Guayaquil (dated May 5, 1834) and calling attention to the claims of the United States which had arisen before the dissolution of the former Republic of Colombia (D. S., 8 Despatches, Colombia, No. 26, June 5, 1835, enclosure). The correspondence thus commenced continued at intervals through 1836, and in 1837 McAfee had some conferences at Bogotá with an agent of the Government of Ecuador, Colonel Urbina, who had authority to discuss the claims and a commercial treaty but did not have full powers (*ibid.*, *passim*). McAfee had both instructions and full powers to negotiate such a treaty. His full power was dated April 21, 1836, and in customary form gave authority "to agree, treat, consult and negotiate of and concerning general commerce and claims of the citizens of the two countries respectively upon the Governments of Ecuador and the United States, and all matters and subjects connected therewith, and to conclude and sign a Treaty or Treaties, Convention or Conventions touching the premises" (D. S., 2 Credences, 246). His instructions were dated in part the same day and in part the following July 18 (D. S., 15 Instructions, Colombia, 29–35), although the latter never reached him, as the vessel in which the courier traveled was destroyed by fire

(D. S., 15 Instructions, Peru, 21, July 18, 1838). The instructions given to Pickett opened as follows (*ibid.*):

> The President of the United States having been recently apprized by a letter from the President of Ecuador of the disposition of that Government to form a commercial treaty with us upon the most liberal basis, informed that functionary in reply that he was similarly disposed, and that the diplomatic agent about to be sent to Lima would be directed to proceed by the way of Quito and would be authorized to negotiate a treaty with Ecuador. You will consequently repair to Quito by the safest and most expeditious route which, as you have visited that region, may more properly be left to your option than prescribed by this Department.

It thus appears that in 1838 letters were exchanged between the President of Ecuador and President Van Buren. However, no other record or mention of them has been found except in the correspondence between Secretary of State Forsyth and Seth Sweetser, consul at Guayaquil, who was in the United States in 1838 (Forsyth to Sweetser, March 12, 1838, D. S., 9 Instructions to Consuls, 271; Sweetser to Forsyth, March 15 and April 19, 1838, D. S., 1 Consular Despatches, Guayaquil).   In the letter last mentioned Sweetser wrote, "You may assure the President that I will present in person the letter for Don Vicente Rocafuerte the Chief Magistrate of the republic of Ecuador on my arrival."

The Status of Pickett

For the purpose of the negotiation of this treaty, Pickett was an Agent of the Executive, appointed by President Van Buren on June 15, 1838, without nomination to the Senate.

On June 6, 1838, President Van Buren sent to the Senate the nomination of James C. Pickett "to be chargé d'affaires of the United States near the Government of the Peru-Bolivian Confederation, in the place of James B. Thornton, deceased" (James B. Thornton, of New Hampshire, was appointed Chargé d'Affaires to the Republic of Peru as successor to Samuel Larned on June 15, 1836); that nomination of Pickett was confirmed by the Senate three days later (Executive Journal, V, 118, 120), and the commission to Pickett was issued on June 9, 1838.

While that nomination was pending, President Van Buren sent to the Senate the following message regarding the negotiation of this treaty with Ecuador, dated June 7 and received in the Senate June 8 (*ibid.*, 119):

> Having received satisfactory assurances from the Government of Ecuador of its desire to negotiate a treaty of commerce on the most liberal principles, in place of the expired treaty made with the Republic of Colombia, heretofore regulating our intercourse with Ecuador, it is my design to give the requisite authority for that purpose to the charge d'affaires of the United States about to be appointed for Peru, with instructions to stop in Ecuador on his way to Lima as the agent of the United States to accomplish that object. The only additional charges to be incurred will be the expense of his journey from Panama to Quito, and from thence to the place of embarkation for Lima, to be paid out of the foreign intercourse fund. I make this communication to the Senate, that an opportunity may be afforded for the expression of an opinion, if it shall be deemed necessary, on the exercise of such a power by the Executive without applying to the Senate for its approbation and consent. In debate it has been sometimes asserted that this

power, frequently exercised without question or complaint and leading to no practical evil, as ro arrangement made under such circumstances can be obligatory upon the United States without being submitted to the approbation of the Senate, is an encroachment upon its rightful authority. It appears to have been considered that the annual appropriation of a gross sum for the expenses of foreign intercourse is intended, among other objects, to provide for the cost of such agencies, and that the authority granted is the same as that frequently given to the Secretary of State to form treaties with the representatives or agents of foreign Governments, upon the granting of which the Senate never have been consulted.

Desiring in this and in all other instances to act with the most cautious respect to the claims of other branches of the Government, I bring this subject to the notice of the Senate, that if it shall be deemed proper to raise any question, it may be discussed and decided before and not after the power shall have been exercised.

The foregoing message, on its receipt, was referred to the Committee on Foreign Relations (*ibid.*, 120), and that was the end of it. No report was made and no action was taken, and in the absence of Senate action, instructions were given to Pickett regarding the negotiation of this treaty, in the preamble of which he is described as "a citizen of the said States".

Just why such a message was sent to the Senate by President Van Buren it is not easy to imagine. Assuming the confirmation and appointment of Pickett as Chargé d'Affaires to the Peru-Bolivian Confederation, he was a duly commissioned diplomatic officer of the United States. There were, of course, precedents for the nomination of the same individual to two missions, one being the case of William Pinkney, who was nominated in 1816 as Minister to Russia "with a special mission to the King of the Two Sicilies", and whose nomination to the first post was confirmed and to the second first rejected and then confirmed (Executive Journal, III, 32, 35, 45, 46); but the message of President Van Buren regarding the mission of Pickett to Ecuador was not a nomination at all; it is perhaps to be considered as a statement of Executive intention designed to forestall possible future criticism, and doubtless the then recent congressional debate in 1831 over the mission to Turkey (see Wriston, Executive Agents in American Foreign Relations, 237–58) was in mind. The author cited makes the following comment regarding the presidential message of June 8, 1838 (*ibid.*, 259–60):

This message is very difficult to explain. Pickett was not the first treaty negotiator sent by Van Buren without the approbation of the Senate. Indeed, in the preceding month Nathaniel Niles had been instructed and empowered to make a treaty with Sardinia without any notice having been given to the Senate. Why, after so many years of quiet on the topic, why, after he had made use of such agencies before, Van Buren should pitch upon this occasion for such a message is a mystery. It is the more puzzling because there had never been any complaint at the use of a person in the diplomatic service to make a treaty with a country other than that to which he was regularly accredited. The only complaints had come when a man was taken from private life, or when a new mission was instituted in a recess. It is possible that Van Buren, with the deliberate notion of gaining the consent of the Senate to a precedent, purposely selected a case where the arguments in opposition would be weakest. That, however, is merely conjecture. Equally interesting is the fact that the Senate made no gesture of any kind. Tazewell and Tyler were gone. There was no one who had this subject peculiarly upon his heart; there was no political capital

to be made of an act which was not done. The matter went to the committee
on foreign relations and there it slumbered. Pickett went to Ecuador and
signed a treaty, June 13, 1839, describing his status as "a citizen" of the United
States.

However, the mission of Nathaniel Niles, which is referred to by
the author cited, presented some other features which are described
in the notes to Document 86, the treaty with Sardinia of November
26, 1838.

91

SAMOA : NOVEMBER 5, 1839

Commercial Regulations, signed by the chiefs of the Samoan Islands at Apia November 5, 1839. Original in English and (doubtless) also in Samoan.

Commercial Regulations made by the principal Chiefs of the Samoa group of islands after full consideration in Council on the 5th day of November /39

1ˢᵗ

All foreign Consuls duly appointed and received in Samoa shall be protected and respected both in their persons and property, and all foreigners obtaining the consent of the Government and conforming to the Laws shall receive the protection of the Government.

2ⁿᵈ

All foreign vessels shall be received into the ports and harbours of Samoa for the purpose of obtaining supplies and for Commerce, and with their officers and crews, so long as they shall comply with these regulations, and behave themselves peaceably shall receive the protection of the Governt

3ʳᵈ

The fullest protection shall be given to all foreign ships and vessels which may be wrecked, and any property saved shall be take possession of by the Consul of the Country to which the vessel belongs, who will allow a salvage or portion of the property so saved to those who may aid in saving and protecting the same, and no embezzlement will be permitted under any circumstances whatever. The effects of all deceased persons shall be given up to the Consul of the Nation to which they may have belonged.

4ᵗʰ

Any person guilty of the crime of murder upon any foreigner shall be given up without delay to the Commander of any public vessel of the Nation to which the deceased may have belonged, upon his demanding the same.

241

5th

Every vessel shall pay a port charge of $5 for anchorage and water, before she will be allowed to receive refreshments on board, and shall pay for pilotage in and out the sum of $7. before she leaves the harbour, and pilots shall be appointed subject to the approval of the Consuls.

6th

No work shall be done on shore, nor shall any natives be employed on board vessels on the Sabbath day under a penalty of *ten dollars*, unless under circumstances of absolute necessity.

7th

All trading in spirituous or landing the same is strictly forbidden: any person offending shall pay a fine of twenty five dollars, and the vessel to which he belongs, shall receive no more refreshments. Any spirituous liquors found on shore shall be seized and destroyed.

8th

All deserters from vessels will be apprehended, and a reward paid of $8 viz $5 to the person who apprehends him and $3 to the Chief of the district in which he may be apprehended on his delivery to the proper officer of the vessel. No Master shall refuse to receive such deserter under a penalty of $25.

Deserters taken after the vessel has sailed shall be delivered up to the Consul to be dealt with as he may think fit. Any person who entices another to desert, or secretes a deserter or in any way assists him shall be subject to a penalty of $5. or one month's hard labour on the public roads.

9th

No Master shall land a passenger without permission of the Government under a penalty of $25. and no individual shall be permitted to land or reside in Samoa without special permission of the Government. Any one so landing shall be compelled to leave by the first opportunity.

10th

If a sick person be left on shore from any vessel for the recovery of his health, he shall be placed in charge of the Consul, who shall be responsible for his sick expenses and will send him away by the first opportunity after his recovery.

11th

Any seamen remaining on shore after 9 Oclock at night, shall be made a prisoner of until the next morning, when he shall be sent on board, and shall pay a fine of $5.

12th

All fines to be paid in specie or its equivalent, or be commuted by the Government at the rate of one months hard labour on the public roads for $5.

13th

Should the Master of any vessel refuse to comply with any of these regulations a statement of the case shall be furnished to the Consul of the Nation to which he belongs and redress sought from thence.

14th

All Magistrates or Chiefs of districts where vessels or boats may visit, shall enforce the rules and regulations relative to the landing of foreigners and apprehension of deserters or pay such a fine as the Malo shall impose.

15th

For carrying into effect the foregoing rules and regulations, the Chiefs and Tula-fale of the respective districts shall meet and elect one of their number to act as a Magistrate or judge to execute the laws.

16th

These regulations shall be printed promulgated, and a copy furnished to the Master of each vessel visiting these islands.

Done in Council at the port of Apia on the island of Upulo this fifth day of November A D 1839

Witnesses	MALIETOA X
CHAS WILKES *Comdg Ex Ex.*	TAMALANGI X
	MATETAU X
	PEEA X
J. C. WILLIAMS *U.S Consul*	TOOA X
	MOLI X
W C CUNNINGHAM *H B M Consul*	SAGA X
Novr 5th 1839	

The foregoing Commercial rules and regulations having been signed by the chiefs in my presence and submitted to me—I consider them just and proper and shall forward to the American Government a copy of the same for the information of all Masters of vessels visiting the Samoa or Navigator group of islands.

U.S Ship Vincennes Harbour of Apia Island of Upulo Navigator group November 6th 1839

(signed)   CHARLES WILKES
Comdg Ex. Ex U.S of America

The foregoing rules and regulations having been submitted to me by the chiefs, I highly approve of the same.

(signed)   W C. CUNNINGHAM
H B M Vice Consul For the Navigator group

APIA UPULO *November 5ᵗʰ 1839*

NOTES

The chief authority regarding the commercial regulations above printed is Wilkes, Narrative of the United States Exploring Expedition (1838–42), which is described in these notes and which is here cited as "The Narrative".

In any technical sense it would perhaps not be possible to say that these regulations, signed by the chiefs of the Samoan Islands, were an international act, although at the time Samoa was not at all subject to any extrinsic authority (Samoan questions in international relations up to 1900 are fully treated in The Foreign Policy of the United States in Relation to Samoa, by George Herbert Ryden).

The form of the regulations is somewhat like that of a decree or order in council; they are not phrased like an agreement. However, they were proposed by a United States naval officer, Lieutenant Charles Wilkes; it was at his instance that they were accepted and signed; they were first written in English; they treat of matters which are frequently the subject of conventions, such as the duties and rights of consuls; they undoubtedly were regarded by the native chiefs who signed them as being of a promissory nature; and, indeed, they contain clauses reading somewhat like mutual promises (salvage, clause 3; rewards, clause 8).

Strict consistency perhaps would not permit the inclusion of such a document in this collection; but the historical interest of the paper is sufficient to warrant the exception, if it be an exception.

THE SOURCE TEXT

No original document is available as a source text for the commercial regulations printed above. The text here printed has been collated with a copy of the regulations enclosed with the despatch of Wilkes to the Secretary of the Navy under date of November 6, 1839, on board "U.S. Ship Vincennes Harbour of Apia Island of Upolu

Navigator group", in which he wrote as follows (Naval Records and Library, 1 Wilkes Exploring Expedition, No. 53):

On my arrival at this harbour on the 26th Ult^{o}, I ascertained that although these islands are frequently visited by Whaling Vessels for supplies no port regulations or Laws existed for their protection.

I accordingly invited a meeting of the Chiefs of this group at this place on the 5th Inst. when the Commercial rules and regulations of which the enclosed marked N° 1 is a copy, were considered and adopted by the Chiefs, and will I have no doubt afford ample protection to all vessels visiting this group, and also secure the Natives from imposition. They are to be printed in both languages, and copies furnished to the Masters of vessels visiting these islands.

Deeming it much to the interest of those engaged in the Whale fishery that we should have a Consul resident here—I appointed Jno C Williams Esqr of this island, Acting U S Consul until the pleasure of the Government should be known. And I trust that the appointment may be confirmed as Mr Williams is every way qualified for the situation, intends to reside permanently on the island, and will do much to facilitate the supplies required by Whaling Vessels, and prevent difficulties which occur between them and the Natives, Also to prevent desertion and apprehend deserters, as this has become a great evil.

It seems that the regulations must have been drawn up in the language of Samoa as well as in English, but only the English text is available. With some slight variances and omitting the certificate of the British vice consul the regulations are printed in The Narrative, II, 453–55, and also in Colvocoresses, Four Years in a Government Exploring Expedition, 367–69; but they do not appear to have been published at the time in the United States, although it seems that they were printed in Samoa in the year 1840 (*ibid.*). They are printed in British and Foreign State Papers, XXXIII, 52–54, a volume published in 1859.

There is another copy of the regulations in the archives of the Navy Department (Wilkes Exploring Expedition, area 9). That copy, which also omits the certificate of the British vice consul, seems to be of a later date. It has a postscript, signed "Manoa Head Chief of the harbor of Pago Pago", and dated 1853, to the effect that the regulations had been carried out in that port since their first adoption in 1839 and would continue to be observed.

An allusion to these regulations and to those of Fiji (Document 93) appears in this paragraph from an article in Niles' Weekly Register, LXII, 261, June 25, 1842, on the "South Sea Exploring Expedition":

Several of the principal groups and islands in the Pacific Ocean have been visited, examined, and surveyed; a friendly intercourse and protective commercial regulations established with the chiefs and natives; aggressions on our citizens and commerce redressed, and a justly merited punishment meted out in some flagrant cases of unprovoked and cold-blooded murder.

The Discussions

Wilkes reached Rose Island, the most eastern of the Samoan Group, or Navigator Islands, as they were then commonly called, on October 7, 1839; he visited Manua and reached the harbor of Pago Pago, Tutuila, on October 11; after spending some days there, he arrived at Apia, Upolu, on October 26. The ceremony of the discus-

sion of the commercial articles is thus described (The Narrative, II, 107–9):

On the 4th of November, a fono was held, according to the appointment made with Malietoa, in the fale-tele of Apia. All the officers who could be spared from the ships were ordered to attend. Old Pea, the chief of Apia, seemed to be the master of ceremonies on the occasion. Clean mats were spread for the chiefs, and chairs and benches borrowed from the missionaries' houses were placed for us, opposite to them. All the highest chiefs of the "Malo" party were present, except Pea of Manono, and two minor chiefs of Savaii. Malietoa presided. His whole demeanour was dignified, composed, and thoughtful. His personal appearance has already been spoken of, and the form of his head, his white hair, and dignified bearing, again reminded us of General Jackson. He is slender and tall, although somewhat bent by age. It was to be regretted that his dress was ill chosen, and rather detracted from the respect he would have inspired had he appeared in his native garb; he wore pantaloons, a round jacket, and a pink and white striped cotton shirt.

Tooa, the nephew of Malietoa, who acted as spokesman, and whose countenance betokened the interest he felt in the business, attracted attention in the second degree. Then came Mole, the son of Malietoa, Maletau, their general, the most renowned leader in the war of Aana, and Tai-ma-le-lagi, Malietoa's brother. There were also present a number of chiefs of less distinction, among whom was old Pea of Apia; although he was compelled to take his place, yet he did not fail to be conspicuous, not merely by his personal appearance, but by his officiousness.

The proceedings were conducted with great ceremony, but there was a marked difference between this fono, and the solemnity of our Indian councils. The Samoan assembly appeared more quiescent, the proceedings exhibited more refinement, and the customs partook of an Asiatic character.

In all such meetings a rigid order of precedence, that seems well understood by every one, is established; all conversation is carried on in a whisper; no one is seen standing in the presence of a superior, and sitting with outstretched legs is considered indecorous. Articles were never passed over a person, and no native ever ventured to come in contact with a chief.

The background on the side of the natives was filled up with inhabitants from different parts of the island.

On the opposite side of the building, the officers of the squadron and the missionaries formed a numerous group. Among the latter, was our friend Mr. Williams and his son, whom I had appointed to act as consul until the pleasure of the government of the United States was known, and whom it was intended to present in this capacity to the meeting, in order that he might be recognised formally by the chiefs. Messrs. Heath, Mills, and Wilson were also present; and Mr. Heath, who was believed to be best acquainted with the Samoan language, was kind enough to officiate as our interpreter.

The object I had in view, in requesting the fono to be called, was to procure the formal enactment of laws and regulations which might secure to our whale-ships a certainty of protection and security, and at the same time to prevent impositions being practised by them upon the native government, of which, as has been stated, complaint had been made. To the breach of these laws, it was intended that the penalty of a fine should be attached, in order to secure obedience to them.

The meeting being organized, I in the first place presented Mr. John Williams, as the consul of the United States, whom the chiefs recognised as such with great willingness and satisfaction.

We then entered upon the discussion of the proposed regulations, which were adopted in a form which promises to be mutually beneficial, being highly advantageous to them, and at the same time insuring a certainty of security to American vessels that may visit the island they could not before enjoy.

The account of the visit of the Wilkes Expedition to the Samoan Islands is in The Narrative, II, 65–162, preceded by a map; it includes much interesting information regarding the region and its

inhabitants and the work of the missionaries among them; the estimate given of the population at the time is as follows (p. 137):

The entire population of the group is estimated at 56,600, of whom 14,850 have embraced Christianity, and 12,300 attend the schools. These numbers are thus distributed:

Islands.	Population.	Professors of Christianity.	Pupils.
Eastern Group	2, 000	150	150
Tutuila	8, 000	2, 200	1, 900
Upolu	25, 000	8, 000	6, 200
Savaii	20, 000	4, 000	3, 700
Manono	1, 100	400	230
Apolima	500	100	120
Total	56, 600	14, 850	12, 300

The whole number of foreign missionaries is eleven, of whom one resides in Tutuila, six in Upolu, three in Savaii, and one in Manono.

The Wilkes Expedition

The United States Exploring Expedition (1838–42) or the Wilkes Expedition, as it is now generally called, was in the strictest sense official; it was authorized by act of Congress (May 14, 1836, 5 Statutes at Large, 27–29); that statute provided—

That the President of the United States, be, and he hereby is authorized, to send out a surveying and exploring expedition to the Pacific ocean and [the] South seas, and for that purpose to employ a sloop of war, and to purchase or provide such other smaller vessels as may be necessary and proper to render the said expedition efficient and useful, and for this purpose the sum of one hundred and fifty thousand dollars be, and the same is hereby appropriated, out of any money in the Treasury not otherwise appropriated, and in addition thereto, if necessary, the President of the United States is authorized to use other means in the control of the Navy Department, not exceeding one hundred and fifty thousand dollars for the objects required.

The expenses of the expedition, which appear to have amounted to over $900,000, were paid from the United States Treasury; the expedition was commanded by Lieutenant Charles Wilkes, U.S.N.; the vessels under his orders were the sloops of war *Vincennes* and *Peacock*, the storeship *Relief*, the brig *Porpoise*, and the tenders *Sea Gull* and *Flying Fish*. The elaborate instructions given to Wilkes were from the Secretary of the Navy (James K. Paulding) under date of August 11, 1838; they are printed in The Narrative, I, xxv–xxxii, and also in House Report No. 160, 28th Congress, 2d session, serial 468, as follows:

Navy Department,
August 11, 1838.

Sir,
The Congress of the United States, having in view the important interests of our commerce embarked in the whale-fisheries, and other adventures in the great Southern Ocean, by an Act of the 18th of May, 1836, authorized an Expedition to be fitted out for the purpose of exploring and surveying that sea, as well to deter-

mine the existence of all doubtful islands and shoals, as to discover and accurately fix the position of those which lie in or near the track of our vessels in that quarter, and may have escaped the observation of scientific navigators. Liberal appropriations have been made for the attainment of these objects, and the President, reposing great confidence in your courage, capacity, and zeal, has appointed you to the command of the Expedition, requiring you to proceed to the performance of the duties of that station with the vessels placed under your orders, consisting of the sloops of war Vincennes and Peacock, the ship Relief, the brig Porpoise, and tenders Sea-Gull and Flying-Fish.

As soon as these vessels are in every respect ready, you will accordingly take your departure from Norfolk, and shape your course to Rio Janeiro, crossing the line between longitude 18° and 22° W., and keeping within those meridians to about latitude 10° S., with a view to determine the existence of certain *vigias* or shoals laid down in the charts as doubtful, and whose position, should they be found to exist it is deemed useful to the interests of our commerce to ascertain.

At Rio Janeiro, where you will replenish your supplies, taking special care to furnish yourself with a sufficiency of all those articles which are considered the best preventives and remedies for the scurvy. You will determine the longitude of that place, as well as of Cape Frio; after which, you will either detach a vessel, or proceed with your whole squadron, to make a particular examination of Rio Negro, which falls into the South Atlantic about latitude 41° S., with a view to ascertain its resources and facilities for trade.

Having completed this survey, you will proceed to a safe port or ports in Terra del Fuego, where the members of the scientific corps may have favourable opportunities of prosecuting their researches. Leaving the larger vessels securely moored, and the officers and crews occupied in their respective duties, you will proceed with the brig Porpoise, and the tenders, to explore the southern Antarctic, to the southward of Powell's Group, and between it and Sandwich Land, following the track of Weddell as closely as practicable, and endeavouring to reach a high southern latitude; taking care, however, not to be obliged to pass the winter there, and to rejoin the other vessels between the middle of February and beginning of March. The attention of the officers left at Terra del Fuego, will, in the mean time, be specially directed to making such accurate and particular examination and surveys of the bays, ports, inlets, and sounds, in that region, as may verify or extend those of Captain King, and be serviceable in future to vessels engaged in the whale-fisheries, in their outward and homeward-bound passages.

You will then, on rejoining the vessels at Terra del Fuego, with all your squadron, stretch towards the southward and westward as far as the Ne Plus Ultra of Cook, or longitude 105 W., and return northward to Valparaiso, where a store-ship will meet you in the month of March, 1839. Proceeding once more from that port, you will direct your course to the Navigator's Group, keeping to the southward of the place of departure, in order to verify, if possible, the existence of certain islands and shoals, laid down in the charts as doubtful, and if they exist, to determine their precise position, as well as that of all others which may be discovered in this unfrequented track. When you arrive in those latitudes where discoveries may be reasonably anticipated, you will so dispose your vessels as that they shall sweep the broadest expanse of the ocean that may be practicable, without danger of parting company, laying-to at night in order to avoid the chance of passing any small island or shoal without detection.

It is presumed you will reach the Navigator's Group some time in June, 1839. You will survey this group, and its harbours, with all due care and attention. If time will permit, it will be well to visit the Society Islands, and examine Eimeo, which, it is stated, possesses a convenient harbour.

From the Navigator's Group, you will proceed to the Feejee Islands, which you will examine with particular attention, with the view to the selection of a safe harbour, easy of access, and in every respect adapted to the reception of vessels of the United States engaged in the whale-fishery, and the general commerce of these seas; it being the intention of the government to keep one of the squadron of the Pacific cruising near these islands in future.

After selecting the island and harbour best adapted to the purposes in view, you will use your endeavours to make such arrangements as will insure a supply of

fruits, vegetables, and fresh provisions, to vessels visiting it hereafter, teaching the natives the modes of cultivation, and encouraging them to raise hogs in greater abundance.

These objects will, it is presumed, occupy you until the latter end of October; and when attained as far as possible, you will proceed to the port of Sydney, where adequate supplies may be obtained. From thence you will make a second attempt to penetrate within the Antarctic region, south of Van Diemen's Land, and as far west as longitude 45° E., or to Enderby's Land, making your rendezvous on your return at Kerguelen's Land, or the Isle of Desolation, as it is now usually denominated, and where you will probably arrive by the latter end of March, 1840.

From the Isle of Desolation you will proceed to the Sandwich Islands, by such route as you may judge best, from the information you may acquire from such sources as fall in your way.

A store-ship from the United States will meet you here, with a supply of provisions, in the month of April, 1840.

Thence you will direct your course to the northwest coast of America, making such surveys and examinations, first of the territory of the United States on the sea-board, and of the Columbia river, and afterwards along the coast of California, with special reference to the Bay of St. Francisco, as you can accomplish by the month of October following your arrival.

You will then proceed to the coast of Japan, taking in your route as many doubtful islands as possible; and you have permission to pass through the Straits of Sangar into the Sea of Japan, where you may spend as much time as is compatible with your arrival at the proper season in the Sea of Sooloo or Mindoro.

Of this sea you will make a particular examination, with a view to ascertain whether there is any safe route through it, which will shorten the passage of our vessels to and from China.

It is enjoined on you to pay very particular attention to this object, in order that you may be enabled to furnish sailing instructions to navigators. It may be also advisable to ascertain the disposition of the inhabitants of the islands of this archipelago for commerce, their productions and resources.

Having completed this survey, you will proceed to the Straits of Sunda, pass through the Straits of Billiton, which you will examine, and thence to the port of Singapore, where it is probable you may arrive about the beginning of April, 1841, and where you will meet a store-ship from the United States.

Having completed this service, it is presumed the objects of your enterprise will be accomplished, and you will accordingly, after receiving your supplies at Singapore, return to the United States by the Cape of Good Hope, taking such a course as may be most likely to further the great purposes of the Expedition.

During your stay in the southern latitudes, should the dysentery or any other fatal epidemic make its appearance among your crews, you have leave to proceed to the northward, until the disease shall either disappear, or be so mitigated, as to admit of the resumption of your surveys.

The Department does not feel the necessity of giving any special directions for preserving the health of those under your command, confiding in your own experience, the care and precautions of the able surgeons with whom you are provided, and in the conviction you must feel, that on the health of your crews must depend the success of the enterprise.

In the prosecution of these long and devious voyages, you will necessarily be placed in situations which cannot be anticipated, and in which, sometimes your own judgment and discretion, at others, necessity, must be your guide. Among savage nations, unacquainted with, or possessing but vague ideas of the rights of property, the most common cause of collision with civilized visiters, is the offence and the punishment of theft. You will therefore adopt every possible precaution against this practice, and in the recovery of the stolen property, as well as in punishing the offender, use all due moderation and forbearance.

You will permit no trade to be carried on by the squadron, with the countries you may visit, either civilized or savage, except for necessaries or curiosities, and that under express regulations established by yourself, in which the rights of the natives must be scrupulously respected and carefully guarded.

You will neither interfere, nor permit any wanton interference with the customs, habits, manners, or prejudices, of the natives of such countries or islands as you may visit; nor take part in their disputes, except as a mediator, nor commit any

act of hostility, unless in self-defence, or to protect or secure the property of those under your command, or whom circumstances may have placed within reach of your protection.

You will carefully inculcate on all the officers and men under your command, that courtesy and kindness towards the natives, which is understood and felt by all classes of mankind; to display neither arrogance nor contempt, and to appeal to their good-will, rather than their fears, until it shall become apparent that they can only be restrained from violence by fear or force.

You will, on all occasions, avoid risking the officers and men unnecessarily on shore, at the mercy of the natives. Treachery is one of the invariable character-istics of savages and barbarians; and very many of the fatal disasters which have befallen preceding navigators, have arisen from too great a reliance on savage pro-fessions of friendship, or overweening confidence in themselves.

Much of the character of our future intercourse with the natives of the lands you may visit, will depend on the impressions made on their minds by their first intercourse with your vessels.

It is the nature of the savage, long to remember benefits, and never to forget inju-ries; and you will use your best endeavours wherever you may go, to leave behind a favourable impression of your country and countrymen. The Expedition is not for conquest, but discovery. Its objects are all peaceful; they are to extend the empire of commerce and science; to diminish the hazards of the ocean, and point out to future navigators a course by which they may avoid dangers and find safety.

An Expedition so constituted, and for such purposes, armed for defence, not conquest, and engaged in pursuits in which all enlightened nations are equally interested, has a right to expect the good-will and good offices of the whole civi-lized world. Should our country, therefore, be unhappily involved in war during your absence, you will refrain from all acts of hostility whatever, as it is confi-dently believed none will be committed against you. So far from this being the case, it is not to be doubted that even hostile nations will respect your purposes, and afford every facility to their accomplishment.

Finally, you will recollect, that though you may frequently be carried beyond the sphere of social life, and the restraints of law, yet that the obligations of justice and humanity are always and every where equally imperative in our intercourse with men, and most especially savages; that we seek them, not they us; and that if we expect to derive advantages from the intercourse, we should endeavour to confer benefits in return.

Although the primary object of the Expedition is the promotion of the great interests of commerce and navigation, yet you will take all occasions, not incom-patible with the great purposes of your undertaking, to extend the bounds of science, and promote the acquisition of knowledge. For the more successful attainment of these, a corps of scientific gentlemen, consisting of the following persons, will accompany the Expedition, and are placed under your direction.

Mr. Hale, Philologist.
Mr. Pickering,} Naturalists.
Mr. Peale,
Mr. Couthouy, Conchologist.
Mr. Dana, Mineralogist.
Mr. Rich, Botanist.
Mr. Drayton,} Draughtsmen.
Mr. Agate,
Mr. Brackenridge, Horticulturist.

The hydrography and geography of the various seas and countries you may visit in the route pointed out to you in the preceding instructions, will occupy your special attention; and all the researches connected with them, as well as with astronomy, terrestrial magnetism, and meteorology, are confided exclusively to the officers of the navy, on whose zeal and talents the Department confidently relies for such results as will enable future navigators to pass over the track traversed by your vessels, without fear and without danger.

No special directions are thought necessary in regard to the mode of conducting the scientific researches and experiments which you are enjoined to prosecute, nor

is it intended to limit the members of the corps each to his own particular service. All are expected to co-operate harmoniously in those kindred pursuits, whose equal dignity and usefulness should insure equal ardour and industry in extending their bounds and verifying their principles.

As guides to yourself and to the scientific corps, the Department would, however, direct your particular attention to the learned and comprehensive Reports of a committee of the American Philosophical Society of Philadelphia, the Report of a Committee of the East India Marine Society, of Salem, Massachusetts; and to a communication from the Naval Lyceum of New York, which accompany, and are to be regarded as forming a part of these instructions, so far as they may accord with the primary objects of the Expedition, and its present organization. You will, therefore, allow the gentlemen of the scientific corps the free perusal of these valuable documents, and permit them to copy such portions as they may think proper.

The Russian Vice-Admiral Krusenstern, has transmitted to the Department memorandums relating to the objects of this Expedition, together with the most improved charts of his atlas of the Pacific Ocean, with explanations, in three volumes.   These are also confided to your care; and it is not doubted that the friendly contributions of this distinguished navigator will essentially contribute to the success of an enterprise in which he takes so deep an interest.

You will prohibit all those under your command from furnishing any persons not belonging to the Expedition, with copies of any journal, charts, plan, memorandum, specimen, drawing, painting, or information of any kind, which has reference to the objects or proceedings of the Expedition.

It being considered highly important that no journal of these voyages, either partial or complete, should be published, without the authority and under the supervision of the government of the United States, at whose expense this Expedition is undertaken, you will, before you reach the waters of the United States, require from every person under your command the surrender of all journals, memorandums, remarks, writings, drawings, sketches, and paintings, as well as all specimens of every kind, collected or prepared during your absence from the United States.

After causing correct inventories of these to be made and signed by two commissioned officers, and by the parties by whom they were collected or prepared, you will cause them to be carefully sealed by the said officers, and reserved for such disposition as the Department may direct.

You will adopt the most effectual measures to prepare and preserve all specimens of natural history that may be collected, and should any opportunities occur for sending home by a vessel of war of the United States, copies of information, or duplicates of specimens, or any other material you may deem it important to preserve from the reach of future accident, you will avail yourself of the occasion, forwarding as frequently as may be done with safety, details of your voyage and its most material events, at the same time strictly prohibiting all communications except to this Department, from any person attached to the Expedition, referring to discoveries, or any circumstances connected with the progress of your enterprise.

It is believed that the officers under your command require no special advice or direction from this Department.   Bearing in mind, as they no doubt will, that the undertaking which they are about assisting to accomplish, is one that necessarily attracts the attention of the civilized world, and that the honour and interests of their country are equally involved in its results, it is not for a moment doubted that in this, as on all other occasions, they will so conduct themselves, as to add to the reputation our navy has so justly acquired at home and abroad.

With the best wishes for the success of the Expedition, and the safe return of yourself and your companions,

I am, very respectfully,

(Signed)   J. K. PAULDING.

To Lieutenant CHARLES WILKES,
   Commanding the Exploring and Surveying Expedition, &c.

P. S.   The accompanying printed list of English words, drawn up by Mr. Gallatin, and received from the War Department since these instructions were

prepared, are intended for Indian vocabularies, which can be filled up as circumstances permit, taking care that the same words be used in all of them.

(Signed)   J. K. PAULDING.

It is to be observed that in respect of treaties or agreements Wilkes had no special directions; and his instructions from the Secretary of the Navy contained merely a brief reference to the Samoan Islands.

The Wilkes expedition sailed from Norfolk on August 18, 1838; after nearly four years the *Vincennes*, with Captain Wilkes, arrived at New York on June 10, 1842; a report of June 25, 1846, of the Joint Committee on the Library (Senate Document No. 405, 29th Congress, 1st session, serial 477) contains the following summary of the results of the expedition:

The equipment and sailing of the expedition, however, were delayed by various causes until August, 1838, when the sloops-of-war Vincennes and Peacock, the brig Porpoise, the store-ship Relief, and the tenders Sea Gull and Flying Fish were placed under the command of Lieutenant (now commander) Wilkes.

The commander was furnished with general instructions, to be observed in the long and devious voyages contemplated. He was particularly enjoined to ascertain the existence of islands and shoals marked on the charts as doubtful; and, if found to exist, he was to determine their precise position. He was directed to make such accurate and particular examinations and surveys of various rivers, bays, ports, inlets, sounds, islands, and reefs as might be serviceable to vessels engaged in the whale fishery, and to our commerce generally. He was particularly directed to survey the Feejee and Navigator groups, and to select an island and harbor in the former, which might answer as a place of refuge and supply to our commercial marine. The government, at the same time, expressed their intention to keep a national vessel cruising near these islands in future. He was directed to examine and survey the northwest coast of America, including as well the river Columbia as the seaboard of Oregon and California; to proceed to the coast of Japan, examining carefully the sea of Sooloo, with a view to furnish sailing instructions to our navigators; and to ascertain the disposition of the inhabitants of this archipelago for commerce, as also their productions and resources. Beside all this, and much more, he was to employ two seasons in efforts to penetrate within the antarctic region, in order to ascertain the existence of the great polar continent which was supposed to extend south of Australia. The hydrography and geography of the various seas and countries visited by the squadron, during their four years' cruise, were recommended to the special attention of the commander; and all the researches connected with them, as well as the astronomical, magnetic, barometric, and meteorological observations, were confided to the officers of the squadron, whose talents and acquirements were fully adequate to these demands.

It will readily be perceived, from this brief abstract of the instructions, how wide was the field of nautical enterprise thus marked out—how various, arduous, important, and hazardous the duties imposed upon the squadron; that the faithful performance of these duties could not fail to give credit and honor to the commander and his officers, and to yield immense advantages to the navigation and commerce of the country, by adding largely to its security and extension. Subordinate to these primary objects of the expedition was the promotion of science generally, and particularly the increase of knowledge in the various departments of natural history. In order to the successful prosecution of these purposes, a corps of scientific gentlemen was appointed, who accompanied the expedition under the direction of the commander.

Thus, the expedition was organized upon a scale commensurate with the dignity of the government, the importance of the objects contemplated, and the duty which a nation, liberal, wealthy, and commercial as our own, owed to the interests of commerce, and the common cause of learning.

The country had a right to expect from the expedition honorable and advantageous results; and the committee do not hesitate to say that all such expectations have been fully realized.

The examinations and surveys are numerous, extensive, exact, minute, and beautifully executed.   They furnish a great mass of most important information to our commerce, and greatly diminish the perils of navigation.   Appended to this report will be found a list of all the separate surveys made during the cruise, also a list of the charts finished and published at the commencement of the year, and of those which remain to be engraved and printed.   These surveys will be so condensed as to be represented on one hundred and five coppers or sheets, on which will be two hundred and forty-nine charts of groups, islands, harbors, reefs, &c.   Surveys and charts have been made of some islands, harbors, and reefs not known hitherto, of many which had not before been surveyed, and of others which, though previously known and surveyed, were not accurately and minutely described on any chart.   A great many doubtful points in the geography of the Pacific ocean have been determined.   The coasts of Oregon and California, the river Sacramento, the Columbia river, and Puget's sound have been carefully surveyed, and the interior has been penetrated and explored to a great distance. The Feejees, the least known of the Pacific groups, the most extensive, the most valuable for commerce, fertile, with numerous and convenient harbors, comprising nearly one hundred and fifty islands, one of which contains about four thousand square miles, the whole group being described as "a labyrinth of lofty islands and coral reefs," have been thoroughly explored and made known.   Formerly, many disastrous wrecks occurred among these islands.   But we already know that the labors of the expedition have given security to our vessels trading in those seas.   Letters from American navigators, engaged in the important trade in biche-da-mar, sandal-wood, tortoise shell, &c., which these islands afford, testify to the great value of the chart of them which Captain Wilkes has made, and the advantages resulting to our commerce from the presence and conduct of the squadron among this group.   A letter from Captain Osborn, received in May, 1841, says: "Thanks to your excellent chart, I have been enabled to sail night and day by it, without fear of reefs and shoals.   I have been enabled to have three and four biche-da-mar houses in operation at one time, by which I soon filled up, and made a much shorter voyage than was ever before made."

Many of these surveys were accomplished under circumstances of great hardship and danger.   The officers and men were frequently required, for this purpose, to engage in boat service, where they were exposed, not only to the discomforts usually attending such service, but to all the perils of the ocean in unknown regions, to storms and burning heats, from which they had no protection but such as they carried in their boats—frequently with short and hard fare, and for periods exceeding the time ordinarily required for a voyage across the Atlantic, during which the labor was severe and incessant.   Some of the boats of the squadron, during their stay among the Feejee islands, were absent from their respective ships as long as forty days in one expedition, under instructions not to land on any inhabited island, and always at night, or when natives were near them, to have their boarding nettings up, and a watch of two men and an officer. The cruise occupied three years and ten months, during which the squadron sailed 87,780 miles.   While among the Feejee islands, the boats of one of the ships sailed 8,225 miles, not including passages from the ship to the shore and harbor surveys.   Seven hundred miles of the coast of Oregon and California were surveyed, besides the rivers, harbors, and bays.

The antarctic explorations required all the energies of stout hearts and manly frames, and all the devices of nautical skill.   There are no adventures, even amidst the seaman's hazardous life, so exciting and perilous as those which the squadron pursued amidst the wild and desolate scenes of the polar ocean.   There they discovered land, and sailed along its frozen barrier for 1,500 miles, amidst storms and islands of ice, which constantly threatened their destruction.

The little schooner Flying Fish reached latitude 70°14' south, nearly the highest point reached by Captain Cook.

During the stay of the squadron at the Sandwich islands, Captain Wilkes scaled the summit of Launa Loa, and surveyed its crater, carrying the pendulum and other philosophical instruments to the summit—a height of 14,000 feet.

All these hardships and labors were suffered and performed with a cheerfulness, and indeed an enthusiasm, which secured success, and reflected the highest honor upon the officers and men.   The committee think they are entitled to and hope they will yet receive some distinct mark of their country's approbation.

In other countries, such voyages have procured honors and rewards for the officers engaged in them. The French government made D'Urville an admiral; Ross was knighted, and the subordinate officers were advanced one grade. The committee believe the services of the officers of our expedition to have been, at least, equally meritorious.

The gentlemen of the scientific corps are entitled to equal praise for their zeal and devotion to the service entrusted to them. When these reports shall all be published, they will furnish a contribution of the highest importance to science, which will justify the expenditure so liberally made by the government, and give reputation to those who risked many of the perils, and shared in many of the hardships, of one of the longest and most laborious voyages of discovery ever made. The collection of specimens of natural history was often attended with difficulty and peril, and not unfrequently articles of rarity and value were obtained only by the expenditure of the private funds of the civilian and the officer. These collections in the various departments of natural history are exceedingly rich, various, and valuable. In whatever country they visited, the scientific corps, frequently in company with parties of officers, penetrated the forests and climbed the mountains wherever practicable. Every department of natural history—all that could illustrate the history of the different races of men they met with—their migrations, languages, physical or moral characteristics—received the most earnest attention. They made frequent and long excursions into the interior of several countries. Mr. Drayton travelled along the Columbia river as far as the Blue Mountains; another party—among whom were Messrs. Peale, Dana, Rich, Agate, and Brackenridge—went from Fort Vancouver, southward, across the land to San Francisco; a third party left one of the ships at Fort Nesqually, travelling east to Fort Colville, thence southeast to the head waters of the Kooskooske river, &c. Mr. Hale made considerable excursions in New Holland, New Zealand, and Oregon, and returned from California overland to the United States. Dr. Pickering was a bold explorer, and made numerous excursions in Brazil and elsewhere.

The interior of the Polynesian islands was thoroughly explored, and some of the scientific corps even passed from the Pacific coast across the Cordilleras of the Andes to the sources of the Amazon river.

The herbarium of the expedition contains about 50,000 specimens, and 10,000 species; the number of *new* genera and species being 2,000. The filices, or ferns, alone number 800 species, of which one-third are new, having never yet been published or described in any botanical work. They are double in number those collected by any similar voyage of discovery. Between eight and nine hundred species of plants are cultivated at the green-house, under the charge of Mr. Brackenbridge, the horticulturist, many of which are new. Eleven hundred and fifty-six different kinds of seeds were obtained during the expedition, and two hundred and five living plants were brought home, and are now in the green house.

In ornithology and mammalia more than 2,000 specimens and 1,000 species were collected, of which about 130 are new species. Much important information has been obtained as to the geographical distribution, &c., of the varieties in this department, as well as in botany.

The committee have been furnished with the following list of species collected in other departments of natural history:

Fishes, 829; reptiles, 140; crustacea, 900; insects, 1,500; shells, 3,000; zoophytes, exclusive of corals, 300; corals, 450.

Of these, the number of new species is nearly as follows:

Fishes, 500, of which 5 are believed to be new genera; reptiles, 40; crustacea, 600; insects, 500; shells, about 350; zoophytes, exclusive of corals, 200; corals, 100.

Nearly 2,000 zoological drawings were made during the cruise by Messrs. Drayton, Agate, and Dana.

The whole of these collections constitute of themselves, a valuable national museum.

THE NARRATIVE

The act of August 26, 1842 (5 Statutes at Large, 534), provided for the publication of "an account of the discoveries made by the Exploring Expedition, under the command of Lieutenant Wilkes of the United States navy", and for the printing of 100 copies thereof for the United States. Distribution of copies of the work, chiefly to other Governments, was directed by the joint resolution of February 20, 1845 (*ibid.*, 797).

That official edition is a quarto. As finally planned it comprised twenty-four volumes and eleven atlases, but certain of the volumes were not published (see Poore, A Descriptive Catalogue of the Government Publications, 500). The first five volumes contain the narrative; the remaining volumes are devoted to the scientific results of the expedition. One of them, volume 17, was not published until 1874, although the five narrative volumes appeared in 1844. The publication was the subject of various congressional reports (e.g., Senate Report No. 391, 35th Congress, 2d session, serial 994).

Wilkes secured copyright on the five volumes of his narrative and under that privilege printed 250 copies of the quarto edition, 100 copies of which, with the publication date 1844 and bearing on the half-title page the words "By authority of Congress", were for the Government, and the remaining 150 copies of which, with the publication date 1845 and bearing the notice of copyright on the verso of the title page, were reserved by Wilkes for "presentation to my friends, and for sale".

Another edition of the narrative, an octavo, was published by Captain Wilkes in 1845 (see his letter of January 28, 1845, in House Report No. 160, 28th Congress, 2d session, serial 468, and Senate Document No. 405, 29th Congress, 1st session, serial 477, p. 11); the volumes of the octavo edition do not have the same pagination as the corresponding volumes of the quarto. Various other editions of the narrative were published between 1845 and 1856. It is the quarto, or official edition, which is cited in these notes.

SAMOA

Samoa, an island group in the South Pacific, consists of about fourteen islands lying between latitude 13° and 15° south and between longitude 168° and 173° west of Greenwich. The islands lying east of the meridian of 171° west longitude belong to the United States, and, together with Swains Island, situated approximately 200 miles north of the Samoan group, comprise the political entity of American Samoa; those west of that meridian constitute the Territory of Western Samoa (the former German Colony of Samoa), administered by New Zealand under a mandate of the League of Nations.

The total area of American Samoa is approximately 60 square miles, and the population in 1930 numbered 10,055. The principal island is Tutuila, area 40.2 square miles, containing Pago Pago Bay, the "best and safest harbor in the South Seas", on which is situated the United

States naval station and the seat of government. The islands of eastern Samoa were formerly officially designated "United States Naval Station, Tutuila", but they are now known in acts of Congress as "American Samoa".

The total area of Western Samoa is approximately 1,133 square miles, with a population estimated June 30, 1930, at 45,065. The principal islands are Savai'i (Savaii), area 703 square miles, and Upolu, area 430 square miles. Apia, a port on the island of Upolu, is the administrative center.

The Samoan group lies at the crossroads of several well-established steamship routes. The sailing distance from Pago Pago to San Francisco is 4,150 nautical (4,779 statute) miles; to Honolulu 2,276 nautical miles; and to Sydney, Australia, 2,377 nautical miles.

Treaty Series No. 153
8 Statutes at Large, 552–59
18 *ibid.*, pt. 2, Public Treaties, 387–91

92

HANOVER : MAY 20, 1840

Treaty of Commerce and Navigation, signed at Berlin May 20, 1840.
Original in French and English.
Submitted to the Senate June 24, 1840. (Message of June 22, 1840.)
Resolution of advice and consent July 15, 1840. Ratified by the
United States July 28, 1840. Ratified by Hanover November 4,
1840. Ratifications exchanged at Berlin November 14, 1840. Pro-
claimed January 2, 1841.

Les Etats-Unis d'Amérique et Sa Majesté le Roi de Hanôvre également animés du désir d'étendre autant que possible les relations commerciales et l'échange des produits entre leurs Etats respectifs sont convenus dans ce but de conclure un Traité de Commerce et de Navigation.

A cet effet le Président des Etats-Unis d'Amérique a muni de pleins-pouvoirs, Henry Wheaton, Leur Envoyé Extraordinaire et Ministre Plénipotentiaire près sa Majesté le Roi de Prusse; et Sa Majesté le Roi de Hanôvre a muni des mêmes pouvoirs, le Sieur Auguste de Berger, Son Envoyé Extraordinaire et Ministre Plénipotentiaire près Sa Majesté le Roi de Prusse, Lieutenant-Général, Chevalier Grand-Croix de l'ordre des Guelphes, de l'aigle rouge de Prusse, de l'ordre pour le mérite de Oldenburg &c

The United States of America and His Majesty the King of Hanover, equally animated by the desire of extending as far as possible the commercial relations between, and the exchange of the productions of their respective States, have agreed, with this view, to conclude a Treaty of Commerce and Navigation.

For this purpose, the President of the United States of America has furnished with full-powers, Henry Wheaton, Their Envoy Extraordinary and Minister Plenipotentiary near His Majesty the King of Prussia; and His Majesty the King of Hanover has furnished with the like full powers, le Sieur Auguste de Berger, His Envoy Extraordinary and Minister Plenipotentiairy near His Majesty the King of Prussia, Lieutenant-General, Knight Grand-Cross of the order of Guelph, the red eagle of Prussia, the order of

&c &c lesquels Plénipotentiaires après avoir échangé leurs dits pleins-pouvoirs, trouvés en bonne et due forme, ont arrêté et signé, sous la réserve de la ratification, les articles suivans:

merit of Oldenburg &c, who after exchanging their said full-powers, found in good and due form, have concluded and signed, subject to ratification, the following articles:

ART: 1.

Il y aura entre les territoires des Hautes Parties Contractantes liberté et reciprocité de commerce et de navigation.

Les habitants de leurs états respectifs pourront, réciproque- ment, entrer avec ou sans leurs vaisseaux et cargaisons, dans les ports, places, eaux et rivières des territoires de chacune d'Elles, partout où le commerce étranger est permis.

Ils seront libres de s'y arrêter et résider dans quelque partie que ce soit des dits territoires, pour y vaquer à leurs affaires, et de louer et occuper des maisons et magazins pour leur négoce, pour- vu qu'ils se soumettent aux lois tant générales que spéciales, réla- tives au droit d'y résider et d'y faire le commerce.

En se conformant aux lois et règlemens en vigueur, ils pour- ront, eux-mêmes, diriger libre- ment leurs propres affaires dans tous les territoires soumis à la juridiction de chacune d'Elles, tant pour ce qui a rapport à la consignation et à la vente en gros et en détail de leurs denrées et marchandises, que pour ce qui regarde le chargement, décharge- ment et expédition de leurs bâti-

ART: 1.

There shall be between the ter- ritories of the High Contracting Parties a reciprocal liberty of commerce and navigation.

The inhabitants of their re- spective states shall mutually have liberty to enter, with or with- out their ships, and cargoes, the ports, places, waters and rivers of the territories of Each Party wherever foreign commerce is permitted.

They shall be permitted to so- journ and reside in all parts what- soever of said territories, in order to attend to their affairs, and also to hire and occupy houses and ware-houses, for the purposes of their commerce, provided they submit to the laws as well general as special, relative to the right of residing and trading.

Whilst they conform to the laws and regulations in force, they shall be at liberty to manage them- selves their own business in all the territories subject to the jurisdic- tion of Each Party, in respect to the consignment, and sale of their goods, by wholesale or retail, as with respect to the loading, un- loading and sending off their ships, or to employ such agents and brokers as they may deem

mens, ou d'employer tels agents et courtiers qu'ils trouveront convenables;—ils seront dans tous ces cas, traités comme les citoyens ou sujets du pays dans lequel ils résident; néamoins il est bien entendu, qu'ils restent assujettis aux dits lois et règlemens, aussi en ce qui regarde les ventes en gros et en détail.

Ils auront pleine liberté de recourir aux tribunaux de justice pour leurs affaires litigeuses aux mêmes conditions qui seront accordées par la loi et l'usage aux citoyen ou sujet du pays et d'employer dans leurs procès, pour la défence de leurs droits, tels avocats avoués ou autres agens qu'ils trouveront convenables de choisir.

proper, they being, in all these cases, to be treated as the citizens or subjects of the country in which they reside, it being nevertheless understood that they shall remain subject to the said laws and regulations also in respect to sales by wholesale or retail.

They shall have free access to the tribunals of justice in their litigous affairs on the same terms which are granted by the law and usage of the country to native citizens or subjects, for which purpose they may employ in defence of their rights such advocates, attornies and other agents as they may judge proper.

Art: 2.

Il ne sera imposé d'autres ni de plus forts droits ou charges sur les vaisseaux Hanôvriens dans les ports des Etats-Unis que ceux payables dans les mêmes ports par les vaisseaux des Etats-Unis; ni dans les ports du Royaume de Hanôvre sur les vaisseaux des Etats-Unis que ceux qui sont payables dans les mêmes ports par des vaisseaux Hanôvriens.

Les privilèges accordés par cet article aux vaisseaux des Hautes Parties Contractantes respectives ne seront applicables qu'aux vaisseaux construis dans leurs territoires respectifs, ou légalement condamnés comme de prises de guerre, ou confisqués pour la vio-

Art: 2.

No higher or other duties shall be imposed in any of the ports of the United States on Hanoverian vessels, than those payable in the same ports by vessels of the United States; nor in the ports of the Kingdom of Hanover on the vessels of the United States than shall be payable in the same ports on Hanoverian vessels.

The privileges secured by the present article to the vessels of the respective High Contracting Parties shall only extend to such as are built within their respective territories, or lawfully condemned as prize of war, or adjudged to be forfieted for a breach of the mu-

lation des lois municipales de l'une ou de l'autre des parties, et appartenant exclusivement à leurs citoyens ou sujets respectifs, et desquels le capitaine, les sous-officiers et les deux tiers de l'équipage seront des citoyens ou sujets du pays auquel le vaisseau appartient.

Les mêmes droits seront payés sur l'importation dans les ports des Etats-Unis des articles provenant du sol ou de l'industrie du Royaume de Hanôvre ou de tout autre pays de la Confédération Germanique et du Royaume de Prusse, n'importe de quels ports des pays susmentionnés que ces vaisseaux sortent, si ces mêmes articles sont importés dans les vaisseaux des Etats-Unis, ou dans les vaisseaux Hanôvriens; et les mêmes droits seront payés sur l'importation dans les ports du Royaume d'Hanôvre des articles provenant du sol ou de l'industrie des Etats-Unis ou de tout autre pays du continent de l'Amérique et des Antilles, n'importe de quels ports des pays susmentionnés que ces vaisseaux sortent, si ces mêmes articles sont importés dans les vaisseaux Hanôvriens ou dans les vaisseaux des Etats-Unis.

Les mêmes droits seront payés et les mêmes primes accordées sur l'exportation aux Etats-Unis, des articles, provenant du sol ou de l'industrie du Royaume de Hanôvre ou de tout autre pays de la Confédération Germanique et

nicipal laws of Either of the Parties, and belonging wholly to their citizens or subjects respectively, and of which the Master, officers and two thirds of the crew shall consist of the citizens or subjects of the Country to which the vessel belongs.

The same duties shall be paid on the importation into the ports of the United States of any articles, the growth, produce or manufacture of the Kingdom of Hanover, or of any other Country belonging to the Germanic Confederation and the Kingdom of Prussia, from whatsoever ports of the said country the said vessels may depart, whether such importation shall be in vessels of the United States or in Hanoverian vessels; and the same duties shall be paid on the importation into the ports of the Kingdom of Hanover, of any articles, the growth, produce or manufacture of the United States and of every other country of the Continent of America and the West-India islands, from whatsoever ports of the said countries the vessels may depart whether such importation shall be in Hanoverian vessels or the vessels of the United States.

The same duties shall be paid and the same bounties allowed on the exportation of any articles, the growth, produce or manufacture of the Kingdom of Hanover, or of any other country, belonging to the Germanic Confederation

du Royaume de Prusse, si ces mêmes articles sont exportés dans les vaisseaux des Etats-Unis ou dans les vaisseaux Hanôvriens qui sortent de ports Hanôvriens; et les mêmes droits seront payés et les mêmes primes accordées sur l'exportation au Royaume de Hanôvre des articles provenant du sol ou de l'industrie des Etats-Unis et de tout autre pays du continent de l'Amérique et des Antilles, si ces mêmes articles sont exportés dans les vaisseaux Hanôvriens ou dans ceux des Etats-Unis, qui sortent des ports des Etats-Unis.

and the Kingdom of Prussia, to the United States, whether such exportation shall be in vessels of the United States or in Hanoverian vessels, departing from the ports of Hanover, and the same duties shall be paid and the same bounties allowed on the exportation of any articles, the growth, produce or manufacture of the United States and of every other country on the Continent of America and the West-India islands, to the Kingdom of Hanover, whether such exportation shall be in Hanoverian vessels or in vessels of the United States, departing from the ports of the United States.

Art: 3.

Il ne sera imposé d'autres ni de plus forts droits sur l'importation aux Etats-Unis des articles provenant du sol ou de l'industrie du Royaume d'Hanôvre, et il ne sera imposé d'autres ni de plus forts droits sur l'importation dans le Royaume de Hanôvre, des articles provenant du sol ou de l'industrie des Etats-Unis, que ceux qui sont ou seront imposés sur le mêmes articles provenant du sol ou de l'industrie de tout autre pays étranger.

Il ne sera imposé d'autres ni de plus forts droits dans les Etats-Unis sur l'exportation des articles de marchandise au Royaume de Hanôvre ou dans le Royaume de Hanôvre sur l'exportation des

Art: 3.

No higher or other duties shall be imposed on the importation into the United States of any articles, the growth, produce or manufacture of the Kingdom of Hanover and no higher or other duties shall be imposed on the importation into the Kingdom of Hanover of any articles, the growth, produce or manufacture of the United States, than are or shall be payable on the like articles, being the growth, produce or manufacture of any other foreign country.

No higher or other duties and charges shall be imposed in the United States, on the exportation of any articles to the Kingdom of Hanover, or in Hanover, on the exportation of any articles to the

articles de marchandise aux Etats-Unis que ceux qui sont ou seront imposés sur l'exportation des mêmes articles à tout autre pays étranger.

Il ne sera imposé sur l'exportation ou sur l'importation des articles provenant du sol ou de l'industrie des Etats-Unis ou du Royaume de Hanôvre, à la sortie ou à l'entrée du même Royaume ou des Etats-Unis, aucune prohibition qui ne soit pas également applicable à toute autre nation.

Art: 4.

Les articles précédens ne sont pas applicables au commerce ou à la navigation de côte ou de cabotage des Hautes Parties Contractantes que l'une et l'autre se réservent exclusivement à ses propres citoyens ou sujets.

Art: 5.

Il ne sera accordé par l'une et par l'autre des Parties Contractantes, ni par aucune compagnie, corporation ou agent, agissant en son nom et par son autorité, aucune priorité ou préférence, quelconque, pour l'achat d'aucun objet de commerce, légalement importé, à cause ou en considération de la nationalité du navire qui aurait importé les dits objets, soit qu'il appartient à l'une des parties, soit à l'autre.

United States, than such as are or shall be payable on the exportation of the like articles to any other foreign country.

No prohibition shall be imposed on the exportation or importation of any articles, the growth, produce or manufacture of the United States, or the Kingdom of Hanover, to or from the ports of said Kingdom or of the said United States, which shall not equally extend to all other nations.

Art: 4.

The preceding articles are not applicable to the coasting trade and navigation of the High Contracting Parties which are respectively reserved by Each exclusively to its own citizens or subjects.

Art: 5.

No priority or preference shall be given by Either of the Contracting Parties, nor by any company, corporation or agent, acting on their behalf, or under their authority in the purchase of any article of commerce lawfully imported, on account or in in reference to the national character of the vessel, whether it be of the one party or of the other in which such article was imported.

ART: 6.

Les Parties Contractantes se sont accordé mutuellement la faculté de tenir dans leurs ports respectifs, des consuls, vice-consuls, agens ou commissaires de leur choix, qui jouiront des mêmes privilèges et pouvoirs dont jouissent ceux des nations les plus favorisées; mais dans le cas, ou les dits consuls, veuillent faire le commerce, ils seront soumis aux mêmes lois et usages, auxquels sont soumis les particuliers de leur nation à l'endroit où ils resident.

Les consuls, vice-consuls, et agens commerciaux auront le droit, comme tels, de servir de juges et d'arbitres dans les différens qui pourraient s'éléver entre les capitaines et les équipages des bâtimens de la nation, dont ils soignent les interêts sans que les autorités locales puissent y intervenir, à moins que la conduite des équipages ou du capitaine ne troublât l'ordre ou la tranquillité du pays, ou que les dits consuls, vice-consuls ou agens commerciaux, ne requissent leur intervention pour exécuter ou maintenir leurs décisions.

Il est néanmoins bien entendu que cette espèce de jugement ou d'arbitrage, ne saurait, pourtant priver les parties contendantes du droit qu'elles ont, à leur retour, de recourir aux autorités judiciaires de leur pays.

ART: 6.

The Contracting Parties grant to Each other the liberty of having, Each in the ports of the other, consuls, vice-consuls, agents and commissaries of their own appointment, who shall enjoy the same privileges and powers as those of the most favored nations; but if any of the said consuls, shall carry on trade, they shall be subjected to the same laws and usages to which private individuals of their nation are subjected in the same place.

The consuls, vice-consuls and commercial agents shall have the right, as such, to sit as judges and arbitrators in such differences as may arise between the masters and crews of the vessels belonging to the nation, whose interests are committed to their charge, without the interference of the local authorities, unless the conduct of the crews or of the Captain should disturb the order or tranquillity of the country; or the said consuls, vice-consuls or commercial agents should require their assistance to cause their decisions to be carried into effect or supported.

It is, however, understood, that this species of judgment or arbitration shall not deprive the contending parties of the right they have to resort on their return, to the judicial authority of their own country.

Les dits consuls, vice-consuls, ou agens commerciaux sont autorisés à requérir l'assistance des autorités locales pour la recherche, l'arrestation, la détention et l'emprisonnement des déserteurs des navires de guerre et marchands de leur pays.

Ils s'adressent pour cet objet aux tribunaux, juges et officiers compétens et réclameront par écrit les déserteurs susmentionnés, en prouvant par la communication des régistres des navires, ou rôles d'équipage, ou par d'autres documens officiels, que de tels individus ont fait partie des dits équipages et cette réclamation ainsi prouvée—l'extradition ne sera point refusée.

De tels deserteurs, lorsqu'ils auront été arrêtés, seront mis à la disposition des dits consuls, vice-consuls ou agents commerciaux et pourront être enfermés dans les prisons publiques, à la réquisition et aux frais de ceux qui les réclament pour être envoyés aux navires, auxquels ils appartenaient, ou à d'autres de la même nation. Mais s'ils ne sont pas renvoyés dans l'espace de trois mois, à compter du jour de leur arrestation, ils seront mis en liberté, et ne seront plus arrêtés pour la même cause. Toutefois, si le déserteur se trouvait avoir commis quelque crime ou délit, il pourra être sursis à son extradition, jusqu'à ce que le tribunal

The said consuls, vice-consuls and commercial agents are authorized to require the assistance of the local authorities for the search, arrest and imprisonment of the deserters from the ships of war, and merchant vessels of their Country.

For this purpose they shall apply to the competent tribunals, judges and officers, and shall, in writing, demand said deserters, proving by the exhibition of the registers of the vessels, the muster-rolls of the crews, or by any other official documents, that such individuals formed part of the crews; and on this claim being thus substantiated, the surrender shall not be refused.

Such deserters, when arrested, shall be placed at the disposal of the said consuls, vice-consuls, or commercial agents, and may be confined in the public prisons, at the request and cost of those who shall claim them, in order to be sent to the vessels to which they belong, or to others of the same country. But if not sent back within three months from the day of their arrest, they shall be set at liberty and shall not be again arrested for the same cause. However if the deserter shall be found to have committed any crime or offence, his surrender may be delayed until the tribunal, before which his case shall be pending, shall have pronounced

nanti de l'affaire aura rendu sa sentence et que celle-ci ait reçu son exécution.

ART: 7.

Les citoyens ou sujets de chacune des Parties Contractantes, auront dans les états de l'autre, la liberté de disposer de leurs biens-meubles et immeubles, soit par vente, donation, testament ou autrement.

Leurs héritiers, étant sujets ou citoyens de l'autre Partie Contractante, succéderont à leurs biens, soit en vertu d'un testament ou *ab intestato*.

Ils pourront en prendre possession, soit en personne, soit par d'autres agissant en leur place, et en disposeront à leur volonté, en ne payant d'autres droits que ceux auxquels les habitants du pays, où se trouvent les dits biens, sont assujettis en pareille occasion.

En cas d'absence des héritiers, on prendra provisoirement des dits biens les mêmes soins qu'on aurait pris en pareille occasion des biens de natifs du pays, jusqu'à ce que le propriétaire légitime ait agrée des arrangements pour recueillir l'héritage.

S'ils s'élèvent des contestations entre différens prétandans ayant droit à la succession, elles seront decidées en dernier ressort, selon les lois et par les juges du pays où la succession est vacante.

its sentence, and such sentence shall have been carried into effect.

ART: 7.

The citizens or subjects of Each Party shall have power to dispose of their personal property within the jurisdiction of the other, by sale, donation, testament or otherwise.

Their personal representatives, being citizens or subjects of the other Contracting Party, shall succeed to their said personal property, whether by testament or *ab intestato*.

They may take possession thereof, either by themselves or by others acting for them, at their will, and dispose of the same, paying such duties only as the inhabitants of the country wherein the said personal property is situate, shall be subject to pay in like cases.

In case of the absence of the personal representatives, the same care shall be taken of the said property as would be taken of the property of a native in like case, until the lawfull owner may take measures for receiving it.

If any question should arise among several claimants to which of them the said property belongs, the same shall be finally decided by the laws and judges of the country wherein it is situate.

Si par la mort de quelque personne possédant des biens fonds sur le territoire de l'une des Parties Contractantes, ces biens fonds venaient à passer à un citoyen ou sujet de l'autre partie; celui-ci, si par sa qualité d'étranger il est inhabile à les posséder, obtiendra un délai convenable pour les vendre, et pour en retirer le produit sans obstacle, et exempts de tout droit de détraction de la part du gouvernement des états respectifs.

Les capitaux et fonds que les citoyens ou sujets des parties respectives, en changeant de demeure, voudront faire sortir de l'endroit de leur domicile, seront aussi exempts de tout droit de détraction ou d'émigration de la part des gouvernemens respectifs.

ART: 8.

L'ancien et barbare droit de naufrage sera entièrement aboli à l'égard des sujets ou citoyens des deux Parties Contractantes.

Au cas que quelque vaisseau appartenant à l'une des Parties Contractantes aurait fait naufrage, échoué, ou souffert quelque autre avarie sur les côtes ou sous la domination de l'autre, les sujets ou citoyens respectifs recevront, tant pour eux que pour les vaisseaux et effets, la même assistance qui aurait été fournie aux habitants du pays où l'accident arrive.

Where, on the decease of any person, holding real estate within the territories of one Party, such real estate would, by the laws of the land descend on a citizen or subject of the other were he not disqualified by alienage, such citizen or subject shall be allowed a reasonable time to sell the same, and to withdraw the proceeds without molestation, and exempt from all duties of *détraction* on the part of the Government of the respective States.

The capitals and effects which the citizens or subjects of the respective parties, in changing their residence, shall be desirous of removing from the place of their domicil, shall likewise be exempt from all duties of *détraction* or emigration on the part of the respective Governments.

ART: 8.

The ancient and barbarous right to wrecks of the sea shall be entirely abolished with respect to the property belonging to the citizens or subjects of the Contracting Parties.

When any vessel of Either Party shall be wrecked, stranded or otherwise damaged on the coasts, or within the dominions of the other, their respective citizens or subjects shall receive, as well for themselves as for their vessels and effects, the same assistance which would be due to the inhabitants of the country where the accident happens.

Ils payeront seulement les mêmes charges et droits de sauvetage, auxquels les dits habitants auraient été assujettis en pareil cas.

Si la réparation du vaisseau exigeait que la cargaison fût déchargée en tout ou en partie, ils ne payeront aucun impôt, charge ou droit, de ce qui sera rembarqué et remporté, qui ne soit ou sera payé en pareil cas par les vaisseaux nationaux de leurs cargaisons.

Toutefois il est entendu, que si pendant la réparation d'un vaisseau, la cargaison était déchargée et gardée dans un dépôt, destinés à recevoir les marchandises, dont les droits n'ont pas encore été payés, la cargaison ne pourra pas être exemptée des charges et droits dûs aux entrepreneurs des dépôts susmentionnés.

ART: 9.

Le présent Traité sera en vigueur pendant douze ans à dater de ce jour; et au delà de ce terme jusqu'à l'expiration de douze mois après que le Gouvernement des Etats-Unis d'une part, ou celui du Hanôvre de l'autre, aura annoncé à l'autre son intention de le terminer.

ART: 10.

Le présent Traité sera approuvé et ratifié par le Président des Etats-Unis d'Amérique par et avec l'avis et le consentement du Sénat des dits Etats; et par Sa

They shall be liable to pay the same charges and dues of Salvage as the said inhabitants would be liable to pay in a like case.

If the operations of repair shall require that the whole or any part of the cargo be unloaded, they shall pay no duties of custom, charges or fees, on the part which they shall reload and carry away, except as are payable in the like cases by national vessels.

It is nevertheless understood that if, whilst the vessel is under repair, the Cargo shall be unladen, and kept in a place of deposite, destined to receive goods, the duties on which have not been paid, the Cargo shall be liable to the charges and fees lawfully due to the keepers of such warehouses.

ART: 9.

The present Treaty shall be in force for the term of twelve years from the date hereof: and further until the end of twelve months after the Government of the United States on the one part or that of Hanover on the other, shall have given notice of its intention of terminating the same.

ART: 10.

The present Treaty shall be approved and ratified by the President of the United States of America by and with the advice and consent of Their Senate;

Majesté le Roi de Hanôvre; et les ratifications en seront échangées en la ville de Berlin dans l'espace de dix mois, à dater de ce jour ou plutôt si faire se peut.

En foi de quoi les Plénipotentiaires respectifs ont signé les articles ci-dessus, tant en francais qu'en anglais et y ont apposé leurs sceaux, déclarant toutefois que la signature dans ces deux langues ne doit pas, par la suite, être citée comme exemple, ni, en aucune manière, porter préjudice aux Parties Contractantes.

Fait par quadruplicata en la cité de Berlin le vingt du mois de Mai, l'an de grâce mille huit-cent et quarante et la soixante-quatrième de l'Indépendance des Etats-Unis d'Amérique.

[Seal] HENRY WHEATON
[Seal] AUGUSTE DE BERGER

and by His Majesty the King of Hanover; and the ratifications thereof shall be exchanged at the city of Berlin, within the space of ten months from this date, or sooner if possible.

In faith whereof the respective Plenipotentiaries have signed the above articles as well in French as in English, and have affixed thereto the Seals of their arms, declaring at the same time that the signature in the two languages shall not hereafter be cited as a precedent, nor in any manner prejudice the Contracting Parties.

Done in quadruplicate at the city of Berlin the twentieth day of May in the year of our Lord, one thousand eight-hundred and forty and the sixty-fourth of the Independance of the United-States of America.

[Seal] HENRY WHEATON
[Seal] AUGUSTUS DE BERGER

NOTES

In the testimonium clause of the treaty it is said that it was "done in quadruplicate". There are two signed originals in the treaty file, one of which was received from the archives of the Legation of the United States at Berlin in 1875. The other, with which the text here printed has been collated, is bound with the duplicate United States instrument of ratification of July 28, 1840, and the original proclamation of January 2, 1841.

The treaty file includes the attested Senate resolution of July 15, 1840 (Executive Journal, V, 302–3), and the protocol, in French, of the exchange of ratifications at Berlin on November 14, 1840, as well as the instrument of ratification on the part of Hanover. The document last mentioned, written in German, is of somewhat unusual form in that it does not include the full text of the treaty in either language but merely, in French and in English, the opening words of Article 1 and the concluding words of the testimonium clause. Such a form is so seldom found in the ratifications of bilateral treaties

that its text is here printed (translation from the German, omitting the signature, countersignature, etc.):

Ernest Augustus, by the Grace of God King of Hanover, Royal Prince of Great Britain and Ireland, Duke of Cumberland, Duke of Brunswick and Lüneburg, etc:

We have been moved to have concluded at Berlin on May 21 of the current year, 1840, a Treaty of Navigation and Commerce by the Plenipotentiary named by Us to that end with the Plenipotentiary of the Free States of North America, the articles and provisions of which begin with the following words:

in the French text:

ART. 1. Il y aura entre les territoires des Hautes Parties Contractantes liberté et réciprocité de commerce et de navigation, etc.

and in the English text:

ART. 1. There shall be between the territories of the High Contracting Parties a reciprocal liberty of commerce and navigation, etc.

And end with the following words:

in the French text:

ne doit pas par la suite être citée comme exemple, ni, en aucune manière, porter préjudice aux Parties Contractantes.

and in the English text:

shall not hereafter be cited as a precedent, nor in any manner prejudice the Contracting Parties.

Since We have now examined this agreement and found the same in accord with Our intentions, We therefore hereby accept and ratify the same in all points and promise faithfully to carry out the same and also to cause the same to be fulfilled by Our Government.

In witness whereof We have drawn up the present document of ratification thereof, have signed the same with Our own hand, and have caused to be affixed hereto Our royal seal.

Given at Hanover on the fourth of November of the year one thousand eight hundred and forty, and of Our reign the fourth.

Doubtless two of the four signed originals of the treaty were for the Government of Hanover, and presumably in them the King of Hanover is named first throughout, with the signatures of the Plenipotentiaries in corresponding order; but in view of the form of the Hanoverian instrument of ratification this cannot be definitely stated. In each of the two originals which are in the treaty file the United States of America is named first and the signature of Henry Wheaton precedes that of Auguste de Berger.

No mention is made of papers accompanying this treaty when it was submitted to the Senate with the presidential message of June 22, 1840 (Executive Journal, V, 295); some of the instructions and correspondence, however, did so accompany the treaty and are printed in Senate Confidential Document G, 26th Congress, 1st session (Regular Confidential Documents, XI, 347–75). That document is cited hereafter in these notes for writings which have not been found in the archives of the Department of State. On the other hand, certain

items of relevant correspondence hereafter cited are not printed in that document.

With his despatch of September 13, 1875 (D. S., 9 Despatches, Germany, No. 171), J. C. Bancroft Davis, then Minister at Berlin, transmitted to the Department of State some eighteen original documents found in the archives of his Legation; among them were four now in this treaty file, namely, a signed original of the treaty, the full power of the King of Hanover under date of August 8, 1839, to Auguste de Berger to negotiate and sign the treaty, the full power of August 7, 1840, to Henry Wheaton to exchange the ratifications, and the protocol of exchange of ratifications of November 14, 1840.

At no time was there a regular diplomatic representative of either the United States or Hanover residing at the capital of the other Government; this treaty was negotiated on behalf of the United States by Henry Wheaton, then Minister to Prussia.

THE TEXTS

There are some slight differences between the texts of the two originals in the treaty file, both in the French and in the English. Some of these are mere matters of capitalization; others are matters of punctuation, all of which seem quite immaterial. In what may be called the other original, that is, the one not here used for collating, various marks of punctuation, mostly commas, here printed, are omitted; and in about the same number of cases a comma or semicolon, not here appearing, is inserted. In the French text there are two instances of variant spellings. The differences in wording are five, all in the English text: In the "other original" the opening words of Article 2 are "No higher or other duties or charges"; in Article 2, instead of reading "whatsoever ports of the said country", the wording is "whatsoever port of the said countries"; in Article 5 "on account or" reads "on account of or" and "in in reference to" (obviously an error) reads "in reference to"; and in Article 9 "on the other" reads "on the other part".

In the testimonium clause of the treaty, while it is mentioned that the articles were signed in the two languages, there is added a declaration that "the signature in the two languages shall not hereafter be cited as a precedent, nor in any manner prejudice the Contracting Parties", a phrase which appears in slightly different wording in the testimonium clause of the convention of September 30, 1800, with France (Document 25); but here the French language was not that of either of the parties. Similar expressions are to be found in two other treaties of about this period with German states (Prussia, May 1, 1828, Document 62; Hesse, March 26, 1844, Document 106).

After the signature of the treaty the Hanoverian Government proposed that upon the exchange of ratifications it should be declared that the French text of the treaty "should be considered as conclusive of any question that might arise as to the true intent & meaning of the compact" (D. S., 2 Despatches, Prussia, No. 154, July 8, 1840); the proposal was not finally pressed (*ibid.*, No. 163, November 14,

1840), as this Government "believed that the consent of the Senate is indispensable to such a condition, which could not be obtained in time for the exchange of ratifications within the period stipulated by the Treaty" (D. S., 14 Instructions, Prussia, 35–36, August 14, 1840).

THE FULL POWERS

In this case it appears that the original full powers were exchanged. The full power given to Henry Wheaton, Minister to Prussia, was under date of December 15, 1837; its language had been in part suggested by him (D. S., 1 Despatches, Prussia, No. 49, October 11, 1837; 14 Instructions, Prussia, 24, December 15, 1837); its clause of substance included the following (D. S., 2 Credences, 286):

to meet & confer with any person or persons, furnished with like powers on the part of the Kingdom of Hanover, & of the Grand Duchy of Oldenberg, the Duchy of Brunswick, & of any other State or States that may join the Commercial & Custom's Union, formed by them, or any or either of them, & with him or them to negotiate, conclude & sign a Convention or Conventions, Treaty or Treaties of Commerce & Navigation.

With the foregoing language may be contrasted that of an earlier full power given to Wheaton under date of June 7, 1837, which was more limited as to its subject matter but more extensive in respect of the parties (*ibid.*, 272):

to meet & confer with any person or persons furnished with like powers on the part of the States composing the Zoll-Verein and those included in the Hanoverian Union or any or either of them, and any other independent State or States of Germany, with the exception of Austria; and with him or them to negotiate, conclude, and sign a Convention or Conventions, Treaty or Treaties, for the removal or modification of the duties charges, or restrictions which now impair or obstruct the trade of the U.S. with those States or any or either of them in the article of Tobacco.

A full power of later date, February 9, 1838, authorized negotiations on the subject of a treaty of navigation and commerce with plenipotentiaries "of His Majesty the King of Prussia, & the other German States associated, or which may hereafter be associated with Prussia in a Union of Commerce and Customs" (*ibid.*, 293).

The original full power given by the King of Hanover under date of August 8, 1839, to Sieur Auguste de Berger, to negotiate and conclude the treaty, is in the file; it reads as follows (translation from the French, omitting signatures, etc.):

We, Ernest Augustus, by the Grace of God King of Hanover, Prince of the United Kingdom of Great Britain and Ireland, Duke of Cumberland, Duke of Brunswick and Lüneburg, etc.

Having deemed it desirable and useful to enter into negotiation for the conclusion of a treaty of commerce and navigation between the Kingdom of Hanover and the United States of North America; for those reasons We have on Our part authorized and appointed, as also by the present full powers We authorize and appoint, the Sieur Auguste de Berger, Our Envoy Extraordinary and Minister Plenipotentiary near His Majesty the King of Prussia, Lieutenant General of Our armies, Knight Grand Cross of Our Order of the Guelphs, to enter into the negotiation for the conclusion of such a treaty with the plenipotentiary ap-

pointed or to be appointed for that purpose on the part of the Government of the United States of North America, and to arrange the provisions and the articles thereof, reserving to Us Our definitive ratification thereof, it being Our will, moreover, to approve all that Our said Plenipotentiary shall have stipulated and concluded in conformity with the instructions which he has received or which he shall receive from Us.

In faith whereof We have signed these presents with Our own hand and have caused to be affixed thereto Our royal seal. Done at the Royal Chateau of Hanover August 8, 1839.

Also in the treaty file, as above mentioned, is the original full power given to Wheaton under date of August 7, 1840, to exchange the ratifications, which seems not to have been recorded.

The Negotiations

In the instruction to Wheaton of December 15, 1837 (D. S., 14 Instructions, Prussia, 24), he was authorized to assume for the basis of the treaty with Hanover, the treaty with Prussia of 1828 (Document 62)—

with this important difference, however, that no stipulation shall be inserted placing the vessels of Hanover and of the States that may be joined in the Treaty & their cargoes, engaged in the *indirect* trade to the United States, upon the footing of American vessels and their cargoes. In that respect you will be guided by the Treaty of 1815 [Document 35] between the United States and Great Britain.

Wheaton then pointed out the practical difficulties in his despatch of February 28, 1838 (D. S., 1 Despatches, Prussia, No. 65):

I beg leave to state that on examining the regulations by which our commercial intercourse is now governed with the Kingdom of Hannover & the Grand Duchy of Oldenburg, with a view to carry into execution your Instructions relating to the proposed negotiation with those States, I find that there is a material difference between the privileges already extended to the Navigation of Hannover and of Oldenburg respectively in the ports of the United States.

By the President's Proclamation of the 1 July, 1828 [4 Statutes at Large, 815–16], it is declared that so much of the Several acts of Congress imposing duties on the tonnage of vessels & the importation of goods as imposed a discriminating duty of tonnage between the vessels of Hannover & those of the United States, & between goods imported into the United States in Hannoverian & United States vessels, are suspended & discontinued *so far as respects the produce or manufactures of Hannover*, the suspension to continue so long as the reciprocal exemption of the vessels of the United States & the merchandise laden therein shall be continued in the ports of Hannover.

By the President's Proclamation of the 18 Sept. 1830 [*ibid.*, 814–15], it is declared that so much of the Acts of Congress imposing discriminating duties on the tonnage of vessels & importation of goods shall be suspended & discontinued so far as respects the vessels of the Grand Dukedom of Oldenburg, & the produce, manufactures, & merchandise imported into the United States in the same from Oldenburg, & *from any other foreign country whatsoever*.

This difference in the concessions made to the Navigation of these two Countries appears to have arisen from the difference in the provisions of the two Acts of [January 7,] 1824 and [May 24,] 1828 [4 Statutes at Large, 2–3, 308–9], the latter extending to the *indirect trade*, which is not within the purview of the former.

As the Instructions contained in your Despatch, No. 14 [of December 15, 1837, cited above], require me to be guided by our Convention of 1815 with Great Britain [Document 35] in respect to *the indirect trade*, a difficulty may possibly arise in the negotiation growing out of this question. Hannover will probably

demand a participation in the indirect trade, whilst Oldenburg may not be willing to give up a privilege already secured to her by the Act of Congress of 1828 and the President's Proclamation.

Under these circumstances, I shall continue the negotiation separately with Hannover, should Oldenburg finally insist upon retaining the privilege she already enjoys under the Acts of Congress & the President's Proclamation.

In a postscript there was added the view of the Government of Hanover:

Since the above was written the Hannoverian minister at this Court has intimated to me that his Government would probably insist upon the right to carry to the United States in Hannoverian vessels *coming directly from the ports of Hannover*, not only the productions & manufactures of Hannover, but those of the other countries of Germany, in order to equalize the advantages which our vessels would have in carrying return cargoes of those articles in exchange for the bulky freights of our staples brought to Europe, whilst the Hannoverian vessels would be confined to the transportation of the linens & other fabrics of Hannover & Brunswick, & in effect excluded from both branches of the carrying trade.

Indeed, as Wheaton pointed out in a private letter of March 6, 1838, to President Van Buren (printed in Senate Confidential Document G, 26th Congress, 1st session, heretofore cited), "the Hanoverians may at any time (though they do not seem to be aware of it) entitle themselves, under the act of 1828, to bring to the United States, not only their own produce, but that of *any other foreign country*, in Hanoverian vessels."

To those and similar representations (D. S., 1 Despatches, Prussia, No. 68, March 21, 1838) Secretary of State Forsyth yielded, writing on May 10, 1838 (D. S., 14 Instructions, Prussia, 26–27):

As no material inconvenience appears likely to arise, under the circumstances, from yielding to Hanover, a participation, to the extent you propose, in the indirect trade for her shipping, the President has consented that, if you should deem it essential to the negotiation of a treaty that such a concession should be made, you may stipulate that the vessels of both Hanover and Oldenburg shall be permitted to bring into the United States the produce or manufactures of any of the countries of Germany. For this privilege the United States must have, as the only equivalent Hanover and Oldenburg can give, the privilege of carrying all articles the growth or manufacture of this Continent and the West India islands.

The basis thus proposed was that adopted in the treaty (Article 2, third and fourth paragraphs); a proposed most-favored-nation clause similar to Article 9 of the treaty with Prussia was dropped after it met with objections when the Plenipotentiary of Hanover sought to add words intended to include the "indirect trade" if the treaties then existing with Prussia and the Hanseatic Republics (Documents 62 and 59; see also Document 63) were prolonged (D. S., 2 Despatches, Prussia, No. 138, October 12, 1839; 14 Instructions, Prussia, 32–34, December 12, 1839; also the despatch of Wheaton of May 20, 1840, No. 148, and enclosures, not found in the archives, but printed in Senate Confidential Document G, 26th Congress, 1st session, heretofore cited). More liberal provisions were written a few years later in Articles 1 and 7 of the treaty with Hanover of June 10, 1846 (Document 121).

THE GERMANIC CONFEDERATION

In Article 2 of this treaty there appears twice the expression, "the growth, produce or manufacture of the Kingdom of Hanover, or of any other Country belonging to the Germanic Confederation and the Kingdom of Prussia".

The Kingdom of Hanover was one of the members of the Germanic Confederation (1815–66), which at this time included not only Austria and Prussia, but more than thirty other states besides Hanover; a summary statement regarding the Germanic Confederation is in the notes to Document 59, with a list of the states members thereof.

It may be supposed that the specific mention of the Kingdom of Prussia in the above-quoted expression was intended to include those domains of Prussia which, as such, did not belong to the Germanic Confederation; to the constitutive act of that Confederation (the text of which, in German, with a French translation, is in British and Foreign State Papers, II, 114–36) the King of Prussia and the Emperor of Austria were parties only "for all their possessions formerly belonging to the German Empire".

At the time of this treaty there had theretofore been made by the United States treaties with three other members of the Germanic Confederation, namely, those with the Hanseatic Republics of December 20, 1827, and June 4, 1828 (Documents 59 and 63), with Prussia of May 1, 1828 (Document 62), and with Austria of August 27, 1829 (Document 66). Treaties had previously been made with Prussia in 1785 and 1799 (Documents 13 and 24).

Hanover was not at this time, or until 1851, a party to the German Zollverein or Customs Union, as to which see also the notes to Document 59.

Hanover and Great Britain were united under the same crown from 1714 (George I) to 1837 (William IV). Formerly an electorate, Hanover became a kingdom as a result of the Congress of Vienna. Following the war of 1866 between Austria and Prussia, Hanover became a province of Prussia by decree of September 20, 1866.

FIJI : JUNE 10, 1840

Commercial Regulations, signed by native chiefs of the Fiji Islands at various places therein, June 10, 1840, and on various other dates. Original in English and Fijian.

Feejee Regulations.

Commercial Regulations made by the Kings and Principal Chiefs of the Feejee group of Islands, after full consideration in Council on the Tenth day of June, 1840.

ARTICLE I.

All foreign Consuls duly appointed and received in the Feejee group of Islands shall be protected and respected both in their persons and property; and all foreigners obtaining the consent of the Government, and conforming to the laws, shall receive the protection of the King and Chiefs.

ARTICLE 2.

All foreign vessels shall be received into the ports and harbours of the Feejees for the purpose of obtaining supplies and for commerce, and with their officers and crews, so long as they shall comply with these regulations, and

Na Vono Vei ra na kai Viti, kai ra na kai Vavalagi e lakomai ki Viti.

Na vono ni veivoli sa-kanaka ko i ra na tui kai ra na turaga levu ni vanua ko Viti me ra vakamuria. Ka ra a bosea ki na ai na nona ka tini ni siga ni vula ko Juni, 1840.

NA VONO 1.

Ko i ra na matanivanua qimaga mai Vavalagi sa lesia me raica e Viti nai valavala ni kai Viti kai na kai Vavalagi, e na vakaruruga ka caka vinaka va na yagodra kai na nodra yau: ka e na caka vinaka na tui kai ra na turaga vei ra na kai Vavalagi qimaga, sa vinaka va na turaga na nodra tiko e Viti, kevaka e ra vakamuria na vono.

NA VONO 2.

Na waqa ni Vavalagi qimaga e ruku va na dua na daveta, me kele va na matana e Viti, me volivoli, e na sega ni tarovi ra; ka na caka vinaka na tui kai ra na turaga vei ra na turaga kai ra na lewe ni waqa, kevaka e ra

behave themselves peaceably, shall receive the protection of the King and Chiefs.

ARTICLE 3.

The fullest protection shall be given to all foreign ships and vessels which may be wrecked, and any property saved shall be taken possession of by the Master of the Vessel, who will allow a salvage or portion of the property so saved to those who may aid in saving and protecting the same, and no embezzlement will be permitted under any circumstances whatever. The effects of all persons deceased shall be given up to the Consul of the Nation to which they may have belonged.

ARTICLE 4.

Any person guilty of the crime of Murder upon any foreigner shall be given up without delay to the Commander of any Public Vessel of the Nation to which the deceased may belong, upon his demanding the same, or be punished on shore.

ARTICLE 5.

Every vessel shall pay a port charge of Three Dollars for Anchorage to the King, before she will be allowed to receive refreshments on board, and shall pay for pilotage in and out the sum of Seven Dollars, before she leaves the harbor; and Pilots shall be appointed subject to the approval of the Consuls.

vakamuria na vono qo, ka valavala vinaka.

NA VONO 3.

Kevaka e na voca e dua na waqa ni Vavalagi, e na caka vinaka sara ki na, ka na karona vata na yau me lewa ki na na turaga ni waqa; ka e na sauma ko koya vei ra e veivukei koya, me kua ni ca na yau: ka e na segai sara ni vakalaiva me butako. E na kauta na yau ni kai Vavalagi qimaga e mate e Viti va na matanivanua ni nona vanua.

NA VONO 4.

Kevaka e na ravu e dua na yatamata, ka mate ki na e dua na kai Vavalagi, e na kauta sara na yatamata ravuravu va na turaga ni waqa ni vanua i koya ka sa mate, se moku ga e vanua.

NA VONO 5.

E na sauma na waqa qimaga na tola e tolu va na tui ai na kelekele ni waqa, ka e na qai vinaka me kauta na voli ki waqa; ka ai na sa kelekele ga va na matana, e na sauma na tola e vitu ai na vakarukuma na waqa, ka na vakatikora na yatamata vakaruku waqa e na vinaka va na matanivanua sa lesia.

ARTICLE 6.

All trading in spirituous liquors, or landing the same is strictly forbidden. Any person offending shall pay a fine of Twenty-five Dollars, and the Vessel to which he belongs shall receive no more refreshments. Any spirituous liquors found on shore shall be seized and destroyed.

ARTICLE 7.

All deserters from Vessels will be apprehended, and a reward paid of Eight Dollars, viz:—Five Dollars to the person who apprehended him, and Three Dollars to the Chief of the district in which he may be apprehended, on his delivery to the proper officer of the Vessel. No Master shall refuse to receive such deserter under a penalty of Twenty-five Dollars. Deserters taken after the Vessel has sailed shall be delivered up to the Consul to be dealt with as he may think fit. Any person who entices another to desert, secretes a deserter, or in any way assists him shall be subject to a penalty of Five Dollars.

NA VONO 6.

Sa tabu sara me voli yaqona, ka sa tabu me kau ki vanua; kevaka e na ta vakamuria na vono qo e dua na yatamata, e na sauma ko koya na tola e ruasagavulu ka mani lima, ka e na sega ni volia tale ga e dua na ka va na waqa e tiko ki na ko koya. Kevaka e na kunea e vanua e dua na yaqona, e na kauta ka biuta laivi.

NA VONO 7.

Kevaka e na dro mai na waqa e dua na yatamata, e na kauti koya tale ki na, ka e na sauma ki na na tola e walu; e lima na tola va na yatamata e tauri koya, ka tolu na tola va na turaga ni vanua e na tauri koya ki na, ai na sa kauti koya va na turaga ni waqa. Kevaka e na kanaka e dua na turaga ni waqa, me kua ni tiko tale ga e nona waqa na yatamata ka dro ka sa kauta tale ki na, e na sauma ki na ko koya na tola e ruasagavulu ka mani lima. Kevaka e na dro e dua na yatamata, ka na qai kunei koya ai na sa soko na nona waqa, e na kauti koya va na matanivanua me veitali koya ki na. Kevaka e na vecevece e dua na yatamata mai vanua me dro mai waqa e dua na yatamata, se vuni koya, se vukei koya ai na dua na ka, e na sauma ko koya na tola e lima.

ARTICLE 8.

Any seaman remaining on shore after Nine o'clock at night, shall be made a prisoner of until the next morning, when he shall be sent on board and shall pay a fine of Five Dollars.

ARTICLE 9.

Should the Master of any Vessel refuse to comply with any of these regulations, a statement of the case shall be furnished to the Consul of the Nation to which he belongs and redress sought from thence.

ARTICLE 10.

All Magistrates or Chiefs of Districts, when vessels or boats may visit, shall enforce the regulations and rules relative to the apprehension of Deserters, or pay such a fine as the Principal Chief shall impose.

ARTICLE 11.

These regulations shall be printed, promulgated, and a Copy furnished to the Master of each vessel visiting these Islands.

Done in Council by the Principal Kings and Chiefs of the Feejee Group this 10th day of June, A.D., 1840.

The foregoing rules and regulations having been signed by the King and Chiefs in my presence,

NA VONO 8.

Kevaka e na tiko e vanua e dua na yatamata mai na waqa ka malua me sivi a kenai ka ciwa ni hora ai na bogi, e na tauri koya, ka ai na sa bogibogi e na qai kauti koya ki waqa, ka e na sauma ko koya na tola e lima.

NA VONO 9.

Kevaka e na ta vakamuria na vono qo e dua na turaga ni waqa, e na vakarogotaka va na matanivanua sa lesia me lewa ki na, me sauma ki na ko koya.

NA VONO 10.

Na matanivanua qimaga se na turaga ni vanua e na qai ki na na waqa vanua se na velovelo, e ra na tanaka me vakamuria sara na vono va na yatamata e dro mai na nona waqa; se kauta nai sau e na kanaka na turaga levu.

NA VONO 11.

E na vola na vono qo, ka vakatusa va na vei korokoro, ka kauta e dua va na turaga ni waqa qimaga e lakomai ki Viti.

Sa bosea na vono qo ko i ra na tui kai ra na turaga ni Viti ai na nona ka tini ni vula ko Juni, 1840.

his
Ko ⋈ TANOA.
mark

and submitted to me, I consider them just and proper, and shall forward to the American government a Copy of the same for the information of all Masters of Vessels visiting the Feejee group of Islands.

United States Ship Vincennes,
    Harbour of Bau,
        June 10, 1840.

CHARLES WILKES,
    Commanding U. States
        Exploring Expedition.

In presence of
    WILLIAM L. HUDSON,
        Commanding U.S.
          Ship Peacock

CADR. RINGGOLD,
    Commanding U.S.
        Brig Porpoise.

R. R. WALDRON,
    U. States' Navy.

B. VANDERFORD, *Pilot.*

In the Ms. the signatures of all the principal chiefs of the group follow.[1]

NOTES

The chief authority regarding the commercial regulations above printed is Wilkes, Narrative of the United States Exploring Expedition (1838–42), which is described in the notes to Document 91 and which is here cited as "The Narrative" (referring to the quarto, or official, edition).

In any technical sense it would perhaps not be possible to say that these regulations, signed by native chiefs of the Fiji Islands, were an international act, although at the time those native rulers of Fiji were not at all subject to any extrinsic authority; Fiji was not under any civilized sovereign until 1874, when British rule commenced.

The form of the regulations is somewhat like that of a decree or order in council; they are not phrased like an agreement. However, they were proposed by a United States naval officer, Lieutenant Charles Wilkes; it was at his instance that they were accepted and signed; they were first written in English; they treat of matters which are frequently the subject of conventions, such as the duties

---

[1] This sentence is written on the print from which the text is taken.

and rights of consuls; they undoubtedly were regarded by the native chiefs who signed them as being of a promissory nature; and, indeed, they contain clauses reading somewhat like mutual promises (salvage, clause 3; rewards, clause 7).

Strict consistency perhaps would not permit the inclusion of such a document in this collection; but the historical interest of the paper is sufficient to warrant the exception, if it be an exception.

These commercial regulations were copied from those written at Samoa some months earlier (Document 91), but five of the sixteen articles of the Samoan regulations (6, 9, 10, 12, and 15) were omitted.

The Source Text

No original document is available as a source text for the commercial regulations printed above. The texts here printed have been collated with the printed copy of the regulations which appears to have been enclosed with the despatch of Wilkes to the Secretary of the Navy under date of August 10, 1840, on board the "U S Ship Vincennes Fegee Islands" (Naval Records and Library, 2 Wilkes Exploring Expedition, No. 70); that long despatch reports the activities of the expedition in the Fiji Islands during a period of more than three months from the date of arrival (May 7, 1840); the passages thereof which deal with the regulations are here extracted:

Tanoa King of Bou [Bau] the most powerful and influential chief of the group visited the ship and was received with every mark of respect it laid in my power to give him. Although his character is notoriously bad, yet he has always shewn himself a great friend to the whites. After some talk with him I prevailed upon him to adopt a set of Rules and Regulations for the Government of his people and those who should visit his territories; and made him and his attendants some presents. They were all extremely gratified with the ship it being the largest they had ever seen, and excited their astonishment not a little.

. . . .

On the 5th of June I proceeded in the Flying Fish to Somo Somo where resides the third most powerful Chief of the group who readily adopted the Rules and Regulations.

. . . .

On my return to Ovolou I found by a report from Captain Hudson that he had executed the duties assigned him, effected the signing of Rules and Regulations by the Chiefs of Rewa and the M'Bua district.

. . . .

Captain Hudson had been [in June] as far as Muthuata on the North shore, carrying the survey to that place. The Chief of that district had adopted the Rules and Regulations.

. . . .

Enclosed herewith I send you a printed copy of the Rules and Regulations adopted by five different Chiefs of these islands.

With some slight variances the English text of the regulations is printed in The Narrative, III, 431–32; but they do not appear to have been published at the time in the United States; the date of the text in The Narrative is May 14, 1840, when the regulations were signed by Tanoa, the most important of the native chiefs; the date in

the text printed above (and in the headnote here) is June 10, 1840, one of the four dates of signature by other chiefs (May 18, June 7, June 10, and June 24). In British and Foreign State Papers, XXXIII, 54–56 (published in 1859), the English text is also printed under date of May 14, 1840.

An allusion to these regulations and to those of Samoa (Document 91) appears in this paragraph from an article in Niles' Weekly Register, LXII, 261, June 25, 1842, on the "South Sea Exploring Expedition":

Several of the principal groups and islands in the Pacific Ocean have been visited, examined, and surveyed; a friendly intercourse and protective commercial regulations established with the chiefs and natives; aggressions on our citizens and commerce redressed, and a justly merited punishment meted out in some flagrant cases of unprovoked and cold-blooded murder.

THE REGULATIONS

The United States Exploring Expedition (1838–42) reached the Fiji group of islands early in May 1840 and remained in that region for more than three months.

During that visit the commander of the expedition, Lieutenant Charles Wilkes, U.S.N., obtained the assent and signatures of various native chiefs to the commercial regulations, the text of which is printed above. It appears that identic documents were signed by various individuals or groups of individuals at different times and at different places; but the record is not altogether complete.

Wilkes gives this account of the meeting with Tanoa, King of Ambau (or Bau), held on board the *Vincennes* in the harbor of Levuka off the island of Ovolau on May 13, 1840, at which the regulations were approved, the day before their signature (The Narrative, III, 59–60):

After presenting him [Tanoa] to the officers, and receiving the rest of his suite, I led him to the after part of the deck, where mats were laid down, and we all seated ourselves to hold a council; for I was anxious to finish first the business for which I had particularly sought the interview: this was to procure the adoption of rules and regulations for the intercourse with foreign vessels, similar to those established in the Samoan Group the year preceding. David Whippy became my interpreter, but Tanoa had too much dignity about him to receive the interpretation through Whippy alone, although he understood all that he said perfectly, for Whippy speaks their language well; but he had his "speech-explaining counsellor," Malani-vanua Vakanduna, or prime minister, who was a remarkably good-looking, intelligent man. Whippy gave his name as Korotumbavalu, and said that he had great influence with the king. It was amusing to see their mode of conducting the business, and to understand that Tanoa's dignity would be offended by holding discourse with our friend Whippy as interpreter; not, however, (as it was explained to me by Tubou Totai,) from any objection he had to Whippy, but it would be derogatory to his rank and station.

On the production of the rules and regulations, Tanoa seemed rather confused, and at first appeared dull and stupid; this I imputed to his ava drinking, in which they had all indulged to excess the night before. He did not seem to comprehend the object of them, or, as the interpreter expressed it, "could not take the idea." This is not to be wondered at, when it is considered that this was the first act of the kind he had been called upon to do. Tubou Totai being a traveller of some note, readily understood their meaning, and through his explanations Tanoa soon comprehended the object, and listened with attention

(his whole suite sitting around) to the reading of them, sentence by sentence; after which he made signs of understanding them, and gave his approval and consent to having them established, and the next day signed them, by making his mark. (See Appendix V.) That which he was to keep I had rolled up and put into a bright round tin case, which he seemed to regard with great pride.

Although I did not anticipate much immediate good from these regulations, yet I was well satisfied they would be of use in restraining the natives as well as masters of ships, and in securing a better understanding between them; at any rate it was a beginning, and would make them feel we were desirous of doing them justice. I talked to him much, through the interpreter, of the necessity of protecting the whites, and of punishing those who molest and take from them their goods in case of shipwreck. He listened to me very patiently, and said, "he had always done so; that my advice was very good, but he did not need it; that I must give plenty of it to his son Seru, and talk hard to him; that he would in a short time be king, and needed it."

A later conversation with Tanoa is thus reported (*ibid.*, 62):

He talked a great deal of the regulations he had signed. I was desirous of knowing whether he fully understood them, which I found he did. I then asked him if it would not be better for his son Seru to sign them also, as he is understood to be the acting chief; he said "no," that his signing was quite sufficient, and made them binding on all the dependencies of Ambau. He desired me, when his son Seru paid me a visit, to talk hard to him, and give him plenty of good advice, for he was a young man, and frisky; but he himself was old, and saw things that were good and bad. He said Seru would visit me in a few days, when he returned, as they could not both leave Ambau at the same time.

No single authority was supreme at the time in the Fiji Islands. Wilkes writes on the subject as follows (*ibid.*, 64):

The Feejee Group is composed of seven districts, and is under as many principal chiefs, viz.:

1st. Ambau.	5th. Somu-somu.
2d. Rewa.	6th. Naitasiri.
3d. Verata.	7th. Mbua.
4th. Nuthuata.	

All the minor chiefs on the different islands are more or less connected or subject to one of these, and as the one party or the other prevails in their wars, they change masters. War is the constant occupation of the natives, and engrosses all their time and thoughts.

Efforts accordingly were made to have the regulations accepted by other native chiefs. On May 18 Captain Hudson on the *Peacock* obtained the signature of the King of Rewa, whose name was Kania, and his chiefs (*ibid.*, 118). The chiefs of Somu-somu on the island of Vuna signed on June 10; the name of the King at that place is given as Tui Thakau (*ibid.*, 165–67); those signatures were obtained by Wilkes. On June 7 various native chiefs, under the auspices of Captain Hudson of the *Peacock*, signed the regulations at a place called Mbua (*ibid.*, 225). Another acceptance of the articles was obtained by the same officer on June 24 from the King and chiefs of Muthuata (*ibid.*, 243). According to another account some eleven chiefs signed the regulations in the presence of Wilkes and others on the *Vincennes* in the harbor of "Ban" (Bau, Mbau, or Ambau) on June 10, 1840 (Colvocoresses, Four Years in a Government Exploring Expedition, 370); but it does not seem possible to reconcile that

statement as to date and place with the account of Wilkes (cf. The Narrative, III, 165).

One early instance of the application of the regulations is to be mentioned. Two British war vessels were at Rewa during the visit of Wilkes in 1840, the ship *Sulphur*, Captain Belcher, and the schooner *Starling*, Lieutenant Kellet; the native chiefs deemed the regulations applicable as against the *Sulphur*, although they were not intended to apply to vessels of war at all. Wilkes gives the following account of the matter (The Narrative, III, 191–92, June 13–14, 1840):

I was not a little amused at Captain Belcher's account of the effect of the regulations as operating upon his vessel. The chiefs required him to pay port-charges, and in default thereof refused to give him any supplies. In drawing up the Rules and Regulations for the trade, it had never occurred to me to mention men-of-war as being free, feeling assured that they would all very readily give five times the amount of the articles required in presents. But it appears that Captain Belcher did not think proper to make the customary present, and the chiefs refused to allow any supplies to go to his vessel until he should comply with the rules. This incensed the captain, and caused him to take offence at the missionaries, who he supposed prevented the supplies from being sent. I well knew, however, that they were guiltless. He likewise broke out into strong invectives against the chiefs, declaring that it was impossible they could understand the rules, &c., although the whole proceeding showed they were not only conversant with their meaning, but also with the power they had in their hands of compelling the visiter to pay.

The Wilkes Expedition

Some account of the Exploring Expedition of 1838–42, or the Wilkes Expedition as it is now generally called, is in the notes to Document 91. The elaborate instructions which Wilkes received from the Secretary of the Navy under date of August 11, 1838, are there cited and quoted in full.

In respect of treaties or agreements Wilkes was given no special directions; but regarding the Fiji Islands this was written:

From the Navigator's Group, you will proceed to the Feejee Islands, which you will examine with particular attention, with the view to the selection of a safe harbour, easy of access, and in every respect adapted to the reception of vessels of the United States engaged in the whale-fishery, and the general commerce of these seas; it being the intention of the government to keep one of the squadron of the Pacific cruising near these islands in future.

The account given by Wilkes of the visit of the Exploring Expedition to the Fiji Islands is elaborate and contains much information of all kinds regarding the region and its inhabitants (The Narrative, III, 45–384); his despatch of August 10, 1840, to the Secretary of the Navy (cited above), includes the following:

Our stay among this group of islands, has afforded us an opportunity of obtaining a great deal of information relative to the products, and the habits, manners, Customs and Character of the Natives. I now proceed to give you a summary of the information obtained at this group which the limits of this communication will permit.

This group of islands is comprised within the latitudes of 16° and 19° 30′ South, and longitudes of 178° west to 177° East, being about three hundred miles in an east and west direction, and two hundred and ten North and South.

The number of inhabited islands is Sixty five, that of uninhabited eighty nine, which are occasionally visited by the Natives for the purpose of fishing. They are of volcanic formation, diversified surface, mostly mountainous, and broken

into deep and fruitful vallies, with a few rivers, the largest of some thirty or forty miles course, and available for canoes.

The population of the whole group is about One hundred and thirty five thousand Souls.

The group is divided into five large districts, each under the government of separate Chiefs, who are frequently engaged in war for supremacy and territory. That of Bow is the most powerful; three fifths of the islands are subject to it.

The Chiefs have the power of life and death, which is frequently exercised, and for trivial causes.

The smaller islands are nearly depopulated owing to heavy exactions by the Chiefs, which if not complied with, result in the slaughter of the men and children, and captivity of the women, who are taken as slaves by the Chiefs and frequently sold for a musket or whales teeth.

The Soil is a loam mixed with vegetable matter; extremely productive, and well adapted to the cultivation of Cotton, Coffee, Sugar Cane, vegetables, fruits and the usual productions of the tropical climates. Timber abounds in some of the islands, such as pine, ironwood, bread fruit &c. The pine is thought to equal that of New Zealand for ships spars. It is of large growth.

The climate is salubrious, enjoying the whole year round a delightful temperature. The winter months passed during our stay: Mean temperature 78°.

Few diseases seem to exist among them, and those cutaneous affections.

They have but two stormy months February and March, at which time gales are frequent from the NW, and violent.

Commerce and Trade at the Fegee Islands, is carried on by a few American and English vessels. They procure about four thousand pounds of tortoise shell annually. Cocoanut Oil, Provisions, Shells and Indian Curiosities are exchanged for Muskets, powder, lead, whales teeth, vermillion, Cottons, Cutlery, and bottles. Beche la Mar has been taken in large quantities by American Vessels only. The Natives are employed to collect it from the reefs, and cure it when it is taken to the Chinese Markets. The only vessel now engaged in the business has obtained a cargo valued at twenty thousand dollars. Six months are required to procure such a cargo. In 1835 and 1836 five cargoes were taken, since which time there has only been one annually.

Sandal wood formally an important article of trade, has been exhausted.

This group is a great resort for Whales during the months of July, Aug, and September, and when our Chart is completed, it will open a new and profitable ground for this fishery. Without the necessary directions to avoid the dangers, it would be extremely hazardous to attempt. Our Whalers have been hitherto confined to the Sea around and in the vicinity, and although hundreds of whales have been seen within the reefs and harbours, I did not hear of a single instance of ones being taken. No vessels have yet ventured to pursue them owing to the want of information relative to the dangers and the hostility of the Natives.

No attempt should be made by any vessel to cruise among the Fegee islands without being well armed and prepared to repel any attack from the Natives. The utmost vigilence is necessary to guard against treachery, and if possible a hostage should be obtained.

The harbours are numerous and safe, that of Ovolou I consider the best, where good pilots can at all times be had and an abundance of Provisions, Wood and Water easily obtained.

The Fegeeans are a strong Athletic, well formed race, an intelligent, observing, ingeneous, and industrious people, but revengeful, treacherous, superstitious and cowardly.

The fear of punishment alone prevents them from more frequent attacks upon the whites who visit them, and who have been killed when found alone merely for their clothing. They are never to be trusted. They are jealous of each other, great thieves and liars, and their only redeeming quality is hospitality.

Many of their Customs are peculiar. Among them is the practice of burying alive the old and diseased by their relatives and friends at their own request; The strangling of women at the death of Chiefs; That of offering Human Sacrifices on the erection of Bonus (Spirit Houses) building canoes &c and afterwards cooking and eating them.

Cannibalism prevails with all its horrors, the Natives availing themselves of any little feud to commit murder, that they may enjoy a feast on human flesh.

Scenes too revolting to repeat have been witnessed by the Missionaries and White residents. Sufficient proof (were it required) has been witnessed by us to place it beyond a doubt that it is done, more to satisfy the cravings of the apetite, than revenge.

Circumcision is practiced. The women are tatoo'd, but not the men, and what is very peculiar the Chiefs receive rank from their Mothers. Polygamy is common among the Chiefs.

The arts are more in advance here than at the other islands. They manufacture earthen ware, and thin mats, tappa, baskets &c are much superior to those found elsewhere.

Their dwellings have many more comforts, and their canoes far excell any that we have seen.

The Tonguese resort here for the purpose of building theirs and adopt the Fegee construction.

They do not worship idols, but believe in spirits. Their mythology is very numerous, and each district differs from the others. Some Animals fish and birds are held sacred, not as spirits, but as the property of Gods.

Each tribe or district has its Gods who are consulted, and to whom offerings are made through the Priest, the office of the latter being hereditary or by special appointment of the Gods through inspiration.

The Priests have great power and are adroit in playing upon the superstitions of the Natives

Several Wesleyan Missionaries and their families have resided here about three years. Much has been done by them in reducing the language to writing and printing a grammar and tracts. As yet however little has been effected towards converting the Natives, and it will require much time and trouble before any impression can be made upon them.

The result of our survey has been the discovery of many new and excellent harbours, many unknown and dangerous reefs, and passages through those already known, with their proper locations, in short every thing that a complete survey and examination of islands, reefs, passages, harbours and anchorages can give, and by stating that there are one hundred and fifty four islands, with extended and broken reefs around and connecting them; fifty distinct and dangerous reefs of large size, and as many harbours that have all been surveyed, and under every disadvantage, from the necessity of avoiding surprise and treachery from the host of Cannibals by whom we were at all times surrounded, you will able to form some idea of our labours.

Fiji Islands

The Fiji Island group in the South Pacific constitutes the British Colony of Fiji and comprises all islands, rocks, and reefs lying between latitude 15° and 22° south and between longitude 177° west and 175° east of Greenwich. It consists of from 200 to 250 islands, of which perhaps 80 are inhabited. The largest is Vitilevu, with an area of 4,053 square miles; next in size is Vanualevu, area 2,128 square miles. The islands of Rotuma, a dependency of Fiji, lie some 220 miles north-northwest of the Fiji Islands. The total area of the Colony (including Rotuma) is 7,083 square miles, and the population on December 31, 1930, was estimated at 182,576. Suva, the capital of the Colony, is situated on the island of Vitilevu.

The sovereignty of the Fiji Islands was ceded to Great Britain by Cakobau, Chief of the Lau Confederacy, and other chiefs, in a deed of cession dated October 10, 1874. The islands of Rotuma were annexed May 13, 1881.

94

CHILE : JULY 7, 1840

*Agreement for the Settlement of the First Case of the Brig "Macedonian".
The agreement was oral. Its terms were embodied in an unsigned and
undated memorandum in Spanish, a copy whereof was delivered to the
Chargé d'Affaires of the United States, and which is printed as stating
the agreement.
Not subject to ratification by the United States. As to ratification by
Chile, see the notes. Not proclaimed.*

[Translation]

Bases del convenio con el Señor Pollard sobre indemnizacion por el dinero perteneciente a los dueños del bergantin Macedonio.

1ª Reconocer el Gobierno 104,000 pesos fuertes.

2ª Intereses de 5p% anual por via de daños y perjuicios desde que se hicieron las presas, hasta el dia que el convenio sea aprobado por el congreso de Chile.

3ª Capitalizar dichos intereses hasta la referida fecha.

4ª Sobre el Capital é intereses pagar el Gobierno un interes anual de 5p%

5ª El pago total hacerlo en siete porciones iguales, una al contado, y las seis restantes en otros tantos años, con mas los intereses vencidos de todo lo que se adeuda en cada año.

6ª El pago de amortizacion e intereses se hará en pesos fuertes

Basis of Agreement with Mr. Pollard for the Indemnity of the Money Belonging to the Owners of the Brig *Macedonian*.

1. The Government is to acknowledge 104,000 hard dollars.

2. Interest of 5 percent per annum in lieu of damages and losses, from the date of the seizure until the date of the approval of this agreement by the Congress of Chile.

3. The said interest up to this date to form a new capital.

4. On the capital and interest the Government will pay an interest of 5 percent per annum.

5. The payment of the whole to be made in seven equal portions, one cash down and the remaining six in an equal number of years, besides the interest due on the sum owing at the end of each year.

6. The payment of the instalments and interest shall be made

o en su equivalente en moneda
corriente con el premio que tengan
los pesos fuertes al tiempo de
hacerse los pagos.

in hard dollars, or in an equivalent in currency with the premium
that the hard dollars may be at
at the time of the payments.

NOTES

The facts in the first case of the *Macedonian* have been thus stated
(Moore, International Arbitrations, II, 1449–50):

President Buchanan on April 28, 1858, communicated to the Senate, in response
to a resolution of the 24th of the preceding month, a report of Mr. Cass, as Secretary of State, together with a voluminous correspondence, in relation to the seizure in the valley of Sitana, in Peru, by the authorities of Chile of the proceeds
of the cargo of the American brig *Macedonian* [Senate Executive Document No.
58, 35th Congress, 1st session, serial 930].   By the papers in question it appeared
that on December 14, 1840, Mr. Forsyth, Secretary of State, inclosed to Richard
Pollard, chargé d'affaires of the United States at Santiago, Chile, a memorial of
Thomas H. Perkins, of Boston.   This memorial represented that in 1818 the
Macedonian, which was owned by John S. Ellery, and commanded by Eliphalet
Smith, sailed from Boston with a valuable cargo belonging to Ellery, Perkins, and
other persons, all citizens of the United States, on a trading voyage to South
America and elsewhere, as might be found expedient.   The brig, after visiting
and trading at several places on the coast of Chile and Peru, proceeded to Callao,
where Captain Smith disposed of the residue of his cargo for about $145,000.   Of
this sum upward of $60,000 in specie was forwarded by Captain Smith, in care of
an agent, to Guamey, to which place the vessel had gone before the receipt of the
money.   Soon afterward Captain Smith himself left Lima with the remaining
$80,000 and upward in specie, and was traveling with it toward Guamey when he
was seized by a party of Chilean soldiers, and carried, together with the money,
on board of the Chilean ship *O'Higgins*, commanded by Lord Cochrane, then
admiral of Chile.   This seizure took place on or about the 5th of April 1819.
After several days' detention, and being compelled to sign a paper relinquishing
all claim to the specie, Captain Smith was released and permitted to go to Guamey,
where he expected to find the $60,000 which had been sent forward in charge of
his agent.   The agent however, having heard of the seizure of Captain Smith by
Lord Cochrane, put the specie on board a French brig called the *Gazelle*, then
lying at Guamey, instead of delivering it on board of the *Macedonian*, where he
feared that Lord Cochrane might seize it.   Lord Cochrane, hearing of the circumstance, captured the French brig and compelled her captain to sign a paper
relinquishing the specie to him, in consideration of his releasing the master and
the vessel.   These two seizures were the subject of a memorial by the persons
interested in the cargo to the Department of State in 1820, and they became the
subject of a negotiation in which the Chilean Government finally offered to admit
the claim for the $80,000 taken from Smith, and part of the claim for the $60,000
taken from the French brig, and to pay the sum of $104,000, with interest, in full
settlement of the claims.   This sum the memoralists signified their willingness
to accept.

The first case of the *Macedonian* is to be carefully distinguished
from the second case of the *Macedonian*.   The second case arose from
a later seizure by Cochrane (in 1821) of other moneys belonging to
Thomas H. Perkins.   That second case of the *Macedonian* was submitted to the arbitration of the King of the Belgians, was decided on
May 15, 1863, and is treated at large in Moore, *op. cit.*, 1450–68.

In his despatch of July 9, 1840, Richard Pollard, Chargé d'Affaires
of the United States at Santiago, wrote of the making of this agreement and its terms as follows (D. S., 5 Despatches, Chile, No. 83):

I have the satisfaction of announcing to you that I have agreed with M.ʳ Tocornal, the acting President of Chile, in the case of the *Macedonian.* The Chilian Government is to pay One hundred & four thousand dollars with interest thereon at 5 per cent per annum from the date of the seizure. The debt thus made is to be paid ⅐ down—say in cash—and the balance in Six equal annual instalments bearing interest at 5 per cent per annum. This is probably as much as I should have insisted on. Lord Cochrane accounted for no more than 104'000 dollars as the amount taken from Captain Smith himself and the French brig. This has been proved to me by a document in the possession of the Chilian Government. Captain Smith says in his statement that he had in his possession $80'000—that $20'000 of it had been hid by a companion of his and that he informed the officer who seized him and his money that he was leaving behind the $20'000—that the officer however left it. It is very remarkable that as eager as Lord Cochrane and his crew were after money that his officer should have left the $20'000 behind if he was informed of its being there. As he did not take it according to the admission of Captain Smith the reasonable presumption is that the Companion and friend of Captain Smith, who was not interrupted by those who seized Smith, saved it—that Smith got it. The translation we had of Lord Cochrane's report was not correct. I have seen the original report. The translation makes him say that he considered from the appearance of the seroons the sum taken from Capt. Smith to be $60'000. The report in truth says that he considered from the appearance of the seroons the sum to be less than $60'000. Certain it is that he accounted for no more than $104000 in the two sums—that taken from Captain Smith added to that taken from the French brig. The law gave the Captors half and half to the Government. The Government received no more for the two captures than $52'000. I accepted of 5 per cent interest because that is the legal interest of the Country. I had been under the impression it was 6 per cent. I have provided for the payments to be made in hard dollars. The difference between the Currency of the Country—gold and Cut money—and hard dollars is 8 to 10 per cent—so that I have gained this much by insisting for and succeeding in the agreement to this manner of payment. I have fought a hard battle, as you will have seen by my correspondence with the Chilian Government to obtain the terms I have agreed upon. I trust the agreement I have made will be entirely satisfactory to my Government and those more immediately interested in the claim. Better *could not* be done.

The agreement was oral; its exact date (July 7, 1840) is not given in the despatch quoted; the statement there of the terms of the agreement is incomplete; nothing is said regarding the necessary approval of the agreement by the Congress of Chile; and the date to which the interest was to be calculated and from which the total would bear interest, is left vague. The latter point became one of difference of opinion.

From later despatches it appears that a written memorandum of the agreement was made for the Chilean Foreign Office and that a copy thereof was delivered to Pollard. A copy of that memorandum (in Spanish) was enclosed with the despatch of John S. Pendleton (who arrived at Santiago on May 16, 1842, as the successor of Pollard as Chargé d'Affaires of the United States) dated October 29, 1843 (D. S., 6 Despatches, Chile, No. 16); at the foot of that copy is written the following, signed by Pendleton and dated November 1, 1843:

The above is an exact Copy of a paper filed amongst a parcel, bound up together and endorsed in Mr Pollards hand writing "letters from the Chilien Minister, 1841–42."

It has neither date nor signature, is folded in the shape of an ordinary letter and directed on the back "Al Sr. D. Ricardo Pollard"—Encargado de negocios &c &c" "Oficina" de R.ᵉ E.ᵉ

To this I should add that it is written in a very beautiful hand—as are all the official notes of this Gov^t—being thus evidently a copy by some Clerk in the department—& not written by either the present or previous minister.

On comparison with the other memorandum it will be found substialy if not verbaly an exact copy—and is evidently, the official statement from the Foreign office, of what *it* had recieved as the report of Mr Tocornal in regard to the negotiation between himself and Mr Pollard. There is nothing among said parcel, nor any thing in the correspondence of Mr Pollard, signifying his appobation or *dis*-approbation of the paper

The "other memorandum" referred to in the statement quoted is that handed to Pendleton on October 8, 1842, by Mr. Bello, "translator for the Minister of Foreign Affairs", and enclosed with Pendleton's unnumbered despatch (No. 5) of December 4, 1842 (*ibid.*); it was delivered "as a correct statement of the agreement between Messrs Pollard and Tocornal in the case of the Macedonian" (*ibid.*). The wording of the two papers is the same except for the first two words and the third word from the end, which read "Basis de" and "hacer" in one and "Bases del" and "hacerse" in the other.

Still another copy of the memorandum, which seems to be more carefully written and with which the text here printed has been collated, is one of the numerous and voluminous enclosures with the despatch of Seth Barton, Chargé d'Affaires of the United States, of July 29, 1848 (D. S., 7 Despatches, Chile, No. 7). Barton suggested that the memorandum, being undated, might have been a project prior to the agreement of July 7, 1840, and not a minute of the agreement itself; but it seems clear that that suggestion was unfounded.

The translation of the memorandum which is printed above is that enclosed with Pendleton's despatch of December 4, 1842.

It was the contention of Pollard, after his return to the United States, that the memorandum did not correctly represent the agreement, in that the interest on the new capital sum ran from the date of the approval of the agreement by the Chilean Congress instead of (as Pollard alleged) from July 7, 1840. The submission of the agreement to the Congress of Chile was delayed until after Pendleton had arrived at Santiago as Chargé d'Affaires; further negotiations were necessary; but the substance of the terms of the agreement as written in the memorandum was not changed; and it seems to be the better view that the memorandum correctly embodied the oral agreement made by Pollard. The matter is discussed at length in the despatch of Pendleton of October 29, 1843, cited above.

The form of the law of December 29, 1842, as adopted by the Congress of Chile, is thus given (D. S., 7 Despatches, Chile, No. 7, July 29, 1848, enclosure):

[Translation]

ART? 1º El Gobierno de Chile se obliga a restituir al Gobierno de los Estados Unidos la cantidad de ciento cuatro mil pesos fuertes apresada el año de 1819 por la Escuadra Chilena en el Puerto de Supe y a bordo del bergantin

ARTICLE 1. The Government of Chile undertakes to restore to the Government of the United States the sum of one hundred and four thousand hard dollars seized in 1819 by the Chilean squadron in the port of Supe

"La Gazelle," y reclamada por el Gobierno de los Estados Unidos como propiedad americana.

2º Los intereses de ésta cantidad, a razon de cinco pesos fuertes por ciento al año corridos desde las fechas de los apresamientos hasta la fecha de la presente lei, se capitalizarán y se agregarán a la sobre dicha cantidad de ciento cuatro mil pesos fuertes

3º El Capital que componga la sobredicha partida y los intereses capitalizados, se dividirá en siete porciones iguales, la primera de las cuales se tendrá a disposicion del Gobierno de los Estados Unidos el dos de Enero de 1843; y las otras seis porciones se tendrá asi mismo a disposicion del Gobierno de los Estados Unidos el dia 2 de Enero de los seis años subseguientes, una partida cada año.

4º Se pagará junto con cada una de estas partidas el interes anual que a razon de cinco pesos fuertes por ciento, desde la fecha de la presente lei, corresponda a la suma que hasta la fecha de cada pago se adeude.

and on board the brigantine *La Gazelle*, and claimed by the Government of the United States as American property.

2. The interests on this sum at the rate of five hard dollars per hundred per annum accrued from the date of the seizures to the date of the present law will be capitalized and added to the above-stated sum of one hundred and four thousand hard dollars.

3. The principal, which includes the above-stated item and the interests capitalized, shall be divided into seven equal portions, the first of which shall be at the disposition of the Government of the United States on January 2, 1843; and the other six portions shall likewise be held at the disposition of the Government of the United States on January 2 of the six following years, one portion each year.

4. There shall be paid with every one of these instalments the annual interest which, at the rate of five hard dollars per hundred from the date of the present law, corresponds to the sum which is due at the date of each payment.

However, the question of the date of the "new capital" was again brought forward in 1848 by Barton; he found support for his argument in a draft convention prepared by Pollard and delivered by him to the Minister of Foreign Affairs of Chile on May 25, 1841. The provisions of that unsigned and uninitialed draft covered both the first case of the *Macedonian* and the case of the *Warrior* (Document 96); a Spanish translation of its text was transmitted to Barton by the Minister of Foreign Affairs with his note of July 6, 1848 (D. S., 7 Despatches, Chile, No. 7, July 29, 1848, enclosures); in that note it was stated that it appeared that the English version (written by Pollard) had been sent by the Chilean Foreign Office to Pendleton on November 2, 1843; but Pendleton makes no mention of that circumstance in his despatches. The text of that draft is available only in a Spanish translation, and in a retranslation thereof which follows (D. S., 8 Despatches, Chile, No. 16, November 30, 1849, and enclosures, *passim*):

Agreement Celebrated between Richard Pollard, Chargé d'Affaires of the United States, and the Chilean Minister of Foreign Affairs upon Reclamations Made by the Former upon the Latter.

In the Case of the *Macedonian*

The moneys taken from Captain Smith on the 5th and from the French brig *Gazelle* on the 10th of April, 1819, by Lord Cochrane, will be computed by the Chilean Government in $104,000, with its respective interest at the rate of 5 percent per annum, from the time of its capture to the date of the agreement, the 7th of July, 1840, that is to say, $214,500.

This sum of $214,500 will be paid by the Chilean Government in the following way:

The seventh part cash.

The rest in six equal annual payments, from the 7th of July, 1840, as follows:

$30,643 on the 7th July, 1841
$30,643 on the 7th July, 1842
$30,643 on the 7th July, 1843
$30,643 on the 7th July, 1844
$30,643 on the 7th July, 1845
$30,643 on the 7th July, 1846

The payments will be made in hard dollars or in an equivalent sum in current money of the country.

To the sum of each of these portions of the debt will be added the interest of 5 percent per annum from the 7th of July, 1840, until the actual payment is effected.

Case of the *Warrior*

The Chilean Government will pay $15,000 with its respective interest at 5 percent per annum from the 30th of September, 1840. The payment will be made in the same manner and proportions as in the case of the *Macedonian*.

It is clearly agreed and understood by the parties that the arrangement of the two claims above specified will have no intervention in other claims between both Governments.

It will be seen that by the tenor of that draft of Pollard the date of the "new capital" was fixed at July 7, 1840, and not at the date of the approval of the accord by the Congress of Chile; but that draft was written by Pollard more than ten months after the date of the verbal agreement; more reliance is to be placed on the memorandum in Spanish, which was probably contemporaneous (although this is not certain); and it is certain at least that no other contemporaneous memorandum is of record. Perhaps one cause of the uncertainty was the imperfect rendering of "hasta la referida fecha" (clause 3 of the memorandum of July 7, 1840) by the phrase "up to this date" instead of "up to the date mentioned"; the translation forwarded by Pendleton (printed above) may well have been the same as that used by Pollard.

The view of Barton as to the correct date of the "new capital" was set forth by him in a note to the Chilean Minister of Foreign Affairs dated April 23, 1849, with great elaboration and detail; a copy of that note (D. S., 8 Despatches, Chile, No. 16, November 30, 1849, enclosure 2) fills sixty-five manuscript pages. The claim which Barton put forward in that communication because of the alleged difference in dates, was $28,954 in Chilean currency as of the date of the note, including interest at 12 percent; but Barton left Santiago to return to the United States on May 22, 1849; the claim which he put forward was not further pressed and, so far as appears, did not receive any support or even consideration by the Department of State.

The Negotiations

The negotiations for the settlement of the first case of the *Macedonian* had been long continued. The first diplomatic representative of the United States sent to Chile was Heman Allen, who was appointed Minister Plenipotentiary on January 27, 1823, and who had instructions regarding the claim (D. S., 10 Instructions, U. S. Ministers, 123–25, November 30, 1823). The negotiations were continued by Allen's successors, Samuel Larned, John Hamm, Richard Pollard, and

John S. Pendleton, each of whom had the rank of Chargé d'Affaires. It was John Hamm who negotiated the Treaty of Peace, Amity, Commerce, and Navigation with Chile of May 16, 1832 (Document 73). His full power of October 15, 1830, gave authority to treat "concerning Commerce and Navigation between the United States and the Republic of Chili, and claims of the Citizens of the two Countries respectively upon the Governments of the United States, and the said Republic of Chili" (D. S., 2 Credences, 156); and the full power which was issued to Pendleton on November 30, 1841, referred to "claims of citizens of the United States upon the Government of the said Republic of Chile" (D. S., 3 Credences, 1).

President Tyler made mention of the adjustment of the first case of the *Macedonian* and of the receipt of the first instalment by the claimants in his annual message of December 1843 (Richardson, IV, 257, 263).

The Payments

The "new capital" according to clause 3 of the memorandum of the agreement, which comprised the sum of $104,000 and interest thereon from the date of the seizure until the date of the approval of the agreement by the Congress of Chile (a period of more than twenty-three years), came to $227,397. Despatches of various dates from 1843 to 1849 report the payment of the instalments with interest; the receipt for the final payment is in the note of January 8, 1849, from Chargé d'Affaires Seth Barton to the Minister of Foreign Affairs of Chile, Don Manuel Camilo Vial (D. S., 7 Despatches, Chile, No. 10, April 26, 1849, enclosure).

Treaty Series No. 289
8 Statutes at Large, 560–69
18 *ibid.*, pt. 2, Public Treaties, 634–38

95

PORTUGAL : AUGUST 26, 1840

*Treaty of Commerce and Navigation, signed at Lisbon August 26, 1840.
Original in English and Portuguese.
Submitted to the Senate December 31, 1840. (Message of December 28, 1840.) Resolution of advice and consent February 3, 1841.
Ratified by the United States April 23, 1841. Ratified by Portugal
March 8, 1841. Ratifications exchanged at Washington April 23,
1841. Proclaimed April 24, 1841.
Following the treaty texts are printed six notes (one in part) exchanged
at Lisbon upon or in connection with the signature of the treaty, which
contain declarations properly to be deemed part of the agreement.
Those six notes, which were before the Senate, are thus dated: the
Plenipotentiary of the United States to the Portuguese Minister of
Foreign Affairs ad interim, August 10, 1840; the Plenipotentiary of
Portugal to the Plenipotentiary of the United States, August 24, 1840;
the same to the same, August 26, 1840; the Plenipotentiary of the
United States to the Plenipotentiary of Portugal, August 26, 1840;
the same to the same, August 26, 1840; the Portuguese Minister of
Foreign Affairs ad interim to the Plenipotentiary of the United States,
August 27, 1840. A discussion of those diplomatic exchanges is in-
cluded in the editorial notes to the treaty.*

In the Name of the Most Holy and Undivided Trinity.

The United States of America, and Her Most Faithful Majesty The Queen of Portugal and of the Algarves, equally animated with the desire of maintaining the relations of good understanding which have hitherto so happily subsisted between Their Respective States; of extending, also, and consolidating the commercial intercourse between them; and convinced that this object cannot better be accomplished than by adopting

En Nome da Santissima e Indivisel Trindade.

Os Estados Unidos da America, e Sua Magestade Fidelissima a Raynha de Portugal e dos Algarves, igualmente animados do desejo de manter as relações de boa intelligencia que até aqui tem felizmente subsistido entre Seus Respectivos Estados; e de estender outrosim e consolidar as relações commerciaes entre elles; e convencidos de que este objecto se não póde melhor conseguir do que pela adopção de

the systeme of an entire freedom of navigation, and a perfect reciprocity based upon pinciples of equity equally beneficial to both Countries; have, in consequence, agreed to enter into negotiations for the Conclusion of a Treaty of Commerce and Navigation: and They have appointed as Their Plenipotenciaries for that purpose, to wit: The President of The United States of America, Edward Kavangh, Their Chargé d'Affaires at the Court of Her Most Faithful Majesty; And Her Most Faithful Majesty, The Most Illustrious and Most Excellent John Baptist de Almeida Garrett, First Historiographer to Her said Majesty, of Her Council, Member of the Cortes, Knight of the ancient and most noble order of the Tower an Sword Knight Commander of the order of Christ, Officer of the order of Leopold in Belgium, Judge of the Superior Court of Commerce, Envoy Extraordinary and Minister Plenipotentiary to Her Catholic Majesty: Who, after having exchanged their respective full powers, found to be in due and proper form, have agreed upon, and concluded, the following articles.

ARTICLE 1ˢᵗ·

There shall be, between the Territories of the High Contracting Parties, a reciprocal liberty of Commerce and navigation. The Citizens and Subjects of their

um systema de inteira liberdade de Navegação e perfeita reciprocidade fundada nos principios de equidade igualmente beneficos para ambos os paizes; assentarão, em consequencia, de entrar em negociações para a conclusão de um Tractado de Commercio e Navegação: para cujo fim Nomearão para seus Plenipotenciarios a saber: o Presidente dos Estados Unidos da America, ao Senhor Edward Kavanagh, Encarregado de Negocios dos mesmos Estados n'esta Côrte: E Sua Magestade a Raynha de Portugal ao Illustrissimo e Excellentissimo João Baptista de Almeida Garrett, Seu Chronista Mór, e do Seu Concelho, Deputado da Nação Portugueza, Cavalleiro da Antiga e muito Nobre Ordem da Torre e Espada do Valor Lealdade e Merito, Commendador da Ordem de Christo, Official da de Leopoldo na Belgica, Juiz do Tribunal Superior de Commercio, Enviado Extraordinario e Ministro Plenipotenciario juncto a Sua Magestade Catholica: os quaes, depois de terem communicado, um ao outro, os seus respectivos plenos poderes, que se acharam em boa e devida fórma, ajustaram e concluiram os Artigos seguintes.

ARTIGO 1º

Haverá, entre os Territorios das Altas Partes Contractantes, reciproca liberdade de Commercio e Navecação. Os Cidadões e Subditos dos Seus respectivos

respective States shall, mutually, have liberty to enter the Ports, Places and Rivers of the territories of each party, wherever foreign Commerce is, or shall be, permitted. They shall be at liberty to sojourn and reside in all parts of said Territories, in order to attend to their affairs; and they shall enjoy, to that effect, the same security and protection as natives of the Country wherein they reside, on condition of their submitting to the laws and ordinances there prevailing, and particularly to the regulations in force concerning commerce.

ARTICLE 2ª

Vessels of the United States of America arriving, either laden or in ballast, in the Ports of the Kingdom and Possessions of Portugal; and, reciprocally, Portuguese Vessels arriving, either laden or in ballast, in the Ports of the United States of America, shall be treated, on their entrance, during their stay, and at their departure, upon the same footing as national vessels, coming from the same place, with respect to the duties of Tonnage, light-house duties, pilotage, port-charges, as well as to the fees and perquisites of Public Officers, and all other duties and charges, of whatever kind or denomination, levied upon Vessels of Commerce, in the name or to the profit of the Government, the local authorities, or of any

Estados poderão, mutua e livremente, entrar nos Portos, Logares e Rios dos Territorios de cada uma das Dittas Partes Contractantes, aonde quer que o Commercio estrangeiro é, ou vier a ser, permittido. Terão igualmente liberdade de pousar e residir em qualquer parte dos dittos Territorios, afim de tractar de seus negocios; e gozarão, para esse fim, a mesma segurança e protecção que os naturaes do Paiz onde residem, sob condição de se sujeitarem ás leis e ordens do Governo que ahi regerem, especialmente aos regulamentos commerciaes em vigor.

ARTIGO 2º

Os navios dos Estados Unidos da America que aportarem, carregados ou em lastro, aos Portos do Reino e Possessões de Portugal; e, reciprocamente, os navios Portuguezes, que aportarem, carregados ou em lastro, nos Portos dos Estados Unidos da America, serão tractados, á entrada, durante a sua estada no Porto, e á sahida d'elle, do mesmo modo que os navios nacionaes, vindos de iguaes procedencias, em relação aos direitos de tonelagem, de faróes, pilotagem, e ancoradouro, e bem assim quanto aos emolumentos e propinas das Auctoridades publicas, ou quaesquer outros encargos e direitos, de qualquer natureza ou denominação que sejão, e que costumam levar-se aos navios de Commercio ou, seja por conta do

public, or private establishment, whatsoever.

ARTICLE 3ᵈ·

No higher or other duties shall be imposed on the importation, into the Kingdom and Possessions of Portugal, of any article, the growth, produce or manufacture of the United States of America; and no higher or other duties shall be imposed on the importation, into the United States of America, of any article, the growth, produce or manufacture of the Kingdom and Possessions of Portugal, than such as are, or shall be, payable on the like article, being the growth, produce, or manufacture of any other foreign Country.

Nor shall any prohibition be imposed on the importation or exportation of any article, the growth, produce or manufacture of the United States of America, or of the Kingdom and Possessions of Portugal, to or from, the Ports of the said Kingdom and Possessions of Portugal, or of the said States, which shall not equally extend to all other foreign Nations.

Nor shall any higher or other duties or charges be imposed, in either of the two countries, on the exportation of any articles to the United States of America, or to the Kingdom of Portugal, respectively, than such as are pay-

Governo, das auctoridades locaes, ou de qualquer outro estabelecimento publico ou particular.

ARTIGO 3º

Não se imporão outros nem maiores direitos, na importação, em o Reino de Portugal e suas Possessões, de nenhum genero de producto natural ou de manufactura dos Estados Unidos da America, nem outros ou maiores direitos serão impostos na importação, em os Estados Unidos da America, de genero algum de producção natural ou de manufactura do Reino de Portugal e suas Possessões, alem daquelles que pagão, ou vierem a pagar, iguaes generos de producção natural ou de manufactura de qualquer outro paiz estrangeiro.

Nem se estabelecerá prohibição alguma na importação ou exportação de qualquer genero de producção natural ou manufactura dos Estados Unidos da America, ou do Reino de Portugal e Suas Possessões, respectivamente, em algum d'elles, que do mesmo modo se não estabeleça igualmente para todas as outras Nações Estrangeiras.

Nem se estabelecerão outros ou maiores direitos ou encargos, em qualquer dos dous paizes, sobre a exportação de quaesquer generos para os Estados Unidos da America, ou para o Reino de Portugal, respectivamente, alem dos que

able on the exportation of the like articles to any other foreign Country.

Provided, however, that nothing contained in this Article shall be understood, or intended, to interfere with the stipulation entered into by the United States of America, for a special equivalent, in regard to French wines, in the Convention[1] made by the said States and France, on the fourth day of July, in the year of our Lord one thousand eight hundred and thirty one; which stipulation will expire, and cease to have effect, in the month of February, in the year of our Lord one thousand eight hundred and forty two.

ARTICLE 4th.

The same duties shall be paid, and the same bounties, deductions, or privileges allowed, on the importation, into the Kingdom and Possessions of Portugal, of any article, the growth, produce, or manufacture of the United States of America, whether such importation shall be in Vessels of the said States, or in Portuguese Vessels; and, reciprocally, the same duties shall be paid, and the same bounties, deductions, or privileges allowed, on the importation, into the United States of America, of any article, the growth, produce, or manufacture of the Kingdom and Possessions of Portugal, whether such impor-

se pagão pela exportação de iguaes generos para outro paiz estrangeiro.

Intendendose, todavia, que nada do que neste artigo se contem poderá prejudicar a estipulação admittida pelos Estados Unidos da America, por um equivalente especial, a respeito dos vinhos Francezes, na Convenção[1] celebrada entre os dittos Estados e a França, em quatro de Julho do anno do nascimento de Nosso Senhor Jesu Christo de mil oitocentos e trinta e um: a qual estipulação hade terminar e deixar de ter effeito, no mez de Fevereiro do anno do nascimento de Nosso Senhor Jesu Christo de mil oitocentos e quarenta e dous.

ARTIGO 4º

Pagar-se-hao os mesmos direitos, e serão concedidos os mesmos favores, deducções, ou privilegios pela importação, em o Reino e Possessões de Portugal, de qualquer genero de producção natural ou manufactura dos Estados Unidos da America, quer a ditta importação se faça em navios dos dittos Estados, ou em Navios Portuguezes: e, reciprocamente, se pagarão os mesmos direitos, e serão concedidos os mesmos favores, deducções, e privilegios pela importação, em os Estados Unidos da America, de qualquer genero de producção natural ou manufactura de Portugal e suas Possessões, quer a ditta

---

[1] Document 71.

tation shall be in Portuguese Vessels, or in Vessels of the said States.

ARTICLE 5th.

It is agreed by the High Contracting Parties, that, whenever there may be lawfully imported into all or any of the Ports of the Kingdom and Possessions of Portugal, in Vessels of any foreign country, articles of the growth, produce, or manufacture of a country other than that to which the importing Vessels shall belong, the same privilege shall immediately become common to Vessels of the United States of America, with all the same rights and favors as may, in that respect, be granted to the most favored nation. And, reciprocally, in consideration thereof, Portuguese Vessels shall, thereafter, enjoy, in the same respect, privileges, rights, and favors, to a correspondent extent, in the Ports of the United States of America.

ARTICLE 6th.

All kinds of merchandise and articles of Commerce, which may be lawfully exported or reexported from the Ports of either of the High Contracting Parties to any foreign country, in national vessels, may, also, be exported or re-exported therefrom in Vessels of the other Party, respectively, without paying other or higher duties or charges, of what-

importação seja feita em Navios Portuguezes, ou em Navios dos dittos Estados.

ARTIGO 5º

Convierão as Altas Partes Contractantes, que se, em algum tempo, fôr permittido o importar em todos ou alguns dos Portos o Reino e Possessões de Portugal, em Navios de qualquer Nação Estrangeira, alguns generos de producção natural ou manufactura de outro paiz que não seja aquelle á que os dittos navios pertencerem, o mesmo favor será immediatamente extensivo aos Navios dos Estados Unidos da America, com os mesmos direitos e favores que, para esse fim, forem concedidos á Nação mais favorecida. Em consideração do que, e reciprocamente, os Navios Portuguezes gozarão, d'ahi em diante, e para o mesmo fim, privilegios, direitos e favores, na mesma extenção correspondente, nos Portos dos Estados Unidos da America.

ARTIGO 6º

Toda a sorte de mercadorias e artigos de commercio que legalmente podem ser exportados ou reexportados dos Portos de uma das Altas Partes contractantes, para qualquer paiz estrangeiro, em navios Nacionaes, poderão igualmente ser exportados ou reexportados dos dittos Portos em os navios da Outra Parte, respectivamente, sem pagar outros ou

ever kind or denomination, than if the same merchandise or articles of Commerce were exported or reexported in National Vessels.

And the same bountries and drawbacks shall be allowed, whether such exportation or reexportation be made in Vessels of the one Party or the other.

ARTICLE 7th.

It is expressly understood that nothing contained in this Treaty shall be applicable to the coastwise Navigation of either of the two Countries, which each of the High Contracting Parties reserves exclusively to itself.

ARTICLE 8th

It is mutually understood that the foregoing stipulations do not apply to Ports and Territories, in the Kingdom and Possessions of Portugal, where foreign Commerce and Navigation are not admitted; and that the Commerce and Navigation of Portugal, directly to and from the United States of America and the said Ports and Territories, are, also prohibited.

But, Her Most Faithful Majesty agrees that, as soon as the said Ports and Territories, or any of them, shall be opened to the Commerce or Navigation of any

maiores direitos ou encargos, de qualquer modo ou denominação que sejam, do que se as dittas mercadorias ou artigos de commercio fossem exportados ou reexportados em navios nacionaes.

E conceder-se hão os mesmos favores e deducções de direitos, quer a exportacão ou a reexportação seja feita em navios de uma ou da outra das dittas Partes.

ARTIGO 7º

Fica expressamente intendido que nenhuma das estipulações conthendas no prezente Tractado será applicavel á Navegação costeira, ou de cabotagem, de qualquer dos dous paizes, que cada uma das Altas Partes Contractantes exclusivamente se reserva.

ARTIGO 8º

Fica mutuamente entendido que as precedentes estipulações não são applicaveis aos Portos e Territorios no Reino e Possessões de Portugal, em que não são admittidos o Commercio e Navegação Estrangeiros; e que o Commercio e Navegação de Portugal, directamente dos dittos Portos para os Estados Unidos da America, e dos dittos Estados para os dittos Portos e Territorios, são igualmente prohibidos.

Mas Sua Magestade Fidelissima consente em que, quando, em algum tempo, os dittos Portos e Territorios, ou algum d'elles, vierem a ser abertos ao Com-

foreign Nation, they shall, from that moment, be also opened to the Commerce and Navigation of the United States of America, with the same privileges, rights and favors as may be allowed to the most favored Nation, gratuitously, if the concession was gratuitously made, or on allowing the same compensation, or an equivalent, if the concession was conditional.

mercio ou Navegação de qualquer Nacão Estrangeira, desde esse momento figuem abertos ao Commercio e Navegação dos Estados Unidos da America, com os mesmos privilegios, direitos e favores que fôrem concedidos á Nação mais favorecida, gratuitamente, se a concessão tiver sido gratuita, ou pela mesma compensação ou um equivalente d'ella, se a concessão tiver sido condicional.

ARTICLE 9th.

Whenever the citizens or Subjects of either of the Contracting Parties shall be forced to seek refuge or asylum in any of the Rivers, Bays, Ports, or Territories of the other, with their Vessels, whether Merchant, or of War, through stress of weather, pursuit of Pirates or Enemies, they shall be received and treated with humanity, giving to them all favor, facility and protection for repairing their ships, procuring provisions and placing themselves in a situation to continue their voyage, without obstacle or hindrance of any kind.

ARTIGO 9º

Os Cidadãos e Subditos de qualquer das Partes Contractantes que forem obrigados a procurar refugio ou asilo em algum dos Rios, Bahias, Portos, ou Territorios da Outra, com seus Navios, ou sejão mercantes ou de guerra, por causa do temporal, perseguição de Piratas ou inimigos, serão recebidos e tractados com humanidade, dando-se-lhes todo o favor, facilidade e protecção para reparar os seus navios, procurar mantimentos e pôr-se em estado de continuar a sua viagem, sem nenhum obstaculo ou molestação.

ARTICLE 10th.

The two Contracting Parties shall have the liberty of having, each in the Ports of the other, Consuls, Vice Consuls, Agents, and Commissaries of their own appointment, who shall enjoy the same privileges and powers as those of the most favored Nation.

ARTIGO 10º

As Duas Partes Contractantes terão a liberdade de nomear para os Portos, uma da outra, Consules, Vice Consules, Agentes, e Commissarios os quaes gozarão dos mesmos privilegios e podêres que os da Nação mais favorecida. Mas, antes que qualquer Consul,

But, before any Consul, Vice Consul, Agent, or Commissary shall act as such, he shall, in the usual form, be approved and admitted by the Government to which he is sent.

But, if any such Consuls shall exercise commerce, they shall be submitted to the same laws and usages to which the private Individuals of their Nation are submitted, in the same place, in respect of their Commercial transactions.

And, it is hereby declared that, in case of offense against the laws, such Consul, Vice-Consul, Agent or Commissary may either be punished according to law, or be sent back, the offended Government assigning, to the other, reasons for the same.

The archives and papers of the consulates shall be respected inviolably; and, under no pretext whatever, shall any Magistrate seize, or in any way interfere with, them.

The Consuls, Vice-Consuls, and Commercial Agents, shall have the right, as such, to sit as Judges and arbitrators, in such differences as may arise between the Captains and Crews of the Vessels belonging to the Nation whose interests are committed to their charge, without the interference of the local authorities, unless the Conduct of the Crews, or of the Captains, should disturb the order or the tranquillity, or offend the laws, of the Country;

Vice-Consul, Agente, ou Commissario possa funccionar como tal, será, na devida e usual forma, approvado e admittido pelo Governo do paiz a que é mandado

Mas, se algum d'estes Consules exercitar o commercio, ficará sujeito ás mesmas leis e usos a que são sujeitos os Individuos particulares de sua Nação, nos mesmos logares, relativamente ás suas transacções commerciaes.

E aqui fica declarado, que no caso de offensa contra as leis, o ditto Consul, Vice-Consul, Agente ou Commissario poderá ser, ou punido conforme o direito, ou mandado sair, declarando o Govêrno offendido, ao outro, as rasões do seu procedimento.

Os archivos e papeis dos consulados serão respeitados inviolavelmente, e, por nenhum pretexto, poderá qualquer Magistrado embarga-los, ou, de outro modo, intervir a respeito d'elles.

Os Consules, Vice Consules, e Agentes Commerciaes, terão o direito, como taes, de exercer as funccões de Juizes e arbitros, nas questões que venhão a levantar se entre os Mestres e Companhas dos Navios da Nação cujos interesses lhe são commettidos, sem intervenção das auctoridades locaes, excepto se o procedimento das dittas companhas e Mestres perturbar a ordem ou a tranquillidade, ou offender as Leis, do païz; ou tambem se os

or the said Consuls, Vice-Consuls, or Commercial Agents should require their assistance to cause their decisions to be carried into effect, or supported.

It is, however, understood that this species of judgment, or arbitration, shall not deprive the contending parties of the right they have to resort, on their return, to the Judicial Authorities of their country.

ARTICLE 11th

The said Consuls, Vice-Consuls and Commercial Agents are authorised to require the assistance of the local authorities, for the search, arrest, detention and imprisonment of the Deserters from the ships of War and Merchant Vessels of their Country.

For this purpose, they shall apply to the competent Tribunals, Judges, and Officers, and shall, in waiting,[1] demand the said Deserters, proving by the exhibition of the Registers of the Vessels, the Rolls of the Crews, or by any other Official Documents, that such Individuals formed part of the Crews; and, this reclamation being thus substantiated, the surrender shall be made, without delay.

Such Deserters, when arrested, shall be placed at the disposal of the said Consuls, Vice-Consuls, or Commercial Agents, and may be confined in the public prisons, at

dittos Consules, Vice-Consules ou Agentes Commerciaes requererem o seu auxilio para haver de levar á effeito as suas decisões.

É, com tudo, entendido que esta especie de julgamento, ou arbitragem, de nenhum modo privará os litigantes do direito que teem a recorrer depois ás Auctoridades Judiciaes do seu Paiz.

ARTIGO 11º

Os dittos Consules, Vice-Consules e Agentes Commerciaes são auctorisados a requerer o auxilio das auctoridades locaes, para a busca, prisão, detenção e custodia dos desertores dos navios de guerra e mercantes da sua Nação.

Para este fim, poderão dirigir se aos competentes Tribunaes, Juizes, e Officiaes publicos, e pedirão, por escripto, os ditos Dezertores provando pela exhibição dos Registos dos Navios, matricula dos Marinheiros, ou por qualque outro Documento Official, que taes Individuos pertencião á tripulação d'elles; e documentada assim a reclamação, será feita a entrega sem demora.

Os Dezertores apenas prezos serão postos á disposição dos dittos Consules, Vice-Consules ou Agentes Commerciaes, e poderão ser detidos nas Cadeãs publicas,

[1] This should be "writing", as in the Portuguese text and in the English of the duplicate original.

the request and cost of those who shall claim them, in order to be detained until the time when they shall be restored to the Vessels to which they belonged, or sent back to their own country; by a Vessel of the same Nation, or any other Vessel whatsoever.

But, if not sent back within four months from the day of their arrest, they shall be set at liberty, and shall not be again arrested for the same cause. However, if the Deserter shall be found to have committed any crime or offense, the surrender may be delayed until the Tribunal, before which is case shall be pending, shall have pronounced its sentence, and such sentence shall have been carried into effect.

ARTICLE 12th

The citizens and Subjects of each of the High Contracting parties shall have power to dispose of their personal goods, within the jurisdiction of the other, by Testament, Donation, or otherwise; and their Representatives shall succeed to their said personal goods, whether by testament or *ab intestato*, and may take possession thereof, either by themselves, or by others acting for them, and dispose of the same, at will, paying to the profit of the respective Governments such dues only as the Inhabitants of the country, wherein the said goods are, shall be subject to pay in like cases.

a rógo e á custa dos que os reclamarem, para haverem de ser detidos, atè se restituirem aos navios a que pertencião, ou mandados para o seu païz, por um Navio da mesma Nação, ou por qualquer outro.

Se porem não forem mandados para o seu paiz dentro de quatro mezes contados do dia da prisão, serão postos em liberdade, e não tornarão a ser presos pela mesma causa. Mas, se vier a conhecer-se que o Dezertor commetten algum crime ou offensa contra as Leis do paiz, será demorada a entrega d'elle atè que o Tribunal, a que o caso estiver affecto pronuncie sentença, e a sentença se execute.

ARTIGO 12º

Os Cidadãos e Subditos de cada uma das Altas Partes Contractantes poderam dispôr dos seus bens moveis que se acharem dentro da jurisdicção da outra, por testamento, doação ou por qualquer outro modo; e os seus Representantes poderam succeder nos ditos bens particulares, por Testamento, ou *ab intestato*, e poderam tomar posse d'elles por si ou por seus Procuradores, e dispor livremente dos mesmos, pagando sómente aos respectivos Governos o que os Habitantes do Paiz, em que os dittos bens estiverem, forem obrigados a pagar em iguaes casos.

And where, on the death of any person holding real estate, within the Territories of one of the High Contracting Parties, such real estate would, by the laws of the land, descend on a citizen or Subject of the other Party, who, by reason of alienage, may be incapable of holding it, he shall be allowed the time fixed by the laws of the Country; and, in case the Laws of the Country actually in force may not have fixed any such time, he then shall be allowed a reasonable time to sell, or otherwise dispose of, such real estate, and to withdraw and export the proceeds without molestation, and without paying to the profit of the respective Governements any other dues than those to which the Inhabitants of the Country, wherein said real estate is situated, shall be subject to pay in like cases.

Article 13th

If either Party shall, hereafter, grant to any other Nation any particular favor in Navigation or Commerce, it shall immediately become common to the other party, freely, where it is freely granted to such other Nation, or on yielding the same compensation, or an equivalent, *quam proximè* where the grant is conditional.

E se, por morte de alguma pessoa que possua bens de raiz dentro do Territorio de uma das Altas Partes Contractantes, esses bens de raiz tiverem de passar, conforme as Leis do paiz, a um Cidadão ou Subdito da outra parte, e a ditta Pessoa as não poder possuir por sua qualidade de estrangeiro, sêr-lhe-ha dado o tempo marcado pelas Leis do Paiz; ou se estas o não tiverem marcado ser-lhe-ha dado o tempo rasoavel para vender, ou de qualquer outro modo dispôr dos dittos bens de raïz, e retirar ou exportar o seu producto sem gravame e sem ter de pagar para os respectivos Governos outro algum direito alem dos que, em iguaes casos, são impostos aos Habitantes do païz aonde os dittos bens de raïz fôrem situados.

Artigo 13º

Se uma das Partes Contractantes vier a conceder a qualquer outra Nação qualquer favor particular em Navegação ou em Commercio, o ditto favor será immediatamente extensivo á outra parte, livremente se livremente fôr concedido, ou pela mesma compensação ou por outra equivalente *quam proximè*, se a concessão fôr condicional.

ARTICLE 14th

The United States of America
and Her Most Faithful Majesty,
desiring to make as durable as
circumstances will permit, the relations which are to be established
between the two Parties, by virtue of this Treaty or General Convention of reciprocal liberty of
Commerce and Navigation, have
declared solemnly, and do agree
to the following points:

1st.

The present Treaty shall be in
force for six years from the date
hereof, and further until the end
of one year after either of the
Contracting Parties shall have
given notice to the other, of its
intention to terminate the same:
each of the Contracting Parties
reserving to itself the right of
giving such notice to the other, at
any time after the expiration of
the Said term of six years; and it
is hereby agreed between them
that, on the expiration of one year
after such notice shall have been
received by either from the other
party, this Treaty shall altogether
cease and terminate.

2^{d.}

If any one or more of the citizens or Subjects of either Party
shall infringe any of the Articles
of this Treaty, such citizen or
Subject shall be held personally
responsible for the same; and the
harmony and good correspond-

ARTIGO 14º

Os Estados Unidos da America
e Sua Magestade Fidelissima,
desejando fazer tam duraveis,
quanto as circumstancias o per-
mittão, as relações que vão estabe-
lecer-se entre as Duas Partes,
em virtude deste Tractado ou
Geral Convenção de reciproca
liberdade de Commercio e Navegação, Declarão solemnemente e
consentem nos seguintes pontos.

1º

O Presente Tractado durara e
estará em plena força e vigor por
espaço de seis annos contados da
data d'este, e por um anno mais
depois que uma das Partes Contractantes tiver intimado á Outra
a sua intenção de terminar o
mesmo; reservando se cada uma
das Partes Contractantes o direito de fazer essa intimação em
qualquer tempo depois de ter
expirado o referido termo de seis
annos: e do mesmo modo fica
ajustado entre Ellas, que, um
anno depois de ser recebida por
uma d'Ellas, da Outra Parte, a
ditta intimação, esse Tractado
cessará e terminará inteiramente.

2º

Se um ou mais Cidadãos ou
Subditos de uma das Partes Contractantes infringir qualquer dos
Artigos d'este Tractado, será o
mesmo Cidadão ou Subdito pes-
soalmente responsavel por aquella
infracção, e a boa harmonia, e

ence between the two Nations shall not be interrupted thereby; each Party engaging in no way to protect the Offender, or sanction such violation.

correspondencia entre as duas Nações não será por isso interrompida, obrigando-se cada uma das dittas Partes a não proteger de nenhum modo o Offensor, e a não sanccionar tal violacão.

3ª

If, (which, indeed, cannot be expected,) unfortunately, any of the articles contained in the present Treaty shall be violated or infringed, in any way whatever, it is expressly stipulated, that neither of the contracting Parties will order or authorise any acts of reprisal, nor declare war against the other, on complaints of injuries or damages, until the said Party, considering itself offended, shall first have presented to the other a statement of such injuries or damages, verified by competent proof, and demanded justice and satisfaction, and the same shall have been either refused or unreasonably delayed.

3º

Se, (o que não é de esperar,) infelizmente algum ou algums dos artigos, no presente Tractado conthendos, vier a ser por qualquer modo violado ou infringido, expressamente se estipula que nenhuma das Partes Contractantes poderá ordenar ou auctorizar nenhum acto de represalia, nem declarar guerra á outra, por agravos de injurias ou damnos, até que a ditta Parte, que offendida se considera, tenha primeiro appresentado á outra uma exposição das dittas injurias ou damnos provados por competentes Documentos, e pedido justiça e satisfacção, que ou lhe tinha sido recusada, ou desarresoadamente demorada:

4º

The present Treaty shall be approved and ratified by the President of the United States of America, by and with the advice and consent of the Senate of the Said States, and by Her Mos Faithful Majesty, with the previous consent of the General Cortes of the Nation, and the ratifications shall be exchanged, in the City of Washington, within eight

4º

O Presente Tractado será approvado e ratificado pelo Presidente dos Estados Unidos da America, por e com annuencia e consentimento do Senado dos dittos Estados, e por Sua Magestade Fidelissima, com previo consentimento das Cortes Geraes da Nação, e as ratificações serão trocadas, na Cidade de Washington, no prazo de outo mezes con-

months from the date hereof, or sooner, if possible.

In witness whereof, the respective Plenipotentiaries have signed the same, and have affixed thereto the seals of their arms.

Done in triplicate, in the City of Lisbon, the twenty sixth day of August, in the year of our Lord one thousand eight hundred and forty.

[Seal]   Edward Kavanagh

tados da datta da assignatura, ou antes se possivel fôr.

Em testemunho do que, os respectivos Plenipotenciarios o assignaram, e lhe appozerão o Sêllo de suas armas.

Feito em triplicado, na Cidade de Lisboa, aos vinte-e-seis dias de Agosto do Anno do Nascimento de Nosso Senhor Jesu Christo de mil outocentos e quarenta.

[Seal]   João Baptista de Almeida Garrett.

[*The Plenipotentiary of the United States to the Portuguese Minister of Foreign Affairs ad interim*]

Legation of the United States of America,
Lisbon, August 10, 1840.

The undersigned, chargé d'affaires of the United States of America, and their plenipotentiary duly authorized to conclude a treaty of commerce and navigation between the said States and Portugal, has the honor of communicating to his excellency the Councillor Rodrigo da Fonseca Magalhães, that questions, arising in the pending negotiations, render it highly material that *the ports and territories of this kingdom, from which foreign commerce and navigation are excluded,* should be designated; the undersigned, therefore, has the honor to request that his excellency will do him the favor to give the desired information.

It has been assumed, by both of the negotiators, that the words *"kingdom and possessions of Portugal"* include every territory and place where Portugal claims or exercises sovereignty and jurisdiction. If this assumption be erroneous, will his excellency have the goodness to correct it?

The undersigned avails himself of this occasion to renew to his excellency assurances of his most distinguished consideration.

Edward Kavanagh.

[Translation]

LISBON, *August 24, 1840.*

The undersigned, Plenipotentiary of Her Most Faithful Majesty, has the honor to inform Mr. Edward Kavanagh, Plenipotentiary of the United States of America, that having, according to his promise of yesterday, officially propounded to Her Majesty's Minister and Secretary of State the three points that were necessary to be explained or decided before signing the treaty that was agreed upon yesterday, as well as to render it possible to draft, in a manner satisfactory to both parties, an additional article which should be signed simultaneously and as an integral part of the said treaty, has received the following verbal answer, which he is authorized to communicate officially and which he does now communicate to Mr. Kavanagh, declaring at the same time that this, his answer, may be considered by him as having all the force and positive authority which Mr. Kavanagh could desire.

1. As to the declaration of the equivalent mentioned in the eighth article of the treaty, there is no hesitation in declaring that from henceforward it be considered that an equivalent for opening the ports of Her Majesty's ultramarine possessions to the direct commerce and navigation of the United States of America, shall be an equal admission in the United States of the direct commerce and navigation in Portuguese vessels from the said ports.

2. That as to the ultramarine ports which are now considered closed against foreign commerce, Her Majesty's Government judges it necessary to proceed to important inquiries before a categorical designation of them; but that a definitive resolution will be necessarily taken very soon, when it will be communicated without delay to the Government of the United States of America.

[Clause 3, relating to a proposed additional article and to a conference to be held the next day, is omitted.]

The undersigned avails himself of this occasion to renew to Mr. Kavanagh assurances of his distinguished consideration and particular esteem.

DE ALMEIDA GARRETT

[The same to the same]

[Translation]

LISBON, *August 26, 1840.*

The undersigned, Plenipotentiary of Her Most Faithful Majesty, has orders, in the name of Her Most Faithful Majesty, to declare, in the act of signing his name to the Treaty of Commerce and Navigation negotiated with Mr. E. Kavanagh, Plenipotentiary of the United States of America, that there have been long pending between her Government and the Empire of Brazil, negotiations on a treaty of commerce, the result of which may be the concession of mutual favors in the duties of importation at the customhouses of Portugal and Brazil, on certain articles of the production of the two countries, in conformity with the spirit of the reservation made for that purpose in the Treaty of Separation between Portugal and Brazil.[1]   And this circumstance (of which, from the commencement of the negotiations, the undersigned frankly informed Mr. Kavanagh) being the principal motive that compelled the undersigned to propose that there should be a stipulation (as, in effect, it has been stipulated) for the long period of eight months for the ratification of the present treaty, the Portuguese Government thinks it due to frankness to declare to Mr. E. Kavanagh that, reserving to itself the right of not ratifying the said treaty, if circumstances shall so require, it cannot in such case, if it should so occur, be charged with a want of that good faith of which it has ever given so many proofs.

The undersigned renews on this occasion to Mr. E. Kavanagh assurances of his distinguished consideration and very particular esteem.

DE ALMEIDA GARRETT

To Mr. EDWARD KAVANAGH, *etc., etc., etc.*

[The Plenipotentiary of the United States to the Plenipotentiary of Portugal]

LISBON, *August 26, 1840.*

The undersigned, plenipotentiary of the United States of America, acknowledges receipt of the note addressed to him this day, in which the Chevalier de Almeida Garrett, plenipotentiary of her Most Faithful Majesty, states that he has orders, in her Majesty's name, to declare, in the act of signing the treaty of commerce and naviga-

---

[1] Treaty of August 29, 1825; printed in Portuguese, with an English translation, in British and Foreign State Papers, XII, 674–78.

tion between the said States and Portugal, concluded this day by the respective plenipotentiaries above mentioned, that, in accordance with the spirit of the treaty of separation between Portugal and Brazil, and in pursuance of the reserve therein made, negotiations have been long pending between these two nations, which may result in the concession of mutual favors, in respect to the duties of importation on products of each of the parties in the ports of the other; and that if, circumstances so requiring it, her Majesty's ratification be withheld from the treaty with the United States, this notice is now given, that her Majesty's Government may not hereafter be taxed with want of good faith.

The undersigned, on his part, also declares, in the act of signing the same treaty, that an equal right is also reserved to the Government of the United States of America, if circumstances special to said States shall so require it, to withhold its ratification therefrom.

The undersigned avails himself of this occasion to renew to the Chevalier de Almeida Garrett assurances of his very distinguished consideration.

EDWARD KAVANAGH.

[*The same to the same*]

LISBON, August 26, 1840.

The undersigned, plenipotentiary of the United States of America, declares, in the act of signing the treaty concluded this day between the said States and Portugal—

First. That he considers the words *"kingdom and possessions of Portugal"* as comprehending all territories and places wherein her Most Faithful Majesty's Government exercises or claims sovereignty and jurisdiction.

Second. That he accepts the following paragraph, contained in the note addressed to him on the 24th instant, by the Chevalier de Almeida Garrett, as of the same force and effect as if it were inserted, word for word, in the said treaty:

"Quanto á declaração do equivalente mencionado no artigo 8º do tractado, não ha duvida nenhuma em declarar que desde ja fique considerado como o dito equivalente pela abertura dos portos das possessões ultramarinas de sua Magestade ao commercio e navegação directos dos Estados Unidos da America, a admissão a igual commercio e navegação directos dos ditos portos para os dos ditos Estados, em navios Portugueses." [1]

---

[1] For a translation of this paragraph, see clause 1 of the note of August 24, 1840, above.

The undersigned duly appreciates the engagement of her Majesty's Government to communicate to that of the United States its definitive specification of the ports and territories, in the possessions of Portugal, where foreign commerce shall not be permitted.

On this occasion, the undersigned has the honor of tendering to the Chevalier de Almeida Garrett assurances of his distinguished consideration.

EDWARD KAVANAGH.

_____

[*The Portuguese Minister of Foreign Affairs ad interim to the Plenipotentiary of the United States*]

[Translation]

The undersigned, Minister and Secretary of State for the Interior, charged *ad interim* with the Department of Foreign Affairs, in answer to the note addressed to him on the 10th instant by Mr. Edward Kavanagh, Chargé d'Affaires of the United States of America, in which he requested *that the ports and territories of this Kingdom from which foreign commerce is excluded* might be specified, has the honor to inform him that, having sought the necessary information on that point from the Minister of Finance, His Excellency has officially communicated, under this day's date, that in the ports of Lisbon and Oporto all articles of foreign commerce are admitted to entry, for consumption, on complying with the conditions stated in the *pauta geral* (or general tariff) of the customhouses, with the single exception of prohibited articles, such as *cereaes* (breadstuffs), flour, and others; and that in other ports of the Kingdom where there is a customhouse, foreign commerce is also admitted, but entry is not permitted of articles specified in the first article of the preamble to said *pauta* (or tariff).

The undersigned has also the honor of confirming Mr. Kavanagh in his opinion that there is no doubt that by the words "Kingdom and possessions of Portugal" are designated all territories and places over which the Crown of Portugal exercises or claims sovereignty and jurisdiction.

The undersigned improves this occasion to renew to Mr. Kavanagh assurances of his most distinguished consideration.

RODRIGO DA FONSECA MAGALHÃES

OFFICE OF FOREIGN AFFAIRS, *August 27, 1840.*

NOTES

Upon or in connection with the signature of the treaty six notes were written, which contained declarations which are properly to be deemed part of the agreement; all those notes were before the Senate; but none of them is referred to in either instrument of ratification or in the certificate of exchange of ratifications. A draft in the treaty file indicates that it was at one time contemplated that upon the exchange of ratifications at Washington a protocol or other formal record be made of the second note of the American Plenipotentiary of August 26, 1840; but that course was not followed.

Those six notes are printed above, after the treaty texts, namely, the Plenipotentiary of the United States, Edward Kavanagh, to the Portuguese Minister of Foreign Affairs *ad interim*, Councilor Rodrigo da Fonseca Magalhães, August 10, 1840; the Plenipotentiary of Portugal, Councilor João Baptista de Almeida Garrett, to the Plenipotentiary of the United States, August 24, 1840 (in part); the same to the same, August 26, 1840; the Plenipotentiary of the United States to the Plenipotentiary of Portugal, August 26, 1840; the same to the same, August 26, 1840; the Portuguese Minister of Foreign Affairs *ad interim* to the Plenipotentiary of the United States, August 27, 1840. Copies of those notes were respectively enclosures F, G, I, K, L, and N to the despatch of Kavanagh of August 31, 1840, No. 112, to Secretary of State Forsyth, the text of which is printed below in these notes.

Neither that despatch, however, nor its enclosures, are to be found in the archives of the Department of State; the only available source text for the six notes above printed is Senate Confidential Document B, 26th Congress, 2d session (Regular Confidential Documents, XI, 387–444; that Senate print is hereafter for convenience sometimes cited simply as "Senate B"); accordingly, the three of the six notes which were written in Portuguese are available only in translation and are so printed.

The File Papers

In the final clause of the treaty it is said that it was "done in triplicate". There are two signed originals in the treaty file, in each of which the English text is in the left columns and the Portuguese in the right; and in each of those originals the United States is named first throughout in both texts and the American Plenipotentiary signed at the left.

The two originals in the treaty file were not written by the same scrivener; they are not strictly and literally identical, either in the English text or in the Portuguese. The differences are in number considerable; if variant spellings are included, one might count upwards of forty in the English text and sixty in the Portuguese; but all of them are quite immaterial; a large majority (in both texts) consist of commas, inserted or omitted; some are merely matters of punctuation or writing style; and in each document there are a few slips in spelling; but the two documents hardly differ in wording; the one here used for collating (which is that which is with the duplicate instrument of

ratification of April 23 and the original proclamation of April 24, 1841) has in Article 11 "the said Deserters", which is "said Deserters" in the other, and in the final clause of the Portuguese text "dias de Agosto" instead of "dias do mez de Agosto", but nothing more.

The treaty file is complete; it includes the attested resolution of the Senate of February 3, 1841 (Executive Journal, V, 337), the certificate of the exchange of ratifications at Washington of April 23, 1841, of which there is one example in English and one in Portuguese, and also, as above mentioned, the duplicate instrument of ratification of April 23, 1841, and the original proclamation of April 24, 1841. All the documents are in customary form.

The Portuguese instrument of ratification of March 8, 1841, includes both texts of the treaty, the Portuguese in the left columns; in those texts the Queen of Portugal is named first throughout and the copy of the signature of the Plenipotentiary of Portugal appears at the left.

The papers which accompanied the treaty when it was transmitted to the Senate with the presidential message of December 28, 1840, were "certain letters relating thereto, of which a list is annexed" (Executive Journal, V, 324; probably eleven of the "letters" were the original despatches of Kavanagh), which were printed with the treaty texts in Senate Confidential Document B, 26th Congress, 2d session (Regular Confidential Documents, XI, 387–444).

There are eleven despatches of Edward Kavanagh, Chargé d'Affaires at Lisbon, written during 1839 and 1840, which are printed in the document cited; all of them are lacking from the archives of the Department of State; all are of interest and some of them are of real importance; none of them, so far as has been noticed, is elsewhere printed or available; they comprise, with their enclosures, some thirty-eight printed pages of the document.

This is one of the treaties of the United States which has the invocation, "In the name of the Most Holy and Undivided Trinity"; some comments on the use of that phrase are in the notes to Document 55, the treaty with Sweden and Norway of July 4, 1827.

The Full Powers

A full power to negotiate and sign a commercial convention was transmitted to Edward Kavanagh, Chargé d'Affaires at Lisbon, with the instruction of January 7, 1836 (D. S., 14 Instructions, Portugal, 28–29; printed in Senate B, 53–54); but no record copy thereof appears.

The respective full powers were communicated and certified copies exchanged by the Plenipotentiaries who signed the treaty, during July 1840 (Senate B, 37–39, enclosures B and C to despatch No. 112 of August 31, 1840); but it seems that the original full powers were also exchanged, for the original full power given to the Plenipotentiary of Portugal to negotiate and sign the treaty is in the file;

it is printed in the Portuguese and also in translation in Senate B, 14, 38; the translation reads as follows:

Dona Maria, by the Grace of God Queen of Portugal and of the Algarves, on This and the Other Side of the Sea in Africa, Mistress (*Senhora*) of Guinea and of the Conquest, Navigation, and Commerce of Ethiopia, Arabia, Persia, and of India, etc.

I make known to all who shall see these presents that, desiring to obtain for My subjects all the benefits and advantages which a free commerce with other nations can secure to them, and acknowledging the utility and interest that would result, as well to My subjects as to those of the United States of America, from the conclusion between the two nations of a treaty of commerce which, founded on liberal bases and reciprocal to the respective subjects, should bind more closely the relations of amity that happily exist between them, and should tend to the greater prosperity of the two states: It is My pleasure to appoint, as I do by these presents appoint, as My Plenipotentiary, João Baptista de Almeida Garrett, Deputy of the Portuguese Nation, gentleman of My royal household, of My council, knight of the ancient and most noble Order of the Tower and Sword, of Valor, Loyalty, and Merit, Commander of the Order of Christ, officer of that of Leopold in Belgium, first historiographer of the Kingdom, Judge of the Superior Tribunal of Commerce, and My Envoy Extraordinary and Minister Plenipotentiary near Her Catholic Majesty; in order that, conferring with the plenipotentiary equally appointed for that purpose by the President of the United States of America, he may treat, stipulate, conclude, and sign, with the reserve of ratification, a treaty of commerce and navigation, founded upon principles of a well understood reciprocity of interests for both nations; confiding in the zeal and intelligence of My said Plenipotentiary that he will duly discharge the duties of this important commission.

In faith of which I have ordered these presents, by Me signed and sealed with the great seal of My arms, to be delivered to him.   Given at the [Seal]   Palace of Cintra on the second day of July in the year of the birth of our Lord Jesus Christ one thousand eight hundred and forty.

A Rainha:

Rodrigo da Fonseca Magalhães

The Negotiations

Discussions of the terms of this treaty began early in 1836, when Edward Kavanagh, Chargé d'Affaires at Lisbon, informed the Portuguese Minister of Foreign Affairs of the receipt of his full power (D. S., 13 Despatches, Portugal, No. 12, March 19, 1836). Early instructions to Kavanagh gave him as a "model" the convention with Russia of December 18, 1832 (Document 75; see D. S., 14 Instructions, Portugal, 28–29, January 7, 1836, printed in Senate B); later Secretary of State Forsyth dealt in some detail with the troublesome questions of the colonial and "indirect" trade and with that most difficult of all, the relations between Portugal and Brazil (D. S., 14 Instructions, Portugal, 41–46, May 30, 1836, misdated May 30, 1840, in Senate B):

It is perceived with regret, that, in other respects, the intimations thrown out by the Minister of Foreign Affairs do not indicate so liberal a spirit as this Government had been led to believe would characterise the Commercial arrangements of Portugal under the present dynasty. The limitation of the Treaty to the territories of Portugal on the European Continent and the Azores and Madeira Islands, and the refusal to allow an indirect trade, are objectionable features in the proposed Convention, and not to be silently or readily conceded: but they are not so unexpected or important, that they should be permitted to constitute

any very serious obstruction to the progress of the negotiation. The exception in favor of Brazil, however, proposed to be inserted in the Article placing the Commerce with the United States upon a footing with that of the most favored nations, is a point of vital consequence, and is not to be yielded until it shall be found that all the opposition which you can make to it is ineffectual, and that a treaty cannot be concluded without it. The analogous exception in the treaty between the United States and Brazil [Document 64], it was known at the time it was admitted, would be entirely inoperative during the concurrent existence of the Convention of 1825 between Brazil and Portugal [August 29, 1825; Portuguese text, with English translation, in British and Foreign State Papers, XII, 674–78] and that of 1827 between Brazil and Great Britain [August 17, 1827; English and Portuguese texts in *ibid.*, XIV, 1008–25]. The Convention of 1825 between Brazil and Portugal provides for the admission of the merchandise of those countries in the ports of each other at a duty of fifteen per cent, whilst the duties on the produce of Great Britain imported into Brazil are confined to the same rate in the Convention of 1827 with that country, which will not expire until the year 1842. The treaty between Brazil and the United States places the produce of the latter upon a footing with that of the most favoured nation, the duties upon which consequently cannot, during the existence of the treaties above referred to, exceed the 15 per cent which under those treaties is charged upon the productions as well of Portugal as of Great Britain. Besides, the effect of such a stipulation upon the interests of the United States in a Convention with Brazil is entirely different from that which would be produced by its insertion in a treaty with Portugal; and the assent which was yielded to its introduction in the one case, when the circumstances under which that assent was given are considered, affords but a feeble argument in favor of a similar acquiescence in the other case. It could not be apprehended that the productions of Portugal would come into formidable competition with those of the United States in the markets of Brazil, and the clause referred to was consequently considered in this view as nearly if not quite inoperative: but the case is far different with the produce of the United States and Brazil in the markets of Portugal. Several of the staple productions of the two countries are the same; and, other circumstances being equal, the effect of such a reservation might be to exclude the most important articles of the commerce of the United States altogether from the ports of Portugal, until the supply which could be furnished from Brazil should be exhausted. This is a question in which other nations have comparatively little concern; and it should therefore go but a very short way towards reconciling the United States to such a provision, that it is intended to introduce it into the commercial treaties which may be negotiated with other countries. Nor is the case varied as regards the United States by the former connexion which subsisted between Portugal and Brazil, whatever obligations that connexion or its dissolution may be thought to have imposed upon Portugal. The injurious effect of such a reservation in favor of Brazil upon the commerce of the United States is still the same, as if the exception had been made in favour of any other country, with similar productions and the same extent of trade, between which and Portugal no such connexion had ever existed. It is also to be observed, that the privilege granted to Brazil by the treaty of separation was merely provisional; and whatever necessity may have been supposed by Portugal to exist at that time in favor of its insertion, the reestablishment of it in a new treaty, at this period of time, very much increases the strength of the objection to it on the part of the United States, when it is sought to be introduced as an exception against this country, in a Convention which is to contain on our side no similar exception, but by which the produce of Portugal imported in Portuguese vessels is *in all cases* to be admitted upon a footing with that of the most favored nation. But the Treaty of Separation itself between Portugal and Brazil imposes no obligation on the former to make any exception in favor of the latter, in its Conventions with other nations. That treaty merely provides, that the merchandise of Brazil shall pay in the ports of Portugal a consumption duty of but 15 per cent. The effect of placing the merchandise of another country, then, upon the footing of that of the most favoured nation, would be to confine the duties upon such merchandise to 15 per cent, as was done by Brazil in regard to the produce of Great Britain by the Treaty of 1827 with that country, and as was done by Portugal

in regard to all nations by the decree of April 18' 1834.   The object of the proposed exception would seem to be, not so much to favor Brazil, as to protect the interests of Portugal itself, by leaving the Government at liberty to raise the duties upon the productions of other countries above the rate of 15 per cent when it should see proper.   In this point of view the insertion of the clause alluded to is strongly objectionable, as it would be a departure from an equitable reciprocity, to the disadvantage of the United States, not from any preexisting obligation on the part of Portugal, but from a prospective regard to its own interest [for the Portuguese decree of April 18, 1834, see Collecção de decretos e regulamentos, 3d series, appendix, 51–52].

Upon the grounds now suggested, and upon such others as may strike your own mind, you will strenuously oppose the introduction of the proposed exception: but if, after all, it should become indispensable to yield the point, you will insist upon a provision in the treaty, that if upon experience it should be found by the United States to be adverse to their interests, by seriously interfering with the disposal of any staple article of their produce, they shall be at liberty to put an end to it, by giving to the Portuguese Government previous notice of such intention for some reasonable and specified period.

The conversations which ensued with successive Ministers of Foreign Affairs of Portugal came for some years to no result; but a heated debate in the Portuguese Chamber of Deputies on June 23, 1840, on the state of the commercial relations between the United States and Portugal, and a resulting change in the Ministry of Foreign Affairs, gave a new impetus to the negotiations; and a full power to the Portuguese Plenipotentiary issued on July 2, 1840 (despatch of July 11, 1840, No. 108, and enclosures; printed in Senate B).   Within two months the treaty was signed.   The report of the negotiations is in the despatch of Kavanagh of August 31, 1840 (No. 112), which follows in full substance (but without its various enclosures, some of which are printed elsewhere in these notes); the original of that despatch is lacking in the archives of the Department of State and the only print thereof noticed is the Senate document cited, which is not generally available:

In my Nos. 110 and 111 I had the honor of informing you that, on the 26th instant, I had signed, with the Portuguese plenipotentiary, a treaty of commerce and navigation between the United States and Portugal.   A duplicate thereof was forwarded yesterday with my No. 111; and I now enclose the original, with translations and copies of correspondence during the progress and at the close of the negotiations, with such explanations as may be necessary to a general understanding of the circumstances attending the transaction.

Desirous of avoiding all needless details in regard to the many and serious difficulties that presented themselves, on both sides, during the negotiation, I shall, at the outset, merely remark that the conferences commenced on the 10th of July, and were continued, with some intermediate delays, to the 26th of August.

I was well aware, from the commencement, of what was frequently repeated— that this negotiation would be exceedingly embarrassed by the existing state of the relations of Portugal with all other foreign nations, with none of whom, excepting Brazil, were any treaties of commerce and navigation acknowledged by *her* as subsisting in full force; and that the utmost circumspection would be used in assenting to stipulations which might be claimed by others without proper equivalent.

Assurances were frequently given, that, in regard to the United States, so far as they alone were concerned, no objection existed to adopt, without any material modification, the draught that I had presented in March, 1836, (which, in pursuance of your instructions, was based on the treaty of 1828 [1832] with Russia [Document 75];) but that, considering the actual posture of affairs, the interests of Portugal might be seriously compromised by yielding especially the indirect trade and commerce with her colonies.

I am well satisfied that, in view of all circumstances, and admitting a disposition on the part of the ministry to forward the negotiation, it would not have been concluded, but for the decided manifestation of opinion by an influential portion of the Senate, of which mention has been made in my former despatches.

With these preliminary observations, I now proceed to a review of the several stipulations in the treaty.

Articles 1, 2, 3, 4, 6, 7, 9, and 13, contain, substantially, all the provisions embraced in articles 1, 2, 5, 6, 7, and 8 of the before-named treaty with Russia: the 3d and 4th of the latter, having reference to indirect trade, were omitted; but, as they are general in their terms, and embrace other points interesting to commerce, their omission has been supplied by several special provisions.

It will be seen that a reservation has been made in favor of French wines, in accordance with the convention of July, 1831, between the United States and France [Document 71].

The 5th article provides that as soon as the indirect trade to the kingdom and possessions of Portugal shall be allowed to any other foreign nation, it shall immediately become common to the United States; and, in consideration thereof, Portugal is to be thereafter entitled to the same privilege, on equal terms, in our ports.

The 8th article applies to the colonial trade, and provides that, whenever it shall be conceded to any other foreign nation, it shall become common to the United States, on the same terms; freely, if freely granted to such nation, or on paying the same equivalent, if the concession was conditional.

However, you will perceive in the correspondence between the Portuguese plenipotentiary and myself (G, L,) that any future discussion as to the nature or character of such equivalent is avoided, and that the question has been settled in advance of the contingency on which it might arise.

Such was the only manner in which, after several conferences, the points involved in the 5th and 8th articles could be adjusted.

Articles 10 and 11 relate to the appointment, powers, and duties of consuls, vice-consuls, and commercial agents.

The 12th secures the rights of heirs to personal and real estate within the jurisdiction of either of the contracting parties, of which they are not citizens or subjects.

The 13th is a transcript from the treaty with Russia.

The 2d and 3d clauses of the 14th article were inserted at the special request of the Portuguese plenipotentiary: they are copied *verbatim* from our treaty with Brazil [Document 64, Article 33].

So far from having been unmindful of your instructions in regard to stipulations concerning the rights of belligerents and neutrals in time of war, the subject was frequently adverted to, until the Portuguese plenipotentiary informed me that his Government preferred leaving the question open for future negotiation.

Such are the stipulations of the treaty which is submitted for the consideration and approval of the President. It now remains to add, that, after every article as it therein stands had been mutually agreed to, one difficulty that had attended the negotiation from the commencement remained to be adjusted in a manner satisfactory to both parties; and it is explained in what follows.

The relations *claimed by Portugal* as still existing with Brazil, under the treaty of separation of 1825 [cited above], with the reciprocal engagements alleged to have been thereby contracted for the grant of exclusive favors to the produce of each in the ports of the other, were stated at the very first of our conferences, and they threatened frequently to interrupt the negotiation altogether. Many propositions were submitted, on both sides, at different times, to obviate any prejudice that might arise to the interests of the United States by assenting to a stipulation recognising a prior right, on the part of Brazil, to any special favor for its produce in the kingdom and possessions of Portugal.

It was at first proposed to insert a proviso analogous to that which was introduced into our treaty of 1828 with Brazil [Document 64], and which acknowledged an exception in favor of Portugal: this proposition, being rejected, was repeated in various forms; but none of them appeared to offer a sufficient guaranty against possible prejudice to many of our staple productions, such as cotton, tobacco, and rice, which are also common to Brazil.

Notwithstanding the opinion of individual members of the ministry in regard to the inexpediency of making such an exception in the treaty with us, and their avowed unbelief that any such measure would be reciprocated on the part of Brazil, still the popular feeling towards such an object, the interests of a numerous class of wealthy merchants, and the opinions of some distinguished personages, who, notwithstanding the experience of the past, still cling to the hope of a reunion, either absolute or in a modified form, between the two countries, constrained them to insist on a point which, it was stated, would, until circumstances were changed, be rigidly adhered to in the settlement of their commercial relations with all other foreign countries.

It was repeatedly asserted, (and such became my own conviction,) that no treaty would receive the approbation of the present Chamber of Deputies, and perhaps of the Senate, without such a reserve.

In pursuance of an agreement between the Portuguese plenipotentiary and myself, the question was finally waived until all the other parts of the treaty should have been arranged, in the expectation that a separate or additional article might be so framed as to overcome the difficulty.

Several projects for that purpose were then successively presented by both of us, without success; and I thought it advisable to adhere to one that I had delivered on the 7th of August, (see copy D,) and, so far as its provisions went, to regard it as an ultimatum. Numerous amendments were offered, that I felt it my duty to reject.

The Portuguese ultimatum (see translation E) was considered inadmissible; and, all arguments having been exhausted, I notified the Portuguese plenipotentiary, on the 23d of August, that I had come to the conclusion that it was best to suspend the negotiation; and, in retiring from the conference-room, I stated that I should embark in a vessel that was then ready to sail for the United States.

In the evening, he wrote a private note, informing me that he had consulted with the members of the cabinet, and that on the following day I might expect to receive an official communication on the question at issue.

Accordingly, on the 24th, the note, of which G is a translation, was sent to me, and its last paragraph contains the promised communication: it requested me to postpone my departure for one day, and to meet, in conference, the Minister of Foreign Affairs, himself, and another gentleman, whose name was not mentioned, but I readily knew that it was the Duke de Palmella.

Annexed is a copy of my answer (H.)

The unexpected absence of the duke at his country seat rendered it necessary to send a messenger for him; and, on his arrival, being requested to name the time and place for the proposed interview, I appointed the same day (25th instant.)

At our meeting, the discussion of the Brazilian question was renewed; and, finding the same opposition to my draught (D) of an additional and separate article, I remarked that it was useless to pursue the matter any further; but, as I was preparing to leave the room, the duke, with the assent of the Minister of Foreign Affairs, offered a compromise to this effect: that our treaty, as it then stood, should be signed without any specific reference to Brazil; but that, as a special minister had been sent to Rio de Janeiro in May last, with instructions to negotiate with that empire for the revival or reinforcement of the treaty of 1825, or for the conclusion of a new one based thereon; and as the result of that mission would be known before long, and would enable her Majesty's Government to act definitively before the expiration of the time fixed for the exchange of the ratification of the treaty with the United States, he proposed, as the only means that then occurred to him of removing existing difficulties, that the Portuguese plenipotentiary, in the act of signature, should deliver to me an official note, declaring that the Portuguese Government might withhold its ratification from our treaty, without incurring the charge of want of good faith, if, in the mean time, a convention were made with Brazil granting any favors to the produce of the latter, inconsistent with the stipulations entered into with the United States.

I agreed to consider this proposal, and, having maturely weighed it in all its bearings, I agreed, on the following day, (the 26th,) to accept it; reserving to the

Government of the United States a reciprocal right to withhold its ratification also, if circumstances special to the United States should so require it.

A translation and copy of the two notes exchanged for that purpose are annexed, marked I and K.

With these reservations, the treaty was signed.

Deeming it proper that the ports and territories of Portugal, where foreign commerce is not permitted, should be specified, I addressed the note F to the Minister of Foreign Affairs; the translations G and N are answers to that inquiry, and the copy L refers to the same point.

The new political constitution having introduced a change in the denomination of the several portions of the monarchy, and as we had no precedent to guide us in that respect, I inquired of the Minister of Foreign Affairs, in my said note F, whether the words *"kingdom and possessions of Portugal"* included every territory and place where Portugal claims or exercises sovereignty and jurisdiction. The translation N contains his answer; but, as it was not received before the signature of the treaty, I added to my note L the declaration therein made as to my understanding of the comprehensiveness of the terms.

As the papers annexed are numerous, and as some of them have not been referred to, I take leave to add an index of their contents:

A is a copy of a note addressed to the Portuguese plenipotentiary after his appointment had been notified to me.

B is a translation of a note from the Portuguese plenipotentiary, with a certified copy of his full power.

C is a copy of a note to the Portuguese plenipotentiary, enclosing a certified copy of my full power.

D is a copy of the final draught of an additional article proposed to the Portuguese plenipotentiary on the 7th of August, 1840, in regard to Brazil.

E is a translation of the final draught on the same subject, proposed by the Portuguese plenipotentiary.

F is a copy of my note to the Minister of Foreign Affairs, requesting him to specify *the ports and territories of Portugal from which foreign commerce is excluded,* and inquiring whether the words *"kingdom and possessions of Portugal"* include every territory and place where Portugal claims or exercises sovereignty and jurisdiction.

G is a translation of a note addressed to me by the Portuguese plenipotentiary; in which he states—1st. The equivalent to be rendered by the United States, whenever the commerce of the Portuguese colonies shall have been opened to them; 2d. That his Government will soon definitively resolve as to the ports and territories where foreign commerce shall be interdicted, and that a communication, in that respect, will be made to the Government of the United States; 3d. That his Government, desirous that a negotiation, which on all other points had been so amicably adjusted, might not be rendered useless, invites me to delay my departure, in the hope that a satisfactory arrangement may be made of the Brazilian question.

H is a copy of my answer to the third clause of the foregoing note.

I is a translation of the note presented to me by the Portuguese plenipotentiary, in the act of signing the treaty, reserving to the Portuguese Government the right of withholding its ratification of the treaty on certain contingencies therein mentioned.

K is a copy of my answer to the foregoing, reserving a similar right to the Government of the United States.

L is a copy of my note delivered to the Portuguese plenipotentiary in the act of signing the treaty; in which I declare—1st. My understanding of the comprehensiveness of the words *"kingdom and possessions of Portugal;"* 2d. My acceptance of the first clause in his note G, as to the equivalent to be rendered by the United States whenever the Portuguese colonies shall be opened to their commerce.

M is a copy of my note to the Minister of Foreign Affairs, informing him of the signature of the treaty.

N is a translation of a note from the Minister of Foreign Affairs, in answer to that part of my note F requesting that *the ports and territories of Portugal from which foreign commerce is excluded* be specified. He also confirms my understanding in regard to the words *"kingdom and possessions of Portugal."*

O is a translation of the answer of the Minister of Foreign Affairs to my note M, informing him that the treaty had been signed.

These are all the explanations that occur to me at this time; but it will be an agreeable duty to add others that may be deemed necessary.

Of the enclosures to the foregoing despatch, A, B, and C are unimportant and not here printed (the full power of the Plenipotentiary of Portugal appears above, in translation); similarly, D, E, part of G, and H, relating to the proposed additional article in regard to Brazil, which failed, are omitted; F, G (in part), I, K, L, and N, are printed above (and in that order), following the treaty texts; M and O are notes of courtesy and are not printed.

In another despatch of August 31, 1840 (No. 113; printed in Senate B, 46–47) the same writer gives the background of the negotiations as he saw it:

The negotiation which resulted in the treaty of the 26th instant, between the United States and Portugal, was embarrassed, as I have already mentioned, by the existing state of the relations of the latter with all other foreign nations; inasmuch as she contends that all former commercial conventions with them, excepting Brazil, have either expired by their own limitation, or have otherwise ceased to have effect. She thus endeavors to place herself in a position to make new terms, and to found her future commercial intercourse with all, upon principles of perfect independence and real reciprocity.

Her treaties with England for the two last centuries are warning beacons in the new course which she is endeavoring to pursue. They are monuments of weakness and folly on the one side, and of dictatorial exaction on the other.

There has lately been, and there still exists, a mutual disposition on the part of the Portuguese and British ministries to resume the negotiations for a commercial convention, that had nearly approached a successful termination at the epoch of the revolution, in September, 1836; and a hope is cherished that, in addition to liberal and well-defined stipulations in regard to commerce, Portugal may thus be able also to obtain a specific surrender of most, if not all, of the odious privileges and exemptions, both political and commercial, enjoyed or claimed by British subjects within her jurisdiction, in virtue of ancient compacts; all of which, with the exception of the commercial convention of 1810, are asserted by Great Britain to exist in full force.

Portugal, on her part, admitting the binding effect of all former stipulations affecting the political alliance of the two countries, insists that those privileges and exemptions can no longer be rightfully claimed, in consequence of repeated infractions, on the part of Great Britain, of the expressed or implied conditions on which they were founded. This, however, is the remonstrance of the weak against the strong.

Causes that have been heretofore explained, having directed the attention of the Portuguese ministry, in an especial manner, to the United States, and having produced a general conviction of the expediency of treating with them, without awaiting the issue of proposals made or received by other nations who might think themselves entitled, by courtesy or otherwise, to a prior adjustment of their future relations, negotiations were commenced between the Portuguese plenipotentiary and myself; and, throughout their continuance, frequent and significant intimations were given by British agents, in quarters where they would be appreciated, that all concessions in favor of the commerce and navigation of the United States would, in virtue of the treaty of 1654, and of others subsequent, immediately become common to British subjects, without any new equivalent therefor.

Thus may be explained the caution used by the Portuguese negotiator, and his unwillingness, whatever his disposition might otherwise be, to assent unreservedly to stipulations that might hereafter be granted to England as conditions for the renunciation of the degrading privileges that the latter still pretends to claim.

However, the fifth and eighth articles of our treaty provide for an eventual and equitable adjustment in regard to the indirect trade and the colonial commerce.

You will have seen, in my No. 112, that the ratification by the Queen's Government is made to depend, in a great measure, on the result of the negotiations that had been pending at Rio de Janeiro.

In British and Foreign State Papers, I, part 1, 462–563, are printed the texts of "Treaties of Alliance and Commerce between Great Britain and Portugal; subsisting between the Two Powers in 1814." Included therein are the commercial treaty of February 19, 1810, and the treaty of July 20, 1654, to which specific reference is made in the foregoing despatch.

EARLIER NEGOTIATIONS WITH PORTUGAL

While a claims agreement between the two countries was made on January 19, 1832 (Document 72), this was the first formal treaty to go into force between the United States and Portugal. In his despatch No. 113, of August 31, 1840, Kavanagh enclosed (in translation) an interesting memorandum regarding earlier negotiations, written perhaps by an official of the Portuguese Foreign Office and reading as follows (Senate B, 47–48):

In 1783 Doctor Franklin negotiated at Paris a treaty containing twenty-four articles, with Don Vincente de Souza, the representative of Portugal at that Court. Upon this treaty Luiz Pinto de Souza (afterwards Viscount de Balsamão), on the 16th of November in the same year, made a report in which he condemned the provision therein made that American vessels should pay in the ports of Portugal no higher duties than those of the most favored nation; because in such case they would be placed on the footing of national vessels, in consequence of favors enjoyed by those of England; that there would be no corresponding reciprocity in behalf of Portuguese vessels in the United States, which at that time had treaties of commerce with only France and Holland and had not granted to vessels of these two nations privileges equal to those which were enjoyed by their own.

Discussions upon a treaty of commerce were afterwards continued, at The Hague, between D. João de Almeida de Mello de Castro (afterwards Count das Galvêas) and Mr. John Adams.

In 1786 Luiz Pinto de Souza renewed these negotiations, at London, with Mr. Adams and Mr. Jefferson. The French Revolution and the extraordinary events that accompanied it caused a suspension until 1823, when they again commenced, at Lisbon, between General Dearborn and the Count de Lapa, the latter of whom had been named Plenipotentiary by his Most Faithful Majesty.

These negotiators agreed upon four articles, viz: 1st. Mutual liberty of commerce to the citizens and subjects of the two nations, respectively. 2d. Equality of tonnage, light, anchorage, and other port charges. 3d. Equality of duties on cargoes, whether imported in Portuguese or American vessels, to the same rate as paid on similar produce of other nations. 4th. Respecting consuls and their powers.

The *desembargador*, José Xavier Mozinho da Silveira, Administrator General of the Customhouse, was heard upon these questions, and the royal *junta do commercio* was also consulted.

In December 1823 Mozinho reported that Portugal had learned, to her cost (alluding probably to the treaty of 1810 with England), the value of treaties of reciprocity—a principle just in itself, but ruinous in practice when one nation has but little navigation and the other much—when one is industrious and the other not. While he denies being a partisan of the system of restrictions, he takes it for granted that the nation is not yet in a situation to dispense with those helps which foster commerce and navigation.

The despatch mentioned (*ibid.*, 46–47) concludes with this paragraph regarding the foregoing memorandum:

I have not thought it amiss to annex the translation of a memorandum (A) regarding former negotiations between the United States and Portugal, inasmuch as the facts which it details belong to the diplomatic history of the two countries. It was procured at Lisbon.   The writer has studiously avoided any illusion to British interference and intrigue, which have ever been active in our diplomatic intercourse with Portugal.

Mention is also to be made of the act "to exempt the vessels of Portugal from the payment of duties on tonnage" (4 Statutes at Large, 517) and of the proclamation of October 11, 1837, under that statute, for the levy and payment of such duties, "as if the said act . . . had not been passed" (*ibid.*, 820).

96

CHILE : DECEMBER 10, 1840

Agreement for the Settlement of the Case of the Brig "Warrior". The agreement was oral. Its terms are stated in despatches of the Chargé d'Affaires of the United States and in a law enacted by the Congress of Chile. The papers printed as stating the agreement are extracts from two despatches of Richard Pollard, Chargé d'Affaires of the United States, dated, respectively, December 10, 1840, to Secretary of State Forsyth, and October 1, 1841, to Secretary of State Webster.

[Excerpt from despatch of December 10, 1840]

I have agreed with the Chilian Minister in the case of the Brig Warrior. The account of the claimants is $15'868. I have agreed to take the round sum of $15'000. I consider this a very fortunate adjustment on my part. The Warrior had no cargo on board, was pursuing no particular voyage; she went into the port of Coquimbo and would probably have remained there or gone to and remained in the port of Valparaiso had she not been detained by the Governor of Coquimbo.

[Excerpt from despatch of October 1, 1841]

I continue to labour upon the subject of the claims. That in the case of the *Warrior* is now before the congress for its action. The agreement like that in the case of the *Macedonian*, divides the amount, Fifteen thousand dollars, into seven parts; one of which to be paid so soon as it has the sanction of Congress and the remaining six parts in six equal annual instalments. I endeavoured to secure the payments in hard dollars but could not succeed: though, I succeeded in having an interest of about fifteen hundred dollars added to the sum of original agreement, Fifteen thousand dollars; so that the amount recovered in the case will be $16'500. The instalments to bear an interest of five per cent per annum. The law of the appropriation by the Congress I will forward to you so soon as I receive it. The agreement I have made in this case is undoubtedly highly advantageous on our part; and will assuredly be received by the claimants as something unexpected, far above their hope, more than satisfactory, and particularly gratifying.

NOTES

The exact date of the oral agreement for the settlement of the case of the *Warrior*, reached between Richard Pollard, Chargé d'Affaires of the United States, and Joaquin Tocornal, Minister of Foreign Relations of the Republic of Chile, cannot be stated with certainty. The date taken, December 10, 1840, is the date of despatch No. 86 from Pollard, an excerpt from which is printed above (D. S., 5 Despatches, Chile). The earliest report of the terms of the agreement is in despatch No. 93 from Pollard of October 1, 1841, the relevant portion of which is also printed above (*ibid.*).

With his despatch of November 25, 1841 (*ibid.*, No. 95), Pollard enclosed a copy, with a translation, of the note addressed to him by the Chilean Minister of Foreign Relations, dated November 12, 1841, and a copy of his answer of November 15, which follow:

[Translation]

SANTIAGO,
12 de Noviembre de 1841.

Tengo de honor de participar a V. S., para su debida inteligencia, que el proyecto de lei pasado al Congreso Nacional sobre la indemnizacion de los perjucios sufridos por el bergantin american Warrior, ha sido aprobado y sancionado con esta fecha en los terminos siguientes—

"Articulo 1ᵣᵒ La Republica de Chile se constituye deudora de la suma de Quince mil pesos (moneda corriente) a los Estados-Unidos de America en razon de perjuicios sufridos por el bergatin americano Warrior, detenido en Coquimbo el año 1820.

2ᵒ Se dividirá la dicha suma de quince mil pesos en siete partes; la primera de las cuales se pagará al contado inmediatamente que se apruebe este ajuste por el Congreso; y las otras seis en otros tantos años contados desde la fecha del primer pago.

3ᵒ Se pagarán asimismo interes, a razon de un cinco por cento anual, por toda la suma desde el 30 de Setiembre de 1839 hasta la fecha del pago de la primera séptima parte; por las seis séptimas partes restantes hasta el pago de la segunda; y asi sucesivamente por las cantidades no pagadas hasta la total extencion de la deuda.

4ᵒ Dichos interes se satisfarán en cado pago que se haya de las

SANTIAGO,
12th November, 1841.

SIR: For your due intelligence I have the honor of informing you that the project of law passed to the National Congress, upon the indemnification for the prejudices suffered by the American brig *Warrior*, has been approved and sanctioned, of this date, in the following terms:

ARTICLE 1. The Republic of Chile constitutes itself debtor to the amount of fifteen thousand dollars (current money) to the United States of America on account of prejudices suffered by the American brig *Warrior*, detained in Coquimbo in the year 1820.

2. The said sum of fifteen thousand dollars will be divided in seven parts, the first of which will be paid in hand immediately that the adjustment may be approved by the Congress, and the other six parts in so many other years, counting from the date of the first payment.

3. Interest will be paid in this manner: at 5 percent annually for the whole sum from the 30th September, 1839, until the payment of the first seventh part; for the other six parts remaining, until the payment of the second; and thus successively for the parts not paid until the total extinction of the debt.

4. Said interest shall be satisfied at each payment made of

porciones en que se divide la cantidad total de los quince mil pesos convenidos, en razon de lo devengado en cada periodo."

Con este motivo renuevo las protestas de mi particular consideracion con que soi
    De V. S. Atento Seguro Servidor.
        R. L. YRARRÁZAVAL.

Señor ENCARGADO DE NEGOCIOS
    DE LOS ESTADOS-UNIDOS DE
    AMÉRICA.

the portions into which the entire sum of fifteen thousand dollars is divided, according to what will be due at each period.

Having thus informed you, I renew the protests of my particular consideration, with which I am
    Your obedient servant,
        R. L. YRARRÁZAVAL

The CHARGÉ D'AFFAIRES
    OF THE UNITED STATES OF
    AMERICA

SANTIAGO, *November 15, 1841*

SIR: I have just had the honor to receive your note of the 12th, accompanying a copy of the law passed by the Chilean Congress in the case of the *Warrior*.

The law conforms to the agreement between us, and, of course, is accepted by me on the part of my Government.

I have the honor to be most respectfully
    Yo: Ob^t Servt

                      RICH^d POLLARD

To, The Hon: RAMON LUIS YRARRÁZAVAL
    Minister of Foreign Relations for the Republic of Chile.

Reference is also to be made to the fact that a draft convention was prepared by Pollard, the provisions of which covered both the first case of the *Macedonian* (see Document 94) and the case of the *Warrior*. That unsigned draft was delivered by Pollard to the Minister of Foreign Relations of Chile on May 25, 1841; its text (retranslation) is printed in the notes to Document 94. According to its tenor, interest in the case of the *Warrior* would have run from September 30, 1840, instead of September 30, 1839, the date fixed by the statute, which was doubtless the agreed date.

THE CASE OF THE "WARRIOR"

The facts in the case of the *Warrior* were stated in a note (undated) addressed and seemingly delivered to the Minister of Foreign Relations of Chile by Heman Allen, American Minister, a copy of which was enclosed with the despatch of Allen of November 5, 1825 (D. S., 1 Despatches, Chile, No. 22), from which the following is extracted:

From the affidavit and protest of the master of that vessel, it appears to be clearly established, that the brig *Warriour*, whilst in the execution of a lawful commerce, arrived at the port of Coquimbo on the 23. of August 1820:—that, the next day the Vice Admiral of the Navy of Chile, Lord Cochrane, caused her to be rigidly searched, and impressed her men and boats for the embarkation of troops, retaining six of said men on board his squadron:—that, when remonstrated with by the master of said vessel, for such injurious treatment, he replied, "that, the crisis of his affairs demanded it," and went to sea with the six men he had thus impressed:—that, the said vessel being thus destitute of hands, and in a port where seamen could not be had, the said master was compelled to leave her in charge of his first officer, with orders how to act, and proceeded to Lima in another vessel on the affairs of his voyage:—that, after a lapse of several months, and finding that his orders were not obeyed, he returned to Coquimbo on the 24. of February 1821. and thereupon, found, that soon after his departure the Commandant of the port came on board with a party of soldiers, unshipped the rudder, which, with her ballast and sundry articles of her cargo, were taken ashore, as he said by order

of the Governour of that place:—that, after this, the said commandant demanded the boat belonging to the said vessel, which being necessary to her safety and convenience, the demand was not complied with; whereupon, the officer left in charge of said vessel, was seized by a party of soldiers, by the order of said commandant, conveyed to a guard house on shore, and was there suspended by the heels for the term of eleven hours, so that his life was greatly despaired of, and that the representation thereof, to the Governour of that place produced no redress or satisfaction:—that, on or about the 12. of November of the same year, the said Governour ordered every person on board said vessel, except the first officer thereof, to appear, before him, on shore, which being complied with, during their absence the said commandant, with a party of soldiers again went on board said vessel, made prisoner of the said first Officer, put him under guard, on shore, and then plundered the said vessel of a large quantity of her provisions, stores, ship's furniture, books &c to the amount of about six hundred dollars; and, that afterwards, when the said Master remonstrated with the said Governour for the detention and outrage committed on his vessel and crew, he alleged "it was done on suspicion of his having furnished the enemies of Chile with arms," and that he could not release the said vessel without the order of his government, which was not made known until the 12. of April of the same year 1821. when the said vessel was released and restored to the Master.

. . . .

For these injuries, and the consequent detention of the vessel for the term of seven months and nineteen days, during which her rudder and ballast were removed to the shore, the undersigned claims of the government of Chile, in behalf of the owners, the sum of fifteen thousand, eight hundred and sixty eight dollars.

THE SETTLEMENT

The claim for the seizure and detention of the brig *Warrior* at Coquimbo in 1820 had been the subject of discussion between the two Governments since the time of its presentation by Heman Allen, Minister Plenipotentiary, the first diplomatic representative of the United States at Santiago. The amount claimed was "about $16,000" (D. S., 14 Instructions, U. S. Ministers, 93, instructions to John Hamm of October 15, 1830). The negotiations were continued by Allen's successors, Samuel Larned, John Hamm, and Richard Pollard, each of whom had the rank of Chargé d'Affaires. It was John Hamm who negotiated the Treaty of Peace, Amity, Commerce, and Navigation with Chile of May 16, 1832 (Document 73). His full power of October 15, 1830, gave authority to treat "concerning Commerce and Navigation between the United States and the Republic of Chili, and claims of the Citizens of the two Countries respectively upon the Governments of the United States, and the said Republic of Chili" (D. S., 2 Credences, 156).

President Tyler made mention of the adjustment in the case of the *Warrior* in his annual message of December 6, 1842 (Richardson, IV, 194, 198).

The agreed instalments, with interest, were duly paid. The report of the final payment is in the despatch of Chargé d'Affaires William Crump of October 18, 1847 (D. S., 6 Despatches, Chile, No. 11).

Treaty Series No. 275
8 Statutes at Large, 570–71
18 *ibid.*, pt. 2, Public Treaties, 611–12

97

PERU : MARCH 17, 1841

Convention Regarding the Claims of Certain Citizens of the United States, signed at Lima March 17, 1841, with a modification proposed by the Congress of Peru October 21, 1845. Original in English and Spanish. Submitted to the Senate January 11, 1842. (Message of January 10, 1842.) Resolution of advice and consent January 5, 1843, and resolution of advice and consent of the same date to the exchange of ratifications at any time prior to December 20, 1843. Approved by the Congress of Peru, on condition, October 21, 1845. Proposed modification submitted to the Senate May 26, 1846. Resolution of advice and consent thereto and to the ratification and exchange of ratifications at any time within two years, May 29, 1846. Ratified by the United States June 1, 1846. Ratified by Peru October 8, 1846. Ratifications exchanged at Lima October 31, 1846. Proclaimed January 8, 1847.

The texts of the modification proposed October 21, 1845, as written in the respective instruments of ratification, are printed after the texts of the convention as signed.

As to the ratification of January 12, 1843, on the part of the United States, the provisional ratification (of 1843) on the part of Peru, without date, the exchange of said ratifications at Lima July 22, 1843, and the proclamation of February 21, 1844, all of which proved ineffectual, see the notes following the treaty texts.

The United States of America and the Republic of Peru, desirous of consolidating permanently, the good understanding and friendship now happily existing between the parties, have resolved to arrange and terminate their differences and pretensions, by means of a Convention that shall determine exactly, the responsibilities of Peru, with respect to the claims of certain citizens of the United States against her: And with this intention, the

Deseando la República del Perú y los Estados-Unidos de América consolidar de un modo permanente, la buena correspondencia y amistad que felizmente reinan entre ambas partes, han resuelto transijir y terminar sus diferencias y pretensiones por medio de un convenio que determine con precision, las responsabilidades del Perú, acerca de las sumas que le han reclamado varios ciudadanos de los Estados-Unidos: y con este fin han nombrado S E. el Presi-

329

President of the United States has appointed James C. Pickett, Chargé d'Affaires of said States, near Peru, and His Excellency the President of the Republic of Peru, has appointed Don Manuel del Rio, Principal Officer of the Department of Finance, Acting Minister of the same Department and Supernumerary Councillor of State; and both Commissioners, after having exchanged their powers, have agreed upon and signed the following articles:

Article I.

The Peruvian Government, in order to make full satisfaction for various claims of citizens of the United States, on account of seizures, captures, detentions, sequestrations and confiscations of their vessels, or for the damage and destruction of them, of their cargoes, or other property, at sea, and in the ports and territories of Peru, by order of said Government of Peru, or under its authority,—has stipulated, to pay to the United States, the sum of three hundred thousand dollars, which shall be distributed among the claimants, in the manner and according to the rules that shall be prescribed by the Government of the United States.

Article II.

The sum of three hundred thousand dollars, which the Government of Peru has agreed to

dente del Perú, a Don Manuel del Rio, Oficial Mayor del Ministerio de Hacienda encargado de su despacho, y Consejero de Estado suplente, y el Presidente de los Estados-Unidos, á Don Santiago C. Pickett, Encargado de Negocios de los mismos Estados-Unidos cerca del Perú; y ambos comisionados, despues de haber canjeado sus poderes han ajustado y firmado los articulos siguientes:

Articulo I.

El Gobierno Peruano, para satisfacer totalmente diferentes reclamos entablados por varios ciudadanos de los Estados-Unidos, por apresamientos, capturas, detenciones, secuestros y confiscaciones de sus buques, ó por el perjuicio ó destruccion que han sufrido en ellos ó sus cargamentos ú otras propiedades, así en el mar como en los puertos y territorio del Perú, en virtud de órdenes del Gobierno Peruano, ó bajo de su autoridad, se compromete á pagar á los Estados-Unidos, la cantidad de trescientos mil pesos, la que será distribuida entre los interesados del modo y en conformidad con los arreglos que establezca el Gobierno de los Estados-Unidos.

Articulo II

La cantidad de trescientos mil pesos, que el Gobierno Peruano se compromete á pagar por el

pay, in the preceding article, shall be paid at Lima, in ten equal annual instalments of thirty thousand dollars each, to the person or persons that may be appointed by the United States, to receive it. The first instalment shall be paid on the first day of January, in the year one thousand eight hundred and forty four, and an instalment on the first day of each succeeding January, until the whole sum of three hundred thousand dollars shall be paid.

ARTICLE III.

The Peruvian Government agrees also, to pay interest on the before mentioned sum of three hundred thousand dollars, at the rate of four per centum per annum, to be computed from the first day of January one thousand eight hundred and forty two, and the interest accruing on each instalment, shall be paid with the instalment. That is to say; interest shall be paid on each annual instalment, from the first day of January one thousand eight hundred and forty two.

ARTICLE IV.

All the annual payments made on account of the three hundred thousand dollars, shall be paid in hard dollars of the same standard and value as those now coined at the Mint in Lima, and the annual payments, as well as the accruing interest, may be

articulo anterior, será entregada en Lima en diez plazos anuales ó iguales de treinta mil pesos cada uno, á la persona ó personas autorizadas para percibirla. El primer pago se hará el dia primero de Enero del año de mil ochocientos cuarenta y cuatro, y los demas, succesivamente en igual cantidad en cada primero de Enero, hasta que quede satisfecha asi enteramente, la total suma de trescientos mil pesos.

ARTICULO III.

El Gobierno Peruano conviene tambien, en pagar los intereses sobre la predicha cantidad de trescientos mil pesos, al cuatro por ciento al año, los que empezaran á correr desde el dia primero de Enero de mil ochocientos cuarenta y dos, pagandose los intereses correspondientes á cada anualidad, al tiempo de ejecutar el pago de esta. Es decir: que los intereses se pagarán sobre cada anualidad, desde el dia primero de Enero de mil ochocientos cuarenta y dos.

ARTICULO IV.

Todos los pagos que se hagan anualmente á cuenta de los trescientos mil pesos, se ejecutarán en pesos fuertes, de la misma ley y valor de los que se acuñan actualmente en la Casa de Moneda de Lima, y tanto las anualidades, como el importe de los intereses,

exported from Peru, free of all duty whatever.

se esportarán libres de todo derecho, sea de la clase que fuese.

ARTICLE V.

There shall not be demanded of the Government of Peru, any other payment or indemnification, on account of any claim of the citizens of the United States, that was presented to it by Samuel Larned Esquire, when Chargé d'Affaires of the United States, near Peru. But the claims subsequent to those presented by Mʳ Larned, to the Government of Peru, shall be examined and acted upon, hereafter.

ARTICULO V.

No se exijirá al Gobierno del Perú otro pago ni indemnizacion, por ningun reclamo de los ciudadanos de los Estados Unidos, que le haya sido presentado por Don Samuel Larned cuando era Encargado de Negocios de los Estados Unidos cerca del Perú: Pero los reclamos ulteriores á los presentados por el Señor Larned al Gobierno del Perú, serán examinados y resueltos posteriormente

ARTICLE VI.

It is further agreed, that the Peruvian Government shall have the option of paying each annual instalment, when it is due, with orders on the Custom House at Callao, which shall be endorsable in sums of any amount, and receivable in the Treasury, as cash, in payment of duties on importations of all kinds; and the orders shall be given in such a manner as, that in case similar orders shall be at a discount in the market, the full value of each annual payment shall be secured and made good to the United States, as though it had been paid in cash, at the time of its falling due; and any loss occasioned by discount, or delay in the collection, shall be borne and made good by the Peruvian Government.

ARTICULO VI.

Se conviene ademas, que el Gobierno Peruano tendrá el derecho de pagar la cantidad de cada plazo anual á su vencimiento, en ordenes endosables contra la Aduana del Callao, en sumas de cualquiera monto, y admisibles en el Tesoro, como dinero efectivo, en pago de derechos sobre importaciones de toda especie; y dichas ordenes se librarán de tal manera, que en el caso que las de igual clase estén á descuento, se asegure y haga efectivo á los Estados Unidos, el percibo integro de la cantidad anual, como si sele hubiera entregado en dinero á la fecha de su vencimiento, siendo por cuenta del Gobierno del Perú, cualquiera pérdida que se sufra en realizarla, por razon de descuento ó tiempo consumido en la amortizacion.

ARTICLE VII.

This Convention shall be ratified by the contracting parties, and the ratifications shall be exchanged within two years from its date, or sooner, if possible, after having been approved by the President and Senate of the United States, and by the Congress of Peru. In witness whereof, the respective Commissioners have signed the same, and affixed thereto their seals.

Done in triplicate at the City of Lima, this seventeenth day of March, in the year of Our Lord one thousand eight hundred and forty one.

J. C. PICKETT   [Seal]
MANUEL DEL RIO   [Seal]

ARTICULO VII.

Este convenio será ratificado por las partes contratantes, y las ratificaciones seran canjeadas en el termino de dos años contados desde esta fecha, ó antes, si fuese posible, despues de haber obtenido la aprobacion del Congreso del Perú, y del Presidente y Senado de los Estados Unidos. En fé de lo cual los respectivos comisionados lo han firmado y Sellado.

Dado por triplicado en la Ciudad de Lima á diez y siete dias de Marzo del año del Señor de mil ochocientos cuarenta y uno.

MANUEL DEL RIO   (un sello)
J. C. PICKETT   (un sello)

[Modification]

. . : the first annual instalment of thirty thousand dollars on account of the principal of the debt recognized thereby and to which the second article relates, should begin from the 1st of January, 1846, and the interests on this annual sum, according to Article III, should be calculated and paid from the 1st of January, 1842.

. . . la primera anualidad de treinta mil pesos por cuenta del capital reconocido como deuda por esta causa, y de que habla el articulo II°, corra y se entienda desde primero de Enero de mil ochocientos cuarenta y seis y los intereses de esta anualidad, segun el articulo III° se abonen desde primero de Enero del pasado año de mil ochocientos cuarenta y dos, corriendo en todo lo demas con arreglo á estas modificaciones las estipulaciones del convenio.

NOTES

In the final clause of the convention it is said that it was "done in triplicate". Precisely what procedure was adopted on the signature of the convention is uncertain. The despatch of James C.

Pickett, Chargé d'Affaires to Peru, of March 31, 1841 (D. S., 6 Despatches, Peru, No. 38), referring to the convention, says, "I now transmit the original, in English and Spanish." The signed original which is in the treaty file is in English only; on it is written, "With M⸢ʳ⸣ Pickett's N⸢º⸣ 38", the despatch above mentioned; and that original is embodied in the original proclamation of February 21, 1844, with which is bound the duplicate United States instrument of ratification of January 12, 1843, both of which instruments mention the convention as "hereunto annexed". Moreover, the green ribbon binding the papers runs under the seals of both the proclamation and the ratification. Accordingly, the present arrangement of the papers could not be of later date than that on which the seal was affixed to the proclamation, presumably the textual date thereof.

Despite this, however, President Polk in his message to the Senate of May 26, 1846, printed below, stated "that the original convention approved by them [the Senate] was sent to Peru, and was exchanged for the other original, ratified by General Vivanco, which is now in the Department of State." That statement seems clearly erroneous, as the instrument of ratification of 1843 (quoted in part below) which was confirmed by General Vivanco is in the treaty file and does not include an original of the convention, but a copy of the text in Spanish. Moreover, with that presidential message was transmitted a copy of the convention, certified as "carefully collated with the original on file in the Department of State", and that copy is in English, corresponding with the original in the treaty file.

Certainly an original in English was sent to the Senate with the presidential message of January 10, 1842 (Executive Journal, VI, 10); no order to print was passed until the following December 27 (*ibid.*, 157); only the treaty was then ordered printed and only the English text is in the print (Senate Confidential Document, December 27, 1842, 27th Congress, 3d session, Regular Confidential Documents, XVIII, 139–41); almost certainly the very document now in the treaty file was the original sent to the Senate in 1842, for it bears marks of printer's ink characteristic of papers ordered printed by the Senate. Perhaps the fact that that original was in 1846 (as it still is) with *an* instrument of ratification (the duplicate United States ratification of January 12, 1843) led to the confused and mistaken notion that it was with the Peruvian ratification of 1843; with such a false start one might well go on to further error and imagine that in 1843 the Department of State had resorted to the extraordinary procedure of incorporating in the original United States instrument of ratification and sending to Lima the only signed original of the convention then in Washington; it is certain that nothing of that sort took place; the instruction to Pickett of January 23, 1843 (quoted below), is evidence that the customary and settled practice was then followed.

The convention was unquestionably signed in both languages. Perhaps Pickett neglected to enclose the original in Spanish with his despatch of March 31, 1841, which did not go forward for some weeks (D.S., 6 Despatches, Peru, No. 40, May 8, 1841); perhaps the original

in Spanish was mislaid or lost after it reached the Department of State; one cannot know.

The Spanish text above printed is from that one of the duplicate Peruvian instruments of ratification of October 8, 1846, which is endorsed, "With Mr. Jewett's Nº 14." As the printed texts show, the *alternat* was duly observed.

THE FULL POWERS

The full power to James C. Pickett for the negotiation and signature of this convention was under date of June 15, 1838; it mentioned the "Government of the Peru-Bolivian Confederation", a union which had no existence after January 1839 (see the notes to Document 82); its clause of substance was as follows (D. S., 2 Credences, 304):

Know Ye, that for the purpose of confirming between the United States and the Peru-Bolivian Confederation perfect harmony and good correspondence and of removing all grounds of dissatisfaction, and reposing special trust and confidence in the integrity, prudence and abilities of James C. Pickett, appointed Chargé d'Affaires of the United States near the government of the said Peru-Bolivian Confederation, I have invested him with full and all manner of power and authority for and in the name of the United States to meet and confer with any person or persons duly authorized by the Government of the Peru-Bolivian Confederation, being furnished with like power and authority, and with him or them to agree, treat, consult and negotiate of and concerning the general commerce between the United States and the Peru-Bolivian Confederation and of all matters and subjects connected therewith, and concerning the claims of indemnity of citizens of the United States on the late government of Peru or on the government of the Peru-Bolivian Confederation, and of citizens of the Peru-Bolivian Confederation on the government of the United States; and to conclude and sign a Treaty or Treaties, Convention or Conventions touching the premises, transmitting the same to the President of the United States for his final ratification by and with the advice and consent of the Senate of the United States.

The original full powers to negotiate the convention were perhaps exchanged. A copy and translation of that given to the Plenipotentiary of Peru were enclosed with the despatch of Pickett of March 31, 1841 (D. S., 6 Despatches, Peru, No. 38); the translation reads as follows:

The Citizen Agustin Gamarra, Grand Marshal, Restorer of Peru, Well Deserving of the Country in a Heroic and Eminent Degree, Decorated with the Medals of the Liberating Army, of Junin, of Ayacucho and Ancachs; with That of Restorer by the General Congress; Generalissimo of the Sea and Land Forces, President of the Republic of Peru, etc.

Whereas the Chargé d'Affaires of the Republic of the United States of America, being competently authorized and instructed, as he states, by his Government, has proposed an arrangement to be based upon the principles of equity and good faith, touching the claims pending between that Government and this, of and concerning wrongs and injuries that certain citizens of the aforesaid States have often alleged, and for seizures and other causes, asserting a right to compensation and indemnification, of and concerning which claims an official discussion has been carried on with various agents of the Government of the United States, sometimes defending, sometimes controverting the justice of them: Therefore, we have resolved to commission Don Manuel del Rio, Supernumerary Councilor of State and Acting Minister of Finance, for the purpose that, after examining

the nature of the propositions made by the Chargé d'Affaires of the United States, he may make an arrangement of the said claims, accepting, according to his instructions, the most reasonable and equitable offer, and conclude *ex aequo et bono* a convention which may determine the responsibility as to the amount and conditions of the payment of the sum that he shall consider it proper to be acknowledged in favor of the Government of the United States for the final and liquidated amount of the claims pending.

In witness whereof we have issued these presents, signed, sealed, and countersigned by the Minister of State of Government and Foreign Affairs. Done in the Palace of the Government at Lima the twenty-seventh day of February, one thousand eight hundred and forty-one.

[Seal]

AGUSTIN GAMARRA

M. FERREYROS

Two original full powers issued by the Peruvian Government and giving authority to exchange the ratifications of this convention are among the documents relating thereto. Each was given to Don Manuel del Rio, the Peruvian Plenipotentiary who signed the convention. That under date of July 17, 1843, is in the treaty file; the other is dated October 5, 1846, and is with a despatch of November 10, 1846 (D. S., 7 Despatches, Peru, No. 14).

THE FIRST RATIFICATIONS

Two attempts were made to put this convention into force, the first of which failed. The unusual procedure adopted and the corresponding number of documents in the treaty file are to be explained.

By Article 7 of the convention the ratifications thereof were to be exchanged within two years from its date of signature, or, in other words, by March 17, 1843; the place of exchange was not stated. There was delay in both capitals.

The convention was submitted to the Senate on January 11, 1842, with certain accompanying correspondence, which was not printed; but the convention was not acted on until nearly a year later, in the following session, when the usual Senate resolution of advice and consent was adopted on January 5, 1843 (see Executive Journal, VI, 10, 146, 157, 162); it was then obvious that the exchange of ratifications could hardly take place within the time allotted. Accordingly, on the same date another resolution of the Senate was adopted (*ibid.*, 162), authorizing the exchange of ratifications at any time prior to December 20, 1843. That resolution reads as follows:

Whereas the time limited by the seventh article of the treaty between the United States of America and the Republic of Peru, concluded at the city of Lima on the 17th day of March, in the year of our Lord one thousand eight hundred and forty-one, may expire before an exchange of ratifications shall take place: Be it therefore

Resolved (two-thirds of the Senators present concurring), That the Senate advise and consent to the exchange of ratifications of the treaty aforesaid at any time prior to the twentieth day of December next, whenever the same can be effected, and the said ratification, when made, shall be deemed and taken to have been regularly exchanged, the limitation in said treaty to the contrary notwithstanding.

Both attested Senate resolutions of January 5, 1843, are in the file.

Ratification on the part of the United States followed on January 12, 1843, and the instrument was transmitted to Peru for exchange. The duplicate of that instrument of ratification is in the treaty file; it is in customary form and has annexed to it the signed original of the convention, which, as has been said, is in English only.

That duplicate United States instrument of ratification of January 12, 1843, has the countersignatures of two Secretaries of State, Daniel Webster and Abel P. Upshur. Secretary of State Webster retired from office on May 8, 1843, after having served for more than two years; Abel P. Upshur, Secretary of the Navy, was Secretary of State *ad interim* from June 24 to July 23, 1843, was commissioned Secretary of State on July 24, 1843, and held that office until his death on February 28, 1844; his countersignature of the instrument of ratification of January 12, 1843, was perhaps added to that of Webster at the time of the first proclamation of the convention, February 21, 1844.

In transmitting the United States instrument of ratification to Peru for exchange, Secretary of State Webster wrote under date of January 23, 1843 (D. S., 15 Instructions, Peru, 32–34):

Herewith you will receive the President's ratification of the Convention with Peru of the 17th of March, 1841, providing for the adjustment of claims of citizens of the United States upon that government. The instrument was submitted to the Senate at the beginning of the last session of that body, but was not finally disposed of until the fifth instant. It is apprehended, therefore, that the arrival of this communication at Lima may be retarded until after the expiration of the time limited for the exchange of the ratifications. Should this be the result, however, it is presumed that there would still be no hesitation on the part of the Peruvian government in effecting the exchange. If any indications of such a disposition should appear, you may say that the President laid the treaty before the Senate at the earliest moment after it was received in the United States, but that the business pending in that body, both Executive and Legislative, has been of a character so uncommon and so engrossing, as to have rendered it impracticable to bestow upon the Convention, in season, the consideration which its importance demanded. You will see by the Resolution a copy of which is enclosed, that the Senate have anticipated and provided for the contingency which has been alluded to. Under the power to effect the exchange which is herewith sent you, your authority is complete to act for that purpose at any time previously to the 20th of December, next. If the exchange should take place subsequently to the 17th of March, you will take care that the power of the person who may act in behalf of Peru, is coëxtensive with your own. I also transmit a form of a certificate of exchange which will be signed in duplicate, being first translated into Spanish. You will place the English copy with our ratification and the Spanish copy must accompany the ratification of Peru.

A clause in the Convention requires for it the approval of the Congress of Peru previously to its ratification by the Executive head of that Republic. If this sanction should not have been given and should in the existing state of things there still be deemed indispensable, you need not detain the bearer of this letter unless there shall be great probability that the subject will speedily be acted upon by the Peruvian Legislature. If, however, there should not have been a material change in the political affairs of that Country since the 8th of August, last, it is supposed that the person exercising the functions of President of Peru will deem himself authorized to ratify the Convention without submitting it to the consideration of the Congress of that Republic. Under all the circumstances, it is not deemed necessary at present that any steps should be taken on our part with a view to a new Convention for the purpose of extending the time within which the exchange may take place.

In acknowledging the receipt of that instruction on July 4, 1843, Pickett wrote (D. S., 6 Despatches, Peru, No. 81, July 8, 1843):

I am endeavoring to get the Convention ratified by the Peruvian Government, but am not yet able to say whether I shall succeed or not. It depends entirely on the Supreme Director, Gen. Vivanco. There has been no session of the Peruvian Congress since 1840 and there is no prospect of one before the month of April next.

Ratification on the part of the Government of Peru followed. The original of that instrument of ratification, which is in the file, includes the Spanish text of the convention only; it is without date; but it appears to have been signed prior to March 17, 1843. Its form is quite unusual, as will be seen from the following translation from the Spanish of its final clause:

Whereas, having seen and examined the preceding adjustment, I hereby approve it in all and each of its parts, recognizing for the Government the amount of debt and the other obligations imposed by the articles mentioned, pledging therefor the national faith and justice, notwithstanding the full power with which the Minister of the United States was provided for the purpose and in virtue whereof he has acted in the business, may have been framed for the purpose of negotiating with the Government of General Santa Cruz, which ruled this country, giving to it an illegal form and annexing it to that which was called the Peru-Bolivian Confederation; for as much as the wish of the Government of the United States to make an equitable settlement of the matter, with a view to preserve the good and friendly relations which very happily subsist between the two states, is sufficiently known, the Government deems its duty to contribute on its part as much as possible to strengthen those mutual bonds of harmony and good understanding, and the present convention and ratification are to be submitted within the term stipulated in the seventh article for the final approbation of the National Congress.

MANUEL MENENDEZ

M. FERREYROS

In transmitting that Peruvian instrument of ratification of the convention Pickett commented as follows (*ibid.*, No. 82, July 24, 1843):

It has not been approved by the Peruvian Congress, there having been no session of that body, but has been ratified by the constitutional President, Don Manuel Menendez, and his ratification has been confirmed by the present Executive, who exercises legislative power, at discretion: The ratification is sufficient therefore, I apprehend, for every purpose.
In N⁰ 4, of the inclosures, you will perceive that the Peruvian Government asks, that the payment of the first instalment may be postponed one year, and in N⁰ 5, I admit that the request is reasonable, provided Peru will pay interest, at the rate of twelve per cent. per annum, during the delay, which is promised in N⁰ 6. This is the commercial interest of the country and is not regarded here as usurious. Six per centum is the interest fixed by law, but twelve is not illegal and is paid by the Government, under similar circumstances.

.   .   .   .

What influenced me greatly, in receiving favorably, the proposition to postpone, was, that in my conversations with the Minister of Foreign Affairs, I was apprehensive, from the nature of his remarks, that had I treated it as inadmissible, he would have contended for the letter of the Convention, alleging the approval of the Congress to be indispensable; and as that body does not meet until April 1844, the Convention could not be ratified, and the claims would be in no better situation than they were before it was signed. You will observe that I have not in any manner committed myself, respecting the proposed postponement, the ratification being absolute and unconditional.

It is to be observed, however, that that ratification is not "absolute and unconditional", but provisional, for it contains the statement that both the convention and the ratification would be submitted within the term stipulated in Article 7, or, in other words, by March 17, 1843, "for the final approbation of the National Congress"; and by the terms of Article 7 approval by the Congress of Peru was expressly made a condition precedent to the exchange of ratifications. Doubtless if such approbation had been duly given, it would have related back and authorized the ratification; but it was not given, and there was no meeting of the Peruvian Congress from 1840 until April 1845 (D. S., 6 Despatches, Peru, No. 112, April 5, 1845).

However, the then Executive of Peru authorized the exchange of the ratifications. There are two original documents in the treaty file which give such authority. The first is in the nature of an order or decree of July 16, 1843, and reads in translation as follows:

Notwithstanding the fact that the date of the preceding ratification is not indicated, since it must be assumed that it took place within the stipulated period, as before its expiration the President and Minister who authorize it ceased to exercise their administrative functions, and the said convention being thus validly ratified; and having ordered that it be vested with all the necessary formalities in order that it may go into effect; let the exchange of the ratifications take place without any hindrance because of the fact that the period has expired which was designated for that purpose in Article 7 nor because the approval of Congress is lacking, as that body has been unable to meet in opportune time, and because, moreover, the Government under the present circumstances exercises the legislative powers demanded by the needs of the state.

Done in the Palace of the Director at Lima July 16, 1843. Sealed with the seal of the Republic and countersigned by the Minister of Foreign Relations.

M. Y. DE VIVANCO

By order of His Excellency:
    FELIPE PARDO

The second of the two documents mentioned bears date one day later, July 17, 1843, and is a full power to exchange the ratifications, though in rather unusual form, reading thus in translation:

Manuel Ygnacio de Vivanco, Provisional Supreme Director of the Republic, Brigadier General of Its Armies, etc.

Whereas the Chargé d'Affaires of the United States, Mr. J. C. Pickett, has stated that he is authorized by his Government to exchange the ratifications of the convention between Peru and the United States concluded in this city March 17, 1841, whereby the differences which existed between the two nations because of financial claims brought by citizens of the United States, were settled; and the said convention having been ratified by Peru, without prejudice to the legality of the said ratification on account of the fact that the date on which it took place was not expressed therein, as it must be assumed that it was within the term stipulated, because before the expiration thereof the President and Minister who authorized it ceased to exercise their administrative functions, nor that it was not submitted for the approval of the National Congress, because that body was unable to meet in opportune time; and as the Government, moreover, is under the present circumstances exercising the legislative powers which the needs of the nation demand: Therefore, and having ordered that steps be taken for the exchange of the ratifications in order that the above convention may have its full effects, I authorize the Senior Auditor of the *Accountant General*, Manuel del Rio, to have the said exchange take place in this city within six days, or sooner if possible.

Done in the Palace of the Director at Lima July 17, 1843, and sealed with the seal of the Republic and countersigned by the Minister of Foreign Relations.

                                                              M. Y. DE VIVANCO

By order of His Excellency:
    FELIPE PARDO

In that state of the papers the ratifications were exchanged at Lima on July 22, 1843, and the original of the certificate or act of the exchange of ratifications, in Spanish and in customary form, is in the file.

Following that exchange the convention was proclaimed by President Tyler under date of February 21, 1844; the original of that proclamation is in the file; it embodies the signed original of the convention and is bound with the duplicate United States instrument of ratification of January 12, 1843; that proclamation is in customary form.

THE SECOND RATIFICATIONS

The foregoing proceedings of ratification, of the exchange of ratifications, and of proclamation all proved ineffectual; for not long thereafter the Government of Peru declared the ratification on the part of Peru to be "insufficient"; and the Department of State was so informed by the despatch of Pickett of December 3, 1844 (D. S., 6 Despatches, Peru, No. 105), in which he wrote:

I have now to inform you that the government at Lima calling itself *constitutional*, has decided that the ratification of the Convention of the 17th of March 1841, for the adjustment of the North American claims, is insufficient, because it was ratified by Gen. Vivanco, whose government is declared to have been a usurpation and all its acts to be null, and because it has not been approved by the Peruvian Congress, as it is provided it shall be.

All this affected reverence for constitutional forms, is but a subterfuge, the object being, I have no doubt, either to avoid the payment of the claims entirely or to postpone it indefinitely. There has been no Congress to approve the Convention, but being ratified by two executive chiefs, Mr Menendez and Gen. Vivanco, the ratification could not have been more formal or more effectual.

Following the submission of the convention to the Peruvian Congress, that body on October 21, 1845, approved the same, but with the condition quoted in the Senate resolution of May 29, 1846, printed below.

The official notification of the action of the Congress of Peru was given by a note of the Peruvian Minister of Foreign Affairs to Chargé d'Affaires Albert Gallatin Jewett under date of November 15, 1845 (D. S., 7 Despatches, Peru, No. 4, November 27, 1845, enclosure); that note, in translation, was among the papers later sent to the Senate, and its text is printed below.

Another submission to the Senate, another ratification on the part of each Government, another exchange of ratifications, and another proclamation thus became necessary.

The presidential message of May 26, 1846, with a full statement of the facts, submitted to the Senate "the amendment . . . thus proposed by the Congress of Peru", as follows (Executive Journal, VII, 76–78):

A convention was concluded at Lima, on the 17th March, 1841, between the United States and the republic of Peru, for the adjustment of claims of our citizens upon that Republic. It was stipulated by the seventh article of this convention that "it shall be ratified by the contracting parties, and the ratifications shall be exchanged within two years from its date, or sooner, if possible, after having been approved by the President and Senate of the United States, and by the Congress of Peru."

This convention was transmitted by the President to the Senate for their consideration during the extra session of 1841; but it did not receive their approbation until the 5th January, 1843. This delay rendered it impracticable that the convention should reach Lima before the 17th March, 1843, the last day when the ratifications could be exchanged under the terms of its seventh article. The Senate, therefore, extended the time for this purpose until the 20th December, 1843.

In the mean time, previous to the 17th March, 1843, General Menendez, the constitutional President of Peru, had ratified the convention, declaring, however, in the act of ratification itself (which is without date), that "the present convention and ratification are to be submitted within the time stipulated in the seventh article for the final approbation of the National Congress." This was, however, rendered impossible from the fact that no Peruvian Congress assembled from the date of the convention until the year 1845.

When the convention arrived at Lima, General Menendez had been deposed by a revolution, and General Vivanco had placed himself at the head of the Government. On the 16th July, 1843, the convention was ratified by him in absolute terms, without the reference to Congress which the constitution of Peru requires, because, as the ratification states, "under existing circumstances the Government exercises the legislative powers demanded by the necessities of the state." The ratifications were accordingly exchanged at Lima on the 22d July, 1843, and the convention itself was proclaimed at Washington by the President on the 21st day of February, 1844.

In the mean time General Vivanco was deposed, and on the 12th October, 1843, the Government then in existence published a decree declaring all his administrative acts to be null and void, and, notwithstanding the earnest and able remonstrances of Mr. Pickett, our chargé d'affaires at Lima, the Peruvian Government have still persisted in declaring that the ratification of the convention by Vivanco was invalid.

After the meeting of the Peruvian Congress in 1845, the convention was submitted to that body, by which it was approved on the 21st October last, "with the condition, however, that the first installment of thirty thousand dollars on account of the principal of the debt thereby recognized, and to which the 2d article relates, should begin from the first day of January, 1846, and the interest on this annual sum, according to article 3d, should be calculated and paid from the first day of January, 1842; following in all other respects besides this modification the terms of the convention."

I am not in possession of the act of the Congress of Peru containing this provision, but the information is communicated through a note under date of the 15th November, 1845, from the minister of foreign affairs of Peru to the chargé d'affaires of the United States at Lima. A copy of this note has been transmitted to the Department of State both by our chargé d'affaires at Lima and by the Peruvian minister of foreign affairs, and a copy of the same is herewith transmitted.

Under these circumstances, I submit to the Senate for their consideration the amendment to the convention thus proposed by the Congress of Peru, with a view to its ratification. It would have been more satisfactory to have submitted the act itself of the Peruvian Congress, but, on account of the great distance, if I should wait until its arrival another year might be consumed, whilst the American claimants have already been too long delayed in receiving the money justly due to them. Several of the largest of these claimants would, I am informed, be satisfied with the modification of the convention adopted by the Peruvian Congress.

A difficulty may arise in regard to the form of any proceeding which the Senate might think proper to adopt, from the fact that the original convention approved by them was sent to Peru, and was exchanged for the other original, ratified by

General Vivanco, which is now in the Department of State. In order to obviate this difficulty as far as may be in my power, I transmit a copy of the convention, under the seal of the United States, on which the Senate might found any action they may deem advisable.

I would suggest that should the Senate advise the adoption of the amendment proposed by the Peruvian Congress, the time for exchanging the ratifications of the amended convention ought to be extended for a considerable period, so as to provide against all accidents in its transmission to Lima.

The papers which accompanied that message were printed with it in Senate Confidential Document No. 6, 29th Congress, 1st session (Regular Confidential Documents, XVIII, 783–89); the certificate with the copy of the convention transmitted is of such unusual form that it is here printed:

James K. Polk, President of the United States of America,

To all to whom these presents shall come, greeting:

I certify that the writing hereunto attached is a true and faithful copy, carefully collated with the original on file in the Department of State, of a convention concluded between the United States of America and the republic of Peru, signed at the city of Lima on the seventeenth day of March, in the year of our Lord one thousand eight hundred and forty-one.

In testimony whereof, I, James K. Polk, President of the United States, have hereunto subscribed my name, and caused the seal of the United States to be affixed. Done at the city of Washington, this twenty-sixth [L.S.] day of May, A.D. 1846, and of the independence of the United States of America the seventieth.

JAMES K. POLK.

The other accompanying paper was the note (in translation) of the Peruvian Minister of Foreign Affairs, José Gregorio Paz y Soldan, to Albert G. Jewett, Chargé d'Affaires of the United States, dated November 15, 1845, as follows:

The undersigned, Minister of Foreign Relations, has received the communication of the 13th instant in which the Chargé d'Affaires of the United States informs him that he intends to transmit by the first vessel from Callao to Panamá the correspondence which has taken place respecting the fulfilment of the convention of March 17, 1841, and he in consequence requests that the answer containing the information which he solicited on this subject may be sent to him before the 25th of the present month.

The convention above mentioned having been submitted to the Congress for its information and deliberation upon it, it is not to be denied that the only answers which the Chargé d'Affaires has received to his repeated communications on the subject, from the undersigned, have been confined to the announcement of this fact, with the promise to remind the Chambers of the urgent necessity of giving preference to the consideration of an affair which has been so diligently and actively prosecuted. This is precisely what the undersigned has done, because it is all that lies within the sphere of his duties; and it is the same which he would still do, had not his continued exertions fortunately caused the legislative power to vary the state of the affair in question. This change permits him now to employ language more positive and peremptory. Congress at length, by a law of the 21st of October last, which was, however, not sent to this Department until the 11th instant, approved in all respects the said convention, with the condition, however, that the first annual instalment of thirty thousand dollars on account of the principal of the debt recognized thereby, and to which the second article relates, should begin from the 1st of January, 1846, and the interest on this annual sum, according to Article 3, should be calculated and paid from the 1st of January, 1842; following, in all other respects besides this modification, the terms of the convention.

Now, according to the seventh article of the convention, it should be ratified by the contracting parties, and the ratifications should be exchanged within the term of two years from the date of its conclusion, or earlier if it be possible, after having obtained the approval of the Congress of Peru and of the President and Senate of the United States. As the latter condition has been already fulfilled, as the want of the exchange of the ratifications—a formality which should be absolutely fulfilled within the term prescribed for the validity of contracts—arose not only from our disturbances, but also from the circumstance that the approval by the Government of the United States arrived after the two years stipulated, and as this serious circumstance might have been sufficient to invalidate the convention and cause it to be regarded as not made, had we not desired to promote harmony and to manifest a benevolent deference towards the Government of the United States, the time is now come for the exchange of the ratifications; and in order that it may be effected the undersigned desires to know whether the Chargé d'Affaires of the United States is duly authorized thereto.

The undersigned repeats to the Chargé d'Affaires of the United States the assurances of his distinguished consideration.

On May 29, 1846, the Senate unanimously adopted the following resolution (Executive Journal, VII, 81):

Whereas the seventh article of the convention between the United States of America and the Republic of Peru concluded at Lima the 17th March, 1841, require that the ratifications by the contracting parties should be exchanged within two years from its date, which provision was not observed by the said parties, owing to delays in the ratification rendering such exchange impracticable within the time stipulated; and whereas it appears by the message of the President of the United States of the 26th instant, and by a communication from the minister of foreign affairs of the Republic of Peru of the 15th November, 1845, that the duly constituted authorities of that Republic did, on the 21st of October, 1845, by law approve "in all respects the said convention, with the condition, however, that the first annual instalment of thirty thousand dollars on account of the principal of the debt recognized thereby, and to which the second article relates, should begin from the 1st of January, 1846, and the interest on this annual sum, according to article third, should be calculated and paid from the 1st of January, 1842, following in all other respects besides this modification the terms of the convention": Therefore,

Resolved (two-thirds of the Senators present concurring), That the Senate advise and consent that the first annual instalment of thirty thousand dollars shall begin on the 1st January, 1846, instead of 1st January, 1844, as required by the second article of the convention between the United States of America and the Republic of Peru concluded at Lima the 17th March, 1841, and that an instalment of thirty thousand dollars be paid on the first day of each succeeding January until the whole sum of three hundred thousand dollars shall be paid, with interest on each instalment as stipulated in the third article of the said convention; and that the ratification and exchange of ratifications of the said convention, and of the modification to which the advice and consent of the Senate are hereby given, shall be valid if made at any time within two years from this day.

Ratification on the part of the United States followed under date of June 1, 1846. A duplicate of that instrument of ratification is in the file; it includes a printed text of the convention, in English only, and is in the following form:

James K. Polk, President of the United States of America,

To all and singular who shall see these presents, Greeting:

Whereas a Convention between the United States of America and the Republic of Peru, was concluded and signed at Lima by their respective Plenipotentiaries,

on the seventeenth day of March, in the year of our Lord one thousand eight hundred and forty one, which Convention is word for word as follows:

[Here follows a printed text of the convention]

And whereas the seventh article of the said Convention required that the ratification of the contracting parties should be exchanged within two years from its date, which provision was not observed by the said parties owing to delays in the ratification rendering such exchange impracticable within the time stipulated:

And whereas it appears that the duly constituted authorities of the Republic of Peru did, on the 21st of October, 1845, by law approve in all respects the said Convention, with the condition, however, that the first annual instalment of thirty thousand dollars on account of the principal of the debt recognized thereby and to which the second article relates, should begin from the 1st of January, 1846, and the interests on this annual sum, according to Article III, should be calculated and paid from the 1st of January, 1842:

And whereas the Senate of the United States by their resolution of the 29th ultimo, two thirds of the Senators then present concurring, did advise and consent "that the first annual instalment of thirty thousand dollars shall begin on the 1st January, 1846, instead of the 1st January, 1844, as required by the second article of the Convention between the United States of America and the Republic of Peru, concluded at Lima on the 17th March, 1841; and that an instalment of thirty thousand dollars be paid on the first day of each succeeding January, until the whole sum of three hundred thousand dollars shall be paid, with interest on each instalment as stipulated in the third article of said Convention; and that the ratification and exchange of the ratifications of the said Convention and of the modification to which the advice and consent of the Senate are hereby given shall be valid, if made at any time within two years from this day":

Now therefore, I, James K. Polk, President of the United States of America, having seen and considered the said Convention, together with the modification herein above mentioned, do, in pursuance of the aforesaid advice and consent of the Senate, by these presents, accept, ratify and confirm the same and every article and clause thereof.

In faith whereof, I have caused the seal of the United States to be hereunto affixed. Given under my hand at the City of Washington, the first
[Seal]   day of June A D 1846, and of the Independence of the United States the seventieth.

JAMES K. POLK

By The President:
    JAMES BUCHANAN
        Secretary of State

On June 1, 1846, Secretary of State Buchanan transmitted to Chargé d'Affaires Jewett the United States instrument of ratification of the same date. From the instructions then written the following is extracted (D. S., 15 Instructions, Peru, 48–51):

Herewith I transmit you a copy of our Convention with Peru of the 17th March, 1841, with the modification proposed by the Peruvian Congress and ratified by the President, by and with the advice and consent of the Senate. I regret that you had not procured and transmitted to this Department a copy of the act of Congress itself. In its absence, the President and Senate, as you will perceive, have adopted the modification according to the language employed by the Peruvian Minister of Foreign Relations in his note to you of the 15ᵗʰ November, last.

You will lose no time in proposing to that Minister, according to his own suggestion, an exchange of the ratifications of this Convention. A corresponding copy of the Convention with a similar modification ratified by the President of Peru ought to be exchanged with you for the copy herewith transmitted. This you will have accomplished with the least possible delay, consistently with the forms of courtesy proper to be observed on such occasions.

To provide against contingencies, a Power to exchange the ratifications (which is herewith transmitted) has been given to Commander William W. McKean of the United States Navy and Stanhope Prevost, Esquire, our Consul at Lima, to be used in case of your absence.

I also send you a copy of the President's Message to the Senate of the 26th ultimo with the accompanying documents on which the proceedings of that Body were founded.

After consulting the principal claimants under the Convention, I found they were not only willing but anxious that it should be ratified with the modification proposed by the Congress of Peru. Their consent to this modification has been reduced to writing and is now on file in this Department.

The next document to be mentioned is the Peruvian instrument of ratification of October 8, 1846, which includes the Spanish text of the convention only. Two originals of that instrument are in the treaty file; one of them has the seal impressed, the other the pendant seal in the then customary silver box; the latter is doubtless "the elegantly prepared book, containing a copy of the Convention", which is mentioned in the despatch of January 9, 1847 (D. S., 7 Despatches, Peru, No. 16); in the text of the convention therein included, the preamble is wholly omitted; otherwise the two originals are identic in all essentials; it is with the text included in the former, which was transmitted with the despatch of Jewett of November 10, 1846 (D. S., 7 Despatches, Peru, No. 14), that the Spanish text here printed has been collated. After that text is the following (translation):

Therefore, this convention having received the approval of Congress, with the provision that the first annuity of thirty thousand pesos on account of the capital recognized as a debt for this cause, and which is referred to in Article 2, let it be in effect and so understood as from January 1, 1846, and let the interest on this annuity, according to Article 3, be paid from January 1 of the past year of 1842, the stipulations of the convention being effective in all other respects in accordance with these modifications; and in consideration of the fact also that the variations indicated, which were brought to the notice of the Government of the United States, have been concluded and approved by the President and Senate of the Union, as appears from the note of the Minister of State of the same dated June 1 of the current year, I have decided to ratify it *in toto*, exercising the power granted to me by attribution 16 of Article 87 of the Constitution, and therefore the amounts of debts and other obligations which are stated in the inserted articles, with the modifications indicated, are recognized by the Government, the national credit and justice being pledged for this purpose.

Done at Lima October 8, 1846.

RAMON CASTILLA

JOSÉ G. PAZ Y SOLDAN

The certificate or act of the exchange of ratifications at Lima on October 31, 1846, is in Spanish and in customary form, mentioning, however, "the modification later made by the Congress of Peru and accepted by the President and Senate of the United States".

The form of the proclamation of the convention by President Polk under date of January 8, 1847, is somewhat adapted to the peculiar circumstances of the case; like the United States instrument of ratification of June 1, 1846, it includes a printed text of the convention in English only; it follows the form of that instrument in the paragraph preceding and in the two paragraphs following the convention

text; but in lieu of the recital regarding the action of the Senate, is the following:

And whereas the said Convention and the aforesaid modification thereof have been duly ratified, and the respective ratifications of the same were exchanged in the City of Lima on the thirty first day of October last, by Albert G. Jewett on the part of the United States and Manuel del Rio on the part of the Republic of Peru. . . .

The texts of the modification proposed on October 21, 1845, as written in the respective instruments of ratification (of the United States, June 1, 1846; of Peru, October 8, 1846) are printed above, following the texts of the convention as signed.

The Claims Settlement

In his despatch enclosing the convention (D. S., 6 Despatches, Peru, No. 38, March 31, 1841) Pickett wrote of its terms as follows:

The sum stipulated to be paid by Peru, is three hundred thousand dollars, the same that my predecessors in this Legation, Mr. Larned and Mr. Thornton offered to take, & their proposition being known at Washington and not disapproved, as far as I am informed, I suppose it to have been sanctioned. The Convention (Article 5th) embraces those claims only that were presented by Mr. Larned. Samuel F. Tracy's claim for 104.559 dollars and one or two others of not much importance, are reserved for future arrangement. This article (the 5th) does not appear in the Convention, as I draughted it, but it shews clearly enough, I think, that the 300.000 dollars are applicable to the old claims only. The Peruvian Commissioner being about to leave Lima, to be absent some months, it was important to conclude the matter, at once, there being but little time for discussion. I accepted his article, therefore, with a slight alteration.

I inserted the 4th article, which provides that the annual payments shall be made in dollars of the standard and value of those now coined at the Mint in Lima, because at Cuzco, they coin silver containing one third alloy, and it may happen that before the claims are paid, the coinage here may be adulterated.

The 6th article provides that Peru shall have the option of paying the instalments, as they fall due, in Orders on the Custom House at Callao, and this provision ensures their payment, in all probability, for although it may never be convenient for the Government to pay in cash, yet it could not refuse, with any decency, to pay in Custom House paper.

The instalments are very moderate in amount, and a long time is allowed for the commencement and completion of the payments. Mr. Larned offered to allow ten years, with instalments, the first to be paid at the end of five years, & Mr. Livingston, in a despatch dated the 30th of January 1833, suggests a credit of eight or nine years, with interest, at the rate of four per centum.

The compromise may not be a very good one, yet I am of opinion, that it is preferable to a prolonged and vexatious negotiation or a resort to hostile or unfriendly measures, for the purpose of obtaining satisfaction. The Peruvian Commissioner declared the inability of his Government to meet punctually, larger payments than thirty thousand dollars annually, or to commence paying, conveniently, earlier than the year 1844, alleging that the country is already overwhelmed with debt and responsibilities: And knowing this to be true, it appeared to me better, to give my assent to what seemed to be practicable, than to defeat the object, by insisting too pertinaciously, upon what was desirable. Peru, impoverished as she has been and seems destined to continue to be, by interminable and exhausting civil conflicts, is utterly unable to meet her pecuniary engagements. Her public debt, foreign and domestic, amounts to not less than thirty millions of dollars, one half or more of which is due to British creditors, who are getting to be very impatient, for they have not received a dollar, for many years.

The very imperfect condition in which I have found the documents relating to the claims, has influenced me, in some degree, in deciding to accept the 300.000 dollars, as it did Mr. Larned and Mr. Thornton, I have no doubt. The claims have, in general, been very carelessly and unskillfully prepared, unless many of the papers have been lost, and I have no reason to suppose they have been. In some cases, it is impracticable to ascertain the amount claimed, and in some, the facts set forth are very inadequately supported by proofs. The fate of a portion of them, therefore, would, before an arbitrator, be doubtful, at least; and the Peruvian Government, I understand, had resolved to propose an arbitration, if a compromise had not taken place. This proposition could not have been rejected, I suppose, by the U. States, and if the claims had been submitted to an arbitrator, the delays, expense and perplexities incident to such a course, together with the uncertainty of the nature of the final award, would perhaps, have made, at last, a compromise less favorable even than the one effected, acceptable to the claimants. The sum to be paid will give a dividend of about seventy per centum, probably, on the original amount of the claims, including neither interest nor damages. I once thought that this amount would not be much under 600.000 dollars but it will not reach 450.000, probably. [The total awards were $421,432.41.]

An account of the negotiations leading up to this convention and of the American claims thereby settled is in Moore, International Arbitrations, V, 4591–4607.

The convention (before its modification) was communicated to Congress on March 20, 1844 (Richardson, IV, 282); and in execution of Article 1 of the convention the act of August 8, 1846 (9 Statutes at Large, 80–81), made it the duty of the Attorney General, then John Y. Mason, to adjudicate the claims, which were, in fact, passed on by his successor, Attorney General Nathan Clifford.

Under date of August 7, 1847, the list of the twenty-six awards made by the Attorney General was duly transmitted to the Secretary of State. Those awards aggregated, without interest, $421,432.41; the claims rejected amounted to $76,094.25 (Moore, *op. cit.*, 4603–7).

By the terms of this convention as amended, the ten annual instalments were payable on January 1 of each year from 1846 to 1855, inclusive, with interest on each instalment from January 1, 1842. Thus the first payment, due on January 1, 1846, was $34,800. The annual payments increased by $1,200 each year, so that the instalment due in 1855 was $45,600, the equivalent of $30,000 plus thirteen years' interest at 4 percent.

The convention did not go into force until October 31, 1846, and the first instalment of $30,000, though without interest, was paid in February 1847. There were occasional delays; but from the despatches of various dates from 1847 to 1855 (D. S., 8–11 Despatches, Peru; see also 15 Instructions, Peru, *passim*), it appears that all the instalments were paid with interest by 1855, and in some cases additional interest was paid because of delay. The volumes entitled "An Account of the Receipts and Expenditures of the United States for the Year . . ." (vols. 20–28) show that the total amount collected at the Treasury was $397,028.62; the amounts are summarized at page 104 of Senate Executive Document No. 38, 44th Congress, 2d session, serial 1720.

Some of the payments were made in "hard dollars" (Article 4); others in their equivalent in currency; the optional method of payment in orders on the customhouse at Callao (Article 6) was not, it

seems, used by the Government of Peru except in 1848 (see Senate Executive Document No. 58, 31st Congress, 1st session, serial 561, dated June 28, 1850).

While the first instalment of $30,000 was paid to the Chargé d'Affaires at Lima, subsequent payments were made pursuant to the arrangement adopted in 1847 for the transfer of the sums received at Lima to the United States Treasury, which is thus described (D. S., 15 Instructions, Peru, 56–58, September 18, 1847):

An arrangement has been made between this Department and the Navy Department, under which you will be relieved from the necessity of receiving the instalments as they become due from the Peruvian Government. Under this arrangement, these will be received by Messrs Edward McCall & Co, Navy Agents of the United States at Lima, and will be expended there for the use of the Navy; whilst the Secretary of the Navy will cause the same amount to be deposited in the Treasury of the United States for the use of the claimants under the Convention with Peru. You will be furnished with a copy of my letter to Messrs McCall & Co of the 24th March. last, which will afford you all the necessary information on this subject.

98

SULU : FEBRUARY 5, 1842

Agreement Made by the Sultan of Sulu at Sooung (Jolo) February 5,
1842. Original in English.
Not subject to ratification and not proclaimed.
Immediately following this headnote is printed the text of the agreement,
including transliteration of the written Arabic characters, which are
treated in the notes. The agreement is reproduced in facsimile facing
pages 350 and 351.

[Seal]

I as-Sultân Muhammad Jamâlul-Kirâm Sultan of Sooloo, for the
purpose of encouraging trade with the poeple of the United States of
America, do promise hereby and bind myself, that I will afford full
protection to all Vessels of the United States, and their Commanders
and Crews, Visiting any of the Islands of my dominions, and they shall
be allowed to trade, on the terms of the most favored Nation, and
recieve such provisions and necessaries as they may be in want of.

2$^{dly\cdot}$ In Case of Shipwreck or Accident to any Vessel I will afford
them all the assistance in my power, and protect the persons and
property of those wrecked, and afford them all the assistance in my
power for its preservation and safe keeping, and for the return of the
Officers and Crews of said Vessels to the Spanish Settlements or
wherever they may wish to proceed.

3dly That any one of my subjects who shall do any injury or harm
to the Commanders or Crews belonging to American Vessels—shall
recieve such punishment as his Crime Merits.

In witness whereof I have hereunto set my hand and seal in presence
of the Dattos and Chiefs at Sooung.

Island of Sooloo, February 5th 1842.

[Seal]   [Seal]

Datu muluk MANDARSHÂH
Datu MUHAMMAD FUDALUN

Witnesses.

CHARLES WILKES. *Comd. Expg. Expd^r*
W^m L HUDSON *Late Comd^n U S Ship Peacock*
R. R. WALDRON *Purser U.S. Exp^n Expedition*

THE ARABIC CHARACTERS

Professor C. Snouck Hurgronje, of Leiden, has been good enough to write the following paragraphs by way of comment on the original document:

At the top of the first page is written *as-Sultân Muhammad Jamâlul-Kirâm*. Although there are attached to the *m* of *Kirâm* some scribbles (perhaps representing a formula of benediction, which I am unable to decipher) such as are sometimes used to conclude signatures in Arabic characters, the writing of the name seems to me to be that of a secretary, not the sign manual of the Sultan. *Jamâlul-Kirâm*, "the beauty of the noble ones", is a composition of Arabic words which sounds rather ridiculous to Arabic ears as a proper name but may make an impression of solemnity on Mohammedans without Arabic erudition.

The seal at the left contains the following words: line 1, *as-shâhid;* line 2, *li'amr al-malik al-imâm;* line 3, *as-Sultân Muhammad;* line 4, *Jamâlul-Kirâm;* line 5, "year [probably] 1257" (which would correspond with 1841–42 A.D.).

The words in the first two lines of the large seal are Arabic, but they do not give a genuine Arabic expression: line 1, "The witness"; line 2, "to the order of the King, the Sovereign." They seem to imply that this seal is the witness that the following order has been issued by the King. Perhaps we might translate *as-shâhid* here by "certification".

On the second page there is a small seal of the same Sultan containing the words: line 1, *as-Sultân;* line 2, *Muhammad Jamâl;* line 3, *ul-Kirâm.* Persons of high position sometimes have a large seal for important and a smaller one for familiar purposes, but generally in one document only one of them is used.

Under the small seal are the names (not signatures, because they are written plainly by the same hand) of (1) *Datu muluk Mandarshâh* and (2) *Datu Muhammad Fudalun. Datu muluk* means datu of the Government, the man's name being *Mandarshâh.*

The Sulu language belongs to the family of the Philippine languages, in a wider sense to the Indonesian family of languages, which includes almost all the hundred or more languages of Netherland India, the Federated Malay States, the Straits Settlements, and the vernacular of a part of the population of Madagascar. Owing to the adoption of the Mohammedan creed by the inhabitants of the Sulu Archipelago, they took to the Arabic alphabet, and like all Mohammedan peoples they borrowed a great number of Arabic words, especially terms of religion and law, which they always pronounce and sometimes even write with a corruptive adaptation to the sounds of their mother tongue. The frequent contact of the Sulu people with North Borneo and to a certain degree with Singapore introduced also a good many Malay words into the Sulu vernacular. Nevertheless, the morphology and the bulk of the *copia verborum* of the Sulu are quite distinct from, although cognate with, Malay; with Arabic the Sulu language has not the slightest affinity.

ٱلسُّلْطَان محمد جمال الكرَام

Sultan of Soo Loo.

For the purpose of encouraging trade
with the People of the United States
of America. do promise hereby and
bind Myself. that I will afford
full protection to all Vessels of the
United States. and their Commanders
and Crews, Visiting any of the Islands
of My dominions, And they Shall
be allowed to trade. on the terms of
the Most favoured Nation, and receive
Such Provisions and Necessaries
as they May be in want of.

2ly. In case of Shipwreck or Accident
to any Vessel I will afford them all
the assistance in my Power. and
protect the Persons and Property
of those Wrecked, and afford
them all the assistance in my
Power for its Preservation and Safe
keeping; and for the return of
the Officers and Crews of Said
Vessels to the Spanish Settlements
or Wherever they May wish to Proceed,

3rd That any one of my.
Subjects who Shall do any
injury or harm to the
Commanders

Commanders or Crews belonging to
American Vessels. Shall receive
Such Punishment as his Crime Merits—

In Witness whereof I have hereunto.
Set My hand and Seal in Presence
of the Dattos and Chiefs at Soong—
Island of Sooloo.
February 5th 1842.

دتو ملك مندى شاه

Witnesses.
Charles Wilkes
Command. Expg. Exptn.

دتو حمد فضلن

W. L. Maddox Late Cand a Ship Reedok

R. R. Waldron
Purser U.S. Ex. Expedition

The original name of Sulu seems to have been *Sulug* (pronounced *Sooloog*), the final consonant having been dropped by foreigners. The Sulu people did not drop the final consonant, but they have the habit of eliding *l* between two vowels in words of their own speech; so they pronounce the name of their island and of their archipelago *Soog*. This word in their spelling system occurs in two different forms: سوغ and سوݣ, some of them reproducing the sound *g*, which does not occur in Arabic writing, by Arabic غ, others adopting therefor the Arabic letter *k*, provided for the purpose with a diacritical point. In the first spelling (سوغ) this word differs from *Soong* only by the different diacritical points; thus *Soog*, the native name of Sulu, may easily be misread into *Soong* or *Sooung*, as it is once written in the document.

NOTES

This agreement made by the Sultan of Sulu on February 5, 1842, is reproduced in facsimile facing pages 350 and 351. The text is printed, including transliteration of the written Arabic characters, immediately following the headnote.

The Sulu Archipelago

The Sulu Archipelago comprises the southernmost island groups of the Philippines, extending from Mindanao to Borneo and separating the Sulu Sea from the Celebes Sea. If it be defined as including Basilan Island, the Sulu Archipelago extends about 250 statute miles from Basilan Strait on the northeast to Alice Channel on the southwest. The line described in the convention of January 2, 1930, between the United States and Great Britain, delimiting the boundary between the Philippine Archipelago and the State of North Borneo (Treaty Series No. 856), passes to the south, the west (in Alice Channel), and the northwest of Sibutu and adjacent islands at the southwest extremity of the Sulu Archipelago.

The name "Sulu" (Sulug or Soog) was written "Xolo" (probably pronounced sō-lō or shō-lō) by the early Spaniards, who later spelled it "Joló" (pronounced hō-ló). "Sulug" means "sea current" and refers to the tidal currents which are characteristic of the Sulu Sea, including those flowing through the numerous passages between the islands and over the shoals of the entire Sulu Archipelago, flowing from the Celebes Sea northward and westward into the Sulu Sea with velocities up to 2 and even 6 knots, and ebbing in the reverse direction. Modern aids to navigators give for each important channel the number of hours and minutes after the meridian passage of the moon when the tide flows in, and when the ebb tide sets out. As the unusually strong tidal currents are an important factor in the life of these seafaring people, the name "Sulu" appropriately applies to the entire archipelago.

The name "Sulu" (or the alternative "Jolo") has been applied (*a*) to the archipelago; (*b*) to a political province coextensive with the archipelago according to a restricted definition; (*c*) to 1 of 3 major groups of islands; (*d*) to a subgroup thereof; (*e*) to the largest island of that group; (*f*) to the chief town on that island; and (*g*) to the sea comprised between the Sulu Archipelago and the islands of Mindanao, Negros, Panay, Palawan, and Borneo.

In present usage the name "Sulu" is almost universally applied to the sea, the archipelago, and the province; "Jolo" is frequently employed in reference to the major island group and subgroup thereof, to the island, and to the town, but especially to the latter. Since the final Spanish conquest and occupation of the archipelago in 1876, the name "Jolo" has become so intimately associated with the town as to be preferred to the name Sulu in that connotation (Saleeby, History of Sulu, 133).

The archipelago, geographically considered, consists of three principal groups—Basilan on the northeast, Sulu in the center, and Tawi-tawi on the southwest. The Sulu group comprises the Samal or Balangingi Islands, Sulu proper, the Pangutaran, and the Tapul Islands—all of which are listed as separate major groups by some authorities. The archipelago, thus defined, comprises more than 300 islands, with a total area of approximately 1,200 square miles and a population numbering 300,000.

The Basilan group, from a political or administrative viewpoint, has been a part of Mindanao, or of its district or province of Zamboanga, since 1861. Basilan has therefore never comprised a part of what later became the Province of Sulu, which embraced all the rest of the Sulu Archipelago.

CHARACTER OF THE AGREEMENT

It may perhaps be doubted whether this agreement made on February 5, 1842, by the Sultan of Sooloo (or Sulu, as now spelled) is properly to be regarded as an international act. Over the Philippines generally the sovereignty of Spain was then recognized; but the effective occupation of the islands by Spain was not complete, such occupation of the Sulu Archipelago did not then exist, and the extent of Spanish jurisdiction was uncertain.

As early as 1578 a Spanish expedition was sent to Sulu, and intermittent hostilities continued until 1638, when a Spanish garrison was established (Saleeby, History of Sulu, 164–77). A treaty was made in 1646 (*ibid.*, 178); but the Spanish troops were soon withdrawn from the region (see Barrows, History of the Philippines, 175–84). In 1726 a treaty was made between Spain and the Sultan of Sulu for trade and other purposes (Montero y Vidal, Historia de la piratería, I, 258–59). A treaty of peace and friendship with Spain was made in 1737 (the Spanish text is in *ibid.*, II, appendices, 3–6; an English summary is in Saleeby, *op. cit.*, 180); and a Jesuit mission was established in Jolo in 1747 (Barrows, *op. cit.*, 200); but hostilities did not cease (Saleeby, *op. cit.*, 181–92). There was a treaty between Spain

and Sulu in 1805, and there were Spanish expeditions in 1823 and 1827 (*ibid.*, 193); but all those events and agreements led to nothing final. "In spite of innumerable expeditions, Spain's occupation of South Mindanao and the Sulu archipelago was limited [1847] to the presidio of Zamboanga. She had occupied this strategic point continuously since the reëstablishment of Spanish power in 1763" (Barrows, *op. cit.*, 240). The same author writes that "Spain's maintenance of Zamboanga was insufficient to sustain her claims of sovereignty over the Sulu and Tawi-Tawi groups" (*ibid.*, 241); and he considers that the arrival in the Philippines in 1848 of three Spanish vessels of war with steam power was the fact which was "destined to revolutionize Moro relations" (*ibid.*, 243). These "were the first steam gunboats the Philippine Government ever employed. Steam was certainly destined to mark a new epoch, one which saw the beginning of the end of Moro piracy" (Saleeby, *op. cit.*, 199).

Various documents are to be mentioned as relevant to the question of Spanish sovereignty over the Sulu Archipelago in the nineteenth century. On September 23, 1836, there were signed at Jolo "Capitulations of Peace, Protection, and Commerce" (Spanish text and English translation in British and Foreign State Papers, XXIV, 807–11; the latter also in Saleeby, *op. cit.*, 196–99); the language of that treaty is perhaps vague enough to permit it to be regarded on the one hand as creating a Spanish protectorate and on the other, a limited alliance between Spain and the Sultan of Sulu (see the documents printed in *ibid.*, 321–43). Reference is made therein to the concurrent agreement regarding duties to be paid by vessels and also to the second clause of the "capitulations" of 1737. At the same time there was signed an agreement regarding the dues to be paid by Jolo vessels in Manila and Zamboanga and by Spanish vessels in Jolo; there is nothing in the form or substance of that agreement implying Spanish sovereignty over the Sulu Archipelago, but rather the contrary. An English translation of the articles (there dated September 22, 1836) is in Senate Document No. 136, 56th Congress, 1st session, serial 3851, pages 11–12, and also in Saleeby, *op. cit.*, 194–96; the Spanish text is in Montero y Vidal, Historia de la piratería, II, appendices, 43–47.

An agreement between France and the Sultan of Sulu was signed on April 23, 1843, at Jolo, on behalf of France by two officers of the French corvette *La Favorite;* its three articles included a most-favored-nation clause, and their terms in general did not differ very materially from those of this agreement of February 5, 1842 (the text, in French, is in De Clercq, Recueil des traités de la France, V, 48; a Spanish translation is in Montero y Vidal, Historia de la piratería, II, appendices, 47–48).

The French mission to China of 1844 was headed by De Lagrené, Minister Plenipotentiary of the King of the French; but that Plenipotentiary had instructions other than those which resulted in the French Treaty of Commerce with China which was signed on October 24, 1844. The story of the efforts of France to obtain the island of Basilan, west of Mindanao, as a commercial and naval base, somewhat

similar to Macao and Hong Kong, has been told by M. Guizot, who was Minister of Foreign Affairs of France at the time.

While De Lagrené considered that Basilan formed part of the Sulu Archipelago, he wholly denied any Spanish sovereignty over either Sulu generally or Basilan in particular. A French squadron under Admiral Cécille visited Basilan, and there the assent of the native chiefs to French sovereignty was obtained by De Lagrené by a declaration of January 13 and a convention of January 20, 1845. De Lagrené and Cécille next sought to obtain the cession of the rights of the Sultan to the island of Basilan; but the council of the Sultan rejected their proposed treaty because no cash payment could be made at the time. De Lagrené wrote to Guizot (translation):

> All that I could obtain was a letter written to me to state that the council was ready to subscribe to the cession of Basilan for one hundred years for a payment of one hundred thousand dollars cash and provided that the taking possession of the island should take place within a period of six months.

De Lagrené had acted in accordance with his instructions; but the protests of Spain and the diplomatic and political situation of France in 1845 induced the French Government to decide to abandon the enterprise. Montero y Vidal gives a Spanish translation of the proposed treaty under date of February 20, 1845, and of the declaration or letter signed by the Sultan of Sulu on the following day (Historia de la piratería, II, appendices, 48–50). That author states that the treaty was signed, and argues that it was void for lack of seals (*ibid.*, I, 381). That a definitive agreement was made is also stated by Barrows (*op. cit.*, 241), who gives the purchase price as one million dollars; but the account of Guizot seems more authoritative (see Oliphant, La Chine et le Japon, I, i–xxxi, introduction by Guizot; the work is a French translation of Oliphant, Narrative of the Earl of Elgin's Mission to China and Japan).

Next in chronological order is the treaty of May 29, 1849, made in the name of the Queen of Great Britain by Sir James Brooke, in eight articles; that document, on the part of the Sultan of Sulu, is a complete denial of Spanish sovereignty; the Sultan "occupies the throne and governs the territories of Sulu"; there is a mutual most-favored-nation clause as to residence and commerce; British subjects may acquire property in the archipelago of Sulu; into the ports thereof British ships of war may freely enter; piracy is to be suppressed; and by Article 7 the Sultan is to make no cession of territory and no acknowledgment of subjection to any other power without the consent of Her Britannic Majesty; but the treaty was to be ratified and was not ratified by Great Britain, for reasons which are variously stated (see Baring-Gould and Bampfylde, A History of Sarawak, 337, note 1; also St. John, Rajah Brooke, xii–xiv); accordingly that treaty failed to go into force. The text of the treaty, with certain correspondence, is in Saleeby, *op. cit.*, 345–53 (see also *ibid.*, 201–6); a Spanish translation is in Montero y Vidal, Historia de la piratería, II, appendices, 50–52 (see also *ibid.*, I, 420–25). According to the Spanish translation, the treaty was signed on behalf of Great Britain not only by Brooke but by "Jome Copey"; this is an attempted trans-

literation or rendering of the words "Home Copy"; similarly "Mm. Copey y Brooke" appear in Montero y Vidal, Historia general de Filipinas, III, 625).

The Treaty of Jolo of April 19, 1851, followed the taking and destruction of Jolo by Spanish forces late in January 1851 and was duly ratified by Spain. It is an elaborate document of seventeen articles, signed by the Sultan of Sulu and other chiefs on the one part and by the Military and Political Governor of Zamboanga on the part of Spain; its provisions (Spanish text) include very formal recognition of Spanish sovereignty over the island of Jolo and its dependencies by right of conquest and of ancient and recent treaties, a prohibition of future treaties with European powers, the adoption of the Spanish flag, and the protection of dynastic and other vested rights and subsidies for the Sultan and certain others (Spanish text in Montero y Vidal, Historia de la piratería, II, appendices, 52–61). In Saleeby, *op. cit.*, 209–14, are printed English translations of the two texts of the treaty, Spanish and Sulu; the differences are material.

Another campaign against Sulu took place in 1876, in which Spain was completely victorious (*ibid.*, 221–25); it was followed by the treaty of July 20, 1878, written in Spanish and Sulu; according to the Spanish text "the sovereignty to Spain over all the archipelago of Sulu and its dependencies is indisputable"; but various rights of the Sultan were preserved, especially in places not occupied by Spain. Translations of both texts are in *ibid.*, 227–31, again showing material differences, which had repercussions in 1899 (see Senate Document No. 136, 56th Congress, 1st session, serial 3851, pp. 34–41). Shortly prior to the treaty of 1878 (January 22), the Sultan of Sulu ceded his territorial rights and claims in Borneo to the British North Borneo Company (Saleeby, *op. cit.*, 225–26). The interrelation of the two questions of Sulu and Borneo in the diplomatic history of the period is interestingly discussed by De Croizier in his preface to Gibert, L'Espagne et la question de Bornéo et de Joló.

On March 11, 1877, a protocol between Spain, Great Britain, and Germany respecting the freedom of commerce and navigation in the Sulu Archipelago was signed at Madrid; by that protocol complete freedom of trade with places in the archipelago not occupied by Spain, was recognized, and it was provided that Spanish taxes and other regulations were applicable only to places occupied (the French text, with two earlier notes, is in British and Foreign State Papers, LXVIII, 494–99; English translations of the protocols of 1877 and 1885 are in Saleeby, *op. cit.*, 367–73).

In a debate in the Spanish Cortes on December 21, 1881, it was remarked by M. Silvela, former Minister of State, that in notes of November 7, 1873, and February 20, 1874, the Government of Great Britain stated that that Government had never recognized and did not recognize the sovereignty of Spain over Jolo (Gibert, L'Espagne et la question de Bornéo et de Joló, 25).

By the protocol of March 7, 1885, signed at Madrid on behalf of Great Britain, Germany, and Spain (text in French in British and Foreign State Papers, LXXVI, 58–60), the two former powers recog-

nized the sovereignty of Spain over the Sulu Archipelago, as there
defined, both in respect of those parts then effectively and those not
then effectively occupied by Spain; and Spain renounced in favor of
Great Britain all claim of sovereignty over those parts of Borneo and
certain adjacent islands which belonged or which had belonged to the
Sultan of Sulu; and various provisions of the protocol of March 11,
1877, were reaffirmed.

As to the protocols of 1877 and 1885, see also Moore, Digest, I,
268, 532, and V, 351–52.

It is obvious that in 1842 the sovereignty of Spain over the Sulu
Archipelago could not be deemed beyond debate or question.

As to the independent status of the Sultan of Sulu, Lieutenant
Charles Wilkes, U.S.N., commanding the Exploring Expedition, who
was responsible for the making of this agreement of February 5,
1842, seems to have had no doubt; extracts from his account of the
expedition, quoted hereafter in these notes, describe the system of
government of the Sultan and its regulations concerning trade, with
no allusion to Spanish sovereignty; and Wilkes had stopped at Manila
and Zamboanga immediately prior to his visit to Sulu, regarding
which he had particular instructions; and, referring to the pirates of
the Sulu Sea, he wrote, "The treaty that I made with the Sultan, if
strictly enforced on the first infraction, will soon put an end to all
the dangers to be apprehended from them" (Narrative of the United
States Exploring Expedition, V, 388; that work, which is described
in the notes to Document 91, is hereafter cited as The Narrative).

It seems clear also that the Sultan of Sulu at the time considered
his Government as sovereign; the agreement is not written with words
of dependence, but the contrary. The covenant for "trade, on the
terms of the most favored Nation", the mention of "the Spanish Settlements", and indeed the whole text (which was written by Wilkes)
indicate that there was no thought of lack of complete power to
make an international agreement.

Whether the Spanish authorities at the time knew of this agreement made by the Sultan of Sulu is an interesting point; it would
perhaps be necessary to examine both the Manila and the Madrid
archives to determine the question; but the visit of Wilkes to Sulu is
not mentioned by the Spanish historian, Montero y Vidal, in either
his Historia general de Filipinas or his Historia de la piratería malayo-
mahometana; and that visit is not mentioned in Saleeby, History
of Sulu, or in Barrows, History of the Philippines.

But there is no positive evidence that the Government of the
United States ever regarded this agreement as an international act
in force; there could hardly, in any case, have been any question of
ratification; the agreement contains no engagement or promise whatever on the part of the United States; no occasion appears to have
arisen for its application; perhaps it was not considered at all or
even known; the agreement seems never to have been officially printed,
except in The Narrative; no mention of it has been found in any of
the various congressional reports and documents treating of the
Wilkes Expedition; there is no record of it in the Department of State;
the fact that the original document is in the Library of Congress,

without any record of its source, indicates that it was used in connection with the publication of The Narrative (which was under the direction of the Joint Committee on the Library) and that it was never in the hands of Wilkes' superiors; in that case the text of the agreement could hardly have been available in Washington until 1844, when The Narrative was published; Wilkes there calls the agreement a "treaty"; but the only allusion to it which has been noticed in his official despatches to the Secretary of the Navy is the following (Naval Records and Library, 2 Wilkes Exploring Expedition, No. 102, February 25, 1842):

> I remained at anchor a day and a half at that place ["the Port of Caldera at the entrance of the Strait of Basilan"] in order to make observations for dip and intensity, and survey the harbour, and then passed over to, and through the Sooloo archipelago, and anchored off the town of Soong in the island of Sooloo the residence of the Sultan or Rajah. I remained here three days, having had friendly intercourse with the Sultan and Datto or Prime Minister, and obtained from him the terms on which he would receive American vessels in writing, and also a written guaranty to afford all who should have the misfortune to fall into difficulties or be shipwrecked at his islands protection for lives and property.

Despite the doubtful character of the agreement as an international act, its historical interest warrants its inclusion in this collection, particularly in view of the later history of the Philippine Islands and the agreement of August 20, 1899, with the Sultan of Sulu (see Senate Document No. 136, 56th Congress, 1st session, serial 3851).

The Original Document

The original of this agreement is in the Division of Manuscripts of the Library of Congress (indexed under Sooloo; United States 1840–50); the document is a folio of four pages, the agreement being written on the first recto and first verso thereof. When the document was deposited with the Library of Congress and from what source, does not appear.

This agreement with the Sultan of Sulu is printed in volume 5 of The Narrative at page 565 of the quarto edition and at page 532 of the octavo edition. In the latter the final line in Arabic characters is reproduced upside down. The agreement is also printed in British and Foreign State Papers, XXXIII, 51–52 (published in 1859).

The Negotiations

The agreement was negotiated or obtained by Lieutenant Charles Wilkes, U.S.N., toward the close of the Exploring Expedition under his command (1838–42), now generally known as the Wilkes Expedition; in The Narrative a chapter is devoted to Sulu, prefaced by a map of the "Sooloo Sea and Archipelago" (vol. 5, ch. IX, pp. 343–90); in the following account, extracts from The Narrative are quoted.

Wilkes left Manila Bay on the *Vincennes* on the evening of January 21, 1842, visited Caldera, which he describes as "a small port on the southwest side of Mindanao, about ten miles from Samboangan [Zamboanga], where the governor resides", and anchored off the town of Soung (Jolo, on the island of that name) on the morning of February 4. Of his reception by the Sultan of Sulu on that day Wilkes writes:

Lieutenant Budd was immediately despatched with the interpreter to call upon the Datu Mulu or governor, and to learn at what hour we could see the Sultan. When that officer reached the town, all were found asleep; and after remaining four hours waiting, the only answer he could get out of the Datu Mulu was, that he supposed that the Sultan would be awake at three o'clock, when he thought I could see him.

.   .   .   .

At the appointed time, Captain Hudson and myself went on shore to wait upon the Sultan. On our approach to the town, we found that a great proportion of it was built over the water on piles, and only connected with the shore by narrow bridges of bamboo. The style of building in Sooloo does not differ materially from that of the Malays. . . .

We passed for some distance between the bridges to the landing, and on our way saw several piratical prahus apparently laid up. Twenty of these were counted, of about thirty tons burden, evidently built for sea-vessels, and capable of mounting one or two long guns. We landed at a small streamlet, and walked a short distance to the Datu's house, which is of large dimensions and rudely built on piles, which raise it about six feet above the ground, and into which we were invited.

.   .   .   .

The dais was occupied by the Datu who is, next to the Sultan, the greatest man of this island. He at once came from it to receive us, and had chairs provided for us near his sanctum. After we were seated, he again retired to his lounge. The Datu is small in person, and emaciated in form, but has a quick eye and an intelligent countenance.

.   .   .   .

We now learned the reason why the Sultan could not be seen: it was Friday, the Mahomedan Sabbath, and he had been at the mosque from an early hour. Lieutenant Budd had been detained, because it was not known when he would finish his prayers; and the ceremonies of the day were more important than usual, on account of its peculiar sanctity in their calendar.

Word had been sent off to the ship that the Sultan was ready to receive me, but the messenger passed us while on our way to the shore. After we had been seated for a while, the Datu asked if we were ready to accompany him to see the Sultan; but intimated that no one but Captain Hudson and myself could be permitted to lay eyes on him. Being informed that we were, he at once, and in our presence, slipped on his silken trousers, and a new jacket, covered with bell-buttons; put on his slippers, strapped himself round with a long silken net sash, into which he stuck his kris, and, with umbrella in hand, said he was ready. He now led the way out of his house, leaving the motley group behind, and we took the path to the interior of the town, towards the Sultan's. The Datu and I walked hand in hand, on a roadway about ten feet wide, with a small stream running on each side. Captain Hudson and the interpreter came next, and a guard of six trusty slaves brought up the rear.

When we reached the outskirts of the town, about half a mile from the Datu's, we came to the Sultan's residence, where he was prepared to receive us in state. His house is constructed in the same manner as that of the Datu, but is of larger dimensions, and the piles are rather higher. Instead of steps, we found a ladder, rudely constructed of bamboo, and very crazy. This was so steep that it was necessary to use the hands in mounting it. I understood that the ladder was always removed in the night, for the sake of security. We entered at once into the presence-chamber, where the whole divan, if such it may be called, sat in arm-chairs, occupying the half of a large round table, covered with a white cotton cloth. On the opposite side of the table, seats were placed for us. On our approach, the Sultan and all his council rose, and motioned us to our seats. When we had taken them, the part of the room behind us was literally crammed with well-armed men. A few minutes were passed in silence, during which time we had an opportunity of looking at each other, and around the hall in which we were seated. The latter was of very common workmanship, and exhibited no signs of oriental magnificence. Overhead hung a printed cotton cloth, forming a kind of tester, which covered about half of the apartment. In other places

the roof and rafters were visible. A part of the house was roughly partitioned off, to the height of nine or ten feet, enclosing, as I was afterwards told, the Sultan's sleeping apartment, and that appropriated to his wife and her attendants.

The Sultan is of the middle height, spare and thin; he was dressed in a white cotton shirt, loose trousers of the same material, and slippers; he had no stockings; the bottom of his trousers was worked in scollops with blue silk, and this was the only ornament I saw about him. On his head he wore a small coloured cotton handkerchief, wound into a turban, that just covered the top of his head. His eyes were bloodshot, and had an uneasy wild look, showing that he was under the effects of opium, of which they all smoke large quantities. His teeth were as black as ebony, which, with his bright cherry-coloured lips, contrasted with his swarthy skin, gave him anything but a pleasant look.

On the left hand of the Sultan sat his two sons, while his right was occupied by his councillors; just behind him, sat the carrier of his betel-nut casket. The casket was of filigree silver, about the size of a small tea-caddy, of oblong shape, and rounded at the top. It had three divisions, one for the leaf, another for the nut, and a third for the lime. Next to this official was the pipe-bearer, who did not appear to be held in such estimation as the former.

I opened the conversation by desiring that the Datu would explain the nature of our visit, and tell the Sultan that I had come to make the treaty which he had some time before desired to form with the United States. (The Sultan, on the visit of one of our merchant-vessels, had informed the supercargo that he wished to encourage our trade, and to see the vessels of the United States coming to his port.)

The Sultan replied, that such was still his desire; upon which I told him, I would draw one up for him, that same day. While I was explaining to him the terms, a brass candlestick was brought in with a lighted tallow candle, of a very dark colour, and rude shape, that showed but little art in the manufacture. This was placed in the centre of the table, with a plate of Manilla cigars. None of them, however, were offered to us, nor any kind of refreshment.

Our visit lasted nearly an hour. When we arose to take our leave, the Sultan and his divan did the same, and we made our exit with low bows on each side.

I looked upon it as a matter of daily occurrence for all those who came to the island to visit the Sultan; but the Datu Mulu took great pains to make me believe that a great favour had been granted in allowing us a sight of his ruler. On the other hand, I dwelt upon the condescension it was on my part to visit him, and I refused to admit that I was under any gratitude or obligation for the sight of His Majesty the Sultan Mohammed Damaliel Kisand, but said that he might feel grateful to me if he signed the treaty I would prepare for him.

"Wilkes' *Damaliel Kisand* must be a writer's error for *Jamâlul-Kirâm*. His *Datu Mulu* wants a *k* at the end and means datu of the Government" (letter of Professor Snouck Hurgronje to the editor, March 28, 1932).

Nothing further appears regarding the drawing up of the agreement and its signature on the following day, February 5, 1842. Wilkes reports his departure on February 6 as follows:

On the 6th, having concluded the treaty : : : and the other business that had taken me to Sooloo, we took our departure for the Straits of Balabac, the western entrance into this sea, with a fine breeze to the eastward. By noon we had reached the group of Pangootaaraang.

The Narrative, in the chapter mentioned, contains also a historical account of the islands and a description of the piratical activities of the natives, as well as much other interesting information. Certain of the observations of Wilkes regarding the population, trade, government, etc., are here quoted:

Few if any of the Sooloos can write or read, though many speak Spanish. Their accounts are all kept by the slaves. Those who can read and write are,

in consequence, highly prized. All the accounts of the Datu of Soung are kept in Dutch, by a young Malay from Ternate, who writes a good hand, and speaks English, and whom we found exceedingly useful to us. He is the slave of the Datu, who employs him for this purpose only. He told us he was captured in a brig by the pirates of Basillan, and sold here as a slave, where he is likely to remain for life, although he says the Datu has promised to give him his freedom after ten years.

.   .   .   .

The government of the Sooloo Archipelago is a kind of oligarchy, and the supreme authority is vested in the Sultan and the Ruma Bechara or trading council. This consists of about twenty chiefs, either datus, or their next in rank, called orangs, who are governors of towns or detached provinces. The influence of the individual chiefs depends chiefly upon the number of their retainers or slaves, and the force they can bring into their service when they require it. These are purchased from the pirates, who bring them to Sooloo and its dependencies for sale. The slaves are employed in a variety of ways, as in trading prahus, in the pearl and biche de mar fisheries, and in the search after the edible birds'-nests.

.   .   .   .

According to our estimates, and the information we received while at Sooloo, the island itself does not contain more than thirty thousand inhabitants, of which the town of Soung may have six or seven thousand. The whole group may number about one hundred and thirty thousand. I am aware, however, that it is difficult to estimate the population of a half-civilized people, who invariably exaggerate their own strength; and visiters are likewise prone to do the same thing. The Chinese comprise about an eighth of the population of the town, and are generally of the lower class. They are constantly busy at their trades, and intent upon making money.

At Soung, business seems active, and all, slaves as well as masters, seem to engage in it. The absence of a strong government leaves all at liberty to act for themselves, and the Ruma Bechara gives unlimited freedom to trade. These circumstances promote the industry of the community, and even that of the slave, for he too, as before observed, has a life interest in what he earns.

Soung being the residence of the Sultan, as well as the grand depôt for all piratical goods, is probably more of a mart than any of the surrounding towns. In the months of March and April it is visited by several Chinese junks, who remain trading until the beginning of the month of August. If delayed after that time, they can scarcely return in safety, being unable to contend with the boisterous weather and head winds that then prevail in the Chinese seas. These junks are said to come chiefly from Amoy, where the cottons, &c., best suited for the Sooloos are made. Their cargoes consist of a variety of articles of Chinese manufacture and produce, such as silk, satin goods, cottons, red and checked, grass-cloth clothing, handkerchiefs, cutlery, guns, ammunition, opium, lumber, china and glass-ware, rice, sugar, oil, lard, and butter. In return for this merchandise they obtain camphor, birds'-nests, rattans, biche de mar, pearls and pearl-shells, cocoa, tortoise-shell, and wax; but there is no great quantity of these articles to be obtained perhaps not more than two or three cargoes during the season. The trade requires great knowledge of the articles purchased, for the Chinese and Sooloos are both such adepts in fraud, that great caution and circumspection are necessary.

The duties on importation are not fixed, but are changed and altered from time to time by the Ruma Bechara. The following was stated to me as the necessary payments before trade could be carried on.

A large ship, with Chinese on board, pays	$2, 000
" without " " " "	1, 800
Small ships,	1, 500
Large brig,	1, 000
Small brig,	500
Schooners,	from 150 to 400

This supposes them all to have full cargoes. That a difference should be made in a vessel with or without Chinamen, seems singular; but this, I was told, arose

from the circumstance that English vessels take them on board, in order to detect and prevent the impositions of the Sooloos.

. . . .

Although I have described the trade with Sooloo as limited, yet it is capable of greater extension; and had it not been for the piratical habits of the people, the evil report of which has been so widely spread, Sooloo would now have been one of the principal marts of the East. The most fertile parts of Borneo are subject to its authority. There all the richest productions of these Eastern seas grow in immense quantities, but are now left ungarnered in consequence of there being no buyers. The cost of their cultivation would be exceedingly low, and I am disposed to believe that these articles could be produced here at a lower cost than any where else.

Besides the trade with China, there is a very considerable one with Manilla in small articles, and I found one of our countrymen engaged in this traffic, under the Spanish flag. To him I am indebted for much information that his opportunities of observation had given him.

. . . .

Many statements have been made and published relative to the piracies committed in these seas, which in some cases exceed, and in others fall short, of the reality. Most of the piratical establishments are under the rule, or sail under the auspices of the Sultan and Ruma Bechara of Sooloo, who are more or less intimately connected with them. The share of the booty that belongs to the Sultan and Ruma Bechara, is twenty-five per cent. on all captures, whilst the datus receive a high price for the advance they make of guns and powder, and for the services of their slaves.

Professor Snouck Hurgronje remarks as follows on terms used by Wilkes in the foregoing observations: *"Rumah Bichara* is pure Malay and means not 'trading council' but 'house of deliberation' or 'council house'. In Batavia the town hall is called *Gedong Bichara*, *Gedong* being a synonym of *Rumah* (house)" (letter to the editor, March 28, 1932). "The use by Wilkes of the word *orangs*, for some of the chiefs, is due to an odd misunderstanding. That word occurs in similar forms in nearly all Indonesian languages; it means simply 'man'; to designate officials it must be accompanied by an adjective or genitive definition (e.g., *orang kaya*, 'eminent men'), or something analogous, which is here omitted" (letter to the editor, August 18, 1933).

THE WILKES EXPEDITION

Some account of the Exploring Expedition of 1838–42, or the Wilkes Expedition as it is now generally called, is in the notes to Document 91. The elaborate instructions which Wilkes received from the Secretary of the Navy under date of August 11, 1838, are there cited and quoted in full.

In respect of treaties or agreements Wilkes was given no special directions; but regarding the "Sea of Sooloo or Mindoro" this was written:

Of this sea you will make a particular examination, with a view to ascertain whether there is any safe route through it, which will shorten the passage of our vessels to and from China.

It is enjoined on you to pay very particular attention to this object, in order that you may be enabled to furnish sailing instructions to navigators. It may be also advisable to ascertain the disposition of the inhabitants of the islands of this archipelago for commerce, their productions and resources.

Treaty Series No. 119
8 Statutes at Large, 572–77
18 *ibid.*, pt. 2, Public Treaties, 315–20

99

GREAT BRITAIN : AUGUST 9, 1842

The Webster-Ashburton Treaty. Treaty to Settle and Define the Boundaries between the Territories of the United States and the Possessions of Her Britannic Majesty in North America, for the Final Suppression of the African Slave Trade, and for the Giving Up of Criminals Fugitive from Justice, in Certain Cases, signed at Washington August 9, 1842. Original in English.
Submitted to the Senate August 11, 1842. Resolution of advice and consent August 20, 1842. Ratified by the United States August 22, 1842. Ratified by Great Britain October 5, 1842. Ratifications exchanged at London October 13, 1842. Proclaimed November 10, 1842.
Following the treaty text are printed three notes written at Washington on the date of the signature of the treaty and in connection therewith; two of these are from Lord Ashburton, Her Britannic Majesty's Minister Plenipotentiary on Special Mission, to Daniel Webster, Secretary of State, and one is from the latter to the former.

A Treaty to settle and define the Boundaries between the Territories of the United States and the possessions of Her Britannic Majesty, in North America: For the final Suppression of the African Slave Trade: and For the giving up of Criminals fugitive from justice, in certain cases.

Whereas certain portions of the line of boundary between the United States of America and the British Dominions in North America, described in the second article of the Treaty of Peace[1] of 1783, have not yet been ascertained and determined, notwithstanding the repeated attempts which have been heretofore made for that purpose, and whereas it is now thought to be for the interest of both Parties, that, avoiding further discussion of their respective rights, arising in this respect under the said Treaty, they should agree on a conventional line in said portions of the said boundary, such as may be convenient to both Parties, with such equivalents and compensations, as are deemed just and reasonable:—And whereas by the Treaty[2] concluded at Ghent, on the 24th day of December, 1814,

---

[1] Document 11. [2] Document 33.

between the United States and His Britannic Majesty, an article was agreed to and inserted of the following tenor, viz⁀ "Art. 10.— whereas the Traffic in Slaves is irreconcilable with the principles of humanity and justice: And whereas both His Majesty and the United States are desirous of continuing their efforts to promote its entire abolition, it is hereby agreed that both the contracting Parties shall use their best endeavors to accomplish so desirable an object": and whereas, notwithstanding the laws which have at various times been passed by the two Governments, and the efforts made to suppress it, that criminal traffic is still prosecuted and carried on: And whereas the United States of America and Her Majesty the Queen of the United Kingdom of Great Britain and Ireland, are determined that, so far as may be in their power, it shall be effectually abolished:—And whereas it is found expedient for the better administration of justice and the prevention of crime within the Territories and jurisdiction of the two Parties, respectively, that persons committing the crimes hereinafter enumerated, and being fugitives from justice, should, under certain circumstances, be reciprocally delivered up: The United States of America and Her Britannic Majesty, having resolved to treat on these several subjects, have for that purpose appointed their respective Plenipotentiaries to negotiate and conclude a Treaty, that is to say: the President of the United States has, on his part, furnished with full powers, Daniel Webster, Secretary of State of the United States; and Her Majesty the Queen of the United Kingdom of Great Britain and Ireland, has, on her part, appointed the Right honorable Alexander Lord Ashburton, a peer of the said United Kingdom, a member of Her Majesty's most honorable Privy Council, and Her Majesty's Minister Plenipotentiary on a Special Mission to the United States; who, after a reciprocal communication of their respective full powers, have agreed to and signed the following articles:

ARTICLE I.

It is hereby agreed and declared that the line of boundary shall be as follows: Beginning at the monument at the source of the river S⁀ Croix, as designated and agreed to by the Commissioners under the fifth article of the Treaty [1] of 1794, between the Governments of the United States and Great Britain; thence, north, following the exploring line run and marked by the Surveyors of the two Governments in the years 1817 and 1818, under the fifth article of the Treaty of Ghent,[2] to its intersection with the river S⁀ John, and to the middle of

---

[1] Document 16; and see also Documents 22 and 23.
[2] Document 33.

the channel thereof: thence, up the middle of the main channel of the said river St John, to the mouth of the river St Francis; thence up the middle of the channel of the said river St Francis, and of the lakes through which it flows, to the outlet of the Lake Pohenagamook; thence, southwesterly, in a straight line to a point on the northwest branch of the river St John, which point shall be ten miles distant from the mainbranch of the St John, in a straight line, and in the nearest direction; but if the said point shall be found to be less than seven miles from the nearest point of the summit or crest of the highlands that divide those rivers which empty themselves into the river Saint Lawrence from those which fall into the river Saint John, then the said point shall be made to recede down the said northwest branch of the river St John, to a point seven miles in a straight line from the said summit or crest; thence, in a straight line, in a course about south eight degrees west, to the point where the parallel of latitude of 46°25′ north, intersects the southwest branch of the St John's; thence, southerly, by the said branch, to the source thereof in the highlands at the Metjarmette Portage; thence, down along the said highlands which divide the waters which empty themselves into the river Saint Lawrence from those which fall into the Atlantic Ocean, to the head of Hall's Stream; thence, down the middle of said Stream, till the line thus run intersects the old line of boundary surveyed and marked by Valentine and Collins previously to the year 1774, as the 45th degree of north latitude, and which has been known and understood to be the line of actual division between the States of New York and Vermont on one side, and the British Province of Canada on the other; and, from said point of intersection, west along the said dividing line as heretofore known and understood, to the Iroquois or St Lawrence river.

Article II.

It is moreover agreed, that from the place where the joint Commissioners terminated their labors under the sixth article of the Treaty of Ghent,[1] to wit: at a point in the Neebish Channel, near Muddy Lake, the line shall run into and along the ship channel between Saint Joseph and St Tammany Islands, to the division of the channel at or near the head of St Joseph's Island; thence, turning eastwardly and northwardly, around the lower end of St George's or Sugar Island, and following the middle of the channel which divides St George's from St Joseph's Island; thence, up the east Neebish channel, nearest to

---

[1] Document 33.

St George's Island, through the middle of Lake George;—thence, west of Jonas' Island, into St Mary's river, to a point in the middle of that river, about one mile above St George's or Sugar Island, so as to appropriate and assign the said Island to the United States; thence, adopting the line traced on the maps by the Commissioners, thro' the river St Mary and Lake Superior, to a point north of Ile Royale in said Lake, one hundred yards to the north and east of Ile Chapeau, which last mentioned Island lies near the northeastern point of Ile Royale, where the line marked by the Commissioners terminates; and from the last mentioned point, southwesterly, through the middle of the Sound between Ile Royale and the northwestern mainland, to the mouth of Pigeon river, and up the said river to, and through, the north and south Fowl Lakes, to the Lakes of the height of land between Lake Superior and the Lake of the Woods; thence, along the water-communication to Lake Saisaginaga, and through that Lake; thence, to and through Cypress Lake, Lac du Bois Blanc, Lac la Croix, Little Vermilion Lake, and Lake Namecan, and through the several smaller lakes, straights, or streams, connecting the lakes here mentioned, to that point in Lac la Pluie, or Rainy Lake, at the Chaudière Falls, from which the Commissioners traced the line to the most northwestern point of the Lake of the Woods;—thence, along the said line to the said most northwestern point, being in latitude 49° 23′55″ north, and in longitude 95°14′38″ west from the Observatory at Greenwich; thence, according to existing treaties,[1] due south to its intersection with the 49th parallel of north latitude, and along that parallel to the Rocky Mountains. It being understood that all the water-communications, and all the usual portages along the line from Lake Superior to the Lake of the Woods; and also Grand Portage, from the shore of Lake Superior to the Pigeon river, as now actually used, shall be free and open to the use of the citizens and subjects of both countries.

Article III.

In order to promote the interests and encourage the industry of all the inhabitants of the countries watered by the river St John and its tributaries, whether living within the State of Maine or the Province of New Brunswick, it is agreed that, where, by the provisions of the present treaty, the river St John is declared to be the line of boundary, the navigation of the said river shall be free and open to both Parties, and shall in no way be obstructed by either: That all the produce of the forest, in logs, lumber, timber, boards, staves, or shingles, or of agricul-

---

[1] See Documents 40 and 56.

ture not being manufactured, grown on any of those parts of the State of Maine watered by the river Sᵗ John, or by its tributaries, of which fact reasonable evidence shall, if required, be produced, shall have free access into and through the said river and its said tributaries, having their source within the State of Maine, to and from the seaport at the mouth of the said river Sᵗ John's, and to and round the Falls of the said river, either by boats, rafts, or other conveyance: That when within the Province of New Brunswick, the said produce shall be dealt with as if it were the produce of the said province: That, in like manner, the inhabitants of the Territory of the Upper Sᵗ John determined by this Treaty to belong to her Britannic Majesty, shall have free access to and through the river for their produce, in those parts where the said river runs wholly through the State of Maine: provided always, that this agreement shall give no right to either party to interfere with any regulations not inconsistent with the terms of this treaty which the Governments, respectively, of Maine or of New Brunswick, may make respecting the navigation of the said river, where both banks thereof shall belong to the same Party.

ARTICLE IV.

All grants of land heretofore made by either Party, within the limits of the territory which by this Treaty falls within the dominions of the other Party, shall be held valid, ratified, and confirmed to the persons in possession under such grants, to the same extent as if such territory had by this Treaty fallen within the dominions of the Party by whom such grants were made: And all equitable possessory claims, arising from a possession and improvement of any lot or parcel of land by the person actually in possession, or by those under whom such person claims, for more than six years before the date of this Treaty, shall, in like manner, be deemed valid, and be confirmed and quieted by a release to the person entitled thereto, of the title to such lot or parcel of land, so described as best to include the improvements made thereon; and in all other respects the two contracting Parties agree to deal upon the most liberal principles of equity with the settlers actually dwelling upon the Territory falling to them, respectively, which has heretofore been in dispute between them.

ARTICLE V.

Whereas, in the course of the controversy respecting the disputed Territory on the northeastern boundary, some moneys have been received by the authorities of Her Britannic Majesty's Province of New

Brunswick, with the intention of preventing depredations on the forests of the said Territory, which moneys were to be carried to a fund called the "Disputed Territory Fund", the proceeds whereof, it was agreed, should be hereafter paid over to the Parties interested, in the proportions to be determined by a final settlement of boundaries: It is hereby agreed, that a correct account of all receipts and payments on the said fund, shall be delivered to the Government of the United States, within six months after the ratification of this Treaty; and the proportion of the amount due thereon to the States of Maine and Massachusetts, and any bonds or securities appertaining thereto, shall be paid and delivered over to the Government of the United States; and the Government of the United States agrees to receive for the use of, and pay over to the States of Maine and Massachusetts, their respective portions of said Fund: And further to pay and satisfy said States, respectively, for all claims for expenses incurred by them in protecting the said heretofore disputed Territory, and making a survey thereof, in 1838; the Government of the United States agreeing with the States of Maine and Massachusetts to pay them the further sum of three hundred thousand dollars, in equal moieties, on account of their assent to the line of boundary described in this Treaty, and in consideration of the conditions and equivalents received therefor, from the Government of Her Britannic Majesty.

ARTICLE VI.

It is furthermore understood and agreed, that for the purpose of running and tracing those parts of the line between the source of the S⁺ Croix and the S⁺ Lawrence river, which will require to be run and ascertained, and for marking the residue of said line by proper monuments on the land, two Commissioners shall be appointed, one by the President of the United States, by and with the advice and consent of the Senate thereof, and one by Her Britannic Majesty: and the said commissioners shall meet at Bangor, in the State of Maine, on the first day of May next, or as soon thereafter as may be, and shall proceed to mark the line above described, from the source of the S⁺ Croix to the river S⁺ John; and shall trace on proper maps the dividing line along said river, and along the river S⁺ Francis, to the outlet of the Lake Pohenagamook; and from the outlet of the said Lake, they shall ascertain, fix, and mark by proper and durable monuments on the land, the line described in the first article of this Treaty; and the said Commissioners shall make to each of their respective Governments a joint report or declaration, under their hands and seals, designating such line of boundary, and shall accompany such report or declaration with maps certified by them to be true maps of the new boundary.

Article VII.

It is further agreed, that the channels in the river St Lawrence, on both sides of the Long Sault Islands and of Barnhart Island; the channels in the river Detroit, on both sides of the Island Bois Blanc, and between that Island and both the American and Canadian shores; and all the several channels and passages between the various Islands lying near the junction of the river St Clair with the lake of that name, shall be equally free and open to the ships, vessels, and boats of both Parties.

Article VIII.

The Parties mutually stipulate that each shall prepare, equip, and maintain in service, on the coast of Africa, a sufficient and adequate squadron, or naval force of vessels, of suitable numbers and descriptions, to carry in all not less than eighty guns, to enforce, separately and respectively, the laws rights and obligations of each of the two countries, for the suppression of the Slave Trade, the said squadrons to be independent of each other, but the two Governments stipulating, nevertheless, to give such orders to the officers commanding their respective forces, as shall enable them most effectually to act in concert and coöperation, upon mutual consultation, as exigencies may arise, for the attainment of the true object of this article; copies of all such orders to be communicated by each Government to the other respectively.

Article IX.

Whereas, notwithstanding all efforts which may be made on the coast of Africa for Suppressing the Slave Trade, the facilities for carrying on that traffic and avoiding the vigilance of cruisers by the fraudulent use of flags, and other means, are so great, and the temptations for pursuing it, while a market can be found for Slaves, so strong, as that the desired result may be long delayed, unless all markets be shut against the purchase of African negroes, the Parties to this Treaty agree that they will unite in all becoming representations and remonstrances, with any and all Powers within whose dominions such markets are allowed to exist; and that they will urge upon all such Powers the propriety and duty of closing such markets effectually at once and forever.

Article X.

It is agreed that the United States and Her Britannic Majesty shall, upon mutual requisitions by them, or their Ministers, Officers, or authorities, respectively made, deliver up to justice, all persons who, being charged with the crime of murder, or assault with intent to

commit murder, or Piracy, or arson, or robbery, or Forgery, or the utterance of forged paper, committed within the jurisdiction of either, shall seek an asylum, or shall be found, within the territories of the other: Provided, that this shall only be done upon such evidence of criminality as, according to the laws of the place where the fugitive or person so charged, shall be found, would justify his apprehension and commitment for trial, if the crime or offence had there been committed: And the respective Judges and other Magistrates of the two Governments, shall have power, jurisdiction, and authority, upon complaint made under oath, to issue a warrant for the apprehension of the fugitive or person so charged, that he may be brought before such Judges or other Magistrates, respectively, to the end that the evidence of criminality may be heard and considered; and if, on such hearing, the evidence be deemed sufficient to sustain the charge it shall be the duty of the examining Judge or Magistrate, to certify the same to the proper Executive Authority, that a warrant may issue for the surrender of such fugitive. The expense of such apprehension and delivery shall be borne and defrayed by the Party who makes the requisition, and receives the fugitive.

ARTICLE XI.

The eighth article of this Treaty shall be in force for five years from the date of the exchange of the ratifications, and afterwards until one or the other Party shall signify a wish to terminate it. The tenth article shall continue in force until one or the other of the Parties shall signify its wish to terminate it, and no longer.

ARTICLE XII.

The present Treaty shall be duly ratified, and the mutual exchange of ratifications shall take place in London, within six months from the date hereof, or earlier if possible.

In Faith whereof, we, the respective Plenipotentiaries, have signed this Treaty, and have hereunto affixed our Seals.

Done, in duplicate, at Washington, the ninth day of August, Anno Domini one thousand eight hundred and forty-two.

DAN¹ WEBSTER   ASHBURTON
    [Seal]   [Seal]

[*Her Britannic Majesty's Minister Plenipotentiary on Special Mission, to the Secretary of State*]

WASHINGTON 9ᵗʰ August 1842

SIR,   It appears desirable that some explanation between us should be recorded by correspondence respecting the fifth Article of the Treaty signed by us this day for the settlement of Boundaries between Great Britain and the United States.

By that Article of the Treaty it is stipulated, that certain payments shall be made by the Government of the United States to the States of Maine and Massachusetts.   It has of course been understood that my negotiations have been with the Government of the United States, and the introduction of terms of agreement between the General Government and the States would have been irregular and inadmissible, if it had not been deemed expedient to bring the whole of these transactions within the purview of the Treaty.   There may not be wanting analogous cases to justify this proceeding, but it seems proper that I should have confirmed by you, that my Government incurs no responsibility for these engagements, of the precise nature and object of which I am uninformed, nor have I considered it necessary to make enquiry concerning them.

I beg, Sir, to renew to you the assurances of my high consideration

ASHBURTON

The Honᵇˡᵉ DANIEL WEBSTER
&c &c &c

———

[*The Secretary of State to Her Britannic Majesty's Minister Plenipotentiary on Special Mission*]

DEPARTMENT OF STATE,
Washington, Augt. 9, 1842.

Lord ASHBURTON,
&ᶜ, &ᶜ, &ᶜ

MY LORD: I have the honor to acknowledge the receipt of your note of the 9ᵗʰ of August, with respect to the object and intention of the 5ᵗʰ article of the treaty.   What you say in regard to that subject is quite correct. It purports to contain no stipulation on the part of Great Britain, nor is any responsibility supposed to be incurred by it, on the part of your Government.

I renew, my Lord, the assurance of my distinguished consideration.

DANˡ WEBSTER.

[Her Britannic Majesty's Minister Plenipotentiary on Special Mission, to the Secretary of State]

WASHINGTON *9ᵗʰ August 1842*

SIR, By the 3ʳᵈ article[1] of the Convention which I have this day signed with you there is an agreement for the reciprocal delivery in certain cases of criminals fugitive from justice, but it becomes necessary that I should apprize you that this article can have no legal effect within the Dominions of Great Britain until confirmed by Act of Parliament.[2] It is possible that Parliament may not be in Session before the Exchange of the ratifications of the Convention, but its sanction shall be asked at the earliest possible period and no doubt can be entertained that it will be given. In Her Majesty's territories in Canada, where cases for acting under this convention are likely to be of more frequent occurrence, the Governor General has sufficient power under the authority of local legislation, and the Convention will there be acted upon, so soon as its ratification shall be known, but it becomes my duty to inform you of the short delay which may possibly intervene in giving full effect to it where the confirmation by Parliament becomes necessary for its execution.

I beg, Sir, to renew to you the assurance of my high consideration

ASHBURTON

The Honᵇˡᵉ DANIEL WEBSTER
&c &c &c

NOTES

Following the treaty text are printed three notes which were exchanged between the Plenipotentiaries of the two Governments on August 9, 1842, the date of the signature of the treaty. The two notes of Lord Ashburton are from the originals in D.S., 21 Notes from the British Legation; the note of Secretary of State Webster is from the record copy in D.S., 6 Notes to the British Legation, 273. Those three notes were among the papers accompanying the treaty when it was submitted to the Senate with the presidential message of August 11, 1842 (Executive Journal, VI, 118–24; Senate Document No. 1, 27th Congress, 3d session, serial 413, hereafter usually cited as "published correspondence"); but they were not mentioned in the Senate resolution of advice and consent (Executive Journal, VI, 131) or referred to in either instrument of ratification.

The Senate proceedings were not prolonged; the treaty was reported from the Committee on Foreign Relations on August 15, and the final vote (yeas 39, noes 9) was had five days later (*ibid.*, 124–31);

[1] I.e., Article 10 of the Webster-Ashburton Treaty. As to the convention first signed, see the editorial notes.
[2] The act of Parliament is 6 and 7 Victoria, ch. 76, August 22, 1843.

a resolution of August 30 provided for the removal of the injunction of secrecy "as soon as the ratifications of the said treaty shall have been exchanged and it shall have been proclaimed by the President" (*ibid.*, 145); the "speeches and remarks" are printed in Congressional Globe, XII, appendix.

The treaty was communicated to Congress with the annual message of December 6, 1842 (Richardson, IV, 194–209); the papers with the message included those accompanying the treaty when it was submitted to the Senate (Senate Document No. 1, 27th Congress, 3d session, serial 413, pp. 19–145; House Document No. 2, 27th Congress, 3d session, serial 418, pp. 17–143).

The File Papers

The Department of State file of this treaty is complete. It is stated in the final clause of the treaty that it was done "in duplicate"; the signed original in the file forms part of the duplicate United States instrument of ratification of August 22, 1842, and of the proclamation of November 10. The other three essential papers are also in the file, namely, the attested Senate resolution of August 20 (Executive Journal, VI, 131), the British instrument of ratification of October 5, and the certificate of the exchange of ratifications at London, signed by Edward Everett, Minister at London, and Lord Aberdeen, British Secretary of State for Foreign Affairs, on October 13, 1842. All the documents mentioned are in customary form.

The British instrument of ratification shows that the principle of the *alternat* was duly observed. In the text of the treaty therein included Her Britannic Majesty is named first throughout, and the signature of Lord Ashburton appears at the left.

One very unusual feature of this treaty file is that it contains the quill pen with which the treaty was signed by Daniel Webster. On December 27, 1927, that pen was presented to the Department of State by Mrs. Archibald Hopkins (Charlotte Everett Hopkins), granddaughter of Edward Everett, who was American Minister at London at the time of the Webster-Ashburton Treaty and who in 1852 became Secretary of State upon the death of Webster, who had in 1850, under President Fillmore, for the second time accepted that office. In his letter of acknowledgment and appreciation of January 6, 1928, Secretary of State Kellogg wrote to Mrs. Hopkins: "The pen, together with your letter of presentation, has been placed in the box which contains the original treaty and will thereby become a part of the permanent treaty records of the Department."

The Full Powers

The "reciprocal communication of their respective full powers", mentioned in the preamble of the treaty, appears to have taken place, in part, during the "preliminary conferences" mentioned in the note of Lord Ashburton of June 13, 1842 (published correspondence, 34). That was the opening note of the formal correspondence between the two Plenipotentiaries and was written after Ashburton had been in

Washington for more than two months, as he arrived there on April 4 and was presented to President Tyler on April 6. The extent of the authority of Ashburton in regard to the northeastern boundary question was stated in the letters of Webster to the Governors of Maine and Massachusetts, dated April 11 (*ibid.*, 64–66), to be "to treat for a conventional line, or line by agreement, on such terms and conditions, and with such mutual considerations and equivalents, as may be thought just and equitable, and that he is ready to enter upon a negotiation for such conventional line, so soon as this Government shall say it is authorized and ready, on its part, to commence such negotiation." Webster's note to Ashburton of June 17 (*ibid.*, 38) refers in similar language to the authority of the latter in relation to the question of the northeastern boundary, mentions the announcement thereof as having been made "on his arrival at Washington", and speaks of "Lord Ashburton having been charged by the Queen's Government with full powers to negotiate and settle all matters in discussion between the United States and England".

The full power of Ashburton was written in very sweeping terms; a copy thereof, which omits the name of the British Plenipotentiary, is in D.S., 21 Notes from the British Legation, as follows:

Victoria R

Victoria &c To all and singular to whom these presents shall come Greeting Whereas for the better treating of and arranging certain matters which are now in discussion, or which may come into discussion, between Us and Our Good Friends the United States of America We have judged it expedient to invest a fit person with full Power to conduct the said discussion on our part: Know ye therefore that We reposing especial Trust and confidence in the Wisdom, Loyalty, Diligence, and Circumspection, of our Right Trusty and Well-beloved &c have named, made, constituted, and appointed, as We do by these presents, name, make, constitute, and appoint, him Our undoubted Commissioner Procurator, and Plenipotentiary Giving to him all manner of power and authority to treat adjust and conclude, with such Minister or Ministers as may be vested with similar power and authority on the part of Our said Good Friends the United States of America any Treaty or Agreement that may tend to the attainment of the above mentioned end, and to sign for Us, and in Our Name, every-thing so agreed upon and concluded and to do and transact all such other matters as may appertain to the finishing of the aforesaid work, in as ample manner and form, and with equal force and efficacy as We ourselves could do, if Personally present. Engaging and Promising upon Our Royal Word that whatever things shall be so transacted and concluded by Our said Commissioner Procurator and Plenipotentiary, shall be agreed to, acknowledged, and accepted by Us in the fullest manner, and that We will never suffer, either in the whole, or in part, any person whatsoever to infringe the same, or act contrary thereto. In Witness whereof We have caused the Great Seal of Our United Kingdom of G⁺ Britain and Ireland to be affixed to these Presents, which We have Signed with our Royal Hand. Given at Our Court at Windsor Castle the eighteenth day of January, in the year of our Lord One Thousand Eight Hundred and Forty Two, and in the Fifth Year of Our Reign

While the note of Webster of June 17, 1842, above mentioned, states that he was "duly authorized" to treat for a conventional line for the northeastern boundary, his full power was not issued until August 1 (D.S., 3 Credences, 19). While in customary form, its terms of substance were also very broad, as follows:

Know Ye, That I have given and granted, and do hereby give and grant to Daniel Webster, Secretary of State of the United States, full power and authority, and also general and special command, to meet and confer with Her Britannic Majesty's Minister, Special and Extraordinary, of and concerning all matters in controversy or in discussion between the said United States and the Government of Her Britannic Majesty, or respecting the interests of the two Nations; and to conclude and sign a treaty or treaties, convention or conventions touching the premises, for the final ratification of the President of the United States, by and with the advice and consent of the Senate thereof.

THE EARLIER FORM OF THE AGREEMENT

As first drawn up and signed on August 9, 1842, the agreement between the two Governments was embodied in two instruments, a treaty and a convention. On the following day, August 10, but under date of August 9, the clauses of those two instruments were combined into one, the treaty here printed as the Webster-Ashburton Treaty.

In the earlier form the separate treaty ("to settle and define the Boundaries between the possessions of Her Britannic Majesty in North America and the territories of the United States") comprised eight articles, which corresponded to Articles 1–7 and 12 of the Webster-Ashburton Treaty; the ratification and testimonium clauses were differently worded; and the preambles of the treaty and of the convention first signed were combined, with slight changes, in the later form.

In the earlier form the convention (of five articles, "for the final suppression of the African Slave Trade, and for the giving up of criminals, fugitive from justice, in certain cases") contained as its Articles 1–3, Articles 8–10 of this treaty. Article 4 of the convention was the same as Article 11 of this treaty except that it provided that the first two articles of the convention (or Articles 8 and 9 of this treaty) "shall be in force for five years" and thereafter until either party should desire to terminate them, whereas the similar clause in Article 11 of this treaty relates only to Article 8. Article 5 of the convention contained the ratification clause of Article 12.

On August 9 Lord Ashburton wrote various despatches to Lord Aberdeen, Secretary of State for Foreign Affairs, two of which enclosed, respectively, the treaty and the convention signed that day (Library of Congress, Ashburton Papers, facsimiles from the Public Record Office, London, Foreign Office Records, America, 5, vols. 378, 379, 380; hereafter cited as "Ashburton Papers"). Despatch No. 17, which enclosed the treaty, has this as its opening paragraph:

I have much satisfaction in informing your Lordship that my tedious negotiation for the settlement of Boundaries between Her Majesty's Dominions and the United States of America is at last closed. The Treaty was signed this day by Mr Webster the Secretary of State and myself, and it will be submitted for ratification to the Senate tomorrow. The original accompanies this Despatch, and I have also the honor of inclosing a Copy for your Lordship's information.

Despatch No. 18 (*ibid.*) enclosed the convention, and its first paragraph reads thus:

167951°—vol. 4—34——26

I have the honour of herewith transmitting in original, accompanied by a copy, a Convention signed this day with Mr Webster, Secretary of State of the United States, for the joint measures agreed to be undertaken between the two countries for the suppression of of the Slave trade, and containing also an agreement for the reciprocal delivery in certain cases of criminals fugitive from justice. I hope that the terms of the Convention will be satisfactory to Her Majesty's Government.

Ashburton's explanation of the change of form and his statement regarding the making of the "consolidated" treaty are in his despatch of August 13 (*ibid.*, despatch No. 23), as follows (see Tyler, Letters and Times of the Tylers, II, 224–25):

I had the honor of sending by the messenger Wright in the Great Western Steamer the original Treaty and Convention signed here on the 9th instant, with the Secretary of State. The Treaty being for the settlement of Boundaries, and the Convention to provide for further measures for the prevention of the Slave Trade, and the extradition of Criminals fugitive from Justice.

The morning after the departure of the Courier, it was suggested from quarters entitled to weight and consideration [President Tyler], that it was desirable that these separate instruments should be thrown into one. This was immediately done, and I have now the honor of transmitting Copy of the one Treaty so consolidated. As I have no remaining messenger here I thought it most prudent to take the original in my own custody on returning home by H.M.S. Warspite, now waiting in New York harbour. As this Treaty will in no case have to be published or acted upon at home before ratification, I trust this alteration will occasion no inconvenience. The reasons assigned for it seemed to me well founded although I abstain for the present from discussing them. It may be well, if your Lordship sees no objection, that the signatures of Mr Webster to the Treaty and convention be cancelled in the presence of Mr Everett. [No such cancelation is mentioned in the despatches from London.]

This change delayed for one day the communication to the Senate of all the papers relating to our negotiations. They were presented there with a Message from the President the 11th instant, and after reading the Treaty and a portion of the papers they were ordered to be printed, and the question of ratification will be discussed in the early part of next week. I am under no great apprehension as to the result, although in the present excited state of parties no perfect reliance can be placed on any thing. I am told that there will certainly be opposition arising from some interests not being perfectly satisfied, but the general opinion in and out of Congress is, to make a settlement and I trust the conditions when they become known will prove acceptable. When all the correspondence and Treaty are printed together it is not unlikely that the Senate may publish them, relieving their members from their usual obligation of secresy, and thus satisfying the impatience of the public.

It is generally expected and seems indeed almost certain that Congress will be prorogued the 22d without passing the Tariff bill, or making any further provision for the exhausted State of the Treasury.

No record of the treaty and convention first signed has been found in the archives of the Department of State. In the earlier form the agreement does not appear ever to have been printed, although various writers have commented on the change (e.g., Ephraim Douglass Adams, "Lord Ashburton and the Treaty of Washington", in American Historical Review, XVII, 764–82). Copies of the treaty and convention first signed are among the Ashburton Papers, with Ashburton's despatches above cited (Nos. 17 and 18).

It is to be observed that the second of the two notes of Ashburton of August 9, 1842, which are printed above following the treaty text, refers to Article 3 of the convention, which in the final form of the

agreement became Article 10 of this treaty. The mention in the first note of Ashburton of August 9, 1842, of Article 5 of the treaty, while referring, when written, to Article 5 of the treaty as first signed, is equally a reference to Article 5 of the treaty in its final form.

THE SCOPE OF THE NEGOTIATIONS

When this treaty was made, and for years thereafter, it was generally known as the Treaty of Washington, and was so styled in legislation and in diplomatic correspondence; but now the agreement usually called the Treaty of Washington is that of May 8, 1871, with Great Britain; and this treaty, from the names of its negotiators, Secretary of State Daniel Webster for the United States and Lord Ashburton, Her Britannic Majesty's Minister Plenipotentiary on Special Mission, for Great Britain, is commonly known as the Webster-Ashburton Treaty.

On December 27, 1841, Lord Aberdeen, British Secretary of State for Foreign Affairs, informed Edward Everett, American Minister at London, that Her Majesty's Government had decided to send "a special Minister to the United States" and that "Lord Ashburton would go with full powers to make a definitive arrangement on every point in discussion between the two countries. He [Lord Aberdeen] was aware of the difficulty of some of them, particularly what had incorrectly been called the right of search, which he deemed the most difficult of all; but he was willing to confide this and all other matters in controversy to Lord Ashburton's discretion" (D.S., 49 Despatches, Great Britain, No. 5, December 31, 1841).

The negotiations covered almost all the then pending differences between the United States and Great Britain; the northwestern boundary from the Rocky Mountains to the Pacific was left to the future (see the treaty of June 15, 1846, with Great Britain); but this treaty, in Article 1, dealt with the northeastern boundary from the source of the River St. Croix to the St. Lawrence River and, in Article 2, with the line from the foot of Neebish Rapids (between Lake Superior and Lake Huron) to the Lake of the Woods. These provisions, with those of earlier treaties and the decisions reached thereunder, meant that there was a definitive agreement as to the Canadian boundary from the mouth of the St. Croix to the Rocky Mountains; for the declaration of 1798 (Document 23) had fixed the line of the St. Croix River; the proceedings (Document 42) under Article 6 of the Treaty of Ghent (Document 33) had determined the line in the St. Lawrence and in Lakes Ontario, Erie, and Huron; and the line from the Lake of the Woods to the Rocky Mountains had been described in terms of geography by Article 2 of the convention of October 20, 1818 (Document 40); and there had also been a decision as to the islands in Passamaquoddy Bay and the Bay of Fundy (Document 39). The clauses of Articles 3–6 of this treaty form part of the northeastern boundary agreement; and those of Article 7, for free passage, of the frontier accord as a whole.

The suppression of the African slave trade was the subject of Articles 8 and 9 of this treaty; the extradition clauses of Article 10

were intended particularly to meet cases of fugitives from justice on one side or the other of the Canadian frontier; and the notes exchanged during the course of the negotiations made the case of the *Caroline* a closed incident, dealt with the general question involved in such cases as that of the *Creole*, and discussed impressment. In no legal sense are those exchanges to be deemed part of the agreement of the treaty; but at the time they (or at least some of them) were politically indispensable adjuncts of the treaty.

That correspondence, with numerous other papers, accompanied the message of President Tyler of August 11, 1842, transmitting the treaty to the Senate; the papers are printed in Senate Document No. 1, 27th Congress, 3d session, serial 413, pages 19–145. That document, as above stated, is herein generally cited as "published correspondence"; the same papers, but with different pagination, are in House Document No. 2, 27th Congress, 3d session, serial 418, pages 17–143.

The literature regarding the Webster-Ashburton Treaty is abundant; a recent account of the negotiations, with many citations and a valuable bibliographical note of the sources for the life and work of Daniel Webster, is in American Secretaries of State and Their Diplomacy, V, 12–53, 339–48 (by Clyde Augustus Duniway).

ARTICLE 1

The provisions of Article 1 of the Webster-Ashburton Treaty, with which are to be read those of Articles 3–6, are a conventional settlement of what had long been known as the "northeastern boundary question", which had troubled the relations of the two Governments for many years. During the decade following the decision of the King of the Netherlands of January 10, 1831 (as to which, see the notes to Document 58), discussion of the northeastern boundary question between the two Governments continued; the diplomatic exchanges during the administrations of Presidents Jackson and Van Buren were voluminous (see Blue Books, 1838, 1840, 1843, North American Boundary, "Correspondence Relating to the Boundary between the British Possessions in North America and the United States of America, under the Treaty of 1783"); there were "many projects and counterprojects, and in the mean time [1839–42] new but independent surveys were made by both governments" (Moore, International Arbitrations, I, 141; the last report, dated March 28, 1842, of the survey made by the United States is in House Document No. 31, 27th Congress, 3d session, serial 420; in the Blue Book of 1840, pt. 2, is the report of the British Commissioners, Lieutenant Colonel Richard Zachariah Mudge and George William Featherstonhaugh, of April 16, 1840, with maps; and in the Blue Book of 1842 are the supplementary reports, of November 28, 1840, with a profile, and of February 11, 1842, with a map, of Captain W. E. Delves Broughton and James D. Featherstonhaugh, who completed the British survey); but nothing resulted from any of those negotiations and discussions (see Moore, *op. cit.*, 138–46, and the writings there cited). The act of March 3,

1839 (5 Statutes at Large, 355–56), is of itself evidence of the grave possibilities that existed (see also the acts of July 20, 1840, and February 27, 1841, *ibid.*, 402, 413–14).

Indeed, "something like a border war", known as the "Restook war", broke out in 1838–39 (Moore, *op. cit.*, 145–46); a memorandum of terms for avoiding "hostile collision", which had, however, "but the force of recommendation on the provincial authorities and on the government of the State" of Maine, and which was signed on February 27, 1839, by Secretary of State Forsyth and the British Minister at Washington, Henry S. Fox, was transmitted to Congress on the day of its date (Richardson, III, 521–27; D.S., 6 Notes to the British Legation, 104–6); it was followed by an arrangement between New Brunswick and Maine, negotiated by General Winfield Scott, who had been sent to the region for the purpose; declarations were signed on the part of New Brunswick (March 23) and on the part of Maine (March 25, 1839), by which "Sir John Harvey [Lieutenant Governor of New Brunswick] bound himself not to seek, without renewed instructions to that effect from his Government, to take military possession of the territory, or to expel from it by military force, the armed civil posse, or the troops of Maine. On the part of Maine it was agreed by her Governor [John Fairfield] that no attempt should be made, without renewed instructions from the Legislature, to disturb by arms the Province of New Brunswick in the possession of the Madawaska settlement, or interrupt the usual communications between that and the Upper Provinces. As to possession and jurisdiction, they were to remain unchanged, each party holding, in fact, possession of part of the disputed territory, but each denying the right of the other to do so. With that understanding Maine was, without unnecessary delay, to withdraw her military force, leaving only, under a Land Agent, a small civil posse, armed or unarmed, to protect the timber recently cut, and to prevent further depredations" (note of Forsyth to Fox, March 25, 1840; D.S., 6 Notes to the British Legation, 160–67; Richardson, III, 582–86; see Scott, Memoirs of Lieut.-General Scott, II, 331–51; for the declarations and previous correspondence, see House Document No. 169, 26th Congress, 1st session, serial 366).

In 1841 there was a change of administration in both countries; Daniel Webster became Secretary of State under President William Henry Harrison on March 6, 1841, and continued in office under President Tyler from April 6, 1841; the Earl of Aberdeen succeeded Viscount Palmerston at the British Foreign Office on the following September 3, when Sir Robert Peel became Prime Minister in lieu of Lord Melbourne; the negotiations between the Governments under their new administrations took a different form, were of wider scope, and were successful.

A summary account of the northeastern boundary question is contained in the notes to the convention with Great Britain of September 29, 1827 (Document 58), to which, and to the writings there cited, reference is made.

In the Joint Report upon the Survey and Demarcation of the Boundary between the United States and Canada from the Source

of the St. Croix River to the St. Lawrence River, submitted to the Secretary of State on October 30, 1924, and published under the authority of the International Boundary Commissioners in 1925, is a "Historical Sketch of the Genesis of the International Boundary from the Source of the St. Croix River to the St. Lawrence River", covering the period from the bull of Pope Alexander VI in 1493 to the Webster-Ashburton Treaty of 1842 (appendix I, 269–94), with a map (facing p. 270) showing graphically the claims of the United States and Great Britain at various dates.

In Paullin, Atlas of the Historical Geography of the United States, are maps showing the various lines of the international boundary from time to time proposed and agreed upon, from the St. Lawrence River to the Bay of Fundy (plates 89, 90, 91A, 91C, 92A, 92B, 93A, and 93D). The relevant text in the work cited is at pages 52–62.

In a report prepared for the Department of State in 1906 by Chandler P. Anderson, entitled "Canadian Questions: Northern Boundary of the United States", there is incorporated a condensed history of the chief points in dispute in the controversy known as the "northeastern boundary question", of the negotiations, and of the settlement by Article 1 of this treaty. That report was written for Secretary of State Root in connection with the negotiations that resulted in the treaty with Great Britain of April 11, 1908; certain extracts therefrom (pp. 8–13, 20) follow:

This portion of the boundary [from the mouth of the St. Croix River to the St. Lawrence River] as originally described in the provisional peace articles of 1782 [Document 7], and repeated in Article II of the Definitive Treaty of Peace of 1783 [Document 11], is divided into a northern and an eastern boundary. . . .

Unfortunately, no map showing the location of the boundary line as agreed upon was annexed to these treaties, and the line was not even marked on any maps mutually accepted by the negotiators. This was doubtless due to the fact that most of the region through which the line was to run had never been surveyed, so that very little was known about it and the existing maps were understood to be inaccurate. The exact location of the boundary, therefore, was left to be determined by applying the general description of the boundary as defined in the treaty to the topographical conditions as afterwards ascertained.

When this came to be done it was found that the conditions assumed by the treaty description as existing were in many respects inaccurately stated, and disputes arose as to the location of this portion of the line throughout almost its entire length. As stated by President Jefferson in his annual message of October 17, 1803:

"A further knowledge of the ground in the northeastern and northwestern angles of the United States has evinced that the boundaries established by the Treaty of Paris between the British territories and ours in those parts were too imperfectly described to be susceptible of execution." (Richardson's Messages and Papers of the Presidents, Vol. I, p. 359.)

The first dispute to be taken up for settlement was the identity of the River St. Croix named in the treaty, and Commissioners were appointed under Article V of the Treaty of 1794 [the Jay Treaty, Document 16] "to decide what river is the River St. Croix intended by the treaty." . . . A full history of the proceedings and the controversy will be found in Moore on International Arbitrations, volume 1, pages 1–143. [A still more complete account is in Moore, International Adjudications, Modern Series, I and II.]

The Commissioners agreed upon the river now known as the St. Croix, and on October 25, 1798, rendered their decision so declaring and describing with par-

ticularity the course of this river to its source.   Maps in duplicate surveyed under the direction of the Commissioners, showing the river thus identified as the St. Croix, were signed by the Commissioners and filed with their decision.   [See Document 23 and the notes thereto regarding the original map of the Commissioners.]

It will be noted that Article V of the Treaty of 1794 [the Jay Treaty, Document 16], above referred to, required the Commissioners to particularize the latitude and longitude of the mouth and of the source of the river. Owing to the delays in the field work, however, difficulties arose in executing this requirement, and in 1798 "an explanatory article to the Treaty of November 19, 1794" [Document 22], was concluded, releasing the Commissioners from particularizing the latitude and longitude of the source of the river, and agreeing instead that they might describe the river "in such other manner as they may judge expedient," and "that no uncertainty may hereafter exist on this subject" it was further agreed that the two Governments should concert measures "to erect and keep in repair a suitable monument at the place ascertained and described to be the source of the said River St. Croix."   The location of the source of the River St. Croix on the map filed by the Commissioners fulfilled these requirements and a monument was thereafter erected on the spot indicated as the source.   In thus determining the identity of the St. Croix and locating its source the location of that portion of the eastern boundary "to be drawn along the middle of the St. Croix" from its mouth to its source was settled, and at the same time the starting point was established for the rest of the eastern boundary, which, by the terms of the treaty, was to be drawn from the source of that river directly north to the "highlands" at the northwest angle of Nova Scotia.

It still remained, however, to determine what constituted the "highlands" and "the northwest angle of Nova Scotia" referred to in the treaty description, which were matters in dispute.

By reference to the treaty [of 1783, Document 11] it will be found that the northwest angle is defined as "that angle which is formed by a line drawn due north from the source of the St. Croix River to the Highlands" and the "highlands" were referred to as "the said Highlands which divide those rivers that empty themselves into the River St. Lawrence from those which fall into the Atlantic Ocean."

It is evident from the description that the negotiators of the treaty, in defining this portion of the boundary, assumed that there was a well-defined ridge or height of land throughout this region forming a watershed between the St. Lawrence and the Atlantic.   When an attempt was made to actually locate the line, however, it was found that no such well-defined highlands existed at a point due north of the source of the St. Croix, and consequently that the location of the northwest angle of Nova Scotia, which was to be formed by a line drawn due north from the source of the St. Croix to such "highlands," could not be accurately determined under the treaty description.

This defect in the description also prevented the location of that portion of the northern line starting at this unlocated angle, from which the line was to run "along the said Highlands * * * to the northwesternmost head of Connecticut River."

Difficulties were also presented in locating the farther end of this section of the line on account of the uncertainty as to which of several branches should be taken as the "northwesternmost head of Connecticut River."

Through the greater part of the region between these two points a height of land can be traced, dividing the waters flowing into the St. Lawrence from those flowing into the Atlantic, but without a starting point accurately fixed at either end of the line it was difficult to determine the exact location of even that portion of the boundary.   The boundary described in the Treaty of 1783 [Document 11] was intended to conform as near as might be to the previously established boundaries along the southern borders of the Provinces of Quebec and Nova Scotia. The southern boundary of Quebec as then established ran along the highlands from the Bay of Chaleurs to the source of the Connecticut River, but this height of land was not mutually regarded as accurately fulfilling the requirements of the treaty description, and ultimately the boundary through this entire region became involved in the dispute.

The location of the line along the Connecticut River from its "northwestern-most head" to the 45th degree of north latitude was also dependent upon the determination of which of the several heads should be taken as the starting point, and that, as above stated, was one of the questions in dispute. On the part of the United States it was claimed that the most westerly branch, known as "Hall's Stream," was the one intended. It, appeared, however, that this branch did not join the main river until it had passed below the 45th parallel, and therefore if this branch was selected a line along the 45th parallel would not strike the Connecticut River at all. For that reason, among others, it was urged on the part of Great Britain that Hall's Stream should be rejected and a more easterly branch selected, joining with the main part of the Connecticut River considerably farther up.

From the Connecticut River at the 45th degree of north latitude to the St. Lawrence the description of the boundary was:

> "From thence, by a line due west on said latitude, until it strikes the river Iroquois or Cataraquy."

This section of the line was certainly described with sufficient accuracy to avoid any dispute as to its exact location, but here again difficulties arose, for it was found that the treaty line did not follow the old established boundary as actually laid down in 1774 between the Provinces of New York and Quebec, which boundary the negotiators of the treaty had intended to adopt. . . .

The 45th parallel had been fixed along this portion of the line as the boundary between the Provinces of New York and Quebec by a grant from James I in 1606, and again by royal proclamation in 1763, and finally it was confirmed as the boundary on August 12, 1768, by an order in council.

Between the years 1771 and 1774 this portion of the line was surveyed and monumented and thereafter was known as the "Valentine and Collins line," from the names of the surveyors surveying it. Their survey was intended to lay the line along the 45th parallel, and it was supposed that this had been accomplished, and the line as laid out was accepted and vested interests on each side had been acquired in reliance upon it, and at the time of the Treaty of Peace it was established in full force.

No question seems to have arisen with respect to the accuracy of its location until 1818, when in the autumn of that year the British and American surveyors, acting under the Commission appointed by the Treaty of Ghent for the settlement of this boundary, discovered that at the Connecticut River, and also at Lake Champlain, the true parallel lay about three-fourths of a mile south of the old line. At Rouses Point in Lake Champlain, which was only about one-fourth of a mile south of the old line and therefore north of the true parallel, the United States had at that time constructed a fort at a cost of about a million dollars, which would be thrown into Canadian territory if the old line was abandoned as the boundary and the 45th parallel established instead.

At other points also the old line varied considerably both to the north and south of the 45th parallel, although it was found to coincide with it at the St. Lawrence River. . . .

Such, in brief, were the chief points of dispute along this portion of the boundary from the St. Croix to the St. Lawrence, which developed into the controversy known as the "Northeastern Boundary Question."

.   .   .   .

A detailed description of the Valentine and Collins line will be found in Birdseye's Revised Statutes of New York, first edition, pages 2744–2746, and third edition, Volume III, page 3320. See also New York State Laws of 1892, chapter 678, section 5.

The results of the Webster-Ashburton Treaty, in respect of the northeastern boundary question, have been thus summed up by an eminent Canadian geographer (James White, "Boundary Disputes and Treaties", in Canada and Its Provinces, VIII, 826–27):

Summing up the results of the Ashburton Treaty, it is evident that, in the north-eastern portion of the territory, Great Britain got all that she could claim

by virtue of possession, and more; that she obtained much more than she could claim under the letter of the Treaty of Paris; and that she obtained nearly 900 square miles of territory in the basin of the upper St John over and above that awarded by the king of the Netherlands. She conceded an area of 150 square miles in the basin of the upper Connecticut River. She also conceded a strip between the 45th parallel and the 'old line' with an area of 73 square miles, but, as the 'old line' is in places south of the 45th parallel, she received, east of St Regis, a strip containing 11½ square miles. So far as these 'strips' were concerned, the United States and Great Britain had valid titles by virtue of occupation, and the *concessions* were simply validations. In addition to the foregoing the Ashburton settlement ended a controversy that had disturbed the relations of the two countries for nearly sixty years; that had, on several occasions, brought two great nations to the verge of war; and that had seriously interfered with commercial intercourse. Finally, it is worthy of note that the commission appointed to adjust the respective claims of New Brunswick and Quebec to the area west of the 'due north line' awarded to Great Britain by the Ashburton Treaty, reported in 1848, six years later, 'that a tract of country lies between the north highlands westward of the due north line, and the line of the United States, which, *according to the strict legal rights of the two provinces, belongs to neither*, . . . and which, in 1763, formed part of the ancient territory of Sagadahock.' This 'tract of country' was confirmed to Great Britain by the Ashburton Treaty.

The Northeastern Boundary Negotiations

While the negotiations were carried on at Washington by Secretary of State Daniel Webster and Lord Ashburton, those negotiations, so far as they concerned the northeastern boundary, were in a very real sense participated in by commissioners of Maine and of Massachusetts appointed at the suggestion and request of President Tyler. In the letters of Webster to the Governors of Maine and Massachusetts dated April 11, 1842 (published correspondence, 64–66), it was expressly stated that no conventional line would be agreed on "without the assent of such commissioners"; and the first formal note written on the northeastern boundary question was that of Ashburton to Webster of June 13, 1842, the day on which Webster had his first conference with the commissioners of the two States, who were Edward Kavanagh, Edward Kent, John Otis, and William Pitt Preble, for Maine, and Abbott Lawrence, John Mills, and Charles Allen, for Massachusetts (*ibid.*, 34–37, 71, 72).

Massachusetts had property interests which were affected by any settlement of the northeastern boundary, for in the public lands of Maine a half interest was reserved by Massachusetts upon the separation (act of June 19, 1819, Laws of the Commonwealth of Massachusetts, 1819, 248–60; and act of March 3, 1820, 3 Statutes at Large, 544); and the frontier in dispute was very largely that of Maine, though partly that of New Hampshire, Vermont, and New York. Indeed, the Legislature of the State of Maine did not consider that the Government of the United States possessed "the constitutional power to conclude any such negotiation without the assent of Maine" (published correspondence, 70), a view which was also expressed by the Legislature of Massachusetts (*ibid.*, 64); that theory should doubtless be considered in the light (*inter alia*) of Article 5 of the Treaty of Ghent (Document 33) and the proceedings thereunder, and particularly of the fact that under that article and the convention

of September 29, 1827 (Document 58), a reference had been made of the northeastern boundary question to arbitration by the King of the Netherlands.

That constitutional theory, moreover, had been explicitly supported by the Federal Government during the negotiations with Great Britain which followed the decision of the King of the Netherlands of January 10, 1831, regarding the northeastern boundary, and the subsequent refusal of the Senate, on June 23, 1832, to accept that award; the British Government at various times and in varied language had been officially informed that "under the peculiar structure of our political system, the Federal Government cannot alienate any portion of the territory of a State, without its consent" (Secretary of State Forsyth to Sir Charles R. Vaughan, D.S., 6 Notes to the British Legation, 18, April 28, 1835). President Jackson in 1832 had had negotiated and signed an agreement between the United States and the State of Maine providing for the relinquishment to the United States of any rights of that State in the disputed territory; the text of that agreement is printed in the notes to Document 58, which should be consulted generally; that agreement, however, failed to go into force, owing to the decision of the Maine Legislature that a referendum thereon would be necessary (see Burrage, Maine in the Northeastern Boundary Controversy, ch. X). So far as the Executive could decide such a question, the constitutional view of the State of Maine had been accepted by the Government of the United States, although the extreme Maine view, which went so far as to maintain that the convention of September 29, 1827, with Great Britain (Document 58) "tended to violate the Constitution of the United States and to impair the sovereign rights and powers of the State of Maine, and that Maine is not bound by the Constitution to submit to the decision, which is or shall be made under that convention" (Resolves of Maine, 1831, 245, resolve of February 28, 1831), was not supported at Washington (D.S., 6 Notes to the British Legation, 16, April 28, 1835):

> If the distinguished Arbiter agreed upon had found himself able to come to a decision upon the subject satisfactory to his own judgment, the Government of the United States would not have hesitated for a moment, whatever might have been its opinion of the justice of such decision, to have united with His Majesty's Government in carrying it fully and immediately into effect.

In a long letter to Governor Kent, of Maine, dated March 1, 1838, reviewing the history of the northeastern boundary negotiations up to that time, Secretary of State Forsyth thus restated the constitutional principles involved as seen by President Van Buren; and it is to be noted that "imperious public necessity" was mentioned as a possible ground of competence (to negotiate a cession) which otherwise the Federal Government would lack (D.S., 29 Domestic Letters, 336–66; Richardson, III, 442–59):

> The principles which have hitherto governed every successive administration of the Federal Government, in respect to its powers and duties in the matter, are—
> 1st That it has power to settle the boundry line, in question, with Great Britain, upon the principles and according to the stipulations of the treaty of

1783, either by direct negotiation, or, in case of ascertained inability to do so, by arbitration; and that it is its duty to make all proper efforts to accomplish this object by one or the other of those means.

2ᵈ That the General Government is not competent to negotiate, unless perhaps on grounds of imperious public necessity, a conventional line involving a cession of territory to which the state of Maine is entitled, or the exchange thereof for other territory not included within the limits of that State, according to the true construction of the treaty without the consent of the State.

In these views of his predecessors in office, the President fully concurs, and it is his design to continue to act upon them.

In the similar letters of Webster to the Governors of Maine and Massachusetts dated April 11, 1842 (D.S., 32 Domestic Letters, 288–91; published correspondence, 64–66), were these paragraphs:

The opinion of this Government upon the justice and validity of the American claim has been expressed, at so many times, and in so many forms, that a repetition of that opinion is not necessary. But the subject is a subject in dispute. The Government has agreed to make it matter of reference and arbitration; and it must fulfil that agreement, unless another mode for settling the controversy should be resorted to, with the hope of producing a speedier decision. The President proposes, then, that the Governments of Maine and Massachusetts should, severally, appoint a Commissioner or Commissioners empowered to confer with the authorities of this Government upon a Conventional line, or line by agreement, with its terms, conditions, considerations and equivalents, with an understanding that no such line will be agreed upon without the assent of such commissioners.

This mode of proceeding, or some other which shall express assent before hand, seems indispensable, if any negotiation for a Conventional line is to be had, since if happily, a treaty should be the result of the negotiation, it can only be submitted to the Senate of the United States for ratification.

The Legislature of Massachusetts had previously (March 3, 1842) granted plenary power to "the governor, with the advice and consent of the council, . . . to adopt such measures to secure the rights and interests of the Commonwealth in said territory, and to produce an honorable and satisfactory adjustment as the emergency may demand"; under that authorization the three commissioners of Massachusetts were named (Acts and Resolves Passed by the Legislature of Massachusetts, 1839–42, 564; published correspondence, 63–64, 66–69); Webster was formally notified by the Secretary of State of Massachusetts of their appointment (D.S., Northeastern Boundary, envelope 18, letter of John P. Bigelow of May 28, 1842).

The Legislature of Maine was summoned in extra session; and a preamble and five resolutions were adopted on May 26, which included the following (Acts and Resolves Passed by the Legislature of Maine, 1842, 111; published correspondence, 69–71):

Resolved, That there shall be chosen, by ballot, in convention of both branches of the legislature, four persons who are hereby constituted and appointed commissioners, on the part of this state, to repair to the seat of government of the United States, and to confer with the authorities of that government touching a conventional line, or line by agreement, between the state of Maine and the British provinces, having regard to the line designated by the treaty of 1783 as uniformly claimed by this state, and to the declarations and views expressed in the foregoing preamble, and to give the assent of this state to any such conventional line, with such terms, conditions, considerations and equivalents as they shall deem consistent with the honor and interests of the state; with the understanding that no such line be agreed upon without the unanimous assent of such commissioners.

President Tyler was formally notified by the Governor of Maine (John Fairfield) of the election of the four commissioners of Maine (published correspondence, 69, letter of May 27, 1842).

By a resolution of the Legislature of New Hampshire of June 23, 1842, the Senators and Representatives of that State in Congress were requested "to take such measures as may be necessary, during the pending negotiations at Washington relative to the Northern and North Eastern Boundary of the United States, to best sustain the rights of this State to the territory over which we have always heretofore claimed and exercised jurisdiction" (Laws of New Hampshire, June 1842, 599). That resolution, however, was not communicated to President Tyler until July 15, 1842, when the northeastern boundary had been settled as between Webster and Ashburton, with full satisfaction of the claim of New Hampshire; and the participation of the New Hampshire delegation in Congress in the proceedings appears to have been limited to the submission, on July 19, 1842, of a brief statement citing certain documents and papers (see published correspondence, 99–102).

Aside from the formal exchanges of June 17, 1842 (*ibid.*, 38), the written negotiations regarding the northeastern boundary comprised four notes (*ibid.*, 34–37, 39–56), three of Ashburton (June 13, June 21, and July 11) and one of Webster (July 8), with which is to be read its enclosure, the letter of the Maine commissioners to Webster of June 29 (*ibid.*, 72–80); also to be mentioned is a second letter of the Maine commissioners to Webster of July 16 (*ibid.*, 84–91), which, while dated after the accord of the two Plenipotentiaries, was doubtless drafted before the terms thereof were communicated. Moreover, during the period of the correspondence there were informal communications of one sort and another (see *ibid.*, 77, 79).

There was expressed a common desire to avoid "the interminable discussion on the general grounds on which each party considers their claims respectively to rest"; notwithstanding this, a considerable portion of the correspondence was argumentative, with historical and geographical references.

In his first note, of June 13, Ashburton gave no precise indication of a line to be proposed; but he spoke of the portion of the disputed territory which might come to Great Britain as being "as worthless for any purposes of habitation or cultivation as probably any tract of equal size on the habitable globe"; and he even suggested that Great Britain would have given up the controversy "if it were not for the obvious circumstance of its connecting the British North American provinces". That necessity of intercolonial communication was the admitted basis of any agreement for a conventional line; it is mentioned in each of the two above-cited letters of the Maine commissioners and is spoken of with emphasis in the note of Webster, who acknowledged "the general justice and propriety of this object" and agreed that "a conventional line ought to be such as to secure it to England".

Ashburton made the first proposal in his note of June 21, after a formal conference on June 18, of which there is no protocol. He

proposed a line north from the source of the St. Croix to the St. John (the line of 1817–18, regardless of its deviation from the true north), and the line of the St. John "up to some one of its sources" (a somewhat ambiguous expression, but meaning approximately up to the source of the southwest branch as mentioned in Article 1 of the treaty), except for a deviation on the right bank so as to include in New Brunswick the whole of the Madawaska settlement, which extended on both sides of the river "from the mouth of the Madawaska up to that of the Fish river"; and with that boundary he was willing to engage that "all lumber and produce of the forest of the tributary waters of the St. John's shall be received freely without duty, and dealt with in every respect like the same articles of New Brunswick", to agree to the old Valentine and Collins line from the Connecticut to the St. Lawrence, and also to accept the American contention as to the source of the Connecticut.

The note of Webster of July 8 presented and supported the counterproposal of Maine (see the letter of the Maine commissioners of June 29). The yielding of any territory on the south side of the St. John so as to include the Madawaska settlement in New Brunswick was definitely rejected. The counterproposal of boundary, with the concurrence of the commissioners of Massachusetts and with the condition that the United States would furnish to the two States "an equivalent", was the main channel of the St. John (from the crossing point of the due-north line from the source of the St. Croix) to a point three miles above the mouth of the Madawaska; thence straight to the outlet of Long Lake; thence westerly by a direct line to the point where the St. Francis enters Lake Pohenegamook; and thence, continuing the same line, to the highlands dividing the waters of the River du Loup from those of the St. Francis (the various *loci* may be conveniently seen on the map in Moore, International Arbitrations, I, between pp. 148 and 149); and while it was intimated that equivalents to some extent might be found if territorial cessions by Great Britain were possible, such as the island of Grand Manan, the islands in Passamaquoddy Bay, or a portion of the so-called strip between the north line and the St. John, it was understood that the British Plenipotentiary was without power to consent thereto.

The last note written before the verbal accord was that of Ashburton of July 11. He intimated that he would yield on the question of the Madawaska settlement; but he made it clear that he could not and would not yield as to the territory north and east of the St. Francis, which was British territory under the line proposed by the King of the Netherlands; Ashburton's final instructions as to the northeastern boundary had definitely limited him to that line (Ashburton Papers, instruction No. 8, May 26, 1842).

Thus the correspondence ended; as Ashburton urged, it was succeeded by conferences, of which there is no formal record. Sending to the Maine commissioners the note of Ashburton of July 11, Webster wrote on July 12 that he would soon meet with them, "being very desirous of making progress in the business in which we are engaged,

and satisfied that the various parties in interest are as well prepared now to come to a decision as they are likely to be at any time hereafter" (published correspondence, 81).

The position as it was left by the correspondence was this: North from the source of the St. Croix to the St. John and thence as far up the St. John as a point just beyond the mouth of the Madawaska, there was common ground; the portion of the region north of the St. John and between the St. Francis and the Madawaska which Maine had demanded, Ashburton had positively refused; for any agreement to be reached it was essential that that part of the claim of Maine should be abandoned; there was left for discussion an area which may be described as bounded on its three sides by a line as follows: (*a*) along the upper St. John from the mouth of the St. Francis to Metjarmette [1] portage (the line proposed by Ashburton); (*b*) along the highlands from that portage north to a point about due west of the entrance to Lake Pohenegamook; and (*c*) thence to and through that lake and down the St. Francis to the St. John. The result was that the claim of Maine to any territory between the St. Francis and the Madawaska north of the St. John was given up; and the remaining area in dispute was divided. One may learn something of the verbal discussions from the despatches of Ashburton of July 28 and August 9 (Nos. 15 and 17, quoted below).

An accord on the northeastern boundary was reached by the negotiators for the two Governments just prior to July 15, 1842. That it had not been reached by July 13 appears from Ashburton's despatch No. 13 of that date, as follows (Ashburton Papers):

The last Despatch which I had the honor of addressing your Lordship the 29th of last month N⁰ 10 on the subject of my negotiations relating to the North Eastern Boundary must have conveyed expectations of an earlier and more satisfactory settlement than I regret to say, I have, with every exertion on my part, been hitherto able to realize. Delay and difficulties have resulted from the present condition of this Government and from the pertinacious resistance of the Commissioners from the North by whom that Government is in this business guided and over-ruled. If I were not warned by the past from over-confidence, I should say that two or three days more could not fail to bring us to a settlement and to the outlines of a convention, but I fear that it may be on rather less favorable terms, than I had given your Lordship to expect. I now proceed to state what has occurred on this subject since I last wrote.

The written proposals submitted by me having circulated among the Commissioners from Maine and Massachusetts, I soon learned that although they differed much among themselves about some parts of them, they all concurred with great earnestness on the one point that we were not to be permitted to cross the St John, nor consequently to save the southern portion of the Madawaska settlements. I was assured by the best-informed and by the best-disposed persons from New England, that the Commissioners would not dare to return to their own country after making such a concession, and finding indirectly that our pretensions in this respect would be considered extravagant in the Senate, and through the whole country, I made up my mind not further to press this part of our claim, especially as I had no equivalent to offer in territory, and I thought it neither prudent nor expedient to offer any in money.

The Commissioners from Maine submitted to the Secretary of State an answer to my proposals, and after keeping it some time the latter sent it to me with his own formal reply, as no regular communications could take place between the

[1] Now spelled "Metgermette".

Commissioners and me. Your Lordship will find these two papers inclosed.
As these discussions began to be talked of abroad, as it was rumoured that serious
differences existed, and as I was sensible that injury might arise from drawing
the public press into the controversy, I lost no time and sent Mʳ Webster my
note the day after the receipt of his.   It is also enclosed herewith.   [The three
enclosures to this despatch are (*a*) Webster to Ashburton, July 8, 1842 (published
correspondence, 44–50); (*b*) the Maine commissioners to Webster, June 29, 1842
(*ibid.*, 72–80); (*c*) Ashburton to Webster, July 11, 1842 (*ibid.*, 50–56).]

These papers will shew your Lordship the present state of this question, and
require little explanation.   You will see that I invite personal conference in preference to a long desultory controversial correspondence because at this advanced
period of the Session, and in the state of parties here, delay might wholly defeat
our object, and there can be no doubt that, with some at least, that defeat is
much desired.

It will be observed that the informal memorandum of the Maine Commissioners
contains some rather coarse insinuations which would hardly have passed unnoticed, if presented in any other form.   Your Lordship will see that, though I
thought it best to give them no direct attention, they induced me to state our
sense of our own rights in rather a firmer tone than I otherwise should have done,
and I have reason to believe that this has been of service towards accelerating a
termination of these discussions.

I can hardly now hope to communicate by this packet any final settlement of
this question.   Various rumours will of course reach Europe, as to the probability
of any settlement whatever.   I am not myself apprehensive of not coming to
some terms within the limits of my powers, but the difficulties of my task have certainly increased, owing to the character of the persons who influence this negotiation, and of those whose duty it is more immediately to conduct it with me.   I
trust your Lordship will be assured that it has not failed to receive from me the
most anxious and cautious attention.

July 14 is almost certainly the exact date of the agreement reached
by the two Plenipotentiaries regarding the northeastern boundary.
In the archives of the Department of State is an annotated copy of
the second edition of Dashiell's Map, the edition which was issued
after the award of the King of the Netherlands of January 10, 1831,
regarding the northeastern boundary; Dashiell's Map, which was
based, in its watercourses and its disputed boundary lines, on Map
A of the convention of September 29, 1827 (Document 58, the notes
to which, particularly p. 356, should be consulted), showed, as originally issued in 1830, the northeastern boundary lines as claimed by
the two countries, drawn in green for the United States and in red for
Great Britain; the second edition of that map (of which the archives
of the Department of State contain some fifty examples, of one or
the other of the editions) added a yellow line as the line "of the
Arbiter" or the line suggested by the King of the Netherlands; the
annotated copy mentioned is signed "W. S. Derrick" in the upper
margin; it has, in the handwriting of William S. Derrick, then a senior
clerk and soon afterwards Chief Clerk of the Department of State,
the notation, "The blue ink marks the proposed conventional line.
14 July, 1842"; the signature and the notation are written in the same
blue ink as is the line drawn to show the northeastern boundary according to the Webster-Ashburton Treaty; the evidence is convincing that that copy of Dashiell's Map was annotated by Derrick on
July 14, 1842, to show the agreement of Webster and Ashburton then
reached (see "An Annotated Dashiell's Map", in American Historical
Review, XXXVIII, 70–73); and it may be added that it was William

S. Derrick who took to London for exchange the United States instrument of ratification of the Webster-Ashburton Treaty, with authority, if occasion arose, to act in place of Everett in making the exchange (D.S., 15 Instructions, Great Britain, 58–59; 3 Credences, 26).

In his letters of July 15 to the commissioners of Maine and Massachusetts, enclosing a statement of the proposed line of the northeastern boundary in almost the exact language of Article 1 of the treaty, Webster wrote as follows (published correspondence, 81–83; a draft in Webster's handwriting is in D.S., Northeastern Boundary, envelope 18):

You have had an opportunity of reading Lord Ashburton's note to me of the 11th of July. Since that date I have had full and frequent conferences with him respecting the eastern boundary, and believe I understand what is practicable to be done on that subject, so far as he is concerned. In these conferences he has made no positive or binding proposition, thinking perhaps it would be more desirable, under present circumstances, that such proposition should proceed from the side of the United States. I have reason to believe, however, that he would agree to a line of boundary between the United States and the British provinces of Canada and New Brunswick, such as is described in a paper accompanying this (marked B), and identified by my signature [see published correspondence, 83–84; D.S., Northeastern Boundary, envelope 18, a draft copy with interlineations and corrections].

In establishing the line between the monument and the St. John, it is thought necessary to adhere to that run and marked by the surveyors of the two Governments in 1817 and 1818. There is no doubt that the line recently run by Major Graham is more entirely accurate; but, being an *exparte* line, there would be objections to agreeing to it without examination, and thus, another survey would become necessary. Grants and settlements, also, have been made, in conformity with the former line, and its errors are so inconsiderable that it is not thought that their correction is a sufficient object to disturb these settlements. Similar considerations have had great weight in adjusting the line in other parts of it.

The territory in dispute between the two countries contains 12,027 square miles, equal to 7,697,280 acres.

By the line described in the accompanying paper, there will be assigned to the United States 7,015 square miles, equal to 4,489,600 acres; and to England 5,012 square miles, equal to 3,207,680 acres.

By the award of the King of the Netherlands, there was assigned to the United States 7,908 square miles, 5,061,120 acres; to England 4,119 square miles, 2,636,160 acres.

The territory proposed to be relinquished to England, south of the line of the King of the Netherlands, is, as you will see, the mountain range, from the upper part of the St. Francis river to the meeting of the two contested lines of boundary, at the Metjarmette Portage, in the highlands, near the source of the St. John's. This mountain tract contains 893 square miles, equal to 571,520 acres. It is supposed to be of no value for cultivation or settlement. On this point you will see, herewith, a letter from Captain Talcott, who has been occupied two summers in exploring the line of the highlands, and is intimately acquainted with the territory. The line leaves to the United States, between the base of the hills and the left bank of the St. John, and lying along upon the river, a territory of 657,280 acres, embracing, without doubt, all the valuable land south of the St. Francis and west of the St. John. Of the general division of the territory, it is believed it may be safely said that while the portion remaining with the United States is, in quantity, seven twelfths, in value it is at least four fifths of the whole. [For the letter of Captain Talcott, see published correspondence, 84.]

Nor is it supposed that the possession of the mountain region is of any importance, in connexion with the defence of the country or any military operations. It lies below all the accustomed practicable passages for troops into and out of Lower Canada; that is to say, the Chaudière, Lake Champlain, and the Richelieu, and the St. Lawrence. If an army, with its *materiel*, could possibly pass into

Canada over these mountains, it would only find itself on the banks of the St. Lawrence *below* Quebec; and, on the other hand, it is not conceivable that an invading enemy from Lower Canada would attempt a passage in this direction, leaving the Chaudière on one hand and the route by Madawaska on the other.

If this line should be agreed to, on the part of the United States, I suppose that the British minister would, as an equivalent, stipulate, first, for the use of the river St. John, for the conveyance of the timber growing on any of its branches, to tide water, free from all discriminating tolls, impositions, or inabilities of any kind, the timber enjoying all the privileges of British colonial timber. All opinions concur that this privilege of navigation must greatly enhance the value of the territory and the timber growing thereon, and prove exceedingly useful to the people of Maine. Second: That Rouse's Point, in Lake Champlain, and the lands heretofore supposed to be within the limits of New Hampshire, Vermont, and New York, but which a correct ascertainment of the 45th parallel of latitude shows to be in Canada, should be surrendered to the United States.

It is probable, also, that the disputed line of boundary in Lake Superior might be so adjusted as to leave a disputed island within the United States.

These cessions on the part of England would enure partly to the benefit of the States of New Hampshire, Vermont, and New York, but principally to the United States. The consideration on the part of England, for making them, would be the manner agreed upon for adjusting the eastern boundary. The price of the cession, therefore, whatever it might be, would in fairness belong to the two States interested in the manner of that adjustment.

Under the influence of these considerations, I am authorized to say, that if the commissioners of the two States assent to the line as described in the accompanying paper, the United States will undertake to pay to these States the sum of two hundred and fifty thousand dollars, to be divided between them in equal moieties; and, also, to undertake for the settlement and payment of the expenses incurred by those States for the maintenance of the civil posse, and also for a survey which it was found necessary to make.

The line suggested, with the compensations and equivalents which have been stated, is now submitted for your consideration. That it is all which might have been hoped for, looking to the strength of the American claim, can hardly be said. But, as the settlement of a controversy of such duration is a matter of high importance, as equivalents of undoubted value are offered, as longer postponement and delay would lead to further inconvenience, and to the incurring of further expenses, and as no better occasion, or perhaps any other occasion, for settling the boundary by agreement, and on the principle of equivalents, is ever likely to present itself, the Government of the United States hopes that the commissioners of the two States will find it to be consistent with their duty to assent to the line proposed, and to the terms and conditions attending the proposition.

The President has felt the deepest anxiety for an amicable settlement of the question, in a manner honorable to the country, and such as should preserve the rights and interests of the States concerned. From the moment of the announcement of Lord Ashburton's mission, he has sedulously endeavored to pursue a course the most respectful towards the States, and the most useful to their interests, as well as the most becoming to the character and dignity of the Government. He will be happy if the result shall be such as shall satisfy Maine and Massachusetts, as well as the rest of the country. With these sentiments on the part of the President, and with the conviction that no more advantageous arrangement can be made, the subject is now referred to the grave deliberation of the commissioners.

Both Maine and Massachusetts gave their formal assent to the proposal, subject to certain conditions. The assent of the commissioners of Massachusetts is dated July 20, 1842 (D.S., Northeastern Boundary, envelope 18; published correspondence, 92–93), and concludes as follows:

Whether the national Boundary, suggested by you, be suitable or unsuitable; whether the compensations that Great Britain offers to the United States for the territory conceded to her, be adequate or inadequate; and whether the Treaty,

which shall be effected, shall be honorable to the Country, or incompatible with its rights and dignity,—are questions, not for Massachusetts, but for the General Government, upon its responsibility to the whole country, to decide. It is for the State to determine, for what equivalents she will relinquish to the United States her interests in certain lands in the Disputed Territory, so that they may be made available to the Government of the United States, in the establishment of the North-Eastern Boundary, and in a general settlement of all matters in controversy, between Great Britain and the United States. In this view of the subject, and with the understanding that by the words, "the nearest point of the highlands", in your description of the proposed line of boundary, is meant, the nearest point of the crest of the highlands; that the right to the free navigation of the river Saint John shall include the right to the free transportation thereupon of all products of the soil as well as of the forest; and that the pecuniary compensation to be paid by the Federal Government to the State of Massachusetts, shall be increased to the sum of one hundred and fifty thousand dollars, the State of Massachusetts, through her Commissioners, hereby relinquishes to the United States her interest in the lands, which will be excluded from the dominion of the United States, by the establishment of the Boundary aforesaid.

The conditions stated on behalf of Massachusetts were all met by the terms of the treaty; the words "the nearest point of the summit or crest of the highlands" are in Article 1 (they are indeed in the print of the paper "B" in published correspondence; but in the draft copy thereof "summit or crest of the" are interlined, and at the end of the same sentence "summit or crest" replace "dividing highlands"); "produce . . . of agriculture" is included in Article 3; and the sum to be paid to Maine and Massachusetts "in equal moieties" (Article 5) is $300,000.

The assent of the commissioners of Maine was under date of July 22 (D.S., Northeastern Boundary, envelope 18; published correspondence, 93–99); its concluding paragraph and the memorandum therein mentioned are in these terms:

We are, now, given to understand that the Executive of the United States, representing the sovereignty of the Union, assents to the proposal, and that this Department of the Government at least is anxious for its acceptance, as, in its view, most expedient for the general good. The Commissioners of Massachusetts have already given their assent, on behalf of that Commonwealth. Thus situated, the Commissioners of Maine, invoking the spirit of attachment and patriotic devotion of their State to the Union, and being willing to yield to the deliberate convictions of her Sister-States as to the path of duty, and to interpose no obstacles to an adjustment which the general judgment of the Nation shall pronounce as honorable and expedient, even if that judgment shall lead to a surrender of a portion of the birth-right of the People of their State, and prized by them because it is their birth-right, have determined to overcome their objections to the proposal, so far as to say, that if, upon mature consideration, the Senate of the United States shall advise, and consent to, the ratification of a Treaty, corresponding in its terms with your proposal, and with the conditions in our Memorandum accompanying this note, marked A, and identified by our signatures, they, by virtue of the power vested in them by the Resolves of the Legislature of Maine, give the assent of that State to such Conventional line, with the terms, conditions and equivalents herein mentioned.

(A)

The Commissioners of Maine request that the following provisions, or the substance thereof, shall be incorporated into the proposed Treaty, should one be agreed on:

1st That the amount of the "disputed territory fund" (so called) received by the authorities of New Brunswick, for timber cut on the disputed territory, shall be paid over to the United States, for the use of Maine and Massachusetts, in

full, and a particular account rendered; or a gross sum to be agreed upon by the Commissioners of Maine and Massachusetts shall be paid by Great Britain, as a settlement of that fund; and that all claims, bonds and securities taken for timber cut upon the territory be transfered to the Authorities of Maine and Massachusetts:

2ᵈ That all grants of land, within that portion of the disputed territory conceded to Great Britain, made by Maine and Massachusetts, or either of them, shall be confirmed; and all equitable possessory titles shall be quieted to those who possess the claims; and we assent to a reciprocal provision for the benefit of settlers falling within the limits of Maine. And we trust that the voluntary suggestion of the British Minister, in regard to John Baker and any others, if there be any similarly situated, will be carried into effect, so as to secure their rights:

3ᵈ That the right of free navigation of the St John, as set forth in the proposition of Mr Webster on the part of the United States, shall extend to, and include, the products of the soil, in the same manner as the products of the forest; and that no toll, tax or duty be levied upon timber coming from the territory of Maine.

The conditions of Maine were also embodied in the treaty text; Article 5 deals with the "Disputed Territory Fund"; by Article 4 grants of land in the disputed territory are confirmed; and the clauses of Article 3 are broad enough to cover the provisions desired by the commissioners of Maine regarding the navigation of the St. John River. The "voluntary suggestion of the British Minister, in regard to John Baker", is referred to below.

A statement of the agreement reached on the northeastern boundary question (Articles 1 and 3–6 of the treaty) was part of the note of Webster of July 27, which set forth the entire boundary settlement (Articles 1–7), with a detailed description of the line "proposed to be agreed to" (Articles 1 and 2). The answering note of Ashburton of July 29 gave his assent; there remained only the drafting of certain of the articles, some of which had been already written (see published correspondence, 58–62).

In the presidential message to the Senate of August 11 the assent of the two States to the boundary clauses was prominently mentioned. That message, which deals with the whole negotiation and which was written by Daniel Webster (The Writings and Speeches of Daniel Webster, XII, 21), follows (published correspondence, 19–25):

I have the satisfaction to communicate to the Senate the results of the negotiations recently had in this city with the British minister special and extraordinary.

These results comprise—

1st. A treaty to settle and define the boundaries between the territories of the United States and the possessions of her Britannic Majesty in North America, for the suppression of the African slave-trade, and the surrender of criminals, fugitive from justice, in certain cases.

2d. A correspondence on the subject of the interference of the colonial authorities of the British West Indies with American merchant vessels driven by stress of weather, or carried by violence, into the ports of those colonies.

3d. A correspondence upon the subject of the attack and destruction of the steamboat Caroline.

4th. A correspondence on the subject of impressment.

If this treaty shall receive the approbation of the Senate, it will terminate a difference respecting boundary which has long subsisted between the two Governments—has been the subject of several ineffectual attempts at settlement, and has sometimes led to great irritation, not without danger of disturbing the

existing peace. Both the United States and the States more immediately concerned, have entertained no doubt of the validity of the American title to all the territory which has been in dispute; but that title was controverted, and the Government of the United States had agreed to make the dispute a subject of arbitration. One arbitration had been actually had, but had failed to settle the controversy; and it was found, at the commencement of last year, that a correspondence had been in progress between the two Governments for a joint commission, with an ultimate reference to an umpire or arbitrator, with authority to make a final decision. That correspondence, however, had been retarded by various occurrences, and had come to no definite result when the special mission of Lord Ashburton was announced. This movement on the part of England afforded, in the judgment of the Executive, a favorable opportunity for making an attempt to settle this long-existing controversy by some agreement or treaty, without further reference to arbitration. It seemed entirely proper that, if this purpose were entertained, consultation should be had with the authorities of the States of Maine and Massachusetts. Letters, therefore, of which copies are herewith communicated, were addressed to the Governors of those States, suggesting that commissioners should be appointed by each of them, respectively, to repair to this city and confer with the authorities of this Government, on a line by agreement or compromise, with its equivalents and compensations. This suggestion was met by both States in a spirit of candor and patriotism, and promptly complied with. Four commissioners on the part of Maine, and three on the part of Massachusetts, all persons of distinction and high character, were duly appointed and commissioned, and lost no time in presenting themselves at the seat of the Government of the United States. These commissioners have been in correspondence with this Government during the period of the discussions; have enjoyed its confidence and freest communications; have aided the general object with their counsel and advice; and, in the end, have unanimously signified their assent to the line proposed in the treaty.

Ordinarily, it would be no easy task to reconcile and bring together such a variety of interests in a matter in itself difficult and perplexed; but the efforts of the Government in attempting to accomplish this desirable object have been seconded and sustained by a spirit of accommodation and conciliation on the part of the States concerned, to which much of the success of these efforts is to be ascribed.

Connected with the settlement of the line of the northeastern boundary, so far as it respects the States of Maine and Massachusetts, is the continuation of that line along the highlands to the northwesternmost head of Connecticut river. Which of the sources of that stream is entitled to this character, has been matter of controversy, and is of some interest to the State of New Hampshire. The King of the Netherlands decided the main branch to be the northwesternmost head of the Connecticut. This did not satisfy the claim of New Hampshire. The line agreed to in the present treaty follows the highlands to the head of Hall's stream, and thence down that river, embracing the whole claim of New Hampshire, and establishing her title to 100,000 acres of territory more than she would have had by the decision of the King of the Netherlands.

By the treaty of 1783, the line is to proceed down the Connecticut river to the 45th degree of north latitude and thence west, by that parallel, till it strikes the St. Lawrence. Recent examinations having ascertained that the line heretofore received as the true line of latitude between those points was erroneous, and that the correction of this error would not only leave, on the British side, a considerable tract of territory heretofore supposed to belong to the States of Vermont and New York, but also Rouse's point, the site of a military work of the United States; it has been regarded as an object of importance, not only to establish the rights and jurisdiction of those States up to the line to which they have been considered to extend, but also to comprehend Rouse's point within the territory of the United States. The relinquishment by the British Government of all the territory south of the line heretofore considered to be the true line, has been obtained; and the consideration for this relinquishment is to enure, by the provisions of the treaty, to the States of Maine and Massachusetts.

The line of boundary, then, from the source of the St. Croix to the St. Lawrence, so far as Maine and Massachusetts are concerned, is fixed by their own consent, and for considerations satisfactory to them; the chief of these considerations being the privilege of transporting the lumber and agricultural products grown and raised in Maine on the waters of the St. John's and its tributaries down that river to the ocean, free from imposition or disability. The importance of this privilege, perpetual in its terms, to a country covered at present by pine forests of great value, and much of it capable hereafter of agricultural improvement, is not a matter upon which the opinion of intelligent men is likely to be divided.

So far as New Hampshire is concerned, the treaty secures all that she requires; and New York and Vermont are quieted to the extent of their claim and occupation. The difference which would be made in the northern boundary of these two States, by correcting the parallel of latitude, may be seen on Tanner's maps (1836), new atlas, maps Nos. 6 and 9. [A copy of that atlas is in the Division of Maps, Library of Congress; it is entitled "New Universal Atlas Containing Maps of the various Empires, Kingdoms, States and Republics of the World With a special map of each of the United States, Plans of Cities &c. Comprehended in seventy sheets and forming a series of One Hundred and Seventeen Maps Plans and Sections", by H. S. Tanner, Philadelphia, 1836.]

From the intersection of the 45° of north latitude with the St. Lawrence, and along that river and the lakes to the water communication between Lake Huron and Lake Superior, the line was definitively agreed on by the commissioners of the two Governments, under the 6th article of the treaty of Ghent. But between this last-mentioned point and the Lake of the Wood[s], the commissioners acting under the 7th article of that treaty found several matters of disagreement, and therefore made no joint report to their respective Governments. The first of these was Sugar island, or St. George's island, lying in St. Mary's river, or the water communication between Lakes Huron and Superior. By the present treaty this island is embraced in the territories of the United States. Both from soil and position, it is regarded as of much value.

Another matter of difference was the manner of extending the line from the point at which the commissioners arrived, north of Isle Royale, in Lake Superior, to the Lake of the Woods. The British commissioner insisted on proceeding to Fond du Lac, at the southwest angle of the lake, and thence, by the river St. Louis, to the Rainy Lake. The American commissioner supposed the true course to be, to proceed by way of the Dog river. Attempts were made to compromise this difference, but without success. The details of these proceedings are found at length in the printed, separate reports of the commissioners [cited below].

From the imperfect knowledge of this remote country, at the date of the treaty of peace, some of the descriptions in that treaty do not harmonize with its natural features, as now ascertained. "Long Lake" is nowhere to be found under that name. There is reason for supposing, however, that the sheet of water intended by that name, is the estuary, at the mouth of Pigeon river. The present treaty, therefore, adopts that estuary and river, and afterward pursues the usual route, across the height of land by the various portages and small lakes, till the line reaches Rainy Lake; from which the commissioners agreed on the extension of it to its termination, in the northwest angle of the Lake of the Woods. The region of country on and near the shore of the lake, between Pigeon river on the north, and Fond du Lac and the river St. Louis on the south and west, considered valuable as a mineral region, is thus included within the United States. It embraces a territory of four millions of acres, northward of the claim set up by the British commissioner under the treaty of Ghent. From the height of land at the head of Pigeon river, westerly to the Rainy Lake, the country is understood to be of little value, being described by surveyors, and marked on the map, as a region of rock and water.

From the northwest angle of the Lake of the Woods, which is found to be in latitude 45°23′55″ north, existing treaties require the line to be run due south to its intersection with the 45th parallel, and thence along that parallel, to the Rocky mountains. [As in Article 2 of the treaty, the latitude is 49°23′55″ north, and the line runs south to the 49th parallel; but the erroneous figures are in all

the official prints of the message: the Senate document here cited; Executive Journal, VI, 121; Richardson, IV, 166; and House Document No. 2, 27th Congress, 3d session, serial 418, p. 20.]

After sundry informal communications with the British minister upon the subject of the claims of the two countries to territory west of the Rocky mountains, so little probability was found to exist of coming to any agreement on that subject at present, that it was not thought expedient to make it one of the subjects of formal negotiation, to be entered upon between this Government and the British minister, as part of his duties under his special mission.

By the treaty of 1783, the line of division along the rivers and lakes, from the place where the 45th parallel of north latitude strikes the St. Lawrence, to the outlet of Lake Superior, is invariably to be drawn through the middle of such waters, and not through the middle of their main channels. Such a line, if extended according to the literal terms of the treaty, would, it is obvious, occasionally intersect islands. The manner in which the commissioners of the two Governments dealt with this difficult subject, may be seen in their reports. But where the line, thus following the middle of the river, or water course, did not meet with islands, yet it was liable sometimes to leave the only practicable navigable channel altogether on one side. The treaty made no provision for the common use of the waters by the citizens and subjects of both countries.

It has happened, therefore, in a few instances, that the use of the river, in particular places, would be greatly diminished, to one party or the other, if, in fact, there was not a choice in the use of channels and passages. Thus, at the Long Sault, in the St. Lawrence, a dangerous passage, practicable only for boats, the only safe run is between the Long Sault islands and Barnhart's island, all which belong to the United States on one side, and the American shore on the other. On the other hand, by far the best passage for vessels of any depth of water, from Lake Erie into the Detroit river, is between Bois Blanc, a British island, and the Canadian shore. So again there are several channels or passages, of different degrees of facility and usefulness, between the several islands in the river St. Clair, at or near its entry into the lake of that name. In these three cases, the treaty provides that all the several passages and channels shall be free and open to the use of the citizens and subjects of both parties.

The treaty obligations subsisting between the two countries for the suppression of the African slave-trade, and the complaints made to this Government within the last three or four years, many of them but too well founded, of the visitation, seizure, and detention of American vessels on that coast, by British cruisers, could not but form a delicate and highly important part of the negotiations which have now been held.

The early and prominent part which the Government of the United States has taken for the abolition of this unlawful and inhuman traffic, is well known. By the tenth article of the treaty of Ghent, it is declared that the traffic in slaves is irreconcilable with the principles of humanity and justice, and that both his Majesty and the United States are desirous of continuing their efforts to promote its entire abolition; and it is thereby agreed that both the contracting parties shall use their best endeavors to accomplish so desirable an object. The Government of the United States has, by law, declared the African slave-trade piracy; and at its suggestion other nations have made similar enactments. It has not been wanting in honest and zealous efforts, made in conformity with the wishes of the whole country, to accomplish the entire abolition of the traffic in slaves upon the African coast; but these efforts and those of other countries directed to the same end have proved, to a considerable degree, unsuccessful. Treaties are known to have been entered into some years ago between England and France, by which the former power, which usually maintains a large naval force on the African station, was authorized to seize, and bring in for adjudication, vessels found engaged in the slave-trade under the French flag. [Citations of certain acts mentioned in this and the following paragraph are in the notes below, under the heading "Article 8".]

It is known that, in December last, a treaty was signed in London by the representatives of England, France, Russia, Prussia, and Austria, having for its professed object, a strong and united effort of the five powers to put an end to the traffic. This treaty was not officially communicated to the Government of

the United States, but its provisions and stipulations are supposed to be accurately known to the public. It is understood to be not yet ratified on the part of France.

No application or request has been made to this Government to become party to this treaty; but the course it might take in regard to it, has excited no small degree of attention and discussion in Europe, as the principle upon which it is founded, and the stipulations which it contains, have caused warm animadversions and great political excitement.

In my message at the commencement of the present session of Congress, I endeavored to state the principles which this Government supports respecting the right of search and the immunity of flags. Desirous of maintaining those principles fully, at the same time that existing obligations should be fulfilled, I have thought it most consistent with the honor and dignity of the country, that it should execute its own laws, and perform its own obligations, by its own means and its own power. The examination or visitation of the merchant vessels of one nation, by the cruisers of another, for any purpose, except those known and acknowledged by the law of nations, under whatever restraints or regulations it may take place, may lead to dangerous results. It is far better, by other means, to supersede any supposed necessity, or any motive, for such examination or visit. Interference with a merchant vessel by an armed cruiser, is always a delicate proceeding, apt to touch the point of national honor, as well as to affect the interests of individuals. It has been thought, therefore, expedient, not only in accordance with the stipulations of the Treaty of Ghent, but at the same time as removing all pretext on the part of others for violating the immunities of the American flag upon the seas, as they exist and are defined by the law of nations, to enter into the articles now submitted to the Senate.

The treaty which I now submit to you, proposes no alteration, mitigation, or modification of the rules of the law of nations. It provides simply that each of the two Governments shall maintain on the coast of Africa a sufficient squadron to enforce, separately and respectively, the laws, rights, and obligations of the two countries, for the suppression of the slave-trade.

Another consideration of great importance has recommended this mode of fulfilling the duties and obligations of the country. Our commerce along the western coast of Africa is extensive, and supposed to be increasing. There is reason to think that, in many cases, those engaged in it have met with interruptions and annoyances, caused by the jealousy and instigation of rivals engaged in the same trade. Many complaints on this subject have reached the Government. A respectable naval force on the coast is the natural resort and security against further occurrences of this kind.

The surrender to justice of persons who, having committed high crimes seek an asylum in the territories of a neighboring nation, would seem to be an act due to the cause of general justice, and properly belonging to the present state of civilization and intercourse. The British provinces of North America are separated from the States of the Union by a line of several thousand miles; and, along portions of this line, the amount of population on either side is quite considerable, while the passage of the boundary is always easy.

Offenders against the law, on the one side, transfer themselves to the other. Sometimes, with great difficulty, they are brought to justice, but very often they wholly escape. A consciousness of immunity, from the power of avoiding justice in this way, instigates the unprincipled and reckless to the commission of offences; and the peace and good neighborhood of the border are consequently often disturbed.

In the case of offenders fleeing from Canada into the United States, the Governors of States are often applied to for their surrender; and questions of a very embarrassing nature arise from these applications. It has been thought highly important, therefore, to provide for the whole case by a proper treaty stipulation. The article on the subject in the proposed treaty is carefully confined to such offences as all mankind agree to regard as heinous, and destructive of the security of life and property. In this careful and specific enumeration of crimes, the object has been to exclude all political offences, or criminal charges, arising from wars or intestine commotions. Treason, misprision of treason, libels, desertion from military service, and other offences of similar character, are excluded.

And, lest some unforeseen inconvenience or unexpected abuse should arise from the stipulation, rendering its continuance, in the opinion of one or both of the parties, not longer desirable, it is left in the power of either to put an end to it at will.

The destruction of the steamboat Caroline at Schlosser, four or five years ago, occasioned no small degree of excitement at the time, and became the subject of correspondence between the two Governments. That correspondence having been suspended for a considerable period, was renewed in the spring of the last year, but, no satisfactory result having been arrived at, it was thought proper, though the occurrence had ceased to be fresh and recent, not to omit attention to it on the present occasion. It has only been so far discussed, in the correspondence now submitted, as it was accomplished by a violation of the territory of the United States. The letter of the British minister, while he attempts to justify that violation upon the ground of a pressing and overruling necessity, admitting, nevertheless, that, even if justifiable, an apology was due for it, and accompanying this acknowledgment with assurances of the sacred regard of his Government for the inviolability of national territory, has seemed to me sufficient to warrant forbearance from any further remonstrance against what took place, as an aggression on the soil and territory of the country.

On the subject of the interference of the British authorities in the West Indies, a confident hope is entertained, that the correspondence which has taken place, showing the grounds taken by this Government, and the engagements entered into by the British minister, will be found such as to satisfy the just expectation of the people of the United States.

The impressment of seamen from merchant vessels of this country by British cruisers, although not practised in time of peace, and, therefore, not at present a productive cause of difference and irritation, has, nevertheless, hitherto been so prominent a topic of controversy, and is so likely to bring on renewed contentions at the first breaking out of an European war, that it has been thought the part of wisdom now to take it into serious and earnest consideration. The letter from the Secretary of State to the British minister explains the ground which the Government has assumed, and the principles which it means to uphold. For the defence of these grounds, and the maintenance of these principles, the most perfect reliance is placed on the intelligence of the American people, and on their firmness and patriotism, in whatever touches the honor of the country, or its great and essential interests.

The negotiations on subjects other than the northeastern boundary question are to some extent discussed elsewhere in these notes.

Ashburton's report of the northeastern boundary settlement is contained in two of his despatches; that of July 28, 1842, is the first; it has references of interest to the position of the "Delegates from the North" (Ashburton Papers, despatch No. 15):

It is with much satisfaction that I have now the honor of informing your Lordship that I have at last settled the terms of the Convention of Boundaries from the River St Croix to the Lake of the Woods. The Convention itself will be ready in a day or two, and I hope to be able to send a Copy home by the Great Western Steamer in the course of next week. In the mean-time the substance will be found in a letter received this morning by me from Mr Webster, of which Copy is inclosed [Webster to Ashburton, July 27, 1842, published correspondence, 58–61].

After last addressing your Lordship on this subject by my Despatch of the 13th inst^t, N° 13., the negotiations continued formally with the Secretary of State, but informally with the Delegates from the North who were more immediately concerned. You will have seen that I had already given up the Madawaska settlement on the South of the St John's, but that I had hoped to retain the upper part of that River as a boundary. At this point I made my stand for some time, but finding the Maine commissioners obstinate, supported by all their deputation in Congress, and, as I believe, really ready to return home re infectâ, I yielded to the mediation of a third party and consented to an intermediate line between the Highlands, as claimed by America, and the River. This was still resisted for some time; but on the 22^d inst^t the Commissioners from Maine and Massachu-

setts signified their consent in their notes to the Secretary of State forwarded by him to me, of which your Lordship will find copies inclosed [*ibid.*, 92–99]. Two of the four Commissioners from Maine are returned home little satisfied with what has been done, and complaining of having been forced by their associates, and I am bound to add that the public of this place generally consider the terms severe, in as far as they are, imperfectly, known to them. The prevailing idea is, that the Netherlands Boundary was the utmost possible pretention on our part; and they listen unwillingly to the explanation that we yield otherwise a large equivalent for the additional strip given to us, to give a better width to our line on the St Lawrence. I trust however that when the whole case with the correspondence comes before the Senate, the convention will be approved and ratified. I hear, as is common in such cases, of some murmurs and threats, but I can not say I am seriously apprehensive of the result. Much will however depend upon the Senate being satisfied on other subjects.

I must ask your Lordship's permission to defer until I send a correct Copy of the Treaty my observations more in detail on its provisions, being at this time very much occupied with this and other parts of my duties, and being anxious that no time should be lost in bringing what may be done before the Senate whose session cannot be much further prolonged

In the mean-time the inclosed map marked with red ink will give some idea of the line agreed, as also of the proportionate division of the country between the Highlands and the upper St John. It will be seen that it removes the boundary completely from the Crest of the Hills over-looking the St Lawrence to their feet towards the River St John, and that in no part it will run nearer than 50 miles from Quebec. I have been obliged to give rather an unsatisfactory description of the line from want of more perfect surveys, but this I shall have hereafter to explain.

It will be seen in the notification of Maine and Massachusetts that they make the addition of the words "produce of the soil" to those of "produce of the forest" in the article for the navigation of the St John, a condition of their assent. I did not think it prudent to object to this, although I made this alteration unwillingly. The persons here connected with New Brunswick attach no importance to it, the articles are few which can be so admitted, and they are now actually admitted duty free, so that the inhabitants of Maine will only obtain by the stipulation of Treaty, what they now enjoy by sufferance. I added to the word produce the word "unmanufactured" which would exclude flour, although no flour can come from Maine which gets supplied from the Middle States, and I stipulate for a right to call for proof of origin, if it should be necessary.

I congratulate your Lordship upon the favorable prospect of at last terminating this tedious controversy on terms which will, I trust, be approved by Her Majesty's Government. In the course of another fortnight I hope to be able to turn my steps towards home. I am rather in doubt at present whether I shall remain here during the discussion of this business in the Senate but I shall be guided in this respect entirely by what may on consideration appear most conducive to the public service.

The "inclosed map marked with red ink", which is mentioned in the foregoing despatch, was a reduced copy, but with minor modifications resulting principally in simplification, of a map, marked "Map A", which was prepared by, and which accompanied the report of, Lieutenant Colonel Richard Zachariah Mudge, of the Royal Engineers, and George William Featherstonhaugh, the British Commissioners appointed on July 9, 1839, to examine and survey the territory in dispute; it is entitled "Map of that portion of Her Majesty's Colonies of New Brunswick and Lower Canada the Title to Which is Disputed by the Government of the U. States with Parts of the Adjacent Country The Rise and Course of the Rivers, with the direction of the Highlands, and their elevation above the Sea, . . . to accompany a report of the investigation of that Country which

the R^t Hon^e Viscount Palmerston G.C.B. Her Majesty's Principal
Secretary of State directed to be made A.D. 1839". The facsimile
in the Ashburton Papers shows the line of the boundary only from
Lake Pohenegamook (not named) to the Metjarmette portage;
another line, to the west, marks the "highlands" for the corresponding distance; the line of the boundary was drawn apparently on the
theory that the "seven miles" clause of Article 1 would come into
play, for the shortest distance between the "point on the northwest
branch of the river St John" and the line of the "highlands", as shown
on that facsimile, is from 13 to 15 miles, and between that "point"
and the St. John River, 7 miles or less. The facsimile is on a scale,
not indicated, of about 30 miles to an inch (1:1,900,800); and the
Commissioners' map, marked "Map A", is on a scale, shown graphically, of about 15 miles to an inch (1:950,400). In their printed report, dated April 16, 1840, the Commissioners describe the preparation
of their map (see Blue Book, 1840, North American Boundary, pt.
2, "Correspondence Relating to the Boundary between the British
Possessions in North America and the United States of America,
under the Treaty of 1783"; a copy thereof is in D.S., Northeastern
Boundary, envelope 19½).

The other despatch of Ashburton to be quoted in this connection is
one of August 9, 1842 (Ashburton Papers, despatch No. 17), which
transmitted the treaty (in its earlier form; but as the article numbers
mentioned are the same, the fact is not here material). Except for
its opening paragraph, previously quoted, and for two others relating
respectively to the boundary "further west" and to the clauses of
Article 7, which are quoted below, that despatch is here set forth:

My correspondence since I have been here will have made your Lordship acquainted with the difficulties which have in succession attended these negotiations,
arising mainly from the variety of persons and interests which it was necessary
to consult and consider. I shall feel well rewarded for my trouble and anxiety
should the final result be honored by Her Majesty's approbation. I believe
the terms as well calculated as circumstances would permit for securing the
interests of the Colonies; but above all I am persuaded of the importance of arriving, on terms not inconsistent with those interests, and with the honor of the
country, at some settlement of these border dissentions, which it is very evident
could not have been suffered long to continue without endangering the maintenance of peace, and rendering at all times the presence of a considerable military
force necessary on the frontier. There are parts of this Treaty which it becomes
my duty to accompany with some explanations, and I proceed to submit them to
your Lordship in the order in which they present themselves.

Starting from the monument at the Source of the St Croix, the North line to
its intersection with the St John's is declared, "to follow the exploring line run
"and marked by the Surveyors of the two Governments in the years 1817 and 1818
"under the fifth Article of the Treaty of Ghent". It had been long known in the
Province as well as in Maine that this North line had been incorrectly run, and
last year Major Graham a distinguished officer of Engineers of the United States,
marked a new line, which was generally believed to be correct. This would, by
becoming gradually wider as it departed from the monument, have taken from
New Brunswick about half a mile at the St John's near the falls, and as the strip
of land is there narrow, the difference was important. All the grants and occupations of land had been formed on the basis of the old imperfect line, and for the
same reason that we give up a more considerable strip on the 45th parallel of
Latitude, I pressed the justice and convenience of this arrangement, and it was
conceded.

Proceeding up the St John's from the intersection of the North Line, the river forms the boundary and it divides the Madawaska settlements. Here there are a number of small Islands in the river, which the Commissioners will have to distribute. They will have to be guided by what is deemed to be the "main channel" but there will be nevertheless occasional questions of doubt. We have promised that our Commissioners shall deal with these questions equitably, and with the least possible contention; consulting where it can be done, the interests of the inhabitants with whose farms the islands, which are not generally large, may be connected [cf. British and Foreign State Papers, XXXIII, 769].

Following the river upwards, there lives at its fork with the St Francis, a man named Baker, who has a mill, and about 100 acres of land. He has been an active partisan and agitator on the part of Maine, and the Maine Commissioners fearing that his situation as a British subject might expose him to difficulties, made many efforts to throw his property within the Maine line. As this was in every respect objectionable, and seeing the object they were aiming at, I got over the difficulty by a voluntary promise, not put into the Treaty, that, if Baker wishes to leave the Province, and is not able to find at once a purchaser for his property, it shall be taken over at a reasonable price. I have written to this effect a letter to Governor Kent one of the Maine Commissioners. This engagement must if necessary be fulfilled, and that rather liberally, but not extravagantly. I do not know what the expence of so doing may amount to, but I think it cannot well exceed a thousand pounds. Care has been taken to give security to the settlers generally whose titles arising from possession are not always strictly legal, and it is believed that the provision for this purpose will be found effectual.

The Boundary further proceeds up the St Francis to the outlet of the Lake Pohenagamook, and from thence in a straight line to a given point on the North-west branch of the River St John. This was the most difficult and is the least clearly defined part of these Boundaries. When in the course of negotiation Maine would not yield, as I had at one time hoped, the line of the Upper St John, and I refused to take that of the Crest of the Highlands, a middle line was after much discussion consented to, which would about divide the territory then in dispute, and bring our boundary every-where off the Hills which might over-look the Valley of the St Lawrence into the Valley of the St Johns. There were no maps to enable us to define with the desired accuracy this line, and there was no time for even the roughest survey: we therefore took the map which seemed most accurate, and which could not have been made with any purpose to mislead, and we described the point as intended, on the presumption that the map was accurate. A copy of this map will accompany the treaty. To guard myself however against the possibility that this point on the north-west branch of the St John's might run too far into the Highlands, the reservation was made, that it should recede to within seven miles thereof, should that be the case. It is my belief that the result of the survey, and final determination of this line will be satisfactory, but I must admit that this part of our work has not been as perfectly and accurately executed, as it would have been, if we could have had proper maps. I trust however that every precaution has been taken which the circum-stances of the case admitted, considering always that it was highly desirable, that no further delay for the purpose of obtaining more correct information should be interposed.

The remainder of the line to St Regis requires no explanation. It was agreed that the hilly ground at the Head of Connecticut River, should be conceded to New Hampshire, and the strip of land by the 45th degree of Latitude, to New York and Vermont, and I had the satisfaction of learning that these concessions, while they were acceptable to the several States concerned, are considered as doing no injury whatever to Canada.

. . . .

That Article of the Treaty which concedes to those parts of the State of Maine watered by the St John's and its tributaries, the free conveyance of their produce by that River, was the subject of many repeated discussions with the Deputies from Maine. The only part to which I had any objection was, the adding the words "agricultural produce" to the produce of the forest, but seeing that the Deputies, on signifying their consent to the Boundary, on leaving Washington made this a part of their consent, I did not think it expedient further to resist. Although I

objected for some time to have this condition forced upon me, I do not consider it to be of much importance, and I am confirmed in this opinion by that of the best-informed persons of the Province. The unmanufactured produce of Agriculture is in fact now admitted free of duty, and consists mainly in potatoes and onions, and the merchants of St John's consider with reason that the prosperity of their port and shipping depends mainly in making it the general mart of the great river on which it is situated.

The Article 5 which engages for the distribution of the fund called, the Disputed Territory Fund, confirms only what would be fairly due, if no notice were taken of this subject in the Treaty. This fund arises from monies received for Lumber cut on the Disputed Territory, and which was always promised to be held and ultimately distributed according to the stipulations of this article. When the account is made up as directed, the portion fairly belonging to Maine will be to be paid, deducting the charges applicable thereto. I would recommend that this be done rather liberally. Real charges of collection or recovery must be made, but I have promised that there shall be no general charge of Salaries to the Warden or others. I have no correct information of the probable amount of this fund but it can not exceed from five to ten thousand pounds.

I have only further to observe that this Treaty of boundaries will only require one Commissioner on each side with such assistants as each may think necessary. The marking the old line and the distribution of the Islands in the St John will be attended with little difficulty, but the running the straight line from the Lake Pohenagamook through the wilderness will take more time. This can not now be done until next summer, and I would recommend our Commissioner being instructed to do this work so as to avoid, if possible, contention, and I am assured that the American officer shall have the same conciliatory instructions.

I shall communicate to the Governor General of Her Majesty's North American Provinces, a copy of this Treaty, recommending that the communication may be considered as confidential, until he is informed from home of its ratification.

The negotiations for this Treaty of Boundaries were connected with a settlement of claims and accounts between the General Government and the States of Maine and Massachusetts. With these we had nothing to do, and I much objected to let any notice be taken of them in the Treaty, but there were great difficulties arising from leaving them out and not giving to this settlement the sanction of the Treaty. The subject is accordingly introduced in the 5th Article, but I thought it expedient to exchange notes [of August 9, 1842, printed above immediately following the treaty text] with the Secretary of State, copies of which accompany this Despatch to explain that Great Britain is without interest or responsibility in the subject of that Article.

Three engagements of the British Government, collateral to the treaty, are mentioned in the foregoing despatch. Two of them, it seems, were promises made verbally by Ashburton: first, that with questions of doubt regarding small islands in the St. John River the British Commissioner under Article 6 would "deal . . . equitably, and with the least possible contention; consulting where it can be done, the interests of the inhabitants with whose farms the islands . . . may be connected"; and, secondly, that in the settlement of the Disputed Territory Fund, pursuant to Article 5, "there shall be no general charge of Salaries to the Warden or others."

The other collateral engagement related to the real property of an American citizen, John Baker, which was located on the New Brunswick side of the St. John; "the voluntary suggestion of the British Minister, in regard to John Baker", was mentioned in the conditions with the assent of the Maine commissioners to the boundary clauses (July 22, 1842, quoted above); the engagement entered into was evidenced by a letter from Ashburton to Edward Kent, one of the Maine commissioners and previously (1838 and 1841) Governor of

Maine. This is spoken of by Ashburton as "a voluntary promise, not put into the Treaty", and was to the effect "that, if [John] Baker wishes to leave the Province [of New Brunswick], and is not able to find at once a purchaser for his property, it shall be taken over at a reasonable price." It seems that no copy of that letter from Ashburton to Kent was sent by the former to London; and no record thereof has been found in the archives of the Department of State, in the Maine archives in the State Library at Augusta, in the collections of the Maine Historical Society at Portland, in the archives of the Province of New Brunswick, or in the papers of the New Brunswick Historical Society at St. John. It is to be added that no necessity for the fulfilment of the engagement regarding the property of John Baker arose, for Baker remained a resident of New Brunswick until his death in the year 1868 (see Thomas Albert, Histoire du Madawaska, 223–24, and Resolves of Maine, 1895, ch. 114).

The remarks regarding "this map" in the despatch last quoted are somewhat obscure; with the despatch in the Ashburton Papers is a copy of the Mudge and Featherstonhaugh map that is identical in its map base with the copy, in the same papers, of the map transmitted with Ashburton's despatch of July 28; it is marked to show the line of the treaty as well as the lines of the rival claims, and it bears in its lower margin an annotated legend; but the "point on the Northwest branch of the River St John" is about 17 miles farther upstream, and the line connecting it with Lake Pohenegamook and with the southwest branch runs much nearer the highlands, than as drawn on the copy with Ashburton's despatch No. 15, of July 28; the statement in the despatch of August 9 that "A copy of this map will accompany the treaty" presumably can refer only to the enclosure with the despatch; and it seems that by "the map which seemed most accurate" Ashburton meant the Mudge and Featherstonhaugh map.

The Maps Known in 1842 [1]

There were two maps which, because of the lines drawn on them, had a great influence on the official representatives of Maine and were persuasive in inducing their assent to the conventional line of the northeastern boundary which is described in Article 1 of the Webster-Ashburton Treaty.

One of those two maps was the Steuben-Webster copy of Mitchell's Map, which is briefly described in the notes to Document 58 (vol. 3, pp. 338–40, 350–51) and a facsimile reproduction of which is in a pocket inside the back cover of volume 3.

Neither historically nor legally was the line on that Steuben-Webster Map any evidence whatever of the intent of the negotiators of the treaties of 1782 and 1783 or of the meaning of the boundary provisions there written; Baron Steuben had no part in those negotia-

[1] The paragraphs under this heading are in large part based upon the studies of Colonel Lawrence Martin, including in particular the draft of his unpublished book on Mitchell's Map, the manuscript of which the editor of these volumes has read (see vol. 3, p. 328, footnote 1).

tions; he did not visit Europe after his arrival here in 1777; and there is no evidence to show where he obtained his copy of Mitchell's Map or who was responsible for the line on it or when that line was drawn.

Of even more importance at the time was the so-called "red-line map". Jared Sparks, the historian, wrote to Secretary of State Webster from Cambridge, Massachusetts, on February 15, 1842, as follows (D.S., Miscellaneous Letters, January–February 1842):

I have deliberated for some time on the propriety of communicating to you the substance of this letter, but at length, believing it important that you should possess a knowledge of all the facts respecting the subject to which it alludes, I have concluded to waive the scruples that have hitherto operated on my mind.

While pursuing my researches among the voluminous papers relating to the American Revolution in the *Archives des Affaires Etrangères* in Paris, I found in one of the bound volumes an original letter from Dr. Franklin to Count de Vergennes, of which the following is an exact [1] transcript.

"Passy, *6 Dec. 1782*

"Sir, "I have the honor of returning herewith the map your Excellency sent me yesterday. I have marked with a strong red line, according to your desire, the limits of the United States as settled in the preliminaries between the British & American plenipotentiaries.

"With great respect, I am, &c.

"B. Franklin."

This letter was written six days after the preliminaries were signed, and if we could procure the identical map, mentioned by Franklin, it would seem to afford conclusive evidence as to the meaning affixed by the commissioners to the language of the Treaty on the subject of the boundaries. You may well suppose, that I lost no time in making inquiry for the map, not doubting that it would confirm all my previous opinions respecting the validity of our claim. In the geographical department of the Archives are sixty thousand maps & charts, but so well arranged, with catalogues & indexes, that any one of them may be easily found. After a little research in the American division, with the aid of the keeper, I came upon a map of North America by D'Anville, dated 1746, in size about eighteen inches square, on which was drawn a *strong red line* throughout the entire boundary of the United States, answering precisely to Franklin's description. The line is bold & distinct in every part, made with red ink, and apparently drawn with a hair pencil, or a pen with a blunt point. There is no other coloring on any part of the map.

Imagine my surprise on discovering, that this line runs wholly south of the St. John's, and between the head waters of that river and those of the Penobscot & Kennebec. In short, it is exactly the line now contended for by Great Britain, except that it concedes more than is claimed. The north line, after departing from the source of the St. Croix, instead of proceeding to Mars Hill, stops far short of that point, and turns off to the west, so as to leave on the British side all the streams which flow into the St. John's between the source of the St. Croix & Mars Hill. It is evident, that the line, from the St. Croix to the Canadian highlands, is inteded to exclude *all the waters* running into the St. John's.

---

[1] The transcript is not exact, even in wording, as it omits the word "thirteen"; the text of the note (from a facsimile of the original) in the French archives, follows (all but the signature is in the hand of William Temple Franklin):

Passy, *6 Decr 1782*

Sir, I have the honour of returning herewith the Map your Excellency sent me Yesterday. I have marked with a Strong Red Line, according to your desire, the Limits of the thirteen United States, as settled in the Preliminaries between the British & American Plenipotentiarys.

With great Respect, I am Sir, Your Excellency's most obed^t & most humble Servant

B Franklin

His Ex^cy Count de Vergennes

There is no positive proof, that this map is actually the one marked by Franklin, yet, upon any other supposition, it would be difficult to explain the circumstances of its agreeing so perfectly with his description, and of its being preserved in the place where it would naturally be deposited by Count de Vergennes. I also found another map in the Archives, on which the same boundary was traced in a dotted red line with a pen; apparently copied from the other.

I enclose herewith a map of Maine, on which I have drawn a strong black line corresponding with the red one above mentioned.

Thus the map which was sent by Sparks to Webster was *not* a facsimile or example of the D'Anville Map of North America of 1746 which Sparks saw at Paris, but was, as he wrote, "a map of Maine". That map, on which is written "With Mr Sparks' letter of 15th Feby 1842", is now with the original letter in the archives of the Department of State. It is approximately 14 inches wide and 23 inches high, measured within the neat lines, and is drawn on a scale of about 15 miles to an inch (1:950,400). The black line on it starts at the source of the St. Croix River and runs first roughly northwest and then roughly west, with various curves, to the highlands near the source of the southwest branch of the St. John, and thence along the highlands to a point near the source of the Arnold River, a southern tributary of Lake Megantic. The map is entitled:

Map of Maine Constructed from the most Correct Surveys With Sectional Distances and Elevations, or Level, of the St Croix River, from Calais Bridge. Deduced from the States Survey, Made by W. Anson, Civil Engineer, in 1836. Engraved & Published by S. H. Colesworthy, Portland. Revised 1840 Edition.

A search recently made in the French archives for the map which Jared Sparks saw at Paris in 1841 has not been successful.

As evidence, the D'Anville Map must also be ruled out. The conclusion of Sparks that the map that he saw was the one sent by the Count de Vergennes to Benjamin Franklin on December 5 and returned by the latter on December 6, 1782, is based on these circumstances: (*a*) that the map seen was in the *Archives des Affaires Etrangères;* (*b*) that on it was drawn a red line purporting to show the entire boundary of the United States; and, perhaps, (*c*) that no other map with the requisite red line was then found in those archives. But a red line may be drawn on a map by anyone, and frequently is; and for a map to be missing from governmental archives after a lapse of more than half a century subsequent to the occasion of its use, is neither surprising nor without precedent; there is nothing whatever to connect the map which Sparks saw either with the transmittal of a map by Vergennes or with the drawing of a line thereon by Franklin or with the note of the latter of December 6, 1782; the conclusion reached by Sparks that the D'Anville Map was the Vergennes-Franklin map was at best no more than an unsupported and improbable surmise.

The remarks of Sir Robert Peel in the House of Commons on March 21, 1843, are in point (Hansard, 3d series, LXVII, 1248):

We made inquiries, in 1826 and 1827, into the maps in the foreign office at Paris, for the purpose of throwing light upon the intentions of the negotiators of 1783. A strict search was made for any documents bearing in any [way] upon the disputed question, but at that time neither letter nor map could be found. How-

ever, there were afterwards discovered, by a gentleman engaged in writing a history of America, a letter and a certain map, supposed by him to be the map referred to in the letter.   In answer to our first inquiry, as I have already stated, no such map could be discovered.

.   .   .   .

On subsequent inquiry, at Paris, we found a map, which must be the map referred to by Mr. Jared Sparkes.   There is placed upon that map a broad red line, and that line marks out the boundary as claimed by the British.   It is probably a map by M. d'Anville, of 1746, and there can be no doubt but that it is the map referred to by Mr. Jared Sparkes; but we can trace no indication of connection between it and the despatch of Dr. Franklin.   To say that they were connected is a mere unfounded inference.

During the same debate (March 22, 1843) Disraeli stated that he had seen the D'Anville Map and that on it the "strong red line . . . blotted out no inconsiderable portion of the State of Main, which could occupy but a very small space in a map of North America, eighteen inches square" (*ibid.*, 1305).

Also to be quoted in this connection is the comment of the Canadian geographer, James White (*op. cit.*, 821):

In these days, when the matter is of academic interest only, calm judgment indicates the value of the map as evidence as nil.   There was no connection between the map and the letter; no note on the latter to indicate that the accompanying map was in the archives; a red line such as was indicated on the map could have been drawn by any one, at any time; to assume that Franklin, one of the ablest men that the American colonies had produced, would draw such a line was to credit him with incredible stupidity and ignorance respecting the acts of state, maps, etc., of the previous twenty years.

However, the two maps which have been mentioned, that is to say, the Steuben-Webster copy of Mitchell's Map and the map of Maine with the black line on it, "corresponding with the red" of the D'Anville Map, were exhibited to the Maine authorities by Jared Sparks in May 1842 (Adams, Life and Writings of Jared Sparks, II, 400–3); and at least the "red-line map" (i.e., the black-line map) and probably the Steuben-Webster copy of Mitchell's Map also, were shown by Webster to the Maine commissioners while they were in Washington.

Moreover, it would not be unreasonable to assume that the Steuben-Webster copy of Mitchell's Map was before Senators of the United States from August 17 to 20, 1842, during the discussion of the Webster-Ashburton Treaty.   Certainly, the "red-line map" which Sparks had taken to Maine was then before the Senate (Congressional Globe, XII, appendix, pp. 16, 61).

Each of the maps discussed above is to be distinguished from the Faden Map of 1785, a copy of which was stated to have been transmitted to the Maine commissioners by Webster (published correspondence, 77).

The different editions of Faden's Map of North America, with full-size facsimile portions from four of them and a reduced facsimile of the whole of one, are described by Lieutenant Colonel Dudley A. Mills (United Empire, the Royal Colonial Institute Journal, new series, II, 700–2); and regarding "Featherstonhaugh's Faden" the author cited, who had access to some of the papers of Lord Aberdeen, has this to say (*ibid.*, 702):

Ashburton took with him to Washington a long confidential report by Feather-stonhaugh (Palmerston's Commissioner). In this report is reproduced a map entitled "North America, with the new Discoveries, by William Faden, Geographer to the King, MDCCLXXXV."

The reproduction is an engraving by Wyld evidently made specially for the report in 1841. It is about ¾ the scale of the "Faden 1785", reproduced in this article, and is an entirely different map. Drawing and lettering are quite different. The boundary line according to the British claim is engraved and hand coloured.

It was this map which Ashburton showed to the Maine Commissioners who called it (in their letter of June 29) "a small map of small pretentions."

The same author states that both the Sparks map and the Steuben-Webster copy of Mitchell's Map were shown at Washington to Ashburton "at the last moment" and that because of them Ashburton assented to the decision to combine the two instruments first signed on August 9, into the single instrument of the Webster-Ashburton Treaty (*op. cit.*, 694, 700, 703); Ashburton wrote on February 7, 1843, "that *probably* but for this discovery there would have been no treaty, and if the secret had been known to me earlier I could not have signed it" (Jennings, Correspondence and Diaries of John Wilson Croker, II, 400–401).

Another copy of Mitchell's Map which has at times (erroneously) been regarded as having evidentiary value is the so-called "Record Office Map", which is also described in the notes to Document 58 (vol. 3, pp. 346–47). That copy appears to have come to light in the British archives in 1841 or 1842. Nothing but supposition in any way connects the map or the line drawn on it with the events of 1782 and 1783 (see Mills, *op. cit.*, 700). The map is not authenticated at all; and the line drawn on it is not, as alleged, one "exactly conforming to the British claim" (Featherstonhaugh, Observations upon the Treaty of Washington, 100), for that line from the source of the St. Croix runs somewhat south of due west.

The Record Office Map was certainly within the knowledge of the British Government before the negotiations of Webster and Ashburton were concluded, and more probably before they were begun; but the story that "an exact account of its lines and marks" was sent to Ashburton by a special messenger some time about June 1842 (Greville, A Journal of the Reign of Queen Victoria from 1837 to 1852, II, 102) is improbable on its face; it has no support in any other writing, official or otherwise, that has been examined, and should not be accepted without further evidence (see Fitzmaurice, Life of William, Earl of Shelburne, III, 324–25, and Sparks, "The Treaty of Washington", in North American Review, LVI, 472–73).

The utmost that can be said regarding the various red lines thus far mentioned is that on the three maps, the Steuben-Webster Map, the D'Anville Map, and the Record Office Map, they are of a rather curious and unexplained general similarity.

Two maps which are well authenticated as connected with the events of 1782 and 1783 and which, taken either separately or together, are evidence directly opposed to the British contention regarding the Maine boundary, are the Jay Map and the King George Map, both

of which are copies of Mitchell's Map; these are also described and commented on in the notes to Document 58 (vol. 3, pp. 341–46).

Neither of those two maps was available to this Government in 1842. The Jay Map was brought to light in 1843 (see Gallatin, A Memoir on the North-eastern Boundary, . . . Illustrated by a Copy of the "Jay Map", *passim*). One vainly wonders why the researches of Albert Gallatin and others had failed to include inquiry regarding the papers of John Jay and examination of them.

The other of those two evidentiary maps, the King George Map, was available in 1842, but it was not then available to the Government of the United States, and in a very curious sense it seems not to have been available to the British Government of 1842. Palmerston knew of the King George Map and so did G. W. Featherstonhaugh; Aberdeen, it appears, did not, nor did Ashburton, until after the negotiation of the Webster-Ashburton Treaty. In his confidential despatch of March 31, 1843, Edward Everett, then Minister at London, wrote (D.S., 50 Despatches, Great Britain):

> If the discovery of Mr Spark's Map at Paris was a singular incident, the bringing to light of Mr Oswald's [the King George Map] at London is much more singular. Lord Aberdeen assured me that he was not aware of its existence, till after the Conclusion of the Treaty, and the stir made about Franklin's map; and Lord Ashburton was equally ignorant of it till his return. It was, however, brought from the British Museum to the Foreign Office in Lord Palmerston's time, and was known to him and to Mr Featherstonhaugh. In whose custody it has been since the change of Ministry, so that it did not come to Lord Aberdeen's knowledge I was not told; very likely in that of Mr Featherstonhaugh himself, who has been employed till lately, as a sort of general Agent for the Boundary question. Be this as it may, I was truly rejoiced at Lord Aberdeen's voluntary disclaimer of all previous knowledge of it, and so I said to him; for I could not have reconciled with that candor and good faith for which I have always given him credit, his repeated assurance to me, last summer, that there was no plan or map in their possession bearing on the question, not previously made known, had he all the time been aware of the Existence of this very remarkable Map, which I consider a far clearer and stronger Evidence in our favor, than any thing else of the kind which has ever been adduced.

Also to be mentioned is the letter which Ashburton wrote to Webster from London on April 28, 1843, in which the statement was made "that the discoveries here are quite recent, and were wholly unknown to me when I was at Washington" (The Writings and Speeches of Daniel Webster, XVIII, 191).

It seems, however, that the King George Map was in the British Museum for a decade prior to 1839, and presumably available to any inquiring student of the northeastern boundary question.

In 1829 the British Museum was in possession of three English copies and one French copy of Mitchell's Map which had come from the library of George III (Catalogue of Maps, Prints, Drawings, etc., Forming the Geographical and Topographical Collection Attached to the Library of His Late Majesty King George the Third, and Presented by His Majesty King George the Fourth to the British Museum, I, 27).

That the King George Map was one of those maps then in the British Museum is not to be doubted.

On March 27, 1839, the proceedings in the House of Commons included remarks by Sir Charles Grey regarding a copy of Mitchell's Map, dated 1755, which "showed the true line", and a French edition of 1756, one of which (or both) could be seen at the British Museum. Later Sir Charles Grey said that any honorable gentleman "who went to the British Museum could see it [the map] there in eight sheets". Sir Robert Peel and Viscount Palmerston took part in the debate; the latter "understood" that it was left to him "to make inquiry on the subject, and bring forward the map if it could conveniently be had" (Hansard, 3d series, XLVI, 1226–28); the map was had, but it was not brought forward.

Two days later, on March 29, 1839, a letter in the following terms (Library of Congress, facsimiles from the Public Record Office, London, Foreign Office Records, America, 5, vol. 340) was written by Mr. (later Sir) Anthony Panizzi, then keeper of printed books and later principal librarian of the British Museum, to Viscount Palmerston, who was British Secretary of State for Foreign Affairs from 1830 to September 3, 1841, except for a brief interval in 1834–35:

Mitchell's Map of America having been mentioned with some degree of importance I beg to inform Your Lord Ship that there are several copies of it in this Library, one of them with MS notes pointing out the boundary between England & America "as described by Mr Oswald" I have locked it up to prevent its being indiscriminately perused & I now take the liberty of privately mentioning the fact, that your Lordship may be aware of the existence of a document which coming from the collection of H M. George III may not be useless. We are forbidden to allow any article to go out of the B.M.; but with a warrant from Your Lordship as Secretary of State I suppose the Trustees would order me to take the document to any place Your Lordship might be pleased to order.

The order, "By Her Majesty's Command", to the trustees of the British Museum to deliver the map in question to Her Majesty's Principal Secretary of State at the Foreign Office followed on April 1, 1839 (*ibid.*).

Another letter of Panizzi to Palmerston, of April 1, 1839, the substance of which is quoted below, shows that Palmerston's attention was very forcibly called to the significance of the King George Map (*ibid.*):

Your Lordship asked yesterday who Mr Oswald was? As this may not be useless for Your Lordship to know I beg to write a few lines on the subject. Mr Richard Oswald was a merchant in the city before being a Commissioner to negotiate the preliminaries of peace in 1783; had lived long in America and is said to have been intimately acquainted with her wants, commerce, circumstances & *localities*. He was a great friend of Lord Shelburne and soon acquired the entire confidence and friendship of Franklin who was most anxious to negotiate with him in preference to Mr Grenville, for he (Oswald) seemed rather negotiating (in my opinion) for the United States than for England. Oswald died old at his seat in Auchincru[i]v[e], Ayrshire on the 6th of nov. 1784. It appears from Franklin's correspondence that this English negotiator was anxious that the Americans should have Canada (to which the Americans were not adverse) conceiving that it would be a cause of future quarrels, and being of opinion that it was ceded by France in the hope of weakening England, and that he had always thought so. It seems also that Lords Shelburne & Rockingham were not very averse to it, but Mr Fox was startled at the proposition. I forgot to mention that Mr Oswald bailed Laurens, the American, out of prison, that he had great influence with them all.

Now, My Lord, this is the person who signed the preliminaries of peace on the 30ᵗʰ of nov. 1782, the second article of which was verbatim transferred to the definitive treaty of the 3ᵈ of sept. 1783, and as he seems to have cared so little about Canada he is not unlikely to have given up more than he ought on that side, chiefly as it appears from one of Franklin's letters that Mʳ Oswald was only intent on obtaining what he conceived requisite for his country on the south, but was willing to yield to the American demands east north & west. He is therefore likely to have knowingly agreed to the boundary as traced in the map which Your Lordship has seen   I hope to be excused for having taken the liberty of troubling Your Lordship with this letter written in a great hurry & more prolix than I thought at first it would be; but it may not be altogether useless that Your Lordship should know these facts.

So the King George Map, available and unnoticed for the ten years from 1829 to 1839, became, when noticed in 1839, unavailable except to certain British officials.

In any view, the facts are extraordinary enough.   The denials of Aberdeen of knowledge on his part of the King George Map until after the signing of the treaty are very explicit and sweeping, and the high character of that statesman lends credence to them; while it is not impossible that the permanent officials of the British Foreign Office knew at that time of the King George Map, even though Aberdeen did not, such a hypothesis is difficult to accept; but if neither Aberdeen nor those officials then had such knowledge, it follows that Viscount Palmerston made no disclosure of the King George Map either to his subordinates or to his successor, the Earl of Aberdeen (see Mills, *op. cit.*, 699).

The tentative articles between the United States and Great Britain which were agreed on between Benjamin Franklin and John Jay on the part of the United States and Richard Oswald on the part of Great Britain, and which were sent to London from Paris on October 8, 1782 (Wharton, Diplomatic Correspondence, V, 805–8), give, in Article 1, two descriptions of the same point, one as the northwest angle of Nova Scotia and the other as the source of the St. John River.   The treaty of November 30, 1782, gives two descriptions of the same point, one as the northwest angle of Nova Scotia and the other as the point at the terminus of a line drawn due north from the source of the St. Croix River to the highlands.   Accordingly, in the minds of the negotiators of 1782 the source of the St. John River was identical with the point in the highlands at the terminus of the line drawn due north from the source of the St. Croix; and that point is marked on those two evidentiary maps, the Jay Map and the King George Map, as located at the headwaters of the Madawaska, which is thus identified as being the northwest angle of Nova Scotia, as being the source of the St. John River, and as being also the terminus in the highlands of the line drawn due north from the source of the St. Croix.

One fact which no one in the United States concerned with the negotiations of 1842 or with the previous official consideration of the northeastern boundary question seems to have known, was the diversity and successive dates of the various English editions of Mitchell's Map (see the notes to Document 58, vol. 3, pp. 331–33).   The statement in the decision of the King of the Netherlands in 1831 (*ibid.*,

362) to the effect that "one would vainly attempt to explain why, if the intention was to retain the ancient provincial boundary, Mitchell's Map, published in 1755 and consequently anterior to the proclamation of 1763 and to the Quebec Act of 1774, was precisely the one used in the negotiation of 1783", was not questioned, then or later; if it had been appreciated (as might easily have been learned in London) that the date of the first edition of Mitchell's Map (1755) had been retained in successive English editions for two decades (the latest English edition was published in 1775), and that the differences of substance between the first and later editions were noteworthy, the historical and legal argument of the American case would have been much strengthened; but Mitchell's Map was thought of as a single English publication, sufficiently described in two words.

Other maps are to be mentioned. Of the "Carte du Canada" (first issued in 1703) of Guillaume de l'Isle (Del Isle, Delisle) there were at least fourteen printings; the author of the map became "Premier Géographe du Roi" in 1718, and one of the editions of his map, though dated 1703, gives him that title; it was a copy of the 1783 (eighth) edition of the "Carte du Canada" (in the collections of the New York Historical Society) which Daniel Webster examined in 1842 and to which Albert Gallatin referred in 1843 as one of the only "two French maps published in those years [1783–84], on which the boundary of the United States is attempted to be traced" which he had seen (Gallatin, A Memoir on the North-eastern Boundary, 45); more important here is the 1781 (seventh) edition (by Dezauche), a copy of which (in the Harvard College Library) has recently been brought to light by the researches of Judge John Bassett Moore; of that map Colonel Lawrence Martin writes:

One is astonished to observe that the seventh or 1781 edition, represented in America by the Harvard copy, was not used by the Department of State between 1783 and 1842 in the negotiations with Great Britain respecting our northeast boundary. This 1781 edition differs from those of 1745 and 1783 in showing a northern boundary of Maine some distance north of the St. John River in the position where the United States maintained that the frontier should be. Being made by one of the outstanding mapmakers of the time, who subsequently (1790) became the royal geographer of France, and being published a full year before the peace negotiations of 1782, this seventh edition of the "Carte du Canada" was a potential item of boundary evidence of high quality.

The surmise that the boundaries drawn on the 1783 French edition of Mitchell's Map (showing the northeastern frontier of the United States in accord with the American claim up to 1842) were based on the line drawn by Franklin for Vergennes on December 6, 1782, may now be regarded as a reasonable inference from known facts; that map was made in 1783 by Le Rouge, the royal geographer of France at the time; it seems highly probable that such an official would have had made available to him, and would have relied on, the latest information of the French Foreign Office; and certainly the line drawn by Franklin was such information; that map has printed on its face a statement to the effect that the limits of the United States and of the other powers had been traced, in March 1783, according to the last treaty of peace; and now that it seems clearly proved (by discoveries

in the Madrid archives, presently to be stated) that the line drawn by Franklin is approximately the line of the French Mitchell of 1783, one may well conclude that the one was copied from the other; but during the period when the northeastern boundary question was open the French Mitchell of 1783 was not cited or mentioned on behalf of the United States (the 1756 and 1776 French editions of Mitchell's Map were discussed in the St. Croix River Arbitration; see Moore, International Adjudications, Modern Series, II, 42, 254).

The line of "the Limits of the thirteen United States" as fixed by the peace preliminaries of November 30, 1782 (Document 7), was drawn by Franklin for Vergennes six days later; at that time France's ally, Spain, as the neighbor of the United States west of the Mississippi and in the Floridas (and with extensive claims in the region east of the Mississippi to the north of the Floridas), had a more direct and immediate interest in the boundary terms of the Treaty of Peace between the United States and Great Britain than did even France herself, as ally of the United States.

The Spanish Ambassador at Paris at the time was the Count de Aranda. In the diary of that diplomat it is recorded that on August 3, 1782, he presented to John Jay a French copy of Mitchell's Map for use in the Spanish-American negotiations (Juan F. Yela Utrilla, España ante la independencia de los Estados Unidos, 2d ed., II, 355). Among the photostats from the Spanish archives which are in the Library of Congress are various despatches from Aranda, in Paris, to the Spanish Secretary of State for Foreign Affairs (Floridablanca), in Madrid. These have been identified and translated by Professor Samuel Flagg Bemis. In one of those despatches, dated January 1, 1783 (thus twenty-six days after Franklin drew the "Limits of the thirteen United States" for Vergennes), Aranda refers to the Anglo-American preliminaries of November 30, 1782, and transmits a map which he says is identical with the one which Aranda and Jay had been using, or, in other words, is a French edition of Mitchell's Map; that despatch contains the following sentence (free rendering from the Spanish; *Legajo* 6609, Doc. 2362, pp. 871–77, *Archivo Histórico Nacional*):

Now I send a map identical with that which I sent you when I began to treat here with Mr. Jay, and it is marked in accordance with the articles of the said treaty with England which Franklin marked on another copy of the same map belonging to M. de Vergennes.

The map sent by Aranda with his despatch of January 1, 1783, has now been (almost certainly) identified as being that in the *Archivo Histórico Nacional*, "in the *sección de Estado* under number 1 of the collection of maps, of the file 3,397, where it is segregated like the others for its better conservation" (D.S., file 852.412/19, translation of a note verbale from the Ministry of State, April 28, 1933, enclosure to despatch No. 18 from Madrid of June 13, 1933); that map is of the fourth impression of the third French edition of Mitchell's Map.

The line drawn on that map is a contemporaneous transcription of the line drawn by Franklin on December 6, 1782; and that transcription agrees substantially with the line engraved on the 1783 edition of

Mitchell's Map, though lacking its minor errors; it is thus also in accord with the American claim up to 1842. A photograph of that map, showing clearly the Aranda transcription of the Franklin line of December 6, 1782, is now in the Library of Congress, and a photostat thereof is in the archives of the Department of State.

THE LINE OF ARTICLE 1 AS NOW DEMARCATED

The boundary between the United States and Canada from the source of the St. Croix River to the St. Lawrence River, as now demarcated, is described in complete detail in the elaborate joint report of the International Boundary Commission made pursuant to Article 3 of the treaty with Great Britain signed at Washington on April 11, 1908; that report was transmitted to the Secretary of State on October 30, 1924, and was printed at Washington in 1925; the technical description of the boundary line will be found in that work at pages 138–266.

The existing line is drawn on a series of maps consisting of 61 sheets with an index sheet, arranged and numbered from sheet 1 at the St. Lawrence River to sheet 61 at the source of the River St. Croix. The scale of sheets 8 to 13 and 24 to 33 is 1:6,000, that of sheets 41 to 57 is 1:12,000, and that of the remaining sheets is 1 : 24,000.

Those maps, copies of which are obtainable from the office of the International Boundary Commission in Washington, are entitled "International Boundary from the St. Lawrence River to the Source of the St. Croix River". They are variously dated from June 23, 1922, to October 16, 1924.

The following statement regarding those maps is from the joint report of the International Boundary Commission (pp. 135–37):

The charts upon which the commissioners have marked the boundary line from the source of the St. Croix to the St. Lawrence River, in accordance with the above, are topographic maps prepared from the surveys made by the field force of the commission. They consist of a series of 61 sheets arranged and numbered as shown on the accompanying map. They have been engraved on copper plates and printed from stone, and the engraved plates will be preserved by the two Governments as permanent records of the work. The four official sets of maps, two for each Government, which bear the commissioners' signatures, are transmitted in portfolios and form a part of this report. The copies of the maps for public distribution are identical with the originals, except that there appear on each map the word "Copy" and the date of publication, and the commissioners' signatures are in facsimile.

The size of each sheet is 23 by 35 inches inside the border. The belt of topography shown has an average width of 1¼ miles. The conventional signs used to represent the various topographic features are those adopted by the United States Board of Surveys and Maps. The boundary line, monuments, culture, and lettering appear in black; relief (20-foot contour lines) in brown; drainage in blue; and timber in green. The maps are constructed on the polyconic projection on scales of 1:6,000, 1:12,000 and 1:24,000, depending on the detail required to show clearly the location of the boundary line. At the top of each map are the title, the number of the sheet, the names of the commissioners, and copies of the seals of the two countries; and in the lower right-hand corner is the commissioners' certificate, which reads as follows:

We certify that this map is one of the quadruplicate set of sixty-one (61) maps adopted under Article III of the Treaty between Great Britain and

the United States, signed at Washington April 11, 1908, and that we have marked thereon the Boundary Line as re-established by the Commissioners designated above, in accordance with the provisions of the said Article.
Signed (date of signature).
(Signed)   J. J. McArthur,   (Signed)   E. Lester Jones,
    His Britannic Majesty's Commissioner.   United States Commissioner.

In addition to the above, each sheet bears the necessary scales and explanatory notes, and the names of the chiefs of parties and their assistants who were responsible for the field work shown thereon.

  .   .   .   .

A limited edition of the maps has been printed for each Government for distribution, either in the form of complete sets or individual maps.   In the United States, copies of the report and maps are on file in the Library of Congress and in all other libraries designated by the Government as "depository libraries"; that is, those which receive all United States Government publications.   In Canada they are on file in the Dominion archives, in the libraries of the Dominion Parliament and of the Provincial Legislative Assemblies, and in university and reference libraries throughout the country.

The deviations of the Valentine and Collins line of 1771–74 from the true parallel of 45° north, appear in full detail on sheets 1 to 8 of the maps of the International Boundary Commission; see also Paullin, *op. cit.*, plate 93D.

ARTICLE 2

By Article 2 of the Definitive Treaty of Peace with Great Britain of September 3, 1783 (Document 11), the boundary from the point where, after passing north through the middle of Lake Huron, it comes "to the Water Communication between that Lake [Huron] and Lake Superior", is described as follows:

thence through Lake Superior Northward of the Isles Royal & Phelipeaux to the Long Lake; Thence through the Middle of of said Long-Lake, and the Water Communication between it & the Lake of the Woods, to the said Lake of the Woods; Thence through the said Lake to the most Northwestern Point thereof.

No steps were taken by the two Governments to describe more in detail or to survey or map any part of the boundary above described until the proceedings of Commissioners appointed for that purpose under the Treaty of Ghent (Document 33).   Article 7 of that treaty deals with that part of the boundary "which extends from the water communication between Lake Huron and Lake Superior to the most North Western point of the Lake of the Woods", and reads as follows:

It is further agreed that the said two last mentioned Commissioners after they shall have executed the duties assigned to them in the preceding Article, shall be, and they are hereby, authorized upon their oaths impartially to fix and determine according to the true intent of the said Treaty of Peace of one thousand seven hundred and eighty three, that part of the boundary between the dominions of the two Powers, which extends from the water communication between Lake Huron and Lake Superior to the most North Western point of the Lake of the Woods;—to decide to which of the two Parties the several Islands lying in the Lakes, water communications, and Rivers forming the said boundary do respectively belong in conformity with the true intent of the said Treaty of Peace of one thousand seven hundred and eighty three, and to cause such parts of the said boundary as require it to be surveyed and marked.   The said Com-

missioners shall by a Report or declaration under their hands and seals, designate the boundary aforesaid, state their decision on the points thus referred to them, and particularize the Latitude and Longitude of the most North Western point of the Lake of the Woods, and of such other parts of the said boundary as they may deem proper. And both parties agree to consider such designation and decision as final and conclusive. And in the event of the said two Commissioners differing, or both or either of them refusing, declining, or wilfully omitting to act, such reports, declarations or statements shall be made by them or either of them, and such reference to a friendly Sovereign or State shall be made in all respects as in the latter part of the fourth Article is contained, and in as full a manner as if the same was herein repeated.

The line described by the same Commissioners, acting under Article 6 of the Treaty of Ghent, from near St. Regis, Franklin County, New York, up the St. Lawrence River and through Lakes Ontario, Erie, and Huron, terminated "at the foot of the Neebish Rapids" pursuant to the declaration of June 18, 1822 (Document 42). The boundary required to be surveyed and marked under Article 7 of the Treaty of Ghent was doubtless intended to run from that point at the foot of the Neebish Rapids to the northwesternmost point of the Lake of the Woods. Owing, however, to the language used in Articles 6 and 7 of the Treaty of Ghent, there was an important question as to the jurisdiction of the Commissioners under Article 7, which has been thus described (Anderson, Canadian Questions: Northern Boundary of the United States, 35–36):

As above stated, the Commissioners under the sixth article had carried the line to a point in the St. Mary's River just below the foot of Neebish Rapids, and owing to the entire absence of any reference to the continuation of the line through the connecting waters between Lakes Huron and Superior in the description of the boundary in the treaties of 1782 and 1783, a serious question presented itself as to the jurisdiction of the Commissioners under Article VII to continue the line through the St. Mary's River. Under Article VI the Commissioners were empowered to designate the boundary only "*to* the water communication between that Lake (Huron) and Lake Superior," and under Article VII they were authorized to determine the boundary "*from* the water communication between Lake Huron and Lake Superior," etc., and they were required to designate the boundary "in conformity with," in the one case, and "according to," in the other, the true intent of the Treaty of 1783, which, as above stated, contained no reference to the course of the line through this particular waterway. The omission was the more noticeable because the boundary was particularly described in that treaty as running along the middle of the waterways between Lakes Ontario and Erie, and between Lakes Erie and Huron. The Commissioners decided, however, that this omission was a mere inadvertence, and they interpreted the true intent of the treaty to be that the line was to continue through the middle of this water communication from Lake Huron to Lake Superior.

A full account of the proceedings of the Commissioners under Article 7 of the Treaty of Ghent is in Moore, International Arbitrations, I, 171–95.

Originals of the separate reports of the American and British Commissioners under Article 7 of the Treaty of Ghent are in the archives of the Department of State. They are printed, with supporting documents, maps, etc., in House Document No. 451, 25th Congress, 2d session, serial 331. The original journal of the Commissioners (who acted also under Article 6 of the Treaty of Ghent), which

is in the archives of the Department of State, ends with the record of
June 22, 1822; some extracts of later date are in the report of the
British Commissioner; copies of the journal record for most of the
proceedings from November 1821 on are enclosures to five letters to
the Secretary of State from Joseph Delafield, Agent of the United
States (D.S., Boundary, Article 7, Treaty of Ghent, letters of January
15, 1822, March 13, 1824, November 17, 1824, November 15, 1826,
and November 6, 1827); the copies from Delafield (the two latest of
which are certified as "true copy") cover the meetings from November 12, 1821, to January 3, 1822, inclusive, and also all the meetings
from February 16, 1824, to the final adjournment, except those held
at Albany on November 1 and 2, 1825; thus the original journal in the
archives of the Department of State, plus the copies from Delafield,
forms a complete record except for the two days last mentioned; for
the period beginning October 23, 1826, the journal of the Commissioners is printed in British and Foreign State Papers, LVII, 803–23;
a facsimile of the original journal in the British archives for the period
from June 22, 1822, to October 23, 1826, has recently been obtained
and is now in the archives of the Department of State.

The Commissioners adjourned *sine die* on October 27, 1827, and
their reports were delivered and exchanged at New York on December
25 or 26, 1827 (D.S., Boundary, Article 7, Treaty of Ghent, letter of
Joseph Delafield of December 26, 1827); the Commissioners reached
no complete agreement on the entire boundary from the foot of the
Neebish Rapids to the Lake of the Woods; and while they did agree
as to certain portions of the line, their agreement as to those portions
was not strictly binding; a decision of the Commissioners under
Article 7 of the Treaty of Ghent was required to be complete in order
to be final and conclusive.

There were two points as to which the Commissioners did not agree;
the first of these involved the island in St. Marys River (between
Lake Huron and Lake Superior) known as St. George's or Sugar
Island, "reported to contain 25920 acres of very fertile land" (see
Moore, *op. cit.*, 173–80); the second point of difference was as to the
boundary from a point in Lake Superior about nine miles northeast
from Isle Royale ("one hundred yards to the north and east of a small
island named . . . Chapeau [Ile Chapeau, now Gull Island]") to
Rainy Lake, at a point below Kettle Falls, a distance of about two
hundred miles as the crow flies; but while the formal reports of the
Commissioners differed widely in their respective proposals as to this
portion of the line, they had very nearly come to an accord during
their discussions (see *ibid.*, 182, 188–89); and the proposition of the
British Commissioner, Anthony Barclay, "to take a water line commencing in the mouth of Pigeon River, and thence proceeding to
Rainy Lake, with a stipulation that the Grand Portage route should
be made free and common for the use of both parties" (declined by
the American Commissioner, Peter B. Porter, because of lack of
power; see *ibid.*, 182) is substantially the equivalent of the relevant
clauses of Article 2 of the Webster-Ashburton Treaty (see Paullin, *op.
cit.*, 57–58, and plate 91B).

Considering the boundary line from its point of termination as fixed under Article 6 of the Treaty of Ghent, namely, at a point in the Neebish Channel near Muddy Lake, and thence to the Lake of the Woods, the result of the labors of the Commissioners under Article 7 of the Treaty of Ghent may be thus stated:

From the said terminating point of the boundary as fixed under Article 6 of the Treaty of Ghent to another point in the middle of "Saint Marys River" about one mile above St. George's or Sugar Island there was a divergence of view, owing to the difference regarding the island mentioned (although for a distance of about six miles from the point of beginning, between St. Tammina or Tammany, now Neebish, and St. Joseph Islands, the line was agreed on and is indicated on maps I and II of the Commissioners); but from about one mile above Sugar Island, through the Sault Ste. Marie and across Lake Superior to a point north of Isle Royale, the Commissioners reached agreement and described the line as follows (British and Foreign State Papers, LVII, 804, journal of the Commissioners, October 23, 1826):

That in the opinion of the Commissioners the following described line, which is more clearly indicated by a series of maps prepared by the surveyors, and now on the files of this Board, by a line of black ink, shaded on the British side with red and on the American side with blue, is, so far as the same extends, the true boundary intended by the Treaties of 1783 and 1814. That is to say:—Beginning at a point in the middle of St. Mary's River, about one mile above the head of St. George's or Sugar Island, and running thence westerly through the middle of said river, passing between the groups of islands and rocks which lie on the north side and those which lie on the south side of the Saut de Ste. Marie as exhibited on the maps, thence through the middle of said river between Points Iroquois and Gros Cap, which are situated on the opposite main shores at the head of the River St. Mary's, and at the entrance into Lake Superior; thence in a straight line through Lake Superior, passing a little to the south of Ile Carreboeuf, to a point in said lake 100 yards to the north and east of a small island named on the map Chapeau, and lying opposite and near to the north-eastern point of Ile Royale.

From the point mentioned in Lake Superior near Isle Royale to the northwesternmost point of the Lake of the Woods there was partial disagreement and partial agreement of the Commissioners; and the result is thus described (Anderson, *op. cit.*, 37–38):

From the point above Isle Royal in Lake Superior to a point at the foot of Chaudière Falls [now Kettle Falls] in Lac la Pluie, or Rainy Lake, the Commissioners were unable to agree as to the location of the line. The treaty descriptions required that the line, after passing north of Isles Royal and Phelippeaux in Lake Superior, should go "to Long Lake; thence through the middle of said Long Lake to the water communication between it and the Lake of the Woods, to the said Lake of the Woods." It was found that there was no lake in that region known as Long Lake, but that there were four separate routes which the line might follow, any one of which, in the absence of the others, would have been regarded as sufficiently fulfilling the requirements of the treaty description. The northernmost of these was through the River Kamanistiquia, for which the American Commissioner contended. The southernmost one, which the British Commissioner selected, was through Fond du Lac or St. Louis River. The two intermediate ones were the Grand Portage route and the Pigeon River route, which latter was a few miles to the north of the other.

From the foot of Chaudière Falls [now Kettle Falls] to the most northwestern point of the Lake of the Woods the Commissioners agreed upon the location of the

line, which they marked as before on the maps surveyed and prepared under their direction.   A detailed description of the portions thus agreed upon is set out in the records of their proceedings as follows:

"Beginning at a point in Lac La Pluie, close north of island marked No. 1, lying below the Chaudière falls of lake Namecan; thence down this channel, between the islets marked No. 2 and No. 3; thence, down the middle of said channel, into Lac La Pluie, westward of island No. 4; thence, through the said lake, close to the south point of island No. 5; thence, through the middle of said lake, north of island No. 6, and south of island No. 7; thence through the middle of said lake, to the north of islet No. 8, and south of islands No. 9, No. 10, No. 11, and between islands No. 12 and No. 13; thence, south of islands No. 14 and No. 15; thence, through the middle of said lake, north of a group of islands, No. 16; thence, south of a group of rocks, No. 17; thence, south of a group of islets, No. 18; thence, north of an islet, No. 19; thence, through the middle of said lake, to the south of island No. 20, and all its contiguous islets; thence, south of island No. 21, and midway between islands No. 22 and No. 23; thence, southwest of island No. 24; thence, north of island No. 25; thence, through the middle of said lake, to its *sortie*, which is the head of the Rivière La Pluie; thence, down the middle of said river, to the Chaudière falls, and having a portage on each side; thence, down the middle of said falls and river, passing close south of islet No. 26; thence, down the middle of said Rivière La Pluie, and passing north of islands, No. 27, No. 28, No. 29 and No. 30; thence, down the middle of said river, passing west of island No. 31; thence, east of island No. 32; thence, down the middle of said river, and of the Manitou rapid, and passing south of No. 33; thence, down the middle of said river, and the Long Sault rapid, north of island No. 34, and south of islets No. 35, No. 36, and No. 37; thence, down the middle of said river, passing south of island No. 38; thence, down the middle of said river, to its entrance between the main land and Great Sand Island, into the Lake of the Woods; thence, by a direct line to a point in said lake, one hundred yards east of the most eastern point of island No. 1; thence, northwestward, passing south of islands No. 2 and No. 3; thence, northwestward of island No. 4, and southwestward of islands No. 5 and No. 6; thence, northward of island No. 7, and southward of islands No. 8, No. 9, No. 10, and No. 11; thence, through the middle of the waters of this bay, to the northwest extremity of the same, being the most northwestern point of the Lake of the Woods.   And from a monument erected in this bay, on the nearest firm ground to the above northwest extremity of said bay, the courses and distances are as follows, viz: 1st. N., 56° W., 156.5½ feet; 2d. N., 6° W., 861½ feet; 3d. N., 28° W., 615.4 feet; 4th. N., 27° 10′ W., 495.4 feet; 5th. N., 5° 10′ E., 1,322½ feet; 6th. N., 7° 45′ W., 493 feet; the variation being 12° east.   The termination of this 6th or last course and distance, being the above said most northwestern point of the Lake of the Woods, as designated by the 7th article of the treaty of Ghent; and being in the latitude forty-nine degrees twenty-three minutes and fifty-five seconds north of the equator; and in longitude, ninety-five degrees fourteen minutes and thirty-eight seconds west from the observatory at Greenwich."

"The Chaudière falls of lake Namecan" (Namakan), at the entrance to Lac la Pluie or Rainy Lake, are now known as Kettle Falls.   They are shown on sheet 14 of the maps of the International Boundary Commission, hereafter described, and are at approximately 48°30′ north and 92°38′ west; these Chaudière Falls are to be distinguished from the other falls of the same name mentioned in the above description of the line as being in Rivière la Pluie or Rainy River.

In so far as the Commissioners under Article 7 of the Treaty of Ghent agreed upon a line, that line was followed and adopted in Article 2 of the Webster-Ashburton Treaty; and in so far as those Com-

missioners did not agree upon a line, the boundary was described in
Article 2 of this treaty, which added that from the northwesternmost
point of the Lake of the Woods the line should run, in accordance with
Article 2 of the treaty of 1818 (Document 40), "due south to its intersection with the 49ᵗʰ parallel of north latitude, and along that parallel
to the Rocky Mountains."

The negotiations of 1842 regarding what was then called "the
North West boundary", a term hardly appropriate now, met with
little difficulty; the question, in comparison with that of the northeastern boundary, was minor; there is little doubt that the Plenipotentiaries reached a general accord on the subject along with that
on the northeastern boundary, for in the letter of Webster to the
commissioners of Maine and Massachusetts of July 15, 1842 (quoted
above), he wrote that it was probable "that the disputed line of boundary in Lake Superior might be so adjusted as to leave a disputed
island [Sugar Island] within the United States"; and in his note dated
the next day Ashburton wrote to Webster as follows (D.S., 21 Notes
from the British Legation; published correspondence, 56–58):

The Commissioners [under Article 7 of the Treaty of Ghent] who failed in
their endeavours to make this settlement, differed on two points

First, as to the appropriation of an island called Sᵗ George's [or Sugar] Island,
lying in the water communication between Lake Huron and Lake Superior; and

Secondly, as to the boundary through the water-communications from Lake
Superior to the Lake of the Woods.

The first point I am ready to give up to you, as you are no doubt aware that
it it is the only object of any real value in this controversy. The island of Sᵗ
George's is reported to contain 25920 acres of very fertile land, but, the other
things connected with these boundaries being satisfactorily arranged, a line shall
be drawn so as to throw this Island within the limits of the United States.

In considering the second point, it really appears of little importance to either
party how the line be determined through the wild country between Lake Superior
and the Lake of the Woods, but it is important that some line should be fixed and
known.

The American Commissioner asked for the line from Lake Superior up the
River Kamanastiguia to the Lake called Dog Lake, which he supposed to be the
same as that called Long Lake in the Treaties, thence through Sturgeon Lake to
the Lac La Pluie, to that point where the two lines assumed by the Commissioners
again meet.

The British Commissioner, on the other hand, contended for a line from the
Southwestern extremity at a point called Le fond du Lac to the middle of the
mouth of the estuary or Lake of Sᵗ Louis River, thence up that river through
Vermilion river to Lac La Pluie.

Attempts were made to compromise these differences, but they failed, apparently more from neither party being willing to give up the Island of Sᵗ George's,
than from much importance being attached to any other part of the case.

Upon the line from Lake Superior to the Lake of the Woods both Commissioners
agreed to abandon their respective claims and to adopt a middle course, for which
the American Commissioner admitted that there was some ground of preference.
This was from Pigeon river, a point between the Kamanastiguia and the fond du
Lac, and although there were differences as to the precise point near the mouth
of the Pigeon river where the line should begin, neither party seem to have
attached much importance to this part of the subject.

I would propose that the line be taken from a point about six miles south of
Pigeon river where the Grand portage commences on the Lake, and continued
along the line of the said Portage alternately by Land and Water to Lac la Pluie:
the existing route by land and by water remaining common to both parties.
This line has the advantage of being known and attended with no doubt or
uncertainty in running it.

Coupled with the concession of Sugar Island were certain conditions of free passage; the relevant paragraphs of the foregoing note are quoted below under the heading "Article 7".

In dealing with these questions of boundary and passage Ashburton was aided by Anthony Barclay, British Commissioner under Articles 6 and 7 of the Treaty of Ghent, from whom he "received much useful advice and assistance". Webster had before him a letter written by Joseph Delafield, who had been agent of the United States under the articles mentioned; and he also received information from James Ferguson, who had served as astronomical surveyor during the proceedings under Article 7 of that treaty, and from Robert Stuart, who was agent for the Ottawa and Chippewa Indians and acting superintendent of the Michigan Superintendency (see published correspondence, 102–6). Delafield and Ferguson had each explored the country between Lake Superior and the Lake of the Woods; Stuart pointed out *inter alia* that the treaty with the Chippewa tribe of Indians of August 5, 1826 (7 Statutes at Large, 290–93), provided for grants of land on Sugar Island.

Webster's answer of July 27 (D.S., 6 Notes to the British Legation, 239–46; published correspondence, 58–61) stated the whole boundary settlement (Articles 1–7 of the treaty); his wording descriptive of the boundary here in question is that of Article 2; the line of that article differs slightly from the proposal of Ashburton in that the boundary from Lake Superior to the Lake of the Woods begins at the mouth of Pigeon River and not at "a point about six miles south" thereof. As to this Webster wrote as follows:

It is desirable to follow the description and the exact line of the original treaty as far as practicable. There is reason to think that "Long Lake", mentioned in the Treaty of 1783, ment merely the estuary of the Pigeon river, as no lake called "Long lake", or any other water strictly conforming to the idea of a lake, is found in that quarter. This opinion is strengthened by the fact that the words of the Treaty would seem to imply that the water intended as "Long Lake", was immediately joining Lake Superior. In one respect an exact compliance with the words of the Treaty is not practicable. There is no continuous water communication between Lake Superior and the Lake of the Woods, as the Lake of the Woods is known to discharge its waters through the Red River of the north into Hudson's Bay. The dividing height or ridge between the eastern sources of the tributaries of the Lake of the Woods and the western sources of Pigeon River appears, by authentic maps, to be distant about forty miles from the mouth of Pigeon River, on the shore of Lake Superior.

It is not improbable that in the imperfection of knowledge which then existed of those remote countries, and perhaps misled by Mitchell's map, the negotiators of the Treaty of 1783 supposed the Lake of the Woods to discharge its waters into Lake Superior. The broken and difficult nature of the water communication from Lake Superior to the Lake of the Woods renders numerous portages necessary; and it is right that these water communications and these portages should make a common highway, where necessary, for the use of the subjects and citizens of both Governments.

The assent of Ashburton (note of July 29; D.S., 21 Notes from the British Legation; published correspondence, 61–62) was general, going to the whole of the terms stated by Webster. His note opens with these sentences:

I have attentively considered the statement contained in the letter you did me the honor of addressing me on the 27ᵗʰ of this month, of the terms agreed to for the settlement of Boundaries between Her Majesty's Provinces and the United States, being the final result of the many conferences we have had on this subject. This settlement appears substantially correct in all its parts, and we may now proceed without further delay to draw up the Treaty. Several of the Articles for this purpose are already prepared and agreed, and our most convenient course will be to take and consider them singly.

Certain paragraphs of the presidential message to the Senate of August 11, 1842 (quoted above), refer to the clauses of Article 2 of the treaty.

THE MAPS OF ARTICLE 2

In the journal of the Commissioners for October 22, 1827, is the following account of the maps prepared under Article 7 of the Treaty of Ghent (printed in British and Foreign State Papers, LVII, 817–19; text here from a "true copy", enclosure to the letter of Joseph Delafield, Agent of the United States, dated November 6, 1827, D.S., Boundary, Article 7, Treaty of Ghent; a few punctuation points lacking in that paper have been supplied, and the style of its centered headings is not followed; and the bracketed numbers here of the last eight maps are from the print cited, as in the manuscript copy those eight maps are not numbered):

Such Maps as were not completed at the last meeting of the Board were directed to be filed in quadruplicate, and they are hereby filed as of October 23ᵈ 1826.

Subjoined is a descriptive list of Maps prepared under the 7th. Article of the Treaty of Ghent.

The following are signed by Mʳ Thompson as Principal Surveyor to the Board

No. 1. Part of Muddy Lake, part of St Tammany and St Josephs Islands, being part of the 6th Article

No. 2. Part of St Tammanys, St Georges and St Josephs Islands, the West, middle and East Neebish Rapids, and part of the lesser and greater Lakes George and the termination of the 6th Article.

No. 3. Part of St George's Island, and of the lesser and greater Lakes George.

No. 4. Part of St. George's Island, part of the Greater Lake George and part of the St Marys River, and the Isles of the Sugar Rapids.

No. 5. Part of St Mary's River, with the Isles of the Falls of St. Marys.

No. 6. Part of the River St. Mary.

No. 7. Part of the River St. Mary and its Sortie from Lake Superior.

No. 8. Lake Superior.

No. 9. The Estuary or Lake of the River St. Louis and part of the River.

No. 10. Part of the River St. Louis.

No. 11. Part of the River St Louis and of the Rivierre aux Embarras.

No. 12. Part of the Rivierre aux Embarras, the Height of Land Portage, part of Vermillion River, and Vermillion Lake.

No. 13. The Grand Portage, the Estuary of the Pigeon River, the Pigeon River, South and North Fowl Lakes Lac d'original and Mountain Lake, arrow River and part of Arrow Lake.

No. 14. Part of Arrow Lake, Rose or Mud Lake, south and North Lakes of the Height, Lac des Pierres a Fusil Chain of Brooks, Rapids and Lakes, Lake Saganagah Swamp and Cypress Lakes and part of Knife Lake

No. 15. Part of Knife Lake, Carp and Birch Lakes, Lac des Bois Blanc, Crooked and Iron Lakes, part of Lac la Croix, and part of Namekan River and an extra Map of Lac la Croix.

No. 16. Part of Vermillion River, Crane Lake, part of Lac la Croix, Loons narrow Lake, lesser Vermillion and sand point Lakes.

No. 17. Part of Namekan River.

No. 18. Part of Namekan River, Namekan Lake and part of the Rainy Lake.
No. 19. Part of the Rainy Lake and River.
No. 20. Part of the Rainy River.
No. 21. A Bay of the Rainy Lake.
No. 22. South East part of the Lake of the Woods.
No. 23. North East Bay of the Lake of the Woods.
No. 24. Part of the Rainy River and of the Lake of the Woods.
No. 25. The North west corner of the Lake of the Woods.
No. 26. The North Part of the Lake of the Woods.
The following Maps are signed by Mr James Ferguson as principal Surveyor to the Board.
[No. 27A.] A Map Containing Part of Muddy Lake, part of St Josephs Island, the termination of the 6th. Article, St Tammany's and St. George's Island, Lesser and greater Lakes George; West, middle and East Neebish Rapids. part of St. Marys River and the Isles of the Sugar Rapids.
[No. 28B.] A Map Containing Part of St. Marys River to its Sortie from Lake Superior and the Islands of the Falls of St Mary.
[No. 29C.] A Map Containing Part of Lake Superior, being Islands Royale and Paté and other Islands, and the Estuary of the Pigeon River.
[No. 30D.] A Map Containing The Grand Portage, Pigeon River, Pakaqua, Sagagan, Lac du Cog, part of Moose Sagagan and part of Arrow River.
[No. 31E.] A Map Containing Part of Arrow River, Arrow Lake, part of Moose Lake, Lac a la Montagne, Lac a la Rose, A.ja.wa.wa. Satagan Lakes, part of Flint Lake
[No. 32F.] A Map Containing Part of Flint Lake, chain of Rivers, Rapids and Lakes Lake Sais-a-gin-cga and Chain of Waters going Northwestward.
[No. 33G.] A Map Containing Chain of Rivers and Lakes leading to Sturgeon Lake, and part of Rivierre Maligne.
[No. 34H.] A Map Containing Part of Rivierre Maligne, Lac la Croix and River Namekan to Lake Namekan.
Two complete sets of the above Maps were delivered to each of the Commissioners.

The maps signed by the Commissioners, which are in the archives of the Department of State, correspond to those thus listed and described in the journal of the Commissioners; but the maps which in that list are numbered 1 to 26, inclusive, are numbered I to XXVI. Map XIV has with it a subchart, not mentioned in that list, showing Lake Kaseiganagah,[1] and there is also with map XV a subchart called in the list "an extra map of Lac la Croix"; and the eight maps corresponding to those which in the list are given bracketed numbers from 27A to 34H are numbered 1 to 8, inclusive. Thus, besides the two subcharts, there are in all thirty-four maps or charts, here referred to as maps I to XXVI and maps 1 to 8 respectively.

Signed maps XVI and XVIII are lacking in the archives of the Department of State; certified copies thereof were obtained in 1869 from the British Government. The statement of Chandler P. Anderson in the matter (*op. cit.*, 42–43) follows. His remark that the missing originals of maps XVI and XVIII "have not yet been found" (written in 1906) remains true in 1934:

In 1869 copies of charts Nos. XIII, XIV (with subchart attached), XV (with subchart attached), XVI, and XVIII of this series, certified to be correct copies by Col. Henry James, of the Royal Engineers, under date of February 5, 1869, were obtained from the British Government for the purpose of replacing the corresponding charts which were then missing from the American set. These certified copies, however, as has since appeared, were not reproductions of the

---

[1] So on the map; now "Saganaga".

British original treaty charts, but of another set of charts on file in the Foreign Office marked "incomplete set," the charts comprising which are apparently exact duplicates of the American treaty charts except that the boundary line as laid down in 1842 by Webster and Ashburton is not marked on them and they do not bear their signatures. The certified copies from this set, therefore, do not show the boundary line and have no treaty value.

When the question of the demarcation of this portion of the boundary came up for consideration before the Joint High Commission in 1898 Sir Richard Cartwright, one of the Canadian Commissioners, produced a series of maps indicating a continuous boundary line, marked in black, through the connecting waters all the way from Lake Superior to Chaudière Falls. These maps, he stated, had been copied from the originals in London by the Ordinance Office there. On them was shown the indorsement: "Map of Boundary. Agreed to by Treaty August 9, 1842. (Signed) Ashburton. Daniel Webster." The signatures of Barclay and Porter, Commissioners under the Treaty of Ghent, were also shown. Mr. Kasson, who was the American member of the Joint High Commission subcommittee on the boundary question, reported the existence of these maps to the Department of State in a letter to Mr. Adee, dated October 5, 1898, in which he says:

> "I am forced to believe that duplicates of these maps, with the original certificates of the negotiators of the Treaty of 1842, must exist somewhere in the Department of State."

Prior to that time for a number of years the fact that Webster and Ashburton had marked on maps any portion of the line west of Lake Superior had been lost sight of in the absence of any maps showing this portion of the line in the series filed with the Treaty of 1842 in the Department of State, and it had been assumed that no such maps existed. . . .

Upon Mr. Kasson's report, however, a search was instituted and three of the missing maps—Nos. XIII, XIV (with an unnumbered submap attached), and XV (also with an unnumbered submap attached) of the series—were discovered in the Library of Congress [and are now in the archives of the Department of State], but the other two missing originals of the series (Nos. XVI and XVIII) were not with them and have not yet been found.

The boundary as shown on the original charts now on file in the Department of State is incomplete west of Lake Superior, from Lac la Croix to the Chaudière Falls in Rainy Lake.

The line drawn on certain of their maps by the Commissioners under Article 7 of the Treaty of Ghent was "a line of black ink, shaded on the British side with red and on the American side with blue"; that line appears on the following thirteen maps, namely, maps I, II, V–VIII, XVIII–XX, XXIV, XXV, and maps 1 and 2.

All the maps and both subcharts were signed by the Commissioners, Peter B. Porter and Anthony Barclay, and by one or other of the surveyors, David Thompson (maps I–XXVI and the two subcharts) and James Ferguson (maps 1–8). Over the signatures of those officials on the thirty-four maps is the following certificate (which varies immaterially on the different maps):

A true Map of part of the Survey, under the 7th Article of the Treaty of Ghent, made by order of the Commissioners

Over the corresponding signatures on the subcharts is written:

A true Copy of the Map made, and presented, by Mr James Ferguson, American Principal Surveyor, to the Commission, and certified, and signed by him, and the Commissioners; this Copy being intended to exhibit the course of a certain Line described by the British Commissioner for a proposed Boundary, as set forth in the Journal of the Board, under date of the 23rd of October 1826

Maps I to XXVI each have also the following certificate, signed by S. Thompson, draftsman and assistant surveyor:

I hereby certify this Map is a True Copy of the original filed by order of the Board of Commissioners under the 6 & 7th Articles of the Treaty of Ghent.

The above certificate does not appear on maps 1 to 8, which are simply inscribed "George W. Whistler. U.S. Artillery. Draftsman & Assist. Surveyor", or on the subcharts.

On maps 1 and 2 is lettered "Scale of two Inches to one Mile Geographic [1:36,450]"; on map 3 is lettered "Scale of one Inch to one Mile Geographic"; and on maps 4 and 5 the scale is shown graphically (1:32,081; about 2 inches to 1 mile). The various scales of the remaining maps and subcharts, though not indicated thereon, have been determined; they are, for the maps designated, roughly as follows: maps 6–8, 2 inches to 1 mile; maps I–VII, 4 inches to 1 mile; map VIII, 1 inch to 7.9 miles; and maps IX–XXVI, 1 inch to 1 mile. The scale of the subchart with map XIV is about 2 inches to 1 mile, and that of the subchart with map XV is about 1⅓ inch to 1 mile.

The maps vary somewhat in size; most of them are from 47 to 52 inches by 27 to 31 inches, or thereabouts; maps XXIII and XXV are slightly narrower, and map XXVI is 47 by 15 inches; the subchart with map XIV is about 23 by 18 inches, and that with map XV, about 29 by 20 inches.

Facsimiles of those thirty-six maps, in black and white and somewhat reduced, are in Moore, International Arbitrations, VI; they are numbered in that collection 26 to 61, inclusive. The arrangement there, however, differs from the order of the list in the journal of the Commissioners; and the reproductions of maps XIII, XIV, and XV and of the subcharts to maps XIV and XV are from certified copies; at the time that that work was published the signed examples of those three maps and of the two subcharts had not been found and were not available in the Department of State archives.

While Article 2 of this treaty makes no mention of the signing of maps, the Plenipotentiaries, Webster and Ashburton, signed certain of the maps of the Commissioners under Article 7 of the Treaty of Ghent; those so signed which are now in the archives of the Department of State are the following: map 1 (27A of the list in the journal of the Commissioners) and maps II, III, IV, VIII, XIII, XIV, and XV, and also the subcharts of maps XIV and XV; and maps XVI and XVIII were also signed by Webster and Ashburton, as an examination of the maps in the British archives, made in 1906, disclosed; but, as has been stated, the archives of the Department of State do not include originals of those two maps. The whole number of maps signed by the respective Plenipotentiaries was thus twelve.

The twelve signed maps show the line of 1842 all the way from the point in the Neebish Channel near Muddy Lake as far as Chaudière (Kettle) Falls, except for a short stretch (less than three miles) of St. Marys River; on those six of the maps so signed (III, IV, XIII, XIV, XV, and XVI) which have no line of the Commissioners under Article 7 of the Treaty of Ghent, a red-ink line (except on map III, where

the line is of black pencil) was drawn to indicate the boundary of the Webster-Ashburton Treaty; on the four maps (II, VIII, XVIII, and 1) having a partial line of the Commissioners, that line was completed; the completing line is similarly of red ink, except on map II, where it is of black pencil; on one of the two subcharts (XIV) the red-ink line is drawn over what is doubtless the original line in black; on the other (XV) it is drawn over a faint black-pencil line.

Each map signed has as a certificate over the signatures of the Plenipotentiaries, "Map of boundary agreed to [or "upon"] by Treaty, August 9th 1842"; and beside the line of 1842 drawn on each signed map is written "Boundary under the Treaty of Washington".

The short stretch of the boundary up St. Marys River which is not shown on the maps signed by Webster and Ashburton appears as part of the line of the Commissioners on map V and similarly on map 2; those two maps are thus within the words of Article 2 where it speaks of "adopting the line traced on the maps by the Commissioners" from a point about one mile above Sugar Island through St. Marys River and Lake Superior "to a point north of Ile Royale . . . where the line marked by the Commissioners terminates"; also within those words are maps VI and VII, each of which shows a part of the line of the Commissioners through St. Marys River, though neither shows any portion of the boundary which is not drawn on the maps signed by Webster and Ashburton; but map I is geographically without the treaty words quoted, as the line of the Commissioners thereon is wholly below Sugar Island.

Four other maps of the Commissioners under Article 7 of the Treaty of Ghent (not signed by Webster and Ashburton) are adopted by Article 2 of this treaty; these are maps XIX, XX, XXIV, and XXV; they (with map XVIII) show the line northwestward from the point at Chaudière (Kettle) Falls "from which the Commissioners traced the line to the most northwestern point of the Lake of the Woods".

The red line, clearly intended as the line of the treaty, is drawn on maps 3 and 6; but those two maps were not signed by Webster and Ashburton and do not show any line of the Commissioners; and the remaining maps, namely, maps IX, X, XI, XII, XVII, XXI, XXII, XXIII, XXVI, and maps 4, 5, 7, and 8, a total of thirteen, show no boundary line at all, either of the Commissioners or of Webster and Ashburton.

It appears that the first suggestion for the adoption by the negotiators of this treaty of the maps prepared by the Commissioners under Article 7 of the Treaty of Ghent was made by Ashburton, who wrote thus to Webster on July 29 (D.S., 21 Notes from the British Legation; published correspondence, 61–62):

I would beg leave to recommend that as we have excellent charts of the country, through which the Boundary which failed of being settled by the Commissioners under the 7th Article of the Treaty of Ghent is partially marked, that it would be advisable to make good the delineation on those charts, which would spare to both parties the unnecessary expence of New Commissioners, and a new survey.

It further appears that that one of the two sets of the maps signed by Webster and Ashburton which was the set for the British Government, was obtained by Ashburton from Anthony Barclay, who had been British Commissioner under Articles 6 and 7 of the Treaty of Ghent. In that one of his despatches of August 9, 1842, to Aberdeen which enclosed the early or first form of the signed treaty (Ashburton Papers, despatch No. 17) Ashburton wrote as follows:

The Boundaries further west require little explanation. I enclose copies of two notes [of July 16 and 29, 1842, published correspondence, 56–58, 61–62] which I have addressed to Mr Webster upon the subject of them. Mr A. Barclay, who acted as British Commissioner under the 6th and 7th Articles of the Treaty of Ghent having furnished me with a set of very perfect Charts of the Country, the line as settled by the Treaty is marked upon them. It will be observed that St George's Island between Lake Huron and Lake Superior, which was in dispute, has been allotted to the United States, and that the line in dispute from Lake Superior to Rainy Lake, (Lac la Pluie) has been fixed at Pigeon River, and thence along the Grand Portage to Rainy Lake. The Pigeon River seemed to answer best to the words of the Treaty of 1783, but it will be seen that there is a stipulation that both parties shall use the line of the Portage, which leaves Lake Superior a few miles south of Pigeon river, and that this Portage as well as our Boundary runs to the South of Hunter's Island. I ascertained, that our North-western fur traders do not commonly use the Grand portage for their communications, but that they prefer the route by the Kaministiguia. They will however have the option of using the Grand portage should they prefer returning to it. It is my duty here to add, that in this part of my work, I have received much useful advice and assistance from Mr Barclay.

The Line of Article 2 as Now Demarcated

As now demarcated, the line of Article 2 of the Webster-Ashburton Treaty is to be considered in two parts.

The first part, from the foot of Neebish Rapids through the water communication between Lake Huron and Lake Superior and across Lake Superior to the mouth of Pigeon River, is a portion of the water boundary between the United States and Canada (i.e., the boundary in the St. Lawrence River and through the Great Lakes).

The demarcation of that entire water boundary was entrusted to the International Waterways Commission pursuant to Article 4 of the treaty of April 11, 1908, with Great Britain; and the resulting demarcation is shown on a series of charts entitled "International Boundary between the United States and Dominion of Canada through the Saint Lawrence River and Great Lakes as Ascertained and Reestablished by the International Waterways Commission Pursuant to Article 4 of the Treaty between the United States and Great Britain Signed April 11, 1908, in 30 Sheets Including an Index Sheet".

Sheets 1 to 23, inclusive, of this series, cover that portion of the boundary dealt with by Article 6 of the Treaty of Ghent, namely, from the point where the 45th degree of north latitude strikes the River St. Lawrence to the water communication between Lake Huron and Lake Superior; sheets 21 to 29, inclusive, show the boundary through the water communication between Lake Huron and Lake Superior and continuing through Lake Superior to the mouth of Pigeon River at the western shore of that lake.

The scale of sheets 22, 23, 24, 26, and 29 is 1:20,000; of sheets 21 and 27, 1:60,000; of sheet 25, 1:10,000; and of sheet 28, 1:300,000.

Some further reference to that series of charts will be found in the notes to Document 42.

The second part of the line of Article 2 of the Webster-Ashburton Treaty is the boundary between the United States and Canada from the Lake of the Woods to Lake Superior. As now demarcated, that line is shown on a series of maps, consisting of 36 sheets with an index sheet, which accompanied the joint report of the International Boundary Commission made pursuant to Article 5 of the treaty of April 11, 1908, with Great Britain.

Sheet 1 shows the northwesternmost point of the Lake of the Woods and also the turning point adopted in lieu thereof, pursuant to Article 1 of the treaty of February 24, 1925; the remaining sheets show the line continuing from the Lake of the Woods to the mouth of Pigeon River. The scale of sheets 1 and 2 is 1:62,500, of sheets 3 to 28, 1:24,000, and of sheets 29 to 36, 1:6,000.

Those maps, copies of which are obtainable from the office of the International Boundary Commission in Washington, are entitled "International Boundary from the Northwesternmost Point of Lake of the Woods to Lake Superior". They are variously dated from January 16, 1928, to February 27, 1930.

The following statement regarding those maps is from the joint report of the International Boundary Commission (pp. 104–6):

The charts upon which the commissioners have marked the boundary line from the Northwesternmost Point of Lake of the Woods to Lake Superior, in accordance with the above provisions of the treaty of 1908, are topographic maps prepared from the surveys made by the field force of the commission. They comprise a series of 36 sheets arranged and numbered as shown on the index map. . . . They have been engraved on copper plates and printed from lithographic stones. The engraved plates will be preserved by the two Governments as permanent records of the work. The four official sets of maps, two sets for each Government, signed by the commissioners, are transmitted in atlas form with this report. The maps for distribution to the public are identical with those of the official sets except that they bear the word "Copy," the year of publication, and the commissioners' signatures in facsimile.

The size of each map, inside the border, is 23 by 35 inches. The conventional signs used to represent the topographic features are those adopted by the United States Board of Surveys and Maps. The boundary line, monuments and other culture, and lettering appear in black, relief (contour lines) in brown, drainage in blue, and timber in green. The maps are constructed on the polyconic projection on scales of 1:6,000, 1:24,000, and 1:62,500, the scale depending upon the detail needed to show clearly the location of the boundary line with respect to important topographic features. Insert maps of the very narrow boundary channels are shown on 1:3,000, 1:6,000, 1:10,000, and 1:12,000 scales. A contour interval of 5 feet is used on the inserts and on the Pigeon River maps. On the rest of the maps a 10-foot interval is used. At the top of each sheet are the title, the number of the sheet, the names of the commissioners, and copies of the seals of the two countries. In the lower right corner is the commissioners' certificate, which reads as follows:

Sheet 1—
We certify that this map is one of the quadruplicate set of thirty-six (36) maps prepared under Article V of the Treaty between Great Britain and the United States of America, signed at Washington, April 11, 1908, and that we have marked hereon the Boundary Line as reestablished by the Com-

missioners designated above, in accordance with the provisions of Article V of the Treaty of 1908 and Article I of the Treaty between the United States and His Britannic Majesty, in respect of the Dominion of Canada, signed at Washington, February 24, 1925.

Signed, January 16, 1928

(Signed)   J. D. CRAIG   (Signed)   E. LESTER JONES
   His Britannic Majesty's Commissioner   United States Commissioner

Sheet 2—typical of sheets 2–36—

We certify that this map is one of the quadruplicate set of thirty-six (36) maps prepared under Article V of the Treaty between Great Britain and the United States of America, signed at Washington, April 11, 1908, and that we have marked hereon the Boundary Line as reestablished by the Commissioners designated above, in accordance with the provisions of the said Treaty.

Signed, January 16, 1928

(Signed)   J. D. CRAIG   (Signed)   E. LESTER JONES [1]
   His Britannic Majesty's Commissioner   United States Commissioner

.   .   .   .

A limited edition of the maps has been printed for each Government for distribution to other governmental agencies having use for them, to libraries, and to others interested in the exact location of any part of the international boundary line.   In the United States, copies of the report and maps are on file in the Library of Congress and in other libraries designated by the Government as "depository libraries"—that is, those which receive all United States Government publications.   In Canada they are on file in the Dominion Archives, in the libraries of the Dominion Parliament and of the provincial legislative assemblies, and in university and reference libraries throughout the country.

The elaborate report of the International Boundary Commission, dated October 27, 1931 (accompanied by "Triangulation and Traverse Sketches"), entitled "Joint Report upon the Survey and Demarcation of the Boundary between the United States and Canada from the Northwesternmost Point of Lake of the Woods to Lake Superior", was printed at Washington in 1931; the "Description and Definition of the International Boundary Line from the Northwesternmost Point of Lake of the Woods to Lake Superior" is there printed at pages 113–87.   With other pertinent material, that work includes five appendices, namely: (1) "Historical Sketch of the Early Explorations of the Region along the International Boundary from Lake Superior to Lake of the Woods" (with bibliography), pages 189–206; (2) "Negotiations and Treaties Pertaining to the Boundary Previous to the Treaty of 1908" (with two maps), pages 207–12; (3) "Original Survey of the Boundary from the Northwesternmost Point of Lake of the Woods to Lake Superior", pages 213–19; (4) "Elevations and Descriptions of Bench Marks", pages 220–27; (5) "Geographic Positions and Descriptions of Triangulation and Traverse Stations" (with index), pages 228–613.

THE MOST NORTHWESTERN POINT OF THE LAKE OF THE WOODS

In the peace of 1782–83 with Great Britain (Documents 7 and 11) the "most Northwestern Point" of the Lake of the Woods was named as a point of the boundary between the United States and Canada

---

[1] Sheets 26–36 are signed by James H. Van Wagenen as United States Commissioner.

whence the line was to run "on a due West Course to the River Mississippi" (Article 2 of the treaty of September 3, 1783); the framers of the peace of 1782–83 relied on Mitchell's Map; the quoted language was consistent therewith, as on that map the Lake of the Woods (drawn as of elliptical form and in simple outline) appears as if lying to the east of the Mississippi, the upper reaches of which are not shown because of the Hudson Bay inset (see the reproduction of Mitchell's Map in the pocket in the back cover of volume 3); but the source of the Mississippi lies well to the south of the Lake of the Woods, a fact which was surmised soon after 1783; no attempt was ever made to locate a line running due west from the Lake of the Woods (Paullin, *op. cit.*, 57); by Article 5 of the unratified convention with Great Britain of May 12, 1803 (D.S., Unperfected A1; American State Papers, Foreign Relations, II, 584–85), the boundary "in this Quarter" was "declared to be the shortest Line which can be drawn between the North west Point of the Lake of the Woods, and the nearest Source of the River Mississippi"; but, owing to the cession of Louisiana, the Senate excepted Article 5 in its resolution of advice and consent to that convention (Executive Journal, I, 463–64), which failed to go into force; and by Article 2 of the convention with Great Britain of October 20, 1818 (Document 40), it was provided—

that a Line drawn from the most North Western Point of the Lake of the Woods, along the forty Ninth Parallel of North Latitude, or, if the said Point shall not be in the Forty Ninth Parallel of North Latitude, then that a Line drawn from the said Point due North or South as the Case may be, until the said Line shall intersect the said Parallel of North Latitude, and from the Point of such Intersection due West along and with the said Parallel shall be the Line of Demarcation between the Territories of the United States, and those of His Britannic Majesty.

The Commissioners under Article 7 of the Treaty of Ghent (quoted earlier in these notes) were required thereby to "particularize the Latitude and Longitude of the most North Western point of the Lake of the Woods"; that task those Commissioners performed; and their determination of the location of that point was adopted in the Webster-Ashburton Treaty and remained accepted until the treaty with Canada of February 24, 1925 (Treaty Series No. 720).

Regarding the surveys of 1824 and 1825 the following paragraphs are extracted from the Joint Report of the International Boundary Commission (previously cited) dated October 27, 1931 (p. 107):

In 1824 David Thompson, surveyor and astronomer for the British Government, received instructions from the commissioners under Article VII of the treaty of Ghent to determine the "most northwestern point" of Lake of the Woods originally named in the treaty of peace, 1783, as the point to which the international boundary was to run westward through the waterways from Lake Superior. Accordingly, in the course of his surveys of the western and northern portions of Lake of the Woods in 1824, Thompson selected, monumented, and determined the astronomical positions of three points which, in his opinion, came nearest to meeting the requirements of the treaty—a point in Northwest Angle Inlet; a second point in Monument Bay, east and a little north of Northwest Angle Inlet; and a third in Portage Bay still farther north. Another point

which was later to be given consideration as the probable site of the Northwestern-most Point was at Rat Portage (Kenora), where an extensive series of astronomical observations had been made by Thompson during the previous year.

As a result of Thompson's work it was apparently realized that it would be necessary, in finally selecting the "most northwestern point," to choose between Rat Portage and the locality of the first point marked by Thompson in 1824, near the head of Northwest Angle Inlet. Accordingly, in the following year, 1825, Dr. J. L. Tiarks, astronomer for the British Government, inspected these two localities and decided that a point nearly a mile north of Thompson's monument in Northwest Angle Inlet was the true "most northwestern point" of Lake of the Woods. Tiarks's astronomic determination of the position of this point placed it in latitude 49°23'55", longitude 95°14'38".

The method used in 1825 in determining the point in question is thus explained (Reports upon the Survey of the Boundary . . . from the Lake of the Woods to the Summit of the Rocky Mountains, pp. 80–81; Senate Executive Document No. 41, 44th Congress, 2d session, serial 1719, p. 22):

I have before me the reports of Dr. I. L. Tiarks, astronomer (November 18, 1825), and David Thompson, surveyor (October, 1824), who were employed by the British Government to determine the northwest point, and whose reports were adopted at the time by the commissioner on the part of the United States.

From these reports, it appears that a question arose between the angle at the Rat Portage [1] and the northern point of the bay, now known as the Northwest Angle.

This question was settled by Tiarks in favor of the latter, on the principle that the northwest point was that point at which, if a line were drawn in the plane of a great circle, making an angle of 45° with the meridian, such a line would cut no other water of the lake. He therefore determined the relative position of the two points in question by means of their latitude and longitude; the latitudes were fixed by means of the sextant, and the longitude by the mean of several chronometer determinations.

From the same publication (p. 53) the following paragraph is quoted as showing the waters regarded as the Lake of the Woods: [2]

The Lake of the Woods is a name usually applied to a group of four lakes lying on the northern boundary of the United States, and nearly in a right line with Lakes Superior and Winnipeg. These four lakes, numbering from the northwest, are the Lac Plat, the Clear Water, the White Fish, and the Lake of the Sand Hills; the latter, by common usage, has adopted the name Lake of the Woods. The official sanction to this title was given by the commissioners under the sixth and seventh articles of the treaty of Ghent, in fixing the northwest point, and it is, therefore, useless, at this late day, to inquire into the extent and significance of the original term. It is, however, a little difficult to understand the process of reasoning by which those commissioners, while including the Clear Water and the Lake of the Sand Hills under the general title, yet rejected the Lac Plat.

---

[1] Shown on map XXVI of those signed by the Commissioners under Article 7 of the Treaty of Ghent approximately at north latitude 49°46' and west longitude 94°39' and, according to the configuration of the area, very near Keewatin, Ontario. On those maps, however, the longitudes in this vicinity are generally somewhat more than five minutes too far west. Rat Portage, a village now known as Kenora, lies about five minutes of longitude east of Keewatin (see the index sheet of the series of maps of the International Boundary Commission showing the line from the Lake of the Woods to Lake Superior); at that latitude a five-minute difference in longitude is equal to approximately 3.7 statute miles; from station to station on the Canadian Pacific Railway the distance is 3.1 miles.

[2] Alternatively "Kaminitik" on the maps of the Commissioners under Article 7 of the Treaty of Ghent.

Map VI (7) in the back of the document last cited shows clearly what waters were comprised in the Lake of the Woods as the Boundary Commission of 1872–76 defined it. Lac Plat of that map is Shoal Lake on the index map (published in 1930) of the series of the International Boundary Commission showing the line from the Lake of the Woods to Lake Superior (heretofore referred to and described). Clear Water Lake and White Fish Lake appear to be now included in Whitefish Bay of the Lake of the Woods.

On Map XXV of the Commissioners under Article 7 of the Treaty of Ghent appears the point fixed and agreed on as "The North-western Point"; and that point is stipulated in terms of latitude and longitude (as astronomically determined in 1825) in Article 2 of the Webster-Ashburton Treaty.

The United States Northern Boundary Commission of 1872–76 (see the act of March 19, 1872, 17 Statutes at Large, 43), which had in charge the determination and demarcation of the boundary line "between the Lake of the Woods and the Rocky Mountains", identified the northwesternmost point from a reference mark placed by Thompson in 1824, which was used by Dr. Tiarks in 1825 in determining the latitude and longitude of the northwesternmost point itself (see Joint Report dated October 27, 1931, p. 110, footnote 8).

The treaty with Great Britain of April 11, 1908, provided "for the more complete definition and demarcation of the international boundary between the United States and the Dominion of Canada"; Articles 5 and 6 thereof deal with the line from Pigeon River to the northwesternmost point of the Lake of the Woods, and thence to the Rocky Mountains. In connection with the survey of 1912 under the treaty of April 11, 1908, it was found necessary to redetermine the northwesternmost point from the records of the survey of 1872, as no trace of the reference monument erected in 1824 could be found (*ibid.*, 110).

At the same time there were discovered certain undesirable features in the boundary due south from the northwesternmost point (*ibid.*, 107, 109):

the fact was definitely established by the surveys made in 1912 under the treaty of 1908 that the straight course of boundary running due south from the Northwesternmost Point was intersected at five points by the winding course of boundary which follows the deep-water channel of Northwest Angle Inlet, thereby leaving two small areas of United States waters entirely surrounded by Canadian waters, a territorial delimitation neither intended nor desired by either Government.

The commissioners acting under the treaty of 1908 therefore agreed that the southernmost point of intersection of these lines, as determined in 1912, should be permanently fixed and monumented and were prepared to recommend to the two Governments, as they later did, that this point be adopted in lieu of the original Northwesternmost Point specified in Articles V and VI of the treaty of 1908, so as to eliminate from the general line of demarcation between the two countries the intersecting portions of the boundary north of this point.

By Article 1 of the treaty with Canada of February 24, 1925 (Treaty Series No. 720), provision was made for the adoption of the most southerly point of intersection of the channel with the meridian

of the northwesternmost point, stipulated as being in latitude 49°23′ 04″.49 north and longitude 95°09′11″.61 west. This point is 4,785 feet south of the original northwesternmost point and 2,522 feet north of monument No. 925 on the meridian line (Joint Report dated October 27, 1931, p. 112).

Reference is also to be made to the map on page 108 of the report last cited, which shows the position of the point adopted in 1925 in lieu of the original northwesternmost point and also the five intersections of the channel with the line due south from the original point.

TURNING POINT AND MONUMENTS

The point fixed by the treaty of 1925 in lieu of the original northwesternmost point is now known as Turning Point No. 1 of the boundary from the Lake of the Woods to Lake Superior. It is marked, not at the point itself, but only by reference points on the land. The turning point at the east end of this portion of the boundary, at the mouth of the Pigeon River, in Lake Superior, is Turning Point No. 1797 (*ibid.*, 155).

As now monumented, the monuments on the meridian due south of the northwesternmost point of the Lake of the Woods, to the 49th parallel, are the last-numbered monuments of the portion of the United States–Canada boundary from the Gulf of Georgia to the northwesternmost point of the Lake of the Woods. The monuments on this meridian are Nos. 913 to 925, inclusive. The most northerly monument on this line, No. 925, is 2,522 feet (768.8 meters) due south of the point which was fixed by the treaty of 1925 in lieu of the original northwesternmost point (*ibid.*, 112, 114).

COORDINATES OF THE NORTHWESTERNMOST POINT AND OF THE POINT ADOPTED IN
1925 IN LIEU THEREOF

Description	Latitude (north)	Longitude (west)
Astronomic determination of the "most northwestern point" by Dr. J. L. Tiarks, 1825	49°23′55″	95°14′38″
Position of the same point relocated in 1912 as closely as possible from the records of the Boundary Commission of 1872–76	49°23′51″.70	95°09′11″.63
Redetermination of the same point on the North American datum of 1927	49°23′51″.35	95°09′11″.36
Point adopted in lieu of the northwesternmost point of the Lake of the Woods by the treaty with Canada of February 24, 1925, Article 1	49°23′04″.49	95°09′11″.61
Position of the same point (Turning Point No. 1) on the North American datum of 1927 [1]	49°23′04″.14	95°09′11″.34

[1] "The geographic coordinates used by the two Governments in the treaty of 1925 to define the location of this point . . . were based on the original North American datum which, since the treaty of 1925, has been superseded by the North American datum of 1927, the geodetic datum on which all geographic positions of this section of the international boundary line are based" (*ibid.*, 114, footnote).

ARTICLE 5

The Disputed Territory Fund had its origin in acts of jurisdiction by the authorities of the Province of New Brunswick within the disputed territory south of the St. John; timber cut there (in part, at least, by trespassers without color of right) was by those authorities seized and sold; the proceeds were "carried to a separate account, the disposal of which awaits the adjustment of the boundary" (Sir Charles R. Vaughan, British Minister at Washington, to Viscount Palmerston, Secretary of State for Foreign Affairs, March 12, 1834); the Secretary of State (Louis McLane) was notified by the British Minister that "the proceeds of the sale of timber unlawfully cut down, are carried to account, and the possession of them will finally be appropriated to the party to which the territory may be adjudged by the settlement of the boundary question" (February 28, 1834); Sir Archibald Campbell, Lieutenant Governor of New Brunswick, wrote on January 20, 1834, to the British Minister that "every sixpence arising from seizures in the disputed territory has been invariably paid over to the Receiver General of the Province, by whom a separate fund, and separate account of all such monies is regularly kept" (see Blue Book, 1838, North American Boundary, pt. B, "Proceedings and Correspondence Relating to the Pretensions of the States of Maine, Massachusetts and New Hampshire, and to the Question of Jurisdiction within the Disputed Territory from 1831 to 1837", pp. 24–35).

It thus appears, as Ashburton wrote in that paragraph of his despatch No. 17 of August 9, 1842 (quoted above), which deals with the Disputed Territory Fund, that the engagement regarding it "confirms only what would be fairly due, if no notice were taken of this subject in the Treaty"; but the accounting and settlement required a longer period than the six months stipulated; correspondence from 1843 to 1845 is printed in House Document No. 110, 29th Congress, 1st session, serial 483, pp. 46–78.

After further exchanges between the two Governments the "Disputed Territory Fund" was finally adjusted and settled between the Provincial Government of New Brunswick and agents of the States of Maine (John Hodsdon) and Massachusetts (George W. Coffin); an agreement of settlement was signed at Fredericton on September 29, 1846. The amount paid over to the agent of Massachusetts for the use of the two States was $14,893.45 (£3,723 8s. 3½d. currency); the bonds delivered came to £8,700 2s. 10d., subject, apparently, to credits of £2,113 3s. 1d. An acquittance to the Government of the United States was signed by the Governors of Massachusetts and Maine on March 31, 1847 (D.S., Northeastern Boundary, envelope 18; see 36 Domestic Letters, 121, November 3, 1846, letters of Secretary of State Buchanan to the Governors of the two States). The settlement was deemed a "substantial fulfilment of the obligations contracted by the British Government under the 5th article of the treaty of Washington" (D.S., 7 Notes to the British Legation, 155–57, April 21, 1847).

The incorporation in Article 5 of the agreement of the Government of the United States "with the States of Maine and Massachusetts" to pay the claims of those States for expenses and $300,000 in addition "on account of their assent to the line of boundary described in this Treaty" was quite anomalous.   Lord Ashburton was concerned about "the introduction of terms of agreement between the General Government and the States" and in a private note to Webster of August 2 wrote as follows (Curtis, Life of Daniel Webster, II, 117):

But, my dear sir, my rest is disturbed by your money clause in our treaty, from which you must somehow contrive to relieve it.   I cannot with any propriety be a party to an agreement that the United States shall pay money to the States of Maine and Massachusetts.   This must, it seems to me, be done by a statement to Congress, of the existence of such an arrangement, with which it would be most impertinent that Great Britain should interfere.   I certainly knew that there was to be a payment, but until yesterday I had no idea that this was to make any part of the treaty with us.   Further, I foresee endless difficulties and delays from this ill-contrived arrangement.   The treaty must pass the lower as well as upper House, and what would require only a few days may be prolonged for as many months.   One M. C. to whom this secret was known told me that it might not be of importance with respect to amount, but that a great constitutional question was involved, viz., the question of Jay's treaty over again.   I am sure this course will involve us in difficulties, setting aside the consideration that there is really an absurdity in putting into a treaty with us your bargain with the States.   I must, my dear sir, beg you will make some other arrangement for these payments.

While the clauses remained in the treaty, by the notes of Ashburton and Webster signed with the treaty and printed above following the text it was expressly agreed that the British Government "incurs no responsibility for these engagements".

The act of March 3, 1843 (5 Statutes at Large, 623), appropriated $300,000 for the payment to Maine and Massachusetts under Article 5 of the treaty and sums of $206,934.79 for the expenses of Maine and $10,792.95 for those of Massachusetts; and by the act of June 17, 1844 (*ibid.*, 681, 695), there was a further appropriation of $80,000 to satisfy the claims of Maine.

ARTICLE 6

The act of March 3, 1843, "for carrying into effect" this treaty (5 Statutes at Large, 623), contained provisions in aid of the execution of Article 6 thereof and made an appropriation of $15,000 for salaries and expenses.

The Commissioners appointed under Article 6 to run, trace, and mark the line from the source of the St. Croix River to the St. Lawrence River were Albert Smith for the United States and Lieutenant Colonel James Bucknall Bucknall Estcourt for Great Britain.   A full account of the work of those Commissioners, entitled "Original Survey and Demarcation of the Boundary under the Treaty of 1842", is appendix 3 (pp. 322–36) to the joint report of the International Boundary Commission submitted to the Secretary of State on October 30, 1924, and heretofore cited.   The joint report of the Commissioners under Article 6 of this treaty was dated June 28, 1847,

and is printed in the work mentioned at pages 309–14; its text is also in Richardson, IV, 171–77; an original is in the Department of State archives (for the instructions to the British Commissioner and other correspondence, see British and Foreign State Papers, XXXIII, 763–806).

However, the maps, drawings, and tables prepared under the direction of the Commissioners and duly authenticated by them and intended to be deposited in the archives of the Department of State were destroyed by fire in 1848; and pursuant to the act of August 12, 1848 (9 Statutes at Large, 284, 297), "reconstructed" maps, on a scale of 2 inches to the mile instead of the original scale of 4 inches to the mile, were prepared by Lieutenant Colonel James D. Graham, U.S.A. (House Executive Document No. 132, 39th Congress, 1st session, serial 1263).   That "reconstructed" series comprises thirty maps showing the boundary from the source of the St. Croix River to the St. Lawrence River, with an index map, besides five maps of islands in the River St. John and four sheets of "Side Work connected with the Survey of the Boundary".   Several sets of those maps are in the archives of the Department of State.

In a letter of Commissioner Smith to Secretary of State Buchanan of April 20, 1848 (*ibid.*, p. 5), reporting the destruction of the American maps by fire, the following statement is made regarding the duplicate maps for the British Government:

Duplicates of the maps duly authenticated have been placed in the British archives at London, which, although they have not the topography of the country so fully laid down upon them as it was upon our own, represent, with equal exactness, the survey of the boundary itself.   Should it be deemed expedient to procure copies of them, access to these archives for that purpose would undoubtedly be permitted, and the object accomplished at small expense; and when completed, these copies could be authenticated by the joint commissioners in accordance with the provisions of the treaty.

There are not, however, in the Department of State archives any original maps of the Commissioners under Article 6 of the Webster-Ashburton Treaty.

The distribution of the islands in the St. John River was the subject of a verbal promise by Ashburton (mentioned in his despatch No. 17, of August 9, 1842, quoted and referred to above); it appears that no difficulty was encountered in that regard by the Commissioners under Article 6; the islands were "distributed to Great Britain or to the United States, as they were found to be on the right or left of the deep channel"; and the one doubtful case was "apportioned to the United States because the majority of the owners were ascertained to reside on the United States side of the river" (joint report of the Commissioners, Richardson, IV, 172).

Certain questions arising under Article 1, which were considered during the demarcation of the boundary under Article 6, are to be mentioned.

From the source of the St. Croix north to the St. John River, a distance of 77.6 miles, "the exploring line run and marked by the Surveyors of the two Governments in the years 1817 and 1818",

which was adopted as the boundary line between the two points, had been found by Major Graham during the survey authorized by the United States in 1840, to deviate "first to the east and then to the west until, when the St. John River was reached, the exploring line was nearly half a mile west of the true north line" (Joint Report of the International Boundary Commission submitted October 30, 1924, and heretofore cited, p. 293; and see sheets 58 to 61 of the maps of the International Boundary Commission).

The terminus (on the northwest branch of the River St. John) of the straight line running "southwesterly" from the outlet of Lake Pohenegamook, was found to be about twelve miles from the St. Lawrence watershed (Joint Report of the International Boundary Commission, above cited, p. 328); so the "seven miles" clause of Article 1, which, on the condition stated, required that point to "be made to recede down the said northwest branch", proved to have no application (see the joint report of the Commissioners under Article 6, in Richardson, IV, 173).

ARTICLE 7

The clauses of Article 7 for "free and open" passage of various channels were a part of the boundary negotiation, although the line through the waters in question had been previously fixed, pursuant to Article 6 of the Treaty of Ghent (see Document 42). In his despatch No. 17, of August 9, 1842 (cited above), Ashburton wrote regarding Article 7 as follows:

> By reference to the proceedings of the Commissioners appointed to execute the 6th and 7th Articles of the Treaty [of Ghent] it will be seen that it was demanded on the part of Great Britain that provision should be made to give greater freedom for the navigation of the St Lawrence through the rapids of the Long Sault and Barnhardt's Island, and also through the various Islands in the channel connecting the River St Clair with the Lake of that name. Mr Webster desired to add also the channels of the river Detroit to which I was assured by Mr Barclay, who was well acquainted with the case, there could be no objection, and which could not be well refused. All this is provided for by the VII Article of this Treaty. These several channels and passages have all been used by the two parties as now agreed for, but apprehensions of obstruction were entertained, and in the case of the Long Sault threatened. The person sent here by Sir Charles Bagot to give me information respecting the Canadian frontier attached considerable importance to this part of the subject.

In the note of Ashburton of July 16, 1842 (D.S., 21 Notes from the British Legation; published correspondence, 56–58), dealing primarily with the "North West boundary", were these paragraphs:

> In making the important concession on this boundary of the Isle St George, I must attach a condition to it of accommodation, which experience has proved to be necessary in the navigation of the Great Waters which bound the two Countries; an accommodation which can, I apprehend, be no possible inconvenience to either. This was asked by the British Commissioner in the course of the attempts of compromise above alluded to, but nothing was done because he was not then prepared, as I am now, to yield the property and sovereignty of St George's Island.
> The first of these two cases is at the head of Lake St Clair, where the river of that name empties into it from Lake Huron. It is represented that the channel

bordering the United States' coast in that part is not only the best for navigation, but with some winds is the only serviceable passage. I do not know that under such circumstances the passage of a British vessel would be refused; but on a final settlement of boundaries, it is desirable to stipulate for what the Commissioners would probably have settled had the facts been known to them.

The other case of nearly the same description occurs on the St Lawrence some miles above the boundary at St Regis. In distributing the islands of the River by the Commissioners Barnharts Island and the Long Sault Islands were assigned to America. This part of the river has very formidable rapids, and the only safe passage is on the Southern or American side between those Islands and the main land. We want a clause in our present treaty to say that for a short distance, viz: from the upper end of upper Long Sault Island to the lower end of Barnhart's Island, the several channels of the river shall be used in common by the Boatmen of the two Countries.

In the answer of Webster of July 27 (D.S., 6 Notes to the British Legation, 241; published correspondence, 58–61), which set forth the terms of the whole boundary settlement (Articles 1–7), was the following:

Besides agreeing upon the line of division through these controverted portions of the boundary, you have suggested also, as the proposed settlement proceeds upon the ground of compromise and equivalents, that boats belonging to Her Majesty's subjects may pass the falls of the Long Saut in the St. Lawrence, on either side of the Long Saut Islands; and that the passages between the islands lying at or near the junction of the river St. Clair, with the lake of that name, shall be severally free and open to the vessels of both countries. There appears no reasonable objection to what is requested in these particulars; and on the part of the United States it is desirable, that their vessels, proceeding in from Lake Erie into the Detroit river, should have the privilege of passing between Bois Blanc, an island belonging to England, and the Canadian shore, the deeper and better channel belonging to that side.

The formal assent of Ashburton of July 29 to the boundary settlement (D.S., 21 Notes from the British Legation; published correspondence, 61–62) included these remarks on the clauses for free passage, noting the inadvertent omission of mention of Barnhart Island by Webster:

The stipulations for the greater facility of the navigation of the River St Lawrence, and of two passages between the upper Lakes, appear evidently desirable for general accomodation, and I can not refuse the reciprocal claim made by you to render common the passage from Lake Erie into the Detroit River. This must be done by declaring the several passages in those parts free to both parties.

I should remark also, that the free use of the navigation of the Long Sault passage on the St Lawrence, must be extended to below Barnhardt's Island, for the purpose of clearing those Rapids.

Also to be read in this connection are two paragraphs of the presidential message of August 11, 1842 (quoted above), submitting the Webster-Ashburton Treaty to the Senate.

The various islands and channels mentioned in Article 7 appear on sheets 1 and 15–19, inclusive, of the charts of the International Waterways Commission (listed and described in vol. 3, pp. 74–75).

ARTICLE 8

The first agreement between the United States and Great Britain regarding the suppression of the slave trade was written in Article 10 of the Treaty of Ghent of December 24, 1814 (quoted in the preamble of this treaty; see Document 33).

"The question of visit and search has been much discussed in connection with efforts to suppress the African slave trade" is the opening sentence of a learned treatment of the diplomatic and legal phases of the subject during the nineteenth century (Moore, Digest, II, 914–51). A few of those efforts are here to be mentioned (see *ibid.*, 922–29, *passim*).

By the act of May 15, 1820 (3 Statutes at Large, 600–1), "slave trading was declared to be piracy and to be punishable with death. This act was general in its language, and was designed to enable the United States to join in the movement then on foot to assimilate the slave trade to piracy, both in the measure of its punishment and the method of its repression. This movement, however, did not succeed, owing to the opposition to opening the way to the establishment of the practice of visitation and search in time of peace" (Moore, *op. cit.*, 922). A convention between the United States and Great Britain signed at London on March 13, 1824, for the suppression of the slave trade, and including clauses for the mutual right of visit and search in certain waters (American State Papers, Foreign Relations, V, 319–22) was somewhat amended in the Senate (*ibid.*, 361–62); one of those amendments was not acceptable to the British Government and the convention failed (*ibid.*, 364–65); a convention between the United States and the Republic of Colombia for the same purpose, signed at Bogotá on December 10, 1824, was rejected by the Senate (*ibid.*, 733–35).

Between France and Great Britain conventions for the suppression of the slave trade were in force (November 30, 1831, and March 22, 1833; British and Foreign State Papers, XVIII, 641–44, and XX, 286–301); to those agreements the United States had declined to adhere; against the Quintuple Treaty signed at London on December 20, 1841, by representatives of Great Britain, Austria, France, Prussia, and Russia (*ibid.*, XXX, 269–300; not ratified by France), Lewis Cass, then Minister to France, had protested (February 13, 1842), and his course had been approved by Secretary of State Webster in an instruction of April 5, 1842 (D.S., 14 Instructions, France, 272–75). An instructive work which should be consulted generally is The Right of Search and the Slave Trade in Anglo-American Relations, 1814–1862, by Hugh G. Soulsby; the three opening chapters thereof deal with the period up to 1843.

In the message of August 11, 1842 (quoted above), with which this treaty was submitted to the Senate, various paragraphs were devoted to the subject of the African slave trade and the clauses of Article 8 for "joint cruising".

In his annual message of December 6, 1842 (Richardson, IV, 194–209), wherewith the Webster-Ashburton Treaty was communi-

cated to Congress, President Tyler observed that "Next to the settlement of the boundary line . . . the question which seemed to threaten the greatest embarrassment was that connected with the African slave trade." Reference was then made to Article 10 of the Treaty of Ghent, and the message continued:

In the enforcement of the laws and treaty stipulations of Great Britain a practice had threatened to grow up on the part of its cruisers of subjecting to visitation ships sailing under the American flag, which, while it seriously involved our maritime rights, would subject to vexation a branch of our trade which was daily increasing, and which required the fostering care of Government. And although Lord Aberdeen in his correspondence with the American envoys in London expressly disclaimed all right to detain an American ship on the high seas, even if found with a cargo of slaves on board, and restricted the British pretension to a mere claim to visit and inquire, yet it could not well be discerned by the Executive of the United States how such visit and inquiry could be made without detention on the voyage and consequent interruption to the trade. It was regarded as the right of search presented only in a new form and expressed in different words, and I therefore felt it to be my duty distinctly to declare in my annual message to Congress [of December 7, 1841; *ibid.*, 74–89] that no such concession could be made, and that the United States had both the will and the ability to enforce their own laws and to protect their flag from being used for purposes wholly forbidden by those laws and obnoxious to the moral censure of the world. Taking the message as his letter of instructions, our then minister at Paris felt himself required to assume the same ground in a remonstrance which he felt it to be his duty to present to Mr. Guizôt, and through him to the King of the French, against what has been called the "quintuple treaty"; and his conduct in this respect met with the approval of this Government. In close conformity with these views the eighth article of the treaty was framed, which provides "that each nation shall keep afloat in the African seas a force not less than 80 guns, to act separately and apart, under instructions from their respective Governments, and for the enforcement of their respective laws and obligations." From this it will be seen that the ground assumed in the message has been fully maintained at the same time that the stipulations of the treaty of Ghent are to be carried out in good faith by the two countries, and that all pretense is removed for interference with our commerce for any purpose whatever by a foreign government. While, therefore, the United States have been standing up for the freedom of the seas, they have not thought proper to make that a pretext for avoiding a fulfillment of their treaty stipulations or a ground for giving countenance to a trade reprobated by our laws. A similar arrangement by the other great powers could not fail to sweep from the ocean the slave trade without the interpolation of any new principle into the maritime code. We may be permitted to hope that the example thus set will be followed by some if not all of them. We thereby also afford suitable protection to the fair trader in those seas, thus fulfilling at the same time the dictates of a sound policy and complying with the claims of justice and humanity.

A Senate resolution of December 27, 1842 (of very unusual substance and wording), included a request for "such information upon the negotiation of the African squadron articles as will show the origin of such articles and the history and progress of their formation." The paragraph of the presidential message of January 9, 1843, which dealt with that part of the resolution, reads thus (see Richardson, IV, 215–20):

These articles were proposed to the British minister by the Secretary of State under my express sanction and were acceded to by him and have since been ratified by both Governments. I might without disrespect speak of the novelty of inquiring by the Senate into the history and progress of articles of a treaty through a negotiation which has terminated, and as the result of which these articles have

become the law of the land by the constitutional advice of the Senate itself.   But I repeat that those articles had their origin in a desire on the part of the Government of the United States to fulfill its obligations, entered into by the treaty of Ghent, to do its utmost for the suppression of the African slave trade, and to accomplish this object by such means as should not lead to the interruption of the lawful commerce of the United States or any derogation from the dignity and immunity of their flag.   And I have the satisfaction to believe that both the Executive, in negotiating the treaty of which these articles form part, and the Senate, in advising to its ratification, have effected an object important to the Government and satisfactory to the people.

Agreement in principle on such clauses as those of Article 8 was reached at an early stage of the negotiations (subject to further instructions from London).   In his despatch No. 6, of May 12, 1842, Ashburton wrote as follows (the extract here quoted and the enclosed report of Commanders Bell and Paine are printed in British and Foreign State Papers, XXXII, 566–72; see *ibid.*, 565–66; and for the despatch of April 25 and the instruction of May 26, 1842, see *ibid.*, XXXI, 708–9, 711–12):

On the important subject of effectually suppressing the Slave Trade by cooperation, I hope I am making very valuable progress.   Your Lordship will find herewith the report of the 2 American naval officers in reply to certain queries put to them by the Secretary of State on the subject of the African Slave Trade, and the best means of suppressing it.   This is a most valuable document.   It is written by men of honour, impartiality, and experience, and will show, I believe, that they agree with the general view of the best informed persons of our own country on this subject.   With this business I trust your Lordship's instructions in reply to my last despatches will enable me to proceed.   Nothing has been done towards framing the Article for cooperation, but it is intended to engage for the employment of a given joint force, leaving to the commanders of it the settlement of their plans of acting.   Mr. Webster seemed to think the amount of force to be employed rather large, but had no objection to The United States supporting their half of it.   I apprehend that, with respect to the amount of this force, I may safely leave them to please themselves.

The report of Commanders Charles H. Bell and John S. Paine, U.S.N., on the slave trade of the west coast of Africa, dated May 10, 1842, and Commander Paine's account of the agreement signed on March 11, 1840, at Sierra Leone, by Commander William Tucker, R.N., and himself, which this Government disapproved, are printed in published correspondence, 107–15.
Regarding that report of May 10, 1842, Ashburton wrote in his despatch of May 12 (Ashburton Papers, despatch No. 6):

The report I send in the original, and your Lordship will not fail to observe the part intended to be erased at the Department of State before it is presented to Congress.   As this has been communicated with rather a careless confidence, it will hardly be fair to make it public without perfecting the erasure.

The paragraph containing the erasure, as printed in published correspondence, 113, with the words stricken here added in parentheses, follows (the omitted phrases are not in the signed report in D.S., Miscellaneous Letters, May–July 1842):

We are of opinion that a squadron should be kept on the coast of Africa to co-operate with the British, or other nations interested in stopping the slave-

trade; and that the most efficient mode would be for vessels to cruise in couples, one of each nation. (with an understanding that either of the cruisers may examine a suspicious vessel so far as may be necessary to determine her *national* character; while any further search would be only pursued by the vessel having a right from the laws of nations or from existing treaties.)

Regarding Article 8 of the treaty Ashburton wrote in one of his despatches of August 9, 1842 (Ashburton Papers, despatch No. 18), as follows:

Your Lordship will perceive in the clause for Joint Cruizing that the minimum of force engaged to be furnished by America is reduced to eighty instead of one hundred guns as first intended. I rather approved this reduction from an apprehension that the Senate might think the force promised too large, considering that Congress this year have been rather economical in their Navy estimates. It is however named as a minimum and may and probably will be increased. The Secretary of the Navy assures me that he has made selection of a very good and discreet commander for this service, and the Lords of the Admiralty will no doubt attend to the same thing, that conciliation and effective cooperation may be secured. Lieutenant Payne who formerly acted satisfactorily with our officers on the African coast will command one of the ships, but was not of sufficient rank to command in chief. This agreement for joint cruizing is to continue for five years and further until notice for its discontinuance from either party.

Section 6 of the act of March 3, 1843, "for carrying into effect" this treaty (5 Statutes at Large, 623), made it the duty of the President, "in execution of the provisions of the eighth article of said treaty, to apply so much of the naval appropriations as may be necessary therefor, to the preparation, equipment, and maintenance of the naval force therein stipulated to be employed on the coast of Africa by the United States."

In an instruction of August 8, 1843, from Secretary of State Upshur to Edward Everett, Minister at London, it was stated that this Government had "proceeded to execute our part of that stipulation, by sending to that [African] coast four vessels carrying more than eighty guns" (D.S., 15 Instructions, Great Britain, 106–20; quoted in Moore, Digest, II, 941); but for the execution of Article 8 generally and the results, see Soulsby, *op. cit.*, 118 *et seq.*

Discussion of the question of visit and search in connection with the suppression of the slave trade was not ended until 1858 (see *ibid.* and Moore, *op. cit.*, 931–46).

ARTICLE 9

"In consequence of an informal understanding with the British Government in 1843, these remonstrances [under Article 9] are not to be made jointly, but by each nation separately" (D.S., 15 Instructions, Brazil, 119–25, September 27, 1845); it seems that on only one occasion was any such remonstrance made on behalf of this Government; on December 19, 1845, Henry A. Wise, Minister to Brazil, "sought an interview . . . with Senhor de Abreu, the Brazilian Minister for Foreign Affairs, and called his attention to the obligations of this Government under the ninth article of the treaty of Washington. Mr. Wise especially disclaimed any intention to

interfere with the domestic policy of Brazil, and desired to be understood only in the sense of making a separate friendly representation of the desire of the United States that Brazil should, by her own means, and in her own way, arrest the foreign Slave Trade to her dominions, and destroy the market for slaves in her territory. Senhor de Abreu made a note of these representations, receiving them without displeasure or objection" (D.S., 7 Notes to the British Legation, 166–68, September 2, 1847; see 14 Despatches, Brazil, No. 37, December 23, 1845); there are other references to Article 9 of the Webster-Ashburton Treaty in the archives volume of instructions last cited (Secretary of State Upshur to George H. Proffit, August 1, 1843, pp. 87–96; Secretary of State Calhoun to Henry A. Wise, May 25, 1844, pp. 100–5; Secretary of State Buchanan to David Tod, June 11, 1847, pp. 147–52; Secretary of State Webster to Robert C. Schenck, May 8, 1851, pp. 186–89).

Correspondence with the British Government on the subject of Article 9 was not extensive (see D.S., 7 Notes to the British Legation, 70–72, July 31, 1845; two notes from Pakenham to Buchanan, of June 25, 1845, and February 9, 1846, are in D.S., 23 Notes from the British Legation; see also British and Foreign State Papers, XXXIV, 967, 978–80, 991–92, and XXXVI, 738–46).

ARTICLE 10

While the clauses of Article 10 are not limited in their territorial applicability, they were considered to be particularly important and necessary in respect of fugitives from justice on one side or the other of the Canadian border. Certain paragraphs of the presidential message to the Senate of August 11, 1842 (quoted above), are to be read in this connection.

Early in the negotiations Webster proposed extradition clauses, in general very similar to those of Article 10 of the treaty (Ashburton Papers, despatch No. 5, April 28, 1842, and enclosure); in that draft the extraditable crimes included those of Article 10, except "assault with intent to commit murder"; but they also included "mutiny and revolt on board ship" (the words "on board ship" being added at the suggestion of Ashburton); but the British Government objected to the inclusion of the crime of mutiny because of its possible applicability to slaves, as in the case of the *Creole* (see *ibid.*, despatch No. 12, June 29, 1842).

In a despatch of August 9, 1842 (*ibid.*, despatch No. 18), Ashburton made the following comments regarding the extradition article:

In the clause for the extradition of criminals your Lordship will perceive that I have altogether omitted mutiny in any shape.   It is a crime most proper to be guarded against in such a Convention, but as the subject gave rise to controversy in considering its possible application to slavery, it has been thought expedient to omit it.

Being sensible that this part of the Convention can have no practical effect in the British dominions until confirmed by Act of Parliament, your Lordship will find herewith the copy of a note [of August 9, 1842; printed above, the third of the notes immediately following the treaty text] addressed by me to Mr Webster on this point.   I thought this mode of explanation preferable to noticing the circumstance in the Convention itself.

In Canada or any other Colony where the Governor has power for this purpose under Colonial law the article will be executed so soon as the ratification of this Convention is notified to him from home. Indeed the Governor General of the North American Provinces has been in the practice of frequently delivering up fugitives, although without reciprocity from the neighbouring states. In a letter recently received from him, he appears to attach much importance to the establishing a regular system of extradition for the repression of crime and disorderly conduct on the frontier. It will be seen that this article is revocable at will, which is perhaps desirable to ensure practical reciprocity, but I have little apprehension of any disposition to abrogate it so long as the countries remain at peace.

Legislation on the part of the United States in aid of the extradition clauses was not at the time deemed necessary (see Moore, Digest, IV, 271); the act of March 3, 1843, "for carrying into effect" this treaty (5 Statutes at Large, 623), contains no reference to Article 10; the earliest statute of the United States dealing with extradition is the act of August 12, 1848 (9 *ibid.*, 302–3); that legislation appears to have been suggested by Secretary of State Buchanan (see his interesting letter of May 31, 1848, to Joseph R. Ingersoll, Chairman of the Committee on the Judiciary of the House of Representatives; Moore, The Works of James Buchanan, VIII, 73; D.S., 6 Report Book, 254–55).

The confirmatory statute essential for "the Dominions of Great Britain", as stated in the formal note of Ashburton of August 9, 1842, and in the despatch above quoted, was duly enacted (6 and 7 Victoria, ch. 76) and was communicated to Secretary of State Upshur on September 29, 1843 (British and Foreign State Papers, XXXIII, 906).

The provisions of Article 10 of the Webster-Ashburton Treaty (with those of later international acts) were considered by the Supreme Court of the United States in the recent extradition case of *Factor* v. *Laubenheimer* (December 4, 1933; 54 Supreme Court Reporter, 191–206).

The "Caroline"

The famous case of the *Caroline* is treated and discussed, with elaborate citation of authority, in Moore, Digest, II, 24–30, 409–14; VI, 261–62; VII, 919–20; see also Moore, International Arbitrations, III, 2419–28, regarding the claim of Alexander McLeod. The following statement is extracted from Moore, Digest, II, 409–11 (and see the following, there cited: House Document No. 64, 25th Congress, 2d session, serial 322; House Document No. 74, 25th Congress, 2d session, serial 323; House Document No. 302, 25th Congress, 2d session, serial 329; House Document No. 183, 25th Congress, 3d session, serial 347; House Document No. 33, 26th Congress, 2d session, serial 383; House Report No. 162, 26th Congress, 2d session, serial 388; House Document No. 128, 27th Congress, 2d session, serial 403; Senate Document No. 99, 27th Congress, 3d session, serial 415):

During the insurrection in Canada in 1837 sympathetic commotions occurred at various places in the United States, especially along the Canadian border. The Government of the United States adopted active measures for the enforce-

ment of the neutrality laws, but the difficulties of the situation were increased by the course of the insurgents, who, when defeated, sought refuge in the United States, where they endeavored to recruit their forces. In December, 1837, meetings were held in Buffalo, in the State of New York, by McKenzie and Rolfe, the leaders in the insurrection, who made a public appeal for arms, ammunition, and volunteers. On the 28th of the month, the United States marshal for the northern district of New York, who had proceeded to Buffalo for the purpose of suppressing violations of neutrality, reported that he had found 200 or 300 men, mostly from the American side of the Niagara River, encamped on Navy Island, in Upper Canada, armed and under the command of "General" Van Rensselaer, of Albany, and that the encampment had received accessions till it numbered about 1,000 men, well armed. This expedition had been organized at Buffalo after McKenzie's arrival, and warrants had been issued for the arrest of the men, but could not be served. There was also an encampment at Black Rock.

On the 29th of December occurred the destruction of the *Caroline*. This vessel was a small steamer employed by the men at Black Rock and on Navy Island in communicating with the mainland. According to the deposition of the master, the *Caroline* left Buffalo on the 29th of December for the port of Schlosser, which was also in New York. On the way he caused a landing to be made at Black Rock and the American flag to be run up. After the steamer left Black Rock a volley of musketry was fired at her from the Canadian side, but without injuring her. She then landed "a number of passengers" at Navy Island, and arrived at Schlosser about 3 o'clock p.m. Subsequently, in the same afternoon, she made two more trips to Navy Island, and returned finally to Schlosser about 6 o'clock p.m. During the evening about 23 persons, all citizens of the United States, came on board and asked to be permitted to "remain on board all night." At midnight about 70 or 80 armed men boarded the steamer and attacked the persons on board with muskets, swords, and cutlasses. The "passengers and crew," of whom there were in all 33, merely endeavored to escape. After this attack the assailing force set the steamer on fire, cut her loose, and set her adrift over the Niagara Falls. Only 21 of the persons on board had since been found, and one of these, Amos Durfee, was killed on the dock by a musket ball. Several others were wounded. Twelve were missing. After the *Caroline* was set adrift beacon lights were seen on the Canadian side, and cheering was heard, and it was not doubted that the assailants belonged to the British force at Chippewa. Such was the statement made by the master. It was generally reported and believed at the time that the men said to be missing lay wounded in the steamer, and were sent with her over the falls. It was subsequently ascertained, however, on further investigation that of the persons on board the only ones missing were Durfee and the cabin boy, Johnson, popularly known as "Little Billy," both of whom were shot as they were leaving the steamer; that Van Rensselaer's forces had made some use of Grand Island, and had fired some shots into Canada while the main forces lay at Navy Island and before the *Caroline* went to Schlosser; that two persons from the *Caroline* were carried by the attacking force into Canada, but were afterward set at liberty, and that that force acted under the command of Col. A. N. McNab, of Chippewa, who was acting under the orders of his superior officer.

On receiving information as to this occurrence, Mr. Forsyth, who was then Secretary of State, addressed a note to Mr. Fox, the British minister at Washington, saying that the destruction of property and assassination of citizens of the United States on the soil of New York, when the President was endeavoring to allay excitement and prevent any unfortunate occurrence on the frontier, had produced "the most painful emotions of surprise and regret," and that the incident would be made the "subject of a demand for redress." General Scott was sent to the frontier, with letters to the governors of New York and Vermont, requesting them to call out the militia. On the 6th of February, Mr. Fox communicated to Mr. Forsyth a letter from Governor Head, and while avowing that the force that destroyed the *Caroline* was under the command of Colonel McNab, declared that the piratical character of the *Caroline* seemed to be fully established; that the ordinary laws of the United States were not at the time enforced along the frontier, but were openly overborne; and that the destruction of the *Caroline*

was an act of necessary self-defense.[1]   On the 22d of May, 1838, Mr. Stevenson, then minister of the United States at London, presented a demand for reparation. Its receipt was acknowledged by Lord Palmerston on the 6th of June, with a promise of consideration.

In March, 1841, a sudden turn was given to the discussion by the arrest and imprisonment on a charge of murder, in the State of New York, of Alexander McLeod, who had, as it appears, while under the influence of liquor, boasted of having taken an effective part in the destruction of the *Caroline*.   Lord Palmerston then avowed responsibility, on the part of Her Majesty's Government, for the destruction of the steamer, as a public act of force, in self-defense, by persons in Her Majesty's service, and on this ground demanded McLeod's release. McLeod was ultimately tried, and was acquitted on proof of an alibi.

There can be no doubt that the steamer *Caroline* (of 46 tons; 71 feet long) was being illegally employed in aid of Van Rensselaer and his associates, the "patriots", as they styled themselves; the expedition which destroyed the *Caroline* during the night of December 29, 1837, was headed by Commander Andrew Drew, R.N., who had under him a force of forty-five, in five boats, and who was acting under the orders of Colonel Allan Napier McNab (House Document No. 302, 25th Congress, 2d session, serial 329, *passim*); the various *loci* of the affair were within small compass; Schlosser, where the *Caroline* was moored, was no more than a landing place and a storehouse with a tavern adjacent, located on the right or American side of Niagara River, less than three miles above the falls (the site of the old and then abandoned Fort Schlosser was somewhat lower down; see *ibid*. and also Lossing, Pictorial Field Book of the War of 1812, 379–82, with map); Chippawa, on the Canadian shore, lies nearly opposite, the river being there about a mile and a half wide; just above is Navy Island (Canadian), at the mouth of Chippawa Channel, about six hundred yards from the Canadian shore on the one side and about the same distance from the north end of Grand Island (American) on the other (see the chart of Upper Niagara River from Lake Erie to the Falls, War Department, Corps of Engineers, 1931, Catalogue No. 312).

The case of the *Caroline* was within the negotiations of Webster and Ashburton, though not mentioned in the treaty.   Notes were exchanged regarding it, which were submitted to the Senate and form part of the published correspondence (pp. 126–38); the first, with enclosures, was that of Webster to Ashburton of July 27, 1842; this was answered on the following day; and the exchanges were concluded by the note of Webster of August 6.   The texts which follow are, for the notes of Webster, from D.S., 6 Notes to the British Legation, 246–47 (without enclosures, which are here copied respectively from *ibid*., 201–10, and from Richardson, IV, 75–77) and 259–61, and for that of Ashburton, D.S., 21 Notes from the British Legation.   The result of the correspondence was to "make this subject, as a complaint of violation of territory, the topic of no further discussion between the two Governments".

---

[1] The note of Secretary of State Forsyth, dated January 5, 1838, and the letter of Sir Francis Bond Head, Lieutenant Governor of the Province of Upper Canada, with enclosures thereto and the covering note of the British Minister at Washington, are printed in House Document No. 302, 25th Congress, 2d session, serial 329, pp. 2–16.

[*Mr. Webster to Lord Ashburton*]

DEPARTMENT OF STATE,
Washington, 27ᵗʰ July, 1842.

Lord ASHBURTON,
&ᵒ, &ᵒ, &ᵒ

MY LORD: In relation to the case of the "Caroline", which we have heretofore made the subject of conference, I have thought it right to place in your hands an extract of a letter from this Department to Mʳ Fox, of the 24ᵗʰ of April, 1841, and an extract from the message of the President of the United States to Congress at the commencement of its present session. These papers you have, no doubt, already seen; but they are, nevertheless, now communicated, as such a communication is considered a ready mode of presenting the view which this Government entertains of the destruction of that vessel.

The act of which the Government of the United States complains is not to be considered as justifiable or unjustifiable, as the question of the lawfulness or unlawfulness of the employment in which the "Caroline" was engaged may be decided the one way or the other. That act is of itself a wrong, and an offence to the sovereignty and the dignity of the United States, being a violation of their soil and territory—a wrong for which, to this day, no atonement, or even apology, has been made by Her Majesty's Government. Your Lordship cannot but be aware that self-respect, the consciousness of independence and national equality, and a sensitiveness to whatever may touch the honor of the country—a sensitiveness which this Government will ever feel and ever cultivate—make this a matter of high importance, and I must be allowed to ask for it your Lordship's grave consideration.

I have the honor to be, my Lord, your Lordship's most obedient servant,

DANˡ WEBSTER.

[Enclosure 1—Extract from note of April 24, 1841]

The Undersigned has now to signify to Mʳ Fox that the Government of the United States has not changed the opinion which it has heretofore expressed to Her Majesty's Government, of the character of the act of destroying the "Caroline". It does not think that that transaction can be justified by any reasonable application or construction of the right of self-defence under the laws of nations. It is admitted that a just right of self-defence attaches always to nations, as well as to individuals, and is equally necessary for the preservation of both. But the extent of this right is a question to be judged of by the circumstances of each particular case; and when its alleged exercise has led to the commission of hostile acts, within the territory of a power at peace, nothing less than a clear and absolute necessity can afford ground of justification. Not having, up to this time, been made acquainted with the views and reasons, at length, which have led Her Majesty's Government to think the destruction of the "Caroline" justifiable as an act of self-defence, the Undersigned, earnestly renewing the remonstrance of this Government against the transaction, abstains, for the present, from any extended discussion of the question. But it is deemed proper, nevertheless, not to omit, to take some notice of the general grounds of justification, stated by Her Majesty's Government, in their instruction to Mʳ Fox.

Her Majesty's Government have instructed Mʳ Fox to say, that they are of opinion, that the transaction, which terminated in the destruction of the "Caroline", was a justifiable employment of force, for the purpose of defending the British Territory from the unprovoked attack of a band of British rebels and American pirates, who, having been "permitted" to arm and organize themselves within the territory of the United States, had actually invaded a portion of the territory of Her Majesty.

The President cannot suppose that Her Majesty's Government, by the use of these terms, meant to be understood as intimating, that those acts, violating the laws of the United States, and disturbing the peace of the British territories, were done under any degree of countenance from this Government, or were regarded by it with indifference; or, that under the circumstances of the case, they could have been prevented, by the ordinary course of proceeding. Although he regrets, that by using the term "permitted", a possible inference of that kind might be

raised, yet such an inference, the President, is willing to believe, would be quite unjust to the intentions of the British Government.

That on a line of frontier, such as separates the United States from Her Britannic Majesty's North American Provinces, a line long enough to divide the whole of Europe into halves, irregularities, violences, and conflicts should sometimes occur, equally against the will of both Governments, is certainly easily to be supposed. This may be more possible, perhaps, in regard to the United States, without any reproach to their Government, since their institutions entirely discourage the keeping up of large standing armies in time of peace, and their situation happily exempts them from the necessity of maintaining such expensive and dangerous establishments. All that can be expected, from either Government, in these cases, is good faith, a sincere desire to preserve peace and do justice, the use of all proper means of prevention, and, that if offences cannot, neverthless, be always prevented, the offenders shall still be justly punished. In all these respects, this Government acknowledges no delinquency in the performance of its duties.

Her Majesty's Government are pleased, also, to speak of those American citizens, who took part with persons in Canada, engaged in an insurrection against the British Government, as "American pirates". The Undersigned does not admit the propriety or justice of this designation. If citizens of the United States fitted out, or were engaged in fitting out, a military expedition from the United States, intended to act against the British Government in Canada, they were clearly violating the laws of their own country, and exposing themselves to the just consequences, which might be inflicted on them, if taken within the British Dominions. But notwithstanding this, they were, certainly, not pirates; nor does the Undersigned think that it can advance the purpose of fair and friendly discussion, or hasten the accommodation of national difficulties so to denominate them. Their offence, whatever it was, had no analogy to cases of piracy. Supposing all that is alleged against them to be true, they were taking a part in what they regarded as a civil war, and they were taking a part on the side of the rebels. Surely, England herself has not regarded persons thus engaged as deserving the appellation which Her Majesty's Government bestows on these citizens of the United States.

It is quite notorious, that for the greater part of the last two centuries, subjects of the British crown have been permitted to engage in foreign wars, both national and civil, and in the latter in every stage of their progress; and yet it has not been imagined that England has at any time allowed her subjects to turn pirates. Indeed in our own times, not only have individual subjects of that crown gone abroad to engage in civil wars, but we have seen whole regiments openly recruited, embodied, armed, and disciplined, in England, with the avowed purpose of aiding a rebellion against a nation, with which England was at peace; although it is true, that subsequently, an Act of Parliament was passed to prevent transactions so nearly approaching to public war, without license from the crown [59 George III, ch. 69, July 3, 1819].

It may be said, that there is a difference between the case of a civil war, arising from a disputed succession, or a protracted revolt of a colony against the mother country, and the case of the fresh outbreak, or commencement of a rebellion. The Undersigned does not deny, that such a distinction may, for certain purposes, be deemed well founded. He admits, that a Government, called upon to consider its own rights, interests, and duties, when civil wars break out in other countries, may decide on all the circumstances of the particular case, upon its own existing stipulations, on probable results, on what its own security requires, and on many other considerations. It may be already bound to assist one party, or it may become bound, if it so chooses, to assist the other, and to meet the consequences of such assistance. But whether the revolt be recent, or long continued, they who join those concerned in it, whatever may be their offence against their own country, or however they may be treated, if taken with arms in their hands, in the territory of the Government, against which the standard of revolt is raised, cannot be denominated Pirates, without departing from all ordinary use of language in the definition of offences. A cause which has so foul an origin as piracy, cannot, in its progress, or by its success, obtain a

claim to any degree of respectability, or tolerance, among nations; and civil wars, therefore, are not understood to have such a commencement.

It is well known to M.ʳ Fox, that authorities of the highest eminence in England, living and dead, have maintained, that the general law of nations does not forbid the citizens or subjects of one Government, from taking part in the civil commotions of another. There is some reason indeed, to think, that such may be the opinion of Her Majesty's Government at the present moment.

The Undersigned has made these remarks, from the conviction that it is important to regard established distinctions, and to view the acts and offences of individuals in the exactly proper light. But it is not to be inferred, that there is, on the part of this Government any purpose of extenuating, in the slightest degree, the crimes of those persons, citizens of the United States, who have joined in military expeditions against the British Government in Canada. On the contrary, the President directs the Undersigned to say, that it is his fixed resolution that all such disturbers of the national peace, and violators of the laws of their country, shall be brought to exemplary punishment. Nor will the fact, that they are instigated and led on to these excesses, by British subjects, refugees from the Provinces, be deemed any excuse or palliation; although it is well worthy of being remembered, that the prime movers of these disturbances on the borders are subjects of the Queen who come within the territories of the United States, seeking to enlist the sympathies of their citizens, by all the motives which they are able to address to them, on account of grievances, real or imaginary. There is no reason to believe that the design of any hostile movement from the United States against Canada, has commenced with citizens of the United States. The true origin of such purposes and such enterprises is on the other side of the line. But the President's resolution to prevent these transgressions of the laws is not, on that account, the less strong. It is taken, not only in conformity to his duty under the provisions of existing laws, but in full consonance with the established principles and practice of this Government.

The Government of the United States has not, from the first, fallen into the doubts, elsewhere entertained, of the true extent of the duties of neutrality. It has held, that however it may have been in less enlightened ages, the just interpretation of the modern law of Nations is, that neutral States are bound to be strictly neutral; and that it is a manifest and gross impropriety for individuals to engage in the civil conflicts of other States, and thus to be at war, while their Government is at peace. War and peace are high national relations, which can properly be established or changed only by nations themselves.

The United States have thought, also, that the salutary doctrine of non-intervention by one Nation with the affairs of others is liable to be essentially impaired, if, while Government refrains from interference, interference is still allowed to its subjects, individually or in masses. It may happen indeed, that persons choose to leave their country, emigrate to other regions, and settle themselves on uncultivated lands, in territories belonging to other States. This cannot be prevented by Governments, which allow the emigration of their subjects and citizens; and such persons, having voluntarily abandoned their own country, have no longer claim to its protection, nor is it longer responsible for their acts. Such cases, therefore, if they occur, show no abandonment of the duty of neutrality.

The Government of the United States has not considered it as sufficient, to confine the duties of neutrality, and non-interference, to the case of Governments, whose territories lie adjacent to each other. The application of the principle may be more necessary in such cases, but the principle itself, they regard as being the same, if those territories be divided by half the globe. The rule is founded in the impropriety and danger, of allowing individuals to make war on their own authority, or, by mingling themselves in the belligerent operations of other Nations, to run the hazard of counteracting the policy, or embroiling the relations, of their own Government. And the United States have been the first, among civilized Nations, to enforce the observance of this just rule of neutrality and peace, by special and adequate legal enactments. In the infancy of this Government, on the breaking out of the European wars, which had their origin in the French Revolution, Congress passed laws with severe penalties, for preventing the citizens of the United States from taking part in those hostilities.

By these laws, it prescribed to the citizens of the United States what it understood to be their duty, as neutrals, by the law of Nations, and the duty, also, which they owed to the interest and honor of their own country.

At a subsequent period, when the American Colonies of a European Power took up arms against their Sovereign, Congress, not diverted from the established system of the Government by any temporary considerations, not swerved from its sense of justice and of duty, by any sympathies which it might naturally feel for one of the Parties, did not hesitate, also, to pass acts applicable to the case of Colonial insurrection and civil war. And these provisions of law have been continued, revised, amended, and are in full force at the present moment. Nor have they been a dead letter, as it is well known, that exemplary punishments have been inflicted on those who have transgressed them. It is known, indeed, that heavy penalties have fallen on individuals, citizens of the United States, engaged in this very disturbance in Canada, with which the destruction of the "Caroline" was connected. And it is in Mr Fox's knowledge also, that the act of Congress of March 10th 1838, was passed for the precise purpose of more effectually restraining military enterprises, from the United States into the British Provinces, by authorizing the use of the most sure, and decisive preventive means. The Undersigned may add, that it stands on the admission of very high British authority, that during the recent Canadian troubles, although bodies of adventurers appeared on the border, making it necessary for the people of Canada to keep themselves in a state prepared for self-defence, yet that these adventurers were acting by no means in accordance with the feeling of the great mass of the American People, or of the Government of the United States. [The neutrality laws of the United States to which reference is made in this and preceding paragraphs are cited and discussed in Moore, Digest, VII, 1010–14; for the act of March 10, 1838, see 5 Statutes at Large, 212–14.]

This Government, therefore, not only holds itself above reproach in every thing respecting the preservation of neutrality, the observance of the principle of non-intervention, and the strictest conformity, in these respects, to the rules of international law, but it doubts not that the world will do it the justice to acknowledge that it has set an example, not unfit to be followed by others, and that by its steady legislation on this most important subject, it has done something to promote peace and good neighborhood among Nations, and to advance the civilisation of mankind.

The Undersigned trusts, that when Her Britannic Majesty's Government shall present the grounds at length, on which they justify the local authorities of Canada, in attacking and destroying the "Caroline", they will consider, that the laws of the United States are such as the Undersigned has now represented them, and that the Government of the United States has always manifested a sincere disposition to see those laws effectually and impartially administered. If there have been cases in which individuals, justly obnoxious to punishment, have escaped, this is no more than happens in regard to other laws.

Under these circumstances, and under those immediately connected with the transaction itself, it will be for Her Majesty's Government to show, upon what state of facts, and what rules of national law, the destruction of the "Caroline" is to be defended. It will be for that Government to show a necessity of self-defence, instant, overwhelming, leaving no choice of means, and no moment for deliberation. It will be for it to show, also, that the local authorities of Canada,— even supposing the necessity of the moment authorized them to enter the territories of the United States at all,—did nothing unreasonable or excessive; since the act justified by the necessity of self-defence, must be limited by that necessity, and kept clearly within it. It must be shewn that admonition or remonstrance to the persons on board the "Caroline" was impracticable, or would have been unavailing; it must be shewn that daylight could not be waited for; that there could be no attempt at discrimination, between the innocent and the guilty; that it would not have been enough to seize and detain the vessel; but that there was a necessity, present and inevitable, for attacking her, in the darkness of the night, while moored to the shore, and while unarmed men were asleep on board, killing some, and wounding others, and then drawing her into the current, above the cataract, setting her on fire, and, careless to know whether there might not be in her the innocent with the guilty, or the living with the dead, committing her

to a fate, which fills the imagination with horror. A necessity for all this, the Government of the United States cannot believe to have existed.

All will see, that if such things be allowed to occur, they must lead to bloody and exasperated war; and when an individual comes into the United States from Canada, and to the very place, on which this drama was performed, and there chooses to make public and vainglorious boast of the part he acted in it, it is hardly wonderful that great excitement should be created, and some degree of commotion arise.

This Republic does not wish to disturb the tranquillity of the world. Its object is peace, its policy, peace. It seeks no aggrandizement by foreign conquest, because it knows that no foreign acquisitions could augment its power and importance so rapidly as they are already advancing, by its own natural growth, under the propitious circumstances of its situation. But it cannot admit, that its Government has not both the will and the power to preserve its own neutrality, and to enforce the observance of its own laws upon its own citizens. It is jealous of its rights, and among others, and most especially, of the right of the absolute immunity of its territory, against aggression from abroad; and these rights it is the duty and determination of this Government fully and at all times to maintain; while it will at the same time, as scrupulously, refrain from infringing on the rights of others.

The President instructs the Undersigned to say, in conclusion, that he confidently trusts, that this, and all other questions of difference between the two Governments, will be treated by both, in the full exercise of such a spirit of candor, justice, and mutual respect, as shall give assurance of the long continuance of peace between the two countries.

The Undersigned avails himself of this opportunity to assure Mr Fox of his high consideration.

DANl WEBSTER.

[Enclosure 2—Extract from presidential message of December 7, 1841]

I regret that it is not in my power to make known to you an equally satisfactory conclusion in the case of the *Caroline* steamer, with the circumstances connected with the destruction of which, in December, 1837, by an armed force fitted out in the Province of Upper Canada, you are already made acquainted. No such atonement as was due for the public wrong done to the United States by this invasion of her territory, so wholly irreconcilable with her rights as an independent power, has yet been made. In the view taken by this Government the inquiry whether the vessel was in the employment of those who were prosecuting an unauthorized war against that Province or was engaged by the owner in the business of transporting passengers to and from Navy Island in hopes of private gain, which was most probably the case, in no degree alters the real question at issue between the two Governments. This Government can never concede to any foreign government the power, except in a case of the most urgent and extreme necessity, of invading its territory, either to arrest the persons or destroy the property of those who may have violated the municipal laws of such foreign government or have disregarded their obligations arising under the law of nations. The territory of the United States must be regarded as sacredly secure against all such invasions until they shall voluntarily acknowledge their inability to acquit themselves of their duties to others. And in announcing this sentiment I do but affirm a principle which no nation on earth would be more ready to vindicate at all hazards than the people and Government of Great Britain. If upon a full investigation of all the facts it shall appear that the owner of the *Caroline* was governed by a hostile intent or had made common cause with those who were in the occupancy of Navy Island, then so far as he is concerned there can be no claim to indemnity for the destruction of his boat which this Government would feel itself bound to prosecute, since he would have acted not only in derogation of the rights of Great Britain, but in clear violation of the laws of the United States; but that is a question which, however settled, in no manner involves the higher consideration of the violation of territorial sovereignty and jurisdiction. To recognize it as an admissible practice that each Government in its turn, upon any sudden and unauthorized outbreak which, on a frontier the extent of which renders it impossible for either to have an efficient

force on every mile of it, and which outbreak, therefore, neither may be able to suppress in a day, may take vengeance into its own hands, and without even a remonstrance, and in the absence of any pressing or overruling necessity may invade the territory of the other, would inevitably lead to results equally to be deplored by both. When border collisions come to receive the sanction or to be made on the authority of either Government general war must be the inevitable result. While it is the ardent desire of the United States to cultivate the relations of peace with all nations and to fulfill all the duties of good neighborhood toward those who possess territories adjoining their own, that very desire would lead them to deny the right of any foreign power to invade their boundary with an armed force. The correspondence between the two Governments on this subject will at a future day of your session be submitted to your consideration; and in the meantime I can not but indulge the hope that the British Government will see the propriety of renouncing as a rule of future action the precedent which has been set in the affair at Schlosser.

[Lord Ashburton to Mr. Webster]

WASHINGTON *28 July 1842*

SIR. In the course of our conferences on the several subjects of difference which it was the object of my mission to endeavour to settle, the unfortunate case of the Caroline, with its attendant consequences, could not escape our attention; for although it is not of a description to be susceptible of any settlement by a convention or treaty, yet being connected with the highest considerations of national honour and dignity it has given rise at times to deep excitement, so as more than once to endanger the maintenance of peace.

The note you did me the honour of addressing me the 27 inst: reminds me that however disposed your Government might be to be satisfied with the explanations which it has been my duty to offer, the natural anxiety of the public mind requires that these explanations should be more durably recorded in our correspondence, and you send me a copy of your note to Mr Fox, Her Britannic Majesty's minister here, and an extract from the speech of the President of the United States to Congress, at the opening of the present session, as a ready mode of presenting the view entertained on this subject by the Government of the United States.

It is so far satisfactory to perceive that we are perfectly agreed as to the general principles of international law applicable to this unfortunate case. Respect for the inviolable character of the territory of independent nations is the most essential foundation of civilization. It is useless to strengthen a principle so generally acknowledged by any appeal to authorities on international law, and you may be assured, Sir, that Her Majesty's Government set the highest possible value on this principle, and are sensible of their duty to support it by their conduct and example for the maintenance of peace and order in the world. If a sense of moral responsibility were not a sufficient surety for their observance of this duty towards all nations, it will be readily believed that the most common dictates of interest and policy would lead to it in the case of a long conterminous boundary of some thousand miles with a country of such great and growing power as the United States of America, inhabited by a kindred race, gifted with all its activity and all its susceptibility on points of national honour.

Every consideration therefore leads us to set as highly as your Government can possibly do this paramount obligation of reciprocal respect for the independent territory of each. But however strong this duty may be it is admitted by all writers, by all Jurists, by the occasional practice of all nations, not excepting your own, that a strong overpowering necessity may arise, when this great principle may and must be suspended. It must be so for the shortest possible period, during the continuance of an admitted overruling necessity, and strictly confined within the narrowest limits imposed by that necessity. Self defence is the first law of our nature and it must be recognised by every code which professes to regulate the condition and relations of man. Upon this modification, if I may so call it, of the great general principle, we seem also to be agreed, and on this part

of the subject I have done little more than repeat the sentiments, though in less forcible language, admitted and maintained by you in the letter to which you refer me.

Agreeing therefore on the general principle and on the possible exception to which it is liable, the only question between us is whether this occurrence came within the limits fairly to be assigned to such exception, whether, to use your words, there was "that necessity of self-defence, instant, overwhelming, leaving no choice of means" which preceded the destruction of the Caroline, while moored to the shore of the United States. Give me leave to say, Sir, with all possible admiration of your very ingenious discussion of the general principles which are supposed to govern the right and practice of interference by the people of one country in the wars and quarrels of others, that this part of your argument is little applicable to our immediate case. If Great Britain, America, or any other country suffer their people to fit out expeditions to take part in distant quarrels, such conduct may, according to the circumstances of each case, be justly matter of complaint, and perhaps these transactions have generally been in late times too much overlooked or connived at. But the case we are considering is of a wholly different description, and may be best determined by answering the following question. Supposing a man standing on ground where you have no legal right to follow him has a weapon long enough to reach you, and is striking you down and endangering your life, How long are you bound to wait for the assistance of the authority having the legal power to relieve you? or, to bring the facts more immediately home to the case, if cannon are moving and setting up in a battery which can reach you and are actually destroying life and property by their fire, If you have remonstrated for some time without effect, and see no prospect of relief, when begins your right to defend yourself, should you have no other means of doing so, than by seizing your assailant on the verge of a neutral territory?

I am unwilling to recall to your recollection the particulars of this case, but I am obliged very shortly to do so, to shew what was at the time the extent of the existing justification, for upon this entirely depends the question whether a gross insult has or has not been offered to the Government and people of the United States.

After some tumultuous proceedings in Upper Canada, which were of short duration and were suppressed by the Militia of the Country, the persons criminally concerned in them took refuge in the neighbouring state of New York, and with a very large addition to their numbers openly collected, invaded the Canadian territory taking possession of Navy Island.

This invasion took place the 16th of December 1837; a gradual accession of numbers and of military ammunition continued openly, and though under the sanction of no public authority, at least with no public hinderance until the 29th of the same month, when several hundred men were collected, and twelve pieces of ordnance, which could only have been procured from some public store or arsenal, were actually mounted on Navy Island and were used to fire within easy range upon the unoffending inhabitants of the opposite shore. Remonstrances, wholly ineffectual were made; so ineffectual indeed that a Militia regiment, stationed on the neighbouring American island, looked on without any attempt at interference, while shots were fired from the American island itself. This important fact stands on the best American authority; being stated in a letter to Mr Forsyth of the 6th of Feby 1838, of Mr Benton, attorney of the United States, the gentleman sent by your Government to enquire into the facts of the case, who adds, very properly, that he makes the statement "with deep regret and mortification". [The letter of Nathaniel S. Benton, United States Attorney for the Northern District of New York, is printed in House Document No. 302, 25th Congress, 2d session, serial 329, pp. 36–39.]

This force, formed of all the reckless and mischievous people of the border, formidable from their numbers and from their armament, had in their pay and as part of their establishment this steamboat Caroline, the important means and instrument by which numbers and arms were hourly increasing. I might safely put it to any candid man acquainted with the existing state of things, to say whether the military commander in Canada had the remotest reason on the 29th of December to expect to be relieved from this state of suffering by

the protective intervention of any American authority. How long could a Government, having the paramount duty of protecting its own people, be reasonably expected to wait for what they had then no reason to expect? What would have been the conduct of American officers—what has been their conduct under circumstances much less aggravated? I would appeal to you, Sir, to say whether the facts which you say would alone justify this act, viz: " a necessity of self defence, instant, overwhelming, leaving no choice of means and no moment for deliberation", were not applicable to this case in as high a degree as they ever were to any case of a similar description in the history of nations.

Nearly five years are now past since this occurrence, there has been time for the public to deliberate upon it calmly, and I believe I may take it to be the opinion of candid and honourable men, that the British officers who executed this transaction and their Government who approved it, intended no slight or disrespect to the sovereign authority of the United States. That they intended no such disrespect, I can most solemnly affirm, and I trust it will be admitted that no inference to the contrary can fairly be drawn even by the most susceptible on points of national honour.

Notwithstanding my wish that the explanations I had to make might not revive in any degree any feelings of irritation, I do not see how I could treat this subject without this short recital of facts, because the proof that no disrespect was intended is mainly to be looked for in the extent of the justification.

There remains only a point or two which I should wish to notice, to remove in some degree the impression which your rather highly coloured description of this transaction is calculated to make. The mode of telling a story often tends to distort facts, and in this case more than in any other it is important to arrive at plain unvarnished truth.

It appears from every account that the expedition was sent to capture the Caroline when she was expected to be found on the British ground of Navy island, and that it was only owing to the orders of the rebel leader being disobeyed, that she was not so found. When the British officer came round the point of the island in the night, he first discovered that the vessel was moored to the other shore. He was not by this deterred from making the capture, and his conduct was approved. But you will perceive that there was here most decidedly the case of justification mentioned in your note, that there should be "no moment left for deliberation". I mention this circumstance to shew also that the expedition was not planned with a premeditated purpose of attacking the enemy within the jurisdiction of the United States, but that the necessity of so doing arose from altered circumstances at the moment of execution.

I have only further to notice the highly coloured picture drawn in your note of the facts attending the execution of this service. Some importance is attached to the attack having been made in the night and the vessel having been set on fire and floated down the falls of the river, and it is insinuated rather than asserted that there was carelessness as to the lives of the persons on board. The account given by the distinguished officer who commanded the expedition distinctly refutes or satisfactorily explains these assertions. The time of night was purposely selected as most likely to ensure the execution with the least loss of life, and it is expressly stated that, the strength of the current not permitting the vessel to be carried off, and it being necessary to destroy her by fire, she was drawn into the stream for the express purpose of preventing injury to persons or property of the inhabitants at Schlosser [see House Document No. 302, 25th Congress, 2d session, serial 329].

I would willingly have abstained from a return to the facts of this transaction, my duty being to offer those explanations and assurances which may lead to satisfy the public mind and to the cessation of all angry feeling, but it appeared to me that some explanation of parts of the case, apparently misunderstood, might be of service for this purpose.

Although it is believed that a candid and impartial consideration of the whole history of this unfortunate event will lead to the conclusion that there were grounds of justification as strong as were ever presented in such cases, and above all that no slight of the authority of the United States was ever intended, yet it must be admitted that there was in the hurried execution of this necessary service a violation of territory, and I am instructed to assure you that Her

Majesty's Government consider this as a most serious fact, and that far from thinking that an event of this kind should be lightly risked, they would unfeignedly deprecate its recurrence. Looking back to what passed at this distance of time, what is perhaps most to be regretted is that some explanation and apology for this occurrence was not immediately made: this with a frank explanation of the necessity of the case might and probably would have prevented much of the exasperation and of the subsequent complaints and recriminations to which it gave rise.

There are possible cases in the relations of nations as of individuals, where necessity which controls all other laws may be pleaded, but it is neither easy nor safe to attempt to define the rights or limits properly assignable to such a plea. This must always be a subject of much delicacy, and should be considered by friendly nations with great candour and forbearance. The intentions of the parties must mainly be looked to, and can it for a moment be supposed that Great Britain would intentionally and wantonly provoke a great and powerful neighbour?

Her Majesty's Government earnestly desire that a reciprocal respect for the independent jurisdiction and authority of neighbouring states may be considered among the first duties of all Governments, and I have to repeat the assurance of regret they feel that the event of which I am treating should have disturbed the harmony they so anxiously wish to maintain with the American people and Government.

Connected with these transactions there have also been circumstances of which I believe it is generally admitted that Great Britain has also had just ground to complain. Individuals have been made personally liable for acts done under the avowed authority of their Government; and there are now many brave men exposed to personal consequences for no other cause than having served their country. That this is contrary to every principle of international law it is useless for me to insist. Indeed it had been admitted by every authority of your Government; but, owing to a conflict of laws, difficulties have intervened much to the regret of those authorities in giving practical effect to these principles; and for these difficulties some remedy has been by all desired. It is no business of mine to enter upon the consideration of them, nor have I sufficient information for the purpose, but I trust you will excuse my addressing to you the enquiry, whether the Government of the United States is now in a condition to secure in effect and in practice the principle which has never been denied in argument, that individuals acting under legitimate authority are not personally responsible for executing the orders of their Government. That the power when it exists will be used on every fit occasion I am well assured, and I am bound to admit that looking through the voluminous correspondence concerning these transactions, there appears no indisposition with any of the authorities of the federal government under its several administrations to do justice in this respect in as far as their means and powers would allow.

I trust, Sir, I may now be permitted to hope that all feelings of resentment and ill will resulting from these truly unfortunate events may be buried in oblivion, and that they may be succeeded by those of harmony and friendship which it is certainly the interest and I also believe the inclination of all to promote.

I beg, Sir, you will be assured of my high and unfeigned consideration.

ASHBURTON

The Honble DANIEL WEBSTER
&c &c &c

[*Mr. Webster to Lord Ashburton*]

DEPARTMENT OF STATE,
*Washington, 6*th *Augt., 1842.*

Lord ASHBURTON,
&c, &c, &c

Your Lordship's note of the 28th of July, in answer to mine of the 27th, respecting the case of the "Caroline", has been received, and laid before the President.

The President sees with pleasure that your Lordship fully admits those great principles of public law, applicable to cases of this kind, which this Government

has expressed; and that on your part, as on ours, respect for the inviolable character of the territory of independent States is the most essential foundation of civilization. And while it is admitted, on both sides, that there are exceptions to this rule, he is gratified to find that your Lordship admits that such exceptions must come within the limitations stated and the terms used in a former communication from this Department to the British Plenipotentiary here. Undoubtedly it is just, that while it is admitted that exceptions growing out of the great law of self-defence do exist, those exceptions should be confined to cases in which the "necessity of that self-defence is instant, overwhelming, and leaving no choice of means, and no moment for deliberation."

Understanding these principles alike, the difference between the two Governments is only whether the facts in the case of the "Caroline" make out a case of such necessity for the purpose of self-defence. Seeing that the transaction is not recent, having happened in the time of one of his predecessors; seeing that your Lordship, in the name of your Government, solemnly declares that no slight or disrespect was intended to the sovereign authority of the United States; seeing that it is acknowledged that, whether justifiable or not, there was yet a violation of the territory of the United States, and that you are instructed to say that your Government considers that as a most serious occurrence; seeing, finally, that it is now admitted that an explanation and apology for this violation was due at the time, the President is content to receive these acknowledgments and assurances in the conciliatory spirit which marks your Lordship's letter, and will make this subject, as a complaint of violation of territory, the topic of no further discussion between the two Governments.

As to that part of your Lordship's note which relates to other occurrences springing out of the case of the "Caroline", with which occurrences the name of Alexander McLeod has become connected, I have to say that the Government of the United States entirely adhere to the sentiments and opinions expressed in the communications from this Department to Mr Fox. This Government has admitted, that for an act committed by the command of his sovereign, *jure belli*, an individual cannot be responsible, in the ordinary courts of another State. It would regard it as a high indignity if a citizen of its own, acting under its authority, and by its special command, in such cases, were held to answer in a municipal tribunal, and to undergo punishment, as if the behest of his Government were no defence or protection to him.

But your Lordship is aware that, in regular constitutional Governments, persons arrested on charges of high crimes can only be discharged by some judicial proceeding. It is so in England; it is so in the colonies and provinces of England. The forms of judicial proceeding differ in different countries, being more rapid in some and more dilatory in others; and, it may be added, generally more dilatory, or at least more cautious, in cases affecting life, in Governments of a strictly limited than in those of a more unlimited character. It was a subject of regret that the release of McLeod was so long delayed. A State court, and that not of the highest jurisdiction, decided that, on summary application, embarrassed as it would appear, by technical difficulties, he could not be released by that court. His discharge, shortly afterwards, by a jury, to whom he preferred to submit his case, rendered unnecessary the further prosecution of the legal question. It is for the Congress of the United States, whose attention has been called to the subject, to say what further provision ought to be made to expedite proceedings in such cases; and, in answer to your Lordship's question towards the close of your note, I have to say that the Government of the United States holds itself not only fully disposed, but fully competent, to carry into practice every principle which it avows or acknowledges, and to fulfil every duty and obligation which it owes to foreign Governments, their citizens, or subjects.

I have the honor to be, my Lord, with great consideration, your obedient servant,

DAN¹ WEBSTER.

In the presidential message of August 11, 1842 (quoted above), submitting the Webster-Ashburton Treaty to the Senate, mention was made of the correspondence "upon the subject of the attack and

destruction of the steamboat Caroline"; and in a paragraph devoted to the subject it was said that the note of Ashburton of July 28 had seemed "sufficient to warrant forbearance from any further remonstrance against what took place, as an aggression on the soil and territory of the country".

The first report of Ashburton on the "settlement" of the case of the *Caroline* was in his despatch of July 28, 1842 (Ashburton Papers, despatch No. 14), which enclosed copies of the first two of the three notes above quoted, with this comment:

Although the question of boundaries forms the material and most substantial part of the differences which I am expected to settle here, your Lordship is aware that there are other subjects in which the public here take great interest. Of these the case of the Caroline is the principal; it has occupied the public mind for nearly five years, and what is called a *settlement* of it is expected, and indeed without it there is reason to apprehend that there would be a general indisposition to settle any thing else. I have attempted this by a letter to the Secretary of State of which a copy is enclosed, as is also the copy of a letter from him to me asking explanations on the subject. I have reason to believe that it will be considered satisfactory here, and I have only to hope that it may not be disapproved by your Lordship. This task was one of some delicacy You will perceive that I have interwoven the degree of apology which I thought the case required with a decided justification of what was done. Indeed, although the explanation is intended for the public eye, I have said no more than what I really think was due, and what is necessary to guard against future violations of territory, from which in this part of the world we have at least as much to fear as our neighbours.

The remaining case of the Creole will, I fear, be attended with more difficulty. This I shall undertake tomorrow; and the whole of this correspondence will go before the Senate at the same time with our treaties.

I am assured that the bills referred to in my note to Mr Webster which are to give power to the Executive to deal with cases similar to those of Mr McLeod and Mr Hogan, are likely to pass through Congress before the session ends.

A later despatch, of August 9, 1842 (*ibid.*, despatch No. 19), further reported on the subject, enclosing a copy of the third of the exchanges above quoted; in that despatch Ashburton wrote as follows:

In my despatch of the 28ᵗʰ of last month, I had the honour of sending your Lordship copy of my letter to Mr Webster on the subject of the case of the Caroline, and I have now to add a copy of his reply. This subject of angry controversy may now be considered as so far set at rest, and I hope in a manner which your Lordship will approve.

I wish I could make as favourable a report of the state of things growing out of this event, and referred to in the latter part of my and Mr Webster's letters. Your Lordship has been informed that a Bill had passed the Senate, giving power to the Executive to relieve persons in the situation of Mr McLeod and Mr Hogan from personal persecution arising from their public service. This bill has made some progress in the House of Representatives, and I am assured that it will pass before the session ends; but there is much unfinished business before the House and much party irritation and general confusion, arising from the controversy between the President and the Legislature; and I am consequently not without apprehension that this important measure may be lost in the crowd; not so much from any objection to it, as from neglect and from the want of any person to look after public business.

It will be seen that the principles which govern cases of this description are fully admitted by the Secretary of State, but experience has proved that, owing to the conflicting complication of federal and State law, there is not that power which he maintains there is, to give practical effect to his own principles. The public mind being satisfied as to the case of the Caroline, I am not very apprehensive of any recurrence of these vindictive proceedings; but at the same time

there can be no security, so long as there is no power in the hands of that branch of the Government which is alone responsible to foreign nations, and to which alone foreign nations can apply.　I am assured, and I believe, that all persons connected with this Government are sensible of this difficulty, and that they will see that it be ultimately satisfactorily settled.

It appears, moreover, that the note of Ashburton to Webster of July 28, 1842, which has been quoted above, was altered from its first form. In his despatch of August 13, 1842 (*ibid.*, marked "Separate"), Ashburton wrote thus:

> By my despatch Nº 14 of the 28ᵗʰ ultº I had the honour of sending your Lordship copy of my note to Mʳ Webster on the subject of the Caroline.　It was on consideration thought expedient to suppress a paragraph of that note, which related to the question of compensation to the owner of the vessel.　I have therefore to ask your Lordship's permission to substitute the accompanying corrected copy of that note, and to request that the former may be cancelled. There is no other difference between these copies but the omission of the paragraph above referred to.

A comparison of the corrected copy of the note of July 28—that is to say, the text above printed—with that originally written, shows that the change made was the omission of a few lines, quoted below, which appeared toward the close of the note as the final sentences of the paragraph beginning "Although it is believed" and immediately following the words "to which it gave rise":

> If the Boat which was destroyed could by any fair construction of the case have been considered as the private property of a citizen bonâ fide and innocently employed by him as a passage vessel, compensation for its loss might perhaps have been admitted, but it is notorious that it was part and parcel of the armament of the insurgent force, and I have reason to know, that the property in part, if not wholly, was in British subjects.　Under such circumstances no question of compensation could be entertained or expected.

The proposed statute to cover such cases as that of McLeod was duly enacted (act of August 29, 1842, 5 Statutes at Large, 539–40).

The "Creole"

One of the subjects of the negotiations was, as phrased by Webster, "the better security of American vessels driven by accident or carried by force into the British West India ports".　Various incidents had occurred to bring the question forward.　An account of them is in Moore, Digest, II, 350–61 (for the subsequent arbitration proceedings, see Moore, International Arbitrations, IV, 4349–78).　The most important, the most recent, and the most sensational case was that of the *Creole;* and the general subject, Ashburton wrote, gave him, for a time, "more trouble than all the other questions taken together".

In each of the authorities last cited there is quoted from Senate Executive Document No. 103, 34th Congress, 1st session, serial 824, the opinion rendered in the case of the *Creole* by Joshua Bates, umpire of the Mixed Commission under the convention between the United

States and Great Britain of February 8, 1853.   From that opinion the following statement of the circumstances of the case is extracted:

The American brig Creole, Captain Ensor, sailed from Hampton Roads, in the State of Virginia, on the 27th October, 1841, having on board one hundred and thirty-five slaves, bound for New Orleans.   On the 7th November, at nine o'clock in the evening, a portion of the slaves rose against the officers, crew, and passengers, wounding severely the captain, the chief mate, and two of the crew, and murdering one of the passengers; the mutineers, having got complete possession of the vessel, ordered the mate, under threat of instant death should he disobey or deceive them, to steer for Nassau, in the island of New Providence, where the brig arrived on the 9th November, 1841.

The American consul was apprised of the situation of the vessel, and requested the governor to take measures to prevent the escape of the slaves, and to have the murderers secured.   The consul received reply from the governor, stating that under the circumstances he would comply with the request.

The consul went on board the brig, placed the mate in command in place of the disabled master, and found the slaves all quiet.

About noon twenty African soldiers, with an African sergeant and corporal, commanded by a white officer, came on board.   The officer was introduced by the consul to the mate as commanding officer of the vessel.

The consul, on returning to the shore, was summoned to attend the governor and council, who were in session, who informed the consul that they had come to the following decision:

"1st. That the courts of law have no jurisdiction over the alleged offences.

"2d. That, as an information had been lodged before the governor, charging that the crime of murder had been committed on board said vessel while on the high seas, it was expedient that the parties, implicated in so grave a charge, should not be allowed to go at large, and that an investigation ought therefore to be made into the charges, and examinations taken on oath; when, if it should appear that the original information was correct, and that a murder had actually been committed, that all parties implicated in such crime, or other acts of violence, should be detained here until reference could be made to the Secretary of State to ascertain whether the parties should be delivered over to the United States Government; if not, how otherwise to dispose of them.

"3d. That as soon as such examinations should be taken, all persons on board the Creole, not implicated in any of the offences alleged to have been committed on board that vessel, must be released from further restraint."

Then two magistrates were sent on board.   The American consul went also. The examination was commenced on Tuesday, the 9th, and was continued on Wednesday, the 10th, and then postponed until Friday, on account of the illness of Captain Ensor.   On Friday morning it was abruptly, and without any explanation, terminated.

On the same day, a large number of boats assembled near the Creole, filled with colored persons armed with bludgeons.   They were under the immediate command of the pilot who took the vessel into the port, who was an officer of the government, and a colored man.   A sloop or larger launch was also towed from the shore and anchored near the brig.   The sloop was filled with men armed with clubs, and clubs were passed from her to the persons in the boats.   A vast concourse of people were collected on shore opposite the brig.

During the whole time the officers of the government were on board they encouraged the insubordination of the slaves.

The Americans in port determined to unite and furnish the necessary aid to forward the vessel and negroes to New Orleans.   The consul and the officers and crews of two other American vessels had, in fact, united with the officers, men, and passengers of the Creole to effect this.   They were to conduct her first to Indian quay, Florida, where there was a vessel of war of the United States.

On Friday morning, the consul was informed that attempts would be made to liberate the slaves by force, and from the mate he received information of the threatening state of things.   The result was, that the attorney general and other officers went on board the Creole.   The slaves, identified as on board the vessel concerned in the mutiny, were sent on shore, and the residue of the slaves were

called on deck by direction of the attorney general, who addressed them in the following terms: "My friends," or "my men, you have been detained a short time on board the Creole for the purpose of ascertaining what individuals were concerned in the murder. They have been identified, and will be detained. The rest of you are free, and at liberty to go on shore, and wherever you please."

The liberated slaves, assisted by the magistrates, were then taken on board the boats, and when landed were conducted by a vast assemblage to the superintendent of police, by whom their names were registered. They were thus forcibly taken from the custody of the master of the Creole, and lost to the claimants.

While the treaty contains no clauses regarding the rights of the parties in such cases as that of the *Creole*, a suggestion in that regard had been made by Webster at a very early stage of the negotiations (Ashburton Papers, despatch No. 5, April 28, 1842, enclosure, "Projected clause by Mr Webster to secure the American Vessels in their passage down the Atlantic to the Gulf of Mexico"), as follows:

And it is further agreed, that if any Ship belonging to the subjects or citizens of either country being engaged in any lawful trade or commerce, and bound on a lawful voyage, without any intent to violate the laws of either country, shall, by stress of weather, shipwreck, or danger of enemies or pirates, be driven to seek shelter in any of the ports of the other country, or be carried into the same by unlawful force, usurpation or mutiny, or revolt of the persons on board the same, the said ship shall be entitled to security and protection during her necessary stay in such port; and the owner or owners thereof shall be permitted to possess and hold said vessel, and all on board thereof, and to depart therewith on their voyage, without obstruction or interference of the local authorities, and without inquiry into the character or condition of persons or things on board thereof, except so far as may be necessary to ascertain the authenticity of her papers and the legality of her voyage. And the owner or owners, or their agents, shall be at liberty to refit and repair damages, and to purchase suitable and necessary provisions, supplies, and refreshments for the voyage; and in case of mutiny or revolt, the owner or owners, or their agents, or the Consul of the country to which the vessel belongs, shall be properly aided in all lawful attempts to restore the authority of the master, and to enable said vessel to proceed on her voyage.

The British Government, however, was unable "to see our way towards the proposal of any stipulations by treaty for this purpose". This decision, Ashburton reported, was "evidently a great disappointment, as it left unsatisfied the President himself and a large party in Congress, connected with the interests of the South" (*ibid.*, despatch No. 12, June 29, 1842).

Ashburton reported on the *Creole* case and on the argument in one of his despatches of August 9, 1842 (*ibid.*, despatch No. 20), with which were enclosed copies of the notes exchanged. The text of that despatch is as follows:

In the course of my correspondence I have been anxious to impress upon your Lordship's attention my apprehensions that the Creole case would prove my main difficulty here. Not indeed the case itself, for that is easily answered, but the claim made from all quarters for some security for the great and extensive American coasting trade passing through the Florida channel between the Atlantic states and the waters of the Mississippi, and in the narrow and dangerous part of that channel exposed to dangers arising from a novel condition of things in our small Bahama islands.

Expectations have by all parties been entertained that this was one of the things to be *settled*, and I need not inform your Lordship that in this country, if you have to treat of matters otherwise important, great and extensive interests cannot safely be neglected.

My anticipations were fully confirmed when, my other questions being settled, this was pressed upon me; and it has for the last ten days given me more trouble than all the other questions taken together. Plans have been suggested, and expressions and promises weighed, and as late as yesterday I was not without apprehension of my whole negotiation failing, from the want of means to make some explanation to pacify a large portion of the Senate and the President himself. Perceiving my difficulties, I have for some time endeavoured to leave the whole question to be discussed in London, confining myself to some general expressions of good will; and how it has at last been disposed of your Lordship will see in my correspondence with Mᵣ Webster, of which copies are herewith enclosed.

Mᵣ Webster's very elaborate argument is, as you may suppose, mainly calculated to cover his popularity in the South. My answer was intended to evade any engagement while I maintained our general principles with respect to slavery. In considering this answer, I trust it will not be forgotten that my object was to escape from a difficulty, and not to embark officiously in a discussion for which I had very inadequate powers or means. To say something conciliatory was indispensable for the safety of other objects, and I am not aware that what I have promised with reference to the conduct of the Governor of the Bahamas until some more satisfactory settlement of the general question, is open to much objection. A full consideration of that general question I shall not here attempt, but it may be of service, while the subject is fresh in my recollection, to state how it stands in the opinions of people here.

The immediate case of the Creole is thus disposed of. The slaves once out of the ship are not to be claimed. This principle is as amply admitted as we could wish, provided always that the authorities do nothing to provoke or instigate them to leave the ship.

Upon the case of the criminals there is no difference of opinion. It is admitted that America had no right to claim criminals anywhere, and it is now understood and admitted that the Crown had no power to deliver them up if it had been desired to do so.

The argument turns therefore entirely upon the question of responsibility arising from any officious interference by the Colonial authorities. In the case of the Creole there is the strongest possible evidence that there was not only no such interference, but that the Attorney general of the Island, by his cautious conduct in this respect showed that in his opinion no such interference would be justifiable.

Mᵣ Webster's very elaborate argument comes at last to this single question—what are the rights and immunities of ships of one country in the harbours or waters of another, more especially when coming there involuntarily? It will be seen that the very broad principle is maintained that the ship so situated is still for all essential purposes to be considered as in its own country. That the municipal officers of the place have no right to take cognizance of the state of persons or things on board, so long as no offence be committed against the laws of the place: That the Captain of such a ship exercising any degree of discipline over crew or passengers cannot be called to account; and Mᵣ Webster would carry this irresponsibility even to cases of murder. He does not deny the right of the municipal authority to see to the regulations of the harbour, or to the sanatory laws, or to the prevention of smuggling, or to the satisfaction of any contract or engagement with people on the shore; but any interference with the condition of persons or things beyond what is necessary for these purposes, where a vessel not intending to unload may by accident be driven into the port of a friendly neighbour, is held to be officious and unjustifiable.

This is an important question and must be left to jurists who are competent to answer it. I state the case merely to record what it is that our differences in this respect rest upon. If Mᵣ Webster's reasoning be admitted even to a more limited extent than he would carry it, there will be no difficulty in giving all the satisfaction required by America.

In the case of a vessel driven by distress or violence into Nassau, the practical principle would be that any slave leaving the ship would be free; that no aid could be afforded by British law to establish any right of property in persons. But on the other hand the authorities would have no right officiously to enquire into the state of things on board, so long as there was no offence committed

against the laws of the place and harbour: In other words that the simple fact
being known that there were slaves on board a vessel so situated, should not of
itself call for or justify municipal interference.   This seems to me after stripping
the question of all popular irrelevant matter on both sides what our lawyers will
have to consider.   I do not pretend to dispose of such grave subjects; but confining myself to their practical application to the state of things known to me in
this country, I am bound to add my opinion that some arrangement of this description within the limits mentioned by me, will be necessary for the avoidance
of future quarrels, and that the interests of the great Southern coasting trade of
America render the demand for this extent of security reasonable.   It must be
recollected that the instances of slaves carried by ship loads from port to port are
few and likely hereafter to be fewer, but that most of the small coasters have a
slave or two on board, and the vexation would be endless if the knowledge of this
fact were to make it a duty of the Colonial authorities to intrude on every
occasion.

Three notes were exchanged dealing with the general subject and
with the case of the *Creole;* they were before the Senate (published
correspondence, 116–25).   The texts which follow are from D.S., 6
Notes to the British Legation, 247–59, 272–73, and 21 Notes from the
British Legation; the first note is that of Webster to Ashburton of
August 1, the next the answering note of Ashburton of August 6,
and finally the conclusion of the discussion in the note of Webster of
August 8.   The question of "the better security of American vessels
driven by accident or carried by force into British West India ports"
remained for further consideration, with, however, a specific engagement on the part of the British Government "that instructions shall
be given to the Governors of Her Majesty's Colonies on the Southern
borders of the United States to execute their own laws with careful
attention to the wish of their Government to maintain good neighbourhood; and that there shall be no officious interference with American vessels driven by accident or by violence into those ports.   The
laws and duties of hospitality shall be executed, and these seem neither
to require nor to justify any further inquisition into the state of
persons or things on board of vessels so situated, than may be indispensable to enforce the observance of the municipal law of the Colony
and the proper regulation of its harbours and waters" (for the suggestions of President Tyler of changes in the wording of the concluding
paragraphs of the note of Ashburton of August 6, 1843, see Tyler,
Letters and Times of the Tylers, II, 221–24):

[*Mr. Webster to Lord Ashburton*]

DEPARTMENT OF STATE,
Washington, August 1, 1842.

Lord ASHBURTON,
&ᶜ, &ᶜ, &ᶜ

MY LORD: The President has learned with much regret, that you are not
empowered by your Government to enter into a formal stipulation for the better
security of vessels of the United States, when meeting with disasters in passing
between the United States and the Bahama Islands, and driven, by such disasters,
into British ports.   This is a subject which is deemed to be of great importance,
and which cannot, on the present occasion, be overlooked.

Your Lordship is aware that several cases have occurred within the last few
years which have caused much complaint.   In some of these cases compensation
has been made by the English Government for the interference of the local authorities with American vessels having slaves on board, by which interference

these slaves were set free.   In other cases, such compensation has been refused. It appears to the President to be for the interest of both countries that the recurrence of similar cases in future should be prevented as far as possible.

Your Lordship has been acquainted with the case of the "Creole", a vessel carried into the port of Nassau last winter by persons who had risen upon the lawful authority of the vessel, and, in the accomplishment of their purpose, had committed murder on a person on board.

The opinions which that occurrence gave occasion for this Government to express, in regard to the rights and duties of friendly and civilized maritime States, placed by Providence near to each other, were well considered, and are entertained with entire confidence.   The facts in the particular case of the "Creole" are controverted: positive and officious interference by the colonial authorities to set the slaves free being alleged on one side, and denied on the other.

It is not my present purpose to discuss this difference of opinion as to the evidence in the case as it at present exists, because the rights of individuals having rendered necessary a more thorough and a judicial investigation of facts and circumstances attending the transaction, such investigation is understood to be now in progress, and its result, when known, will render me more able than at this moment to present to the British Government a full and accurate view of the whole case.   But it is my purpose, and my duty, to invite your Lordship's attention to the general subject, and your serious consideration of some practical means of giving security to the coasting trade of the United States against unlawful annoyance and interruption along this part of their shore.   The Bahama Islands approach the coast of Florida within a few leagues, and, with the coast, form a long and narrow channel, filled with innumerable small islands and banks of sand, and the navigation difficult and dangerous, not only on these accounts, but from the violence of the winds and the variable nature of the currents.   Accidents are of course frequent, and necessity often compels vessels of the United States, in attempting to double Cape Florida, to seek shelter in the ports of these islands.   Along this passage, the Atlantic States hold intercourse with the States on the Gulf and the Mississippi, and through it the products of the valley of that river (a region of vast extent and boundless fertility) find a main outlet to the sea, in their destination to the markets of the world.

No particular ground of complaint exists as to the treatment which American vessels usually receive in these ports, unless they happen to have slaves on board; but, in cases of that kind, complaints have been made, as already stated, of officious interference of the colonial authorities with the vessel, for the purpose of changing the condition in which these persons are, by the laws of their own country, and of setting them free.

In the Southern States of this Union slavery exists by the laws of the States and under the guarantee of the Constitution of the United States; and it has existed in them for a period long antecedent to the time when they ceased to be British colonies.   In this state of things, it will happen that slaves will be often on board coasting vessels, as hands, as servants attending the families of their owners, or for the purpose of being carried from port to port.   For the security of the rights of their citizens, when vessels having persons of this description on board are driven by stress of weather, or carried by unlawful force, into British ports, the United States propose the introduction of no new principle into the law of nations.   They require only a faithful and exact observance of the injunctions of that code, as understood and practised in modern times.

Your Lordship observes that I have spoken only of American vessels driven into British ports by the disasters of the seas, or carried in by unlawful force.   I confine my remarks to these cases, because they are the common cases, and because they are the cases which the law of nations most emphatically exempts from interference.   The maritime law is full of instances of the application of that great and practical rule, which declares that that which is the clear result of necessity ought to draw after it no penalty and no hazard.   If a ship be driven by stress of weather into a prohibited port, or into an open port, with prohibited articles on board, in neither case is any forfeiture incurred.   And what may be considered a still stronger case, it has been decided by eminent English authority, and that decision has received general approbation, that if a vessel be driven, by

necessity, into a port strictly blockaded, this necessity is good defence, and exempts her from penalty [see the *Charlotta*, decided in 1810 by Sir William Scott; Edwards, 252–53; 165 English Reports, 1099–1100].

A vessel on the high seas, beyond the distance of a marine league from the shore, is regarded as part of the territory of the nation to which she belongs, and subjected exclusively to the jurisdiction of that nation. If, against the will of her master or owner, she be driven or carried nearer to the land, or even into port, those who have, or ought to have, control over her, struggling all the while to keep her upon the high seas, and so within the exclusive jurisdiction of her own Government, what reason or justice is there in creating a distinction between her rights and immunities, in a position thus the result of absolute necessity, and the same rights and immunities before superior power had forced her out of her voluntary course?

But, my Lord, the rule of law, and the comity and practice of nations, go much further than these cases of necessity, and allow even to a merchant vessel coming into any open port of another country voluntarily, for the purposes of lawful trade, to bring with her, and keep over her, to a very considerable extent, the jurisdiction and authority of the laws of her own country, excluding, to this extent, by consequence, the jurisdiction of the local law. A ship, say the publicists, though at anchor in a foreign harbor, preserves its jurisdiction and its laws. It is natural to consider the vessels of a nation as parts of its territory, though at sea, as the State retains its jurisdiction over them; and, according to the commonly received custom, this jurisdiction is preserved over the vessels, even in parts of the sea subject to a foreign dominion.

This is the doctrine of the law of nations, clearly laid down by writers of received authority, and entirely conformable, as it is supposed, with the practices of modern nations.

If a murder be committed on board of an American vessel, by one of the crew upon another or upon a passenger, or by a passenger on one of the crew or another passenger, while such vessel is lying in a port within the jurisdiction of a foreign State or Sovereignty, the offence is cognizable and punishable by the proper court of the United States, in the same manner as if such offence had been committed on board the vessel on the high seas. The law of England is supposed to be the same.

It is true that the jurisdiction of a nation over a vessel belonging to it, while lying in the port of another, is not necessarily wholly exclusive. We do not so consider or so assert it. For any unlawful acts done by her while thus lying in port, and for all contracts entered into while there, by her master or owners, she and they must doubtless be answerable to the laws of the place. Nor, if her master or crew, while on board in such port, break the peace of the community by the commission of crimes, can exemption be claimed for them. But, nevertheless, the law of nations, as I have stated it, and the statutes of Governments founded on that law, as I have referred to them, show that enlightened nations, in modern times, do clearly hold that the jurisdiction and laws of a nation accompany her ships, not only over the high seas, but into ports and harbors, or wheresoever else they may be water-borne, for the general purpose of governing and regulating the rights, duties, and obligations of those on board thereof, and that, to the extent of the exercise of this jurisdiction, they are considered as parts of the territory of the nation herself.

If a vessel be driven by weather into the ports of another nation, it would hardly be alleged by any one that, by the mere force of such arrival within the waters of the State, the law of that State would so attach to the vessel as to affect existing rights of property between persons on board, whether arising from contract or otherwise. The local law would not operate to make the goods of one man to become the goods of another man. Nor ought it to affect their personal obligations, or existing relations between themselves; nor was it ever supposed to have such effect, until the delicate and exciting question which has caused these interferences in the British islands arose. The local law in these cases dissolves no obligations or relations lawfully entered into or lawfully existing, according to the laws of the ship's country. If it did, intercourse of civilized men between nation and nation must cease. Marriages are frequently celebrated in

one country in a manner not lawful or valid in another; but did any body ever doubt that marriages are valid all over the civilized world, if valid in the country in which they took place? Did any one ever imagine that local law acted upon such marriages, to annihilate their obligation, if the parties should visit a country in which marriages must be celebrated in another form?

It may be said that, in such instances, personal relations are founded in contract, and therefore to be respected; but that the relation of master and slave is not founded in contract, and therefore is to be respected only by the law of the place which recognises it. Whoever so reasons encounters the authority of the whole body of public law, from Grotius down; because there are numerous instances in which the law itself presumes or implies contracts; and prominent among these instances is the very relation which we are now considering, and which relation is holden by law to draw after it mutuality of obligation.

Is not the relation between a father and his minor children acknowledged, when they go abroad? And on what contract is this founded, but a contract raised by general principles of law, from the relation of the parties?

Your Lordship will please to bear in mind, that the proposition which I am endeavoring to support is, that by the comity of the law of nations, and the practice of modern times, merchant vessels entering open ports of other nations, for the purpose of trade, are presumed to be allowed to bring with them, and to retain, for their protection and government, the jurisdiction and laws of their own country. All this, I repeat, is presumed to be allowed; because the ports are open, because trade is invited, and because, under these circumstances, such permission or allowance is according to general usage. It is not denied that all this may be refused; and this suggests a distinction, the disregard of which may perhaps account for most of the difficulties arising in cases of this sort; that is to say, the distinction between what a State may do if it pleases, and what it is presumed to do, or not to do, in the absence of any positive declaration of its will. A State might declare that all foreign marriages should be regarded as null and void, within its territory; that a foreign father, arriving with an infant son, should no longer have authority or control over him; that, on the arrival of a foreign vessel in its ports, all shipping articles and all indentures of apprenticeship, between her crew and her owners or masters, should cease to be binding. These, any many other things equally irrational and absurd, a sovereign State has doubtless the power to do. But they are not to be presumed. It is not to be taken for granted, *ab ante*, that it is the will of the sovereign State thus to withdraw itself from the circle of civilized nations. It will be time enough to believe this to be its intention, when it formally announces that intention, by appropriate enactments, edicts, or other declarations. In regard to slavery within the British territories, there is a well-known and clear promulgation of the will of the sovereign authority; that is to say, there is a well-known rule of her law. As to England herself, that law has long existed; and recent acts of Parliament establish the same law for the colonies.[1] The usual mode of stating the rule of English law is, that no sooner does a slave reach the shore of England, than he is free. This is true; but it means no more than that, when a slave comes within the exclusive jurisdiction of England, he ceases to be a slave, because the law of England positively and notoriously prohibits and forbids the existence of such a relation between man and man. But it does not mean that English authorities, with this rule of English law in their hands, may enter where the jurisdiction of another nation is acknowledged to exist, and destroy those rights, obligations, and interests, lawfully existing under the authority of such other nation. No such construction, and no such effect, can be rightfully given to the British law. It is true that it is competent to the British Parliament, by express statute provision, to declare that no foreign jurisdiction of any kind should exist, in or over a vessel, after its arrival voluntarily in her ports. And so she might close all her ports to the ships of all nations. A State may also declare, in the absence of treaty stipulations, that foreigners shall not sue in her courts, nor travel in her territories, nor carry away funds or goods received for debts. We need not

---

[1] The act of August 28, 1833, which took effect August 1, 1834 (3 and 4 William IV, ch. 73).

inquire what would be the condition of a country that should establish such laws, nor in what relation they would leave her towards the States of the civilized world. Her power to make such laws is unquestionable; but, in the absence of direct and positive enactments to that effect, the presumption is that the opposites of these things exist. While her ports are open to foreign trade, it is to be presumed that she expects foreign ships to enter them, bringing with them the jurisdiction of their own Government, and the protection of its laws, to the same extent that her ships, and the ships of other commercial States, carry with them the jurisdiction of their respective Governments into the open ports of the world; just as it is presumed, while the contrary is not avowed, that strangers may travel in a civilized country, in a time of peace, sue in its courts, and bring away their property.

A merchant vessel enters the port of a friendly State, and enjoys while there the protection of her own laws, and is under the jurisdiction of her own Government, not in derogation of the sovereignty of the place, but by the presumed allowance or permission of that sovereignty. This permission or allowance is founded on the comity of nations, like the other cases which have been mentioned; and this comity is part, and a most important and valuable part, of the law of nations, to which all nations are presumed to assent until they make their dissent known. In the silence of any positive rule, affirming or denying or restraining the operation of foreign laws, their tacit adoption is presumed to the usual extent. It is upon this ground that courts of law expound contracts according to the law of the place in which they are made; and instances almost innumerable exist, in which, by the general practice of civilized countries, the laws of one will be recognised and often executed in another. This is the comity of nations; and it is upon this, as its solid basis, that the intercourse of civilized States is maintained.

But while that which has now been said is understood to be the voluntary and adopted law of nations, in cases of the voluntary entry of merchant vessels into the ports of other countries, it is nevertheless true that vessels in such ports, only through an overruling necessity, may place their claim for exemption from interference on still higher principles; that is to say, principles held in more sacred regard by the comity, the courtesy, or indeed the common sense of justice of all civilized States.

Even in regard to cases of necessity, however, there are things of an unfriendly and offensive character, which yet it may not be easy to say that a nation might not do. For example, a nation might declare her will to be and make it the law of her dominions, that foreign vessels, cast away on her shores, should be lost to their owners, and subject to the ancient law of wreck. Or a neutral State, while shutting her ports to the armed vessels of belligerants, as she has a right to do, might resolve on seizing and confiscating vessels of that description, which should be driven to take shelter in her harbors by the violence of the storms of the ocean. But laws of this character, however within the absolute competence of Governments, could only be passed, if passed at all, under willingness to meet the last responsibility to which nations are subjected.

The presumption is stronger, therefore, in regard to vessels driven into foreign ports by necessity, and seeking only temporary refuge, than in regard to those which enter them voluntarily, and for purposes of trade, that they will not be interfered with; and that, unless they commit, while in port, some act against the laws of the place, they will be permitted to receive supplies, to repair damages, and to depart unmolested.

If, therefore, vessels of the United States, pursuing lawful voyages from port to port, along their own shore, are driven by stress of weather, or carried by unlawful force, into English ports, the Government of the United States cannot consent that the local authorities in those ports shall take advantage of such misfortunes, and enter them, for the purpose of interfering with the condition of persons or things on board, as established by their own laws. If slaves, the property of citizens of the United States, escape into the British territories, it is not expected that they will be restored. In that case the territorial jurisdiction of England will have become exclusive over them, and must decide their condition. But slaves on board of an American vessel, lying in British waters, are not within the exclusive jurisdiction of England, or under the exclusive operation of English law; and this founds the broad distinction between the cases. If persons, guilty of

crimes in the United States, seek an asylum in the British dominions, they will not be demanded until provision for such cases be made by treaty: because the giving up of criminals, fugitive from justice, is agreed and understood to be a matter in which every nation regulates its conduct according to its own discretion. It is no breach of comity to refuse such surrender.

On the other hand, vessels of the United States, driven by necessity into British ports, and staying there no longer than such necessity exists, violating no law, nor having intent to violate any law, will claim, and there will be claimed for them, protection and security, freedom from molestation, and from all interference with the character or condition of persons or things on board. In the opinion of the Government of the United States, such vessels, so driven and so detained by necessity in a friendly port, ought to be regarded as still pursuing their original voyage, and turned out of their direct course only by disaster, or by wrongful violence; that they ought to receive all assistance necessary to enable them to resume that direct course; and that interference and molestation by the local authorities, where the whole voyage is lawful, both in act and intent, is ground for just and grave complaint.

Your Lordship's discernment and large experience in affairs cannot fail to suggest to you how important it is to merchants and navigators engaged in the coasting trade of a country so large in extent as the United States, that they should feel secure against all but the ordinary causes of maritime loss. The possessions of the two Governments closely approach each other. This proximity, which ought to make us friends and good neighbors, may, without proper care and regulation, itself prove a ceaseless cause of vexation, irritation, and disquiet.

If your Lordship has no authority to enter into a stipulation by treaty for the prevention of such occurrences hereafter as have already happened, occurrences so likely to disturb that peace between the two countries which it is the object of your Lordship's mission to establish and confirm, you may still be so far acquainted with the sentiments of your Government as to be able to engage that instructions shall be given to the local authorities in the islands, which shall lead them to regulate their conduct in conformity with the rights of citizens of the United States, and the just expectations of their Government, and in such manner as shall, in future, take away all reasonable ground of complaint. It would be with the most profound regret that the President should see that, whilst it is now hoped so many other subjects of difference may be harmoniously adjusted, nothing should be done in regard to this dangerous source of future collisions.

I avail myself of this occasion to renew to your Lordship the assurances of my distinguished consideration.

DAN! WEBSTER.

[*Lord Ashburton to Mr. Webster*]

WASHINGTON *August 6. 1842*

SIR You may be well assured that I am duly sensible of the great importance of the subject to which you call my attention in the note which you did me the honour of addressing me the 1st Instant, in which you inform me that the President had been pleased to express his regret that I was not empowered by my government to enter into a formal stipulation for the better security of vessels of the United States when meeting with disasters in passing between the United States and the Bahama islands, and driven by such disasters into British ports.

It is, I believe, unnecessary that I should tell you that the case of the Creole was known in London a few days only before my departure. No complaint had at that time been made by Mr Everett. The subject was not therefore among those which it was the immediate object of my mission to discuss. But at the same time I must admit that from the moment I was acquainted with the facts of this case, I was sensible of all its importance, and I should not think myself without power to consider of some adjustment of and remedy for a great acknowledged difficulty, if I could see my way clearly to any satisfactory course, and if I had not arrived at the conclusion, after very anxious consideration, that for the reasons which I will state, this question had better be treated in London where it will have a much increased chance of settlement on terms likely to satisfy the interests of the United States.

The immediate case of the Creole would be easily disposed of; but it involves a class and description of cases which, for the purpose of affording that security you seek for the trade of America through the Bahama channel, brings into consideration questions of law, both national and international, of the highest importance; and to increase the delicacy and difficulty of the subject, public feeling is sensitively alive to everything connected with it.   These circumstances bring me to the conviction that although I really believe that much may be done to meet the wishes of your Government, the means of doing so would be best considered in London where immediate reference may be had to the highest authorities on every point of delicacy and difficulty that may arise.   Whatever I might attempt would be more or less under the disadvantage of being fettered by apprehensions of responsibility, and I might thereby be kept within limits which my Government at home might disregard.   In other words I believe you would have a better chance in this settlement with them than with me.   I state this after some imperfect endeavours by correspondence to come at satisfactory explanations. If I were in this instance treating of ordinary material interests, I should proceed with more confidence, but anxious as I unfeignedly am that all questions likely to disturb future good understanding between us should be averted, I strongly recommend this question of the security of the Bahama channel being referred for discussion in London.

This opinion is more decidedly confirmed by your very elaborate and important argument on the application of the general principles of the law of nations to these subjects; an argument to which your authority necessarily gives great weight, but in which I would not presume to follow you with my own imperfect means.   Great Britain and the United States, covering all the seas of the world with their commerce, have the greatest possible interest in maintaining sound and pure principles of international law, as well as the practice of reciprocal aid and good offices in all their harbours and possessions.   With respect to the latter it is satisfactory to know that the disposition of the respective Governments and people leaves little to be desired with the single exception of those very delicate and perplexing questions which have recently arisen from the state of slavery; and even these seem confined, and likely to continue to be confined, to the narrow passage of the Bahama channel.   At no other part of the British possessions are American vessels with slaves ever likely to touch, nor are they likely to touch there otherwise than from the pressure of very urgent necessity.   The difficulty therefore, as well as the desired remedy, is apparently confined within narrow limits.

Upon the great general principles affecting this case we do not differ.   You admit that if slaves, the property of American citizens, escape into British territories, it is not expected that they will be restored, and you may be well assured that there is no wish on our part that they should reach our shores, or that British possessions should be used as decoys for the violators of the laws of a friendly neighbour.

When these slaves do reach us, by whatever means, there is no alternative. The present state of British law is in this respect too well known to require repetition, nor need I remind you that it is exactly the same with the laws of every part of the United States, where a state of slavery is not recognised; and that the slave put on shore at Nassau would be dealt with exactly as would a foreign slave landed under any circumstances whatever at Boston.

But what constitutes the being within British dominion, from which these consequences are to follow?   Is a vessel passing through the Bahama channel, and forced involuntarily either from storm or mutiny into British waters to be so considered?   What power have the authorities of those islands to take cognisance of persons or property in such vessels?   These are questions which you, Sir, have discussed at great length and with evident ability.   Although you have advanced some propositions which rather surprize and startle me, I do not pretend to judge them; but what is very clear is that great principles are involved in a discussion, which it would ill become me lightly to enter upon, and I am confirmed by this consideration in wishing that the subject be referred to where it will be perfectly weighed and examined.

It behoves the authorities of our two Governments well to guard themselves against establishing by their diplomatic intercourse false precedents and prin-

ciples, and that they do not for the purpose of meeting a passing difficulty, set examples which may hereafter mislead the world.

It is not intended on this occasion to consider in detail the particular instances which have given rise to these discussions; they have already been stated and explained. Our object is rather to look to the means of future prevention of such occurrences. That this may be obtained I have little doubt, although we may not be able immediately to agree on the precise stipulations of a treaty. On the part of Great Britain there are certain great principles too deeply rooted in the consciences and sympathies of the people for any minister to be able to overlook. And any engagement I might make in opposition to them would be instantly disavowed. But at the same time that we maintain our own laws within our own territories we are bound to respect those of our neighbours, and to listen to every possible suggestion of means of averting from them every annoyance and injury. I have great confidence that this may be effectually done in the present instance; but the case to be met and remedied is new and must not be too hastily dealt with. You may however be assured that measures so important for the preservation of friendly intercourse between the two countries shall not be neglected.

In the mean time I can engage that instructions shall be given to the Governors of Her Majesty's Colonies on the Southern borders of the United States to execute their own laws with careful attention to the wish of their Government to maintain good neighbourhood; and that there shall be no officious interference with American vessels driven by accident or by violence into those ports. The laws and duties of hospitality shall be executed, and these seem neither to require nor to justify any further inquisition into the state of persons or things on board of vessels so situated, than may be indispensable to enforce the observance of the municipal law of the Colony and the proper regulation of its harbours and waters.

A strict and careful attention to these rules applied in good faith to all transactions as they arise will, I hope and believe, without any abandonment of great general principles, lead to the avoidance of any excitement or agitation on this very sensitive subject of slavery, and consequently of those irritating feelings which may have a tendency to bring into peril all the great interests connected with the maintenance of peace.

I further trust that friendly sentiments, and a conviction of the importance of cherishing them, will on all occasions lead the two countries to consider favourably any further arrangements which may be judged necessary for the reciprocal protection of their interests.

I hope, Sir, that this explanation on this very important subject will be satisfactory to the President, and that he will see in it no diminution of that earnest desire, which you have been pleased to recognise in me, to perform my work of reconciliation and friendship; but that he will rather perceive in my suggestion in this particular instance that it is made with a well founded hope of thereby better obtaining the object we have in view.

I beg to renew to you, Sir, the assurances of my high consideration.

ASHBURTON

Honble DANIEL WEBSTER
&c &c &c
_____

[*Mr. Webster to Lord Ashburton*]

DEPARTMENT OF STATE,
Washington, Augt. 8, 1842.

Lord ASHBURTON,
&c, &c, &c

MY LORD: I have the honor to acknowledge the receipt of your Lordship's note of the 6th instant, in answer to mine of the 1st, upon the subject of a stipulation for the better security of American vessels driven by accident or carried by force into the British West India ports.

The President would have been gratified if you had felt yourself at liberty to proceed at once to consider of some proper arrangement, by formal treaty, for this object; but there may be weight in the reasons which you urge for referring such mode of stipulation for consideration in London.

The President places his reliance on those principles of public law which were stated in my note to your Lordship, and which are regarded as equally well-founded and important; and on your Lordship's engagement that instructions shall be given to the Governors of Her Majesty's colonies to execute their own laws with careful attention to the wish of their Government to maintain good neighborhood, and that there shall be no officious interference with American vessels driven by accident or by violence into those ports; that the laws and duties of hospitality shall be executed, and that these seem neither to require nor to justify any further inquisition into the state of persons or things on board of vessels so situated than may be indispensable to enforce the observance of the municipal law of the colony, and the proper regulation of its harbors and waters. He indulges the hope, nevertheless, that, actuated by a just sense of what is due to the mutual interests of the two countries, and the maintenance of a permanent peace between them, Her Majesty's Government will not fail to see the importance of removing, by such further stipulations, by treaty or otherwise, as may be found to be necessary, all cause of complaint connected with this subject.

I have the honor to be, with high consideration, your Lordship's obedient servant,

DAN! WEBSTER.

In the presidential message of August 11, 1842 (quoted above), submitting the Webster-Ashburton Treaty to the Senate, mention is made of the correspondence "on the subject of the interference of the colonial authorities of the British West Indies with American merchant vessels driven by stress of weather, or carried by violence, into the ports of those colonies"; and in the next to the final paragraph of the message the hope is expressed that the correspondence "and the engagements entered into by the British minister, will be found such as to satisfy the just expectation of the people of the United States."

IMPRESSMENT

Lord Ashburton did not have authority to treat on the subject of impressment; he asked for such power and was refused; his suggestion was not for a formal treaty engagement, but for a statement in a British note. His case was very forcibly put; what he wrote to Lord Aberdeen follows (Ashburton Papers, despatch No. 7, May 12, 1842):

It cannot have escaped your Lordship's observation that, in all discussions with the Government of this Country respecting maritime rights and the practice at sea of visiting & searching or otherwise, the apprehension always uppermost in the public mind is, that they may in some way or other lead to that impressment of Seamen during any future War, which was the source of so much dissention during the last. All Pamphlets and speeches on those subjects of my negotiations here having the remotest reference to maritime affairs point to this result, and the very sensitive feelings of all classes are kept in a state of irritation by imputations wholly unfounded. Considering the object of my mission here to be not only the settlement of existing differences, but the establishment, if possible, of a more wholesome state of the public mind, by which future differences may be averted, I feel it to be my duty to call your Lordship's attention to this subject.

It becomes further necessary, because a proposition has been made to me by M\[r\] Webster, which, without your authority, I am not able to answer. In settling the various subjects, which, if we succeed, he will have to present to the Senate and to the Public, it is important for me, as well as to him, to give to the whole the greatest character of popularity. Nothing would so much contribute to this, as having something satisfactory to say on the subject of Impressment. It would go far to ensure success to our other negotiations, and, which is more important, remove the most serious cause of animosity and ill will. It is not

proposed to make any Treaty on this subject, but the question is, whether I may say in a note to Mr Webster, that in the event of our being engaged in a war in which the United States shall be neutral, impressment from her Merchant Vessels navigating the *High Seas* will not be practised, provided that provision be made by Law or other competent regulation, that during such War no subject of the Crown be entered into the Merchant Service of America, that shall not have been resident at least five years in the United States,—Mr Webster adds "being *naturalized*" but I believe this word had better be omitted as it brings forward the troubled question of naturalization and allegiance.

Mr Webster's proposition is in a form to render it reciprocal, and the proper form will be to be considered. The substance, as affecting us is stated above. I have used the words on the *High Seas* to avoid any minute discussions as to what may be done in our own waters and harbours or in the narrow Seas, as also the question what are *narrow* seas. The grace of the concession would be much impaired by any minute definitions on these matters.

The general subject of Impressment has been so often discussed, that I should not feel justified in going over the common ground, but there are some considerations so peculiarly applicable to the actual state of this singular Country, that I trust your Lordship will excuse my calling your attention to them.

We take our Seamen from a common stock of nearly undistinguishable Individuals.

Impressment, as a system, is an anomaly hardly bearable by our own people. To the foreigner it is undeniable tyranny, which can only be imposed upon him by force, and submitted to by him so long as that force continues. Our last war, and the perils in which at some periods of that War we were involved, may perhaps have justified violence. America was comparatively weak, and was forced for some years to submit. She afterwards declared her own War, and there can be no doubt that it was mainly, if not wholly occasioned by Impressment. But the proportions of Power are altered. The population of America has more than doubled since the last War, and that War has given her a Navy which she had not before. A navy very efficient in proportion to its extent.

Under these circumstances can Impressment ever be repeated? I apprehend nobody in England thinks it can. Here there can be no doubt that the first exercise of this practice would produce War. Is it not then better to surrender with a good grace a pretended right, while the surrender may bring you some credit, than to maintain what you will have no power to execute. Further you may obtain some compensatory stipulation respecting the period of years during which the subject shall reside before he becomes a Citizen, although it must be admitted that this condition is open to much evasion.

I am aware that this question in some degree involves that conflict prevailing between the Laws of the two Countries with respect to Allegiance. We maintain its indefeasibility; America, the contrary. The simple stipulation that Sailors shall not be taken from Ships on the High Seas, seems to me to evade conveniently the decision of the more general principle which would otherwise obtrude itself.

This question in one shape or other is not easily avoided. It was observed by Mr Clay in the Senate, a short time before he left it, that England burthened with a surplus population, of which she promoted by every means the emigration, sent to this Country, through various channels, annually, from 80 to 100.000 people, for the most part in indigent circumstances. The most destitute of these hang about the Sea Ports; but will the Mother Country, when so much pleased to be rid of them, insist on retaining their Allegiance? I believe I should not overstate the number of Persons living in these states, but owing, according to our Laws, allegiance to Great Britain, at a million.

I find on enquiry that the naturalization Laws of the United States require a constant residence of five years in the Country, before an Alien can acquire the rights of Citizenship. He must also make a declaration, two years before the expiration of the five, of his renunciation of other Allegiance, and of his intention to become a citizen of the States. I am assured that these restrictions are more likely to be made more stringent than to be relaxed, as the numbers and the conduct of these newly acquired Citizens begin to render them objects of much jealousy.

But without pursuing further these observations, which I trust your Lordship will excuse, I hope you will be of opinion that a favorable answer may be given to Mᵣ Webster on the subject of Impressment. If it can otherwise be done with safety, I have only to repeat that it would be of great benefit to the general success of our negotiations, and abundantly productive of future harmony and good will.

Aberdeen flatly refused to accede to the suggestion of Ashburton; Her Majesty's Government "would consider that assent as tantamount to an absolute and entire renunciation of the indefeasible right inherent in the British Crown to command the allegiance and services of its subjects, where ever found; for such it would be in fact, however that renunciation might be apparently limited, or modified" (*ibid.*, instruction No. 9, June 3, 1842). While accepting the directions given, Ashburton in reply justified his suggestion in his despatch of June 29 (*ibid.*, despatch No. 11):

I had the honour of receiving your Lordship's despatch of the 3ᵈ instant, № 9, on the subject of my proposal to be permitted to make some satisfactory answer to the wish expressed by the Secretary of State of the United States to enter into some arrangement respecting the practice of Impressment from American vessels on the High Seas which had been the cause of so much animosity between the two Countries. I collect from your Lordship's instructions that, notwithstanding your desire to promote the success of the negotiations by which the settlement of differences here is to be effected, a concession of the description proposed appeared to involve the abandonment of rights and principles which could under no circumstances be consented to. I have in consequence of this view of the case made verbally to Mᵣ Webster the communication which it required.

Although this question is so settled I trust your Lordship will excuse my offering a few observations in vindication of myself in making a suggestion which seems to have been considered as new and as leading for the first time to the abdication of the rights of the British Crown and to the surrender by Her Majesty of the allegiance and services of her subjects wherever found.

Whatever may be the importance of this question, and I would by no means deny that it is most important, I beg to remind your Lordship that it has been repeatedly in discussion between the two Governments, and has at no time that I can find been considered in the light of the abandonment of a great principle, whatever other difficulties may have attended it.

In 1803 this subject was considered by Lord Hawkesbury and Mᵣ Rufus King, the American Minister, and referred by the former to Lord Sᵗ Vincent the then First Lord of the Admiralty, with an assurance that he, Lord Hawkesbury, would be satisfied with whatever the first Lord of the Admiralty would consent to, and an article was prepared which finally was rejected because Mᵣ King refused to confine the exemption from Impressment to the *High Seas*—a restriction which, your Lordship will observe, was contained in Mᵣ Webster's proposal. It does not appear that any party in this case considered any important prerogative of the Crown to be drawn in question. [As to the negotiations of 1803, see the letter of Rufus King, Minister at London, to Secretary of State Madison, dated July 1803, American State Papers, Foreign Relations, II, 503–4.]

The transaction above referred to was in time of war, but after the entire restoration of peace I find in 1818 the British Plenipotentiaries, Lord Ripon and Mᵣ Goulburn, proposing to the American Plenipotentiaries, Messʳˢ Gallatin and Rush, a formal Treaty, in the 4ᵗʰ article of which the right of Impressment is explicitly renounced on the High Seas. This proposed Treaty again failed on another ground, viz: that there were circumstances which then prevented America from making corresponding regulations respecting the enlistment of seamen; but here again no person seems to have thought that any great principle was involved in the settlement of an obvious cause of international disputes. [As to the negotiations of 1818, so far as they treated of impressment, see *ibid.*, IV, 383–97, *passim.*]

167951°—vol. 4—34——32

This subject has on various other occasions been discussed with the United States but I cannot find that at any time the Principle now considered so serious was ever made an objection. The impediments to its settlement seem always to have turned upon the details of execution.

I venture to call your Lordship's attention to these circumstances in my justification that I may not be supposed to have been induced by my zeal to promote the success of my immediate negotiations to propose any dangerous novelties or the abandonment of any valued rights.

The result was that the subject of impressment was treated in two notes of the Plenipotentiaries, which were before the Senate and which are part of the published correspondence (pp. 139–45). The first is the note of Webster to Ashburton of August 8 (D.S., 6 Notes to the British Legation, 261–71), containing a very definite and positive statement of the American position; the second is the answering note of Ashburton of August 9, the concluding note of the entire correspondence (D.S., 21 Notes from the British Legation).

[*Mr. Webster to Lord Ashburton*]

DEPARTMENT OF STATE,
Washington, 8ᵗʰ Augt., 1842.

MY LORD: We have had several conversations on the subject of impressment, but I do not understand that your Lordship has instructions from your Government to negotiate upon it, nor does the Government of the United States see any utility in opening such negotiation, unless the British Government is prepared to renounce the practice in all future wars.

No cause has produced, to so great an extent, and for so long a period, disturbing and irritating influences on the political relations of the United States and England, as the impressment of seamen by British cruisers from American merchant vessels.

From the commencement of the French Revolution to the breaking out of the war between the two countries in 1812, hardly a year elapsed without loud complaint and earnest remonstrance. A deep feeling of opposition to the right claimed, and to the practice exercised under it, and not unfrequently exercised without the least regard to what justice and humanity would have dictated, even if the right itself had been admitted, took possession of the public mind of America; and this feeling, it is well known, coöperated most powerfully, with other causes, to produce the state of hostilities which ensued.

At different periods, both before and since the war, negotiations have taken place between the two Governments, with the hope of finding some means of quieting these complaints. At some times, the effectual abolition of the practice has been requested and treated of; at other times, its temporary suspension; and, at other times again, the limitation of its exercise, and some security against its enormous abuses.

A common destiny has attended these efforts; they have all failed. The question stands at this moment where it stood fifty years ago. The nearest approach to a settlement was a convention proposed in 1803, and which had come to the point of signature, when it was broken off in consequence of the British Government insisting that the *narrow seas* should be expressly excepted out of the sphere over which the contemplated stipulations against impressment should extend. The American Minister, Mr. King, regarded this exception as quite inadmissible, and chose rather to abandon the negotiation than to acquiesce in the doctrine which it proposed to establish [see the letter to Rufus King of July 1803, above cited].

England asserts the right of impressing British subjects, in time of war, out of neutral merchant vessels, and of deciding, by her visiting officers, who among the crews of such merchant vessels are British subjects. She asserts this as a legal exercise of the prerogative of the Crown; which prerogative is alleged to be founded on the English law of the perpetual and indissoluble allegiance of

the subject, and his obligation, under all circumstances, and for his whole life, to render military service to the Crown whenever required.

This statement, made in the words of eminent British jurists, shows, at once, that the English claim is far broader than the basis or platform on which it is raised. The law relied on is English law; the obligations insisted on are obligations existing between the Crown of England and its subjects. This law and these obligations, it is admitted, may be such as England may choose they shall be. But then they must be confined to the parties. Impressment of seamen, out of and beyond English territory, and from on board the ships of other nations, is an interference with the rights of other nations; is further, therefore, than English prerogative can legally extend; and is nothing but an attempt to enforce the peculiar law of England beyond the dominions and jurisdiction of the Crown. The claim asserts an extra territorial authority, to the manifest injury and annoyance of the citizens and subjects of other States, on board their own vessels on the high seas.

Every merchant vessel on the seas is rightfully considered as part of the territory of the country to which it belongs. The entry, therefore, into such vessel, being neutral, by a belligerent, is an act of force, and is *prima facie* a wrong, a trespass, which can be justified only when done for some purpose allowed to form a sufficient justification by the law of nations. But a British cruiser enters an American merchant vessel in order to take therefrom supposed British subjects; offering no justification therefor, under the law of nations, but claiming the right under the law of England respecting the King's prerogative. This cannot be defended. English soil, English territory, English jurisdiction, is the appropriate sphere for the operation of English law. The ocean is the sphere of the law of nations; and any merchant vessel on the seas is, by that law, under the protection of the laws of her own nation, and may claim immunity, unless in cases in which that law allows her to be entered or visited.

If this notion of perpetual allegiance, and the consequent power of the prerogative, was the law of the world; if it formed part of the conventional code of nations, and was usually practised like the right of visiting neutral ships for the purpose of discovering and seizing enemy's property, then impressment might be defended as a common right, and there would be no remedy for the evil till the national code should be altered. But this is by no means the case. There is no such principle incorporated into the code of nations. The doctrine stands only as English law—not as national law; and English law cannot be of force beyond English dominion. Whatever duties or relations that law creates between the sovereign and his subjects can be enforced and maintained only within the realm, or proper possessions or territory of the sovereign. There may be quite as just a prerogative right to the property of subjects as to their personal services, in an exigency of the State; but no Government thinks of controlling by its own laws property of its subjects situated abroad; much less does any Government think of entering the territory of another Power, for the purpose of seizing such property, and applying it to its own uses—as laws, the prerogatives of the Crown of England, have no obligation on persons or property domiciled or situated abroad.

"When, therefore," says an authority not unknown or unregarded on either side of the Atlantic [Story, Conflict of Laws, 8th ed., 25], "we speak of the right of a State to bind its own native subjects every where, we speak only of its own claim and exercise of sovereignty over them, when they return within its own territorial jurisdiction, and not of its right to compel or require obedience to such laws, on the part of other nations, within their own territorial sovereignty. On the contrary, every nation has an exclusive right to regulate persons and things within its own territory, according to its sovereign will and public policy."

The good sense of these principles, their remarkable pertinency to the subject now under consideration, and the extraordinary consequences resulting from the British doctrine, are signally manifested by that which we see taking place every day. England acknowledges herself overburdened with population of the poorer classes. Every instance of the emigration of persons of those classes is regarded by her as a benefit. England, therefore, encourages emigration; means are notoriously supplied to emigrants to assist their conveyance, from public funds; and the new world, and most especially these United States, receive the many thousands of her subjects thus ejected from the bosom of their native land by the necessities of their condition. They come away from poverty and distress, in

over-crowded cities, to seek employment, comfort, and new homes, in a country of free institutions, possessed by a kindred race, speaking their own language, and having laws and usages in many respects like those to which they have been accustomed; and a country which, upon the whole, is found to possess more attractions for persons of their character and condition than any other on the face of the globe. It is stated that in the quarter of the year ending with June last, more than twenty-six thousand emigrants left the single port of Liverpool, for the United States, being four or five times as many as left the same port within the same period for the British colonies and all other parts of the world. Of these crowds of emigrants, many arrive in our cities in circumstances of great destitution, and the charities of the country, both public and private, are severely taxed to relieve their immediate wants. In time they mingle with the new community in which they find themselves, and seek means of living—some find employment in the cities; others go to the frontiers, to cultivate lands reclaimed from the forest; and a greater or less number of the residue, becoming in time naturalized citizens, enter into the merchant service, under the flag of their adopted country.

Now, my Lord, if war should break out between England and a European Power, can any thing be more unjust, any thing more irreconcilable to the general sentiments of mankind, than that England should seek out these persons, thus encouraged by her, and compelled by their own condition, to leave their native homes, tear them away from their new employments, their new political relations, and their domestic connexions, and force them to undergo the dangers and hardships of military service, for a country which has thus ceased to be their own country? Certainly, certainly, my Lord, there can be but one answer to this question. Is it not far more reasonable that England should either prevent such emigration of her subjects, or that, if she encourage and promote it, she should leave them, not to the embroilment of a double and a contradictory allegiance, but to their own voluntary choice, to form such relations, political or social, as they see fit, in the country where they are to find their bread, and to the laws and institutions of which they are to look for defence and protection?

A question of such serious importance ought now to be put at rest. If the United States give shelter and protection to those whom the policy of England annually casts upon their shores—if, by the benign influence of their Government and institutions, and by the happy condition of the country, those emigrants become raised from poverty to comfort, finding it easy even to become landholders, and being allowed to partake in the enjoyment of all civil rights—if all this may be done (and all this is done, under the countenance and encouragement of England herself,) is it not high time, my Lord, that, yielding that which had its origin in feudal ideas as inconsistent with the present state of society, and especially with the intercourse and relations subsisting between the old world and the new, England should, at length, formally disclaim all right to the services of such persons, and renounce all control over their conduct?

But impressment is subject to objections of a much wider range. If it could be justified in its application to those who are declared to be its only object, it still remains true that, in its exercise, it touches the political rights of other Governments, and endangers the security of their own native subjects and citizens. The sovereignty of the State is concerned in maintaining its exclusive jurisdiction and possession over its merchant ships on the seas, except so far as the law of nations justifies intrusion upon that possession for special purposes; and all experience has shown that no member of a crew, wherever born, is safe against impressment when a ship is visited.

The evils and injuries resulting from the actual practice can hardly be over-rated, and have ever proved themselves to be such as should lead to its relinquishment, even if it were founded in any defensible principle. The difficulty of discriminating between English subjects and American citizens has always been found to be great, even when an honest purpose of discrimination has existed. But the Lieutenant of a man-of-war, having necessity for men, is apt to be a summary judge, and his decisions will be quite as significant of his own wants and his own power, as of the truth and justice of the case. An extract from a letter of Mr. King, of the 13th of April, 1797, to the American Secretary of State [see American State Papers, Foreign Relations, III, 582–83], shows something of the enormous extent of these wrongful seizures:

"Instead of a few, and these in many instances equivocal cases, I have," says he, "since the month of July past, made application for the discharge from British men-of-war of two hundred and seventy-one seamen, who, stating themselves to be Americans, have claimed my interference. Of this number, eighty-six have been ordered by the Admiralty to be discharged, thirty-seven more have been detained as British subjects or as American volunteers, or for want of proof that they are Americans; and to my applications for the discharge of the remaining one hundred and forty-eight I have received no answer—the ships on board of which these seamen were detained having, in many instances, sailed before an examination was made, in consequence of my application.

"It is certain that some of those who have applied to me are not American citizens, but the exceptions are, in my opinion, few, and the evidence, exclusive of certificates, has been such as, in most cases, to satisfy me that the applicants were real Americans, who have been forced into the British service, and who, with singular constancy, have generally persevered in refusing pay or bounty, though in some instances they have been in service more than two years."

But the injuries of impressment are by no means confined to its immediate subjects or the individuals on whom it is practised. Vessels suffer from the weakening of their crews, and voyages are often delayed, and not unfrequently broken up, by subtraction from the number of necessary hands by impressment. And, what is of still greater and more general moment, the fear of impressment has been found to create great difficulty in obtaining sailors for the American merchant service, in times of European war. Seafaring men, otherwise inclined to enter into that service, are, as experience has shown, deterred by the fear of finding themselves ere long in compulsory military service in British ships of war. Many instances have occurred, fully established in proof, in which raw seamen, natives of the United States, fresh from the fields of agriculture, entering for the first time on shipboard, have been impressed before they made the land, placed on the decks of British men-of-war, and compelled to serve for years before they could obtain their release or revisit their country and their homes. Such instances become known, and their effect in discouraging young men from engaging in the merchant service of their country can neither be doubted nor wondered at. More than all, my Lord, the practice of impressment, whenever it has existed, has produced, not conciliation and good feeling, but resentment, exasperation, and animosity, between the two great commercial countries of the world.

In the calm and quiet which have succeeded the late war—a condition so favorable for dispassionate consideration—England herself has evidently seen the harshness of impressment, even when exercised on seamen in her own merchant service, and she has adopted measures calculated, if not to renounce the power or to abolish the practice, yet at least to supersede its necessity by other means of manning the royal navy, more compatible with justice and the rights of individuals, and far more conformable to the spirit and sentiments of the age.

Under these circumstances, the Government of the United States has used the occasion of your Lordship's pacific mission to renew this whole subject, and to bring it to your notice, and that of your Government. It has reflected on the past, pondered the condition of the present, and endeavored to anticipate, so far as might be in its power, the probable future; and I am now to communicate to your Lordship the result of these deliberations.

The American Government, then, is prepared to say that the practice of impressing seamen from American vessels cannot be allowed to take place. That practice is founded on principles which it does not recognise, and is invariably attended by consequences so unjust, so injurious, and of such formidable magnitude, as cannot be submitted to.

In the early disputes between the two Governments on this so long contested topic, the distinguished person to whose hands were first intrusted the seals of this Department declared, that "the simplest rule will be, that the vessel being American shall be evidence that the seamen on board are such." [See *ibid.*, 574, Secretary of State Jefferson to Thomas Pinckney, Minister at London, June 11, 1792.]

Fifty years' experience, the utter failure of many negotiations, and a careful reconsideration now had of the whole subject, at a moment when the passions are laid, and no present interest or emergency exists to bias the judgment, have fully convinced this Government that this is not only the simplest and best, but the

only rule which can be adopted and observed, consistently with the rights and honor of the United States and the security of their citizens. That rule announces, therefore, what will hereafter be the principle maintained by their Government. In every regularly documented American merchant vessel the crew who navigate it will find their protection in the flag which is over them.

This announcement is not made, my Lord, to revive useless recollections of the past, nor to stir the embers from fires which have been, in a great degree, smothered by many years of peace. Far otherwise. Its purpose is to extinguish those fires effectually, before new incidents arise to fan them into flame. The communication is in the spirit of peace, and for the sake of peace, and springs from a deep and conscientious conviction that high interests of both nations require that this so long contested and controverted subject should now be finally put to rest. I persuade myself, my Lord, that you will do justice to this frank and sincere avowal of motives, and that you will communicate your sentiments, in this respect, to your Government.

This letter closes, my Lord, on my part, our official correspondence; and I gladly use the occasion to offer you the assurance of my high and sincere regard.

DAN! WEBSTER.

Lord ASHBURTON,
&º, &º, &º

[*Lord Ashburton to Mr. Webster*]

WASHINGTON *9ᵗʰ August 1842*

SIR The note you did me the honour of addressing me, the 8ᵗʰ inst. on the subject of impressment shall be transmitted without delay to my government and will, you may be assured, receive from them the deliberate attention which its importance deserves.

The object of my mission was mainly the settlement of existing subjects of difference, and no differences have or could have arisen of late years with respect to Impressment, because the practice has since the peace wholly ceased, and can not consistently with existing laws and regulations for manning Her Majesty's Navy be under present circumstances renewed.

Desirous however of looking far forward into futurity to anticipate even possible causes of disagreement, and sensible of the anxiety of the American people on this grave subject of past irritation, I should be sorry in any way to discourage the attempt at some settlement of it; and although without authority to enter upon it here during the limited continuance of my mission, I entertain a confident hope that this task may be accomplished when undertaken with the spirit of candour and conciliation which has marked all our late negotiations.

It not being our intention to endeavour now to come to any agreement on this subject, I may be permitted to abstain from noticing at any length your very ingenious arguments relating to it, and from discussing the graver matters of constitutional and international law growing out of them. These sufficiently shew that the question is one requiring calm consideration, though I must at the same time admit that they prove a strong necessity of some settlement for the preservation of that good understanding, which I trust we may flatter ourselves that our joint labours have now succeeded in establishing.

I am well aware that the laws of our two Countries maintain opposite principles respecting allegiance to the sovereign. America, receiving every year by thousands the emigrants of Europe, maintains the doctrine suitable to her condition of the right of transferring allegiance at will. The laws of Great Britain have maintained from all time the opposite doctrine. The duties of allegiance are held to be indefeasible, and it is believed that this doctrine, under various modifications, prevails in most, if not in all, the civilized states of Europe.

Emigration, the modern mode by which the population of the world peaceably finds its level, is for the benefit of all, and eminently for the benefit of humanity. The fertile deserts of America are gradually advancing to the highest state of cultivation and production, while the emigrant acquires comfort which his own confined home could not afford him.

If there were any thing in our laws or our practice on either side tending to impede this march of providential humanity we could not be too eager to provide a remedy, but as this does not appear to be the case, we may safely leave this part of the subject without indulging in abstract speculations having no material practical application to matters in discussion between us.

But it must be admitted that a serious practical question does arise, or rather has existed, from practices formerly attending the mode of manning the British navy in times of war. The principle is that all subjects of the Crown are in case of necessity bound to serve their Country, and the seafaring man is naturally taken for the naval service.

This is not, as is sometimes supposed, any arbitrary principle of monarchical Government, but one founded on the natural duty of every man to defend the life of his Country, and all the analogy of your laws would lead to the conclusion that the same principle would hold good in the United States if their geographical position did not make its application unnecessary.

The very anomalous condition of the two countries with relation to each other here creates a serious difficulty. Our people are not distinguishable, and owing to the peculiar habits of sailors, our vessels are very generally manned from a common stock. It is difficult under these circumstances to execute laws which at times have been thought to be essential for the existence of the Country, without risk of injury to others. The extent and importance of those injuries however are so formidable that it is admitted that some remedy should if possible be applied. At all events it must be fairly and honestly attempted. It is true that during the continuance of peace no practical grievance can arise, but it is also true that it is for that reason the proper season for the calm and deliberate consideration of an important subject. I have much reason to hope that a satisfactory arrangement respecting it may be made so as to set at rest all apprehension and anxiety, and I will only further repeat the assurance of the sincere disposition of my Government favourably to consider all matters having for their object the promoting and maintaining undisturbed kind and friendly feelings with the United States.

I beg, Sir, on this occasion of closing the correspondence with you connected with my mission to express the satisfaction I feel at its successful termination, and to assure you of my high consideration and personal esteem and regard.

ASHBURTON

The Honble DANIEL WEBSTER
        &c &c &c

Ashburton's report of the discussion was brief. It is contained in one of his despatches of August 9, 1842 (Ashburton Papers, despatch No. 21), as follows:

Although I had communicated to Mr Webster that I was not prepared or authorised to enter here into any negotiation on the subject of Impressment, he has addressed a very long argument to me upon it, copy of which and of my answer I have the honour of enclosing for your Lordship's information.

I consider the motive for this proceeding to be the presentation of a general mass of popular correspondence to the Senate and to the public on the occasion of our treaty, and to this there can on our part be no objection. Your Lordship will perceive that in my answer I have, in stating my want of powers for this purpose, not discouraged the expectation that something may hereafter be done, and in this I felt justified as well by the desire of making my intercourse here as conciliatory as possible as by the general tenor of my instructions.

In the presidential message of August 11, 1842 (quoted above), submitting the Webster-Ashburton Treaty to the Senate, reference is made to the correspondence on the subject of impressment and, particularly, in the final paragraph of the message, to the note of Webster of August 8.

Treaty Series No. 206
8 Statutes at Large, 578–81
18 *ibid.*, pt. 2, Public Treaties, 490–92

100

MEXICO : JANUARY 30, 1843

Convention Further to Provide for the Payment of Awards in Favor of Claimants under the Convention between the United States and the Mexican Republic of April 11, 1839 (Document 89), signed at Mexico City January 30, 1843. Original in English and Spanish.
Submitted to the Senate February 28, 1843. Resolution of advice and consent March 2, 1843. Ratified by the United States March 13, 1843. Ratified by Mexico February 7, 1843. Ratifications exchanged at Washington March 29, 1843. Proclaimed March 30, 1843.
For reasons set forth in the editorial notes, the texts of the convention here printed are from the signed original thereof which is in the Mexican archives.

Convention further to provide for the payment of awards in favor of claimants under the Convention between the United States and the Mexican Republic of the 11ᵗʰ April 1839.

Whereas by the Convention between the United States and the Mexican Republic of the 11ᵗʰ of April 1839. it is stipulated that if it should not be convenient to the Mexican Government to pay at once the sums found to be due to the Claimants under that Convention,—that Government shall be at liberty to issue Treasury notes in satisfaction of those sums;—and whereas the Government of Mexico anxious to comply with the terms of said Convention and to pay those awards in full, but finds it inconvenient either to pay them in money or to issue the said Treasury notes,

Convencion para mejor asegurar el pago de los fallos en favor de los reclamantes en virtud del Convenio entre la República mexicana y los Estados unidos de 11. de Abril de 1839.

Por cuanto por el Convenio entre la República mexicana y los Estados unidos, de 11. de Abril de 1.839, está estipulado que sino le fuere comodo al Gobierno mexicano satisfacer al contado las cantidades que resultare deudor á virtud de esa Convencion, el mismo tendrá la facultad de emitir libranzas de Tesoreria en pago de esas cantidades; y por cuanto el Gobierno de Mexico deseoso de cumplir con las condiciones de dicho convenio y de pagar estos fallos en su monto total, se encuentra que no le conviene ó pagarlos en dinero, ó emitir dichas libranzas. El Pre-

479

The President of the United States has, for the purpose of carrying into full effect the intentions of the said parties, conferred full powers on Waddy Thompson, Envoy Extraordinary and Minister of the United States to the Mexican Government, and the President of the Mexican Republic has conferred full powers on José Mª de Bocanegra, Minister of Foreign Relations and Government, and Manuel Eduado de Gorostiza, Minister of Finances;

And the said Plenipotentiaries after having exchanged their full powers,—found to be in due form,—have agreed to and concluded the following articles.

ARTICLE 1.ˢᵗ

On the 30ᵗʰ day of April 1843, the Mexican Government shall pay all the interest which may then be due on the awards in favor of claimants under the Convention of the 11.ᵗʰ of April 1839., in gold or silver money, in the city of Mexico.

ARTICLE 2.ᵈ

The principal of the said awards and the interest accruing thereon, shall be paid in five years in equal instalments every three months, the said term of five years to commence on the 30ᵗʰ day of April 1843 aforesaid

sidente de la República mexicana con objeto de llevar á efecto las intenciones de ambos Gobiernos ha conferido Plenos Poderes á los Escelentisimos Señores Don José Maria de Bocanegra, Ministro de Relaciones exteriores y gobernacion, y Don Manuel Eduardo de Gorostiza, Ministro de Hacienda; y el Presidente de los Estados unidos al Honorable Señor Waddy Thompson, Enviado Estraordinario y Ministro Plenipotenciario de dichos Estados cerca del Gobierno de Mexico.

Y dichos Plenipotenciarios despues de haber cambiado sus Plenos Poderes y encontradolos en debida forma, han convenido y concluido los articulos siguientes.

ARTICULO 1º

En el dia 30. de Abril de 1.843. el Gobierno mexicano pagará todo el interes que entonces estuviere vencido sobre los fallos en favor de los reclamantes á virtud del convenio de 11. de Abril de 1.839., en moneda de oro ó en plata, en la Ciudad de Mexico.

ARTICULO 2º

El principal de dichos fallos y el interes que se vaya venciendo sobre ellos, se pagará en cinco años, en pagos iguales de cada tres meses; dicho termino de cinco años comenzará el dia 30. de Abril de 1.843. como está dicho.

ARTICLE 3.ᵈ

The payments aforesaid shall be made in the city of Mexico to such person as the United States may authorize to receive them in gold or silver money. But no circulation, export nor other duties shall be charged thereon, and the Mexican Government takes the risk, charges and expenses of the transportation of the money to the city of Veracruz.

ARTICLE 4.ᵗʰ

The Mexican Government hereby solemnly pledges the proceeds of the direct taxes of the Mexican Republic for the payment of the instalments and interest aforesaid; but it is understood that whilst no other fund is thus specifically hypothecated that the Government of the United States by accepting this pledge does not incur any obligation to look for payment of those instalments and interest to that fund alone.

ARTICLE 5.ᵗʰ

As this new arrangement which is entered into for the accommodation of Mexico, will involve additional charges of freight, commissions &., the Government of Mexico hereby agrees to add two and a half per centum to each of the aforesaid payments on account of said charges.

ARTICULO 3º

Los pagos arriba indicados se harán en la Ciudad de Mexico á la persona que los Estados unidos autorizen á recibirlos en oro ó en plata. Pero no se pagará sobre estas cantidades derecho de circulacion, de exportacion ú otra clase que fuere, sobre el mismo. Y el Gobierno mexicano toma por si el riesgo, cargos y gastos de transportacion del dinero hasta la Ciudad de Veracruz.

ARTICULO 4º

El Gobierno mexicano por este articulo hipoteca solemnemente los productos de contribuciones directas de la República mexicana, para el pago de las cantidades señaladas y su interes; pero se entiende que si bien no se hipoteca ningun otro fondo especialmente, no por esto el Gobierno de los Estados unidos, con aceptar esta hipoteca, contrae ninguna obligacion de limitarse para el pago de estos dividendos y su interes, solamente á este fondo.

ARTICULO 5º

Como este nuevo arreglo que se adopta para la comodidad de Mexico, ha de ocasionar cargos adicionales de fletes, comisiones & &, el Gobierno de Mexico se compromete por la presente á aumentar en un dos y medio por ciento cada uno de dichos pagos á causa de los gastos arriba mencionados.

ARTICLE 6.th

A new Convention shall be entered into for the settlement of all claims of the Government and Citizens of the United States against the Republic of Mexico, which were not finally decided by the late Commission which met in the city of Washington, and of all claims of the Government and citizens of Mexico against the U. States.

ARTICLE 7.th

The ratifications of this Convention shall be exchanged at Washington within three months after the date thereof provided it shall arrive at Washington before the adjournment of the present Session of Congress,—and if not then within one month after the meeting of the next Congress of the United States.

In faith whereof we the Plenipotentiaries of the United States of America, and of the Mexican Republic have signed and sealed these presents.

Done at the city of Mexico on the thirtieth day of January one thousand eight hundred and forty three, and in the sixty seventh year of the Independence of the United States of America, and in the twenty third of that of the Mexican Republic.

[Seal] WADDY THOMPSON
[Seal] J. M^a DE BOCANEGRA
[Seal] M E DE GOROSTIZA

ARTICULO 6º

Se celebrará una nueva Convencion para el arreglo de todas las reclamaciones del Gobierno y Ciudadanos de los Estados unidos contra la República mexicana que no fueron decididas por la última comision que se reunió en la Ciudad de Washington y de todas las reclamaciones del Gobierno mexicano y sus Ciudadanos contra los Estados unidos.

ARTICULO 7º

Esta convencion se ratificará y las ratificaciones serán cangeadas en Washington dentro de tres meses contados desde la fecha, siempre que se reciba en Washington antes del termino de la actual sesion del Congreso; y en caso contrario, las ratificaciones se cangearán dentro de un mes despues de la reunion del procsimo Congreso de los Estados unidos.

En fé de lo cual nosotros los Plenipotenciarios de la República mexicana y de los Estados unidos de America hemos firmado y sellado el presente.

Fecho en la Ciudad de Mexico el dia treinta de Enero del año de mil ochocientos cuarenta y tres, vigesimo tercero de la Yndependencia de la República mexicana y sexagesimo septimo de la de los Estados unidos de America.

[Seal] J. M^a DE BOCANEGRA
[Seal] M E DE GOROSTIZA
[Seal] WADDY THOMPSON.

NOTES

It is the rule of this edition that the primary source text of a treaty or other international act is a signed original thereof when available; ordinarily this is the signed original (or one of the signed originals) in the archives of the Department of State. In the case of this convention the source text used is the signed original in the Mexican archives (a facsimile of which has been received therefrom), and not the signed original in the archives of the Department of State. The reasons for the choice are to be set forth; and for convenience the two signed originals will be called, respectively, the Mexican signed original and the American signed original.

The English text of this convention as written in the American signed original (and as printed below) is extraordinarily inaccurate. The errors of orthography are numerous and gross. The scrivener who wrote that text (and who apparently did not write the Spanish text in either of the signed originals) was surely quite unfamiliar with the English language. In general one can make out what was intended as the wording; but Article 4 as there written is hardly intelligible; it requires some imagination to read "reillement" as "settlement" in Article 6; and without the Spanish text as a guide it would be little more than guesswork to read "late" (or "last") for "sole" in the same article; a text of such a character could not possibly be accepted as the official text of an international act.

On the other hand, the English text of the convention which is written in the Mexican signed original is all that it should be; and it is accordingly that English text which is printed above in the left of the two columns following the headnote. The Spanish text in the right of those two columns is also from the Mexican signed original; of the columns of that document, however, the Spanish text has the left and the English text the right; here the position of the two texts in the American signed original is followed.

Neither in the despatches from Mexico City of Waddy Thompson, who signed the convention as Plenipotentiary of the United States, nor in the presidential message with which the convention was sent to the Senate, nor in the Senate resolution of advice and consent, nor in either instrument of ratification, nor in the certificate of the exchange of ratifications, is there any mention of the character of the English text of the American signed original; no direct reference to the glaring defects of that English text has been found in the archives of the Department of State; a satisfactory explanation of the circumstances must rest in part on inference and in part on guesswork.

The procedure was somewhat hurried at both capitals; the convention was not signed until midnight of its date (see the postscript of the despatch of January 31, 1843, quoted below). The English text in the Mexican signed original was examined and found correct. The English text in the other signed original was assumed to be the same, was accepted without examination or collating, and the document was almost at once sent forward to Washington as the American signed original.

When the American signed original was received at the Department of State, on Sunday, February 26, 1843, time pressed. The session of Congress then holding was to end during the night of March 3 (the following Friday), and without action during that session the convention would have failed in the absence of an extra session of the Senate (see the clauses of Article 7 for the exchange of ratifications).

The convention, that is to say, the American signed original, was sent to the Senate on Tuesday, February 28. It was probably accompanied, in accordance with custom, by a copy of the texts written out for the printer. If so, the English of that copy was a corrected text made in the Department of State with the aid of the Spanish text and lacking most of the errors of the American signed original (but not all; Article 6 has "sole commission"). This is sufficiently evident from the Senate print then made (Senate Confidential Document D, 27th Congress, 3d session, Regular Confidential Documents, XX, 115–19; see Executive Journal, VI, 176). The convention was favored in the Senate; there was no opposition; the resolution of advice and consent was passed unanimously two days after the convention was received. While the original was before the Senate, it is highly probable that no one looked at it, but merely at the print from the accompanying corrected copy.

The United States instrument of ratification is dated March 13, 1843; the English text therein (as appears from a facsimile thereof, obtained from the Mexican archives) is very nearly the English text printed for the Senate, though having "last commission" (in place of "sole commission") in Article 6.

The Mexican instrument of ratification bears date (February 7) only eight days after the convention; its English text (written by the scrivener of the English in the Mexican signed original) follows, with approximate literality, that of the Mexican signed original, the source text here.

The Mexican ratification reached Washington about March 27 (D.S., 4 Notes from the Mexican Legation, March 27, 1843; see also 6 Notes to the Mexican Legation, 158–59, March 28, 1843); the exchange of ratifications followed on March 29, without reference to or mention of textual discrepancies; indeed, the act of exchange, signed by General Almonte, the Mexican Minister at Washington, and by Secretary of State Webster, includes this statement (translation from the Spanish): "They certify that, having exchanged their full powers and finding them in due form, they have exchanged said ratifications on this day, with all due solemnities, after each was duly compared with the other and both with the original example of said convention"; the record is formally perfect; and the slight differences in wording between the texts of the respective ratifications may have been tacitly agreed to be (as they in fact were) of no consequence.

Since the proclamation of the convention the English text which has always been printed, officially and otherwise, as in the Daily National Intelligencer for April 4, 1843, in the Laws of the United States, Bioren & Duane edition, X, 879–83, in volumes 8 and 18 of the Statutes at Large, in Haswell, and in Malloy, has generally

accorded with that of the United States instrument of ratification; in all the publications mentioned, however, Article 6 has more correctly "late commission" and not "last commission" (the reference being to the only commission that had previously sat, namely, that under the convention of April 11, 1839, Document 89). Thus the difference in wording between the published English text and that of the Mexican signed original are very few and minor; in all essentials the two are the same.

The Defective English Text

The English text of the American signed original of the convention, with all its crudities and blunders printed literally, follows:

Conbention Further to provide for the payment of awards in fabor of Claimantss under the Conbention between the United States and the Mexican Republic of the 11. April 1839.

Whereos by the conbention between the United States and the Mexican Republic of the 11. of April 1839. it is stipulated that if it should not be conbenient to the Mexican Gobernment to pay at once the sums found to be due to the claimantss under that Conbention—that Gobernment shall be at liberty to issue Treosury notes in satisfaction of those sums—and whereos the Gobernment of Mexico anxious to comply with the terms of said conbention and to pay those awards in full but finds it inconbenient orther to pay them in money or to issue the said Treosury notes. The President of the United States has for the purpose of carryng into full effects the intentions of the said partees conferred full powars on Waddy Thompson Envoy Extraordinary and Minister of the United States to the mexican Gobernment and the President of the Mexican Republic has conferret full powers on H.E.E. Jose Maria de Bocänegra Minister of forsing relations and Manuel Eduardo de Gorostiza Minister of Finance and the said Plenipotentiarees after having exchanged theer full powers fownd to be in due form—hom agreed to and concluded the following articles

Article 1.

On the 30. day of April 1843. the Mexican Government shall pay all the interest which may then be due on the awards in fabor of claimantes under the Conbention of the 11. of April 1839. in gold or sirber money—in the City of Mexico.

Article 2.

The principal of the said awards and the interest accresing thereon shall be paid in five years in equal instalmentes every three months the said **term of five** years to commence on the 30. day of April 1843, aforesaid.

Article 3.

The paymentes of cresaid shall be made in the city of Mexico to such person as the United States may authorige to receive them in gold or selver money—But no cerculatin export nor other dutees shall be charged thereon—and the Mexican Government to takes the risk charges and expenses of the transportation of the money to the City of Vera Cruz.

Article 4.

The Mexican Gobernment herely solemnly pleoges the procedes of the direct toxes of the mexican Republic for the payment of the instalmants and interest of aresaid, but it is understood that whiest no other fund is, thees specifically hipothecaled that this Gobernment of the United States by accepting this pledge daes not incur any obligation to looke for payment of those instalmentes and interest to that fumdalone.

ARTICLE 5.

As this new arrangement which is entered into for the accommdolim of Mexico will involue additional charges of freigtet commissein &c—The Government of Mexico herely agrees to add 2 & ½ per centum on each of the aforesaid payments on account of said charges.

ARTICLE 6.

A new Convention shall be entered into for the reillement of all claims of the Government &. citices of the United States against the Republic of Mexico which were not finally decidet by the sole commissein which met in the City of Washington and of all claims of the Government and citicens of Mexico aganst the United States.

ARTICLE 7.

The ratifications of this Convention shall be exchanged at Washington urther Three months after the dole therof provided it shall arrive at Washington before the adjournment of the present session of Congres—and if not then urther one month after the meeting of the next Congres of the United States.

In faeth whereof we the Plenipotentiares of the United States of America and of the Mexican Republic have signed and seoled these presents
Done at the City of Mexico on Therteeth day of January in the year of our Lerd one Thausand Eight hundred and forty three and in the sexty seventh year of the Independence of the United States of America and in the Twenty-third of that of the mexican Republic.

[Seal] WADDY THOMPSON
[Seal] J. Mᵃ DE BOCANEGRA
[Seal] M E DE GOROSTIZA

THE SPANISH TEXT

As between the Mexican signed original (the source text here) and the American signed original there are perhaps a dozen slight variances in the Spanish text (the same scrivener wrote the Spanish of both originals and also of the Mexican ratification), besides a few quite immaterial differences in the punctuation; the American signed original has (in the preamble) *pleno* before *efecto* and *partes* for *Gobiernos* and omits (in Article 1) the words *que entonces*. The collating shows otherwise merely variations in style of expression (*á pagar* for *de pagar* in the preamble; *convenio del* for *convenio de* in Article 1; *tomará sobre* for *toma por* in Article 3; *su fecha* for *la fecha* and *serán cangeadas* for *se cangearán* in Article 7; *tercio* for *tercero* and *sesenta y siete* for *sexagesimo septimo* in the final clause).

THE FILE PAPERS

Besides the American signed original of the convention and the facsimiles above mentioned, the file papers include the attested Senate resolution of March 2, 1843 (Executive Journal, VI, 179), the duplicate United States instrument of ratification of March 13, 1843 (which is now a separate paper, not including the texts of the convention, but mentioning the original of the convention as "hereunto annexed", as apparently it formerly was), the certificate (in Spanish) of the exchange of ratifications at Washington on March 29, 1843, and the original proclamation of March 30, 1843, which has within it, as

"hereunto annexed", the signed original of the convention. The Mexican instrument of ratification of February 7, 1843, includes both texts of the convention, the Spanish in the left columns; that instrument was signed by Nicolas Bravo, "General de Division, Benemérito de la Patria y Presidente Sustituto de la República Mexicana"; its words of ratification are these (translation):

Now, therefore, having seen and examined the said convention, and using the power granted to me by the seventh of the bases adopted at Tacubaya, I have ratified, accepted, and confirmed the same; and by these presents I do ratify, accept, and confirm the same and promise to observe and to cause to be faithfully observed all therein contained without permitting any contravention thereof whatsoever.

The "Bases of Tacubaya" were a document of September 28, 1841, issued at that suburb of Mexico City by the principal officers of the army of General Santa Anna; they "became, in effect, the Constitution of the country for the next three years" (Rives, The United States and Mexico, 1821–1848, I, 458); their text is in Dublan y Lozano, Legislatión mexicana, IV, 32–34.

The convention was submitted to the Senate with the following presidential message of February 28, 1843 (Executive Journal, VI, 175–76):

I transmit to the Senate, for its consideration with a view to ratification, a convention further to provide for the payment of awards in favor of claimants under the convention between the United States and the Mexican Republic of the 11th of April, 1839 [Document 89], signed in the City of Mexico on the thirtieth day of last month. A copy of the instructions from the Department of State to the minister of the United States at Mexico relative to the convention, and of the dispatches of that minister to the Department, is also communicated. By adverting to the signatures appended to the original draught of the convention as transmitted from the Department of State to General Thompson, it will be seen that the convention as concluded was substantially approved by the representatives of a large majority in value of the parties immediately interested.

The Senate document included the message and the convention, in both texts, but not the accompanying papers (*ibid.*, 176; Senate Confidential Document D, 27th Congress, 3d session, Regular Confidential Documents, XX, 115–19); as has been mentioned, the English text there printed corrected most of the errors of orthography of the American signed original.

The Senate resolution of advice and consent was unanimously adopted two days after the receipt of the convention (Executive Journal, VI, 179, March 2, 1843).

The Full Powers

It is stated in the preamble of the convention that the full powers of the Plenipotentiaries were exchanged. There does not appear, however, in the despatches or elsewhere, any record of the full powers of the Mexican Plenipotentiaries. That given to General Waddy Thompson, Minister of the United States to Mexico, was under date of October 12, 1842. That full power was in customary form and the authority given was "to agree, treat, consult and negotiate of

and concerning the payment of the awards in favor of claimants under the Convention between the United States and that Republic, of the 11th of April, 1839, and of and concerning claims of citizens of the United States upon the Mexican Government which were not disposed of or acted upon by the Board of Commissioners under the said Convention" (D.S., 3 Credences, 25).

The treaty file contains the original full power given by the Mexican Government under date of February 7, 1843, to Señor Don Juan Nepomuceno Almonte to exchange the ratifications.

A full power for the purpose of the exchange was given to Secretary of State Daniel Webster under date of March 28, 1843 (*ibid.*, 35). Such practice is unusual. Rarely has a full power been given to the Secretary of State to exchange the ratifications of a treaty; authority to make such exchange is deemed to be inherent in the office.

THE NEGOTIATIONS

On February 10, 1842, General Waddy Thompson (whose military title arose from his having been a brigadier general of militia in South Carolina) was appointed Envoy Extraordinary and Minister Plenipotentiary to the Mexican Republic. The early instructions to Thompson dealt with matters other than claims or the payment of the awards under the convention of April 11, 1839 (Document 89). Those two subjects were treated generally in the instructions of September 5, 1842 (D.S., 15 Instructions, Mexico, 206–9), but no very detailed directions were there given; a messenger of the Treasury Department was the bearer of those instructions and took with him a full power running to Thompson (and not, as first contemplated, to an agent of the Treasury Department) to receive payment of the awards under the convention of 1839 (D.S., 3 Credences, 20, August 6, 1842). A letter from Secretary of State Daniel Webster to the Secretary of the Treasury (Walter Forward) of July 26, 1842, had expressed the following views regarding the meaning of Article 6 of the convention of April 11, 1839 (D.S., 32 Domestic Letters, 387–89):

I have the honor to acknowledge the receipt of your letter of the 5th inst. . . . requesting the opinion of this Department as to the meaning intended to be given to the phrase 'Treasury notes', by the 6th. Article of the Convention.

A reference to the history of the Convention will, it is believed be sufficient to illustrate that meaning. The convention between the two Governments which was signed on the 10th. of September, 1838 [for the English text of which, see the notes to Document 89], stipulated that the Mexican Government should issue in payment of the awards which might be made, certificates of debt to such an amount as, according to their price in the London market, would be sufficient to discharge such awards. This Convention was not ratified by the Mexican Government, upon the alleged ground, as the preamble to the Second Convention states, that the consent of the King of Prussia to act as Arbiter could not be obtained. That preamble states further that the new Convention was to be equally advantageous to citizens of the United States as the former one, but more convenient to Mexico. This Department has no doubt that these terms in the preamble were intended to be significant, and that the 6th article of the Convention cannot be understood without a reference to them. If, then, the contingency should happen which is mentioned in that article, namely, if it should not be convenient for the Mexican Government to pay at once (in cash) the amounts found due, and it should avail itself of the privilege of issuing Treasury notes

then, the United States ought not to be requested to receive funds of that description in discharge of the awards unless, while they may constitute a more convenient medium of payment for Mexico than cash, they shall still be equally advantageous or valuable to those in whose favor awards have been made. The words of the preamble which have been quoted may justly be considered as tantamount to a condition to this effect. It would seem that the convenience of that government, for which the second Convention was intended to provide, had reference to an extension of the time, within which it was to satisfy the awards, and did not contemplate that they were to be paid in a depreciated currency; since it would be idle to go through the trouble and expence of liquidating debts, under a doubt, nevertheless, whether, when liquidated, they would receive substantial payment.

There are circumstances which may affect the value of the Mexican Treasury notes, which it may be necessary for the agent of the Treasury Department to regard. The Mexican government ought not to expect us to receive Treasury notes of any other than the usual character which such paper bears. A Treasury note is an Exchequer Bill, a negotiable obligation of the Government, binding the Government to payment of principal and interest. With us, as giving greater facility to their use, they are made receivable for public dues, and it was with reference, probably, to this practice of this Government that the Mexican Treasury notes were required to have this character. But this is not all, that is necessary to constitute a Treasury note, in the common understanding of such an instrument. There is necessarily a promise, or undertaking to pay in money at some time; otherwise it would be obvious, that payment by means of such a medium would be liable to become quite illusory, as paper, with nothing to give it value but mere receivability for public dues, might be issued in such quantity as to render its value nearly nominal. The Mexican Government should also cause the Treasury notes which it may offer to be subdivided into convenient amounts, say from one to five hundred dollars and such fractions as may be necessary to cover particular awards, so that those of the claimants or their assigns, who may choose to offer the notes in payment of duties according to the Convention, may be accomodated. It may also be necessary for the interests of the claimants that the notes should express on their face that they are issued pursuant to the Convention, and that their receivability at the Mexican maratime Custom Houses should not be confined to the payment of duties on importations or exportations by citizens of the United States, or on productions of the United States.

It is to be presumed that the Government of Mexico will concur in the views here expressed, respecting the manner of payment of the awards; since no doubt can exist that both Governments looked to a full and substantial payment and satisfaction, of whatever sums should be awarded to the Claimants.

It appears, moreover, from his early despatches, that Thompson was well informed as to what basis of arrangement regarding the payment of the awards under the convention of 1839 would be satisfactory to those in whose favor they were made; and he reported to the Department that he thought a favorable arrangement was possible (D.S., 11 Despatches, Mexico, No. 4, July 30, 1842; No. 5, August 16, 1842; September 10, 1842).

Upon receipt of that news, further instructions were sent, which are quoted below. These were of October 13, 1842, and were signed by Fletcher Webster as Acting Secretary of State (D.S., 15 Instructions, Mexico, 210–12):

The President directs me to acquaint you that he is gratified with the favorable opinion which you express respecting the payment by the Mexican government of the awards under the Convention of the 11th of April, 1839. The intelligence was the more acceptable as it was quite unexpected, serious difficulties having been apprehended in the equitable adjustment of the business. It is the duty and the determination of this government not to sacrifice the rights of the claimants. It is also its duty towards Mexico as a power with which we are and desire

to continue in amity, to accommodate her in regard to the ultimate satisfaction of the claims, in every way which may be compatible with the rights of the interested parties. Consequently, if in your judgment the Mexican government cannot conveniently pay the awards in cash and if its obligations should not be of substantial value, you may make an overture for the conclusion of a new convention, providing for the payment of the awards by instalments in cash, with interest on the amount now due and on the deferred payments, also payable in cash. The particulars of the treaty are confided to your discretion, but you are referred, generally to the accompanying copies of Conventions with The Two Sicilies and with Spain upon a similar subject [see Documents 74 and 78].

When you shall have finally settled the business of the awards, you may make an overture for the adjustment of the claims which were not disposed of by the Board of Commissioners and the arbiter appointed under the Convention of the 11th of April, 1839. It is deemed best to leave to your discretion also the terms of this overture. Being yourself on the spot and understanding the position as well as the capacity of the Mexican Government in relation to the final settlement and discharge of these claims, you will be better able to judge as to the most expeditious and surest mode of obtaining a real satisfaction for them. You will be careful in the communications which you shall make, to hold no such language as may lead that government to suppose that any relinquishment or abatement of the just demands of our citizens is to be made, on any consideration whatever. In treating with Mexico on these matters and proposing arrangements at this time, we are to be considered as doing and not receiving favors, and no proposals on her part, having in view a reduction of the amounts of liquidated claims in consideration of such payments, must be admitted.

In treating for the settlement of the claims which were not acted on by the late Mexican Commission, you will not propose nor assent to any proposition for another mixed commission such as the late one under the Convention of the 11th of April, 1839. If the Mexican Government shall insist upon such an arrangement, you will suspend the negotiations and inform the department, which will then give you further instructions. It will be much to your credit if you shall be able to conclude an arrangement upon the matters now entrusted to your management which shall be satisfactory in its results and procure at last a payment in money or such other satisfactory provision as may be of importance to the United States and the claimants and satisfy all the demands of our citizens upon Mexico. The responsibility is a serious one and I must remind you that you are to deal with a government which is not wanting in the arts of diplomacy and that many complaints are made of evasion and procrastination in the fulfilment of its engagements.

You will keep the department constantly informed of the progress and state of the negotiations and in cases of serious doubt on your part as to any particular step, you had better communicate at once with the department and await its opinion.

A full power, authorizing you to conclude treaties upon the subjects adverted to, is now transmitted.

In the meantime, however, Thompson had begun negotiations; the result of these was a proposal of the Mexican Government regarding which Thompson reported in his despatch of November 8, 1842, as follows (D.S., 11 Despatches, Mexico, No. 7):

I was invited on Sunday the 15ᵗʰ [16th] of October to an interview with President Santa Anna; but nothing more occurred at that interview than general professions of good faith and honest intentions on the part of Mexico accompanied with the declaration of a positive inability to comply with the terms of the convention of April 1839. I was however, invited to an interview with the Minʳˢ of For. Relations & of the Treasury on the next Thursday [October 20] the result of this Conference was a sort of provisional arrangement by which the Mexican Govᵗ was to be bound provided it was agreed to by my Government. I distinctly stated that I had no powers to enter into a new Convention, but that if propositions were made to me which I thought it expedient to accede to—I would

submit them to my Gov^t; but that neither I, nor my Gov^t should be regarded in any way compromitted. . . .

After a long conference [on November 4, 1842] it was agreed that I should submit to my Gov^t the propositions contained in the note of Mr Bocanegra No 8 [quoted below in translation.]

I was instructed by you to receive, with favor a proposition to pay these awards in coin, in annual instalments, with interest payable annually or semi annually. In a paper [lacking] which you sent me drawn up by F. S. Key, Esqre, I was directed to grant an indulgence of five years, and in a similar paper [lacking] drawn up by Mr Gilpin, I was instructed to grant an indulgence of nine years—and nothing was said of guarantees. You will perceive that the terms secured are infinitly more favorable **to** the claimants. It is proper that I should state to you that the whole of the duties on imports as well as exports with the exception of 11⅓ pc are already hypothecated to other creditors, some of them American Citizens. To have insisted, therefore, upon the issuing of the Treasury notes would not only have been in vain, but would have given rise to various conflicts of liens, and some of those with our own citizens. I know that some of these notes have been refused to be purchased here at 40 cents in the dollar,—and if so large an additional amount had been issued, I am quite sure they would not have been worth 25. p.c as the fund out of which they were to be paid was otherwise appropriated & the obligation was altogether indefinite, no time of payment being fixed.

Those of the claimants who reside here are highly gratified with the proposed arrangement, and the opinion of all intelligent men with whom I have conversed is that it will double the value of the awards.

By the 1st Clause you will perceive that the ground taken in the note of Mr de Bocanegra that the interest should neither be paid, nor bear interest until the whole of the principal was paid is abandoned, & the interest is to be paid first. Strange as it may seem it is the universal rule in Mexico, that the principal is first paid, & it was with no little difficulty that they were induced to surrender this point.

By the 2nd Clause five years are allowed to pay off the whole debt and interest; but it is to be paid in quarterly instalments. The advantages of this mode of payment are 1st—it increases the rate of interest; 2nd the claimants, many of whom are in necessitous circumstances will be continually receiving a portion of their money; 3^d, & the most important,—the payments will be in small sums, & I do not doubt they will be punctually paid. The Govenmt can always command the amount required to meet these instalments; but it can rarely command three, or four hundred thousand dollars at any one time. I believe I could have obtained the promise of more prompt payment; but I thought the true interest of those concerned would be more promoted by such an arrangement, as would secure the payment punctually, than by promises which would not be fulfilled. If the first payments are made, as I think they will be, these claims must be available at par,—and, besides this, I consented to grant another year in consideration of the relinquishment of export duties, & the payment of the interest, in the first instance.

By the 3^d Clause provision is made that in case of failure to pay any of the instalments, it shall bear an interest of 18. p.c. I first demanded an interest of 15. p.c,—on the whole debt; but it was said, and with much force, that the penalty should not attach to the payment of what was not actually due, but only to that which was due & not paid.

By the 4th Clause it is provided that there shall be no charge of circulation & export duties, which will be a saving of 5½ p.c. I required that the money should be paid in Vera Cruz, to which it was replied, that the Government could only pay at its Treasury which was in this City. The only difference will be the charge of transportation which is 1. p.c

By the 5th clause the whole of the direct taxes which amount, as they inform me, to $6.000.000—are pledged for these payments

By the 6th clause provision is made for a new convention for the settlement of all of our claims which were not adjudicated by the late commission

Altho' I was not instructed to provide for this I felt it my duty to do so and the more as nothing is obligatory on my Governmt which it does not approve. The Mexican Gov^t regarded all these claims as precluded by the late convention but they have yielded that point. I was very certain that if some provision

was not now made for those claims, that they would be irrevocably lost. Any future negotiation with this Govt. would have been out of the question, and if they had been isolated from the awards they would not, *per se,* have justified measures of coercion. They are not of such a character of manifest and indisputable justice, and very far from being so, in their amounts, as to have justified such a course. I knew too that anxious as I, (as well as the claimants,) was for some such change of the terms of the convention as would ultimatly secure their demands on this Govenmt—that Mexico was much more so; and that therefore in consideration of the indulgence given for the payment of the awards—that such a provision for the outstanding claims would be agreed to. I therefore insisted, in my conferences as well as in my notes Nos 9 & 10 as a preliminary condition to any relaxation of terms of the Convention of '39—upon a provision for the settlement of those claims.

I have no idea what claims the Govt of Mexico can have upon that of the US:—perhaps you may know. It was impossible that at the moment I was asking redress of injuries from this Govemnt,—I could refuse the same measure of redress to Mexico. I was induced to commit this Governmt, in advance to the terms of a new Convention from the consideration, that if it was known here that our Governmt desired in the least such a measure they would not have conceded terms so advantageous. They have no idea that any such thing is desired, or that I had any instructions on the subject—, and I beg that it may not transpire so as to reach the ears of Genl Almonte, or there may yet be difficulty.

If any other guarantees or any alterations of the terms occur to you, and you will suggest them to me—I believe that I can secure them.

I would suggest that my instructions should be drawn up in such a way, that I may exhibit them if necessary. You can write me privately any modifications of those instructions which you may deem fit. I think it important that your Despatch should arrive at the earliest possible moment. As far as any calculation can be made on a governmt so unsettled and revolutionary, I do not doubt the punctual payment of the instalments, and if so, the stock must be worth, at least, par value, for, besides the abundant security which is provided—it has the guaranties of the two Governmts—our own & Mexico, and draws an interest of 8. p.c payable quarterly—equal to 9. p.c payable annually.

As I have been instructed to receive with favor, terms much less advantageous, I do not deem it necessary to urge upon you any reasons for acceding to these propositions. But it may not be so with others. It will then be considered that a payment, at once, in coin was out of the question; equally so, was the issuing of Treasury notes, as the whole of the fund for their payment was exhausted, and with only an indefinite obligation to pay, or, rather an acknowledgment of indebtedness without any fixed time for the payment of even the accruing interest—they would have possessed but little value. The only other alternative left would have been coercion by war or blockade,—Would this have secured the immediate payment? It might,—in vengeance & blood,—but not in money.

The proposals of the Mexican Government were contained in a note addressed by the Minister of Foreign Relations to Thompson under date of November 5, 1842, and were in the following terms (D.S., 11 Despatches, Mexico, No. 7, enclosure 8, extract, translation):

1. At the conclusion of the first three months following the date of a new convention, there shall be paid all interest accrued on the amount of the claims already allowed.

2. The principal, together with the interest accruing, shall be paid in five years, in equal instalments every three months. The said five years shall not begin to be counted from the date of the convention, but from the expiration of the first three months in which interest is paid, as above stated.

3. If the Mexican Government should for any reason fail to pay, for the period of one month, any one of the instalments, interest shall accrue to the said instalment at the rate of 10 percent in addition to the 8 percent provided in the convention, until the instalment is paid.

4. The said payments shall be made in the city of Mexico, but the Mexican Government shall levy no export or circulation dues on these sums.

5. All the direct taxes of the Government of Mexico are formally pledged to the payment of the aforesaid instalments.

6. A new convention shall be arranged for the decision and settlement of all claims of the American Government and citizens against the Government of Mexico which were not decided by the Commission which met at Washington, and of all claims of the Mexican Government and citizens against the Government of the United States.

The counterproposal of the United States was sent to Thompson with the instructions of December 30, 1842, which included the following comments (D.S., 15 Instructions, Mexico, 216–19):

it has been decided by the President that a Convention should be entered into confined to the simple object of paying the awards. A draught of one is accordingly now transmitted based mainly upon the overture contained in the note of M⸢r⸣ de Bocanegra to you of the 5th ult.

In the first article the payment of the interest has been required within three months from the signature instead of three months from the date of the Convention. This has been done in order that the sense might be clear and undoubted. If (as is understood, and presumed to be the case) President Santa Anna can, under the existing state of things in that country, ratify the Convention without requiring for it the previous sanction of the Mexican Congress, yet our experience gives us cause to apprehend that there may be delay in effecting an exchange of the ratifications at least to the full term to be allowed for that purpose. This would unreasonably retard the first payment of the interest if it should not take place until three months from that time. We wish to make it certain that the interest due shall be paid, without fail, in three months from the time you put your signature to the treaty.

The second article requires that the five years within which the payments of the principal and interest are to be completed, shall also begin at the expiration of three months from the signature by the Plenipotentiaries.

By the third article it is stipulated that the Mexican Government shall provide an escort sufficient to protect the money in its transit from the capital to the coast. This provision is considered to be essential, as the necessity for the protection is notorious, and although the reason assigned for making the payments at Mexico and not at Vera Cruz may be a good one, it is not sufficient to exempt that government from the obligation, as it alone has the right, to insure in the way proposed, a safe passage for the treasure to the coast.

No article has been admitted founded upon M⸢r⸣ de Bocanegra's fourth [third] proposition, because it is conceived that such an article would imply at least an apprehension on the part of this government that the payments would not be punctually made. It is deemed best that the Mexican government should not have any cause to suppose that such an apprehension is entertained. Indeed, the fixed feeling of this Government is that while allowing to Mexico such a time as she herself has requested for the payment of these awards, nothing must be allowed to interrupt that payment in the manner stipulated.

In the fourth article the pledge of the Mexican direct taxes is accepted, but a proviso is added that by this acceptance the government of the United States incurs no obligation to look to that source alone or to rely upon it for payment. The necessity for this proviso, considering the frequent changes in the persons administering the Mexican Government and in its policy, will, I presume, be obvious to you.

The ratifications are to be exchanged within ten months from the signature. If the Convention should not be received here in season to be considered by the Senate of the United States at its present session, the term mentioned will suffice to enable that body to dispose of it at its next session. At all events it is thought to be indispensable that the Compact should be ratified by the Mexican government before it is sent to the United States for that purpose.

It cannot be anticipated that the Mexican government will seriously object to these modifications of the terms which it offered through Mr de Bocanegra,

especially as the only important one is favorable to Mexico. The President, however, confidently relies upon your skill to answer any objections which may be made, and hopes that through your means this difficult and delicate business may at length be adjusted to the satisfaction of all parties.

It is not thought expedient to give you any instructions at present in regard to the claims which were not disposed of by the Commission under the Convention of the 11th of April, 1839.   That subject may properly be matter for a separate Convention.   It is under consideration, and you will hear from this Department respecting it, at an early day.

The American draft enclosed with the foregoing instructions of December 30, 1842, was in a preamble and five articles, with the usual final clauses.   From the message of President Tyler to the Senate of February 28, 1843 (quoted above), it seems that the "original" of the draft, with the signatures of a majority in value of the parties in interest appended, was sent to the Senate; that paper is not now available; but a copy of the draft, "which appears to be in the same handwriting as the instruction" of December 30, 1842, has been obtained from the archives of the Embassy at Mexico City (despatch No. 2032, November 22, 1932, enclosure).

The differences between the American draft and the convention as signed are described generally in the despatch of January 31, 1843, which is quoted below.

The wording of the preamble was somewhat altered; slight changes were made in the language of Articles 1, 2, and 4.   For the provision in Article 3 of the draft that "at every payment, the Mexican government engages to furnish an escort sufficient to protect the conveyance of the money to the sea-coast" was substituted a clause of assumption of risk and expenses.   Article 5 of the convention was new; and Article 5 of the draft, which provided simply for the exchange of the ratifications within ten months from the signature, appears in quite different form as Article 7 of the convention; but Article 6 of the convention, providing for a future settlement of all claims of each Government and its citizens against the other, substantially as written in clause 6 of the proposals of the Mexican Government, did not appear in the American draft in any form.

The despatch of Thompson transmitting the treaty was dated January 31, 1843, and is unnumbered (D.S., 11 Despatches, Mexico). The final paragraph here quoted therefrom is a postscript which, unlike the body of the despatch, is in the hand of Thompson himself. It appears that there was haste in the final preparation of the treaty for signature and that it was not signed until about midnight:

I said to you in my last that in one week after receiving your instructions I would be able to conclude a New convention which I have this day accomplished in just one week after the arrival of Mr. Southall.   You will see that I have changed the preamble.   I was instructed by you that I was to make the Mexican government understand that this new arrangement, for the convenience of Mexico, and it was not therefore proper that it should have been stated as having been done for the accommodation of the claimants, and besides I thought that if we should hereafter be forced to coerce the payments that it would be done with more grace after this second indulgence, than if this new arrangement appeared to have been entered into at the desire of the creditors.   You will also perceive

that instead of an escort which would have envolved an additional charge to the claimants without furnishing any additional security that it is provided that the money is to be transported to Vera Cruz at the risk as well as *charge* of the Mexican Government   You will also see that 2½ per cent is added for the payment of commissions &c.   This I thought no more than right, for if the money had all been paid at once under the terms of the Convention of 1839—it could have been carried home in a Ship of War, and many of these charges would have been avoided. Upon the whole there can be no doubt that the interest of the claimants has been promoted, In which I feel some pride as these claims when I came here were not worth twenty cents on the dollar, and I regard them now as worth par value.   I deeply regret however that the 10 per cent penalty clause was stricken out by your orders.   I should have expressly stated that this clause was not to be considered as granting any additional indulgence.   I regret still more that I was not authorized to include in this convention, all the undecided claims, and I anticipate difficulties about them.

You will see that a clause is added for the future settlement of those claims which whilst it actually imposes no obligations on either Government which did not before exist is in my judgement important.

.   .   .   .

The late hour of the night must be my excuse for a postscript.   The convention was not signed until 12 oclock and these (the most formal of all people) have to make a report to the President and then he approves the Treaty—and I should have had to delay sending it for two days and there is now no time to spare for it to arrive at Washgton and besides they say that the Treaty of 1839 made at Washington was not ratified until after it was sent here.   The ratification will however been sent by the first opportunity to Genl. Almonte and cannot be a matter of the least consequence

ARTICLE 6

Article 6 of this convention contemplated a new convention for the settlement of claims between the two countries, not only claims of citizens of each country against the Government of the other, but also claims of the respective Governments as such.

Under date of November 20, 1843, a convention, in seventeen articles, designed to carry out those provisions, was signed at Mexico City (see House Document No. 158, 28th Congress, 2d session, serial 466; the original is D.S., Unperfected H2).   Articles 1 to 15 of that convention provided somewhat elaborately for the determination of the claims of citizens of Mexico against the United States and of claims of citizens of the United States against Mexico.   Provision was made for a board of four commissioners to sit at Mexico City to consider such claims and also for an umpire, to be named by the King of Belgium, to pass on cases in which the commissioners were equally divided in opinion and on cases referred to the umpire under the convention of April 11, 1839 (Document 89), but not decided.   Article 17 provided for the exchange of ratifications within three months from the date of signature.   Article 16 is quoted below.

The Senate accepted that convention, but with certain amendments (Executive Journal, VI, 228–29).   The time for the exchange of ratifications was made six months from the date of signature instead of three; Washington was substituted for Mexico City as the place of meeting of the board of commissioners; and Article 16, containing provisions in respect of governmental claims and reading as follows in the English text, was stricken:

Whereas, the High Contracting Parties to this Convention desire to remove all causes of complaint between the two countries, and therefore to provide for the adjustment of all claims, which the two governments may have against each other, it is further agreed: That all claims which the two governments may have against each other, of a pecuniary character, shall be presented to the government, against which such claim is made; and if reparation is not made within six months, the same shall be immediately referred to the arbiter provided for in the 7th Article of this Convention, and who is to decide, in case of difference, the claims of the citizens of the two countries. His decision in these cases shall be final and conclusive, and all such cases shall be decided within one year after they are submitted to him, and according to the principles hereinbefore expressed. And all such cases as involve the good name and national honor of either of the two countries, shall be treated diplomatically, and in the manner usual amongst nations in the settlement of questions of international right; and more especially it is understood that it is not intended to submit to the aforesaid umpire the question of Boundaries between the two countries, which shall be arranged according to the stipulations of existing treaties between the said countries.

Subject to those amendments President Tyler ratified the convention on February 15, 1844 (the original instrument of ratification is in the archives); but the Mexican Government withheld its ratification from the convention as amended, and accordingly it did not go into force.

By Articles 14 and 15 of the Treaty of Guadalupe Hidalgo of February 2, 1848, the United States discharged Mexico from all unliquidated claims of American citizens "which may have arisen previously to the date of the signature" of that treaty and agreed to pay such claims to the extent of $3,250,000. That obligation of the United States was duly fulfilled under the act of March 3, 1849 (9 Statutes at Large, 393–94; see Moore, International Arbitrations, II, 1249–86).

Article 7

The provisions of Article 7 regarding the time limited for the exchange of ratifications of this convention are very unusual. It is first provided that the exchange should take place at Washington within three months from the date of the convention (or by April 30, 1843), if the document should "arrive at Washington before the adjournment of the present Session of Congress". That clause obviously required very early ratification of the convention on the part of the Mexican Government, which, indeed, took place eight days after the signature.

The session of Congress then holding was the short session, which was at that time (and until the going into force of sections 1 and 2 of the Twentieth Amendment to the Constitution on October 15, 1933) required by law to terminate not later than March 4 of the odd-numbered year; so a period of less than five weeks was allowed for the receipt in Washington of despatches from Mexico City; in the then state of communications between the United States and Mexico, that was a rather scant limit; but in this case the provision mentioned became effective as the convention was received on February 26; the Senate resolution of advice and consent was adopted on March 2,

1843, and the ratifications were duly exchanged on March 29, within two months from the date of signature of the convention.

A further provision of Article 7, to take care of possible delay in the receipt of the document at Washington, was to the effect that the exchange should then take place "within one month after the meeting of the next Congress of the United States"; that provision would have allowed, in the absence of an extra session of Congress, something over eleven months for the exchange of ratifications, counting from the date of signature.

Payment of the American Claims

The claims of American citizens, payment of which was agreed to be made by this convention, were those adjudicated under the convention of April 11, 1839 (Document 89), the notes to which should be consulted. A full and authoritative history of those claims is in Moore, International Arbitrations, II, 1209–86, with numerous citations.

While all the claims presented under the convention of April 11, 1839, had not been adjudicated, the amount of the awards thereunder reached $2,026,139.68. Pursuant to the acts of June 12, 1840 (5 Statutes at Large, 383–84), and of September 1, 1841 (*ibid.*, 452), certificates were issued by the Secretary of the Treasury to the claimants for the amounts of their respective awards, which generally bore 5 percent interest.

It had been found impossible by the Government of Mexico to carry out the provisions for the payment of the awards which were contained in the convention of April 11, 1839; the interest payment due on April 30, 1843, according to Article 1 of this convention, and the first three instalments of principal and interest payable under Article 2 (on July 30 and October 30, 1843, and January 30, 1844), were duly met; for the two following instalments, the fourth and fifth, a receipt was given to the Mexican Government by the agent of the United States, Emilio Voss, in the sum of $274,664.67; but it seems that the money was not in fact paid, and Voss himself later suspended payment; the facts of the matter are complex and obscure (D.S., 12 Despatches, Mexico, January 25, 1845, to January 10, 1846, *passim*). Some of the correspondence regarding the payments is printed with a report of Secretary of State Calhoun under date of February 14, 1845, transmitted to the House of Representatives by President Tyler on February 17 (House Document No. 144, 28th Congress, 2d session, serial 466). According to the figures of the Secretary of the Treasury (*ibid.*, 24), the principal sum due was $2,016,149.98, and each instalment due included principal in the sum of $100,807.49 plus an "amount of interest constantly decreasing by the diminution of the principal". The act of March 3, 1845 (5 Statutes at Large, 752–65), contained the following (p. 765):

For paying the April and July instalments of the Mexican indemnities due in eighteen hundred and forty-four, the sum of two hundred and seventy-five thousand dollars: *Provided,* It shall be ascertained to the satisfaction of the

American Government, that said instalments have been paid by the Mexican Government to the agent appointed by the United States to receive the same in such manner as to discharge all claim on the Mexican Government, and said agent to be a delinquent in remitting the money to the United States.

Owing to the language of the proviso quoted, President Polk did not feel warranted in directing payment to be made to the claimants, as he considered the subject involved "in much mystery", and suggested further legislation (Richardson, IV, 392, message of December 2, 1845); further correspondence was transmitted with the presidential message of February 18, 1846 (House Document No. 133, 29th Congress, 1st session, serial 483).

No further payments were made by the Mexican Treasury under this convention; the fourth and fifth instalments were finally taken up by the United States Treasury, pursuant to the act of August 10, 1846 (9 Statutes at Large, 85, 94), which appropriated $320,000 for that purpose. That date, it may be observed, is after the commencement of the war with Mexico (*ibid.*, 9–10, May 13, 1846).

By Article 13 of the Treaty of Guadalupe Hidalgo of February 2, 1848, the United States assumed the obligation to pay the balance of the liquidated claims under this convention and the convention of April 11, 1839 (Document 89), an obligation for which appropriation was duly made by the act of July 29, 1848 (*ibid.*, 265).

NEW GRANADA : FEBRUARY 9, 1843

Convention for the Settlement of Claims Arising Out of the Confiscation of Part of the Cargo of the Schooner "By Chance", signed at Bogotá February 9, 1843. Original in Spanish.
Not subject to ratification by the United States. As to ratification by New Granada, see the notes. Not proclaimed.

[Translation]

Los infrascritos, á saber, Mariano Calvo de parte del Gobierno de la Nueva Granada, en virtud de autorizacion especial que este le ha conferido, y José Gooding de Los Estados Unidos de America, en virtud de nombramiento y autorizacion del Soř Encargado de Negocios de dicho Gobierno cerca del de la Nueva Granada, Honorable Guillermo M Blackford hemos convenido en que los reclamos á que ha dado motivo la decomisacion de la parte perteneciente á ciudadanos de los Estados Unidos en el cargamento de la Goleta Norte Americana "By Chance" que tubo lugar en Panamá en anos Anteriores, y cuyos reclamos se hallaban pendientes ante el Gobierno Granadino, queden transijidos de la manera que espresan los articulos siguientes.

The undersigned, to wit, Mariano Calvo on the part of the Government of New Granada, in virtue of special authority confided to him, and Joseph Gooding, of the United States of America, in virtue of an appointment and authority conferred by the Honorable William M. Blackford, Chargé d'Affaires of the United States, have agreed that the claims arising out of the confiscation of the part of the cargo belonging to citizens of the United States, of the schooner *By Chance*—which confiscation took place some years ago and which claims have been pending before the Government of New Granada—shall be adjusted in the manner prescribed in the following articles.

ARTICULO 1º El Gobierno de la Nueva Granada se obliga á pagar á la orden del Soř Encargado de Negocios de los Estados Unidos, Honorable Guillermo M Black-

ARTICLE 1. The Government of New Granada stipulates to pay to the order of the Honorable William M. Blackford, Chargé d'Affaires of the United States, ten

499

ford los diez Mil ciento cincuenta pesos, que los Señores Icaza, Sweetser y Compañia, embarcaron en Guayaquil para Panamá en la Goleta Norte Americana "By Chance" por cuenta del Sõr Alejandro Ruden Junior, y á que asciende la propiedad de ciudadanos Norte Americanos que fué decomisada por la aduana de Panamá, como perteneciente al cargamento de dicha Goleta; es á saber; tres mil doscientos pesos en Onzas de Oro; Seis Mil quinientos cincuenta pesos en plata y cien Cargas de cacao, que se regulan á cuatro pesos cada una; cuyo pago se compromete á hacer en la misma clase de monedas en que se decomisaron, es decir la primera partida de tres mil doscientos pesos en Onzas de Oro; tres mil en moneda de plata de ley de once dineros ó en onzas Granadinas, y el resto en plata de cordon, verificandolo por duodecimos partes en cada una de los doce meses del Año economico que empesará en 1º de Setiembre del corriente Año.

Artículo 2º Asi mismo se obliga el Gobierno de la Nueva Granada á satisfacer sobre dicha suma de diez mil ciento cincuenta pesos, el interes correspondiente á razon de un seis por ciento annual, que correrá desde el dia en que fué embargada en panamá hasta aquel en que se efectue el pago de cada instala-

thousand one hundred and fifty dollars ($10,150), which Messrs. Icaza, Sweetser & Co. embarked at Guayaquil for Panamá on board the American schooner *By Chance*, on account of Mr. Alexander Ruden, Jr., being the amount belonging to citizens of North America confiscated by the customhouse of Panamá and forming part of the cargo of said schooner, that is to say, three thousand two hundred dollars ($3,200) in doubloons, six thousand five hundred and fifty dollars ($6,550) in silver, and one hundred cargoes of cocoa, which is valued by the undersigned at four dollars ($4) per cargo—which payment the said Government stipulates to make in the same description of coin that was confiscated, viz, the first-mentioned three thousand two hundred dollars in doubloons, three thousand dollars in standard silver, and the residue in Granadan silver coin, the said payment to be made in twelve equal monthly instalments commencing the 1st of September of the current year.

Article 2. The Granadan Government also agrees to pay upon the said ten thousand one hundred and fifty dollars, the accruing interest, at the rate of 6 percent per annum from the date of the seizure at Panamá until the day of the respective payments, this being the indemnification agreed upon for all damages and

mento respectivamente; siendo esta la indemnizacion que ortorga por todos los daños y perjuicios que puedan haberse ocasionado á los ciudadanos de los Estados Unidos interesados, quienes no conservarán derecho alguno para intentar ninguna nueva reclamacion

losses that may have been caused to the citizens of the United States interested, who are barred from any further claim in the premises.

ARTICULO 3º Tanto el pago del capital, como el de los intereses se verificará en los terminos espresados en los articulos Anteriores, en la Tesoreria general de la Republica.

ARTICLE 3. The payment of the principal, as well as that of the interest, as specified in the above articles, shall be made out of the General Treasury of the Republic.

ARTICULO 4º El presente conbenio será presentado por el Poder Ejecutivo de la Nueva Granada al Congreso Nacional de la Misma Republica en su proxima reunion del corriente Año, á fin de que previa su aprobacion vote la cantidad necesaria para que tenga efecto.

ARTICLE 4. This convention shall be presented by the Executive Power of New Granada to the National Congress of the Republic at the approaching session of this year, that they may approve the same and appropriate the necessary funds.

En fé de lo dicho nosotros los infrascritos hemos firmado dos ejemplares de este convenio, ambas de un mismo tenor y forma, en Bogotá á nueve de Febrero de Mil ochocientos cuarenta y tres.

In testimony whereof we, the undersigned, have executed two copies of this convention, of the same tenor and date, in Bogotá, this ninth day of February, one thousand eight hundred and forty-three.

MARIANO CALVO
JOSÉ GOODING

MARIANO CALVO
JOSEPH GOODING

NOTES

An original of this convention, in Spanish, is in D.S., Colombian Claims, folder *By Chance;* it is with that original that the Spanish text above printed has been collated; the English translation of the convention above printed is from that with the despatch of William M. Blackford, Chargé d'Affaires at Bogotá, dated February 17, 1843 (D.S., 10 Despatches, Colombia, No. 8). The translation is, on the whole, well enough, though rather summary here and there.

The convention was submitted to the Congress of New Granada on March 9, 1843. It received congressional approval on the following May 29, and the decree of execution and promulgation, which includes the text of the convention, was dated June 16, 1843 (Codificación nacional de Colombia, X, 306–8). Reference to the settlement was made in the annual message of President Tyler of December 1843 (Richardson, IV, 263).

THE FULL POWERS

Three Chargés d'Affaires of the United States treated at Bogotá regarding the case of the *By Chance*. The first in point of time, Robert B. McAfee, had a full power dated March 30, 1833, to negotiate for a treaty of amity, commerce, and navigation, but in that authorization there is no mention of claims (D.S., 2 Credences, 199).

The successor of McAfee was James Semple, who had a full power dated January 9, 1838, to treat regarding commerce and navigation (*ibid.*, 288), and also a full power dated February 4, 1839, "to agree, treat, consult and negotiate of and concerning claims of citizens of the United States upon the governments of the Republic of New Granada and of the late Republic of Colombia, and all matters and subjects connected therewith" (*ibid.*, 308). The successor of Semple was William M. Blackford, who also had two full powers. The first was dated May 17, 1842, regarding commerce and navigation (D.S., 3 Credences, 15). The second was dated August 12, 1843 (after the date of this convention), for negotiations with Ecuador; its subject was "claims of the citizens of the two countries respectively upon the governments of the United States and the Republic of Ecuador, and of citizens of the United States upon the government of the late Republic of Colombia, and all matters and subjects connected therewith" (*ibid.*, 48); but all the full powers mentioned were in customary form, contemplating treaties or conventions to be submitted to the Senate. Sufficient authorization for Blackford (or for either of his predecessors) to negotiate and sign a convention of this nature is to be found in his instructions.

Ordinarily a diplomatic officer would not be empowered to delegate his authority to sign an agreement with another Government to a "commissioner", as was done in this case; but the circumstances here were somewhat unusual. Liability had been admitted; the task of the Commissioners was to agree on the amount thereof. The procedure adopted was that suggested by the Government of New Granada. The Government of the United States acquiesced in the course taken, and its diplomatic representative at Bogotá collected the payments made under the convention.

Joseph Gooding, who signed the convention on behalf of the United States, was designated (in January 1843) by William M. Blackford, Chargé d'Affaires of the United States, as Commissioner "to act on behalf of the American claimants" (D.S., 10 Despatches, Colombia, No. 7, January 20, 1843); Gooding was "long a resident" of Bogotá and "owns the greater part of this claim, and has a power of At-

torney, from those who own the residue" (*ibid.*, No. 5, December 23, 1842); nothing appears as to the form of his appointment.

The Commissioner who signed the convention on behalf of New Granada, Mariano Calvo, acted, according to the preamble, "in virtue of special authority confided to him"; the congressional act of approval of May 29, 1843, uses the words "en virtud de nombramiento y especial autorización del Poder Ejecutivo" (Codificación nacional de Colombia, X, 306); the appointment was reported to have been made by "the Secretary of the Treasury" (D.S., 10 Despatches, Colombia, No. 7, January 20, 1843); nothing further is of record.

THE "BY CHANCE"

The schooner *By Chance*, of New Bedford, Massachusetts, Hiram Covell, master, sailed from her home port on September 6, 1833, on a sealing and shelling voyage in the Pacific, with a cargo of merchandise which included nine boxes and one hogshead of tobacco, weighing in all 1,900 pounds. On March 10, 1834, the *By Chance* anchored at Paita, discharged part of her cargo, and took on other merchandise for Guayaquil, where she arrived on April 11. She sailed from that port on April 26 for Panamá, after taking on board, with other cargo, about $30,000 in gold and silver. Of the specie $9,950, and of the cargo fifty bags of cocoa, belonged to Alexander Ruden, Jr., an American citizen. Upon arrival at Panamá on May 15, 1834, a manifest of the cargo, including "the exact quantity of Tobacco", was delivered. Learning, however, that there might be some difficulty on account of the tobacco, the master of the *By Chance* took his vessel some distance out of port. During that evening permission was obtained from the customhouse to land the cargo from Guayaquil. The specie was brought ashore; the port charges, $126, were paid; and the *By Chance* proceeded on her voyage.

The collector of the customs at Panamá, however, seized all the property landed, on the ground that the *By Chance* had tobacco on board and that the captain of that vessel intended to land the same contrary to law; and despite judicial proceedings which followed at Panamá, at Cartagena, and at Bogotá, the property was not restored (D.S., 8 Despatches, Colombia, No. 19, September 19, 1834; No. 29, December 4, 1835, and enclosures). In the despatch last cited Robert B. McAfee, Chargé d'Affaires at Bogotá, wrote that on December 2, 1835, "the supreme court here decided that they had no power to reverse the decision of the court at Carthagena, thus leaving the money and goods seized at *Panama* confiscated, the agent for the claimants leaves on tomorrow in despair after expending near four thousand dollars".

THE NEGOTIATIONS

The American claim was first presented to the Government of New Granada by the note of McAfee of September 5, 1834 (*ibid.*, No. 19, September 19, 1834, enclosure C). McAfee continued, without success, to press the claim during his residence at Bogotá, which terminated in the summer of 1837.

The negotiations were continued by the successor of McAfee as
Chargé d'Affaires, James Semple, who was commissioned on October
14, 1837, and who had instructions in the case of the *By Chance*
(D.S., 15 Instructions, Colombia, 42–51, January 9, 1838).   The
diplomatic correspondence which ensued during the next few years
was extensive.   One cause of the delay was the impeachment of the
judges of the court at Cartagena who pronounced the sentence of
condemnation.   They were brought to trial on May 20, 1839, and
were acquitted (D.S., 9 Despatches, Colombia, No. 19, May 28,
1839).

Semple was absent from New Granada from May 28, 1839, to
March 17, 1840 (*ibid.*, No. 20, July 25, 1839; No. 24, March 20, 1840).
During this period a note of the New Granadan Secretary of State
for Foreign Affairs, Pedro Alcántara Herrán, dated June 21, 1839,
stated that he was authorized by his Government "to enter into
equitable arrangements" concerning the claims (*ibid.*, No. 21, September 15, 1839, enclosure).   On April 30, 1840, Semple transmitted
to the Government of New Granada a statement of the claims of
American citizens interested in the cargo of the *By Chance*, from which
it appears that the interest of Alexander Ruden, Jr. (who had been
consul at Paita from October 12, 1837), was in large part that of
agent, as the statement was thus itemized (*ibid.*, No. 26, July 1, 1840,
enclosure):

Henry Patto_____	$3000. 00
Hussey & Mackey_____	6600. 00
George Hussey_____	81. 37
W. H. Bowne_____	60. 00
Alexᴿ Rudin_____	600. 00
Edward Ewen_____	274. 75
	$10616. 12
Fifty pᴿ ct. damages_____	5308. 06
Six years interest_____	3821. 80
Total_____	$19745. 98

The correspondence continued, however, without result, until on
February 28, 1842, the New Granadan Secretary of State for Foreign
Affairs, Mariano Ospina, wrote as follows (*ibid.*, No. 45, March 2,
1842, enclosure, translation):

Having laid before the Executive the note of the Honorable Chargé d'Affaires
of the United States dated 17th January last, asking an early arrangement of the
claims heretofore made concerning the confiscation of certain property of North
Americans, taken from the schooner *By Chance* in 1834, he has resolved to appoint
Mr. Francisco Montoya on the part of New Granada to conclude with Mr.
Semple an arrangement of this matter to be submitted to the approaching Congress.   As soon as the previous formalities shall have been complied with, full
powers will be furnished to Mr. Montoya to proceed in the negotiation.

Within a few weeks after the date of that note, however, Semple
left Bogotá.   His successor as Chargé d'Affaires was William M.
Blackford, who was commissioned on February 10, 1842, and who
reached Bogotá on September 10 following.   The first instructions

to Blackford, of May 20, 1842, referred in general terms to pending claims and to the fact that the negotiations regarding them had been interrupted by the "civil war which had until very recently prevailed for some time in that country" (D.S., 15 Instructions, Colombia, 76–80).

A decree of the Congress of New Granada of June 27, 1842, dealt generally with the claims against that Government (D.S., 10 Despatches, Colombia, No. 3, October 20, 1842). On December 13, 1842, Blackford was informed that the commissioner to consider the claim in the case of the *By Chance* would be appointed by the Secretary of the Treasury (*ibid.*, No. 5, December 23, 1842). In the despatch cited Blackford wrote:

> I believe there will be no difficulty now, in effecting an adjustment of the claim of the "By Chance". I am assured that the Commissioner will be appointed in a few days—Mʳ Joseph Gooding—an intelligent American, long a resident of this city—owns the greater part of this claim, and has a power of Attorney, from those who own the residue. I intend to appoint him the Commissioner on our part. He is, thoroughly, acquainted with the case, and, as his interest is largely involved, I may safely trust the matter in his hands.

Nothing has been found in the despatches or elsewhere regarding the form of the appointment of the Commissioners or the exact date on which they were named. In his despatch of January 20, 1843 (*ibid.*, No. 7), Blackford wrote as follows:

> Since my despatch of the 6ᵗʰ Inst., the Secretary of Foreign Affairs has informed me of the appointment, by the Secretary of the Treasury, of a Commissioner to adjust the claim of the "By Chance". I have, accordingly, appointed Mr. Gooding to act on behalf of the American claimants. The Commissioners will meet next week—and I hope that, in my next, I shall have it in my power to communicate the result of their conference.

It thus appears that the discussions of the terms of the convention which was signed by the two Commissioners could have lasted only a few days, as the date of the convention is February 9, 1843. In his despatch of February 17, 1843, transmitting the original of the convention and a translation thereof, Blackford wrote as follows (*ibid.*, No. 8):

> In my communication, of the 20ᵗʰ ultimo, I informed you of the appointment of Commissioners, by the Granadian Government and myself, respectively, to adjust the claim in the case of the "By-Chance". I have now the honor to transmit, herewith, the copy of a Convention, signed by the said Commissioners, on the 9ᵗʰ of the present month, in which it is stipulated that the Government of New Granada is to pay, in twelve, equal, monthly Instalments, the amount of specie and other property, taken from the "By-Chance", together with Interest; at the rate of six pr. centum, pr. annum, from the date of the seizure until paid.
>
> As Mʳ Gooding, the Commissioner named by me, owns the whole of the Claim, except the amount of the Cocoa, and two or three hundred Dollars of the specie, I have, of course, but to ratify the convention, though I think the Granadian Government should have been made to pay, at least Twenty pr cent damages, in addition to the Interest—and I do not doubt such was their expectation. But, most unaccountably, the British Commissioner waived the claim for damages, and was content with the lawful Interest, on the portion of money, taken from the "By Chance", which belonged to British subjects, and, of course, Mʳ Gooding had to agree to the same terms.

PAYMENT

Blackford reported that on May 29, 1843, the Congress of New Granada appropriated the amount stipulated to be paid under the convention (D.S., 10 Despatches, Colombia, No. 11, June 3, 1843; see Codificación nacional de Colombia, X, 306–8). The payments stipulated in the convention were duly made, the final instalment having been paid on August 2, 1844 (D.S., 10 Despatches, Colombia, No. 28, November 29, 1844, enclosure).

Although by the terms of the convention the interested claimants were "barred from any further claim in the premises", a further claim seems to have been presented to the Commission under the convention with Colombia of February 10, 1864; it was adjudged not valid (Moore, International Arbitrations, II, 1418, case 47).

SIMILAR CONVENTIONS

A convention in terms very similar to this was signed on the same date, February 9, 1843, for the payment of $17,000 for claims of British subjects in respect of a portion of the cargo of the *By Chance* (Codificación nacional de Colombia, X, 302–3); and on May 12, 1843, a convention was signed for the payment of $4,483.31¼ in respect of the similar claims of French citizens (*ibid.*, 304–5).

102

BRAZIL : JUNE 12, 1843

Convention for the Adjustment of the Claim for the Detention and Seizure of the Schooner "John S. Bryan", signed at Rio de Janeiro June 12, 1843. Original in Portuguese.
Not subject to ratification by the United States. As to ratification by Brazil, see the notes. Not proclaimed.

[Translation]

Os abaixo assignados, Commissarios devidamente nomeados pelo Governo de Sua Magestade o Imperador do Brasil, e pelo Enviado Extraordinario e Ministro plenipotenciario do Governo dos Estados Unidos d'America, para liquidar as perdas, damnos, e lucros cessantes motivados pela detenção e apresam^{to} da Escuna Americana—Johon S. Bryan—, que teve lugar na Provincia do Pará em Junho de 1836—, tem ajustado e convencionado a mencionada Liquidação da maneira seguinte:

Por indemnisação total do valor da Escuna—Johon S. Bryan—, seu carregamento, fretes, Estalias, Soldadas, despesas ordinarias e extraordinarias, cambios, juros, &ª &ª_____26:000$000

Cuja quantia de vinte e seis contos de reis, em dinheiro de Notas circulantes, deverá ser paga pelo Governo de Sua Megestade o Imperador do Brasil em Apolices da divida publica pelo preço

The undersigned Commissioners, duly appointed by the Government of His Imperial Majesty and by the Envoy Extraordinary and Minister Plenipotentiary of the United States of America to liquidate the losses, damages, and suspended profits arising from the detention and seizure of the American schooner *John S. Bryan*, which took place in the Province of Pará in June 1836, have adjusted and agreed to the following liquidation and indemnity:

For indemnity, entire value of the schooner *John S. Bryan*, her cargo, freights, [demurrage], pay roll, ordinary and extraordinary expenses, exchange, interest, etc., etc., Rs. 26,000$000.

Which sum of twenty-six thousand milreis is to be paid in money of current notes by the Government of His Imperial Majesty the Emperor of Brazil in stock of public debt at the price current

que correrem no mercado no dia em que se verificar o pagamento.

O Governo dos Estados Unidos d'America, pelo seu Representante nesta Corte, ha de garantir ao do Brasil o pagamento a os interessados nesta Reclamação, por isso que a Soma liquidada e convencionada será posta, do modo expressado, á desposição do mesmo Representante do Governo dos Estados Unidos.

A presente convenção e ajuste de Liquidação fica em tudo dependente da Approvação e ratificação do Governo de Sua Magestade O Imperador do Brasil.

E para que assim conste, nós os respectivos Commissarios Liquidantes fixemos e assignamos a preste por duplicata

Rio de Janeiro 12 de junho de 1834—aliás de 1843.

João Miž Lóur. Vianna
Commissario Brasileiro

João Gardner
Commissario Americano

in the market on the day of payment.

The Government of the United States of America by its representative at this Court is to guarantee to Brazil the payment to those interested in this claim, for which purpose the sum agreed upon and liquidated shall be placed at the disposal of the representative of the United States.

The present convention for adjustment remains altogether subject to the approval and ratification of His Imperial Majesty the Emperor of Brazil.

And in faith thereof we, the undersigned Commissioners, signed the present in duplicate.

Rio de Janeiro, 12 June 1834, alias 1843.

João Miž Lóur. Vianna
Brazilian Commissioner

John Gardner
American Commissioner

NOTES

The source text of this convention is the original in the Portuguese language which is in D.S., Brazilian Claims, folder *John S. Bryan;* there is with that original a translation thereof, which is also printed above.

The Full Powers

The negotiations in the case of the *John S. Bryan* were conducted at Rio de Janeiro on behalf of this Government by William Hunter, Chargé d'Affaires and, from September 13, 1841, Minister to Brazil. Hunter had a full power dated July 3, 1834 (D.S., 2 Credences, 225–26), which granted authority—

for and in the name of The United States, to meet and confer with any person or persons authorized by the said Regency being furnished with like power and authority, and with him or them to agree, treat, consult and negotiate of and

concerning commerce and navigation between the United States and Brazil, and of claims of the citizens and subjects of the two countries respectively upon the Governments of Brazil and the United States, and all matters and subjects connected therewith, and to conclude and sign a treaty or treaties, Convention or conventions touching the premises, transmitting the same to the President of The United States for his ratification by and with the advice and consent of the Senate of The United States.

Doubtless even without that full power sufficient authority for Hunter to negotiate and sign a convention of this nature is to be found in his instructions.

The convention, however, was signed not by Plenipotentiaries of the two Governments but by Commissioners appointed in October 1842, respectively by the American Minister to Brazil and by the Brazilian Secretary of State for Foreign Affairs. The Commissioner who signed the convention on behalf of the United States was John Gardner, a merchant of Rio de Janeiro, a citizen of the United States, and the agent of the claimants (D.S., 12 Despatches, Brazil, No. 12, November 8, 1842, enclosure). Nothing appears as to the form of the appointment of Gardner.

Ordinarily a diplomatic officer would not be empowered to delegate his authority to sign an agreement with another Government to a "commissioner", as was done in this case, but the circumstances here were somewhat unusual. Liability had been admitted; the task of the Commissioners was to agree on the amount thereof. The procedure adopted was that suggested by the Government of Brazil. The Government of the United States approved the course taken (see Richardson, IV, 263). The procedure here closely resembles that followed in the case of the agreement with New Granada of February 9, 1843, regarding the claim in the case of the schooner *By Chance* (Document 101).

The Commissioner who signed the convention on behalf of Brazil, João M. L. Vianna, was a merchant of Rio de Janeiro (D.S., 12 Despatches, Brazil, No. 12, November 8, 1842) and, according to the preamble of the convention, had been "duly appointed by the Government of His Majesty the Emperor of Brazil"; nothing appears of record as to the form of that appointment.

THE "JOHN S. BRYAN"

The following statement of the facts in the case of the *John S. Bryan* is collected from the various records in the archives of the Department of State.

The schooner *John S. Bryan*, of about 100 tons, Thomas Perkins Pingree of Salem, Massachusetts, owner, Chaplin Conway, master, sailed from Boston on December 4, 1835. She was under orders to proceed to Pará, Brazil, unless that port should be under blockade on account of the rebellion in the Province of Pará against the Brazilian Government, in which case she was to proceed to Cayenne or Maranhão.

The vessel arrived off the coast of Brazil, within fifty miles of Pará, where information was received that that port was under blockade;

accordingly, but chiefly because of damage sustained by his vessel in a severe gale, Conway decided to put into Macapá, a port on one of the mouths of the Amazon, to make repairs; she arrived at Macapá on January 7, 1836.

While at Macapá, at the solicitation of the authorities of that place, the cargo, which consisted of salt and other necessaries, was sold to the inhabitants (who were represented as being in distress for want of provisions), with the exception of certain ammunition which was on board and which was sold to the Governor of Macapá for the use of the Brazilian Government. A certificate was given for the value of the ammunition, which it was arranged was to be set against the duties payable to the Brazilian authorities on the cargo.

A return cargo was put on board the vessel, the loading of which was completed on January 29, 1836. Captain Conway received from the authorities at Macapá certificates regarding the goods delivered by him and also regarding the return cargo shipped, and was ordered to sail for the island of Tatuoca (a small island about fifteen geographical miles northward from Pará, on the eastern side of Pará River; see chart No. 887 of the United States Hydrographic Office), the rendezvous of the blockading squadron, for the purpose of paying the customary import and export duties.

On February 6, 1836, when on the point of sailing for Tatuoca, the vessel was taken by an officer and a file of soldiers acting under instructions from the President of the Province; and when she sailed on February 15 that detachment was on board. The *John S. Bryan* arrived at Tatuoca on February 22; a court of inquiry was shortly thereafter ordered by the President of Pará to examine into the circumstances of the voyage and to decide whether or not the vessel was subject to seizure. Over two months elapsed before the court brought in its report, which was in the form of a sentence against the master of the vessel, fining him in the amount of Rs. 356$700 for having contraband (ammunition) on board, although, as above stated, the ammunition had been sold for the use of the Brazilian Government. The vessel and cargo were otherwise cleared.

The Government of Brazil obtained possession of the city of Pará on May 13, 1836; the master of the *John S. Bryan* paid the penalty above mentioned and the duties in full. It was found that the schooner, in order to render her safe for the passage home, required considerable overhauling and repairs, and a permit was obtained from the proper authorities to land the cargo so that this might be done. Before discharging was commenced, however, the vessel was seized on June 23, 1836, by the "Juiz de Direito", who announced that he annulled the previous proceedings; the crew was dismissed and a guard was placed on board. Captain Conway immediately commenced legal proceedings against the "Juiz de Direito" for the detention and seizure of the vessel and cargo, and a protest was duly entered before the American consul at Pará. Neither the vessel nor the cargo was restored.

THE NEGOTIATIONS

While legal proceedings were still pending in Brazil this claim was called to the attention of the Government of the United States by the communication of Charles J. Smith, American consul at Pará, to Secretary of State Forsyth, dated July 24, 1836 (D.S., 1 Consular Despatches, Pará, No. 16). Forsyth transmitted a copy of that despatch to William Hunter, Chargé d'Affaires to Brazil (Minister from September 13, 1841; D.S., 2 Credences, 353), with his instruction dated August 30, 1836, and directed him to take the matter up with the Brazilian Government (D.S., 15 Instructions, Brazil, 28–31).

The proceedings which had been instituted in the Brazilian courts resulted in the "acquittal" of the ship and cargo; an appeal at the instance of the Brazilian Government was pending; and Hunter preferred to await the result of that appeal before approaching the Government of Brazil (D.S., 10 Despatches, Brazil, No. 49, January 17, 1837). However, Hunter appears to have mentioned the matter informally; and in his despatch of January 31, 1837 (*ibid.*, No. 50), he states that he had communicated the contents of the instructions of August 30, 1836, to Montezuma (the counsel for the claimants), "who is in consequence greatly encouraged and confirmed in his intended course".

In May 1837 Montezuma (Francisco Gê Acayaba de Montezuma) became Secretary of State for Foreign Affairs of Brazil; after he took office Hunter conferred with him on the case of the *John S. Bryan;* but although Montezuma adhered to the opinion he had previously given (as counsel), favorable to the claimants, he was unwilling to act upon the case until the decision of the Court of Appeals (D.S., 11 Despatches, Brazil, No. 56, July 7, 1837).

The Court of Appeals unanimously decided in favor of the claimants, and upon the grounds of Montezuma's arguments. However, as Secretary of State for Foreign Affairs, he was unwilling to take up the question of indemnity and the amount thereof, stating that there were other judicial stages which might be traversed, first in the nature of a rehearing before the Court of Appeals and finally an appeal to the Supreme Court at Bahia; and he even questioned the want of authentication of certain papers (*ibid.*, No. 58, August 29, 1837).

In September 1837 there was a change of Government in Brazil, and Antonio Peregrino Maciel Monteiro became Secretary of State for Foreign Affairs in place of Montezuma.

On November 27, 1837, Hunter addressed to Monteiro a note elaborately reciting the facts and arguing the law (D.S., 11 Despatches, Brazil, No. 66, December 16, 1837, enclosure). This brought no result; there was further delay and postponement of consideration; and there were further instructions from Washington to press for a settlement (D.S., 15 Instructions, Brazil, 64–65, June 26, 1839).

The correspondence went on at Rio de Janeiro with successive Brazilian Secretaries of State for Foreign Affairs; the position taken by this Government was that nothing remained but adjustment of

the sum to be paid and payment. A statement of the claim, as presented on May 4, 1840, was as follows (D.S., 12 Despatches, Brazil, No. 108, May 14, 1840, enclosure, translation):

Claim made by John Gardner on behalf of the owners and insurers of the American schooner *John S. Bryan* against the Brazilian Government for the seizure of the said schooner at Macapá on February 15, 1836, which vessel was condemned at Pará and then ordered to be restored by decision of the Court of the Supreme Council of Justice, Military, and Admiralty, and approved in the Chancellery of the Empire on December 12, 1837, for the schooner, its cargo, and costs.

For the value of the schooner and its cargo as shown by the document submitted by the Government of the United States, $11,-
012.75 at the rate of 1$750 for each dollar_____ 19, 272, 312
For the profit on the cargo of the said schooner of $5,147.72 at the rate of 1$750 for each dollar, amounting to Rs. 9,008$510, estimated
at 20 percent_____ 1, 801, 702
For the expenses incurred for lawyers, attorneys, and the agencies
supporting the rights of the parties_____ 1, 800, 000
                                                                ───────────
                                                   Rs. 22, 874. 012

Interest on this amount from June 23, 1836, to the day of its liquidation.
Rio de Janeiro, May 2, 1840.
                                                        JOHN GARDNER

National commissioners were appointed by the Government of Brazil in 1840 and in 1842 to examine this and other claims, but no decision was reached; definitive action was not taken until October 15, 1842, when Aureliano de Souza e Oliveira Coutinho, then Brazilian Secretary of State for Foreign Affairs, wrote as follows (*ibid.*, No. 12, November 8, 1842, enclosure 6, translation):

in regard to the matter of the other reclamation on account of the schooner *John S. Bryan*, the Imperial Government, although it does not consider that claim to be perfectly established, yet, from respect to the decisions of the tribunals of the country, has resolved to nominate as Commissioner on its part a merchant of this city, John Martins Lorenzo Vianna, who, in conjunction with the American commissioner to be appointed by Mr. Hunter, may decide upon the liquidations of the damages which the claimant in that case has suffered, upon the inspection of such demonstrative accounts as may be to them presented, as has been the practice in all such cases, submitting the result to the approbation of the Imperial Government for its information and ulterior decision.

Under date of October 24, 1842, Hunter addressed a note to Coutinho expressing satisfaction at the appointment of Vianna and nominating as the Commissioner on the part of the United States and the individual claimants, John Gardner, a merchant of Rio de Janeiro and a citizen of the United States (*ibid.*). No record has been found in the archives of the Department of State of any formal commissions issued to Vianna or to Gardner in the premises.

The adjustment of the claim for 26,000 milreis and the signature of this convention of June 12, 1843, followed.

The Emperor of Brazil gave his approval to the adjustment; and under date of June 21, 1843, Secretary of State for Foreign Affairs Paulino José Soares de Souza wrote as follows to Hunter (*ibid.*, No. 22, July 9, 1843, enclosure, translation):

The undersigned, of the Council of His Majesty the Emperor, Minister and Secretary of State for Foreign Affairs, has the honor to make known to Mr. William Hunter, Envoy Extraordinary and Minister Plenipotentiary of the United States of America, that having submitted to the consideration of His Majesty the convention signed by the Brazilian and American Commissioners, named by their respective Governments, for the purpose of liquidating the damages sustained by the schooner *John S. Bryan,* detained and proceeded against as prize in the Province of Pará in the year 1836, the same August Seignior has seen fit to give his imperial approbation to the adjustment in this case made by the said Commissioners, by ordering the payment of the sum of twenty-six thousand milreis (Rs. 26,000$000), the amount assessed as damages by the aforesaid Commissioners in the matter aforesaid, as soon as the necessary funds therefor shall be granted by the General Assembly.

The undersigned immediately directed himself to the Secretary of the Treasury, to the end of having brought to a complete result the aforesaid imperial resolve, which he communicates to Mr. Hunter as another proof of the consideration to which the Brazilian Government deems the representations of the Government of the United States entitled, when they are founded on justice and substantiated by documents.

The imperial approbation was expressed in the decree of June 19, 1843, of which the following is a translation (*ibid.*, No. 8, February 10, 1844, enclosure):

It is My imperial desire to approve of the convention made between the Commissaries named for liquidating the claims against the American schooner *John S. Bryan* detained and taken as prize in the Province of Pará in the year 1836 and which with this convention followed by a copy and signed by Paulino José Soares de Souza, of My Council, Minister and Secretary of State for Foreign Affairs, for the purpose of verifying its respective payment, in conformity with the same, so soon as the necessary funds shall be granted for the purpose by the General Legislative Assembly.   The said Minister and Secretary of State has thus understood it and expedites in consequence the necessary despatches.

Palace at Rio de Janeiro, 19th June, 1843.

Mention of the settlement of the case of the *John S. Bryan* was made by President Tyler in his annual message of December 1843 (Richardson, IV, 263).

During the next three years various and repeated efforts were made by the American Ministers to Brazil, George H. Profitt and Henry A. Wise (commissioned respectively on June 7, 1843, and February 8, 1844), to obtain payment of the liquidated amount of the claim with interest from the date of the settlement; but the General Legislative Assembly did not appropriate the necessary funds; and it was not until May 20, 1846, that payment was finally made and the net proceeds remitted to the claimants (D.S., 15 Despatches, Brazil, No. 46, June 19, 1846).   At the time of receiving payment of the principal, protest was made by Gardner, the agent of the claimants, for interest thereon from June 12, 1843 (*ibid.*, enclosure).

The interest demanded was not paid and became the subject of a claim under the convention with Brazil of January 27, 1849; that claim also included the expenses incurred in the prosecution of the original claim.   The total of the claim then made by Thomas Perkins

Pingree, as of January 13, 1851, was Rs. 21,413$486, or, at 1,900 reis to the dollar, $11,270.25. The Commissioner under the convention of 1849 and the act of March 29, 1850 (9 Statutes at Large, 422–23), awarded the sum of $3,292.07 in all, being interest at 6 percent on the original adjustment of Rs. 26,000$000 from June 12, 1843, to May 20, 1846, the date of payment, $2,444.91, plus $847.16, interest on $2,444.91 from May 20, 1846, to March 1, 1852, the date of the expiration of the Commission under the convention of January 27, 1849; the claim for expenses was disallowed (see D.S., Brazilian Claims, folder *John S. Bryan;* also Moore, International Arbitrations, V, 4613–14).

Treaty Series No. 89
8 Statutes at Large, 580–83
18 *ibid.*, pt. 2, Public Treaties, 247–48

103

FRANCE : NOVEMBER 9, 1843

*Convention for the Surrender of Criminals, signed at Washington
November 9, 1843. Original in English and French.
Submitted to the Senate December 15, 1843. (Message of December
12, 1843.) Resolution of advice and consent February 1, 1844.
Ratified by the United States February 2, 1844. Ratified by France
January 22, 1844. Ratifications exchanged at Washington April 12,
1844. Proclaimed April 13, 1844.*

Convention for the surrender of Criminals between the United States of America and His Majesty the King of the French.

The United States of America and His Majesty the King of the French having judged it expedient, with a view to the better administration of justice, and to the prevention of crime within their respective territories and jurisdictions, that persons charged with the crimes hereinafter enumerated, and being fugitives from justice, should, under certain circumstances, be reciprocally delivered up; the said United States of America and His Majesty the King of the French have named as their Plenipotentiaries to conclude a Convention for this purpose; that is to say, the President of the United States of America, Abel P. Upshur, Secretary of State of the United States; and His Majesty the King of the

Convention pour l'extradition de Criminels entre les Etats Unis d'Amérique et Sa Majesté le Roi des Français.

Les Etats Unis d'Amérique et Sa Majesté le Roi des Français ayant jugé convenable, en vue d'une meilleure administration de la justice, et pour prévenir les crimes dans leurs territoires et jurisdictions respectifs, que les individus accusés des crimes ci-après énumérés, et qui se seraient soustraits par la fuite aux poursuites de la justice, fussent, dans certaines circonstances, réciproquement extradés; les Etats Unis d'Amérique et Sa Majesté le Roi des Français ont nommé pour leurs Plénipotentiaires, à l'effet de conclure dans ce but, une Convention; savoir, le President des Etats Unis d'Amérique, Abel P. Upshur, Secretaire d'Etat des Etats Unis; et Sa Mejesté le Roi des Français, le Sieur Pageot,

515

French, the Sieur Pageot, Officer of the Royal Order of the Legion of Honor, his Minister Plenipotentiary, *ad interim*, in the United States of America; who, after having communicated to each other their respective full powers, found in good and due form, have agreed upon and concluded the following articles:

ARTICLE I.

It is agreed that the High Contracting Parties shall, on requisitions made in their name, through the medium of their respective Diplomatic Agents, deliver up to justice persons who, being accused of the crimes enumerated in the next following article, committed within the jurisdiction of the requiring party, shall seek an asylum, or shall be found within the territories of the other: *Provided,* That this shall be done only when the fact of the commission of the crime shall be so established as that the laws of the country in which the fugitive or the person so accused shall be found would justify his or her apprehension and commitment for trial, if the crime had been there committed.

ARTICLE II.

Persons shall be so delivered up who shall be charged, according to the provisions of this Convention, with any of the following crimes, to wit: murder, (comprehending the crimes designated in the French Penal Code by the

Officier de l'Ordre Royal de la Légion d'honneur, son Ministre Plénipotentiaire, par interim, auprès les Etats Unis d'Amérique; lesquels après s'être communiqué leurs pleins pouvoirs respectifs, trouvés en bonne et due forme, ont arrêté et conclu les articles suivants:

ARTICLE I.

Il est convenu que les hautes parties contractantes, sur les réquisitions faites en leur nom par l'intermédiaire de leurs Agents Diplomatiques respectifs seront tenus de livrer en justice les individus qui, accusés des crimes énumérés dans l'article suivant, commis dans la juridiction de la partie requérante, chercheront un asile, ou seront rencontrés dans les territoires de l'autre, pourvu que cela n'ait lieu que dans le cas où l'existence du crime sera constatée de telle manière que les lois du pays, où le fugitif ou l'individu, ainsi accusé, sera rencontré, justifieraient sa détention et sa mise en jugement, si le crime y avait été commis.

ARTICLE II.

Seront livrés en vertu des dispositions de cette Convention, les individus qui seront accusés de l'un des crimes suivants, savoir: meurtre, (y compris les crimes qualifiés dans le Code Penal Français, d'assassinat, de par-

terms, assassination, parricide, infanticide, and poisoning,) or with an attempt to commit murder, or with rape, or with forgery, or with arson, or with embezzlement by public officers, when the same is punishable with infamous punishment.

ARTICLE III.

On the part of the French Government, the surrender shall be made only by authority of the Keeper of the Seals, Minister of Justice; and on the part of the Government of the United States, the surrender shall be made only by authority of the Executive thereof.

ARTICLE IV.

The expenses of any detention and delivery effected in virtue of the preceding provisions, shall be borne and defrayed by the Government in whose name the requisition shall have been made.

ARTICLE V.

The provisions of the present Convention shall not be applied in any manner to the crimes enumerated in the second article, committed anterior to the date thereof, nor to any crime or offence of a purely political character.

ARTICLE VI.

This Convention shall continue in force until it shall be abrogated by the contracting parties, or one of them; but it shall not be abro-

ricide, d'infanticide, et d'empoisonnement,) ou tentative de meurtre, ou viol, ou faux, ou incendie, ou soustractions commises par les depositaires publics, mais seulement dans le cas où elles seront punies de peines infamantes.

ARTICLE III.

L'extradition ne sera effectuée, de la part du Gouvernement Français que sur l'avis du Ministre de la Justice, Garde des Sceaux, et de la part du Gouvernement des Etats Unis, l'extradition ne sera effectuée que sur l'ordre de l'Exécutif des Etats Unis.

ARTICLE IV.

Les frais de toute détention et extradition opéreés en vertu des articles précédents seront supportés et payés par le Gouvernement au nom duquel la réquisition aura été faite.

ARTICLE V.

Les dispositions de la présente Convention ne s'appliqueront en aucune manière aux crimes énumérés dans l'article II., commis antérieurement à sa date, ni aux crimes ou delits purement politiques.

ARTICLE VI.

Cette Convention continuera d'être en vigueur jusqu'à ce qu'elle soit abrogée par les parties contractantes, ou l'une d'elles; mais

gated except by mutual consent, unless the party desiring to abrogate it shall give six months' previous notice of his intention to do so. It shall be ratified, and the ratifications shall be exchanged within the space of six months, or earlier, if possible.

In witness whereof, the respective Plenipotentiaries have signed the present Convention in duplicate, and have affixed thereto the seal of their arms.

Done at Washington, the ninth day of November, Anno Domini one thousand eight hundred and forty-three.

[Seal]   A P Upshur
[Seal]   A Pageot.

elle ne pourra être abrogée que d'un consentement mutuel, à moins que la partie qui désirerait l'abroger ne donne avis, six mois d'avance, de son intention de le faire. Elle sera ratifiée, et les ratifications en seront échangées, dans l'espace de six mois, ou plustôt, si faire se peut.

En foi de quoi, les Plénipotentiaires respectifs ont signé la présente Convention en double, et y ont apposé le sceau de leurs armes.

Fait à Washington, le neuvième jour de Novembre, l'an de grace mil huit cent quarante trois.

A Pageot   [Seal]
A P Upshur   [Seal]

NOTES

It is said in the convention that it was signed in duplicate. The signed original in the file has the English text written in the left columns and the French in the right; as the printed texts show, the United States is named first therein throughout; but the two Plenipotentiaries signed the texts in alternate order, corresponding with the languages. All the usual papers are in the file, and they are in customary form, including the attested Senate resolution of February 1, 1844 (Executive Journal, VI, 230), the duplicate United States instrument of ratification of the following day, the act of the exchange of ratifications at Washington on April 12, in English, and the original proclamation of April 13, 1844. The French instrument of ratification contains the text of the convention in both languages, the French in the left columns; in each text therein the King of the French is named first throughout, the copies of the signatures of the two Plenipotentiaries appearing under each text in alternate order, corresponding with the languages.

The Senate resolution of advice and consent was first adopted on January 19, 1844, by a vote of 35 to 5, then reconsidered, and finally adopted by 30 to 15, exactly two thirds of the Senators present (*ibid.*, 220, 230).

It appears that no papers accompanied this convention when it was transmitted to the Senate with the presidential message of Decem-

ber 12, 1843 (*ibid.*, 194; Senate Confidential Document No. 1, 28th Congress, 1st session, Regular Confidential Documents, XVIII, 221–23).

THE FULL POWERS

The preamble of the convention makes the usual mention of the communication of the full powers. Nothing further appears of record regarding the full power of the French Plenipotentiary other than the mention in the French instrument of ratification of his "special full powers".

The full power given to Secretary of State Upshur was dated October 24, 1843, and was in customary form, authorizing him "to treat of and concerning the extradition of persons, fugitive from justice, charged with crimes in certain cases" (D.S., 3 Credences, 57).

THE NEGOTIATIONS

The proposal for an extradition convention between the two countries was made on behalf of the Government of France by the Minister Plenipotentiary *ad interim* at Washington, Alphonse Joseph Yves Pageot, in his note to Secretary of State Webster of April 21, 1843 (D.S., 12 Notes from the French Legation). In that note the French Minister referred to extradition conventions concluded by France with Switzerland in 1828, with Belgium in 1834, with Sardinia in 1838, and with Great Britain on February 13, 1843. The basis proposed for a convention with the United States was Article 10 of the Webster-Ashburton Treaty (Document 99). The proposal was at once accepted in principle by this Government (D.S., 6 Notes to the French Legation, 73–74, April 26, 1843). A few days later, on May 8, 1843, Daniel Webster retired from office.

There is very little of record regarding the negotiations, which were brought to a conclusion on behalf of the United States by Secretary of State Upshur. It is to be observed, however, that the enumeration of extraditable crimes mentioned in Article 2 of this convention differs both in inclusion and in omission from that of Article 10 of the Webster-Ashburton Treaty; and it appears that the crimes of robbery and burglary were not included in the convention because of the difficulty of translation of the French "vol" (D.S., 12 Notes from the French Legation, April 4, 1844). To remedy this defect an additional article was signed on behalf of the two Governments on April 15, 1844, but that article failed to go into force. Final agreement in the matter was reached by the additional article of February 24, 1845 (Document 112), the notes to which should be consulted.

EXTRADITION PROCEDURE

Extradition procedure under this convention was discussed shortly after it went into force. A note from the French Minister dated June 28, 1844, reads in part as follows (D.S., 12 Notes from the French Legation, translation):

The convention of November 9 having left to each Government the task of determining the forms in cases of extradition, I am charged, Sir, to request you to inform me of the provisions which the Federal Government will adopt in that regard. As to France, the Government of the King will require only that the request for extradition be made officially through the diplomatic channel and accompanied by an order of arrest or by some judicial act [the French is *jugement;* the following words in parentheses are in English in the original] (warrant, verdict, true bill, or indictment) stating clearly the nature of the acts with which the individual whose extradition is demanded is charged, as well as his nationality.

To that note Secretary of State Calhoun replied on July 10 (D.S., 6 Notes to the French Legation, 81–82) that he saw "no objection whatever to the course of proceeding proposed to be adopted on the part of the King's Government" and enclosed a copy of a communication from Attorney General Nelson of July 8, 1844, which reads in substance as follows (D.S., Miscellaneous Letters, July–August 1844; Opinions of Attorneys General, IV, 330–31):

The Treaty with France providing for the surrender of persons accused of the crimes therein enumerated, and fleeing within the jurisdictions of the United States and France respectively, prescribes as well the mode and manner, as the evidence upon which such surrender shall be made.

The mode and manner prescribed is:

"Requisitions made in the name of the respective parties through the medium of their respective Diplomatic Agents."

The evidence upon which its is to be done is:

"Only when the fact of the commission of the crime shall be so established, "as that the laws of the country in which the fugitive or the person so accused "shall be found, would justify his or her apprehension, and committment for "trial, if the crime had been there committed."

With reference to the mode and manner to be pursued, as preliminary to the surrender; there can be no difficulty. The Treaty is explicit on the subject, and the suggestion contained in Mr Pageot's note is accurately conformed to it.

In regard to the degree of evidence, which may be required to establish the fact of the commission of the crime, of which the person demanded may be accused, there is much difficulty. No rule more explicit or certain than that contained in the Treaty itself can indeed be prescribed. Cases as they occur, will necessarily depend upon the laws of the several States in which the fugitive may be arrested or found. That which may be sufficient to justify the apprehension and committement in one State, may not be regarded as sufficient in another. All that can be stipulated for therefore is, that in every case that may be presented to this Government, all proper and lawful means will be used to bring about the surrender demanded. In practice there will be found no difficulty, whilst an attempt to particularize might exclude the very means of redress most effectual to accomplish the object in the view of the contracting parties.

Upon principle, I do not think that a mere warrant for the arrest of an accused party, *without the evidence upon which it was granted,* would be sufficient to justify the imprisonment of a citizen.

A *Verdict* would—so also an Indictment and True Bill ought, I should think, to be regarded as *prima facie* evidence of guilt. But as I remarked before, this will depend on the law of the jurisdiction, in which the accused party may be found,—and must be referred to the judgment of the United States officer, whose aid may be invoked in execution of the Treaty.

The provisions of the Treaty with England on this subject are more full, though substantially the same with those in the Treaty with the King of the French. To shew the liberal principles upon which that Treaty has been carried into execution, I beg leave to refer to my opinion, in the case of Christina Cochrane [*ibid.*, 201–15], a printed copy of which is inclosed.

In view of the whole subject, I am of opinion, that whilst the mode of making the demand may be stipulated, and that suggested by Mr Pageot is unexception-

able,—it is impracticable to prescribe any rule of evidence, more definite, than that contained in the Treaty itself. Its provisions can be effectuated only by a *bona fide* effort in every case to arrest and surrender the guilty accused.

Statutory provisions regarding extradition (and interstate rendition) are now to be found in United States Code, title 18, chapter 20, sections 651–68; embodied therein are provisions of earlier enactments, such as the acts of August 12, 1848 (9 Statutes at Large, 302–3), and of June 22, 1860 (12 *ibid.*, 84), which were included in Revised Statutes, sections 5270–77.

104

VENEZUELA : FEBRUARY 26 AND 29
AND MARCH 1, 1844

Arrangement for the Settlement of the Case of the Brig "Morris". Note of the Chargé d'Affaires of the United States, Allen A. Hall, to the Secretary of State for Foreign Affairs of Venezuela, Francisco Aranda, dated February 26, 1844, in English. Note of the latter to the former, dated February 29, 1844, in Spanish. Note of the former to the latter, dated March 1, 1844, in English. Those three notes were written at Caracas.

As to ratification, see the editorial notes following the texts of the diplomatic exchanges. Not proclaimed.

[*The Chargé d'Affaires of the United States to the Secretary of State for Foreign Affairs of Venezuela*]

LEGATION OF THE UNITED STATES
Caracas, February 26, 1844

SIR   In pursuance of the verbal agreement concluded upon in our informal conversation on Saturday, I have now the honor to say to you, that I will agree to recommend to the favorable consideration of the Government of the United States, a proposition from the Government of Venezuela to pay eighteen thousand dollars, Spanish, as its proportion of the indemnity claimed in the case of the Brig Morris—said sum of eighteen thousand dollars to be paid by the Government of Venezuela so soon as official information of the assent of the Government of the United States to said arrangement shall be received in Caracas.

I have the honor to be, Sir, with great respect, Your obedient servant,

ALLEN A. HALL

Hon. F. ARANDA
    Secretary of State for Foreign Affairs.

523

*[The Secretary of State for Foreign Affairs of Venezuela to the
Chargé d'Affaires of the United States]*

[Translation]

REPUBLICA DE VENEZUELA
Caracas Febrero 29 de 1844

DEPARTAMENTO DE ⎫
RELACIONES EXTERIORES⎭

SEÑOR: De acuerdo con lo Convenido en nuestra conferencia de 24 del corriente y de lo que V.S. se ha servido expresar en su comunicacion de 26 del mismo mes, he recibido órden de S.E. el Presidente de la República para proponer, como arreglo definitivo de lo que se ha cobrado á Venezuela por indemnizacion á los dueños y cargadores del Bergantin Morris, la entrega de diez y ocho mil pesos fuertes en esta Capital tan luego como se reciba el anso oficial competente de haber sido admitida esta proposicion por el Gobierno de los Estados Unidos; bien entendido, que este arreglo tiene por objeto poner término á la negociacion de una manera amistosa, sin admitir aquellos principios en que no ha podido convenir el Gobierno de Venezuela, y que deberá someterse á la aprobacion del Congreso de la República sin la cual no puede tener efecto.

Aprovecho esta ocasion para reiterar á V.S. las seguridades de la distinguida consideracion con

REPUBLIC OF VENEZUELA,
Caracas, 29 February, 1844.

DEPARTMENT OF STATE ⎫
FOR FOREIGN AFFAIRS⎭

SIR: In conformity with the understanding come to at our last interview, of 24th instant, and with what you have been pleased to state in your communication of 26th of same month, I have been ordered by His Excellency the President of the Republic to propose, as a definitive settlement of the claim made on Venezuela for indemnity to the owners of brig *Morris* and cargo, the payment of eighteen thousand round dollars, in this city, as soon as official and competent information shall have been received of the acceptance of this proposal by the Government of the United States; it being well understood that this arrangement has for its object the termination of this business in a friendly manner, without admitting those principles with which the Government of Venezuela has not been able to coincide, and that this proposal must be submitted to the approbation of Congress, without which it cannot be carried into effect.

I improve this opportunity to reiterate to you, Sir, the assurances of the distinguished con-

que tengo la honra de ser de V.S. atento S.S.

FRANCISCO ARANDA.

sideration with which I have the honor to be your attentive servant.

FRANCISCO ARANDA.

ALLEN A. HALL, Esq.,
*Chargé d'Affaires of the
United States.*

[The Chargé d'Affaires of the United States to the Secretary of State for Foreign Affairs of Venezuela]

LEGATION OF THE UNITED STATES
Caracas, March 1st 1844

SIR   I have the honor to acknowledge the receipt of your note of yesterday, and to say, that the proposition therein contained is hereby accepted—subject to the approbation of my Government. With all proper respect for the opinions entertained by the Venezuelan Government, and the motives by which it has been actuated on this occasion, I entertain not a doubt, that, in strict justice, and upon universally received principles of International Law, a much larger sum than that now proposed to be paid might be claimed of Venezuela by the Government of the United States.   But I have pleasure in believing, that under the influence of those feelings of unfeigned good will, which, I trust, will be admitted to have uniformly characterized the conduct of the United States towards the people of Venezuela, my Government will accept, in a spirit of liberal and amicable compromise, the offer now made by the Venezuelan Government with a view to settle definitively the claim in the case of the Brig Morris.

I have the honor to be, Sir, with great respect, your obdt. servt.

ALLEN A. HALL

Hon. F. ARANDA
Secretary of State for Foreign Affairs.

NOTES

The agreement for this settlement was first reached orally on Saturday, February 24, 1844.   In his despatch of March 2, 1844, Allen A. Hall, Chargé d'Affaires of the United States at Caracas, recounted his discussions since the previous December of the case of the brig *Morris* with the Secretary of State for Foreign Affairs of Venezuela,

Francisco Aranda, and wrote of their conclusion as follows (D.S., 2 Despatches, Venezuela, No. 31):

Although I considered the negotiation broken off, there were in this explanatory and justificative statement some very singular misconceptions of fact as well as of law which I was unwilling to let pass without correction. I had accordingly prepared a notice of them, when, during a call at my house, Mr Aranda adverted to the case of the Morris and asked me whether the matter could not be amicably adjusted by the payment of a sum in gross, as Venezuela's proportion proportion of the indemnity, without reference to the principles involved in the case or to any particular items in the account. I replied I thought it might, and proposed $20,000—Spanish dollars. This he would not agree to, but after some hesitation on his part the sum of $18,000 was finally agreed upon:—the arrangement to be subject to your approval, and the money to be paid so soon as I am officially notified of it. Under this arrangement the proportions of the three States will be as follows:

Venezuela	$18.000
New Granada	31.500
Ecuador	13.500

Total amount of indemnity	$63.000,

which sum will cover,

1. Full value of Brig	6.000
2. Full freight on entire cargo	6.414
3. Invoice price of Owners' part of cargo	6.982
4. Do Do of Backus' do do	7.530
5. Passage money	500
	$27.426
6. Int. from date of capture, 19 yrs	31.265
	$58.691
7. Leaving for damages	4.309
	$63.000

The amount of damages is not so large as with propriety might have been insisted upon, but that, it appears to me, is more than counterbalanced by the immediate cash payment which Venezuela agrees to make of her entire proportion. It is surely better for the claimants to take the eighteen thousand dollars cash in hand offered now than to have the whole matter postponed another year.

Notes were then written to set forth the terms of the settlement reached; first that of February 26, 1844, from the Chargé d'Affaires of the United States to the Venezuelan Secretary of State for Foreign Affairs; then the answering note of February 29; and finally the note of Hall of March 1. Copies of those three notes (and a translation of the second) are enclosures to the despatch cited; and the texts printed above have been collated with those enclosures.

The "Morris"

The facts in the case of the brig *Morris* are summarized in the notes to the convention of November 5, 1844, with New Granada (Document 110), which was negotiated on behalf of the United States by William M. Blackford, Chargé d'Affaires at Bogotá.

The case of the *Morris* was mentioned in Article 3 of the convention with Colombia of November 25, 1829 (Document 67), but was then left open for future adjustment.

The liability of the former Republic of Colombia, in this as in other cases, devolved upon the three successor Republics in the proportions of 50 percent for New Granada, 28½ percent for Venezuela, and 21½ percent for Ecuador (Moore, Digest, V, 559–61; see also the notes to Document 67); the amount of the claim was a matter of negotiation in each case, as it had not been fixed.

The negotiations at Bogotá regarding the case of the *Morris* were being carried on at the same time as those at Caracas; early in March 1844 Hall received a letter from Blackford at Bogotá "in which he states, that he has virtually concluded a Convention with the Government of New Granada, in the case of the Morris, which he has no doubt will be carried into effect" (D.S., 2 Despatches, Venezuela, No. 32, March 8, 1844); the terms of the convention with New Granada as set forth in that despatch do not differ from those of the convention of November 5, 1844 (Document 110); and in the despatch cited Hall did not fail to point out that the settlement which he had reached with the Government of Venezuela was proportionately more favorable to the claimants than that reached by Blackford with the Government of New Granada.

The reason for the delay in signing the convention of November 5, 1844, with New Granada, for some eight months after it was "virtually concluded", is thus reported (D.S., 2 Despatches, Venezuela, No. 36, June 27, 1844):

Mr Blackford writes me, that the chancess of getting an appropriation by the late Congress of New Granada of their proportion of the Morris indemnity were so utterly hopeless, that, at the pressing instance of the Executive, he agreed to postpone the signing of the Convention until Congress should adjourn.

The adjustment of the claim in the case of the *Morris*, so far as it concerned the Republic of Ecuador, was made by the convention with Ecuador of February 9, 1850, to the notes to which reference is made.

RATIFICATION

The arrangement made by Hall with the Government of Venezuela for the settlement of the case of the *Morris* was at once approved by the Government of the United States. Secretary of State Calhoun wrote to Hall under date of April 25, 1844, as follows (D.S., 1 Instructions, Venezuela, 47–48):

Your despatches N°s 31 and 32 have been received. The information which they communicate in regard to the adjustment of the claim in the case of the brig Morris, is acceptable and I lose no time in acquainting you that the terms of that adjustment are approved by the President. They have also been approved by the agent of Mr H. H. Williams, who is understood to be the principal claimant in the case.

You will consequently inform the Venezuelan government that the government of the United States, actuated by a spirit of compromise and by a desire to bring this long pending subject to a close, and thereby to remove one of our few causes

of complaint against that government, is willing to receive the sum offered, as a full indemnification on the part of Venezuela.

When the money is paid, if, from the papers and vouchers in your possession you should be satisfied that Mr H. H. Williams is in fact the principal claimant, and that in the prosecution of the claim he has represented the other claimants, you may remit the amount as he may direct, being careful, however, to require such acknowledgements from him as will secure the department from any future accountability in the matter. If, on the contrary, you should doubt the propriety of paying the money at once to Mʳ Williams or to his order, you will remit the same to the United States either in good bills, payable to the order of the department, or in specie, to be deposited to its credit at the port where the vessel which brings the specie may arrive.

The Government of Venezuela was duly informed on June 10, 1844, of the approval of the settlement by this Government. However, the Congress of Venezuela, to which the arrangement had been submitted with a recommendation by the Executive for favorable and immediate attention, had adjourned (apparently on May 23, 1844) without making the appropriation requisite for carrying the adjustment into effect; and Hall protested at the delay (D.S., 2 Despatches, Venezuela, No. 36, June 27, 1844, and enclosures).

Within less than four months the affair was brought to a conclusion by payment of the agreed sum on behalf of Venezuela without legislative appropriation. The payment was reported by Hall in his despatch of October 10, 1844, from which the following is extracted (*ibid.*, No. 41):

I have pleasure in informing you that the Morris claim has been paid. The Executive could not direct it to be done in the absence of an appropriation by Congress. But the National Bank, after consultation with him, agreed to anticipate the action of Congress, and to advance the money to Mʳ Caduc, the authorized agent of Mʳ Williams. To such an arrangement I could see no objection, more particularly as Mʳ Caduc came out with full powers from Mʳ Williams to arrange the matter in any way he might deem expedient. It is virtually a payment by the Government, and while it relieves the Executive will be of great advantage to the owner of the claim.

Being perfectly satisfied that Mʳ Williams is "in fact the principal claimant, and that in the prosecution of the claim he has represented the other claimants," I have in conformity with the instructions contained in your despatch of the 25th of April, disposed of the amount as directed by him, first, however, taking from him such acknowledgments as will secure your Department from any further accountability in the matter.

Reference to the settlement was made in the presidential messages to Congress of December 3 and December 10, 1844 (Richardson, IV, 340, 353).

Treaty Series No. 53
8 Statutes at Large, 584–89

105

NEW GRANADA : MARCH 6, 1844

Postal Convention, signed at Bogotá March 6, 1844. Original in English and Spanish.
Submitted to the Senate May 13, 1844. (Message of May 7, 1844.)
Resolution of advice and consent June 12, 1844. Ratified by the United States June 28, 1844. Ratified by New Granada December 1, 1844. Ratifications exchanged at Bogotá December 20, 1844. Proclaimed February 22, 1845.

Postal Convention between the United States of North America and the Republic of New Granada.

The Republics of the United States of North America, and of New Granada, being desirous of drawing more closely the relations existing between the two countries and of faciliting the prompt and regular transportation of the correspondence of the United States across the Isthmus of Panamá, have agreed to conclude a Postal Convention—for which purpose, his Excellency the President of the United States named, as a Plenipotentiary, William M. Blackford, their Chargé d'Affaires at Bogotá, and his Excellency the President of New Granada, Joaquin Acosta, Colonel of Artillery and Secretary of State for Foreign Affairs—who have agreed upon the following articles.

Convencion Postal entre la Republica de la Nueva Granada y los Estados Unidos del Norte America.

Deseando las Republicas de la Nueva Granada y de los Estados Unidos del Norte America facilitar y estrechar mas las relaciones entre los dos pueblos, y la pronta y regular conduccion de las correspondencias de los Estados Unidos al travez del Istmo de Panamá han convenido en celebrar una Convencion de correos; para lo cual su Escelencia el Presidente de la Nueva Granada nombró como Plenipotenciario al Coronel de Artilleria Joaquin Acosta, Secretario de Estado del Despacho de Relaciones Esteriores, y su Exelencia el Presidente de los Estados Unidos al Señor Guillermo M. Blackford, su Encargado de Negocios en Bogotá: los que acordaron los articulos siguientes.

ARTICLE 1

The Packet vessels of war of the Republic of the United States will disembark at Chagres or Porto-bello, the sealed bag or packet, which may contain the letters and newspapers, destined to cross the Isthmus of Panamá, which said bag or packet shall be delivered to the postmaster, of one or the other of these places, by whom it shall be forwarded to Panamá, for the consideration of thirty dollars for each trip—provided the weight of the bag or packet should not exceed one hundred pounds, and in the proportion of twelve dollars more for each succeeding hundred pounds, which sum shall be paid though the excess should not amount to one hundred pounds.

ARTICLE 2.

With respect to the letters and newspapers the said vessels may have on board, which shall not be intended to cross the Isthmus, but to be delivered at any point on the Atlantic coast of New Granada, the practice, established conformably to the New Granadian rates of postage, shall be continued.

ARTICLE 3.

The Consul, or other Agent, of the United States at Panamá shall receive the bag, unopened, and, after delivering to the Post office all the correspondence, ex-

ARTICULO 1º

Los buques de guerra correos de la República de los Estados Unidos desembarcarán en Chagres ó en Porto-belo la balija ó paquete cerrado que contenga las correspondencias é impresos destinados á atravesar el Istmo de Panamá; la cual balija ó paquete será entregada al respectivo Administrador de correos y dirijida por el a Panamá, mediante la indemnizacion de treinta pesos fuertes por cada viaje, siempre que el peso de la balija ó paquete no exediere de cien libras, y en la proporcion de doce pesos fuertes mas por cada cien libras de exceso, que se pagaran aun cuando el exceso del peso no llegare a cien libras.

ARTICULO 2º

Respecto de la correspondencia é impresos que conduzcan los mencionados buques y que vengan destinados, no á atravezar el Istmo, sino a ser entregados en cualesquiera puntos de su litoral Atlantico, se continuará la practica establecida, conforme á la tarifa de correos de la Nueva Granada.

ARTICULO 3º

El Cónsul ú otro Ajente de los Estados Unidos en Panamá recibirá la balija cerrada y, a excepcion de sus propias cartas, entregará en la administracion de

cept letters to himself, directed to Panamá or other points of the Granadian Territory, (which correspondence shall be subjected to the usual rates of postage established in New Granada), he shall retain the remainder to be forwarded to its destination as soon as an opportunity occurs.

ARTICLE 4.

The Post Office at Panamá will charge itself likewise with forwarding the mail bag or packet, which it may receive from the Consul or other Agent of the United States, to the Post office of Chagres or Porto bello, at which place it shall be delivered to the Consul, or other Agent, of the United States, or, in their default, to the Commander of the vessel of war, calling for it, under the same conditions stipulated in the 1ᵗ Article.

ARTICLE 5.

The Consul, or other Agent, of the United States residing at Panamá, shall be the person whose duty it is to pay for the carriage of the bag, across the Istmus, as well when he receives it from the Post office at Panamá after it has crossed the Isthmus, as when he delivers it to the said Post Office to be sent to Chagres, or Porto Bello.

correos toda la correspondencia dirijida a Panamá ú otros puntos del territorio granadino (la cual pagará el porte de la tarifa de correos de la Nueva Granada), reservandose la restante para remitirla á su destino cuando haya oportunidad.

ARTICULO 4º

La administracion de correos de Panamá se encargará igualmente de enviar la balija ó paquete de correspondencia, que le entregue el Consul ú otro Agente de los Estados Unidos, para ser conducida á la Administracion de correos de Chagres, ó Porto-belo de donde se derijirá al Consul ú otro Ajente de los Estados Unidos, ó si no lo hubiere á los respectivos Comandantes de buques de guerra, que la demandaren, bajo las mismas condiciones estipulados en el Articulo 1º

ARTICULO 5º

El Cónsul ú otro Ajente de los Estados Unidos residente en Panamá, será la persona encargada de satisfacer el porte que haya devengado la balija, tanto al recibirla de la administracion de correos de Panamá despues de que haya atravezado el Istmo, como al entregarsela para ser conducida a Chagres, ó Porto-belo.

ARTICLE 6.

The said packet vessels which shall or may be established, will bring to the Ports of New Granada at which they may touch—and will also take from them to those of the United States—all official and private letters and newspapers, without any compensation whatever—Granadian vessels will be subject to the same conditions if, at any time, it may be thought advisable to contribute with them to the establishment of a line of packets between the ports of the United States and those of New Granada.

ARTICLE 7.

The packet vessels of war of the United States will also carry, free of charge, all the official or private letters and newspapers, which may be delivered to them, from one port of New Granada to another at which they may touch.

ARTICLE 8.

If the Government of the United States should think fit to employ steamers, as packets, between New Granada and the said United States—the coals which may be brought for the use of such vessels shall then enjoy, in the Granadian Ports, the same exemptions, as to introduction and deposite, which may have been granted in said ports to the

ARTICULO 6º

Los mencionados buques correos que se establezcan, ó en adelante se establecieren, traerán á aquellos puertos de la Nueva Granada en que tocaren, y llevarán de estos á los de los Estados Unidos toda la correspondencia asi oficial, como particular, y los impresos sin percibir porte alguno. A las mismas condiciones quedarán sujetos los buques granadinos, si alguna vez se juzgare oportuno contribuir con ellos al establecimiento de alguna linea de buques correos entre los puertos granadinos y los de los Estados Unidos.

ARTICULO 7º

Tambien llevaran gratuitamente los buques de guerra correos de los Estados Unidos toda la correspondencia oficial, ó particular, y los impresos que se les confiaren, de un puerto á otro de la Nueva Granada en que tocaren.

ARTICULO 8º

Si el Gobierno de los Estados Unidos tuviere por conveniente destinar al servicio de correos entre la Nueva Granada y dichos Estados algunos buques de vapor, los carbones que se traigan para el uso de tales buques, disfrutarán entonces en los puertos Granadinos las mismas excenciones, relativas a introduccion y deposito, que se hayan otorgado en

coals destined for the steamers of any other power.

ARTICLE 9.

The Republics of the United States and of New Granada, being desirous of avoiding all interpretacions, contrary to their intentions, declare, that any advantage, or advantages, that one or the other power may enjoy, from the foregoing stipulations, are and ought to be understood in virtue and as in compensation of the obligations they have just contracted in the present postal convention.

ARTICLE 10.

For the purpose of carrying into effect the provisions of the present Convention as soon as possible, the two high contracting parties have agreed, that said provisions shall begin to be enforced immediately after the Governor of the Province of Panamá has official knowledge that the present convention has been ratified by the Government of New Granada, and that the Consul, or other agent, of the United States shall have communicated to him that it has been also ratified by the Government of that Republic.

los mencionados puertos a los carbones destinados para el uso de los buques de vapor de cualquiera otra potencia.

ARTICULO 9º

La Republica de la Nueva Granada y la de los Estados Unidos deseando evitar toda interpretacion contraria á sus intenciones, declaran que cualquier ventaja ó ventajas que la una ó la otra potencia reporten de las estipulaciones anteriores, son y deben entenderse en virtud y como compensacion de las obligaciones que acaban de contraer en la presente convencion postal.

ARTICULO 10º

Con el objeto de que las estipulaciones de la presente convencion se lleven a efecto lo mas pronto que sea posible, las dos altas partes contratantes han convenido en que dichas estipulaciones principiarán a cumplirse inmediatamente que el Gobernador de la provincia de Panamá sepa oficialmente la ratificacion de la presente convencion por parte del Gobierno de la Nueva Granada, y que el Consul ú otro Agente de los Estados Unidos le haya comunicado igual ratificacion prestada por el Gobierno de la ultima Republica.

ARTICLE 11.	ARTICULO 11º
The present Convention shall remain in force and vigor for the term of eight years, to be counted from the day on which the exchange of the ratifications may be made—which shall take place in Bogotá as soon as possible— and shall continue in the same force and vigor for another term of four years more; and so on, always for another term of four years more, until one of the two Governments shall give the other six months notice of its wish that the same shall terminate.	La presente Convencion permanecerá en fuerza y vigor por el termino de ocho años contados desde el dia del canje de sus ratificaciones, que se verificará en Bogota lo mas pronto que sea posible, y continuará con la misma fuerza y vigor por otro termino de cuatro años mas, y asi sucsesivamente siempre por un termino de otros cuatro años mas, hasta que uno de los dos Gobiernos notifique al otro, con anticipacion de seis meses, su voluntad de que termine la convencion.
In faith whereof the Plenipotentiaries of the two Republics have signed and sealed the present Convention in Bogotá, on the sixth day of the month of March, in the year of our Lord one thousand eight hundred and forty four.	En fé de lo cual los plenipotenciarios de las dos Republicas han firmado y sellado la presente Convencion en Bogotá a los seis dias del mes de Marzo del año del Señor de mil ochocientos cuarenta y cuatro.
Wᵐ M BLACKFORD [Seal] JOAQUIN ACOSTA [Seal]	JOAQUIN ACOSTA [Seal] Wᵐ M BLACKFORD [Seal]

NOTES

The former (sometimes called "Great") Republic of Colombia included New Granada, Venezuela, and Ecuador, a union from which Venezuela withdrew in 1829 and Ecuador in 1830. There followed, in November 1831, the founding of the "State of New Granada", which, in May 1834, adopted as its official designation the title, "Republic of New Granada". In 1858 the title was changed to the "Granadan Confederation"; by a *Pacto de Unión* of 1861 the title was changed to the "United States of Colombia"; and in 1885 the present designation, the "Republic of Colombia", was adopted (Robertson, History of the Latin-American Nations, 359–84).

Some comments on the early relations between the United States and the Republic of Colombia are in the notes to Document 47, the Treaty of Peace, Amity, Navigation, and Commerce signed at Bogotá October 3, 1824.

THE FILE PAPERS

There are two signed originals of the convention in the file, each of which has the English text written in the left columns and the Spanish in the right; as the printed texts show, the *alternat* was duly observed.

The original with which the text here printed has been collated is that which is with the duplicate United States instrument of ratification of June 28, 1844, and the original proclamation of February 22, 1845; on that original is written, "With Mͬ Blackford's Nͦ 22"; that despatch, of March 8, 1844, is quoted below.

The two signed originals are not literally and exactly alike in either the English or Spanish text; a few of the differences between them are such trifles as capitalization, spelling, and punctuation style; mostly they are matters of commas inserted or omitted in the one original as compared with the other; none of them is of any consequence; the only differences in wording are in the English text of Articles 8 and 11; the words "think fit" and "day on which" in one original read, respectively, "think it fit" and "day in which" in the other.

The treaty file contains the usual papers, in customary form; these include the attested Senate resolution of June 12, 1844 (Executive Journal, VI, 321), and the certificate of the exchange of ratifications at Bogotá on December 20, 1844, one example in English and one in Spanish; the instrument of ratification on the part of New Granada of December 1, 1844, includes both texts of the convention, the Spanish in the left columns.

The presidential message of May 7, 1844, submitting the convention to the Senate (Executive Journal, VI, 275), was accompanied by copies of "a correspondence between the Department of State and the Chairman of the Committee on Commerce in the Senate, and between the same Department and Mr. Blackford, the chargé d'affaires of the United States at Bogotá, who concluded the convention on the part of this Government" (printed in Senate Confidential Document No. 13, 28th Congress, 1st session, Regular Confidential Documents, XX, 143–54); some of those papers are quoted below.

THE NEGOTIATIONS

By the act of March 3, 1843 (5 Statutes at Large, 630–45), there was appropriated (p. 643):

> For defraying the expenses attending the conveyance and forwarding, by land, and of the receipt and delivery, of mails, letters and despatches at and between Chagres and Panama, including the compensation to an agent of the United States at each of said places for the above purposes, one thousand dollars, to be expended under the direction of the Secretary of State.

Under date of March 14, 1843, the following instructions were sent to William M. Blackford, then Chargé d'Affaires at Bogotá (D.S., 15 Instructions, Colombia, 82–83):

> You will probably have noticed that Congress at its late session passed an appropriation to defray the expenses of transmitting letters from and for the United States between Chagres and Panama. It is presumed that the authorities of New Granada will not object to the establishment for that purpose, of

an occasional post between those places, under the direction of agents of this
government.   It would be proper, however, for you to converse with the Minister
for Foreign Affairs upon the subject and explain to him the purposes and views
of this government in regard to it.   We would of course be willing, that any
proper regulations having for their object the prevention of frauds upon the
revenue of New Granada by the persons engaged in the carriage of the mails
should be imposed by that Government.   Early intelligence of the result of your
interview with the Minister will be acceptable to the Department.

Without any further authority, and without any full power, Blackford negotiated and signed this convention and reported as follows
(D.S., 10 Despatches, Colombia, No. 22, March 8, 1844):

In my despatch Nº 12., I mentioned that the Granadian Government declined
entering upon any arrangement, with respect to the transportation, across the
Isthmus, of the mails carried to Chagres, by the American Packets, until the
result of a negotiation, then in progress in London, between its Chargé d'Affaires
and the British Ministry, should be known.   A short time since, in answer to
an enquiry touching the issue, or progress, of this negotiation, I was informed
by the Secretary of Foreign Relations, that it had entirely failed, in consequence
of the unreasonable demands of the British Government, and that he was now
ready and anxious to receive any overture, I might feel authorised to make on
the subject.
The despatch of the Department, of the 4ᵗʰ [14th] March last, being far from
explicit in its terms, I felt somewhat at a loss to know what answer to make to
this invitation.   Impressed with the importance of securing, upon equitable
terms, the agency of the Granadian Post in carrying our mails, and believing
that the present was a favorable moment, for the attainment of this object, I
determined, after mature reflection, though not specially instructed to do so, to
enter upon the negotiation.   I therefore presented a memorandum of an agreement on the subject.   It was considered fair and liberal and was acceded to
without any alteration, and upon its basis a Convention—which I have the honor
herewith to transmit—was framed, and signed on the 6ᵗʰ Inst.
The sum, stipulated to be paid for the transportation of each mail, is less
than that which it would cost to despatch it by a special messenger—and even
if it were not, the convenience and greater speed and safety of transmission by
the Post, would be more than equivalent to the additional expense.   In no country, is the mail considered so sacred as in this—nor, having respect to the physical
obstacles, is there any in which it is carried with more regularity.   Though
large sums, in specie, are constantly remitted, there has never occurred but one
instance of robbery of the mail, and that was perpetrated, by a Guerrilla Chief,
at the head of a military corps.
You will observe that the bag is not to be opened by the Granadian authorities,
but to be handed to the Consul, or other agent of the United States, and that
the agency of the Post is confined to its transportation from Chagres to Panama
and from Panama to Chagres.   The maximum weight stipulated is, perhaps,
sufficient to cover any amount of correspondence which may occur for some time.
Should it not, however, I have provided that the excess shall be charged at a
very moderate rate.
Aware that the establishment of a line of Packets, by the Government, was not
with a view to profit, and that the vessels to be employed would be ships of War,
I had no hesitation in agreeing that the Granadian mails should be carried from
one port of this country to another, or to the United States, free of charge.   This
liberality—whilst it will be attended with no inconvenience on our part—is
highly appreciated by this Government, inasmuch as a Postal Convention, just
concluded here by the Chargé d'Affaires of France, stipulates that the French
Packets are to receive half the rates of the Postage now established, for carrying
letters between the ports of the country—By the same Convention, it is provided
that a postage of one Real—or twelve and a half cents—is to be charged on each
single letter, contained in the French mail, carried across the Isthmus by the
Granadian Post.   I need not indicate to you, the greater liberality of the provisions of the Convention enclosed.

The President and Secretary of Foreign Relations have both manifested the most lively solicitude that the Packets should touch at Carthagena, before proceeding to Chagres, and I most respectfully, but earnestly renew the recommendation to that effect, which I took the liberty heretofore to make.

The very little additional time, which this enlargement of the plan will require—the advantages which a regular communication with the United States will afford to persons in trade, in the opportunities of a safe and direct transmission of letters and Specie—and the importance of counteracting the injurious influence, which the monthly communication afforded by the Steam Packets of England and France, cannot fail to exert upon our commerce with New Granada—are considerations, which, without a conscious dereliction of duty, I cannot omit, upon all proper occasions, to press upon the attention of the Department

I would respectfully suggest that the Packets should sail, at least once a month, and on a stated day, that the time of their arrival at Carthagena might be anticipated with some degree of certainty

In order to save time, I have stipulated, in case the Government at Washington approve of the Convention, that its provisions should go into effect so soon as that fact is communicated to the Governor of Panama, by the Consul of the United States for that Port. This arrangement will give efficacy to the Convention some months sooner, than if the approval were required to be first communicated to the authorities here.

I feel conscious that I have assumed some responsibility in thus concluding a Convention, in the absence of specific instructions upon the subject—But I am equally convinced that I have made an arrangement as favorable to the United States, as could be expected or desired. I have endeavored to carry out what I inferred to be the wishes and designs of the Government, in the best manner possible, and I hope my proceedings in the premises will receive your approbation—or, at least, that my motives will be properly appreciated.

I could have wished, that the arrangement had been of a less formal character—but, according to the views of the Secretary, it could be effected in no other way than by a Convention.

Ratification of the convention "by both Houses of the Granadian Congress" was reported under date of the following May 1 (*ibid.*, No. 24).

Blackford was informed of the approval of the Senate and of the ratification by President Tyler by the instruction of June 29, 1844, which enclosed the United States instrument of ratification and a full power for the exchange of ratifications (D.S., 15 Instructions, Colombia, 88–89; 3 Credences, 93, June 28, 1844).

Chagres and Porto Bello

The two ports on the north or Atlantic side of the Isthmus of Panama which are named in the convention are Chagres and Porto Bello (Portobelo), both now in the Province of Colón of the Republic of Panama. At the time of this convention Chagres, now a comparatively small town, was the most important port on the Atlantic side of the Isthmus. It lies at the mouth of the Chagres River, about eight miles west-southwest of Colón, which became the port of the region upon the completion of the Panama Railroad in 1855 and is situated at the Caribbean end of the Panama Canal. Chagres was discovered by Columbus in 1502 and was opened for traffic with Panamá, on the Pacific coast, by way of the Chagres River, in the sixteenth century.

Portobelo or Porto Bello, on the bay of the same name, which Columbus discovered in 1502, is twenty miles northeast of Colón; Portobelo dates from 1584 and was formerly an important commercial city; it is the terminus of an old paved road from Panamá.

A LATER STATUTE

The act of March 3, 1847 (9 Statutes at Large, 187–88), made provision for the transportation of the mail by steamships of not less than 1,500 tons and of not less than 1,000 horsepower, from "New York to New Orleans, twice a month and back, touching at Charleston, (if practicable,) Savannah and Havana; and from Havana to Chagres and back, twice a month"; for the service last named, the steamer might be of 600 tons; the vessels were to be commanded by officers of the Navy, with passed midshipmen as watch officers; and they were to carry agents of the Postmaster General in charge of the mails. The annual message of President Polk of December 7, 1847, remarked upon the construction of steamers under the statute cited (see Richardson, IV, 561).

POSTAL CONVENTIONS

Arrangements with foreign post offices were authorized by statute as early as 1792 (1 Statutes at Large, 239) and are made under statutory authority now (act of June 8, 1872, 17 Statutes at Large, 304, sec. 167; Revised Statutes, sec. 398; United States Code, title 5, ch. 6, sec. 372).

Postal conventions are not now and, except for five instances in the past, of which this convention is one, never have been submitted to the Senate as treaties. Postal conventions are approved and ratified by the President and pass under the Great Seal; their texts are printed in the Statutes at Large but they are not proclaimed; as documents they are in the custody of the Postmaster General and are not in the archives of the Department of State. The number of postal conventions printed in the Statutes at Large to volume 47 is about 280; they fill some 2,500 printed pages.

As mentioned, there are of record five postal conventions which have been submitted to the Senate and which, accordingly, are exceptions to the general practice stated, as follows: this convention with New Granada of March 6, 1844; the convention with Great Britain of December 15, 1848; the convention with Mexico of July 31, 1861, which was submitted to the Senate August 1, 1861 (Executive Journal, XI, 497), but which did not go into force; the convention with Mexico of December 11, 1861; and the convention with Costa Rica of June 9, 1862, which was submitted to the Senate July 12, 1862 (*ibid.*, XII, 398), but which did not go into force.

There are included in this edition those three postal conventions mentioned above which went into force pursuant to the customary treaty procedure of submission to the Senate, ratification on each part, exchange of ratifications, and proclamation, namely, this convention with New Granada of March 6, 1844, the convention with Great Britain of December 15, 1848, and the convention with Mexico of December 11, 1861.

Treaty Series No. 170
9 Statutes at Large, 818–20
18 *ibid.*, pt. 2, Public Treaties, 422–23

106

GRAND DUCHY OF HESSE : MARCH 26, 1844

Convention for the Mutual Abolition of the Droit d'Aubaine and Taxes on Emigration, signed at Berlin March 26, 1844. Original in French and English.
Submitted to the Senate May 13, 1844. (Message of May 11, 1844.) Resolution of advice and consent June 12, 1844. Ratified by the United States June 22, 1844. Ratified by Hesse October 8, 1844. Ratifications exchanged at Berlin October 16, 1844. Question of the exchange of ratifications submitted to the Senate December 23, 1844. Resolution of advice and consent to the exchange of ratifications January 13, 1845. Proclaimed May 8, 1845.

Convention pour l'abolition mutuelle du droit d'aubaine et des taxes sur l'émigration entre les Etats-Unis d'Amérique et le Grand Duché de Hesse.

Les Etats-Unis d'Amérique, d'une part, et Son Altesse Royale le Grand Duc de Hesse, de l'autre part, désirant également d'ecarter les restrictions qui existent actuellement dans leurs territoires sur l'acquisition et l'aliénation des biens par leurs citoyens et sujets respectifs, sont convenus dans ce but d'entrer en negotiation.

Pour atteindre ce but désirable le Président des Etats-Unis d'Amérique a muni de pleins pouvoirs le Sieur Henry Wheaton, leur Envoyé extraordinaire et ministre plenipotentiaire près la Cour de Sa Majesté le Roi de Prusse, et Son Altesse Royale le Grand Duc de Hesse a muni de

Convention for the mutual abolition of the droit d'aubaine and taxes on emigration between the United States of America and the Grand Duchy of Hesse.

The United States of America, on the one part, and His Royal Highness the Grand Duke of Hesse, on the other part, being equally desirous of removing the restrictions which exist in their territories upon the acquisition and transfer of property by their respective citizens and subjects have agreed to enter into negotiation for this purpose.

For the attainment of this desireable object, the President of the United States of America has conferred full powers on Henry Wheaton, their Envoy extraordinary and minister plenipotentiary at the Court of His Majesty the King of Prussia, and His Royal Highness the Grand Duke of

539

pleins pouvoirs Monsieur le Baron de Schaeffer-Bernstein, Son Chambellan, Colonel et Aide-de-Camp, et Son ministre Résident près Sa Majesté le Roi de Prusse, lesquels, après avoir échangés leurs pleins pouvoirs, trouvés en bonne et due forme, ont arrêtés les articles suivans:

Hesse upon Baron Schaeffer Bernstein, His Chamberlain, Colonel, Aide-de-Camp, and minister resident near His Majesty the King of Prussia, who, after having exchanged their said full powers, found in due and proper form, have agreed to the following articles:

ART. 1

Toute espèce de droit d'aubaine, droit de retraite et droit de détraction ou impôt d'emigration, est et demeurera aboli entre les deux Parties Contractantes, leurs Etats, citoyens et sujets respectifs.

ART. 1

Every kind of droit d'aubaine, droit de retraite, and droit de détraction, or tax on emigration, is, hereby, and shall remain abolished, between the two Contracting Parties, their States, citizens, and subjects, respectively.

ART 2

Si par la mort de quelque personne possédant des immeubles ou biens-fonds sur le territoire de l'une des Parties Contractantes, ces immeubles ou biens-fonds venaient à passer selon les lois du pays, à un citoyen ou sujet de l'autre Partie, celui-ci, si par sa qualité d'étranger il est inhabile à les posséder, obtiendra un délai de deux ans, qui, d'après les circonstances, pourra être convénablement prolongé, pour les vendre, et pour en retirer le produit sans obstacle, et exempte de tout droit de retenue, de la part du Gouvernement des Etats respectifs.

ART. 2

Where, on the death of any person, holding real property within the territories of one Party, such real property would, by the laws of the land, descend on a subject or citizen of the other, were he not disqualified by alienage, such citizen or subject shall be allowed a term of two years to sell the same, which term may be reasonably prolonged according to circumstances, and to withdraw the proceeds thereof, without molestation, and exempt from all duties of detraction on the part of the Government of the respective States.

Art. 3.

Les citoyens ou sujets de chacune des Parties Contractantes, auront dans les Etats de l'autre, la liberté de disposer de leurs biens mobiliers, soit par testament, donation ou autrement, et leurs heritiers étant citoyens ou sujets de l'autre Partie Contractante, succéderont à leur biens, soit en vertu d'un testament, ou ab intestato, et ils pourront en prendre possession, soit en personne, soit par d'autres agissant en leur place, et en disposeront à leur volonté, en ne payant d'autres droits que ceux auxquels les habitans du pays où se trouvent les dits biens sont assujettis en pareille occasion.

Art. 4.

En cas d'absence des heritiers, on prendra, provisoirement, des dits biens mobiliers ou immobiliers, les mêmes soins qu'on aurait pris en pareille occasion des biens des natifs du pays jusqu'à ce que le propriétaire légitime, ou la personne qui a le droit de les vendre, d'après l'article 2, ait agreé des arrangemens pour recueiller l'héritage ou en disposer.

Art. 5.

S'il s'élève des contestations entre différens pretendans ayant droit à la succession, elles seront décidées en dernier ressort, selon les lois et par les juges du pays, où la succession est vacante.

Art. 3

The citizens or subjects of each of the Contracting Parties shall have power to dispose of their personal property within the States of the other, by testament, donation, or otherwise; and their heirs, being citizens or subjects of the other Contracting Party, shall succeed to their said personal property, whether by testament or ab intestato, and may take possession thereof, either by themselves or by other acting for them, and dispose of the same at their pleasure, paying such duties only as the inhabitants of the country, where the said property lies, shall be liable to pay in like cases.

Art. 4

In case of the absence of the heirs, the same care shall be taken provisionally, of such real or personal property, as would be taken in a like case of property belonging to the natives of the country, until the lawful owner, or the person who has a right to sell the same, according to article 2, may take measures to receive or dispose of the inheritance.

Art. 5.

If any dispute should arise between different claimants to the same inheritance, they shall be decided, in the last resort, according to the laws, and by the judges of the country where the property is situated.

ART. 6.

Cette Convention sera ratifiée par le Président des Etats-Unis d'Amérique par et avec l'avis et le consentement de leur Sénat et par Son Altesse Royale le Grand Duc de Hesse, et les ratifications en seront échangés à Berlin dans l'espace de six mois, à dater de ce jour, ou plutôt, si faire se peut.

En foi de quoi les plenipotentiaires respectifs ont signés les articles ci-dessus, tant en Français qu'en Anglais et y ont apposé leurs sceaux, déclarant toutefois que la signature dans ces deux langues ne doit pas, par la suite, être citée comme exemple, ni en aucune manière, porter prejudice aux Parties Contractantes.

Fait par quadruplicata en la ville de Berlin, le vingt-Six du mois de Mars l'an de grace mille huit cent quarante quatre et la soixante huitième de l'Independance des Etats-Unis d'Amérique.

HENRY WHEATON
[Seal]

ART. 6

This Convention shall be ratified by the President of the United States of America, by and with the advice and consent of their Senate, and by His Royal Highness the Grand Duke of Hesse, and the ratifications shall be exchanged at Berlin within the term of six months from the date of the signature hereof, or sooner, if possible.

In faith of which the respective Plenipotentiaries have signed the above articles, both in French and English and have thereto affixed their seals declaring, nevertheless that the signing in both languages shall not, hereafter, be cited as a precedent, nor in any way, operate to the prejudice of the Contracting Parties.

Done in quadruplicata in the city of Berlin, on the twenty sixth day of March in the year of our Lord one Thousand Eight Hundred and Forty Four, and the Sixty eighth of the Independance of the United States of America.

B^{on} DE SCHAEFFER BERNSTEIN
[Seal]

NOTES

In the final clause of this convention it is said that it was "done in quadruplicata". There is but one signed original in the treaty file, in which the French text is written in the left columns; the United States of America is named first throughout in both texts, and the Plenipotentiary of the United States signed at the left.

In the testimonium clause of the convention, after mention of the fact of the signing in French and English, it is declared that "the signing in both languages shall not, hereafter, be cited as a precedent, nor in any way, operate to the prejudice of the Contracting Parties."

In slightly different wording this clause appears in the convention with France of September 30, 1800 (Document 25); but here the French language was not that of either of the parties; similar expressions are to be found in two other treaties of this period with German States, written in French as well as in English (Prussia, May 1, 1828, Document 62; Hanover, May 20, 1840, Document 92).

The usual papers are in the file. They include the attested Senate resolution of June 12, 1844 (Executive Journal, VI, 320), the duplicate United States instrument of ratification of June 22, 1844, and the original proclamation of May 8, 1845. There are two similar originals of the protocol of the exchange of ratifications at Berlin on October 16, 1844. That protocol is written in French and does not contain the customary specific statement of the comparison of texts. It is signed on the part of the United States by Theodore S. Fay, Chargé d'Affaires *ad interim* of the United States ("in the absence of Mr. H. Wheaton"), and on the part of the Grand Duchy of Hesse by Baron Schaeffer Bernstein.

The instrument of ratification by the Grand Duke of Hesse of October 8, 1844, is written in German and includes both texts of the convention, the French in the left columns. Throughout those texts the Grand Duke of Hesse is named first, and the copy of the signature of the American Plenipotentiary appears under the English text.

This convention and that with Württemberg of April 10, 1844 (Document 107), were both submitted to the Senate with the presidential message of May 11, 1844, accompanied by copies of certain correspondence, which was printed (Executive Journal, VI, 275–76); but the Senate print is not now available.

THE EXCHANGE OF RATIFICATIONS

Also in the file is the attested resolution of the Senate of January 13, 1845 (Executive Journal, VI, 379). The occasion of that resolution was the fact that the ratifications of the convention were not exchanged at Berlin "within the term of six months from the date of the signature" or by September 26, 1844. The exchange did not take place until the following October 16.

That delay resulted in the following presidential message to the Senate of December 23, 1844 (*ibid.*, 363):

The messenger who lately bore to Berlin the ratified copy of the Convention for the mutual abolition of the *droit d'aubaine* and taxes on emigration between the United States of America and the Grand Duchy of Hesse, has just returned to Washington, bearing with him the exchange copy [instrument of ratification] of said Convention. It appears that the exchange of ratifications did not take place until the 16th day of October, twenty days after the period fixed by the Convention itself for that purpose. This informality, which, it would seem, was occasioned by the absence from Berlin of the plenipotentiary from Hesse, and by the time necessarily required for the preparation of the document, has been waived by the representative of that Government.

This subject is now submitted for the consideration of the Senate.

Despite the clear language of that presidential message the Senate resolution of January 13, 1845, which follows, seems to have been drawn under a misapprehension of the facts (*ibid.*, 379):

Whereas the time limited by the sixth article of the convention for the mutual abolition of the *droit d'aubaine* and taxes on emigration between the United States of America and the Grand Duchy of Hesse has expired before an exchange of ratifications has taken place, as provided for by the said article, be it therefore

Resolved (two-thirds of the Senators present concurring), That the Senate advise and consent to the exchange of ratifications of the convention aforesaid at any time prior to the fourth day of July next, whenever the same shall be offered by the Grand Duchy of Hesse; and the said ratifications shall be deemed and taken to have been regularly exchanged, the limitation contained in said convention to the contrary notwithstanding.

Under the terms of that resolution it appears to be assumed that the exchange of ratifications had not taken place; but that exchange had in fact been effected on October 16, 1844, twenty days after the time allowed by the convention. The consent of both Governments was sufficient to waive the time limit. Strictly, the action of the Government of the United States was perhaps not complete and perfect without the advice and consent of the Senate thereto; and such advice and consent, in whatever language phrased, would relate back to the date of the exchange, as indeed the language used in the Senate resolution did, although on its face it contemplated a subsequent exchange of ratifications.

The proceedings thus taken Secretary of State Calhoun did not deem sufficient; he wrote on January 23, 1845, enclosing a copy of the Senate resolution of January 13 and instructing Henry Wheaton, Minister to Prussia, as follows (D.S., 14 Instructions, Prussia, 88–89):

You, will, therefore, on the receipt of these instructions, lose no time in taking proper steps to secure the formal sanction of the Government of Hesse to the act of the exchange of the ratifications of the Convention aforesaid, which took place on the 16th of October last;—which, when obtained, you will transmit hither, without delay, to enable the President to proclaim the Convention at an early period. The difficulty is one of mere form, and the mode of executing these instructions is left to your good judgment and experience in diplomatic matters. It is not even deemed necessary to give you any new power beyond the authority which this despatch conveys.

It is not doubted that the Plenipotentiary of Hesse was satisfied in his own mind that his Government would approve of what he had done; and it is not improbable that this may already have taken place, upon the communication by him, to his Government, of the facts of the case. If this conjecture prove to be well-founded, it is conceived that an official announcement of any such action would be sanction sufficient to satisfy the Senate, and enable the Executive to proclaim the Convention,—and to supersede the necessity of exchanging formal certificates. The mode of effecting the object in view, as I have already said, will be left entirely to your discretion.

Such abundant caution was perhaps unnecessary; it might reasonably have been decided to issue the proclamation at once on the ground that the Government of the Grand Duchy of Hesse had waived any question of the time limit by the ratification of October 8, 1844 (some days after the term of six months had expired), followed by exchange of ratifications.

However, the instructions were duly carried out by Wheaton; he formally communicated the Senate resolution to the Minister Resident at Berlin of the Grand Duke of Hesse, Baron Schaeffer Bernstein, and requested a formal approval of the act of exchange of ratifications by the Grand Ducal Government; this resulted in due course in a note from the Minister of the Grand Duchy under date of March 19, 1845, in which he wrote (translation):

His Royal Highness has ordered that I declare hereby in His name that He formally sanctions the act of the exchange of ratifications of the above-mentioned convention which took place at Berlin on October 16, 1844, adding the assurance that the Grand Ducal Government will consider itself completely bound by that treaty, which it will cause to be executed and observed with exactitude in its whole extent.

This procedure was duly communicated by Wheaton to the Secretary of State (D.S., 3 Despatches, Prussia, No. 261, March 26, 1845); and the proclamation issued on the following May 8.

The Full Powers

It appears that in this case the original full powers were exchanged; that given to the Plenipotentiary of the Grand Duke of Hesse is in the file and reads as follows (translation from the German):

Ludwig II, by the grace of God Grand Duke of Hesse and the Rhine, etc., etc., hereby proclaims and declares:

As We have most graciously designated and commissioned Our Minister Resident at the Royal Prussian Court, Chamberlain, Aide-de-Camp, and Colonel on the General Staff, Commander, First Class, of Our Order of Ludwig, etc., etc., Baron Friedrich Ferdinand Wilhelm Schaeffer von Bernstein, to conduct negotiations with the plenipotentiaries of the Government of the United States of America, in accordance with Our instructions, concerning a convention on liberty to emigrate without paying emigration tax, and formally to conclude and sign such a convention, subject to ratification by Us, We hereby give him full power, charge, and command to do so.

In faith whereof this authorization which has been drawn up has been signed by Us, and Our state seal has been affixed thereto.

Darmstadt, March 5, 1844.

[Seal]   Ludwig

Du Thil

Authorization for the Minister Resident of the Grand Duchy of Hesse at the Royal Prussian Court, Chamberlain, Aide-de-Camp, and Colonel on the General Staff, Baron Schaeffer von Bernstein, to negotiate and conclude a convention with the United States of America concerning liberty to emigrate without payment of emigration tax.

That full power and also one of the two examples of the protocol of exchange of ratifications of this convention were among the original documents transmitted to the Department of State by J. C. Bancroft Davis, Minister to Germany, with his despatch of September 13, 1875 (D.S., 9 Despatches, Germany, No. 171).

Under date of November 18, 1843, there were given to Henry Wheaton, Minister to Prussia, six identic full powers to treat with the respective Plenipotentiaries of the Kings of Saxony, Bavaria, and

Württemberg, the Elector of Hesse, and the Grand Dukes of Hesse and of Baden, the subject of which was (D.S., 3 Credences, 61):

> the removal of all obstructions to emigration from the one country to the other, or to the withdrawal from the one country, by the citizens or subjects of the other, of any property which may have been transferred to them by gift, contract, or will,—or which they may have inherited *ab intestato;* for affording increased security or accommodation, in regard to person or property—to the citizens or subjects of the one country trading, travelling, or residing in the other; and for securing to each party the right to have Consuls resident in the dominions of the other, and establishing the rights and privileges to which such Consuls shall be entitled.

THE NEGOTIATIONS

This is one of five very similar conventions negotiated with various German states at about the same time (1844–46) by Henry Wheaton, then Minister to Prussia, namely, this convention with the Grand Duchy of Hesse of March 26, 1844, and those with the Kingdom of Württemberg of April 10, 1844 (Document 107), with the Kingdom of Bavaria of January 21, 1845 (Document 111), with the Kingdom of Saxony of May 14, 1845 (Document 115), and with the Duchy of Nassau of May 27, 1846 (Document 120). (The convention signed on May 2, 1846, with Hesse-Cassel, did not go into force.) The five conventions have the same general purposes; in some cases their provisions differ slightly *inter se;* but most of the language is the same in all; however, this convention is in French and English, while the others are in English and German.

The effect of the provisions of these five conventions is substantially the same as that of Article 7 of the treaty with Hanover of May 20, 1840 (Document 92); but their form is quite different. Two distinct though not wholly unrelated subjects are dealt with. The first is the right of succession by the nationals of the one country, either in cases of testacy or intestacy, to property located within the jurisdiction of the other. In Article 1 of each of these five conventions, differing in that regard from Article 7 of the treaty with Hanover, specific mention is made of the *droit d'aubaine*, the *droit de détraction*, and the *droit de retraite*, which are mutually abolished.

The principle of the mutual abolition of the *droit d'aubaine* and similar levies was nothing novel. Various treaties of the United States, beginning with the Treaty of Amity and Commerce with France of February 6, 1778 (Document 1), and many European treaties, had embodied it. It is said that by 1789 France alone had concluded treaties with sixty-six states dealing with the *droit d'aubaine* (Weiss, Traité élémentaire de droit international privé, 332).

The *aubain* was a foreigner, not naturalized. The *droit d'aubaine*, in the sense in which the expression is here used, was the right by virtue of which the state became vested with all the real and personal property of such an alien, deceased, which was located in its territory, to the exclusion of all otherwise entitled thereto either by reason of intestacy or under a will of the decedent (see Wheaton, International Law, 8th ed., par. 82).

A less harsh rule than that of the *droit d'aubaine* was the *droit de détraction*. This was a levy of a certain percentage of the value of property of the deceased alien, or its proceeds, upon removal or exportation thereof from the state of its location (Surville and Arthuys, Cours élémentaire de droit international privé, 5th ed., 158).   An example of a convention abolishing the *droit d'aubaine* but containing provisions for the exercise of the *droit de détraction* is that between France and Hesse-Darmstadt of July 27, 1779 (Von Martens, Recueil des principaux traités, 1st ed., II, 29–33); and Calvo says that the *droit de détraction* was sometimes called the *droit de retraite, de sortie, de gabelle,* or *d'émigration* (Le droit international, 5th ed., II, 14, par. 526).

The abolition of all taxes on emigration went far enough to reach another and quite different class of cases; a tax on the possessions of emigrants leaving the one country for the other is a tax paid by the nationals of the country levying it, and not one affecting the property of aliens; and as between the German states and the United States the mutuality of abolition thereof was one of words only, because of the large emigration from Germany to America then going on.

The five conventions here considered treat exclusively of the subjects mentioned; and none of them contains any clause of termination or denunciation; in each respect they are unlike earlier treaties with German states (the Hanseatic Republics, Document 59, Article 7; Prussia, Document 62, Article 14; Hanover, Document 92, Article 7).

As early as March 14, 1836, Wheaton had been instructed to negotiate conventions with certain German states on these and other subjects (D.S., 14 Instructions, Prussia, 7–10; 2 Credences, 248–49, March 16, 1836); but those instructions were suspended soon afterward (D.S., 14 Instructions, Prussia, 10, June 14, 1836), following the action of the Senate in refusing consent to the treaty with Switzerland of March 6, 1835 (Executive Journal, IV, 559, June 11, 1836); but on July 15, 1840, the Senate accepted without question the convention with Hanover of May 20, 1840 (Document 92; see Article 7).

Referring to his earlier instructions and to the action of the Senate, Wheaton wrote in his despatch of June 14, 1843 (D.S., 3 Despatches, Prussia, No. 226):

In my Despatch, No. 143, dated the 31 March, 1840, I had the honor to report to the Department a proposition, on the part of the Saxon Government, for the mutual abolition of the *droit d'aubaine* & *droit de détraction* between the Kingdom of Saxony & the U. States.

I had long before been instructed to commence negotiations with several of the minor German States (& among others with Saxony, embracing this with some other matters) which I was subsequently directed to discontinue, in consequence of the Senate having refused to ratify a similar Convention, concluded by Mr. Livingston, in Paris, with the minister of the Swiss Confederation.   As the Senate has, since that time, ratified the Convention concluded by me with Hanover, the 7th article of which embraces such a stipulation as that now in question, it is to be presumed that the same objection no longer exists in the opinion of the Senate.

These odious prohibitions & taxes on the acquisition & transfer, by the citizens & subjects of one country of property situated in another, or on the sale of their property by the citizens & subjects of one country emigrating to another,

which originated in the barbarous ages of the feudal system, when man was chained to the soil on which he grew, have been almost universally abolished by compact, & the common consent of most civilized nations—almost every commercial Treaty, concluded by the United States with foreign Powers, contains a stipulation for that purpose.   It is a matter of very considerable importance with respect to our intercourse with Germany, & the vast emigration constantly going on from this country to the U. States.   In all the German States, where it is not otherwise provided by Treaty, a tax is levied on all property sold, & the proceeds of which are carried out of the country by Emigrants, which amounts, in most instances, to ten *per centum* on the capital thus transferred.   That amount would consequently be gained to the U. States by the proposed stipulations; & I cannot perceive that we should lose more than we should gain by the free disposition of property by testament or inheritance, on both sides; as, if there be many cases accurring of persons dying in the U. States, & leaving heirs in Germany, there are also probably as many cases of naturalized Germans, resident in the U. States, who are entitled to inherit the property of their relations deceased in Germany.

Should the same view of the matter be taken by the Department, I beg leave to suggest that the necessary instructions & full Powers may be sent to me, to conclude Conventions for this purpose with any persons duly authorized on the part of the following German sovereigns:—

> His Majesty the King of Saxony.
> His Majesty the King of Bavaria.
> His Majesty the King of Wurtemberg.
> His Royal Highness the Elector of Hesse.
> His Royal Highness, the Grand Duke of Hesse.

The request of Wheaton for full powers and instructions was granted (D.S., 14 Instructions, Prussia, 70–71, November 18, 1843); he was furnished with powers to treat with the Kings of Saxony, of Bavaria, and of Württemberg, the Elector of Hesse-Cassel, and the Grand Dukes of Hesse and of Baden; he was to take as his "general guide" the provisions of the treaties with Prussia, the Hanseatic Republics, and Hanover.

Nothing appears as to the details of the negotiations of this convention and of that with Württemberg, signed a few days later (April 10, 1844; Document 107); both were transmitted with the same despatch of the latter date (D.S., 3 Despatches, Prussia, No. 244).

THE GRAND DUCHY OF HESSE

At the time of this convention the Grand Duchy of Hesse (Hesse-Darmstadt, since 1866 known generally simply as Hesse) was a member of the Germanic Confederation (1815–66).   A summary account of that Confederation, with a list of the members thereof, is in the notes to Document 59, the convention with the Hanseatic Republics of December 20, 1827.   The Grand Duchy of Hesse was also party to the German Zollverein or Customs Union, as to which, also, see the notes to Document 59.

Following the war between Austria and Prussia of 1866, in which other German states took part (Hesse on the side of Austria), Hesse in 1867 entered the North German Confederation, but only for the territories of the Grand Duchy north of the Main; and in 1871 Hesse became one of the States of the German Empire.

Treaty Series No. 373
8 Statutes at Large, 588–91
18 *ibid.*, pt. 2, Public Treaties, 809–10

107

WÜRTTEMBERG : APRIL 10, 1844

Convention for the Mutual Abolition of the Droit d'Aubaine and Taxes on Emigration, signed at Berlin April 10, 1844. Original in English and German.
Submitted to the Senate May 13, 1844. (Message of May 11, 1844.) Resolution of advice and consent June 12, 1844. Ratified by the United States June 22, 1844. Ratified by Württemberg September 18, 1844. Ratifications exchanged at Berlin October 3, 1844. Proclaimed December 16, 1844.

Convention for the mutual abolition of the droit d'aubaine and taxes on emigration between the United States of America and His Majesty the King of Wurttemberg.

The United States of America and His Majesty the King of Wurttemberg having resolved, for the advantage of their respective citizens and subjects, to conclude a convention for the mutual abolition of the droit d'aubaine & taxes on emigration, have named for this purpose their respective Plenipotentiaries, namely the President of the United States of America has conferred full powers on Henry Wheaton their Envoy extraordinary and Minister plenipotentiary at the Royal Court of Prussia and His Majesty the King of Wurttemberg upon Baron de Maucler, His Captain of the Staff and chargé d'affaires at the said Court, who, after having

Vertrag über die gegenseitige Aufhebung von Heimfalls- (Fremdling-) Recht und Auswanderungs-Steuern zwischen den vereinigten Staaten von Nord-America und Seiner Majestät dem König von Württemberg.

Nachdem die vereinigten Staaten von Nord-Amerika und Seine Majestät der König von Württemberg beschlossen haben: zum Besten der beiderseitigen Staats-Angehörigen einen Vertrag über gegenseitige Aufhebung von Heimfalls- (Fremdling-) Recht und Auswanderungs-Steuern abzuschließen, so sind dazu von beiden Seiten Bevollmächtigte ernannt worden, nämlich von Seiten des Präsidenten der vereinigten Staaten von Nord-Amerika Herr Heinrich Wheaton, nordamerikanischer außerordentlicher Gesandter und bevollmächtigter Minister am Königlich Preußischen Hofe und von Seiten Seiner Majestät des Königs von Würt-

549

exchanged their said full powers, found in due and proper form, have agreed to & signed the following Articles:

temberg Freiherr von Maucler, Hauptmann im Generalstabe und Geschäftsträger Seiner Majestät am Königlich Preussischen Hofe, welche Bevollmächtigte nach vollzogener Auswechselung ihrer gegenseitig in richtiger und gehöriger Form befundenen Vollmachten nachstehende Artikel festgesetzt und unterzeichnet haben:

ART. 1. Every kind of droit d'aubaine, droit de retraite, and droit de détraction or tax on emigration, is, hereby, and shall remain abolished between the two contracting Parties, their States, citizens & subjects respectively.

ART. 1. Jede Art von Heimfalls- (Fremdling-) Recht, Nachsteuer und Abzugsrecht, oder Auswanderungs-Steuer ist und bleibt aufgehoben zwischen beiden abschliessenden Theilen, ihren beiderseitigen Staaten und Staats-Angehörigen.

ART. 2. Where, on the death of any person holding real property within the territories of one Party, such real property would, by the laws of the land, descend on a citizen or subject of the other were he not disqualified by alienage, such citizen or subject shall be allowed a term of two years to sell the same,—which term may be reasonably prolonged, according to circumstances,—and to withdraw the proceeds thereof, without molestation, & exempt from all duties of detraction.

ART. 2. Wenn durch den Tod irgend eines Besitzers von Immobilien oder Grund-Eigenthum, welche sich auf dem Gebiete des einen der abschließenden Theile befinden, diese Immobilien oder Grund-Eigenthum nach den Gesetzen des Landes auf einen Staats-Angehörigen des anderen Theils übergehen sollten, so wird diesem, wenn er durch seine Eigenschaft als Fremder zum Besitze derselben unfähig ist, ein Aufschub von zwei Jahren gewährt—welcher Termin nach Umständen in angemessener Weise verlängert werden kan̄—um dieselben zu verkaufen und um den Ertrag davon ohne Anstand und frei von jeder Abzugs-Steuer zu beziehen.

ART. 3. The citizens or subjects of each of the contracting Parties shall have power to dispose of their personal property within the States of the other, by testament, donation, or otherwise, and their heirs, legatees, and donees, being citizens or subjects of the other contracting Party, shall succed to their said personal property, and may take possession thereof, either by themselves, or by others acting for them,—and dispose of the same at their pleasure, paying such duties only as the inhabitants of the country where the said property lies, shall be liable to pay in like cases.

ART. 4. In case of the absence of the heirs, the same care shall be taken, provisionally, of such real or personal property, as would be taken in a like case of property belonging to the natives of the country until the lawful owner, or the person who has a right to sell the same according to Article 2., may take measures to receive or dispose of the inheritance.

ART. 3. Den Staats-Angehörigen eines jeden der abschließenden Theile soll in den Staaten des anderen die Freiheit zustehen: über ihre beweglichen Güter durch Testament, Schenkung, oder auf andere Weise zu verfügen und deren Erben ab intestato oder Rechts-Nachfolger durch Testament oder Schenkung sollen, wenn sie Staats-Angehörige des anderen der beiden abschließenden Theile sind, ihnen in dem Besitze ihrer beweglichen Güter folgen, auch— in Person sowohl als durch Andere, welche an ihrer Stelle handeln— davon Besitz ergreifen und nach Gutdünken damit schalten können, ohne andere Steuern zu bezahlen als solche, welchen die Einwohner des Landes, worin sich die genannten Güter befinden, bei gleichem Anlasse unterworfen sind.

ART. 4. Im Falle der Abwesenheit der Erben wird man hinsichtlich der erwähnten beweglichen oder unbeweglichen Güter provisorisch ganz dieselbe Sorgfalt anwenden, welche man bei gleichem Anlasse hinsichtlich der Güter der Eingeborenen angewendet hätte, bis der gesetzmäßige Eigenthümer, oder Derjenige, welcher nach Art. 2. das Recht hat: dieselben zu verkaufen, Anordnungen zu treffen für gut finden wird: um die Erbschaft anzutreten oder darüber zu verfügen.

ART. 5. If any dispute should arise between different claimants to the same inheritance, they shall be decided in the last resort, according to the laws, and by the judges of the country where the property is situated.

ART. 6. All the stipulations of the present convention shall be obligatory in respect to property already inherited or bequeathed, but not yet withdrawn from the country where the same is situated at the signature of this convention.

ART. 7. This convention is concluded subject to the ratification of the President of the United States of America,—by & with the advice and consent of their Senate, and of His Majesty the King of Wurttemberg, and the ratifications thereof shall be exchanged at Berlin, within the term of twelve months from the date of the signature hereof, or sooner if possible.

In witness whereof, the respective Plenipotentiaries have signed the above Articles, as well in

ART. 5. Wenn sich Streitigkeiten zwischen verschiedenen rechtlichen Anspruch auf die Erbschaft habenden Prätendenten erheben, so werden dieselben in letzter Instanz nach den Gesetzen und von den Richtern des Landes entschieden werden, in welchem das Object der Erbschaft sich befindet.

ART. 6. Sämmtliche in gegenwärtigem Vertrage enthaltencn Bestimmungen sollen auch in Ansehung solcher Vermögens Theile verbindliche Kraft haben, welche zur Zeit der Unterzeichnung des gegenwärtigen Vertrags bereits angefallen, jedoch noch nicht wirklich exportirt sind.

ART. 7. Gegenwärtiger Vertrag ist abgeschlossen worden, vorbehaltlich der Ratifikation des Präsidenten der vereinigten Staaten von Nord-Amerika—nach und mit dem Rathe und der Einwilligung des nordamerikanischen Senats und vorbehaltlich der Ratification Seiner Majestät des Königs von Württemberg und es soll die Auswechselung der Ratifications-Urkunden innerhalb zwölf Monaten vom Tage der Unterzeichnung des gegenwärtigen Vertrags an gerechnet, oder früher wenn es möglich ist, zu Berlin stattfinden.

In Urkund dessen haben die beiderseitigen Bevollmächtigten obenstehende Artikel sowohl in

English as in German, and have thereto affixed their seals.	englischer als deutscher Sprache unterzeichnet und ihre Siegel beigedrückt.
Done in triplicata in the city of Berlin on the tenth day of April, One Thousand Eight Hundred & forty four, in the sixty eighth year of the Independance of the United States of America, and the twenty-eighth of the Reign of His Majesty the King of Wurttemberg.	Ausgestellt in drei Exemplaren zu Berlin den zehnten April Ein Tausend Acht Hundert Vier und Vierzig, im acht und sechszigsten Jahre der Unabhängigkeit der vereinigten Staaten von Nord-Amerika, und im acht und zwanzigsten Jahre der Regierung Seiner Majestät des Königs von Württemberg.
[Seal] HENRY WHEATON	[Seal] FREIHERR VON MAUCLER.

NOTES

In the final clause of this convention it is said that it was "done in triplicata". There is but one signed original in the treaty file, in which the English text is written in the left columns; the United States of America is named first throughout in both texts, and the Plenipotentiary of the United States signed at the left.

The usual papers are in the file; they include the attested Senate resolution of June 12, 1844 (Executive Journal, VI, 319–20), the duplicate United States instrument of ratification of June 22, 1844, and the original proclamation of December 16, 1844. There are two similar originals of the protocol of the exchange of ratifications at Berlin on October 3, 1844. The protocol is written in French and does not contain the customary specific statement of the comparison of texts.

The instrument of ratification by the King of Württemberg of September 18, 1844, is written in German and includes both texts of the convention, the German in the left columns. Throughout those texts the King of Württemberg is named first, and the copy of the signature of the American Plenipotentiary appears under the English text.

This convention and that with Hesse of March 26, 1844 (Document 106), were both submitted to the Senate with the presidential message of May 11, 1844, accompanied by copies of certain correspondence, which was printed (Executive Journal, VI, 275–76); but the Senate print is not now available.

THE NEGOTIATIONS

As to the negotiations and content of this and the four other very similar conventions with various German states of about the same period (1844–46), the notes to Document 106, the convention with Hesse of March 26, 1844, should be consulted.

The provisions of Article 6 of this convention do not appear in that with Hesse of March 26, 1844 (Document 106), or in that with Bavaria of January 21, 1845 (Document 111).

THE FULL POWERS

It appears that in this case the original full powers were exchanged; that given to the Plenipotentiary of the King of Württemberg is in the file and reads as follows (translation from the French):

We, William, by the grace of God King of Württemberg, hereby make known:
The Government of the United States of North America having indicated its desire, through its Envoy Extraordinary and Minister Plenipotentiary near the Royal Court of Prussia, Mr. Henry Wheaton, to conclude a convention with the Crown of Württemberg for the reciprocal abolition of the right of *aubaine* and the right of *détraction*, and We being disposed to join him in such purpose, We have appointed Our Plenipotentiary, the Baron de Maucler, Our Captain of the General Staff and Chargé d'Affaires near the Royal Court of Prussia, and We have authorized him to enter into pourparlers with the Plenipotentiary appointed by the United States of North America on the subject indicated above and to conclude with him a treaty subject to Our ratification.
In faith whereof we have signed this full power and have caused to be apposed thereto Our royal seal.
Done at Stuttgart the 20th of March, 1844, in the twenty-eighth year of Our reign.

[Seal] WILHELM

The Minister of Foreign Affairs,
 COUNT DE BECOLDINGEN
By order of the King:
 The Secretary of State,
 GOES

That full power and also one of the two examples of the protocol of exchange of ratifications of this convention were among the original documents transmitted to the Department of State by J. C. Bancroft Davis, Minister to Germany, with his despatch of September 13, 1875 (D.S., 9 Despatches, Germany, No. 171).

As to the full power of the Plenipotentiary of the United States, see the notes to the convention of March 26, 1844, with Hesse (Document 106).

THE KINGDOM OF WÜRTTEMBERG

At the time of this convention the Kingdom of Württemberg was a member of the Germanic Confederation (1815–66). A summary account of that Confederation, with a list of the members thereof, is in the notes to Document 59, the convention with the Hanseatic Republics of December 20, 1827. The Kingdom of Württemberg was also party to the German Zollverein or Customs Union, as to which, also, see the notes to Document 59.

The Kingdom of Württemberg was not within the North German Confederation of 1867, which followed the war of 1866 between Austria and Prussia, participated in by various other German states on one side or the other, among which was Württemberg on the side of Austria; but the Kingdom of Württemberg became one of the States of the German Empire from 1871.

108

NEW GRANADA : APRIL 22, 1844

Convention for the Settlement of the Claim Arising Out of the Loss of Part of the Cargo of the Schooner "Henrietta", signed at Bogotá April 22, 1844. Original in Spanish.
Not subject to ratification by the United States. As to ratification by New Granada, see the notes. Not proclaimed.

[Translation]

Los infrascritos á saber: el Encargado de Negócios de los Estados Unidos Guillermo M. Blackford, y el Secretario de Relaciones Esteriores de la Nueva Granada Joaquin Acosta, hemos convenido en que la reclamacion á que ha dado motivo la pérdida de la parte perteneciente á un ciudadano de los mencionados Estados Unidos en el cargamento de la goleta granadina Henrieta, que tuvo lugar á consecuencia del aprezamiento de dicho buque verificado por la goleta de guerra tambien granadina "La Calamar" el 4 de Octubre de 1841; y cuya reclamacion se hallaba pendiente ante el Gobierno de la Nueva Granada, quede transijida de la manera que espresan los articulos siguientes:

The undersigned, to wit, William M. Blackford, Chargé d'Affaires of the United States, and Joaquin Acosta, Secretary for Foreign Relations of New Granada, have agreed that the claim which arose out of the loss of the part of the cargo belonging to a citizen of the United States, of the Granadan schooner *Henrietta*, which occurred in consequence of the capture of the said vessel by the Granadan schooner of war *Calamar* on the 4th of October, 1841, and which claim has been pending before the Government of New Granada, shall be settled as stipulated in the following articles.

ARTICULO 1º. El Gobierno de la Nueva Granada se obliga á pagar á la órden del Señor Encargado de Negócios de los Estados Unidos la suma de mil doscientos cuarenta y tres pesos ($1,243.) pertenecientes al ciudadano de

ARTICLE 1. The Government of New Granada stipulates to pay to the order of the Chargé d'Affaires of the United States the sum of twelve hundred and forty-three dollars ($1,243) due to John Hugg, a citizen of the said United States,

555

los mencionados Estados Unidos Juan Hugg por el valor de los efectos de su propiedad que conducia la goleta Henrieta cuando fué aprezada por la Calamar. Estos mil doscientos cuarenta y tres pesos ($1,243) proceden del valor siguiente: por treinta y tres fardos de algodon del peso de nueve mil doscientas veinte y cuatro libras, al precio de un real la libra, mil ciento cincuenta y tres pesos ($1,153); y por un bocoy con sesenta gallones de aceite de coco al precio de un peso y cuatro reales cada gallon, noventa pesos ($90). El pago se hará en plata corriente por quintas partes en cada uno de los cinco primeros meses del año económico que empezará el primero de Setiembre próximo venidero.

ARTICULO 2º. Igualmente se obliga el Gobierno de la Nueva Granada á satisfacer sobre dicha suma de mil doscientos cuarenta y tres pesos ($1,243) el interes correspondiente á razon de un seis por ciento anual, que correrá desde el dia en que fué aprezada la goleta Henrieta hasta aquel en que se efectúe el pago de cada partida respectivamente; siendo esta la indemnizacion que otorga por todos los daños y perjuicios que puedan haberse ocasionado al mencionado ciudadano de los Estados Unidos, que no conservará derecho alguno para intentar ninguna nueva reclamacion sobre este particular.

for the value of the goods belonging to him which were on board the schooner *Henrietta* when captured by the *Calamar*, this sum of twelve hundred and forty-three dollars ($1,243) being for indemnity as follows: for thirty-three bales of cotton, weighing nine thousand two hundred and twenty-four pounds, at one real (12½ cents) per pound, eleven hundred and fifty-three dollars ($1,153), and for one cask containing sixty gallons of cocoa oil, at one dollar and a half per gallon, ninety dollars ($90)—the payment to be made in current silver, by five instalments, one in each of the first five months of the fiscal year which will commence on the 1st of September next.

ARTICLE 2. The Government of New Granada also obliges itself to pay upon the said sum of twelve hundred and forty-three dollars ($1,243), accruing interest at the rate of 6 percent per annum, to be calculated from the day on which the schooner *Henrietta* was captured to that on which payment of each respective instalment is made— this being compensation granted for all losses and damages which may have been caused to the said citizen of the United States, who shall have no right to prefer any new claim in the premises.

ARTICULO 3º. Tanto el pago del capital como el de los intereses se verificará, en los términos espresados en los articulos anteriores, en la Tesoreria Jeneral de la República.

ARTICLE 3. The payment of the capital, as well as of the interest, shall take place according to the tenor of the foregoing articles at the General Treasury of the Republic.

ARTICULO 4º. El presente convenio será presentado por el Poder Ejecutivo de la Nueva Granada al Congreso nacional de la misma República en su presente reunion, á fin de que previa su aprobacion vote la cantidad necesaria para que tenga efecto.

ARTICLE 4. The present convention shall be presented by the Executive Power of New Granada to the National Congress of the said Republic during its present session, to the end that, having ratified the same, it may appropriate the sum necessary to carry it into effect.

En fé de lo dicho nosotros los infrascritos hemos firmado dos ejemplares de este convenio, ambos de un mismo tenor, en Bogotá á veinte y dos de Abril de mil ochocientos cuarenta y cuatro.

In faith of which we, the undersigned, have signed two copies of this convention, both of the same tenor, in Bogotá, on this twenty-second April, one thousand eight hundred and forty-four.

Wᵐ M. BLACKFORD
JOAQUIN ACOSTA

Wᵐ M. BLACKFORD
JOAQUIN ACOSTA

NOTES

The original of this convention, in Spanish, is in D.S., Colombian Claims, folder *Henrietta;* and it is with that original that the Spanish text above printed has been collated. The English translation of the convention above printed is from that with the despatch of William M. Blackford, Chargé d'Affaires to New Granada, of May 1, 1844 (D.S., 10 Despatches, Colombia, No. 24).

There is no mention of full powers either in the despatches or in the convention; but as to the authority of Blackford to negotiate regarding claims, see the notes to Document 101.

This convention was for the settlement of the claim of John Hugg, a citizen of the United States, for the loss of certain bales of cotton and a cask of oil; these formed part of the cargo of the Granadan schooner *Henrietta*, which, on October 4, 1841, during the civil war between two factions of New Granada, was captured by the constitutional squadron under the command of Commodore Forro (D.S., Colombian Claims, folder *Henrietta*).

Hugg's original claim was as follows:

9,224 pounds of cotton at 15 cents a pound_____ $1, 383. 60
1 cask containing 60 gallons of cocoanut oil at $1.50 a gallon_____ 90. 00

    Total_____ $1, 473. 60

Regarding the adjustment of the claim Blackford, in his despatch above cited, wrote as follows:

> The amount of indemnity obtained is nearly as much as the claimant demanded. The price—fifteen cents—at which he had valued the cotton, was objected to as exorbitant. Upon enquiry, I found it was extravagant, and proposed to reduce the price to twelve and a half cents per pound, which proposition was agreed to.

The amount stipulated in the convention, $1,243, was payable in current silver in five instalments, one in each of the first five months of the fiscal year commencing September 1, 1844, with interest at 6 percent from the date of the capture of the *Henrietta* until the respective dates of payment.

The Congress of New Granada appropriated the money due under the convention (D.S., 10 Despatches, Colombia, No. 25, June 14, 1844); and on November 1, 1844, Blackford wrote (*ibid.*, No. 27) that he had received "about two thirds of the sum" awarded to Hugg. There is no record in the despatches of the payment of the balance; however, Blackford left Bogotá on December 24, 1844, and his successor did not arrive there until December 1, 1845 (*ibid.*, No. 29, December 23, 1844; 11 *ibid.*, December 4, 1845); and it is likely that the balance was paid in the interval, perhaps directly to Hugg, whose residence was in Cartagena (10 *ibid.*, No. 27).

Notwithstanding this settlement, a claim in respect of the cargo of the *Henrietta* was presented to the Commission under the convention with Colombia of February 10, 1864; but it was adjudged not valid (Moore, International Arbitrations, II, 1418, case 21).

Treaty Series No. 45
8 Statutes at Large, 592–605
18 *ibid.*, pt. 2, Public Treaties, 116–28

109

CHINA : JULY 3, 1844

Treaty of Peace, Amity, and Commerce, with tariff of duties, signed at Wang Hiya (in the outskirts of Macao) July 3, 1844. Original in English and Chinese.
Submitted to the Senate December 10, 1844. Resolution of advice and consent January 16, 1845. Ratified by the United States January 17, 1845. Ratified by China August 15, 1844 (see the notes as to the Chinese ratification). Ratifications exchanged at Poon Tong (Pwan Tang), a village now within Canton, December 31, 1845. Proclaimed April 18, 1846.
The English text of the treaty, with the accompanying tariff, is first printed; then follows the Chinese text of the treaty, with the tariff; the Chinese texts of both the treaty and the tariff are reproduced in facsimile, page for page from original documents, but in left-to-right order of pagination; as to the collating of the texts of both the treaty and the tariff, see the notes.

The United States of America, and The Ta Tsing Empire, Desiring to establish firm, lasting, and sincere friendship between the two Nations, have resolved to fix, in a manner clear and positive, by means of a treaty or general convention of peace, amity, and commerce, the rules which shall in future be mutually observed in the intercourse of their respective countries:—For which most desirable object, the President of the United States has conferred full powers on their Commissioner Caleb Cushing, Envoy Extraordinary and Minister Plenipotentiary of the United States to China; and the August Sovereign of the Ta Tsing Empire on his Minister and Commissioner Extraordinary Tsiyeng, of the Imperial House, a vice Guardian of the Heir Apparent, Governor-general of the Two Kwang, and Superintendant General of the trade and foreign intercourse of the five ports.

And the said Commissioners, after having exchanged their said full powers, and duly considered the premises, have agreed to the following articles.

Article I.

There shall be a perfect, permanent, universal peace, and a sincere and cordial amity, between the United States of America on the one part, and the Ta Tsing Empire on the other part, and between their people respectively, without exception of persons or places.

559

Article II.

Citizens of the United States resorting to China for the purposes of commerce will pay the duties of import and export prescribed in the Tariff, which is fixed by and made a part of this Treaty. They shall, in no case, be subject to other or higher duties than are or shall be required of the people of any other nation whatever. Fees and charges of every sort are wholly abolished, and officers of the revenue, who may be guilty of exaction, shall be punished according to the laws of China. If the Chinese Government desire to modify, in any respect, the said Tariff, such modifications shall be made only in consultation with consuls or other functionaries thereto duly authorized in behalf of the United States, and with consent thereof. And if additional advantages or privileges, of whatever description, be conceded hereafter by China to any other nation, the United States, and the citizens thereof, shall be entitled thereupon, to a complete, equal, and impartial participation in the same.

Article III.

The citizens of the United States are permitted to frequent the five ports of Kwangchow, Amoy, Fuchow, Ningpo and Shanghai, and to reside with their families and trade there, and to proceed at pleasure with their vessels and merchandize to and from any foreign port and either of the said five ports, and from either of the said five ports to any other of them. But said vessels shall not unlawfully enter the other ports of China, nor carry on a clandestine and fraudulent trade along the coasts thereof. And any vessel belonging to a citizen of the United States, which violates this provision, shall, with her cargo, be subject to confiscation to the Chinese government.

Article IV.

For the superintendence and regulation of of the concerns of the citizens of the United States doing business at the said five ports, the government of the United States may appoint Consuls, or other officers, at the same, who shall be duly recognized as such by the officers of the Chinese government, and shall hold official intercourse and correspondence with the latter, either personal or in writing, as occasions may require, on terms of equality and reciprocal respect. If disrespectfully treated or aggrieved in any way by the local authorities, said officers on the one hand shall have the right to make representation of the same to the superior officers of the Chinese Government, who will see that full inquiry and strict justice be had in the

premises; and on the other hand, the said Consuls will carefully avoid all acts of unnecessary offence to, or collision with, the officers and people of China.

ARTICLE V.

At each of the said five ports, citizens of the United States lawfully engaged in commerce, shall be permitted to import from their own or any other ports into China, and sell there, and purchase therein, and export to their own or any other ports, all manner of merchandize, of which the importation or exportation is not prohibited by this Treaty, paying the duties which are prescribed by the Tariff hereinbefore established, and no other charges whatsoever.

ARTICLE VI.

Whenever any merchant-vessel belonging to the United States shall enter either of the said five ports for trade, her papers shall be lodged with the Consul, or person charged with affairs, who will report the same to the commissioner of customs; and tonnage duty shall be paid on said vessel at the rate of five mace per ton, if she be over one hundred and fifty tons burden; and one mace per ton if she be of the burden of one hundred and fifty tons or under, according to the amount of her tonnage as specified in the register; said payment to be in full of the former charges of measurement and other fees, which are wholly abolished. And if any vessel, which having anchored at one of the said ports, and there paid tonnage duty, shall have occasion to go to any others of the said ports to complete the disposal of her cargo, the Consul, or person charged with affairs, will report the same to the commissioner of customs, who, on the departure of the said vessel will note in the port-clearance that the tonnage duties have been paid, and report the same to the other custom-houses; in which case on entering another port the said vessel will only pay duty there on her cargo, but shall not be subject to the payment of tonnage duty a second time.

ARTICLE VII.

No Tonnage duty shall be required on boats belonging to citizens of the United States, employed in the conveyance of passengers, baggage, letters, and articles of provision, or others not subject to duty to or from any of the five ports. All cargo-boats, however, conveying merchandize subject to duty shall pay the regular tonnage duty of one mace per ton, provided they belong to citizens of the United States, but not if hired by them from subjects of China.

ARTICLE VIII.

Citizens of the United States for their vessels bound in shall be allowed to engage pilots, who will report said vessels at the passes and take them into port; and when the lawful duties have all been paid they may engage pilots to leave port. It shall also be lawful for them to hire at pleasure, servants, compradors, linguists, and writers, and passage or cargo boats, and to employ laborers, seamen, and persons for whatever necessary service for a reasonable compensation to be agreed on by the parties, or settled by application to the consular officer of their government, without interference on the part of the local officers of the Chinese government

ARTICLE IX.

Whenever merchant vessels belonging to the United States shall have entered port, the Superintendent of Customs, will, if he see fit, appoint custom-house officers to guard said vessels, who may live on board the ship or their own boats, at their convenience; but provision for the subsistence of said officers shall be made by the superintendent of customs, and they shall not be entitled to any allowance from the vessel or owner thereof; and they shall be subject to suitable punishment for any exaction practiced by them in violation of this regulation

ARTICLE X.

Whenever a merchant-vessel belonging to the United States shall cast anchor in either of said ports, the supercargo, master, or consignee, will, within forty-eight hours deposit the ship's papers in the hands of the consul, or person charged with the affairs of the United States; who will cause to be communicated to the superintendant of customs, a true report of the name and tonnage of such vessel, the names of her men, and of the cargo on board; which being done, the superintendent will give a permit for the discharge of her cargo.

And the master, supercargo, or consignee, if he proceed to discharge the cargo without such permit, shall incur a fine of five hundred dollars; and the goods so discharged without permit shall be subject to forfeiture to the Chinese government. But if the master of any vessel in port desire to discharge a part only of the cargo, it shall be lawful for him to do so, paying duties on such part only, and to proceed with the remainder to any other ports.

Or, if the master so desire, he may, within forty-eight hours after the arrival of the vessel, but not later, decide to depart without breaking bulk; in which case he will not be subject to pay tonnage or other du-

ties or charges, until on his arrival at another port he shall proceed to discharge cargo, when he will pay the duties on vessel and cargo according to law. And the tonnage-duties shall be held to be due after the expiration of said forty-eight hours.

ARTICLE XI.

The Superintendent of Customs, in order to the collection of the proper duties, will, on application made to him through the Consul, appoint suitable officers, who shall proceed, in the presence of the captain, supercargo, or consignee, to make a just and fair examination of all goods in the act of being discharged for importation, or laden for exportation, on board any merchant vessel of the United States. And if dispute occur in regard to the value of goods subject to an ad valorem duty, or in regard to the amount of tare, and the same cannot be satisfactorily arranged by the parties, the question may, within twenty-four hours, and not afterwards, be referred to the said Consul to adjust with the Superintendent of Customs.

ARTICLE XII.

Sets of standard balances, and also weights and measures, duly prepared, stamped, and sealed, according to the standard of the custom-house at Canton, shall be delivered by the Superintendents of customs to the consuls at each of the five ports, to secure uniformity, and prevent confusion in measures and weights of merchandize

ARTICLE XIII.

The tonnage duty on vessels belonging to citizens of the United States shall be paid on their being admitted to entry. Duties of import shall be paid on the discharge of the goods, and duties of export on the lading of the same. When all such duties shall have been paid, and not before, the Superintendant of Customs shall give a port-clearance, and the Consul shall return the ship's papers, so that she may depart on her voyage. The duties shall be paid to the shroffs authorized by the Chinese government to receive the same in its behalf. Duties payable by merchants of the United States shall be received, either in sycee silver or in foreign money, at the rate of exchange as ascertained by the regulations now in force. And imported goods, on their resale or transit in any part of the empire, shall be subject to the imposition of no other duty than they are accustomed to pay at the date of this Treaty

ARTICLE XIV.

No goods on board any merchant vessel of the United States in port are to be transhipped to another vessel, unless there be particular occasion therefor; in which case the occasion shall be certified by the Consul to the Superintendant of Customs, who may appoint officers to examine into the facts, and permit the transhipment. And if any goods be transhipped without such application, inquiry and permit, they shall be subject to be forfeited to the Chinese Government.

ARTICLE XV.

The former limitation of the trade of foreign nations to certain persons appointed at Canton by the government, and commonly called hong-merchants, having been abolished, citizens of the United States engaged in the purchase or sale of goods of import or export, are admitted to trade with any and all subjects of China without distinction; they shall not be subject to any new limitations, nor impeded in their business by monopolies or other injurious restrictions.

ARTICLE XVI.

The Chinese Government will not hold itself responsible for any debts which may happen to be due from subjects of China to citizens of the United States, or for frauds committed by them: but citizens of the United States may seek redress in law; and on suitable representation being made to the Chinese local authorities through the Consul, they will cause due examination in the premises, and take all proper steps to compel satisfaction. But in case the debtor be dead, or without property, or have absconded, the creditor cannot be indemnified according to the old system of the co-hong so called. And if citizens of the United States be indebted to subjects of China, the latter may seek redress in the same way through the Consul, but without any responsibility for the debt on the part of the United States.

ARTICLE XVII.

Citizens of the United States residing or sojourning at any of the ports open to foreign commerce, shall enjoy all proper accommodation in obtaining houses and places of business, or in hiring sites from the inhabitants on which to construct houses and places of business, and also hospitals, churches and cemeteries. The local authorities of the two Governments shall select in concert the sites for the foregoing objects, having due regard to the feelings of the people in the location thereof: and the parties interested will fix the rent by mutual agreement, the proprietors on the one hand not demanding any exorbitant

price, nor the merchants on the other unreasonably insisting on particular spots, but each conducting with justice and moderation. And any desecration of said cemeteries by subjects of China shall be severely punished according to law.

At the places of anchorage of the vessels of the United States, the citizens of the United States, merchants, seamen, or others sojourning there, may pass and repass in the immediate neighborhood; but they shall not at their pleasure make excursions into the country among the villages at large, nor shall they repair to public marts for the purpose of disposing of goods unlawfully and in fraud of the revenue.

And, in order to the preservation of the public peace, the local officers of government at each of the five ports, shall, in concert with the Consuls, define the limits beyond which it shall not be lawful for citizens of the United States to go.

Article XVIII.

It shall be lawful for the officers or citizens of the United States to employ scholars and people of any part of China without distinction of persons, to teach any of the languages of the Empire, and to assist in literary labors; and the persons so employed shall not, for that cause, be subject to any injury on the part either of the government or of individuals: and it shall in like manner be lawful for citizens of the United States to purchase all manner of books in China

Article XIX.

All citizens of the United States in China, peaceably attending to their affairs, being placed on a common footing of amity and goodwill with subjects of China, shall receive and enjoy, for themselves and everything appertaining to them, the special protection of the local authorities of Government, who shall defend them from all insult or injury of any sort on the part of the Chinese. If their dwellings or property be threatened or attacked by mobs, incendiaries, or other violent or lawless persons, the local officers, on requisition of the Consul, will immediately dispatch a military force to disperse the rioters, and will apprehend the guilty individuals, and punish them with the utmost rigor of the law.

Article XX.

Citizens of the United States who may have imported merchandize into any of the free ports of China, and paid the duty thereon, if they desire to re-export the same, in part or in whole, to any other of the said ports, shall be entitled to make application, through their Consul,

to the Superintendant of Customs, who, in order to prevent frauds on the revenue, shall cause examination to be made by suitable officers to see that the duties paid on such goods, as entered on the custom-house books, correspond with the representation made, and that the goods remain with their original marks unchanged, and shall then make a memorandum in the port-clearance, of the goods, and the amount of duties paid on the same, and deliver the same to the merchant; and shall also certify the facts to the officers of customs of the other ports. All which being done, on the arrival in port of the vessel in which the goods are laden, and everything being found on examination there to correspond, she shall be permitted to break bulk and land the said goods, without being subject to the payment of any additional duty thereon. But if, on such examination, the superintendent of customs shall detect any fraud on the revenue in the case, then the goods shall be subject to forfeiture and confiscation to the Chinese Government.

Article XXI.

Subjects of China who may be guilty of any criminal act towards citizens of the United States, shall be arrested and punished by the Chinese authorities according to the laws of China: and citizens of the United States,who may commit any crime in China, shall be subject to be tried and punished only by the Consul, or other public functionary of the United States, thereto authorized according to the laws of the United States. And in order to the prevention of all controversy and disaffection, justice shall be equitably and impartially administered on both sides.

Article XXII.

Relations of peace and amity between the United States and China being established by this Treaty, and the vessels of the United States being admitted to trade freely to and from the five ports of China open to foreign commerce, it is further agreed that in case at any time hereafter, China should be at war with any foreign nation whatever, and for that cause should exclude such nation from entering her ports, still the vessels of the United States shall not the less continue to pursue their commerce in freedom and security, and to transport goods to and from the ports of the belligerent parties, full respect being paid to the neutrality of the flag of the United States: Provided that the said flag shall not protect vessels engaged in the transportation of officers or soldiers in the enemy's service; nor shall said flag be fraudulently used to enable the enemy's ships with their cargoes to enter the ports of China; but all such vessels so offending shall be subject to forfeiture and confiscation to the Chinese Government.

ARTICLE XXIII.

The Consuls of the United States at each of the five ports open to foreign trade, shall make annually to the respective Governors-general thereof, a detailed report of the number of vessels belonging to the United States which have entered and left said ports during the year, and of the amount and value of goods imported or exported in said vessels, for transmission to and inspection of the Board of Revenue.

ARTICLE XXIV.

If citizens of the United States have special occasion to address any communication to the Chinese local officers of government, they shall submit the same to their consul, or other officer, to determine if the language be proper and respectful, and the matter just and right; in which event he shall transmit the same to the appropriate authorities for their consideration and action in the premises. In like manner, if subjects of China have special occasion to address the consul of the United States, they shall submit the communication to the local authorities of their own Government, to determine if the language be respectful and proper and the matter just and right; in which case the said authorities will transmit the same to the Consul or other officer for his consideration and action in the premises. And if controversies arise between citizens of the United States and subjects of China, which cannot be amicably settled otherwise, the same shall be examined and decided conformably to justice and equity by the public officers of the two nations acting in conjunction.

ARTICLE XXV.

All questions in regard to rights, whether of property or person, arising between citizens of the United States in China shall be subject to the jurisdiction, and regulated by the authorities of their own Government. And all controversies occurring in China between citizens of the United States and the subjects of any other government, shall be regulated by the treaties existing between the United States and such governments respectively, without interference on the part of China.

ARTICLE XXVI.

Merchant vessels of the United States lying in the waters of the five ports of China open to foreign commerce, will be under the jurisdiction of the officers of their own government, who, with the masters and owners thereof, will manage the same without control on the part of China. For injuries done to the citizens or the commerce of the

United States by any foreign power, the Chinese Government will not hold itself bound to make reparation. But if the merchant-vessels of the United States, while within the waters over which the Chinese government exercises jurisdiction, be plundered by robbers or pirates, then the Chinese local authorities, civil and military, on receiving information thereof, will arrest the said robbers or pirates, and punish them according to law, and will cause all the property which can be recovered, to be placed in the hands of the nearest consul, or other officer of the United States, to be by him restored to the true owner. But if, by reason of the extent of territory and numerous population of China, it should, in any case, happen that the robbers cannot be apprehended, or the property only in part recovered, then the law will take its course in regard to the local authorities, but the Chinese government will not make indemnity for the goods lost.

Article XXVII.

If any vessel of the United States shall be wrecked or stranded on the coast of China, and be subjected to plunder or other damage, the proper officers of government on receiving information of the fact, will immediately adopt measures for their relief and security; and the persons on board shall receive friendly treatment, and be enabled at once to repair to the most convenient of the free ports, and shall enjoy all facilities for obtaining supplies of provisions and water. And if a vessel shall be forced in whatever way to take refuge in any port other than one of the free ports, then in like manner the persons on board shall receive friendly treatment, and the means of safety and security.

Article XXVIII.

Citizens of the United States, their vessels and property, shall not be subject to any embargo; nor shall they be seized or forcibly detained for any pretense of the public service; but they shall be suffered to prosecute their commerce in quiet, and without molestation or embarrassment.

Article XXIX.

The local authorities of the Chinese Government will cause to be apprehended all mutineers or deserters from on board the vessels of the United States in China, and will deliver them up to the consuls or other officers for punishment. And if criminals, subjects of China, take refuge in the houses or on board the vessels of citizens of the United States, they shall not be harbored or concealed, but shall be delivered up to justice, on due requisition by the Chinese local officers addressed to those of the United States.

The merchants, seamen, and other citizens of the United States, shall be under the superintendance of the appropriate officers of their government. If individuals of either nation commit acts of violence and disorder, use arms to the injury of others, or create disturbances endangering life, the officers of the two governments will exert themselves to enforce order, and to maintain the public peace by doing impartial justice in the premises

ARTICLE XXX.

The superior authorities of the United States and of China, in corresponding together, shall do so in terms of equality, and in the form of mutual communication (*cháu hwui*). The Consuls, and the local officers civil and military, in corresponding together, shall likewise employ the style and form of mutual communication (*cháu hwui*). When inferior officers of the one government address superior officers of the other, they shall do so in the style and form of memorial (*shin chin*). Private individuals, in addressing superior officers, shall employ the style of petition (*pin ching*). In no case shall any terms or style be suffered which shall be offensive or disrespectful to either party. And it is agreed that no presents, under any pretext or form whatever, shall ever be demanded of the United States by China, or of China by the United States.

ARTICLE XXXI.

Communications from the government of the United States to the court of China shall be transmitted through the medium of the Imperial Commissioner charged with the superintendance of the concerns of foreign nations with China, or through the Governor-general of the Liang Kwang, that of Min and Cheh, or that of the Liang Kiang.

ARTICLE XXXII.

Whenever ships of war of the United States, in cruizing for the protection of the commerce of their country, shall arrive at any of the ports of China, the commanders of said ships and the superior local authorities of Government, shall hold intercourse together in terms of equality and courtesy, in token of the friendly relations of their respective nations. And the said ships of war shall enjoy all suitable facilities on the part of the Chinese Government in the purchase of provisions, procuring water, and making repairs if occasion require.

Article XXXIII.

Citizens of the United States, who shall attempt to trade clandestinely with such of the ports of China as are not open to foreign commerce, or who shall trade in opium or any other contraband article of merchandize, shall be subject to be dealt with by the Chinese Government, without being entitled to any countenance or protection from that of the United States; and the United States will take measures to prevent their flag from being abused by the subjects of other nations, as a cover for the violation of the laws of the Empire.

Article XXXIV.

When the present convention shall have been definitively concluded, it shall be obligatory on both Powers, and its provisions shall not be altered without grave cause; but, inasmuch as the circumstances of the several ports of China open to foreign commerce are different, experience may show that inconsiderable modifications are requisite in those parts which relate to commerce and navigation: in which case, the two Governments will, at the expiration of twelve years from the date of said convention, treat amicably concerning the same, by the means of suitable persons appointed to conduct such negotiation.

And when ratified, this Treaty shall be faithfully observed in all its parts by the United States and China, and by every citizen and subject of each. And no individual State of the United States can appoint or send a minister to China to call in question the provisions of the same.

The present Treaty of peace, amity, and commerce, shall be ratified and approved by the President of the United States, by and with the advice and consent of the Senate thereof, and by the August Sovereign of the Ta Tsing Empire, and the ratifications shall be exchanged, within eighteen months from the date of the signature thereof, or sooner if possible.

In Faith Whereof, We, the respective Plenipotentiaries of the United States of America, and of the Ta Tsing Empire, as aforesaid, have signed and sealed these Presents.

Done at Wang Shia, this third day of July, in the year of our Lord Jesus Christ, one thousand eight hundred and forty-four; and of Taoukwang, the twenty-fourth year, fifth month, and eighteenth day.

C. Cushing   [Seal]   [Signature and seal of Tsiyeng]

The Tariff of duties to be levied on imported and exported merchandise at the Five Ports.

The duties which it is agreed shall be paid upon goods, imported and exported by the United States, at the Custom houses of Canton, Amoy, Fuchow, Ningpo, and Shang-Hai, are as follows, the articles being arranged in Classes. viz.

EXPORTS

Class 1st   Alum, Oils &c

		Taels	Mace	Candareens
Alum i.e. white alum formerly white alum & blue stone	pr 100 catties	0	1	0
Anniseed oil, not formerly contained in the Tariff	do	5	0	0
Cassia oil do do do	do	5	0	0

Class 2nd   Tea, Spices &c.

		Taels	Mace	Candareens
Tea, formerly divided into fine & native black, and fine & native green	do	2	5	0
Anniseed star	do	0	5	0
Musk	Catty	0	5	0

Class. 3.   Drugs.

		Taels	Mace	Candareens
Capoor Cutchery	pr 100 catties	0	3	0
Camphor	do	1	5	0
Arsenic under different Chinese names	do	0	7	5
Cassia	do	0	7	5
Cassia buds, not formerly contained in the Tariff	do	1	0	0
China Root	do	0	2	0
Cubebs, not formerly in Tariff	do	1	5	0
Galingal	do	0	1	0
Hartall	do	0	5	0
Rhubarb	do	1	0	0
Turmeric	do	0	2	0

Class. 4.   Sundries.

		Taels	Mace	Candareens
Bangles, not formerly in Tariff	do	0	5	0
Bamboo screens & Bamboo ware	do	0	2	0
Corals, native or false corals not formerly in Tariff	do	0	5	0
Crackers & fire works formerly classed as rockets	do	0	7	5
Fans (feather fans &c) not formerly in the Tariff	do	1	0	0
Glass. Glassware of all kinds, formerly classed as native crystal ware	do	0	5	0
Glass beads or false pearls	pr 100 catties	0	5	0
Kittisols or Paper umbrellas	do	0	5	0
Marble, Marble slabs not formerly in Tariff	do	0	2	0
Rice paper pictures	do	0	1	0
Paper fans	do	0	5	0
Pearls (false) not formerly in Tariff	do	0	5	0

Class. 5.   Painters Stores. &c.

		Taels	Mace	Canda- reens
Brass leaf	pr 100 catties	1	5	0
Gamboge	do	2	0	0
Red lead	do	0	5	0
Glue, as Fish glue, Cowhide glue &c	do	0	5	0
Paper. Stationery	do	0	5	0
Tin foil	do	0	5	0
Vermillion	do	3	0	0
Paintings (large paintings) formerly divided into large & small paintings	Each	0	1	0
White lead	pr 100 Catties	0	2	5

Class 6.   Wares of various Kinds.

Bone & Horn ware	do	1	0	0
China ware, fine & coarse, formerly classed as fine, native coarse and middling	do	0	5	0
Copper ware & Pewter ware	per 100 Catties	0	5	0
Manufactures of wood, furniture &c	do	0	2	0
Ivory ware, All carved ivory work included, formerly divided into ivory and ivory carving	do	5	0	0
Lacquered ware	do	1	0	0
Mother of pearl ware	do	1	0	0
Rattan ware. Rattan & Bamboo work	do	0	2	0
Sandal wood ware	do	1	0	0
Gold & Silver ware, formerly divided into Gold ware & Silver ware	do	10	0	0
Tortoise shell ware	do	10	0	0
Leather trunks & Boxes	do	0	2	0

Class 7.   Canes &c.

Canes & walking sticks of all kinds	pr 1.000 pieces	0	5	0

Class 8.   Articles of clothing.

Wearing Apparel, whether of Cotton, Woolen, or Silk; formerly divided into Cotton clothing, Woolen do, Silk & Satin do & Velvet	pr 100 Catties	0	5	0
Boots and Shoes, whether of leather, Satin or otherwise	do	0	2	0

Class 9.   Fabrics of Hemp, Cotton &c

Grass cloth and all cloths of Hemp or linen	per 100 Catties	1	0	0
Nankeen & all cloths of cotton formerly not in the Tariff	do	1	0	0

Class 10.   Silk, Fabrics of silk &c

Raw silk of any Province	do	10	0	0
Coarse or refuse silk	do	2	5	0
Organzine of all kinds	do	10	0	0
Silk ribbon & thread	do	10	0	0
Silk & satin fabrics of all kinds; as Crape, Lutestrings &c &c. formerly classed as Silks & Satins	do	12	0	0
Silk & Cotton mixed fabrics	do	3	0	0

Heretofore a further charge per piece has been levied, the whole duty is now to be paid in one sum, & the further charge is abolished

Class 11.　Carpeting, Matting &c

		Taels	Mace	Canda- reens
Mats of all kinds, as of straw, Rattan, Bamboo &c _____ pr 100 Catties		0	2	0

Class 12.　Preserves &c.

		Taels	Mace	Candareens
Preserved ginger & fruits of all kinds _____ pr 100 Catties		0	5	0
Soy _____ do		0	4	0
Sugar, White & Brown _____ do		0	2	5
Sugar Candy, all kinds _____ do		0	3	5
Tobacco prepared & unprepared &c of all kinds_ do		0	2	0

Class 13.　Unenumerated Articles.

All articles which it has not been practicable to
enumerate herein specifically are to be charged
a duty of five per cent ad valorem.

Class 14.　Gold & Silver.

Coin & Gold & Silver.　Duty free.

Class 15.　Bricks, Tiles and Building Materials.

Duty free.

IMPORTS.

Class 1st　Wax, Saltpetre &c

		Taels	Mace	Candareens
Wax foreign, as Beeswax also called tile wax ____ pr 100 Catties		1	0	0
Oil of Rose Mallows _____ do		1	0	0
Saltpetre foreign _____ do		0	3	0
This article is only allowed to be sold to the Government merchants: formerly this regulation did not exist.				
Soaps foreign as perfumed soap _____ do		0	5	0

Class 2.　Spices & Perfumes.

		Taels	Mace	Candareens
Gum Benzoin & Oil of Benzoin _____ do		1	0	0
Sandal Wood _____ do		0	5	0
Pepper Black _____ do		0	4	0
All other articles of this class not specifically mentioned herein to pay a duty of 10 pr cent ad valorem.				
Perfumery, 5 pr ct ad valorem.				

Class 3.　Drugs.

		Taels	Mace	Candareens
Assafoetida _____ do		1	0	0
Camphor superior quality, that is, pure, formerly classed as good & inferior _____ pr Catty		1	0	0
Camphor, inferior quality, a refuse, formerly uncleaned Camphor _____ do		0	5	0
Cloves, Superior quality (Picked) _____ pr 100 Catties		1	5	0
Do　inferior　do　(Mother cloves) _____ do		0	5	0
Cow Bezoar _____ pr Catty		1	0	0
Cutch _____ pr 100 Catties		0	3	0
Gambier _____ do		0	1	5
Areca nut _____ do		0	1	5

		Taels	Mace	Canda-reens
Ginseng (foreign) superior quality &c	pr 100 Catties	38	0	0
Do inferior do &c	do	3	5	0
Of every hundred catties of foreign Ginseng of whatever sort, one fifth part is to be considered as of superior quality, & four fifths of inferior quality.				
Gum Olibanum	do	0	5	0
Myrrh	do	0	5	0
Mace or flower of nutmeg	do	1	0	0
Quicksilver	do	3	0	0
Nutmegs 1st quality	do	2	0	0
Do 2nd do, or coarse	do	1	0	0
Putchuk	do	0	7	5
Rhinoceros horns	do	3	0	0

Class 4. Sundries.

		Taels	Mace	Canda-reens
Flints	pr 100 Catties	0	0	5
Mother of pearl shells	do	0	2	0

Class. 5. Dried Meats &c.

		Taels	Mace	Canda-reens
Birds nests 1st quality Mandarin	do	5	0	0
Do 2nd do ordinary	do	2	5	0
Do 3d do with feathers	do	0	5	0
Bicho de Mar 1st do black	do	0	8	0
Do 2nd do white	do	0	2	0
Sharks fins 1st do white	do	1	0	0
Do 2nd do black	do	0	5	0
Stockfish called dried fish	do	0	4	0
Fish Maws not formerly in Tariff	do	1	5	0

Class 6. Painters Stores.

		Taels	Mace	Canda-reens
Cochineal	do	5	0	0
Smalts	do	4	0	0
Sapan Wood	do	0	1	0

Class 7. Woods, Canes &c.

		Taels	Mace	Canda-reens
Rattans	do	0	2	0
Ebony	do	0	1	5

All other imported woods, as red wood, Satin wood, yellow wood, not specifically enumerated, to pay a duty of 10 pr ct ad valorem.

Class 8. Clocks Watches &c.

Clocks,
Watches,
Telescopes
Glass panes, & crystal ware of all kinds,
Writing desks,
Dressing cases,
Jewelry of Gold & Silver,
Cutlery, Swords &c,
All the foregoing, & any other miscellaneous articles of the same description 5 pr ct ad valorem.

Class. 9. Gold & silver

Bullion & specie. Duty free

Class 10.   Cotton & Fabrics of Cotton &c.

		Taels	Mace	Canda-reens
Canvas, from 75 to 100 Chih long & 1 Chih 7 tsun to 2 Chih 2 tsun wide	pr piece	0	5	0
Cotton, allowing 5 pr ct for tare	pr 100 Catties	0	4	0
Long white cloth, 75 to 100 Chih long & 2 Chih 2 tsun to 2 Chih 6 tsun wide, formerly divided into superior, and inferior fine Cotton cloth	pr piece	0	1	5
Cambrics & Muslins, from 50 to 60 Chih long, & 2 Chih 9 tsun to 3 Chih 3 tsun wide	do	0	1	5
Cottons, grey & unbleached domestic &c, from 75 to 100 Chih long & 2 Chih to 2 Chih 9 tsun wide, formerly classed as coarse long cloths	do	0	1	0
Twilled cottons grey same dimensions	do	0	1	0
Chintz & Prints of all kinds from 60 to 75 chih long & from 1 chih 9 tsun to 2 chih 2 tsun wide, formerly called ornamented or flowered cloths	do	0	2	0
Cotton yarn & cotton thread	pr 100 Catties	1	0	0
Linen, fine, not formerly in the Tariff, from 50 to 75 chih long & 2 chih 1 tsun to 2 chih 7 tsun wide	pr piece	0	5	0
Bunting	pr chang	0	0	1½

All other imported articles of this class, as ginghams, pulicats, dyed cottons, velveteens, Silk & cotton mixtures, coarse linen, & mixtures of linen & cotton, &c &c. 5 pr ct ad valorem.

Class 11.   Fabrics of Silk, Woolen &c.

		Taels	Mace	Canda-reens
Handkerchiefs, large, above 2 chih 6 tsun	Each	0	0	1½
Do small under 2 chih 6 tsun	do	0	0	1
Gold & silver thread, superior or real	pr Catty	0	1	3
Do do inferior or imitation	do	0	0	3
Broad cloth, Spanish stripe &c from 3 chih 6 tsun to 4 chih 6 tsun wide	pr Chang	0	1	5
Narrow cloths, as Long ells, Cassimeres &c. formerly classed as narrow Woolens	do	0	0	7
Camlets. (Dutch)	do	0	1	5
Do	do	0	0	7
Imitation Camlets or bombazettes	do	0	0	3½
Woolen Yarn	pr 100 Catties	3	0	0
Blankets	Each	0	1	0

All other fabrics of wool or of mixed wool & cotton, wool & silk &c 5 pr ct ad valorem.

Class 12.   Wines &c.

		Taels	Mace	Canda-reens
Wine & Beer in qt bottles	pr 100	1	0	0
D do " p't do	do	0	5	0
Do do " cask	pr 100 Catties	0	5	0

Class 13.   Metals.

		Taels	Mace	Canda-reens
Copper foreign, in pigs &c	pr 100 Catties	1	0	0
Do wro't as Sheets, rods &c	do	1	5	0
Iron foreign, unmanufactured as in pigs	do	0	1	0
Do manufactured, as in bars, rods &c	do	0	1	5
Lead foreign, in pigs or manufactured	do	0	2	8
Steel foreign of every kind	do	0	4	0
Tin, foreign	do	1	0	0

		Taels	Mace	Canda-reens
Tin plates, formerly not in the Tariff_____	pr 100 Catties	0	4	0

Spelter, (included under lead), is only permitted
to be sold to Government merchants.

All unenumerated metals as Zinc, Yellow Copper
&c, 10 pr ct ad valorem.

Class 14.   Jewelry.

		Taels	Mace	Canda-reens
Cornelians_____	pr 100 stones	0	5	0
Cornelian beads_____	pr 100 Catties	10	0	0

Class 15.   Skin, Teeth, Horns &c.

		Taels	Mace	Canda-reens
Bullock & Buffalo's horns_____	pr 100 Catties	2	0	0
Cow & Ox hides tanned & untanned_____	do	0	5	0
Sea Otter Skins_____	Each	1	5	0
Fox Skins, large_____	do	0	1	5
Do small_____	do	0	0	7½
Tiger, Leopard & Martin Skins_____	do	0	1	5
Land Otter, Raccoon & Shark Skins_____	pr 100	2	0	0
Beaver Skins_____	do	5	0	0
Hare, Rabbit & Ermine Skins_____	do	0	5	0
Sea Horse teeth_____	pr 100 Catties	2	0	0
Elephants teeth 1st quality whole_____	do	4	0	0
Do 2nd do broken_____	do	2	0	0

Class 16.   Unenumerated

All new goods, which it has not been practicable
to enumerate herein, a duty of 5 pr ct ad valorem

Class 17.   Rice & other Grain.

duty free

CONTRABAND;   Opium.

SHIPPING DUES;

These have been hitherto charged on the measurement of the ships length & breadth at so much pr *chang;* but it is now agreed to alter this system, & charge according to the registered statement of the number of tons of the ships burden, On each ton (reckoned equal to the cubic contents of 122 tow) a shipping charge of 5 mace is to be levied; & all the old charges of measurement, entrance & port clearance fees, daily & monthly fees &c. are abolished.

C. CUSHING   [Seal]   [Signature and seal of TSIYENG]

茲中華

大清國亞美理駕洲

大合眾國欲堅定兩國誠實永遠友睦之條約及太平和好貿易

之章程以為兩國日後遵守成規是以

大清

大皇帝特派

欽差大臣太子少保兩廣總督部堂總理五口通商善後事宜辦理

外國事務宗室者

大合眾國

大伯理璽天德特派

欽差全權大臣駐中華顧聖　各將所奉便宜行事之

上諭及欽奉全權之

敕諭公同較閱照驗俱屬善當因將議明各條款臚列於左

　一嗣後

大清與

大合眾國及兩國民人無論在何地方均應互相友愛真誠和好

　共保萬萬年太平無事

　一合眾國來中國貿易之民人所納出口入口貨物之稅餉俱

照現定例冊不得多於各國一切規費全行草除如有海關

胥役需索中國照例治罪倘中國日後欲將稅例更變須與

合眾國領事等官議允如另有利益及於各國合眾國民人

應一體均沾用昭平允

一嗣後合眾國民人俱准其挈帶家眷赴廣州福州廈門寧波

上海共五港口居住貿易其五港口之船隻裝載貨物互相

往來俱聽其便但五港口外不得有一船駛入別港擅自遊

奕又不得與沿海奸民私相交易如有違犯此條禁令者應

按現定條例將船隻貨物俱歸中國入官

一合眾國民人既准赴五港口貿易應須各設領事等官管理

本國民人事宜中國地方官應加欵接遇有交涉事件或公

文往來或會晤面商務須兩得其平如地方官有欺藐該領

事各官等情准該領事等將委曲申訴中國大憲秉公查辦

但該領事等官亦不得率意任性致與中國官民動多牴牾

一合眾國民人在五港口貿易除中國例禁不准攜帶進口出

口之貨物外其餘各項貨物均准其由本國或別國販運進

口售賣並准其將中國貨物販運出口赴本國或別國售賣

均照現定條例納餉不得另有別項規費

一凡合眾國船隻赴五港口貿易者均由領事等官查驗船牌

報明海關按所載噸數輸納船鈔計所載貨物在一百五十

噸以上者每噸納鈔銀五錢不及一百五十噸者每噸納鈔

銀一錢所有以前文量及各項規費全行裁革或有船隻進

口已在本港海關納完鈔銀因貨未全銷復載往別口轉售

者領事等官報明海關於該船出口時將鈔已納完之處在

紅牌內註明並行文別口海關查照俟該船進別口時止納

貨稅不輸船鈔以免重徵

一凡合眾國民人在各港口以本國三板等船附搭客商運帶

行李書信及例不納稅之零星食物者其船隻均不須輸納

船鈔外若載有貨物即應按不及一百五十噸之數每噸納

銀一錢若雇用內地艇隻不在按噸納鈔之例

一凡合眾國民人貿易船隻進口准其自雇引水赴關隘處所

報明帶進俟稅鈔全完仍令引水隨時帶出其雇覓跟隨買

辦及延請通事書手雇用內地艇隻搬運貨物附載客商或

添雇工匠廝役水手人等均屬事所必需例所不禁應各聽

其便所有工價若干由該商民等自行定議或請各領事官

酌辦中國地方官勿庸經理

一合衆國貿易船隻到口一經引水帶進即由海關酌派妥役

隨船管押該役或搭坐商船或自雇艇隻隨同行走均聽其

便其所需食用由海關按日給銀不得需索商船絲毫規費

違者計贓科罪

一合衆國商船進口或船主或貨主或代辦商人限二日之內

將船牌貨單等件呈遞本國領事等官存貯該領事即將船

名人名及所載噸數貨色詳細開明照會海關方准領取牌

照開艙起貨倘有未領牌照之先擅行起貨者即罰洋銀五

百大圓並將擅行卸運之貨一概歸中國入官或有商船進

口止起一分貨物者按其所起一分之貨輸納稅餉未起之

貨均准其載往別口售賣倘有進口並未開艙即欲他往者

限二日之內即行出口不得停留亦不徵收稅餉船鈔均俟

到別口發售再行照例輸納 倘進口貨船已逾二日之限即須輸納船鈔 仍由海關填發紅牌知照別口以免重徵

一合眾國商船販貨進口出口均將起貨下貨日期呈報領事

等官由領事等官轉報海關屆期派委官役眼同該船主貨

主或代辦商人等秉公將貨物驗明以便按例徵稅若內有

估價定稅之貨或因議價高下不等除皮多寡不齊致有辦

論不能了結者限該商於即日內稟報領事官俾得通知海

關會商酌奪若稟報稽遲即不為准理

一合眾國各口領事官處應由中國海關發給丈尺秤碼各一

副以備丈量長短權衡輕重之用即照粵海關

部頒之式蓋戳鐫字五口一律以免參差滋弊

一合眾國商船進口後於領牌起貨時應即將船鈔交清其進

口貨物於起貨時完稅出口貨物於下貨時完稅統俟稅鈔

全完海關給發紅單由領事官驗明再行發還船牌准該商

船出口回國其完納稅銀由中國官設銀號代納或以紋銀

納餉或以洋銀折交均照現定章程辦理其進口貨物由中

國商人轉販內地者經過各關均照舊例納稅不得另有加
增

一合眾國商船停泊口內不准互相剝貨倘有必須剝過別船
者由該商呈報領事官報明海關委員查驗明確方准剝運
倘不稟明倏輒行剝運者即將其剝運之貨一併歸中國
入官

一各國通商舊例歸廣州官設洋行經理現經議定將洋行名
目裁撤所有合眾國民人販貨進口出口均准其自與中國
商民任便交易不加限制以杜包攬把持之弊

一中國商人遇有拖欠合眾國人債項或誆騙財物聽合眾國
　人自向討取不能官為保償若控告到官中國地方官接到
　領事官照會即應秉公查明催追還欠尚欠債之人實已身
　亡產絕誆騙之犯實已逃匿無踪合眾國人不得執洋行代
　賠之舊例呈請著賠若合眾國人有拖欠誆騙華商財物之
　事彷照此例辦理領事官亦不保償
一合眾國民人在五港口貿易或久居或暫住均准其租賃民
　房或租地自行建樓並設立醫館禮拜堂及殯葬之處必須
　由中國地方官會同領事等官體察民情擇定地基聽合眾

國人與內民公平議定租息內民不得擡價掯勒遠人勿許

強租硬占務須各出情願以昭公允倘墳墓或被中國民人

毀掘中國地方官嚴拿照例治罪其合眾國人泊船寄居處

所商民水手人等止准在近地行走不准遠赴內地鄉村任

意閒遊尤不得赴市鎮私行貿易應由五港口地方官各就

民情地勢與領事官議定界址不許踰越以期永久彼此相

安

一准合眾國官民延請中國各方士民人等教習各方語音並

帮辦文墨事件不論所延請者係何等樣人中國地方官民

等均不得稍有阻撓陷害等情并准其採買中國各項書籍

一嗣後合眾國民人在中國安分貿易與中國民人互相友愛
地方官自必時加保護令其身家全安並查禁匪徒不得欺
凌騷擾倘有內地不法匪徒逞兇放火焚燒洋樓掠奪財物
領事官速即報明地方官派撥兵役彈壓查拿併將焚搶匪
徒按例嚴辦

一合眾國民人運貨進口既經納清稅餉倘有欲將已卸之貨
運往別口售賣者稟明領事官轉報海關檢查貨稅底簿相
符委員驗明實係原包原貨並無拆動抽換情弊即將其貨

若干担已完稅若干之處填入牌照發該商收執一面行文
別口海關查照俟該船進口查驗符合即准開艙出售免其
重納稅餉若有影射夾帶情事經海關查出罰貨入官

一嗣後中國民人與合眾國民人有爭鬭詞訟交涉事件中國
民人由中國地方官捉拿審訊照中國例治罪合眾國民人
由領事等官捉拿審訊照本國例治罪但須兩得其平秉公
斷結不得各存偏護致啓爭端

一合眾國現與中國訂明和好五處港口聽其船隻往來貿易
倘日後另有別國與中國不和中國止應禁阻不和之國不

准來五口交易其合眾國人自往別國貿易或販運其國之

貨物前來五口中國應認明合眾國旗號便准入港惟合眾

國商船不得私帶別國一兵進口及聽受別國商人賄囑換

給旗號代為運貨入口貿易倘有犯此禁令聽中國查出拿

辦

一每屆中國年終分駐五港口各領事官應將合眾國一年出

入口船隻貨物數目及估定價值詳細開報各本省總督轉

咨

戶部以憑查驗

一合眾國民人因有要事向中國地方官辦訴先稟明領事等
官查明稟内字句明順事在情理者即為轉行地方官查辦
中國商民因有要事向領事等官辦訴先稟明地方官查明
稟内字句明順事在情理者即為轉行領事等官查辦倘遇
有中國人與合眾國人因事相爭不能以和平調處者即須
兩國官員查明公議察奪

一合眾國民人在中國各港口自因財產涉訟由本國領事等
官訊明辦理若合眾國民人在中國與別國貿易之人因事
爭論者應聽兩造查照各本國所立條約辦理中國官員均

不得過問

一 合眾國貿易船隻進中國五港口灣泊仍歸各領事等官督
同船主人等經管中國無從統轄倘遇有外洋別國凌害合
眾國貿易民人中國不能代為報復若合眾國商船在中國
所轄內洋被盜搶刦者中國地方文武官一經聞報即須嚴
拿強盜照例治罪起獲原贓無論多少均交近地領事等官
全付本人收回但中國地廣人稠萬一正盜不能緝獲或有
盜無贓及起贓不全中國地方官例有處分不能賠還贓物

一 合眾國貿易船隻若在中國洋面遭風觸礁擱淺遇盜致有

損壞沿海地方官查知即應設法拯救酌加撫卹俾得駛至

本港口修整一切採買米糧汲取淡水均不得稍為禁阻如

該商船在外洋損壞漂至中國沿海地方者經官查明亦應

一體撫卹妥為辦理

一合眾國民人貿易船隻財物在中國五港口者地方官均不

得強取威脅如封船公用等事應聽其安生貿易免致苦累

一合眾國民人間有在船上不安本分離船逃走至內地避匿

者中國地方官即派役拿送領事等官治罪若有中國犯法

民人逃至合眾國人寓館及商船潛匿者中國地方官查出

即行文領事等官捉拿送回均不得稍有庇匿至合眾國商

民水手人等均歸領事等官隨時稽查約束倘兩國人有倚

強滋事輕用火器傷人致釀鬥殺重案兩國官員均應執法

嚴辦不得稍有偏狗致令眾心不服

一嗣後中國大臣與合眾國大臣公文往來應照平行之禮用

照會字樣領事等官與中國地方官公文往來亦用照會字

樣申報大憲用申陳字樣若平民稟報官憲仍用稟呈字樣

均不得欺藐不恭有傷公誼至兩國均不得互相徵索禮物

一合眾國日後若有國書遞達中國

朝廷者應由中國辦理外國事務之

欽差大臣或兩廣閩浙兩江總督等大臣將原書代

奏

一嗣後合眾國如有兵船巡查貿易至中國各港口者其兵船
之水師提督及水師大員與中國該處港口之文武大憲均
以平行之禮相待以示和好之誼該船如有採買食物汲取
淡水等項中國均不得禁阻如或兵船損壞亦准修補

一合眾國民人凡有擅自向別處不開關之港口私行貿易及
走私漏稅或攜帶鴉片及別項違禁貨物至中國者聽中國

地方官自行辦理治罪合眾國官民均不得稍有袒護若別

國船隻冒合眾國旗號做不法貿易者合眾國自應設法禁

止

一和約一經議定兩國各宜遵守不得輕有更改至各口情形

不一所有貿易及海面各款恐不無稍有變通之處應俟十

二年後兩國派員公平酌辦又和約既經

批准後兩國官民人等均應恪遵至合眾國中各國均不得遣員到

來另有異議

以上關涉太平和好貿易海面各款條約應俟各大臣奏明

大清

大皇帝批准

大合衆國

大伯理璽天德既得各國選舉國會長公會大臣議定允肯批准限

以十八個月即將兩國

君上批准之條約互換若能早互換尤為善美茲將現定條約先由

大清國

欽差大臣太子少保兩廣總督部堂總理五口通商善後事宜辦理

外國事務宗室者

大合眾國

欽差全權大臣駐中華顧聖　鈐蓋關防印信書名畫押以昭信摅

須至和約者

道光

五月十八日即

七月初三　日在望廈鈐蓋關防

我主耶穌基理師督降生後紀年之一千八百四十四年

[Seal]

C. CUSHING

今將廣州福州厦門寧波上海各關合眾國出進口貨

物議定應完稅則分類開列於後

計開

出口油蠟礬礦類

礬石 即白礬 原例作青白礬   每百觔   壹錢

八角油 原例並未賅載   每百觔   伍兩

桂皮油 原例並未賅載   每百觔   伍兩

出口香料椒茶類

茶葉 原例分細細土夷茶松茶兩款   每百觔   貳兩伍錢

八角	麝香	出口藥材類	三籟	樟腦	信石 即砒石 一名人言 又名砒礵	桂皮	桂子 原例並未賅載	冷飯頭 即土茯苓
每百觔 伍錢	每觔 伍錢		每百觔 叁錢	每百觔 壹兩伍錢	每百觔 柒錢伍分	每百觔 柒錢伍分	每百觔 壹兩	每百觔 貳錢

土珊瑚 即假珊瑚 原例並未賅載	竹簾 各樣竹器同例	手釦 即燒料釦 原例並未賅載	出口雜貨類	黃薑	大黃	石黃	良薑	澄茄 即華澄茄 原例並未賅載
每百觔 伍錢	每百觔 貳錢	每百觔 伍錢		每百觔 貳錢	每百觔 壹兩	每百觔 伍錢	每百觔 壹錢	每百觔 壹兩伍錢

花竹響爆等類	原例作爆竹	每百觔	伍錢　柒分
毛扇	即鸞毛等扇　原例並未賍載	每百觔	壹兩
玻璃片玻璃鏡燒料等物	原例作土琉璃	每百觔	伍錢
土珠	即草珠	每百觔	伍錢
雨遮	即紙雨傘	每百觔	伍錢
雲石	即花石片　原例並未賍載	每百觔	貳錢
蓮紙花	原例作紙蓮花	每百張	壹錢
紙扇		每百觔	伍錢
假珠	原例並未賍載	每百觔	伍錢

出口顏料膠漆紙劄類	銅箔	藤黃	紅丹	土膠	紙類	錫箔	砥磲	畫工
			原例作黃丹	即魚膠牛皮膠各等同例	各色同例 原例作各色紙			大油漆畫 原例分大油畫兩款
	每百觔 壹兩伍錢	每百觔 貳兩	每百觔 伍錢	每百觔 伍錢	每百觔 伍錢	每百觔 伍錢	每百觔 叁兩	每件 壹錢

海珠壳器 即雲母壳器 原例並未賬載	漆器 各等同例	牙器 各樣素雕象牙物件同例 原例分作雕花牙器牙器兩款	雜木器 即家内所用物器	銅器錫器 各等一例	磁器 粗細各樣同例 原例分作粗細中土磁器四款	骨器角器 各樣同例	出口器皿箱盒類	鉛粉	
每百觔 壹兩	每百觔 壹兩	每百觔 伍兩	每百觔 貳錢	每百觔 伍錢	每百觔 伍錢	每百觔 壹兩		每百觔 貳錢 伍分	

籐籃籐席及籐竹諸貨　原例作籐竹絲器　每百觔　貳錢

檀香木器　各樣同例　原例作檀香器　每百觔　壹兩

金銀器各樣　原例分作累絲金器銀器兩款　每百觔　拾兩

玳瑁器　每百觔　拾兩

皮箱皮槓等物　原例作皮箱　每百觔　貳錢

出口竹木籐椰類　原例作籐鞭桿

竹竿鞭竿　各等同例　每千條　伍錢

出口衣帽靴雜類

衣服　布衣絨衣絲衣各等同入一例　原例分作綢布衫衣各色呢羅呢衫衣各色前絨衫衣四款　每百觔　伍錢

絲帶及絲線各樣	湖絲經及各等絲經	天蠶絲 即區粗絲	湖絲土絲各等同例	出口紬緞絲絨類	紫花布 棉屬諸布同例 原例並未賅載	夏布 蘇屬諸類布疋同例	出口布疋花幔類	靴鞾 皮緞各樣同例
每百觔	每百觔	每百觔	每百觔		每百觔	每百觔		每百觔
拾兩	拾兩	貳兩伍錢	拾兩		壹兩	壹兩		貳錢

絹縐紗綾剪絨及各等紬緞 原例作各色紬緞　　每百觔　拾貳兩

絲棉雜貨 如棉紬及絲毛各樣　　每百觔　叁兩

向來各種紬緞論疋另行加稅今統歸一例徵收

不再另加

出口氈羢毯席類

席 如草席籐席竹席各等同例　　每百觔　貳錢

出口糖菓食物類

糖薑及各樣糖菓 原例作蜜餞糖菓　　每百觔　伍錢

豉油 即醬油類　　每百觔　肆錢

白糖黃糖各樣　每百觔　貳錢伍分

氷糖　各省氷糖同例　每百觔　叁錢伍分

生熟烟水烟黃烟孖古烟各等同例　每百觔　貳錢

凡出口貨有不能賅載者即論價值若干每百兩

抽銀伍兩

金銀洋錢及各樣金銀類免稅

瓦磚瓦片等造屋之料免稅

進口油蠟礬礦類

洋蠟　即蜜蠟又名磚蠟　每百觔　壹兩

蘇合油 每百觔 壹兩

洋硝 此物不准亂賣只准賣與官商 原例無 每百觔 叄錢

洋靦 即番靦 原例作靦 每百觔 伍錢

進口香椒類 每百觔 壹兩

安息香安息油 每百觔 壹兩

檀香 每百觔 伍錢

胡椒 每百觔 肆錢

凡屬進口香料等貨例未賖載者即按價值若干

每百兩抽銀拾兩進口香水油按價值若干每百兩

抽銀伍兩

進口藥材類	阿魏	上等冰片 清的 原例作好低冰片	下等冰片 坭的 原例作冰片坭	上等丁香即子丁香	下等丁香即母丁香	牛黃	兒茶
	每百觔 壹兩	每觔 壹兩	每觔 伍錢	每百觔 壹兩伍錢	每百觔 伍錢	每觔 壹兩	每百觔 叁錢

檳榔膏	每百觔	壹錢伍分
檳榔	每百觔	壹錢伍分
上等洋參　除淨參鬚的　原例作人參	每百觔	叁拾捌兩
下等洋參　即　洋參鬚　原例作人參鬚　每百觔按上參二成下參八成折算	每百觔	捌兩
乳香	每百觔	伍錢
没藥	每百觔	伍錢
豆蔻花　即玉果花　原例並未賅載	每百觔	壹兩
水硪	每百觔	叁兩
上等豆蔻　即玉菓	每百觔	貳兩

品名	說明	單價
下等豆蔻	即草蔻連壳的.	每百觔　壹兩
木香	原例作好低木香	每百觔　柒錢伍分
犀角		每百觔　叁兩
進口雜貨類		
火石		每百觔　伍分
珠海壳	即雲母壳	每百觔　貳錢
進口醃臘海味類		
上等燕窩	官燕	每百觔　伍兩
中等燕窩	常燕	每百觔　貳兩伍錢

下等燕窩毛燕　　　每百觔　伍錢

上等海參黑的　　　每百觔　捌錢

下等海參白的　　　每百觔　貳錢

上等魚翅白的　　　每百觔　壹兩

下等魚翅黑的　　　每百觔　伍錢

柴魚 即乾魚類　　　每百觔　肆錢

魚肚 原例並未賍載．　每百觔　伍錢

進口顏料膠漆紙劄類

呼嘸米　　　　　　每百觔　伍兩

洋青即大青　每百觔　肆兩

蘇木　每百觔　壹錢

進口竹木籐椰類

沙籐　每百觔　貳錢

烏木　每百觔　壹錢伍分

凡進口木料如紅木紫檀木黃楊木等例不賍載

者俱按價值若干每百兩抽銀拾兩

進口鏡鐘標玩類

自鳴鐘

時辰標

千里鏡

玻璃片及各樣玻璃水晶器

寫字盒

梳粧盒

各樣金銀首飾

各鋼鐵器刀劍等物

以上各貨及同類雜貨即論價值若干每百兩抽
銀伍兩　凡進口金銀類各樣金銀洋錢錠錁免

稅

進口布疋花幔類

帆布　即嗶布　長柒丈半至拾丈　闊壹尺七寸至貳尺貳寸　每疋　伍錢

棉花　每百觔除皮五觔　每百觔　肆錢

白洋布　長柒丈半至拾丈　闊貳尺貳寸至貳尺陸寸原例分作二等西洋布兩款　每疋　壹錢伍分

白袈裟布　長伍丈至陸丈　闊貳尺玖寸至叁尺叁寸　每疋　壹錢伍分

原色洋布　長柒丈半至拾丈　闊貳尺玖寸　原例作西洋粗布　每疋　壹錢

原色斜紋布　長柒丈半至拾丈　闊貳尺至貳尺玖寸　每疋　壹錢

印花布　長陸丈至柒丈半　闊壹尺玖寸至貳尺貳寸　原例作錦花被面　每疋　貳錢

棉紗　原例作棉綫　每百觔　壹兩

蘇布白色幻細洋竹布　長伍太至柒文半　闊貳尺壹寸至貳尺柒寸　原例並未載　每疋　伍錢

羽布　每文　壹分伍厘

此外凡屬進口棉布類如柳條巾旗方巾顏色布

剪絨布絲棉布毛棉布又粗蘇布半棉半蘇布絲

蘇布毛蘇布等即論價值若干每百觔抽銀五兩

進口紬緞絲絨類

大手帕　四方長闊在貳尺陸寸之上　每條　壹分伍厘

小手帕　四方長闊在貳尺陸寸之下　每條　壹分

上等金銀線 即真金銀的	每劤	壹錢叁分
下等金銀線 即僞金銀的	每劤	叁分
大呢 即哆囉呢闊叁尺陸寸至肆尺陸寸 原例作瑣難喇	每丈	伍分錢
小呢 即嗶嘰番紀之類 原例作小絨	每丈	柒分
羽緞	每丈	壹錢伍分錢
羽紗	每丈	柒分
羽紬	每丈	叁分伍厘
絨線	每百劤	叁兩
洋白氈	每條	壹錢

凡進口絨貨例未賅載者如素毛絲毛綿毛等即

以價值若干每百兩抽銀伍兩

進口酒果食物類

洋酒 裝玻璃瓶大的　　　每百瓶　壹兩

洋酒 裝玻璃瓶小的　　　每百瓶　伍錢

洋酒 裝桶的　　　　　　每百觔　伍錢

進口銅鐵鉛錫類

洋生銅 如銅磚之類　　　每百觔　壹兩

洋熟銅 如銅扁銅條之類　每百觔　壹兩伍錢

洋生鐵 如鐵磚之類	每百觔 壹錢
洋熟鐵 如鐵條之類	每百觔 伍分
洋生鉛 黑白同例 白鉛止准賣給官商	每百觔 貳錢捌分
洋熟鉛	每百觔 肆錢
洋生鋼各樣	每百觔 肆錢
洋錫 即畨錫	每百觔 壹兩
馬口鐵 即錫扁 原例並未賅載	每百觔 肆錢

凡屬進口銅鐵鉛錫等類如白銅黃銅等例未賅載者即按價值若干每百兩抽銀拾兩

進口珍珠寶石類

品名	單位	價
瑪瑙石片	每百片	伍錢
瑪瑙珠	每百觔	拾兩
進口纓皮牙角羽毛類		
水牛角 原例作藥角	每百觔	貳兩
熟牛皮	每百觔	伍錢
海龍皮 即海虎皮	每條	壹兩
大狐狸皮	每條	壹錢伍分
小狐狸皮	每條	柒厘伍分
虎皮豹皮貂皮等	每條	壹錢伍分

獺皮貉貛皮沙魚皮等		每百條　貳兩
海騾皮等		每百條　伍兩
兔皮灰鼠皮銀鼠皮等		每百條　伍錢
海馬牙	原例並未賅載	每百觔　貳兩
上等象牙	不碎的牙	每百觔　肆兩
下等象牙	碎的牙	每百觔　貳兩

凡屬進口新貨例內不能賅載者即按價值若干每百兩抽銀伍兩

又進口洋米洋麥五穀等皆免稅

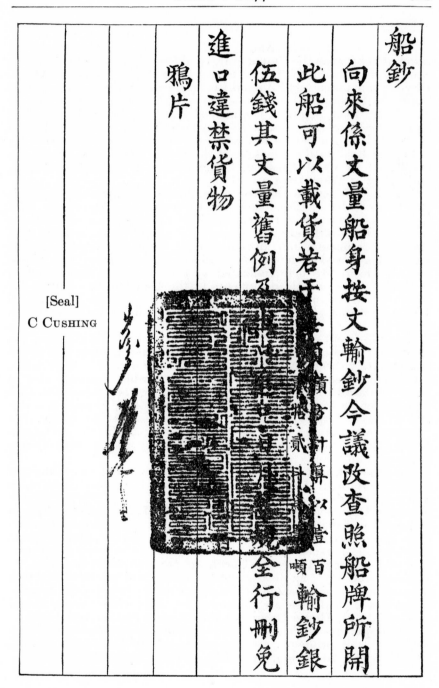

船鈔

向來係丈量船身按丈輸鈔今議改查照船牌所開

此船可以載貨若干...噸...計算以一百...噸...輸鈔銀

伍錢其文量舊例及...全行刪免

進口達禁貨物

鴉片

[Seal]
C Cushing

NOTES

This Treaty of Peace, Amity, and Commerce was the first treaty negotiated between the United States and China and one of the earliest agreements between the United States and a country of the Far East. Eleven years previously Edmund Roberts, Special Agent of the United States, had negotiated unsuccessfully with Cochinchina and had, on March 20, 1833, signed a commercial treaty with the Kingdom of Siam (Document 76); but since that mission of Roberts the United States had contracted no formal treaty engagement with a country of the Far East until the making of this treaty with China, which was negotiated by Caleb Cushing, Commissioner of the United States, and signed at Wang Hiya on July 3, 1844.

The English text of this treaty, with the accompanying tariff, is first printed above; then follows the Chinese text of the treaty, with the Chinese version of the tariff. The Chinese texts of both the treaty and the tariff are reproduced in facsimile, page for page from original documents, but in left-to-right order of pagination; the signature and seal of the United States Commissioner on the Chinese text, however, are here indicated in type and not reproduced in facsimile. The original documents in the Department of State file of this treaty, including the source texts for the English and Chinese versions printed above, are described in detail in the notes which follow.

The indifferent use of the terms "treaty" and "convention" is again illustrated by this agreement, which has always, and quite appropriately, been styled a treaty; but in its preamble there is the expression "treaty or general convention", which appears also in various treaties with countries of Latin America beginning with that with Colombia of October 3, 1824 (Document 47); Articles 2, 5, 13, and 22 have "this Treaty"; Article 34, in its first paragraph, has "present convention" and "said convention", and in the next paragraph "this Treaty"; the paragraph following has "present Treaty of peace, amity, and commerce".

The papers which accompanied this treaty when it was submitted to the Senate with the presidential message of December 10, 1844, as well as those subsequently transmitted on January 9, 1845, are printed in Senate Document No. 67, 28th Congress, 2d session, serial 450; in response to a Senate resolution of February 14, copies of three instructions and of two letters of President Tyler to the Emperor of China (one a letter of credence) were transmitted with the presidential message of February 21 (Senate Document No. 138, 28th Congress, 2d session, serial 457); an abstract of the treaty and copies of two despatches were communicated to Congress with the presidential message of January 22, 1845 (Senate Document No. 58, 28th Congress, 2d session, serial 450; House Document No. 69, same session, serial 464).

The despatches of Caleb Cushing cited in these notes, except when noted as "not printed", are printed in Senate Document No. 67, 28th Congress, 2d session, serial 450.

The Signed Originals

The despatches of Caleb Cushing, the Commissioner of the United States who negotiated this treaty, are clear in their statements that in each text four originals of the treaty proper (separate from the tariff of duties) were signed on July 3, 1844.

In his despatch of July 8, 1844 (D.S., 2 Despatches, China, No. 72), Cushing wrote of "the several copies, four in English and four in Chinese [meaning eight documents], completed and ready for signature"; with his despatch of August 2 (*ibid.*, No. 81; received December 6, 1844), he transmitted "by the barque Sappho and the favor of Augustine Heard Esquire, one of the originals of the Treaty of Wang-Sheah, together with the Tariff, which is to be considered as annexed to and a part of the same"; he added that the treaty "was executed in English & in Chinese, four copies of each language, of which two [of each] were retained by Tsiyeng and two by myself." On the arrival of Cushing at Washington on January 4, 1845 (*ibid.*, No. 99; not printed), after the completion of his mission, he wrote to Secretary of State Calhoun "to place in your hands a duplicate original of the Treaty with China concluded at Wang Hiya on the 3rd of July last".

Each English text and each Chinese text of the treaty, when signed, was a separate paper; each original of the treaty in the file and each "original" mentioned in the despatches, is one manuscript which combines two documents as signed, one English and one Chinese; the fact is clear, as in each original the kind of paper with the English script is not the same as that bearing the Chinese characters; so an "original" of the treaty means an English text and a Chinese text, both separately signed and now bound together.

Those two originals of the treaty proper which Cushing retained for his own Government are in the file; in each the English text is first, followed by the Chinese text; the pages of the latter are in the usual Chinese order, so that the final page of the Chinese is immediately after (in left-to-right order of pagination) the final page of the English. One of those originals forms part of the duplicate United States instrument of ratification of January 17, 1845; the other, that which Cushing brought with him (endorsed in pencil as received January 4, 1845), is embodied in the original proclamation of April 18, 1846.

As between the two English texts of the treaty proper in the two documents above mentioned, the number of minor differences, aside from capitalization, is large, running to something over two hundred; some few are matters of spelling and of punctuation or writing style, or involve the use of a singular for a plural or vice versa, or a transposition of words; the large majority of the total are commas inserted or omitted in the one document as compared with the other; no one of these appears to raise any arguable difference in meaning. Those variances which are strictly of wording seem of as little consequence as all the rest; but they are listed here, the second column giving the wording here printed, and the third that of the other of those two signed originals:

Article or clause	Original here printed	Proclaimed original
Article 1	be a perfect	be perfect
	permanent, universal	permanent, and universal
Article 2	in the Tariff	by the Tariff
	made a part	made part
Article 3	either of the said five ports	either of said five ports
Article 4	of the citizens	of citizens
Article 6	will note	shall note
Article 10	with the affairs	with affairs
	held to be due	held due
Article 11	to an ad valorem	to ad valorem
Article 12	consuls at each	Consuls of each
	in measures and weights	in the measure and weight
Article 17	peace, the local officers	peace, local officers
Article 19	with subjects	with the subjects
	dwellings or property	dwellings or their property
Article 20	free ports	five ports
	on such examination	on examination
Article 22	and for that cause should	and should for that cause
Article 24	officer	functionary
Article 25	jurisdiction, and	jurisdiction of and
Article 27	at once to repair	to repair at once
	free ports	five ports
Article 28	seized or forcibly	seized and forcibly
Article 30	the one government	the Government
Article 31	of the Liang Kiang	of Liang-Kang
Article 34	this Treaty shall	the treaty shall
Final clauses	and of the	and the

The choice as a source text (English) of one or the other of the two originals mentioned is not without difficulty; there is something to be said each way; precedent has controlled the decision; the source text here of the English text is that original which forms part of the duplicate United States instrument of ratification; that original was the one first received by this Government; it was that document which was sent to the Senate; more important perhaps is the fact that it was the source text for the official contemporaneous pamphlet print of the treaty (a copy of which is in the file) and for the Statutes at Large (8 Statutes at Large, 592–605; 18 *ibid.*, pt. 2, Public Treaties, 116–28), as comparison shows; the text printed in Haswell is obviously a composite, based on the two documents; and Malloy copies Haswell.

It should be said here that a third signed original of the treaty proper is also in the file; that document is bound in yellow silk and is of similar form and arrangement to the other two; it is endorsed in pencil as received on April 18, 1846; it has added to it the Chinese ratification.

The English text in that document is not identical with that in either of the other two originals, though it is much nearer to the text of the original which is now with the original proclamation; the writing of the American scriveners and their collating (if any) of the various originals, was done with extraordinary carelessness; comparison

of this third original with that now with the duplicate United States instrument of ratification (the source text here) reveals more than three hundred discrepancies, aside from matters of capitalization; it is true that most of them are of the minor nature of those above described, the vast majority being cases of commas; but they are none the less quite inexcusable. Those that are differences of wording (omitting cases of obvious slips in one document or the other, such as "the the", or a plural for a singular) are listed here, the second column giving the wording here printed, and the third column that of the third signed original mentioned:

Article or clause	Original here printed	Yellow silk original
Article 1	be a perfect	be perfect
	permanent, universal	permanent and universal
Article 2	in the Tariff	by the Tariff
	made a part	made part
Article 3	either of the said five ports	either of said five ports
Article 4	of the citizens	of citizens
Article 6	will note	shall note
Article 10	with the affairs	with affairs
	held to be due	held due
	of said forty-eight	of forty eight
Article 11	to an ad valorem	to ad-valorem
Article 12	custom-house at Canton, shall	custom house shall
	consuls at each	Consuls of each
	in measures and weights	in the measure and weight
Article 17	the proprietors	the Chinese proprietors
	peace, the local officers	peace, local officers
Article 19	with subjects	with the the subjects
	dwellings or property	dwellings or their property
Article 22	and for that cause should	and should for that cause
Article 24	officer	functionary
Article 25	jurisdiction, and	jurisdiction of and
Article 27	of government	of the Government
	at once to repair	to repair at once
Article 31	of the Liang Kwang	of Liang Kwang
Final clauses	and of the	and the

In all three of the signed originals of the treaty above mentioned the Chinese texts appear to be literally identical, except that the fifth from the last character of Article 29 is omitted in the original which forms part of the original proclamation; the document used for reproduction here is the third or "yellow silk" original; the choice was made merely because of the greater physical adaptability of that document for the reproduction process.

Another Chinese text of the treaty in the file is one written wholly, and very beautifully, on white silk; it has no signatures or seals; no English text is with it and no tariff; its text is not written page for page or column for column with the other documents; its dating clause, while the same, is written in part in a fuller form than in the three signed originals; but its characters seem otherwise identical, except that two are transposed in Article 13 and two are omitted, seemingly by an error of the scribe, in Article 16.

Much care appears to have been taken to have no arguable discrepancies in the Chinese text of the treaty; Cushing wrote as follows on the subject in his despatch of August 19, 1844 (D.S., 2 Despatches, China, No. 86; printed in part):

Question has occurred among British subjects in China, whether the document, which the Chinese Government has communicated to its officers at the Five Ports, purporting to be the Chinese counterpart of the British Supplementary Treaty, and which has thus become public, is or is not a faithful copy. It has been translated by Mr Medhurst, and also by Dr Bridgman; and their translations differ very materially from the official English counterpart. The official Chinese counterpart in the hands of the British Government not having yet been published, it cannot be known whether this difference is to be ascribed, as some think, to want of care in the English interpreters, by reason of which the provisions of the Chinese counterpart do not correspond to those of the English, or whether, as others think, to interpolation on the part of the Chinese.

It seems a harsh construction to suspect the Chinese of such an act; but the possibility of it is inferred from the circumstance that such frauds are known to have been practised, in sundry cases, by Chinese officials, for the purpose of concealing the true facts of a case from the Emperor or from the people.

To guard against the inconvenience of a possible step of this kind, I have adopted the expedient, which is customary among the Chinese themselves, namely, having the characters of the original document numbered, and that number placed on record for remembrance and future observation. To this end, I annex hereto a memorandum, in which is set down the number of characters in each principal division of the Chinese original counterparts of the Treaty Wang-Hiya.

The "Memorandum of the Number of Characters in the Chinese Counterpart of the Treaty of Wang-Hiya" which was enclosed with that despatch, gives the following figures, which examination of the originals of the treaty shows to be accurate:

Preamble	154	Article 20	137
Article 1	40	Article 21	82
Article 2	102	Article 22	140
Article 3	109	Article 23	54
Article 4	116	Article 24	126
Article 5	86	Article 25	74
Article 6	172	Article 26	162
Article 7	88	Article 27	101
Article 8	127	Article 28	47
Article 9	76	Article 29	153
Article 10	229	Article 30	93
Article 11	131	Article 31	49
Article 12	60	Article 32	91
Article 13	140	Article 33	94
Article 14	72	Article 34	94
Article 15	65	Conclusion	165
Article 16	130	Date	46
Article 17	209		
Article 18	70	Total	3,982
Article 19	98		

THE TARIFF OF DUTIES

There are in the file three original examples of the document headed "The Tariff of duties to be levied on imported and exported merchandise at the Five Ports"; while separate documents, the three tariffs correspond with the three signed originals of the treaty; one of them

accompanied the original which Cushing transmitted to the Department of State (received December 6, 1844); one of them, endorsed as received on January 4, 1845, was with the original which Cushing brought to the United States; and the third is endorsed as having been "With the Emperor's ratified copy of Treaty", or, in other words, with the "yellow silk" original. In each of these three originals of the tariff both the English and the Chinese texts are signed and sealed by Cushing and by the Chinese Commissioner, Tsiyeng.

The collating of the English texts of these three tariffs shows quite a number of the same sort of careless differences that might be expected from the discrepancies among the originals of the treaty proper; but in the tariffs these are generally of at least as little consequence, as they are almost all merely such variances in the form of such lists as might be expected from unskilled or negligent copyists.

The original used as the source text for the English of the tariff here printed is that example which is marked as having been with the "yellow silk" original of the treaty proper.

The reason for the choice is that, of the three tariffs, the one here adopted as the source text contains an English text which on the whole is much more carefully and clearly written than that in either of the other two; in two or three instances its wording is more precise or complete; moreover, examination of the Chinese text of the tariff shows that the figures of rates in this example are generally more accurate (cf. the rates with the supplementary treaty of October 8, 1843, between China and Great Britain, in British and Foreign State Papers, XXXI, 141–45); thus the duty on the export of "Coarse or refuse silk" (class 10) is given as 2 taels in the first of the three tariffs received at the Department of State and is so printed in the Statutes at Large and generally; the correct figure, as written in the English of the other two examples of the tariff and in the Chinese text of all three, is 2 taels and 5 mace (2½ taels). In class 10 of the import duties the width of chintz is given in the English of the first two examples as "2 chih 9 tsun to 3 chih 3 tsun wide" and has been generally so printed; in the third example it is correctly "1 chih 9 tsun to 2 chih 2 tsun wide", as in all the Chinese texts. The import duty on "Linen, fine" (class 10), is given as 5 mace "per hundred catties" in the first example of the tariff received at the Department of State; this is obviously erroneous; the rate should be "per piece", as it is in the other English texts and in the Chinese and as it has always been printed. In the same item the width of the linen is given generally in the prints heretofore as "1 chih 9 tsun to 2 chih 2 tsun wide", and thus the English text reads in two of the three examples of the tariff; in the other, the one "With the Emperor's ratified copy", which is here used as the source text, there is written "2 chih 1 tsun to 2 chih 7 tsun wide"; this agrees with the Chinese of all three examples. Accordingly, for the sake of greater accuracy, the latest of the three originals of the tariff is here taken for the source text of the English thereof; and it is to be added that the contemporaneous official separate print of the treaty and tariff of duties, a copy of which is in the file, gives the *rates* of duties in the tariff as in that original, though it does not follow that text in stating the "widths" in class 10 of imports.

However, the rate on the import of flints (class 4) is correctly 5 candareens, as in the three Chinese examples and in the first two of the English, and has so always been printed; it is written incorrectly 5 mace in the third example of the English; the correct figure is given in the tariff here printed.

The Chinese text of the tariff which is reproduced above is from the same document as that used as the source text of the English; but the three Chinese texts of the tariff appear to be identical in characters and also similarly written page for page and column for column.

Not only was each tariff a separate document from the treaty originals proper, but its signing and sealing (in four examples, English and Chinese) took place between two and three weeks after the date of the treaty (see despatch No. 80, enclosure 2, quoted below); strictly speaking, there were originally eight tariff documents, four in English and four in Chinese; each of the three examples in the file is a combined manuscript of two papers.

The United States Ratification

As has been said, the duplicate United States instrument of ratification of January 17, 1845, which is in the file, has annexed to it that one of the signed originals of the treaty which was received by the Department of State on December 6, 1844, enclosed with Cushing's despatch of August 2 (D.S., 2 Despatches, China, No. 81). The ratification is in customary form; presumably the original thereof included both texts of the treaty proper; whether a copy of the tariff of duties was also annexed or included cannot be determined; no mention thereof is made in the wording of the ratification.

The Chinese Ratification

In an unofficial letter of Tsiyeng to Cushing under date of August 18, 1844, the Chinese Commissioner wrote (D.S., 2 Despatches, China, August 24, 1844, enclosure, translation; not printed):

All the articles of the treaty on a former occasion I, the Minister, transmitted to the Emperor, and I have received for reply that the August Sovereign has delivered it over to the Ministers of the Privy Council, together with the appropriate Board (of War), for them speedily to deliberate thereon and report to the Throne. But the articles of the treaty are numerous and the distance great; and it cannot be avoided but that there be some delay. It may be calculated that at the earliest, by the end of this month (September 10), and at the latest, before mid-autumn (26 September), the reply of the Board of War may reach Canton. So soon as the communication from the Board arrives, I, the Minister, will, as in duty bound, immediately send information thereof and also address a flying despatch to each of the ports, that they may, as is expedient, manage accordingly.

When the August Sovereign has put the vermilion pencil to the treaty, then it will be necessary to wait till the day when the ratification of the treaty by the President of your honorable nation comes back, at which time the ratifications will be exchanged in due form.

Announcement of the ratification of the treaty by the Emperor of China was made by Commodore Foxhall A. Parker, commanding the United States naval forces, East India Station, by his despatch of September 16, 1844 (D.S., 2 Despatches, China); similar information was contained in the despatch of Fletcher Webster of September 26 (*ibid.*); each of those despatches enclosed a translation of a note of Tsiyeng, the Chinese Commissioner, to Cushing under date of September 9, 1844, communicating the fact of the imperial ratification. From that note the following is extracted:

Ke Ying, of the Imperial House, Governor General of the two Kwang, a Director of the Board of War, a Vice Guardian of the Heir Apparent, Minister and Commissioner Extraordinary of the Ta Tsing Empire, makes this communication: I, the Minister, on a former occasion met the honorable Envoy at Macao face to face and negotiated and settled every article (of a treaty) for the future regulation of the lawful and just commerce of the United States, and on the 5th month and 24th day (9 July) of the present year respectfully made up a despatch thereof and memorialized the Emperor. Upon the 6th month and 30th day (13 August) I received the intelligence that the August Emperor had delivered over the same to the Ministers of the Privy Council, together with the appropriate boards, speedily to deliberate thereon and report to the Throne. Now the Ministers of the Privy Council, together with the respective boards, have communicated to me, the Minister, that to every article of that which we have deliberated upon, they have replied to article by article, "grant it be done". Upon the 7th month and 2d day (15 August) I addressed the Emperor and have (since) received (as follows): "It is the imperial pleasure to ratify the negotiations. *By the Emperor.*"
Now a communication from the Board of Revenue has come to hand informing me, the Minister, of the ratification, besides severally addressing the Governors General and Lieutenant Governors of each of the Provinces of Fuh Keen, Che Keang, and Keang Soo, and the (Tartar) General of Fuh Chow, that they manage in respectful conformity thereto. I also, as behooveth me, address the honorable Envoy, that he may in the same manner conform thereto and issue his orders requiring the merchants, citizens, etc., of the United States that they absolutely and carefully adhere to the treaty and each quietly attend to his own duty, carrying on his commerce without transgressing (the treaty) in the slightest degree, in order that our peace and harmony may be firmly established forever. That this may be the case, I devoutly hope.

The despatch of Fletcher Webster above mentioned enclosed also a translation of an unofficial note of Tsiyeng to Cushing, received September 9, 1844, stating that directions had been given for the carrying out of the treaty at the five ports and including this language: "But having received the treaty ratified by the Emperor, I now respectfully receive and hold that copy till the arrival of the one (ratified) by your honorable nation, when they will be exchanged".

There is no doubt whatever that the provisions of the treaty were operative in China in September 1844, and that it had received the imperial ratification on August 15, 1844, the 24th year, 7th month, and 2d day of Tao-kuang.

The Chinese ratification, however, is dated (erroneously) a year later, the 25th year, 7th month, and 2d day of Tao-kuang, or August 4, 1845; the ratification is written in fourteen Chinese characters preceding the Chinese text of that signed original of the treaty above

described as the "yellow silk" original; the contemporaneous translation thereof in the file reads literally as follows:

Taou Kwang the 25th year, 7th month, and 2nd day, (Aug. 4th A.D. 1845) (We the great ministers of State members of the Privy Council) reverently received the Imperial Ratification. [Here are written the two final Chinese characters of the ratification.] "E. E."
"I Ratify these Deliberations."

Faithful translation. The parenthesis is supplied from authority.

PETER PARKER
Secretary & Interpreter to the Legation

Dr. Arthur W. Hummel, Chief of the Division of Orientalia, Library of Congress, has been good enough to examine the Chinese ratification; Dr. Hummel writes that the first column thereof (twelve characters) reads "Tao-kuang, 25th year, 7th month, 2d day", the second column (two characters), "Imperial Indorsement", and that the third column (two large characters in red) means "Let it be as recommended", adding that this is a phrase used by the Emperor to indicate ratification; and regarding the Parker translation Dr. Hummel states that the two final Chinese characters, with their English phonetic ("E.E.") equivalent, were there added to indicate that the ratification was "signed" with the phrase "Let it be as recommended."

The date written in the original Chinese ratification is due to an error of the scribe, who wrote "25th" instead of "24th"; in the record copy of the Parker translation in the archives of the American Legation (D.S., Legation Archives, China, No. 199, p. 19) correction has been made of "24th" for "25th" and "1844" for "1845"; though the other corresponding change from August 4 to August 15 was overlooked; and the copy in Chinese of the ratification on the following page of that volume, reads "24th"; that copy omits the two final Chinese characters above mentioned, and it has an extra character in its first column, which, Dr. Hummel writes, "in no way alters the meaning". Also to be quoted is the following statement of Dr. Hummel:

In the Library of Congress are reprints, in the Chinese language, of the actual court records of that period. These clearly state that Ke-ying memorialized the Throne about the treaty on July 28, 1844, and that the treaty received imperial ratification (in the 24th year, 7th month, 2d day) August 15, 1844. Moreover, for the period, August 4, 1845, these records say nothing about any dealings with the United States. The real dates then are as follows: signed by the two Plenipotentiaries July 3, 1844; Ke-ying memorialized the Throne July 28, 1844; ratified by the Emperor August 15, 1844.

OTHER FILE DOCUMENTS

The file contains the attested resolution of the Senate of January 16, 1845 (Executive Journal, VI, 385). The act of the exchange of ratifications is described and quoted below in the discussion of the exchange of ratifications.

It has been mentioned that one of the originals of the treaty proper is embodied in the original proclamation of April 18, 1846; that docu-

ment is in customary form, but it does not include and makes no mention of the tariff of duties, which was before the Senate and which has always been printed with the text of the treaty.

The Exchange of Ratifications

Regarding the exchange of ratifications Cushing wrote as follows in his despatch of August 19, 1844 (D.S., 2 Despatches, China, No. 86; printed in part):

I have not thought it expedient to make any formal stipulation as to the mode of exchanging ratifications of the Treaty of Wang-Hiya, in case it should receive the confirmation of the two Governments; but it is understood that the exchange may take place at the Bogue,[1] if there be at the time a Minister from the United States in China; but otherwise at Canton.

It is also expected that the Treaty will practically go into effect, so soon as it shall have been ratified by the Emperor of China. This will be the voluntary act of the Chinese Government, and done for our benefit; and as the new stipulations consist of advantages conceded to the United States, and the provisions of which are to be executed in China, there can be no cause of objection to it on the part of the merchants of the United States or their Government.

The Imperial Commissioner has already sent notice to the Free Ports of the conclusion of the Treaty. I presume, when he shall have received intelligence of the ratification of the Treaty by the Emperor, he will communicate a copy of the Treaty to the public officers of those Ports, as he did in the case of the British Supplementary Treaty.

Alexander H. Everett, of Massachusetts, was appointed Commissioner to China on March 13, 1845 (D.S., 3 Credences, 117); under date of April 15, 1845, he was given instructions to exchange the ratifications of this treaty, a full power for that purpose, and also (April 16) a full power to negotiate a commercial treaty with Japan, similar to one which had been issued to Caleb Cushing under date of August 14, 1844 (D.S., 1 Instructions, China, 34–35; 3 Credences, 99, 127–28); en route to China Everett became ill at Rio de Janeiro and delegated his authority to exchange the ratifications to Commodore James Biddle, U.S.N., commanding the United States squadron in the East Indies (D.S., 3 Despatches, China, No. 5, September 28, 1845).

Commodore Biddle duly exchanged the ratifications on December 31, 1845; his despatch of that date (*ibid.*, No. 1) from Canton reported the exchange, which took place " at 1 o'clock this day at the Country residence of a friend [of Tsiyeng, namely, 'Pun Ting Kwa, the Mandarine'] immediately upon the River [Canton] and about two miles above this city " (*ibid.*, Nos. 1 and 2), as follows:

I have the honor to inform you that the ratifications of the Treaty of Peace, Amity, and Commerce between the United States and China concluded at Wang Hiya in July 1844 were this day duly exchanged. The Commissioner on the part of the Emperor of China was Ke Ying the Governor General of the Provinces of Kwang Tung and Kwang Se. I delivered to him the ratification of the Treaty by the President of the United States, receiving from him the ratification by His Imperial Majesty. I shall take an early opportunity of forwarding to the United States His Majesty's ratification.

---

[1] The Bogue, or Boca Tigris (Tiger's Mouth), is the more navigable channel at the mouth of the Canton (or Pearl) River, rather more than half way from Macao to Canton. The equivalent in Chinese characters (variously transcribed "hu-mên" and "fu-mun") means "tiger's gate".

With the despatch mentioned of December 31, 1845, is an original of the act of exchange of ratifications, in English and Chinese, each text signed and sealed by the representatives of the two Governments. The English text of that document follows, omitting indication of the seals and also of the signature of Tsiyeng, whose seal and signature thereon are similar to those shown on the facsimile of the treaty:

Now We James Biddle Commander in Chief of the Naval forces, and Acting Minister and Commissioner, to China, of the United States of America, and Ke Ying of the Imperial House, general Superintendant of the free trade of the Five Ports, Governor General of the Two Kwang Provinces, director of the Board of War, Vice High Chancellor, a vice guardian of the Heir apparent, Minister and Commissioner extraordinary, of the Ta Tsing Empire, each having taken the Treaty negotiated and settled at Wang Hiya on the 3ᵈ day of July in the year of our Lord one thousand eight hundred and forty-four, and of Taou Kwang the twenty fourth year, fifth month and eighteenth day, with all suitable solemnity and after due comparison of the ratified copies each with the other & both with the original examples of the said Treaty, have this day exchanged them.

In witness whereof, we have this day signed this act in duplicate and have sealed the same with our respective seals, and signs manuel at Pwan Tang, Canton
Taou Kwong 25ᵗʰ yr. 12ᵗʰ m. 3ᵈ day
Dec. 31ˢᵗ A.D. 1845.

JAMES BIDDLE

In his despatch No. 416, of May 19, 1932, Consul General Joseph W. Ballantine thus reported from Canton regarding the name appearing as "Pwan Tang" in the English text of the act of the exchange of ratifications of December 31, 1845:

From inquiries I have made among Chinese I have come to the conclusion that the person referred to by Commodore Biddle as "Pun Ting Kwa, the Mandarine" was Poon Shi-shing (Mandarin transliteration P'an Shih-ch'eng) (潘士成).

He was a friend of His Excellency Ch'i Ying (耆英), Viceroy of the two Kwang Provinces, and of other high officials and was one of the four conspicuously wealthy men of the time. Poon was a salt merchant, and held the important post of Salt Commissioner.

Mr. Poon owned considerable property in Poon Tong (P'an T'ang in Mandarin) (泮塘), a village which was situated on the river about two miles southwest of the Viceroy's Yamen, and which has now been absorbed into the city of Canton. Presumably on account of the inconvenience experienced in those days by foreigners in calling upon Chinese officials, it was arranged to have the ratifications exchanged at Mr. Poon's residence in the village of Poon Tong, since it was directly accessible to boats.

In that despatch of Consul General Ballantine was enclosed "a sketch map of Canton showing the location of Poon Tong Village in relation to the city and the Pearl River".

THE FULL POWERS

The Imperial Commissioner of the Government of China who was charged with the negotiations is named in the preamble of the treaty as "Tsiyeng"; in the despatches and elsewhere his name is frequently written Ke Ying (or Keying); the latter style appears in the Treaty

of Nanking (between China and Great Britain) of August 29, 1842 (British and Foreign State Papers, XXX, 389–402); Dr. Hummel writes on the point as follows:

> The forms, "Ke Ying", "Keying", and "Tsiyeng" are all western attempts at transcribing the same person's name, 耆英, now generally romanized Ch'i Ying. The older spellings were employed before the days of any established system of romanizing Chinese words, so that each westerner wrote as seemed best to him! Hearing a *Cantonese* pronounce it, it sounded like the first part of our word "keep", hence he wrote "Ke" for the first sound. But when pronounced by a *Pekinese* it sounded like the first part of our word "cheer", hence he wrote "Tsi", to give the idea that it is *aspirated*. This latter rendering is also closer to the Manchu original.

A formal communication of the full powers of the Chinese Commissioner was made in his note to Cushing of July 14, 1844 (D.S., 2 Despatches, China, No. 77, July 19, 1844, enclosure, with copy of original and translation), in which he wrote:

> KeYing, of the Imperial House, Governor General of the two Kwang Provinces, a Director of the Board of War, a Vice Guardian of the Heir Apparent, Minister and Commissioner Extraordinary of the Ta Tsing Empire, communicates a respectful copy (of his imperial appointment as Commissioner).
> It has been granted me upon my official table to open a communication from the Board of War containing, from the Inner Council (Nuy Kō), a copy of an imperial order they had received, viz:
> KeYing has already been appointed to the office of Governor General of the two Kwang Provinces. Let the appropriate business relating to the free trade of every Province be altogether delivered over to the said Governor General to conduct. Cause to be delivered over to him the seals of Minister and Commissioner Extraordinary, that if it occur that there be any correspondence issued relating to the free commerce at the ports of the different Provinces, cause it to be granted him to affix this seal, in order to manifest careful attention thereto.
> By order of the Emperor.
> With becoming obedience I have, as behoveth me, to communicate this respectful copy (of my commission) for the information of the honorable Envoy, that he may respectfully thereto conform. As is requisite, I make this communication.
> The foregoing communication is to Cushing. Envoy Extraordinary and Minister Plenipotentiary of the United States of America.
> Taou Kwang, 24th year, 5th month, 29th day (July 14, 1844).

The full power of Cushing is mentioned in his instructions (D.S., 1 Instructions, China, 14–18, May 8, 1843; Senate Document No. 138, 28th Congress, 2d session, serial 457); but no copy thereof is of record, and nothing appears in the despatches regarding the communication thereof to the Chinese Commissioner.

The Negotiations

The opening chapters of the work of Dr. Tyler Dennett, Americans in Eastern Asia (pp. 1–171), give an admirable account of the background of this treaty, of the surrounding circumstances, and of the commercial interests involved. Under the command of Commodore Lawrence Kearny, U.S.N., the East India Squadron visited Chinese waters in 1842–43; various despatches from Commodore Kearny to the Secretary of the Navy during that period are in Senate Docu-

ment No. 139, 29th Congress, 1st session, serial 473, with other papers; these include correspondence with the Governor General at Canton regarding claims (some of which were settled), trade, future relations of the two countries, and a possible treaty (see Dennett, *op. cit.*, 108–11, 124–27, 326–27). One chapter is given to the mission of Cushing in Fuess, Life of Cushing (I, 397–454).

In his message to Congress of December 30, 1842, President Tyler referred to the treaty made by China with Great Britain during that year and to other then recent events in the Far East and recommended an appropriation "for the compensation of a commissioner to reside in China" (Richardson, IV, 211–14). By the act of March 3, 1843 (5 Statutes at Large, 624), forty thousand dollars was "appropriated and placed at the disposal of the President of the United States, to enable him to establish the future commercial relations between the United States and the Chinese empire on terms of national equal reciprocity".

On March 3, 1843, Edward Everett, then Minister at London, was nominated as Commissioner to China and confirmed (Executive Journal, VI, 190–91); but Everett at once declined the appointment; following this, Caleb Cushing, who had been a Representative in Congress from Massachusetts since 1835 and whose nomination as Secretary of the Treasury had been thrice rejected by the Senate on March 3, 1843 (*ibid.*, 186–90), was appointed. Cushing received two commissions, one as "Commissioner of the United States of America to China" and the other as "Envoy Extraordinary and Minister Plenipotentiary of the United States of America to the Court of China". Those commissions, in customary form, were under date of May 8, 1843 (D.S., 3 Credences, 41–42); they were recess appointments; the nomination sent to the Senate and which was duly confirmed, was only as Commissioner (Executive Journal, VI, 193, 352); and the subsequent commission as Commissioner issued accordingly under date of June 17, 1844 (D.S., 3 Credences, 88).

The instructions of Secretary of State Webster regarding the mission, also under date of May 8, 1843, contained the following (D.S., 1 Instructions, China, 5–13; Senate Document No. 138, 28th Congress, 2d session, serial 457):

It now remains for this Department to say something of the political objects of the Mission, and the manner in which it is hoped those objects may be accomplished. It is less necessary, than it might otherwise be, to enter into a detailed statement of the considerations which have led to the institution of the Mission, not only as you will be furnished with a copy of the President's communication to Congress, recommending provision to be made for the measure, but also as your connexion with Congress has necessarily brought those considerations to your notice and contemplation.

Occurrences happening in China within the last two years have resulted in events which are likely to be of much importance as well to the United States as to the rest of the civilized world. Of their still more important consequences to China herself, it is not necessary here to speak. The hostilities which have been carried on between that Empire and England, have resulted, among other consequences, in opening four important ports to English commerce, viz: Amoy, Ning-po, Shang-hai, and Fow-chow-fow.

These ports belong to some of the richest, most productive, and most populous provinces of the Empire; and are likely to become very important marts of

commerce. A leading object of the Mission in which you are now to be engaged, is to secure the entry of American ships and cargoes into these ports, on terms as favorable as those which are enjoyed by English merchants. It is not necessary to dwell, here, on the great and well known amount of imports of the productions of China into the United States. These imports, especially in the great article of tea, are not likely to be diminished. Heretofore they have been paid for in the precious metals, or, more recently, by bills drawn on London. At one time, indeed, American paper, of certain descriptions, was found to be an available remittance. Latterly, a considerable trade has sprung up in the export of certain American manufactures to China. To augment these exports, by obtaining the most favorable commercial facilities, and cultivating, to the greatest extent practicable, friendly commercial intercourse with China, in all its accessible ports, is matter of moment to the commercial and manufacturing, as well as the agricultural and mining, interests of the United States. It cannot be foreseen how rapidly, or how slowly, a people of such peculiar habits as the Chinese, and apparently so tenaciously attached to their habits, may adopt the sentiments, ideas, and customs of other nations. But if prejudiced and strongly wedded to their own usages, the Chinese are still understood to be ingenious, acute, and inquisitive. Experience, thus far, if it does not strongly animate and encourage efforts to introduce some of the arts and the products of other countries into China, is not, nevertheless, of a character, such as should entirely repress those efforts. You will be furnished with accounts, as accurate as can be obtained, of the history and present state of the export trade of the United States to China.

As your Mission has in view only friendly and commercial objects, objects, it is supposed, equally useful to both countries, the natural jealousy of the Chinese, and their repulsive feeling towards foreigners, it is hoped may be in some degree removed or mitigated by prudence and address on your part. Your constant aim must be to produce a full conviction on the minds of the Government and the people that your Mission is entirely pacific; that you come with no purposes of hostility or annoyance; that you are a messenger of peace, sent from the greatest Power in America to the greatest Empire in Asia, to offer respect and good will, and to establish the means of friendly intercourse. It will be expedient, on all occasions, to cultivate the friendly dispositions of the Government and people, by manifesting a proper respect for their institutions and manners, and avoiding, as far as possible, the giving of offence, either to their pride or their prejudices. You will use the earliest, and all succeeding occasions, to signify that the Government which sends you has no disposition to encourage, and will not encourage, any violation of the commercial regulations of China, by citizens of the United States. You will state, in the fullest manner, the acknowledgment of this Government, that the commercial regulations of the Empire, having become fairly and fully known, ought to be respected by all ships, and all persons, visiting its ports; and if citizens of the United States, under these circumstances, are found violating well known laws of trade, their Government will not interfere to protect them from the consequences of their own illegal conduct. You will, at the same time, assert and maintain, on all occasions, the equality and independence of your own country. The Chinese are apt to speak of persons coming into the Empire from other nations as tribute bearers to the Emperor. This idea has been fostered perhaps by the costly parade embassies of England. All ideas of this kind, respecting your Mission, must, should they arise, be immediately met by a declaration, not made ostentatiously, or in a manner reproachful towards others, that you are no tribute bearer; that your Government pays tribute to none; and expects tribute from none; and that even as to presents, your Government neither makes nor accepts presents. You will signify to all Chinese authorities, and others, that it is deemed to be quite below the dignity of the Emperor of China, and the President of the United States of America to be concerning themselves with such unimportant matters as presents from one to the other; that the intercourse between the heads of two such Governments should be made to embrace only great political questions, the tender of mutual regard, and the establishment of useful relations.

It is of course desirable that you should be able to reach Pekin, and the Court and person of the Emperor, if practicable. You will accordingly at all times signify this as being your purpose and the object of your Mission; and perhaps it may be well to advance as near to the capital as shall be found practicable,

without waiting to announce your arrival in the country. The purpose of seeing the Emperor in person must be persisted in as long as may be becoming and proper. You will inform the officers of the Government that you have a letter of friendship from the President of the United States to the Emperor, signed by the President's own hand, which you cannot deliver except to the Emperor himself, or some high officer of the Court in his presence. You will say, also, that you have a commission conferring on you the highest rank among representatives of your Government; and that this, also, can only be exhibited to the Emperor, or his chief officer. You may expect to encounter, of course, if you get to Pekin, the old question of the *Kotou.*

In regard to the mode of managing this matter, much must be left to your discretion, as circumstances may occur. All pains should be taken to avoid the giving of offence, or the wounding of the national pride; but, at the same time, you will be careful to do nothing which may seem, even to the Chinese themselves, to imply any inferiority on the part of your Government, or any thing less than perfect independence of all Nations. You will say that the Government of the United States is always controlled by a sense of religion and of honor; that Nations differ in their religious opinions and observances; that you cannot do any thing which the religion of your own country, or its sentiments of honor, forbid; that you have the most profound respect for His Majesty the Emperor; that you are ready to make to him all manifestations of homage which are consistent with your own sense; and that you are sure His Majesty is too just to desire you to violate your own duty; that you should deem yourself quite unworthy to appear before His Majesty as peace bearer from a great and powerful Nation, if you should do any thing against religion or against honor, as understood by the Government and people in the Country you come from. Taking care thus in no way to allow the Government or people of China to consider you as tribute bearer from your Government, or as acknowledging its inferiority, in any respect, to that of China, or any other Nation, you will bear in mind, at the same time, what is due to your own personal dignity and the character which you bear. You will represent to the Chinese authorities, nevertheless, that you are directed to pay to His Majesty the Emperor the same marks of respect and homage as are paid by your Government to His Majesty the Emperor of Russia, or any other of the great Powers of the world.

A letter, signed by the President, as above intimated, and addressed to the Emperor, will be placed in your hands. As has been already stated, you will say that this letter can only be delivered to the Emperor, or to some one of the great officers of State, in his presence. Nevertheless, if this cannot be done, and the Emperor should still manifest a desire to receive the letter, you may consider the propriety of sending it to him, upon an assurance that a friendly answer to it shall be sent, signed by the hand of the Emperor himself.

It will be no part of your duty to enter into controversies which may exist between China and any European State; nor will you, in your communications, fail to abstain altogether from any sentiment, or any expression, which might give to other Governments just cause of offence. It will be quite proper, however, that you should, in a proper manner, always keep before the eyes of the Chinese the high character, importance, and power of the United States. You may speak of the extent of their territory, their great commerce spread over all seas, their powerful navy, every where giving protection to that commerce, and the numerous schools and institutions established in them, to teach men knowledge and wisdom. It cannot be wrong for you to make known, where not known, that the United States, once a country subject to England, threw off that subjection, years ago, asserted its independence, sword in hand, established that independence, after a seven years' war, and now meets England upon equal terms upon the ocean and upon the land. The remoteness of the United States from China, and still more the fact that they have no colonial possessions in her neighborhood, will naturally lead to the indulgence of a less suspicious and more friendly feeling, than may have been entertained towards England, even before the late war between England and China. It cannot be doubted that the immense power of England in India must be regarded by the Chinese Government with dissatisfaction, if not with some degree of alarm. You will take care to show strongly how free the Chinese Government may well be from all jealousy arising from such causes towards the United States. Finally, you will signify, in decided terms, and a

positive manner, that the Government of the United States would find it impossible to remain on terms of friendship and regard with the Emperor, if greater privileges, or commercial facilities, should be allowed to the subjects of any other Government, than should be granted to citizens of the United States.

It is hoped and trusted that you will succeed in making a treaty such as has been concluded between England and China; and if one containing fuller and more regular stipulations could be entered into, it would be conducting Chinese intercourse one step further towards the principles which regulate the public relations of the European and American States.

Cushing sailed from Norfolk on August 5, 1843, by way of Gibraltar; he visited various Mediterranean ports and Aden; he reached Bombay on November 15; there he embarked on the U.S. frigate *Brandywine* on November 26 and landed at Macao on February 27, 1844 (D.S., 1 Despatches, China, Nos. 1–32, *passim;* not printed).

The Chinese Government, through Paul S. Forbes, consul of the United States at Canton, had previously been informed of the intention of the Government of the United States to send a mission to China; and it was the expectation and desire of Cushing, in accordance with his instructions, to proceed to Peking (Peiping) for the negotiations.

Within a few days after reaching Macao Cushing communicated to Ching, the Acting Governor General of the two Kwangs, the fact of his arrival; a somewhat lengthy correspondence with this official ensued; the notes of Cushing to Ching, like his notes to Tsiyeng throughout the negotiations, were written in Chinese as well as in English, both originals (D.S., 1 Despatches, China, No. 38, March 10, 1844; not printed); the Chinese Government did not approve of the proposal of Cushing to proceed to Peking; and instructions thence were awaited.

On May 10, 1844, Cushing received formal notice from Ching of the appointment of Tsiyeng (who had been the ranking Chinese Plenipotentiary during the negotiation of the treaty of 1842 between China and Great Britain) as Governor General of the two Kwangs and as Imperial Commissioner; the despatch of Cushing announcing this fact was under date of May 15 (D.S., 1 Despatches, China, No. 59; not printed), in which he wrote:

I enclose here with copies of two letters of great importance from the Governor General and of my reply.

These letters announce the appointment of Keying, who conducted the commercial negociations with Sir Henry Pottinger, as Commissioner, with powers to conclude a Treaty with the United States, and his speedy arrival at Canton, in the double capacity of Commissioner and of Governor General of the two Kwangs.

They also signify the continued unwillingness of the Court to receive the Legation at Peking.

Ching's letter of the ninth with its enclosure of copies of his instructions from the Court was delivered to me on the twelfth instant by a deputation of civil and military officers of rank, namely Kisheo, a general of the second class under the Mantchu banner, wearing a red button and a peacocks feather—Ching Ying, a Che-Fu, or Magistrate of a Fu, wearing a blue button, and Tung Leën, a Tung Che, that is Assistant Magistrate of a Heën, wearing a crystal button.

They were accompanied, also, by Woo Ting Heën, an aide de camp of the Acting Governor General.

Doubtless one object of a delegation so respectable was to show some attention to the Legation, though I presume it was still more its object to endeavour to give an imposing authority to the "Imperial Pleasure" as documents from the Court are somewhat affectedly denominated.

Among the enclosures to that despatch was a translation of a communication of His Excellency, Ching, quoting extracts from communications of the Privy Council of the Imperial Cabinet; another and more formal communication from Ching transmitted "the imperial pleasure", the translation whereof by Dr. Peter Parker is headed "Three Communications of the Imperial Will respectfully transcribed". These include statements regarding the authority of Tsiyeng to negotiate and are in the following form:

We, great Ministers of State, members of the Privy Council
(Keun Ke Ta Chin), communicate that upon Taou Kwang, 24th year, 2d moon, and 22d day (9 April, 1844) we received the imperial mandate that Ching had memorialized the Throne relative to the American Envoy's entering Peking; but America never as yet having gone through with presenting tribute, then hastily proceeding to Teen Tsin, it will be necessary to require its immediate return. As to the request to negotiate and settle commercial regulations, it will also be necessary to deliver over to the original deliberator (Ke Ying), the great Minister of State, to negotiate and settle them. Certainly there exists no cause at the north for hastily proceeding to Teen Tsin, requiring the appointment of another High Commissioner to negotiate with him. The great Minister of State, Ke Ying, the original deliberator, has been appointed Governor General of the two Kwang Provinces and is coming post to Canton.

Enjoin upon the said Envoy quietly to wait at Canton and by no means to esteem it a light matter to agitate disorder, which is an important concern. Take this mandate and at (the speed of) four hundred le per day (133 miles), make it known. Respect this.

We, great Ministers of State, members of the Privy Council, communicate that on Taou Kwang, 24th year, 3d moon, and 5th day (22 April) we received the imperial mandate that whereas Ching has memorialized the Throne that the American still again importunately requests to enter Peking and is willing by the inner rivers to make the journey, etc.; cause the said Lieutenant Governor again to issue a clear edict respecting the treaty to be deliberated upon and which it is desired to negotiate with an Imperial High Commissioner, that now Ke Ying has been appointed to the office of Governor General of the two Kwangs, and also, as before, the seals of Imperial Commissioner have been delivered over to him. The said nation's Envoy quietly waiting at Yue (Canton) may properly negotiate with him. If absolutely he desires to come to the mouth of the Pei-ho, to Teen Tsin, there is no Imperial High Commissioner there, and he will not be able to negotiate a treaty, and positively he must return again to Canton to negotiate with Ke Ying, and why unnecessarily take the voyage?

Let the said Lieutenant Governor receive this imperial pleasure, then clearly explain that neither by sea nor land can it be permitted him to enter Peking, but let there be orders for him to wait for the Imperial Commissioner at Canton. It is not permitted to do otherwise.

Take this mandate and at the speed of five hundred le (166 miles) per day, order it to be known. Respect this.

Upon the same day the 內閣, Nuy Kō (Imperial Cabinet), received the imperial edict (stating) that Ke Ying now having been appointed to the office of Governor General of the two Kwang Provinces—the supplementary appropriate

business relating to the free commerce of every Province, let all be delivered over to the said Chief Agent and cause the seals of Imperial High Commissioner again to be delivered to him, and if it occur that he have to manage the business of free commerce and the correspondence of the ports of each Province, he is in like manner permitted to affix the seal, using great precaution. Respect this.

Other translations of the three foregoing "communications of the Imperial Will" (D.S., 2 Despatches, China, No. 60, May 15, 1844, enclosures) substitute "By the Emperor" for the closing words, "Respect this."

The Chinese Commissioner, Tsiyeng, proceeded to Macao by way of Canton, sending to Cushing three letters in the meantime, dated April 29, May 31, and June 9 (*ibid.*, No. 66, June 13, 1844, enclosures).

The first interview between the Commissioners took place on June 18. The treaty was signed fifteen days later, on July 3. The discussions regarding its terms lasted for less than two weeks; some explanation of the speed of the negotiations is given in despatch No. 73, of July 9, 1844, from which the following is extracted (*ibid.*):

There is another important consideration, which gave a peculiar character to this correspondence and which appears still more distinctly in certain semi-official correspondence between Tsiyeng and myself, copies of which I transmit in a separate despatch. The Chinese Ministers became thoroughly satisfied at our personal interviews, and still more in the course of the correspondence, that it was not the policy or the wish of the United States to take territory from China, to extort money payments or in any other respect to wound the national pride or injure the political interests of the Empire, and that though capable of being a dangerous enemy to China, we preferred to be her friend, and that, in fine, the object of my mission was what it professed to be on the face of it, an amicable arrangement of the terms of future intercourse, commercial and political, on principles honourable and just, as well to China as to the United States.

These circumstances serve in some degree to account for the great expedition with which the negociations proceeded. Their despatch was facilitated also by the solicitude of Tsiyeng to return to Canton.

And it was still further promoted by the desire of the Chinese Minister to conclude every thing with the United States before the arrival of the French Legation.

And while due allowance must of course be made for the politeness of diplomatic expressions, the views of Cushing find support in the stated attitude of the Chinese Commissioner; first to be quoted is an extract from one of the so-called "official" communications of Tsiyeng (*ibid.*, No. 73, enclosure M1, of June 29, 1844, translation; printed in part):

I received some days since Your Excellency's communication of the 21st instant and the residue of the draft of the treaty, with which I have made myself fully acquainted. Your Excellency is unwilling to take possession of any of the territory belonging to China, but desires to have the United States and China treat each other with respect, cordiality, and justice. In truth, this conduct is vastly different from that of the English taking and keeping possession of Hong Kong, and therefore the deliberations upon the schedule of the treaty will be very unlike those upon the original draft of the English treaty. When I first had the honor of an interview with Your Excellency, I learned that you had come hither with the simple purpose (of cultivating) good will; and this draft of the treaty confirms me in that idea. Since Your Excellency has the laudable intention and is heartily desirous of firmly establishing a treaty by which the people of our respective countries will be protected hereafter in peace, I also am of the same mind, and my pleasure thereat is not small.

Another note in point in this connection is "semi-official", that of July 2, 1844, from the Chinese Commissioner (*ibid.*, No. 74, July 10, 1844, enclosure D1, translation; not printed), in which this was written:

By your extremely kind reception of the sentiments of my former notes the conditions of the treaty between our respective nations have been brought to a speedy settlement. Justice and rectitude must manifestly dwell in Your Excellency's heart; and in your transaction of business equity is strictly maintained. Unspeakable are my emotions of joy and gratitude.

The Treaty of Peace, now agreed upon, will soon be concluded, and we both ought equally to rejoice and offer congratulations. I have prepared a repast of fruits and tea, and beg Your Excellency will, at four o'clock tomorrow, come to enjoy festivities and friendly converse at my residence, in token of the future tranquillity, peace, and joy that await our two nations. May these bonds of friendship be perpetual.

Under date of June 21 Cushing submitted a project of a treaty, regarding which he wrote to the Chinese Commissioner as follows (*ibid.*, No. 73, enclosure A1):

At the interview which I had the honor to hold with your Excellency on the 19th instant, it was agreed that Messrs Wang, Chow, and Pwan, in behalf of your Excellency and Messrs Webster, Bridgman and Parker, in my behalf, should meet together at a subsequent hour on the same day, and arrange the time and mode of proceeding to the business with which we are charged by our respective Governments.

These Gentlemen met accordingly; when Messrs Wang, Chow and Pwan stated that your Excellency was ready to enter at once upon the consideration of a Treaty between our respective countries, and desired me to present a *projet* of such a treaty as would be satisfactory to the United States.

I cannot refuse to meet your Excellency's proffer in the spirit of promptitude and frankness, in which it was made, though, in assuming this responsibility without any previous discussion of preliminaries, I place myself at some disadvantage.

I have the honor, therefore, to submit to your Excellency the minutes of a proposed Treaty, which covers all questions, except two or three, of a special nature, and of great importance, which I desire to present to your Excellency separately at an early day.

It is proper for me to state briefly the principles on which this *projet* of Treaty has been prepared.

1. The United States is to treat with China on the basis of cordial friendship and firm peace.

2. We do not desire any portion of the territory of China, nor any terms or conditions whatever, which shall be otherwise than just and honorable to China as well as the United States.

My Government would be happy to treat with China on the further basis of perfect reciprocity in all commercial relations. All the ports of the United States are open to foreign commerce, and we do not impose any duties on exports. But I am well aware of the Emperor's wish to limit the commerce of foreign nations to five ports of the Empire, and to retain the general system of duties in the establishment of which your Excellency was a principal agent. In the spirit of amity towards China, the United States acquiesces in the view of this subject, which it has pleased the Emperor to adopt. And, accordingly, I have drawn up the minutes of a Treaty adapted to this exceptional state of facts, only proposing such articles as may procure to the Citizens of the United States a free and secure commerce in the ports open to the nations of the West.

It will occur to your Excellency to remark that some of the articles are different from those contained in the commercial treaties recently concluded with England. A single fact constitutes the cause of this difference. Those two treaties are based on the fact of the possession of Hong-Kong by Great Britain; and the commercial provisions have relation to this primary idea. The United States

does not seek any such possession in China, and is therefore constrained to propose new articles of commercial regulation, for the security of citizens of the United States, residing or prosecuting trade in China.

I have to make the further remark, that in drawing up these minutes, I have not looked to the side of the United States alone. I felt that it would not be honorable in dealing with your Excellency to take a partial view of the subject. I have inserted a multitude of provisions in the interest and for the benefit of China. In a word, I have sought to present the draught of a Treaty, which, as already intimated, shall be, in all parts, alike just and honorable to China and to the United States.

I am sure your Excellency's candor will do justice to the motives which have actuated me in this matter; and I can give the assurance that I will consider in the same candor any modifications which your Excellency may propose.

I will communicate the Tariff for annexation to morrow.

No copy of that draft or "minutes" of a treaty is with the despatches; details of the text were discussed by the three representatives of each Government deputed for that purpose by the Commissioners; one of the three deputed by Cushing was Daniel Fletcher Webster, better known as Fletcher Webster; he was Secretary of the Mission (D.S., 3 Credences, 40), was the son of Daniel Webster, and had been Chief Clerk of the Department of State; he had been authorized to act as Commissioner in event of the death or disability of Cushing (D.S., 1 Instructions, China, 1–4). Dr. Elijah Coleman Bridgman and Dr. Peter Parker were missionaries; the latter was both physician and clergyman; each of them translated many of the documents of the negotiations; each signed at times as Joint Chinese Secretary to the Legation; Dr. Parker was later (1855) appointed Commissioner to China; regarding the services of Drs. Bridgman and Parker, Cushing wrote as follows (D.S., 2 Despatches, China, No. 101, January 25, 1845; not printed; see also Dennett, *op. cit.*, 142–43):

But the most indispensable branch of assistance in the Mission, and that involving most expense, was for translation & interpretation, chiefly in Chinese & Tartar for intercourse with the Chinese Government, and in Portuguese for intercourse with the authorities of Macao. These duties were performed chiefly by Drs E. C. Bridgman and Peter Parker, American Missionaries in China, and by Mr Stanislas Herniss.

. . . .

On Messrs Bridgman, Parker, and Herniss, especially, there devolved a great amount of writing, as well as of intellectual labor.

Drs Bridgman & Parker are of that most praiseworthy & meritorious class of men, who devote themselves to the propagation of the Gospel in pagan lands, and deservedly stand among the highest in estimation of the American Missionaries in the East. They were preeminently useful to the Legation, not only as interpreters & translators, but also as *advisers*, by reason of their long & exact knowledge of China.

Drs Bridgman & Parker also officiated as chaplains to the Legation, in the performance of religious services at the residence of the Legation on the Lord's Day.

The negotiations otherwise proceeded in two forms of correspondence between Cushing and Tsiyeng, the "official" correspondence, which is enclosed with despatch No. 73, and the "semi-official" correspondence, which is enclosed with despatch No. 74, both of which have been cited.

It does not appear that any very material changes were made in the American draft; Cushing's own account of the mode in which the negotiations were conducted is in his despatch No. 72, of July 8, 1844 (D.S., 2 Despatches, China), in which he wrote:

By way of preface to copies of the correspondence connected with the Treaty of Wong Sha, I proceed to lay before you a brief account of the mode in which the negociations between the Imperial Commissioner and myself were conducted.

On the 16th instant Tsiyeng arrived at the Chinese village outside the barrier of Macao, called by the Portuguese Casa Branca; and on the 17th. he passed the barrier, and took lodgings for himself and suite at a Chinese temple dedicated to the Lady of Mercy, situated in a village within the barrier, but without the walls, of Macao. This village is designated by two Chinese words, which are pronounced Mong Ha in the provincial dialect of Canton, Wang Ha (or Ya) in the dialect of Nanking, and Wang Sha at the Court.

The temple had been fitted up with some degree of taste for the reception of the Imperial Commissioner and the numerous soldiers, followers and servants, with which, according to the usage of men of his rank in China, he was attended.

Accompanying the Commissioner, as his advisers and assistants, were three Chinese officers of distinction, namely Hwang, the Treasurer of the Province, Chow, a member of the Han-lin college, and Pwan, Circuit judge of the Province. Two of these persons, Hwang and Pwan, by means of their long residence at Canton, and their general intelligence, and one of them, Pwan, by reason of his parentage, he being the son of an opulent Hong merchant, are understood to possess very liberal views in regard to the foreign relations of China.

On the 18th. in conformity with previous notice, the Imperial Commissioner, together with Hwang, Chow and Pwan, and their respective suites, came to the residence of the Legation, to make a visit of ceremony and to be introduced to the Legation and to the officers of the American Squadron.

The Commissioner was received and entertained by me with suitable regard to the dignity of my Government, but the interview was, at his request, a purely friendly one, no business being transacted, the time being passed in conversation, in expressions of mutual esteem, and in exchange of assurances of the reciprocal good will of the United States and China. On the ensuing day, the 19th. I proceeded, accompanied by the gentlemen of the Legation and by Commodore Parker and several officers of the squadron, to Wang Sha to return his visit. We were received and entertained in the most friendly and hospitable manner; but no business was transacted, further than to agree that Messrs Webster, Bridgman and Parker, on my part, and Messrs. Hwang, Chow and Pwan, on the part of the Imperial Commissioner, should meet again during the evening of the same day and arrange the course of negociation.

At each of these interviews every thing was conducted on a footing of perfect equality and of course no questions of etiquette arose.

At the interview of the evening Messrs. Hwang, Chow and Pwan made known the readiness of the Imperial Commissioner to proceed at once to the discussion of the articles of a Treaty between China and the United States.

Accordingly, on the 21st I communicated to Tsiyeng the *projet* of a Treaty, and, by agreement between us, Messrs. Webster Bridgman and Parker, on the one side, and Messrs Hwang, Chow, and Pwan on the other met together for a number of days in succession, partly at my house in Macao, and partly at Wang Sha, and discussed and modified this *projet*, in behalf of myself and Tsiyeng respectively, until it assumed the form of the Treaty as concluded and signed on the third instant at Wang Sha.

Meanwhile on the 24th Tsiyeng and myself had an interview of business at the residence of the Legation, in which interview the principles of the Treaty and Sundry incidental questions were briefly discussed.

All the points discussed on this occasion will appear in the written correspondence, which ensued, it being understood that for the purpose of putting on record our respective views the interview should be deemed an informal one, and that we should proceed to re-discuss the several matters in question, in written communications.

Of the different subjects touched upon at this time, there is occasion for me to refer, in this place, to two only, in anticipation of what appears in the copies of correspondence.

One is the question of my proceeding to Peking. In this interview Tsiyeng avowed distinctly that he was not authorised either to obstruct or facilitate my proceeding to the Court, but that if I persisted in the purpose of going there, at this time, he had no power to continue the negociation of the Treaty.

In a despatch appropriated to this matter I shall have occasion to show the bearing and effect of this declaration of the Imperial Commissioner

At the same interview it was agreed by us that Hwang in behalf of the Chinese, and Dr. Parker in behalf of the Americans, should constitute a commission, to arrange and agree upon suitable provisions for the security of the foreign factories at Canton.

On this subject, also, I shall have occasion to address a separate communication to the Department.

After the conclusion of the business interview of the day Tsiyeng dined at the house of the Legation, in company with the American Ladies residing in Macao.

You will observe that the correspondence between Tsiyeng and myself, pending the negociations, is of two descriptions, many of the questions being discussed in semi-official communications, which were distinguished from the others, not only by the size and form of the letters, but by the absence of the style of official correspondence, and, also, by being uniformly addressed in Manchu.

At length, on the 3ᵈ of July, the articles of the Treaty being all fixed, and the several copies, four in English and four in Chinese, completed and ready for signature, I repaired by agreement to Wang Sha, where four originals of the Treaty were signed and sealed in the presence of Commodore Parker and several gentlemen of the Legation, and of the Chinese accompanying, or in attendance upon, Tsiyeng.

After the execution of the Treaty, we partook of an entertainment and exchanged congratulations on the speedy and happy issue of the negociation; and the next day the Commissioner left Wang Sha for Canton.

It now remains to complete the details of the Tariff, to be annexed to this Treaty, after which it will be ready for transmission to the Department.

It is clear that the tariff schedules were not completed until some days after the signature of the treaty proper; and as the Chinese Commissioner left for Canton on July 4, they were not signed by Cushing until July 22 and then, it seems, were sent to Canton for signature and sealing by Tsiyeng, to whom Cushing wrote on that date as follows (D.S., 2 Despatches, China, No. 80, July 31, 1844, enclosure 2):

I have the honor to acknowledge the receipt of your Excellency's communication of the 9th instant, covering a draught of the Tariff in Chinese to be annexed to the Treaty of Wang-Shia: all which I have examined and find to be in accordance with the terms as arranged at the time of the signature of said Treaty. I have therefore caused to be prepared a counterpart in English; and have affixed my seal and signature to four copies in each language as in the case of the Treaty, two to be retained by your Excellency and two by myself.

Cushing wrote this very full explanation of his reasons for deciding against attempting negotiations at Peking (*ibid.*, No. 76, July 15, 1844):

From the contents of sundry despatches preceeding this you will have gathered the general reasons for my consenting to negociate at Macao, instead of Peking. But I am desirous to lay these before you in a more specific form.

It is to be observed, in the first place, that the Imperial Government entertains the strongest repugnance to receiving embassies of the Western Governments. It's policy, so far as regards these, is one of seclusion. It has no proper depart-

ment of Foreign affairs. It sends no embassies of its own to Europe or America. It is accustomed to receive only tribute-bearing embassies from various minor states in Asia, which recognize, in different degrees of submission, the supremacy of the Ta Tsing Empire.

When European Embassies here made their way to Peking, they have been compelled (with the single exception of that of Lord Macartney) to submit to the degrading acts of vassalage and of religious worship, which the forms of the Tartar Court exact from all men; or, refusing this, they have been compelled to leave Peking without being presented to the Ta Howang Tei. If received, they are expected to remain only a few weeks, and in no case have they succeeded in transacting any important public business at Peking.

This general policy of the Tartar Court has been fortified by recent events; the war with Great Britain having rendered the Court more averse than ever to admit Embassies from the Western States.

Accordingly the Imperial Government, immediately on receiving notice from the American Consul at Canton that the United States had appointed a Minister to China, made known to him, and through him to the Government of the United States, that it was unwilling the American Minister should go to Peking.

The views of the Chinese Government in this respect were communicated to me by the Acting Governor General soon after my arrival at Macao, as the correspondence already transmitted by me to the Department will show at length.

I struggled against these objections until intelligence was officially communicated to me of the appointment of Tsiyeng as Imperial Commissioner and of his being actually on his way to Canton.

To have left Macao after receiving this intelligence would have subjected me to the imputation of fleeing from, and as it were evading, a meeting with Tsiyeng; and such an imputation would have constituted a serious difficulty (if not an insuperable one) in the way of successful negociation at the North.

Independently of this consideration, I deemed it of the highest importance to the interests of the United States to be able to treat with Tsiyeng. It would have been vain to expect to meet with any other Chinese statesman equally well disposed and equally competent to conduct the negociation in behalf of China.

At Canton also were other statesmen likely to be associated with Tsiyeng, who (as the result showed) were better informed on foreign affairs and possessed of better feelings towards the United States, than any persons to be found at the North.

And though my instructions required me to employ all proper efforts to reach Peking, yet going thither after all was but the means to an end, that end being the establishment of the commercial interests of the United States in China on a satisfactory footing of advantage, confidence friendship and permanency. To attain this end was the indispensable object; the means were a matter of choice according to circumstances.

Add to which, that in the actual disposition of the Chinese Government on this subject to go to Peking at all with the free consent of that Government had become a matter requiring negociation, to be discussed with some Minister at some point on the Coast; for it is to be remembered that Peking is an inland city and that no foreigner can obtain the means of conveyance in China or subsistence on the roads, without the consent of the Government.

I could not anywhere expect to find a negociator on this question more friendly than Tsiyeng.

With these reflections present to my mind it only needed to consider further whether I should endeavour to force my way to Peking, or at least by demonstration of force at the mouth of the Pih-ho attempt to intimidate the Imperial Government into conceding to me free access to the Court. In regard to this it is to be observed that, owing to the extraordinary delays of the St. Louis on her way here, I had no means of making any serious demonstration of force at the North prior to the time when Tsiyeng arrived at Canton on his way to Macao, there to meet me and negociate a Treaty.

And with an Imperial Commissioner near at hand, ready and willing to treat, would it have been expedient or even justifiable to enter upon acts of hostility with China in order if possible to make Peking the place of negociation?

To do so, would be, as already remarked, to sacrifice the end for the sake of the means.

Even the European Law of Nations, with all it's provisions in behalf of diplomatic Ministers, and the assertion of the duty of every Government to receive and negociate with them, yet admits that the Government to which a minister is sent may well refuse to receive him at the Court, provided it appoints some other convenient place, and some suitable person, for the negociations. (Vattel. b. IV, ch. 5. S. 65) And I felt well assured that the United States would not sanction the performance of acts of hostility against China for the object of placing a resident Minister at Peking, and still less for the object of a Minister being received and entertained for a brief period at the Court.

Such was the state of the question when Tsiyeng arrived at Macao, and avowed his readiness at once to enter upon the negociation of a Treaty of Amity and Commerce, satisfactory to the United States.

In the communication he had made to Mr. Forbes on the subject of the Legation, he had assumed that no Treaty could or would be made with the United States, on the ground that the Imperial Government had, of it's own motion, opened the new ports to all nations, and conferred on them the same rights and privileges, which the English had obtained by Treaty; all which had been repeated in the correspondence of Ching with myself.

But this ground the Imperial Government had now abandoned, professing it's readiness to make all reasonable concessions to the United States and to assure these concessions by Treaty.

At the same time Tsiyeng declared, either verbally or in writing, that if I chose to proceed to Peking he could not, according to his instructions, treat with me at all; that he had no commission to throw any impediments in the way of my proceeding to the North, but, on the other hand, that he was not authorised to afford me any facilities; that if I treated with him here, China would deal with the United States as a sincere and trusting friend; but that if I insisted upon going to Peking, in the face of the strong indisposition of the Court, I must take my chance as to my reception there, with the probability of all the substantial objects of my Mission being lost on a question of Court Ceremony, even if no worse event ensued, of possible collision, or at least ill will, between the two Governments.

These facts being clearly understood I could not doubt as to my duty in the case.

The interests of the United States in China are commercial, not political, and it was the primary purpose of my mission to make satisfactory arrangements for the prosecution of our commerce with this Country under new and more favourable circumstances.

All this was now within my reach. To sacrifice it, to run the risk of losing it altogether, and to peril our public peace as well as our commerce upon the question of being received at Peking was a proceeding, which, it seemed to me, neither my Government, nor any portion of the people of the United States would justify or approve.

For I have never disguised from myself the serious difficulties, which I might encounter in forcing my way to Peking, and if voluntarily admitted there, the difficulties, almost equally serious, connected with the question of presentation at Court. On the one hand I had come to a fixed resolution not to perform the acts of prostration to the Emperor, nay I had acquired so firm a conviction of the servile as well as idolatrous character of the ceremony of prosternation, that I had determined not to entertain question on the subject. On the other hand, I did not well see how the United States could make war on China to change the ceremonial of the Court. And for this reason, it had always been, with me, an object of great solicitude to dispose of all the commercial questions by Treaty before venturing on Peking.

If it should be suggested that it would have been better for me to have proceeded at once to the North without stopping at Macao, I reply that this was impracticable at the time of my arrival, with the Brandywine alone, before the Southerly Monsoon had set in, and without any steamer; that if at any time I had gone to the North in the view of negociating there I should have been wholly dependant on the Chinese for the means of lodging and subsisting on shore, and even for the means of landing at the mouth of the Pih-ho; that only at Macao could I treat independently, and that here of necessity must all the pecuniary and

other arrangements of the Mission be made, and the supplies obtained for the Squadron.

Such are the considerations and the circumstances, which induced me to consent to forego proceeding to Peking.

Treating here I have secured for the United States the two great objects of my Mission, namely—In the first place, a Treaty of Amity and Commerce on the most favourable conditions; and, in the second place, the friendship and good will of the Imperial Government.

And, in regard to Peking itself, I have obtained the means of direct correspondence between the two Governments immediately, and an express engagement, that, if hereafter a Minister of the French, or any other Power, should be admitted to the Court, the same privilege shall be accorded to the United States.

If the conclusion of the whole matter be one less agreeable to my own feelings of pride or curiosity, it is, at any rate, the most important and useful to my country and will therefore, I trust, prove satisfactory to the President.

The "express engagement" mentioned in the next to the final paragraph above quoted was contained in the note of Tsiyeng of June 29, 1844, in which he wrote (D.S., 2 Despatches, China, No. 73, enclosure O1, translation):

Hereafter if the ministers of Western nations are admitted to Peking, then the ministers of your honorable country in China will rightfully, with becoming etiquette, and without partiality, be received at the North. My August Sovereign treats all men with equal and perfect equity and will never make distinctions among the nations of the West, esteeming and favoring some more and others less.

EXTRATERRITORIALITY IN CHINA

Various articles of the treaty (especially Articles 21 and 25) give judicial powers to consuls or other officers of the United States. A statute in aid of these provisions was recommended by President Tyler in his message to Congress of January 22, 1845 (Senate Document No. 58, 28th Congress, 2d session, serial 450; House Document No. 69, same session, serial 464). One of the two despatches of Cushing printed with that message (No. 97, September 29, 1844) discusses the question of extraterritoriality at length.

Reference here can be made only to the earliest statute on the subject, which was the act of August 11, 1848 (9 Statutes at Large, 276–80); there are later statutes, treaties, and regulations; the numerous phases of the general subject have been much discussed in learned treatises and elsewhere (see Moore, Digest, II, 644–53; Haswell, 1279–85).

A recent and important official document is the "Report of the Commission on Extra-territoriality in China", signed at Peking on September 16, 1926, by the representatives of thirteen powers, including the United States (China, No. 3, 1926; Cmd. 2774); and the work of Professor Willoughby, Foreign Rights and Interests in China, deals elaborately with the question, particularly in the second volume.

ARTICLES 30 AND 31

The subject of communications between the two Governments is dealt with in Articles 30 and 31 of the treaty; it was somewhat elaborately discussed during the negotiations; Cushing's account of

the matter is in his despatch of July 13, 1844 (D.S., 2 Despatches, China, No. 75), which, with the two enclosures therein mentioned, follows:

Heretofore it has been the policy of the Court of Peking not only not to permit resident embassies, but also not to entertain direct communication, by correspondence, with any of the Western Governments, except in the case of Russia.

In proof of the rigour with which this rule has been observed, it deserves to be mentioned, that there is not in the *personnel* of the Chinese Government any Minister or Department corresponding to the Minister or Department of Foreign affairs in Europe.

There are two bureaux at Peking which administer certain affairs belonging to this class. One is the *Le Fan Yuen*, which has charge of the business of this Government with the Mongol and other nomadic tribes on the West and Northwest of China Proper. This bureau is called the Colonial Board in some English publication. It more nearly corresponds both in dignity and functions to our Superintendency of Indian affairs.

The other is the "Le Poo", or as it is commonly called in English, the board of Rites. One of the sections of this Council, Board, or Commission, has charge of the reception of the envoys of certain minor states in the East, which are tributary to the Ta Tsing Empire.

If it were suitable to the dignity of any independent state (which it is not) to address itself to either of these boards, the difficulty would remain that neither of them has jurisdiction of the relations of China to the Western Governments.

It is utterly absurd and inadmissible for China to think of persevering, under the new state of facts which has arisen, in excluding all direct correspondence of Western Governments with the Court.

Indeed, the Chinese Government has made a perceptible advance towards the appointment of a Minister of Foreign affairs, in the very extensive commission it has conferred on Tsiyeng, of General Superintendant, or Administrator of the Foreign Intercourse of the Five Ports, in virtue of which, and of his authority as Imperial Commissioner Extraordinary, he has the power to treat with any and all Foreign Powers.

Situated as China now is, forced into diplomatic relations with Great Britain, the United States and France, such a Ministry cannot fail to grow, erelong, into a proper Department of Foreign affairs.

I proposed and steadily insisted upon some provision of Treaty applicable to this point, but the Imperial Commissioner made much difficulty in regard to it, as you will perceive from the papers annexed hereto, marked (A) and (B.), which consist of a memorandum presented by Tsiyeng and of one presented by myself in reply. It was at length arranged that the Government of the United States shall have the power to correspond with the Court, and that the proper Ministers on the Frontier shall be required to receive and forward all such correspondence, leaving the Minister at Peking, or the board which shall be addressed, *to the choice and discretion of the United States.*

Contemporaneously with the making of this arrangement, it has been construed in one respect by the fact of the reception and transmission of the letter of the President to the Ta Howang Tei, or Emperor, as he is commonly called. That is, the President and the Emperor address each other according to the forms of usage existing between the United States and the Monarchies of Europe.

In regard to communications from the Secretary of State of the United States, I decidedly recommend that they be addressed either to the Nuy Ko, that is the Cabinet, or to the General Council.

There is no individual Minister at Peking to whom they ought to be or can be addressed.

But communications from the President to the Emperor, or from the Secretary of State, directed either to the Cabinet or to the General Council, must, under the provisions of the Treaty of Wang Shia [Article 31], be received at either of the Five Ports, by the Imperial Commissioner, if there be one, or if not by the respective Governors General of the three Provinces in one or the other of which the Five Ports are situated, and forwarded to Peking according to their address. And in this way access to the Chinese Court is at length opened to all the Western Governments, or at least to the United States.

It has been supposed heretofore, erroneously, that a great Minister of State existed at Peking called 'the Grand Colao', whom it was proper for Foreign Governments to address. This error was propagated by Lord Macartney. No such officer or name or office is to be found in the Peking Red Book, which is as full and particular on these subjects as any of the European Red Books, or the American Blue Book.

In fact, when a letter from Lord Castlereagh, some years ago, addressed to "the Great Colao or Prime Minister of the Chinese Empire" was tendered to the Governor General of the two Kwangs for Transmission, that officer refused to receive it, for the general reason that the regulations of the Ta Tsing Empire forbad the receipt of any such communication, as also for the special reason, enlarged upon by the then Emperor, Kia King, that there was no such Minister as the supposed 'Great Colao' (Staunton's Chinese Embassy to the Tourgouth Tartars, ap.) Indeed there is no doubt that Lord MaCartney's error arose from misapprehension, the person whom he dealt with as 'Grand Colao', possibly holding at that time the office of '*Koloi Amban*' (so called in Tartar) and as such having charge of the affairs of the embassies of *tributary states*, in which category, it is well known, the Embassy of Lord Macartney was, with his tacit acquiescence, classed. (Ld. Macartney's private journal).

These circumstances place in the clearest light, not merely the facts of the peculiar organization of the Chinese Government and the jealous care with which all access to it has been barred against the nations of Europe, but also the still more striking fact of the slow progress of Europeans in acquiring a knowledge of the forms of the Chinese Government.

For two hundred years, as the Chinese are accustomed to phrase it, Europeans had had intercourse with China; a dozen European Embassies had visited Peking; a most intelligent and inquisitive British Embassy had just been there; and yet it still remained a mystery to what Minister of State, if any, the Communications of a European Government ought to be addressed, and to this day, I believe, even Great Britain has no direct official intercourse with the Chinese Court.

The Article of the Treaty of Wang Shia and the two Memoranda, with other parts of the correspondence between Tsiyeng and myself seem to settle this question, in so far, certainly, as regards the United States.

[Enclosure A—Translation]

Hitherto China has never established intercourse with the ministers of foreign nations. Properly the Fan Yuen (藩院), or Colonial Board, is the appropriate board for the superintendence of each of the Mang Koo, Mongolian, and Mohammedan tribes. It is the province of the Board of Rites (禮部),

Le Poo, to manage the affairs of Siam, Lew Chew, and Korea and Cochinchina, which have ever been treated as dependent states. All the great nations of the West are altogether upon terms of equality, and it is inexpedient to refer their correspondence to the office for the correspondence of the dependent states of China. I, the Minister, have received the imperial appointment to the office of conducting the appropriate affairs of free commerce at the five ports. All that relates to the despatches of your honorable nation's ministers ought to be referred to the Minister's office to be replied to. If, after the expiration of my term of office, another minister shall receive the superintendence of the appropriate affairs of the five ports, then your honorable nation's minister ought with him to correspond.

If there be no minister appointed, the Governors of the border provinces of the Empire are the highest officers who can with your honorable nation's minister hold communications. To the Board of Censure (都察院), Too Chû

Yuen, it belongs to receive the complaints of citizens of China against its officers. With foreign nations they have never once had intercourse. Moreover, with the affairs of foreign countries at the five ports they have not been fully informed, and how can they manage the complaints of consuls! I, the Minister, therefore think, respecting the several open ports on the coast, that if at Canton, then the

correspondence should be referred to the Governor of Kwang Tung and Kwang Se, at Fuchow, Amoy, and Ningpo, to the Governor General of Chekiang and Fukien, and if at Shang-hae, then refer it to the Governor General of Kiang Nan and Keang Se, all of whom are Chinese ministers of the first class, by whom all on the seaboard is to be regulated.

If the consuls of each port have complaints to make, then let a duly prepared communication be made to the office of the Governor and wait for him justly and equitably to dispose of it. If the affair be small, the Governor can adjudge it; if of magnitude, he can clearly memorialize the Emperor to dispose of it; or if there be a commissioner extraordinary appointed to the general superintendence of the proper business of the five ports, the consul can also complain to him.

(Presented by Tsiyeng June 28, 1844.)

[Enclosure B]

The Government of the United States desires to have a Minister at Peking. If this demand be waived, it becomes indispensably necessary that some other means be provided, by which the Government of the United States may make known it's wishes to that of China. The Secretary of State of the United States will not transact the business of the two nations with a mere Provincial Governor. Nor, if he were willing to do so, would that be satisfactory, because it may well happen that the Government of the United States desires to invoke the interposition of the Imperial Government to correct the errors or chastise the misconduct of some Provincial Governor. And this is quite as important to China as it is to America; for, if the United States should have occasion to redress any wrong, and all access to the court is closed up, so that no communication can be addressed to it, then the United States has no remedy but by recourse to arms. It was in this way that the late war with England came to take place. If the English Government had possessed any means of directly addressing the Court, and thus bringing it's views and wishes to the Knowledge of the Emperor, it would have sought redress from the justice and magnanimity of the Emperor, instead of bringing soldiers into China. I have perfect confidence in the good faith and firmness of Kekungpow;[1] but some one of his successors may be a bad man, and may conduct ill; and it is not for the life of one generation, but for all future time, that we are now arranging the affairs of the two nations. I am sure the Emperor will always do right; but I am equally sure that Provincial Governors will sometimes do wrong. My object, then, in proposing that there be provided some person or board at Peking whom the Government of the United States may address, is because it is one of the means of preventing all occasion or possibility of a breach of peace between China and the United States. Such questions are not a provincial affair, but a national one, because the peace of the whole nation is involved. They must of course come before the Court sooner or later; and it is better they should go to it directly. And if there be any objection to the Li Pu, I propose the Nuy Ko, or the General Council.

(Presented, June 28th 1844 by C Cushing to Tsiyeng)

The intent of Article 31 was that "communications from the President to the Emperor, or from the Secretary of State, directed either to the Cabinet or to the General Council, must, under the provisions of the Treaty of Wang Shia, be received at either of the Five Ports, by the Imperial Commissioner, if there be one, or if not by the respective Governors General of the three Provinces in one or the other of which the Five Ports are situated, and forwarded to Peking according to their address" (despatch No. 75, quoted above). The Viceroyalty

---

[1] Kekungpow, now generally romanized Ch'i kung-pao, refers to "Ke Ying", "Keying", or "Tsiyeng", all variant transcriptions of the same person's name. Ke (Ch'i) is his surname. Kungpow (Kung-pao) is an official title, translated as "Guardian of the Heir Apparent".

of Liangkwang comprised the "Two Kwang" (preamble), the Provinces of Kwangtung and Kwangsi, of the former of which Canton (or "Kwangchow", Article 3) is the capital; Amoy and Foochow are in the Province of Fukien, formerly Min; Cheh, or Chekiang, is the Province in which is located Ningpo; and the Viceroyalty of Liangkiang comprised the Provinces of Kiangsu, Anhwei, and Kiangsi; the first of these is the maritime Province of which Shanghai is a port.

FOREIGN TERMS IN THE TREATY

The "Ta Tsing Empire" is the title given to China in the preamble; the name of "Ta Tsing" or "Great Pure" was that adopted by the Manchu dynasty, which displaced the Ming dynasty in 1644.

Taou Kwang, or Tao-kuang, mentioned in the final clause, was Emperor of China from 1820 to 1850; the date given "of Taoukwang, the twenty-fourth year, fifth month, and eighteenth day" is that of his reign, in years of lunar months; similarly the original Chinese ratification is textually (though erroneously) dated "Taou Kwang the 25th year, 7th month, and 2nd day", which would be August 4, 1845; and the act of the exchange of ratifications is of that same year, the twelfth month and the third day, or December 31, 1845.

The name of the village where the treaty was signed (in the outskirts of Macao) is given variously in the English of the originals as "Wang Hiya" (original with the proclamation; "Hiya" shows an erasure), as "Wang Shia" (original with the duplicate United States ratification; "Shia" shows an erasure, and above is written "Hiya" in pencil), and as "Wang Hea" (original ratified by China). In the despatch of Cushing of July 8, 1844 (D.S., 2 Despatches, China, No. 72), this is written:

on the 17th. [June 1844] he [Tsiyeng] passed the barrier, and took lodgings for himself and suite at a Chinese temple dedicated to the Lady of Mercy, situated in a village within the barrier, but without the walls, of Macao. This village is designated by two Chinese words, which are pronounced Mong Ha in the provincial dialect of Canton, Wang Ha (or Ya) in the dialect of Nanking, and Wang Sha at the Court. [Above the three forms so given are written respectively, in another hand, "Mong-Hah", "Wang-Heah", and "Wang Sheah".]

In the act of exchange of ratifications the name is given as "Wang Hiya", which appears then to have been regarded as the approved transliteration.

The five ports mentioned in Article 3 are "Kwangchow, Amoy, Fuchow, Ningpo and Shanghai". In the tariff the names, except for the first, are the same; there the first is Canton, which is "Kwangchow" or more correctly Kwang-chowfu; in Article 12 there is also mention of Canton.

In Articles 6 and 7 there is used the word "mace" as a unit of payment; and in the tariff the rates are stated in "taels", "mace", and "candareens".

The tael is the term current for the Chinese *liang* or ounce, the *liang* of fine, uncoined silver being the monetary unit. The tael is thus not a coin, but a measure of weight. At the time of this treaty there

was no one standard tael, as each large commercial center had its own; so the equivalent of the tael is variously stated; but the "Haikwan" or customhouse tael is about 585 grains troy; the gold value of that silver tael accordingly varies with the price of silver. As a money of account the tael is divided into 10 mace (*ch'ien*), 100 candareens (*fên*), 1,000 cash (*li*).

Various terms used in the tariff are explained in the regulations annexed to the convention of November 8, 1858 (rule IV); there a *ch'ih* (Chinese foot) was said to be equal to 14.1 English inches; a *ts'un* is one tenth of a *ch'ih*; it was also there agreed that a *chang* of 10 Chinese feet equaled 141 English inches or four yards English less three inches.

In that same rule IV of the regulations annexed to the convention of November 8, 1858, it was agreed that a "catty" was 1⅓ pounds avoirdupois; a catty is one hundredth part of a "picul"; one hundred catties (or one picul) equals, therefore, 133⅓ pounds avoirdupois.

As to Chinese weights and measures generally, see Dingle, Across China on Foot, 399–402. It is there said that the "tow" (final clause of the tariff) contains 629 cubic inches.

The "shroffs" (Article 13) were those employed as experts to inspect and count coins.

The "compradors" (Article 8) were the chief native servants of foreign business houses.

"Sycee silver" (Article 13) is uncoined silver, cast in ingots and marked with the weight and fineness.

The hong merchants (Article 15) were a body of Chinese merchants at Canton who formerly had the monopoly of trading with Europeans. Article 16 mentions the "system of the co-hong"; the practice had been abolished by Article 5 of the Treaty of Nanking of August 29, 1842 (British and Foreign State Papers, XXX, 390; see also *ibid.*, XXXI, 152, regulation 4); a description of the system and its operation is in Dennett, *op. cit.*, 48–51.

THE CANTON REGULATIONS

The subject of the security of foreigners and foreign interests at Canton had been discussed during the negotiations, and a commission consisting of Dr. Peter Parker for the United States and Hwang for China, had been set up to consider the matter (despatch No. 73, quoted above). With his despatch of August 15, 1844, Cushing enclosed a copy, in English and Chinese, of regulations regarding Canton, which appear to have been regarded as in partial execution of the provisions of the treaty (e.g., Article 19); in that despatch Cushing wrote as follows (D.S., 2 Despatches, China, No. 84):

From the contents of previous despatches, you will have inferred how insecure is the present condition of the hongs occupied by the Americans, and indeed by the foreigners generally, in Canton.

Repeated acts of incendiarism on a large scale, attack of the buildings by mobs, and acts of intrusion and insult, have shown the necessity of some provision for the better security of the Foreign Factories.

The Treaty of Wang-Hiya contains ample stipulations *of a general nature* in the interest of the personal safety of Americans.

It seemed to me important, however, that detailed arrangements should be made in part execution of these provisions of the treaty.

Accordingly at one of my interviews with the Imperial Commissioner in Macao I called his attention to the matter; my object being to obtain the consent of the Chinese Government to the extension of the grounds occupied by my countrymen at Canton, the construction of a solid wall around the factories, the closing up of some streets, the erection of gates and the establishment of an efficient and adequate police for the guard of the gates and the repression of the evil disposed persons among the Chinese.

The Imperial Commissioner readily agreed that this question should be satisfactorily arranged and proposed that the Provincial Treasurer Hwang on his part and a suitable person to be designated by me should constitute a commission to frame the requisite regulations.

Assenting to this proposition I authorised Dr. Parker to act in my behalf.

The result is the regulation of which a copy is annexed.

As these regulations affect all the *foreign* Residents at Canton and as I, of course, could not presume to bind them, all, while at the same time the interests of the foreigners, or at least of all but the English are identical, it was agreed that the substance of these regulations should go into operation upon a proclamation to be made by the Imperial Commissioner for that purpose.

Dr. Parker endeavoured also to obtain sites for additional foreign residences on the Island of Hoenan, between Canton and Whampoa, but objections were made to this, although it was agreed that foreigners might rent buildings wherever it should be found safe and convenient.

I anticipate much benefit to the American Residents from these Regulations.

The regulations were written in English and Chinese; the English text which follows is from the copy transmitted with the despatch of August 15, 1844, above quoted; and it is to be noted that the regulations were signed by representatives of the two Governments.

New Regulations for the security of the Citizens of the United States resident at Canton.

The following articles have been deliberated on and settled.

1ˢᵗ The citizens shops in the vicinity of the Thirteen Factories being densely crowded together there is great liability to the calamity of fire, and we must in anticipation guard against it. Hereafter it is permitted to the Merchants and Citizens of Foreign Nations to erect walls on the foundations of their own premises forty cubits high and from one cubit and a half to two cubits thick,[1] all the additional expense of building, labour and materials to be defrayed by the occupants of the Factories.

2ᵈ From the head of Sin Tow Lane (Green Pea Street) on the East and from the entrance of Tsing Yuen Kae (Old China Street) on the West to the River the old wooden fence shall be changed to a strong wall either of stone or brick, the expense thereof to be defrayed by foreign merchants. This is granted to avoid the Chinese in passing and repassing looking through the fence causing disturbances and quarrels.

3ᵈ The three streets Tung Wang Kae (New China Street) Tsin Yuen Kae (Old China Street) and Sin Tow Lan on the North and on the rear of the Factories it is also permitted the Foreign occupants thereof to erect high walls and at the North and South ends of these streets to make strong doors of wood covered with sheet iron.

4ᵗʰ Chinese and Foreigners being mixed up together it is easy for trouble to arise, hereafter therefore at the six gates of the three streets it is right to establish

---

[1] The Chinese text reads "four *chang* high" and "from 1 *ch'ih* and 5 *ts'un* to 2 *ch'ih* thick"; this would be 47 English feet high and about 21 to 28 inches thick.

a military station and posts for sentries who shall constantly dwell there and keep guard.

Men bearing things above and upon their shoulders to traffic with (pedlars) are not permitted in front and on the right and left of the Factories to expose for sale melons, fruits, cakes, et caetera, and likewise all quacks, fortune tellers, barbers, beggars and show-men—and all idlers and the like are not permitted to pass and repass in front and on the right and left of the Factories, obstructing the way and collecting a crowd of idlers. Whoever violates this (regulation) shall be searched out and pursued to the utmost.

In the event of any quarrel or of the calamity of fire these six gates shall be immediately shut and locked and the idlers shall not be permitted to look through and should any bandits insist on violently entering and wrangle with the guards and soldiers the bandits shall be rigorously seized and punished to the utmost. If the soldiers and guards are remiss in expelling them they also shall be severely punished.

The official station at the head of Tung Yuen Kae, (old China Street) a clever and able military officer shall be appointed who shall constantly have command with soldiers and guards attached to him who shall reside there to keep watch. Should any wrangling or trifling disturbance occur, it shall be warded off by the said military officer in charge of the place, but in the event of a riot the said Mandarin shall petition the high officers of Government to lead out police men and soldiers in great numbers and proceed to make investigations and so to manage as to preserve peace.

6th Hence forth the street in front of the Factories is not to be a thoroughfare; the gates at both ends, by order of the Consul may be closed at sunset, and also upon the sabbath, in order that there may be no confusion.

7th If any of the shops in the neighborhood of the Thirteen Factories clandestinely sell ardent spirits to Foreigners to drink, on being found out the said shops shall be closed and the proprietor thereof shall be seized and punished.

8th It is not permitted to throw out and accumulate filth at the head of the streets.

This has long been publickly prohibited, and required that all in front and rear of the Hongs and at the head of the Streets shall be kept pure and clean. Whoever shall throw out and accumulate filth therein, shall, on being found out, be sent to the officers of Government and be tried and punished.

9th The foregoing regulations shall be stereotyped and printed and delivered over to the military officers to be pasted up at the head of each street that all may clearly understand.

Taou Kwang 24th yr. 5th m. 27th day.
July 12th 1844.

HWANG GAN TUNG
PETER PARKER.

Also enclosed with the despatch of August 15, 1844, was a copy of a note of the same date addressed to the Chinese Commissioner, in which Cushing wrote:

Dr Parker has reported to me the regulations, drawn up by the provincial Treasurer Hwang and himself, in virtue of the authority conferred on them by us, respectively at one of our interviews in Macao.

These regulations appear to me to be in the main exceedingly judicious, and well adapted to promote the security of the foreign merchants at Canton, to prevent collisions between them and the Chinese, and to cement the good intelligence of the two Governments.

With two small modifications, therefore, I cheerfully agree to and accept them, on the part of the United States, namely,

First, that the proposed wall be erected at the expense either of the proprietors or occupants; that is, not at the expense of the Chinese Government.

And, secondly, that the inclosure be continued along the water-side.

I am informed by Dr Parker that such was the understanding of himself and of Hwang Ta Jin on the subject; and I presume these modifications will be satisfactory to your Excellency.

THE TREATY OF 1842 BETWEEN CHINA AND GREAT BRITAIN

Allusion was made to the treaty of 1842 between China and Great Britain in the message of President Tyler to Congress of December 30, 1842 (Richardson, IV, 211–14), and in the instructions to Cushing of May 8, 1843, above quoted.   That Treaty of Nanking of August 29, 1842 (English text in British and Foreign State Papers, XXX, 389–402), and the treaty supplementary thereto of October 8, 1843 (English text in *ibid.*, XXXI, 132–56), were to a considerable extent the basis of this treaty; the differences of substance between the respective agreements with Great Britain and the United States were discussed in the despatch of Cushing of July 5, 1844 (D.S., 2 Despatches, China, No. 71), in which he wrote:

I have the honour to enclose to you a copy of the Treaty of Wang Hiya, as signed on the third instant.

On examining this document you will find in the first place that in the description of the contracting parties, the language of the stipulations and the mode of execution, the style of perfect equality between the United States and China has been sedulously observed, and I may add that this has been carefully attended to in the Chinese, as well as in the English Duplicate, of the Treaty.

You will perceive, in the second place, that this Treaty contains many provisions which are not embraced either in the Treaty of Nanking or in the Treaty supplementary thereto, which embraces the Tariff and the Commercial Regulations.

First. The Tariff is amended by the reduction of the duties on some articles of American production and by fixing with greater precision what goods are contraband, or subjects of monopoly.

There is nothing in the English Treaties to limit the power of the Emperor in the exclusion of articles of import or export.

Thus he might render all commercial privileges nugatory, by prohibiting the exportation of tea and silk and the importation of cotton or cotton fabrics; or he might obstruct the commerce in these, or any other articles, by making them the subjects of close monopoly, as is now the case with salt.

This is guarded against in the Treaty of Wang Hia by making the objects of contraband and monopoly a matter of stipulation between the Governments. And no modifications of the Tariff are to be made without the consent of the United States.

Second. By the English Treaties the Consul is security for the payment of duties and is bound to prosecute for all infraction of the revenue laws of China. This is to transfer to the British Government the office and responsibility of paying duties, which involves much of regulation and of form in the prosecution of trade, which experience has already shown to be inconvenient to the subjects, as well as the Government, of Great Britain.   All this is avoided in the Treaty of Wang Hia, by making the duties payable in cash, which is perfectly acceptable to the merchant, and in accordance with the course of business in China.

Third. New provision is made in the amplest manner for the trade from port to port in China.

A ship which having touched at Canton has there paid tonnage duties and discharged a part of her cargo, may proceed with the residue to any other port in China without being subject to the payment of tonnage duty a second time, and goods which have been landed and paid duty at one of the ports of China, may, at any time, be re-exported to any other port of China, without being subject to any further duty.   This latter provision is equivalent to a warehousing system for all the coast of China.

Fourth. Due provision is made for the recognition and personal dignity and security of Consuls, or any other officers, whom the Government of the United States may see fit to appoint for the superintendance of our trade in China.

Fifth. In regard to the payment of duties various provisions are inserted for the convenience of our commerce, with respect to the mode of payment, and

among others, that merchandize may be landed from time to time, as may be convenient, duty being paid on the articles only when they are landed, and that vessels may, within a limited time depart, if they please, without breaking bulk.

Sixth. Citizens of the United States are to have all accomodation, at each of the five ports, not only, as heretofore, in the construction of dwelling houses and magazines, but also of churches, cemeteries and hospitals.

Seventh. Provision is made for the employment by Americans of persons to teach the languages of the Empire, and the purchase of books is legalised; it having been the custom heretofore for the Chinese Government to persecute and oppress such of it's subjects as either gave instruction or sold books to foreigners in China; which circumstance has been a great obstacle to the study of the languages of China, and the acquisition of the means of satisfactory intercourse with it's Government

Eighth. All Americans in China are to be deemed subject only to the jurisdiction of their own Government, both in Commercial matters and in questions of civil right.

I shall have occasion hereafter to enter into these subjects somewhat in detail and to suggest to the President the expediency of recommending to Congress the enactment of laws in this relation, applicable not only to Americans in China, but in Turkey and elsewhere in Asia, where Americans (in common with Europeans) are in like manner exempt from the jurisdiction of the local Government.

Ninth. Citizens of the United States in China, and every thing appertaining to them, are placed under the special protection of the Chinese Government, which engages to defend them from all insult or injury.

If the Chinese Authorities neglect their duty in this respect they of course become responsible for all consequences, on complaint being made to the Government of the United States.

In part execution of this, and other corresponding provisions of the Treaty, particular arrangements are in train for the further security of citizens of the United States residing in Canton, of which a report will be made to you in due time.

Tenth. The vessels of the United States are to come and go freely between the ports of China and those of any other country with which China may happen to be at war, in full security not only for the ship, but for all descriptions of merchandize, the neutrality of our flag and every thing it covers being especially guarantied.

Eleventh. Provision is made for the protection and relief of vessels stranded on the coast of China, or driven by any sort of *vis major*, into whatever port of China; and also for the restitution of property taken by pirates in the seas of China.

Twelfth. Equality in correspondence between civil or military and naval officers of the United States and those of China is stipulated; as also the observance of all courtesy and respect in the correspondence between individual citizens of the United States and officers of the Chinese Government.

Thirteenth. No presents are to be demanded of either Government by the other.

The usage among Asiatic states of giving and receiving presents has been the source of great inconvenience to the United States in those cases even where it has been a mere matter of courtesy.   But as the receipt of presents by the Chinese Government, has always, hitherto, been assumed by the latter as an act of tribute on the part of the Government making such presents, it seemed to be still more desirable to abolish the practice at once by a provision of the Treaty.

14th. Ships of war of the United States and their Commanders are at all times to be courteously received in the ports of China.

It seemed to me that such a provision would secure to our ships of war all such access to the ports of China as may be needful, either for their own relief or for the protection of the merchant ships and citizens of the United States; while it would be inconvenient to go so far as the English have done and engage to keep a ship of war at all times in each of the five ports of China.

Fifteenth. Heretofore no Government (except Russia) has held direct communication with the Court of China.   At the present time even the British Government does not hold correspondence with the Court of Peking.   I insisted upon and obtained a provision for communications between the two Governments.

The article of the Treaty does not specify to *whom* communications from the United States shall be addressed, it being left to the discretion of the American Government to elect whom it will address, not excepting the Emperor.

Upon this point I shall make to you a separate communication, with reference, as well to it's importance, as for the purpose of indicating the parties at Court whom it will be most convenient for the Secretary of State to address, when occasion shall arise.

Sixteenth. In regard to opium, which is not directly mentioned in the English Treaties it is provided by the Treaty of Wang-Hia, that all Citizens of the United States engaged in this or any other contraband trade shall receive no protection from the American Government, nor shall the flag of the United States be abusively employed by other nations as a cover for the violation of the laws of China. Upon this point also, I shall have occassion to address you a separate despatch.

I have thus, in a brief manner indicated some of the peculiar provisions of this Treaty.

Many of them are new and important.

Some of the English news papers have commented, rather boastfully upon the fact that the English arms had opened the ports of China to other nations, and at the same time have, with flippant ignorance, ridiculed the idea of a Mission from the United States, to do that which had been already wholly done by England.

I ascribe all possible honour to the ability displayed by Sir Henry Pottinger in China and to the success which attended his negociations, and I recognise the debt of gratitude which the United States and all other nations owe to England for what she has accomplished in China. From all this much benefit has accrued to the United States.

But, in return, the Treaty of Wang Hia, in the new provisions it makes confers a great benefit on the commerce of the British Empire, for the supplementary Treaty stipulates that any new privileges conceded by China to other nations shall be enjoyed also by England, and there is a similar provision in the Treaty of Wang-Hia; and thus whatever progress either Government makes in opening this vast Empire to the influence of foreign commerce is for the common good of each other and of all Christendom.

The details of the Tariff are not yet completed and some incidental questions remain to be arranged.

I shall dispose of these matters as soon as possible, in order to transmit the Treaty, and all the correspondence, and various other particulars of the negociation, in season, if possible, to be laid before the Senate at the opening of the next session of Congress.

THE LETTERS EXCHANGED

One of the documents entrusted to Commissioner Cushing was a letter from the President of the United States to the Emperor of China; and as Cushing was obliged to abandon his proposed visit to Peking, one of the matters which he arranged with the Chinese Commissioner was the transmittal of that letter to the Emperor of China, for which purpose it was given to Tsiyeng (D.S., 2 Despatches, China, No. 73, enclosures P1, Q1; No. 74, enclosures D1, E1, F1, G1; the latter were not printed).

The style of the letter of President Tyler was quite unusual; the text thereof follows (D.S., 1 Communications to Foreign Sovereigns and States, 270–72; Senate Document No. 138, 28th Congress, 2d session, serial 457; cf. Fuess, *op. cit.*, I, 419–20):

I, John Tyler, President of the United States of America, which States are— Maine, New-Hampshire, Massachusetts, Rhode-Island, Connecticut, Vermont, New-York, New-Jersey, Pennsylvania, Delaware, Maryland, Virginia, North Carolina, South Carolina, Georgia, Kentucky, Tennessee, Ohio, Louisiana, Indiana, Mississippi, Illinois, Alabama, Missouri, Arkansas and Michigan— send you this letter of Peace and Friendship, signed by my own hand.

I hope your health is good. China is a Great Empire, extending over a great part of the World. The Chinese are numerous. You have millions and millions of subjects. The Twenty-six United States are as large as China, though our People are not so numerous. The rising Sun looks upon the great mountains and great rivers of China. When he sets, he looks upon rivers and mountains equally large, in the United States. Our Territories extend from one great ocean to the other,—and on the West we are divided from your Dominions only by the Sea. Leaving the mouth of one of our great rivers, and going constantly towards the setting Sun, we sail to Japan, and to the Yellow Sea.

Now, my words are, that the Governments of two such Great Countries, should be at Peace. It is proper, and according to the will of Heaven, that they should respect each other, and act wisely. I, therefore, send to your Court, Caleb Cushing, one of the wise and learned men of this Country. On his first arrival in China, he will inquire for your health. He has then strict orders to go to Your Great City of Pekin, and there to deliver this letter. He will have with him, Secretaries and Interpreters.

The Chinese love to trade with our People, and to sell them Tea and Silk—for which our People pay Silver, and sometimes other articles. But if the Chinese and the Americans will trade, there should be rules, so that they shall not break your laws, nor our laws. Our Minister, Caleb Cushing, is authorised to make a Treaty, to regulate trade. Let it be just. Let there be no unfair advantage on either side. Let the People trade, not only at Canton, but also at Amoy, Ning-po, Shang-hai, Foo-Choo-foo, and all such other places as may offer profitable exchanges, both to China and the United States; provided they do not break your laws, nor our laws. We shall not take the part of evil-doers. We shall not uphold them that break your laws. Therefore, we doubt not, that you will be pleased that our Messenger of Peace, with this letter in his hand, shall come to Pekin, and there deliver it,—and that Your great officers will, by Your order, make a Treaty with him to regulate affairs of Trade,—so that nothing may happen to disturb the Peace, between China and America. Let the Treaty be signed by Your own Imperial hand. It shall be signed by mine,—by the authority of our Great Council, the Senate.

And so may your health be good, and may Peace reign.

Written at Washington, this twelfth day of July, in the year of Our Lord, one thousand eight hundred and forty-three.

Your Good Friend!

JOHN TYLER.

By the President:
A. P. UPSHUR,
   Secretary of State.

The answering letter of the Emperor of China was transmitted by Tsiyeng to Dr. Peter Parker, who forwarded it to Cushing, then in Washington, by whom it was delivered to the Secretary of State under date of June 21, 1845 (D.S., 2 Despatches, China; not printed). The original is a scroll of heavy yellow silk and brocade, backed with linen, mounted on two wooden rods, and contained in a case of yellow silk; it is written in Chinese and Manchu, with the imperial seal at the top between the two texts. The contemporaneous translation by Dr. Peter Parker (presumably of the Chinese text) was an enclosure to the despatch mentioned and reads literally as follows (the words underscored once being here printed in italics, and those underscored twice, in capitals and small capitals):

The GREAT EMPEROR presents his regards to the PRESIDENT and trusts HE is well.

I the EMPEROR having looked up and received the manifest *Will* of HEAVEN, hold the reins of *Government* over, and sooth and tranquilize, the *Central Flowery Kingdom*, regarding all within & beyond the border seas as one and the same Family.

Early in the Spring the *Ambassador* of *Your Honorable Nation, Caleb Cushing,* having received *Your Letter,* arrived from afar at my *Province* of *Yuè.* He having passed over the vast oceans with unspeakable toil and fatigue, I the EMPEROR not bearing to cause him further inconvenience of travelling by land and water, to dispense with his coming to *Peking* to be presented at *Court,* specially appointed *Ke Ying,* of the IMPERIAL HOUSE, *Minister* and *Commissioner Extraordinary* to repair thither and to treat *Him* with courteous attentions.

Moreover, they having negotiated and settled all things proper, the said *Minister* took the *Letter* and presented it for MY INSPECTION, and YOUR sincerity and friendship being in the highest degree real, & the thoughts and sentiments being with the utmost sincerity & truth kind, at the time of opening & perusing it, my pleasure and delight were exceedingly profound.

All, and every thing, they had settled regarding the *Regulations* of *Commerce,* I the EMPEROR further examined with utmost scrutiny, and found they are all perspicuous, and entirely and perfectly judicious, and forever worthy of adherence.

To *Kwang Chow, Heu Mūn, Fūh Chow, Ning-Po,* and *Shang Hae,* it is alike permitted the *Citizens* of the *United States* to proceed, and according to the articles of Treaty, at their convenience to carry on Commerce.

Now bound by perpetual *Amity* and *Concord* advantage will accrue to the *Citizens* of both *Nations,* which I trust must certainly cause the PRESIDENT also to be extremely well satisfied and delighted.

Taou Kwang.   24th yr. 11th m. and 7th d.   16th Dec. A.D. 1844

Great Seal of the Empire in Chinese and Tartar.

[Signet of the Imperial Will.]

PETER PARKER
Late Chinese Secʸ to the Legation.

With the original document is the following comment (written by Raymond Parker Tenney):

The characters for "President" are used without honorifics, while those for "Emperor" are preceded by the character "Great". The importance of the Emperor is emphasized by the position of the three characters for "The Great Emperor (His Imperial Highness)" at the beginning of the letter. The opening sentence is in colloquial Chinese, as if addressed to an illiterate person. The second sentence requires no comment.

110

NEW GRANADA : NOVEMBER 5, 1844

Convention for the Settlement of the Case of the Brig "Morris", signed at Bogotá November 5, 1844. Original in English and Spanish. Not subject to ratification by the United States. As to ratification by New Granada, see the notes. Not proclaimed.

We, the Undersigned, to wit: William M. Blackford, Chargé d'Affairés of the United States, and Joaquín Acosta, Secretary of Foreign Relations of New Granada, have agreed that the claim arising from the capture of the American brig Morris and cargo by the Colombian privateer Schooner, María Isabel, on the 12th May 1825, which claim has been pending for some years before the Government of New Granada; shall be settled in the manner expressed in the following articles.

Los infrascritos, a saber: el Secretario de Relaciones Esteriores de la Nueva Granada, Joaquin Acosta, i el Encargado de Negocios de los Estados Unidos, Guillermo M. Blackford, hemos convenido que la reclamacion a que dió motivo el apresamiento del bergantin anglo-americano Morris i de su cargamento verificado el 12 de Mayo de 1825 por el corsario colombiano goleta Maria Isabel; i cuya reclamacion se halla pendiente ante el Gobierno de la Nueva Granada algunos años ha, quede transijida de la manera que espresan los artículos siguientes:

ARTICLE THE 1^{rst}

The Government of New Granada obliges itself to pay and hold subject to the order of the Chargé d'Affairés of the United States, or to the order of any other person or persons that may be appointed by the Government of the United States at the instance of the parties interested in

ARTÍCULO 1º

El Gobierno de la Nueva Granada se obliga a pagar a la órden del señor Encargado de Negocios de los Estados Unidos o a la órden de cualquiera otra persona o personas que designe el Gobierno de dichos Estados Unidos a instancias de las partes interesadas en el bergantin Morris

the brig Morris and her cargo,— the sum of twelve thousand seven hundred and fifty six dollars, forty seven and a half cents ($12,756$\frac{47\frac{1}{2}}{100}$). The said amount comprises the following items:— for the value of the brig Morris, three thousand dollars ($3000); for the value of the part of the cargo belonging to the owners of the brig, as per invoice, three thousand four hundred and ninety one dollars, three and a half cents ($3,491$\frac{3\frac{1}{2}}{100}$); for the value of the part of the cargo belonging to Thomas Bachus, as per invoice, three thousand seven hundred and sixty five dollars, forty four cents ($3,765.$\frac{44}{100}$); and for one year's demurrage of the vessel, two thousand five hundred dollars, ($2,500.). This sum shall be paid in the current money of the country,—in nine equal instalments,—at intervals of two months, in such a manner that the total amount shall be paid within the term of eighteen months, to be counted from the day on which the present Convention shall be approved by the Congress of New Granada.

ARTICLE THE 2nd

The Government of New Granada likewise obliges itself to pay, upon the said sum of twelve thousand seven hundred and fifty six dollars, forty seven and a half cents, the accruing interest, at the rate of six per Cent per annum, from the 12th January 1826 until

i en su cargamento la suma de doce mil setecientos cincuenta i seis pesos i cuarenta i siete i medio centavos (12756\frac{47\frac{1}{2}}{100}$). Esta suma proviene de los siguientes valores: por el bergantin Morris tres mil pesos ($3000): por la parte del cargamento perteneciente a los dueños del buque, segun factura, tres mil cuatrocientos noventa i un peso i tres i medio centavos (3491\frac{3\frac{1}{2}}{100}$): por la parte del cargamento perteneciente a Tomás Bachus, segun factura, tres mil setecientos sesenta i cinco pesos i cuarenta i cuatro centavos (3.765\frac{44}{100}$); i por demoras i estadias del buque durante un año, dos mil i quinientos pesos ($2500). La suma total se pagará en moneda corriente del pais por novenas partes iguales cada dos meses, de tal manera que toda ella quede cubierta dentro del término de diez i ocho meses contados desde el dia en que el presente convenio sea aprobado por el Congreso de la Nueva Granada.

ARTÍCULO 2º

Igualmente se obliga el Gobierno de la Nueva Granada a satisfacer sobre dicha suma de doce mil setecientos cincuenta i seis pesos i cuarenta i siete i medio centavos (12756\frac{47\frac{1}{2}}{100}$) el interes correspondiente a razon de un seis por ciento anual que correrá

the day upon which each bi-monthly instalment shall be respectively paid: and this being the compensation that the New Granadian Government grants for all losses and damages which may have been occasioned to all parties interested in the aforesaid brig and cargo, they shall have no right, whatever, to raise in future any new claim upon this matter.

desde el 12 de Enero de 1826, hasta el dia en que se efectúe el pago de cada partida bimestral respectivamente; siendo esta la indemnizacion que otorga por todas las pérdidas i perjuicios que puedan haberse ocasionado a cuantas personas estuvieren interesadas en el mencionado bergantin i su cargamento, quienes no conservarán derecho alguno para intentar en ningun tiempo ninguna nueva reclamacion sobre este particular.

ARTICLE THE 3rd

The payment of the capital, as well as that of the interest, shall take place, in the manner stated, in the preceeding articles, at the General Treasury of the Republic.

ARTÍCULO 3º

Así el pago del capital como el de los intereses, se verificará en la Tesorería Jeneral de la República i en los términos espresados en los artículos anteriores.

ARTICLE THE 4th

This Convention shall be presented by the Executive Power of New Granada to the National Congress of the same Republic, in its aproaching session, in order that, after approving of it, it may vote the necesary amount for carrying it into effect.

In faith of which, we, the Undersigned, have subscribed our names to two copies of this Convention, in Bogotá, on the fifth November one thousand eight hundred and forty four.

Wᵐ M. BLACKFORD
JOAQUIN ACOSTA

ARTÍCULO 4º

Este convenio será presentado por el Poder Ejecutivo de la Nueva Granada al Congreso nacional de la misma República en su próxima reunion, a fin de que, prévia su aprobacion, vote la cantidad necesaria para que tenga efecto.

En fé de lo dicho nosotros los infrascritos hemos firmado dos ejemplares de este convenio en Bogotá a cinco de Noviembre de mil ochocientos cuarenta i cuatro.

JOAQUIN ACOSTA
Wᵐ M. BLACKFORD

NOTES

The original of this convention, with which the texts here printed have been collated, is in two papers, one in each language, in D.S., Colombian Claims, folder *Morris*. As may be seen from the printed texts, the principle of the *alternat* was observed.

Under the procedure adopted, the convention was not subject to ratification by the United States; it was "approved by the Congress of New Granada in a legislative decree" of April 19, 1845 (D.S., 11 Despatches, Colombia, No. 5, January 16, 1846, enclosure, note of the Secretary of Foreign Relations of New Granada of January 14, 1846; Codificación nacional de Colombia, XI, 43). There is no record or mention of full powers; but as to the powers of the Chargé d'Affaires of the United States, William M. Blackford, see the notes to Document 101, the convention with New Granada of February 9, 1843, in the case of the *By Chance*.

The "Morris"

The brig *Morris* belonged to Richard H. Douglass and Henry H. Williams, citizens of the United States, and was registered at Baltimore; with Williams as master, the *Morris* sailed from Santiago, Cuba, about March 31, 1825, for Gibraltar; when in sight of "the rock", the *Morris* was captured on May 12, 1825, by the Colombian privateer *Maria Isabella*, Captain Doutant, and was taken into Puerto Cabello; some of the passengers were Spaniards; part of the cargo and a sum in specie on board were Spanish; the remaining cargo was, it seems, American, and no part thereof was claimed to be contraband. The Admiralty Court at Puerto Cabello acquitted the vessel and also the cargo, so far as it was American; but there was delay, owing to appeal proceedings, and both vessel and cargo were sold. The claim made was for the value of the vessel and of all the cargo, for the specie, and for freight, demurrage, and interest; the facts and the law of the case are elaborately discussed in the enclosures to the despatch of William M. Blackford, Chargé d'Affaires at Bogotá, of February 2, 1844 (D.S., 10 Despatches, Colombia, No. 20).

The Settlement

The case of the *Morris* was mentioned in Article 3 of the convention with Colombia of November 25, 1829 (Document 67), but was then left open for future adjustment.

The liability of the former Republic of Colombia, in this as in other cases, devolved upon the three successor Republics in the proportions of 50 percent for New Granada, 28½ percent for Venezuela, and 21½ percent for Ecuador (Moore, Digest, V, 559–61; see also the notes to Document 67). The amount of the claim was a matter of negotiation in each case, as it had not been fixed.

Venezuela first agreed to a lump-sum settlement in the amount of $18,000, which was paid (see Document 104).

The negotiations which, after prolonged delay and previous discussions, resulted in the settlement with New Granada of the case of the

Morris, were carried on at Bogotá by William M. Blackford, Chargé d'Affaires of the United States, and Joaquín Acosta, Secretary of Foreign Relations of New Granada. Following various notes Blackford proposed a definite sum, abandoning certain items; it was that proposal which was accepted and was embodied in this convention; and the action of Venezuela in making a lump-sum settlement on a somewhat more liberal basis of liability appears to have been of influence; for although agreement here was "virtually concluded" in February or early March 1844, when the arrangement with Venezuela could not have been known at Bogotá, that arrangement anticipated this convention by some eight months (see the correspondence of Blackford with Allen A. Hall, Chargé d'Affaires at Caracas, quoted in the notes to Document 104).

The proposal made by Blackford and the course of the argument are thus set forth in the despatch of Blackford of February 2, 1844 (D.S., 10 Despatches, Colombia, No. 20):

Our first conference was held on the 10th January. The evidence, on both sides was produced and collated and many incidental points discussed and decided I found the Secretary [of Foreign Relations] frank and liberal, and I am constrained to say that an examination of the evidence, contained in the original papers of the case, considerably modified the opinion I had formed upon the *ex parte* testimony in my possession

I deemed it my duty to contend for the operation of the Treaty of Bogotá [that with Colombia of October 3, 1824, Document 47], at the date of the capture of the Morris, and supported the position, in my despatch [meaning note to the Secretary of Foreign Relations] of the 22[d] of Decr. by such arguments as I could command. I confess, however, that I was not satisfied with my own reasoning, and had no authorities to cite in support of my doctrine. Acting in good faith, therefore, I abandoned the point insisted upon—viz. that the Treaty of Bogotá should be considered in force from the date of its last ratification and not merely from the date of the Exchange of Ratifications. As the capture occurred upon the 12th & the Exchange of ratifications not until the 27th of May, 1825, the liberal provisions of the Treaty were consequently admitted to be inapplicable.

In the second conference, the question was presented, whether I would adhere to the judicial sentences in the case, or rely upon the general principles of the Law of Nations. In view of all the circumstances, I considered it to be safer to claim as a basis for the settlement, the first decision of the Admiralty Court of Puerto Cabello, pronounced on the 6th July 1825. This decision acquitted the Brig and the greater part of the cargo, as American property—upon the condition, however, that Captain Williams should produce to the Court a certified copy of the clearance of the Brig, from the Custom House of S[t] Iago de Cuba. Within the time specified Williams presented a document of a character somewhat suspicious, certainly, but—which was pronounced by the Court to be satisfactory. The condition of the sentence of the 6th July 1825 having thus been fulfilled, the Brig and the acquitted part of the cargo should at once have been restored to the owners. It was not, however, until the 12th of January, 1826. that the court declared itself satisfied and decreed restitution.

Unfortunately, Williams appealed from this last sentence, because no damages had been awarded to him. The captors also appealed, on account of supposed partiality of the Judge, and on the further ground of the alleged spurious character of the document from the S[t] Iago de Cuba Custom House. This appeal of Williams—which is no where mentioned in his various statements—is the fact, upon which the Secretary bases his resistance to the claim for Demurage, and led me to put down that item smaller than I should otherwise have done. I do not know that a claim for Demurage could justly be demanded at all, but for the fact, which, I think, is sufficiently proven, that the clearance—the want of which prevented the Brig & neutral part of the Cargo from being unconditionally acquitted by the Sentence of 6th July '25—had been given by Capt. Williams,

with the rest of his papers, to the Commander of the Privateer & was by the latter suppressed or destroyed.

Having failed to cover the case by the provisions of the Treaty of Bogotá, as heretofore stated, I could not deny that the capture of the Morris was not in violation of the Laws of Nations. This admission, of course, implied a surrender of all claim to the Spanish property & money on board, and likewise for Freight. There were circumstances of subsequent outrage on the part of the Captors, and vexatious delays in the adjudication of the case. The whole of the judicial proceedings—conformable as they may have been to the Constitution and laws of Colombia—appear strange when compared with the administration of Justice in our own country. On the other hand, it must be admitted, that the conduct of Capt. Williams, at the time of the capture & subsequently, was somewhat calculated to excite suspicion. In more than one instance, during the progress of the Trial, and especially by his appeal from the sentence of 12th Jany 1826 he seriously compromised his interests. He seems to have been badly advised.

Taking into consideration every circumstance connected with the case, and having reference to the deplorable state of the finances of New Granada,—to the probable temper of the two Houses of Congress—and to the obstacles which each succeeding year added to a satisfactory adjustment of the claim, and believing that the present favorable dispositions of the Executive afforded an opportunity which might not speedily again present itself, I determined to present a modified demand for indemnity—as follows.

1. For value of Brig _____ $6. 000
2. For value of owner's part of Cargo, as pr Invoice _____ 6. 982. 07
3. For value of Backus' part of Cargo as pr Invoice _____ 7. 530. 88
4. For Demurage, one year _____ 5. 000. 00

                                                                     $25, 512. 95

5. Interest at 6 pr cent from 12th Jany 1826 til paid say 18 years _____ $27. 554. 59

                                                                      $53. 067. 54

The proportionate part of this Government being one half, the amount she would have to pay, at this time, is about $26,533.77.

I am fully aware that this is an amount, much below what the parties interested have, heretofore, claimed, and may be less than that to which, in strict justice, they are entitled. In offering to receive it, I acted for the best interests of the claimants—to have demanded more I believe would have led to the rejection of the whole claim. My instructions leave the management of the whole affair to my discretion and I have, to the best of my ability, followed the dictates of that discretion. I trust the Department, on a review of all the circumstances, will be pleased to approve of my conduct.

As to the argument this is to be said: By the treaty with Colombia of October 3, 1824 (Document 47, Article 12), free ships made free goods; that treaty was clearly not in force on the date of the capture (May 12, 1825), as the date of the exchange of ratifications was fifteen days later; the argument for the controlling character of the date of the "last ratification" (that by Colombia, March 26, 1825) was quite untenable, though made pursuant to instructions (of February 12, 1839, quoted in Moore, Digest, V, 245); but the point might well have been pressed that, as between the two Governments, the date of signature was the essential date (see the authorities cited, *ibid.*, 244); and another point, hardly raised at all, was that, even if the treaty with Colombia of 1824 did not govern the case, it still was ruled by that with Spain of 1795, which also provided for "free ships, free goods" (Document 18, Article 15; confirmed, as to such a case

as that of the *Morris*, by Article 12 of the treaty with Spain of February 22, 1819, Document 41; see the notes to Document 47, vol. 3, pp. 187–88, and Moore, International Arbitrations, II, 1574–75).

PAYMENT

The nine instalments due under the convention were duly paid; but there were difficulties of remittance, with premiums for gold ranging from 7½ to 14 percent (D.S., 11 Despatches, Colombia, No. 4, January 16, 1846; No. 6, February 19, 1846; No. 19, June 3, 1846; No. 39, January 16, 1847; No. 46, April 23, 1847; No. 51, November 1, 1847).

Notwithstanding this settlement, a further claim in respect of the brig *Morris* was made before the Commission under the convention of February 10, 1864, with the United States of Colombia, but was adjudged not valid (Moore, International Arbitrations, II, 1418, case 37).

The settlement with Ecuador of the case of the *Morris* was made by the convention of February 9, 1850, the notes to which should be consulted.

Treaty Series No. 16
9 Statutes at Large, 826-29
18 *ibid.*, pt. 2, Public Treaties, 41-42

111

BAVARIA : JANUARY 21, 1845

Convention for the Mutual Abolition of the Droit d'Aubaine and Taxes on Emigration, signed at Berlin January 21, 1845. Original in English and German.
Submitted to the Senate February 26, 1845. (Message of February 24, 1845.) Resolution of advice and consent, with amendment, March 15, 1845. Ratified by the United States March 18, 1845. Ratified by Bavaria September 3, 1845. Ratifications exchanged at Berlin November 4, 1845. Proclaimed August 15, 1846.

Convention for the mutual abolition of the droit d'aubaine, and taxes on emigration, between the United States of America, and His Majesty the King of Bavaria

The United States of America and His Majesty, the King of Bavaria, having agreed for the advantage of their respective citizens and subjects, to conclude a Convention for the mutual abolition of the droit d'aubaine and taxes on emigration, have named, for this purpose, their respective Plenipotentiaries, namely: the President of the United States of America has conferred full powers on Henry Wheaton, their Envoy Extraordinary, and Minister Plenipotentiary at the Royal Court of Prussia, and His Majesty, the King of Bavaria, upon Count Maximilian von Lerchenfeld-Koefering, His Chamberlain, Envoy Extraordinary and Minis-

Vertrag über die gegenseitige Aufhebung von Heimfalls-(Fremdlings-) Recht, und Auswanderungs-Steuern zwischen den vereinigten Staaten von Nord-America und Sr Majestät dem König von Bayern.

Nachdem die vereinigten Staaten von Nord-Amerika und Sr Majestät der König von Bayern übereingekommen sind, zum Besten der beiderseitigen Staats-Angehörigen einen Vertrag über gegenseitige Aufhebung von Heimfalls (Fremdlings-) Recht, und Auswanderungssteuern abzuschliessen, so sind hiezu von beiden Seiten Bevollmächtigte ernannt worden, als nämlich von Seiten des Präsidenten der vereinigten Staaten von Nord-Amerika, Herr Heinrich Wheaton, nordamerikanischer ausserordentlicher Gesandter, und bevollmächtigter Minister am königlich preussischen Hofe, und von Seiten Sr Majestät des Königs von Bayern, Allerhöchst dessen

671

ter Plenipotentiary at the Royal Prussian Court, Commander of the Royal Order of the Knights of St. George, of the Order for Merit in Civil Service of the Bavarian crown, of St. Michael, Grand Cross of the Russian Imperial Order of St. Anne of the first Class, of the Royal Prussian Order of the Red Eagle of the first Class, Commander Grand Cross of the Royal Swedish Order of the North Star and Great Commander of the Royal Greek Order of the Saviour,—who after having exchanged their said full powers, found in due and proper form, have agreed to and signed the following Articles:

Gesandten und bevollmächtigten Minister am königlich preussischen Hofe, Graf Maximilian von Lerchenfeld-Koefering, Commandeur des königlichen Ritterordens vom heiligen Georg, der königlichen Civil-Verdienstorden der bayrischen Krone, und vom heiligen Michael, Grosskreuz des kaiserlich russischen St. Annenordens I Classe in Diamanten, des königlich preussischen rothen Adlerordens I Classe in Diamanten, Commandeur Grosskreuz des königlich schwedischen Nordstern-Ordens und Gross-commenthur des königlich griechischen Erlöser-Ordens,—welche Bevollmächtigte, nach vollzogener Auswechslung ihrer, in guter und gehöriger Form befundenen Vollmachten nachstehende Artikel festgesetzt und unterzeichnet haben:

ART. I

Every kind of droit d'aubaine, droit de retraite and droit de détraction or tax on emigration is hereby, and shall remain abolished between the two Contracting Parties, their States, citizens and subjects respectively.

ART. I

Jede Art von Heimfalls- (Fremdling) Recht, Nachsteuer und Abzugsrecht, oder Auswanderungssteuer, ist und bleibt aufgehoben zwischen beiden abschliessenden Theilen, ihren beiderseitigen Staaten und Staats-Angehörigen.

ART II

Where, on the death of any person holding real property within the territories of one Party, such real property would, by the laws of the land, descend on a citizen or subject of the other, were he not disqualified by alien-

ART. II

Wenn durch den Tod irgend eines Besitzers von Immobilien oder Grundeigenthum, welche sich auf dem Gebiete des einen der abschliessenden Theile befinden, diese Immobilien oder Grundeigenthum nach den Ge-

age, such citizen or subject shall be allowed a term of two years to sell the same, which term may be reasonably prolonged according to circumstances, and to withdraw the proceeds thereof, without molestation, and exempt from all duties of detraction.

Art. III

The citizens or subjects of each of the Contracting Parties shall have power to dispose of their[1] personal property within the States of the other, by testament, donation, or otherwise, and their heirs, legatees, and donees, being citizens or subjects of the other Contracting Party, shall succeed to their said[1] personal property, and may take possession thereof, either by themselves, or by others acting for them, and dispose of the same at their pleasure, paying such duties only as the inhabitants of the country where the said property lies shall be liable to pay in like cases.

setzen des Landes auf einen Staats-angehörigen des andern Theils übergehen sollen, so wird diesem, wenn er durch seine Eigenschaft als Fremder zum Besitze derselben unfähig ist, ein Aufschub von zwei Jahren gewährt, welcher Termin nach Umständen in angemessene Weise verlängert werden kann, um dieselben zu verkaufen, und um den Ertrag davon ohne Anstand und frei von jeder Abzugssteuer zu beziehen.

Art. III

Den Staatsangehörigen eines jeden der abschliessenden Theile soll die Freiheit zustehen, über ihr bewegliches Vermögen in den Staaten des Andern durch Testament, Schenkung oder auf andere Weise zu verfügen, und ihre im Unterthans-oder Staatsbürgerverbande des andern contrahirenden Theiles stehenden Erben, Legatarien und Donatarien sollen in dieses bewegliche Vermögen succediren, davon entweder selbst oder durch Stellvertreter Besitz nehmen und darüber nach Gutdünken verfügen können, ohne andere Abgaben zu entrichten, als soche, welchen die Einwohner des Landes, worin sich das genannte Vermögen befindet, in derleÿ Fällen unterworfen sind.[2]

---

[1] The words "real and" appear here in the treaty as signed; see the note regarding Article 3.
[2] As to the German text of this article, see the note regarding Article 3.

ART. IV

In case of the absence of the heirs, the same care shall be taken, provisionally, of such real or personal property as would be taken in a like case of property belonging to the natives of the country, until the lawful owner, or the person who has a right to sell the same according to Art. II, may take measures to receive or dispose of the inheritance.

ART. IV

Im Fall der Abwesenheit der Erben, wird man hinsichtlich der erwahnten, beweglichen oder unbeweglichen Güter provisorisch ganz dieselbe Sorgfalt anwenden, welche man bei gleichem Anlasse hinsichtlich der Güter der Eingebornen angewendet hätte, bis der gesetzmässige Eigenthümer oder derjenige, welcher nach Art. II das Recht hat, dieselben zu verkaufen, Anordnungen zu treffen, für gut finden wird, um die Erbschaft anzutreten, oder darüber zu verfügen.

ART. V.

If any dispute should arise between different claimants to the same inheritance, they shall be decided in the last resort according to the laws, and by the judges of the country where the property is situated.

ART. V.

Wenn sich Streitigkeiten zwischen verschiedenen rechtlichen Anspruch auf die Erbschaft habenden Prätendenten erheben, so werden dieselben in letzter Instanz nach den Gesetzen und von den Richtern des Landes entschieden werden, in welchem das Object der Erbschaft sich befindet.

ART. VI

But this Convention shall not derogate in any manner from the force of the laws already published, or hereafter to be published by His Majesty, the King of Bavaria, to prevent the emigration of His subjects.

ART. VI

Durch die Bestimmungen des gegenwärtigen Vertrags sollen jedoch auf keiner Weise diejenigen Gesetze entkräftet werden, welche durch Sr Majestät den König von Bayern bezüglich der Verhinderung der Auswanderung Allerhöchst dessen Unterthanen bereits erlassen worden sind, oder in der Folge zu erlassen wären.

Art. VII

This Convention is concluded subject to the ratification of the President of the United States of America, by and with the advice and consent of their Senate, and of His Majesty, the King of Bavaria, and the ratifications thereof shall be exchanged at Berlin within the term of fifteen months from the date of the signature hereof, or sooner if possible.

In witness whereof, the respective Plenipotentiaries have signed the above articles, as well in English as in German, and have thereto affixed their seals.

Done in quadruplicata in the city of Berlin on the Twenty First day of January, one Thousand, Eight Hundred and Forty Five, in the sixty ninth year of the Independence of the United States of America, and the nineteenth of the reign of His Majesty, the King of Bavaria.

[Seal] Henry Wheaton

Art. VII

Gegenwärtiger Vertrag ist abgeschlossen worden, vorbehaltlich der Ratification des Präsidenten der vereinigten Staaten von Nord-America nach und mit dem Rathe und der Einwilligung des nordamerikanischen Senats und vorbehaltlich der Ratification Sr Majestät des Königs von Bayern, und es soll die Auswechslung der Ratifications-Urkunden innerhalb fünfzehn Monaten vom Tage der Unterzeichnung des gegenwärtigen Vertrags an gerechnet oder früher, wenn es möglich ist, zu Berlin statt finden.

Urkundlich dessen die beiderseitigen Bevollmächtigten obenstehende Artikel sowohl in englischer als teutscher Sprache unterzeichnet, und ihre Siegel beigedrückt haben.

Ausgestellt in 4 Exemplaren zu Berlin den Ein und Zwanzigsten Januar, Ein Tausend, acht hundert, vierzig und fünf, im 69ten Jahr der Unabhängigkeit der vereinigten Staaten von America und im 19ten Jahr der Regierung Sr Majestät des Königs von Bayern.

[Seal] Graf v Lerchenfeld

NOTES

In the final clause of this convention it is said that it was "done in quadruplicata". There are two signed originals in the treaty file. In each of these the English text is written in the left columns, the United States of America is named first throughout both texts, and the Plenipotentiary of the United States signed at the left. In neither original is the German script used.

The usual papers are in the file. They include the attested Senate resolution of March 15, 1845 (Executive Journal, VI, 447–48), the duplicate United States instrument of ratification of March 18, 1845, and the proclamation of August 15, 1846. The protocol of the exchange of ratifications at Berlin on November 4, 1845, is written in French and, while not including any specific statement as to the comparison of texts, contains a clause to the effect that the two participants, Henry Wheaton, Minister to Prussia, and Count Maximilian von Lerchenfeld, the Bavarian Minister to Prussia, had found the ratifications in good and due form.

The instrument of ratification by the King of Bavaria of September 3, 1845, is written in German and includes both texts of the convention, the German in the left columns; the German script is used. Throughout those texts the King of Bavaria is named first, and the copy of the signature of the American Plenipotentiary appears under the English text.

The texts of this convention printed above have been collated with that one of the two originals which is with the original proclamation. The differences between the two originals are trifling and of no importance whatever. The original here used for collating omits five commas which are in the other document and contains one comma which it omits. The original convention which is apart from the proclamation was one of the enclosures to the despatch of J. C. Bancroft Davis, Minister to Germany, of September 13, 1875 (D.S., 9 Despatches, Germany, No. 171). Another of the enclosures to that despatch was the Bavarian full power given to Count von Lerchenfeld under date of November 22, 1844, to negotiate and sign the convention, to which further reference is made below.

When this convention was submitted to the Senate with the presidential message of February 24, 1845, it was accompanied by a copy of the relevant portion of a despatch from Henry Wheaton, Minister to Prussia, of January 21, 1845, which was printed (Senate Confidential Document No. 6, 28th Congress, 2d session, Regular Confidential Documents, XX, 231–35).

THE NEGOTIATIONS

As to the negotiations and content of this and four other very similar conventions with various German states of about the same period (1844–46), the notes to Document 106, the convention with Hesse of March 26, 1844, should be consulted.

THE FULL POWERS

It appears that in this case the original full powers were exchanged; the full power of Henry Wheaton is described in the notes to Document 106, the convention with Hesse of March 26, 1844; that given to the Plenipotentiary of the King of Bavaria is in the file, reading as follows (translation from the French):

We, Louis, by the grace of God King of Bavaria, Count Palatine of the Rhine, Duke of Bavaria and in Swabia, etc., etc., desiring to facilitate more and more

the relations between our subjects and those of the Republic of the United States of America, and responding to the overtures which have been made to us on this subject, We have authorized and We authorize by these presents Our Chamberlain, Envoy Extraordinary and Minister Plenipotentiary near His Majesty the King of Prussia, Count Maximilian of Lerchenfeld-Koefering, Commander of Our Order of St. George, of the Orders of the Crown of Bavaria and of St. Michael, Chevalier of the Order of St. Anne of the first class in diamonds, of the Order of the Red Eagle of the first class in diamonds, Grand Commander of the Order of the Saviour, and Commander of the Order of the North Star, to conclude with the Minister Plenipotentiary of the Republic of the United States of America at the Court of His Majesty the King of Prussia, Mr. Henry Wheaton, authorized for this purpose, a convention for the abolition of rights of *aubaine*, of *détraction*, and other similar ones existing down to this day, between Our states and those of the Republic, subject to Our subsequent ratification. In faith whereof we have signed the present full powers and have caused to be affixed thereto Our royal seal. Done at Munich the twenty-second of November, the year of grace eighteen hundred and forty-four, and of Our reign the nineteenth.

Louis   [Seal]

Le Baron de Gise
By Order of His Majesty the King:
The Private Secretary,
Gessele

Full powers for the Count of Lerchenfeld-Koefering, Envoy Extraordinary and Minister Plenipotentiary of His Majesty the King of Bavaria near His Majesty the King of Prussia.

ARTICLE 3

This convention was negotiated by Henry Wheaton, Minister to Prussia; in his despatch of January 21, 1845, transmitting the convention, was this paragraph (D.S., 3 Despatches, Prussia, No. 257):

> As the stipulations of this Convention are substantially, & almost literally the same with the Conventions on the same subject with Wurtemberg & Hesse Darmstadt, which have received the sanction of the Senate, it appears to require no particular observations except as to the sixth Article. This Article was proposed by the Bavarian negotiator, & as the same reservation is found in the last clause of the 14th Article of our Treaty of 1828 with Prussia [Document 62], I saw no sufficient reason to object to its insertion.

No mention was made of the fact that Article 3 of this convention, differing from those of the same period (1844–46) with Hesse, Württemberg, Saxony, and Nassau (Documents 106, 107, 115, and 120), refers to "real and personal property"; the other four conventions mentioned refer in the respective corresponding articles of each to "personal property" only.

The Senate resolution of advice and consent amended Article 3 by striking out the words "real and"; the resolution reads as follows (Executive Journal, VI, 447):

> *Resolved (two-thirds of the Senators present concurring)*, That the Senate advise and consent to the ratification of the convention for the mutual abolition of the *droit d'aubaine* and taxes on emigration between the United States of America and His Majesty the King of Bavaria, concluded at Berlin on the 24th [21st] day of January, 1845, with the following amendment: Strike out from the third article the words "real and."

It is to be observed that the Senate resolution referred only to the English text of the convention; in Article 3 of the English text the words "real and" appear twice; there can be no doubt that it was the intention of the Senate resolution to strike out the two words in each case where they appear in Article 3.

The United States instrument of ratification of March 18, 1845, according to the duplicate in the treaty file, contained the paragraphs quoted below; it is of course to be supposed that the original ratification transmitted for exchange did not refer to the original convention as "annexed" but rather to its text incorporated in the instrument of ratification:

Whereas, a Convention for the mutual abolition of the droit d'aubaine and taxes on emigration, between the United States of America and His Majesty the King of Bavaria, was concluded and signed in the City of Berlin, by their respective Plenipotentiaries, on the twenty-first day of January, in the year of Our Lord one thousand eight hundred and forty-five, the original of which Convention, being in the English and German languages, is hereunto annexed;

And whereas, the Senate of the United States by their Resolution of the fifteenth instant, two-thirds of the Senators present concurring, did advise and consent to the ratification of the said Convention, with the following amendment, viz: "strike out from the third article the following words, 'real and'":

Now, therefore, be it known, that I, James K. Polk, President of the United States, in pursuance of the aforesaid advice and consent of the Senate, do hereby ratify and confirm the said Convention, and every article and clause thereof.

The United States instrument of ratification was transmitted to Wheaton with the instruction of March 27, 1845, in which, after reference to the Senate amendment, it was stated that "The President would have had no hesitation in ratifying the Convention as it stood"; and a full power to exchange the ratifications was enclosed (D.S., 14 Instructions, Prussia, 92–94).

Wheaton acknowledged receipt of the instrument of ratification by his despatch of May 11, 1845 (D.S., 3 Despatches, Prussia, No. 266); and on November 5, 1845, he reported that the amendment proposed by the Senate "after long deliberation, has been at last assented to by the Bavarian Government" and that the ratifications had been exchanged on the date of his despatch (*ibid.*, No. 276). According to the protocol of exchange the date was November 4.

The Bavarian instrument of ratification was very carefully drawn, beginning, as is customary, with the name and titles of the King of Bavaria, followed by a clause regarding the signature of the convention; then appears the full text thereof in English and in German as originally signed.

After the texts is a clause of specific and accurate reference to the amendment of the Senate, incorporating a revised German text of Article 3 of the convention to correspond to the English so amended. It includes a statement that no objection had been found to the Senate amendment and concludes with words of acceptance and ratification of the convention subject to the changes in Article 3. The clause mentioned reads in the German and in translation as follows:

[Translation]

Nachdem nun dieser Vertrag die Zustimmung des Senats der vereinigten Staaten, jedoch mit der Modifikation, erhalten hat, daß in dem dritten Artikel des Englischen Textes die Worte "real and" hinwegbleiben sollen, und von Uns gegen diese Modifikation, welcher gemäß der deutsche Text des benannten Artikels folgende Faßung anzunehmen hätte:

Now as this treaty has received the assent of the Senate of the United States, with the modification, however, that in the third article of the English text the words "real and" shall be suppressed, and as no objection has been found by Us to this modification, according to which the German text of the said article would acquire the following wording:

[Here follows the German text of Article 3 as printed above]

nichts zu erinnern gefunden worden ist, so genehmigen und ratifiziren Wir obigen, aus sieben Artikeln bestehenden Vertrag in allen seinen Punkten und Klauseln unter den bezeichneten Abänderungen des dritten Artikels und versprechen, denselben getreulich beobachten zu lassen.

accordingly, We accept and ratify the aforesaid treaty, drawn up in seven articles, in all its points and clauses, subject to the indicated changes in the third article, and We promise that the same shall be faithfully observed.

The Bavarian Government thus in the most formal manner accepted the Senate amendment; and as that amendment in terms referred only to the English text of the convention, that Government recast the German text of Article 3, making it somewhat simpler, but conforming to the amended English text. It is that revised German text of Article 3, as taken from the Bavarian instrument of ratification, which is printed above; and in the corresponding English text of Article 3 the words "real and" occurring twice in the article as signed, before the words "personal property", are of course omitted, as they were stricken from the text by the agreement of both Governments. The German text of Article 3 as originally signed reads as follows:

ARTIKEL III.

Den Staatsangehörigen eines jeden der abschliessenden Theile soll in den Staaten des andern die Freiheit zustehen, über ihre beweglichen und unbeweglichen Güter durch Testament, Schenkung oder auf andere Weise zu verfügen, und deren Erben durch Testament, oder ab intestato, oder durch Schenkung hiezu berechtigt, sollen, wenn sie die Standesangehörige des andern der beiden abschliessenden Theile sind, ihnen in dem Besitze dieser ihrer beweglichen und unbeweglichen Güter folgen, auch in Person sowohl, als durch andere, welche an ihrer Stelle handeln, davon Besitz ergreifen, und nach Gutdünken damit schalten können, ohne andere Steuern zu bezahlen, als solche, welche die Einwohner des Landes, worin sich die genannten Güter befinden, bei gleichem Anlasse unterworfen sind.

Notwithstanding the very careful procedure of the Bavarian Government, and acting under a complete misapprehension of the facts, Secretary of State Buchanan instructed the Minister at Berlin, Henry Wheaton, under date of April 25, 1846, as follows (D.S., 14 Instructions, Prussia, 95–97):

In my despatch N⁰ 68, of the 27th March, 1845, you were apprised that the Senate advised and consented to the ratification of the Convention for the mutual abolition of the Droit d'aubaine and taxes on Emigration, between the United

States and Bavaria, with an amendment, striking out from the 3ʳᵈ Article the words "real and", and a copy of the Resolution of the Senate accompanied that despatch. This Convention has not yet been proclaimed by the President, because of the absence, in the exchange copy sent home by you, of any reference to the amendment, and of the retention in the text of the words "real and", which has excited some surprise. It is thought best, under the circumstances, to place the copy in the hands of your successor, who will take it with him to Berlin, that its place may be supplied by another copy, executed in conformity with the Senate's amendment; the mode of doing which, will be left to your discretion.

Such instructions were naturally highly embarrassing to one so learned in international law and procedure as was Henry Wheaton. None the less, he endeavored to carry them out. After a verbal discussion with the Bavarian Minister, Wheaton wrote him a note proposing the striking out of the two words "real and" and of the corresponding German words "und unbeweglichen" in the German text of Article 3 of the convention as contained in the Bavarian instrument of ratification. To that note of July 9, 1846, the Bavarian Minister replied on the following day, pointing out very correctly that the established usage of European diplomacy had been followed by his Government, that the convention had already been published in Bavaria in the Bulletin of the Laws, as amended, and that to strike out the words in the convention text would change the sense of the ratification.

Nothing more could be done by Wheaton in the matter, and he accordingly enclosed copies of his correspondence with the Bavarian Minister with his despatch of July 11, 1846 (D.S., 3 Despatches, Prussia, No. 290), in which he wrote as follows:

Your Despatch, No. 71, was handed to me by Mr. Donelson, on his arrival here, & I immediately endeavoured to execute your instructions respecting the Convention with Bavaria for the mutual abolition of the *droit d aubaine* & taxes on emigration.

Had I been aware, at the time when the ratifications of this Convention were exchanged, that the United States had adopted any peculiar practice, different from that which is sanctioned by the general usage of nations, for the exchange of the ratification of Treaties, I should certainly have endeavored to conform to it, on this occasion. But in that case it would have been necessary that the form of the Instrument of Ratification, on our part, should have been the counterpart of that of Bavaria; that is, that it should have recited the Convention, omitting the words proposed by the Senate, & agreed by the Bavarian Government, to be stricken out of the original.

This was not the fact. Our ratification recited the Convention as it was originally concluded, & the Bavarian government has already proclaimed it as the law of the land in its dominions, omitting the words rejected by the Senate.

Both the Bavarian Instrument of ratification & our own applied to the original text of the Convention. To efface or alter that text, in any respect, would be to change the effect of the ratifications which are applied to the Convention as it originally stood, & by which each of the high contracting parties agrees to strike out the two words in question, & the Convention is thus ratified with this alteration.

The Bavarian government has proclaimed the Convention, first striking out these words. It has done this without asking our consent, which, with all due respect, is *implied* in the tenor of the Instrument of Ratification. If the Bavarian government could lawfully do this, it seems evident that the American government may do the same.

But as the Department appears to be under a different impression, I applied myself to endeavor to execute your Instructions, by ascertaining how far the Bavarian Minister at this Court, by whom the Convention was negotiated & the ratifications exchanged, felt himself authorized to consent to the alteration desired by the Department.

The result of this application will appear from the enclosed copy of my correspondence with the Minister on this subject. It will be perceived from his letter to me that, though he feels fully authorized to declare that we are at liberty to do the same thing which the Bavarian Government has done, that is, to strike out from the Convention the two words in question, before it is proclaimed by the President as the Law of the land, he perceives serious objections in point of form to striking out these words in the Copy of the Convention recited in the Instrument of ratification, by which the sense of the ratification would be essentially changed.

With the strongest desire to fulfil the intentions of the Department in this respect, I confess myself quite at a loss how to accomplish this task. I would therefore beg leave respectfully to suggest that the object may be attained by your striking out the words in question, before the Convention is proclaimed, in the same manner as the Bavarian government has done.

For this purpose I shall re-deliver the Instrument of Ratification to Mr. Donelson, in order that the necessary Instructions may be given to him as to the disposition to be made of it.

With that despatch is a printed copy of the pages of the official Bavarian promulgation of the convention, which includes Articles 1 to 6 thereof, in German and in English; Article 3 of the former is the revised text, and Article 3 of the latter omits the words "real and".

Wheaton left Berlin on the following July 23, and in response to the request of his successor, Andrew J. Donelson, for instructions, Secretary of State Buchanan wrote under date of August 14, 1846, as follows (D.S., 14 Instructions, Prussia, 102–4):

A strange mistake has most probably occurred, in regard to the terms in which the King of Bavaria has ratified the Convention of the 21st January, 1845. Not understanding the German language myself, I was obliged to trust to the information of the Translator or some other clerk in the Department; and when I wrote my despatch to Mr Wheaton of the 25th April last, I firmly believed that the Bavarian ratification contained no assent to the amendment which had been adopted by the Senate. It was for the purpose of having this supposed mistake corrected, that you carried back the copy of the Convention to Berlin.

I am now informed by the note of Count Lerchenfeld to Mr Wheaton, of the 10th July last, that the ratification of the King has recognised and adopted the amendment of the Senate. Mr Wheaton, doubtless believing that I had a knowledge of this fact, has construed my instructions to him literally, and has endeavored to have the words "real and" actually expunged from the text of the Convention! This would have been highly improper, and would have changed the true history of the transaction. The amendment of the Senate is, to "strike out from the third article the following words,—' real and' "; but this is never understood literally.

If, therefore, upon examination, you shall ascertain that the Bavarian ratification, in terms, assents to the amendment of the Convention adopted by the Senate, you will return it to the Department by the first good opportunity, so that it may be proclaimed by the President.

I would thank you, also, to read this Despatch to Count Lerchenfeld.

To that instruction, however, there was added the following postscript, in accordance with which the convention was proclaimed the following day:

Upon a consideration of all the circumstances, and especially of the fact that the King of Bavaria has published the Convention officially, in conformity with the amendment of the Senate, the President has determined to issue the Proclamation on his part, without further delay.

The strange sequel to the confusion which had arisen in the matter was that in the original proclamation no reference whatever is made to the Senate amendment. In the technical sense President Polk proclaimed the convention in disregard of the Senate amendment. The original proclamation, in which is embodied the original convention as signed, reads as follows:

By the President of the United States of America.

A PROCLAMATION:

Whereas, a Convention between the United States of America and His Majesty the King of Bavaria, was concluded and signed at Berlin, by their respective Plenipotentiaries, on the twenty-first day of January, one thousand eight hundred and forty-five, which Convention, being in the English and German languages, is, word for word, as follows:

[Here follows the original convention]

And whereas, the said Convention has been duly ratified on both parts, and the respective ratifications of the same were exchanged at Berlin, on the fourth day of November, one thousand eight hundred and forty-five, by Henry Wheaton, Envoy Extraordinary and Minister Plenipotentiary of the United States, and the Count Maximilian von Lerchenfeld, Chamberlain of His Majesty the King of Bavaria, and His Envoy Extraordinary and Minister Plenipotentiary near the Court of His Majesty the King of Prussia, on the part of their respective Governments:

Now, therefore, be it known, that I, James K. Polk, President of the United States of America, have caused the said Convention to be made public, to the end that the same and every clause and article thereof may be observed and fulfilled with good faith, by the United States and the citizens thereof.

In witness whereof, I have hereunto set my hand, and caused the Seal of the United States to be affixed.

[Seal] Done at the City of Washington, this fifteenth day of August, in the year of Our Lord, one thousand eight hundred and forty-six; and of the Independence of the United States, the seventy-first.

JAMES K. POLK

By the President:
JAMES BUCHANAN
    Secretary of State.

However, in the original of the convention which is embodied in the original proclamation, the words "real and" in the English text of Article 3 (twice) have around them a line drawn with a red crayon pencil, not in red ink as has been stated (Haswell, 46; followed by Malloy, I, 57); but no indication of change is there made in the German text; and in the other original of the convention in the treaty file there is no line drawn at all.

In 9 Statutes at Large, Article 3 of the convention appears at page 827; the German text there printed is that first signed; the words "und unbeweglichen" (twice) are in parentheses, as are the words "real and" (twice) in the English, with a footnote reading, "The words in parentheses are, in the Original Treaty, encircled in red ink"; all of which is erroneous.

In 18 Statutes at Large (pt. 2, Public Treaties, 41) and in the Treaty Series print of the convention (1913), neither of which has the German text, the English of Article 3 correctly omits the words "real and".

THE KINGDOM OF BAVARIA

At the time of this convention the Kingdom of Bavaria was a member of the Germanic Confederation (1815–66). A summary account of that Confederation, with a list of the members thereof, is in the notes to Document 59, the convention with the Hanseatic Republics of December 20, 1827. The Kingdom of Bavaria was also party to the German Zollverein or Customs Union, as to which, also, see the notes to Document 59.

The Kingdom of Bavaria was not within the North German Confederation of 1867, which followed the war of 1866 between Austria and Prussia, participated in by various other German states on one side or the other, among which was Bavaria, on the side of Austria; but the Kingdom of Bavaria became one of the States of the German Empire from 1871.

Treaty Series No. 91
8 Statutes at Large, 617
18 *ibid.*, pt. 2, Public Treaties, 248–49

112

FRANCE : FEBRUARY 24, 1845

Additional Article to the Convention of November 9, 1843 (Document 103), signed at Washington February 24, 1845. Original in English and French.
Submitted to the Senate February 27, 1845. (Message of February 26, 1845, read March 5, 1845; see Executive Journal, VI, 425.) Resolution of advice and consent March 12, 1845. Ratified by the United States May 5, 1845. Ratified by France June 17, 1845. Ratifications exchanged at Paris June 21, 1845. Proclaimed July 24, 1845.

Additional Article.

The crime of Robbery, defining the same to be, the felonious and forcible taking from the person of another, of goods, or money to any value, by violence or putting him in fear;—and the crime of Burglary, defining the same to be, breaking and entering by night into a mansion house of another with intent to commit felony; and the corresponding crimes included under the French law in the words *vol qualifié crime,*—not being embraced in the second article of the convention [1] of Extradition concluded between the United States of America and France, on the ninth of November, 1843, it is agreed, by the present article, between the high contracting parties,—that persons charged with those crimes shall be respectively

Article Additionel.

Le crime de *Robbery*, consistant dans l'enlèvèment forcé et criminel, effectué sur la personne d'autrui, d'argent, ou d'effets, d'une valeur quelconque, à l'aide de violence, ou d'intimidation; et le crime de *Burglary*, consistant dans l'action de s'introduire nuitamment et avec effraction, ou escalade, dans l'habitation d'autrui, avec une intention criminelle; et les crimes correspondants prévus et punis par la loi française, sous la qualification de vols commis avec violence ou menaces, et de vols commis dans une maison habité, avec les circonstances de la nuit, et de l'escalade ou de l'effraction,—n'étant pas compris dans l'article 2 de la convention [1] d'Extradition conclue entre les États Unis d'Amérique et la France, le

[1] Document 103.

delivered up, in conformity with the first article of the said convention; and the present article when ratified by the parties, shall constitute a part of the said convention, and shall have the same force as if it had been originally inserted in the same.

In witness whereof, the respective plenipotentiaries have signed the present article, in duplicate, and have affixed thereto the seal of their arms.

Done at Washington, this twenty-fourth of February, 1845.

J. C. CALHOUN [Seal]

9 Novembre, 1843,—il est convenu, par le présent article entre les hautes parties contractantes, que les individus accusés de ces crimes, seront respectivement livrés, conformément à l'art 1ᵉʳ de la dite convention; et le présent article, lorsqu'il aura été ratifié par les parties, fera partie de la dite convention et aura la même valeur que s'il y avait été originairement inscrit.

En foi de quoi, les Plénipotentiaires respectifs ont signe, en double, le présent article, et y ont apposé le sceau de leurs armes.

Fait à Washington, le vingt quatre Février, 1845.

A PAGEOT [Seal]

NOTES

The usual papers in customary form are in the treaty file. They include the original additional article, in English and French, with the English in the left columns; the attested resolution of the Senate of March 12, 1845 (Executive Journal, VI, 435); the duplicate United States instrument of ratification of May 5, 1845; the certificate, in English, of the exchange of ratifications at Paris on June 21, 1845; and the original proclamation of July 24, 1845. The French instrument of ratification of June 17, 1845, contains no opening recital and has the French text in its left columns.

The presidential message of February 26, 1845, submitting the additional article to the Senate, was that of President Tyler. That message was received in the Senate a day after its date, but was not read until the following March 5, during the administration of President Polk (*ibid.*, 425); no papers were transmitted with the message, which contained the statement that the additional article "will be found to contain the amendments suggested by the resolution of the Senate of the 15th of June last" (*ibid.*, 346, which is quoted below).

THE NEGOTIATIONS

Prior to the exchange of ratifications of the extradition convention with France of November 9, 1843 (Document 103), the French Minister Plenipotentiary *ad interim* wrote to Secretary of State

Calhoun as follows (D.S., 12 Notes from the French Legation, April 4, 1844, translation):

The Government of the King has observed with regret that the crime of "vol" was not included in this convention. It considers that the difficulty of translation which led to this omission is not insurmountable and proposes that it be introduced therein by means of an additional article; the expressions which might be employed to that end would be "vol qualifié crime par les lois françaises" and designated in American law as "robbery and burglary"; or "vol criminel", to be translated by "criminal theft", putting in parentheses the crimes designated by American law as "robbery and burglary"; or finally the English expressions "robbery and burglary" might be simply translated by those of "vol qualifié" or "vol qualifié crime".

The answering note of April 5 stated that "it is not apprehended that there will be any serious difficulty in meeting the wishes of His Majesty the King of the French in regard to the proposed additional article" (D.S., 6 Notes to the French Legation, 79).

On the day of the exchange of ratifications of the convention of November 9, 1843, a full power was issued to Secretary of State Calhoun in the customary form (D.S., 3 Credences, 70, April 12, 1844); the original of that document is in the treaty file of the convention of 1843.

An additional article was drawn up accordingly and signed on April 15, 1844, in English and French (Treaty Series No. 90), as follows:

Additional Article.

The crimes of *Robbery* and *Burglary* not being embraced in the 2nd article of the convention of Extradition concluded between France and the United States of America on the ninth of November, 1843, it is agreed by the present article, between the high contracting parties, that persons charged with those crimes shall be respectively delivered up, in conformity with the 1st article of the said Convention, and the present article, when ratified by the parties shall constitute a part of the said convention, and shall have the same force as if it had been originally inserted in the same.

In witness whereof, the respective Plenipotentiaries have signed the present article, in duplicate, and have affixed thereto the seal of their arms.

Done at Washington, this fifteenth day of April, 1844.

J. C. CALHOUN
[Seal]

Article Additionel.

Le crime de *vol qualifié* n'étant pas compris dans l'article 2 de la Convention d'Extradition conclue entre la France et les Etats Unis d'Amérique, le 9 Novembre 1843, il est convenu, par le présent article, entre les hautes parties contractantes, que les individus accusés de ce crime seront respectivement livrés, conformément à l'article 1er de la dite convention, et le présent article, lorsqu'il aura été ratifié par les parties, fera partie de la dite convention, et aura la même valeur que s'il y avait été originairement inscrit

En foi de quoi, les Plénipotentiaires respectifs ont signé, en double, le présent article, et y ont apposé le sceau de leurs armes.

Fait à Washington le quinze Avril, 1844.

A PAGEOT
[Seal]

That additional article was transmitted to the Senate with the presidential message of April 22, 1844 (Executive Journal, VI, 256); accompanying it was a translation of the note of April 4, 1844, above cited (Senate Confidential Document No. 4, 28th Congress, 1st session).

Document 112

The Senate resolution of advice and consent on June 15, 1844 (Executive Journal, VI, 346), amended the article by striking out the words "the crimes of robbery and burglary" and inserting the following:

The crime of robbery, defining the same to be the felonious and forcible taking from the person of another of goods or money to any value, by violence or putting him in fear; and the crime of burglary, defining the same to be breaking and entering by night into a mansion-house of another with intent to commit felony, and the corresponding crimes included under the French law in the words *"vol, qualifié crime."*

Nothing appears in the Senate resolution regarding the French text or its wording; and the procedural difficulty thus created was met by the drawing up and signing of the additional article of February 24, 1845, which embodies the Senate proposal in both texts.

113

TEXAS : MARCH 1 TO DECEMBER 29, 1845

Annexation of Texas. Joint resolution of the Congress of the United States, March 1, 1845. Joint resolution of the Congress of Texas, June 23, 1845. Ordinance of the Convention of Texas, July 4, 1845. Joint resolution of the Congress of the United States, December 29, 1845. Other proceedings are described in the editorial notes.

[*Joint Resolution of the Congress of the United States, March 1, 1845*]

28th Congress, Second Session. {Begun and held at the city of Washington, in the District of Columbia, on Monday the second day of December, eighteen hundred and forty-four.

Joint Resolution for annexing Texas to the United States.

Resolved by the Senate and House of Representatives of the United States of America in Congress assembled, That Congress doth consent that the territory properly included within, and rightfully belonging to the Republic of Texas, may be erected into a new state, to be called the state of Texas, with a republican form of government, to be adopted by the people of said republic, by deputies in Convention assembled, with the consent of the existing government, in order that the same may be admitted as one of the states of this Union.

2. And be it further resolved, That the foregoing consent of Congress is given upon the following conditions, and with the following guarantees, to wit: *First*—said state to be formed, subject to the adjustment by this government of all questions of boundary that may arise with other governments; and the constitution thereof, with the proper evidence of its adoption by the people of said republic of Texas, shall be transmitted to the President of the United States, to be laid before Congress for its final action, on or before the first day of January, one thousand eight hundred and forty-six. *Second*—said state, when admitted into the Union, after ceding to the United States all public edifices, fortifications, barracks, ports and harbors, navy and navy-yards, docks, magazines, arms, armaments, and all other property and means pertaining to the public defence belonging to said republic of Texas, shall retain all the public funds, debts, taxes, and dues of every kind which may belong to or be due and owing

689

said republic; and shall also retain all the vacant and unappropriated lands lying within its limits, to be applied to the payment of the debts and liabilities of said republic of Texas; and the residue of said lands, after discharging said debts and liabilities, to be disposed of as said state may direct; but in no event are said debts and liabilities to become a charge upon the government of the United States. *Third—* New states, of convenient size, not exceeding four in number, in addition to said state of Texas, and having sufficient population, may hereafter, by the consent of said state, be formed out of the territory thereof, which shall be entitled to admission under the provisions of the federal constitution. And such states as may be formed out of that portion of said territory lying south of thirty-six degrees thirty minutes north latitude, commonly known as the Missouri compromise line, shall be admitted into the Union with or without slavery, as the people of each state asking admission may desire. And in such state or states as shall be formed out of said territory north of said Missouri compromise line, slavery, or involuntary servitude, (except for crime,) shall be prohibited.

3. And be it further resolved, That if the President of the United States shall in his judgment and discretion deem it most advisable, instead of proceeding to submit the foregoing resolution to the Republic of Texas, as an overture on the part of the United States for admission, to negotiate with that Republic; then, Be it resolved, that a state, to be formed out of the present Republic of Texas, with suitable extent and boundaries, and with two representatives in Congress, until the next apportionment of representation, shall be admitted into the Union, by virtue of this act, on an equal footing with the existing states, as soon as the terms and conditions of such admission, and the cession of the remaining Texan territory to the United States shall be agreed upon by the governments of Texas and the United States: And that the sum of one hundred thousand dollars be, and the same is hereby, appropriated to defray the expenses of missions and negotiations, to agree upon the terms of said admission and cession, either by treaty to be submitted to the Senate, **or by** articles to be submitted to the two Houses of Congress, as the President may direct.

J W JONES
Speaker of the House of Representatives.
WILLIE P. MANGUM
President, pro tempore, of the Senate.

Approv'd March 1. 1845

JOHN TYLER

[*Joint Resolution of the Congress of Texas, June 23, 1845*]

Joint Resolution Giving the consent of the existing Government to the Annexation of Texas to the United States.

Whereas the Government of the United States hath proposed the following terms, guarantees and conditions on which the people and Territory of the Republic of Texas may be erected into a new State to be called the State of Texas, and admitted as one of the States of the American Union, to wit: "Resolved by the Senate and House of "Representatives of the United States of America in Congress "assembled, That Congress doth consent that the territory properly "included within and rightfully belonging to the Republic of Texas "may be erected into a new State, to be called the State of Texas, "with a Republican form of Government, to be adopted by the people "of said Republic, by deputies in Convention assembled, with the "consent of the existing Government, in order that the same may be "admitted as one of the States of this Union.   2. And be it further "resolved, That the foregoing consent of Congress is given upon the "following conditions, and with the following guarantees, to wit: "First, said State to be formed subject to the adjustment by this "Government of all questions of boundary that may arise with other "Governments, and the Constitution thereof, with the proper evidence "of its adoption, by the people of said Republic of Texas, shall be "transmitted to the President of the United States, to be laid before "Congress for its final action, on or before the first day of January "one thousand eight hundred and forty six.   Second, said State when "admitted into the Union, after ceding to the United States all public "edifices, fortifications, barracks, ports, and harbors, navy and navy-"yards, docks, magazines, arms, armaments and all other property "and means pertaining to the public defence, belonging belonging to "the said Republic of Texas, shall retain all the public funds, debts, "taxes and dues of every kind which may belong to or be due and "owing said Republic, and shall also retain all the vacant and unap-"propriated lands lying within its limits, to be applied to the pay-"ment of the debts and liabilities of said Republic of Texas, and the "residue of said lands, after discharging said debts and liabilities, to "be disposed of as said State may direct: but in no event are said "debts and liabilities to become a charge upon the Government of "the United States.   Third, new States of convenient size, not "exceeding four in number, in addition to said State of Texas, and "having sufficient population, may hereafter, by the consent of said "State, be formed out of the territory thereof, which shall be entitled

"to admission under the provision of the Federal Constitution. And "such States as may be formed out of that portion of said territory "lying south of thirty-six degrees thirty minutes north latitude, "commonly known as the Missouri compromise line, shall be admitted "into the Union, with or without Slavery, as the people of each State "asking admission may desire. And in such State or States as shall "be formed out of said territory north of said Missouri compromise "line, slavery or involuntary servitude (except for crime) shall be "prohibited." And whereas, by by said terms, the consent of the existing Government of Texas is required,—Therefore,

Be it resolved by the Senate and House of Representatives of the Republic of Texas in Congress assembled, That the Government of Texas doth consent that the People and Territory of the Republic of Texas may be erected into a new State to be called the State of Texas, with a Republican form of Government to be adopted by the People of said Republic, by Deputies in Convention assembled, in order that the same may be admitted as one of the States of the American Union; and said consent is given on the terms, guarantees, and conditions set forth in the Preamble to this Joint Resolution.

Section 2. Be it further resolved, That the Proclamation of the President of the Republic of Texas, bearing date May fifth eighteen hundred and forty five, and the election of deputies to set in Convention, at Austin, on the fourth day of July next for the adoption of a Constitution for the State of Texas, had in accordance therewith, hereby receives the consent of the existing Government of Texas.

Sec. 3. Be it further resolved, That the President of Texas is hereby requested, immediately, to furnish the Government of the United States, through their accredited Minister near this Government, with a copy of this Joint Resolution, also to furnish the Convention to assemble at Austin on the fourth of July next a copy of the same. And the same shall take effect from and after its passage.

JOHN M. LEWIS
Speaker of the House of Representatives

K. L. ANDERSON
President of the Senate

Approved June 23ᵈ 1845

ANSON JONES

[*Ordinance of the Convention of Texas, July 4, 1845*]

An Ordinance.

Whereas the Congress of the United States of America has passed resolutions providing for the Annexation of Texas to that Union, which resolutions were approved by the President of the United States on the first day of March One thousand eight hundred and forty five; and Whereas the President of the United States has submitted to Texas, the first and second Sections of the said Resolution, as the basis upon which Texas may be admitted as one of the States of the said Union; and Whereas the existing Government of the Republic of Texas has assented to the proposals thus made, the terms and conditions of which are as follow,

Joint Resolution For annexing Texas to the United States.

Resolved by the Senate and House of Representatives of the United States of America in Congress assembled That Congress doth consent, that the territory, properly included within and rightly belonging to the Republic of Texas may be erected into a new State, to be called the State of Texas, with a republican form of Government, to be adopted by the people of said Republic, by Deputies in Convention assembled, with the consent of the existing Government, in order that the same may be admitted as one of the States of this Union.

2nd. And be it further Resolved, That the foregoing consent of Congress is given upon the following conditions, and with the following guarantees, to wit:

1st. Said State to be formed, subject to the adjustment by this Government of all questions of boundary, that may arise with other Governments, and the Constitution thereof with the proper evidence of its adoption by the people of said Republic of Texas, shall be transmitted to the President of the United States, to be laid before Congress, for its final action, on or before the first day of January, One thousand eight hundred and forty six.

Second. Said State when admitted into the Union, after ceding to the United States all public edeficies, fortifications, barracks, ports and harbors, navy and navy yards, docks, magazines, arms and armaments and all other property and means pertaining to the public defence belonging to the said Republic of Texas, shall retain all the public funds, debts, taxes, and dues of every kind which may belong to or be due & owing to the said Republic; and shall also retain all the vacant and unappropriated lands lying within its limits, to be applied to the payment of the debts and liabilities of said Republic of Texas, and the residue of said lands, after discharging said debts and liabilities, to be disposed of as said State may direct, but in no event are said debts and liabilities to become a charge upon the Government of the United States.

Third. New States of convenient size not exceeding four in number, in addition to said State of Texas, and having sufficient population, may hereafter, by the consent of said State, be formed out of the territory thereof, which shall be entitled to admission under the provisions of the Federal Constitution. And such States as may be formed out of that portion of said Territory lying South of thirty six degrees thirty minutes North latitude, commonly known as the Missouri compromise line, shall be admitted into the Union, with or without Slavery, as the people of each State asking admission may desire. And in such State or States as shall be formed out of said Territory, North of said Missouri Compromise line, slavery or involuntary servitude (except for crime) shall be prohibited.

Now, in order to manifest the assent of the people of this Republic as required in the above recited portions of the said Resolutions; We, the Deputies of the people of Texas in Convention assembled, in their name and by their Authority, do ordain and declare, that we assent to and accept the proposals, conditions and guarantees contained in the first and second Sections of the Resolution of the Congress of the United States aforesaid.

TH⁰ J. RUSK, *President.*

PHIL' M. CUNY
H. G. RUNNELS
ROBERT M. FORBES
SAM LUSK
JN⁰ CALDWELL
JOSE ANTONIO NAVARRO
GEO' M. BROWN
GUSTAVUS A. EVERTS
LEMUEL DALE EVANS
J. B. MILLER
R. E. B. BAYLOR
J. S. MAYFIELD.
R. BACHE
JAMES LOVE
Wᵐ L. HUNTER
JOHN D. ANDERSON
ISAAC PARKER
P. O. LUMPKIN
FRANCIS MOORE Jʳ
ISAAC W. BRASHEAR
ALEXANDER MᶜGOWAN

ISAAC VAN ZANT
S HOLLAND
EDWARD CLARK
GEO' W. SMYTH
JAMES ARMSTRONG
FRANCIS M. WHITE
JAMES DAVIS
GEORGE T. WOOD
G. W. WRIGHT
H. R. LATIMER
JOHN M. LEWIS
JAMES SCOTT
ARCHIBALD MᶜNEILL
A. C. HORTON
ISRAEL STANDEFER
JOS' L. HOGG
CHAˢ S. TAYLOR
DAVID GAGE
HENRY J. JEWETT
CAVITT ARMSTRONG
JAMES BOWER

ALBERT H. LATIMER
Wᵐ C. YOUNG
J. PINCKNEY HENDERSON
NICHOLAS H. DARNELL
EMERY RAINS
A. W. O. HICKS
JAMES M. BURROUGHS

H. L. KINNEY
WILLIAM L. CAZNEAU
A. S. CUNNINGHAM
ABNER S. LIPSCOMB
JOHN HEMPHILL
VAN R. IRION.

Adopted.   July 4th 1845

Attest

JAˢ H. RAYMOND
Secretary of the Convention

CITY OF AUSTIN REPUBLIC OF TEXAS *July 5th 1845*

I certify the foregoing is a correct copy of the Ordinance as adopted and signed by the Members of the Convention on Yesterday, July 4th 1845.

JAˢ H RAYMOND
Secretary of the Convention

[*Joint Resolution of the Congress of the United States, December 29, 1845*]

29th Congress.
1st Session.
{ Begun and held at the city of Washington, in the District of Columbia, on Monday, the first day of December, eighteen hundred and forty-five.

Joint Resolution for the admission of the state of Texas into the Union.

Whereas, the Congress of the United States, by a Joint Resolution approved March the first, eighteen hundred and forty-five, did consent that the territory properly included within, and rightfully belonging to the Republic of Texas, might be erected into a new state, to be called *The State of Texas*, with a republican form of government, to be adopted by the people of said republic, by deputies in Convention assembled, with the consent of the existing government, in order that the same might be admitted as one of the states of the Union; which consent of Congress was given upon certain conditions specified in the first and second sections of said Joint Resolution: And whereas, the people of the said Republic of Texas, by deputies in Convention assembled, with the consent of the existing government, did adopt a Constitution and erect a new state, with a republican form of government, and in the name of the people of Texas, and by their authority, did ordain and declare, that they assented to and accepted the proposals, conditions, and guarantees contained in said first and second

167951°—vol. 4—34——46

sections of said resolution: And whereas the said Constitution, with the proper evidence of its adoption by the people of the republic of Texas, has been transmitted to the President of the United States, and laid before Congress, in conformity to the provisions of said Joint Resolution:

Therefore

Resolved by the Senate and House of Representatives of the United States of America in Congress assembled, That the state of Texas shall be one, and is hereby declared to be one, of the United States of America, and admitted into the Union on an equal footing with the original states, in all respects whatever.

Section 2. And be it further resolved, That until the representatives in Congress shall be apportioned according to an actual enumeration of the inhabitants of the United States, the state of Texas shall be entitled to choose two representatives.

JOHN W DAVIS
Speaker of the House of Representatives.

G. M. DALLAS.
President of the Senate.

Approved December 29ᵗʰ 1845.

JAMES K POLK

NOTES

The source texts of the four documents printed above are the following: the joint resolution of the Congress of the United States approved March 1, 1845, from the original in the archives of the Department of State; the joint resolution of the Congress of Texas approved June 23, 1845, from the certified copy in D.S., 2 Despatches, Texas, No. 31, June 23, 1845, enclosure 2; the ordinance of the Convention of Texas of July 4, 1845, from the certified copy in *ibid.*, No. 31 [33], July 6, 1845, enclosure; the joint resolution of the Congress of the United States approved December 29, 1845, from the original in the archives of the Department of State (each original joint resolution of the Congress of the United States bears the customary certification of origin, "I certify that this Joint Resolution originated in the House of Representatives", signed by B. B. French, Clerk).

Other proceedings had at Washington, D.C., at Washington, Texas (for a time the seat of government of the Republic of Texas; a town in Washington County, on the Brazos, about sixty miles northwest of Houston), and at Austin (the capital of the Republic of Texas pursuant to an act of the Congress of Texas of January 14, 1839, and the present capital of the State of Texas), are described below.

The Treaty of Annexation

On April 12, 1844, a treaty of annexation between the United States of America and the Republic of Texas was signed at Washington in the following terms (D.S., Unperfected R3):

A Treaty of Annexation, concluded between the United States of America and the Republic of Texas.

The people of Texas having, at the time of adopting their constitution, expressed by an almost unanimous vote, their desire to be incorporated into the Union of the United States, and being still desirous of the same with equal unanimity, in order to provide more effectually for their security and prosperity; and the United States, actuated solely by the desire to add to their own security and prosperity, and to meet the wishes of the Government and people of Texas, have determined to accomplish, by treaty, objects so important to their mutual and permanent welfare:

For that purpose, the President of the United States has given full powers to John C. Calhoun, Secretary of State of the said United States, and the President of the Republic of Texas has appointed, with like powers, Isaac Van Zandt and J. Pinckney Henderson, citizens of the said Republic: and the said plenipotentiaries, after exchanging their full powers, have agreed on and concluded the following articles:

Article I.

The Republic of Texas, acting in conformity with the wishes of the people and every department of its government, cedes to the United States all its territories, to be held by them in full property and sovereignty, and to be annexed to the said United States as one of their Territories, subject to the same constitutional provisions with their other Territories. This cession includes all public lots and squares, vacant lands, mines, minerals, salt lakes and springs, public edifices, fortifications, barracks, ports and harbours, navy and navy-yards, docks, magazines, arms, armaments and accoutrements, archives and public documents, public funds, debts, taxes and dues unpaid at the time of the exchange of the ratifications of this treaty.

Article II.

The citizens of Texas shall be incorporated into the Union of the United States, maintained and protected in the free enjoyment of their liberty and property, and admitted, as soon as may be consistent with the principles of the federal constitution, to the enjoyment of all the rights, privileges and immunities of citizens of the United States.

Article III.

All titles and claims to real estate, which are valid under the laws of Texas, shall be held to be so by the United States; and measures shall be adopted for the speedy adjudication of all unsettled claims to land, and patents shall be granted to those found to be valid.

Article IV.

The public lands hereby ceded shall be subject to the laws regulating the public lands in the other Territories of the United States, as far as they may be applicable; subject, however, to such alterations and changes as Congress may from time to time think proper to make. It is understood between the parties that if, in consequence of the mode in which lands have been surveyed in Texas, or from previous grants or locations, the sixteenth section cannot be applied to the purpose of education, Congress shall make equal provision by grant of land elsewhere. And it is also further understood, that, hereafter, the books, papers and documents of the General Land Office of Texas shall be deposited and kept at such place in Texas as the Congress of the United States shall direct.

ARTICLE V.

The United States assume and agree to pay the public debts and liabilities of Texas, however created, for which the faith or credit of her government may be bound at the time of the exchange of the ratifications of this treaty; which debts and liabilities are estimated not to exceed, in the whole, ten millions of dollars, to be ascertained and paid in the manner hereinafter stated.

The payment of the sum of three hundred and fifty thousand dollars shall be made at the Treasury of the United States within ninety days after the exchange of the ratifications of this treaty, as follows: Two hundred and fifty thousand dollars to Frederick Dawson, of Baltimore, or his Executors, on the delivery of that amount of ten per cent. bonds of Texas: One hundred thousand dollars, if so much be required, in the redemption of the Exchequer bills which may be in circulation at the time of the exchange of the ratifications of this treaty. For the payment of the remainder of the debts and liabilities of Texas, which, together with the amount already specified, shall not exceed ten millions of dollars, the public lands herein ceded and the nett revenue from the same are hereby pledged.

ARTICLE VI.

In order to ascertain the full amount of the debts and liabilities herein assumed, and the legality and validity thereof, four commissioners shall be appointed by the President of the United States, by and with the advice and consent of the Senate, who shall meet at Washington, Texas, within the period of six months after the exchange of the ratifications of this treaty, and may continue in session not exceeding twelve months, unless the Congress of the United States should prolong the time. They shall take an oath for the faithful discharge of their duties, and that they are not directly or indirectly interested in said claims at the time, and will not be during their continuance in office; and the said oath shall be recorded with their proceedings. In case of the death, sickness or resignation of any of the commissioners, his or their place or places may be supplied by the appointment as aforesaid or by the President of the United States during the recess of the Senate. They, or a majority of them, shall be authorised, under such regulations as the Congress of the United States may prescribe, to hear, examine and decide on all questions touching the legality and validity of said claims, and shall, when a claim is allowed, issue a certificate to the claimant, stating the amount, distinguishing principal from interest. The certificates so issued shall be numbered, and entry made of the number, the name of the person to whom issued, and the amount, in a book to be kept for that purpose. They shall transmit the records of their proceedings and the book in which the certificates are entered, with the vouchers and documents produced before them, relative to the claims allowed or rejected, to the Treasury Department of the United States, to be deposited therein, and the Secretary of the Treasury shall, as soon as practicable after the receipt of the same, ascertain the aggregate amount of the debts and liabilities allowed; and if the same, when added to the amount to be paid to Frederick Dawson and the sum which may be paid in the redemption of the Exchequer bills, shall not exceed the estimated sum of ten millions of dollars, he shall, on the presentation of a certificate of the commissioners, issue, at the option of the holder, a new certificate for the amount, distinguishing principal from interest, and payable to him or order, out of the nett proceeds of the public lands, hereby ceded, or stock, of the United States, for the amount allowed, including principal and interest, and bearing an interest of three per cent. per annum from the date thereof; which stock, in addition to being made payable out of the nett proceeds of the public lands hereby ceded, shall also be receivable in payment for the same. In case the amount of the debts and liabilities allowed, with the sums aforesaid to be paid to Frederick Dawson and which may be paid in the redemption of the Exchequer bills, shall exceed the said sum of ten millions of dollars, the said Secretary, before issuing a new certificate, or stock, as the case may be, shall make in each case such proportionable and rateable reduction on its amount as to reduce the aggregate to the said sum of ten millions of dollars, and he shall have power to make all needful rules and regulations necessary to carry into effect the powers hereby vested in him.

ARTICLE VII.

Until further provision shall be made, the laws of Texas as now existing shall remain in force, and all executive and judicial officers of Texas, except the President, Vice-President and Heads of Departments, shall retain their offices, with all power and authority appertaining thereto, and the Courts of justice shall remain in all respects as now established and organized.

ARTICLE VIII.

Immediately after the exchange of the ratifications of this treaty, the President of the United States, by and with the advice and consent of the Senate, shall appoint a commissioner who shall proceed to Texas, and receive the transfer of the territory thereof, and all the archives and public property and other things herein conveyed, in the name of the United States. He shall exercise all executive authority in said territory necessary to the proper execution of the laws, until otherwise provided.

ARTICLE IX.

The present treaty shall be ratified by the contracting parties and the ratifications exchanged at the City of Washington, in six months from the date hereof, or sooner if possible.

In witness whereof, we, the undersigned plenipotentiaries of the United States of America and of the Republic of Texas, have signed, by virtue of our powers, the present treaty of Annexation, and have hereunto affixed our seals respectively.
Done at Washington, the twelfth day of April, eighteen hundred and forty-four.

[Seal] J C. CALHOUN   [Seal] ISAAC VAN ZANDT
                             [Seal] J PINCKNEY HENDERSON

That treaty was submitted to the Senate on April 22, 1844, with the presidential message of the same date (Executive Journal, VI, 257–61); and it was rejected by the Senate by a vote of sixteen ayes to thirty-five noes on the following June 8 (*ibid.*, 311–12). Certain papers accompanied the presidential message of April 22, 1844, and also the sixteen later messages to the Senate of various dates from April 26 to June 10 (*ibid.*, *passim*); from most of these the injunction of secrecy was removed during the Senate proceedings; nine of the messages of April and May, with the accompanying papers, were printed at the time in Senate Documents Nos. 341, 345, and 349, 28th Congress, 1st session, serial 435; of the first and last mentioned of those three documents (perhaps of the second also) twenty thousand copies were printed; but the message to the Senate of May 16, 1844 (Executive Journal, VI, 286–87), and the accompanying papers, the Senate refused to print (*ibid.*, 287); with the other papers sent to the Senate they were made public with the presidential message to Congress of June 10 (Richardson, IV, 323–27; House Document No. 271, 28th Congress, 1st session, serial 444).

MEXICO AND TEXAS

At no time had Mexico recognized the independence or separate existence of Texas. The position of Mexico was that "the Department of Texas" was an integral part of Mexico; not until the negotiations of 1845, to which reference is made below, was there any willingness on the part of Mexico to treat on the basis of Texan

independence. Except for a few expeditions, which were of the nature of raids on the one side or the other (see Rives, The United States and Mexico, 1821–1848, I, 477–92), hostilities between the two countries had in fact for some years ceased to be carried on; but no legal or formal basis of peace existed, and recent proposals of mediation and for an armistice had failed (see Senate Document No. 1, 28th Congress, 2d session, serial 449, particularly pp. 29–36, the instruction of Secretary of State Calhoun to Wilson Shannon, Minister to Mexico, of September 10, 1844; the decree of General Santa Anna of June 17, 1843; and the order of General Adrian Woll of June 20, 1844). Under date of May 16, 1844, the following statement of the facts was made to Secretary of State Calhoun by the Plenipotentiaries of the Republic of Texas who signed the treaty of April 12, 1844 (D.S., 1 Communications from Agents of Texas; House Document No. 271, 28th Congress, 1st session, serial 444, pp. 85–86):

LEGATION OF TEXAS
Washington May 16ᵗʰ 1844

The Undersigned &c. &c. in reply to the note of Mʳ Calhoun Secretary of State of the United States of yesterdays date, have the honor to submit for his information the following facts, in relation to the origin and history of the alledged armistice between Mexico and Texas, to which he refers.

By the terms of a convention, concluded between Texas and Great Britain on the 14th of November 1840 [text in British and Foreign State Papers, XXIX, 84–85], the British Government agreed to offer its mediation for the settlement of the difficulties between Mexico and Texas, upon the basis of the recognition of the Independence of Texas by Mexico. In pursuance of this convention, the mediation of Great Britain was tendered to, and declined by Mexico, information of which was communicated to the President of Texas. Afterwards, in the year 1842 representations were made, by Texas to Great Britain, France, and the United States, requesting their joint interposition for the settlement of the difficulties between Mexico and Texas. To this request the Governments of France and the United States indicated their ready willingness to accede. The British Government however for reasons deemed by it sufficient declined to be thus associated, suggesting at the same time that each might act separately. Subsequently the Texian Charge d'Affaires in London, was informed by the Minister of Foreign Affairs of the British Government that the mediation, as before pursued, was utterly hopeless, and that Her Majesty's Charge d'Affaires in Mexico had been directed to propose a *new feature* in the same to Mexico.

In the month of May 1843, in reply to the representations upon the subject, made by Her Britannic Majesty's Charge d'Affaires in Mexico, to Genl. Santa Anna, the latter indicated his willingness to agree to a suspension of hostilities, and to receive Commissioners from Texas to treat on the terms of a peace. This fact was communicated by Her Britannic Majesty's Charge d'Affaires in Texas to the President of Texas, on the 10th of June 1843, who, on the 15th of the same month, issued his proclamation for an armistice [text in *ibid.*, XXXIII, 251], annexing certain stipulations, by which it should be terminated. When these were communicated to Genl Santa Anna, through the British Charge d'Affaires, he declined to assent to them, suggesting that it would be better that the terms, duration &c should be arranged by Commissioners, appointed by the respective Governments, for that purpose. Information of this was communicated to the Texian Government, both, through the British Charge d'Affaires in Texas and in a communication from Genl. Woll to Genl. Houston, in which it was stated, in substance, that he (Genl Woll) was authorized, by Genl Santa Anna, to appoint Commissioners to meet any persons, similarly commissioned by Texas, to arrange the proposed armistice. In pursuance of this the Texian Commissioners were appointed and proceeded to Mexico. They were instructed that no arrangement made by them would be binding until approved by the

President. When the agreement entered into by them was submitted to the President of Texas, he declined approving it. Refering to Texas as a Department of Mexico was a sufficient reason for its prompt rejection, and precluded all possibility of official action under it.

The negotiations having thus terminated; and this agreement being held to be null and void, there is at present no subsisting arrangement of any character between Mexico and Texas.

The Undersigned avail themselves of this occasion to offer to Mᣴ Calhoun renewed assurances of their distinguished consideration.

ISAAC VAN ZANDT
J PINCKNEY HENDERSON

Honorable J. C. CALHOUN
&c. &c. &c.

THE PRESIDENTIAL CAMPAIGN OF 1844

The question of the annexation of Texas became one of the major issues of the presidential campaign of 1844. Henry Clay was nominated by the Whig Party; the party platform said nothing about Texas; but the letter of Clay of April 17, 1844, the Raleigh letter, had declared against annexation, at least at that time. The leading candidate for the Democratic nomination was Martin Van Buren, who received a majority of the votes in the party convention on the first ballot; but Van Buren's letter of April 20, 1844, was also against immediate annexation; and James Knox Polk became the Democratic nominee on a platform which declared "that the re-occupation of Oregon and the re-annexation of Texas at the earliest practicable period are great American measures, which this Convention recommends". A third candidate was James G. Birney, of Ohio, nominated by the Liberty Party on an antislavery platform; and President John Tyler was renominated by still another group, but withdrew on August 21. The result was the election of Polk, who carried New York by a small plurality and had 170 votes in the electoral college against 105 for Henry Clay (see Rives, The United States and Mexico, 1821–1848, I, ch. XXIV, "The Election of Polk", 618–50).

THE SUBMISSION TO CONGRESS

In the meantime President Tyler had presented to Congress the question of the annexation of Texas in his message of June 10, 1844 (Richardson, IV, 323–27); he communicated "for your consideration, the rejected treaty, together with all the correspondence and documents which have heretofore been submitted to the Senate in its executive sessions" (House Document No. 271, 28th Congress, 1st session, serial 444); and he proposed action by the National Legislature in lieu of action by treaty.

It seems that the earliest suggestion that the annexation of Texas might be accomplished by means of a joint resolution of Congress rather than by treaty was made by J. Pinckney Henderson, who, as Acting Secretary of State of the Republic of Texas, wrote the following in the elaborate instructions of December 31, 1836, to Memucan Hunt, who had been appointed Minister Extraordinary of Texas to

the United States (Garrison, Diplomatic Correspondence of Texas, pt. 1, 161–65):

In the event that there should be doubts entertained whether a treaty made with this Government for its annexation to the United States would be ratified by a constitutional majority of the Senate of the United States you are instructed to call the attention of the authorities of that Government to the propriety and practicability of passing a law by both house (in which it would require a bare majority) taking in this Country as a part of her Territory, this law could be passed, (provided Congress has the power to do so) based upon the vote of the people of Texas at the last election but in framing such an act great care should be used in order to secure all of the rights of Texas and its citizens as fully as you are instructed to have them attended to in any treaty which may be made. If such an act is passed you can give that Government the fullest assurance that it will be approved by this Government and people. But inasmuch as this is rather a novel position you will speak of it with great prudence and caution.

The following paragraphs are extracted from the message of President Tyler of June 10, 1844, above cited:

The treaty negotiated by the Executive with the Republic of Texas, without a departure from any form of proceeding customarily observed in the negotiations of treaties for the annexation of that Republic to the United States, having been rejected by the Senate, and the subject having excited on the part of the people no ordinary degree of interest, I feel it to be my duty to communicate, for your consideration, the rejected treaty, together with all the correspondence and documents which have heretofore been submitted to the Senate in its executive sessions. The papers communicated embrace not only the series already made public by orders of the Senate, but others from which the veil of secrecy has not been removed by that body, but which I deem to be essential to a just appreciation of the entire question. While the treaty was pending before the Senate, I did not consider it compatible with the just rights of that body or consistent with the respect entertained for it to bring this important subject before you. The power of Congress is, however, fully competent in some other form of proceeding to accomplish everything that a formal ratification of the treaty could have accomplished, and I therefore feel that I should but imperfectly discharge my duty to yourselves or the country if I failed to lay before you everything in the possession of the Executive which would enable you to act with full light on the subject if you should deem it proper to take any action upon it.

:   :   .   .   .   .   :   :   .   :

So much have I considered it proper for me to say; and it becomes me only to add that while I have regarded the annexation to be accomplished by treaty as the most suitable form in which it could be effected, should Congress deem it proper to resort to any other expedient compatible with the Constitution and likely to accomplish the object I stand prepared to yield my most prompt and active cooperation.

The great question is not as to the manner in which it shall be done, but whether it shall be accomplished or not.

The responsibility of deciding this question is now devolved upon you.

Moreover, while no action was taken at that session of Congress, which adjourned on June 17, 1844, the question of annexation was kept open with the Government of Texas, despite the rejection of the treaty. General Tilghman A. Howard was appointed Chargé d'Affaires to Texas on June 11, 1844; and in the instructions to him of June 18, Secretary of State Calhoun wrote (D.S., 1 Instructions, Texas, 96–100):

The recent rejection of the Treaty of Annexation by the Senate has placed these relations [between the United States and Texas] in a very delicate and

hazardous state;—and the great object of your mission is to prevent, by every exertion in your power, the dangerous consequences to which it may lead.

The first step towards the accomplishment of so desirable a result, will be to satisfy the government of Texas that the loss of the Treaty does not necessarily involve the failure of the great object which it contemplated. It is now admitted that what was sought to be effected by the Treaty submitted to the Senate, may be secured by a joint resolution of the two houses of Congress incorporating all its provisions. This mode of effecting it will have the advantage of requiring only a majority of the two houses, instead of two thirds of the Senate. A joint resolution for this purpose has accordingly been introduced by Mr McDuffie of South Carolina in the Senate, and was laid on the table by a vote of 19 to 27 (many members being absent) on the ground that there was not sufficient time to act on it. Three of the absentees and also three who voted to lay on the table, were known to be favorable to annexation, which shows that, in a full Senate, and supposing the other absentees unfavorable, but two Senators are required to constitute a majority of the whole number.

In the other House the indications are still more favorable; as appears by the votes to which the President's recent Message communicating the Treaty and accompanying documents to that body, gave rise. On the motion to lay the Message and Documents on the table, the vote stood 66 yeas to 118 nays, and on that to suspend the rules with a view to the printing of 15.000 extra copies, it stood 108 yeas to 79 nays. All of which would seem to indicate that there is already a majority in the House in favor of annexation. In addition to these facts, it may be safely stated from the indications in the country, that amongst the people, a far larger proportion is in favor of annexation, and that it is still on the increase. On this point, however, it is not deemed necessary to enlarge; as your residence here during the past winter with all the facilities for ascertaining the state and current of public opinion, will enable you to sustain its correctness from your own information. Indeed, the force of the popular sentiment in favor of annexation is believed to be so strong as to afford just ground to hope that, on consulting with their Constituents, it will induce a sufficient number to make a majority, especially from the South and West, to vote for the measure, and you may assure the Government of Texas that the President is resolved to call an extra session of Congress whenever there is cause to believe that there is a sufficient change to secure the passage of a Joint Resolution by both Houses.

The importance of satisfying the Government of Texas that the non-approval of the Treaty does not involve the loss of annexation, and that there is still reasonable ground to hope for its success, is based on the belief that the government and people of Texas are so deeply devoted to the measure that they will not abandon it so long as there is any reasonable hope of its success. In this belief we cannot feel that we are mistaken. The evidences they have given of such a disposition are so numerous and strong, that we cannot permit ourselves to doubt. Indeed, an opposite conclusion would imply that they were not only insensible to the feelings and sympathies which belong to a common origin, but blind to their own safety and prosperity. The danger is that the revulsion of disappointed hopes highly excited, may be seized upon by an interested and wily diplomacy, and made the means of seducing them to seek and form other alliance with the Power, which there is reason to fear has been eagerly watching the favorable opportunity.

Of all the results which could follow, this, in the end, would be the most disastrous to Texas,—to the United States and to the whole American continent. The Government of Texas would be blind, indeed, not to see that Great Britain, in seeking its alliance, seeks it for purposes purely selfish. She looks to her interests exclusively,—not to the interests of Texas:—and that whatever motive may be held out, the result, in the end, must be abject submission and degradation on the part of Texas. Such has ever been the fate of the smaller in alliances between them and larger communities; and in none would the connection be followed by more oppressive consequences than between Texas and Great Britain. Their interests would be opposite in many and important particulars. Her vast East Indian possessions exercise a controlling influence over her in all commercial questions in which their interests come in conflict with the products of this continent. To those she has already sacrificed her West India Islands; and it would

be the height of folly for Texas, as a dependent community, to expect a better fate. The enlightened Chief Magistrate of the Republic of Texas [General Samuel Houston] has too much intelligence not to see that this would be the consequence of such an alliance; and too much patriotism to seek it while one hope remained of incorporating that Republic into our glorious Union. He has already acquired too much fame to hazard it by a step which Texas would long deplore, and which in after times could not fail to impair his just renown, while, on the other hand, by successfully carrying out the measure with which he is so intimately identified, he would fill the measure of his country's glory and his own.

In regard to the orders which have been heretofore given to the officers in command of the military and naval force of the United States in the Gulph of Mexico and on the frontiers of Texas, you may assure the government of Texas that there will be no material change, except that the communications made to it by the officer commanding the military as well as the naval force, will be made through the Chargé d'Affaires of the United States.

You will consider these as constituting the general outline of your instructions. Much must be left to your judgement and discretion as to the means and matters most proper to be employed in securing the attachment of the Government and people of Texas, in removing existing and preventing future causes of discontent and alienation and of advancing the great object of annexation, so essential to the peace and safety of both countries. In conclusion you may give assurance that annexation has been defeated at the present time mainly by the controlling influence of temporary causes, but that the measure has taken so deep and general a hold on the public mind that it must ultimately triumph, should it not be abandoned by the Government and People of Texas.

The Joint Resolution of March 1, 1845

Part of the annual presidential message to Congress of December 3, 1844, at the opening of the ensuing session (Richardson, IV, 334–52), was devoted to the question of Texas; the concluding paragraphs on the subject were these:

Other considerations of a controlling character influenced the course of the Executive. The treaty which had thus been negotiated had failed to receive the ratification of the Senate. One of the chief objections which was urged against it was found to consist in the fact that the question of annexation had not been submitted to the ordeal of public opinion in the United States. However untenable such an objection was esteemed to be, in view of the unquestionable power of the Executive to negotiate the treaty and the great and lasting interests involved in the question, I felt it to be my duty to submit the whole subject to Congress as the best expounders of popular sentiment. No definitive action having been taken on the subject by Congress, the question referred itself directly to the decision of the States and people. The great popular election which has just terminated afforded the best opportunity of ascertaining the will of the States and the people upon it. Pending that issue it became the imperative duty of the Executive to inform Mexico that the question of annexation was still before the American people, and that until their decision was pronounced any serious invasion of Texas would be regarded as an attempt to forestall their judgment and could not be looked upon with indifference. I am happy to inform you that no such invasion has taken place; and I trust that whatever your action may be upon it Mexico will see the importance of deciding the matter by a resort to peaceful expedients in preference to those of arms. The decision of the people and the States on this great and interesting subject has been decisively manifested. The question of annexation has been presented nakedly for their consideration. By the treaty itself all collateral and incidental issues which were calculated to divide and distract the public councils were carefully avoided. These were left to the wisdom of the future to determine. It presented, I repeat, the isolated question of annexation, and in that form it has been submitted to the ordeal of public sentiment. A controlling majority of the people and a large majority of the States have declared in favor of immediate annexation. Instructions have thus come up to both branches of Congress from their respective constituents in

terms the most emphatic. It is the will of both the people and the States that Texas shall be annexed to the Union promptly and immediately. It may be hoped that in carrying into execution the public will thus declared all collateral issues may be avoided. Future Legislatures can best decide as to the number of States which should be formed out of the territory when the time has arrived for deciding that question. So with all others. By the treaty the United States assumed the payment of the debts of Texas to an amount not exceeding $10,000,000, to be paid, with the exception of a sum falling short of $400,000, exclusively out of the proceeds of the sales of her public lands. We could not with honor take the lands without assuming the full payment of all incumbrances upon them.

Nothing has occurred since your last session to induce a doubt that the dispositions of Texas remain unaltered. No intimation of an altered determination on the part of her Government and people has been furnished to the Executive. She still desires to throw herself under the protection of our laws and to partake of the blessings of our federative system, while every American interest would seem to require it. The extension of our coastwise and foreign trade to an amount almost incalculable, the enlargement of the market for our manufactures, a constantly growing market for our agricultural productions, safety to our frontiers, and additional strength and stability to the Union—these are the results which would rapidly develop themselves upon the consummation of the measure of annexation. In such event I will not doubt but that Mexico would find her true interest to consist in meeting the advances of this Government in a spirit of amity. Nor do I apprehend any serious complaint from any other quarter; no sufficient ground exists for such complaint. We should interfere in no respect with the rights of any other nation. There can not be gathered from the act any design on our part to do so with their possessions on this continent. We have interposed no impediments in the way of such acquisitions of territory, large and extensive as many of them are, as the leading powers of Europe have made from time to time in every part of the world. We seek no conquest made by war. No intrigue will have been resorted to or acts of diplomacy essayed to accomplish the annexation of Texas. Free and independent herself, she asks to be received into our Union. It is a question for our own decision whether she shall be received or not.

The two Governments having already agreed through their respective organs on the terms of annexation, I would recommend their adoption by Congress in the form of a joint resolution or act to be perfected and made binding on the two countries when adopted in like manner by the Government of Texas.

In order that the subject may be fully presented in all its bearings, the correspondence which has taken place in reference to it since the adjournment of Congress between the United States, Texas, and Mexico is herewith transmitted [Senate Document No. 1, 28th Congress, 2d session, serial 449].

The joint resolution of March 1, 1845, the text of which is the first of the four documents printed above (following the headnote), originated in the House of Representatives; as passed there on January 25 by a vote of 120 to 98, it included sections 1 and 2 only; section 3 was added in the Senate, which on February 27, by 27 votes to 25, adopted the resolution thus amended; the House of Representatives concurred in the amendment on February 28 by 132 votes to 76; and on March 1 the resolution was approved by President Tyler (5 Statutes at Large, 797–98; the debates on the measure are in Congressional Globe, XIV, and appendix, *passim;* see also Benton, Thirty Years' View, II, 632–38).

It will be observed that those clauses of the joint resolution of March 1, 1845, on which action was based and taken (sections 1 and 2) differed from the provisions of the defeated treaty of annexation in certain important features. Under the treaty it was contemplated

that Texas would become temporarily a territory of the United States; the public lands were ceded, and the United States assumed the public debts of Texas to the extent of $10,000,000. Under the joint resolution Texas was to be admitted as a State, and the State of Texas retained all the vacant and unappropriated lands, to be applied to the payment of the debts and liabilities of the Republic of Texas, which were not to become a charge upon the Government of the United States.

THE COMMUNICATION TO TEXAS

With the first annual message of President Polk to Congress of December 2, 1845, there were transmitted most of the correspondence between the Department of State and the Chargé d'Affaires to Texas during the year 1845 (beginning with March 3) and various other papers relevant to the question of the annexation of Texas. The message and the accompanying papers are printed in Senate Document No. 1, 29th Congress, 1st session, serial 470, and also in House Document No. 2 of that Congress and session, serial 480. The first of those two documents is hereafter generally cited as "published correspondence".

In its final form the joint resolution of March 1, 1845, authorized two entirely different modes of procedure; by sections 1 and 2 the consent of Congress to the erection of a new State, the State of Texas, to be admitted into the Union "with the consent of the existing government" of the Republic of Texas, was given under certain conditions; a constitution of the new State was to be adopted by "deputies in Convention assembled" and by the people; that constitution was to be transmitted to the President of the United States to be laid before Congress by January 1, 1846; all questions of boundary with "other governments" were for the United States to adjust; there were provisions regarding public buildings and property, public funds, public lands, and public debts; new States might be formed out of the territory in question with the consent of Texas; and the Missouri Compromise line of 1820 (36°30' north; sec. 8 of the act of March 6, 1820, 3 Statutes at Large, 545-48) was made applicable to any such States.

By section 3 of the joint resolution, as an alternative, the President was authorized, in lieu of submitting sections 1 and 2 to the Republic of Texas "as an overture on the part of the United States for admission", to negotiate with the Government of Texas for the admission of a State "with suitable extent and boundaries", and for "the cession of the remaining Texan territory to the United States"; and "the terms of said admission and cession" were to be framed "either by treaty to be submitted to the Senate, or by articles to be submitted to the two Houses of Congress, as the President may direct".

The term of President Tyler was about to expire; but he decided to act at once, and to act under sections 1 and 2 of the joint resolution (see Tyler, Letters and Times of the Tylers, II, 364–65); and the following instructions were sent to Andrew Jackson Donelson, Chargé d'Affaires to Texas (who had been appointed on September 16, 1844, following the death of Tilghman A. Howard on August 16), under

date of March 3, 1845 (D.S., 1 Instructions, Texas, 107–11; published correspondence, 32–34):

I herewith transmit to you a copy of the Joint Resolutions adopted by Congress for the annexation of Texas to the United States.

You will perceive that they consist of two distinct parts; the one embraced in the first and second sections, being the original Resolution as it passed the House of Representatives; the other, included in the third and last, being the amendment made by the Senate and subsequently adopted by the House. The former contains certain specific propositions for the admission of Texas into our Union; the latter gives a discretionary power to the President, if he should deem it advisable, to enter into negotiations with the Republic, as prescribed in the section itself, instead of submitting to its acceptance or rejection the proposals contained in the former.

The President has deliberately considered the subject, and is of opinion that it would not be advisable to enter into the negotiations authorized by the amendment of the Senate, and you are accordingly instructed to present to the government of Texas, as the basis of its admission, the proposals contained in the Resolution as it came from the House of Representatives.

It is not deemed necessary to state at large the grounds on which his decision rests. It will be sufficient to state briefly that the provisions of the Resolution as it came from the House, are more simple in their character; may be more readily and with less difficulty and expense, carried into effect, and that the great object contemplated by them is much less exposed to the hazard of ultimate defeat.

That they are more simple in their character a very few remarks will suffice to show. According to the Resolution as it came from the House, nothing more is necessary than that the Congress of Texas should be called together, its consent given to the provisions contained in it, and the adoption of a Constitution by the people in Convention to be submitted to the Congress of the United States for its approval in the same manner as when one of our own territories is admitted as a State. On the contrary, according to the provisions of the Senate's amendment, the Congress of Texas must, in like manner, be convened;—it must then go through the slow and troublesome process of carving a State out of a part of its territory;—afterwards it must appoint agents or commissioners to meet similar agents or commissioners to be appointed on our part, to discuss and agree on the terms and conditions on which the State shall be admitted, and on the cession of the remaining territory to the United States, and after all this, and not before, the people of the said State must call a Convention, frame a Constitution and then present it to the Congress of the United States for its approval, but which cannot be acted on until the terms agreed upon by the negotiators, and which constitute the conditions on which the State is to be admitted, shall have been ratified.

That they may be more readily and with less difficulty and expense, carried into effect, is plain from the fact that the details are fewer and less complex. It is obvious that the numerous and complicated provisions contained in the amendment of the Senate must involve much time and difficulty in their execution; while, as to the expense, the appropriation of $100.000 provided for by it, is a clear additional cost over and above that attendant on the execution of the Resolution of the House.

But the decisive objection to the Amendment of the Senate is, that it would endanger the ultimate success of the measure. It proposes to fix, by negotiation between the Governments of the United States and Texas, the terms and conditions on which the State shall be admitted into our Union, and the cession of the remaining territory to the United States. Now, by whatever name the agents conducting the negotiation may be known, whether they be called commissioners, Ministers or by any other title, the compact agreed on by them in behalf of their respective governments would be a Treaty;—whether so called or designated by some other name. The very meaning of a Treaty is a compact between independent States founded on negotiation. And if a treaty (as it clearly would be) it must be submitted to the Senate for its approval and run the hazard of receiving the votes of two thirds of the members present, which could hardly be expected, if we are to judge from recent experience. This, of itself, is considered by the President as a conclusive reason for proposing the Resolution of the House, instead of the amendment of the Senate, as the basis of annexation.

But it may be objected that the Resolution of the House prescribes no means of rendering its provisions acceptable to the government and people of Texas, in case they should prove unsatisfactory. The objection, however, is more apparent than real; for although none are expressly provided, it cannot be doubted that the Congress of Texas may propose whatever amendments it may think essential, and transmit them to the government of the United States for its consideration and agreement; and, if adopted, to be binding on both parties, a far more satisfactory mode, in all probability, of obtaining the mutual consent of both, than that of negotiating through commissioners or other agents; while it is exempt from the decisive objections to which this is liable.

But it is deemed by the President of great importance that the Resolution should be adopted by the Government of Texas without amendment; so as to avoid the hazards and contingencies incident to delay; and you are accordingly instructed to use your best exertions to effect this object. Should you fail in this, you will next endeavor to induce the Congress of Texas to substitute, in place of amendments, separate and distinct propositions, expressive of their views of what the provisions of the Resolution ought to be, accompanied by a strong address setting forth their reasons at length, and expressing their reliance on the justice of the government of the United States for their adoption. If both fail, it will then remain for the Congress of Texas to amend the Resolutions as above suggested.

The President also directs me to instruct you to proceed with as little delay as possible to the seat of the government of Texas and to urge speedy and prompt action on the subject. Time is important, and not a day ought to be lost. The last hope on the part of any foreign power which may feel disposed to defeat annexation, will be to act upon the Government of Texas; and it can scarcely be doubted from the feelings expressed on the part of one of the leading European Powers against the measure, that no effort will be spared to induce Texas to reject the proposals contained in the Resolution. Your prudence, intelligence, activity and influence are confidently relied on to counteract the attempt.

President Polk adopted the decision of his predecessor; the instructions to Donelson signed by Secretary of State Buchanan on March 10, 1845, the day he took over the duties of his office, differed somewhat in their reasoning from those of March 3, 1845, but were to the same effect (D.S., 1 Instructions, Texas, 112–17; published correspondence, 35–38):

You will have received, ere this can reach you, the despatch of Mr Calhoun, the late Secretary of State, of the third instant, instructing you "to present to the government of Texas, as the basis of its admission, the proposals contained in the Resolution as it came from the House of Representatives." President Tyler having thus determined to adopt the two first of the series of Resolutions instead of the alternative presented by the third, it became the duty of the President to devote his attention to this important question at as early a moment as possible. This has been done, and his deliberations have resulted in a clear and firm conviction that it would be inexpedient to reverse the decision of his predecessor.

Whilst the President does not concur in the opinion of his predecessor, that under the third Resolution the terms of admission and cession which might be agreed upon by commissioners of the respective governments would necessarily be a Treaty which must, under the Constitution, be submitted to the Senate for their advice and consent, yet he is sensible that many of the sincere friends of Texas may entertain this opinion. Should that prove to be the case in the two Houses of Congress, members sincerely friendly to the admission of Texas would be compelled to vote against the adoption of such articles of Union under the conviction that they could only be constitutionally submitted to the Senate. This might create a division among the friends of the measure which would prove fatal to its success.

The President prefers the two first Resolutions, because they will, in his judgement, the most speedily and certainly secure the admission of Texas into the Union. These Resolutions pursue the usual course adopted by Congress in pre-

paring the way for the admission of new States, so far as the existing relations between the two Republics will permit. Should Texas assent to the terms and conditions proposed by them, the faith of the Government of the United States then becomes pledged for her admission into the Union, and the Act of Congress redeeming this pledge will follow as a necessary consequence. The President can perceive no good reason why this Union so long desired by the people of the two Republics may not be consummated within a brief period after the commencement of the next session of Congress. Nothing can prevent this happy result but the determination of Texas to change and modify the conditions presented by these Resolutions, and you cannot too earnestly warn the government of that Republic against the unhappy consequences which may flow from such a policy. Should any of these conditions appear to be unreasonable, she may rely with confidence upon the well known justice and liberality of her sister States to change or modify them after she shall have been restored to the bosom of our Republican family. The great object now to be accomplished, that which far transcends all other objects in importance, is her prompt admission into the Union. This once accomplished, all other subordinate questions can be easily and satisfactorily arranged between the parties. The President confidently trusts that the Government of Texas may take this view of the subject and not suffer the reünion between the two countries to be delayed or defeated by the interposition of minor questions which in the natural course of events will settle themselves hereafter.

Should Texas refuse her assent to the terms and conditions of the two first Resolutions or present new conditions for the acceptance of Congress, we are then again at sea and the success of the great measure may be placed in jeopardy. These new conditions may become the subject of earnest and angry debate before Congress,—the friends of the admission of Texas may be divided in opinion regarding them, and thus the great work of union may be almost indefinitely postponed. Should the Congress of the United States, after a debate which may be protracted until near the termination of the next session, reject all or any of the conditions which may be proposed by Texas, these must be again referred back for the decision of the Government of that Republic. This must produce long delay in her admission into the Union. Indeed nothing could be more tedious and embarrassing than such an exchange of conditions and propositions between the Legislative authorities of the two Governments, and nothing would have a stronger tendency to produce angry discussions which might end in estrangement. The two Governments might thus involve themselves in an inextricable labyrinth of confusion, and be finally compelled to commence the great work anew which may now so happily and so soon be completed. The confident expectation of the President that Texas would postpone all minor questions and consent to an immediate admission into the Union on the terms proposed, was one of the prevailing reasons for his preference of the two first Resolutions.

But cannot a mode be suggested entirely consistent with the immediate admission of Texas into the Union by which she may obtain all that she can reasonably desire? If it should be objected to that portion of the conditions proposed which necessarily deprives her of her revenue from customs without furnishing her the means of paying her debts incurred in the war of independence, that she would thus be forced into a condition of continued insolvency; this objection may be easily avoided. Both national honor and national justice forbid that the Government of the United States should place her in such a position. But the remedy for this evil is plainly pointed out by the relative condition of the two countries. Whilst the President cannot consent that this government should assume the debts of Texas, nothing is more easy than for her Convention to make a distinct and independent proposition to the Government of the United States, the almost certain acceptance of which by Congress would relieve her from this embarrassment.

The public lands of Texas ought unquestionably to belong to the United States. This is equally due to the prosperity of Texas and to that of the other States within whose limits there are public lands. Our land system has worked admirably in practice and has met the approbation of the world. Equal and exact justice to all the States requires that all the public lands should be subject to the control of the Federal Government and that they should be administered under an uniform system. Besides, the peace of the whole country as well as the security of Texas, demands that this Government alone should possess the power of

extinguishing the Indian title within her limits and have the absolute and exclusive control over the Camanches and other fierce and warlike tribes which now roam over her territory.   The United States must incur the expense and bear the burden of our wars with these tribes, and they ought therefore to possess the power of preserving peace and regulating all our relations with them.   In short, it is indispensable that our Indian policy should be extended over Texas.

Under these circumstances, why may not the Convention which will assemble to form a Constitution for Texas submit a distinct proposition to Congress to cede to the United States all her public lands and the exclusive jurisdiction over the Indians within her limits, in consideration of a fair and adequate sum of money. The amount may be the subject of future agreement.   Whilst this would enable Texas to pay her debts, it would extend our land system and our Indian system to territory which they ought to embrace.   Such a proposition would be so just and reasonable in itself, so consonant with the established policy of the United States and so beneficial to Texas, that scarcely a doubt exists but that it would receive the sanction of Congress.   The President would strongly recommend it to Congress, in the confident hope that it would receive the approbation of that enlightened body.   Presented as a distinct proposition, in no manner connected with the question of admission and after this question shall have been decided favorably, he does not apprehend that it would encounter any serious opposition. But if this were made a condition of admission, members who are honestly and conscientiously hostile to the measure might oppose it for the purpose of defeating or delaying the accomplishment of an object which they deem injurious to the country.

In every aspect in which the President has viewed this subject he believes that the paramount question of admission can be best settled and the just rights of Texas can be best secured by her acceptance, without qualification, of the terms and conditions proposed by the first two resolutions, and he therefore confidently expects that you will exert your well known ability and energy to secure this auspicious result by every honorable means within your power.

I herewith transmit to you the copy of a note, dated on the 6th instant, addressed to this Department by General Almonte, the Envoy Extraordinary and Minister Plenipotentiary of the Mexican Republic, together with a copy of my answer of this date.   These notes require no comment.   They will speak for themselves.   You will perceive that they furnish a powerful additional reason, in support of the arguments already advanced, why Texas should consent to be admitted into the Union without proposing any embarrassing conditions which might render long delay inevitable.

The protest of the Mexican Minister and the reply thereto of Secretary of State Buchanan, mentioned in the final paragraph of the foregoing instructions, are quoted below in these notes.

Donelson received his instructions (both those of March 3 and of March 10) at New Orleans on March 24, 1845, and returned to Washington, Texas, where he arrived on Sunday, March 30.   A new administration had been in office in Texas since December 9, 1844; Anson Jones, who had been Secretary of State under President Samuel Houston, had become President, and Ashbel Smith, Secretary of State; but Smith, while at the seat of Government of Texas on the arrival of Donelson, had been granted leave and departed for England on a special mission early in April 1845.   During his absence Ebenezer Allen, Attorney General, was Acting Secretary of State of Texas.

Just before the arrival of Donelson at Washington, Texas, the Chargés d'Affaires of France and Great Britain, Comte de Saligny and Captain Charles Elliot, had invited the Government of Texas to accept the good offices of their two Governments "for an early and honorable settlement of their difficulties with Mexico, upon the basis

of the acknowledgment of the independence of Texas by that Republic"; the terms proposed by Texas (dated March 29, 1845) as a basis for negotiation were these (D.S., 2 Despatches, Texas, No. 31, June 23, 1845, enclosure 5, pamphlet entitled "Correspondence Relating to a Treaty of Peace between Mexico and Texas, upon the Basis of an Acknowledgment of the Independence of the Latter"; see published correspondence, 87–90):

1. Mexico consents to acknowledge the Independence of Texas.
2. Texas engages that she will stipulate in the treaty not to annex herself or become subject to any country whatever.
3. Limits and other conditions to be matter of arrangement in the final treaty.
4. Texas will be willing to remit disputed points respecting territory and other matters to the arbitration of umpires.

The episode and its results are described in Smith, The Annexation of Texas, 407–13, 421–41, 449–56, and in Rives, The United States and Mexico, 1821–1848, I, 704–10. The action of the Mexican Congress in favor of accepting the proposals for negotiation became definitive on May 17, 1845, but was in any case too late; for that action was not proclaimed in Texas until June 4, the day fixed for the election of delegates to a National Convention to act on the proposals of the United States; and by that time acceptance by Texas of the proposals of the United States was as certain as any future event could be. The proclamation of June 4, 1845, which also declared a cessation of hostilities, is printed in published correspondence, 81–82.

Under date of March 31 Donelson communicated the joint resolution of the Congress of the United States of March 1, 1845, to the Government of Texas with the following note (D.S., 2 Despatches, Texas, April 3, 1845, enclosure; published correspondence, 48–51). The original of the note of Donelson is in the Texas State Library; the text here printed has been collated with a facsimile thereof; the two variances between the text here and that of the cited archives copy which are slips of the scrivener of the latter are indicated in the footnotes; other variances are mentioned below; the print in published correspondence was from the archives copy, but has a few slight errors (the written copy of the joint resolution of March 1, 1845, which was the enclosure to Donelson's note, was not certified):

WASHINGTON, TEXAS,
31ˢᵗ March, 1845.
The undersigned, Chargé d'Affaires of the United States, has the honor to transmit herewith to the Hon. Ebenezer Allen, Attorney General of the Republic of Texas and Charged *ad interim* with the direction of the Department of Foreign Affairs, the joint resolution which has been recently adopted by the Congress of the United States, for the annexation of Texas to the Union.

This important measure has thus been brought to the consummation so confidently anticipated, by the undersigned in his communication of the 10th December last, to this Government: And he trusts that it may be received as a just response to the wishes of the people of Texas, alike honorable to both countries, and worthy of the reciprocally national interests which have so long demanded it.

It now remains for the Government and people of Texas, by their acceptance and ratification of the provisions contained in this joint resolution, to finish the great work of annexation; and to assume their station as an independent, equal, and sovereign member of the American Confederacy, as soon as the constitutional requirements usual in the admission of new states. can be complied with.

Anxious to execute the trust devolved upon him by the resolution referred to in the manner best calculated to secure its objects, and with the least inconvenience and delay to Texas, the President of the United States has instructed the undersigned to inform this Government that he has selected as the basis of the action yet necessary on the subject, the first and second sections of the resolution—leaving out of view the remaining or third section. This last section, as the Hon. Mʳ Allen is aware, was added as an amendment, and leaves optional with the President a resort to the means it creates for an adjustment of the terms of annexation on a basis different from that offered in the first and second sections, which constituted the bill as it originally came to the Senate from the House of Representatives. It was doubtless intended to place in the hands of the President the means of obviating such objections as Texas might possibly make to the details of the propositions contained in the two preceding sections, but in doing so it complicates the process, and is otherwise productive of disadvantages so considerable as to induce the President not to rely upon it as the most appropriate or practicable mode of securing to Texas a speedy admission into the Union.

It is obvious, that if the discretionary power contemplated by the third section were resorted to, the action on the part of this Government, which can now settle the question of annexation would be deferred until the new negotiation to be made by commissioners, or ministers, on the part of the respective Governments, could be known. But this is not all. The negotiation thus made, even when ratified by Texas, would not be conclusive. It would still have to undergo a similar reference to the Government of the United States where it would again be liable to alteration or amendment, and this in its turn necessarily referrible back again to this Government, might involve the subject in inextricable confusion, and could not fail to be productive of danger to the measure, and of irritation to those friendly relations in other respects which so happily prevail between the two countries.

Such difficulties will be avoided by adhering to the proposals contained in the first and second sections. By those proposals, the door is at once opened for the admission of Texas into the Union in the manner that has been customary with the other territories of the United States, varied only by the peculiar relations which the two Republics have maintained as separate nations. If Texas now accepts those proposals, from that moment she becomes virtually a state of the Union, because the faith of the United States will be pledged for her admission, and the act of Congress necessary to redeem the pledge, is obliged to follow as soon as she presents a republican form of Government. All, then, that is necessary upon this basis, is for this Goverᵗ, after expressing its assent to the proposals submitted to it, to call a convention of the people to clothe their deputies with the power necessary to amend their constitution, and adapt the Government created by it, to the new circumstances under which it will be placed by annexation to the Union.

On the grounds, therefore, of more directness and simplicity in the process, whereby time and much expenditure of money will be saved—and of the entire avoidance of all further risks resulting from possible differences attending efforts to obtain terms more suitable to the separate views of the respective Governments—it has been thought best, by the President of the United States, as before stated, to rest the question on the joint resolution, as it came from the House of Representatives, which contains propositions complete and ample, as an overture to Texas, and which, if adopted by her, places the reunion of the two countries beyond the possibility of defeat.

This great question, then, is in the hands of Texas. It depends upon herself, whether she will be restored to the bosom of the Republican family, and, taking her station with the other sisters of the confederacy, will cooperate with them in advancing the cause of free government; or whether, standing aloof from them, she is to run the hazards of a separate career, at a period in the affairs of the world, when the friends of a different system of Government are urged by the most powerful motives to resist the extension of the republican principle.

The undersigned doubts not that there are objections to the terms proposed, which, under ordinary circumstances, ought to be obviated before a basis which admits them is adopted. But the circumstances are not ordinary, and the objections, when weighed in the scale of importance, with the magnitude of the inter-

ests involved in the success of the measure, become secondary in their character, and may well be postponed, until the natural course of events removes them. If annexation should now be lost, it may never be recovered. A patriotic and intelligent people, in the pursuit of a measure of general utility, if they commit a partial mistake, or inflict temporary injury,[1] were never known to fail in making the proper reparation. If they have, in this instance, made proposals of union to Texas, on terms which deprive her of means that should be exclusively hers, to enable her to pay the debt contracted in the war for her independence, it has been accidental; and no assurance, from the undersigned, can be needed to give value to the anticipation that such an error will be corrected, whenever it is communicated to the Government of the United States.

It is objected, that Texas, in surrendering her revenue from customs, parts with the ability to put into efficient organization her state government. This objection must result from an undue examination of the expenditures which the United States, on the other hand, will make in the many improvements necessary on the sea coast of Texas, to protect and facilitate her commerce, in the removal of obstructions in her numerous bays and rivers, and in the military organization necessary to guard her extensive frontier against the inroads of a foreign enemy. When expenditures for these and many other internal objects are drawn from the Treasury of the Union, and not from that of Texas, it will be seen that the remaining means for the support of the state government will not only be as great as they now are, but rapidly increased by the influx of population; and the growing capacity resulting from the superabundance of their rich productions.

So, also, on the part of the United States, it was objected that the cession of the unappropriated lands, ought to have been made by Texas, for a fair consideration, to enable the Federal Government to extend her[2] Indian policy over the various tribes within her limits. The right to extinguish the Indian title to these lands, seems almost a necessary consequence of the obligation to regulate the trade and intercourse with them, and to keep them at peace with each other and with us; and the absence of any provision to this effect in the terms proposed, constituted a serious obstacle in the minds of many sincerely friendly to the measure. Yet so strong was the desire to put the question beyond the possibility of defeat; and to leave with Texas the means of discharging her national debt, that they nevertheless recorded their votes in its favor.

But reference is made to such objections, not to ascertain their justness or unjustness[3] on this occasion; but to remark, on the part of the United States, that much was conceded to obtain the passage of the resolution. And it was also believed, that a like spirit would induce Texas to overlook minor considerations relying on that high sense of honor and magnanimity which governs both the people and the representatives of the United States to secure to her hereafter all that she can reasonably desire to place her on the most favorable footing with the other members of the Union. It was this belief that mainly induced the President of the United States, to give the instructions which have controlled this communication from the undersigned, adopting as the basis of action, for finishing the work of annexation, the joint resolution as it originally passed the House of Representatives.

With these observations, the question is now submitted to the Hon. Mr Allen, under the confident hope, that this Government will see the necessity of prompt and decisive action, whereby the measure may obtain the constitutional sanction of Texas. And the undersigned takes this occasion to renew to Mr Allen, an expression of the distinguished consideration, with which he has the honor to be

His very obt hbl sevt

A J DONELSON

Hon. EBENEZER ALLEN,
Attorney General of Texas, &c., &c., &c.

---

[1] Written "injuries" in the archives copy.

[2] Written "their" in the archives copy.

[3] In published correspondence this word is "invalidity", which is written in pencil over "unjustness" in the archives copy of the note.

In his subsequent writings Anson Jones stated that the foregoing note of Donelson of March 31, 1845, was not formally presented until nearly two weeks later (Jones, Letters Relating to the History of Annexation, 14; Jones, Memoranda and Official Correspondence, 103); Jones further intimated that "Major Donelson made various alterations in the original paper after the 1st of April, resuming it for that purpose" (*ibid.*). Those statements of Jones have been accepted by various authorities (Smith, *op. cit.*, 442, footnote 15; Middleton, "Donelson's Mission to Texas in Behalf of Annexation", in Southwestern Historical Quarterly, XXIV, 275, footnote 31); the evidence is to be examined.

Regarding the delivery of the note, Donelson specifically states that he presented it on the morning of its date, March 31; the final paragraph of the despatch of Donelson of April 1, 1845, as printed in the Senate document here cited as published correspondence (p. 48) is to the effect that a copy of the note of March 31 is enclosed, and Donelson adds: "I prepared it [the note] in the few hours I could command, the night of my arrival [March 30], and presented it the next morning [March 31]." There is nothing in Donelson's despatches to indicate that he deemed the delivery of the note on the day of its date as other than formal and definitive; and Donelson makes no mention of any changes in the text of his note subsequent to its presentation.

In the original of the despatch last cited, following the signature of Donelson, there is a paragraph which is not printed in published correspondence; that paragraph reads as follows (D.S., 2 Despatches, Texas):

I am disappointed in being able to send the copy referred to of my letter to this Government. The original draft, to save time, I sent to Gen¹ Houston—and that to the Government which I expected to copy at the Department of State, I am just informed has been sent to Mʳ Allen who with Judge Ochletree the Secretary of the Treasury is at Montgomery. At this latter place then the whole subject is now under *caucus* consideration and by the return of the *express*, either mine or the Governments, something important may be anticipated.

Thus no copy of the note of March 31, 1845, was enclosed with the despatch of Donelson of April 1, for there were at the time only two examples of that note; the copy retained by Donelson had been sent to General Houston; the original, delivered to the Department of State, had been sent to Allen at Montgomery.

There is still another relevant paragraph of Donelson's correspondence which is not printed in published correspondence. This is the opening paragraph of his despatch of April 3 (D.S., 2 Despatches, Texas; see published correspondence, 51); that omitted paragraph reads as follows:

I have just obtained from the State Department here the copy of the communication referred to in my last despatch, which, for reasons, therein stated, I could not copy myself. I am looking hourly for the return of my express to Gen¹ Houston, who with the actᵍ Secʸ of state, and the Secʸ of the Treasury, Judge Ocheltree, have had a day at least to deliberate upon the proposals offered by the United States.

Accordingly, it was the copy of the note of March 31 which Donelson received on April 3 from the Department of State of Texas (and which had been made from the original) which he enclosed with his despatch of that date.   That copy, written in a clerkly hand very different from the writing of Donelson and very different from the writing of the original note, is not only now with his despatch of April 3 (which was received on April 21), but is marked "With Mr Donelson's letter of 3ᵈ Apl."

There are available for examination and comparison three manuscripts of the note of March 31, 1845: first, a facsimile of the original thereof in eight pages (the source text of the print here); secondly, the copy with the despatch of Donelson of April 3, 1845, here referred to as the archives copy; and thirdly, a facsimile of the record copy in a manuscript volume entitled "Foreign Letters to Department, 1844, 5 and 6", II, 69–73, which is in the Texas State Library.

Certain of the corrections and interlineations in the original note were obviously made when it was first written and before its delivery. These (perhaps eight in number) need not here be considered.   Of the other changes two were undoubtedly made after the writing of the copy of April 3, and these perhaps comprise all the "various alterations" referred to by Anson Jones.   They are as follows:

Paragraph	As first written	As altered
Five	thus concluded	thus made
Twelve	an equal	the most favorable

Besides those two changes there are three others which possibly were made after the delivery of the note on March 31, 1845; but if so, the time of their making was the brief period between the return of the original note from Montgomery (presumably on April 2) and the time when the copy of April 3 was sent forward by Donelson. As possibilities they are here listed; the state of the available manuscripts rather supports the view that only one of the three (paragraph 9) is a probability:

Paragraph	As first written	As altered
Six	adopt	adapt
Nine	assertion	anticipation
Twelve	justice and injustice	justness or unjustness

In any case the "various alterations" were of very little consequence.   Donelson may have deemed them too minor to mention in a despatch.

Subsequent Proceedings

What may perhaps be regarded as the first step toward action by Texas on the annexation proposals of the United States contained in sections 1 and 2 of the joint resolution of March 1, 1845, was the issu-

ance of a proclamation by the President of Texas on April 3, 1845, for the filling of two vacancies in the Texan Congress by elections on April 26 in Fort Bend and Bexar Counties (D.S., 2 Despatches, Texas, No. 18, April 12, 1845; the text of the proclamation is in the Texas National Register, Washington, Texas, April 24, 1845, a copy of which is with despatch No. 21, of April 29, 1845); under section 3 of Article 1 of the Texan Constitution of 1836 the members of the House of Representatives were "chosen annually, on the first Monday of September", and held "their offices one year from the date of their election"; so the terms of those to be elected on April 26 were to expire on the following September 1 (see Thorpe, The Federal and State Constitutions, VI, 3532).

Sections 1 and 2 of the joint resolution of March 1, 1845, required the assent of Texas to admission into the Union; various conditions were laid down; *inter alia* "the consent of the existing government" was to be given; a constitution was to be adopted "by deputies in Convention assembled" and "by the people of said republic of Texas" and was to be "transmitted to the President of the United States, to be laid before Congress for its final action" by January 1, 1846.

The independent Republic of Texas was to end its separate existence and to become a part of the United States of America; the treaty method of accomplishing that result, which perhaps might be called the normal method, had failed, for reasons extrinsic to Texas; very naturally, the then existing constitution and laws of Texas contained no provisions appropriate for the required action; resort to first principles was necessary.

At the outset there was, not unnaturally, some doubt and hesitation in the minds of the officials of Texas as to the procedure to be adopted. President Jones is reported as saying "that his past impression had been in favor of a call of Congress, but that he did not know but under the circumstances of the case, as now presented, a more judicious course would be a reference of the subject at once to the people for the purpose of obtaining the convention to effect the changes which would be necessary for admission into the Union. He however added that the gravity of the subject required him not to act in haste, and that although he had a decided opinion he would dwell awhile on it until he was aided by the advice of his Cabinet" (D.S., 2 Despatches, Texas, April 1, 1845, from Andrew J. Donelson; published correspondence, 47–48).

On the other hand, the Attorney General of Texas, Ebenezer Allen, expressed the extraordinary view (which he very soon abandoned) "that he was decidedly opposed to a call of Congress, alleging that the whole subject was extraconstitutional, and one which the President could as well dispose of, as Congress" (*ibid.*). Donelson himself was willing either that the President of Texas "would call Congress at an early day, or designate a day for the people to choose Delegates to a convention to decide upon the terms of admission, and if adopted, to make the necessary Constitutional changes in the Government", and he drafted a note in that sense as a reply to his communication of the American proposals (in the same despatch, but omitted in published correspondence).

Moreover, Donelson found that the views of the members of the Government of Texas on the merits of the offer of the United States were at least lukewarm and probably even hostile thereto. "It is very likely that President Jones and many of the high officials in Texas would have preferred independence to annexation" (Rives, *op. cit.*, I, 710). In his despatch of April 3 Donelson wrote, "Affairs do not wear the encouraging aspect I would desire, but there are no conclusive indications against the acceptance of the proposals" (D.S., 2 Despatches, Texas; published correspondence, 51–52); and he found that General Samuel Houston, whom he visited at Montgomery, was "adverse to the basis selected for the admission of Texas into the Union". Houston would have preferred negotiations under the alternative provisions of section 3 of the joint resolution of March 1, 1845. Donelson left Houston "under a full conviction that if the adoption of our proposals depended upon his vote, it would be lost" (D.S., 2 Despatches, Texas, No. 18, April 12, 1845; the relevant portion of the despatch is omitted in published correspondence, 52).

However, the official attitude of President Jones toward the proposals of the United States remained perfectly correct. His decision as to the procedure was both to call an extra session of the Texan Congress and to call a convention; and the decision to call an extra session of Congress was reached with very little delay. Donelson was informed of it on April 12, 1845, just thirteen days after his arrival at the seat of Government. In his despatch of that date Donelson wrote (*ibid.*):

Returned to this place I have had to day a long and interesting interview with President Jones. He informs me that although he is of the same opinion with Gen¹ Houston in his belief that the United States should have offered Texas more liberal terms, he will interpose no obstacle to their submission to Congress and the people—and that he will call Congress at an early day in order that they may apportion the Districts for the election of the deputies to the convention which will be necessary to test the ratification of the proposals and to make the corresponding changes in the Govᵗ.

Despite the apparent difficulties, it cannot be said that the fate of the proposals of the United States depended on the negotiations between Donelson and the officials of the Texan Government. Indeed, such negotiations as were had were of comparatively minor importance. The circumstances of the time, the history of the previous ten years, the terms of the American offer, the very nature of the question presented, the crucial importance of the answer, all these made a decision by the body of the people[1] of Texas imperative; any executive decision was precluded (see generally Smith, The Annexation of Texas, ch. XX, 432–61; Middleton, "Donelson's Mission to Texas in Behalf of Annexation", in Southwestern Historical Quarterly, XXIV, 247–91; and Middleton, "The Texas Convention of 1845", in *ibid.*, XXV, 26–62).

---

[1] The population of Texas in 1845, exclusive of Indians, was perhaps about 100,000 (Wooten, A Comprehensive History of Texas, II, 760). The vote on annexation on October 13, 1845 (incomplete), was 4,254 for and 267 against, a ratio of nearly 16 to 1.

The proclamation for the meeting of the Congress of Texas on June 16, 1845, at Washington, Texas, was issued on April 15, as follows (D.S., 2 Despatches, Texas, No. 19, April 16, 1845, enclosure, broadside; published correspondence, 54–55):

By the President of the Republic of Texas.

A PROCLAMATION.

WHEREAS, since the close of the last session of Congress, a Joint Resolution respecting the Annexation of Texas to the United States has, by their Congress been adopted, authorizing the President of the United States to select the alternative of two certain propositions contained in the said Joint Resolution as the basis for consummating the proposed annexation:

And whereas, the President of the United States has selected the *first* and *second* sections of the Resolution as such basis, and notified this Government thereof, which sections are as follows, viz:

[Here follows the text of sections 1 and 2 of the joint resolution of March 1, 1845]

And whereas, the premises, requiring the solemn deliberation and action of the Representatives of the people, form an extraordinary occasion for convening the Congress of the Republic,

Therefore, be it known, that I, ANSON JONES, President of the Republic of Texas, by virtue of the power vested in me by the Constitution, do, by these presents, require that the Senators and Representatives to Congress of this Republic, shall assemble in special session, at the Town of Washington, in the County of Washington, on *Monday,* the *sixteenth day of June* next ensuing, then and there to receive such communications as may be made to them, and to consult and determine on such measures as in their wisdom may be deemed meet for the welfare of Texas.

In testimony whereof, I have caused the Great seal of the Republic to be hereunto affixed. Done at the Town of Washington, this (L.S.) fifteenth day of April, in the year of our Lord one thousand eight hundred and forty-five, and of the Independence of the Republic the tenth.

ANSON JONES.

By the President,
   EBEN'R ALLEN.
    Acting Secretary of State.

In the absence of any express provision of law for the calling of a convention, President Jones acted by issuing a proclamation on May 5, 1845, in which he went no further than to "recommend to the citizens of Texas" the election on June 4, 1845, of deputies to a National Convention of Texas, with a specific apportionment of delegates or deputies by counties. The difficult problem of representation in the Convention was thus solved by that instrument and was not, as had been previously suggested, left to the Congress of Texas for decision; and as will be seen from the text of the proclamation, which follows, the date of the meeting of the Convention (July 4, 1845) and its purposes, were similarly and merely recommended (published correspondence, 63–64):

By the President of the Republic of Texas.

A PROCLAMATION.

Whereas the people of Texas have evinced a decided wish that prompt and definite action should be had upon the proposition for annexation recently submitted by the government of the United States to this government, and that a convention should be assembled for this purpose; and

Whereas it is competent for the people alone to decide finally upon the proposition for annexation, and, "by deputies in convention assembled," to adopt a constitution with a view to the admission of Texas as one of the States of the American Union; and

Whereas no authority is given by the constitution of this republic to any branch of the government to call a convention and to change the organic law—this being a right reserved to the people themselves, and which they alone can properly exercise—

Therefore, be it known that I, Anson Jones, President of the republic of Texas, desirous of giving direction and effect to the public will, already so fully expressed, do *recommend* to the citizens of Texas that an election for "deputies" to a convention be held in the different counties of the republic on Wednesday, the fourth day of June next, upon the following basis, viz: Each county in the republic to elect one deputy, irrespective of the number of voters it contained at the last annual elections; each county voting at that time three hundred, and less than six hundred, to elect two deputies; each county voting at that time six hundred, and less than nine hundred, to elect three deputies; and each county voting at that time nine hundred and upwards, to elect four deputies; which basis will give to the county of Austin two, Bastrop one, Bexar two, Brazoria two, Brazos one, Bowie one, Colorado one, Fayette two, Fannin two, Fort Bend one, Goliad one, Galveston two, Gonzales one, Harris, three, Harrison three, Houston two, Jackson one, Jasper one, Jefferson one, Lamar two, Liberty two, Matagorda one, Montgomery four, Milam one, Nacogdoches three, Red River three, Robertson two, Rusk one, Refugio one, Sabine one, San Augustine two, Shelby two, San Patricio one, Travis one, Victoria one, and Washington three deputies; and that the said deputies so elected do assemble in convention at the city of Austin, on the "fourth of July" next, for the purpose of considering the proposition for the annexation of Texas to the United States, and any other proposition which may be made concerning the nationality of the republic, and, should they judge it expedient and proper, to adopt, provisionally, a constitution to be submitted to the people for their ratification, with the view to the admission of Texas, as a State, into the American Union, in accordance with the terms of the proposition for annexation already submitted to this government by that of the United States. And the chief justices of the respective counties aforesaid will give due notice of the said elections, appoint a presiding officer in the several precincts, who will appoint the judges and clerks of said elections, and have the same conducted according to the constitution and laws regulating elections, and make due return thereof.

In testimony whereof, I have caused the great seal of the republic to be hereunto affixed.

      Done at Washington, this fifth day of May, in the year of our Lord [L.S.]   one thousand eight hundred and forty-five, and of the independence of the republic the tenth.

ANSON JONES.

By the President:
    EBENEZER ALLEN,
        Attorney General and acting Secretary of State.

On June 4, 1845, deputies to the National Convention were elected; on the same day President Jones proclaimed the acceptance by the Government of Mexico of the conditions preliminary to a treaty of peace and declared a cessation of hostilities (the proclamation is printed in published correspondence, 81–82).

On June 16, 1845, the President of Texas submitted to the Texan Congress the annexation proposals of the United States and communicated the proclamation of June 4 (for the text of the presidential message, see *ibid.*, 74–76); two days later the declaration of the Government of Mexico of May 19, 1845, was submitted to the Senate of Texas, which, on June 21, unanimously rejected the proposed "pre-

liminary Treaty with Mexico" (D.S., 2 Despatches, Texas, No. 31, June 23, 1845; the presidential message of June 18, 1845, to the Senate of Texas, with the accompanying papers, is in the pamphlet cited above, enclosure 5 to that despatch; see published correspondence, 87–90).

The joint resolution of the Congress of Texas, unanimously passed on June 21 and approved on June 23, 1845, the text of which is the second of the four documents printed above (following the headnote), consented to the terms of the joint resolution of the Congress of the United States of March 1, 1845, and consented also to the proclamation of President Jones of May 5, 1845, for a National Convention (D.S., 2 Despatches, Texas, No. 31, June 23, 1845, enclosure 2); the covering note transmitting that joint resolution on the date of its approval, follows (*ibid.*, enclosure 1; published correspondence, 84):

DEPARTMENT OF STATE,
Washington, 23ᵈ June 1845.

The Undersigned Attorney General of the Republic of Texas, charged, *ad interim*, with the direction of the Department of State, by order of His Excellency, the President, has the honor of transmitting to the Hon. Mʳ Donelson, Chargé d'Affaires of the United States near this Government, the enclosed copy of a Joint Resolution, adopted by both Houses of the Congress of Texas, on the 21st. Inst., and this day received and approved by the President—declaring the consent of the existing government of this Republic, to the terms of the proposition for annexation tendered by the United States through the Hon. Mʳ Donelson, on the 31st. of March Ultimo, to the Government and People of Texas.

To all true friends of the great cause of annexation, and especially to the Hon. Mʳ Donelson, whose energies and tallents have been so ably and faithfully devoted to the success of that cause through the several stages of its recently triumphant progress, it must be peculiarly gratifying to observe the harmony and unanimity with which this Resolution has passed the two houses of Congress and received the Executive approval.

Rejecting the idea of separate nationality, although commended to to their choice by the proffered recognition of their independence by Mexico, and the countenance of powerful European Sovereignties, the people of this country have thus evinced by most decided manifestations, their strong but natural preference for the advantages of a voluntary incorporation into the American Union,—and their strong attachment to the free institutions of that great and glorious Republic.

Among the features of this Resolution, it must be gratifying to the Hon. Mʳ Donelson and his Government to observe that provision, whereby the acts of the Convention, to meet on the 4th proximo, are clothed with all the sanctions, which can result from the concurring approval and consent of the Executive and the Representatives of the people; and not less gratifying, the undersigned trusts, will be the assurance necessarily resulting from the premises, that the various steps yet to be taken on the part of this Republic to perfect, so far as depends upon her, the measure of annexation upon the proposed basis, will be adopted with the same promptness and fidelity, which have distinguished her preceeding movements in the great cause; and in that confiding spirit of firm reliance upon the magnanimity and generosity of the United States, which has ever characterized the policy of her Government and the dispositions of her people.

The undersigned renews to Mʳ Donelson, the assurances of his high regard and remains

His most Obedient Servant

EBNʳ ALLEN.

Hon. A. J. DONELSON
Chargé d'Affaires of the U. States etc etc etc

The ordinance adopted by the Convention of Texas on July 4, 1845, the text of which is the third of the four documents printed above (following the headnote), passed with "but one dissenting voice" and was signed unanimously (D.S., 2 Despatches, Texas, No. 31 [33], July 6, 1845); a certified copy was transmitted to Donelson by the President of the Convention, General Thomas J. Rusk, under date of July 5, and by Donelson to Secretary of State Buchanan (*ibid.*, enclosures). The note of transmittal to Donelson reads thus (*ibid.*, enclosure; published correspondence, 98):

Hon! A J DONELSON
    Chargé d'Affaires of United States &c &c &c &c
SIR The undersigned President of the Convention assembled at this place for the purpose of forming a State Constitution for the State of Texas, preparatory to her admission as one of the States of the United States of America, by order of said Convention, has the honor herewith to transmit to you a properly certified copy of an Ordinance adopted by the Convention on Yesterday (July 4th 1845).
I have the honor to be with the highest respect Mr Donelson's Obedient Servant
                                                    THO J RUSK
    CITY OF AUSTIN REPUBLIC OF TEXAS *July 5th 1845*

On July 7, 1845, the Convention of Texas adopted a resolution requesting the stationing of United States troops in Texas; a certified copy thereof was transmitted to Donelson by Thomas J. Rusk, President of the Convention, with a covering note of the same date; the texts which follow are from *ibid.*, No. 34, July 7, 1845, enclosures (published correspondence, 100–1):

                                        CONVENTION ROOM
                                    Austin, Texas July 7th 1845
His Excellency A J DONELSON
    Chargé d'Affaires of United States &c &c &c
SIR By order of the Convention I have the honor herewith to transmit to your Excellency the enclosed copy of a Resolution adopted by the Honorable Convention this day
Very respectfully Your Excellencys most obedient servant
                                        THO J RUSK *President.*

Resolution Relative to the introduction of the United States forces into Texas.

Be it resolved by the Deputies of the people in Convention assembled, That the President of the United States of America is hereby authorized and requested to occupy and establish posts without delay upon the frontier and exposed positions of this Republic, and to introduce for such purpose and defence of the territory and people of Texas, such forces as may be necessary and advisable for the Same.
Adopted in Convention at the city of Austin Republic of Texas July 7th 1845.
                                                    THO J RUSK
    Attest
        JAS H RAYMOND
            Secretary of the Convention.

The Convention of Texas on August 27, 1845, unanimously adopted a constitution for the State of Texas; the text of that instrument is in published correspondence, 117–37, and also in House Document

No. 16, 29th Congress, 1st session, serial 482. Sections 5 and 6 of Article 13 contained these provisions:

Sec. 5. Immediately after the adjournment of this convention, the President of the republic shall issue his proclamation directing the chief justices of the several counties of this republic, and the several chief justices and their associates are hereby required, to cause polls to be opened in their respective counties, at the established precincts, on the second Monday of October next, for the purpose of taking the sense of the people of Texas in regard to the adoption or rejection of this constitution; and the votes of all persons entitled to vote under the existing laws or this constitution shall be received. Each voter shall express his opinion, by declaring by a *"viva voce"* vote for "the constitution accepted," or "the constitution rejected;" or some words clearly expressing the intention of the voter; and, at the same time, the vote shall be taken in like manner for and against annexation. The election shall be conducted in conformity with the existing laws regulating elections; and the chief justices of the several counties shall carefully and promptly make duplicate returns of said polls; one of which shall be transmitted to the secretary of state of the republic of Texas, and the other deposited in the clerk's office of the county court.

Sec. 6. Upon the receipt of said returns, or on the second Monday of November [1] next, if the returns be not sooner made, it shall be the duty of the President, in presence of such officers of his cabinet as may be present, and of all persons who may choose to attend, to compare the votes given for the ratification or rejection of this constitution; and, if it shall appear from the returns that a majority of all the votes given is for the adoption of the constitution, then it shall be the duty of the President to make proclamation of that fact; and thenceforth this constitution shall be ordained and established as the constitution of the State, to go into operation and be of force and effect from and after the organization of the State government under this constitution; and the President of this republic is authorized and required to transmit to the President of the United States duplicate copies of this constitution, properly authenticated, together with certified statements of the number of votes given for the ratification thereof, and the number for rejection—one of which copies shall be transmitted by mail, and one copy by a special messenger, in sufficient time to reach the seat of government of the United States early in December next.

By the first quoted of those two sections of the Texas Constitution the voting under the proclamation which was directed to be issued was to take place on "the second Monday of October next", or October 13, 1845. Each voter was to express his opinion for the acceptance or rejection of the constitution and also for or against "annexation". Moreover, section 13 of Article 13 of the constitution expressly directed that the ordinance of July 4, 1845, "shall be attached to this constitution, and form a part of the same". The question of annexation could not have been more clearly put before the people of Texas.

The proclamation of the President of Texas issued pursuant to Article 13, section 5, of the Texas Constitution was dated August 28, 1845, and reads as follows (from a facsimile of the original in the Texas State Library):

By the President of the Republic of Texas.

A Proclamation.

Whereas, the Convention of Deputies assembled at the City of Austin on the fourth day of July, ultimo, in accordance with the provisions of a Joint Resolution adopted by the Congress of the United States, presenting to the Govern-

[1] November 10, 1845.

ment and people of Texas, an overture for annexation, and in accordance with the Executive Proclamation issued on the fifth of May last, did, on the twenty-seventh day of August instant, adopt the subjoined Constitution, conformably to the terms and requirements of the Joint Resolution aforesaid, for the organization and Government of the State of Texas: and

Whereas, the Convention did, on the 27th. instant, adopt an ordinance in relation to Colonization Contracts, which is also subjoined—

Now, therefore, be it known, that I, Anson Jones, President of the Republic of Texas, in accordance with the provisions of the fifth section of the thirteenth Article of the Constitution aforesaid, do require and direct the Chief Justices—or, in their absence, the Associate Justices, of the several Counties of the Republic, to cause polls to be opened at the established precincts in their respective, counties on the second Monday, (the 13th day) of October next, for the purpose of taking the sense of the people of Texas in regard to the ADOPTION OR REJECTION of the said Constitution; also, for the purpose of taking the expression of their opinions FOR or AGAINST annexation: the election to be conducted, the votes taken, and returns made in conformity with the existing laws regulating elections, and the rules prescribed in the fifth section aforesaid, the votes of the electors will, also, then and there be taken on the adoption or rejection of the aforesaid ordinance, and returns thereof made in conformity with the third section of the same.

In testimony whereof, I have caused the Great Seal of the Republic to be hereunto affixed.

Done at the City of Austin, this twenty-eighth day of August, in [Seal] the year of our Lord, one thousand eight hundred and forty five, and of the Independence of the Republic the tenth.

ANSON JONES

By the President:
EBN ALLEN
Secretary of State.

The vote was accordingly had on October 13, 1845; on the following November 10 two proclamations were issued by the President of Texas, Anson Jones. One of these called for elections on December 15 of State officers and members of the State Legislature (House Document No. 16, 29th Congress, 1st session, serial 482, pp. 25–26); the other, the text of which follows, proclaimed the adoption of the State Constitution (*ibid.*, 27; text here collated with a facsimile of the original in the Texas State Library):

By the President of the Republic of Texas

A PROCLAMATION.

Whereas, in accordance with a proclamation issued on the 28th day of August [1] last, polls were opened in the established precincts of the several Counties of this Republic, on Monday the 13th of October, ultimo, for the purpose of taking the sense of the people of Texas in regard to the ratification or rejection of the Constitution, adopted by the Convention of Deputies, at the City of Austin, on the 28th day of August [1] last; and,

Whereas, by Article Thirteenth of the said Constitution, it is made the duty of the Executive on or before the second Monday of November, Instant, to compare the votes given for the ratification or rejection of the same, and to proclaim the result;

Therefore, be it known, that I, Anson Jones, President of the Republic of Texas, having this day examined and compared the returns of votes given for the adoption and rejection of said Constitution, do hereby declare and proclaim,

---

[1] In the original appears "September" crossed out, with "August" above; the copy sent to Congress by President Polk on December 9, 1845, has "September"; so does the print cited; the word should be "August".

that a majority of all the votes polled, is for the adoption of the same, and that henceforth the said Constitution is ordained and established by the people of Texas for their governance, to go into operation and to be of force and effect, from and after the organization of the State Government under it.

In testimony whereof, I have hereunto caused the Great Seal of the Republic to be affixed.

[Seal]   Done at the City of Austin, this tenth day of November, in the year of our Lord one thousand eight hundred and forty-five, and of the Independence of the Republic, the tenth.

ANSON JONES

By the President:
JOSEPH C. ELDREDGE
      Act'g Secretary of State.

One error of date in the text of the foregoing proclamation is to be noted; the adoption of the Texas Constitution by the Convention at Austin was on August 27 (not 28), 1845.

The first annual message of President Polk to Congress, under date of December 2, 1845 (Richardson, IV, 385–416), contained this paragraph regarding the proceedings for annexation (pp. 386–87):

In pursuance of the joint resolution of Congress "for annexing Texas to the United States," my predecessor, on the 3d day of March, 1845, elected to submit the first and second sections of that resolution to the Republic of Texas as an overture on the part of the United States for her admission as a State into our Union. This election I approved, and accordingly the chargé d'affaires of the United States in Texas, under instructions of the 10th of March, 1845, presented these sections of the resolution for the acceptance of that Republic. The executive government, the Congress, and the people of Texas in convention have successively complied with all the terms and conditions of the joint resolution. A constitution for the government of the State of Texas, formed by a convention of deputies, is herewith laid before Congress. It is well known, also, that the people of Texas at the polls have accepted the terms of annexation and ratified the constitution. I communicate to Congress the correspondence between the Secretary of State and our chargé d'affaires in Texas, and also the correspondence of the latter with the authorities of Texas, together with the official documents transmitted by him to his own Government. The terms of annexation which were offered by the United States having been accepted by Texas, the public faith of both parties is solemnly pledged to the compact of their union. Nothing remains to consummate the event but the passage of an act by Congress to admit the State of Texas into the Union upon an equal footing with the original States. Strong reasons exist why this should be done at an early period of the session. It will be observed that by the constitution of Texas the existing government is only continued temporarily till Congress can act, and that the third Monday of the present month is the day appointed for holding the first general election. On that day a governor, a lieutenant-governor, and both branches of the legislature will be chosen by the people. The President of Texas is required, immediately after the receipt of official information that the new State has been admitted into our Union by Congress, to convene the legislature, and upon its meeting the existing government will be superseded and the State government organized. Questions deeply interesting to Texas, in common with the other States, the extension of our revenue laws and judicial system over her people and territory, as well as measures of a local character, will claim the early attention of Congress, and therefore upon every principle of republican government she ought to be represented in that body without unnecessary delay. I can not too earnestly recommend prompt action on this important subject. As soon as the act to admit Texas as a State shall be passed the union of the two Republics will be consummated by their own voluntary consent.

The papers accompanying the presidential message just cited are printed in Senate Document No. 1, 29th Congress, 1st session, serial 470, and also in House Document No. 2 of that Congress and session, serial 480.

On December 9, 1845, the following presidential message was sent to Congress (Richardson, IV, 416; also, with the accompanying papers, in House Document No. 16, 29th Congress, 1st session, serial 482):

I communicate herewith a letter received from the President of the existing Government of the State of Texas, transmitting duplicate copies of the constitution formed by the deputies of the people of Texas in convention assembled, accompanied by official information that the said constitution had been ratified, confirmed, and adopted by the people of Texas themselves, in accordance with the joint resolution for annexing Texas to the United States, and in order that Texas might be admitted as one of the States of that Union.

The papers communicated with the foregoing presidential message were a letter of Anson Jones to President Polk of November 10, 1845, and its enclosures. Those enclosures were (*a*) duplicate certified copies of the Constitution of Texas; (*b*) copies of the two Texan proclamations of November 10, 1845, which have been previously mentioned in these notes; (*c*) a letter of Joseph C. Eldredge, Acting Secretary of State of Texas, dated November 10, 1845, transmitting (*d*) a certificate of the same date signed by Eldredge. The letter stated in the message of President Polk to be from "the President of the existing Government of the State of Texas", and the communication signed by Joseph C. Eldredge, Acting Secretary of State of the Republic of Texas, with the certificate of the vote therewith transmitted, follow (*ibid.*):

EXECUTIVE DEPARTMENT
City of Austin, Nov. 10ᵗʰ 1845

SIR. I have the honor to transmit you, herewith, a copy of the "Constitution of the State of Texas," with the proper evidence of its adoption by the people of this Republic, to be laid before the Congress of the United States for its final action in accordance with the provisions of the "Joint Resolution for annexing Texas to the United States."

I have the honor to be with the highest respect Your most ob⸱ Servant

ANSON JONES

To His Excellency JAMES K. POLK
President of the United States.

REPUBLIC OF TEXAS,
Department of State November 10ᵗʰ 1845

SIR: I have the honor to transmit you herewith, an authenticated statement, of the results of elections held in this Republic, on the 13th October ultimo, for the ratification or rejection of "Annexation" and the Constitution adopted by the Convention for the "State of Texas"; so far as returns of said elections have been made to this Department.

I have the honor to be With great respect Your Obedient Servant

JOSEPH C. ELDREDGE
Acting Secretary of State

To His Excellency JAMES K. POLK
President of the United States.

726   *Document 113*

[Enclosure]

REPUBLIC OF TEXAS, *Department of State.*

The undersigned, Acting Secretary of State, hereby certifies, that at an election held in the several Counties of the Republic, on the thirteenth day of October, ultimo. for taking the sense of the people of Texas in regard to the ratification or rejection of Annexation in accordance with the "Joint Resolution for annexing Texas" and for the adoption or rejection of the "Constitution of the State of Texas," adopted in Convention on the 28th [27th], August, ultimo; it appears from returns of elections received at this Department up to the date hereof, that Four thousand, two hundred and fifty four (4.254) votes were polled in favor of Annexation: and two hundred and sixty seven (267) against it: for the adoption of the Constitution, Four thousand, one hundred and seventy four (4.174) votes and for its rejection, Three hundred and twelve (312) votes.

    In testimony whereof, I have hereunto affixed my hand and official seal at the city of Austin, this tenth day of November. A.D. 1845.

[Seal]

JOSEPH C. ELDREDGE

The letter and enclosures from President Jones to President Polk had been received by the latter on "Saturday evening", December 6 (D.S., Miscellaneous Letters, November–December 1845, Polk to Buchanan, December 8); those papers (transmitted to the House of Representatives) are now in the Library of Congress; it is with the examples in those House papers that the foregoing texts of the letters of Anson Jones and Eldredge and of the certificate of the latter have been collated; the letter and certificate of Eldredge are each headed "(Duplicate)", and the two proclamations of November 10, 1845, are each headed "[Copy—The printed original sent to the Senate.]".

The "Joint Resolution for the admission of the state of Texas into the Union", the text of which is the last of the four documents printed above (following the headnote), became law on December 29, 1845 (9 Statutes at Large, 108); on the same day "An Act to extend the Laws of the United States over the State of Texas, and for other Purposes" was approved (*ibid.*, 1–2); authenticated copies of the two statutes were sent on the same evening by special messenger with a covering letter from President Polk "to President Jones of Texas" (Diary of James K. Polk, I, 148); annexation was complete; organization of the State Government followed (see Middleton, "The Texas Convention of 1845", in Southwestern Historical Quarterly, XXV, 59–60).

THE PROCEDURE IN TEXAS

The steps taken in Texas for annexation (which have been mentioned above) subsequent to the communication on March 31, 1845, of the joint resolution of the Congress of the United States of March 1, 1845, pursuant to the decision of President Tyler, followed by President Polk, to proceed under sections 1 and 2 of that joint resolution, were these:

(a) The proclamation of the President of Texas, dated April 3, 1845, for the filling of vacancies in the Congress of Texas.

(b) The proclamation of the President of Texas, dated April 15, 1845, for the meeting in extra session of the Congress of Texas at Washington, Texas, on June 16, 1845.

(*c*) The proclamation of the President of Texas, dated May 5, 1845, for the election on June 4, 1845, of deputies to a National Convention and calling the National Convention to meet on July 4, 1845, at Austin, Texas.

(*d*) The election on June 4, 1845, of deputies to the National Convention of Texas.

(*e*) The proclamation of the President of Texas, dated June 4, 1845, of the acceptance by the Government of Mexico of the conditions preliminary to a treaty of peace, and declaring a cessation of hostilities.

(*f*) The message of the President of Texas of June 16, 1845, to the Texan Congress, submitting the annexation proposals of the United States and communicating the proclamation of June 4, 1845.

(*g*) The message of the President of Texas of June 18, 1845, to the Texan Senate, submitting the declaration of the Government of Mexico of May 19, 1845.

(*h*) The rejection by the Senate of Texas on June 21, 1845, of the proposed agreement with Mexico.

(*i*) The joint resolution of the Congress of Texas, approved June 23, 1845, consenting to sections 1 and 2 of the joint resolution of the Congress of the United States of March 1, 1845, and also to the proclamation of the President of Texas of May 5, 1845.

(*j*) The communication to the Government of the United States of the joint resolution of the Congress of Texas of June 23, 1845.

(*k*) The ordinance of the Convention of Texas of July 4, 1845, assenting to sections 1 and 2 of the joint resolution of the Congress of the United States of March 1, 1845.

(*l*) The communication to the Government of the United States of the ordinance of the Convention of Texas of July 4, 1845.

(*m*) The resolution of the Convention of Texas of July 7, 1845, requesting the stationing of United States troops in Texas.

(*n*) The communication to the Government of the United States of the resolution of the Convention of Texas of July 7, 1845.

(*o*) The adoption by the Convention of Texas on August 27, 1845, of a constitution for the State of Texas.

(*p*) The proclamation of the President of Texas, dated August 28, 1845, calling for the voting of the people of Texas on the proposed constitution and on annexation, on October 13, 1845.

(*q*) The vote of the people of Texas on the proposed constitution and on annexation, on October 13, 1845.

(*r*) The proclamation of the President of Texas, dated November 10, 1845, of the adoption of the constitution.

(*s*) The proclamation of the President of Texas, dated November 10, 1845, calling for elections on December 15, 1845, of State officers and members of the State Legislature.

(*t*) The communication to the President of the United States of the constitution adopted for Texas and of the vote of the people of Texas on adoption thereof and on annexation.

THE INTERMEDIATE STATUS

The ordinance of the Convention of Texas of July 4, 1845, together with the joint resolution of the Congress of Texas of the previous June 23, constituted as complete assent to the proposals of the United States for annexation as representative institutions could give; the Executive, the Congress, and the Convention, with almost literal unanimity, had all formally rejected independence and had formally accepted annexation and admission of the State of Texas into the Union; and the Convention, on July 7, 1845, had invited the introduction into Texas of the armed forces of the United States.

However, under the terms of sections 1 and 2 of the joint resolution of the Congress of the United States of March 1, 1845, certain other

steps were required; a constitution of the State of Texas was to be framed, was to be adopted by the people, and was to be transmitted to the President of the United States, to be laid before Congress, whereupon "final action" was to be taken; time was required for these proceedings, which were not consummated until December 29, 1845; and although there was and could be no doubt that they would all be duly accomplished, such proceedings could hardly be regarded as formalities; a vote of the people adopting a State constitution is by no means a formality, even if its result be a foregone conclusion.

The status of Texas intermediate July 4 and December 29, 1845, was *sui generis;* it was one within a twilight zone between independence and statehood.

The views of the Government of the United States as to the then status of Texas were expressed in connection with the possible necessity of defense of Texas (in view of the position of Mexico) and in connection with the reception of diplomatic representatives of Texas at Washington.

Diplomatic relations between the United States and Mexico had been suspended; upon the passage of the joint resolution of March 1, 1845, the Mexican Minister at Washington, General Juan N. Almonte, had, under date of March 6, protested in the name of his Government and requested his passports in the following terms (D.S., 4 Notes from the Mexican Legation, translation; published correspondence, 38–39):

The undersigned, Envoy Extraordinary and Minister Plenipotentiary of the Mexican Republic, has the honor to address the Honorable John C. Calhoun, Secretary of State of the United States of America, with the object of making known to him the profound regret with which he has seen that the general Congress of the Union has passed a law giving its consent and admitting (prestando su consentimiento y admitiendo) into the American confederacy the Mexican Province of Texas.

The undersigned had flattered himself with the idea that on this question the good judgment and sound counsels of the citizens most distinguished and most intimately acquainted with the conduct of the public affairs of this Republic would have prevailed in the deliberations of the Legislative body and of the Executive of the Union. Unfortunately, however, it has been otherwise; and, contrary to his hopes and his most sincere prayers, he sees consummated, on the part of the American Government, an act of aggression the most unjust which can be found recorded in the annals of modern history, namely, that of despoiling a friendly nation like Mexico of a considerable portion of her territory.

For these reasons the undersigned, in compliance with his instructions, finds himself required to protest, as he does in fact protest, in the most solemn manner, in the name of his Government, against the law passed on the 28th of the last month by the general Congress of the United States and approved on the 1st of the present month by the President of these States, whereby the Province of Texas, an integrant portion of the Mexican territory, is agreed and admitted (se consiente y admite) into the American Union. The undersigned, moreover, protests in the name of his Government that the said law can in no wise invalidate the rights on which Mexico relies to recover the above-mentioned Province of Texas, of which she now holds herself unjustly despoiled; and that she will maintain and uphold those rights at all times by every means which may be in her power.

The undersigned will say in conclusion, to the Honorable Secretary of State of the United States, in order that he may be pleased to communicate it to the President of these States, that in consequence of this law against which he has just protested, his mission near this Government has ceased from this day.

Wherefore the undersigned prays the Honorable Secretary of State to be pleased to deliver him his passports, as he has made arrangements to leave this city without delay, for New York.

On March 10 Secretary of State Buchanan thus replied to the Mexican protest (D.S., 6 Notes to the Mexican Legation, 185–86; published correspondence, 39):

The Undersigned, Secretary of State of the United States, has received the note of General Almonte, the Envoy Extraordinary and Minister Plenipotentiary of the Mexican Republic of the 6th instant, addressed to his predecessor, the Hon. John C. Calhoun, protesting, in the name of his Government, against the resolution of the late Congress for annexing Texas to the United States: and he has submitted the same to the President.

In answer, the Undersigned is instructed to say, that the admission of Texas as one of the States of this Union, having received the sanction both of the legislative and Executive Departments of the government, is now irrevocably decided, so far as the United States are concerned. Nothing but the refusal of Texas to ratify the terms and conditions on which her admission depends, can defeat this object. It is, therefore, too late at present to re-open a discussion which has already been exhausted, and again to prove that Texas has long since achieved her independence of Mexico, and now stands before the world, both *de jure* and *de facto*, as a sovereign and independent State amid the family of nations. Sustaining this character and having manifested a strong desire to become one of the members of our Confederacy, neither Mexico nor any other nation will have just cause of complaint against the United States for admitting her into this Union.

The President nevertheless sincerely regrets that the Government of Mexico should have taken offence at these proceedings; and he earnestly trusts that it may hereafter be disposed to view them in a more favorable and friendly light. Whilst entering upon the duties of the Presidential office, he cheerfully declares in advance, that his most strenuous efforts shall be devoted to the amicable adjustment of every cause of complaint between the two Governments, and to the cultivation of the kindest and most friendly relations between the sister Republics.

The Mexican Minister of Foreign Relations, Luis Gonzaga Cuevas, had likewise written to the American Minister to Mexico, Wilson Shannon, under date of March 28, 1845, that "diplomatic relations between the two countries cannot be continued" (D.S., 12 Despatches, Mexico, No. 10, April 6, 1845, enclosure 1, translation; see Rives, *op. cit.*, I, 699–702).

In the instructions to Donelson of May 23, 1845 (D.S., 1 Instructions, Texas, 119–21; published correspondence, 40–41), this was written:

Anticipating the receipt of the note to be addressed to you by the Acting Secretary of State of Texas to which your letter of the 6th instant refers, I shall proceed to present you the views of the President on the subject to which it relates. You state its substance to be "an earnest expression of the wish of the Government of Texas, that as soon as their assent is given to the terms contained in the Joint Resolution for their admission as a State, the troops of the United States may be marched to some suitable point on the Western frontier for the purpose of guarding the inhabitants against Mexican or Indian incursion" and of being employed within the territory of Texas for this purpose, should occasion require.

I am instructed by the President to inform you that, as soon as the Existing Government and the Convention of Texas shall have accepted the terms proposed to them in the two first sections of the "Joint Resolution for annexing Texas to the United States," he will then consider it to be both his right and his duty to employ the army in defending that State against the attacks of any foreign Power.

This shall be done promptly and efficiently, should any emergency render it necessary. In order to be prepared for such a contingency, a force of three thousand men shall immediately be placed upon the border, prepared to enter Texas and to act without a moment's delay. It would be the most crying injustice towards the people of Texas for the United States to stand by and refuse to extend a helping hand to sustain them against an invasion brought upon them by their free determination to annex their own glorious Republic to the American Union, in compliance with a solemn Resolution of Congress.

It would be useless to inquire what would be the precise condition of Texas during the intermediate period, after she shall have accepted the terms of the Joint Resolution, but before her actual admission into the Union. In many respects she will be in a position similar to that occupied by Mississippi, Illinois and other States, after they had complied with the previous conditions required by Acts of Congress, but before they had been formally received into the family of States. Like them, Texas will then have conformed to every preliminary requisition of Congress; and like them, Texas, in execution of the public faith, will be admitted as a matter of course by the passage of a brief Bill for that purpose, with a preamble reciting the facts which render this inevitable. That no obstacle can prevent this happy consummation, is as certain as that Congress have never yet violated any of their engagements.

Under these circumstances, Texas, before her formal admission into the Union will, in the opinion of the President, have become in fact one of our States, at least in such a degree as to render it obligatory on him to defend her against foreign invasion.

More detailed and elaborate were the instructions of June 15, 1845 (D.S., 1 Instructions, Texas, 123–27; published correspondence, 42–45, with two paragraphs omitted):

It appears from them [Donelson's despatches] that Mexico has already seven thousand troops on the Rio Grande,—that Captain Elliott [British Chargé d'Affaires to Texas] has declared to many of the citizens of Texas "that a rejection of the proposals now offered by him for the independence of Texas will be followed immediately by an invasion from Mexico," and "that as soon as he is informed that he cannot defeat annexation, he will be apt to find means of conveying secret intelligence to the commander of the Mexican troops on the Rio Grande, who it is reasonable to conclude will be prepared at once to resume the war upon Texas." You, also, express the opinion that "a war with Mexico is inevitable.

Under these circumstances, you very properly ask the question, "should Mexico take possession of the country between the Nueces and the Rio Grande, or come still further East within the Texan territory, before a Convention can express the requisite ratification of our proposals, are the United States to stand still and see the country thus invaded without interposing protection!

In answer to this important question, I shall proceed to present to you the views of the President upon the subject.

There are many reasons why it is preferable that Texas should drive the intruders from her territory until after the Convention shall have accepted the terms of our Joint Resolution. Of her ability and her will to perform this service, no man acquainted with her history can doubt. Her citizens are brave, they can endure the climate at this hot season of the year, and it will redound to their glory to ask no aid in defending her territory until this duty shall clearly devolve upon the United States. Besides, it is impossible that our troops can now reach the scene of action in time to render her any assistance in expelling the intruders before the 4th of July, the day of the meeting of the Convention. The expenses of such an expedition must eventually be borne by the United States. If an attempt should be made to dismember the territory of Texas as it existed when the Joint Resolution for annexation passed Congress, at the moment when her people and authorities are deliberating upon these proposals, most certainly the strongest obligation would be imposed upon the American Congress to indemnify her for the charges of repelling the invasion. In performing this duty, she will be acting for the benefit of our whole country and preserving her territory in the same condition it was when we offered to receive her into the American Union. The

President cannot doubt for a moment but that after annexation, the troops employed in this service will be placed upon precisely the same footing as troops would be who had been regularly called out under the authority of the Act of Congress to repel an invasion of any of the existing States.

Should the Congress of Texas consent to the terms of annexation, and the Convention be prevented from holding its session on the fourth of July, or be afterwards disturbed in its peaceful deliberations by an actual invasion of their territory by Mexico;—in either event, the President would feel himself bound at once to repel such an invasion. An unanimous or nearly an unanimous vote of her Congress in favor of annexation, would afford conclusive evidence that the people of Texas are anxious for the reünion of the two Republics. Under such circumstances, it would degrade the character of the United States to suffer this great measure to be defeated against the will of the people of both countries, by the machinations of foreign Governments and the control they exercise over Mexico. The moment that the Convention of Texas shall ratify the terms of annexation, the substantial engagements of both parties will then have been completed; and nothing would remain to be done but her mere formal admission as a State into the Union, in obedience to these solemn engagements. Now if the will of the people of Texas should be rendered manifest by the vote of her Congress, and a Mexican invasion, instigated by foreign nations for the express purpose of defeating annexation should prevent the Convention from assembling or disturb it afterwards in its peaceful deliberations, the President would have had no difficulty in acting as he would have done had the Convention been permitted to assemble and adopt our Joint Resolution and in ordering the troops of the United States to repel such an invasion. This contingency the President trusts, however, may not occur; and if it should, the Convention ought to meet at the earliest practicable moment and proceed to ratify the Resolutions of our Congress and adopt a Constitution.

The President will immediately send an express to General Taylor, the commanding officer at Fort Jesup, with an order to him from the Secretary of War to march the troops collected at that post to the Sabine. There shall be as little delay as possible in this movement. The moment that the Convention of Texas shall have accepted and ratified the terms of annexation proposed by the American Congress, the President, for the purposes of defence, will consider her territory as belonging to the United States. You are, therefore, hereby authorized in that event forthwith to send an express to our commanding officer on the Sabine, communicating to him the information, and he will be directed to move to such points as yourself and the authorities of Texas shall deem most expedient. Captain Stockton will be ordered with the fleet now under his command (and other vessels of war will be attached to it) to repair to the mouth of the Sabine for the purpose of transporting the American troops to the positions where they shall, in your opinion and that of these authorities, be most required.

Similar orders will be issued both to our commanding officer on the Sabine and to Captain Stockton, to be executed in case the Convention shall be prevented from assembling or be disturbed in its peaceful deliberations by a Mexican invasion, after the Texan Congress shall have accepted the terms of annexation proposed by the American Congress.

I herewith transmit to you copies of orders just received and this day issued by the Navy Department to Commodore R. F. Stockton, commanding the squadron off Galvezton, and of orders from the War Department to Brigadier General Z. Taylor, commanding the first Department at Fort Jesup.

I also transmit copies of orders dated to-day and this moment received from the Treasury Department to Captains Foster and Prince of the United States revenue marine.

I regret that I have not time before the departure of the messenger, to express to you as I could desire, the feelings of indignation which the conduct of Captain Elliott has excited throughout this country. These are not confined to any party, but pervade the whole community. One of its good effects has been to render us, to a very great extent, an united people on the question of annexation. It is scarcely possible that his conduct can be approved by his government. Without entering upon the inquiry how far the British government had a right to interfere in preventing the people of Texas from consenting to annexation, no

impartial man can doubt but that Captain Elliott in his efforts has transcended all reasonable bounds. To assume the character of a secret negotiator of the government of Texas with Mexico, in a hostile spirit towards the United States; to conceal his agency in this matter by pretending that he had left Galvezton for Charleston, when his destination was Vera Cruz; and then to prevail upon Mexico to consent to the independence of Texas on condition that Texas should never annex herself to the United States; these acts taken together are at war with all the modern usages of diplomacy and with the character of the British government, which is generally bold and frank if not always just in its policy towards foreign nations. He has not even for a moment succeeded in his efforts at concealment, and he will find that his transparent cunning will only tend to make him ridiculous. But what is far worse on his part, by obtaining the consent of Mexico to the independence of Texas, he has deprived that power of the only miserable pretext which it had for a war against the United States, whilst he has fomented among the Mexican people a spirit of hostility against us which may plunge that ill-fated country into such a war.

The final instructions, of August 7, 1845, authorized Texan volunteers to be mustered into the service of the United States, while stating that the President of the United States had no authority to call out the militia of Texas. These passages are extracted therefrom (D.S., 1 Instructions, Texas, 128–31; not in published correspondence):

Intelligence has reached the President, which has an appearance of authenticity, not to be disregarded, that the Mexicans are approaching the frontier of Texas in considerable force; that General Paredes with seven thousand men is at San Luis Potosi, and that General Arista, with three thousand, principally cavalry, is in position on or near the Rio del Norte; and that these troops are destined for the invasion of Texas, with or without a declaration of war against the United States.

The Government and people of Texas by their Delegates in Convention, having accepted the conditions of annexation proposed in the first and second sections of the joint Resolution of the Congress of the United States on that subject, the President considers it to be his constitutional duty to repel a hostile invasion of Texas, with all the means at his disposal.

The troops under General Taylor have proceeded to the points on the frontier of Texas, at which it was supposed they could act most efficiently in the attainment of this object. Orders have been also given to Commodore Conner to employ the naval forces under his command, in coöperation with the troops. The regular force which could be transferred on this duty with the reinforcements which will immediately be ordered to report to the officer commanding, may not be sufficient to resist so imposing a force as that, which, it is believed, is about to invade Texas.

The President has no authority to call out the militia of Texas, but he has entire confidence in the patriotism and bravery of those gallant men, nor does he doubt their enthusiastic readiness to coöperate with their brethren from the United States in repelling the invaders of their own soil. Their coöperation may become necessary. In view of this necessity, the President instructs you to place yourself without delay, in communication with the government of Texas, and to propose, that volunteers may be invited to join the United States troops under the command of General Taylor, organized and officered by officers of their own selection, to be mustered into the service of the United States in such numbers as the United States commanding general may deem necessary. The information received by the President, is believed to be authentic, and is such that he cannot disregard, but the superior opportunities enjoyed by the government of Texas and by General Taylor on the frontier, may satisfy them that the danger of invasion is not imminent. In that event, it is not desired that volunteers should be called from their homes into actual service.

Apprehending that there may be a deficiency of arms and ammunition in Texas, the President has ordered them to be placed in depôt at Galvezton, subject to General Taylor's orders, in sufficient quantity for ten thousand men. They

will be furnished to the Texan volunteers under such regulations as may issue from the War Department for their return when the men are discharged.   Rations will be issued to the volunteers while mustered in service of the United States. But there is no appropriation from which the President can have these troops paid.   There is, however, no reason to doubt, that troops thus employed will be placed by Congress upon precisely the same footing as troops would be who had been regularly called out to repel an invasion of any of the existing States.

You will make it known to the Government of Texas that it is not the wish or purpose of the President to limit the number of men which that government may deem necessary to defend the country; but to guard against misunderstandings which may fatally disturb the harmony of coöperation, it is deemed most advisable that no volunteers shall be mustered into the service of the United States, except such as may be required and approved by the commander of our troops on that service.   All others will act under the authority of Texas.

On September 1, 1845, William D. Lee wrote to the Secretary of State that he had been appointed Acting Chargé d'Affaires of the Government of Texas near the Government of the United States and requested an appointment in order to present his credentials (D.S., 1 Communications from Agents of Texas).   To this communication Secretary of State Buchanan replied under date of September 6, declining to receive Lee and suggesting that he might remain in Washington as "an agent of Texas", to which suggestion Lee replied two days later that he had no authority to act in such capacity (*ibid.*).   From the note of Secretary of State Buchanan the following is extracted (D.S., 6 Notes to the Texan Legation, 82–83):

Your note has been submitted to The President, who, after a careful examination of the subject, has directed me to inform you, that, in his opinion, the State of Texas has now become so intimately indentified with the other States of the Union, that it would not be proper to receive a Chargé d'Affaires from its Government and thus treat it as a foreign nation.   The moment that the Convention of Texas had ratified the terms of annexation proposed by the Congress of the United States, the substantial engagements of both parties were completed, and nothing then remained to be done but her mere formal admission into the Union in compliance with these engagements.   The President has, accordingly, directed the troops of the United States to march into her territory, and has determined to defend it against the forces of Mexico.   Under these circumstances, Texas has already in his judgement, become in fact, if not in form, one of our States, at least so far as to render it obligatory on him to protect her against foreign invasion.   It would, therefore, it appears to him, be inconsistent with these relations to receive a public minister from her Government as though she were still a stranger.

It is certain, however, that the Government of Texas yet retains all the powers that it formerly possessed except such as would be inconsistent with the engagements of the respective parties to consummate annexation.   It is still both the right and duty of that Government to repel a Mexican invasion, and should such an event occur, it would be extremely convenient, if not absolutely necessary, to have an agent of Texas in the City of Washington.   Other circumstances might be adverted to which would render this highly proper.   Whilst, therefore, the President cannot receive you in a diplomatic character, he will be much gratified should you determine to remain in this City as an agent of Texas.   In that capacity, you may render essential service to both countries.

In arriving at these conclusions the President requests me to assure you of his sincere regard for the President of Texas and his regret that he has not been able to comply with his wishes in regard to your reception.

The opinion of Buchanan had been in favor of the reception of Lee; but his view had been overruled; the subject was considered at a

Cabinet meeting of the same date as the foregoing note of September 6, 1845; the interesting discussion had and the decision made are thus reported (Diary of James K. Polk, I, 17–20):

The President laid before the Cabinet a letter [of] appointment from the President of Texas (by Mr. Allen, Secretary of State of Texas) to Mr. Lee as acting Chargé d'affaires of Texas to the U. States. He also laid before the Cabinet the instructions of the President of Texas to Mr. Lee which had been furnished by Mr. Lee to Mr. Buchanan. . . . During Mr. Buchanan's absence of half an hour the President read to the Cabinet Mr. Lee's letter of appointment, and instructions. The President expressed his opinion to be against receiving Mr. Lee in his diplomatic character, and the Cabinet were engaged in conversation on the subject when Mr. Buchanan returned. The President informed Mr. Buchanan that the papers had been read to the Cabinet. Mr. Buchanan had, on presenting Mr. Lee's application to the President to be accredited as Chargé d'affaires of Texas to the United States two days ago, intimated the opinion that Texas was so far to be regarded as an independent Nation as to make it proper to receive Mr. Lee as her accredited Minister to this Government. The President in a short note to Mr. Buchanan had expressed a different opinion. The President repeated that opinion in substance as follows. He said after what had transpired he could not regard Texas as a foreign State. Texas by her Congress and Convention had, in the most solemn forms, accepted the terms of annexation offered to her by the U. States; that from that moment the compact of Union between Texas & the U. States was complete, and that he considered Texas as being now virtually a part of our own country. We had so treated Texas by sending our squadron to the Gulf and our army to her Western border, to defend her territory & people against the threatened Mexican invasion. If we now receive a foreign Minister from Texas, we recognize her as a foreign State, and it would be difficult to justify the sending our army into her territory to defend her, claiming it to be a part of our own country. The President asked Mr. Buchanan if we received and accredited this Minister, if we could make a Treaty with him. To which Mr. B. replied we could, but it could only last until the act of Congress was passed admitting Texas as one of the States of the Union. The President remarked, if we received this Minister, we must to all intents and purposes admit that Texas was a foreign State, and so regarding her, if we could make a Treaty for a limited time with her there would be nothing to restrain us from making any other Treaty with her; and that, in either case, it would be wholly inconsistent with the ground which the Cabinet had unanimously taken when it was ordered to send our army into Texas to defend her, regarding her as a part of our own country & the faith of the country pledged to protect and defend her. All the Cabinet concurred with the President in these views; the Secretary of War expressing himself strongly on the subject. Mr. Buchanan said although his opinion was unchanged he would not insist upon it. A conversation of some length took place, when it was agreed that the Minister (Mr. Lee) could not be received & accredited as chargé d'affaires. The President, with the concurrence of the Cabinet, directed that Mr. Buchanan should address a letter to Mr. Lee, in courteous & friendly terms, explaining to him why he could not be recognized in the official character of chargé de affaires but that the Government would confer with him as the agent of Texas, as they would with the agent of one of the States of the Union having business at Washington; that any information he desired to communicate would be received, and in turn any information deemed important to Texas or relating to annexation would be communicated to him.

An elaborate argument on the subject was subsequently addressed to the Secretary of State by Colonel David S. Kaufman, who had been appointed Chargé d'Affaires of the Republic of Texas (D.S., 1 Communications from Agents of Texas). The text of that note appears below. No answer to it was written; practical considerations were of more weight than the juridical aspects of the question which Kaufman presented:

LEGATION OF TEXAS
Washington 23ᵈ Sept. 1845.

The undersigned has the honor to inform the Hon: Mʳ Buchanan, Secretary of State of the United States, that he has been appointed by his Excellency the President of Texas, Chargé d'Affaires of the Government of Texas near the Government of the United States, and, but for the tenor of Mʳ Buchanan's note of the Sixth Inst. addressed to my immediate predecessor, the Hon: W. D. Lee, the undersigned would ask for the appointment of a time when he might have the honor of presenting his letter of credence.

In your communication of the date above alluded to, you state, that, it is the opinion of the President, that, "the *State of Texas* has now become so intimately identified with the other States of the Union that it would not be proper to receive a Chargé d'Affaires from its Government and thus treat it as a foreign Nation."

After the expression of an opinion thus decided, on the part of his Excellency, it might be considered indelicate in the undersigned to urge a reconsideration of the question, and it would place his Government in a position that he would not have it occupy. He will not do so of his own responsibility. On this subject he will await the instructions of his Government.

The decision thus made, in regard to the reception of my immediate predecessor however, seems to place the government which I have the honor to represent in so singular an attitude before the world, *The attitude of ignorance of its present relations with the United States,* that I feel it due to it, as well as to myself, to vindicate it from that charge.

The kind, friendly, and confidential relations which exist between the two Governments, to be blended shortly in "a more perfect Union", will I trust authorize me to do so with a frankness and freedom that I might not otherwise indulge in; at the same time assuring the Hon Mʳ Buchanan, that, whatever may be the course his Government may finally pursue in regard to this matter, as far as Texas is concerned, it can throw no impediment in the way of the final consummation of the great American question of Annexation.

By the provisions of "a joint resolution for annexing Texas to the United States", the first and second sections of which were selected and presented to the consideration of the Government of Texas, certain duties were required to be performed by the "existing Government" of Texas, by "Deputies in Convention" assembled, and by "the people" themselves in their original sovereign capacity. The *existing Government* of Texas was to give *its consent* to the proposed change, The *deputies in Convention* were to form a Constitution of a Republican Character, and *the People* themselves were to approve said Constitution, and the evidence of their approval of the same was to be sent to the President of the United States, on or before the first day of January 1846, to be by him laid before your Congress for its final action.

All these conditions have to be complied with on the part of the *Government*, the *Convention*, and the *people* of Texas before it can be said with propriety that Texas has "ratified the terms of Annexation proposed by the Congress of the United States."

Now how many of these "Powers of the State" have performed the duties required of them preliminary to a *further* action on the part of the United States Congress? But *one* of the *three*. The existing Government has given its consent but as far as we are informed, the Convention has not yet adopted a State Constitution, and *certain it is* that the People, *in whom and whom alone*, not only by the theory of all popular governments, but by an express provision of our Constitution, is vested the right to abolish one form of Government and erect another in its stead, have not yet ratified that Constitution.

"All political power is inherent in the *people* and they have at all times an inalienable right to alter their Government in such manner as they may think proper" Declaration of rights—Constitution of Texas.

It may be argued that the People have in this instance effected the Change through their Deputies or Representatives in Convention assembled, but this argument is untenable, as the joint resolution above referred to plainly draws a distinction between "the Deputies in Convention" assembled "and the *people* of said Republic of Texas." If the universal practice of submitting amendments of the Constitutions of States of the American Union to the People for their

ratification or rejection, be right or expedient, how much more so is it when not only the whole Constitution of Texas is proposed to be changed, but her Nationality itself merged in that of another.

But the joint resolution on this point is explicit, and it is the "Law of Union" for both Governments.

It is true as remarked by Mᵣ Buchanan that "the Convention had (has) ratified the terms of Annexation proposed by the Congress of the United States."

Composed as that honorable body is, of so much of the talent, integrity, and patriotism of the Land, they have done, and will do every thing in their power to consummate so desirable an object. They have "Ordained and declared that they assent to and accept the proposals contained in the first and second sections" of the joint resolution above referred to. Now so far as the first and 2ⁿᵈ sections are concerned, the ordinance of the Convention was unnecessary and supererogatory. It travelled out of the record, although it did much good in quieting the public mind by the extraordinary and gratifying unanimity evinced in favor of this interesting measure. A simple reading of said Sections will however satisfy every mind that this was not a duty prescribed by them. The formation of a State Constitution is all that they require.

This view of the question, I have no doubt has been, or will be sustained by the Convention itself, for I see in the public prints, that a Committee of that body has recommended that the question, not only of the adoption of the Constitution, but also of Annexation be referred to the People themselves at the Ballot Box, a recommendation which I have no doubt has already been concurred in. More or Less could not have been expected from such a body.

It cannot be said that the People, by electing deputies favorable to annexation, deprived or meant to deprive themselves of a final decision of this question at the Polls. They had not the power to do so by the said joint resolution, nor had they the inclination. This same People, have on the first of this month, elected members for the tenth Congress of Texas, a proceeding which would have been superfluous—not to say treasonable if they had not reserved to themselves the right of finally deciding the question of a Change of Government. Although the first and second Sections do not literally provide for the submission of the question of annexation to the People, yet a decision of that question is substantially involved in the vote upon the adoption of the Constitution. Let us suppose, for instance, that the People should not adopt the Constitution submitted to them, or if adopted, that the same should not be transmitted to the President of the United States on or before the first day of January 1846, would the terms of our admission be complied with, notwithstanding the said Ordinance of the Convention? Clearly not. Indeed the said joint resolution provides that these proceedings shall be had by the Government, the Convention, and the People, before the first day of January 1846, "in order that the same (Texas) *may be* admitted as one of the *States* of the Union." It recognizes no intermediate, no *territorial* State. The moment Texas looses her separate sovereignty she assumes the rank of a sovereign state of the American Confederacy. Your Government requires of Texas no pupilage, no probation. Her sovereignty is never lost. It will only flow in a different channel.

Texas is as yet an Independant Republic. Her Government has given her consent to Annexation and the Convention are in the process of the performance of the duties required of them. During these proceedings, past present and *to come*, Texas maintains her independent and seperate attitude, and will continue to do so until the final consummation of the measure of annexation. Her President continues to discharge his duties, Her courts are now in session by virtue of Authority from the *Republic of Texas*, and a congress was elected at the usual annual Election. Her revenue from imposts as well as direct taxes are still collected as usual, and her gallant army, small though it be, continues ready to defend the Country from aggressions. It is true that the United States has sent a portion of its Army into that Country, but it was by the invitation of the Representatives of the *owners of the soil, the People of Texas*.

The invitation of the Convention was given three days after the ordinance accepting the terms &ᶜ showing conclusively, that the Convention did not conceive that the acceptance by it of the terms of annexation *ipso facto* brought Texas into the Union. Their presence in no way impairs the sovereignty of

Texas. They were there at Nacogdoches in 1836, and yet in that case the sovereignty of Texas was not questioned. In that case as in the present they were there by the consent of the People and for purposes of self defence. The People of the United States have the right to form a more perfect Union with Texas. If she has the right to form a compact of any character with her as an independent power, she has the right to form a *constitutional* compact.

If England and France had a right to form Compacts with her, so has the United States, and no one has a right to question that power, and if they have a right to form this Constitutional Compact, they have a clear right to combine their strength (as is now done) to prevent their rights from being impaired. Indeed when the *Treaty* form of annexation was attempted the Government of the United States obligated itself to protect Texas from invasion *pending the negociation,* and now the United States are ready to protect Texas from invasion during the proceedings necessary to consummate the measure on her part, in order to enable her to complete the work without molestation.

The undersigned sincerely trusts that the foregoing remarks will be received by the Hon: Secretary of State of the United States in the spirit with which they are written, and knows that the utmost harmony and friendship will continue to exist between the two Governments until the now "Lone Star" becomes "one of the *many*" that glitter in the American Constellation.

The undersigned would in conclusion take occasion to remark that the promptitude, energy, and patriotism, with which his Excellency the President of the United States has acted in forwarding the measure of Annexation, have earned for him the admiration and gratitude of the people of Texas.

The undersigned avails himself of this occasion to assure Mr Buchanan of his very high Consideration and has the honor to subscribe himself his

 Very Obedient Servant

             David S. Kaufman

To the Hon: James Buchanan
 Secretary of State

The United States and Texas

The question of Texas may be said to have first become one of interest to the United States with the cession of Louisiana in 1803; the limits of the Province of Louisiana to the west had never been determined; the United States acquired whatever rights France had; and whether Texas was within Louisiana was a matter of political controversy for decades ("Reannexation of Texas" was a slogan of 1844) and has since been the subject of elaborate historical criticism (see Ficklen, "Was Texas Included in the Louisiana Purchase?" in Publications of the Southern History Association, V, 351–87; Paullin, Atlas of the Historical Geography of the United States, 66–68, and plate 95A; Marshall, A History of the Western Boundary of the Louisiana Purchase, 1819–1841, *passim,* and the writings there cited; also, Rives, The United States and Mexico, 1821–1848, I, 1–26). While the Florida Treaty of February 22, 1819, with Spain (Document 41) did not fix or purport to fix the limits of Louisiana, it did determine the frontiers of the United States and Spain on this continent west of the Mississippi; Texas was then definitively within Spanish America; but that treaty of 1819 had hardly gone into force before Mexico became independent and Texas part of Mexican territory.

During the administrations of John Quincy Adams and Andrew Jackson (1825–29 and 1829–37) the acquisition of Texas by arrangement with Mexico was a leading policy of the United States, though

one which was proved to have had no chance of success.   The independence of Texas (1836) was recognized by the United States in 1837 and later by other powers, including Great Britain and France, though not by Mexico (as to the recognition of Texas by European powers, and treaties negotiated, see Rives, *op. cit.*, I, 472).   In 1838 two international agreements were made by the United States with Texas, one regarding claims (Document 84) and one for a partial demarcation of boundary (Document 85); a treaty of commerce with Texas, signed on July 30, 1842, failed because the Senate struck out two articles (see Executive Journal, VI, 188–89).

Proposals by Texas for annexation during the administration of Martin Van Buren (1837–41) and again during the first years of the administration of John Tyler (1841–45) were declined; President Tyler, however, was none the less determined on annexation; the negotiations were renewed under his direction in October 1843; the note of the Plenipotentiaries of Texas who signed the treaty of April 12, 1844 (Isaac Van Zandt and J. Pinckney Henderson) includes a summary of the policy of Texas in the matter of annexation as well as a statement of the public lands and debts (D.S., 1 Communications from Agents of Texas, April 15, 1844):

LEGATION OF TEXAS,
Washington City, April 15ᵗ, 1844.

The undersigned, &c. &c., in reply to the inquiries of Mʳ Calhoun, Secretary of State of the United States, have the honor to submit the following:

In 1836, after the declaration of the independence of Texas, in pursuance of the orders of the convention and the expression of the popular will, the President *ad interim*, by his proclamation, ordered an election to be held throughout the Republic, for the ratification or rejection of the constitution which had been adopted by the convention, and for the expression by the people of their wishes in regard to the Annexation of Texas to the United States.   The result was, that upon a full poll but ninety three votes were given against the Annexation.

Following up this declared wish of the people, the first Congress that assembled, thereafter, passed an act empowering the President to appoint a minister to present the question to the Government of the United States.   The proposition having been declined, it was deemed prudent, in order to facilitate negotiations with other countries, not to press the question of Annexation further, and therefore it was withdrawn.

Subsequently, in 1842, instructions were given for the informal renewal of the negotiations; which, not having been met by a reciprocal action on the part of the United States, were, in August last, again withdrawn, and the attention of the Government of Texas directed to other objects calculated, in its opinion, to secure its safety and advance its prosperity—for the attainment of which reasonable assurances had been received.

Afterwards, on the 16ᵗ October last, the proposition for the formation of a treaty of Annexation was made by this Government, through the late Secretary of State, Mʳ Upshur, to the Government of Texas.   At that time—no arrangement having been concluded, inconsistent with such a step, and the Congress having expressed their approbation of the measure, and every expression of public sentiment fully indicating that the people of Texas were yet desirous to consummate a measure, believed to be promotive of the mutual welfare of both countries, and without which, from motives of policy or necessity, they might be compelled to adopt measures which, it is to be feared, would engender a feeling of unfriendly rivalship, productive of discord and strife and dangerous to their mutual peace and quiet—the President of Texas determined to accede to the proposition, and accordingly empowered the undersigned to adjust the terms of the treaty just concluded.

The undersigned have the most abiding confidence that, should the Annexation be consummated, the same will receive the hearty and full concurrence of the people of Texas. And believing that the fate of this treaty, be the decision whatever it may, will forever decide the question of Annexation—a question, the continued agitation of which has prevented their Government from pursuing vigorously any other policy—they feel the highest gratification that this opportunity has thus been offered. They will not anticipate nor speculate upon the consequences of a rejection. Satisfied, however, that the language, institutions and locality of the two countries have fitted them for becoming members of the same great political family, or fated them to a conflict of interest, which may result in evil consequences, they trust that it may be so determined as to secure the blessings of liberty to both and promote the happiness of mankind.

Upon the subject of the public lands, the undersigned submit a summary statement made from a late report of the Commissioner of the General Land Office to the President of Texas. He estimates the aggregate at_____ 203, 520, 000 acres,
Lands appropriated at_____ 67, 408, 673   "

Remainder, unappropriated, at_____ 136, 111, 327   "

In a report of a committee of the House of Representatives of the Congress of Texas, made to that body on the 12ᵗʰ January, 1841, the debt and liabilities of the Republic are stated to be as follows:

Funded debt bearing 10 per cent. interest_____ $1, 650, 000
Bonds sold and pledged, bearing 10 per cent. interest_____ 1, 350, 000
Treasury notes without interest_____ 3, 000, 000
Debts of various descriptions, say audited drafts and other
   claims without interest_____ 1, 000, 000

   Total_____ $7, 000, 000

This report includes the interest then accrued and a number of unaudited claims, supposed to be valid, which were not computed in the report of the Secretary of the Treasury to the same Congress, which report shows the public debt as less than five millions of dollars.

Since the date above referred to, no further general estimate has been made at the Treasury Department. It is known, however, that the revenues of the Government have nearly equalled its expenditures. So that the debt has not been materially increased, except from the interest which has since accrued.

The undersigned avail themselves of this occasion to offer to Mʳ Calhoun assurances of their distinguished consideration.

Isaac Van Zandt
J Pinckney Henderson

The writings on the various phases of diplomatic history during the years which preceded the annexation of Texas are numerous; there are valuable bibliographies in the works of two leading authorities: Justin H. Smith, The Annexation of Texas; and George Lockhart Rives, The United States and Mexico, 1821–1848.

A historical diagram of Texas is at page 143 of this volume; relevant plates and text in Paullin, Atlas of the Historical Geography of the United States, are cited at page 142.

114

NEW GRANADA : MARCH 29, 1845

Convention for the Settlement of Claims Arising Out of the Seizure of the Schooner "Yankee", signed at Bogotá March 29, 1845. Original in Spanish.
Not subject to ratification by the United States. As to ratification by New Granada, see the notes. Not proclaimed.

[Translation]

Mariano Calvo, comicionado por el Poder Ejecutivo por parte de la Republica de la Nueva Granada, y José Gooding, autorisado debidamente por el Encargado de Negocios de los Estados Unidos del Norte, con el objeto de arreglar los reclamos pendientes sobre la Goleta americana nombrada "Yankee" su Capitan Eliphalet Robbins, hemos celebrado el contrato, cuyo tenor se contiene en los articulos siguientes:—

Mariano Calvo, commissioned by the Executive of New Granada, and Joseph Gooding, duly authorized by the Honorable William M. Blackford, Chargé d'Affaires of the United States, to arrange and settle the claims originating out of the seizure of the American schooner *Yankee*, Captain Eliphalet Robbins, have agreed on the following articles, viz:

ARTICULO 1º El Gobierno de la Nueva Granada tendrá ā la orden i disposicion del Encargado de Negocios de los Estados Unidos, ō de la persona que los reclamantes designen por medio del Secretario de Estado de la Republica de los Estados Unidos, las cantidades que pasan ā espresarse.

ARTICLE 1. The Government of New Granada will hold at the disposal of the Chargé d'Affaires of the United States or such other person as the claimants may request the Secretary of State of the United States to receive the same:

1ª Como compensacion de la prision del Capitan Eliphalet Robbins y como saldo general absoluto por sus salarios, gastos,

1. As remuneration for Captain Eliphalet Robbins' imprisonment, balance of his wages, and indemnity in full of all claims originat-

741

daños i perjuicios, y Derechos de Consulado *Cuatro Mil Pesos* los que se pagarán sin interés alguno en el entrante año économico que comienza en primero de Setiembre proximo.

2ª En el mismo tiempo y por las mismas razones de la partida anterior, *Setecientos setenta y cinco pesos* que se distribuirán en la forma siguiente:—para el Piloto Edward L. Vennard *Doscientos cincuenta pesos*, para los marineros James Ross i Sidney Kelly (*Tres cientos Pesos*) ā *Ciento cincuenta pesos* cada uno, al Cocinero y Despensero Henry Hillman *Doscientos veinte i cinco Pesos*, cuyas cantidades ganan el interés de un Seis por Ciento anual desde primero de Abril de mil ochoCientos treinta y ocho hasta el dia en que se verifique su pago.

3ª Por el valor de la Goleta "Yankee" *Cuatro mil Pesos*, cuya cantidad gana el interés de Seis por ciento anual desde primero de Abril de mil ochoCientos treinta y ocho hasta el dia en que se haga su pago, que será en el año économico que principia en Primero de Setiembre de mil ochoCientos cuarenta y Seis.

4ª Por el saldo del cargamento de la espresada Goleta "Yankee" *Mil ochocientos diez y Seis pesos* ademas de Mil Seis cientos ochenta y cuatro pesos recividos por el Vice Consul de los Estados Unidos en Rio Hacha por el producido de la venta que hizo este Señor en aquella cuidad, cuya suma de Mil

ing out of the seizure of the said schooner *Yankee*, four thousand dollars, which shall be paid without interest in the ensuing economical year that commences on the 1st of September next.

2. At the same time and for the same reasons above stated, seven hundred and seventy-five dollars, to be distributed as follows: to the mate, Edward L. Vennard, two hundred and fifty dollars; to the sailors James Ross and Sidney Kelly, three hundred dollars, or one hundred and fifty dollars each; to the cook and steward, Henry Hillman, two hundred and twenty-five dollars; all which said sums shall bear interest at the rate of 6 percent per annum from the 1st of April, 1838, until payment be made.

3. As value of the schooner *Yankee*, four thousand dollars, which sum shall bear interest at 6 percent per annum from the 1st of April, 1838, until the day payment be made, which shall be in the economical year beginning on the 1st of September, 1846.

4. As balance of the cargo of said schooner *Yankee*, one thousand eight hundred and sixteen dollars over and above one thousand six hundred and eighty-four dollars received by the vice consul of the United States in Riohacha, being proceeds of sales effected by him in that city,

ochocientos diez y seis pesos, gana el interés de Seis por ciento anual desde primero de Abril de mil ochoCientos treinta i ocho hasta que se verifique el pago, que será en el año économico que principia en primero de Setiembre de mil ochoCientos cuarenta y seis.

5ª Por el valor de la mitad del flete del Puerto de Rio Hacha al de Nueva York *Trescientos pesos,* cuya cantidad gana el interés de seis por ciento anual desde primero de Abril de mil ochocientos treinta i ocho hasta que se verifique su pago que será en el año économico que principia en primero de Setiembre de mil ochoCientos cuarenta y seis.

ARTICULO 2ndo José Gooding declara: que las cantidades anteriores satisfacen debida y cumplidamente todos los reclamos que se han hecho i pudieren hacerse por el Gobierno de su nacion ó por alguno ó algunos de los Cuidadanos de la misma al Gobierno de la Nueva Granada, ó ā alguno ó ā algunos de sus cuidadanos por el acontecimiento de la Goleta "Yankee" succedido en el Rio del Hacha en el año de mil ochoCientos treinta y ocho, y por lo mismo queda saldado y cancelado todo cargo, accion ō derecho que haya podido ō pudiere tenerse ō intentarse en el precitado reclamo.

ARTICULO 3º El présente contrato serà presentado al Poder

which said sum of one thousand eight hundred and sixteen dollars shall bear interest at 6 percent per annum from the 1st April, 1838, until payment be made, which shall be in the economical year beginning on the 1st September, 1846.

5. As half freight from the port of Riohacha to that of New York, three hundred dollars, which sum shall bear interest at 6 percent per annum from the 1st April, 1838, until payment be made, which shall be in the economical year that commences on the 1st September, 1846.

ARTICLE 2. Joseph Gooding hereby declares that the above sums shall be a discharge in full of all and every claim or claims that have originated or may hereafter originate out of the seizure of the American schooner *Yankee,* Captain Eliphalet Robbins, in Riohacha in the year 1838.

ARTICLE 3. The present convention shall be submitted to the

Ejecutivo para que le preste su aprobacion y para que se eleve al Congreso Nacional en las presentes sesiones para los fines legales. En fé de lo cual firmamos Dos ejemplares de un mismo tenor y forma en Bogotá ā Veinte y nueve de Marzo del año de mil ochoCientos cuarenta y cinco.

Executive of New Granada for its approbation and presented to Congress, now in sessions, for its sanction.

In faith of which we have signed two of same tenor and date in Bogotá this twenty-ninth day of March in the year one thousand eight hundred and forty-five.

MARIANO CALVO
JOSÉ GOODING

JOSEPH GOODING
MARIANO CALVO

NOTES

The Spanish text of this convention which is printed above has been collated with the signed original document in D.S., Miscellaneous Papers Relative to Claims "on file in Bureau of Rolls and Library . . . August 1, 1887", No. 226. The English translation printed above is from a paper, headed "Translation", which was transmitted to the Secretary of State by Joseph Gooding with his letter of March 29, 1845 (D.S., 11 Despatches, Colombia); that rendering gives the general sense of the convention, but is somewhat summary (e.g., Article 2).

This convention, except, as will hereinafter appear, so much of it as related to the indemnity to the captain of the *Yankee*, was negotiated by Gooding "By virtue of an appointment of our Chargé d'Affaires, the Honb'ẹ Wᵐ M. Blackford dated 23ʳᵈ December 1844, for the special purpose of settling the amount of Indemnity to the claimants in the case of the Schooner 'Yankee' seized at Rio de la Hacha in the year 1838" (*ibid.*). The other negotiator was Mariano Calvo, who "received an appointment from the Granadian Govᵗ for the above purpose" (*ibid.*). There is no original or copy of either of the above-mentioned "appointments" with the despatches.

An earlier convention with New Granada, that of February 9, 1843, in the case of the *By Chance* (Document 101), was also signed by Gooding and Calvo. The circumstances here were somewhat similar to those in the case of the *By Chance*, as liability was admitted. The signers of the convention acted as commissioners to determine the amounts due. Some comments on the powers of Blackford and on the delegation of his authority to Gooding will be found in the notes to Document 101.

THE CASE OF THE "YANKEE"

The facts and circumstances out of which arose the claims settled by this convention are thus set forth in the report of Henry Aaron, vice consul at Riohacha (there appears no record of the appointment of Aaron other than the despatch of Alexander Danouille,

consul at Santa Marta, of April 18, 1834; D.S., 1 Consular Despatches, Santa Marta) to James Semple, Chargé d'Affaires at Bogotá, under date of March 28, 1838 (D.S., 9 Despatches, Colombia, No. 8, September 10, 1838, enclosure):

The American schooner Yankee of Bath [Maine], Eliphalet Robbins arrived in this port from the Island of Saint Thomas on the 22^d of february last past having on board part of a cargo of Merchandise consigned to H. A. Victoria of this city—which were landed and passed thro' this Custom House with the usual and necessary formalities.   The said schooner then proceeded to take on board a cargo of Hacha wood, hides and skins and the captain reported his vessel ready for sea, on the 7th inst.   But on application being made to the custom house by the consignee for her clearance, the collector refused to grant the same alleging as a reason therefor that six bags of peas had been seized on the beach the evening before, and that suspicion falling on the schooner Yankee he considered it his duty to detain the vessel and captain until an investigation of the matter could take place by the proper authorities and which according to the laws of the republic would be summarily done.

On the 9th inst. I received a representation from Capt. Robbins stating that he had received on board his vessel an order from the Judge of this province (Juez letrado de hacienda) to appear before him and declare what had become of five bags of pease which were minus in his stores, he having entered on his provision list on his arrival in this port ten bags, and he having now only five on board.   In obedience thereto he immediately repaired on shore and wouthout hesitation declared that the pease being of no value to him he had sent five bags on shore to his consignee with a note stating that he had done so to make room for storage in the forecastle, not knowing that he had by so doing infringed any law, particularly they being of so small a value: The result of this declaration was that Capt. Robbins was immediately thrown in prison in the common jail of this city—a place of the most filthy and insalubrious nature, amongst vagabonds and criminals of all kinds, his vessel seized and proceedings of a criminal nature instituted against him which may terminate in his utter ruin.   He therefore claimed my protection as an american citizen and an injured man.

I, in accordance with my duty immediate remonstrated on such conduct, towards a man who in my opinion had committed, if any but a verry trifling offence, and requested that he might be liberated from prison on my responsibility. Meanwhile the case was under investigation so that he might be enabled to go on board his vessel and take the necessary care of her, she lying in an open roadstead with her cargo on board of her and exposed to considerable danger but I regret to state that I could not obtain a condescention so trifling

On the 16th inst. Captain Robbins was taken ill in prison and he petitioned the Judge to grant him a temporal release from prison for the purpose of taking medicine which he required, and in reply the Judge decreed that his statement must be corroborated by the surgeon of the military hospital of this city, and that it would also be necessary that he should present a good and sufficient bail. On the following morning the surgeon visited him in jail and declared him to be in ill health and that the situation he was then in was unfit for him being too much exposed to the northerly winds and that to take the requisite medicine it was indispensable his removal to a more convenient dwelling.   This was immediately represented to the Judge together with a notice from Capt Robbins stating that he being an entire stranger here it was not possible for him to find bail in his then state, and as he only required a temporal release for the recovery of his health he trusted that his own responsibility would be deemed sufficient.   To this he received no reply.

I again remonstrated with the Governor of the Province on the cruelty of keeping a man in such a prison whose health required so much care, and that neglected as he was the consequences might be serious which note his excellency transmitted to the Judge from whom on the 20th inst. I received a communication stating that Capt Robbins would be allowed to leave the jail for the purpose of receiving medical assistance on condition that he should retire to a private dwelling or on board his vessel, that he should not take exercise out of doors and that I should be responsible for his person, and give notice of his recovery.   Notwithstanding

the harshness of such terms I immediately stated in reply that for the sake of humanity and relief to a man I considered inocent I would undertake the [?] responsibility—not doubting that on the receipt of this reply which was placed in the hands of the Judge on the following morning the release of Capt Robbins would without delay take place—but up to this date no steps whatever have been taken, and he still remains a prisoner and in the most precarious state of health.

The proceedings (which by the laws of the country ought to have been summarily gone through) are still pending. The vessel a new one and not yet coppered, lying laden in the port, a prey to the weather and worms which will soon render her unfit for sea, himself ill and in a most wretched place stiled a prison, and I as the protector of the rights and interests of american citizens am obliged to witness this cruel treatment without a remedy of a man whom I consider inocent, and whose only crime has been that of landing inocently five bags of pease which by the laws of the country are not of sufficient value to warrant measures so violent.

I have been thus prolix in the narration of all the circumstances so as to place you in possession of a full knowledge of all the particulars of this disagreeable business not doubting but the Capt and owners of the vessel and cargo will claim compensation for damages &c and as I am informed that there is a probability of the proceedings being brought to a conclusion in all the ensuing week I hope to be enabled by next post to transmit you for your satisfaction and government copies of the proceedings and of all communications which have passed on this subject between the authorities of this city and myself which will enable you to judge of the liberal policy extended towards citizens of a nation whose institutions and sentiments are said to sympathise

It was not until May 23, 1838, that sentence was pronounced by the court at Riohacha; after a long recital of the alleged facts, the judgment concluded as follows (*ibid.*, translation):

It is adjudged and decreed, first, that the six bags of peas seized shall be confiscated according to the sixth and eighth paragraphs of the sixteenth article of the decree of the 9th March, 1827; secondly, that the captain shall pay the sum of twenty-five dollars for the peas found short in his ship's stores, according to the fourth paragraph of the fifth article of same decree; thirdly, that it has not been sufficiently proved that Captain Robbins has contravened the laws or that his intention to commit a fraud has been carried into effect. He is therefore accordingly acquitted. And it is further ordered that the vessel which has been detained shall be delivered to the said Captain Robbins, and it is further ordered that the said captain shall pay all the costs and damages occasioned to the Treasury according to law.

Let this judgment be submitted to the superior tribunal for its approval before it is carried into effect.

Although Captain Robbins was "acquitted", he was still detained in jail to await the approval or disapproval by the superior court at Cartagena of the decision of the judge at Riohacha. The judgment of the superior court is signed by three judges and is under date of July 25, 1838; in translation it reads as follows (*ibid.*):

Having diligently examined the case of Eliphalet Robbins, captain of the American schooner *Yankee*, on a charge of having landed, contrary to law, six bags of peas at the port of Riohacha, decided by the Judge of the Treasury of that Province on the 23d May last and sent to this court for its approval or disapproval: By the decision of the said judge the six bags of peas were confiscated and also the small boat in which they were landed, and the captain was condemned to the payment of twenty-five dollars, the value of the five bags of peas which were found short in his ship's stores. He was also acquitted of the charge of fraud but condemned to pay the costs of suit and the damages to the Treasury. The schooner was also acquitted.

It is necessary to consider the three principal points which are comprehended in said sentence in order that we may properly comprehend those points that are naturally connected therewith.

It is clearly proved that on the 6th March last six bags of peas were apprehended in the said port, marked (B), weighing five arrobas each, which were disembarked, without permission from the customhouse, in a small boat with three men, who ran away when they were discovered by the watchman. Consequently the said judge, in accordance with the sixth paragraph of the seventeenth article of the decree of the 9th March, 1827, without further proceedings ought to have confiscated the said six bags of peas without including the small boat because the value of the contraband only amounted to thirty dollars.

In the second place, it is without doubt that the captain of said vessel committed a violation of law in sending on shore without permission from the customhouse five bags of peas; as it appears from the manifest furnished when the vessel was first entered that there were ten bags on board, and from the examination afterwards made there were only found four and about a half, and it appears also from the evidence of the cook of the vessel there had only been used about half a bag since the vessel came into port, from all which it is plain that the five bags had been disembarked or thrown into the water. It was confessed by the captain that he had landed the said five bags of peas and sent them as a present to the consignee of the vessel, Mr. Victoria. Therefore it is evident there was good ground for condemning the captain to pay the value of the five bags of peas found wanting in his vessel. But all these facts could by no means furnish a foundation for proceedings against Captain Robbins or his vessel—neither does the evidence show that the six bags marked (B) were of the provisions of the schooner, and if the judge had from the *beginning* proceeded in the manner he did at *last* there would have been no detention either of the captain or of the schooner, because in all the proof the value of the contraband did not amount to fifty dollars, and of course the supposed smuggler is not liable to be proceeded against, according to the circular of 14th July, 1828, which, besides being according to the decree above recited, is peculiarly applicable to this case, for as this circular is applicable to articles prohibited by law, much more is it applicable to goods not prohibited. Therefore—

In view of all the considerations aforesaid and in conformity with the opinion of the fiscal, doing justice in the name of the Republic and by authority of law, the sentence of the court at Riohacha is and the same is hereby reversed and annulled, except only so much as confiscates the six bags of peas apprehended and to the payment of the value of the five bags of peas which Captain Robbins had disembarked. And it is further ordered and adjudged that the judge who decided this case at Riohacha be condemned to the payment of all the costs and damages of this prosecution, leaving the fiscal of said port at liberty to proceed against the said judge as is made his duty by the first paragraph of the thirty-third article of the law organizing the tribunal. And leaving Captain Robbins at liberty to commence and prosecute any suit or suits which he may think proper for the recovery of damages for the detention of himself and his vessel.

Let a copy of this sentence be sent to the Governor of Riohacha in answer to his note of the 10th instant and a copy also to the Chief Executive Power in answer to the request of the Secretary of the Interior and Foreign Relations.

On August 21, 1838, the sentence of the superior court was carried into effect; Captain Robbins was liberated after an imprisonment of 165 days and notified to receive his vessel. On going on board he found that she had become, by exposure to worms and the weather, unseaworthy, and that a large part of her cargo, being of a perishable nature, was destroyed or so much injured as to be unmarketable. He therefore refused to take possession of the vessel and cargo and entered his protest accordingly.

The Negotiations

The case of the *Yankee* was mentioned in an instruction to James Semple, Chargé d'Affaires at Bogotá, of October 20, 1839 (D.S., 15 Instructions, Colombia, 71–72); but it seems that no claim was presented until the note of November 15, 1844, from William M. Blackford (successor of Semple as Chargé d'Affaires) to Joaquín Acosta, Secretary of Foreign Relations of New Granada, brought the case to the attention of that Government (D.S., 10 Despatches, Colombia, No. 28, November 29, 1844, enclosure).

The Granadan Government admitted the justice of the claim, and the result of the negotiations is thus described in the despatch of Blackford of December 23, 1844 (*ibid.*, No. 29):

> In my last Despatch I mentioned that I had taken up the case of the Schooner "Yankee" & expressed a hope of bringing it to a satisfactory issue. In this, I am happy to say, I was not too sanguine, as I have, this day, settled the claim. . . . I insisted, with some pertinacity, upon the settlement, at once, of the amount of indemnity for the Captain, whilst I expressed my willingness to refer the ascertainment of the sum, to be paid for vessel & Cargo, to commissioners to be respectively appointed. I could not, however be insensible of the force of some of the objections urged by the Secretary against two Conventions in the same case; nor to the danger of Congress rejecting one, or both, if thus made by the Executive in the absence of full official information on the subject. At the same time, I could not consent to submit the amount of the personal damages to the judgment of another. It was finally agreed, in the conference of today, as a matter of compromise, that the whole affair should be referred—but that the Granadian Commissioner should be instructed to grant the sum of Four Thousand Dollars, without interest, to Captain Robbins, as compensation for his imprisonment, wages, expenses &c. I contended, long & earnestly, for a larger sum—but the embarrassed condition of the finances was urged in mitigation of my demand. The amount, no doubt, will be quite satisfactory to Capt. Robbins, who—as well as the other parties—seems to have taken no interest in the claim, since it was first presented.

Payment

The Congress of New Granada duly made an appropriation to cover the provisions of the convention (D.S., 11 Despatches, Colombia, No. 18, June 1, 1846); and the amounts stipulated were duly paid, although the despatches of the period do not give full details; the total, including the interest, came to more than $14,000, current money, which was at some discount under gold at the time (see D.S., 11 Despatches, Colombia, 1846–47, *passim*).

Receipts running to Benjamin A. Bidlack (who had succeeded Blackford as Chargé d'Affaires at Bogotá) for the amounts awarded to Captain Robbins and to the other individuals named in the convention (except Hillman) are of various dates in August and September 1848 (D.S., Miscellaneous Letters, July–September 1848). The claimant in respect of the cargo was the Atlantic Insurance Company, of New York, which had given a power of attorney to Gooding on January 18, 1839, wherein the value of the cargo is given as $5,145 and the amount of the insurance as $3,500; appended to that instrument is a receipt, of March 7, 1848, from Gooding to Bidlack, for the amount of the award for the cargo with interest, or $2,842 (D.S., Miscellaneous Papers . . . No. 226, cited above).

Bidlack died at Bogotá on February 6, 1849 (D.S., 11 Despatches, Colombia, Joseph Gooding to the Secretary of State, February 16, 1849); suspicions expressed by Gooding as to Bidlack's stewardship of the moneys (March 15, 1849, letter pinned to front pages of D.S., 12 Despatches, Colombia) were baseless; the amount of the award in respect of the schooner had been deposited by Bidlack with one Henry Grine, of Bogotá (D.S., Miscellaneous Letters, May–June 1849; letter of J. H. Lunt, May 31, 1849); the proceeds of that award were, it seems, received by Gooding as agent for the New England Marine Insurance Company, of Boston, not long after the death of Bidlack (see D.S., 12 Despatches, Colombia, No. 6, February 2, 1850, from Thomas M. Foote, Chargé d'Affaires).

Treaty Series No. 317
9 Statutes at Large, 830–32
18 *ibid.*, pt. 2, Public Treaties, 690–91

115

SAXONY : MAY 14, 1845

Convention for the Mutual Abolition of the Droit d'Aubaine and Taxes on Emigration, signed at Berlin May 14, 1845. Original in English and German.
Submitted to the Senate December 18, 1845. (Message of December 15, 1845.) Resolution of advice and consent, with amendment, April 15, 1846. Ratified by the United States April 22, 1846. Ratified by Saxony July 14, 1846. Ratifications exchanged at Berlin August 12, 1846. Proclaimed September 9, 1846.

The united States of America on the one part and his Majesty the King of Saxony on the other part being equally desirous of removing the restrictions which exist in their territories upon the acquisition and transfer of property by their respective citizens and subjects, have agreed to enter into negotiations for this purpose.

For the attainment of this desirable object the President of the United States of America has conferred full powers on Henry Wheaton their Envoy extraordinary and Minister plenipotentiary at the Court of His Majesty the King of Prussia, and His Majesty the King of Saxony upon John de Minckwitz His Minister of State, Lieutenant General, Envoy extraordinary and Minister plenipotentiary at the said Court, who, after having exchanged their

Die Vereinigten Staaten von Nord-Amerika einestheils, und Seine Majestät der König von Sachsen anderntheils, von gleichem Wunsche beseelt, die Beschränkungen aufzuheben, welche in Ihren Staatsgebieten bei Erwerbung und Uebereignung von Gütern Seiten Ihrer beiderseitigen Staatsangehörigen bestehen, sind übereingekommen zu diesem Ende in Unterhandlung zu treten.

Um diesen wünchenswerthen Zweck zu erreichen, haben der Präsident der Vereinigten Staaten von Nordamerika, deren außerordentlichen Gesandten und bevollmächtigten Minister am königl. preußischen Hofe Heinrich Wheaton und Seine Majestät der König von Sachsen Allerhöchst-Ihren Staatsminister, General-Lieutenant, außerordentlichen Gesandten und bevollmächtigten Minister am gedachten Hofe Johannes von Minckwitz zu Be-

751

said full powers, found in due and proper form, have agreed to the following articles:

vollmächtigten ernannt, welche, nach erfolgter Auswechselung ihrer, in gehöriger Form befundenen Vollmachten über folgende Artikel sich vereinigt haben.

ART: 1.

Every kind of droit d'aubaine, droit de retraite, and droit de détraction, or tax on Emigration, is hereby and shall remain abolished, between the two contracting Parties, their states, citizens and subjects respectively.

ARTIKEL 1.,

Jede Art von Heimfallsrecht, Abschoß- und Auswanderungs-Steuer ist und bleibt aufgehoben zwischen den beiden abschließenden Theilen, ihren beiderseitigen Staaten und Staatsangehörigen.

ART: 2.

Where, on the death of any person holding real property within the territories of one party, such real property would, by the laws of the land, descend on a citizen or subject of the other, were he not disqualified by alienage,—or where such real property has been devised by last will and testament to such citizen or subject, he shall be allowed a term of two years from the death of such person, which term may be reasonably prolonged according to circumstances,—to sell the same and to withdraw the proceeds thereof without molestation, and exempt from all duties of detraction on the part of the Government of the respective states.

ARTIKEL 2.,

Wenn durch den Tod irgend eines Besitzers von unbeweglichen Gütern, die in den Gebieten des einen Theils liegen, solche unbewegliche Güter durch gesetzliche Erbfolge einem Staatsangehörigen des andern Theils, wenn er nicht wegen seiner Eigenschaft als Fremder zu deren Besitz unbefähigt wäre, zufallen, oder wenn unbewegliches Eigenthum durch testamentarische Verfügung einem solchen Staatsangehörigen bestimmt worden seyn sollte; so soll diesem ein Zeitraum von Zwei Jahren vom Tode des Erblassers an—welche Frist jedoch nach Umständen in billiger Weise verlängert werden kann—zugestanden werden, um die gedachten unbeweglichen Güter verkaufen und den Erlöß ohne Hinderniß und frei von jeder Abzugssteuer Seiten der Regierung eines der beiden Staaten, beziehen zu können.

Art: 3.

The citizens or subjects of Each of the contracting Parties shall have power to dispose of their personal property within the states of the other, by testament, donation or otherwise, and their heirs, being citizens or subjects of the other contracting Party, shall succeed to their said personal property, whether by testament or ab intestato, and may take possession thereof, either by themselves or by others acting for them, and dispose of the same at their pleasure, paying such duties only as the inhabitants of the country, where the said property lies, shall be liable to pay in like cases.

Artikel 3.,

Die Staatsangehörigen eines jeden der abschließenden Theile sollen in den Gebieten des Andern das Recht haben über ihre beweglichen Güter durch Testament, Schenkung oder auf andere Weise zu verfügen, und ihre Erben, wenn sie Staatsangehörige des andern abschließenden Theiles sind, sollen denselben, entweder durch Testament oder *ab intestato* in dem Besitze ihrer gedachten beweglichen Güter folgen und von selbigen, sey es in Person oder durch Andere in deren Namen Handelnde, Besitz ergreifen und nach Gefallen darüber verfügen können, ohne einer andern Abgabe als derjenigen unterworfen zu seyn, welche die Einwohner des Staats worin sich die fraglichen Güter befinden, in gleichen Fällen zu entrichten haben würden.

Art: 4.

In case of the absence of the heirs, the same care shall be taken provisionally of such real or personal property, as would be taken, in a like case, of the property belonging to the natives of the country, until the lawful owner, or the person who has a right to sell the same, according to article 2. may take measures to receive or dispose of the inheritance.

Artikel 4.,

Im Falle der Abwesenheit der Erben, wird man für dergleichen bewegliche oder unbewegliche Güter einstweilen dieselbe Sorge tragen, welche man in einem gleichen Falle rücksichtlich der Güter eines Eingebornen getragen haben würde, bis daß der rechtmäßige Eigenthümer oder derjenige welchem das Recht zusteht, dieselben zu verkaufen, dem Artikel 2. gemäß, Anordnungen die Erbschaft anzutreten oder darüber zu verfügen, getroffen haben wird.

Art: 5.

If any dispute should arise between the different claimants to the same inheritance, they shall be decided, according to the laws and by the judges of the country where the property is situated.

Art: 6.

All the stipulations of the present convention shall be obligatory in respect to property, already inherited, devised, or bequeathed, but not yet withdrawn from the country where the same is situated, at the signature of this convention.

Art: 7.

This convention shall be ratified by the President of the united States of America, by and with the advice and consent of their Senate, and by His Majesty the King of Saxony and the ratifications shall be exchanged at Berlin within the term of eighteen[1] months, from the date of the signature or sooner if possible.

In faith of which, the respective Plenipotentiaries have signed the above Articles, both in Ger-

Artikel 5.,

Wenn sich irgend eine Streitigkeit zwischen verschiedenen dieselbe Erbschaft beanspruchenden Personen erheben sollte, so soll dieselbe in Gemäßheit der Gesetze und durch die Richter desjenigen Staates worin sich die Güter befinden, entschieden werden.

Artikel 6.,

Sämmtliche Bestimmungen dieses gegenwärtigen Vertrags sollen auch verbindlich seyn rücksichtlich derjenigen unbeweglichen oder beweglichen Güter, welche zur Zeit der Vollziehung dieses Vertrags bereits angefallen oder vererbt, aber aus dem Lande, in dem sie sich befinden, noch nicht bezogen worden sind.

Artikel 7.

Dieser Vertrag wird von dem Präsidenten der Vereinigten Staaten von Nordamerika, mit Beirath und Einwilligung Seiten des Senats sowie von Seiner Majestät dem Könige von Sachsen ratificirt, und sollen die Ratificationen zu Berlin binnen achtzehn[1] Monaten vom Tage der Unterzeichnung an gerechnet oder auch früher, sofern es thunlich ist, ausgewechselt werden.

Zu Urkund dessen haben die beiderseitigen Bevollmächtigten die vorstehenden Artikel, sowohl

---

[1] In the treaty as signed this word was "twelve" ("zwölf"), not "eighteen" ("achtzehn"); see the note regarding the exchange of ratifications.

man and English, and have thereto affixed their seals.	in deutscher als englischer Sprache, vollzogen und ihre Siegel beigedrückt.
Done in triplicata in the city of Berlin on the 14th of May, in the year of our Lord one thousand eight hundred and forty five and the sixty ninth of the Independence of the United States of America.	Ausgefertigt in drei Exemplaren zu Berlin, den 14ten May des Jahres der Gnade Ein Tausend, Acht Hundert Fünf und Vierzig, und dem Neun und Sechszigsten der Unabhängigkeit der Vereinigten Staaten von Nordamerika.
HENRY WHEATON [Seal]	J MINCKWITZ [Seal]

NOTES

In the headnote this convention is given the same descriptive title as those of the other four very similar conventions with German states of about the same period (1844–46), namely, with Hesse of March 26, 1844 (Document 106), with Württemberg of April 10, 1844 (Document 107), with Bavaria of January 21, 1845 (Document 111), and with Nassau of May 27, 1846 (Document 120). Properly speaking, this convention has no title; and in the preamble the parties are spoken of as being "desirous of removing the restrictions which exist in their territories upon the acquisition and transfer of property by their respective citizens and subjects".

In the final clause of this convention it is said that it was "done in triplicata". There are two signed originals in the treaty file. In each of these the English text is written in the left columns, the United States of America is named first throughout in both texts, and the Plenipotentiary of the United States signed at the left.

The usual papers are in the file. They include the attested Senate resolution of April 15, 1846 (Executive Journal, VII, 64), the duplicate United States instrument of ratification of April 22, 1846, the original proclamation of September 9, 1846, and the *procès-verbal* of the exchange of ratifications at Berlin on August 12, 1846, a translation of which is printed below.

The instrument of ratification by the King of Saxony of July 14, 1846, is written in German and includes both texts of the convention, the German in the left columns. Throughout those texts the King of Saxony is named first, and the copy of the signature of the American Plenipotentiary appears under the English text.

The texts of this convention printed above have been collated with that one of the two originals which is with the original proclamation. The differences between the two originals are trifling and of no importance whatever. The original here used for collating omits eight commas which are in the other document and contains five commas which it omits.

Three papers in the file are marked as enclosures to the despatch of J. C. Bancroft Davis, Minister to Germany, of September 13, 1875 (D.S., 9 Despatches, Germany, No. 171), namely, an unsigned copy of the *procès-verbal* of the exchange of ratifications, the original Saxon full power, dated July 28, 1846, to Count Charles Vitzthum de Eckstädt to exchange the ratifications, and the original full power of the Saxon Plenipotentiary, given under date of December 17, 1836, to negotiate and sign the convention, to which further reference is made below.

When this convention was submitted to the Senate with the presidential message of December 15, 1845, it was accompanied by a copy of the despatch of Henry Wheaton, Minister to Prussia, of May 14, 1845, which was printed (Senate Confidential Document No. 1, 29th Congress, 1st session, Regular Confidential Documents, XVIII, 463–70). The substance of that despatch appears below.

THE NEGOTIATIONS

As to the negotiations and content of this and the four other very similar conventions with various German states of about the same period (1844–46), the notes to Document 106, the convention with Hesse of March 26, 1844, should be consulted.

The despatch of Wheaton which transmitted this convention is dated on the day of its signature, May 14, 1845, and contains the following (D.S., 3 Despatches, Prussia, No. 267):

I have the honor to enclose a Convention, which I have this day signed with the Minister of Saxony, at this court, for the mutual abolition of the *droit d'aubaine, droit de détraction* and taxes on emigration between the United-States and that Kingdom.

The stipulations of this Convention will be found to correspond substantially with those contained in the treaties, on the same subject, previously negotiated by me with Hesse-Darmstadt, Wurtemberg & Bavaria, which have already been ratified with the advice & consent of the Senate. The only material difference between the present Instrument & the others, is the following:

In the 2ᵈ article of the proposed Convention with Saxony, corresponding with the same article of the Treaties above referred to, the words: "or where such real property has been devised by last Will & Testament to such citizen or subject", have been inserted, in order to provide for the case of a party who might think fit to *devise* his real property, situated in the one country, to a citizen or subject of the other, instead of suffering it to *descend* according to the rules of inheritance established by the local law. The case supposed by the Saxon negotiator was that of a person of Saxon origin, holding lands in the United States, & having relations in Saxony, who would by our law be his heirs by descent, & who might wish to leave his property to some of those heirs in preference to the others, or even to disinherit them altogether, & devise it to some other Saxon subject, from justifiable motives, & in the exercise of that complete dominion which every man ought to have over that which belongs to him. As very few such cases are ever likely to occur, & as the land which might be *devised* to an alien, in this case, must be sold within the term of two years, in the same manner with that which *descends* to an alien, I have perceived no solid objection to this clause, which was proposed, & very strenuously insisted on, by the Saxon negotiator, under the instructions of his Government. Its only possible effect, so far as we are concerned, must be to increase the inducements of Saxon emigrants, who may have become naturalized, or who may have been authorized by special legislative acts, to acquire & hold real property in the United-States, to lay out in land the money they bring with them, instead of investing it in any other mode. The incapacity of Aliens

to *take* lands by descent, & to *hold* them by devise & other modes of purchase, as established by the common law of England, which our ancestors brought with them from that country, is the creature of a barbarous age & of a narrow feudal policy, opposed to the liberal spirit of our republican institutions. Its modification, in the manner proposed by this clause of the 2d Article of the Convention, as to the power of devising lands, restricted as it is by the condition of selling, within a limited time, to a citizen or other person authorized by the local State laws to hold real property, it is presumed will hardly meet with any serious opposition. In fact it amounts to little more than adopting the doctrine of the courts of Equity, by which land, directed to be sold & converted into money, is considered as personal estate which may be devised to an alien independent of Special treaty-stipulations.

Whilst on this subject I may add that it is confidently believed that the advantages gained by the United States under these arrangements with the different German States, in the abolition of the taxes on emigration, are more than equivalent to the concessions made by us, in respect to the power of taking & holding lands in a limited manner. The tax imposed on the funds removed by emigrants who leave this Country, amounts, in Saxony & most of the German States, to ten *per centum* on the capital thus transferred. This amount is so much clear gain to us, in the capital thus brought into our country by the rich peasants, & others, who sell their real property here & emigrate in great numbers to the United States. Indeed we may be said to gain, both by what we get, & by what we give; since the additional capital, brought into our country by the abolition of the taxes on emigration in Germany, is a clear gain, whilst the limited faculty of taking & holding real property in the United-States operates as an inducement to persons of German origin to lay out their funds in that species of property.

Two other mere verbal discrepancies, between the proposed Convention & the others which have already been ratified, remain to be noticed.

In the 5th Article the words: "in the last resort", contained in the corresponding articles of the previous treaties, have been omitted as superfluous & obscuring the sense of the stipulation. This Article is merely affirmative of the general principle of international law applicable to the subject. If the controversies in question are to be determined "according to the laws, & by the judges, "of the country where the property is situated,"—it follows of course that they must be determined "in the last resort", if either party thinks fit to appeal to the court of the last resort.

In the 6th article the word "devised" has been inserted after the word "inherited", in order to make it correspond with the new clause in the 2d Article above mentioned.

The Full Powers

It appears that in this case the original full powers were exchanged. The full power of Henry Wheaton is described in the notes to Document 106, the convention with Hesse of March 26, 1844. That given to the Plenipotentiary of the King of Saxony is in the file. It is to be observed that it is dated more than eight years prior to the signature of the convention. It reads as follows (translation from the French):

We, Frederick Augustus, by the grace of God King of Saxony, etc., etc., etc., desiring to establish on a solid and mutually advantageous basis the relations which happily exist between Our Kingdom and the United States of America, by means of a treaty of friendship, and reposing entire confidence in the zeal, experience, and fidelity of Jean de Minckwitz, Our Minister of State, Brigadier General, and Envoy Extraordinary and Minister Plenipotentiary near the Royal Court of Prussia, etc., We have appointed him and by these presents do give unto him full power, commission, and special command to confer, negotiate, conclude, and sign, according to his instructions, with the plenipotentiary of the United States of America, such treaty, articles, or conventions judged to be necessary for the purpose indicated. Promising to accept, ratify, and cause faithfully to be executed that which Our said Plenipotentiary shall have stipulated, promised, and signed by virtue of such powers.

In faith whereof We have signed these presents and have caused to be affixed thereto the seal with Our arms.

Done at Dresden the seventeenth of December, one thousand eight hundred and thirty-six.

[Seal]   FREDERIC AUGUSTE

HENRI ANTOINE DE ZESCHAU.

THE EXCHANGE OF RATIFICATIONS

As signed, the convention, by Article 7, provided that the ratifications should be exchanged within twelve months from the date of signature, or by May 14, 1846. As the Senate resolution of advice and consent was not adopted until April 15, 1846, an extension of the time was necessary. The Senate amendment, which, strictly speaking, referred to the English text only, merely struck out the word "twelve" in Article 7 and inserted in lieu thereof the word "eighteen" (Executive Journal, VII, 64). The United States instrument of ratification, as appears from the duplicate thereof which is in the treaty file, was in customary form, including the text of the convention in both languages, followed by a recital of the Senate amendment; it reads in substance as follows (cf. the paragraphs of the United States ratification of the convention with Bavaria of January 21, 1845, printed in the notes to Document 111):

Whereas, a Convention for the mutual abolition of the droit d'aubaine, droit de détraction and taxes on emigration, between the United States of America and The Kingdom of Saxony, was concluded and signed at Berlin, by their respective Plenipotentiaries, on the fourteenth day of May, in the year of Our Lord one thousand eight hundred and forty-five, the original of which Convention being in the English and German languages, is hereunto annexed;

And whereas, the Senate of the United States, by their Resolution of the fifteenth day of April, 1846, two-thirds of the Senators then present, concurring, did advise and consent to the ratification of the said Convention, with the following amendment, to wit; "strike out from Article 7. the word 'twelve' and insert— "*eighteen* in lieu thereof":

Now, therefore, I, James K. Polk, President of the United States of America, having seen and considered the said Convention, do, in pursuance of the aforesaid advice and consent of the Senate, by these presents accept, ratify and confirm the same, as amended, and every clause and article thereof.

However, the confusion which arose from the instructions of April 25, 1846, regarding the exchange of ratifications of the convention with Bavaria of January 21, 1845, which is described in the notes to Document 111, caused also some difficulty in the exchange of ratifications of this convention. It appears that Andrew J. Donelson, Minister at Berlin, considered that in conformity with those instructions a change of wording should be made in the texts recited in the Saxon instrument of ratification; and after some delay an instrument of ratification by the King of Saxony was drawn up in which the texts recited contain respectively the words "achtzehn" and "eighteen" instead of "zwölf" and "twelve". Donelson wrote about the matter in his despatch of August 12, 1846, as follows (D.S., 4 Despatches, Prussia, No. 4):

It was not until to day that the exchange of the ratifications of the convention, between us & the Kingdom of Saxony, for the abolition of the droit d'aubaine

&c could be completed. The Plenipotentiary from Saxony, at this Court, the Count Charles Vitzthum, did not feel himself at liberty, without being specially authorised, to make the change in the text of the convention which seemed to be necessary by your № 71 [the instructions of April 25, 1846]: and then, after this authority was obtained, a new cause of delay grew out of the unwillingness of the Saxon Plenipotentiary to sign the protocol of the transaction without again consulting his Government, there being necessarily a disagreement in the copies, produced by the change of the word *eighteen* for the word *twelve*, Art 7, in the Saxon copy, which was not made in our copy. To remedy the inconvenience it was proposed that the Plenipotentiaries should make their protocol state the facts of the case, but to this, although no objection occurred to the Count, he would not assent without receiving the instructions of his Government. Hence the delay which has occurred.

The protocol of this transaction, certifying the exchange in pursuance of the full powers of the respective Plenipotentiaries, is herewith enclosed.

The *procès-verbal* of the exchange of ratifications, which contains a record of the difficulty, reads as follows (translation from the French):

The undersigned, A. J. Donelson, Envoy Extraordinary and Minister Plenipotentiary of the United States of America near His Majesty the King of Prussia, and Charles Count Vitzthum de Eckstaedt, Chargé d'Affaires of His Majesty the King of Saxony near the Government of Prussia, having been charged by their respective Governments to exchange the ratifications of the treaty concluded between the United States of America and Saxony, dated Berlin, May 14, 1845, for the mutual abolition of the *droits d'aubaine et de détraction*, met this day for that purpose at the residence of the said Envoy of the United States.

After having communicated to each other their full powers, found in good and due form, they had first to establish the fact that the Government of the United States not having been able to keep strictly within the term of twelve months fixed in Article 7 of this treaty for the exchange of the ratifications, a conference had been previously held on this subject, in which it was agreed to change this original term of twelve months to eighteen months.

On then comparing the two acts these have been found entirely conformable with the stipulations agreed on, and no other remark has been found necessary, except that, whilst the prolongation of the term above mentioned, fixed for the exchange of the ratifications, has been effected in the Saxon document, by the substitution of the word *"eighteen"* for *"twelve"*, it is mentioned by the Government of the United States in the act of its ratification.

Whereupon the undersigned Plenipotentiaries proceeded to the exchange of the said acts of ratification.

In faith whereof the present *procès-verbal* has been drawn up, signed, and completed in duplicate.

Berlin this 12th day of August, 1846.

[Seal] A J DONELSON
[Seal] CHARLES COMTE VITZTHUM DE ECKSTÄDT.

The original proclamation follows the form of that of the convention with Bavaria of January 21, 1845, which is printed in the notes to Document 111, and makes no mention whatever of the Senate amendment. In the English text of the original convention therein included a pencil line has been drawn around the word "twelve" in Article 7, and the word "eighteen" written above it. The printed English text of the convention has always read "eighteen" and not "twelve"; but the German text in 9 Statutes at Large 832, reads "zwölf".

The Kingdom of Saxony

At the time of this convention the Kingdom of Saxony was a member of the Germanic Confederation (1815–66). A summary account of that Confederation, with a list of the members thereof, is in the notes to Document 59, the convention with the Hanseatic Republics of December 20, 1827. The Kingdom of Saxony was also party to the German Zollverein or Customs Union, as to which, also, see the notes to Document 59.

The Kingdom of Saxony was within the North German Confederation of 1867, which followed the war of 1866 between Austria and Prussia, participated in by various other German states on one side or the other, among which was Saxony, on the side of Austria; and the Kingdom of Saxony became one of the States of the German Empire from 1871.

Treaty Series No. 19
8 Statutes at Large, 606–13
18 *ibid.*, pt. 2, Public Treaties, 48–52

116

BELGIUM : NOVEMBER 10, 1845

Treaty of Commerce and Navigation, signed at Brussels November 10, 1845. Original in English and French.
Submitted to the Senate February 3, 1846. Resolution of advice and consent March 26, 1846. Ratified by the United States March 30, 1846. Ratified by Belgium January 17, 1846. Ratifications exchanged at Washington March 30, 1846. Proclaimed March 31, 1846.

Treaty of Commerce and Navigation between the United States of America and His Majesty the King of the Belgians.

The United States of America, on the one part, and His Majesty the King of the Belgians on the other part, wishing to regulate in a formal manner, their reciprocal relations of commerce and navigation, and further to strengthen through the developement of their interests respectively, the bonds of friendship and good understanding, so happily established between the Governments and People of the two countries; and desiring, with this view, to conclude, by common agreement, a treaty establishing conditions equally advantageous to the commerce and navigation of both states, have, to that effect, appointed as their Plenipotentiaries, namely: The President of the United States Thomas G. Clemson, Chargé d'affaires of the

Traité de Commerce et de Navigation entre Sa Majesté le Roi des Belges et Les Etats-Unis d'Amérique.

Sa Majesté le Roi des Belges d'une part, et les Etats Unis d'amérique d'autre part, voulant régler d'une manière formelle les relations réciproques de commerce et de navigation, et fortifier de plus en plus, par le développement des intérêts respectifs, les liens d'amitié et de bonne intelligence si heureusement établis entre les deux gouvernements et les deux peuples; désirant, dans ce but, arrêter, de commun accord, un traité stipulant des conditions également avantageuses au commerce et à la navigation des deux Etats, ont, à cet effet, nommé pour leurs Plénipotentiaires, savoir: Sa Majesté le Roi des Belges, le Sieur Adolphe Dechamps, officier de l'ordre de Léopold, chevalier de l'órdre de l'aigle rouge de 1ʳᵉ classe, Grand'

United States of America to His Majesty the King of the Belgians—And His Majesty the King of the Belgians, M. Adolphe Dechamps, officer of the order of Leopold., Knight of the order of the red Eagle of the first class, Grand Cross of the order of St Michel of Bavaria, His Minister for Foreign Affairs, a member of the Chamber of Representants, Who, after having communicated to each other their full powers, ascertained to be in good and proper form, have agreed and concluded the following articles.

croix de l'ordre de St Michel de Bavière, Ministre des Affaires Etrangères, membre de la chambre des Représentants, et Son Excellence le Président des Etats-Unis, le Sieur Thomas G. Clemson Chargé d'affaires des Etats-Unis d'amérique près Sa Majesté le Roi des Belges, lesquels après s'être communiqué leurs pleins pouvoirs, trouvés en bonne et due forme, ont arrêté et conclu les articles suivants:

ARTICLE 1

There shall be full and entire freedom of commerce and navigation, between the inhabitants of the two countries; and the same security and protection, which is enjoyed by the citizens or subjects of each country, shall be guarantied on both sides. The said inhabitants, whether established or temporarily residing within any ports, cities or places whatever, of the two countries, shall not, on account of their commerce or industry, pay any other or higher duties, taxes, or imposts, than those which shall be levied on citizens or subjects of the country, in which they may be; and the privileges, immunities and other favours, with regard to commerce or industry, enjoyed by the citizens or subjects of one of the two states, shall be common to those of the other.

ARTICLE 1er

Il y aura pleine et entière liberté de commerce et de navigation entre les habitans des deux pays, et la même sécurité et protection dont jouissent les nationaux, seront garanties des deux parts. Ces habitans ne paieront point, à raison de leur commerce ou de leur industrie, dans les ports, villes, ou lieux quelconques des deux Etats, soit qu'ils s'y établissent, soit qu'ils y résident temporairement, des droits, taxes ou impôts autres ou plus élévés que ceux qui se percevront sur les nationaux; et les privilèges, immunités et autres faveurs dont jouissent en matière de commerce ou d'industrie, les citoyens ou sujets de l'un des deux Etats, seront communs à ceux de l'autre.

ARTICLE II

Belgian vessels, whether coming from a Belgian or a foreign port, shall not pay, either on entering or leaving the ports of the United states, whatever may be their destination, any other or higher duties of tonnage, pilotage, anchorage, buoys, light-houses, clearance, brokerage, or generally other charges whatsoever, than are required from vessels of the United States in similar cases. This provision extends, not only to duties levied for the benefit of the State, but also to those levied for the benefit of provincies, cities, countries, districts, townships, corporations, or any other divisions or jurisdiction, whatever may be its designation.

ARTICLE III.

Reciprocally, vessels of the United States, whether coming from a port of said states, or from a foreign port, shall not pay, either on entering or leaving the ports of Belgium, whatever may be their destination, any other or higher duties of tonnage, pilotage, anchorage, buoys, light-houses, clearance, brokerage, or generally, other charges whatever, than are required from Belgian vessels, in similar cases. This provision extends not only to duties levied for the benefit of the state, but also to those levied for the benefit of provinces, cities, countries, dis-

ARTICLE II.

Les navires Belges venant d'un port Belge ou d'un port étranger, ne paieront point à leur entrée dans les ports des Etats-Unis, ou à leur sortie, quelle que soit leur destination, d'autres ni ,de plus forts droits de tonnage, de pilotage, d'ancrage, de balisage, de feux et de fanaux, d'expédition et de courtage, ni généralement d'autres charges que celles exigées des bâtimens de l'Union dans les mêmes cas. Ce qui précéde s'entend, non seulement des droits perçus au profit de l'Etat, mais encore de tous droits perçus au profit des provinces, villes, arrondissemens, communes, juridictions, corporations &ᵃ, sous quelque terme qu'elles puissent être désignées.

ARTICLE 3.

Réciproquement, les navires des Etats-Unis, venant d'un port national ou d'un port étranger, ne paieront point, à leur entrée dans les ports de Belgique ou à leur sortie, quelle que soit leur destination, d'autres ni de plus forts droits de tonnage, de pilotage, d'ancrage, de balisage, de feux et de fanaux, d'expédition et de courtage, ni généralement d'autres charges, que celles exigées des batimens Belges dans les mêmes cas. ce qui précède s'entend non seulement des droits perçus au profit de l'état, mais encore de tous droits perçus au profit des

tricts, townships, corporations, or any other division or jurisdiction, whatever be its designation.

provinces, villes, arrondissements, communes, juridictions, corporations &ª, sous quelque terme qu'elles puissent être désignés.

Article IV

The restitution by Belgium, of the duty levied by the Governement of the Netherlands, on the navigation of the scheldt, in virtue of the third paragraph, of the ninth article, of the Treaty of April nineteenth, eighteen hundred and thirty nine, is guarantied to the vessels of the United States.[1]

Article 4.

Le remboursement par la Belgique du droit perçu sur la navigation de l'escaut par le gouvernement des Pays-Bas, en vertu du paragraphe troisième de l'article neuf du traité du dix neuf avril mil huit cent trente neuf, est garanti aux navires des Etats Unis.[1]

Article V.

Steam vessels of the united states and of Belgium, engaged in regular navigation, between the United States and Belgium, shall be exempt in both countries, from the payment of duties of tonnage, anchorage, buoys, and lighthouses.

Article 5.

Les bateaux à vapeur Belges et des Etats Unis faisant un service régulier de navigation, entre la Belgique et les Etats Unis, seront exemptés dans l'un et l'autre pays, du paiement des droits de tonnage, d'ancrage, de balisage, de feux et de fanaux.

Article VI.

As regards the coasting trade, between the ports of either country, the vessels of the two nations shall be treated on both sides, on the same footing with the vessels of the most favoured nation.

Article 6.

En ce qui concerne l'exercice du cabotage, (commerce de port à port) les navires des deux nations seront traités, de part et d'autre, sur le même pied que les navires des nations les plus favorisées.

Article VII.

Articles of every description, whether proceeding from the soil,

Article 7.

Les objets de toute nature provenant, soit du sol, soit de

---

[1] See the note regarding Article 4.

industry or warehouses of Belgium, directly imported therefrom, into the ports of the United-States, in Belgian vessels, shall pay no other or higher duties of import, than if they were imported under the flag of said States.

And, reciprocally, articles of every description directly imported into Belgium from the united states, under the flag of the said states, shall pay no other or higher duties, than if they were imported under the Belgian flag.

It is well understood:

1º, that the goods shall have been really put on board, in the ports from which they are declared respectively to come.

2º, that a putting-in at an intermediate port, produced by uncontrollable circumstances, duly proved, does not occasion the forfeiture of the advantage allowed to direct importation.

Article VIII.

Articles of every description, imported into the United States, from other countries than Belgium, under the Belgian flag, shall pay no other, or higher duties whatsoever, than if they had been imported under the flag of the most favoured foreign nation, other than the flag of the country from which the importation is made. And reciprocally, articles of every description, imported

l'industrie, soit des entrepôts de Belgique, importés en droiture de Belgique par navires Belges, dans les ports des Etats Unis d'amérique, ne paieront d'autres ni de plus forts droits d'entrée que s'ils étaient importés en droiture, sous le pavillon des dits Etats.

Et réciproquement, les objets de toute nature importés en droiture en Belgique des Etats Unis d'amérique, sous pavillon de ces Etats, n'acquitteront d'autres ni de plus forts droits que s'ils étaient importés en droiture sous pavillon Belge.

Il est bien entendu:

1º que les marchandises devront avoir été reéllement chargées dans les ports d'où elles auront été déclarées respectivement provenir.

2º que la relâche forcée dans les ports intermédiaires pour des causes de force majeure dûment justifiée, ne fait pas perdre le bénéfice de l'importation en droiture.

Article 8.

Les objets de toute nature importés aux Etats Unis d'ailleurs que de Belgique, sous pavillon Belge, ne paieront d'autres ni de plus forts droits quelconques que si l'importation était effectuée sous le pavillon de la nation étrangère la plus favorisée, autre que le pavillon du pays même d'où l'importation a lieu. Et réciproquement, les objets de toute nature, importés sous pavil-

under the flag of the United States into Belgium from other countries than the United States, shall pay no other or higher duties whatsoever, than if they had been imported under the flag of the foreign nation most favoured, other than that of the country from which the importation is made.

ARTICLE IX.

Articles of every description, exported by Belgian vessels, or by those of the United States of America, from the ports of either country, to any country whatsoever, shall be subjected to no other duties or formalities, than such as are required for exportation, under the flag of the country where the shipment is made.

ARTICLE X.

All premiums, drawbacks, or other favours of like nature, which may be allowed in the states of either of the contracting parties, upon goods imported or exported in national vessels, shall be likewise, and in the same manner, allowed upon goods imported directly from one of the two countries, by its vessels, into the other, or exported from one of the two countries by the vessels of the other to any destination whatsoever.

ARTICLE XI.

The preceding article is, however, not to apply to the importation of salt, and of the produce of

lon des Etats Unis en Belgique, d'ailleurs que des Etats Unis, ne paieront d'autres ni de plus forts droits quelconques que si l'importation était effectuée sous le pavillon de la nation étrangère la plus favorisée, autre que celui du pays même d'ou l'importation a lieu.

ARTICLE 9.

Les objets de toute nature quelconque exportés par navires Belges ou par ceux des Etats-Unis d'amérique des ports de l'un ou de l'autre de ces Etats vers quelque pays que ce soit, ne seront assujettis à des droits ou à des formalités autres que ceux exigés pour l'exportation par pavillon national.

ARTICLE 10.

Les primes, restitutions ou autres faveurs de cette nature qui pourraient être accordées dans les Etats des deux parties contractantes, sur des marchandises importées ou exportées par des navires nationaux, seront aussi et de la même manière accordées aux marchandises importées directement de l'un des deux pays sur ses navires dans l'autre, ou exportées de l'un des deux pays, par les navires de l'autre, vers quelque destination que ce soit.

ARTICLE 11.

Il est néanmoins derogé aux dispositions qui précèdent pour l'importation du sel et des pro-

the national fisheries; each of the two parties reserving to itself, the faculty of granting special privileges, for the importation of those articles, under its own flag.

Article XII.

The high contracting parties agree to consider and to treat as Belgian vessels, and as vessels of the United States, all those which being provided by the competent authority with a passport, Sea Letter, or any other sufficient document, shall be recognised conformably with existing laws, as national vessels in the country to which they respectively belong.

Article XIII.

Belgian vessels and those of United States may, conformably with the Laws of the two countries, retain on board, in the ports of both, such parts of their cargoes as may be destined for a foreign country; and such parts shall not be subjected, either while they remain on board, or upon reexportation, to any charges whatsoever, other than those for the prevention of smuggling.

Article XIV.

During the period allowed by the laws of the two countries respectively for the warehousing of goods, no duties, other than those of watch and storeage, shall be levied upon articles brought from

duits de la pêche nationale, les deux pays se reservant la faculté d'accorder aux importations de ces articles par pavillon national des privilèges spéciaux.

Article 12.

Les hautes parties contractantes conviennent de considérer et de traiter comme navires Belges et comme navires des Etats Unis, tous ceux qui étant pourvus par l'autorité compétente d'un passeport, d'une lettre de mer ou de tout autre document suffisant, seront, d'après les lois existantes, reconnus comme nationaux dans le pays auquel ils appartiennent respectivement.

Article 13.

Les navires Belges et ceux des Etats-Unis, pourront, conformement aux lois des deux pays, conserver à leur bord dans les ports de l'un et de l'autre Etat, les parties de cargaison qui seraient destinées pour un pays étranger, et ces parties, pendant leur séjour à bord, ou lors de leur réexportation, ne seront astreintes à aucuns droits quelconques autres que ceux de surveillance.

Article 14.

Pendant le temps fixé par les lois des deux pays respectivement pour l'entreposage des marchandises, il ne sera perçu aucuns droits autres que ceux de garde et d'emmagasinage sur les objets

either country, into the other, while awaiting transit, re-exportation, or entry for consumption. Such goods shall in no case be subject to higher warehouse charges, or to other formalities, than if they had been imported under the flag of the country.

Article XV.

In all that relates to duties of customs and navigation, the two high contracting parties promise, reciprocally, not to grant any favour, privilege, or immunity to any other state, which shall not instantly become common to the citizens and subjects of both parties, respectively: gratuitously, if the concession or favour to such other state is gratuitous, and on allowing the same compensation or its equivalent, if the concession is conditional.

Neither of the contracting parties shall lay upon goods proceeding from the soil or the industry of the other party which may be imported into its ports, any other or higher duties of importation or reexportation than are laid upon the importation and re-éxportation of similar goods coming from any other foreign country.

importés de l'un des pays dans l'autre en attendant leur transit, leur réexportation ou leur mise en consommation. ces objets, dans aucun cas, ne paieront de plus forts droits d'entrepôt et ne seront assujettis à d'autres formalités que s'ils avaient été importés par pavillon national.

Article 15.

En tout ce qui concerne les droits de douane et de navigation, les deux hautes parties contractantes se promettent reciproquement de n'accorder aucune faveur, privilège ou immunité à un autre Etat, qui ne soit aussi, et à l'instant, étendu à leurs sujets ou citoyens respectifs, gratuitement si la concession en faveur de l'autre Etat est gratuite, et en donnant la même compensation ou l'équivalent si la concession est conditionnelle.

Ni l'une ni l'autre des parties contractantes n'imposera sur les marchandises provenant du sol ou de l'industrie de l'autre partie, qui seront importées dans ses ports, d'autres ni de plus forts droits d'importation ou de réexportation, que ceux qui seront imposés sur l'importation ou la réexportation de marchandises similaires provenant de tout autre pays étranger.

ARTICLE XVI.

In cases of shipwreck, damages at Sea, or forced putting-in, each party shall afford to the vessels of the other, whether belonging to the state or to individuals, the same assistance and protection, and the same immunities, which would have been granted to its own vessels in similar cases.

ARTICLE XVII.

It is moreover agreed between the two contracting parties, that the consuls and Vice consuls of the United States in the ports of Belgium, and, reciprocally, the consuls and Vice-Consuls of Belgium in te ports of the United States shall continue to enjoy all the priveleges, protection and assistance, usually granted to them and which may be necessary for the proper discharge of their functions. The said consuls and Vice Consuls may cause to be arrested and sent back, either to their vessels or to their country, such seamen as may have deserted from the vessels of their nation. To this end, they shall apply in writing to the competent, local authorities, and they shall prove, by exhibition of the vessels crew list, or other document, or, if she shall have departed, by copy of Said documents, duly certified by them, that the seamen whom they claim formed part of the said crew. Upon such demand, thus supported, the delivery of the

ARTICLE 16.

En cas de naufrage, de dommage en mer ou de relâche forcée, chaque partie accordera aux navires, soit de l'Etat ou des particuliers de l'autre pays, la même assistance et protection et les mêmes immunités que celles qui seraient accordées à ses propres navires dans les mêmes cas.

ARTICLE 17

Il est en outre convenu entre les deux parties contractantes que les consuls et Vice-Consuls des Etats-Unis dans les ports de Belgique, et reciproquement les consuls et vice-consuls de Belgique dans les ports des Etats-unis, continueront à jouir de tous les priviléges et de toute la protection et assistance, qui leur sont ordinairement accordés et qui peuvent être nécessaires pour remplir convenablement leurs fonctions. Les dits consuls et vice-consuls pourront faire arrêter et renvoyer soit à bord, soit dans leur pays, les marins qui auraient déserté des batiments de leur nation. À cet effet, ils s'adresseront par écrit aux autorités locales compétentes et justifieront par l'exhibition du rôle d'équipage ou des registres du batiment, ou si le batiment était parti, par copie des dites pièces, dûment certifiée par eux, que les hommes qu'ils réclament faisaient partie du dit équipage. Sur cette demande ainsi justifiée,

deserters shall not be refused. They shall moreover, receive all aid and assistance, in searching for, seizing and arresting such deserters, who shall, upon the requisition and at the expense of the consul or Vice-Consul, be confined and Kept in the prisons of the country until he shall have found an opportunity for sending them home. If, however, such an opportunity should not occur within three months after the arrest, the deserters shall be set at liberty and shall not again be arrested for the same cause. It is, however, understood, that seamen of the country in which the desertion shall occur are excepted from these provisions, unless they be naturalized citizens or subjects of the other country.

la remise ne pourra leur être refusée. Il leur sera donné, de plus, toute aide et assistance, pour la recherche, saisie et arrestation des dits déserteurs, qui seront même détenus et gardés dans les prisons du pays à la réquisition et aux frais du consul ou vice-consuls jusqu'à ce qu'il ait trouvé une occasion de les renvoyer chez eux. Si pourtant cette occasion ne se présentait pas dans un délai de trois mois, à compter du jour de l'arrestation, les déserteurs seront mis en liberté et ne pourront plus être arrêtés pour la même cause. Il est entendu néanmoins que les marins du pays où la désertion aura lieu sont exceptés de la présente disposition à moins qu'ils ne soient naturalisés sujets ou citoyens de l'autre pays.

Article XVIII.

Articles of all Kinds the transit of which is allowed in Belgium, coming from or going to the United states, shall be exempt from all transit duty in Belgium, when the transportation through the Belgian territory is effected on the rail-roads of the state.

Article 18.

Les objets de toute nature dont le transit est permis en Belgique, venant des Etats-Unis ou expédiés vers ce pays, seront exempts de tout droit de transit en Belgique lorsque le transport sur le territoire Belge se fera par les chemins de fer de l'Etat.

Article XIX

The present treaty shall be in force during ten years from the date of the exchange of the ratifications, and until the expiration of twelve months after either of the high contracting parties shall have announced to the other its

Article 19.

Le présent traité sera en vigueur pendant dix ans, à dater du jour de l'échange des ratifications, et au delà de ce terme, jusqu'à l'expiration de douze mois, après que l'une des hautes parties contractantes aura an-

intention to terminate the operation thereof; each party reserving to itself the right of making such declaration to the other, at the end of ten years above mentioned; and it is agreed, that after the expiration of the twelve months of prolongation accorded on on both sides, this treaty and all its stipulations shall cease to be in force.

ce son intention d'en faire cesser les effets; chacune d'elles se reservant le droit de faire à l'autre une telle déclaration à l'expiration des dix ans susmentionnés, et il est convenu qu'après les douze mois de prolongation, accordés de part et d'autre, ce traité et toutes les stipulations qu'il renferme cesseront d'être obligatoires.

ARTICLE XX.

This treaty shall be ratified and the ratifications shall be exchanged at Washington within the term of six months after its date, or sooner if possible; and the treaty shall be put in execution, within the term of twelve months.

In faith whereof, the respective Plenipotentiaries have signed the present treaty, in duplicate, and have affixed thereto their seals, Brussels the tenth of November eighteen hundred & forty five.

[Seal] THOS. G. CLEMSON
[Seal] DECHAMPS

ARTICLE 20.

Ce traité sera ratifié et les ratifications seront échangées à Washington dans le terme de six mois après sa date, ou plustôt si faire se peut, et le traité sera mis à exécution dans le terme de douze mois.

En foi de quoi les Plénipotentiaires respectifs ont signé le présent traité par duplicata et y ont apposé leur Sceau, a Bruxelles le dix Novembre mille huit cent quarante cinq.

[Seal] DECHAMPS
[Seal] THOS. G. CLEMSON

NOTES

This treaty was signed in duplicate; there is one original in the file, in which the English text is written in the left columns. As the printed texts show, the *alternat* was duly observed.

The other papers in the file are in customary form. They include the attested Senate resolution of March 26, 1846 (Executive Journal, VII, 57), the duplicate United States instrument of ratification of March 30, and the original proclamation dated the following day.

There is also in the file (received from the Belgian archives) a certified facsimile of the certificate or act of the exchange of ratifications at Washington on March 30, 1846, drawn up in English. The date of the exchange is also mentioned in the proclamation.

The Belgian instrument of ratification, engrossed on vellum, with illuminated letters, is a beautiful example of calligraphy; it is dated January 17, 1846, and includes both texts of the treaty, the French in the left columns.

The Full Powers

The full power given to Thomas G. Clemson, "Chargé d'Affaires of the United States at the Court of His Majesty the King of Belgium", was under date of September 15, 1845, and in customary form (D.S., 3 Credences, 147). In this case the original full powers were exchanged. That given to the Belgian Plenipotentiary, Adolphe Dechamps, Minister for Foreign Affairs of Belgium, is under date of November 3, 1845, and was enclosed with the despatch of Clemson of November 29, 1845 (D.S., 3 Despatches, Belgium, No. 18). It reads as follows (translation from the French):

We, Leopold, King of the Belgians, desiring to draw up in concert with His Excellency the President of the Republic of the United States of America a treaty of commerce and navigation, and reposing entire confidence in the capacity, the zeal, and the devotion to Our Person of Mr. Adolphe Dechamps, Minister of Foreign Affairs, officer of Our order, decorated with the Order of the Red Eagle, First Class, Grand Cross of the Order of St. Michael of Bavaria, Member of the Chamber of Representatives, We have appointed, commissioned, and deputed him, and we do by these presents, signed by Our hand, appoint, commission, and depute him, Our Plenipotentiary for the purpose of entering into *pourparlers* with him or those who shall be authorized thereunto on the part of His Excellency the President of the Republic of the United States of America, to conclude and sign, after the exchange of the full powers in good and due form, a treaty adapted to attain the end proposed. We give to him full and absolute power to negotiate, draw up, and sign the provisions of the said convention; We promise, on the faith and word of a King, to accept, to hold firm and stable forever, to accomplish, and to execute exactly all that Our said Plenipotentiary shall have stipulated, promised, and signed by virtue of the present full powers, without ever intervening therein for any reason and under any possible pretext, and also to cause to be issued Our letters of ratification thereof in good form and to cause them to be delivered for the purpose of being exchanged within the period which shall be agreed upon. In faith whereof We have ordered that the seal of the State be apposed to these presents.

Done at St. Cloud the third day of the month of November, one thousand eight hundred and forty-five.

LEOPOLD

By the King:
    The Minister of Foreign Affairs,
        DECHAMPS

Two other original full powers are in this treaty file; one is that given to Secretary of State Edward Livingston under date of July 13, 1832, pursuant whereto he negotiated and signed the treaty of January 23, 1833 (which did not go into force); the other is a full power given to Secretary of State Buchanan under date of March 30, 1846, to exchange the ratifications of this treaty. It is not now the practice of the Department of State to issue a full power to the Secretary of State to exchange the ratifications of a treaty. Authority to make such an exchange is deemed to be inherent in the office. Indeed, ratifications of a bilateral treaty are now frequently exchanged without full powers on either side.

The Negotiations

This was the first treaty between the United States and Belgium to go into force; but two treaties between the two countries had previously been signed at Washington, one on January 23, 1833, and one on March 29, 1840; each of those treaties received the advice and consent of the Senate of the United States (Executive Journal, IV, 310; V, 324); President Jackson signed a ratification of the earlier treaty on February 15, 1833, and President Van Buren of the other on January 26, 1841; but neither of those treaties went into force; the Belgian Government was unwilling to ratify the treaty of 1833; and the treaty of 1840 failed to receive the approval of the Belgian Chambers. Apparently the treaty of 1833 was not printed on its submission to the Senate (Executive Journal, IV, 302). The text of the treaty of 1840, English and French, is in Senate Confidential Document A, 26th Congress, 2d session (Regular Confidential Documents, XI, 379–86).

Thomas G. Clemson was appointed Chargé d'Affaires at Brussels on June 17, 1844 (D.S., 3 Credences, 87); the subject of a treaty with the United States was brought forward by the Belgian Minister of Foreign Affairs very soon after the arrival of Clemson at Brussels on October 4 (D.S., 3 Despatches, Belgium, No. 1, October 17, 1844).

The recorded instructions to Clemson contain nothing regarding a treaty, and he had no full power; but in accord with his private instructions he requested that a draft be prepared of a treaty satisfactory to the Belgian Government, which he might forward to Washington. The Belgian project was later communicated, and in the despatch of Clemson transmitting the draft to Secretary of State Buchanan this was written (*ibid.*, No. 10, March 13, 1845):

> Soon after my arrival in Belgium, and in pursuance of private instructions, I requested General Goblet, Minister of Foreign affairs, to prepare such a treaty as it would please the Belgian Government to ratify, with the United States, and that, so soon as received, I would forward it to the Department of State, for the consideration of my Government. I now have the honour of transmitting it to you, hoping that if it should not meet with your entire approbation, you will give me such instructions, for modification, as your judgment may dictate.
>
> The assimilation of our flag with that of Belgium, was an act intended by the Belgian Government as a means of treating, and the difficulties which prevented the ratification of the treaty of 1840, by the Belgian Chambers, arose from the fact, that the "*Loi des droits differentiels*" was at that time being discussed, and not enacted, as has since been the case, so greatly to our advantage.
>
> The document which I send you will strike you as being very similar to the treaty of 1840. There are, however, some changes, which you will remark in reading, or comparing it with that. You will find these changes noted in red ink, in the margin of the copy transmitted. The accompanying note of Genl. Goblet alludes to, & explains the same. The treaty here offered is, in words, one of reciprocity, but in execution, it will be far otherwise, and evidently the advantages will be in favour of the U. States. Our Commerce with Belgium being so much greater, than hers with us, as to place the advantages entirely on our Side. It is hardly necessary for me to dwell upon its merits, in this respect, for they are abundantly manifest.

The note of the Belgian Minister of Foreign Affairs (dated March 30, 1845), a copy and translation of which are with the despatch

mentioned, contains the following explanation of the additions made in the draft to the provisions of the treaty signed on March 29, 1840:

Agreeably to your request I hasten to send you herewith the *avant projet* (first draft) of a treaty between Belgium and the United States which I have caused to be drawn up.

As you will observe, Sir, this *projet* is nearly a literal copy of the treaty of March 29, 1840, rendered complete by some provisions particularly favorable to the navigation of the United States.

These are:

1. Assurance of reimbursement of tolls paid on the Escaut (Scheldt) by American vessels in general [Article 4].

2. The reciprocal abolition of the principal duties of navigation in favor of steam vessels employed in the regular service of navigation between the two countries [Article 5].

3. Exemption from transit duties on articles transported on the railway either from or to the United States, as stipulated in favor of the Zollverein by the treaty of September 1 [Article 18; the text, in French, of the Treaty of Commerce and Navigation between Belgium and the Zollverein of September 1, 1844, is in British and Foreign State Papers, XXXIII, 742–51].

4. Mutual assurance of being treated on the footing of the most favored nation as concerns indirect and coasting trade (*cabotage*) [Articles 8 and 6].

5. The extension of the period of duration of the treaty to ten years [Article 19].

That Belgian draft, in French, is almost literally the same as the French text of the articles of the treaty as signed; the only real difference is the substitution of Washington for Brussels as the place of exchange of ratifications. Under date of September 17, 1845, Secretary of State Buchanan wrote regarding the draft and the negotiation as follows (D.S., 1 Instructions, Belgium, 57–59):

I have the honor to acknowledge the receipt of your despatch, N° 10., of the 13th of March, which reached this Department on the 9th of May. The projêt of a Treaty of Commerce and Navigation, between the United States and Belgium, which accompanied your despatch, has been submitted to the President. With a very few alterations,—and these only to render the sense more explicit,—it is entirely satisfactory to him; and I now transmit, by his direction, a full power, to negotiate and conclude a Convention accordingly. Upon comparing the draft, herewith transmitted with the Projêt, it will be seen what the alterations referred to are. The projêt would have been returned to you sooner; but it was known that the Belgian Chambers would not be in session, and that, therefore, the delay could not retard the final conclusion of the Treaty.

It is unnecessary to refer you to the history of our past negotiations with the Belgian Government, and their unfortunate termination. The two Treaties heretofore proposed by Belgium, and rejected by her Chambers, after they had been ratified by the Senate of the United States, have taught this Government, that they ought not to enter upon a third negotiation without a moral certainty that we shall not again be disappointed. The assurances which you have received, and communicated from the Belgian Government, and especially that from Mr Northomb, leave no room for reasonable doubt upon this subject. Still the recent change of Ministry may have produced a change of policy in regard to the Treaty; and if such should prove to be the case, then a third abortive attempt ought not to be made. Such a result could not fail to excite unfriendly feelings on the part of this Government towards that of Belgium. The passage of the law "des droits differentials" seems to render it highly probable that the Chambers would sanction the Treaty.

It is deemed indispensable, however, that the Treaty, which you may conclude, shall receive the sanction of the whole Treaty-making power of Belgium, before it can be submitted to the Senate of the United States; and that the ratifications of it shall be exchanged at Washington, and not Brussels.

The desire of this Government that the treaty should, before its submission to the Senate, "receive the sanction of the whole Treaty-making power of Belgium", was met. In his despatch of October 30, 1845, acknowledging receipt of the instructions of September 17, Clemson wrote as follows (D.S., 3 Despatches, Belgium, No. 16):

On the 24ᵗʰ I saw Mʳ Deschamps Minister of foreign affairs, and informed him of the receipt of my Despatches, at which he was much gratified.

I asked him, very formally, if with the change of Ministry there had been any change of policy, with regard to the pending negotiations between the United States & Belgium, to which he responded that there had been none; He had made part of the former Ministry, and still retained the same views. He also stated that he was one of those that opposed the last treaty with the United States, because the law called "Le Loi des droits differentiels" was under discussion, and not finished, but that now, that law being in vigour things were entirely changed. It is impossible to receive more positive assurances than I have done, from the Minister of Foreign affairs upon the certainty of the ratification of the treaty, and so far as I am able to judge, not only from the expression of the Ministers, but from collateral evidence I feel morally certain, (without something unforeseen should occur,) that the treaty will be ratified at an early period during the coming session of the chambers.

I have dwelt on several occasions most formally upon the evil consequences that would grow out of a failure on the part of Belgium to ratify this the third attempt, but up to this moment I do not feel the least apprehension on the subject. The King will put his signiature to it before its presentation to the chambers which will be an additional guarantee. Monsieur Beaulieu, the new Belgian Minister resident to the United States, who is to replace Mons. Serruys their former Chargé d'Affaires arrived in Brussels from Lisbon on the 23ᵈ inst. At the request of the Minister of Foreign Affairs he immediately called to see me, and it was then the intention of this Government that he should leave for the United States in the steamer which leaves Liverpool on the 4ᵗʰ of November. In the mean time my Despatches arrived, and the orders to Mʳ Beaulieu were countermanded. He will now remain in Brussels until the treaty has received the benefit of the entire treaty making power of Belgium when he will leave for Washington. In Mr. Beaulieu the United States will receive a Minister of higher rank & with him the finished document so far as Belgium is concerned. It would be difficult to have stronger guarantees or a higher compliment to the United States under the circumstances.

Mr. Deschamps informed me that he would present the treaty to the Chambers at the earliest moment, and he thinks it will be passed by the middle of December. It will also make one of the leading paragraphs in the discourse from the throne at the opening of the Chambers, and I am requested to say on the part of the Minister of Foreign Affairs that a "phrase de sympathie" if introduced by the President in his coming message noticing the good understanding and friendly relations that exist between the United States, and Belgium would be kindly received by this Government.

As far as I can bear evidence from experience of all those in authority, this Government could not entertain more friendly feelings for the United States than those which have at all times been manifested, and which I have always been careful to reciprocate on the part of the United States.

On the 25ᵗʰ Mʳ Deschamps and myself read over the treaty together, when he made & agreed to the alterations which were introduced into the copy you forwarded me from Washington.

The King is now in Paris. As soon as he returns, which will be shortly, we shall be in readiness, and it will be signed. I will here remark that among other things Mr Deschamps stated that he thought the treaty would not have ten voices against it.

The "loi sur les droits différentiels", which is mentioned in the foregoing despatch, was the Belgian law of July 21, 1844. Its text, with various decrees thereunder of the same date, is in Pasinomie Belge, 1844, 3d series, XIV, 109–41. One of those decrees (*ibid.,*

138–39) contained provisions in favor of vessels of the United States not dissimilar to those of Articles 3, 4, and 7 of this treaty.

The despatch transmitting this treaty was dated November 14, 1845. The portions of that despatch which deal with the treaty are as follows (D.S., 3 Despatches, Belgium, No. 17):

Herewith you will recieve the Treaty of Commerce and Navigation, as concluded between the United States, and the King of the Belgians

. . . .

A preamble was necessary to the treaty of Commerce & Navigation; We took that of the treaty of 1840, it was apposite and had already received the approbation of the authorities of the United States.

As you will remark, it was signed on the 10ᵗʰ inst. By refering to the discourse of the King, made at the opening of the Chambers on the 11ᵗʰ, (a copy of which accompanies this Despatch,) you will perceive what consideration is there given to this measure. I need scarce dwell upon the importance of this convention, and particularly the eighth article. I see behind it an almost entire abolishment of the "Droits differentiels", in favour of the United States. All Germany, with its forty millions of inhabitants, will feel its influence, Antwerp being virtually a port of the Zoll Verein. An increased trade in favour of the United States, partly at the expense of the Hanse towns, will be another consequence, and, if I do not much mistake, it will precipitate the action of the Zollverein to enact higher duties on particular articles of English Manufacture, or to the enactment of Differential duties to favour direct trade with the United States.

The papers accompanying the treaty when it was transmitted to the Senate with the presidential message of February 3, 1846, are printed in Senate Confidential Document No. 4, 29th Congress, 1st session, a pamphlet of one hundred pages (Regular Confidential Documents, XVIII, 527–626). Among the papers printed is Clemson's despatch No. 19, the original of which is lacking in the archives of the Department of State. In the print the date of that despatch is given merely as December; it was written on one of the last three days of December 1845. The opening portion of that despatch (but not the enclosures there mentioned) follows:

Herewith you will receive the following documents, viz:

1st. Exposé des motifs accompanying the projet of law relating to the treaty of commerce and navigation concluded between the United States and Belgium the 10th of November, 1845.

2d. Report made by Mons. de Theux in the name of the committee charged to examine the projet of law relating to the same treaty.

3d. A copy of that part of the official paper (the Moniteur) containing the discussion that took place in the Chamber of Representatives on the 16th and 17th instant, on the treaty.

You will perceive that it (the treaty) passed the Chamber of Representatives on the 17th instant by the following vote: seventy-seven members were present when the vote was taken; seventy-three voted in favor, three against, and one refused to vote.

This unexpected majority, amounting almost to unanimity, took every one by surprise, and may be considered as mainly resulting from the previous preparation of the premises, and the able defence made by the minister of foreign affairs, M. Dechamps. I feel convinced that, had it not been urged as it was, the opposition would have been greater, and the majority much smaller. Many voted for the treaty, not because they were in favor of it, but because they thought it would be incompatible with the dignity of Belgium to reject this the third attempt at ratification; others, because its rejection would be a reason why the United States would not choose the port of Antwerp as one of the points on the continent to which a line of steamers might be directed; and this argument had great influence.

Mons. de Theux, the reporter of the committee in the House, told me that he could not succeed in getting all the members of the committee together to consider the measure, so reluctant did some of them feel at committing themselves; and this is the cause alleged by that gentleman for the failure of the treaty of 1840. The opinion obtains here, and I have heard it frequently expressed, that this treaty is not only more advantageous to the United States than either of the two preceding, which were not ratified by Belgium, but much more advantageous to the United States than Belgium.

The opposition in the committee of the Senate has been much more strenuous than that which was manifested in the Chamber. One of the members of the Senate went so far as to say that the minister of foreign affairs ought to be put in judgment for signing such a treaty. The objections appear to have been against the article on transit and the stipulations included in the 7th article. They apprehend that the trade with all transatlantic countries will be carried on through the United States, and entirely in American bottoms; thus not only depriving them of the advantages of direct communication, but injuring their navy, which they are anxious to establish, the increase of which was one of the considerations in the enactment of "la loi des droits différentiels."

Objections were also raised, as well in the Senate as the House, against the fourth article, which stipulates for the restitution by Belgium of the duty levied by the Netherlands on the navigation of the Scheldt, and against the duration of the convention, which would have been more popular had the time been restricted to five instead of ten years.

The Senate met on the evening of the 28th instant, when the treaty was adopted by that body by a unanimous vote, less one refusal.

I enclose the report of the committee of the Senate charged to examine the treaty; and the following is a copy of the note just received from the minister of foreign affairs on the ratification of the treaty:

[Translation: French text omitted]

DEPARTMENT OF FOREIGN AFFAIRS,
Brussels, December 29, 1845.

SIR: You are aware that the Treaty of Commerce and Navigation between Belgium and the United States, signed on the 10th of November last, has been sanctioned by a great majority in the Chamber of Representatives at its meeting on the 17th of this month.

I hasten to inform you, Sir, that the Senate, at its extraordinary meeting yesterday, likewise approved the treaty, by a vote, with one exception, unanimous.

It is also with extreme satisfaction that the Government has witnessed the readiness to examine the treaty and the result of the votes; it cannot be doubted that the members of the Legislature desired, by this demonstration, to efface all trace of the difficulties which previously presented themselves, and to prove that the obstacles which then existed against the execution of an international arrangement arose entirely from causes connected with the interior legislation of the country.

M. Beaulieu, appointed by the King Minister Resident at Washington, finding it impossible to take passage in the packet from England of January 4th, as had been first arranged, will go in the following packet, of February 4th, and will carry the act of the royal ratification.

The eagerness with which the Belgian Government has ratified the treaty of November 10 will, I hope, facilitate the negotiation of the *postal* convention, with which is connected the projected establishment of a line of steamers between New York and Antwerp.

I embrace this occasion, Sir, to renew to you the assurance of my very distinguished consideration.

The Minister of Foreign Affairs,
A. DECHAMPS

ARTICLE 4

By the provisions of Article 4 Belgium guaranteed the restitution to vessels of the United States "of the duty levied by the Governement of the Netherlands, on the navigation of the scheldt" in virtue of Article 9, paragraph 3, of the treaty of April 19, 1839. There were various treaties of that date signed at London. For their texts in

French, see British and Foreign State Papers, XXVII, 990–1003. English translations are in Hertslet, Map of Europe by Treaty, II, 979–1000. To the treaty between the five powers, Great Britain, Austria, France, Prussia, and Russia, on the one part and the Netherlands on the other, and also to the treaty between the five powers and Belgium, were annexed twenty-four articles which, with two others, formed the treaty between Belgium and the Netherlands. Article 9, paragraph 3, reads in translation as follows (*ibid.*, 986–87):

There shall be levied by the Government of the Netherlands upon the navigation of the Scheldt and of its mouths a single duty of 1 florin 50 cents per ton, that is to say, 1 florin 12 cents on vessels which, coming from the high sea, shall ascend the western Scheldt in order to proceed to Belgium by the Scheldt or by the canal of Terneuze; and of 38 cents per ton on vessels which, coming from Belgium by the Scheldt or by the canal of Terneuze, shall descend the western Scheldt in order to proceed to the high sea. And in order that the said vessels may not be subject to any visit nor to any delay or hindrance whatever within the Dutch waters, either in ascending the Scheldt from the high sea or in descending the Scheldt in order to reach the high sea, it is agreed that the collection of the duty above mentioned shall take place by Dutch agents at Antwerp and at Terneuze. In the same manner vessels arriving from the high sea in order to proceed to Antwerp by the western Scheldt, and coming from places suspected in regard to health, shall be at liberty to continue their course without hindrance or delay, accompanied by one health guard, and thus to proceed to the place of their destination. Vessels proceeding from Antwerp to Terneuze, and vice versa, or carrying on in the river itself coasting trade or fishery (in such manner as the exercise of the latter shall be regulated in pursuance of section 6 hereinafter) shall not be subjected to any duty.

RELATIONS WITH BELGIUM

The first diplomatic representative of the United States accredited to Belgium was Hugh S. Legaré, commissioned Chargé d'Affaires on April 14, 1832 (D.S., 2 Credences, 185); the first Belgian representative at Washington was Baron Desiré Behr, Minister Resident, who presented his credentials on June 6, 1832; the following is quoted from Moore, Digest, I, 110:

By the congress of Vienna Belgium and Holland were united, the Belgic provinces being placed under the sovereignty of the King of the Netherlands. In September, 1830, the Belgians declared their independence. October 14, 1831, the plenipotentiaries of Austria, France, Great Britain, Prussia, and Russia, in conference at London, agreed upon twenty-four articles as a basis of a definite arrangement between the two countries. This arrangement was not accepted by the Netherlands, and on November 15, 1831, the plenipotentiaries above mentioned, together with a plenipotentiary of the King of the Belgians, signed at London a treaty by which it was agreed that Belgium should form "an independent and perpetually neutral State." The United States recognized the independence of Belgium by issuing an exequatur to the Belgian consul at New York January 6, 1832.

The French text of the treaty of November 15, 1831, which embodies the articles of October 14, 1831, is, with an English translation, in British and Foreign State Papers, XVIII, 645–64. An English translation is also in Hertslet, Map of Europe by Treaty, II, 858–71.

The treaties of April 19, 1839, which have been cited above, were based upon the articles of October 14, 1831, and the treaty of November 15, 1831; by those treaties of 1839 there was concluded a definitive arrangement of the international status of Belgium, accepted by the Netherlands as well as by the five powers and Belgium.

117

GREAT BRITAIN : NOVEMBER 10 AND 26, 1845

Settlement of Claims. Note of the Right Honorable Richard Pakenham, Envoy Extraordinary and Minister Plenipotentiary of Her Britannic Majesty, of November 10, 1845, to James Buchanan, Secretary of State, with memorandum enclosed. Answering note of the Secretary of State of November 26, 1845. Other proceedings are described in the editorial notes.

[*The Envoy Extraordinary and Minister Plenipotentiary of Her Britannic Majesty to the Secretary of State*]

WASHINGTON *10 November 1845.*

SIR, With reference to what I have already had the honor verbally to communicate to you on the subject of a mutual settlement of certain claims which have been for some time pending between the two Governments with the particulars of which you are already fully acquainted—I now beg leave to place in your hands the enclosed Memorandum explaining the considerations which have induced Her Majesty's Government to suggest the proposed arrangement.

I venture to hope that the views of Her Majesty's Government upon this matter will meet with the cordial concurrence of the Government of the United States.

I take advantage of this opportunity, to renew to you, Sir, the assurance of my high consideration.

R PAKENHAM

The Honble JAMES BUCHANAN
&c &c &c

[Enclosure—Memorandum]

Her Majesty's Government have for some time past had under their anxious consideration the claim of certain British Merchants carrying on trade with the United States for a return of the excess of duties levied on goods imported by them into the United States under the Tariff of 1842, which claim was first brought to the notice of the United States Government by Mr Fox's note [1] of 8. January 1844.

---

[1] Printed in the editorial notes.

The attention of Her Majesty's Government has been no less anxiously directed to the claim advanced by citizens of the United States against the British Government for a return of the excess of duties levied on certain parcels of rough rice imported into England some years since.

These cases which have formed the subject of frequent representations between the two Governments are in many respects parallel, but especially in the essential feature of their connection with the Provisions contained in the 2^d Article of the commercial Convention[1] of 1815. between Great Britain and the United States to which it is mutually affirmed that the levying of the duties complained of on both sides is directly opposed.

Both the cases have been repeatedly and enegetically discussed by the respective Parties but hitherto without any visibly nearer approach to a satisfactory result than when they were first opened.

In each case the Treaty is appealed to with confidence by one Party and its applicability denied by the other. The sums respectively involved are large, and that consideration coupled with the not unreasonable doubts which hang over the subject in both cases seem to justify the tenacity with which each party has defended its own cause and has refused to concede any thing to its opponent.

Under these circumstances it appears to Her Majesty's Government that it would be wise on the part of both Governments to consider whether in this involved and unpromising state of the matter a settlement of it upon equal terms might not be agreed to.

Supposing the United States Government to concur in the propriety of effecting such a settlement, it would seem desirable to avoid reopening discussion on the merits of either of the contested cases but to assume that both are equal, that both present themselves under the same aspect of alleged violation of Treaty engagements strictly and literally taken, and that both have been maintained with equal sincerity and good faith by the respective Parties.

Such is the mode in which the British Government is prepared to treat this matter in case the Government of the United States should signify their concurrence therein, and considering the irritation which protracted discussion on points so serious as the alleged infraction of Treaty stipulations is apt to engender even in the minds of Governments and Nations whose interest and wish it is to maintain the best understanding with each other, Her Majesty's Government trust that the Government of the United States may acquiesce in the mode of adjustment thus proposed.

---

[1] Document 35; see also Documents 40 and 57.

Should this be the case it might be well that in the first place it should be mutually admitted and declared that in the respective acts which gave rise to the controversies which have arisen between the two Governments the view taken by both Parties respectively is mutually believed and acknowledged to have been conscientiously entertained and supported; that nevertheless both Parties admit that their respective views may have been erroneous and that under this admission each is willing to respect the claim to compensation put forward by the opposite party, that seeing however the reasonable doubt which may still be considered to hang over each claim and also that if real injury has resulted from the acts of either Party it has arisen from error and not from intention, each Government shall forego all claims to arrears of interest on the sums which may be found respectively due, and that with this explicit agreement these sums having been first clearly ascertained to the satisfaction of both Governments which shall mutually afford every facility for that object, shall be forthwith paid by each Government to the other for distribution to the claimants, each Government being from the moment that such payment shall have been effected, entirely absolved from all further responsibility on the part of the claimants of the opposite Party.

It appears to Her Majesty's Government that each Government would thus be placed on a footing of entire parity and that both may agree to carry out such an arrangement without any sacrifice of national credit.

This proposal to be considered as conditional, in every respect;—if not accepted on the terms in which it is offered, things would of course return to their original position.

[*The Secretary of State to the Envoy Extraordinary and Minister Plenipotentiary of Her Britannic Majesty*]

DEPARTMENT OF STATE,
Washington, 26ᵗʰ Nov̄., 1845.

The Rt. Honᵇˡᵉ R. PAKENHAM,
&ᶜ., &ᶜ., &c.

SIR: I have had the honor of receiving your note of the 10ᵗʰ instant, together with "the memorandum" presenting the views of Her Britannic Majesty's Government in relation to the mutual claims of the two Governments for refunding the excess of duties which has been levied in the ports of each, in violation of the second article of

the Commercial Convention between the two countries, of the 3ᵈ of July, 1815. The memorandum has been submitted to the President; and I am pleased to inform you that it has received his cordial approbation. He is perfectly willing to terminate the pending questions between the two Governments under this convention, on the terms proposed by the British Government. Indeed, you are aware that, from the very moment I first examined the question, I believed that the claim of the British Government was well-founded, and rested upon the same basis with that of the United States.

The only remaining obstacle is to adjust the claims of the respective Governments on each other according to the principles in which they both concur. It may save trouble in the end if this should be done in the beginning.

The second article of the convention provides that "no higher or other duties shall be imposed on the importation into the United States of any articles the growth, produce, or manufacture of His Britannic Majesty's territories in Europe, and no higher or other duties shall be imposed on the importation into the territories of His Britannic Majesty in Europe of any articles the growth, produce, or manufacture of the United States, than are or shall be payable *on the like articles*, being the growth, produce, or manufacture of any other foreign country." No difficulty exists in specifying the claim of the United States under this provision, because it is confined to the single article of rough rice. Not so the British claim. This is now indefinite; and it is highly desirable that it should be rendered specific, by an enumeration of the articles on which an excess of duty has been levied under the tariff act of 30 August, 1842.[1]

Under the 25ᵗʰ section of this act, it is provided "that nothing in this act contained shall apply to goods shipped in a vessel bound to any port of the United States, actually having left her last port of lading eastward of the Cape of Good Hope, or beyond Cape Horn, prior to the first day of September, 1842; and all legal provisions and regulations existing immediately before the thirtieth day of June, 1842, shall be applied to importations which may be made in vessels which have left such last port of lading eastward of the Cape of Good Hope, or beyond Cape Horn, prior to said first day of September, 1842."

Now no difficulty can exist as to what vessels are embraced by the British claim. It is freely admitted that in regard to these they shall be the same as though this section of the tariff act had expressly embraced vessels "bound to any port of the United States, actually having left their last port of lading" in any of Her "Britannic Ma-

---

[1] 5 Statutes at Large, 548–67.

jesty's territories in Europe" prior to the first day of September, 1842; thus placing them on the identical footing with vessels from "eastward of the Cape of Good Hope or beyond Cape Horn."

The designation of such articles imported in these vessels as are protected from increased duties by the convention between the two countries is the only matter of difficulty. According to this convention and the tariff act, they must be "like articles", "the growth, produce, or manufacture of Her Britannic Majesty's territories in Europe", to those which had been imported into the United States from "any other foreign country," "eastward of the Cape of Good Hope or beyond Cape Horn, prior to the said first day of September, eighteen hundred and forty-two."

I invite you, Sir, to furnish me a list of these articles; and in order to enable you to comply with this request, all the information on the subject in possession of the Treasury Department shall be most cheerfully communicated to you.

The phrase "eastward of the Cape of Good Hope or beyond Cape Horn," has received a settled construction by long practice under our revenue laws. It does not embrace any port of Europe, or any port of Asia or Africa upon the Mediterranean.

I avail myself of this occasion to offer you renewed assurances of my distinguished consideration.

JAMES BUCHANAN.

P.S.—I have the honor of communicating to you, herewith, a copy of the opinion of the Secretary of the Treasury on the subject of this note.[1]

NOTES

The papers printed above are three: the note of November 10, 1845, from the British Minister at Washington (Richard Pakenham), to the Secretary of State (James Buchanan); the memorandum enclosed (D.S., 23 Notes from the British Legation); and the answering note of the Secretary of State of November 26, 1845 (D.S., 7 Notes to the British Legation, 125–27).

Copies of the foregoing papers, with the opinion of the Secretary of the Treasury (Robert J. Walker) of October 17, 1845 (quoted below; House Document No. 169, 29th Congress, 1st session, serial 485, pp. 3–8), were transmitted to Congress with the following message of President Polk of March 23, 1846 (*ibid.*, 1–3; also in Richardson, IV, 424–26):

I transmit, for your consideration, a correspondence between the minister of her Britannic majesty in Washington and the Secretary of State, containing an

[1] For the text of the opinion, see the editorial notes which follow.

arrangement for the adjustment and payment of the claims of the respective governments upon each other, arising from the collection of certain import duties in violation of the second article of the commercial convention of 3d July, 1815, between the two countries; and I respectfully submit to Congress the propriety of making provision to carry this arrangement in effect.

The second article of this convention provides that "no higher or other duties shall be imposed on the importation into the United States of any articles the growth, produce, or manufacture of his Britannic majesty's territories in Europe, and no higher or other duties shall be imposed on the importation into the territories of his Britannic majesty in Europe of any articles the growth, produce, or manufacture of the United States,than are or shall be payable on the like articles, being the growth, produce, or manufacture of any other foreign country."

Previous to the act of Parliament of the 13th of August, 1836, the duty on foreign rough rice imported into Great Britain was two shillings and sixpence sterling per bushel. By this act the duty was reduced to one penny per quarter (of eight bushels) on the rough rice "imported from the west coast of Africa." Upon the earnest and repeated remonstrances of our ministers at London, in opposition to this discrimination against American and in favor of African rice, as a violation of the subsisting convention, Parliament, by the act of 9th July, 1842, again equalized the duty on all foreign rough rice by fixing it at seven shillings per quarter. In the intervening period, however, of nearly six years, large importations had been made into Great Britain of American rough rice, which was subjected to a duty of two shillings and sixpence per bushel; but the importers, knowing their rights under the convention, claimed that it should be admitted at the rate of one penny per quarter, the duty imposed on African rice. This claim was resisted by the British government, and the excess of duty was paid, at the first, under protest, and afterwards, in consequence of an arrangement with the board of customs, by the deposite of exchequer bills.

It seems to have been a clear violation both of the letter and spirit of the convention to admit rough rice, "the growth" of Africa, at one penny per quarter, whilst the very same article, "the growth" of the United States, was charged with a duty of two shillings and sixpence per bushel.

The claim of Great Britain, under the same article of the convention, is founded on the tariff act of 30th August, 1842. Its twenty-fifth section provides "that nothing in this act contained shall apply to goods shipped in a vessel bound to any port of the United States, actually having left her last port of lading eastward of the Cape of Good Hope, or beyond Cape Horn, prior to the first day of September, 1842; and all legal provisions and regulations existing immediately before the 30th day of June, 1842, shall be applied to importations which may be made in vessels which have left such last port of lading eastward of the Cape of Good Hope, or beyond Cape Horn, prior to said first day of September, 1842."

The British government contends that it was a violation of the second article of the convention for this act to require that "articles the growth, produce, or manufacture" of Great Britain, when imported into the United States in vessels which had left their last port of lading in Great Britain prior to the first day of September, 1842, should pay any "higher or other duties" than were imposed on "like articles" "the growth, produce, or manufacture" of countries beyond the Cape of Good Hope and Cape Horn.

Upon a careful consideration of the subject, I arrived at the conclusion that this claim on the part of the British government was well founded. I deem it unnecessary to state my reasons at length for adopting this opinion, the whole subject being fully explained in the letter of the Secretary of the Treasury and the accompanying papers.

The amount necessary to satisfy the British claim cannot at present be ascertained with any degree of accuracy, no individual having yet presented his case to the government of the United States. It is not apprehended that the amount will be large. After such examination of the subject as it has been in his power to make, the Secretary of the Treasury believes that it will not exceed $100,000.

On the other hand, the claims of the importers of rough rice into Great Britain have been already ascertained, as the duties were paid either under protest or in exchequer bills. Their amount is stated by Mr. Everett, our late minister at London, in a despatch dated June 1, 1843, to be £88,886 16s. 10d. sterling, of which £60,006 0s. 4d. belong to citizens of the United States.

As it may be long before the amount of the British claim can be ascertained, and it would be unreasonable to postpone payment to the American claimants until this can be adjusted, it has been proposed to the British government immediately to refund the excess of duties collected by it on American rough rice. I should entertain a confident hope that this proposal would be accepted, should the arrangement concluded be sanctioned by an act of Congress making provision for the return of the duties in question. The claimants might then be paid as they present their demands, properly authenticated, to the Secretary of the Treasury.

The letter of October 17, 1845, written to the President by Robert J. Walker, Secretary of the Treasury, which is referred to in the foregoing presidential message and which was communicated to the British Government with the note of Secretary of State Buchanan of November 26, 1845, has been cited above. It read as follows:

> TREASURY DEPARTMENT,
> *October 17, 1845.*

SIR: I have considered with great care the question submitted by you to me for an opinion and report whether articles shipped from British territories in Europe for this country prior to the first of September, 1842, would be subjected to higher duties than those collected on like articles, also shipped for the United States before that date, from any port eastward of the Cape of Good Hope, or beyond Cape Horn.

The question arises under the *second* article of the convention between the United States and Great Britain, concluded on the third day of July, 1815; continued by that of the 20th of October, 1818, and again by that of the 6th of August, 1827, and the twenty-fifth section of the act of Congress of the 30th of August, 1842, changing and modifying the laws imposing duties on imports.

That article, so far as it applies to this case, is in the following words: "No higher or other duties shall be imposed on the importation into the United States of any articles the growth, produce, or manufacture of his Britannic majesty's territories in Europe, and no higher or other duties shall be imposed on the importation into the territories of his Britannic majesty in Europe of any articles the growth, produce, or manufacture of the United States, than are or shall be payable on the like articles, being the growth, produce, or manufacture of any other foreign country."

The 25th section of the act of Congress is as follows: "That nothing in this act contained shall apply to goods shipped in a vessel bound to any port of the United States, actually having left her last port of lading eastward of the Cape of Good Hope, or beyond Cape Horn, prior to the first day of September, eighteen hundred and forty-two; and all legal provisions and regulations existing immediately before the 30th day of June, eighteen hundred and forty-two, shall be applied to importations which may be made in vessels which have left such last port of lading eastward of the Cape of Good Hope, or beyond Cape Horn, prior to the said first day of September, eighteen hundred and forty-two."

Now if any articles are shipped for the United States from China for instance, and also from British territories in Europe for the United States, prior to the first of September, 1842, can a higher duty be imposed on like articles thus shipped from Great Britain, than on those from China, both being imported here?

By the treaty it was taken for granted, and known to be the fact, that like articles might be of the growth, produce, or manufacture of different countries; and the treaty placed those coming from British territories in Europe at a duty as low as was imposed on such articles imported here from any other foreign country. The right under the treaty was confined to like articles; but so limited, it extended so as to place such articles shipped to the United States from British territories in Europe, and the growth, produce, or manufacture of such territories, on a footing of equality with those of the growth, produce, or manufacture of any other country, without regard to its geographical position. If different countries were not presumed to produce or manufacture like articles, the clause of the treaty would have no operation whatever; and no discrimination is made,

whether the territory is nearer or more remote, but all are embraced in the provisions of the treaty.

The object of the 25th section of the act may have been to prevent the operation of high duties upon those who might have shipped goods from distant ports prior to any knowledge of the probable augmentation of the duties; but this object or purpose of those who introduced this section cannot authorize a violation of the treaty of 1815, by the exaction of higher duties upon articles imported from British territories in Europe, than if the like articles were imported from countries eastward of the Cape of Good Hope or beyond Cape Horn. It is true also that the 25th section authorized an exception from the general rule, and was but temporary in its operation. But the treaty precluded an exception in any case, or for any purpose, or for any period of time, whether of longer or shorter duration. If an exception could be made in one case, it might be made in others; and if a higher duty could be exacted for a month, it might for a year, or for any indefinite period; and if by the United States, by Great Britain also, for the obligations of the treaty were reciprocal; and if one party can make exceptions as to time and place, so may the other. The treaty extended to all cases of importation of like articles; it admitted of no exception, and it operated at all times throughout the whole year, and every part of it, and during the whole period of the duration of the treaty, and at all times was equally and reciprocally obligatory upon both parties to the treaty. If a vessel sails for the United States from China on the 1st of May, 1842, and from Great Britain on the 1st of August, 1842, and both arrive in the port of New York on the 1st of September, or in the same month, both laden with like articles—if lower duties are collected on the articles shipped from China, than on the like articles shipped from British territories in Europe—it is a violation of the second article of the treaty of 1815. But it never was the intention of Congress to violate any provision of that treaty, or of any other treaty. This is demonstrated in the clause of the act of 30th August, 1842, declaring "that nothing herein contained shall be construed or permitted to operate so as to interfere with subsisting treaties with foreign countries;" and full effect can be given to the 25th section of the act by confining its operation to those countries with whom no such treaty existed, and to whom that section would be applied without any violation of the public faith, of treaty obligations, or of the constitution of the Union.

It is, then, my opinion, that articles actually shipped from British territories in Europe, and of their growth, produce, or manufacture, for the United States, prior to the 1st of September, 1842, and imported here, cannot be subjected to a higher duty than that exacted on like articles, "the growth, produce, or manufacture of any other foreign country," shipped, prior to that date, from ports eastward of the Cape of Good Hope, or beyond Cape Horn, and imported here.

In order to bring the articles shipped from British territories in Europe within the protection of the treaty of 1815, they must be of the growth, produce, or manufacture of such British territories, and like articles to those shipped from ports eastward of the Cape of Good Hope, or beyond Cape Horn, and imported here; and they must have been shipped prior to the 1st of September, 1842; the vessel must have sailed to the United States, and the goods have been imported there, and the vessel must have actually left such British port in Europe, as her last port of lading, prior to the 1st of September, 1842, for the United States. When all these circumstances concur, the augmented duty cannot be exacted.

In giving this opinion, it is to be understood that the terms eastward of the Cape of Good Hope or beyond Cape Horn do not embrace any port of Europe, or any port of Asia or Africa, upon the Mediterranean.

Most respectfully,

R. J. WALKER, *Secretary of the Treasury.*

To the PRESIDENT OF THE UNITED STATES.

The deficiency appropriation act of May 8, 1846 (9 Statutes at Large, 6–9), contained the following paragraph:

For refunding certain duties collected under the act of the thirtieth of August, eighteen hundred and forty-two, entitled "An Act to provide Revenue from Imports, and to change and modify existing Laws imposing Duties on Imports, and

for other Purposes," contrary to the terms of the convention of eighteen hundred and fifteen, between Great Britain and the United States, in fulfilment of the agreement lately entered into by the government of the United States and Great Britain, one hundred thousand dollars.

THE ARRANGEMENT

This international act, adjusting the claims on the one side and on the other, is called an "arrangement" in the message of President Polk and an "agreement" in the statute above cited. So far as it concerned American claims against Great Britain, it required no approval on behalf of the United States except that of the Executive; and so far as it concerned British claims against the United States, the admission by the President of their validity was followed by the sanction of the act of Congress providing for their payment.

It is to be noted that the claims on each part were based upon the provisions of the first paragraph of Article 2 of the convention of July 3, 1815 (Document 35). Legislation, first of the one Government and then of the other, had, unintentionally, gone counter to their agreement of 1815; and it seems to have been for this reason that interest on the amounts claimed was mutually waived.

THE CLAIMS

The American claims in respect of the British duty on rough rice had been elaborately discussed from 1839 on; most of the somewhat voluminous correspondence has been printed (see British and Foreign State Papers, XXXIII, 92–145, 300–12); various presidential messages had informed Congress of the question (December 7, 1841, Richardson, IV, 78; December 1843, *ibid.*, 259; June 15, 1844, *ibid.*, 328; see also Senate Document No. 1, 27th Congress, 2d session, serial 395, pp. 47–57, and House Document No. 278, 28th Congress, 1st session, serial 444).

The facts on which the American claims were based are summarized in the presidential message of March 23, 1846 (*supra*). Prior to the British statute of August 13, 1836, the duty on rough rice imported into Great Britain was 2s. 6d. per bushel or, per quarter (eight bushels), one pound sterling; by the statute mentioned (6 and 7 William IV, ch. 60), the duty on such rice from "the West Coast of Africa" was nominal, one penny per quarter; the purpose of the enactment was to benefit the natives of the region in question; the higher duty continued to be applicable to imports of rice from the United States, contrary to the most-favored-nation clause of paragraph 1 of Article 2 of the convention of July 3, 1815 (Document 35), which had been continued in force by the conventions of October 20, 1818 (Document 40, Article 4), and of August 6, 1827 (Document 57, Article 1).

Owing to the representations of this Government, the discrimination was abolished by the statute of July 9, 1842 (5 and 6 Victoria, ch. 47), and had been in fact ended in October 1841 (British and Foreign State Papers, XXXIII, 311); the American claims were for the duties previously paid (or secured to be paid).

Following the arrangement of November 1845, and before the passage of the act of Congress of May 8, 1846, the "Lords Commissioners of Her Majesty's Treasury" gave "directions for the payment of the several claimants on account of the Duties levied on Rough Rice imported into this Country from the United States" (D.S., 23 Notes from the British Legation, May 26, 1846, and enclosure of May 4, 1846); difficulties that led to some delay in payment were, it seems, adjusted (D.S., file 124.416/147, American note of August 6, 1846, enclosure to despatch No. 583 from London, March 21, 1934; D.S., 57 Despatches, Great Britain, No. 11, January 4, 1847, enclosure, British note of December 5, 1846).

The British claims were also founded on paragraph 1 of Article 2 of the convention of July 3, 1815 (Document 35). The British contention was first presented to this Government by a note of the British Minister at Washington, Henry S. Fox, under date of January 8, 1844, as follows (D.S., 21 Notes from the British Legation):

WASHINGTON *January 8th 1844*

The Undersigned, Her Britannick Majesty's Envoy Extraordinary and Minister Plenipotentiary, has been directed by his Government to bring the following Claim of British Merchants, whose Interests have been injuriously affected under the operation of One of the Clauses of the United States Tariff Law of the 29th of August 1842, under the serious consideration of the United States Government.

It was provided by the 25th Section of the aforesaid Tariff Law, that Goods imported in vessels bound to any part of the United States, which had left their Ports of lading, Eastward of the Cape of Good Hope or beyond Cape Horn, prior to the 1st of September 1842, should be subjected only to the lower Rate of Duties specified in the Tariff Regulations existing before the 30th of June 1842; while, on the contrary, like Goods imported into America from British Ports, although likewise shipped prior to the aforesaid date of the 1st of September 1842, were subjected to the heavy additional duties imposed by the Tariff Law of the 29th of August.

But it is stipulated in the 2d article of the Commercial Convention between Great Britain and the United States, concluded in London on the 3d of July 1815, that "no higher or other duties shall be imposed upon the importation into the "United States of any articles, the growth produce or manufacture of His Britan-"nick Majesty's Territories in Europe, than are or shall be payable on the like "articles being the growth produce or manufacture of any other Foreign Country."

The British Importing Merchants, whose Goods, though shipped from British Ports prior to the 1st of September 1842, have been subjected to the heavy duties imposed by the New Tariff,—while like goods imported under like circumstances from other Countries were exempted from the payment of those increased duties,— complain that such discriminating provision of the Tariff Law has affected their interests injuriously and wrongfully, and in violation of the 2d article, above cited, of the Commercial Convention of 1815.

Her Majesty's Government, after due consideration of the representations and complaints addressed to them by the British Merchants whose interests have been thus affected, are of opinion that the complaints are well founded. Her Majesty's Government consider that the Importers of any articles, the growth produce and manufacture of Great Britain, shipped from British Ports prior to the 1st of September 1842, were entitled to the same exemption from the increased duties of the New Tariff, as was granted to the importers of like goods shipped within the same date from Ports Eastward of the Cape of Good Hope or from beyond Cape Horn; and that the withholding such similar exemption from the British Importers, amounts to a violation, although no doubt not so intended, of the Convention of 1815.

The Undersigned is, therefore, instructed to claim from the well known Justice and Good Faith of the United States Government, that all such excess of duties as may have been levied upon those British Merchants whose case comes under the circumstances described in this Note, shall be duly reimbursed to them.

The Undersigned avails himself of this occasion to renew to the Secretary of State of the United States the assurance of his distinguished consideration.

H. S. Fox.

The United States tariff act of August 30, 1842 (5 Statutes at Large, 548–67), was one which generally increased duties on imports; by section 25 of that statute the previous and lower duties were, by exception, made applicable to goods shipped in a vessel bound to the United States which left her last port of lading east of the Cape of Good Hope, or beyond Cape Horn, prior to September 1, 1842. Under the terms of Article 2 of the convention of July 3, 1815, it followed that shipments of like articles which were the growth, produce, or manufacture of British territories in Europe and which were imported in a vessel which left her last port of lading before September 1, 1842, were entitled to a similar privileged exception.

The respective contentions were considered in Cabinet on September 9, 1845, and this account is given (Diary of James K. Polk, I, 21–22):

> The rough rice question, or the violation by Great Brittain of the commercial Treaty between that country & the U. States by levying and collecting higher and other duties on rough Rice imported from the U.S. into Great Brittain, than on the like article imported from the Western coast of Africa, was considered. The Cabinet were unanimously of opinion that the Treaty had been violated. It was stated by the Secretary of State that the excess of duties thus collected was ascertained to be between £88,000 and £89,000 sterling. It appeared that Great Brittain claimed indemnity for an alleged violation of the same treaty by the U.S. by the 25th Section of the Tariff act of 1842; in this, that a discrimination was made in favour of goods shipped prior to 1st Sept., 1845, from places East of the Cape of Goodhope, and beyond Cape Horn, over the like articles shipped from Great Brittain prior to the same day. After discussion the Cabinet was of opinion that the tariff act of 1842 was a violation of the Treaty in this respect; and it was referred to the Secretary of the Treasury to ascertain & report the amt. of excess which had been collected. It was understood that when the amt. was ascertained, Mr. McLane, our Minister at London, should be instructed to adjust the claims on both Sides if practicable.

The opinion of the Secretary of the Treasury of October 17, 1845, which is printed above, was wholly in favor of the British view, pointing out, however, that the increased rates of duty would be contrary to the convention only when they were levied on "like articles to those shipped from ports eastward of the Cape of Good Hope, or beyond Cape Horn".

Following the act of May 8, 1846, steps were taken by the Treasury Department to notify those entitled thereunder to present their claims (Treasury Department, Miscellaneous, 1801–48, 209, May 12, 1846; Treasury Department, Circulars, October 10, 1843–February 4, 1848, 193–96, August 15, 1846; these were respectively enclosures to letters of the Secretary of the Treasury to the Secretary of State of May 13 and August 21, 1846; D.S., Miscellaneous Letters, April–June and July–September 1846); and the British Government was duly informed (D.S., 7 Notes to the British Legation, 140, 146, May 18 and August 24, 1846).

It appears from the account of the receipts and expenditures of the Government for the fiscal year ending June 30, 1847, that the claims paid under the arrangement and the act of May 8, 1846, amounted to $48,014.76 (House Executive Document No. 7, 30th Congress, 1st session, serial 514, pp. 73–75).

Thus the terms of the "memorandum" of November 10, 1845, were fully carried out, though not literally; as suggested in the presidential message of March 23, 1846, quoted above, the claimants were paid direct by the respective Governments instead of the sums being paid by "each Government to the other for distribution to the claimants".

Other claims arising under Article 2 of the convention of July 3, 1815, between the United States and Great Britain, were presented to the Commission under the convention of February 8, 1853, and were allowed or adjusted (Moore, International Arbitrations, IV, 3361–65).

Treaty Series No. 363
9 Statutes at Large, 833–41
18 *ibid.*, pt. 2, Public Treaties, 772–76

118

TWO SICILIES : DECEMBER 1, 1845

Treaty of Commerce and Navigation, signed at Naples December 1, 1845. Original in English and Italian.
Submitted to the Senate January 28, 1846. Resolution of advice and consent April 11, 1846. Ratified by the United States April 14, 1846. Ratified by the Two Sicilies February 28, 1846. Ratifications exchanged at Naples June 1, 1846. Proclaimed July 24, 1846.

The United States of America and His Majesty the King of the Kingdom of the Two Sicilies, equally animated with the desire of mainteining, the relations of good understanding which have hitherto so happily subsisted between their respective States, and consolidating the commercial intercorse between them have agreed to enter in negotiations for the conclusion of a Treaty of commerce and navigation, for which purpose they have appointed Plenipotentiaries, that is to say.

The President of the United States of America

William H. Polk Chargé d'Affaires of the same United States of America to the Court of His Majesty the King of the Kingdom of the Two Sicilies

And His Majesty the King of the Kingdom of the Two Sicilies

D. Giustino Fortunato Knight Grand Cross of the Royal Military Constantinian Order of S^t

Gli Stati Uniti di America e Sua Maestà il Re del Regno delle Due Sicilie, del pari animati dal desiderio di conservare le relazioni di buona corrispondenza che ànno finora felicemente esistito tra'Loro rispettivi Stati, e di estendere e consolidare i rapporti commerciali tra essi, sono convenuti di entrare in negoziazione per la conchiusione di un Trattato di commercio e di navigazione, ed ànno a tale effetto destinato rispettivamente de'Plenipotenziarî, cioè

Il Presidente degli Stati Uniti di America

Il Sig^r Guglielmo H. Polk, Incaricato di Affari degli stessi Stati Uniti di America presso la Corte di S. M. il Re del Regno delle Due Sicilie.

E Sua Maestà il Re del Regno delle Due Sicilie

D. Giustino Fortunato Cavaliere Gran Croce del Militare Reale Ordine Costantiniano di S. Gior-

George, and of Francis the 1ˢᵗ Minister Secretari of State of His said Majesty.

D. Michael Gravina and Requesenz, Prince of Comitini, Knight Grand Cross of the Royal Order of Francis the 1ˢᵗ, Gentleman of the chamber in waiting, and Minister Secretary of State of His said Majesty.

And D. Antonio Spinelli, of Scalea, Commander of the Rˡ Order of Francis the 1ˢᵗ, Gentleman of the chamber of His said Majesty Member of the General Consulta and Surintendant General of the Archives of the Kingdom.

Who after having each others exchanged their full powers, found in good and due forme, have concluded and signed the following Articles

Artᵉ 1.

There shall be reciprocal liberty of commerce and navigation between the United States of America and the Kingdom of the Two Sicilies.

No duty of customs or other impost shall be charged upon any goods, the produce or manufacture of one Country, upon importation by sea or by land from such Country into the other, other or higher than the duty or impost charged upon goods of the same kind, the produce or manufacture of, or imported from, any other country: and the United States of America and His Majesty the King of the

gio, e di quello di Francesco 1º, Ministro Segretario di Stato della M. S.

D. Michele Gravina e Requesenz. Principe di Comitini, Cavaliere Gran Croce di Francesco 1º, Gentiluomo di Camera con esercizio, e Ministro Segretario di Stato della M. S.

E D. Antonio Spinelli, dei Principi di Scalea, Commendatore del Real Ordine di Francesco 1º, Gentiluomo della M. S, Consultore della Consulta Generale, e Soprantendente Generale degli Archivî del Regno

I quali dopo di avere scambiato i loro pieni poteri, trovati in buona e dovuta forma àn conchiuso e sottoscritto gli articoli seguenti.

Artº 1º

Vi sarà reciproca libertà di commercio e di navigazione tra gli Stati Uniti di America ed il Regno delle Due Sicilie, e niun dazio doganale o altra imposizione, sarà caricato sopra qualunque merce di produzione del suolo o dell'industria di un paese, alla importazione per mare o per terra da tale paese nell'altro, diverso o più elevato del dazio o imposizione caricata sulle merci dello stesso genere di produzione, o manifattura importata da qualsivoglia altro Paese.

Gli Stati Uniti di America e S. M. il Re del Regno delle Due Sicilie s'impegnano, perciò, che

Kingdom of the Two Sicilies, do hereby engage, that the subjects or citizens of any other State, shall not enjoy any favour privilege or immunity whatever in matters of commerce and navigation which shall not, also, and at the same time be extended to the subjects or citizens of the other High contracting Party, gratuitously, if the concession in favour of that other State shall have been gratuitous, and in return for a compensation, as nearly as possible of proportionate value and effect, to be adjusted by mutual agreement, if the concessions shall have been conditional.

i Sudditi o Cittadini di alcun altra Potenza, non godranno alcun favore, privilegio o immunità, in materia di commercio o di navigazione, senza estenderlo, egualmente, e nello stesso tempo, a'Sudditi o Cittadini dell'altra Potenza contraente, gratuitamente, se la concessione fatta a favore di tale altro Stato sarà stata gratuita, e mediante un compensamento proporzionato, per quanto sia possibile, di valore e di effetto, da stabilirsi di comune accordo, se la concessione è stata onerosa

ART⁹ 2.

All articles of the produce or manufacture of either country, and of their respective States, which can legally be imported into either country from the other in ships of that other country and thence coming, shall, when so imported, be subject to the same duties, and enjoy the same privileges wheter imported in ships of the one country, or in ships of the other; and in like manner, all goods which can legally be exported or reexported from either country to the other, in ships of that other country, shall, when so exported or rexported be subject to the same duties, and be entitled to the same privileges, drawbacks, bounties and allowances, whether exported in ships of the one country, or in ships of the other.

ART⁹ 2°

Tutte le produzioni del suolo e dell'industria dell'uno e dell'altro Paese, o de'loro rispettivi Stati che possono essere legalmente immesse in uno de'due paesi con legni dell'altro paese e da esso provvenienti, saranno quando verranno così immesse sottoposte agli stessi dazî, e godranno degli stessi privilegî, o che sieno importate con bastimenti dell'uno o con bastimenti dell'altro paese: ed allo stesso modo, tutte le merci che potranno essere legalmente esportate o riesportate da uno de'due paesi nell'altro, con legni dell'altro paese, saranno, quando verranno così esportate o riesportate, sottoposte agli stessi dazî, ed avranno diritto agli stessi privilegî diffalchi, beneficî, concessioni e restituzioni, o che sieno espor-

tate da'legni di un paese o da quelli dell'altro

Art.ᵉ 3.

No duties of tonnage, harbour, light-houses, pilotage, quarantine, or other similar duties, of whatever nature, or under whatever denomination, shall be imposed in either country upon the vessels of the other, in respect of voyages between the United States of America and the Kingdom of the Two Sicilies, if laden, or in respect of any voyage, if in ballast, which shall not be equally imposed in the like cases on national vessels

Art.º 3º

Niun diritto di tonnellaggio, di porto, di fanale o di pilotaggio, quarantena e altri simili o corrispondenti diritti di qualsivoglia natura, e sotto qualsiasi denominazione, sarà imposto in uno de'due paesi sopra i legni dell'altro, in risguardo ai viaggi tra gli Stati Uniti di America, ed il Regno delle Due Sicilie, se carichi, e per qualunque viaggio, se in zavorra, che non sarà egualmente imposto, in casi simiglianti, sopra i legni del proprio paese

Art.ᵉ 4.

It is hereby declared that the stipulations of the present Treaty, are not to be understood as applying to the navigation and carrying trade between one port and another situated in the States of either contracting party, such navigation and trade being reserved exclusively to national vessels. Vessels of either country shall, however, be permitted to load or unload the whole or part of their cargoes at one or more ports in the States of either of the High contracting parties, and then to proceed to complete the said loading or unloading to any other port or ports in the same States.

Art.º 4º

È espressamente dichiarato, che le stipulazioni del presente Trattato, non debbono intendersi come applicabili alla navigazione ed al traffico tra un porto ed un altro situati negli Stati di ciascuna delle Alte Parti contraenti, essendo tale navigazione e traffico, riserbato esclusivamente a'bastimenti nazionali.

I bastimenti de'due paesi, del resto, potranno caricare o discaricare il tutto, o una parte de'loro carichi, in uno o più porti degli Stati di ciascuna delle parti contraenti, e quindi procedere per completare il rimanente del carico o del discarico, in ogni altro porto o porti negli stessi Stati

ART? 5.

Neither of the Two Governments nor any corporation or agent acting in behalf, or under the authority of either Government, shall, in the purchase of any article, which being the growth, produce or manufacture of the one country, shall be imported into the other, give directly or indirectly any priority or preference on account of or in reference to, the national character of the vessel in which such article shall have been imported; it being the true intent and meaning of the High contracting parties, that no distinction or difference whatever shall be made in this respect

ART? 6.

The High contracting Parties engages, in regard to the personal privileges that the citizens of the United States of America shall enjoy in the Dominions of His Majesty the King of the Kingdom of the Two Sicilies, and the subjects of His said Majesty in the United States of America, that they shall have free and undoubted right to travel and to reside in the States of the Two High contracting Parties, subject to the same precautions of Police, which are practiced towards the subjects or citizens of the most favoured Nations

They shall be entitled to occupy dwellings, and warehouses,

ART? 5.

Niuno de'due Governi, nè alcuna corporazione o agente che operi in favore, o sotto l'autorità di ciascuno di essi nella compra di qualunque articolo, il quale essendo produzione o manifattura di un paese, sarà importato nell'altro, darà direttamente o indirettamente alcuna preeminenza preferenza, in risguardo o in rapporto al carattere nazionale del bastimento, in cui tale articolo sarà stato importato; essendo il vero scopo ed intenzione delle Alte parti contraenti, che niuna distinzione o differenza qualunque, sia fatta sotto questo rapporto

ART? 6º

Le Alte Parti contraenti s'impegnano, per risguardo a'personali privilegî, di cui godranno i cittadini degli Stati Uniti di America né Dominî di S. M il Re del Regno delle Due Sicilie, ed i Sudditi della M. S. né detti Stati Uniti di America, che avranno essi libero e non dubbio diritto di viaggiare e risiedere negli Stati delle Due Alte Parti Contraenti, rimanendo sottoposti, soltanto, alle precauzioni di polizia che vengono usate verso i Sudditi o Cittadini delle Nazioni le più favorite

Essi avranno diritto di occupare delle case e de'magazzini, e di

and to dispose of their personal property of every kind and description, by sale, gift, exchange, will, or in any other way whatever, whithout the smallest hindrance or obstacle; and their heirs, or representatives, being subjects or citizens of the other High contracting Party, shall succeed to their personal goods whether by Testament or *ab intestato;* and may take possession thereof, either by themselves, or by others acting for them, and dispose of the same at will, paying to the profit of the respective governments, such dues only as the inhabitants of the country wherein the said goods are, shall be subject to pay in like cases. And in case of the absence of the Heir and representative, such care shall be taken of the said goods, as would be taken of the goods of a native of the same country in like case, until the lawful owner, may take measures for receiving them. And if a question should arise among several claimants as to which of them said goods belong, the same shall be decided, finally, by the laws and judges of the land wherein the said goods are.

They shall not be obliged to pay under any pretence whatever, any taxes or impositions, other or greater than those which are paid, or may hereafter be paid by the subjects or citizens of the most favoured Nations, in the respective States, of the High contracting parties

disporre delle loro proprietà personali di qualunque specie e denominazione, per vendita, donazione, permuta testamento, o in qualunque altro modo, senza il minimo ostacolo o impedimento; ed i loro eredi, essendo sudditi o cittadini dell'altra parte contraente, succederanno a'detti loro beni personali, sia per testamento, sia *ab intestato*, e potranno prenderne possesso, sia da se stessi o per altri agendo per essi, e di disporne a piacimento, pagando a profitto de'rispettivi Governi, quei soli diritti, a'quali gli abitanti del paese ove sono situati tali beni, sarebbero assoggettati in simiglianti circostanze: ed in caso di assenza degli eredi o de'rappresentanti di essi, si prenderà de' detti beni, la stessa cura che sarebbe presa, in simili casi, de'beni de'nativi dello stesso paese, fino a tanto che il legittimo proprietario abbia rinvenuto i mezzi per riceverli E laddove sorgesse quistione tra molti pretendenti per l'appartenenza de'detti beni, la stessa sarà decisa diffinitivamente, secondo le leggi, e da'Giudici del paese ove si trovano i detti beni.

Non saranno essi obbligati a pagare, sotto verun pretesto, altre tasse o imposizioni, diverse o più elevate di quelle che sono pagate o che potranno essere in seguito pagate da' Sudditi o Cittadini delle Nazioni le più favorite ne'rispettivi Stati delle Alte Parti contraenti.

They shall be exempt from all military service whether by land or by sea, from forced loans, and from every extraordinary contribution not general and by law established. Their dwellings, warehouses and all premises apparteining thereto, destined for purposes of commerce or residence shall be respected. No arbitrary search of, or or visit to their houses, and no arbitrary examination or inspection whatever of the books, papers or accounts of their trade shall be made; but such measures shall be executed only in conformity with the legal sentence of a competent tribunal, and each of the Two High contracting Parties engages, that the citizens or subjects of the other residing in their respective States, shall enjoy their property and personal security, in as full and ample manner, as their own citizens or subjects, or the subjects or citizens of the most favoured Nations

Saranno essi esenti da qualunque servizio militare, sia per terra, sia per mare, da'prestiti forzosi e da qualunque contribuzione straordinaria, purchè non sia generale e stabilita dalle leggi. Le loro abitazioni, i magazzini, e tutto ciò che loro appartiene per obbietto di commercio e di residenza, saranno rispettati. Non sarà fatta alcuna arbitraria perquisizione o visita nelle loro abitazioni, e neanche arbitrario esame o ispezione qualunque de'loro libri, carte o conti commerciali; potendo siffatte misure essere soltanto eseguite in forza di sentenza legale di un competente tribunale; ciascuna delle Due Alte Parti contraenti s'impegna, perciò, che i Cittadini o i sudditi dell'altra residenti ne'loro rispettivi Stati, godranno della loro proprietà e sicurezza personale, in tal pieno ed amplo modo, come i loro proprî cittadini e sudditi, o i sudditi o cittadini delle Nazioni le più favorite.

ART.e 7.

The citizens and the subjects of each of the Two High contracting Parties, shall be free in the States of the other, to manage their own affairs themselves, or to commit those affairs, to the management of any persons whom they may appoint as their broker, factor or agent, nor shall the citizens and subjects of the Two High contracting Parties, be restrained in their choice of persons, to act in such capacities, nor shall

ARTº 7º

I cittadini ed i sudditi di ciascuna delle Due Alte Parti contraenti, potranno, negli Stati dell'altra, liberamente trattare i proprî affari da se stessi, o commettere tali affari alla gestione di tutte le persone, ch'essi potranno nominare loro mezzani, fattori o agenti, e non saranno i cittadini ed i sudditi delle Due Alte Parti contraenti, impediti nella scelta delle persone che potranno agire in tale qualità, nè saranno essi ri-

they be called upon to pay any salary, or remuneration to any person, whom they shall not choose to employ.

Absolute freedom shall be given in all cases to the buyer and seller to bargain toghether, and to fix the price of any goods, or merchandize imported into, or to be exported from the States and Dominions of the Two High contracting Parties; save and except generally such cases wherein the Laws and usages of the country, may require the intervention of any special agents, in the States and Dominions, of the High contracting Parties

ART.ᵉ 8.

Each of the Two High contracting Parties, may have in the ports of the other, Consuls, Vice Consuls and Commercial Agents, of their own appointment, who shall enjoy the same privileges, and powers of those of the most favored Nations, but if any such Consuls shall exercise commerce, they shall be submitted to the same Laws and usages, to which the private individuals of their nation are submitted in the same place

The said Consuls, Vice Consuls and Commercial Agents are authorized to require the assistance of the local Authorities for the search, arrest detention and imprisonnement of the deserters from the ships of war, and merchant vessels of their country. For this purpose they shall apply

chiesti di pagare alcun salario o rimunerazione, ad alcuna persona, che non sia da essi scelta.

Assoluta libertà sarà data, in ogni caso, al compratore ed al venditore, di negoziare insieme, e di fissare il prezzo di qualunque effetto o mercanzia immessa negli Stati e ne'Dominî delle Due Alte Parti contraenti, o da essere dai medesimi esportata; salvo, in generale, gli affari, pe'quali, le leggi e le usanze del paese, richieranno l'opera di agenti speciali negli Stati e Dominî delle Due Alte Parti contraenti

ART.ᵒ 8ᵒ

Ciascuna delle Due Alte Parti contraenti, potrà avere, ne'porti dell'altra, de'Consoli, Vice Consoli ed Agenti Commerciali di loro scelta, i quali godranno degli stessi privilegî e poteri, di cui godono quelli delle Nazioni le più favorite, ma nel caso che i detti Consoli volessero esercitare il commercio, saranno soggetti alle stesse leggi ed usi, a'quali sono sottoposti gl'Individui della loro nazione nel paese ove risiedono

I detti Consoli, Vice Consoli ed Agenti Consolari, sono autorizzati a richiedere l'assistenza delle Autorità locali per la ricerca l'arresto, la detenzione e l'imprigionamento de'disertori da navi da guerra e mercantili del loro paese. A tale effetto, essi si rivolgeranno a'tribunali, giudici ed ufficiali

to the competent Tribunals, judges and officers, and shall in writing demand the said deserters, proving by the exhibition of the registres of the vessel, the rolls of the crews, or by other official documents that such individuals formed part of the crews, and this reclamation being thus substantiated, the surrender shall not be refused

Such deserters when arrested shall be placed at the disposal of the said Consuls, Vice Consuls or Commercial Agents, and may be confined in the public prisons, at the request and cost of those who shall claim them, in order to be detained until the time when they shall be restored to the vessels to which they belonged, or sent back to their own country, by a vessel of the same nation, or any other vessel, whatsoever. But if not sent back within four months from the day of their arrest, or if all the expenses of such imprisonment are not defrayed, by the party causing such arrest and imprisonment they shall be set at liberty, and shall not be again arrested for the same cause.

However if the deserter should be found to have committed any crime or offence, his surrender may be delayed until the Tribunal before which his case shall be depending, shall have pronounced its sentence, and such sentence shall have been carried into effect.

competenti, e domanderanno in iscritto i suddetti disertori, provando co'registri del bastimento o ruolo di equipaggio o con altri documenti officiali, che tali Individui abbiano fatto parte de'suddetti equipaggi, e a tal dimanda, così documentata, il disertore non sarà negato

Questi disertori, allorchè arrestati, rimarranno a disposizione de'Consoli, Vice Consoli o Agenti Commerciali, e potranno esser rinchiusi nelle pubbliche carceri, a richiesta e spesa di chi ne faccia la dimanda, per essere ritenuti sino al momento che saranno restituiti al bastimento al quale appartenevano, o inviati nel loro paese su di un bastimento della stessa nazione o di qualsiasi altra; ma, però, se nello spazio di quattro mesi, a contare dal giorno dello arresto, non fossero essi rimandati, o che tutte le spese per tale imprigionamento non sieno pagate dalla parte che à dimandato tale arresto e prigionia, saranno essi messi in libertà, senza che possano quindi essere arrestati di bel nuovo per la stessa ragione

Se però il disertore avesse commesso qualche delitto, la estradizione dello stesso sarà differita fino a tanto che il Tribunale, da cui dipende, abbia emanata la sua sentenza, e che abbia questa avuto il suo effetto

ART? 9.

If any ships of war or merchant vessels be wrecked on the coasts of the States of either of the High contracting parties, such ships or vessels, or any parts thereof, and all furniture and appartenances belonging thereunto, and all goods and merchandize which shall be saved therefrom, or the produce thereof, if sold shall be faithfully restored, with the least possible delay, to the proprietors upon being claimed by them, or by their duly authorized factors; and if there are no such proprietors or factors on the spot, then the said goods and merchandize, or the proceeds thereof as well as all the papers found on board such wrecked ships or vessels, shall be delivered to the American or Sicilian Consul or Vice Consul, in whose district the wreck may have taken place; and such Consul, Vice Consul, proprietors, or factors, shall pay only the expenses incurred in the preservation of the property, together with the rate of salvage and expenses of quarantine which would have been payable in the like case of a wreck of a national vessel; and the goods and merchandize saved from the wreck, shall not be subject to duties, unless cleared for consumption; it being understood, that in case of any legal claim upon such wreck, goods or merchandize, the same shall be referred for decision to the competent tribunals of the Country.

ART? 9º

Se alcun bastimento da guerra o mercantile, farà naufragio sulle coste degli Stati di ciascuna delle Alte Parti contraenti, tali bastimenti o qualunque parte di essi éd attrezzi ed appartenenze de'medesimi, ed ogni altro effetto e mercanzia che sarà salvata da essi, o il prodotto, se venduto, sarà fedelmente restituito, il più presto che si potrà, ai proprietarî, su la di loro richiesta, o di agenti debitamente da loro autorizzati; e se non vi sieno tali proprietarî o agenti sul luogo, allora siffatti effetti e mercanzie, o il di loro prodotto, del pari che tutte le carte ritrovate a bordo de'bastimenti naufragati, saranno consegnate al Console o Vice Console Americano o Siciliano, nel di cui distretto il naufragio à potuto avere luogo; e tale Console o Vice Console, proprietarî o agenti, pagheranno solamente le spese incorse per la conservazione della proprietà, insieme con la rata di salvataggio, e le spese di quarantena che sarebbero pagabili in simil caso di naufragio di un bastimento nazionale, e gli effetti e mercanzie salvate dal naufragio non saranno soggette a dazio, a meno che non sieno esse destinate per consumazione, beninteso che, in caso di qualunque legale reclamo su di tale naufragio, effetti e mercanzie, lo stesso sarà deferito alla decisione dei Tribunali competenti del paese

ART? 10.

The merchant vessels of each of the Two High contracting Parties, which may be forced by stress of weather or other cause into one of the Ports of the other, shall be exempt from all duty of port or navigation paid for the benefit of the State, if the motives which led to take refuge be real and evident, and if no operation of commerce be done by loading or unloading merchandises; well understood however that the loading or unloading, which may regard the subsistance of the crew, or necessary for the reparation of the vessel, shall not be considered operations of commerce, which lead to the payement of duties, and that the said vessels do not stay in Port beyond the time necessary, keeping in wiew the cause which led taking refuge.

ART? 11.

To carry always more fully into effect the intentions of the Two High contracting parties, they agree, that every difference of duty, whether of the ten per cent or other, established in the respective States, to the prejudice of the navigation and commerce of those Nations which have not treaties of Commerce and Navigation with them, shall cease and remain abolished in conformity to the principle es-

ART? 10º

Le navi mercantili di ciascuna delle Due Alte Parti contraenti, che per fortuna di mare o altra cagione fossero costrette ad entrare in uno de'porti dell'altra, vi saranno esentate da ogni diritto di porto o di navigazione solito a pagarsi in beneficio dello Stato, se i motivi che le avranno costrette a rifuggirsi sieno reali ed evidenti, e purchè non facciano esse alcuna operazione di commercio caricando o scaricando delle mercanzie. Beninteso, però, che i caricamenti o discaricamenti risguardanti la sussistenza degli equipaggi o necessarî alla riparazione delle navi, non saranno considerati come operazioni di commercio che diano adito al pagamento de'diritti, e purchè le dette navi, non prolunghino la loro permanenza nel porto, al di là del tempo necessario, avendosi riguardo alle cagioni che le avranno costrette a cercar rifugio.

ART? 11º

Per recare sempre più ad effetto le intenzioni delle Due Alte Parti contraenti, convengono Esse, che ogni differenza di dazio, sia del 10. p %, sia altra stabilita negli stati rispettivi in pregiudizio della navigazione e del commercio delle nazioni che non ànno con Esse Trattati di Navigazione e di Commercio, cesserà e rimarrà abolita, consentaneamente al principio stabilito nel primo Articolo del presente Trattato, tanto sulle produ-

tablished in the 1ˢᵗ Article of
the present Treaty, as well on the
productions of the soil and industry of the Kingdom of the Two
Sicilies, which therefrom shall be
imported in the United States of
America, whether in vessels of
the one, or of the other country,
as on those, which in like manner,
shall be imported in the Kingdom
of the Two Sicilies in vessels of
both countries.

They declare besides, that as
the productions of the soil and
industry of the Two countries,
on their introduction in the ports
of the other, shall not be subject
to greater duties than those which
shall be imposed on the like productions of the most favoured
Nations, so the red and white
wines of the Kingdom of the Two
Sicilies of every kind, including
those of Marsala, which may be
imported directly into the United
States of America, whether in
vessels of the one or of the other
country, shall not pay higher or
greater duties than those of the
red and white wines of the most
favoured Nations. And in like
manner, the Cottons of the United
States of America, which may be
imported directly in the Kingdom of the Two Sicilies, whether
in vessels of the one or other
Nation, shall not pay higher or
greater duties, than the Cottons
of Egypt, Bengal, or those of the
most favoured Nations.

zioni del suolo e della industria
del Regno delle Due Sicilie, che
da esso verranno immesse negli
Stati Uniti di America con legni
dell'uno e dell'altro paese, quanto
sulle produzioni del suolo e
dell'industria degli Stati Uniti di
America, che da essi verranno
parimenti immesse nel Regno
delle Due Sicilie con bastimenti
de'due Paesi.

Dichiarano, inoltre, che non do-
vendo le produzioni del suolo e
dell'industria dei due paesi, nella
loro immissione dall'uno nell'altro, essere assoggettate a dazio
maggiore di quello a cui sono sottoposti i prodotti medesimi delle
Nazioni le più favorite, i vini rossi
e bianchi, perciò, del Regno delle
Due Sicilie, di qualunque sorta,
inclusi quelli di Marsala, che saranno immessi direttamente negli
Stati Uniti di America, con legni
dell'uno o dell'altro paese, non
pagheranno dazî maggiori o più
elevati de'vini rossi o bianchi
delle Nazioni le più favorite. E
similmente, i Cotoni degli Stati
Uniti di America, che verranno
immessi direttamente nel Regno
delle Due Sicilie, con legni del-
l'una o dell'altra Nazione, non pagheranno dazî maggiori, o più elevati de'Cotoni di Egitto, del Ben-
gala, o di quelli delle Nazioni le
più favorite

ART⁹ 12.

The present Treaty shall be in force from this day, and for the term of ten years, and further, until the end of twelve months after either of the High contracting Parties shall have given notice to the other, of its intention to terminate the same; each of the said High contracting Parties, reserving to itself the right of giving such notice, at the end of the said term of ten years, or at any subsequent term

ART⁹ 13.

The present Treaty shall be approved and ratified by the President of the United States of America, by and with the advice and consent of the Senate of the said States, and by His Majesty the King of the Kingdom of the Two Sicilies, and the ratifications shall be exchanged at Naples, at the expiration of six months from the date of its signature, or sooner, if possible

In witness whereof the respective Plenipotentiaires have signed the same, and have affixed thereto the seal of their arms

Done at Naples the first of Dicember in the year one thousand eight hundred and forty five

WILLIAM. H. POLK [Seal]

ART⁹ 12⁹

Il presente Trattato sarà in vigore da questo giorno, e per lo spazio di dieci anni, ed anche fino al termine di dodici mesi, dopo che ciascuna delle Alte Parti contraenti, avrà notificato all'altra, la sua intenzione di porvi termine; riserbandosi ciascuna delle Alte Parti contraenti, il diritto di dare tale conoscenza, alla fine del detto termine di dieci anni, o a qualunque susseguente tempo

ART⁹ 13⁹

Il presente Trattato sarà approvato e ratificato dal Presidente degli Stati Uniti di America, con l'intesa e col consentimento del Senato degli Stati suddetti e da S. M. il Re del Regno delle Due Sicilie, e ne saranno scambiate in Napoli le ratifiche allo spirare di sei mesi dalla data della sottoscrizione, o anche prima, se sarà possibile

In fede di chè, i Plenipotenziarî rispettivi lo àn firmato, e vi ànno apposto il sugello delle loro armi

Fatto in Napoli il primo di Dicembre dell'anno milleottocento quarantacinque

GIUSTINO FORTUNATO [Seal]
IL PRINCIPE DI COMITINI [Seal]
ANTONIO SPINELLI [Seal]

NOTES

The treaty file is complete; the signed original of the treaty is written in English and Italian, with the English in the left columns; in each text the United States of America is named first; as may be seen from the print, the English text was carelessly written, containing quite a few orthographic and other errors.

The other documents in the file are in customary form; they include the attested resolution of the Senate of April 11, 1846 (Executive Journal, VII, 61-62), the duplicate United States instrument of ratification of April 14, the act of the exchange of ratifications at Naples on June 1, which is in English, and the original proclamation of July 24, 1846. The instrument of ratification of the Two Sicilies, under date of February 28, 1846, is in Italian and includes the text of the treaty in both languages, the Italian in the left columns; in each text the King of the Kingdom of the Two Sicilies is named first.

The presidential message submitting this treaty to the Senate was accompanied by "portions of the correspondence (so far as it has been received) in explanation of the treaty", and this was printed (*ibid.*, 39; Senate Confidential Document No. 3, 29th Congress, 1st session, Regular Confidential Documents, XVIII, 495-520).

The Full Powers

In this case the original full powers were exchanged; that given to William H. Polk, "Chargé d'Affaires of the United States at the Court of His Majesty the King of the Kingdom of the Two Sicilies", under date of March 17, 1845, was in customary form; its subject was "the commerce and navigation of the two Countries, and all matters and subjects connected therewith, which may be interesting to the two Nations" (D.S., 3 Credences, 123).

The original full power given to the Plenipotentiaries of the Kingdom of the Two Sicilies is in the treaty file, with a translation thereof as follows (printed in the Senate document cited, pp. 505-6):

Ferdinando II, by the Grace of God King of the Kingdom of the Two Sicilies, of Jerusalem, etc., Duke of Parma, Placentia, Castro, etc., Hereditary Grand Prince of Tuscany, etc., etc., etc.

Considering it proper for the good of Our royal dominions and of Our subjects to second the desire expressed to Us by the Government of the United States of America, We are determined to enter into a negotiation with that Government for the conclusion of a treaty of commerce and navigation on the principle of perfect reciprocity, which, by strengthening and extending the commercial relations already subsisting between the two states, may prove of reciprocal advantage to Our royal subjects and to the citizens of the United States of America. Being desirous to appoint for this purpose persons worthy in all respects of Our entire confidence and to authorize them in a proper manner to discuss, conclude, and subscribe the articles of such a treaty; and knowing from the many clear proofs received, the zeal, wisdom, faithfulness, and fitness which are combined in you, Don Giustino Fortunato, Knight Grand Cross of Our Royal Military Constantinian Order of St. George and of those of Francisco I, and Our Minister Secretary of State; in you, Don Michele Gravina e Requescuz, Prince of Comitini, Knight Grand Cross of Our Royal Order of Francisco I, Our Gentleman of the Chamber in exercise, and Our Minister Secretary of State; and in you, Don Antonio Spinelli, of the Princes of Scalea, Commander of Our

Royal Order of Francisco I, Our Gentleman of the Chamber, Consultore of the General Consulta, and Superintendent General of the Archives of the Kingdom; we have chosen and appointed, as by these present letters we do choose and appoint you, to agree, regulate, and conclude all that may relate to the said treaty. To which effect, with the present full power, We confer on you entire faculty and the necessary authorization to negotiate, conclude, and subscribe in Our name the articles of the said treaty of commerce and navigation. And we promise under Our royal faith and word to hold as approved and ratified and to fulfil exactly all that may be stipulated by you on Our part, with the person who may be furnished by the Government of the United States with equal full powers to negotiate, conclude, and subscribe such treaty.

In faith whereof We have signed with Our own hand the present full power, We have caused the seal of Our royal arms to be affixed to it, and We have had it countersigned by Our Counselor and Minister of State charged with the portfolio of foreign affairs.

Given at Naples, in the palace of Our royal residence, on the 28th day of November, 1845.

[Seal] FERDINANDO

JULIO RUFFO DI CALABRIA

THE EXCHANGE OF RATIFICATIONS

By Article 13 of the treaty the term of six months from the date of signature was allowed for the exchange of ratifications. As the Senate did not act until April 11, 1846, the time remaining for the exchange was brief; the United States instrument of ratification was sent to Naples by Washington Greenhow, as special bearer of despatches; he arrived at Naples on May 28 (D.S., 14 Instructions, Two Sicilies, 37–38; 2 Despatches, Italy: Naples, No. 5, June 2, 1846). In the despatch of William H. Polk last cited, reporting the exchange of ratifications on the last day of the term allowed, he wrote as follows:

Mr Greenhow reached Naples on the morning of 28th May, three days before the expiration of the time limited for the exchange of the ratifications, and on the same day I addressed a note to the Minister of Foreign Affairs informing him that I was prepared to exchange the ratifications at such time and place as he would be pleased to designate. On the following day I received his answer appointing the 1st Inst for that purpose. At the hour designated I attended at the office of Foreign Affairs and after having carefully compared the original and copies, exchanged the ratifications, and herewith transmit the copy delivered to me with the sanction and approval of the King endorsed thereon. When I presented to His Majesty's Plenopotentiaries the special power from the President [of April 14, 1846; D.S., 3 Credences, 169] authorizing me to exchange the ratifications, they informed me that their authority was contained in the original power granted by the King to conduct and conclude the negotiation, which I forwarded to the Department with the Treaty in December last, and by reference to which will be found to be correct.

THE NEGOTIATIONS

William H. Polk, a brother of President Polk, was appointed Chargé d'Affaires at Naples on March 13, 1845. His instructions regarding the negotiation of this treaty were under date of April 24, in the following terms (D.S., 14 Instructions, Two Sicilies, 26–33; Senate Confidential Document No. 3, 29th Congress, 1st session, Regular Confidential Documents, XVIII, 508–11).

The Government of the United States has given the strongest evidence of its desire to maintain the most friendly relations with his Sicilian Majesty, by still

continuing their mission at Naples, although his Majesty has never accredited any Diplomatic Agent to this country [see the notes to Document 74, the convention with the Two Sicilies of October 14, 1832]. This want of mutuality in the relations between the two Governments cannot long continue. The usual courtesy observed between independent nations requires that there should be a reciprocity in their diplomatic intercourse; and you may informally communicate to His Sicilian Majesty's Government, that such is the feeling entertained by the President of the United States.

The successive Representatives of the United States at Naples have been instructed, if possible, to negotiate a commercial Treaty with His Sicilian Majesty's Government. Whilst they have pursued this object with diligence, neither of them has ever yet succeeded even in drawing from the Minister of Foreign Affairs a single note upon the subject. All that has transpired between them, and him, have been informal and unsatisfactory conversations, without any result.

That no obstacle has existed during the last quarter of a century to prevent the Sicilian Government from placing our commercial relations on the same footing with those of England, appears conclusively from the Treaty, signed at London on the 26ᵗʰ September, 1816, between Great Britain and the Two Sicilies [cited *infra*]. Whilst that Treaty, by its Seventh article, and by the "separate and additional article", of the same date, makes a reduction of ten per cent from the amount of the duties payable "upon the total of the merchandize or produc-"tion of the United Kingdom of Great Britain and Ireland, her Colonies, posses-"sions, and dependencies, imported into the States of his said Sicilian Majesty", it expressly provides, *"that nothing in this article shall be construed to prevent the "King of the Two Sicilies from granting, if he shall think proper, the same reduction "of duty to other foreign nations"*. "The same reduction of duty" has been granted to France and Spain; though the commerce of the latter Kingdom, with Naples, is quite insignificant. You will thus perceive that, if an American and a British vessel enter any of the ports of the Two Sicilies together, freighted with similar productions of their respective countries, whilst these American productions are subject to an impost of fifty per cent ad valorem, those of Great Britain are charged with only forty-five per cent. By some strange mistake, the impression seems heretofore to have prevailed, that His Sicilian Majesty was bound by Treaty in such a manner to Great Britain, France, and Spain, as to preclude him from placing the commerce of the United States on the same level with that of these favored nations. You will be furnished with a copy of the Treaty, and separate additional article, of 1816, together with the Decree of His Sicilian Majesty, to give them effect, extracted from MacGregor's Commercial Tariffs and Regulations, &ᶜ volume second.

It appears from a review of the correspondence of Mʳ Boulware—your immediate predecessor—with this Department, that the Governments of Great Britain, and the Two Sicilies, have been for some years engaged in framing a new Commercial Treaty. It was to have been hoped, as well from the early portion of that correspondence, as the enlightened spirit of the age, that Great Britain would no longer have insisted upon the advantage of ten per cent which she had acquired over the United States by the Treaty of 1816. It would seem, however, from Mʳ Boulware's despatch of September 13ᵗʰ 1843, that the Treaty agreed upon between these two Powers, but not yet ratified, still retains this ten per cent advantage in favor of British productions imported in British vessels [see the treaty of April 29, 1845, between Great Britain and the Kingdom of the Two Sicilies, British and Foreign State Papers, XXXIII, 19–31]; although, for the rest, it is a reciprocal Treaty, so far as Navigation is concerned. The final execution of this Treaty has been suspended, to await the result of negotiations still pending between the Governments of France and the Two Sicilies; as it seems to be agreed that Great Britain and France shall be placed upon the same footing; and if French diplomacy can obtain greater concessions than those embraced in the Treaty with Great Britain, these are to become common to both the favored nations. Nay, more; if we have a correct understanding on this subject, these pending Treaties, should they be concluded, would affect, still more injuriously, the interests of the United States than even the Treaties now in existence. At present, although American productions, imported into the Two Sicilies in American vessels, are subject to the unjust discrimination of ten per cent in favor of British and French productions, and navigation, yet a reduction

of 30 per cent is now made from the common rate of duties on American productions, when imported in Sicilian vessels. This discrimination, although intended alone to encourage Sicilian Navigation, operates indirectly in favor of our productions when brought into competition with those of a similar character of Great Britain and France. Should the pending Treaties be finally ratified, it is more than probable that we shall be deprived even of this advantage.

In view of these circumstances, you are instructed, at the earliest convenient moment after your arrival in Naples, to remonstrate respectfully, but strongly, in a diplomatic note, against the grant of any privileges to British and French navigation and commerce, in which the United States shall not equally participate; and to ask that our country shall enjoy the same advantages in the ports of the Two Sicilies, whatever they may be, which shall be extended to these two nations. In a separate note, you will respectfully request that the Sicilian Government may exercise its clear right, reserved under its Treaty with Great Britain; and, by a Royal Decree, grant to American commerce and navigation the same privileges which are now extended to those of Great Britain and France. In making this request, you may state that, the President is anxious to receive an answer in time to be presented to Congress at the commencement of its next Session. He trusts, and believes that this answer will be favorable; but should his confident expectations be disappointed, it will then be for the wisdom of that Body to decide what countervailing discriminations ought, in justice, to be made against the productions of the Two Sicilies, imported into the United States. The ardent desire of the President to cultivate the most friendly relations with the Government of the Two Sicilies, causes him earnestly to hope that, after so long a delay, no necessity may exist to resort to any such commercial retaliation.

The Government of the United States have long desired to conclude a Commercial Treaty with the Two Sicilies;—they have been pursuing this object for years with a steady aim, and it is now time that they should know the final decision of the Sicilian Government upon the subject. They sincerely believe that such a Treaty would be equally beneficial to both Countries. The United States seek no advantages over other nations. All they desire is, a perfect reciprocity in trade. The civilized world is now rapidly advancing towards this great principle; and experience has already demonstrated that its universal prevalence in practice,—so far at least as regards the direct trade,—would be beneficial to all nations. This policy was adopted at an early period by the Government of the United States; and has been developed before the World by the Acts of Congress of March 3^d 1815, January 7th 1824, and May 24th 1828 [3 Statutes at Large, 224; 4 *ibid.*, 2–3, 308–9].

The first of these Acts offers to all nations to admit their vessels laden with their productions, into the ports of the United States on the payment of the same duties of tonnage and import exacted from our own vessels; provided similar advantages shall be extended by them to American vessels. The Act of 1828, abolishes all restrictions in regard to the origin of the productions imported. Under it, the United States offer to throw wide open their ports to the vessels of all nations, with their cargoes—no matter to what country these cargoes may owe their origin—, upon payment of the same duties with our own vessels; provided such nations shall extend similar privileges in their ports, to vessels and cargoes belonging to citizens of the United States.

You are authorised to conclude a Treaty of Commerce and navigation with the Government of the Two Sicilies upon the most liberal principles of reciprocity. It is more than probable, however, that the Sicilian Government would prefer to confine this reciprocity to the direct trade between the two countries, according to the provisions of the Act of March 3^d 1815; and with such a Treaty the United States would be entirely satisfied, provided Great Britain and France should be placed in the same position.

You will find models of a reciprocal Treaty of Commerce, for your guidance, in every variety of form, in Elliott's American Diplomatic Code, now in the Library of your Legation. This will furnish you many precedents; as we have either concluded such Treaties, or made commercial arrangements of the same character, through the intervention of Legislation, with almost every civilized nation.

You can urge convincing arguments to the Government of His Sicilian Majesty, that such a Treaty would be highly advantageous to his Kingdom. Under the

blighting influence of existing restrictions, the direct trade between the two countries is considerably less than it was some years ago; and falls very far short of what it would soon become under a fair reciprocal Treaty. Commerce always flourishes most between Nations whose productions are different; because then they can mutually supply each other's wants. For this very reason, if the existing restrictions were removed, the commerce between the United States and the Two Sicilies, must rapidly increase, greatly for the benefit of both nations. We should then export to that country, our dried, smoked and salted fish; our cotton, rice, tobacco, naval stores, and other articles which I might enumerate, and receive in return their silks, wines, olive oil, fruits, Leghorn hats, sulphur, and crude brimstone, with many other Sicilian commodities. It is lamentable to reflect, that, a commerce which might be so mutually beneficial, is limited to such a comparatively small amount by unwise restrictions. Herewith, you will receive an abstract of this commerce, since the year 1834;—prepared at the Treasury Department.

Great reliance is placed on the zeal, discretion and ability with which you will devote yourself to accomplish the important objects of your mission; and good hopes are entertained that you will prove successful.

Polk reached Naples on July 18, 1845, and was received by the King of the Two Sicilies on August 22; four days later he formally communicated the fact that he had full powers to negotiate a treaty of commerce and navigation; and on September 9 he was informed of the appointment of the Plenipotentiaries of the Two Sicilies (D.S., 2 Despatches, Italy: Naples, No. 1, July 26, 1845; No. 2, September 28, 1845).

Polk submitted as a basis of the proposed agreement the treaty between the United States and Austria of August 27, 1829 (Document 66), with certain other articles "providing for the reduction of present duties exacted on the produce of our Country in this Kingdom" (D.S., 2 Despatches, Italy: Naples, No. 2, September 28, 1845). This course was approved by instructions of November 12, 1845, from which the following paragraphs are excerpted; that communication, however, could not have reached Naples by the date of the signature of this treaty (D.S., 14 Instructions, Two Sicilies, 34–36; printed in the Senate document cited, 511–12):

It would certainly be desirable that you should obtain if possible a stipulation in the proposed Treaty, to reduce the existing duties in the Kingdom of the Two Sicilies on cotton, tobacco, or any other articles, of the production of the United States. This, in your opinion, you will not be able to accomplish, without the grant of equivalents on our part. The fate of the Zoll-Verein Treaty [of March 25, 1844] in the Senate, as well as the embarrassments with other nations with whom we have commercial Treaties, which would result from a reduction of duties by Treaty on the productions of that country, would prevent us from granting this equivalent required. For the present, therefore, you are instructed to conclude a Treaty without insisting upon a reduction of duties in the ports of the Two Sicilies on any of our productions. It is deemed of so much importance to obtain a commercial Treaty on the terms which we have adopted with other nations, that you will not delay its conclusion by insisting on any thing further. A reciprocal reduction of duties on the productions of the two countries may hereafter be accomplished under more propitious circumstances.

You acted correctly in presenting our Treaty with Austria as a model for that with the Neapolitan Government. It is probable, however, as you suggest, that they may not be willing to conclude such a Treaty of general commercial reciprocity with the United States. Their Treaty with Great Britain, which you have forwarded to the Department, is limited to the direct trade, and it is not likely that they will be willing to grant us more extensive privileges.

I would, however, call your special attention to the 11ᵗʰ [14th] article of the Neapolitan Treaty with Great Britain. By this it is provided that the subjects of Great Britain shall continue to enjoy a reduction of ten per cent upon the duties payable according to their Customs' Tariff upon British Merchandize and productions; but it is also stipulated that the same privilege may be granted to other nations. You will insist upon a grant of this privilege to the United States to the full extent in which it is enjoyed by Great Britain; and conclude no treaty which does not clearly embrace such a provision.

There are several Treaties, confined to the direct trade between the United States and foreign countries, to which you may refer as models. I would instance that with Portugal of the 26ᵗʰ August, 1840 [Document 95],—because it is our latest Treaty of this character. I transmit you a copy.

It seems that the discussions between the Plenipotentiaries commenced in October and were verbal (D.S., 2 Despatches, Italy: Naples, No. 4, May 5, 1846). In his despatch of December 1, 1845, transmitting the treaty, Polk reported as follows (Senate Confidential Document No. 3, 29th Congress, 1st session, Regular Confidential Documents, XVIII, 512–14; original not in the archives of the Department of State):

I have the honor to transmit, herewith, for ratification by the President, by and with the advice and consent of the Senate, a treaty of commerce and navigation, which I have this day concluded and signed on the part of the United States with the Kingdom of the Two Sicilies, together with the full powers granted by the King to the plenipotentiaries whose names and seals are thereunto affixed. Throughout the negotiation I have endeavored, and I hope successfully, to confine myself within the limits of my instructions from the Department of State. Every effort was made to secure a treaty of general and perfect reciprocity, embracing the productions of the soil and industry of every nation entering the ports of the Sicilies under the American flag, but without success. The recent treaties between this Kingdom and England [cited above], France [of June 14, 1845; British and Foreign State Papers, XXXIV, 1275–82], and Russia [of September 25, 1845; *ibid.*, 1328–35], restrict their reciprocal commercial intercourse to the direct trade, and it could not be reasonably expected that this government would change its settled policy in this respect, and extend greater advantages to the United States than to other countries.

Prior to the conventions between the Two Sicilies and England, France, and Spain, concluded in 1816 and 1817 [see *ibid.*, V, 586–609], by which these three powers secured for the productions of their respective countries a reduction of *ten per cent.* on the tariff of duties in the ports of this Kingdom, the vessels of the United States frequented all its ports, laden with cargoes the produce of our country, and in return took away cargoes the productions of this country. The privilege of the *ten per cent.* being now equally extended to the United States, there is every reason to believe that the trade between the two countries will revive to the same activity which existed previous to 1816. For twenty-five years or more, an American vessel has been seldom seen to arrive in the port of Naples, though Palermo and Messina have been, and still continue to be, visited by our vessels on their return from Trieste, Marseilles, Genoa, and Leghorn, but it is always without cargoes, and with money or bills to purchase fruit or other produce. Now that our vessels are not subjected to other or higher duties of tonnage than national vessels, and our productions are relieved from all differential duties, it may be expected in future that they will, instead of paying money, be able to exchange commodities. No means have been spared to get reduced the duty on cotton and tobacco; but as this government has, for many years, been steadfastly pursuing the encouragement of the cultivation of these articles, all that has been practicable has been done to reduce the duty on cotton from *twenty ducats* per cantar, which is about one hundred and ninety pounds English weight, to *ten ducats;* and as the duty on tobacco was found to have been reduced in the last year from *twenty-eight ducats* per cantar, which it has for many years paid, to *fifteen ducats*, they could not be induced to make any further diminution. It has not been possible to change their system for the article of tobacco at Naples;

it being a government monopoly, yielding an annual revenue of nearly a million of dollars, they cannot be induced to alter the regulation. I do not think, however, that the consumption of American tobacco is the less on this account, for the persons or company who contract for the exclusive privilege of introducing the article into Naples import large quantities, either directly from the United States, or indirectly, as it suits best where to make their purchases. There exists, also, a differential duty on the exportation of oil between national and the vessels of nations with whom they have no treaty regulations. This will now cease with regard to us, and it may be that vessels of the United States will find freights of *this* and other articles for the north of Europe as well as the United States. The tonnage duty heretofore exacted from American vessels of *forty grains* per ton, and which, according to their manner of measurement, is equal to *forty cents*, is now reduced to *four grains*. This obstacle to many merchant vessels touching the ports of this Kingdom being now removed, is of no small importance when it is considered that from eighty to one hundred of our vessels load annually in Sicily. It may be that the tonnage of only six cents per ton on Sicilian vessels in the United States, and the extra duty of *ten per cent.* levied on the cargoes of vessels belonging to nations with whom we have no fixed commercial regulations, may serve to increase the number of their vessels in the ports of our country, but still they can never reach that of our vessels which will visit the Two Sicilies. The tariffs of each country have not been altered in else than to place each nation on a footing of national, or the most favored. They always answered to any demand for reduction of their duties, "We cannot change ours, increase yours if you think proper." When, however, they will have concluded treaties now in progress with other nations, I am assured their tariff will be revised, and such changes made as may seem advantageous to their new system of liberal commercial intercourse with the world. Being now placed on an equal footing with national vessels, or those of the most favored nations, it depends on our merchants and captains to contend in a field of fair competition, and I believe they will do it successfully, from their known intelligence and activity. You will discover by the twelfth article of the treaty that it takes effect from the day it bears date. This I was induced to adopt by the urgent solicitation of our consul at Palermo. This being the season of the year when American vessels chiefly visit the Kingdom of the Two Sicilies, it was considered desirable to give them the advantages of treaty regulations, which would relieve them from the existing burden of tonnage and other duties; of course, the old rate of duties will be exacted until the treaty shall have been ratified and exchanged by both the contracting parties, as provided by the twelfth article, subject to be refunded.

. . . .

The irregularities of the mails between Naples and Paris, at this particular season of the year, are such as to render the safe transmission of a document, the size of a treaty, very uncertain, and I have therefore deemed it my duty to carry it myself as far as Paris, from whence it can be safely sent to the United States. I will remain a few days only in Paris before returning to Naples.

ARTICLE 12

The provision in Article 12 of the treaty to the effect that it should "be in force from this day", that is to say, the date of signature, is rather unusual. In his despatch of December 1, 1845, above quoted, Polk explains this provision as meaning that "the old rate of duties will be exacted until the treaty shall have been ratified and exchanged . . . subject to be refunded". In his despatch of May 5, 1846 (D.S., 2 Despatches, Italy: Naples, No. 4), there are the following observations on the subject:

A few weeks ago a Sicilian Merchant Vessel returned to Naples, having entered one of the ports of the United States after the 1st day of December, when the new rate of duties are to receive effect, as provided by the 12th Article of the Treaty, and complained that the Vessel and Cargo were subjected to the old

rate of duties. Concerning this complaint I received no official or other communication from the Minister of State, but learned from our worthy and excellent Consul Mr Hammette that some disatisfaction existed and fearing lest the Government might possibly participate in the discontent or had fallen into some error as to the agreed meaning of the 12ᵗʰ Article of the Treaty, I took occasion a few days after, a good opportunity occurring to allude to the circumstance when in conversation with one of the gentlemen who was engaged in the negotiation, and from him learned that the exaction of the old rate of duties was expected, until the ratifications were exchanged, when according to the clearly understood meaning of the 12ᵗʰ Article all duties which had been levied and received by either Government over and above the rate settled by the Treaty, should on application in proper form, being made, be refunded—to which I assented—such being the distinct agreement when the date was fixed from which time the provisions of the Treaty should take quallified effect.

A Treasury Department circular to collectors of the customs, dated August 18, 1846, and having annexed a copy of the proclamation of the treaty, including the English text thereof, contains these paragraphs (D.S., Miscellaneous Letters, July–September 1846, enclosure to letter of the Secretary of the Treasury of August 21, 1846):

The clear and explicit terms employed in the several important stipulations of the treaty, render it unnecessary, in the opinion of the Department, at this time to add detailed instructions in relation to its provisions generally. It, however, becomes expedient, in view of those contained in the first, eleventh, and twelfth articles, so far as they apply to the entry of the wines of Sicily and the duties chargeable thereon, questions in regard to which being now before the Department, to advise you, that the white and red wines of the Kingdom of the Two Sicilies, of every kind, including those of Marsala, imported directly into the United States, whether in vessels of the one or the other country, since the first day of December, 1845, are entitled to entry, and are to be accordingly so admitted, at the lowest rates of duty at which the white and red wines, respectively, of any other country, are admitted, whether in conformity with treaty stipulations between the United States and such country, or otherwise.

The importers of the white or red wines of Sicily, including those of Marsala, entered since the first day of December, 1845, who have paid the rates of duty chargeable on such designated wines under the tariff act of 30th August, 1842, being, by the operation of the said provisions of the treaty, entitled to a return of the excess over the rates at which the white or red wines of some other countries have been admitted within the same period, under the laws or treaty stipulations, you are authorized and directed to issue the usual certified statement for the return of such excess found, on examination, to have been so paid, referring in such statement, and in your accounts of the Customs, to this letter by date, as your authority for the payment.

119

NEW GRANADA : MAY 16, 1846

*Convention for the Final Settlement of the Case of the Brig "Josephine",
signed at Bogotá May 16, 1846. Original in Spanish.
Not subject to ratification by the United States. As to ratification by
New Granada, see the notes. Not proclaimed.*

[Translation]

Los infrascritos, á saber: el Encargado de Negocios de los Estados Unidos Benjamin A. Bidlack, i el Secretario de Estado del Despacho de Relaciones Esteriores de la Nueva Granada Eusebio Borrero habiendonos reunido con el objeto de transar la reclamacion á que ha dado lugar la falta de pago de ciertos resíduos de intereses y otras pérdidas que se dicen sufridas por los interesados en el bergantin americano Josephine; hemos convenido en que la citada reclamacion quede transijida definitivamente de la manera que se espresa en los articulos siguientes:

The undersigned, that is to say, the Chargé d'Affaires of the United States, Benjamin A. Bidlack, and the Secretary of Exterior Relations for New Granada, Eusebio Borrero, having joined for the purpose of settling the claim originating in the nonpayment of certain interest and other losses alleged to have been suffered by those interested in the American brig *Josephine*, have agreed that the said claim shall be settled definitively in the manner following.

ARTÍCULO 1º

El Gobierno de la Nueva Granada se obliga á pagar á la órden del Señor Encargado de Negocios de los Estados Unidos seis mil quinientos sesenta i nueve pesos i catorce centavos de peso ($6,569.14cˢ). en moneda corriente, como única y absoluta indemnizacion por todas las pérdidas i

ARTICLE 1

The Government of New Granada agrees to pay to the order of the Chargé d'Affaires of the United States six thousand five hundred and sixty-nine dollars, fourteen cents ($6,569.14), in the current money, as an absolute indemnification for all losses and prejudices arising out of the claim

813

perjuicios que han dado motivo á la citada reclamacion de los interesados en el Bergantin "Josephine," quienes no conservarán derecho alguno para intentar ninguna nueva reclamacion sobre este particular.

of those interested in the brig *Josephine* not heretofore paid; and they shall have no right to institute any new demand growing out of the circumstances of this case.

ARTÍCULO 2º

La mencionada suma de seis mil quinientos sesenta i nueve pesos i catorce centavos de peso ($6,56.9.14c$) será satisfecha en la Tesoreria Jeneral en tres pagos mensuales, i en la forma siguiente: mil quinientos sesenta i nueve pesos i catorce centavos de peso ($1569.14c$) en el mes de Setiembre próximo: i dos mil i quinientos pesos ($2,500.) en cada uno de los meses de Octubre i Noviembre inmediatos al citado mes de Setiembre en que debe verificarse el primer pago.

ARTICLE 2

The said sum of $6,569.14 shall be paid at the Treasury in three monthly payments in the following manner: $1,569.14 in the month of September next, and $2,500 in each of the months of October and November immediately following the first payment.

ARTÍCULO 3º

Este convenio será presentado por el Poder Ejecutivo de la Nueva Granada al Congreso de la misma en su presente reunion, á fin de que, prévia su aprobacion, vote la cantidad necesaria para que tenga efecto.

ARTICLE 3

This convention shall be presented by the President to the Congress now in session, that it may appropriate the amount required to carry it into effect.

En fé de lo cual, nosotros los infrascritos hemos firmado dos ejemplares de este convenio, ambos de un mismo tenor i forma, en Bogotá á diez i seis de Mayo de mil ochocientos cuarenta i seis.

B A BIDLACK
EUSEBIO BORRERO

In faith of which the undersigned have executed two agreements of this tenor and form in Bogotá this sixteenth of May, one thousand eight hundred and forty-six.

B A BIDLACK
EUSEBIO BORRERO

NOTES

The source text of this convention is the original in D.S., Colombian Claims, folder *Josephine*. There appears to have been no English text; the translation printed, which does not follow the Spanish as closely as might be desired, is from D.S., 11 Despatches, Colombia, No. 20, June 15, 1846, enclosure.

Neither in the convention nor in the despatches is there any mention of full powers. Under date of May 30, 1845, however, Bidlack had been given a full power with authority "to agree, treat, consult and negotiate of and concerning claims of citizens of the United States upon the late Republic of Colombia and the said Republic of New Granada" (D.S., 3 Credences, 141). The approval of the convention by the Congress of New Granada was given by an appropriation of the sum payable thereunder (D.S., 11 Despatches, Colombia, No. 18, June 1, 1846).

The case of the *Josephine* was dealt with in the conventions with Colombia of March 16, 1825, and of November 25, 1829 (Documents 48 and 67); the notes to those conventions should be consulted.

This convention was for the final settlement of the case of the *Josephine* so far as it concerned New Granada. The claim here was for interest from May 25, 1830, to the various dates of payment in 1837 and 1838 of the instalments aggregating approximately $13,-849.31, as mentioned in the notes to Document 67; that interest came to $6,569.14. A further claim for $692.45 for loss on depreciated money was not allowed (D.S., Miscellaneous Letters, April–July 1845, letter of Simeon Toby of May 9, 1845).

The three payments agreed to under the convention were duly made, in "current money", by the Government of New Granada (D.S., 11 Despatches, Colombia, No. 32, December 14, 1846, and No. 37, January 8, 1847); there is a receipt for the entire amount, signed by Simeon Toby, president of the Insurance Company of the State of Pennsylvania, under date of July 23, 1847 (D.S., Colombian Claims, folder *Josephine*).

While a further claim in respect of the *Josephine* was made before the Commission under the convention of February 10, 1864, with the United States of Colombia, it was adjudged not valid (Moore, International Arbitrations, II, 1418, case 23).

Still other conventions dealing with the case of the *Josephine* are that with Venezuela of November 16, 1846, and that with Ecuador of June 15, 1849.

Treaty Series No. 248
9 Statutes at Large, 849–52
18 *ibid.*, pt. 2, Public Treaties, 531–32

120

NASSAU : MAY 27, 1846

Convention for the Mutual Abolition of the Droit d'Aubaine and Taxes on Emigration, signed at Berlin May 27, 1846. Original in English and German.
Submitted to the Senate June 24, 1846. (Message of June 23, 1846.) Resolution of advice and consent July 21, 1846. Ratified by the United States July 23, 1846. Ratified by Nassau July 29, 1846. Ratifications exchanged at Berlin October 13, 1846. Proclaimed January 6, 1847.

Convention for the mutual abolition of the droit d'aubaine and taxes on emigration between the United States of America and His Royal Highness the Duke of Nassau.

The United States of America and His Royal Highness the Duke of Nassau having resolved, for the advantage of their respective citizens and subjects, to conclude a Convention for the mutual abolition of the droit d'aubaine and taxes on emigration, have named for this purpose their respective Plenipotentiaries, namely, the President of the United States of America has conferred full powers on Henry Wheaton, their Envoy Extraordinary and Minister Plenipotentiary at the Royal Court of Prussia, and His Royal Highness the Duke of Nassau, upon His Minister Resident at the

Vertrag ueber die gegenseitige Aufhebung von Heimfalls (Fremdlings) Recht und Auswanderungs-Steuern zwischen den vereinigten Staaten von Nord America und Seiner Koeniglichen Hoheit dem Herzog von Nassau.

Nachdem die Vereinigten Staaten von Nord America und Seiner Koenigliche Hoheit der Herzog von Nassau beschlossen haben: zum Besten der beiderseitigen Staatsangehoerigen einen Vertrag über gegenseitige Aufhebung von Heimfalls (Fremdlings) Recht u. Auswanderungs Steuern abzuschliessen, so sind dazu von beiden Seiten Bevollmaechtigte ernannt worden, nämlich von Seiten des Praesidenten der Vereinigten Staaten von Nord America, Herr Heinrich Wheaton, Nordamericanischer ausserordentlicher Gesandter und bevollmaechtigter Minister am Königlich Preussi-

817

Royal Court of Prussia, Colonel and Chamberlain, Otto Wilhelm Carl von Roeder, Comthur[1] of the 1st Class of the Ducal Order of Henry, the Lion, etc, etc. who, after having exchanged their said full powers, found in due and proper form, have agreed to, and signed, the following articles.

schen Hofe, und von Seiten Seiner Koeniglichen Hoheit des Herzogs von Nassau Hoechstihr Minister-resident am Koeniglich Preus-sischen Hofe, Oberst und Kam-merherr, Otto Wilhelm Carl von Roeder, Comthur[1] 1er Classe des Herzoglichen Ordens Heinrich des Loewen &c. &c. welche Be-vollmaechtigte, nach vollzogener Auswechselung ihrer, gegenseitig in rechtiger und gehoeriger Form befundener Vollmachten, nachste-hende Artikel festgesetzt und un-terzeichnet haben.

ARTICLE I.

Every kind of droit d'aubaine, droit de retraite and droit de dé-traction or tax on emigration is, hereby, and shall remain abol-ished, between the two contract-ing parties, their States, citizens, and subjects respectively.

ARTIKEL I.

Jede Art von Heimfalls (Fremd-lings) Recht, Nachsteuer und Abzugsrecht oder Auswanderungs Steuer, ist und bleibt aufgehoben zwischen beiden abschliessenden Theilen, ihren beiderseitigen Staa-ten und Staats-Angehoerigen.

ARTICLE II.

Where, on the death of any person holding real property with-in the territories of one party, such real property would, by the laws of the land, descend on a citizen or subject of the other, were he not disqualified by alien-age, such citizen or subject shall be allowed a term of two years to sell the same,—which term may be reasonably prolonged, accord-ing to circumstances,—and to withdraw the proceeds thereof,

ARTIKEL II.

Wenn durch den Tod irgend eines Besitzers von Immobilien oder Grundeigenthum, welche sich auf dem Gebiete des einen der ab-schliessenden Theile befinden, diese Immobilien oder Grundei-genthum nach den Gesetzen des Landes auf einen Staatsangehoe-rigen des anderen Theils ueber-gehen sollten, so wird diesem, wenn er durch seine Eigenschaft als Fremder zum Besitze dersel-ben unfaehig ist, ein Aufschub

[1] Or *Komtur*, i.e., "Commander".

without molestation, and exempt from all duties of detraction.

von zwei Jahren gewaehrt, welcher Termin nach Umstaenden in angemessener Weise verlaengert werden kann, dieselbe zu verkaufen und um den Ertrag davon ohne Anstand und frei von jeder Abzugs Steuer zu beziehen.

Article III.

The citizens or subjects of each of the contracting parties shall have power to dispose of their personal property within the States of the other, by testament, donation, or otherwise, and their heirs, legatees and donees, being citizens or subjects of the other contracting party, shall succeed to their said personal property, and may take possession thereof, either by themselves or by others acting for them, and dispose of the same at their pleasure, paying such duties only as the inhabitants of the country where the said property lies, shall be liable to pay in like cases.

Artikel III.

Den Staatsangehoerigen eines jeden der abschliessenden Theile, soll in den Staaten des anderen die Freiheit zustehen, über ihre beweglichen Gueter durch Testament, Schenkung, oder auf andere Weise zu verfuegen, und deren Erben ab-intestato oder Rechtsnachfolger, durch Testament oder Schenkung, sollen wenn sie Staatsangehoerige des anderen der beiden abschliessenden Theile sind, ihnen in dem Besitze ihrer beweglichen Gueter folgen, auch in Person sowohl, als durch Andere, welche an ihrer Stelle handeln, davon Besitz ergreifen und nach Gutduenken damit schalten können, ohne andere Steuern zu bezahlen als solche, welchen die Einwohner des Landes, worin sich die genannten Gueter befinden, bei gleichem Anlasse unterworfen sind.

Article IV.

In case of the absence of the heirs, the same care shall be taken provisionally, of such real or personal property, as would be taken in a like case of property belonging to the natives of the country until the lawful owner, or the person who has a right so sell the

Artikel IV.

Im Falle der Abwesenheit der Erben wird man hinsichtlich der erwähnten beweglichen oder unbeweglichen Gueter provisorisch ganz dieselbe Sorgfalt anwenden, welche man bei gleichem Anlasse, hinsichtlich der Gueter der Eingebornen angewendet hatte, bis

same, according to Article II, may take measures to receive or dispose of the inheritance.

der gesetzmaessige Eigenthuemer, oder derjenige, welcher nach Artikel II das Recht hat: dieselben zu verkaufen, Anordnungen zu treffen für gut finden wird: um die Erbsohaft anzutreten oder darüber zu verfügen.

ARTICLE V.

If any disputes should arise between different claimants to the same inheritance, they shall be decided, in the last resort, according to the laws and by the judges of the country where the property is situated.

ARTIKEL V.

Wenn sich Streitigkeiten zwischen verschiedenen, rechtlichen Anspruch auf die Erbschaft habenden Praetendenten erheben, so werden dieselben in letzter Instanz nach den Gesetzen und von den Richtern des Landes entschieden werden, in welchem das Object der Erbschaft sich befindet.

ARTICLE VI.

All the stipulations of the present Convention shall be obligatory in respect to property already inherited or bequeathed, but not yet withdrawn from the country where the same is situated at the signature of this Convention.

ARTIKEL VI

Sämmtliche, in gegenwaertigem Vertrage enthaltene Bestimmungen, sollen auch in Ansehung solcher Vermögenstheile verbindliche Kraft haben, welche zur Zeit der Unterzeichnung des gegenwaertigen Vertrages bereits angefallen, jedoch noch nicht wirklich expectorirt sind.

ARTICLE VII.

This Convention is concluded subject to the ratification of the President of the United States of America, by and with the advice and consent of their Senate, and of His Royal Highness the Duke of Nassau, and the ratifications thereof shall be exchanged at Berlin, within the term of twelve months from the date of the sig-

ARTIKEL VII.

Gegenwaertiger Vertrag ist abgeschlossen worden, vorbehaltlich der Ratification des Praesidenten der Vereinigten Staaten von Nord America, nach und mit dem Rathe und der Einwilligung des nordamericanischen Senates, und vorbehaltlich der Ratification Seiner Koeniglichen Hoheit des Herzogs von Nassau, und es soll die Aus-

nature hereof; or sooner if possible.

wechselung der Ratifications-Urkunden innerhalb zwoelf Monaten, vom Tage der Unterzeichnung des gegenwaertigen Vertrages an gerechnet, oder früher, wenn es möglich ist, zu Berlin stattfinden.

In witness whereof, the respective Plenipotentiaries have signed the above articles, as well in English as in German and have thereto affixed their seals

In Urkund dessen haben die beiderseitigen Bevollmaechtigten obstehende Artikel, sowohl in englischer als in deutscher Sprache unterzeichnet, und ihre Siegel beigedrueckt.

Done in triplicata, in the city of Berlin, on the 27th day of May one thousand eight hundred and forty-six, in the 70th year of the Independence of the United States of America, and the seventh of the reign of His Royal Highness the Duke of Nassau.

Ausgestellt in drei Exemplaren zu Berlin, den 27^{en} Mai Ein Tausend Acht Hundert Sechs und Vierzig, im siebzigsten Jahre der Unabhaengigkeit der vereinigten Staaten von Nord America, und im siebenten Jahre der Regierung Seiner Koeniglichen Hoheit des Herzogs von Nassau.

HENRY WHEATON
[Seal]

OTTO WILHELM CARL v. RÖDER
[Seal]

NOTES

In the final clause of this convention it is said that it was "done in triplicata". There are two signed originals in the treaty file. In each of these the English text is written in the left columns, the United States of America is named first throughout in both texts, and the Plenipotentiary of the United States signed at the left. In neither original is the German text written in German script.

The usual papers are in the file. They include the attested Senate resolution of July 21, 1846 (Executive Journal, VII, 125), the duplicate United States instrument of ratification of July 23, 1846, and the original proclamation of January 6, 1847. There are two examples of the protocol of the exchange of ratifications at Berlin on October 13, 1846. That act is in French, drawn in simple form, and makes no specific mention of the comparison of texts.

The instrument of ratification by the Duke of Nassau of July 29, 1846, is written in German and includes both texts of the convention, the German in the left columns in German script. Throughout those texts the Duke of Nassau is named first, and the copy of the signature of the American Plenipotentiary appears at the right, under the

English text.   That instrument of ratification is beautifully engrossed on parchment, with illuminated letters.   Its pendant seal is now lacking.

The texts of this convention printed above have been collated with that one of the two originals which is with the original proclamation. The differences between the two originals are trifling and of no importance whatever.   The original here used for collating omits a few commas which are in the other document and contains a few which it omits.

Three papers in the file were enclosures to the despatch of J. C. Bancroft Davis, Minister to Germany, of September 13, 1875 (D.S., 9 Despatches, Germany, No. 171), namely, that original of the convention which is not with the original proclamation, one of the examples of the protocol of the exchange of ratifications, and the original full power of the Plenipotentiary of Nassau given under date of May 20, 1846, to negotiate and sign the convention, to which further reference is made below.

When this convention was submitted to the Senate with the presidential message of June 23, 1846, it was accompanied by the despatch of Henry Wheaton, Minister to Prussia, of May 27, 1846, which has not been found in the archives of the Department of State, but which was printed (Senate Confidential Document No. 10, 29th Congress, 1st session, Regular Confidential Documents, XVIII, 801–5).   The substance of that brief despatch is as follows:

I have the honor to enclose a convention, concluded this day with the Duchy of Nassau, for the mutual abolition of the droit d'aubaine and taxes on emigration, between that State of the Germanic confederation and the United States of America.

The stipulations of this treaty will be found to be identically the same with those of the convention concluded with Wurtemberg, for the same purposes, in 1844, and subsequently ratified by the President with the advice and consent of the Senate [Document 107].

THE FULL POWERS

In the preamble of this convention it is said that the full powers were exchanged.   As stated in the notes to Document 106, Henry Wheaton was given, under date of November 18, 1843, six identic full powers to treat with the respective Plenipotentiaries of Saxony, Bavaria, Württemberg, the Electorate of Hesse, the Grand Duchy of Hesse, and the Grand Duchy of Baden; but no record has been found of any full power issuing to Wheaton to treat with a Plenipotentiary of the Duke of Nassau; and in a private despatch of February 26, 1846 (D.S., 3 Despatches, Prussia), Wheaton wrote that he was still awaiting the necessary full powers to conclude conventions with various German states on the same basis as those already signed.

The full power given to the Plenipotentiary of the Duke of Nassau is in the file.   That document is dated at Wiesbaden, May 20, 1846, and is in unusual form, for it is under the seal of the Ministry of State and is signed by the Minister of State, with, apparently, the attesting signature of another official.   In substance it reads as follows (translation from the German, which is written in German script):

The Most Serene Prince and Lord, Adolph, Duke of Nassau, etc.:

We, most graciously appointed Minister of State at the Ministry of State of His Highness, hereby commission, by virtue of full authority and special instructions graciously given us by His Highness the Duke, the Minister Resident of the Duchy of Nassau at the Court of the Kingdom of Prussia, Colonel and Chamberlain von Röder, at Berlin, as Plenipotentiary from this Duchy for the conclusion of a convention with the United States of North America concerning reciprocal abrogation of the rights of *aubaine* and emigration taxes, promising to ratify everything which he may undertake in this capacity in accordance with the instructions given him.

In faith whereof our signature is affixed, and the ministerial seal.

Wiesbaden, May 20, 1846.

[Seal]   Dungern

The Negotiations

As to the negotiations and content of this and the four other very similar conventions with various German states of about the same period (1844–46), the notes to Document 106, the convention with Hesse of March 26, 1844, should be consulted.

The provisions of this convention are copied almost literally from those of the convention with Württemberg of April 10, 1844 (Document 107).

The Duchy of Nassau

At the time of this convention the Duchy of Nassau was a member of the Germanic Confederation (1815–66). A summary account of that Confederation, with a list of the members thereof, is in the notes to Document 59, the convention with the Hanseatic Republics of December 20, 1827. The Duchy of Nassau was also party to the German Zollverein or Customs Union, as to which, also, see the notes to Document 59.

In the war of 1866 between Austria and Prussia, in which various other German states participated on one side or the other, Duke Adolph of Nassau took the side of Austria; on October 3, 1866, Nassau was formally incorporated into the Kingdom of Prussia.

167951°—vol. 4—34——54

Treaty Series No. 154
9 Statutes at Large, 857–68
18 *ibid.*, pt. 2, Public Treaties, 391–96

121

HANOVER : JUNE 10, 1846

*Treaty of Navigation and Commerce, signed at Hanover June 10, 1846.
Original in German and English.
Submitted to the Senate July 7, 1846. Resolution of advice and consent January 6, 1847. Ratified by the United States January 8, 1847.
Ratified by Hanover March 5, 1847. Ratifications exchanged at
Hanover March 5, 1847. Proclaimed April 24, 1847.*

Die Vereinigten Staaten von America und Seine Majestät der König von Hannover, von gleichem Wunsche beseelt, die Privilegien Ihrer Schifffahrt auf die Grundlage der ausgedehntesten Liberalität zu stellen und auch sonst jede Aufmunterung und Erleichterung zu gewähren, um den Handels-Verkehr zwischen den beiderseitigen Staaten zu vermehren, haben beschlossen, die zwischen denselben zu beobachtenden Regeln durch einen Handels- und Schifffahrts-Vertrag definitiv festzusetzen.

Zu diesem Behufe hat der Präsident der Vereinigten Staaten mit Vollmacht versehen:

den Special-Agenten derselben bei Seiner Majestät dem Könige von Hannover, A. Dudley Mann, und haben Seine Majestät der König von Hannover gleiche Vollmacht ertheilt:

Allerhöchst Ihrem Geheimenrath den Freyherrn Georg Fried-

The United States of America and His Majesty the King of Hanover, equally animated with a desire of placing the privileges of their navigation on a basis of the most extended liberality, and of affording, otherwise, every encouragement and facility, for increasing the commercial intercourse between their respective States, have resolved to settle in a definitive manner the rules which shall be observed between the one and the other by means of a treaty of Navigation and Commerce: For which purpose the President of the United States has conferred full powers on A. Dudley Mann, their special Agent to His Majesty the King of Hanover, and His Majesty the King of Hanover has furnished with the like full powers the Baron George Frederick de Falcke of His privy Council, Knight Grand-Cross of the Royal Guelphick Order, who after exchanging their full powers found in good and due

rich von Falcke, Groskreuz des Königlichen Guelphenordens, welche nach Auswechselung ihrer in guter und gehöriger Form befundenen Vollmachten, die nachstehenden Artikel mit dem Vorbehalte der Ratification abgeschlossen und unterzeichnet haben:

form, have concluded and signed, subject to ratification, the following articles.

Art: 1.

Die hohen contrahirenden Theile kommen überein, daß jedwede Art von Producten, Manufacten oder Waaren irgend eines fremden Landes, welche zu jeder Zeit in den Vereinigten Staaten in deren eigenen Schiffen gesetzlich eingeführt werden darf, auch in Schiffen des Königreichs Hannover soll eingeführt werden dürfen, und daß keine höhere oder andere Abgaben von dem Tonnengehalte oder der Ladung des Schiffs, es mag die Einfuhr in einem Schiffe der Vereinigten Staaten oder in einem Hannoverschen Schiffe geschehen, gehoben werden soll. In gleicher Weise soll jedwede Art von Producten, Manufacten oder Waaren, irgend eines fremden Landes, welche je zur Zeit in das Königreich Hannover in dessen eigenen Schiffen gesetzlich eingeführt werden darf, auch in Schiffen der Vereinigten Staaten eingeführt werden dürfen, und sollen keine höhere oder andere Abgaben von dem Tonnengehalte oder der Ladung des Schiffs, es mag die Einfuhr in Schiffen des einen oder des andern Theils geschehen, erhoben werden.

Art: 1.

The High Contracting Parties agree, that whatever kind of produce, manufacture or merchandise of any foreign country can be, from time to time, lawfully imported into the United-States in their own vessels, may also be imported in vessels of the Kingdom of Hanover, and no higher or other duties upon the tonnage or cargo of the vessel shall be levied or collected whether the importation be made in a vessel of the United States or in a Hanoverian vessel. And in like manner, whatever kind of produce, manufacture or merchandise of any foreign country can be, from time to time, lawfully imported into the Kingdom of Hanover in its own vessels may also be imported in vessels of the United States; and no higher or other duties upon the tonnage or cargo of the vessel shall be levied or collected, whether the importation be made in vessels of the one party or the other.

Alles was von dem einen Theile in dessen eigenen Schiffen nach irgend einem fremden Lande gesetzlich ausgeführt oder wiederausgeführt werden darf, soll in gleicher Weise auch in den Schiffen des andern Theils ausgeführt oder wiederausgeführt werden dürfen; und die nämlichen Abgaben, Vergütungen und Rückzahlungen sollen gehoben und bewilligt werden, es mag die derartige Ausfuhr oder Wiederausfuhr in Schiffen des einen oder des andern Theils geschehen; auch sollen keine höhere oder andere Abgaben irgend einer Art in den Häfen des einen Theils den Schiffen des andern Theils auferlegt werden, als welche in denselben Häfen von den einheimischen Schiffen zu entrichten sind oder sein werden.

Es wird ferner vereinbart, daß kein höherer oder anderer Zoll zu Brunshausen oder Stade an der Elbe von dem Tonnengehalte oder den Ladungen von Schiffen der Vereinigten Staaten erhoben werden soll, als von dem Tonnengehalte und den Ladungen von Schiffen des Königreichs Hannover erhoben wird, und daß die Schiffe der Vereinigten Staaten keinen Lasten, Aufenthalt oder sonstigen Unannehmlichkeiten von den Hannoverschen Behörden bei der Vorbeifahrt an dem obgenannten Orte unterworfen werden sollen, wovon die Schiffe des Königreichs Hannover befreit sind oder werden.

Whatever may be lawfully exported or re-exported by one party in its own vessels to any foreign country, may, in like manner, be exported or re-exported in the vessels of the other. And the same duties, bounties and drawbacks shall be collected and allowed, whether such exportation or re-exportation be made in vessels of the one party or the other.

Nor shall higher or other charges of any kind be imposed in the ports of the one party on vessels of the other, than are or shall be payable in the same ports by national vessels.

And further it is agreed that no higher, or other toll, shall be levied or collected at Brunshausen or Stade on the river Elbe, upon the tonnage or cargoes of vessels of the United States than is levied and collected upon the tonnage and cargoes of vessels of the Kingdom of Hanover and the vessels of the United States shall be subjected to no charges, detention or other inconvenience by the Hanoverian authorities in passing the above mentioned place, from which vessels of the Kingdom of Hanover are or shall be exempt.

ART: 2.

Der vorhergehende Artikel ist nicht anwendbar auf den Küstenhandel und die Küstenfahrt der hohen contrahirenden Theile, welche beiderseits ihren eigenen Unterthanen oder Bürgern ausschließlich vorbehalten werden.

ART: 3.

Von keinem der contrahirenden Theile, noch von, in deren Namen oder unter deren Autorität handelnden Gesellschaften, Corporationen oder Agenten, soll, bei dem Ankaufe irgend eines gesetzlich eingeführten Handels-Artikels, wegen oder bezüglich der Nationalität des Schiffes, in welchem ein solcher Artikel eingeführt worden, es mag dem einen oder dem andern Theile angehören, ein Vorrecht noch Vorzug gegeben werden.

ART: 4.

Das alte und barbarische Strandrecht soll rücksichtlich des den Unterthanen oder Bürgern der hohen contrahirenden Theile gehörenden Eigenthums gänzlich aufgehoben bleiben.

Wenn ein Schiff des einen Theils an den Küsten oder innerhalb der Besitzungen des andern Theils Schiffbruch erlitten hat, gestrandet oder sonst beschädigt ist, so sollen die respectiven Bürger oder Unterthanen, sowohl für sich als für ihre Schiffe und Sachen den nämlichen Beistand erhalten,

ART: 2.

The preceeding article is not applicable to the coasting trade and navigation of the High Contracting Parties, which are respectively reserved by each exclusively to its own subjects or citizens.

ART: 3.

No priority or preference shall be given by either of the Contracting Parties, nor by any company, corporation or agent, acting on their behalf, or under their authority in the purchase of any article of commerce lawfully imported, on account of or in reference to the national character of the vessel, whether it be of the one Party or of the other, in which such article was imported.

ART: 4.

The ancient and barbarous right to wrecks of the sea shall remain entirely abolished with respect to the property belonging to the subjects or citizens of the High Contracting Parties.

When any vessel of either Party shall be wrecked, stranded or otherwise damaged on the coasts, or within the dominions of the other, their respective citizens or subjects shall receive, as well for themselves as for their vessels and effects, the same assistance which would be due to the inhabitants of the

welcher den Einwohnern des Landes, wo der Unfall sich ereignet, gebührt haben würde.

Dieselben sollen gehalten sein, die nämlichen Abgaben und Bergelöhne zu entrichten, welche die besagten Einwohner in einem gleichen Falle zu zahlen schuldig wären.

Wenn die Ausbesserungs-Arbeiten erforderlich machen, daß die Ladung ganz oder zum Theil gelöscht werde, so sollen sie von Demjenigen, was sie wieder einladen und wegführen, keine Zoll-Abgaben, Auflagen oder Gebühren zahlen, außer solchen, welche in gleichem Falle von den einheimischen Schiffen zu entrichten sind.

Es versteht sich jedoch, daß wenn, während das Schiff ausgebessert wird, die Ladung gelöscht und in einer Niederlage für unversteuerte Güter aufbewahrt wird, die Ladung denjenigen Abgaben und Gebühren unterliegen soll, welche den Inhabern solcher Niederlagen gesetzlich zukommen.

Art: 5.

Die durch gegenwärtigen Vertrag den respectiven Schiffen der hohen contrahirenden Theile zugesicherten Privilegien sollen sich nur auf solche Schiffe erstrecken, welche innerhalb ihrer respectiven Gebiete erbaut, oder gesetzlich als Kriegs-Beute condemnirt oder wegen Bruchs der Municipalgesetze des einen oder des andern

country where the accident happens.

They shall be liable to pay the same charges and dues of salvage as the said inhabitants would be liable to pay in a like case.

If the operations of repair shall require that the whole, or any part of the cargo be unloaded, they shall pay no duties of custom, charges or fees, on the part which they shall reload and carry away, except such as are payable in the like case, by national vessels.

It is nevertheless understood, that if, whilst the vessel is under repair, the cargo shall be unladen, and kept in a place of deposite destined to receive goods, the duties on which have not been paid, the cargo shall be liable to the charges and fees lawfully due to the keepers of such warehouses.

Art: 5.

The privileges secured by the present treaty to the respective vessels of the High Contracting Parties shall only extend to such as are built within their respective territories, or lawfully condemned as prize of war, or adjudged to be forfeited for a breach of the municipal laws of either of the High Contracting Parties and be-

der hohen contrahirenden Theile für confiscirt erklärt sind, und welche ihren Unterthanen oder Bürgern ganz gehören.

Es wird ferner stipulirt, daß Schiffe des Königreichs Hannover ihre Mannschaften aus allen Staaten des Deutschen Bundes wählen dürfen, sofern nur der Capitain eines jeden Schiffs Unterthan des Königreichs Hannover ist.

longing wholly to their subjects or citizens.

It is further stipulated, that vessels of the Kingdom of Hanover may select their crews from any of the States of the Germanic Confederation, provided that the master of each be a subject of the Kingdom of Hanover.

ART: 6.

Es sollen keine höhere oder andere Abgaben auf die Einfuhr in die Vereinigten Staaten von Artikeln, welche Erzeugnisse des Bodens oder des Gewerbfleißes des Königreichs Hannover oder seiner Fischereien sind, und keine höhere oder andere Abgaben auf die Einfuhr in das Königreich Hannover von Artikeln, welche Erzeugnisse des Bodens und des Gewerbfleißes der Vereinigten Staaten und ihrer Fischereien sind, gelegt werden, als von den gleichen Artikeln, welche Erzeugnisse des Bodens oder des Gewerbfleißes irgend eines andern fremden Landes oder seiner Fischereien sind, zu entrichten sind oder sein werden.

Es sollen keine höhere oder andere Abgaben und Abgiften in den Vereinigten Staaten auf die Ausfuhr irgend eines Artikels nach dem Königreiche Hannover, noch in Hannover auf die Ausfuhr irgend eines Artikels nach den Vereinigten Staaten gelegt werden, als

ART: 6.

No higher or other duties shall be imposed on the importation into the United States of any articles, the growth, produce or manufacture of the Kingdom of Hanover, or of its fisheries, and no higher or other duties shall be imposed on the importation into the Kingdom of Hanover of any articles, the growth, produce and manufacture of the United States and of their fisheries, than are or shall be payable on the like articles being the growth, produce or manufacture of any other foreign country or of its fisheries.

No higher or other duties and charges shall be imposed in the United States on the exportation of any articles to the Kingdom of Hanover, or in Hanover on the exportation of any articles to the United States, than such as are or shall be payable on the exporta-

diejenigen, welche bei der Ausfuhr der gleichen Artikel nach irgend einem andern fremden Lande zu entrichten sind oder sein werden.

Es soll auf die Einfuhr oder Ausfuhr irgend eines Artikels, welcher Erzeugniß des Bodens oder des Gewerbfleißes des Königreichs Hannover oder seiner Fischereien, oder der Vereinigten Staaten oder ihrer Fischereien ist, aus oder nach den Häfen des besagten Königreichs oder der besagten Vereinigten Staaten, kein Verbot gelegt werden, welches nicht ebenfalls auf alle anderen Mächte und Staaten sich erstreckt.

tion of the like articles to any other foreign country.

No prohibition shall be imposed on the importation or exportation of any articles, the growth, produce or manufacture of the Kingdom of Hanover or of its fisheries or of the United States or their fisheries from or to the ports of said Kingdom or of the said United States, which shall not equally extend to all other powers and states.

ART: 7.

Die hohen contrahirenden Theile verpflichten sich gegenseitig, anderen Nationen in Ansehung der Schifffahrt und der Zoll-Abgaben keine besondere Begünstigung zu verleihen, die nicht sofort auch dem andern Theile zu Gute kommt, welcher dieselbe unentgeltlich genießen soll, wenn die Verleihung unentgeltlich erfolgt war, oder gegen Bewilligung einer möglichst gleichkommenden Vergütung, wenn die Verleihung gegen Bedingungen geschehen war.

ART: 7.

The High Contracting Parties engage mutually not to grant any particular favor to other nations in respect of navigation and duties of customs which shall not immediately become common to the other Party, who shall enjoy the same freely, if the concession was freely made, or on allowing a compensation as near as possible if the concession was conditional.

ART: 8.,

Um durch alle zu seiner Verfügung stehenden Mittel die Handels-Beziehungen zwischen den Vereinigten Staaten und Deutschland zu vermehren, versteht das Königreich Hannover hiemit sich

ART: 8.

In order to augment by all the means, at its bestowal, the commercial relations between the United States and Germany the Kingdom of Hanover hereby agrees to abolish the import duty

dazu, die Eingangs-Abgabe von roher Baumwolle abzuschaffen und auch die bestehenden Durch-gangs-Abgaben von Tabacks-Blättern und Stengeln in Hogsheads oder Fässern, roher Baumwolle in Balesor-Säcken, Wallfischthran in Fässern oder Tonnen und Reis in Tierces oder halben Tierces aufzuheben.

Ferner verpflichtet sich das Königreich Hannover, keine Weserzölle von den vorerwähnten Artikeln zu erheben, welche nach Häfen oder andern Plätzen innerhalb seines Gebiets an der Weser bestimmt sind oder daselbst gelandet werden, und will außerdem, wenn die an besagten Fluß gränzenden Staaten, zu irgend einer Zeit früher oder später sich dazu verstehen, die Abgaben, welche sie von besagten, nach Häfen oder anderen Plätzen innerhalb des Hannoverschen Gebiets bestimmten Artikeln erheben, abzuschaffen, dann das Königreich Hannover bereitwillig die Weserzölle für dieselben, nach den Häfen und Plätzen in solchen Staaten bestimmten Artikel aufheben.

Es versteht sich jedoch, daß die vorbesagten Stipulationen nicht so anzusehen sein sollen, als verböten sie, von den besagten Artikeln eine Abgift zu erheben, welche hinreicht zu Bestreitung der Unkosten wegen Aufrechthaltung der Anordnungen in Betreff von Transit-Gütern. In keinem Falle soll jedoch die derartige Abgift den Betrag von Acht Pfen-

on raw cotton, and also to abolish the existing transit duties upon leaves, stems and strips of Tabacco, in hogsheads or casks, raw cotton in Bales or Bags, whale Oil in casks or barrels, and rice in tierces or half tierces.

And further the Kingdom of Hanover obligates itself to levy no Weser-tolls on the afore mentioned articles, which are destined for, or landed in ports or other places, within its territory on the Weser; and it moreover agrees that if the States bordering upon said river shall consent at any time, however soon, to abolish the duties which they levy and collect upon said articles destined for ports or other places within the Hanoverian territory, the Kingdom of Hanover will readily abolish the Weser-tolls upon the same articles destined for ports and places in such States.

It being understood however that the afore said stipulations shall not be deemed to prohibit the levying upon the said articles a tax sufficient for defraying the expence of maintaining the regulation respecting transit goods. But in no case shall such tax exceed Eight Pfennigs Hanoverian currency (two Cents United States currency,) for one hundred

nigen Hannoversches Geld (zwei Cents in dem Gelde der Vereinigten Staaten) für einhundert Pfund Hannoversches Gewicht (einhundert und vier Pfund Gewicht der Vereinigten Staaten) übersteigen.

Pounds Hanoverian weight (one hundred and four Pounds United States weight.).

Art: 9.

Die hohen contrahirenden Theile gestehen einander die Befugniß zu, jeder in den Häfen des andern, selbst bestellte Consuln, Vice-Consuln, Handels-Agenten und Vice-Handels-Agenten zu unterhalten, welche die nämlichen Privilegien und Befugnisse, wie diejenigen der begünstigten Nationen genießen sollen; wenn jedoch der eine oder der andere der genannten Consuln Handel treiben will, so sollen dieselben den nämlichen Gesetzen und Gebräuchen unterworfen sein, welchen Privatpersonen ihrer Nation in demselben Orte unterliegen.

Die Consuln, Vice-Consuln, Handels- und Vice-Handels-Agenten sollen das Recht haben, als solche bei Streitigkeiten, welche zwischen den Capitains und Mannschaften der Schiffe der Nationen, deren Interessen sie wahrzunehmen beauftragt sind, entstehen mögen, als Richter und Schiedsmänner zu handeln, ohne Dazwischenkunft der Orts-Behörden, wenn nicht etwa das Benehmen der Mannschaften oder des Capitains die Ordnung oder Ruhe des Landes stört, oder die besagten Consuln, Vice-Consuln, Handels-Agenten oder Vice-Handels-Agen-

Art: 9.

The High Contracting Parties grant to each other the liberty of having, each in the ports of the other, consuls, vice-consuls, commercial-agents and vice-commercial-agents of their own appointment, who shall enjoy the same privileges and powers as those of the most favored nations; but if any of the said consuls, shall carry on trade, they shall be subjected to the same laws and usages to which private individuals of their nation are subjected in the same place.

The consuls, vice-consuls, commercial- and vice-commercial-agents, shall have the right, as such, to sit as judges and arbitrators in such differences as may arise between the masters and crews of the vessels belonging to the nation, whose interests are committed to their charge, without the interference of the local authorities, unless the conduct of the crews or of the Captain should disturb the order or tranquillity of the country; or the said consuls, vice-consuls, commercial-agents or vice-commercial-agents should require their assistance to

ten deren Beistand zu Vollziehung oder Aufrechthaltung ihrer Entscheidungen in Anspruch nehmen.

Es versteht sich jedoch, daß diese Art von Urtheil oder schiedsrichterlicher Entscheidung die streitenden Theile nicht des ihnen zustehenden Rechts berauben soll, bei ihrer Zurückkunft an die richterliche Behörde ihres eigenen Landes sich zu wenden.

Die besagten Consuln, Vice-Consuln, Handels-Agenten und Vice-Handels-Agenten sind befugt, den Beistand der Orts-Behörden zu Aufsuchung, Festnehmung und Gefangensetzung der Deserteurs von den Kriegs- und Handels-Schiffen ihres Landes in Anspruch zu nehmen.

Zu diesem Behuf haben sie sich an die competenten Gerichte, Richter und Beamten zu wenden und die besagten Deserteurs schriftlich zu reclamiren, indem sie durch Beibringung der Schiffsregister, der Musterrollen der Mannschaften oder anderer amtlicher Urkunden darthun, daß jene Individuen zu den Mannschaften gehörten, und wenn diese Reclamation also begründet ist, so soll die Auslieferung nicht versagt werden.

Wenn dergleichen Deserteurs festgenommen sind, so sollen sie zur Verfügung der besagten Consuln, Vice-Consuln, Handels-Agenten oder Vice-Handels-Agenten gestellt werden, und können sie, auf Requisition und Kosten Derer, welche sie reclamiren, in

cause their decisions to be carried into effect or supported.

It is however understood that this species of judgment or arbitration shall not deprive the contending parties of the right they have to resort on their return, to the judicial authority of their own country.

The said consuls, vice-consuls, commercial-agents and vice-commercial-agents are authorized to require the assistance of the local authorities for the search, arrest, and imprisonment of the deserters from the ships of war and merchant vessels of their country.

For this purpose they shall apply to the competent tribunals, judges and officers, and shall, in writing, demand said deserters proving by the exhibition of the registers of the vessels, the muster-rolls of the crews, or by any other official documents, that such individuals formed part of the crews, and on this claim being thus substantiated, the surrender shall not be refused.

Such deserters, when arrested, shall be placed at the disposal of the said consuls, vice-consuls, commercial-agents or vice-commercial-agents and may be confined in the public prisons, at the request and cost of those who shall claim them, in order, to be

den öffentlichen Gefängnissen festgehalten werden, um auf die Schiffe, zu welchen sie gehören, oder auf andere desselben Landes, gesandt zu werden. Wenn sie aber binnen drei Monaten vom Tage ihrer Festnehmung an nicht zurückgeschickt sind, so sollen sie in Freiheit gesetzt und wegen desselben Grundes nicht wieder verhaftet werden. Wenn jedoch befunden werden sollte, daß der Deserteur irgend ein Verbrechen oder Vergehen begangen hätte, so kann dessen Auslieferung ausgesetzt werden, bis das Gericht, vor welchem seine Sache anhängig ist, das Urtheil gesprochen haben und dieses Urtheil zur Vollstreckung gebracht sein wird.

sent to the vessels to which they belong, or to others of the same country. But if not sent back within three months from the day of their arrest, they shall be set at liberty and shall not be again arrested for the same cause. However if the deserter shall be found to have committed any crime or offence, his surrender may be delayed until the tribunal, before which his case shall be pending, shall have pronounced its sentence, and such sentence shall have been carried into effect.

Art: 10.

Den Unterthanen und Bürgern der hohen contrahirenden Theile soll erlaubt sein, in allen Theilen der besagten Gebiete sich aufzuhalten und zu wohnen, um ihren Geschäften nachzugehen und auch Häuser und Speicher behuf ihres Handels zu miethen und innezuhaben, vorausgesetzt, daß sie den allgemeinen und besonderen Gesetzen in Betreff des Rechts zu Wohnen und zu Handeln sich unterwerfen.

So lange sie den bestehenden Gesetzen und Verordnungen nachkommen, sollen sie die Freiheit haben, ihre Geschäfte in allen der Botmäßigkeit eines jeden Theils unterworfenen Gebieten, sowohl in Ansehung der Consignation

Art: 10.

The subjects and citizens of the High Contracting Parties shall be permitted to sejourn and reside in all parts whatsoever of the said territories in order to attend to their affairs, and also to hire and occupy houses and warehouses for the purposes of their commerce, provided they submit to the laws, as well general as special, relative to the right of residing and trading.

Whilst they conform to the laws and regulations in force, they shall be at liberty to manage themselves their own business in all the territories subject to the jurisdiction of each party, as well in respect to the consignment and

und des Verkaufs ihrer Waaren en gros oder en détail, als hinsichtlich der Beladung, Ausladung und Absendung ihrer Schiffe selbst wahrzunehmen oder aber nach Belieben Agenten und Makler zu gebrauchen, indem sie in allen diesen Fällen, wie die Bürger oder Unterthanen des Landes, in welchen sie wohnen, zu behandeln sein sollen, wobei es sich jedoch versteht, daß sie den besagten Gesetzen und Verordnungen auch in Ansehung von Verkäufen en gros oder en détail unterworfen bleiben sollen.

Sie sollen in ihren Proceßsachen freien Zutritt zu den Gerichten in gleichem Maaße, wie den eingebornen Bürgern oder Unterthanen nach den Gesetzen und Gebräuchen des Landes zusteht, haben, und zu diesem Zweck für die Vertheidigung ihrer Rechte Advocaten, Procuratoren und andere Agenten nach Gutbefinden gebrauchen dürfen.

Die Bürger oder Unterthanen jedes Theils sollen die Befugniß haben, über ihr persönliches Eigenthum innerhalb der Gerichtsbarkeit des Andern, durch Verkauf, Schenkung, Testament oder sonst zu verfügen.

Wenn ihre Erben Bürger oder Unterthanen des andern contrahirenden Theils sind, so sollen diese in ihr Vermögen durch Testament oder ab intestato nachfolgen.

Sie können davon selbst oder durch für sie handelnde Andere,

sale of their goods, by wholesale or retail, as with respect to the loading, unloading and sending off their ships, or to employ such agents and brokers as they may deem proper, they being in all these cases to be treated as the citizens or subjects of the country in which they reside, it being nevertheless understood, that they shall remain subject to the said laws and regulations also in respect to sales by wholesale or retail.

They shall have free access to the tribunals of justice in their litigious affairs on the same terms which are granted by the law and usage of country to native citizens or subjects, for which purpose they may employ in defence of their rights, such advocates, attornies and other agents as they may judge proper.

The citizens or subjects of each Party shall have power to dispose of their personal property within the jurisdiction of the other, by sale, donation, testament or otherwise.

Their personal representatives, being citizens or subjects of the other Contracting Party shall succeed to their said personal property, whether by testament or ab intestato.

They may take possession thereof, either by themselves, or

nach ihrem Willen, Besitz nehmen und darüber verfügen, indem sie nur diejenige Abgift entrichten, welche die Einwohner des Landes, in welchem das besagte Vermögen befindlich ist, in gleichen Fällen zu bezahlen verbunden sein werden.

Im Fall der Abwesenheit der Erben soll für das besagte Vermögen bis dahin, daß der gesetzliche Eigenthümer Maßregeln zu Empfangnahme desselben treffen kann, die nämliche Sorge getroffen werden, welche für das Vermögen eines Eingebornen in gleichem Falle getragen werden würde.

Wenn zwischen verschiedenen Prätendenten Streit darüber entstehen sollte, wem von ihnen das besagte Vermögen gehöre, so soll selbiger nach den Gesetzen und durch die Richter des Landes, worin selbiges sich befindet, definitiv entschieden werden.

Wo, bei dem Ableben einer innerhalb der Gebiete des einen Theils Grundeigenthum besitzenden Person, dieses Grundeigenthum, nach den Gesetzen des Landes, auf einen Bürger oder Unterthan des andern Theils übergehen würde, wenn derselbe nicht als Fremder unfähig wäre es zu besitzen, so soll einem solchen Bürger oder Unterthan eine angemessene Frist nachgelassen werden, um dasselbe zu verkaufen und den Erlös ohne Beschwerde und frei von allem Abzug von Seiten der Regierung der respec-

by others, acting for them, at their will, and dispose of the same, paying such duty only as the inhabitants of the country wherein the said personal property is situate shall be subject to pay in like cases.

In case of the absence of the personal representatives, the same care shall be taken of the said property as would be taken of the property of a native in like case, until the lawfull owner may take measures for receiving it.

If any question should arise among several claimants to which of them the said property belongs, the same shall be finally decided, by the laws and judges of the country wherein it is situate.

Where, on the decease of any person, holding real estate within the territories of one Party such real estate would, by the laws of the land descend on a citizen or subject of the other were he not disqualified by alienage, such citizen or subject shall be allowed a reasonable time to sell the same, and to withdraw the proceeds without molestation, and exempt from all duties of detraction on the part of the Government of the respective States.

tiven Staaten, aus dem Lande zu
ziehen.

Die Capitalien und Fonds,
welche die Bürger oder Unterthanen der respectiven Theile,
bei Veränderung ihres Aufent-
halts, von ihrem Wohnorte fort-
zubringen wünschen, sollen ebenfalls von allen Abzugs- und Aus-
wanderungs-Abgaben von Seiten
ihrer respectiven Regierungen frei
sein.

ART: 11.

Der gegenwärtige Vertrag soll
auf die Zeit von zwölf Jahren,
vom Tage desselben an, in Kraft
bleiben und ferner bis zum Ab-
laufe von zwölf Monaten nachdem
die Hannoversche Regierung einer
Seits oder die Regierung der
Vereinigten Staaten anderer Seits,
ihre Absicht zu erkennen gegeben hat, denselben zu Ende gehen
zu lassen; jedoch mit der hie-
durch ausdrücklich stipulirten
und vereinbarten Bedingung, daß,
wenn das Königreich Hannover
während der besagten Zeit von
zwölf Jahren sich entschließen
sollte, die bestehende Einfuhr-
Abgabe auf, in Hogsheads oder
Fässern eingebrachte Tabacks-
Blätter, Streifen oder Stengel,
welche Abgabe gegenwärtig einen
Thaler und einen Gutengroschen
von einhundert Pfund Hannoversches Geld und Gewicht (sieben-
zig Cents von hundert Pfund Geld
und Gewicht der Vereinigten
Staaten) nicht übersteigt, zu er-
höhen, die Hannoversche Regierung ein Jahr vor der Ausführung

The capitals and effects which
the citizens or subjects of the respective Parties, in changing their
residence shall be desirous of removing from the place of their
domicil shall likewise be exempt
from all duties of detraction or
emigration on the part of their
respective Governments.

ART: 11.

The present treaty shall continue in force for the term of
twelve years from the date hereof,
and further until the end of twelve
months after the Government of
Hanover on the one part or that
of the United States on the other
part, shall have given notice of its
intention of terminating the same;
but upon the condition hereby
expressly stipulated and agreed,
that, if the Kingdom of Hanover
shall determine, during the said
term of twelve years, to augment
the existing import duty upon
leaves, strips or stems of tabacco,
imported in Hogsheads or
Casks,—a duty which at this
time does not exceed one Thaler
and one Gutengroschen per one
hundred pounds Hanoverian currency and weight (seventy Cents
pr. one hundred pounds United
States currency and weight)—the
Government of Hanover shall
give a notice of one year to the
Government of the United States
before proceeding to do so, and
at the expiration of that year,

dieser Maßregel der Regierung der Vereinigten Staaten davon Nachricht geben und am Ende dieses Jahrs oder alle Zeit nachher die Regierung der Vereinigten Staaten volle Gewalt und Befugniß haben soll, den gegenwärtigen Vertrag durch vorgängige sechsmonatliche Kündigung bei der Hannoverschen Regierung aufzuheben, oder, nach ihrer Wahl, den Vertrag in voller Kraft fortbestehen zu lassen, bis die Wirksamkeit desselben in der im gegenwärtigen Artikel zuerst angegebenen Weise seine Endschaft erreicht hat.

or any time subsequently, the Government of the United States shall have full power and right to abrogate the present treaty by giving a previous notice of six months to the Government of Hanover, or to continue it, (at its option), in full force, until the operation thereof shall have been arrested in the manner first specified in the present article.

ART: 12.

Die Vereinigten Staaten erklären sich bereit, die in den Bestimmungen des gegenwärtigen Vertrags enthaltenen Vortheile und Privilegien auf einen oder mehrere der übrigen Staaten des Deutschen Bundes auszudehnen, welche wünschen möchten, denselben mittelst einer amtlichen Auswechselung von Declarationen beizutreten, vorausgesetzt daß der oder die solche Staaten ähnliche Vergünstigungen, wie sie von dem Königreiche Hannover ertheilt sind, den Vereinigten Staaten ertheilen und den nämlichen Bedingungen, Stipulationen und Verpflichtungen nachkommen und sich unterziehen.

ART: 12.

The United States agree to extend all the advantages and privileges contained in the stipulations of the present treaty to one or more of the other States of the Germanic Confederation, which may wish to accede to them, by means of an official exchange of declarations, provided that such State or States shall confer similar favors upon the said United States to those conferred by the Kingdom of Hanover and observe and be subject to the same conditions, stipulations and obligations.

ART: 13.

Der gegenwärtige Vertrag wird von dem Präsidenten der Vereinigten Staaten von Amerika nach

ART: 13.

The present Treaty shall be approved and ratified by the President of the United States of

und mit Beirath und Zustimmung ihres Senats und von Seiner Majestät dem Könige von Hannover, genehmigt und ratificirt werden; und die Ratificationen sollen in der Stadt Hannover innerhalb des Zeitraums von zehn Monaten vom heutigen Tage an, oder wo möglich früher, ausgewechselt werden, und soll dann der zwischen den hohen contrahirenden Theilen am 20sten Mai 1840 zu Berlin abgeschlossene Handels- und Schifffahrts-Vertrag[1] in allen seinen Absichten und Zwecken null und nichtig werden.

Zu Urkund Dessen haben wir die Bevollmächtigten der hohen contrahirenden Theile, den gegenwärtigen Vertrag unterzeichnet und untersiegelt.

Geschehen, in vierfacher Ausfertigung, in der Stadt Hannover am zehnten Junius des Jahrs unsers Herrn eintausend achthundert sechs und vierzig, im siebenzigsten Jahre der Unabhängigkeit der Vereinigten Staaten von Amerika.

America by and with the advice and consent of their Senate and by His Majesty the King of Hanover; and the ratifications thereof shall be exchanged at the City of Hanover within the space of ten months from this date, or, sooner if possible, when the treaty of commerce and navigation[1] concluded between the High Contracting Parties at Berlin on the 20th day of May 1840 shall become null and void to all intents and purposes.

In faith whereof, We, the plenipotentiaries of the High Contracting Parties, have signed the present treaty and have thereto affixed our seals.

Done in quadruplicate at the City of Hanover on the tenth day of June in the year of our Lord One thousand eight hundred and forty six, & in the seventieth year of the independence of the United States of America.

[Seal]   A. DUDLEY MANN.
[Seal]   GEORGE FREDERICK BARON DE FALCKE

NOTES

As stated in its final clause, this treaty was signed in quadruplicate. There are two originals in the treaty file; in each of them the texts are written in parallel columns, the German at the left; but in the document with which the text here printed has been collated (that original which is with the original proclamation), the President and the United States are named first throughout in both texts and the signature of the American Plenipotentiary comes first; in the other original the order of naming and signing is reversed.

[1] Document 92.

As between the two originals there have been observed a few variances of punctuation, perhaps a dozen, nine in the English and three in the German; all but one of these are matters of commas, and none of them is of the slightest importance.

The other usual papers are in the file and are in customary form; they include the attested resolution of the Senate of January 6, 1847, the duplicate United States instrument of ratification of January 8, 1847, the certificate of the exchange of ratifications at Hanover on March 5, 1847, which is written in English, and the original proclamation of the following April 24. The Hanoverian instrument of ratification of March 5, 1847, is written in German and includes both texts of the treaty, the German in the left columns. Throughout those texts the King of Hanover is named first, and the copy of the signature of the Hanoverian Plenipotentiary precedes that of the American Plenipotentiary.

THE SIGNATURE OF THE TREATY

On the part of the United States this treaty was signed *ad referendum*, not only "subject to ratification", as stated in the preamble, but subject to the approval of the President, who, if he disapproved, was not to be deemed even morally obligated to submit the treaty to the Senate. This course was taken because the Plenipotentiary of the United States did not consider that the agreement was entirely consonant with his instructions.

In his despatch transmitting the treaty, written at London on June 17, 1846, Ambrose Dudley Mann, Special Agent of the United States, who negotiated and signed the treaty, wrote as follows (D.S., 14 Special Agents, German States):

I have the honor to transmit you, by Mr. Fleischmann of Washington City, a copy [original] of the Treaty which I concluded—(subject to the condition contained in the protocol by which it is accompanied)—at Hanover on the 10th inst.

When I made up my last despatch I had determined not to sign the Treaty until it was submitted to your examination, but since then I received a letter from Mr. M'Lane, wherein he expressed an opinion that I could do so with the utmost propriety, if the Hanoverian government would consent, that unless the President approved of it no obligation rested upon him to lay it before the Senate. Under date of May 25 Mr. M'Lane wrote to me to say, "In the dilemma in which you "are placed it appears to me that you may either send the Treaty to Washington "to be signed there, upon the contingency you mention, making a memorandum "or protocol of the arrangement, and relying upon the ratification and exchange "of ratifications to make all right, as they certainly would do; or, I think you "may *sign* the Treaty at Hanover, with the disclosure that your instructions do "not authorize it in the precise form and that your signature is to be taken "subject to the approbation of the President at Washington; that if he dis-"approve, the Treaty may be regarded as not having been signed, and to be "of no validity not even as imposing upon the President any obligation whatever "to send it to the Senate; but that if he approve and the Treaty be ratified by "the Senate it is to be binding. This mode too if adopted must be made the "subject of a protocol to recite the arrangement, and to be mutually signed, "and to accompany the Treaty."

Aware of the importance of getting the Treaty to Washington before the adjournment of Congress, and fearing that I would be disappointed in securing a berth on the steamer which is to leave Liverpool on the 19th inst., I resolved to

sign it at Hanover. It was as late as the 12ᵗʰ before every thing was ready for my departure, from Hanover, but by travelling day and night I was enabled to reach here yesterday.

Of the protocol which was signed concurrently with the treaty itself, there are two originals in the file, each written in English and in the following terms:

> The terms of a new Treaty of Navigation and Commerce having been negociated between the Kingdom of Hanover on the one part and the United States of America on the other part, by the undersigned plenipotentiaries of the respective nations, they proceeded to put the various stipulations into proper form, and after having agreed to it four copies thereof were signed by each and their seals thereunto attached; upon the reservation and condition, however, that the Treaty thus concluded shall be approved by his Excellency the President of the United States. This was agreed to by the Hanoverian Plenipotentiary, inasmuch as the United States Plenipotentiary stated that he did not feel himself authorized, to perfect a Treaty so far as to attach to it his signature unless all the stipulations and provisions therein contained were in the strictest conformity with his instructions. To prevent any possible misunderstanding with reference to the object of this protocol it is hereby distinctly stated, and fully understood by the Hanoverian Plenipotentiary, that if the President of the United States of America should not approve of the Treaty herein referred to, and decline presenting it to the Senate for ratification, said Treaty shall be deemed as possessing no more validity than if it had not been signed by the United States Plenipotentiary: And thus this protocol is concluded.
> Done at Hanover 10ᵗʰ of June 1846.
> [Seal] A. DUDLEY MANN.
> [Seal] GEORGE FREDERICK BARON DE FALCKE

As stated in the despatch of June 17, 1846, above quoted, Mann had at first intended not to sign the treaty at Hanover; he had intended, he wrote in his despatch of May 30, 1846, to "carry with me a Treaty *perfected* by Hanover, with the liberty to sign, or not, as you may determine, after I reach Washington. My signature there is to be regarded as valid, as if executed here." That form of procedure, however, was abandoned in view of the opinion expressed by Louis McLane, then Minister at London, to which Mann referred, to the effect that the procedure finally adopted was proper.

THE FULL POWERS

Aside from the mention in the preamble of the treaty of the exchange of full powers, nothing appears in the despatches or elsewhere regarding them. The instrument given to Mann was under date of March 28, 1846; its clause of substance, mentioning four Governments, was as follows (D.S., 3 Credences, 179):

> Know Ye, That, reposing special trust and confidence in the integrity, prudence, and abilities of A. Dudley Mann, appointed Special Agent of the United States to the Kingdom of Hanover and the Grand Duchy of Oldenburg, also to the Grand Duchy of Mecklenburg Schwerin, and to the Grand Duchy of Mecklenburg Strelitz, I have invested him with full and all manner of power, for, and in the name of, the United States, to meet and confer with any person or persons furnished with like powers on the part of His Majesty the King of Hanover, His Royal Highness the Grand Duke of Oldenburg, His Royal Highness the Grand Duke of Mecklenburg Schwerin, and His Royal Highness the Grand Duke of Mecklenburg Strelitz, or either of said Sovereigns, and with the person

or persons so empowered, to treat, negotiate, conclude, and sign, a convention or conventions, treaty or treaties, of and concerning the commerce and navigation of the respective countries, and all matters and subjects connected therewith, which may be interesting to the parties: Such convention or conventions, treaty or treaties, to be transmitted to the President of the United States for his final ratification, by and with the advice and consent of the Senate thereof.

The Negotiations

At the time of this treaty the United States had no regular diplomatic representative at the capitals of any of the members of the Germanic Confederation except Austria and Prussia. A. Dudley Mann was appointed Special Agent of the United States and was given, under date of March 28, 1846, a full power which has been cited and, in part, quoted above, and also letters of credence, of the same date, addressed to the Ministers of Foreign Affairs of the Kingdom of Hanover, the Grand Duchy of Oldenburg, the Grand Duchy of Mecklenburg-Schwerin, and the Grand Duchy of Mecklenburg-Strelitz (D.S., 3 Credences, 180; similar letters of credence were again given under date of January 9, 1847).

The primary object of the negotiations was the revision of the treaty with Hanover of May 20, 1840 (Document 92, the notes to which should be consulted; that treaty was written in French and English); this treaty took the place of the treaty of 1840, which it terminated (Article 13); the other negotiations were of less importance and were to some extent dependent upon the result with the Government of Hanover. To Mann were given somewhat elaborate instructions under date of March 27, 1846, as follows (D.S., 1 Special Missions, 239–45):

This Department has received information from several sources that His Hanoverian Majesty is desirous to conclude a new commercial treaty with the United States. To meet his wishes, you are herewith furnished with full powers for that purpose. Inasmuch as the Grand Duchy of Oldenburg is united with the Kingdom of Hanover in a commercial league, (the Steuer-Verein,) and as there is reason to believe that the Governments of Mecklenburg Schwerin and Mecklenburg Strelitz may desire to become parties to the same treaty, your full powers embrace all these States.

You are aware that a treaty of commerce and navigation already exists between Hanover and the United States, which was concluded at Berlin on the 20th day of May, 1840. This treaty provides for a perfect freedom and reciprocity in the direct trade between the two countries. Hanover has manifested much anxiety that the indirect trade should also be placed upon the same unrestricted footing. This will be accorded, provided Hanover will yield equivalents for such a concession, which she can do not only without injury, but with benefit to herself.

A perfect reciprocity of navigation and commerce in the direct trade between any two countries is fair and equal. Both parties, to the extent of this trade, be it great or small, ought to be placed upon the same footing of equal competition. Not so with the indirect trade. Should we concede such a privilege to Hanover and the Grand Duchy of Oldenburg, this would confer upon their vessels the advantage of carrying to the United States the productions of all countries for the supply of our twenty millions of people; whilst the reciprocal advantages which our vessels could derive from such an arrangement would be confined to carrying these productions for the supply of the two millions and a quarter of people within that Kingdom and Grand Duchy. This inequality is palpable; and must accrue to the benefit of Hanoverian and Oldenburg commerce and navigation. Such views you will not fail to present to these Governments.

Nevertheless, it is not believed that a concession of this nature on the part of the United States would materially injure our commerce or navigation. Hanover and Oldenburg do not possess within their limits the chief materials for ship building. These they must purchase from abroad. Their vessels are built at great expense, and their present commercial marine is inconsiderable. Besides, under the second article of the existing treaty with Hanover, this trade can only be conducted in vessels built within the United States and that Kingdom; and, in the new treaty which you are authorized to conclude, this provision must be retained. In this manner the ship building interest of our country will be encouraged; because nearly all the vessels which Hanoverian subjects may require to conduct this trade must be built within the United States and purchased from our citizens.

All the articles in our present treaty with Hanover, with two exceptions, may be included in the new treaty, changing their phraseology so as to embrace Oldenburg.

1. Instead of the second article, the first article of our treaty of the 20th December, 1827, with the Hanseatic Republics [Document 59] may be substituted. This article will confer upon Hanover and Oldenburg the same general reciprocity in commerce and navigation, both in the direct and indirect trade with the United States now enjoyed by these Republics. Care must be taken however to insert at the end of this article the provision contained in the second article of our subsisting treaty with Hanover, confining the benefits of the trade to vessels built within the territories of the respective parties.

2. The ninth article of our present treaty with Hanover should be changed so as to substitute ten for twelve years, in accordance with our usual practice.

You are to conclude no treaty, however, unless the Governments of Hanover and Oldenburg shall stipulate for the following equivalents.

Four of our grat staples, cotton, tobacco, rice, and whale oil are not only largely consumed by the population of Hanover and Oldenburg, but are transported through their territories into the heart of Germany, for the consumption of other German States. At present, these articles pay considerable transit duties, to the injury of the United States. Hanover and Oldenburg, in order to promote their own internal trade, and to increase the transportation on their railroads, ought to abolish the transit duties on these and all other articles, the growth, produce, or manufacture of our country. If the Hanoverian and Oldenburg Governments will not consent to abolish these duties, they ought, at the least, to reduce them to such a nominal rate as may be necessary for a mere police regulation.

Without such an abolition or reduction of the transit duties on the four important articles of cotton, tobacco, rice, and whale oil, you are not authorized to conclude a treaty.

The import duty on tobacco in the Kingdom of Hanover and Grand Duchy of Oldenburg is now but 69 cents on the hundred pounds: and a very large amount of American tobacco is consumed in proportion to their population. In the States composing the Zollverein the duty on tobacco is $3.33 per hundred pounds; nearly five times the amount of the Hanoverian and Oldenburg duty. The Consul of the United States to Hanover has informed this Department, that the States of Northern Germany, not belonging to the Zollverein, with a population of about 3,000,000, consume annually about 10,000,000 lbs. of American tobacco; whilst the States embraced within the Zollverein, with a population of twenty-eight millions, consume but 24,000,000 lbs of American tobacco. The protective duty which the latter States levy in favor of their domestic article enabled them to raise about 56 millions of pounds of tobacco for their own consumption.

Prussia and the other States of the Zollverein are extremely anxious that Hanover and Oldenburg should join their league; but the King of Hanover has resolutely resisted this measure. Serious apprehensions are entertained that after his death, and he is now old and infirm, his successor may be prevailed upon to change his father's policy in this particular. In that event, the present low rate of duty on American tobacco would be raised to the standard of the Zollverein; and the tobacco grown in the States of this league would come into competition even in Hanover and Oldenburg with the tobacco of the United States, with this heavy discrimination against the latter. Whereas if Hanover and Oldenburg should conclude a treaty with the United States, stipulating

against any increase in the existing rate of duty on tobacco, this would not only secure to us a continuance of those markets upon the present favorable terms; but, in the end, might constrain the States of the Zollverein to reduce their duty to the same standard. This would certainly be the case if these two States should join the league whilst the treaty remained in force. It would be of the first importance to this great agricultural interest of our country could this object be accomplished.

You are, therefore, instructed not to conclude a treaty with Hanover and Oldenburg, unless the Governments of these countries should stipulate not to increase their present rate of duty on tobacco.

The duties imposed upon all American productions in the Kingdom of Hanover and Grand Duchy of Oldenburg are moderate, when compared with those of the Zollverein. You will, therefore, exert your best efforts to make the stipulation general in regard to all our productions, or as many of them as possible. Cotton is an article which will take care of itself; but still it would be of importance that Hanover and Oldenburg should abolish the duty at present imposed upon raw cotton, and agree to admit it hereafter free.

It is understood that great efforts have been made by Prussia to induce Hanover, Oldenburg, the two Mecklenburgs, and the Hanseatic Republics to join the Zollverein. Should she succeed in accomplishing this object, even with respect to Hanover, the United States would lose much of the trade they at present enjoy with the north of Germany. Besides, the accession of the Kingdom of Hanover to the Zollverein, both from its territorial extent and position, and from its influence, would, most probably, ere long, induce the other northern German States just mentioned to follow its example. In that event, as the policy of the Zollverein is becoming gradually more restrictive, the change might prove eminently prejudicial to American commerce. In regard to the article of tobacco alone, not to mention others, this might eventually lead to the establishment, throughout all those States, of a *regie* such as now exists in France and other European States, both for the sake of revenue and to encourage the growth of the domestic product. These prospective injuries to our commerce may not only be averted, but the present Zollverein may be constrained not to increase, if they should not reduce, their present duties on American productions: provided the Hanse Towns, and the States of Mecklenburg, Hanover, and Oldenburg, stretching as they do along the Baltic and the North Sea, from Prussia to the Netherlands, shall resolutely remain separated from the league. To maintain this separation and the system of low duties generally is the policy of the present King of Hanover; and it is this reason which has, as we understand, prompted his desire to conclude a commercial treaty with the United States, upon the terms which I have indicated. It is proper that this information should be communicated to you; but it is equally proper that you should not impart it to any other person.

You will be furnished with copies of all the papers in the Department necessary to enable you to enforce the views which I have presented; and I am happy to know that your own information on the subject is both minute and extensive.

Should the Governments of Hanover and Oldenburg propose to insert stipulations in the treaty limiting the rates of duty to be imposed in the United States on their productions, you can furnish them with conclusive answers to such a proposition.

In the first place: It may be regarded as doubtful whether, under the Federal Constitution, the right to enter into any such stipulation is embraced in the treaty making power: and it is certain that it could not be carried into effect without the authority of a previous act of Congress.

2. It would encounter insurmountable obstacles in the Senate; and you can cite the proceedings of that body on the Zollverein treaty, in support of this position.

3. It would give rise to claims of foreign Powers, for similar privileges, under existing treaties. Indeed the British Government had intimated their intention to assert such a claim, on the presumption that the Zollverein treaty would be ratified.

4. The contemplated change in our tariff laws would render such a stipulation unnecessary for the benefit of Hanover and Oldenburg.

These reasons to which I have merely adverted, you can develope at greater length.

It may be wise to insert a provision in the treaty to enable the Duchies of Mecklenburg Schwerin and Strelitz to become parties to it hereafter, should they be unwilling to do so at present.

Mann presented his credentials at Hanover on April 30, 1846 (D.S., 14 Special Agents, German States, No. 1), and just a month later wrote as follows regarding the progress of the discussions (*ibid.*, No. 3, May 30, 1846):

Since I had the honor of addressing you, two weeks since I have had frequent interviews with the Hanoverian Minister of Foreign Affairs; and I have ascertained that, although the King is exceedingly anxious to conclude a new Treaty with the United States, upon a basis of the most extended liberality, yet nevertheless he is unwilling to enter into an obligation not to increase the existing import duty on Tobacco. The 19th article of the Treaty, forming the Germanic Confederation [see British and Foreign State Papers, II, 134–35], renders it somewhat questionable in his opinion—notwithstanding it is generally admitted to be a dead letter—whether any German state has a right to subscribe to such a stipulation; and he studiously avoids giving the slightest cause for offence to the Diet at Frankfort.

The King, I understand, as well as his Ministers, with several of whom—and particularly the premier—I have conversed upon the subject, entertain views similar to those expressed in your letter of instructions, relative to the Zollverein; but it is feared that if Hanover were to place herself in a position of apparent hostility to this association, by any overt act, a sympathy would be engendered, however false, in its behalf, that might result adversely to her wishes. If let alone, a recent palpable departure from the principles upon which the Zollverein was established—at least the *professed* principles—will hasten the dissolution of the bond which heretofore has held it together. The Director General of Customs of Prussia has stated *officially* that its object is *finacial*, not *commercial*—a fact that I never doubted, and which I freely expressed to yourself, during the first audience you honored me with, and also to one or more of your predecessors.

The King of Hanover will agree to abolish the *transit* duty upon Tobacco, Cotton, Rice, and Whale Oil; but for the purpose of maintaining efficient police regulations he will reserve the right of levying a tax of, not exceeding, two cents per 100[lbs] weight of each: He will likewise consent to abolish the import duty upon raw cotton. He will further stipulate to place our vessels upon an entire equality, both with respect to their tonnage and their cargoes, with Hanoverian vessels at Stade or Brunshausen; and to collect no "Weser Tolls" on the four articles afore-mentioned destined for Hanoverian ports and landings on the Weser: And he has intimated, at my urgent solicitation, his readiness to abolish the "Weser Tolls" on the said articles passing into other states bordering upon this river as soon as such states—Prussia &c.—shall consent to abolish their Weser Tolls on the same articles passing into Hanover. These tolls are prerogatives of the crown; and they are in perfect keeping with the Rhine Tolls, the Elbe Tolls, and the Danish Sound Tolls. I conceive it, consequently, an object of primary importance to get an expression, by Treaty agreement, of King Ernst's desire to remove them, whenever a similar liberality prevails in the states of the Zollverein; and if he shall yield to my request the preliminary measure will have been taken for the utter abrogation of all these relics of the feudal customs, of robber knights and barons, so detrimental to an extension of our commerce in central and Northern Europe. Our country, whose influence is extending almost with the rapidity of light, will thus have the honor, and the present administration the credit, of breaking up a most unjustifiable system of exactions upon the products of industry; a system which battles against the discoveries by science for facilitating intercourse between nations, and against the genius of the age in which it is our good fortune to live.

The Zollverein has repeatedly taken occasion to speak of its exceeding liberality towards the United States. The hour is hastening, if I be not deceived, when that liberality will be subjected to a searching ordeal! Can it retain its transit

duties—on one or more routes three times as oppressive, (and on none less than double) as those in Hanover; its Elbe tolls; its Rhine tolls; and its Weser tolls, after the generous demonstrations of its sea-board neighbor, covenanted for by formal compact?

If, however, the example of the Kingdom of Hanover is lost upon the Zollverein; if it should persist in burdening our chief staples, transiting its territory, to our customers behind, or outside, its limits, with duties and tolls we should not hesitate in my opinion to retaliate by terminating, after giving the requisite notice, the convention of commerce and navigation with Prussia; a convention which sustains, in an eminent degree, the shipping of that Kingdom, from her large *indirect* carrying under it; and the privileges of which she is desirous of extending to the other states of the league, as a ligament to bind them more closely to, and identify them more intimately with, her own *financial* destiny.

Although I cannot, acting under implicit obedience to my instructions, as you will already have observed, *conclude* a Treaty with Hanover, yet I feel quite confident that I will *perfect* one, as far as that government is concerned, that will be equally satisfactory to you, as the one which you authorized me to make. To obviate the difficulty, with regard to the import duty on Tobacco, His Majesty proposed the following article:—

"It is hereby expressly stipulated and agreed that if the Kingdom of Hanover "shall determine, during the said term of twelve years, to augment the existing "import duty upon leaves, strips, or stems of Tobacco, imported in hogsheads or "casks—a duty which does not exceed one *Thaler* and one *Gutengroschen* per one "hundred pounds Hanoverian currency and weight (seventy cents per one hundred "pounds United States currency and weight) it shall give a notice of one year to "the United States before proceeding to do so; and at the expiration of that time, "or any time subsequently, the United States shall have full power and right to "abrogate the present treaty by giving a previous notice of six months to the "Kingdom of Hanover, or to continue it, at their option, until it shall have been "terminated by limitation."

This provision will, doubtless, have a greater tendency to perpetuate the present moderate Tobacco duty, than a positive obligation on the part of Hanover not to increase it. The transit duties and tolls, once off, can never be re-established, and this much, therefore, we secure at the out-set, while the Crown, upon whomsoever it may descend, will not likely join any league unless the present duty on our staple is continued; or rather, not augmented. It will not consent either during the present King's reign, or afterwards, to risk such an expedient for the sake of revenue when its navigation is to suffer materially thereby. Should the King agree to insert the clause respecting the Weser Tolls, I shall carry with me a Treaty *perfected* by Hanover, with the liberty to sign, or not, as you may determine, after I reach Washington. My signature there is to be regarded as valid, as if executed here. This arrangement I shall the more willingly agree to, as I cannot receive additional instructions from you in time to get the treaty before the Senate, previous to the adjournment of Congress.

The despatch of Mann of June 17, 1846, from London, which transmitted the treaty to Secretary of State Buchanan, and which has been cited above, includes the following report of the result of the negotiations:

Before I put the Treaty into its present form I examined carefully all our reciprocity [commercial] Treaties, at the consulate at Bremen, from the one concluded in 1826 with Denmark [Document 51] to the one just ratified with Belgium [Document 116]; and although I yielded in one or two instances to the opinions of the Hanoverian plenipotentiary I believe the arrangement of the articles, whatever exceptions may be taken to the stipulations which they contain, will be found as little objectionable as any one of them.

The *first* article relates exclusively to Navigation. The indirect carrying is to be reciprocal. Our vessels and their cargoes are to be placed upon the same footing as Hanoverian vessels and their cargoes, with respect to the Stade Tolls; and are to "be subjected to no detention or other inconvenience", (a matter of

much importance to our shipping and mercantile interests) from which the latter are exempt.

The *second* article, reserves the trade upon the coasts, to the contracting parties, respectively.

The *third* article provides that, no priority or preference shall be given by either of the contracting parties, in the purchase of any article of commerce &c. &c. on account of the national character of the vessel &c.

The *fourth* article provides that, the ancient and barborous right to wrecks of the sea shall remain entirely abolished &c. &c.

The *fifth* article stipulates that such vessels only, as are *built* within the respective territories of the contracting parties, and belong exclusively to their citizens or subjects, and of which the master shall be a citizen or subject, shall be deemed national vessels. Hanover is obligated that the crew of a vessel, sailing under her Flag, must consist of subjects or citizens of the states embraced within the Germanic confederation; while the United States are free to sail their vessels as they please. Our Treaties require in nearly, if not in every, instance that the master and three-fourths of the crew of our vessels shall be citizens of the United States. This we have never hesitated about consenting to, inasmuch as it was provided for by law; but before the expiration of the present Treaty I think it is altogether probable that this regulation, or rather statute, may be modified. I am certain, and have been of this belief, for a long time, that it would be the means of building up more rapidly our mercantile marine.

The *sixth* article provides that, no higher or other duties shall be imposed on articles grown in the respective countries, than are imposed on the like articles, imported from other countries, &c. &c.

The *seventh* article obligates the contracting parties not to grant to other countries, favors which they withhold from each other, upon certain conditions.

The *eighth* article binds the King of Hanover to abolish the duty on raw cotton imported into his realm; and also the abolish the transit duties on raw cotton, tobacco, rice, and whale oil. The former amounts to about twenty cents on the 100 ^{lbs}, and the latter to about 13 cents on the 100 ^{lbs}. Instead of stipulating that the transit duty should be abolished on the four articles designated, the "growth and produce of the United States or their fisheries" I preferred saying in "hogsheads or casks, bales or bags" &c. &c., because except a few boxes of Tobacco, they are not exported in any other manner; and the possibility is thus utterly precluded of a *certificate of origin* ever being demanded by the Hanoverian authorities. It seemed necessary to describe "in Hogsheads *or* casks and bales *or* bags" inasmuch as a question might arise whether a *hogshead would be deemed a cask, or a bale a bag.* This article contains another, and in my opinion an infinitely more important stipulation, than any that has been recently expressed or secured by Treaty. I refer to the "Weser Tolls" to which I called your attention in my letter of the 30th ult. The King yielded to my request, as I then believed he would, and consented to precisely such a clause as I desired. I most confidently believe that this will speedily lead, if followed up with energy by our government, to the utter abrogation, in the north of Europe, of all river tolls (including those of the Rhine,) upon our staple products. The Congress of the Zollverein is now in session at Berlin, and if the Treaty is ratified and sent back to me without unnecessary delay—say by the Boston steamer of the 19th July—its influence would, assuredly, be immediate upon that body, and result most favorably to our agriculture and commerce; not only with respect to transit duties and river tolls, but to the import duty on Tobacco.

The *ninth* article relates exclusively to Consuls &c. &c.

The tenth article provides for certain privileges, to be enjoyed by the citizens or subjects of the contracting parties, when residing within the territory of each other.

The *eleventh* article fixes the period at which, and the manner how, the Treaty shall terminate. The Hanoverian government desired that the term be for twelve years. To this I had no weighty objection to interpose; and the less as its length settles, beyond question, the tobacco duty to the almost nominal one of 70 cents on the 100 ^{lbs};—not so much by two cents as the existing one in Great-Britain upon a *single* pound! and which Sir Robert Peel, in his great "*Free Trade*" speech said it was not his intention to reduce!! The liberality of Hanover, which consumes more of our staple in proportion to her population than any state

in Europe, will, by this article, be presented to the view of the commercial nations of the world, and her example serve to shame France, England, &c. &c. out of their inexcusable policy of making an article, which grows in every state of the American Union, a mere convenience for revenue purposes.

The twelfth article permits other states of the Germanic confederation, to become parties to the Treaty, upon certain conditions. This was indispensable with reference to Oldenburg and the Mecklenburgs, and conforms to my instructions, with the exception that they are not named, specifically, which by the by I am not quite sure that you intended they should be. Other states may avail of this article, in the event of a dismemberment of the Zollverein,—Bavaria, for instance, which has no Tobacco interest to protect, with her population of nearly 5,000,000—and consequently abolish their transit duties on our principal products and reduce their import duty to the Hanoverian standard on Tobacco.

I have thus as succinctly, as I well could, stated the object and purport of each of the twelve articles of the Treaty, which I have signed and to which I have attached my seal. As the Treaty was made at Hanover, it seemed to be nothing more than a matter of courtesy, for me to consent to an exchange of ratifications there.

The protocol, should the Treaty be found by you objectionable, in any respect, is sufficiently clear and explicit I am sure, and in which opinion Mr. M'Lane fully concurs, to justify the President in his rejection of the various stipulations of the Treaty. If he should approve, and the Senate should ratify, I distinctly foresee, that the most formidable barriers to the extension of our commercial relations, with the North and centre of Europe, will have been removed.

Proceedings in the Senate

The treaty was received in Washington on July 6, 1846, was approved by the President, and was submitted to the Senate the next day (Executive Journal, VII, 115), as Congress was then in session. Accompanying the treaty were communicated extracts from the despatch of Mann of June 17, 1846 (quoted in large part above; Senate Confidential Document No. 11, 29th Congress, 1st session, Regular Confidential Documents, XXII, 533–41). Later, however, apparently in December 1846, there was also communicated to the Senate the despatch of Mann of September 16, 1846 (which in large part is quoted below), and a private despatch of November 10, 1846 (Senate Confidential Document No. 2, 29th Congress, 2d session, Regular Confidential Documents, XXII, 683–96).

In the Senate there was some opposition and delay. In order to obtain the advice and consent of the Senate the Secretary of State informally consented to a suggested amendment, which was never formally presented and which seems of trifling consequence, for the amendment would merely have limited the term of the treaty to twelve years instead of requiring one year's notice of termination from that time (Article 11); but Congress adjourned on August 10, 1846, without action having been taken. The following instruction in the matter was sent by Buchanan to Mann under date of August 12, 1846 (D.S., 1 Special Missions, 245–47):

Your despatch, not numbered, dated at London on the 17th June last, accompanied by the Treaty which you have concluded with Hanover, was received at this Department on the 6th July. The Treaty was immediately submitted to the President, and received his approbation.

On the 7th day of July, it was communicated by him to the Senate for their consideration. In that Body, it encountered unexpected difficulties and delays. A portion of the Senators are opposed to Treaties of reciprocity, so far as our

indirect trade is concerned; and although the equivalents for this concession contained in the Treaty with Hanover were considered sufficient, yet objection was made to that clause in the 13ᵗʰ [11th] Article, which authorises the Hanoverian Government, at any time, after one years notice to increase the duty on Tobacco.

Although I believe a Constitutional majority of the Senate would have ratified this Treaty without amendment; yet it was postponed from time to time in consequence of these objections and the pressure of other business, until the Session was about to expire. Finally, in order to secure its ratification before the adjournment of Congress, I consented that it might be amended, by limiting its duration absolutely to the term of twelve years, amending it for this purpose, by striking out the clause for its continuance after this period, until one or other of the parties shall have given twelve months' notice of their intention to terminate it.

With this amendment it would have passed the Senate, I believe, unanimously, had they gone into Executive Session during the last day of their sitting. This was prevented by the pressure of Legislative business; and thus not only the Hanover Treaty but several important Executive nominations failed.

You may, in my opinion, confidently assure the Minister for Foreign Affairs of Hanover, that the Treaty will be ratified by the Senate, at an early period of their next Session, either with or without the single amendment, which I have already indicated, limiting its duration absolutely to the term of twelve years.

The President deems it important that you should proceed to Hanover, if this despatch does not find you there, for the purpose of making these explanations. After having performed this duty, you will return immediately to the United States.

Responding to the foregoing instruction, Mann reported very fully upon his discussion of the proposed amendment with the Hanoverian Minister of Foreign Affairs, Baron von Falcke, and at the same time commented at some length upon the views of Senators (D.S., 14 Special Agents, German States, No. 7, September 16, 1846):

I had the honor to receive on the evening of the 12ᵗʰ, instant, your despatch under date of August 12; and with as little delay as possible I had an interview with the Minister of Foreign Affairs of this government and communicated to him the information which had been transmitted to me. He was apparently much surprised that a Convention so entirely one-sided—so immediate in its favorable bearings, (or rather calculated to be so) upon the interests of the United States—should have encountered either opposition or delay in the Senate.

It is fortunate that I stipulated for a period of ten months during which to exchange ratifications, although Congress was in session and not a fourth of that time seemed to be necessary, for carrying the provisions of the Treaty into effect, for I am fully persuaded that, if negotiations had to be re-opened, we should be unsuccessful in securing such benefits as have been stipulated for.

The Minister of Foreign Affairs remarked to me, "we have given to your government, in this Treaty, every thing at our disposal, and in return we get nothing—emphatically nothing—that you have not long since conferred on Mecklenberg Schwerin and on Oldenburg [see the proclamations of September 18, 1830, for Oldenburg, and of April 28, 1835, for Mecklenburg-Schwerin, in 4 Statutes at Large, 814–15, 818]. They, with other states, have the privilege of the *indirect* carrying under the act of Congress of 1828 [see the notes to Document 92], and which Mr. Buchanan in a letter to our Consul at New-York, agreed to confer upon us, provided we would consent to put your vessels upon the same footing, with respect to the Stade Tolls upon the Elbe, of our own."

In reply I stated that both the President and the Secretary of State, properly appreciated the liberal commercial sentiments of the Kingdom of Hanover, as contained in the Convention which had been concluded, but that in a body like the Senate of the United States,—composed of 56 members, coming from every state in the Union,—time was required for deliberation upon all subjects submitted to its consideration, and that the pressure of important business, and other causes as explained by yourself, had occasioned a postponement merely of the ratification, and that for a comparatively short period.

Yesterday I prevailed upon the Minister of Foreign Affairs to ascertain whether the King would accept, in order that you might act understandingly, the amendment to the 11th Article (not 13th as stated in your despatch) which you proposed to make with a view to obviate all objections in the Senate. At a late hour last night, he called at my apartments and said, that he was authorized to assure me that His Majesty, inasmuch as he regarded the contemplated change of no consequence, would cheerfully consent to its being made. Thus you are relieved from any apprehension or responsibility in the premises as concerns Hanover. The Article as amended, if I have understood your views correctly, will read "The present Treaty shall continue in force for the term of twelve years from the date hereof; but upon the express condition," &c. &c. by which the clause "and further until the end of twelve months, after the government of Hanover on the one part or that of the United States on the other part, shall have given notice of its intention of terminating the same," will have been struck out.

I fear that the Treaty is not duly estimated by the Senators from the New-England states, particularly those of Connecticutt, Rhode-Island and Massachusetts. The chief product of our fisheries in the South Sea, it is perceptible to them, and to every body else, is to be free from *transit* duties, whereby every barrel of oil, passing into the Zollverein, will be relieved of a tax of something like 40 cents. This they may, as they undoubtedly do, clearly understand: But have they examined carefully the sixth article, which has such a direct bearing upon the prosperity of that valuable trade and navigation? It is there stipulated that, "No higher or other duties shall be imposed on the importation "into the United States of any articles, the growth, produce, or manufacture of "the Kingdom of Hanover or of its *fisheries;* and no higher or other duties shall "be imposed on the importation into the Kingdom of Hanover of any articles, "the growth, manufacture and produce of the United States *and of their fisheries,* "that are, or shall be payable on the *like articles,* being the growth, produce or "manufacture of ANY OTHER FOREIGN COUNTRY *or its fisheries.*" You must be apprized of the fact, that about 100,000 barrels of Whale Oil, with a large quantity of Whale-Bone, are annually imported from the United States into the ports of Bremen, Hamburgh, and Stettin for consumption in Germany. Prussia is so desirous of monopolizing this lucrative commerce, that she pays a premium of twenty Thalers per last for every ship that is fitted out at her ports, and engages *regularly* in it; and one Thaler (69 cents U.S. Currency) for every barrel of oil which they may bring home. Bremen and Hamburgh are also ambitious to extend their fisheries, and without affording any protection to their merchants they are gradually augmenting this branch of navigation. It must be recollected that Prussia, and the Hanse-Towns, as well as every other member of the Germanic Confederation, stand in the relation of *"Foreign countries"*, and therefore neither of them, while this Treaty would continue in force, could have a preference in the disposal of their product, as respects import duty, over the product of the United States! The northern Senators may oppose, or yield a reluctant support, to the Treaty, but when a great interest of the enterprizing portion of the Union which they represent, is so effectually guarded as the one under consideration, I predict that if its provisions are carried into operation, they or those who may succeed them, will have cause to regret its abrupt abrogation, by the amendment which has been insisted upon. It has been our uniform practice, I believe, to give and require a twelve [months'] notice in discontinuing Conventions with Foreign governments; and the only argument adduced, as I understand, for a departure from it in this instance is, that at the end of the twelve years Hanover could increase the duty on Tobacco and yet enjoy the indirect carrying until the notice was given, which if promptly done, would of course be only for twelve months. Now it is quite certain that if Hanover does not lay an additional burden upon our staple, until the expiration of the specified term, she will not be disposed to adopt such a measure the day thereafter: On the contrary she would have every inducement to let it remain at what it is, provided that she derived any benefit from the Treaty, and without which the United States, with the advantages which they would realize from the abolition of the transit duties and river tolls, could have no motive whatever, for wishing its operations to cease.

When I arrived here I suggested to the Minister of Foreign Affairs, that it was clearly to the interest of Hanover to admit "Paddy", or Rice in the husk, free of duty: He immediately called the attention of the *"Ober Finanzrath"* (upper Finance Councillor) to the subject.   A Report has not yet been made, and I now trust that it will be suspended until the Treaty is returned ratified, in which event, I shall be disappointed if it is not favorable to the measure. The Grand Duke of Oldenburg, from a conversation which I had with him, I am sure will give his assent.   The board of control of the "Steuer-Verein", (Customs-Union) has charge of the matter.   No discrimination can be made in behalf of our Rice, in Hanover and Oldenburg on account of existing Treaties with Holland, &c., but it may be greatly favored by a regulation to impose no duty upon "Paddy".   From Charleston a voyage may be made to the ports on the Ems, the Weser, and the Elbe in about a fourth of the time required from Batavia, and the charge of freight is consequently proportionately less.   It is not South-Carolina alone that would be benefitted by such a concession: The article matures well in Louisiana, and the cultivation under proper encouragement is susceptible of being vastly extended there.   *"Paddy"* is already imported into England from South-Carolina, and after being cleaned, the kernel is invariably much more fresh and sweet, than that which is imported in tierces, after its separation from the husk.

However, at the following session the advice and consent of the Senate were given on January 6, 1847, without qualification, by a vote of 32 yeas to 13 nays, after an amendment to strike out Article 12 had been defeated (Executive Journal, VII, 176).

The Exchange of Ratifications

Authority to exchange the ratifications of the treaty, and the usual full power, were given to Mann (D.S., 1 Special Missions, 248–51, January 9, 1847; 3 Credences, 189).   Before the completion of the procedure, which took place on March 5, 1847, at Hanover, he reported as follows (D.S., 14 Special Agents, German States, No. 8, February 26, 1847):

The triplicate of your despatch, No. 3, was received on the 13th instant, and on the 16th a notification reached me from the Legation of the United States at London, that the Treaty with Hanover accompanied by a despatch from yourself, had been placed in its charge by Gen. Armstrong to be retained subject to my order.   I forthwith despatched a messenger to Mr. Bancroft who returned this morning, discharging satisfactorily the trust confided to him.

Determining to hasten the exchange of ratifications I proceeded to this city without unnecessary delay, and immediately informed the Minister of Foreign Affairs that I should be prepared to complete the object of my mission in five or six days, or so soon as my messenger arrived from London: He remarked that inasmuch as the "Chambers" were in session it was proper that the Treaty should be submitted to them for approval, and that it should be at once laid before them. To-morrow [Friday, February 27] it will be read in this body the first time, and on Tuesday [March 3] it will be definitively disposed of.   These proceedings are for form's sake merely,—no sovereign of Europe being more respectful or courteous to his "States-General" than the one who reigns over this Kingdom.

Article 1

For an account of the important international acts regarding the navigation of the Elbe, see Kaeckenbeeck, International Rivers, 188–92 (see also Von Martens, Nouveau recueil de traités, VI, pt. 2, 588–602; VII, pt. 2, 653–56; IX, 365–69; XIII, 411–12; Nouveau recueil général de traités, V, 292–93, 530–36; VI, 370–72).

The general convention of June 23, 1821, to which various German states, including Hanover, were parties (British and Foreign State Papers, VIII, 953–64, translation), provided for the application to the Elbe of the principles for the free navigation of rivers laid down at the Congress of Vienna; but the Brunshausen or Stade tolls were left to some extent to future negotiations; those resulted in the general convention (Austria, Prussia, Saxony, Hanover, Holstein and Lauenburg, Mecklenburg-Schwerin, Anhalt-Köthen, Anhalt-Dessau, Anhalt-Bernburg, Lübeck, and Hamburg) signed at Dresden on April 13, 1844 (with elaborate annexes and tables), regarding the tolls in question (*ibid.*, XXXII, 20–59, translation; the German text, omitting the articles "not intended for unconditional publicity", is in Von Martens, Nouveau recueil général de traités, VI, 473–525. For the two other agreements regarding the navigation of the Elbe signed at the same time by the same parties, see *ibid.*, 386–472). The provisions of that convention (with some favoring exceptions) were made applicable to British vessels and cargoes by Article 6 of the Treaty of Commerce and Navigation between Great Britain and Hanover signed at London July 22, 1844 (British and Foreign State Papers, XXXII, 8–20).

To the United States (and certain other countries) privileges very similar to those accorded by the last-mentioned treaty were, from October 1, 1844, granted by the ordinance of the King of Hanover dated September 8, 1844, which is thus translated (*ibid.*, 868–69):

Ernest Augustus, by the Grace of God King of Hanover, etc.

Whereas Article 6 of the Treaty of Commerce and Navigation with the British Government grants to British goods and vessels various privileges in reference to the Brunshausen toll, We, in consideration of the relations of commerce and navigation to other states, decree as follows:

§1. The toll upon goods to be levied at Brunshausen shall, from the 1st of next month, be diminished to the amount stated in the above-mentioned treaty.

1. For goods designated in that article, of British, German, or Prussian origin, if they pass the toll line in British, German, Prussian, Swedish, Norwegian, or Belgian vessels.

2. For the like articles, the produce of the United States of North America, if imported into Our Kingdom in ships of those states or of one of the nations named in No. 1.

3. For the like articles of Mexican origin, if imported into Our Kingdom in Mexican vessels or in vessels of one of the nations named in No. 1 or 2.

For proof of claim to the said reduction of duty an official certificate of the origin of the goods is required to be added to the bill of lading.

§2. All additional dues, whether in money or in kind, which have hitherto been levied at Brunshausen, including Our ship toll and the rowers' toll of the town of Stade, are abolished and reduced in accordance with the first section of the Regulations for the Brunshausen Toll agreed to at Dresden on the 13th of April last.

1. For German, Prussian, Swedish, Norwegian, and Belgian vessels and their cargoes, of whatever the latter may consist.

2. For vessels of the United States of North America, so far as the said additional dues have reference to the vessel or would be leviable on goods the produce of the continent of America or of the West Indies and would be imported from thence into Our Kingdom.

3. For Mexican ships, so far as those additional dues would fall on the vessel or would be leviable on goods of Mexican origin and would be imported from thence into Our Kingdom.

§3. From the provisions of the Articles §1 and §2 relative to German vessels and their cargoes, the ships of Hamburg, with their cargoes, are excepted; the principles hitherto applicable to them in regard to the levying of the Brunshausen toll remaining temporarily in force for the same. [This section was abolished by the ordinance of September 26, 1844.]

This ordinance shall be entered in the first part of the Collection of Laws. Hanover, September 8, 1844.

ERNEST AUGUSTUS

SCHULTE
VON FALKE

The Stade or Brunshausen dues were abolished by the general treaty of June 22, 1861, as to vessels of the parties thereto (see De Clercq, Recueil des traités de la France, VIII, 279–94; also British and Foreign State Papers, LI, 27–35), and, as to the American marine, by the treaty between the United States and Hanover of November 6, 1861.

ARTICLE 8

For the act concerning the free navigation of the Weser, signed at Minden September 10, 1823 (Prussia, Hanover, Electoral Hesse, Brunswick, Oldenburg, Lippe, and Bremen), and the separate conventions signed in connection therewith, see Von Martens, Nouveau recueil de traités, VI, pt. 1, 301–40 (other acts relating to the Weser are in *ibid.*, IV, 645–47; VI, pt. 2, 840–53; and in Nouveau recueil général de traités, II, 572–74; see also Kaeckenbeeck, *op. cit.*, 192–94).

The Weser tolls were suspended by the treaty of January 26, 1856 (Prussia, Hanover, Electoral Hesse, and Bremen; Von Martens, Nouveau recueil général de traités, XVI, pt. 1, 440–42).

ARTICLE 12

The agreement by Article 12 to permit accession to "all the advantages and privileges contained in the stipulations of the present treaty" of "one or more of the other States of the Germanic Confederation" (which is also mentioned in Article 5) was specially intended to provide for such accession on the part of the neighboring Grand Duchies of Oldenburg, Mecklenburg-Schwerin, and Mecklenburg-Strelitz. Following the exchange of ratifications of this treaty, Oldenburg so acceded (March 10, 1847), as did Mecklenburg-Schwerin later, though by a more detailed agreement (December 9, 1847); but Mecklenburg-Strelitz, the smaller and less important of the two Mecklenburg Grand Duchies, did not; and no steps were taken toward extending this agreement to other members of the Germanic Confederation.

A summary statement regarding the Germanic Confederation (Deutscher Bund), with a list of the members thereof, is in the notes to Document 59, which include also a brief account of the German Zollverein or Customs Union (Deutscher Zoll- und Handelsverein). Neither Hanover nor any one of the three Grand Duchies mentioned was at the time of this treaty a member of the Zollverein, to which Hanover became party in 1851.

Hanover and Great Britain were united under the same crown from 1714 (George I) to 1837 (William IV). Formerly an electorate, Hanover became a kingdom as a result of the Congress of Vienna. Following the war of 1866 between Austria and Prussia, Hanover became a province of Prussia by decree of September 20, 1866.

ARTICLE 13

Upon the going into force of this treaty (March 5, 1847) the earlier Treaty of Commerce and Navigation (of May 20, 1840) between the United States and Hanover became "null and void" (see Document 92 and also generally the notes thereto).

O